The National Garden Scheme
A company limited by guarantee. Registered in England & Wales. Charity No. 1112664. Company No. 5631421

Registered & Head Office: Hatchlands Park, East Clandon, Guildford, Surrey, GU4 7RT.
01483 211535 www.ngs.org.uk

© The National Garden Scheme 2020

Published by Constable, an imprint of Little, Brown Book Group, Carmelite House, 50 Victoria Embankment,
London EC4Y 0DZ. An Hachette UK Company www.hachette.co.uk www.littlebrown.co.uk

Right: Mary Berry
with Martin McMillan

© Julie Skelton

Who's who

Chairman's message

I write this message in a reflective mood as, after nearly six years as Chairman and a total of fifteen years as a Trustee, my term of office will come to an end in 2020. During that time we have managed to grow the annual donations to our beneficiary charities from £1.75 million in my first year to £3 million in 2019.

I am proud that we continue to offer visitors a unique range of delightful gardens which continue to resonate with the quality, interest and character that have always been the hallmarks of the National Garden Scheme. They are nearly all privately owned and only ever open to visitors under our auspices, offering visitors a very personal experience. I am also very proud that, after opening her garden for 20 years, Mary Berry agreed to become our president in 2016.

Through the fifteen years there has been much change and many highlights. One of which I am also very proud has been our pioneering championing of the health benefits of gardens and gardening, which is now a significant part of our annual donations and our charity's wider activities.

But some things have not changed, most significantly the quality which has underpinned the National Garden Scheme since its foundation in 1927 and will, I am confident, sustain its future growth. It is an organisation built on human engagement and enjoyment; the enjoyment our garden owners have always got out of welcoming visitors and which visitors get out of their experience in a garden. It is a charity rooted in local communities, with the common purpose of making a difference to other people's lives with funds raised and donated. I count myself very privileged to have had the opportunity to lead this wonderful organisation and I wish it well for the future.

Martin McMillan, OBE

Discover the nation's best gardens

The National Garden Scheme gives visitors unique access to exceptional private gardens across England and Wales and raises impressive amounts of money for nursing and health charities through admissions, teas and cake.

Thanks to the generosity of garden owners, volunteers and visitors we have donated over £60 million to nursing and health charities since we were founded in 1927, and in 2019 made total annual donations of £3 million. Last year confirmed the National Garden Scheme's extraordinary dual impact, both within the gardens that open and through the donations made with the funds raised at their open days. As well as their unrivalled horticultural delights and quality, the gardens offer visitors enjoyment, relaxation and confirmation that having access to a garden is good for everybody's health and wellbeing, especially those without their own garden or who have particular health needs.

Originally established to raise funds for district nurses, we are now the most significant charitable funder of nursing in the UK and our beneficiaries include Macmillan Cancer Support, Marie Curie, Hospice UK and The Queen's Nursing Institute. Year by year, the cumulative impact of the grants we are able to give grows incrementally, helping our beneficiaries make their own important contribution to the nation's health and care, and strengthening the partnerships that we have with them all.

With over 3,700 gardens opening across England and Wales in 2020, including 893 new and returning gardens, we hope you enjoy exploring our beautiful gardens this year. Each inspiring space not only provides a unique glimpse into hidden horticultural delights but also the chance to support the health and wellbeing of thousands.

To plant a garden is to invest in tomorrow

Some tips on using your Handbook

This book lists all the gardens opening for the National Garden Scheme between January 2020 and early 2021. It is divided up into county sections, each including a map, calendar of opening dates and details of each garden, listed alphabetically.

Symbols explained

NEW Gardens opening for the first time this year or re-opening after a long break.

◆ Garden also opens on non-National Garden Scheme days. (Gardens which carry this symbol contribute to the National Garden Scheme either by opening on a specific day(s) and/or by giving a guaranteed contribution.)

♿ Wheelchair access to at least the main features of the garden.

🐕 Dogs on short leads welcome.

❀ Plants usually for sale.

NPC Plant Heritage National Plant Collection.

🛏 Gardens that offer accommodation.

☕ Refreshments are available, normally at a charge.

D Garden designed by a Fellow, Member, Pre-registered Member, or Student of The Society of Garden Designers.

🚌 Garden accessible to coaches. Coach sizes vary so please contact garden owner or County Organiser in advance to check details.

Group Visits Group Organisers may contact the County Organiser or a garden owner direct to organise a group visit to a particular county or garden. Otherwise contact our Visitor Development Manager, Linda Shelton, on 01483 213919 or linda@ngs.org.uk.

Children must be accompanied by an adult.

Photography is at the discretion of the garden owner; please check first. Photographs must not be used for sale or reproduction without prior permission of the owner.

Funds raised In most cases all funds raised at our open gardens comes to the National Garden Scheme. However, there are some instances where income from teas or a percentage of admissions is given to another charity.

Toilet facilities are not always available at gardens.

If you cannot find the information you require from a garden or County Organiser, call the National Garden Scheme office on 01483 211535.

2020: In celebration of nursing

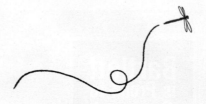

George Plumptre, Chief Executive of the National Garden Scheme, highlights the importance of the charity's annual donations

Originally founded by The Queen's Nursing Institute (QNI) in 1927 to raise money to support district nursing, the National Garden Scheme now has a core group of beneficiaries which make a vital contribution to the nation's community healthcare. As well as the QNI the group includes Macmillan Cancer Support, Marie Curie, Hospice UK, Parkinson's UK and Carer's Trust.

That 2020 has been designated 'Year of the Nurse and Midwife' in celebration of the 200th anniversary of Florence Nightingale's birth, provides a wonderful opportunity to celebrate the significant contribution the National Garden Scheme has made to nursing. With over £60 million donated to-date we are the largest cumulative funder of most of our beneficiaries – a fact which deserves to be more widely known.

Building on this contribution, in 2019 the National Garden Scheme commissioned The King's Fund to produce a report, Investing in Quality: the contribution of large charities to shaping future health and care. The report highlighted the work of the different organisations we support and set out how their joint contribution impacts on the wider landscape of the nation's health and care.

Throughout 2020, as we celebrate the wider world of nursing which the National Garden Scheme has done so much to support, we will be reinforcing the legacy of this report to ensure the maximum recognition for our beneficiaries and to ensure their engagement in the ongoing debate about the future of community nursing and health to which, as The King's Fund report suggests, they will make such a vital contribution.

© Marie Curie, Ben Gold

The impact of our donations to nursing and health

Since our inception, the National Garden Scheme has developed an efficient fundraising formula which allows us to donate 80% of the money raised at our open gardens to nursing and health beneficiaries. It is thanks to the generosity and hard work of our garden owners, and the county teams that support them, that we are able to welcome so many visitors each year and in turn to give so generously.

Our beneficiaries are major contributors to the key areas of community health and care including:

- Nursing people at home so they do not need to be in hospital
- End of life and palliative care for patients and support for their families
- Specialist nursing and care for particular health conditions such as cancer or Parkinson's

Here are some of the incredible things our donations have supported in 2019:

28,000
People living with cancer supported through our funding for Macmillan

200,000
People and their families reached by our support of Hospice UK

1,325
Queen's Nurses supported by our funding

28,495
Unpaid carers and their families reached by our support of Carers Trust

26
Clinical bursaries supported for Marie Curie professionals

450
Additional people living with Parkinson's able to access the support they need to manage their condition

Your visits to our gardens help change lives

In 2019 the National Garden Scheme donated £3 million to nursing and health charities including:

Macmillan Cancer Support £500,000	**Marie Curie** £500,000	**Hospice UK** £500,000
Carers Trust £400,000	**The Queen's Nursing Institute** £250,000	**Parkinson's UK** £185,000
Perennial £130,000	**Mind** £100,000	**Horatio's Garden** £75,000

Thank you

To find out about all our donations visit ngs.org.uk/beneficiaries

Gardens and health: people and communities

Since 2016 when The King's Fund published our ground-breaking report, *Gardens and Health*, we have championed and supported the concept that access to gardens and practical gardening are good for people's health. Hundreds of our garden owners have engaged enthusiastically, either with compelling stories of their own or by opening their gardens to our beneficiaries.

We have made substantial donations to specific charities for health-related garden projects, supporting Horatio's Garden to build gardens for NHS spinal injuries units, the National Autistic Society to build gardens for children and young people living with autism, Leonard Cheshire to build gardens for patients at their residential facilities and Maggie's Centre to add to their portfolio of gardens at their cancer support centres.

In 2019 we also gave donations to KIDS, a charity which supports children with a range of disabilities, to create gardens in Basingstoke and Birmingham, and to Treloar's School and College to create a garden within a new Horticultural and Outdoor Learning Centre at their Hampshire campus.

As well as these specific projects we also support a broad spectrum of people and communities. One of our longest-standing beneficiaries, Perennial, supports gardeners and horticulturalists who have fallen on tough times. We also fund a variety of gardening apprentice and trainee programmes, with the WRAGS scheme, ABF The Soldier's Charity, the Professional Gardener's Trust, the National Botanic Garden, Wales and The Garden Museum. And we fund a range of life-enhancing community garden projects in a scheme that we established a decade ago in memory of the garden writer Elspeth Thompson.

380
Patients benefitted from Horatio's Garden Oswestry

165
Children and young people with disability supported at Treloar School and College

£206,208
donated for grants and bursaries

£245,000
donation to gardens and health beneficiaries

Help open gardens for the future
with a gift in your will

A love of gardens is often inherited from our parents or grandparents. If you love gardens and garden visiting, you can help inspire that passion in future generations by leaving a gift in your will to the National Garden Scheme.

For more information or to speak to our friendly team call **01483 211535**, email **giftinwill@ngs.org.uk** or visit **ngs.org.uk/giftinwill**

The English Garden magazine is delighted to support the National Garden Scheme in 2020

Each sumptuous issue of *The English Garden* features beautiful gardens, many from the The Garden Visitor's Handbook, as well as inspiring borders, gorgeous plants and expert advice to help you create your dream garden.

"*The English Garden* is a constant reminder of the beauty of English gardens. It keeps alive the British tradition of gardening and the passion all gardeners feel for their plants."

- ALAN TITCHMARSH

SUBSCRIBE FROM JUST £19.50
www.chelseamagazines.com/NTEGNG20
or call +44(0)1858 438 833 (quote code NTEGNG20)

Open your garden

"The garden was my delight. I grew up with gardeners and I just love gardens. I was always very much aware that gardens were important and they were for sharing..."

Hazel Hawke, wife of Bob Hawke,
23rd Prime Minister of Australia

The appeal of gardens is universal. They bring joy not just to the gardener who nurtures and shapes them but to all those who have the privilege to visit and discover them. Opening your garden with the National Garden Scheme means that you'll be opening your gate to a community of like-minded garden owners, visitors and volunteers, all passionate about gardens.

Our friendly volunteer team offer all the support you need to open your garden for the National Garden Scheme but it's up to you when you'd like to open and how often. In May 2019 garden owner Shelly Rand opened her garden at 1 Whitehouse Cottages, Essex for the first time.

"At 7pm I was sitting in my garden - my happy place - with my friends and family around me, in the aftermath of my first garden opening. The excited chatter, buzzing with stories of our day, and my permanent smile made me realise that this was always going to be a fun journey, as gardening should be."

Shelly is doing it all again in 2020, with three garden openings in May, June and July.

For many, the joy of sharing their garden with others is motivation enough but, by opening your garden, you will also be helping to raise vital funds for nursing and health charities, contributing to the outstanding impact that the National Garden Scheme makes each year to the nation's health.

Mary Berry, President of the National Garden Scheme, says:

"As President of the National Garden Scheme I am enormously proud of the remarkable amounts of money that our garden openings have helped generate for nursing and health charities. I have always believed that gardens and garden visits can have positive health benefits and our beneficiary partnerships are the living embodiment of that."

Open your garden with the National Garden Scheme

You'll join a community of like-minded individuals, all passionate about gardens, and help raise money for nursing and health charities.

Big or small, if your garden has quality, character and interest we'd love to hear from you to arrange a visit.

Call us on 01483 211535, email hello@ngs.org.uk or visit our website ngs.org.uk for more information.

An evening at the world's greatest glasshouse

Join us for an evening of music, delicious food and fine wines
Thursday, April 30th, 2020, 6.30–9.30pm
Temperate House, Kew

The Royal Botanic Gardens, Kew has generously offered the National Garden Scheme the rare privilege of hosting a glittering soirée in its iconic Temperate House. Mary Berry CBE, President of the National Garden Scheme, will welcome 400 guests to this glamorous fundraising event in the world's greatest Victorian glasshouse. You'll be serenaded by music and enjoy delicious food and wine as you explore the wonders of the building's architecture and its collection of 10,000 plants, many rare and endangered. There'll also be an exciting live auction of exclusive lots, run by legendary auctioneer Nick Bonham, all contributing to the evening's fundraising for this worthy cause.

Knight Frank are the generous lead sponsor, with Freshfields and Candide helping to make this a truly magical, exclusive event. Tickets go on sale in February. For more information and to book tickets go to www.ngs.org.uk/kew.

Be the first to hear about our future ticketed gardens and events by emailing events@ngs.org.uk to be added to the mailing list.

Below: Temperate House, Royal Botanical Gardens, Kew, London © Marianne Majerus

Knight Frank

Found

We sell and let homes of all sizes, from city studios and houses for growing families, to the finest country properties with acres of land and beautiful gardens. Let us surprise you

If you are thinking of moving or would simply like some advice on the market, please do get in touch.

We'd love to help you.

020 3869 4758
knightfrank.co.uk

Connecting people and property, perfectly

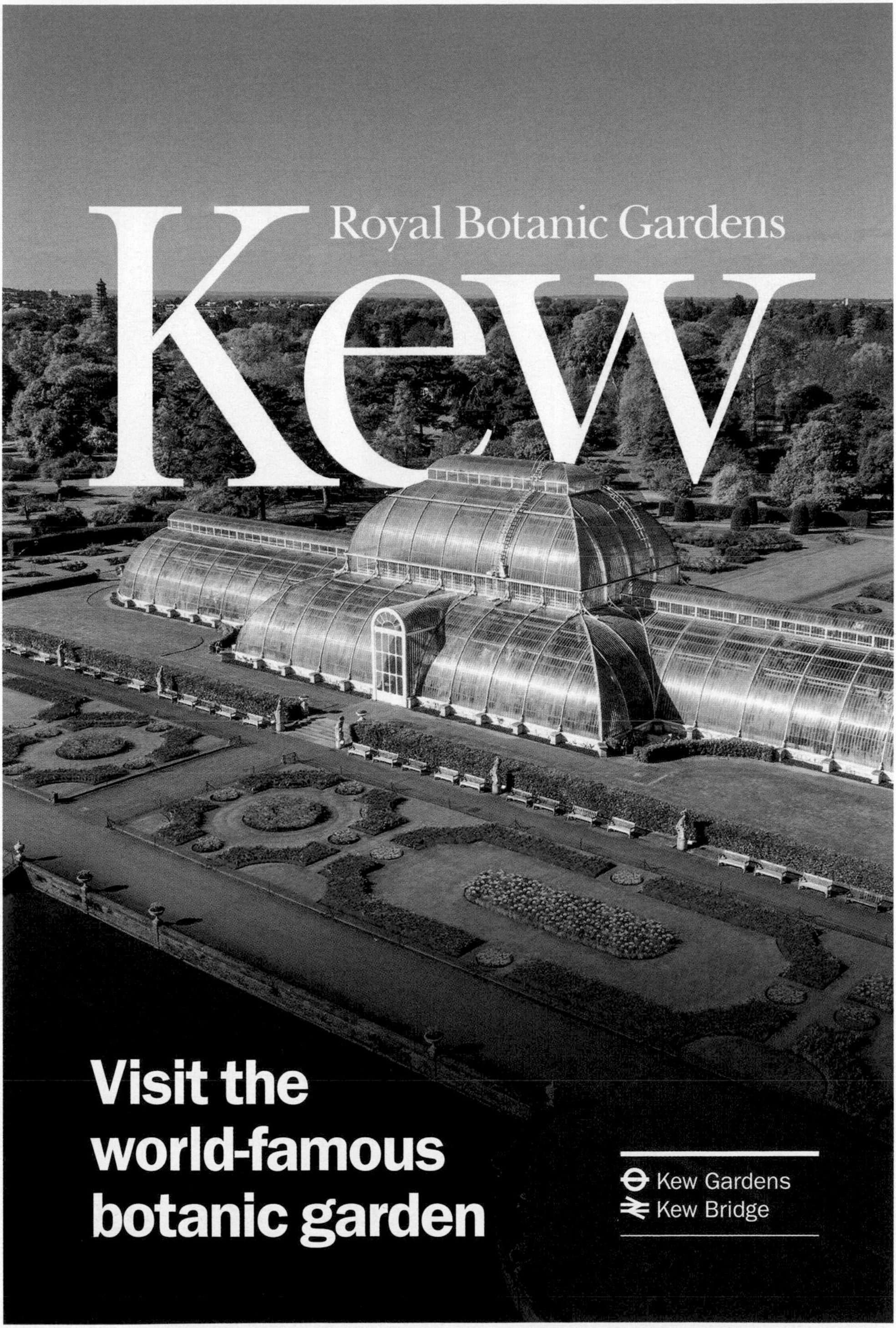

Royal Botanic Gardens

Kew

Visit the world-famous botanic garden

⊖ Kew Gardens
⇄ Kew Bridge

22

PWI
PROPERTY WEALTH INSURANCE

PWI Brokers are proud to partner National Garden Scheme

Help Us Support National Garden Scheme

NATIONAL Open GARDEN SCHEME

25% contribution to **National Garden Scheme** for every policy arranged

* Please Quote Code:
NGS2020

One Policy! One Renewal! All Covered!

We champion correct insurance protection for your individual homes and gardens backed by exceptional insurance cover which cannot be purchased online or by direct insurers.

Take advantage of our expert advice with a no obligation review of your domestic insurance requirements.

*25% Contribution Offer: By arranging your insurance policy through PWI, we will contribute 25% of our earned commission income to the NGS for each policy arranged through PWI and every year you renew the policy. Only available when using the **Promotion Code NGS2020** for new policies arranged during 2020.

We can arrange cover for:

- One policy for your home, property and motor vehicles with one renewal date
- Worldwide cover for all contents
- No restrictive warranties
- Agreed value for motor, jewellery and collections.
- Statues and garden features
- Charitable events, country pursuits and incidental business
- Mechanical vehicles used for gardening
- Bespoke claims management
- Hobbies such as Golf, cycling and country pursuits.

Contact us to see how you can benefit from a Portfolio Insurance policy

☎ **01425 486684**
✉ **keithc@pwinsurance.co.uk**
🌐 **www.pwinsurance.co.uk**

Try 6 issues of COUNTRY LIFE

for just £6 *

The quintessential weekly British magazine

Visit www.countrylifesubs.co.uk/55ac
or call 0330 333 1113 quote code 55ac

Lines open Monday-Saturday, 8am-6pm UK time

BEDFORDSHIRE

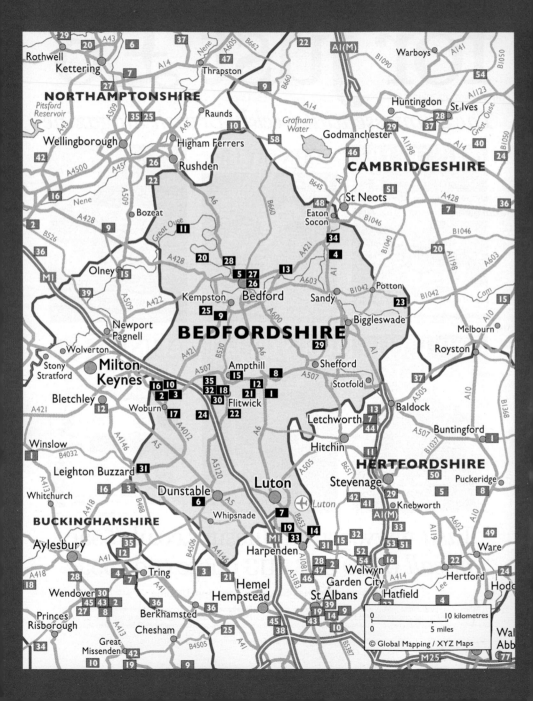

The Birthplace of John Bunyan, it is little wonder the county of Bedfordshire inspired the author of Pilgrim's Progress.

We are delighted to welcome you to the National Garden Scheme in Bedfordshire. This year, 44 garden owners will open their gates to their private havens and share with you their passion, and enthusiasm, for plants and planting schemes.

We begin the season with the National Collection of Snowdrops in February followed by spring bulbs in March and April. You can enjoy beautiful plantings and inspirational designs at numerous gardens throughout the summer, some of which have been featured in national magazines and television. There are themed gardens such as the Alpine garden, the Japanese garden and the Texan garden as well as several walled gardens. A trio of 18th century gardens designed by Capability Brown, Southill Park, Luton Hoo and The Walled Garden at Luton Hoo are also open for the National Garden Scheme in Bedfordshire. We will conclude the year at the end of October with an enchanting, Diwali themed evening of lanterns and diya lamps and a colourful woodland garden. In case of adverse weather, please check our website for any changes to the opening. We look forward to welcoming you.

Volunteers

County Organiser
Indi Jackson
01525 713798
indi.jackson@ngs.org.uk

County Treasurer
Colin Davies
01525 712721
colin1davies1@gmail.com

Press Officer
Hannah Sardar
07590 385911
hannah.sardar@ngs.org.uk

Facebook & Twitter
Hannah Sardar
(as above)

Booklet Co-ordinator
Indi Jackson
(as above)

Photography
Venetia Barrington
07767 668027
venetiajanesgarden@gmail.com

Talks
Kate Gardner
07725 307803
kate.gardener@ngs.org.uk

Assistant County Organisers
Geoff & Davina Barrett
geoffanddean@gmail.com

Ann Davies
annie1davies1@gmail.com

Brenda Hands
brenda.hands@outlook.com

Julie Neilson
julieneilson@outlook.com

[f] @bedfordshire.ngs

Left: The Walled Garden

OPENING DATES

All entries subject to change. For latest information check www.ngs.org.uk

Map locator numbers are shown to the right of each garden name.

February

Snowdrop Festival

Saturday 1st
NEW 127 Stoke Road   31

Sunday 2nd
NEW 127 Stoke Road   31

Sunday 23rd
◆ King's Arms Garden   15

March

Sunday 29th
The Old Rectory,
Westoning   22

April

Sunday 26th
Townsend Farmhouse 32
West Oak   35

May

Saturday 2nd
NEW 127 Stoke Road   31

Sunday 3rd
Secret Garden   28

Saturday 9th
88 Castlehill Road   6

Sunday 10th
NEW 111 Cutenhoe
Road   7

Sunday 17th
The Old Rectory,
Wrestlingworth   23

Sunday 24th
Steppingley Village
Gardens   30

Monday 25th
◆ The Manor House,
Stevington   20
Steppingley Village
Gardens   30

Sunday 31st
Flaxbourne Farm   10
The Old Rectory,
Wrestlingworth   23

June

Saturday 6th
88 Castlehill Road   6
22 Elmsdale Road   9

Sunday 7th
22 Elmsdale Road   9
Southill Park   29

Saturday 13th
NEW Bedford Heights   5
NEW Hollington Farm   12

Sunday 14th
NEW Hollington Farm   12
The Hyde Walled
Garden   14

Saturday 20th
NEW Ash Trees   2
Howbury Hall Garden   13

Sunday 21st
Lindy Lea   18
NEW Royal Oak
Cottage   25

Sunday 28th
Dragons Glen   8
NEW Mill Lane Gardens 21

July

Saturday 4th
22 Elmsdale Road   9

Sunday 5th
22 Elmsdale Road   9
The Hyde Walled
Garden   14
The Old Rectory,
Westoning   22

Saturday 11th
NEW Aspley Guise
Gardens   3

Sunday 12th
NEW Aspley Guise
Gardens   3

Saturday 18th
Walnut Cottage   34

Sunday 19th
NEW Rads End Farm   24
Walnut Cottage   34

Sunday 26th
NEW 111 Cutenhoe
Road   7
Luton Hoo Hotel Golf
& Spa   19

August

Sunday 2nd
NEW Royal Oak Cottage 25

Saturday 8th
NEW 4 St Andrews
Road   26
1a St Augustine's
Road   27

Sunday 9th
NEW 100 High Street   11

Saturday 15th
◆ The Walled Garden   33

Monday 31st
Flaxbourne Farm   10

September

Saturday 12th
40 Leighton Street   17

October

Saturday 24th
Townsend Farmhouse 32

Sunday 25th
◆ King's Arms Garden   15

By Arrangement

Arrange a personalised garden visit with your club, or group of friends, on a date to suit you. See individual garden entries for full details.

10 Alder Wynd   1
NEW 1c Bakers Lane   4
22 Elmsdale Road   9
Howbury Hall Garden   13
NEW Lake End House   16
The Old Rectory,
Wrestlingworth   23
NEW 4 St Andrews
Road   26
1a St Augustine's
Road   27
Secret Garden   28
NEW 127 Stoke Road   31
Walnut Cottage   34

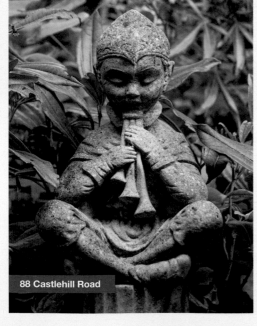

88 Castlehill Road

THE GARDENS

1 10 ALDER WYND

Silsoe, Bedford, MK45 4GQ.
David & Frances
Hampson, 01525 861356,
mail@davidhampson.com. *From
Barton Road, turn into the estate on
Obelisk Way, at the end of Obelisk
Way turn R at the school and then
first L into Alder Wynd, bear R, 10
Alder Wynd is the 1st house on the
R.* **Visits by arrangement June to
Sept for groups of up to 20. Adm
£8 incl refreshments. Off street
parking for 4 vehicles.**
Runners up in 2017 Gardeners
World Competition, 'Small Garden
Category'. The garden demonstrates
what can be achieved in a relatively
small space, 10m x 11m. Created
from scratch in autumn 2014, it is
courtyard in style and formed around
a series of raised beds and oak
structures. Lush plantings of bananas,
gingers, tree ferns, cannas, hosta's,
bamboos, herbaceous perennials and
tetrapanax. This small area has a wide
selection of plants, tetrapanax, roses,
wisteria, clematis, a variety of grasses
and traditional perennials. A water
feature provides a subtle background
noise.
✹ ☙

2 NEW ASH TREES

Green Lane, Aspley Guise, Milton
Keynes, MK17 8EN. Teresa & John
Kennard. *2m J13 M1. Follow signs
to Aspley Guise & yellow arrow signs
from the village square. Green Lane
off Wood Lane. On road parking in
Wood Lane.* **Evening opening Sat
20 June (4-7). Adm £5, chd free.
Light refreshments.**
Music from a group of flautists drifts
through this secluded garden, walled
in with borrowed tree-scape and
hidden in a private lane. Herbaceous
borders, shrubs, trees, bulbs, and fruit
including apricot and peach. There
is a unique garden arch sculpture
created for a Hampton Court show
garden. Seats in quiet spots amongst
the plants. Children and wheelchairs
welcome as are dogs on leads. WC.
Garden is flat with reasonable access
for wheels and walkers.

GROUP OPENING

3 NEW ASPLEY GUISE GARDENS

Spinney Lane, Aspley Guise, Milton
Keynes, MK17 8JT. Alex Ballance.
*SE of Milton Keynes. 1½ m from
M1 J13. Follow rd to Aspley Guise
Sq, turn up Woburn Lane, L into
Spinney Lane, R into Village Hall car
park. Gardens are signed from there.
Blue Badge parking ONLY outside
individual gardens.* **Sat 11, Sun 12
July (2-5). Combined adm £6, chd
free. Home-made teas in Aspley
Guise Village Hall.**

DAWNEDGE LODGE
Phil & Lynne Wallace.

GLADE HOUSE
Alex Ballance & Lindsay Walker.

HOLLYDALE, WOBURN LANE
Mrs Gill Cockle.

Three colourful gardens that are
well stocked with a wide range
of different plants, displayed in a
variety of planting styles. There are
herbaceous borders and shrubs
galore, plus vegetable and herb
gardens, chickens, a fishpond and
greenhouses. All the gardens are a
short stroll from the village hall, where
parking is provided and delicious tea,
coffee and scrumptious home-made
cakes will be on sale. Also available
for sale in the hall and gardens will be
plants, handicrafts, honey and other
handmade items. Partial wheelchair
access to parts of Glade House and
Hollydale gardens. Dawnedge Lodge
is accessible but with some steps.
♿ 🐕 ✹ ☙

4 NEW 1C BAKERS LANE

Tempsford, Sandy,
SG19 2BJ. Juliet & David
Pennington, 01767 640482,
juliet.pennington01@gmail.com.
*Tempsford is 1m N of Sandy on A1.
Station Road is on the E side of the
A1. Bakers Lane is approx 300 yards
down Station Road on L.* **Visits
by arrangement Feb to Oct for
groups of up to 20. Adm £5.**
This is a garden for all seasons with
interesting and unusual plants. It comes
to life with a winter border planted with
colourful Cornus and evergreen shrubs
under planted with snowdrops and
hellebores with gravel areas carpeted
with miniature cyclamen. It develops
through the seasons culminating in

early autumn with a spectacular show
of sun-loving herbaceous plants.
Garden is mainly level with a central
wide paved path. Other paths are
surfaced with slate or bark and are not
suitable. Sorry no dogs.
♿

5 NEW BEDFORD HEIGHTS

Brickhill Drive, Bedford,
MK41 7PH. Graham A. Pavey,
bedfordheights.co.uk/. *Next to
Travelodge in Bedford. Park in
Travelodge carpark in Brickhill Drive.*
**Sat 13 June (10-2). Adm £5, chd
free. Light refreshments.**
Originally built by Texas Instruments,
Texan theme runs throughout the
building and the gardens. The
entrance simulates an arroyo or dry
river bed, and is filled with succulents
and cacti, mixture of grasses and
herbaceous plants, many of which
are Texan natives. There are also
3 courtyard gardens, where less
hardy plants thrive in the frost free
environment. Gardens designed by
Graham A Pavey. No wheelchair
access to two of the courtyards
but can be viewed from a viewing
platform. Sorry no dogs.
♿ 🚗 ☙

6 88 CASTLEHILL ROAD

Totternhoe, Dunstable, LU6 1QG.
Chris & Carole Jell. *Middle End.
Turn R off B489 Aston Clinton
rd. Fronting main rd approx ½ m
through village. Garden is in the
centre of the village.* **Sat 9 May, Sat
6 June (2-5). Adm £5, chd free.**
Diverse planting managed in a natural
and artistic way, creating a feel of
peace and beauty and a wildlife haven.
Roses, clematis, shrubs, trees and
perennials are arranged in glorious
disarray with a gentle plea for chaos.
Sloping on limestone and clay, created
and evolved by the owners over 40
years, this garden enjoys its own micro
climate. Views of Chiltern Hills from the
front garden and field. No access for
wheelchairs. Sorry no dogs.
✹ ☙

7 NEW **111 CUTENHOE ROAD**
Luton, LU1 3NG. Joe & Laura
Carey. *From J10 M1, follow signs
for local traffic towards Stockwood
Park. Take the 1st R at the lights,
into Cutenhoe Road. We're approx
halfway down the hill on L.* **Sun 10
May, Sun 26 July (2-5.30). Adm
£4. Home-made cakes, tea and
home roasted coffee.**
Set into a steep slope, our
contemporary tropical garden is
divided into 6 levels, each planted
with a luscious tropical scheme. Musa
Basjoo, Echiums, Yuccas and a wide
range of euphorbias, bamboos, spring
bulbs and summer flowering perennials
- all nestled in amongst cast rendered
walls and shuttered spiral steps leading
to our vine tunnel and upper deck
with outdoor fireplace and pizza oven.
Steep steps and no wheelchair access.

8 DRAGONS GLEN
17 Great Lane, Clophill, Bedford,
MK45 4BQ. Kate & Andy Gardner.
*Great Lane is situated approx halfway
along the High St almost opp the
Village Primary School. The house is
approx. 500 metres up the lane on the
L.* **Sun 28 June (12-5). Adm £5, chd
free. Home-made teas. Gluten and
dairy free cakes are available at all
garden openings.**
This contemporary garden takes full
advantage of the sloped landscape
and dry conditions of its Greensand
Ridge location to great effect. Dry
shade, herbaceous borders, waterfall
and wildlife pond create distinct
spaces that are linked together
by the oriental influences that run
throughout the garden. This garden
has been featured on BBC Gardeners
World and in Garden News. Partial
wheelchair access due to steep
slopes and steps. Sorry no dogs.
✿ ☕

> We help ordinary
> people open the gates
> to their extraordinary
> private gardens to raise
> impressive amounts
> of money through
> admissions, teas and
> slices of cake!

9 22 ELMSDALE ROAD
Wootton, Bedford, MK43 9JN. Roy
& Dianne Richards, 07733 222495,
roy.richards60@ntlworld.com. *4m
from J13 M1. Join old A421 towards
Bedford, follow signs to Wootton.
Turn R at The Cock PH follow to
Elmsdale Rd.* **Sat 6, Sun 7 June,
Sat 4, Sun 5 July (12-5). Adm £4,
chd free. Home-made teas. Visits
also by arrangement May to Sept
for groups of 10 to 30.**
Topiary garden greets visitors before
they enter a genuine Japanese Feng
Shui garden including bonsai. Large
collection of Japanese plants, Koi
pond, lily pond and a Japanese Tea
House. The garden was created from
scratch by the owners about 20 years
ago and has many interesting features
including Japanese lanterns and the
Kneeling Archer terracotta soldier
from China. Partial wheelchair
access. The Garden is on 2 levels
with gravel type paths but some of
the garden can be viewed from the
lower level.
♿ 🐕 🚗 ☕

10 FLAXBOURNE FARM
Salford Road, Aspley Guise,
MK17 8HZ. Paul Linden,
www.flaxbournegardens.com. *Turn
off at J13 M1 follow signs to Aspley
Guise turn R in village centre & follow
road until you go over the railway line
and we are 250 yards on L.* **Sun 31
May, Mon 31 Aug (12-5). Adm £6,
chd free. Home-made teas.**
A beautiful, entertaining and fun
garden of 3 acres, lovingly developed
with numerous water features, a
windmill, modern arches and bridges,
a small moated castle, lily pond,
herbaceous borders and a Greek
temple ruin. A recently established
jungle garden complete with a three-
way bridge, planted up with tree
ferns, hostas, gunnera and
large bamboos. Crow's nest,
crocodiles, tree house for children.
Huge Roman arched stone gateway.
Wheelchair access to main parts of
the garden.
♿ 🐕 🚗 ☕

11 NEW **100 HIGH STREET**
Odell, Bedford, MK43 7AS. John
& Rosemary. *Park in Village Hall and
walk across.* **Sun 9 Aug (2-5). Adm
£5, chd free. Home-made teas at
the village hall.**
This multi-level garden is set in
about one and a half acres with hard
landscaping that creates a variety of
viewing levels. The garden has mature

trees, an orchard, raised vegetable
and cutting garden, a lawned area
with pergola and herbaceous borders,
prairie style planting with grasses
etc. A pond has both fish and lilies.
Access for wheelchairs may be
difficult. There are steps and gravel.
Sorry no dogs.

12 NEW **HOLLINGTON FARM**
Flitton Hill, Bedford, MK45 2BE.
Mr & Mrs John & Susan Rickatson.
*Off A507 between Clophill &
Ampthill- take Silsoe/ Flitton then
bear R & follow yellow signs.* **Sat 13,
Sun 14 June (2-5.30). Adm £6, chd
free. Home-made teas.**
Two acre country garden. Semi
formal near house with small parterre,
pergola, pond and borders. Planting
is massed perennials, shrubs and
roses. Outer areas are wilder with
mature trees. An option to walk
through a wild flower farm meadow
with views over Mid Beds. Plant sales
and teas. Some steps and steep
slopes. Sorry no dogs.
♿ ✿ ☕

13 HOWBURY HALL GARDEN
Howbury Hall Estate, Renhold,
Bedford, MK41 0JB. Julian Polhill
& Lucy Copeman, 07808 773577,
j_polhill@polhill.com,
www.howburyfarmflowers.co.uk.
*2m E of Bedford. Off A421 A1 - M1
link. Leave A421 at A428/Gt Barford
exit, take A428 to Bedford. Entrance
to house & gardens ½ m on R.
Parking in field. Short walk to garden.*
**Sat 20 June (2-5). Adm £5, chd
free. Home-made teas. Visits also
by arrangement May to Sept for
groups of 20+. Floristry demos
and classes also available with
light lunches or teas.**
A late Victorian garden designed
with mature trees, sweeping lawns
and herbaceous borders. The large
walled garden is a working garden,
where one half is dedicated to
growing a large variety of vegetables
whilst the other is run as a cut flower
business. In the woodland area,
walking towards the large pond, the
outside of a disused ice house can
be seen. Gravel paths and lawns may
be difficult for smaller wheels. Sorry
no dogs.
♿ ☕

King's Arms Gardens

14 THE HYDE WALLED GARDEN

East Hyde, Luton, LU2 9PS. D J J Hambro Will Trust. *2m S of Luton. M1 exit/10a Exit to A1061 towards Harpenden take 2nd on L signed East Hyde. From A1 exit J4 follow A3057 N to r'about 1st L to B653 follow rd to Wheathampstead/Luton to East Hyde.* **Sun 14 June, Sun 5 July (2-5). Adm £5, chd free. Home-made teas.**
Walled garden adjoins the grounds of The Hyde (not open). Extends to approx 1 acre and features rose garden, seasonal beds and herbaceous borders, imaginatively interspersed with hidden areas of formal lawn. An interesting group of Victorian greenhouses, coldframes and cucumber house are serviced from the potting shed in the adjoining vegetable garden. Gravel paths.

15 ◆ KING'S ARMS GARDEN

Brinsmade Road, Ampthill, Bedford, MK45 2PP. Ampthill Town Council, www. ampthilltowncouncil.org.uk/ amenities/kings-arm-garden. *8m S of Bedford. Free parking in town centre. Entrance opp Old Market Place, down King's Arms Yard.* **For NGS: Sun 23 Feb (2-4). Light refreshments. Sun 25 Oct (2.30-4.30). Adm £3, chd free. For other opening times and information, please visit garden website.**
Small woodland garden of about 1½ acres created by plantsman, the late William Nourish. Trees, shrubs, bulbs and many interesting collections throughout the year. Since 1987, the garden has been maintained by 'The Friends of the Garden' on behalf of Ampthill Town Council. Mass plantings of snowdrops and early spring plants in February and beautiful autumn colours in October. Activity for children. Wheelchair access to most of the garden.

16 NEW LAKE END HOUSE

Mill Lane, Woburn Sands, Milton Keynes, MK17 8SP. Mr & Mrs G Barrett, 07831 110959, Geoffanddean@gmail.com. *Directions advised upon arrangement.* **Visits by arrangement May to Sept for groups of 20+. Light refreshemnts and guided tour. Adm £10.**
A large 3 acre lake created on a brown field site, provides sanctuary to a pair of black swans and large number of wild waterfowl. Beds adjacent to lake are planted with colourful perennials, shrubs and trees for yr-round interest. Larger garden sited above the house, with Japanese style ponds, bridges, tea house and rock formations, is further enhanced by several cloud pruned trees and shrubs. Owners, Davina and Geoff are also the inspirational couple who created the Flaxbourne fun garden which opens for the NGS separately.

17 40 LEIGHTON STREET

Woburn, MK17 9PH. Mr & Mrs Ron & Rita Chidley. *On main road leaving Woburn towards Leighton Buzzard. 500yds from centre of village L side of road. Last cottage in a row of 6.* **Sat 12 Sept (2-5). Adm £5, chd free. Home-made teas.**
Large cottage style garden in three parts. There are several 'rooms' with interesting features to explore and many quiet seating areas. There are perennials, climbers, vegetables, shrubs, trees and two ponds with fish. In September colour comes from late summer and autumn with dahlias, fuchsias and grasses and late flowering roses. Many pots and ornaments. Partial wheelchair access. Sorry no dogs.

18 LINDY LEA

Ampthill Road, Steppingley, Bedford, MK45 1AB. Roy & Linda Collins. *On Steppingley Rd between Flitwick & Ampthill. From E L off A507 Ampthill towards Steppingley or from M1 J13 turn R at Millbrook r'about then L at 1st r'about, 1st entrance past Steppingley Hospital entrance.* **Sun 21 June (2-5). Adm £4, chd free. Home-made teas.**
Set within an acre, this garden is a haven for wildlife with two water features, cottage garden style perennial plantings, variety of shrubs and mature trees. There is also a vegetable garden and a sunny terrace furnished with pots and climbers. Some paths may be difficult to negotiate. Sorry no dogs.

19 LUTON HOO HOTEL GOLF & SPA

The Mansion House, Luton Hoo, Luton, LU1 3TQ. Luton Hoo Hotel Golf & Spa, www.lutonhoo.co.uk. *Approx 1m from J10 M1, take London Rd A1081 signed Harpenden for approx ½ m - entrance on L for Luton Hoo Hotel Golf & Spa.* **Sun 26 July (11-4). Adm £5, chd free. Light refreshments. Visitors wishing to have lunch/formal afternoon tea at the hotel must book in advance directly with the hotel.**

The gardens and parkland designed by Capability Brown are of national historic significance and lie in a conservation area. Main features - lakes, woodland and pleasure grounds, Victorian grass tennis court and late C19 sunken rockery. Italianate garden with herbaceous borders and topiary garden. Gravel paths.

20 ◆ THE MANOR HOUSE, STEVINGTON

Church Road, Stevington, Bedford, MK43 7QB. Kathy Brown, www.kathybrownsgarden.com. *5m NW of Bedford. Off A428 through Bromham.* **For NGS: Mon 25 May (1-5). Adm £6, chd free. Home-made teas in Church Rooms next to car park. For other opening times and information, please visit garden website.**

The Manor House Garden has many different rooms, including six art inspired gardens. Early roses and wisteria along with several different Clematis montana will be festooning the walls and pergolas; foxgloves, poppies and peonies providing colour down below. Elsewhere avenues of white stemmed birches, gingko, eucalypts, and metasequoia will take the eye to further parts of the garden. Kathy plans an edible flower workshop followed by a talk on bees mid afternoon. Teas in aid of Sue Ryder. 85% wheelchair access. Disabled WC.

21 NEW MILL LANE GARDENS

Mill Lane, Greenfield, Bedford, MK45 5DG. Pat Rishton. *In the centre of Greenfield off High Street. From Flitwick, Mill Lane is on L in the centre of the village. Parking at the village hall further on, on the R. Room for disabled parking only at each house.* **Sun 28 June (1-5). Combined adm £5, chd free. Home-made teas at 69 Mill Lane.**

> **NEW 13 MILL LANE**
> Shirley Dickinson.

> **NEW 69 MILL LANE**
> Pat Rishton.

> **NEW 70 MILL LANE**
> Lesley Arthur.

Greenfield is an attractive and varied Bedfordshire village close to Flitwick and Ampthill. The village has houses of many different characteristics including several thatches and a recently refurbished village pub. Mill Lane was previously in the centre of a fruit growing area and was apparently famous for its strawberry fields. The three gardens are interesting and varied including cottage garden style perennials, courtyards, fruit gardens and ponds both ornamental and for wildlife. One includes the river Flit. Most of the gardens are accessible to wheelchairs but there are some steps, banks and gravel paths. Plenty of seating provided. 69 Mill Lane fully accessible while the other two are partially accessible. Sorry no dogs.

22 THE OLD RECTORY, WESTONING

Church Road, Westoning, MK45 5JW. Ann & Colin Davies. *2m S of Flitwick, 2m N of M1 J12. Off A5120, ¼ m up Church Rd, next to church.* **Sun 29 Mar, Sun 5 July (2-5.30). Adm £5, chd free. Delicious cream teas and other refreshments in C14 church next door.**

Ancient box and yew hedges surround the colour co-ordinated beds of this 2 acre garden. Spring is greeted by hellebores and daffodils with magnolias blooming in profusion. A rose garden and herbaceous borders complement the flowering trees and shrubs of summer with a stunning display of poppies and cornflowers in the meadow. Come and enjoy

Dragons Glen

the sights and smells of a traditional English garden. Wheelchair access generally good. Sorry no dogs.

23 THE OLD RECTORY, WRESTLINGWORTH

Church Lane, Wrestlingworth, Sandy, SG19 2EU. Josephine Hoy, 01767 631204, hoyjosephine@hotmail.co.uk. *5m E of Sandy, 5m NE of Biggleswade. Wrestlingworth is situated on B1042. 5m from Sandy & 6m from Biggleswade. The Old Rectory is at the top of Church Lane, which is well signed, behind the church.* **Sun 17, Sun 31 May (2-5.30). Adm £6, chd free. Home-made teas. Visits also by arrangement Apr to Sept for groups of 10 to 30.**
4 acre garden full of colour and interest. The owner has a free style of gardening sensitive to wildlife. Beds overflowing with tulips, alliums, bearded iris, peonies, poppies, geraniums and much more. Beautiful mature trees and many more planted in the last 30 years. Incl a large selection of betulas. Gravel gardens, box hedging and clipped balls, woodland garden and wild flower meadows. Wheelchair access maybe restricted to grass paths.

24 NEW RADS END FARM

Higher Rads End, Eversholt, Milton Keynes, MK17 9ED. Carolyn Howell. *If using satnav you may be told you have 'reached your destination' at a T junction, but you haven't. Turn L there. L round Sbend is our gate. Park in field.* **Sun 19 July (2-5). Adm £5, chd free. Home-made teas.**
A country garden with lawns and herbaceous borders surrounding the house. There are also a veg and fruit garden, water garden, bog garden and rough areas. Pergolas and sitting areas with quiet spots. Specimen trees of mulberry and medlar. Some gravel paths.

25 NEW ROYAL OAK COTTAGE

46 Wood End Road, Kempston Rural, Bedford, MK43 9BB. Teresa & Mike Clarke. *From Wood End lane turn L at the Cross Keys, no 46 is on the L after 400yds.* **Sun 21 June, Sun 2 Aug (1.30-5.30). Adm £5, chd free. Home-made teas.**
¾ acre garden created on the land of an old beer house, with wildlife in mind. There are old orchard trees, herbaceous beds, small oriental garden and a vegetable plot. A blue and white border surrounds an old renovated piggery building. Agapanthus and blue hydrangeas a patio speciality. Shallow ponds support newts and other amphibians. The wild flower meadow is Austrian scythed in August. A winding concrete path and grass paths through meadows. Sorry no dogs.

26 NEW 4 ST ANDREWS ROAD

Bedford, MK40 2LJ. David Meghen, 07710 404323, davidmeghen@aol.com. *1½ m from Bedford Station. From Ashburnham Rd, take the 3rd exit on Bromham Rd, 2nd L onto Union St, at the r'about take the 2nd exit on to Ruff St, at the r'about take 2nd exit on to Park Avenue.* **Sat 8 Aug (12-4.30). Combined adm with 1a St Augustine's Road £5, chd free. Home-made teas at 1a St Augustine's Rd. Visits also by arrangement May to Sept for groups of up to 10.**
An elegant, multi-functional urban garden set within a semi-formal layout featuring clipped beech hedges softened by colourful shrubs and perennials and a rose pergola. Focal points have been created to be enjoyed from both within the garden as well from the house.

27 1A ST AUGUSTINE'S ROAD

Bedford, MK40 2NB. Chris Bamforth Damp, 01234 353730/01234 353465, chrisdamp@mac.com. *St Augustine's Rd is on L off Kimbolton Rd as you leave the centre of Bedford.* **Sat 8 Aug (12-4.30). Combined adm with 4 St Andrews Road £5, chd free. Home-made teas. Visits also by arrangement June to Sept for groups of 10 to 30.**
A colourful town garden with herbaceous borders, climbers, a green house and pond. Planted in cottage garden style with traditional flowers, the borders overflow with late summer annuals and perennials including salvias and rudbeckia. The pretty terrace next to the house is lined with ferns and hostas. The owners also make home-made chutneys and preserves which can be purchased on the day. Featured in Garden News, June 2019. The garden is wheelchair accessible.

28 SECRET GARDEN

4 George Street, Clapham, Bedford, MK41 6AZ. Graham Bolton, 07746 864247, bolton_graham@hotmail.com. *3m N of Bedford (not the bypass). Clapham Village High St. R into Mount Pleasant Rd then L into George St. 1st white Bungalow on R.* **Sun 3 May (12.30-5.30). Adm £3.50, chd free. Light refreshments. Visits also by arrangement Apr & May for groups of 10 to 20.**
Profiled in the RHS The Garden, alpine lovers can see a wide collection of alpines in two small scree gardens, front and back of bungalow plus pans. Planting also incl dwarf salix, rhododendrons, daphnes, acers, conifers, pines, hellebores and epimediums. Two small borders of herbaceous salvias, lavenders and potentillas. Alpine greenhouse with rare varieties and cold frames with plants for sale. Partial wheelchair access. No access at the rear of property due to narrow gravel paths but garden can be viewed from the patio.

29 SOUTHILL PARK

Southill, nr Biggleswade, SG18 9LL. Mr & Mrs Charles Whitbread. *3m W of Biggleswade. In the village of Southill. 3m from A1 junction at Biggleswade.* **Sun 7 June (2-5). Adm £5, chd free. Cream teas.**
Southill Park first opened its gates to NGS visitors in 1927. A large garden with mature trees and flowering shrubs, herbaceous borders, a formal rose garden, sunken garden, ponds and kitchen garden. It is on the south side of the 1795 Palladian house. The parkland was designed by Lancelot 'Capability' Brown. A large conservatory houses the tropical collection and a new fernery was added in 2019.

We open the gates to the nation's best gardens, offering a relaxing, memorable and affordable day out. A perfect experience to share with friends and family.

30 STEPPINGLEY VILLAGE GARDENS

Steppingley, Bedford, MK45 5AT. *Follow signs to Steppingley, pick up yellow signs from village centre.* **Sun 24, Mon 25 May (2-5). Combined adm £6, chd free. Home-made teas at Townsend Farmhouse. Classic car show on Mon 25**

MIDDLE BARN
Bruce & Pauline Henninger.

NEW **37 RECTORY ROAD**
Bill & Julie Neilson.

TOP BARN
Tim & Nicky Kemp.

TOWNSEND FARMHOUSE
Hugh & Indi Jackson.
(See separate entry)

WEST OAK
John & Sally Eilbeck.
(See separate entry)

Steppingley is a picturesque Bedfordshire village on the Greensand ridge, close to Ampthill, Flitwick and Woburn. Although a few older buildings survive, most of Steppingley was built by 7th Duke of Bedford between 1840 and 1872. Five gardens in the village offer an interesting mix of planting styles and design to include pretty court yards, cottage garden style perennial borders, ponds, a Victorian well, glass houses, an orchard, vegetable gardens, a herb garden, wild life havens and country views. Live stock include chickens, ducks and fish. Long gravel driveway may be difficult for wheelchairs. Sorry no dogs.

  ♿ ✿ ☕

31 NEW 127 STOKE ROAD

Linslade, Leighton Buzzard, LU7 2SR. Steve Owen, 07973 318383. *Opposite the turn for Rothschild Road.* **Sat 1, Sun 2 Feb, Sat 2 May (10-4.30). Adm £5, chd free. Visits also by arrangement Jan to May for groups of up to 30.** The garden houses the National Collection of Galanthus (snowdrop), with nearly 2,000 different varieties. Most are grown in the garden setting but some specialised ones can be seen on display racks. There is a Japanese themed garden and a raised alpine bed. Other plants grown include daphnes and a collection of over 100 maple trees. The alpine house contains a collection of Primula allionii. Access with care. Sorry no dogs.

♿ NPC ☕

32 TOWNSEND FARMHOUSE

Rectory Road, Steppingley, Bedford, MK45 5AT. Hugh & Indi Jackson. *In Steppingley Village. Follow directions to Steppingley village and pick up yellow signs from village centre.* **Sun 26 Apr (2-5). Combined adm with West Oak £5, chd free. Home-made teas. Evening opening Sat 24 Oct (5.30-8). Light refreshments. Adm £5, chd free. Opening with Steppingley Village Gardens on Sun 24, Mon 25 May (2-5).** Tree lined driveway with young specimens and mature broad leaves rising above swathes of spring bulbs, narcissi, fritillaria, tulips, hyacinths and more. Planted for year round interest, the cottage-garden style herbaceous borders are filled with early perennials, bearded iris and alliums. Pretty cobbled courtyard with a glass house and a Victorian well 30 metres deep,

Lindy Lea

Royal Oak Cottage

viewed through a glass top. Sunday 27 October is a Diwali themed evening with lanterns, diya lamps and flower rangoli; bring a torch. Long gravelled driveway may be difficult for wheelchairs. Sorry no dogs.

❀ ☕

33 ◆ THE WALLED GARDEN

Luton, LU1 4LF. Luton Hoo Estate, www.lutonhooestate.co.uk. *Take A1081. Turn at West Hyde Road (signed for Newmill End). After approx 100 metres turn L through black gates. Follow red signs to Walled Garden.* **For NGS: Sat 15 Aug (9.30-12.30). Adm £5, chd free. Light refreshments. For other opening times and information, please visit garden website.**
The 5 acre Luton Hoo Estate Walled Garden was designed by Capability Brown and established by the notorious Lord Bute in the late 1760s. The Walled Garden now offers a unique opportunity to see conservation and restoration combined with outstanding volunteer involvement in action. The garden continues to be restored, repaired and reimagined for the enjoyment of all. Volunteer garden and local history experts on hand to explain and expand on what you see. An amazing cactus collection and original restored

prop houses. Exhibition of Victorian tools. Walled Garden Shop with ever changing seasonal produce, including our outstanding Estate honey. Disabled parking next to Walled Garden Entrance. A hard path goes through and around the garden.

♿ 🐕 ❀ 🚌 ☕

34 WALNUT COTTAGE

8 Great North Road, Chawston, MK44 3BD. Dave Parker, 07784 792975, dave.parkergnr@gmail.com. *2m S of St Neots. Between Wyboston & Blackcat r'about on S-bound lane of A1. Turn off at McDonalds, at end of filling station forecourt turn L. Off rd parking.* **Sat 18, Sun 19 July (2-6). Adm £5, chd free. Home-made teas. Visits also by arrangement Mar to Sept for groups of 10+.**
Once a land settlement and a 4 acre smallholding. This one acre cottage garden is an oasis of rare, unusual and exotic plants. The owner is a knowledgeable plantsman and has planted over 2000 species of bulbs, perennials, water and bog plants, ferns, grasses, shrubs and trees to give year round interest. Special features include, coppiced Paulownias, giant lilies and a pond. Level grass paths.

♿ 🐕 ❀ 🚌 ☕

35 WEST OAK

50 Rectory Road, Steppingley, Bedford, MK45 5AT. John & Sally Eilbeck. *Steppingley Village. Follow signs to Steppingley from A507 r'about between Ampthill & Flitwick, pick up yellow signs from centre of village.* **Sun 26 Apr (2-5). Combined adm with Townsend Farmhouse £5, chd free. Home-made teas at Townsend Farmhouse. Opening with Steppingley Village Gardens on Sun 24, Mon 25 May.**
An informal garden of approx ¾ acre with open countryside on two sides. It consists of lawns and shrubs with perennial planting including some mature trees.There is a herb garden, greenhouse, vegetable gardens with soft fruit, and small orchard with chickens. The garden has been developed over 30 years by the present owners from a completely bare plot. The garden is approached across a gravel drive and there are some steps. Sorry no dogs.

❀ ☕

BERKSHIRE

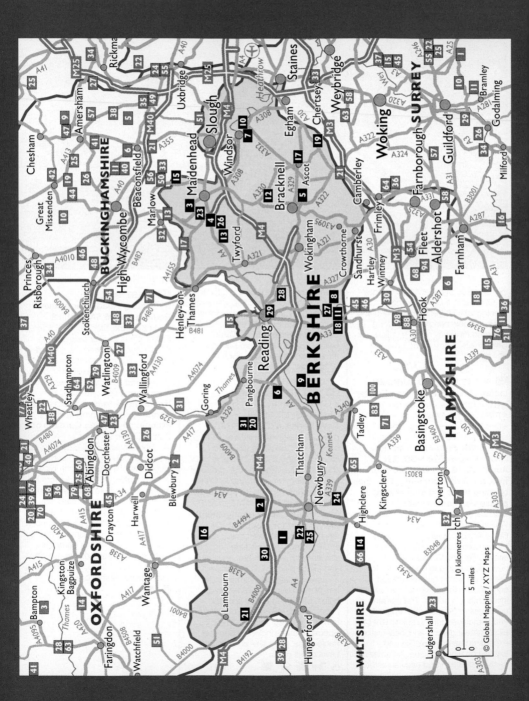

The Royal County of Berkshire offers a wonderful mix of natural beauty and historic landmarks that are reflected in the portfolio of gardens opening for the National Garden Scheme.

The Thames flows right through the county, passing picturesque towns and villages, many of which have beautiful gardens opening in 2020. Private gardens at famous places such as Windsor Castle and Eton College offer rare opportunities for visitors to enjoy gardens not normally open to the public. All are generously opened to raise funds for the nursing and caring charities we support.

Our gardens come in every shape, size and style, and some have been supporting us for many years. Do come along to help us celebrate 60 years of opening at Eton College on 6th June, and to congratulate Caroline and Michael Todhunter who have personally opened their garden at The Old Rectory, Farnborough near Wantage for 50 years (19th April, 17th May, 24th June).

If you are organising a group visit, please see our gardens open 'by arrangement', or if you would like someone locally to give a talk about the National Garden Scheme, contact Angela at angela.oconnell@icloud.com.

Some gardens may capture your interest due to their designers or their historic setting, while most have evolved thanks to the efforts of their enthusiastic owners. We think they all offer moments of inspiration and look forward to welcoming you at a garden soon.

Volunteers

County Organiser
Heather Skinner
01189 737197
heather.skinner@ngs.org.uk

County Treasurer
Hugh Priestley
01189 744349 Fri – Mon
hughpriestley@aol.com

Booklet Co-ordinator
Heather Skinner
(as above)

Talks & Group Visits
Angela O'Connell
01252 668645
angela.oconnell@icloud.com

Assistant County Organisers
Claire Fletcher
claire.fletcher@ngs.org.uk

Carolyn Foster
01628 624635
candrfoster@btinternet.com

Angela O'Connell
(as above)

Graham O'Connell
01252 668645
graham.oconnell22@gmail.com

Rebecca Thomas
01491 628302
rebecca.thomas@ngs.org.uk

Rachel West
07468 707491
rachel.west@ngs.org.uk

f @BerksNationalGardenScheme
🐦 @BerksNGS

© Sussie Bell

Left: The Old Rectory, Farnborough

OPENING DATES

All entries subject to change. For latest information check www.ngs.org.uk
Map locator numbers are shown to the right of each garden name.

February

Snowdrop Festival

Wednesday 5th
◆ Welford Park 30

March

Saturday 7th
Stubbings House 26

Sunday 8th
Stubbings House 26

April

Sunday 19th
Odney Club 15
The Old Rectory, Farnborough 16

Wednesday 22nd
Rooksnest 21

Sunday 26th
Rookwood Farm House 22

Wednesday 29th
Malverleys 14

May

See www.ngs.org.uk for details
◆ Frogmore House & Garden 10

Sunday 10th
Sandleford Place 24

Saturday 16th
Stubbings House 26

Sunday 17th
The Old Rectory, Farnborough 16
Stubbings House 26

Monday 25th
Rookwood Farm House 22

Sunday 31st
Stockcross House 25

June

Saturday 6th
Eton College Gardens 7

Sunday 14th
Farley Hill Place Gardens 8

Sunday 21st
Chieveley Manor 2
Pyt House 20
Willow Tree Cottage 31

Wednesday 24th
The Old Rectory, Farnborough 16
Rooksnest 21

Sunday 28th
Sandleford Place 24
Swallowfield Village Gardens 27

July

Wednesday 1st
Lower Lovetts Farm 13

Sunday 5th
St Timothee 23
NEW Watlington House, Geoff Hill Memorial Garden 29

Wednesday 8th
Lower Lovetts Farm 13

Wednesday 15th
Malverleys 14

Sunday 26th
NEW Jealott's Hill Community Landshare 12

August

Wednesday 5th
St Timothee 23

Monday 31st
Rookwood Farm House 22

September

Sunday 6th
Stockcross House 25

October

Thursday 29th
St Timothee 23

By Arrangement

Arrange a personalised garden visit with your club, or group of friends, on a date to suit you. See individual garden entries for full details.

Boxford House 1
Compton Elms 3
Deepwood Stud Farm 4
Devonia 5
Farley Hill Place Gardens 8
Handpost 11
Old Waterfield 17
The Priory 18
Priory House 19
Rooksnest 21
Rookwood Farm House 22
St Timothee 23
Sandleford Place 24
NEW 7 The Knapp 28

Eton College Gardens

THE GARDENS

Deepwood Stud Farm

❶ BOXFORD HOUSE

Boxford, Newbury, RG20 8DP.
Tammy Darvell, Head
Gardener, 07802 883084,
tammydarvell@hotmail.com. *4m
NW of Newbury. Directions will be
provided on booking.* **Visits by
arrangement May to Sept for
groups of 20+. Adm £10, chd
free. Guided tour & refreshments
included.**
Beautiful large family garden
extensively developed over the
past 7 yrs. Emphasis on roses and
scent throughout the 5 acre main
garden. Old and new orchards,
laburnum tunnel, formal and colourful
herbaceous borders. Handsome
formal terraces, pond, water features
and garden woodland areas. Inviting
cottage garden and productive
vegetable gardens. Partial wheelchair
access, gravel paths and sloping
lawns.

❷ CHIEVELEY MANOR

Chieveley, Nr Newbury, RG20 8UT.
Mr & Mrs CJ Spence. *5m N of
Newbury. From M4 J13, follow signs
for A34 N & immed keep L on to slip
road for Chieveley. At T-junction turn
L into village, after ½ m turn L into
Manor Lane.* **Sun 21 June (2-5).
Adm £5, chd free. Home-made
teas in the adjacent church.
Donation to St Mary's Church,
Chieveley.**
Large garden surrounding listed
house (not open) in the heart of
Chieveley village. Attractive setting
with fine views over stud farm.
Walled garden containing lovely
borders, shrubs and rose garden,
evolving every year. Box parterre
filled with alliums, white geraniums
and lavender. Many viticella clematis
growing through shrubs.

❸ COMPTON ELMS

Marlow Road, Pinkneys Green,
Maidenhead, SL6 6NR. Alison
Kellett, kellettaj@gmail.com.
*Situated at the end of a gravel road
located opp & in between the Arbour
& Golden Ball pubs on the A308.*
**Visits by arrangement Feb to Apr
for groups of 10 to 30. Adm £7.50,
chd free. Refreshments by prior
request.**
A delightful spring garden set
in a sunken woodland, lovingly
recovered from clay pit workings.
The atmospheric garden is filled with
snowdrops, primroses, hellebores and
fritillaria, interspersed with anemone
and narcissi under a canopy of ash
and beech.

❹ DEEPWOOD STUD FARM

Henley Road, Stubbings, Nr
Maidenhead, SL6 6QW. Mr &
Mrs E Goodwin, 01628 822684,
ed.goodwin@deepwood.co.
*2m W of Maidenhead. M4 J8/9
take A404M N. 2nd exit for A4 to
Maidenhead. L at 1st r'about on
A4130 Henley, approx 1m on R.*
**Visits by arrangement Apr to Sept
for groups of 10+. Adm £4.50,
chd free. Refreshments by prior
request.**
4 acres of formal and informal
gardens within a stud farm, so great
roses! Small lake with Monet style
bridge and 3 further water features.
Several neo-classical follies and
statues. Walled garden with windows
cut in to admire the views and horses.
Woodland walk and enough hanging
baskets to decorate a pub! Partial
wheelchair access.

❺ DEVONIA

Broad Lane, Bracknell,
RG12 9BH. Andrew Radgick,
aradgick@btinternet.com. *1m S
of Bracknell. From A322 Horse &
Groom r'about take exit into Broad
Lane, over 2 r'abouts. 3rd house
on L after railway bridge.* **Visits
by arrangement Aug & Sept for
groups of 5 to 20. Adm £5, chd
free.**
Inspirational urban garden, planted for
all season interest with many plants
that survive regardless of the weather,
both current and with climate change
in mind. Contains traditional borders,
prairie planting, and areas with foliage
effects. With three different soil types
and many aspects, this ⅓ acre
garden offers lots of ideas. Particularly
interesting for gardening groups, with
optional guided tour.

6 ◆ ENGLEFIELD HOUSE GARDEN

Englefield, Theale, Reading, RG7 5EN. Mr & Mrs Richard Benyon, 01189 302221, peter.carson@englefield.co.uk, www.englefieldestate.co.uk. *6m W of Reading. M4 J12. Take A4 towards Theale. 2nd r'about take A340 to Pangbourne. After ⅙m entrance on the L.* **For opening times and information, please phone, email or visit garden website.**

The 12 acre garden descends dramatically from the hill above the historic house through woodland where mature native trees mix with Victorian conifers. Drifts of spring and summer planting are followed by striking autumn colour. Stone balustrades enclose the lower terrace, with wide lawns, roses, mixed borders and topiary. Open every Monday from Apr-Sept (10am-6pm) and Oct-Mar (10am-4pm). Please check Englefield website for any changes before travelling. Wheelchair access to some parts of the gardens.

7 ETON COLLEGE GARDENS

Eton, Nr Windsor, SL4 6DB. Eton College. *½m N of Windsor. Parking signed off B3022, Slough Rd. Walk from car park across playing fields to entry. Follow signs for tickets & maps which are sold at gazebo near entrance.* **Sat 6 June (2-5). Adm £6, chd free. Home-made teas in the Fellows Garden.**

A rare chance to visit a group of central College gardens surrounded by historic school buildings, including Luxmoore's garden on a small island in the Thames reached across two attractive bridges. Also an opportunity to explore the fascinating Eton College Natural History Museum and the Museum of Eton Life, and a small group of other private gardens. Plant Sale at Warre House. Sorry, the gardens are not suitable for wheelchairs due to gravel, steps and uneven ground.

8 FARLEY HILL PLACE GARDENS

Church Road, Farley Hill, Reading, RG7 1TZ. Tony & Margaret Finch, 01189 762544, tony.finch7@btinternet.com. *From M4 J11, take A33 S to Basingstoke. At T-lights turn L for Spencers Wood, B3349. Continue 2m, turn L through Swallowfield towards Farley Hill. Garden ½m on R.* **Sun 14 June (2-5). Adm £5, chd free. Home-made teas. Visits also by arrangement June & July for groups of 10+.**

A 4 acre, C18 cottage garden. 1½ acre walled garden with yr-round interest and colour. Well stocked herbaceous borders, large productive vegetable areas with herb garden, dahlia and cutting flower beds. Enjoy wandering around the garden, with spontaneous singing from a Barber's Shop Quartet. Victorian glasshouse recently renovated and small nursery. Plants, lovely cut flowers and produce for sale. Partial wheelchair access.

9 FOLLY FARM

Sulhamstead Hill, Sulhamstead, RG7 4DG. *7m SW of Reading. From A4 between Reading & Newbury (2m W of M4 J12) take road to Sulhamstead at The Spring Inn. Restricted car parking.* **Visits by arrangement for groups up to 12 max. Adm £27.50. Home-made teas. Pre-booking essential, please visit www.ngs.org.uk/ events for information & booking.**

Gardens laid out in 1912 by Sir Edwin Lutyens and Gertrude Jekyll. Garden designs evolved during culmination of their partnership and considered one of their most complex. Extensively restored and replanted by current owners assisted by Dan Pearson. Recently reopened for private small group visits which include approx 1½ hour guided tour and tea and home-made cake. Very limited availability. Please note paths are uneven and there are many sets of steps between areas of the garden. Sorry no children or dogs.

St Timothee

10 ◆ FROGMORE HOUSE & GARDEN

Windsor, SL4 1LU. Her Majesty The Queen. *1m SE of Windsor. Enter via Park Street gate into Long Walk to car parking. Visiting the garden involves 10-15 min walk from Long Walk entrance.* **Pre-booking recommended, please visit www. ngs.org.uk/events for information & booking. Light refreshments. Picnics welcome.**

The private royal garden at Frogmore House on the Crown Estate at Windsor. This beautiful landscaped garden, set in 35 acres with notable trees, lawns, flowering shrubs and C18 lake, is rich in history. It is largely the creation of Queen Charlotte, who in the 1790s introduced over 4,000 trees and shrubs to create a model picturesque landscape. The historic plantings, including tulip trees and redwoods, along with Queen Victoria's Tea House, remain key features of the garden today. The Royal Mausoleum is closed due to long term restoration. Tickets for the garden and also to visit the house are available on the day, cash payment only. House visits with timed tickets are managed by the Royal Collection Trust and may sell out. Wheelchair access is difficult due to gravel paths. Please note Windsor traffic may be halted around 11am for Guard change.

11 HANDPOST

Basingstoke Road, Swallowfield, Reading, RG7 1PU. Faith Ramsay, faith@mycountrygarden.co.uk, www.mycountrygarden.co.uk. *From M4 J11, take A33 S. At 1st T-lights turn L on B3349 Basingstoke Rd. Follow road for 2¾m, garden on L.* **Visits by arrangement May to Sept for groups of 10+. Adm £6.50. Home-made teas.**

4 acre designer's garden with many areas of interest. Features incl two lovely long herbaceous borders attractively and densely planted in six colour sections, a formal rose garden, an old orchard with a grass meadow, pretty pond and peaceful wooded area. Large variety of plants, trees and a productive fruit and vegetable patch. Some gravel areas but largely accessible.

12 NEW JEALOTT'S HILL COMMUNITY LANDSHARE

Wellers Lane, Warfield, Bracknell, RG42 6BQ. David Putt, www. jealottshilllandshare.org.uk. *Enter Wellers Lane off the A330, 1st gateway on R across junction with Penfurzen Lane.* **Sun 26 July (10-4). Adm £4.50, chd free. Light refreshments.**

Jealott's Hill Community Landshare is an inspirational 6 acre multi-purpose community garden. The gardens are tended by the whole local community. The site offers various horticultural activities as well as creating a haven for wildlife. Along with 2 acres of cultivated ground there is a 2 acre wildflower meadow, sensory garden, vineyard and a 450 tree orchard. Wheelchair access to most of the site, please phone 07867 695931 with any queries.

13 LOWER LOVETTS FARM

Knowl Hill Common, Knowl Hill, RG10 9YE. Richard Sandford. *5m W of Maidenhead. Turn S off A4 at Knowl Hill Church into Knowl Hill Common. Past pub & across common to T-junction. Turn L down dead end lane.* **Wed 1, Wed 8 July (10.30-1). Adm £12, chd free. Pre-booking essential, please visit www.ngs.org.uk/events for information & booking. Coffee, tea & cake included.**

A fascinating large modern organic kitchen garden (60m x 30m) with a wildflower meadow and herbaceous border. Wide variety of vegetables and fruit grown for all year-round home consumption and nutritional value. Flowers grown for eating or herbal teas. Lots of interesting growing techniques and tips. Join Richard Sandford for a 'Talk & Walk' event to learn about this amazing garden and how his plant-based diet influences his growing methods. Limited availability so please book early to avoid disappointment.

14 MALVERLEYS

Fullers Lane, East End, Newbury, RG20 0AA. *A34 S of Newbury, exit signed for Highclere. Follow A343 for ½m, turn R to Woolton Hill. Pass school & turn L to East End. After 1m R at village green, then after 100 metres, R onto Fullers Lane.* **Wed 29 Apr, Wed 15 July. Adm £15, chd free. Pre-booking essential, please visit www.ngs.org.uk/**

events for information & booking. Visits are by guided tours at 10.30am, 1pm or 3pm with tea & cake included. Availability is limited, please book early to avoid disappointment.

10 acres of dynamic gardens which have been developed over the last 8 yrs to include magnificent mixed borders and a series of contrasting yew hedged rooms, hosting flame borders, a cool garden, a pond garden and new stumpery. A vegetable garden with striking fruit cages sit within a walled garden, also encompassing a white garden. Meadows open out to views over the parkland. Due to steps and uneven paths, the garden is not suitable for wheelchairs.

15 ODNEY CLUB

Odney Lane, Cookham, SL6 9SR. John Lewis Partnership. *3m N of Maidenhead. Off A4094 S of Cookham Bridge. Signs to car park in grounds.* **Sun 19 Apr (2-6). Adm £5, chd free. Light refreshments.**

This 120 acre site is beside the Thames with lovely riverside walks. A favourite with Stanley Spencer who featured our magnolia in his work. Lovely wisteria, specimen trees, side gardens, spring bedding and ornamental lake. The John Lewis Partnership Heritage Centre will be open, showcasing the textile archive and items illustrating the history of John Lewis and Waitrose. Light refreshments in the Sir Bernard Miller Centre from 2-5pm (Guide dogs only). Wheelchair access with some gravel paths. Dogs on leads please.

Your visits help change lives – since 1927, we've donated over £60 million to nursing and caring charities

16 THE OLD RECTORY, FARNBOROUGH

Nr Wantage, Oxon, OX12 8NX. **Mr & Mrs Michael Todhunter, 01488 638298.** *4m SE of Wantage. Take B4494 Wantage-Newbury road, after 4m turn E at sign for Farnborough. Approx 1m to village, Old Rectory on L.* **Sun 19 Apr, Sun 17 May (2-5); Wed 24 June (11-4). Adm £5, chd free. Home-made teas. Donation to Farnborough PCC.**

In a series of immaculately tended garden rooms, incl herbaceous borders, arboretum, secret garden, roses, vegetables and bog garden, there is an explosion of rare and interesting plants, beautifully combined for colour and texture. Regional Finalist, The English Garden's The Nation's Favourite Gardens 2019. With stunning views across the countryside, it is the perfect setting for the 1749 rectory (not open), once home of John Betjeman, in memory of whom John Piper created a window in the local church. Plants and preserves for sale. Access over some steep slopes and gravel paths.

17 OLD WATERFIELD

Winkfield Road, Ascot, SL5 7LJ. **Hugh & Catherine Stevenson, catherine.stevenson@ oldwaterfield.com.** *6m SW of Windsor to E of Ascot Racecourse. On E side of A330 midway between A329 & A332.* **Visits by arrangement May to Sept for groups of 10 to 20. Adm £4.50, chd free. Home-made teas by prior request.**

Set in 4 acres between Ascot Heath and Windsor Great Park, the original cottage garden has been developed and extended over the past few years. Herbaceous borders, meadow with specimen trees, large productive vegetable garden, orchard and mixed hedging.

18 THE PRIORY

Beech Hill, RG7 2BJ. **Mr & Mrs C Carter, 07957 151534, ljcbryan@gmail.com.** *5m S of Reading. M4 J11, A33 S to Basingstoke. At T-lights, L to Spencers Wood. After 1½m turn R for Beech Hill. After approx 1½m, L into Wood Lane, R down Priory Drive.* **Visits by arrangement May & June for groups of 10 to 30.**

Tea, coffee & cake included. **Adm £10, chd free.**

Extensive gardens in grounds of former C12 French Priory (not open), rebuilt 1648. The mature gardens are in a very attractive setting beside the River Loddon. Large formal walled garden with espalier fruit trees, lawns, mixed and replanted herbaceous borders, vegetables and roses. Woodland, fine trees, lake and Italian style water garden. A lovely garden for group visits.

19 PRIORY HOUSE

Priory Road, Sunningdale, Ascot, SL5 9RQ. **Mrs J Leigh, 07973 746979, rio4jen@gmail.com.** *Approx 4½m SE of Ascot. Take turning opp Waitrose, Ridgemount Rd. Turn 1st L into Priory Rd. Priory House located at end of road. Parking for 15 cars.* **Visits by arrangement May to Sept for groups of 10 to 30. Sorry, no visits in June. Adm £10, chd free. Tea & home-made cake included.**

3 acre garden designed in 1930s by Percy Cane with yr-round interest, colour and fragrance. Ornamental pond, large lawn with shrub borders, yew hedges and rare trees. Lavish borders, vegetable garden, rose garden, rhododendrons, azaleas, daphne, gunnera and Lysichiton americanus by stream. Mature camellias, magnolias, fine shrubs and conifers. A truly exuberant and fragrant, rather than manicured, garden.

20 PYT HOUSE

Ashampstead, RG8 8RA. **Edward & Sarah Ross.** *4m W of Pangbourne. From Yattendon, head towards Reading. Road forks L into a beech wood towards Ashampstead. Keep L & join lower road. ½m turn L after long fence before houses.* **Sun 21 June (2-5). Combined adm with Willow Tree Cottage £5, chd free. Home-made teas in the barn.**

A 4 acre garden planted over the last 10 yrs, around C18 house (not open). Mature trees, yew, hornbeam and beech hedges, pleached limes, modern perennial borders, iris beds, pond, orchard and vegetable garden. Broadly organic, a haven for bees and butterflies, and we also have chickens.

21 ROOKSNEST

Ermin Street, Lambourn Woodlands, RG17 7SB. **garden@rooksnest.net.** *2m S of Lambourn on B4000. From M4 J14, take A338 Wantage Rd, turn 1st L onto B4000 (Ermin St). Rooksnest signed after 3m.* **Wed 22 Apr, Wed 24 June (11-4). Adm £6, chd free. Light refreshments. Last entry 3.30pm. Visits also by arrangement Apr to June for groups of 20 to 30.**

Approx 10 acre, exceptionally fine traditional English garden. Rose garden (redesigned 2017), herbaceous garden, pond garden, herb garden, fruit, vegetable and cutting garden, and glasshouses. Many specimen trees and fine shrubs, orchard and terraces. Garden mostly designed by Arabella Lennox-Boyd. Most areas have step-free access, although surface consists of gravel and mowed grass.

22 ROOKWOOD FARM HOUSE

Stockcross, Newbury, RG20 8JX. **The Hon Rupert & Charlotte Digby, 01488 608676, charlotte@rookwoodhouse.co.uk, www.rookwoodhouse.co.uk.** *3m W of Newbury. M4 J13, A34(S). After 3m exit for A4(W) to Hungerford. At 2nd r'about take B4000 towards Stockcross, after approx ¾m turn R into Rookwood.* **Sun 26 Apr, Mon 25 May, Mon 31 Aug (11-5). Adm £5, chd free. Light refreshments. Visits also by arrangement Apr to Sept for groups of 10+.**

This exciting valley garden, a work in progress, has elements all visitors can enjoy. A rose covered pergola, fabulous tulips, giant alliums, and a recently developed jungle garden with cannas, bananas and echiums. A kitchen garden features a parterre of raised beds, which along with a bog garden and colour themed herbaceous planting, all make Rookwood well worth a visit. Wheelchair access with gravel paths, steps and some steep slopes.

23 ST TIMOTHEE

Darlings Lane, Maidenhead, SL6 6PA. **Sarah & Sal Pajwani, 07976 892667, pajwanisarah@gmail.com.** *1m N of Maidenhead. M4 J8/9 to A404M. 3rd exit onto A4 to Maidenhead. L at 1st r'about to A4130 Henley Rd. After ½m turn R onto Pinkneys Drive. At*

Pinkneys Arms Pub, turn L into Lee Lane, follow NGS signs. **Sun 5 July (11-4.30). Adm £4.50, chd free. Also, 'Talk & Walk' events on Wed 5 Aug, Thur 29 Oct (10.30-12.30). Adm £15. Pre-booking essential, please visit www.ngs.org.uk/ events for information & booking. Home-made teas. Visits also by arrangement May to Aug for groups of 10+.**
Colour themed borders planted for yr-round interest with a wide range of attractive grasses and perennials. Includes a box parterre, wildlife pond, rose terrace, wild areas and mature trees, all set within the 2 acre plot of a 1930s house. Our pre-ticketed 'Talk and Walk' events are planned for Aug (Successional Planting) and Oct (Grasses and the Autumn Garden).
&. ✿ Ⓓ ☕

24 SANDLEFORD PLACE
Newtown, Newbury, RG20 9AY. Mel Gatward, 01635 40726, melgatward@btinternet.com. *House is on A339. 1½m S of Newbury on NW side of Swan r'about at Newtown. Please slow down on approach. Turn L into parking via field gate 50yds beyond entrance.* **Sun 10 May, Sun 28 June (2-6). Adm £5, chd free. Home-made teas.** *Visits also*

by arrangement Apr to Sept for groups of 10+. For group bookings more than a month in advance pre-payment is requested.
A plantswoman's 4 acres, more exuberant than manicured with River Enborne flowing through. Various areas of shrub and mixed borders create a romantic, naturalistic effect. Wonderful old walled garden. Long herbaceous border flanks wildflower meadow. Yr-round interest from early carpets of snowdrops and daffodils, crocus covered lawn, to autumn berries and leaf colour. A garden for all seasons. Guide dogs only.
&. ✿ 🚐 ☕

25 STOCKCROSS HOUSE
Church Road, Stockcross, Newbury, RG20 8LP. Susan & Edward Vandyk. *3m W of Newbury. M4 J13, A34(S). After 3m exit A4(W) to Hungerford. At 2nd r'about take B4000, 1m to Stockcross, 2nd L into Church Rd.* **Sun 31 May, Sun 6 Sept (1-5). Adm £5, chd free. Home-made teas.**
A delightful 2 acre garden set around a Grade II listed former rectory (not open), with an emphasis on naturalistic planting. Romantic wisteria and clematis covered pergola, reflecting pond with folly. New greenhouse. Vegetable garden,

orangery with vines, pond with cascade and small stumpery with ferns. Sculptural elements by local artists. Plants from garden for sale. Partial wheelchair access with some gravelled areas.
&. ✿ ☕

26 STUBBINGS HOUSE
Stubbings Lane, Henley Road, Maidenhead, SL6 6QL. Mr & Mrs D Good, www.stubbingsnursery.co.uk. *2m W of Maidenhead. From A404(M) W of Maidenhead, exit at A4 r'about & follow signs to Maidenhead. At the small r'about turn L towards Stubbings. Take the next L onto Stubbings Lane.* **Sat 7, Sun 8 Mar, Sat 16, Sun 17 May (10-4). Adm £3.50, chd free.**
Parkland garden accessed via adjacent retail nursery. Set around C18 house (not open), home to Queen Wilhelmina of Netherlands in WW2. Large lawn with ha-ha and woodland walks. Notable trees incl historic Cedars and Araucaria. March brings an abundance of daffodils and in May a 60 metre wall of wisteria. Attractions incl a C18 icehouse and access to adjacent NT woodland. Refreshments available in onsite Café. Wheelchair access to a level site with firm gravel paths.
&. 🐕 ✿ ☕

Malverleys

GROUP OPENING

27 SWALLOWFIELD VILLAGE GARDENS

The Street, Swallowfield, **RG7 1QY**. *5m S of Reading. From M4 J11 take A33 S. At 1st T-lights turn L on B3349 signed Swallowfield. In the village follow signs for parking. Purchase tickets & map in Swallowfield Medical Practice car park, opp Crown Pub.* **Sun 28 June (2-5.30). Combined adm £7, chd free. Home-made teas at Brambles.**

5 BEEHIVE COTTAGE
Ray Tormey.

BRAMBLES
Sarah & Martyn Dadds.

BROOKSIDE NURSERY
David Maskell.

5 CURLYS WAY
Carolyn & Gary Clark.

THE FIRS
Harmi Kandohla & Mark Binns.

GREENWINGS
Liz & Ray Jones.

NORKETT COTTAGE
Jenny Spencer.

PRIMROSE COTTAGE
Hilda Phillips.

WESSEX HOUSE
Val Payne.

This year Swallowfield is offering 9 gardens to visit. A number are in the village itself, others are nearby, so there is a mix of walking to some, with those in different directions needing a car or bicycle to reach them comfortably. Whilst each provides its own character and interest, they all nestle in countryside by the Whitewater, Blackwater and Loddon rivers with an abundance of wildlife and lovely views. The garden owners, many of whom are members of the local Horticultural Society, are always happy to chat and share their enthusiasm and experience. Plants for sale. Wheelchair access to many gardens, some have slopes and uneven ground.

Pyt House

28 NEW **7 THE KNAPP**
Earley, Reading, RG6 7DD.
Mrs Ann McKie, 07881 451708,
annmckie@hotmail.co.uk.
*Directions & parking details will
be provided on booking.* **Visits
by arrangement June & July
for groups of 10 to 20. Adm £8.
Home-made teas included.**
A mature garden of third of an acre,
surrounded by tress and divided into
rooms with lawns, mixed borders,
gravel area with box hedging, pond
and an area with natural planting
where beehives are situated. The
garden provides interest for most
of the year, but the highlights are
the David Austen roses, particularly
rambling roses covering sheds,
arches and climbing into the trees.
Wheelchair access across an area
of gravel.

♿ 🐕 ☕

29 NEW **WATLINGTON HOUSE,
GEOFF HILL MEMORIAL
GARDEN**
44 Watlington Street,
Reading, RG1 4RJ.
www.watlingtonhouse.org.uk.
*Limited car parking on site via South
St. Public car parks at Oracle &
Queen's Rd, approx 10 mins walk.*
**Sun 5 July (10.30-5). Adm £3.50,
chd free. Light refreshments.**

An attractive walled garden at
Watlington House, a Grade II *
property, recreated since 2012 using
archival research on site of previous
car park. Clipped panel-pleached
hornbeam, box hedging and pruned
fruit trees give formal structure within
a quadrangle design. Featuring
a shade walk, knot garden, and
colourful herbaceous planting, it
is a calm oasis in a bustling town.
Beautiful flint and brick walled
surround. House dating back to
Medieval times with Jacobean and
Georgian facades. Wheelchair access
to garden on gravel topped paths, but
no access to buildings and WC.

❀ ☕

30 ◆ **WELFORD PARK**
Welford, Newbury, RG20 8HU.
Mrs J H Puxley, 01488 608691,
snowdrops@welfordpark.co.uk,
www.welfordpark.co.uk. *6m NW
of Newbury. M4 J13, A34(S). After
3m exit for A4(W) to Hungerford. At
2nd r'about take B4000, after 4m
turn R signed Welford. Entrance on
Newbury-Lambourn road.* **For NGS:
Wed 5 Feb (11-4). Adm £8, chd
£4. Light refreshments. For other
opening times and information,
please phone, email or visit garden
website.**

One of the finest natural snowdrop
woodlands in the country, approx 4
acres, along with a wonderful display
of hellebores throughout the garden
and winter flowering shrubs. This is
an NGS 1927 pioneer garden on the
River Lambourn set around Queen
Anne House (not open). Also the
stunning setting for Great British Bake
Off 2014 - 2019. Dogs welcome on
leads. Coach parties please book in
advance.

♿ 🐕 🚍 ☕

31 **WILLOW TREE COTTAGE**
Ashampstead, RG8 8RA. Katy
& David Weston. *4m W of
Pangbourne. From Yattendon, head
towards Reading. Road forks L into
beech wood to Ashampstead. Keep
L & join lower road. ½m turn L after
long fence just before houses.* **Sun
21 June (2-5). Combined adm
with Pyt House £5, chd free.
Home-made teas at Pyt House.**
Small pretty cottage garden
surrounding the house (not open) that
was originally built for the gardener of
Pyt House. Substantially redesigned
and replanted in recent yrs. Perennial
borders, vegetable garden, pond
with ducks and chickens. Most of the
garden is accessible by wheelchair.

♿ ❀ ☕

Watlington House, Geoff Hill Memorial Garden

BUCKINGHAMSHIRE

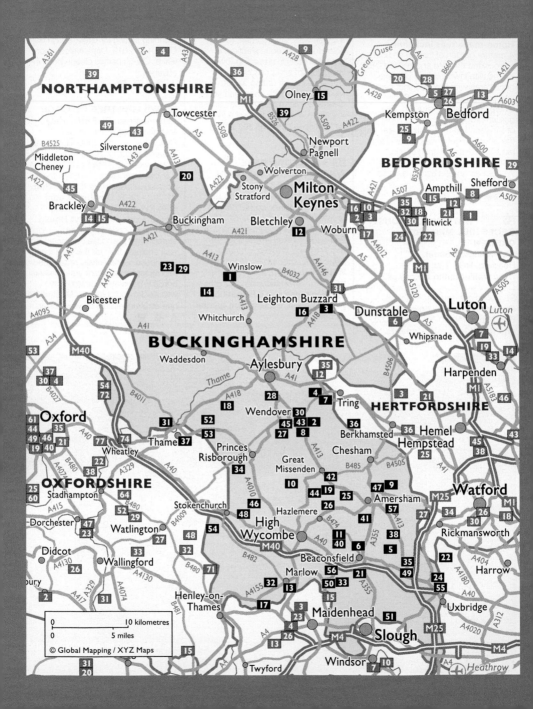

Buckinghamshire has a beautiful and varied landscape; edged by the River Thames to the south, crossed by the Chiltern Hills, and with the Vale of Aylesbury stretching to the north.

This year Buckinghamshire will hold six group openings, many of which can be found in villages of thatched or brick and flint cottages.

Many Buckinghamshire gardens have been used as locations for films and television, with the Pinewood Studios nearby and excellent proximity to London.

We also boast historical gardens including Ascott, Cowper and Newton Museum Gardens, Hall Barn, and Stoke Poges Memorial Gardens (Grade I listed).

Most of our gardens offer homemade tea and cakes to round off a lovely afternoon, visitors can leave knowing they have enjoyed a wonderful visit and helped raise money for nursing and health charities at the same time.

Volunteers

County Organiser
Maggie Bateson
01494 866265
maggiebateson@gmail.com

County Treasurer
Tim Hart
01494 837328
timgc.hart@btinternet.com

Publicity
Sandra Wetherall
01494 862264
sandracwetherall@gmail.com

Booklet Co-ordinator
Maggie Bateson
(as above)

Assistant County Organisers
Janice Cross
01494 728291
janice.cross@ngs.org.uk

Christine D'Netto
christine.dnetto@ngs.org.uk

Judy Hart
01494 837328
judy.elgood@gmail.com

Margaret Higgins
01844 347072
margarethiggins358@gmail.com

Mhairi Sharpley
01494 782870
mhairisharpley@btinternet.com

Stella Vaines
07711 420621
stella@bakersclose.com

 @BucksNGS
 @BucksNGS
 @national_garden_scheme_bucks

Left: 8 Claremont Road

OPENING DATES

All entries subject to change. For latest information check www.ngs.org.uk

Map locator numbers are shown to the right of each garden name.

February

Snowdrop Festival

Saturday 15th
Hollydyke House   25

Sunday 16th
Hollydyke House   25

March

Sunday 22nd
Chesham Bois House   9
Higher Denham
  Gardens   22

April

Sunday 12th
Overstroud Cottage   42

Monday 13th
Rivendell   47

Sunday 19th
Dinton Village
  Gardens   18

Sunday 26th
Aston Clinton Gardens   4
Horatio's Garden   28
Long Crendon
  Gardens   31
Orchard House   41

May

Sunday 10th
◆ Nether Winchendon
  House   37
The Plough   45
Turn End   52

Tuesday 12th
Red Kites   46

Sunday 17th
Overstroud Cottage   42

Sunday 24th
Abbots House   1
Fressingwood   19
Lindengate   30

Monday 25th
◆ Ascott   3
The Claydons   14
Glebe Farm   20
The Plough   45

Sunday 31st
Higher Denham
  Gardens   22
The Manor House   34

June

Sunday 7th
Cublington Gardens   16
Dinton Village
  Gardens   18
Tythrop Park   53
The White House   55

Friday 12th
The Walled Garden   54

Saturday 13th
◆ Cowper & Newton
  Museum Gardens   15
Woodside   57

Sunday 14th
126 Church Green
  Road   12
◆ Cowper & Newton
  Museum Gardens   15
Long Crendon
  Gardens   31
Overstroud Cottage   42
◆ Stoke Poges
  Memorial Gardens   51
Woodside   57

Tuesday 16th
126 Church Green
  Road   12

Thursday 18th
Lords Wood   32

Saturday 20th
Acer Corner   2
NEW Mead Cottage   35
Orchard House   41
11 The Paddocks   43

Sunday 21st
Acer Corner   2
18 Brownswood Road   6
Hillesden House   23
11 The Paddocks   43
NEW Robin Hill   48

Friday 26th
11 The Paddocks   43

Sunday 28th
Aston Clinton Gardens   4
NEW Canal Cottage   7
NEW Chiltern Forage
  Farm   10
Old Park Barn   39

July

Saturday 4th
11 The Paddocks   43
St Michaels Convent   49

Sunday 5th
NEW The Chinnery   11
NEW Oldfields   40
11 The Paddocks   43

Tuesday 14th
Red Kites   46

Wednesday 22nd
NEW 8 Claremont
  Road   13

Saturday 25th
NEW 8 Claremont
  Road   13

Sunday 26th
NEW 8 Claremont
  Road   13

August

Wednesday 5th
Danesfield House   17

Sunday 30th
◆ Nether Winchendon
  House   37

Monday 31st
◆ Ascott   3

September

Saturday 5th
NEW 8 Claremont
  Road   13

Sunday 6th
NEW 8 Claremont
  Road   13
Lindengate   30

By Arrangement

Arrange a personalised garden visit with your club, or group of friends, on a date to suit you. See individual garden entries for full details.

Abbots House   1
Acer Corner   2
Beech House   5
Cedar House   8
Chesham Bois House   9
NEW 8 Claremont
  Road   13
Glebe Farm   20
Hall Barn   21
Hillesden House   23
Hollydyke House   25
NEW Hollytrees   26
Homelands   27
Kingsbridge Farm   29
Lords Wood   32
Magnolia House   33
Montana   36
North Down   38
Old Park Barn   39
Orchard House   41
Overstroud Cottage   42
11 The Paddocks   43
Peterley Corner
  Cottage   44
Red Kites   46
The Shades   50
20 Whitepit Lane   56
Wind in the Willows,
  Higher Denham
  Gardens   22

THE GARDENS

1 ABBOTS HOUSE
10 Church Street, Winslow, MK18 3AN. Mrs Jane Rennie, 01296 712326, jane@renniemail.com. *9m N of Aylesbury. A413 into Winslow. From town centre take Horn St & R into Church St, L fork at top. Entrance 20 metres on L. Parking in town centre & adjacent streets.* Sun 24 May (12-5). Adm £4, chd free. Home-made teas. Visits also by arrangement Apr to July for groups of 5 to 20.
Behind red brick walls a ¾ acre garden on four different levels, each with unique planting and atmosphere. Lower lawn with wisteria arbor and pond, upper lawn with rose pergola and woodland, pool area with grasses, Victorian kitchen garden and wild meadow. Spring bulbs in wild areas and woodland is a major feature in April, remaining areas peak in June/July. Late spring bulbs, water feature and many pots. Experimental wild areas. Some sculptures. Partial wheelchair access, garden levels accessed by steps. Guide dogs and medical-aid dogs only.

2 ACER CORNER
10 Manor Road, Wendover, HP22 6HQ. Jo Naiman, 07958 319234, jo@acercorner.com, www.acercorner.com. *3m S of Aylesbury. Follow A413 into Wendover. L at clock tower r'about into Aylesbury Rd. R at next r'about into Wharf Rd, continue past schools on L, garden on R.* Sat 20, Sun 21 June (2-5). Adm £3.50, chd free. Home-made teas. Visits also by arrangement May to Oct for groups of up to 20.
Garden designer's garden with Japanese influence and large collection of Japanese maples. The enclosed front garden is Japanese in style. Back garden is divided into three areas; patio area recently redesigned in the Japanese style; densely planted area with many acers and roses; and the corner which includes a productive greenhouse and interesting planting.

3 ◆ ASCOTT
Ascott, Wing, Leighton Buzzard, LU7 0PP. The National Trust, 01296 688242, amy@ascottestate.co.uk, www.ascottestate.co.uk. *2m SW of Leighton Buzzard, 8m NE of Aylesbury. Via A418. Buses: 150 Aylesbury - Milton Keynes, 100 Aylesbury & Milton Keynes.* For NGS: Mon 25 May, Mon 31 Aug (12-6). Adm £6, chd £3. Light refreshments. (NT members are required to pay to enter the gardens on NGS days). For other opening times and information, please phone, email or visit garden website.
Combining Victorian formality with early C20 natural style and recent plantings to lead it into the C21, with a recently completed garden designed by Jacques and Peter Wirtz who designed the gardens at Alnwick Castle, and also a Richard Long sculpture. Terraced lawns with specimen and ornamental trees, panoramic views to the Chilterns. Naturalised bulbs, mirror image herbaceous borders, and impressive topiary incl box and yew sundial. Ascott House is closed on NGS Days. Outdoor wheelchairs available from car park. Mobility buggy, prior booking advised.

GROUP OPENING

4 ASTON CLINTON GARDENS
Green End Street, Aston Clinton, Aylesbury, HP22 5JE. *3m E of Aylesbury. From Aylesbury take A41 E. At large r'about, continue straight (signed Aston Clinton). Continue onto London Rd. L at The Bell Pub, parking on Green End St & side roads.* Sun 26 Apr, Sun 28 June (2-5). Combined adm £4, chd free. Home-made teas at Lantern Cottage. Also open Canal Cottage on 28 June only.

101 GREEN END STREET
Sue Lipscomb.

THE LANTERN COTTAGE
Jacki Connell.

These two cottage gardens, one well established and the other having recently undergone a radical redesign by its new owner, share a basis of seasonal interest underpinned by evergreens and perennial planting. At The Lantern Cottage, spring hellebores and an abundance of tulips give way to an early summer display of roses, peonies, bearded iris,

alliums and climbers including various clematis, wisteria and akebia. A wide selection of salvias and herbaceous perennials, mostly raised from seed and cuttings. Pelargoniums provide yr-round colour in the conservatory and the greenhouse is always full! At 101, the new owner took up residence in autumn 2015, quickly establishing raised beds for vegetable production, a number of fruit trees and a variety of soft fruits. There is also a wildlife pond, an arbour overlooking the Victorian greenhouse, plus herbaceous borders, ornamental grasses surrounding a red kite sculpture and varied container planting. Wildlife is encouraged to visit.

5 BEECH HOUSE
Long Wood Drive, Jordans, Beaconsfield, HP9 2SS. Sue & Ray Edwards, raychessmad@hotmail.com. *From A40, L to Seer Green & Jordans for approx 1m, turn into Jordans Way on R, Long Wood Drive 1st L. From A413, turn into Chalfont St Giles, straight ahead until L signed Jordans, 1st L Jordans Way.* Visits by arrangement Mar to Oct. Adm £4, chd free.
2 acre plantsman's garden built up over the last 32 yrs, with a wide range of plants in a variety of habitats providing yr-round interest. Many colourful bulbs, perennials, shrubs, roses. Trees planted for their foliage, ornamental bark and autumn display. Two flowering meadows are always a popular feature. Wheelchair access dependent upon weather conditions.

6 18 BROWNSWOOD ROAD
Beaconsfield, HP9 2NU. John & Bernadette Thompson. *From New Town turn R into Ledborough Lane, L into Sandleswood Rd, 2nd R into Brownswood Rd.* Sun 21 June (2-6). Adm £4, chd free. Home-made teas & gluten free options.
A plant filled garden designed by Barbara Hunt. A harmonious arrangement of arcs and circles introduces a rhythm that leads through the garden. Sweeping box curves, gravel beds, brick edging and lush planting. A restrained use of purples and reds dazzle against a grey and green background. There has been considerable replanning and replanting during the winter.

7 NEW **CANAL COTTAGE**
11 Wharf Row, Buckland Road, Buckland, Aylesbury, HP22 5LJ. Angela Hale. *4m E of Aylesbury. On A41 E of Aylesbury, exit A41 Aston Clinton. R on Lower Ickneild Way, 1st L Buckland Rd (park along here). Wharf Row is end of Buckland Rd. Walk over the bridge, garden entrance is signed.* **Sun 28 June (12-4). Adm £3, chd free. Also open Aston Clinton Gardens.**
A peaceful garden celebrates what can be achieved in a long narrow strip behind a terraced cottage (not open). Recently landscaped to create rooms and feeding places for wildlife. Rockery of seasonal colour and small waterfall opp a dramatic herb garden. A cottage garden of herbaceous borders, leading through shady rose arbour of ferns to pond, and seating area with Mediterranean terracing and many pots.

8 **CEDAR HOUSE**
Bacombe Lane, Wendover, HP22 6EQ. Sarah Nicholson, 01296 622131, sarahhnicholson@btinternet.com. *5m SE Aylesbury. From Gt Missenden take A413 line at Wendover. Take 1st L before row of cottages, house at top of lane. Parking for no more than 10 cars.* **Visits by arrangement Feb to Sept for groups of 10+. Adm £4.50, chd free. Home-made teas.**
A plantsman's chalk garden in the Chiltern Hills with a great variety of trees, shrubs and plants. A sloping lawn leads to a natural swimming pond, with wild flowers including native orchids. A lodge greenhouse and a good collection of half-hardy plants in pots. Local artist sculptures can be viewed. Wheelchair access over gentle sloping lawn.

9 **CHESHAM BOIS HOUSE**
85 Bois Lane, Chesham Bois, HP6 6DF. Julia Plaistowe, 01494 726476, plaistowejulia@gmail.com, cheshamboishouse.co.uk. *1m N of Amersham-on-the-Hill. Follow Sycamore Rd (main shopping centre road of Amersham) which becomes Bois Lane. Do not use SatNav once in lane as you will be led astray.* **Sun 22 Mar (12-5). Adm £4.50, chd free. Home-made teas. Visits also by arrangement Mar to Aug.**
3 acre interesting and lovely garden with primroses, daffodils and

hellebores in early spring. Interesting for most of the year with lovely herbaceous borders, rill with small ornamental canal, walled garden, old orchard with wildlife pond, and handsome trees of which some are topiaried. It is a peaceful oasis. Close to the garden the 800 yr old church can also be visited. Wheelchair access with gravel in front of the house.

10 NEW **CHILTERN FORAGE FARM**
Speen, Princes Risborough, HP27 0SU. Emma Plunket, www.plunketgardens.com. *Directions provided when place on tour is confirmed. Parking in field, suitable footwear is recommended for uneven ground.* **Sun 28 June. Adm £4, chd free. Pre-booking essential, please email emma@plunketgardens.com to book your tour at 3pm or 4.30pm for limited numbers. Light refreshments.**
Two pre-booked tours only by owners of this new project under development in stunning AONB setting. 8 acres of pasture being restored to native hay meadows and planted with fruit trees, soft fruit and perennial vegetables. Creation of wildlife habitats with native planting, dead hedges and green manure.

11 NEW **THE CHINNERY**
Church Road, Penn, High Wycombe, HP10 8NX. Jennie Roberts. *Garden located between The Crown Pub in Penn & Tylers Green Pond on the B474, opp Penn Methodist Church.* **Sun 5 July (2-5). Combined adm with Oldfields £5, chd free. Tea.**
A s-facing, 1 acre garden with mature trees, extensive undulating lawn and full deep herbaceous borders. Formal area using square mature hornbeam, yew and box to give structure (designed by Coworth Park designer). Former home of Lord Dawson of Penn, now home of an artist with wood and metal garden sculpture on display, and an art studio showing art and ceramics for sale (donation to NGS).

12 **126 CHURCH GREEN ROAD**
Bletchley, Milton Keynes, MK3 6DD. David & Janice Hale. *13m E of Buckingham, 11m N of Leighton Buzzard. Off B4034 into*

Church Green Rd, take L turn at mini-r'about. **Sun 14 June (2-6); Tue 16 June (2-5). Adm £4, chd free. Home-made teas.**
A gentle sloping mature garden of ½ acre is a plant lover's delight, which incl a small formal garden, shady areas and mixed borders of shrubs, perennials and roses. Features incl a thatched wendy house, pergola, formal pond, wildlife pond, productive fruit and vegetable garden, two greenhouses and patio.

13 NEW **8 CLAREMONT ROAD**
Marlow, SL7 1BW. Andi Gallagher, 01628 474620. *No parking at garden, but short walk from all town car parks. From town centre walk S on High St, L on Institute Rd, L on Beaufort Gardens & R on Claremont Rd.* **Wed 22, Sat 25, Sun 26 July, Sat 5, Sun 6 Sept (11-4). Adm £3.50, chd free. Home-made teas. Visits also by arrangement June to Sept for groups of up to 10.**
Plants, paintings and pots to see and buy in this small town garden owned by an artist gardener. The unusual house was built in 2015. Gravel paths divide the rectangular beds filled with herbaceous perennials, grasses and ferns. A cow trough water feature and owner's ceramics add surprise. A gate leads to a deliberate wild area with fruit trees and art studio with garden related paintings.

GROUP OPENING

14 **THE CLAYDONS**
East Botolph and Middle Claydon, MK18 2ND. *1½m SW Winslow. In Winslow turn R off High St, by the Bell Pub & follow NT signs towards Claydon House & The Claydons.* **Mon 25 May (2-6). Combined adm £6, chd free. Home-made teas in village hall.**

CLAYDON COTTAGE
Mr & Mrs Tony Evans.

NEW **FLETCHERS**
Mrs Lynda Read.

THE OLD RECTORY
Mrs Jane Meisl.

THE OLD VICARAGE
Nigel & Esther Turnbull.

NEW **WEIR COTTAGE**
Mrs Carol Gould.

Three small villages, originally part of the Claydon Estate with typical north Buckinghamshire cottages and two C13 churches. Weir Cottage a newly laid out and planted garden, the collaboration between mother and daughter. The garden wraps around the C17 black and white thatched cottage (not open) and showcases a palette of spring bulbs, perennials and topiary. Claydon Cottage, a pretty thatched cottage (not open) with an unconventional garden. The Old Vicarage, a large garden on clay with mixed borders, scented garden, dell, shrub roses, vegetables and a natural clay pond. Small meadow area and planting to encourage wildlife and beehives. A free children's quiz. Access via gravel drive. Fletchers is a newly planted relatively small garden behind a pretty cottage (not open). The Old Rectory is a large garden with a wildflower meadow, herbaceous borders, a woodland walk and cloud hedging. No wheelchair access at Weir Cottage.

GROUP OPENING

16 CUBLINGTON GARDENS
Cublington, Leighton Buzzard, LU7 0LF. *5m SE Winslow, 5m NE Aylesbury. From Aylesbury take A413 Buckingham Rd. After 4m, at Whitchurch, turn R to Cublington.* Sun 7 June (2-6). Combined adm £5, chd free. Home-made teas in Biggs Pavilion, Orchard Ground.

CHERRY COTTAGE, 3 THE WALLED GARDEN
Gwyneira Waters.

LARKSPUR HOUSE
Mr & Mrs S Jenkins.

OLD MANOR COTTAGE
Mr & Mrs J Packer.

1 STEWKLEY ROAD
Tom & Helen Gadsby, www.structuredgrowth.co.uk.

A group of diverse gardens in this attractive Buckinghamshire village listed as a conservation area. Cherry Cottage is adapted for wheelchair gardening with raised beds and artificial grass. Larkspur House garden uses a variety of plants and hard landscaping to create distinct areas. Through an Art Nouveau inspired gate there is a large orchard and wildflower meadow. 1 Stewkley Road has a strong focus on home-grown food with an idyllic organic kitchen garden, small orchard and courtyard garden. Old Manor Cottage, a cottage garden with low hedges enclosing secluded seating areas. Partial wheelchair access to some gardens.

15 ◆ COWPER & NEWTON MUSEUM GARDENS
Orchard Side, Market Place, Olney, MK46 4AJ. Anne Kempson, 01234 711833, house-manager@ cowperandnewtonmuseum.org.uk, www.cowperandnewtonmuseum. org.uk. *5m N of Newport Pagnell. 12m S of Wellingborough. On A509. Please park in public car park in East St.* For NGS: Sat 13, Sun 14 June (10.30-4.30). Adm £3.50, chd free. Home-made teas. For other opening times and information, please phone, email or visit garden website.
The tranquil Flower Garden of C18 poet William Cowper, who said 'Gardening was of all employments, that in which I succeeded best', has plants introduced prior to his death in 1800, many mentioned in his writings. The Summer House Garden with Cowper's 'verse manufactory', now a Victorian Kitchen Garden, has new and heritage vegetables organically grown, also a herb border and medicinal plant bed. Features incl lacemaking demonstrations and local artists painting live art on both days. Georgian dancers on Sun. Wheelchair access on mostly hard paths.

Lindengate

17 DANESFIELD HOUSE

Henley Road, Marlow, SL7 2EY. Danesfield House Hotel, 01628 891010, amoorin@danesfieldhouse.co.uk, www.danesfieldhouse.co.uk. *3m from Marlow. On the A4155 between Marlow & Henley-on-Thames. Signed on the LH-side Danesfield House Hotel & Spa.* **Wed 5 Aug (10-4). Adm £4.50, chd free. Cream teas. Pre-booking essential for lunch & afternoon tea.**

The gardens at Danesfield were completed in 1901 by Robert Hudson, the Sunlight Soap magnate who built the house. Since the house opened as a hotel in 1991, the gardens have been admired by several thousand guests each yr. However, in 2009 it was discovered that the gardens contained outstanding examples of pulhamite in both the formal gardens and the waterfall areas. The 100 yr old topiary is also outstanding. Part of the grounds incl an Iron Age fort. Wheelchair access on gravel paths throughout the garden.

GROUP OPENING

18 DINTON VILLAGE GARDENS

Dinton, HP17 8UN. *4m SW Aylesbury, 4m NE Thame. For SatNavs enter HP17 8UQ. ¼m off A418. Please only use turning signed Ford & Dinton for free car park, clearly signed. 5 gardens open in Apr & 7 gardens in June.* **Sun 19 Apr (1-5.30). Combined adm £6, chd free. Sun 7 June (1-5.30). Combined adm £7, chd free. Home-made teas in Dinton Village Hall.**

GRAPEVINE COTTAGE
Anne & Mark Seckington.
Open on Sun 7 June

GREENDALE
S A Eaton.
Open on Sun 19 Apr

NEW **INGLENOOK COTTAGE**
Paul & Moira Offord.
Open on Sun 7 June

INNISFREE
David & Rosemary Jackson.
Open on Sun 7 June

LAVENDER COTTAGE
Sara & Trevor Hopwood.
Open on Sun 7 June

NEW **LILACS**
Marion Baker.
Open on all dates

NEW **THE OLD COACH HOUSE**
Lynn Holloway.
Open on Sun 19 Apr

NEW **WESTLINGTON BARN**
Catherine Crump & Robin Nash.
Open on Sun 7 June

WESTLINGTON FARM
Catherine Brogan.
Open on all dates

WILLOW COTTAGE
Philip & Jennifer Rimell.
Open on Sun 19 Apr

Dinton is a very picturesque, secluded, historic village, set in countryside with views to the Chiltern Hills. A conservation area, it has many pretty, thatched, whitewashed, old cottages and has been featured in the Midsomer Murders TV series. The colourful and interesting gardens range from small, informal cottages through to medium and larger country house styles, each one with a strikingly different character and purpose. All gardens are within easy and peaceful walking distance of the car park and village hall. The beautiful C11/12 Norman church will be open all day and there will be a children's quiz. The Grade I listed building, has an outstanding south doorway and an 800 yr old font. Next to the church is Dinton Hall; this fine many-gabled mansion altered at various periods during its long history, was until the last quarter of the C20 the seat of the Currie family and is now owned by the Vanbergen family. Wheelchair access and dogs allowed to most gardens. WC at village hall.

---

19 FRESSINGWOOD

Hare Lane, Little Kingshill, Great Missenden, HP16 0EF. John & Maggie Bateson. *1m S of Gt Missenden, 4m W of Amersham. From the A413 at Chiltern Hospital, turn L signed Gt & Lt Kingshill. Take 1st L into Nags Head Lane. Turn R under railway bridge, then L into New Rd & continue to Hare Lane.* **Sun 24 May (2-5.30). Adm £4, chd free. Home-made teas.**

Thoughtfully designed and structured garden with yr-round colour and many interesting features. Including

The Old Vicarage, The Claydons

herbaceous borders, a shrubbery with ferns, hostas, grasses and hellebores. Small formal garden, pergolas with roses and clematis. A variety of topiary and a landscaped terrace. A central feature area incorporating water with grasses. Large bonsai collection.

20 GLEBE FARM

Lillingstone Lovell, Buckingham, MK18 5BB. Mr David Hilliard, 01280 860384, thehilliards@talk21.com, www.glebefarmbarn.co.uk. *Off A413, 5m N of Buckingham & 2m S of Whittlebury. From A5 at Potterspury, turn off A5 & follow signs to Lillingstone Lovell.* **Mon 25 May (1-5). Adm £4, chd free.** Home-made teas. **Visits also by arrangement in June for groups of 10 to 20.**

A large cottage garden with an exuberance of colourful planting and winding gravel paths, amongst lawns and herbaceous borders on two levels. Ponds, a wishing well, vegetable beds, a knot garden, a small walled garden and an old tractor feature. Everything combines to make a beautiful garden full of surprises.

21 HALL BARN

Windsor End, Beaconsfield, HP9 2SG. Mrs Farncombe, jenefer@farncombe01.demon. co.uk. *½m S of Beaconsfield. Lodge gate 300yds S of St Mary & All Saints' Church in Old Town centre. Please do not use SatNav.* **Visits by arrangement Feb to Oct. A welcome is given to individual visitors as well as groups. Home-made teas for groups of 10+. Adm £5, chd free.**

Historical landscaped garden laid out between 1680-1730 for the poet Edmund Waller and his descendants. Features 300 year old cloud formation yew hedges, formal lake and vistas ending with classical buildings and statues. Wooded walks around the grove offer respite from the heat on sunny days. One of the original NGS garden openings of 1927. Gravel paths, but certain areas can be accessed by car for those with limited mobility.

GROUP OPENING

22 HIGHER DENHAM GARDENS

Higher Denham, UB9 5EA. *6m E of Beaconsfield. Turn off A412, approx ½m N of junction with A40 into Old Rectory Lane. After 1m enter Higher Denham straight ahead. Tickets for all gardens available at the community hall, 70yds into the village.* **Sun 22 Mar, Sun 31 May (2-5). Combined adm £6, chd free.** Home-made teas in the community hall. Donation to Higher Denham Community CIO (Garden Upkeep Fund).

9 LOWER ROAD
Mrs Patricia Davidson.
Open on Sun 31 May

30 LOWER ROAD
Mr & Mrs Mike Macgowan.
Open on all dates

19 MIDDLE ROAD
Sonia Harris.
Open on all dates

5 SIDE ROAD
Jane Blyth.
Open on all dates

WIND IN THE WILLOWS
Ron James, 07740 177038, r.james@company-doc.co.uk.
Open on all dates
Visits also by arrangement Mar to Oct for groups of 10+.

At least 5 gardens will open in 2020 in the delightful Misbourne chalk stream valley, 4 will open in March and 5 in May. Wind in the Willows has over 350 shrubs and trees, informal woodland and wild gardens incl riverside and bog plantings and a collection of 80 hostas and 12 striped roses in 3 acres. 'Really different' was a typical visitor comment. The garden at 5 Side Road is medium sized with lawns, borders and shrubs, and many features which children will love. An old conifer has been removed and the area replanted for greater interest. 9 Lower Road, opening in May, is a small garden backing onto the river. Recently professionally designed, it is now maturing and has new shrubs. At 30 Lower Road is a well-stocked garden with charm and character including a wartime underground bunker! 19 Middle Road with contrasting dry front and damper back garden is opening this yr in spring when the front garden looks especially good. In May the owner of Wind in the Willows will lead optional

guided tours of the garden starting at 2.30pm and 4pm. Tours last approx 1 hour. Partial wheelchair access to some gardens.

23 HILLESDEN HOUSE

Church End, Hillesden, MK18 4DB. Mr & Mrs R M Faccenda, 01296 730451, suef@faccenda.co.uk. *3m S of Buckingham through Gawcott. Next to church in Hillesden.* **Sun 21 June (2-5). Adm £6, chd free.** **Visits also by arrangement June to Aug for groups of 20 to 30.**

By the superb church Cathedral in the Fields. Lakes, fountains and waterfalls with mature trees. Rose, alpine and herbaceous borders with 80 acres of deer park. Wild flower areas and extensive lakes developed by the owner. Lovely walks and plenty of wildlife. Also a woodland area and vegetable garden with raised beds. The orchard was created 4 yrs ago, and vines were planted 2 yrs ago. All Saints Church is open and well worth a visit. No wheelchair access to lakes.

Your visits help change lives – your generosity helps Marie Curie fund nurses to care for people night and day in their homes, with donations of more than £9 million

25 HOLLYDYKE HOUSE

Little Missenden, HP7 0RD. Bob & Sandra Wetherall, 01494 862264, sandracwetherall@gmail.com. *Off A413 between Great Missenden & Amersham. Parking, please use field adj to house, weather permitting.* **Sat 15, Sun 16 Feb (11.30-3.30). Adm £4, chd free. Light refreshments. Visits also by arrangement Feb & Mar for groups of 10+.**
3 acre garden surrounds Hollydyke House (not open) has yr-round interest. During Feb we hope to see hellebores, crocus and carpets of snowdrops. You will be able to appreciate the structure in winter with the trees, colourful barks, seed heads and grasses. Walk down the road to see more snowdrops surrounding C10 Saxon Church, St John The Baptist. Join a tour to learn about its fascinating history. Please Note: On Sun16 Feb St John the Baptist Church will be closed for services until 12.30pm. Wheelchair access on gravel paths.

26 [NEW] HOLLYTREES

Parish Piece, Holmer Green, High Wycombe, HP15 6SP. Brian Fisher, 07751 720060, brian@the-fishers.org.uk. *From Amersham (3m) or High Wycombe (4m). Follow the A404, signed exit to Holmer Green (Earl Howe Rd).*

After approx ½ m continue over Xrd by pond & Parish Piece is 2nd road on L. **Visits by arrangement Aug & Sept for groups of 10 to 20. Afternoon or evening visits only. Adm £3.50, chd £1. Drinks & light refreshments by prior request.**
A garden that reflects the enthusiasm of a highly qualified, respected and widely travelled plantsman who loves passing on his knowledge. Many unusual hardy plants combine in a unique micro-climate with exotic, tender species such as oleander, to reach a colourful peak in late summer. Also features three beautifully displayed collections; rocks from around the world, old gardening tools and curiosities, and West Indian treasures, which completes a fascinating experience.

27 HOMELANDS

Springs Lane, Ellesborough, Aylesbury, HP17 0XD. Jean & Tony Young, 01296 622306, young.ellesborough@gmail.com. *6m SE of Aylesbury. On the B4010 between Wendover & Princes Risborough. Springs Lane is between village hall at Butlers Cross & the church. Narrow lane with an uneven surface.* **Visits by arrangement Apr to Aug. Adm £4, chd free. Home-made teas.**

Hollytrees

Secluded ¾ acre garden on difficult chalk, adjoining open countryside. Designed to be enjoyed from many seating positions. Progress from semi-formal to wildflower meadow and wildlife pond. Deep borders with all season interest, and gravel beds with exotic late summer and autumn planting.

28 HORATIO'S GARDEN

National Spinal Injuries Centre (NSIC), Stoke Mandeville Hospital, Mandeville Road, Stoke Mandeville, Aylesbury, HP21 8AL. Jacqui Martin-Lof, www.horatiosgarden.org.uk. *The closest car park to Horatio's Garden at Stoke Mandeville Hospital is Car Park B, opp Asda. Free parking on open day.* **Sun 26 Apr (2-5). Adm £5, chd free. Home-made teas in the Garden Room.**
Opened in Sept 2018, Horatio's Garden at the National Spinal Injuries Centre, Stoke Mandeville Hospital is designed by Joe Swift. The fully accessible garden for patients with spinal injuries has been part funded by the NGS. The beautiful space is cleverly designed to bring the sights, sounds and scents of nature into the heart of the NHS. Everything is high quality and carefully designed to bring benefit to patients who often have lengthy stays in hospital. The garden features an incredible garden room designed by architect Andrew Wells. We also have the most wonderful wildflower meadow. Meet the Head Gardener and volunteer team and taste our delicious tea and home-made cake! The garden is fully accessible, having been designed specifically for patients in wheelchairs or hospital beds.

29 KINGSBRIDGE FARM

Steeple Claydon, MK18 2EJ. Mr & Mrs T Aldous, 01296 730224. *3m S of Buckingham. Halfway between Padbury & Steeple Claydon. Xrds with sign to Kingsbridge Only.* **Visits by arrangement Apr to June for groups of 10+. Adm £6, chd free. Home-made teas in our cosy, converted barn.**
Stunning and exceptional 6 acre garden imaginatively created over last 30 yrs. Main lawn is enclosed by softly, curving, colour themed herbaceous borders, and many roses and shrubs interestingly planted with cleverly created landscaping

features. Clipped topiary yews, pleached hornbeams lead out to the ha-ha and countryside beyond. A natural stream with bog plants and nesting kingfishers, meanders serenely through woodland gardens, with many walks. A garden always evolving, to visit again and again.

  ♿ 🐕 ✿ 🚌 ☕

30 LINDENGATE
The Old Allotment Site, Worlds End Garden Centre, Aylesbury Road, Wendover, HP22 6BD. Lindengate Charity, www.lindengate.org.uk. *4m SE of Aylesbury on A413. Turn into Dobbies Garden Centre, Lindengate on LH-side.* **Sun 24 May, Sun 6 Sept (2-4). Adm £4.50, chd free. Home-made teas.**
Lindengate's mission statement is to 'Foster an improved state of mental health and wellbeing through the healing power of nature and horticulture'. The charity's 5 acre site, has been developed into a series of wild spaces in synergy with more formalised gardens and is described as an oasis in a busy world. It successfully supports many people on their road to recovery. The garden has a sensory garden which includes a log wall, stumpery and various sensory experiences including water ball and rill. Accessible refreshments and welfare facilities, and 60% of the site has accessible pathways.

  ♿ 🐕 ✿ 🚌 ☕

GROUP OPENING

31 LONG CRENDON GARDENS
Long Crendon, HP18 9AN. *Long Crendon village is situated on the B4011 Thame-Bicester road, 2m N of Thame. A map showing the location of the gardens will be available at each garden & at Church House in the High St.* **Sun 26 Apr, Sun 14 June (2-6). Combined adm £6, chd free. Home-made teas in the village hall (Apr & June), and for the NGS at Lopemead Farm (June).**

BAKER'S CLOSE
Mr & Mrs Peter Vaines.
Open on Sun 26 Apr

BARRY'S CLOSE
Mr & Mrs Richard Salmon.
Open on Sun 26 Apr

NEW BRINDLES
Sarah Chapman.
Open on all dates

COP CLOSE
Sandra & Tony Phipkin.
Open on Sun 14 June

25 ELM TREES
Carol & Mike Price.
Open on all dates

LOPEMEAD FARM
Wendy Thompson & Bryony Rixon.
Open on Sun 14 June

MANOR HOUSE
Mr & Mrs West.
Open on Sun 26 Apr

TOMPSONS FARM
Mr & Mrs T Moynihan.
Open on Sun 14 June

Sun 26 April: Baker's Close has shrubs and wild area, and 1000's of daffodils, narcissi and tulips will be on display. Barry's Close, a collection of spring flowering trees, borders, pool and water garden. A cottage style organic garden at 25 Elm Trees with spring bulbs, flowering trees and shrubs, pond and orchard area. Manor House, a large garden with views towards the Chilterns, two ornamental lakes, a variety of spring bulbs and shrubs. New for 2020, Brindles, an organic garden with several rooms and incl a natural swimming pool, beehives, vegetables and developing wild flower area. Sun 14 June: A formal courtyard garden at Lopemead Farm with raised beds, vegetables and flower borders. Cop Close with mixed borders, vegetable and cutting garden. Tompsons Farm, a large woodland garden with lake and newly planted borders. Opening again, Brindles where the roses will be out, and 25 Elm Trees, where the herbaceous borders, roses and clematis will feature! Partial wheelchair access to some gardens.

  ♿ 🐕 ✿ ☕

32 LORDS WOOD
Frieth Road, Marlow Common, SL7 2QS. Mr & Mrs Messum, millie-messum@messums.com, www.messums.com. *1½m NW Marlow. From Marlow turn off the A4155 at Platts Garage into Oxford Rd & Chalkpit Lane towards Frieth for 1½m, 100yds past the Marlow Common road turn L opp Valley View Stables.* **Thur 18 June (11-4). Adm £5, chd free. Home-made teas. Visits also by arrangement June to Aug for groups of 20+.**
'An outpost of Old Bloomsbury in Marlow Woods' was how diarist

Frances Partridge described Lords Wood. James and Alex Strachey entertained many of the Bloomsbury Group including Lytton Strachey and Dora Carrington. The 5 acres surrounding the house (not open) showcase sculpture, water features, extensive mature borders, flower and herb gardens, orchard, and woodland walks with spectacular views over the Chilterns. Partial wheelchair access; gravel paths, steep slopes, and open water.

  ♿ 🚌 ☕

33 MAGNOLIA HOUSE
Grange Drive, Wooburn Green, Wooburn, HP10 0QD. Elaine & Alan Ford, 01628 525818, lanforddesigns@gmail.com. *On A4094 2m SW of A40 between Bourne End & Wooburn. From Wooburn Church, direction Maidenhead, Grange Drive is on L before r'about. From Bourne End, L at 2 mini-r'abouts, then 1st R.* **Visits by arrangement Feb to Aug. Light refreshments.**
½ acre garden with mature trees incl large copper beech and large magnolia. Cacti, fernery, stream, ponds, greenhouses, aviaries, 10,000 snowdrops, hellebores, bluebells and over 60 varieties of hosta. Child friendly. Constantly being changed and updated. Combined visit with The Shades maybe possible. Partial wheelchair access.

  ♿ 🐕 ✿ 🚌 🚐 ☕

34 THE MANOR HOUSE
(Off Perry Lane), Bledlow, Nr Princes Risborough, HP27 9PB. The Lord Carrington. *9m NW of High Wycombe, 3m SW of Princes Risborough. ½m off B4009 in middle of Bledlow village. SatNav directions HP27 9PA.* **Sun 31 May (2-4.30). Adm £6, chd free. Tea.**
Paved garden, parterres, shrub borders, old roses and walled kitchen garden. Water garden with paths, bridges and walkways fed by 14 chalk springs, plus 2 acres of landscaped planting. Sculpture garden. Partial wheelchair access as there is stepped access or sloped grass to enter the gardens.

  ♿ ☕

35 NEW MEAD COTTAGE

The Ridgeway, Chalfont St Peter, Gerrards Cross, SL9 8NP. Lyn & John Tweed. *From Gerrards Cross turn L into Austenwood Lane. Take 1st R immed after The Three Oaks into Austenway. The Ridgeway is 1st turning on L. Parking in The Ridgeway is limited.* **Sat 20 June (2-5). Adm £5, chd free. Home-made teas.**
Enter through a hornbeam arch onto a narrow path to a garden that opens out to 2/3 of an acre. The grounds have been redeveloped over 17 yrs, and now the gardens perfectly complement the pretty cottage (not open). Yr-round interest and colour are enjoyed with a huge variety of plants and shrubs around the old oak gazebo, pergola and potager. Many rooms are designed in the garden for you to discover. Wheelchair access on gravel paths.

& �"⚘ ☕

36 MONTANA

Shire Lane, Cholesbury, HP23 6NA. Diana Garner, 01494 758347, montana@cholesbury.net. *3m NW of Chesham. From Wigginton turn R after Champneys, 2nd R onto Shire Lane. From Cholesbury common, turn on Cholesbury Rd by cricket club, take 1st L on to Shire Lane. Montana is 1/2 m down Shire Lane on LH-side.* **Visits by arrangement Mar to July. Adm £3.50, chd free. Home-made teas. Wine (eve visits).**
A peaceful large country garden bursting with rare trees, unusual flowering shrubs and perennials under planted with thousands of bulbs; kitchen garden edged by sweet peas; shade loving plants, small meadow. A gate leads to a mixed deciduous wood with level paths, a fernery planted in an old clay pit, and an avenue of daffodils and acers. Lots of seats to enjoy the atmosphere. Bees and chickens. An un-manicured garden high in the Chiltern Hills. Surrounding fields have been permanent pasture for more than 100 yrs. We can accommodate visits at short notice. Refreshments will be in a covered barn.

& 🐎 ⚘ 🚗 ☕

37 ♦ NETHER WINCHENDON HOUSE

Nether Winchendon, Thame, Aylesbury, HP18 0DY. Mr Robert Spencer Bernard, 01844 290101, Contactus@ netherwinchendonhouse.com,

www.nwhouse.co.uk. *6m SW of Aylesbury, 6m from Thame. Approx 4m from Thame on A418, turn 1st L to Cuddington, turn L at Xrds, downhill turn R & R again to parking by house.* **For NGS: Sun 10 May, Sun 30 Aug (2-5.30). Adm £4, chd free. Home-made teas at church. For other opening times and information, please phone, email or visit garden website.**
Nether Winchendon House has fine and rare trees, set in a stunning landscape surrounded by parkland, with 7 acres of lawned grounds running down to the River Thame. A Founder NGS Member (1927). Enchanting and romantic Mediaeval and Tudor House, one of the most romantic of the historic houses of England and Grade I listed. Picturesque small village with an interesting church. Unfenced riverbank.

& 🐎 🚗 🛏 ☕

38 NORTH DOWN

Dodds Lane, Chalfont St Giles, HP8 4EL. Merida Saunders, 01494 872928. *4m SE of Amersham, 4m NE of Beaconsfield. Opp the green in centre of village, at Costa turn into UpCorner onto Silver Hill. At top of hill fork R into Dodds Lane. North Down is 7th on L.* **Visits by arrangement May to Sept for groups of up to 30. Adm £4.50, chd free. Light refreshments.**
A passion for gardening is evident in this plantswomans lovely 3/4 acre garden which has evolved over the yrs with scenic effect in mind. Colourful and interesting throughout the yr. Large grassed areas with island beds of mixed perennials, shrubs and some unusual plants. Variety of rhododendrons, azaleas, acers and clematis. Displays of sempervivum, alpines, grasses and ferns. Small patio and water feature, greenhouse and an Italianate front patio to owner's design. You can see Milton's Cottage and garden where John Milton wrote Paradise Lost in the village.

⚘ ☕

39 OLD PARK BARN

Dag Lane, Stoke Goldington, MK16 8NY. Emily & James Chua, 01908 551092, emilychua51@yahoo.com. *4m N of Newport Pagnell on B526. Park on High St. A short walk up Dag Lane. Limited disabled parking near garden via Orchard Way.* **Sun 28 June (2-5). Adm £4.50, chd free. Home-made**

teas. **Visits also by arrangement in June for groups of 10+.**
A garden of under 3 acres made from a rough field over 20 yrs ago. Near the house (not open) a series of terraces cut into the sloping site to create the formal garden with long and cross vistas, lawns and deep borders. The aim is to provide interest throughout the yr with naturalistic planting and views borrowed from the surrounding countryside. Beyond is a wildlife pond, meadow and woodland garden. Partial wheelchair access.

& ⚘ ☕

40 NEW OLDFIELDS

Church Road, Penn, High Wycombe, HP10 8NU. Nicki Pritchard. *Parking around Penn Common village green. 5 mins walk.* **Sun 5 July (2-5). Combined adm with The Chinnery £5, chd free.**
Country garden, colourful herbaceous borders with penstemon, hydrangeas, fuschia, roses, geraniums and wisteria. Olive trees on the terrace which has uninterrupted views of the fields and woods. A courtyard filled with wonderful array of potted hostas, planted herbs, a lemon tree, and a selection of old and varying sized filled chimneys.

& 🐎

41 ORCHARD HOUSE

Tower Road, Coleshill, Amersham, HP7 0LB. Mr & Mrs Douglas Livesey, 07740 100342, Jane.livesey88@btinternet.com. *From Amersham Old Town take the A355 to Beaconsfield. Appox 3/4 m along this road at top of hill, take the 1st R into Tower Rd. Parking in cricket club grounds.* **Sun 26 Apr, Sat 20 June (2-5). Adm £5, chd free. Home-made teas in the barn. Visits also by arrangement Apr to June for groups of 10+. Morning or afternoon visits welcome.**
The 5 acre garden incl several wooded areas with eco bug hotels for wildlife. Two ponds with wild flower planting, large avenues of silver birches, a bog garden with board walk, and a wildflower meadow. There is a cut flower garden and a dramatic collection of spring bulbs set amongst an acer glade. Wheelchair access with sloping lawn in rear garden.

& 🐎 ⚘ ☕

42 OVERSTROUD COTTAGE

The Dell, Frith Hill, Gt Missenden, HP16 9QE. Mr & Mrs Jonathan Brooke, 01494 862701, susanmbrooke@outlook.com. *½ m E Gt Missenden. Turn E off A413 at Gt Missenden onto B485 Frith Hill to Chesham Rd. White Gothic cottage set back in lay-by 100yds uphill on L. Parking on R at church.* **Sun 12 Apr, Sun 17 May, Sun 14 June (2-5). Adm £4, chd free. Cream teas at parish church. Visits also by arrangement Apr to Sept for groups of 20 to 30.**
Artistic chalk garden on two levels. Collection of C17/C18 plants including auriculas, hellebores, bulbs, pulmonarias, peonies, geraniums, dahlias, herbs and succulents. Many antique, species and rambling roses. Potager and lily pond. Blue and white ribbon border. Cottage was once C17 fever house for Missenden Abbey. Features incl a garden studio with painting exhibition (share of flower painting proceeds to NGS).

43 11 THE PADDOCKS

Wendover, HP22 6HE. Mr & Mrs E Rye, 01296 623870, pam.rye@talktalk.net. *5m from Aylesbury on A413. From Aylesbury turn L at mini-r'about onto Wharf Rd. From Gt Missenden turn L at the Clock Tower, then R at mini-r'about onto Wharf Rd.* **Sat 20, Sun 21 June (2-5). Evening opening Fri 26 June (5-8.30). Sat 4, Sun 5 July (2-5). Adm £3, chd free. Wine on Fri 26 June only. Visits also by arrangement June & July for groups of 20 to 30. Donation to Bonnie People in South Africa.**
Small peaceful garden with mixed borders of colourful herbaceous perennials, a special show of David Austin roses and a large variety of spectacular named Blackmore and Langdon delphiniums. A tremendous variety of colour in a small area. The White Garden with a peaceful and shady arbour, and The Magic of Moonlight created for the BBC.

44 PETERLEY CORNER COTTAGE

Perks Lane, Prestwood, Great Missenden, HP16 0JH. Dawn Philipps, 01494 862198, dawn.philipps@googlemail.com. *Turn into Perks Lane from Wycombe Rd (A4128), Peterley Corner Cottage is the 3rd house on the L.* **Visits by arrangement May to Aug for groups of 10 to 30. Adm £5, chd free. Light refreshments.**

Mead Cottage

A 3 acre mature garden, incl an acre of wild flowers and indigenous trees. Surrounded by tall hedges and a wood, the garden has evolved over the last 30 yrs. There are many specimen trees and mature roses incl a Paul's Himalaya Musk and a Kiftsgate. A large herbaceous border runs alongside the formal lawns with other borders like heathers and shrubs. The most recent addition is a potager.

45 THE PLOUGH

Chalkshire Road, Terrick, Aylesbury, HP17 0TJ. John & Sue Stewart. *2m W of Wendover. Entrance to garden & car park signed off B4009 Nash Lee Rd. 200yds E of Terrick r'about. Access to garden from field car park.* **Sun 10, Mon 25 May (1-5). Adm £4, chd free. Home-made teas.**
Formal organic garden with open views to the Chiltern countryside. Designed as a series of outdoor rooms around a listed former C18 inn (not open), incl border, parterre, vegetable and fruit gardens, and a newly planted orchard. Delicious home-made teas in our barn and adjacent entrance courtyard. Jams and apple juice for sale, made with fruits from the garden.

46 RED KITES

46 Haw Lane, Bledlow Ridge, HP14 4JJ. Mag & Les Terry, 01494 481474, lesterry747@gmail.com. *4m S of Princes Risborough. Off A4010 halfway between Princes Risborough & West Wycombe. At Hearing Dogs sign in Saunderton turn into Haw Lane, then ¾ m on L up the hill.* **Tue 12 May, Tue 14 July (2-5). Adm £4, chd free. Home-made teas. Visits also by arrangement May to Sept for groups of 20+.**
This much admired 1½ acre Chiltern hillside garden is planted for yr-round interest and is lovingly maintained with mixed and herbaceous borders, wild flower orchard, established pond, vegetable garden, managed woodland area and a lovely hidden garden. Many climbers used throughout the garden which changes significantly through the seasons. Sit and enjoy the superb views from the top terrace.

Horatio's Garden

47 RIVENDELL
13 The Leys, Amersham, HP6 5NP. Janice & Mike Cross. *Off A416. From Amersham take A416 N towards Chesham. The Leys is on L ½ m after Boot & Slipper Pub. Park at Beacon School, 100yds N.* **Mon 13 Apr (2-5). Adm £4, chd free. Home-made teas.**
An established, but always evolving, south-facing garden with different linked areas. A woodland area, gravel area with grasses and pond, bug hotels, fruit and vegetables, herbaceous beds containing a wide variety of shrubs, bulbs and perennials designed to encourage pollinators, surround a circular lawn with a rose and clematis arbour. Many of the plants are propagated for sale.

48 NEW ROBIN HILL
Water End, Stokenchurch, High Wycombe, HP14 3XQ. Caroline Renshaw & Stuart Yates. *2m from M40 J5 Stokenchurch. Turn off A40 just S of Stokenchurch towards Radnage, then 1st R to Waterend & then follow signs.* **Sun 21 June (11-4). Adm £4.50, chd free. Home-made teas.**
1½ acre informal country garden at the start of The Chiltern Hills, open to the views, over its own wildflower meadow. The garden is full of planting with shrubs, perennials and grass borders,

new and established trees, and lots of places to sit and enjoy the views. Wind your way through the paths in the meadow and you can also visit the chickens in the large cherry orchard.

49 ST MICHAELS CONVENT
Vicarage Way, Gerrards Cross, SL9 8AT. Sisters of the Church. *15mins walk from Gerrards Cross station. 10mins from East Common buses. Limited parking at convent.* **Sat 4 July (2-4.30). Adm by donation. Cream teas.**
Recently acquired garden, having been neglected for many years, is now being developed by the Community as a place for quiet, reflection and to gaze upon beauty. Includes a walled garden with vegetables and beehives, a shady woodland dell and a recently built chapel. Colourful borders, beds and mature majestic trees. Come and see how the garden is developing and growing! A garden for quiet reflection with hidden corners and boundless beauty.

50 THE SHADES
High Wycombe, HP10 0QD. Pauline & Maurice Kirkpatrick, 01628 522540. *On A4094 2m SW of A40 between Bourne End & Wooburn. From Wooburn Church,*

direction Maidenhead, Grange Drive is on L before r'about. From Bourne End, L at 2 mini-r'abouts, then 1st R. **Visits by arrangement Feb to Aug. Combined visit with Magnolia House. Light refreshments at Magnolia House.**
The Shades drive is approached through mature trees, areas of shade loving plants, beds of shrubs, 60 various roses and herbaceous plants. The rear garden with natural well surrounded by plants, shrubs and acers. A green slate water feature and scree garden with alpine plants completes the garden. Partial wheelchair access.

51 ♦ STOKE POGES MEMORIAL GARDENS
Church Lane, Stoke Poges, Slough, SL2 4NZ. South Bucks District Council, 01753 523744, memorial.gardens@ chilternandsouthbucks.gov. uk, www.southbucks.gov.uk/ stokepogesmemorialgardens. *1m N of Slough, 4m S of Gerrards Cross. Follow signs to Stoke Poges & from there to the Memorial Gardens. Car park opp main entrance, disabled visitor parking in the gardens. Weekend disabled access through churchyard.* **For NGS: Sun 14 June (1.30-4.30). Adm £4.50, chd free. Home-made**

teas. **For other opening times and information, please phone, email or visit garden website.**
Unique 20 acre Grade I registered garden constructed 1934-39. Rock and water gardens, sunken colonnade, rose garden, 500 individual gated gardens. Lovely autumn colours around the gardens and especially in the rock garden. Guided tours every half hour. Guide dogs only.

52 TURN END
Townside, Haddenham, Aylesbury, HP17 8BG. Margaret & Peter Aldington, **turnendgarden@gmail.com, , www.turnend.org.uk.** *3m NE of Thame, 5m SW of Aylesbury. Exit A418 to Haddenham. Turn at Rising Sun to Townside. Street parking very limited. Please park in village with consideration for residents. See Turn End website for parking info.* **Sun 10 May (2-5). Adm £4.50, chd free. Home-made teas.**
Grade II registered series of garden rooms each with a different planting style enveloping architect's own Grade 2* listed house (not open). Dry garden, formal box garden, sunken gardens and mixed borders around curving lawn, all framed by ancient walls and mature trees. Bulbs, irises, wisteria, roses, ferns and climbers. Courtyards with pools, pergolas, secluded seating, and Victorian Coach House. Open studio with displays and demonstrations by creative artists.

53 TYTHROP PARK
Kingsey, HP17 8LT. Nick & Chrissie Wheeler. *2m E of Thame, 4m NW of Princes Risborough. Via A4129, at T-junction in Kingsey turn towards Haddenham, take L turn on bend. Parking in field on L.* **Sun 7 June (2-5.30). Adm £7, chd free. Home-made teas.**
10 acres of garden surrounds a C17 Grade I listed manor house (not open). This large and varied garden blends traditional and contemporary styles, featuring pool borders rich in grasses with a green and white theme, walled kitchen/cutting garden with large greenhouse at its heart, box parterre, deep mixed borders, water feature, rose garden, wildflower meadow, and many old trees and shrubs.

54 THE WALLED GARDEN
Wormsley, Stokenchurch, High Wycombe, HP14 3YE. Wormsley Estate. *Leave M40 at J5. Turn towards Ibstone. Entrance to estate is ¼ m on R. NB: 20mph speed limit on estate. Please do not drive on grass verges.* **Fri 12 June (10-3). Adm £7, chd free. Pre-booking essential, please visit www.ngs.org.uk/events for information & booking. Home-made teas.**
The Walled Garden at Wormsley Estate is a 2 acre garden providing flowers, vegetables and tranquil contemplative space for the family. For many years the garden was neglected until Sir Paul Getty purchased the estate in the mid-1980s. In 1991 the garden was redesigned by the renowned garden designer Penelope Hobhouse. The garden has changed over the years, but remains true to the original brief. Wheelchair access to grounds, please ensure you confirm upon booking.

55 THE WHITE HOUSE
Village Road, Denham Village, UB9 5BE. Mr & Mrs P G Courtenay-Luck. *3m NW of Uxbridge, 7m E of Beaconsfield. Signed from A40 or A412. Parking in village road. The White House is in centre of village, opp St Mary's Church.* **Sun 7 June (2-5). Adm £6, chd free. Cream teas.**
Well established 6 acre formal garden in picturesque setting. Mature trees and hedges with River Misbourne meandering through lawns. Shrubberies, flower beds, rockery, rose garden and orchard. Large walled garden. Herb garden, vegetable plot and Victorian greenhouses. Wheelchair access with gravel entrance and path to gardens.

56 20 WHITEPIT LANE
Flackwell Heath, High Wycombe, HP10 9HS. Trevor Jones, 01628 524876, **trevorol4969@gmail.com.** *¾ m E Flackwell Heath, 4m High Wycombe. From M40 J3 (west bound exit only) take 1st L, 300yds T-junction turn R, 300yds turn L uphill to centre of Flackwell Heath, turn L ¾ m, garden 75yds on R past mini-r'about.* **Visits by arrangement May to Aug for groups of up to 10. Weeks 10-16 May, 21-27 June, 19-25 July, 9-15 Aug for am, pm & eve visits. Adm £7, chd free. Light refreshments**
included.
The front garden has a seaside type landscape with timber groynes and a rock pool. The rear garden is long and thin with colour from Apr to Oct, containing many unusual plants, with steps and bridges over two ponds. Amongst the plants are a large Banana, an Albizia, Grevillea's, Callistemon's Abutilon, Salvia's and several Alstroemeria's. The beds are filled with mixed shrubs and herbaceous plants. Many rare and unusual plants and a garden railway.

57 WOODSIDE
23 Willow Lane, Amersham, HP7 9DW. Elin & Graham Stone. *On A413, 1m SE from Old Amersham, between Barley Lane & Finch Lane. The garden is the last but one, on the RH-side. Limited parking, please park with consideration to neighbours.* **Sat 13, Sun 14 June (2-5). Adm £3.50, chd free. Light refreshments & delicious home-made cakes.**
A small cottage garden, created on s-facing slope, integrating a circular lawn, lily pond, gravel paths and steps to a curved clematis and rose pergola. Rose beds and abundant humped borders. In contrast, a secret naturally arching, woodland path winds past a stumpery, a shade area and wildlife hedging leading to a kitchen garden and a bee hotel. Hidden seating areas abound. Artist's Studio. Features incl dragon flies, wildlife habitat, fernery, regular through-year evolution of potted decorative plants, and a very effective 8 monthly composting process.

Your visits help change lives – we've donated over £17 million to Macmillan Cancer Support since 1984

CAMBRIDGESHIRE

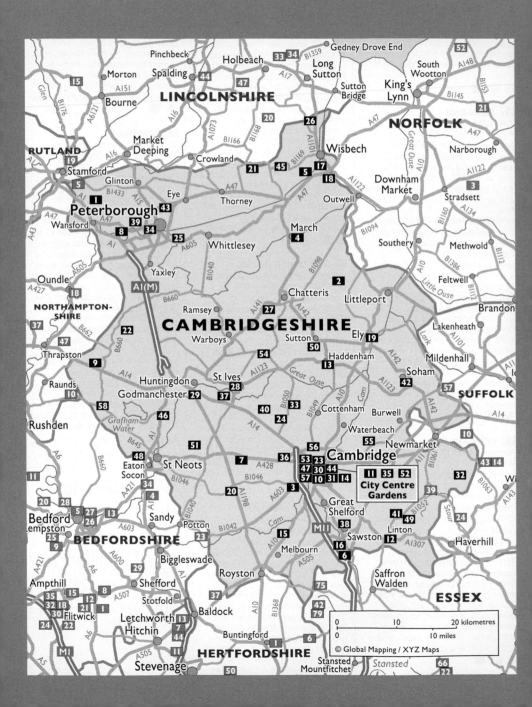

Historic cathedral cities, wide open skies and unique fenland landscapes make Cambridgeshire a special place to visit.

Our generous gardeners invite you to come and take a closer look at gardens to delight and surprise.

From the splendid college gardens in the city of Cambridge to rural idylls in isolated hamlets, the County has something to suit all tastes.

Stroll around our group gardens and be inspired by their diversity and interest. Explore spaces planned for the dry East Anglian climate and others on rich fenland soil. See the contemporary and the historic; small town courtyards, large country gardens and those maintained for wildlife and the environment. Be inspired by innovative and creative ideas and talk to our enthusiastic and knowledgeable gardeners.

Some are open by arrangement where your host will happily share plant knowledge, anecdotes and plant passions with you - so long as you have time to listen!

Begin the year with a visit to our early Spring gardens in February, enjoy a summer afternoon with friends or family, relax and unwind with good tea and cake in the surroundings of a beautiful garden. End with the spectacular autumn colours of trees and trees.

Whenever you visit, you can be sure that you will receive a warm welcome and a memorable day out.

Volunteers

County Organiser
Pam Bullivant
01353 667355
pam.bullivant@ngs.org.uk

Deputy County Organiser
Jenny Marks
07956 049257
jenny.marks@ngs.org.uk

County Treasurer
Nicholas Kyberd
01954 200568
n.kyberd@ntlworld.com

Booklet Coordinator
Jenny Marks
(As above)

Publicity
Penny Miles
01954 201415
penny.miles@ngs.org.uk

Social Media
Hetty Dean
hetty.dean@ngs.org.uk

Assistant County Organisers
Nicholas Kyberd
(as above)

Annette White
01638 730876
annette.white@ngs.org.uk

John Wylde
07973 523437
john.wylde@ngs.org.uk

National Garden Scheme Cambs
@GardenCambs
cambsngs

Left: Music Maze and Garden

OPENING DATES

All entries subject to change. For latest information check www.ngs.org.uk

Extended openings are shown at the beginning of the month.

Map locator numbers are shown to the right of each garden name.

January

Daily
Robinson College 47

February

Daily
Robinson College 47

Snowdrop Festival

Saturday 15th
NEW Caldrees Manor 6

Sunday 16th
Clover Cottage 12

Sunday 23rd
Clover Cottage 12

March

Daily
Robinson College 47

Sunday 1st
Clover Cottage 12

Sunday 29th
Music Maze and Garden 41

April

Daily to Sunday 19th
Robinson College 47

Sunday 5th
Kirtling Tower 32
Netherhall Manor 42
Trinity College Fellows' Garden 52

Sunday 19th
Churchill College 11
Fitzwilliam College 23
NEW Little Puffers 34

Monday 20th
NEW Little Puffers 34

Sunday 26th
◆ Docwra's Manor 15
Farm Cottage 20
Staploe Gardens 48

May

Sunday 3rd
Netherhall Manor 42

Saturday 9th
Chaucer Road Gardens 10

Sunday 10th
Chaucer Road Gardens 10
Farm Cottage 20
◆ Ferrar House 22
NEW Milton Hall 39

Sunday 17th
Sutton Gardens 50

Thursday 21st
Wild Rose Cottage 55

Friday 22nd
NEW 28 Houghton Road 28

Saturday 23rd
High Bank Cottage 26
NEW Little Oak 33

Sunday 24th
Cambourne Gardens 7
College Farm 13
Farm Cottage 20
High Bank Cottage 26
NEW 28 Houghton Road 28
NEW Little Oak 33

Monday 25th
NEW Little Oak 33

Sunday 31st
Island Hall 29

June

Every Monday to Friday from Monday 29th
Robinson College 47

Saturday 6th
Cottage Garden 14
Staploe Gardens 48
Twin Tarns 54

Sunday 7th
Barton Gardens 3
Catworth, Molesworth & Brington Gardens 9
Duxford Gardens 16
Ely Open Gardens 19
The Old Rectory 45
Staploe Gardens 48
Twin Tarns 54

Saturday 13th
Abbots Barn 1
NEW 28 Houghton Road 28

Sunday 14th
Abbots Barn 1
Elm House 18
Lucy Cavendish College 35

Saturday 20th
45 Beaver Lodge 4

Sunday 21st
45 Beaver Lodge 4
Farm Cottage 20
Green End Farm 24
Madingley Hall 36
Streetly End & West Wickham Gardens 49

Saturday 27th
NEW Ashdene 2
NEW Little Oak 33

Sunday 28th
NEW Ashdene 2
King's College Fellows' Garden and Provost's Garden 30
Kirtling Tower 32
NEW Little Oak 33
Mary Challis Garden 38

July

Daily
Robinson College 47

Saturday 4th
NEW Bramley Cottage 5
38 Norfolk Terrace Garden 44
Trinity Hall - Wychfield 53
Wrights Farm 58

Sunday 5th
NEW Bramley Cottage 5

Farm Cottage 20
Green End Farm 24
NEW 38 Kingston Street 31
38 Norfolk Terrace Garden 44
Wrights Farm 58

Saturday 11th
NEW Top Farm 51

Sunday 12th
NEW Top Farm 51

Sunday 19th
Farm Cottage 20

August

Daily to Friday 14th
Robinson College 47

Sunday 2nd
◆ Elgood's Brewery Gardens 17
Netherhall Manor 42

Sunday 9th
Netherhall Manor 42

Sunday 16th
Duxford Gardens 16
Wrights Farm 58

Saturday 22nd
45 Beaver Lodge 4

Sunday 23rd
45 Beaver Lodge 4
Castor House 8

Saturday 29th
Wolfson College Garden 57

September

Daily
Robinson College 47

Saturday 5th
The Night Garden 43

Saturday 12th
The Night Garden 43

Saturday 19th
The Night Garden 43

October

Every Monday to Friday
Robinson College 47

Your visits help change lives – your generosity has supported unpaid carers through donations to Carers Trust totalling over £4 million since 1996

Castor House

THE GARDENS

1 ABBOTS BARN

Southorpe, Stamford, PE9 3BX.
Carl & Vanessa Brown. *5m SE of Stamford, 8m W of Peterborough. On entering Southorpe Village from A47, 1st house on left.* Sat 13, Sun 14 June (1-5.30). Adm £5, chd free. Home-made teas. Vegan and gluten-free catered for.
2-acre garden surrounding converted Georgian barn. Large 'family' garden with herbaceous borders and wild flower meadow, allotment-sized vegetable plot, orchard, mediterranean gravel garden with mulberry tree, large glasshouse, 20 year-old woodland with mown grass paths, beach garden, wildlife pond, large courtyard garden with garden-sized croquet lawn, cutting flower garden, gravel/pergola walkways. We maintain the garden using organic methods, providing a rich wildlife habitat. Children of all ages welcome.

2 NEW ASHDENE

Wisbech Road, Manea, March, PE15 0HB. Mr & Mrs David White, www.endeavourtandt.com. *From direction of A142/ A141. After 5m, in Manea, turn from Station Rd into Wisbech Rd. The garden is opp Festival Close. Please call to arrange a visit on these dates.* 01354 688252, endeavourtandt@outlook.com. Sat 27, Sun 28 June (10.30-4). Adm £4, chd free. Home-made teas
When you enter this one acre garden be prepared to be amazed. The garden has a valley, medieval ruin, wibbly wobbly tree house, secret paths, a large pond, African hut, winter garden and, in the summer, tropical borders with bananas, palms, cannas and many other exotic plants. There are many quirky ideas and unusual features in the garden and it is intended as a garden for all seasons. Short gravel drive to enter garden. Access on level grass with some bark paths.

GROUP OPENING

3 BARTON GARDENS

High Street, Barton, Cambridge, CB23 7BG. *3½ m SW of Cambridge. Barton is on A603 Cambridge to Sandy Rd, ½ m for J12 M11.* Sun 7 June (2-5). Combined adm £5, chd free. Home-made teas in Barton Church, Village Hall (June). The White Horse Inn (118 High St) serves meals.

FARM COTTAGE
Dr R M Belbin.
(See separate entry)

GLEBE HOUSE
David & Sue Rapley.

114 HIGH STREET
Meta & Hugh Greenfield.

11 KINGS GROVE
Mrs Judith Bowen.

2 MAILES CLOSE
Mr Patrick Coulson.

31 NEW ROAD
Drs D & M Macdonald.

Varied group of large and small gardens reflecting different approaches to gardening. Farm Cottage: large landscaped cottage garden with herbaceous beds and themed woodland walk. Glebe House: a 1 acre mature, partly wooded and walled garden with large (unfenced) duck pond. Italianate style courtyard garden. Landscaped secret garden with gazebo. Cedar clad Artist Studio, Paintings, prints, cards & gifts for sale by Sue Rapley Art - www.suerapley.co.uk proceeds to NGS charities.114 High Street: small cottage garden with an unusual layout comprising several areas incl vegetables, fruit and a secret garden. 31 New Road: large, wildlife friendly cottage garden with a good show of spring flowers, mature shrubs, trees and a kitchen garden. The Six Houses: recently renovated gardens, incl winter and dry gardens, lovely spring bulbs and a small wood. 2 Mailes Close: L shaped Garden completely renovated 3 years ago with herbaceous border, veg and fruit areas. 11 Kings Grove: a garden developed from a wilderness since 1992 with a lawn, flowers and shrub area and a fruit area. The White Horse Inn (118 High Street) serves meals. Some gardens have gravel paths.

4 45 BEAVER LODGE

Henson Road, March, PE15 8BA.
Mr & Mrs Maria & Paul Nielsen Bom, 01354 656185, beaverbom@gmail.com. *A141 to Wisbech rd into March, turn L into Westwood Ave, follow rd leading to Henson Rd, turn R. Property opp school playground.* Sat 20, Sun 21 June, Sat 22, Sun 23 Aug (10.30-4). Adm £3, chd free. Home-made teas. Visits also by arrangement May to Sept for groups of up to 30.
An Oriental garden with large numbers of bonsai both large and small and different types of acer, pagodas, oriental statues, water features and pond with Koi carp create a peaceful and relaxing atmosphere. The garden is divided into different rooms one of which has the Mediterranean feel with Tree Ferns, Lemon trees, Bougainvilleas and a great variety of plants and water fountain. With a collection of more than 120 bonsai trees, different acer, pond, water features and oriental statues and pagoda.

5 NEW BRAMLEY COTTAGE

Barton Road, Wisbech St Mary, Wisbech, PE13 4RP. Jim & Mel Wakefield, 01945 410554, melaniewright061@btinternet.com. *Coming towards Wisbech St Mary from Wisbech, when you have come through a sweeping RH bend we are the 1st house on the R.* Sat 4, Sun 5 July (10-5). Adm £5, chd free. Light refreshments. Visits also by arrangement Mar to Oct for groups of 20+. Evenings and weekends only.
This garden has been built over the last twelve years from an area of brambles and rubbish. it is an adult garden with structures of a rose arch and a wisteria and laburnum arch. It has an antique water bowser used as a planter and various quirky pieces that we like. On display also will be a selection of vintage horticultural machinery and hand tools.

6 NEW CALDREES MANOR

Abbey Street, Ickleton, Saffron Walden, CB10 1SS. *In the centre of Ickleton on Abbey Street. Parking for 30 cars at village hall. From M11 J10, A505 East, then through Duxford village, signed Ickleton. From Saffron Walden, via Gt Chesterford.* Sat 15 Feb, Sat 17 Oct (10-4).

Adm £5, chd free. Home-made teas in Ickleton Village Hall. C19 Manor House (not open) with extensive formal gardens, lakes and streams, over 120 varieties of Acer Palmatum, many specimen trees, a Japanese garden, orchard, woodland walks, wildlife garden and wild flower meadow. As well as snowdrops in late winter, the garden has been designed to peak in spring and autumn. Some gravel, and a few steps.

GROUP OPENING

7 CAMBOURNE GARDENS
Great Cambourne, CB23 6AH. 8m W of Cambridge on A428. From A428: take Cambourne junction into Great Cambourne. From B1198, enter village at Lower Cambourne & drive through to Great Cambourne. Follow NGS signs via either route to start at any garden. **Sun 24 May (11-5). Combined adm £6, chd free. Home-made teas. Teas and cakes at 13 Monkfield Lane; coffee and biscotti at 43 Monkfield Lane; cold drinks at 18 Foxhollow.**

13 FENBRIDGE
Lucinda and Tony Williams.

18 FOXHOLLOW
Babs & Bob Cox.

14 GRANARY WAY
Jackie Hutchinson.

88 GREENHAZE LANE
Darren & Irette Murray.

8 LANGATE GREEN
Steve & Julie Friend.

5 MAYFIELD WAY
Debbie & Mike Perry.

14 MILLER WAY
Geoff Warmington, 01954710152, laine.april@btinternet.com. Visits also by arrangement.

43 MONKFIELD LANE
Tony & Penny Miles.

A unique and inspiring modern group, all created from new build in just a few years. This selection of eight demonstrates how imagination and gardening skill can be combined in a short time to create great effects from unpromising and awkward beginnings. The grouping includes foliage gardens with collections of carnivorous pitcher plants and hostas; a suntrap garden for play, socialising and colour; gardens with ponds and many other beautiful borders

showing their owners' creativity and love of growing fine plants well. One inspiring garden features a tiny space split between a recreation of a beach complete with bar serving cold drinks, contrasted with a miniature Moroccan riad. The group's largest garden features carefully considered borders, a wildlife pond and vegetable garden. Cambourne is one of Cambridgeshire's newest communities, and this grouping showcases the happy, vibrant place our village has become. No garden is more than 18 years old, and most are much younger.

8 CASTOR HOUSE
2, Peterborough Road, Castor, Peterborough, PE5 7AX. Ian & Claire Winfrey, ian@winfrey.co.uk, www.castorhousegardens.co.uk. 4m W of Peterborough. House on main Peterborough Rd in Castor. Parking in paddock off Water Lane. **Sun 23 Aug (2-5). Adm £6, chd free. Home-made teas. Visits also by arrangement June to Sept for groups of 20+.** 12 acres of gardens and woodland on a slope, terraced and redesigned 2010. Italianate spring fed ponds and stream gardens. Potager with greenhouse and exotic borders. Willow arbour and woodland garden. Peony and prunus walk. Rose and cottage gardens, 'Hot' double border, stumpery. Orchard in walled gardens. Only partial access for wheelchairs due to sloping nature of the garden.

GROUP OPENING

9 CATWORTH, MOLESWORTH & BRINGTON GARDENS
Molesworth, Huntingdon, PE28 0QD. 10m W of Huntingdon. A14 W for Molesworth & Brington exit at J16 onto B660. **Sun 7 June (2-6). Combined adm £4, chd free. Home-made teas at Molesworth House and Yew Tree Cottage.**

32 HIGH STREET
Colin Small.

MOLESWORTH HOUSE
John Prentis.

YEW TREE COTTAGE
Christine & Don Eggleston.

Molesworth House is an old rectory garden with everything that you'd both expect and hope for, given its Victorian past. There are surprising corners to this traditional take on a happy and relaxed, yet also formal garden. Yew Tree Cottage, informal garden approx 1 acre, complements the C16 building (not open) and comprises flower beds, lawns, vegetable patch, boggy garden, copses and orchard. Plants in pots and hanging baskets. High Street, Catworth is a long narrow garden with many rare plants including ferns, herbaceous borders, woodland area and wildlife pond. Partial wheelchair access.

Kings College, Fellows' Garden

© Simon Baylis

GROUP OPENING

10 CHAUCER ROAD GARDENS
Cambridge, CB2 7EB. *1m S of Cambridge. Off Trumpington Rd (A1309), nr Brooklands Ave junction. Parking available at MRC Psychology Dept on Chaucer Rd.* **Sat 9, Sun 10 May (2-5). Combined adm £7, chd free. Home-made teas at Upwater Lodge.**

11 CHAUCER ROAD
Mark & Jigs Hill.

12 CHAUCER ROAD
Mr & Mrs Bradley.

UPWATER LODGE
Mr & Mrs George Pearson, 07890 080303, jmp@pearson.co.uk.
Visits also by arrangement May & June.

11 Chaucer Road is a ¾ acre Edwardian garden that has changed rapidly over the ensuing 110 yrs. A rock garden with pond and large weeping Japanese maple dates from about 1930. 12 Chaucer Road is a half acre town garden with mature trees, Japanese themed garden and unusually for this part of the world, some impressive ericaceous planting. Upwater Lodge is an Edwardian academic's house with 7 acres of grounds. It has mature trees, fine lawns, old wisterias, and colourful borders. There is a small, pretty potager with a selection of fruits, and a well maintained grass tennis court. A network of paths through a wooded area lead down to a dyke, water meadows and a small flock of rare breed sheep. Enjoy a walk by the river and watch the punts go by. Buy home-made teas and sit in the garden or take them down to enjoy a lazy afternoon with ducks, geese, swans and heron on the riverbank. Cakes made with garden fruit where possible. Swings and climbing ropes. Plant stall possible but please email to check. Some gravel areas and grassy paths with fairly gentle slopes.

11 CHURCHILL COLLEGE
Storey's Way, Cambridge, CB3 0DS. University of Cambridge, www.chu.cam.ac.uk/about/grounds-gardens/. *1m from M11 J13. 1m NW of Cambridge city centre. Turn into Storeys Way*

from Madingley Rd (A1303), or from Huntingdon Rd (A1307). Parking on site. **Sun 19 Apr (2-5). Combined adm with Fitzwilliam College £5, chd free. Home-made teas in College Buttery.**
42 acre site designed in 1960s for foliage and form, to provide year round interest in peaceful and relaxing surrounds with courtyards, large open spaces and specimen trees. 10m x 5m orchid house, herbaceous plantings. Beautiful grouping of Prunus Tai Haku (great white cherry) trees forming striking canopy and drifts of naturalised bulbs in grass around the site. The planting provides a setting for the impressive collection of modern sculpture. Orchid house, Sculptures, trees, bulbs, landscape. The greenhouse is restricted in size.

12 CLOVER COTTAGE
50 Streetly End, West Wickham, CB21 4RP. Mr Paul & Mrs Shirley Shadford, 01223 893122, shirleyshadford@live.co.uk. *3m from Linton, 3m from Haverhill & 2m from Balsham. From Horseheath turn L, from Balsham turn R, thatched cottage opposite triangle of grass next to old windmill.* **Every Sun 16 Feb to 1 Mar (2-4). Adm £2.50, chd free. Light refreshments. Free hot drinks in the summerhouse. Opening with Streetly End & West Wickham Gardens on Sun 21 June (12-5). Visits also by arrangement Feb to June.**
In winter find a flowering cherry tree, borders of snowdrops, aconites, iris reticulata, hellebores and miniature narcissus throughout the packed small garden which has inspiring ideas on use of space. Pond and arbour, raised beds of fruit and vegetables. In summer arches of roses and clematis. Hardy geraniums, delightful borders of English roses and herbaceous plants. Snowdrops, hellebores and spring flowering bulbs for sale for the snowdrop festival , plants also for sale in June. NO WHEELCHAIRS, PRAMS, PUSHCHAIRS, WHEELED WALKERS OR DOG ACCESS TO THE GARDEN AT ALL.

13 COLLEGE FARM
Station Road, Haddenham, Ely, CB6 3XD. Sheila & Jeremy Waller, www.primaveragallery.co.uk. *From Stretham & Wilburton, at Xrds in Haddenham, turn R. Pass the church & exactly at the bottom of the hill, turn L down narrow drive, with a mill wheel on R of the drive.* **Sun 24 May (2-5).**

Adm £6, chd free.
40 acres around an intact Victorian farm. Walks, galleries, flower and sculpture cattle yard. Roses, wild flowers, water plants, foxgloves and plantings of trees, hedges and fruit trees, amongst ponds and through meadows, add colour and structure. Splendid fen views, lovely water features and ancient ridge and furrow pasture land. Original farm buildings, outside galleries and inside galleries full of extraordinary British paintings, art and craft. Abundant wildlife. Interesting wild flowers - e.g. Jack go to bed at noon and Salsify. Wheelchair access is only possible around the garden near the house, but not through the gallery, farm, milking parlour and many of the walks.

14 COTTAGE GARDEN
79 Sedgwick Street, Cambridge, CB1 3AL. Rosie Wilson, 01223 570890, p.wilson34@ntlworld.com. *From town centre or park & ride, go down Mill Rd over railway bridge. If driving take 2nd L Cavendish Rd, then 2nd R which leads into Sedgwick St.* **Sat 6 June (2-5.30). Adm £3.50, chd free. Home-made teas. Visits also by arrangement June & July for groups of up to 10.**
Long narrow and planted in the cottage garden style with over 40 roses some on arches and growing through trees. Particularly planned to encourage wildlife with small pond, mature trees and shrubs. Perennials and some unusual plants interspersed with sculptures. Large number of roses. Some growing through trees and over arches.
☕

15 ♦ DOCWRA'S MANOR
2 Meldreth Road, Shepreth, Royston, SG8 6PS. Mrs Faith Raven, 01763 260677, faithraven@btinternet.com, www.docwrasmanorgarden.co.uk. *8m S of Cambridge. ½m W of A10. Garden is opp the War Memorial in Shepreth. King's Cross-Cambridge train stop 5 min walk.* **For NGS: Sun 26 Apr (2-5). Adm £5, chd free. Home-made teas. For other opening times and information, please phone, email or visit garden website.**
2½ acres of choice plants in a series of enclosed gardens. Tulips and Judas trees. Opened for the NGS for more than 40yrs. The garden

is featured in great detail in a book published 2013 'The Gardens of England' edited by George Plumptre. Garden open Weds & Fri 10-5, 1st Sun in the month 2-5. Unusual plants. Wheelchair access to most parts of the garden, gravel paths.

GROUP OPENING

16 DUXFORD GARDENS
Bustlers Cottage, 26 St Peters Street, Duxford, CB22 4RP. *Most gardens are close to the centre of the village of Duxford. S of the A505 between M11 J10 & Sawston. One garden in Ickleton, between Duxford and Saffron Walden.* Sun 7 June (2-6). Combined adm £7, chd free. Sun 16 Aug (2-6). Combined adm £5, chd free. Home-made teas at one of the churches in the village (tea and cake) and at Bustlers Cottage (for cream teas if fine). Venues will be clearly signed.

6 THE BIGGEN
Mrs Bettye Reynolds.
Open on all dates

9 THE BIGGEN
Valerie Bennett.
Open on Sun 7 June

BUSTLERS COTTAGE
John & Jenny Marks.
Open on Sun 7 June

NEW **CLODERTON HOUSE**
Mark Titcomb.
Open on Sun 7 June

NEW **GIFU**
Cali Holberry.
Open on Sun 7 June

2 GREEN STREET
Mr Bruce Crockford.
Open on Sun 7 June

NEW **5 GREEN STREET**
Jenny Shaw.
Open on Sun 7 June

NEW **28 GREEN STREET**
Gordon Lister.
Open on Sun 16 Aug

16 ICKLETON ROAD
Claire James.
Open on Sun 7 June

NEW **26 PETERSFIELD ROAD**
Robert & Josephine Smit.
Open on Sun 16 Aug

31 ST PETER'S STREET
Mr David Baker.
Open on Sun 7 June

Several gardens new to the NGS, of different sizes and characters. Two openings. In June nine gardens, from the charming small cottage garden at 2 Green Street to two gardens in the Biggen running down to the river showing how differently similar spaces can be gardened. The sunny aspects at 16 Ickleton Road, and further into Ickleton, Gifu at 3 Birds Close, have interesting and unusual planting, as does 31 St Peters Street also with its rockery in front of the house. Bustlers Cottage has an acre of cottage garden and Cloderton House is surrounded by farmland, with orchard, formal

gardens and wild flower meadow. 5 Green Street's walled garden contains lawn, pergolas, various beds and vegetables. In August there is an opportunity to revisit one of the gardens in the Biggen and see the 30 varieties of dahlias at 28 Green St at their best. The innovative green walls in the new garden at 26 Petersfield Rd are vibrant with colour. A village scarecrow festival is planned to coincide with the June garden opening. Some gravel paths and a few steps, mostly avoidable.

Wrights Farm

17 ◆ ELGOOD'S BREWERY GARDENS

North Brink, Wisbech, PE13 1LW.
Elgood & Sons Ltd, 01945 583160,
info@elgoods-brewery.co.uk,
www.elgoods-brewery.co.uk.
*1m W of town centre. Leave A47
towards Wisbech Centre. Cross river
to North Brink. Follow river & brown
signs to brewery & car park beyond.*
**For NGS: Sun 2 Aug (12-4). Adm
£4, chd free. Light refreshments.
For other opening times and
information, please phone, email or
visit garden website.**
Approx 4 acres of peaceful garden
featuring 250 yr old specimen trees
providing a framework to lawns,
lake, rockery, herb garden and maze.
Wheelchair access to Visitor Centre
and most areas of the garden.

18 ELM HOUSE

Main Road, Elm, Wisbech,
PE14 0AB. Mrs Diana Bullard.
*2½ m SW of Wisbech. From A1101
take B1101, signed Elm, Friday
Bridge. Elm House is ⅓ m on L, well
signed.* **Sun 14 June (1-5). Adm £4,
chd free. Home-made teas.**
Walled garden with arboretum,
many rare trees and shrubs, mixed
perennials C17 house (not open).

New 3 acre flower meadow. Children
welcome. Guide dogs only please.

GROUP OPENING

19 ELY OPEN GARDENS

Ely, CB6. *14m N of Cambridge.
Parking at Barton Rd car park, Tower
Rd, (adjacent to 42 Cambridge
Rd); the Grange Council Offices; St
Mary's St. These within easy reach
of most of the gardens. A map
given at first garden visited.* **Sun 7
June (12-6). Combined adm £6,
chd free. Home-made teas at 42
Cambridge Road & 14 Lynn Road.**

**BISHOP OF HUNTINGDON'S
GARDEN**
Dagmar, Bishop of Huntingdon.

THE BISHOP'S HOUSE
The Bishop of Ely.

42 CAMBRIDGE ROAD
Mr & Mrs J & C Switsur.

12 CHAPEL STREET
Ken & Linda Ellis.

NEW 38 CHAPEL STREET
Peter & Julia Williams,
01353 659161,
peterrcwilliams@onetel.com.
Visits also by arrangement Mar

to Oct for groups of up to 20.
Individuals welcome. On-site
parking for 2 cars only. Teas by
arrangement.

5B DOWNHAM ROAD
Mr Christopher Cain.

17B HILLS LANE
Mr & Mrs John & Alison Eden-
Eadon.

A delightful and varied group of
gardens in an historic Cathedral
city: The Bishop's House adjoins Ely
Cathedral and has mixed planting with
a formal rose garden, wisteria and
more. Local artist displaying and selling
work. The Bishop of Huntingdon's
garden is for family and entertaining.
Lawns, herbaceous borders, an
orchard and more! 12 Chapel Street,
a small town garden, reflecting the
owners varied gardening interests,
from alpines to herbaceous and
vegetables all linked with a railway! 38,
Chapel St has year round interest and
is bursting with unusual and interesting
planting. 42 Cambridge Road, a
secluded town garden has colourful
herbaceous borders, roses, shrubs
and trees. 17b Hills Lane, a tiny garden
with no grass! Paving and raised beds
show how the owners have made their
garden manageable for older people,
or people with limited mobility. 5b

Abbot's Barn

BUG HOTEL Made by CAITLIN and DAD

Downham Road shows how to rise to the challenge of a small interestingly shaped area. Careful planting has created a tranquil area. Wheelchair access to areas of most gardens.

20 FARM COTTAGE

18 High Street, CB23 7BG. Dr R M Belbin. *Barton. On A603 Cambridge to Sandy Rd, ½ m for J12 M11.* **Sun 26 Apr, Sun 10, Sun 24 May, Sun 21 June, Sun 5, Sun 19 July (2-5). Adm by donation. Opening with Barton Gardens on Sun 7 June.** A landscaped cottage garden with courtyard and peripheral woodland and walled garden. On the dates below, visitors will be asked to record their names, make a voluntary contribution in the NGS box and receive an entry leaflet giving guidance on the walk round a mature garden together with some philosophical messages about how to gain the most from the journey through life.

21 FENLEIGH

Inkerson Fen, Off Common Rd, Throckenholt, PE12 0QY. Jeff & Barbara Stalker, barbarastalker@gmail.com. *2m from Gedney Hill. Turn R on to B1166 take next R into Common Rd following NGS signs approx 1m. From Parson Drove on B1166 turn L into Common Rd following NGS signs approx 3m.* **Visits by arrangement. Light refreshments.** Set in 4 acres incl 2 acre paddock. Quirky areas for easy maintenance. A fish pond dominates the garden surrounded with planting. Seating and two permanent gazebos if the weather is inclement. Patio with pots and raised beds, BBQ area containing ferns and acers. Small wooded area, poly tunnels and corners of the garden for wildlife. Large grass area for family fun and games.

22 ◆ FERRAR HOUSE

Little Gidding, Huntingdon, PE28 5RJ. Mrs Susan Capp, 01832 293383, info@ferrarhouse.co.uk, www.ferrarhouse.co.uk. *Take Mill Rd from Great Gidding (turn at Fox & Hounds) then after 1m turn R down single track lane. Car Park at Ferrar House.* **For NGS: Sun 10 May (10.30-5). Adm £4, chd free. Home-made teas. For other opening times and information, please phone, email or visit garden website.** A peaceful garden of a Retreat House with beautiful uninterrupted views across meadows and farm land. Adjacent to the historic Church of St John's it was here that a small religious community was formed in the C17. The poet T. S. Eliot visited in 1936 and it inspired the 4th of his Quartets named Little Gidding. Lawn and walled flower beds with a walled vegetable garden. Games on the lawn. Traditional wooden garden games, tea and home-made cakes, plant stall. History talks in Church. WC accessible at Ferrar House.

23 FITZWILLIAM COLLEGE

University of Cambridge, Storey's Way, Cambridge, CB3 0DG. Master & Fellows, www.fitz.cam.ac.uk. *1m NW of Cambridge city centre. Turn into Storey's Way from Madingley Rd (A1303) or from Huntingdon Rd (A1307). Free parking on site.* **Sun 19 Apr (2-5). Combined adm with Churchill College £5, chd free. Cafe open for drinks and snacks.** Traditional topiary, borders, woodland walk, lawns from the Edwardian period are complemented by modern planting and wild meadow. The avenue of limes, underplanted with spring bulbs, leads to The Grove, the 1813 house once belonging to the Darwin Family (not open). Some ramped pathways.

24 GREEN END FARM

Over Road, Longstanton, Cambridge, CB24 3DW. Sylvia Newman, www.sngardendesign.co.uk. *From A14 take the direction of Longstanton At the r'about, take the 2nd exit At the next r'about, turn L (this shows a dead end on the sign) We're a couple of hundred metres on L.* **Sun 21 June, Sun 5 July (1-5). Adm £4, chd free. Home-made teas. and refreshments.** A developing garden that's beginning to blend well with the farm. An interesting combination of new and established spaces interlinked with a design eye. An established orchard with beehives; two wildlife ponds. An outside kitchen, productive kitchen and cutting garden. Doves, chickens and sheep complete the picture!

25 NEW 6 HEMINGFORD CRESCENT

Stanground, Peterborough, PE2 8LL. Michael & Nick Mitchell, 07880 871763, michaelandnick64@gmail.com. *South side of city centre. 10 minutes drive from A1M. Take Whittlesey Rd B1092. Coming out of town look for Apple Green petrol stn on L. Turn into Coneygree Rd. Follow road round, Hemingford Crescent is the 6th turning on R.* **Visits by arrangement May to Sept for groups of up to 20. Adm £5, chd free. Light refreshments.** Medium sized city garden. Inspired by our travels to Morocco, Egypt and India. Mixture of exotic planting, shrubs and perennials. Various seating areas including an outside dining area and an enclosed moroccan/egyptian room. Raised beds and pond area. Michael is an artist and his work is available for viewing. Partial wheelchair access. No dogs.

26 HIGH BANK COTTAGE

Kirkgate, Tydd St Giles, Wisbech, PE13 5NE. Mrs F Savill. *Heading from Wisbech, North Cambs. A1101 take turn signed Tydd St Giles. Parking at Tydd St Giles golf & country club, a few minutes walk from the garden. www.pure-leisure.co.uk/parks/tydd-st-giles/overview/.* **Sat 23, Sun 24 May (10.30-4). Adm £4, chd £1. Light refreshments.** The garden is a tranquil oasis from the hurry of life. A cottage garden, mainly, but it has many mature trees and shrubs. It is separated into different areas with seating so that the views of the garden can be appreciated. There are two ponds, one of which has fish, and a river bank with areas for wildlife, and also an allotment. Please supervise children closely. NGS discretionary ticket holders £2. Coffee/tea, home-made cakes and biscuits available to purchase. Also, plants and garden related craft items. Meals are available at the golf course. There are gravelled areas, and some steps. The brick paths are uneven, and all of these areas can be slippery when wet.

27 HORSESHOE FARM

Chatteris Road, Somersham, Huntingdon, PE28 3DR. Neil & Claire Callan, 01354 693546, nccallan@yahoo.co.uk. *9m NE of St Ives, Cambs. Easy access from the A14. Situated on E side of B1050, 4m N of Somersham Village. Parking for 8 cars in the drive.* **Visits by arrangement May to July for groups of up to 20. Adm £4, chd free. Home-made teas.**
This ¾ acre plant-lovers' garden has a large pond with summer-house and decking, bog garden, alpine troughs, mixed rainbow island beds with over 30 varieties of bearded irises, water features, a small hazel woodland area, wildlife meadow, secret corners and a lookout tower for wide Fenland views and bird watching. Featured in WI Life, Amateur Gardening and Garden News.

28 NEW 28 HOUGHTON ROAD

St Ives, PE27 6RH. Julie Pepper. *On the A1123, western edge of St Ives. Garden on L as you enter St Ives from Huntingdon. Please call to arrange a visit on these dates: 07788 657568.* **Fri 22, Sun 24 May, Sat 13 June (12-5.30). Adm £3, chd free. Home-made teas. Cold drinks, gluten free options.**
Step into the peace and tranquility of Acer heaven, created by designer Julie. Among more than 60 Acers, of which there are 43 varieties, you will also find a patio area set out as a room for outside dining and relaxation. There is much use of dramatic accent planting, punctuated with sculpture, artifacts, water feature, seating areas, bonsai, hostas, trees, ferns and many other interesting plants.

29 ISLAND HALL

Godmanchester, PE29 2BA. Mr Christopher & Lady Linda Vane Percy, www.islandhall.com. *1m S of Huntingdon (A1). 15m NW of Cambridge (A14). In centre of Godmanchester next to free Mill Yard car park.* **Sun 31 May (10.30-5). Adm £4.50, chd free. Home-made teas in the 'Fisherman's Lodge' on the Island set within the grounds.**
3-acre grounds. Tranquil riverside setting with mature trees. Chinese bridge over Saxon mill race to embowered island with wild flowers. Garden restored in 1983 to mid C18

formal design, with box hedging, clipped hornbeams, parterres, topiary, good vistas over borrowed landscape and C18 wrought iron and stone urns. The ornamental island has been replanted with Princeton elms (ulmus americana). Mid C18 mansion (not open).

30 KING'S COLLEGE FELLOWS' GARDEN AND PROVOST'S GARDEN

Queen's Road, Cambridge, CB2 1ST. Provost & Scholars of King's College. *In Cambridge, the Backs. Entry by gate at junction of Queen's Rd & West Rd. Parking at Lion Yard 10mins walk, or some pay & display places in West Rd & Queen's Rd.* **Sun 28 June (2-5). Adm £4, chd free. Home-made teas.**
Fine example of a Victorian garden with rare specimen trees. With a small woodland walk and a kitchen/allotment garden created in 2011 and a rose pergola and herbaceous border created in 2013. Now with an exciting sub-tropical border and a new Rond Pont entrance feature celebrating the mathematicians who studied and researched at King's over the centuries. Gravel paths.

31 NEW 38 KINGSTON STREET

Cambridge, CB1 2NU. Wendy & Clive Chapman. *Central Cambridge. A603 Gonville Place R into Mill Rd, L at St Barnabus Church to Gwydir St, L to Hooper St, R into Kingston St. From Ring Rd A1134 West up Mill Rd over railway bridge R at St Barnabus Church.* **Sun 5 July (2-5). Adm £2, chd free. Also open 38 Norfolk Terrace Garden.**
A courtyard garden with contrasts between deep shade and sunlit areas. Our aim is to provide year round colour. Raised beds and pots of various sizes with a range of perennial and annual planting. Small step into garden.

32 KIRTLING TOWER

Newmarket Road, Kirtling, Newmarket, CB8 9PA. The Lord & Lady Fairhaven. *6m SE of Newmarket. From Newmarket head towards village of Saxon Street, through village to Kirtling, turn L at war memorial, signed to Upend, entrance is signed on the L.* **Sun 5 Apr, Sun 28 June (11-4). Adm £5,**

chd free. **Light refreshments at the Church throughout the day. Selection of delicious hot and cold food, sandwiches, cakes, tea and coffee.**
Surrounded by a moat, formal gardens and parkland. In the spring there are swathes of daffodils, narcissi, crocus, muscari, chionodoxa and tulips. Closer to the house, vast lawn areas Secret and Cutting Gardens. In the summer the Walled Garden has superb herbaceous borders with anthemis, hemerocallis, geraniums and delphiniums. The Victorian Garden is filled with peonies. Views of surrounding countryside. A Classic car display will be in attendance. The Arcadia Recorder Group will be playing in the walled garden. A variety of plant and craft stalls on both dates as well as a display of Stonework from the Fairhaven Stoneyard. Many of the paths and routes around the garden are grass - they are accessible by wheelchairs, but can be hard work if wet.

33 NEW LITTLE OAK

66 Station Road, Willingham, Cambridge, CB24 5HG. Mr & Mrs Eileen Hughes, www.littleoak.org. uk/garden/index.html. *4m N of A14 J29 near Cambridge. Easy to find on the main road in the village.* **Sat 23, Sun 24 May (1-5). Home-made teas. Evening opening Mon 25 May (6-9). Sat 27, Sun 28 June (1-5). Home-made teas. Adm £4.50, chd free.**
New for 2020 Michael and Eileen welcome you to our 1 acre garden. Featuring a 50' Laburnum Walk with perennial borders, ponds, Cottage Garden, Fruit Cage, Kitchen Garden/greenhouses/growing tunnels, Orchard, Mediterranean and Rose Garden, Coppice and Chickens. Weather permitting, Michael will demonstrate wood turning using a pole lathe in the coppice throughout afternoon openings. Home-made teas (afternoon openings only). Main garden is wheelchair accessible Driveway parking for disabled use only.

34 NEW LITTLE PUFFERS

13 Apsley Way, Longthorpe, Peterborough, PE3 9NE. Mr Keith Richardson. *Take the turning to Longthorpe off the A47. Apsley Way is in the middle of the village*

between 'The Fox and Hounds' Pub & Longthorpe church. **Sun 19, Mon 20 Apr (2-5). Adm £4, chd £2. Tea.** Years ago my wife and I built the layout of the back garden around our model railway. we added structural evergreens, fragrant shrubs, a clipped topiary hen and early flowering bulbs. A viewing platform with colourful pots leads to a wooden bridge over the track to the lawn. Sit awhile on the sunny patio enjoying a small trickling pond, home to three fat frogs. Children welcome, no dogs please. working model railway.

35 LUCY CAVENDISH COLLEGE

Lady Margaret Road, Cambridge, CB3 0BU. *1m NW of Gt St Mary. College situated on the corner of Lady Margaret Rd & Madingley Rd (A1303). Entrance off Lady Margaret Rd.* **Sun 14 June (2-5). Adm £3.50, chd free.**
The gardens of 4 late Victorian houses have been combined and developed over past 25yrs into an informal 3 acre garden. Fine mature trees shade densely planted borders. An Anglo Saxon herb garden is situated in one corner. The garden provides a rich wildlife habitat.

36 MADINGLEY HALL

Cambridge, CB23 8AQ. **University of Cambridge, 01223 746222, reservations@madingleyhall.co.uk, www.madingleyhall.co.uk.** *4m W of Cambridge. 1m from M11 J13.* **Sun 21 June (2.30-5.30). Adm £5, chd free. Home-made teas.**
C16 Hall (not open) set in 8 acres of attractive grounds landscaped by Capability Brown. Features incl landscaped walled garden with hazel walk, alpine bed, medicinal border and rose pergola. Historic meadow, topiary, mature trees and wide variety of hardy plants.

37 ◆ THE MANOR, HEMINGFORD GREY

Hemingford Grey, PE28 9BN. Mrs D S Boston, 01480 463134, diana_boston@hotmail.com, www.greenknowe.co.uk. *4m E of Huntingdon. Off A14. Entrance to garden by small gate off river towpath. Limited parking on verge halfway up drive. Parking near house also limited. Otherwise please park in village/.* **For opening times and information, please phone, email or visit garden website.**
Garden designed and planted by author Lucy Boston, surrounds 12th Century manor house on which Green Knowe books based (house open by appt). 3 acre 'cottage' garden with topiary, snowdrops, old roses, extensive collection of irises incl Dykes Medal winners and Cedric Morris varieties, herbaceous borders with mainly scented plants. Meadow with mown paths. Enclosed by river, moat and wilderness. Late May splendid show of irises followed by the old roses. Care is taken with the planting to start the year with a large variety of snowdrops and to extend the flowering season with colour through to the first frosts from unusual annuals. The garden is interesting even in winter with the topiary. Gravel paths but wheelchairs are encouraged to go on the lawns.

38 MARY CHALLIS GARDEN

68 High Street, Sawston, Cambridge, CB22 3BG. **A M Challis Trust Ltd, www.challistrust.org.uk.** *5m SE of Cambridge. Passageway between 60 High St & 66 High St (Billsons Opticians).* **Sun 28 June (1-5). Adm £3, chd free. Home-made teas.**
Gifted to Sawston in 2006, this 2 acre garden is maintained by volunteers to benefit wildlife and for the local community. Winter/spring long border, drifts of crocuses, snowdrops and aconites in spring; very colourful summer flowerbeds. Woodland, specimen trees, pond, raised vegetable beds, orchard, vine house, wild flower meadow and beehives. Featured in Cambridgeshire Journal 'The Lost Garden'. Open year round: 9.30-12.30am Tues, Thurs & Sat; 2-4pm summer and 1-3pm winter on Suns. House and museum open every Tue 10-12am and for Open Gardens. Paths and lawns accessible by wheelchair from car-park.

39 NEW MILTON HALL

Milton Park, Milton, Peterborough, PE6 7AG. **Lady Isabella Naylor-Leyland.** *Please use entrance off A47, shared with Peterborough, (Milton), Golf Club* **Sun 10 May (10.30-5.30). Adm £5, chd free. Cream teas.**
20 acres of pleasure grounds laid out by Humphrey Repton in 1791 including lake, mature trees, extensive lawns, hard gravel paths, historic orangery. Enclosed walled Italian garden and kitchen garden. Teas served in orangery all day. Garden very level and well serviced by hard gravel surfaced paths.

Trinity College, Fellows' Garden

© Simon Baylis

40 5 MOAT WAY

Swavesey, CB24 4TR. Mr & Mrs N Kyberd, 01954 200568, n.kyberd@ntlworld.com. *Off A14, 2m beyond Bar Hill. Look for School Lane/Fen Drayton Rd, at mini r'about turn into Moat Way, no.5 is approx 100 metres on L.* **Visits by arrangement June & July for groups of up to 10. Adm £4, chd free.**
Colourful garden filled with collection of trees, shrubs and perennials. Large patio area displaying many specimen foliage plants in planters, incl pines, hostas and acers.

41 MUSIC MAZE AND GARDEN

Troy Green, 2A Nine Chimneys Lane, Balsham, Cambridge, CB21 4ES. Mr & Mrs Jim & Hilary Potter, 01223 891211, hppotter@btinternet.com, www.balshammaze.org.uk. *In centre of Balsham just off High St. 3m E of A11, 12m S of Newmarket & 10m SE of Cambridge. Car parking in the High St or the Church car park. 2 disabled spaces in Nine Chimneys Lane.* **Sun 29 Mar (1-5). Adm £5, chd £2. Home-made teas. Visits also by arrangement Apr to Oct for groups of 10 to 20. Allow 2 hours. Min £70 incl refreshments.**
Two acres of garden with spring bulbs, mixed borders, raised vegetable beds, gravel garden, large duck pond, wild flower meadow, an orchard, modern sculptures and human sundial. A yew Music Maze was planted in 1993 with golden yew (Taxus elegantissima) in the shape of a treble clef, overlooked by a viewing hill. Mature and new trees. In the maze there are over 1500 trees. Two paved areas form the shape of French horns which enclose an alpine garden and a mobile fountain. Refreshments by Macmillan Cancer Support, overlooking duck pond. Children's swings and sandpit. Hard paths around formal garden area. Ltd wheelchair access to grassland areas. Fine in dry weather with a good driver.

42 NETHERHALL MANOR

Tanners Lane, Soham, CB7 5AB. Timothy Clark. *6m Ely, 6m Newmarket. Enter Soham from Newmarket, Tanners Lane 2nd R 100yds after cemetery. Enter Soham from Ely, Tanners Lane 2nd L after War Memorial.* **Sun 5 Apr, Sun 3 May, Sun 2, Sun 9 Aug (2-5). Adm £3, chd free. Home-made teas.**
Elegant garden 'touched with antiquity'. Good Gardens Guide 2000. Unusual garden appealing to those with historical interest in individual collections of plant groups: March-old primroses, daffodils, Victorian double flowered hyacinths & first garden hellebore hybrids. May-old English tulips, Crown Imperials. Aug-Victorian pelargonium, heliotrope, calceolaria, dahlias. Author-Margery Fish's Country Gardening & Mary McMurtrie's Country Garden Flowers Historic Plants 1500-1900. The only bed of English tulips on display in the country. Author's books for sale. Featured on Gardeners' World three times. Flat garden with two optional steps. Lawns.

43 THE NIGHT GARDEN

37 Honeyhill, Paston, Peterborough, PE4 7DR. Andrea Connor, 07801 987905, andrea.connors@ntlworld.com. *From A47 Soke Parkway at J19. Take exit N on Topmoor Way. R at next r'about (3rd exit) to Paston Ridings, over the speed humps. Take 4th L to Honeyhill. 1st R into car park. No.37 at top L corner.* **Evening opening Sat 5, Sat 12, Sat 19 Sept (7-10). Adm £5, chd free. Light refreshments in garden, or house if weather inclement. Visits also by arrangement Aug to Oct for groups of 5 to 20.**
Small town garden with shrubs, roses,

Elm House

clematis, colourful bedding plants and Ash tree for shade, seclusion and privacy. Many Salvias for 'wellbeing'. Arches and trellis give height, water adds tranquility. At dusk, the solar-powered lighting gradually transforms the space into an enchanting magical world. Sit and enjoy the gradual transformation from seating areas at the ends of the garden. Night time garden lighting brings an unusual dimension, transforming the experience, hence suggested evening visiting times. Light refreshments: incl tea, coffee, glass of wine. £3 donation appreciated.

44 38 NORFOLK TERRACE GARDEN

Cambridge, CB1 2NG. John Tordoff & Maurice Reeve. *Central Cambridge. A603 East Rd turn R into St Matthews St to Norfolk St, L into Blossom St & Norfolk Terrace is at the end.* **Sat 4 July (11-6). Sun 5 July (11-6), also open 38 Kingston Street. Adm £3, chd free. Light refreshments.**
A small, paved courtyard garden in Moroccan style. Masses of colour, backed by oriental arches. An ornamental pool done in patterned tiles. The garden won third prize in the 2018 Gardener's World national competition. It is also included in the book 'The Secret Gardens of East Anglia'.The owners' previous, London garden, was named by BBC Gardeners' World as 'Best Small Garden in Britain'. There will also be a display of recent paintings by John Tordoff and handmade books by Maurice Reeve.

45 THE OLD RECTORY

312 Main Road, Parson Drove, Wisbech, PE13 4LF. Helen Roberts, 01945 700415, yogahelen@talk21.com. *SW of Wisbech. From Peterborough on A47 follow signs to Parson Drove L after Thorney Toll. From Wisbech follow the B1166 through Levrington Common.* **Sun 7 June (11-4). Adm £4, chd free. Home-made teas. Visits also by arrangement for groups of 10+.**
Walled Georgian cottage garden of 1 acre, opening into wild flower meadow and paddocks. Long herbaceous border, 3 ponds one with a flavour of Monet! We like to think this garden has a romantic feel. No hills but lovely open Fen views. Also a par 3 golf hole if you fancy a putt!

46 23A PERRY ROAD

Buckden, St Neots, PE19 5XG. David & Valerie Bunnage, 01480 810553, d.bunnage@btinternet.com. *5m S of Huntingdon on A1. From A1 Buckden roundabout take B661, Perry Rd approx 300yds on left.* **Visits by arrangement Apr to Sept. Adm £4, chd free. Light refreshments. Donations appreciated.**
Approx 1 acre garden consisting of many garden designs including Japanese interlinked by gravel paths. Large selection of acers, pines, rare and unusual shrubs. Also interesting features, a quirky garden. Plantsmans garden for all seasons, small bog garden. WC. Coaches welcome.

47 ROBINSON COLLEGE

Grange Road, Cambridge, CB3 9AN. Warden and Fellows, www.robinson.cam.ac.uk/about-robinson/gardens/national-gardens-scheme. *Garden at main Robinson College site, report to Porters' Lodge. There is only on-street parking.* **Daily weekdays 10-4, weekends 2-4. Closed Sat 18 April-Mon 29 June, Sat 15 Aug, Tue 1 Sept and Sun 4 Oct. Adm £4, chd free. Check website for details**
10 original Edwardian gardens are linked to central wild woodland water garden focusing on Bin Brook with small lake at heart of site. This gives a feeling of park and informal woodland, while at the same time keeping the sense of older more formal gardens beyond. Central area has a wide lawn running down to the lake framed by many mature stately trees with much of the original planting intact. More recent planting incl herbaceous borders and commemorative trees. Please report to Porters' Lodge on arrival to pay for entry and guidebook. No picnics. Children must be accompanied at all times. NB from time to time some parts, or occasionally all, of Robinson College gardens may be closed for safety reasons involving work by contractors and our maintenance staff. Please report to Porters' Lodge on arrival for information. Ask at Porters' Lodge for wheelchair access.

GROUP OPENING

49 STREETLY END & WEST WICKHAM GARDENS

West Wickham, CB21 4RP. *3m from Haverhill & 3m from Linton. Clover Cottage, Streetly End is opp grass triangle next to old windmill. 25 High Street, West Wickham CB21 4RY is approx. 100 yards from T junction on the left.* **Sun 21 June (12-5). Combined adm £3.50, chd free. Light refreshments at Clover Cottage.**

CLOVER COTTAGE
Mr Paul & Mrs Shirley Shadford.
(See separate entry)

25 HIGH STREET
Mrs Jane Scheuer.

Find at Clover Cottage, Streetly End, arches of roses, clematis and many varieties of geraniums, and raised fruit and vegetable beds. Delightful pond and borders of English roses, climbers and herbaceous plants. Ferns and shade plants under an old tree, with views over open countryside from the summer house in the sunken white garden. This small garden has an inspiring use of space. 25 High Street, West Wickham is a charming informal cottage garden to ramble, wander and relax in, with many routes through borders and pathways. Plants are allowed to self-seed and hybridise freely. Several interesting and unusual shrubs and herbaceous perennials from many continents. Regret no dogs. Regret no access for dogs, wheelchairs, prams, pushchairs, or wheeled walkers.

GROUP OPENING

50 SUTTON GARDENS

Sutton, Ely, CB6 2QQ. *6m W of Ely. From A142 turn L at r'about on to B1381 to Earith. Parking at Brooklands Centre 1 km on R.* **Sun 17 May (2-6). Combined adm £6, chd free. Home-made teas at 19 The Row.**

NEW 8 HADDOCK'S RISE
Mr William England.

61 HIGH STREET
Ms Kate Travers & Mr Jon Megginson.

THE OLD BAPTIST CHAPEL
Janet Porter & Steve Newton.

19 THE ROW
Alistair & Jane Huck.

NEW 89 THE ROW
Andrew Thompson.

A very varied group of gardens in this attractive village. The Old Baptist Chapel is a new garden being created around an C18 Baptist chapel, recently converted to a family home. Display board of site history. 61 The High Street is a small shaded garden with a host of features: interesting trees, herb and vegetable plots, two greenhouses, and boxes for birds, bats and bugs. 19 The Row is a long 3/4 acre family garden, started 25 yrs ago. Decking, seating, summer house, shed with green roof, pond, sculpture, some unusual trees, shrubs, perennials, fruit and vegetables. Wildlife area with long grass. 89 The Row is a medium sized garden on a slight slope with a variety of planted areas including mature trees, shrubs, fernery and herbaceous with an emphasis on scented plants. Vegetable plot and a wide variety of fruit trees. 8 Haddocks Rise is a small but densely planted garden. Still maturing with trees, roses and shrubs and splashes of colour throughout the year.

51 NEW TOP FARM

High Street, Toseland, St Neots, PE19 6RX. Mandy & Steve Hill. *1½m from A428; 9m from Black Cat round'about on A1; 5½m from St Neots. Leave the A1 & drive towards Cambridge along the A428. Turn L at yellow sign. Or, from St Neots, drive towards Great Paxton. Turn R at yellow sign.* **Sat 11, Sun 12 July (11-4). Adm £4, chd free. Home-made teas.**
Planted from scratch in 2016, on heavy clay, the garden now comprises a number of different areas. The main garden has long herbaceous borders in different colour schemes either side of a gravel path with rose covered pergolas. Other areas include a large vegetable garden and cut flower bed, a natural pond with informal planting for shade, and a paddock with fruit trees and wild flowers.

52 TRINITY COLLEGE FELLOWS' GARDEN

Queens Road, Cambridge, CB3 9AQ. Master and Fellows of Trinity College, www.trin.cam. ac.uk/about/gardens. *Short walk from city centre. At the Northampton St/Madingley Rd end of Queens Rd close to Garrett Hostel Lane.* **Sun 5 Apr (1-4). Adm £4, chd free. Home-made teas. Special dietary requirements are usually catered for.**
Interesting historic garden of about 8 acres with impressive specimen trees, mixed borders, drifts of spring bulbs and informal lawns with notable influences throughout from Fellows over the years. Across the gently flowing Bin Brook to Burrell's Field you will find some modern planting styles and plants nestled amongst the accommodation blocks in smaller intimate gardens. Members of the Gardens Department will be on hand to answer any questions and serve home-made cakes, tea and coffee. There will also be some plant sales. Wheelchair access - some gravel paths.

  ⅁ ✻ ☕ 🍷

53 TRINITY HALL - WYCHFIELD

Storey's Way, Cambridge, CB3 0DZ. The Master & Fellows, www.trinhall.cam.ac.uk/about/gardens/. *1m NW of city centre. Turn into Storey's Way from Madingley Rd (A1303) & follow the yellow NGS signs. Limited on-road parking is available.* **Sat 4 July (11-3). Adm £3.50, chd £1. Home-made teas. Donation to MIND.**
A beautiful large garden that complements the interesting and varied architecture. The Edwardian Wychfield House and its associated gardens contrast with the recent contemporary development located off Storey's Way. Majestic trees, roses and herbaceous perennials, shady under storey woodland planting and established lawns, work together to provide an inspiring garden. Plant sale. Tea and home-made cakes. Some gravel paths.

  ⅁ 🐎 ✻ 🍷

54 TWIN TARNS

6 Pinfold Lane, Somersham, PE28 3EQ. Michael & Frances Robinson, 07938 174536, mikerobinson987@btinternet.com. *Easy access from the A14. 4m NE of St Ives. Turn onto Church St. Pinfold Lane is next to the church. Please park on Church Street as access is narrow & limited.* **Sat 6, Sun 7 June (1-5). Adm £4, chd free. Cream teas. Visits also by arrangement May to Aug.**

One-acre wildlife garden with formal borders, kitchen garden and ponds, large rockery, mini woodland, wild flower meadow (June/July). Topiary, rose walk, greenhouses. Character oak bridge, veranda and tree-house. Adjacent to C13 village church.

55 WILD ROSE COTTAGE

Church Walk, Lode, Cambridge, CB25 9EX. Mrs Joy Martin, 01223 811132, joymartin123@outlook.com. *From A14 take the rd towards Burwell turn L into Lode & park on L after 150 metres. Walk straight on between thatched cottages to the archway of Wild Rose Cottage.* **Evening opening Thur 21 May (6-8). Adm £8, chd free. Wine. Food and drink available at 'The Shed'. Visits also by arrangement Apr to Sept.**
A real cottage garden overflowing with plants. Gardens within gardens of abundant vegetation, roses climbing through trees, laburnum tunnel, a daffodil spiral which becomes a daisy spiral in the summer. Circular vegetable garden and wildlife pond. Described by one visitor as a garden to write poetry in! It is a truly wild and loved garden where flowers in the vegetable circle are not pulled up! Geese, a dog, circular vegetable garden, wild life pond, and wild romantic garden! Lots of little path ways.

56 THE WINDMILL

10 Cambridge Road, Impington, CB24 9NU. Pippa & Steve Temple, 07775 446443, mill.impington@ntlworld.com, www.impingtonmill.org. *2½ m N of Cambridge. Off A14 at J32, B1049 to Histon, L into Cambridge Rd at T-lights, follow Cambridge Rd round to R, the Windmill is approx 400yds on L.* **Visits by arrangement Apr to Sept. Adm £5, chd free. Light refreshments incl coffee/tea/wine and nibbles by arrangement.**
A previously romantic wilderness of 1½ acres surrounding windmill, now filled with bulbs, perennial beds, pergolas, bog gardens, grass bed and herb bank. Secret paths and wild areas with thuggish roses maintain the romance. Millstone seating area in smouldering borders contrasts with the pastel colours of the remainder of the garden. Also 'Pond Life' seat, 'Tree God' and amazing compost area! The Windmill - an C18 smock on C19 tower on C17 base on C16

foundations - is being restored. Guide dogs only.

57 WOLFSON COLLEGE GARDEN

Barton Road, Cambridge, CB3 9BB. *On SW side of Cambridge. From M11 J12, take A603 into Cambridge. Wolfson College is approx 2m from J12, on L.* **Sat 29 Aug (12-3.30). Adm £4, chd free.**
Gardens are a series of lawned courtyards forming a set of garden 'rooms', and some stunning Herbacious borders. The beds and borders contain a wide variety of plants and shrubs which provide structure, colour and interest through the year. Several courts reflect a Chinese influence in the design and planting with many rare small Acers and Chinese trees. The retention of some majestic trees from the original site helps to give an atmosphere of maturity and permanence to a garden which has developed greatly over the last 30yrs. The borders contain many ornamental grasses (of all types) and

'naturalistic plantings' combined with Exotic plants such as Bananas, Cannas, a huge variety of Salvias and late summer colour. There is also Topiary galore (Penguin, Roadrunner, Cat etc etc !). Please come and see our wonderful gardens. Phil. Head Gardener.

58 WRIGHTS FARM

Tilbrook Road, Kimbolton, Huntingdon, PE28 0JW. Russell & Hetty Dean. *13m SW of Huntingdon. ¼ m W of Kimbolton on the B645. Do not follow sat nav.* **Sat 4, Sun 5 July, Sun 16 Aug (11-5). Adm £5, chd free. Home-made teas.**
A new garden started in 2013, set within 4 acres. Varied borders with bee and butterfly friendly planting. Formal walled vegetable garden with raised beds, potting shed and greenhouses. Mediterranean style courtyard with dry garden. Paved entrance area with plenty of pots. Tropical hot border good in August. Riverside paths and seating areas with open countryside views.

Caldrees Manor

CHESHIRE & WIRRAL

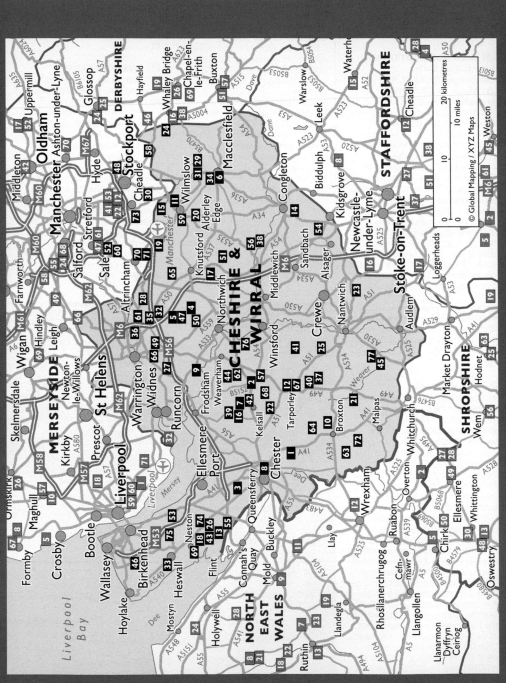

The area of Cheshire and Wirral comprises what are now the four administrative regions of West Cheshire and Chester, East Cheshire, Warrington and Wirral, together with gardens in the south of Greater Manchester, Trafford and Stockport.

The perception of the area is that of a fertile county dominated by the Cheshire Plain, but to the extreme west it enjoys a mild maritime climate, with gardens often sitting on sandstone and sandy soils and enjoying mildly acidic conditions.

A large sandstone ridge also rises out of the landscape, running some 30-odd miles from north to south. Many gardens grow ericaceous-loving plants, although in some areas, the slightly acidic soil is quite clayey. But the soil is rarely too extreme to prevent the growing of a wide range of plants, both woody and herbaceous.

As one travels east and the region rises up the foothills of the Pennine range, the seasons become somewhat harsher, with spring starting a few weeks later than in the coastal region.

As well as being home to one of the RHS's major shows, the region's gardens include two National Garden Scheme 'founder' gardens in Arley Hall and Peover Hall, as well as the University of Liverpool Botanic Garden at Ness.

Below: Bollin House

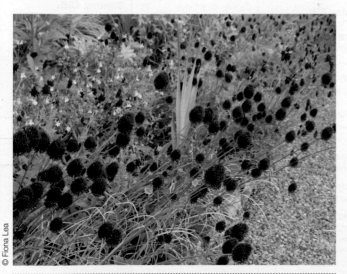

© Fiona Lea

@National Garden Scheme Cheshire & Wirral   CheshireWirrNGS

Volunteers

County Organiser
Janet Bashforth
01925 349895
jan.bashforth@ngs.org.uk

County Treasurer
Andrew Collin
01513 393614
andrewcollin@btinternet.com

Booklet Co-ordinator
John Hinde
0151 353 0032
johnhinde059@gmail.com

Assistant County Organisers
Graham Beech
01625 402946
gb.ngs@talktalk.net

Sue Bryant
0161 928 3819
suewestlakebryant@btinternet.com

Jean Davies
01606 892383
mrsjeandavies@gmail.com

Linda Enderby
07949 496747
linda.enderby@ngs.org.uk

Sandra Fairclough
0151 342 4645
sandra.fairclough@tiscali.co.uk

Juliet Hill
01829 732804
t.hill573@btinternet.com

Romy Holmes
01829 732053
romy@bowmerecottage.co.uk

Richard Goodyear
01270 528944
goodyear.pickford@btinternet.com

Mike Porter
01925 753488
porters@mikeandgailporter.co.uk

OPENING DATES

All entries subject to change. For latest information check www.ngs.org.uk

Map locator numbers are shown to the right of each garden name.

February

Snowdrop Festival

Sunday 16th
West Drive Gardens 73

Saturday 22nd
Briarfield 13

Sunday 23rd
Briarfield 13
Bucklow Farm 17

April

Saturday 11th
Poulton Hall 53

Sunday 12th
Poulton Hall 53

Sunday 19th
Briarfield 13
Long Acre 37

Saturday 25th
◆ Ness Botanic
Gardens 43

May

Saturday 2nd
Brooke Cottage 15
◆ Mount Pleasant 42

Sunday 3rd
Brooke Cottage 15
Manley Knoll 39
◆ Mount Pleasant 42
Tirley Garth Gardens 68

Thursday 7th
◆ Cholmondeley Castle
Gardens 21

Saturday 9th
64 Carr Wood 19
◆ Lane End Cottage
Gardens 35

Sunday 10th
◆ Abbeywood Gardens 2
◆ Lane End Cottage
Gardens 35
◆ Stonyford Cottage 62

Wednesday 13th
◆ Tatton Park 65

Saturday 16th
Inglewood 33
The Old Parsonage 47

Sunday 17th
Inglewood 33
The Old Parsonage 47
Tirley Garth Gardens 68

Sunday 24th
73 Hill Top Avenue 30
Manley Knoll 39
Rowley House 56
34 Stanley Mount 60
Tattenhall Hall 64

Saturday 30th
Clemley House 22
10 Statham Avenue 61

Sunday 31st
NEW Brook Farm 14
Hall Lane Farm 27
Mayfield House 40
Sandymere 57
10 Statham Avenue 61
Tirley Garth Gardens 68

June

Saturday 6th
Drake Carr 24
◆ Peover Hall
Gardens 51
Willaston Grange 74

Sunday 7th
Drake Carr 24
The Homestead 32
◆ Peover Hall
Gardens 51
West Drive Gardens 73

Wednesday 10th
◆ Tatton Park 65

Saturday 13th
Ashmead 6

Sunday 14th
Ashmead 6
Bucklow Farm 17
60 Kennedy Avenue 34
Mayfield House 40
24 Old Greasby Road 46

Friday 19th
Twin Gates 69

Saturday 20th
Cheriton 20
18 Highfield Road 29
NEW Milford House
Farm 41

Sunday 21st
Bowmere Cottage 12
Cheriton 20
18 Highfield Road 29
Long Acre 37

Saturday 27th
NEW Abbey Gate
College 1
All Fours Farm 4
◆ Bluebell Cottage
Gardens 9
17 Poplar Grove 52

Sunday 28th
All Fours Farm 4
Ashton Grange 7
◆ Bluebell Cottage
Gardens 9
Burton Village
Gardens 18
17 Poplar Grove 52

July

Saturday 4th
8a Warwick Drive 71

Sunday 5th
8a Warwick Drive 71

Thursday 9th
5 Cobbs Lane 23

Saturday 11th
5 Cobbs Lane 23

Sunday 12th
The Homestead 32
Rowley House 56
NEW Tiresford 67

Saturday 18th
Stretton Old Hall 63
NEW 26 Warwick Drive 70
Wirral Hospice St
John's 75

Sunday 19th
NEW Norley Bank
Farm 44
15 Park Crescent 49
Stretton Old Hall 63
NEW 26 Warwick Drive 70
Wirral Hospice St
John's 75

Sunday 26th
◆ Abbeywood Gardens 2
The Firs 25

August

Saturday 1st
21 Scafell Close 58
Thorncar 66

Sunday 2nd
◆ Arley Hall & Gardens 5
The Firs 25
73 Hill Top Avenue 30
21 Scafell Close 58

Saturday 8th
Laskey Farm 36

Sunday 9th
Laskey Farm 36

September

Saturday 5th
NEW Milford House
Farm 41
◆ Mount Pleasant 42
39 Osborne Street 48

Sunday 6th
◆ Mount Pleasant 42
39 Osborne Street 48

Saturday 12th
◆ Lane End Cottage
Gardens 35

Sunday 13th
◆ Lane End Cottage
Gardens 35

October

Sunday 11th
◆ The Lovell Quinta
Arboretum 38

February 2021

Saturday 20th
Briarfield 13

Sunday 21st
Briarfield 13

Sunday 28th
Bucklow Farm 17

By Arrangement

Arrange a personalised garden visit with your club, or group of friends, on a date to suit you. See individual garden entries for full details.

THE GARDENS

1 NEW ABBEY GATE COLLEGE

Saighton Grange, Saighton, Chester, CH3 6EN. The Governors of Abbey Gate College, www.abbeygatecollege.co.uk. *4m SE of Chester. Take A41 towards Whitchurch. At far end of Waverton turn R to Saighton Grange at the end of village.* **Sat 27 June (10-4). Adm £4, chd free. Home-made teas.**
6½ acres of garden designed by Inigo Triggs for the 2nd Duke of Westminster in 1901. Redesigned for the 4th Duchess during the 1960's by Russell, of Castle Howard fame. Now undergoing third development. Spring garden with magnolias, daffodils and bluebell woodland walk, but development continues to introduce later flowering plants to extend the season.

2 ◆ ABBEYWOOD GARDENS

Chester Road, Delamere, Northwich, CW8 2HS. The Rowlinson Family, 01606 889477, info@abbeywoodestate.co.uk, www.abbeywoodestate.co.uk. *11m E of Chester. On the A556 facing Delamere Church.* **For NGS: Sun 10 May, Sun 26 July (10-4). Adm £6, chd free. Restaurant in Garden.** For other opening times and information, please phone, email or visit garden website.
Superb setting near Delamere Forest. Total area 45 acres incl mature woodland, new woodland and new arboretum all with connecting pathways. Approx 4½ acres of gardens surrounding large Edwardian House. Vegetable garden, exotic garden, chapel garden, pool garden, woodland garden, lawned area with beds.

3 ADSWOOD

Townfield Lane, Mollington, CH1 6LB. Ken & Helen Black, 01244 851327, keneblack@outlook.com, www.kenblackclematis.com. *3m N of Chester. From Wirral take A540 towards Chester. Cross A55 at r'about, past Wheatsheaf PH, turn L into Overwood Lane. At T junction turn R into Townfield Lane. Parking will be signed.* **Visits by arrangement Mar to Oct for groups of 5 to 30. Specific requests for demonstrations can be discussed. Adm £6, chd free. Home-made teas.**
A cottage garden with several borders packed with a wide range of bulbs, perennials, climbers and English roses.The garden is planted with over 100 varieties of clematis with many more grown in containers. There is a small woodland garden, wildlife pond and a raised ornamental fish pond. There are several seating areas including a garden pavilion. There are no steps but the front drive and some of the garden paths are gravelled and side access to the garden is quite narrow.

4 ALL FOURS FARM

Colliers Lane, Aston by Budworth, Northwich, CW9 6NF. Mr & Mrs Evans. *M6 J19, take A556 towards Northwich. Turn immed R, past The Windmill Pub. Turn R after approx 1m, follow rd, garden on L after approx 2m. We're happy to allow direct access for drop off & collection for those with limited mobility.* **Sat 27 June (10-4). Home-made teas. Sun 28 June (10-4). Light refreshments. Adm £5, chd free.**
A traditional and well established country garden with a wide range of roses, hardy shrubs, bulbs, perennials and annuals. You will also find a small vegetable garden, pond and greenhouse as well as vintage machinery and original features from its days as a working farm. The garden is adjacent to the families traditional rose nursery. The majority of the garden is accessible by wheelchair.

5 ◆ ARLEY HALL & GARDENS

Northwich, CW9 6NA. Viscount Ashbrook, www.arleyhallandgardens.com. *10m from Warrington. Signed from J9 & 10 (M56) & J19 & 20 (M6) (20 min from Tatton Park, 40 min to Manchester). Please follow the brown tourist signs.* **For NGS: Sun 2 Aug (10-5). Adm £9, chd £4. Light refreshments in The Gardener's Kitchen Cafe. All refreshments available. For other opening times and information, please visit garden website.**
Arley has been lovingly created by the same family over 550 years and is famous for its double herbaceous border, thought to be the oldest in Europe. Other outstanding features of the garden are the avenue of ilex columns, walled garden, pleached lime avenue, victorian rootree and informal Grove and Woodland Walk. A garden of great atmosphere, interest and vitality throughout the seasons.

Your visits help change lives – we are the largest single funder of the Queen's Nursing Institute

6 ASHMEAD

2 Bramhall Way, off Gritstone
Drive, Macclesfield, SK10 3SH.
Peter & Penelope McDermott,
01625 434200, penelope.
mcdermott@pmsurveying.plus.
com. *1m W of Macclesfield. Turn
onto Pavilion Way, off Victoria Rd ,
then immed L onto Gritstone Drive.
Bramhall Way first on R.* **Sat 13,
Sun 14 June (1-5). Adm £4, chd
free. Home-made teas. Visits also
by arrangement Apr to June for
groups of 10 to 30.**
1/8 acre suburban cottage garden,
featuring plant packed mixed borders,
rock gardens, kitchen garden, island
beds, water feature, pond. The
garden demonstrates how small
spaces can be planted to maximum
effect to create all round interest.
Extensive range of plants favoured
for colours, texture and scent. Pots
used in a creative way to extend and
enhance borders.

7 ASHTON GRANGE

Grange Road, Ashton Hayes,
Chester, CH3 8AE. Martin and
Kate Slack, 01829 759172,
kateslack1@icloud.com. *8m E of
Chester. Grange Rd is a single track
road off the B5393, by the village
sign at the North end of Ashton
Hayes.* **Sun 28 June (2-5). Adm
£6, chd free. Home-made teas.
Visits also by arrangement May
to Aug for groups of 10 to 30. Not
accessible for large coaches.**
Ashton Grange has a traditional
country house garden with sweeping
lawns, herbaceous borders, kitchen
garden and unusual trees. You can
wander through mature woodland,
see tree carvings, visit the wildflower
meadow with lovely views and sit by
a large wildlife pond. The garden and
woodland extend to 9 acres and this
year there will be access to a new
three acre native woodland planted in
2018. Wheelchair access is possible
to most parts of the garden, but
woodland paths could be difficult.
Limited parking for wheelchair users
is available.

8 150 BARREL WELL HILL CHESTER

Boughton, Chester, CH3 5BR. Mrs
Christine Browne, 01244 329988,
wta@cawyld.co.uk. *On riverside
3/4 m E of Chester off A5115.
Proceeding towards Chester, the
turning is on L after St Paul's Church.*

**Visits by arrangement May to Aug
for groups of 5 to 30. Adm £4,
chd free. Light refreshments. to
be agreed on booking.**
Spectacular terraced garden with
views over the River Dee to the
Meadows and Clwyd Hills. Informal
cottage style garden on historic site
by the Martyrs Memorial. Lawns
running down to the river, prolific
shrub and flower beds, productive
vegetable patch and soft and hard
fruit areas, springs, stream and lily
pond. You can arrange to come by
boat. Not suitable for wheelchairs or
children under eight due to steps and
unprotected drop into river. Access
via steps down from road or up from
the river.

9 ◆ BLUEBELL COTTAGE GARDENS

Lodge Lane, Dutton, WA4 4HP.
Sue Beesley, 01928 713718,
info@bluebellcottage.co.uk,
www.bluebellcottage.co.uk. *5m
NW of Northwich. From M56 (J10)
take A49 to Whitchurch. After 3m
turn R at T-lights towards Runcorn/
Dutton on A533. Then 1st L. Signed
with brown tourism signs from A533.*
**For NGS: Sat 27, Sun 28 June (10-
5). Adm £5, chd free. Home-made
teas. For other opening times and
information, please phone, email or
visit garden website.**
South facing country garden wrapped
around a cottage on a quiet rural lane
in the heart of Cheshire. Packed with
thousands of rare and familiar hardy
herbaceous perennials, shrubs and
trees. Unusual plants available at
adjacent nursery. The opening dates
coincide with the peak of flowering
in the herbaceous borders. Regional
Finalist, The English Garden's The
Nation's Favourite Gardens 2019.
Some gravel paths. Wheelchair
access to 90% of garden. WC is not
fully wheelchair accessible.

10 BOLESWORTH CASTLE

Tattenhall, CH3 9HQ. Mrs
Anthony Barbour, 01829 782210,
dcb@bolesworth.com,
www.bolesworth.com. *8m S of
Chester on A41. Enter through
Chowley Lodge on A41. Postcode:
CH3 9DU.* **Visits by arrangement
Apr & May for groups of 10+.
Adm £5, chd free.**
The Spring garden on The Rock
Walk above Castle, planted with
superb collection of Rhododendrons,

Camellias and specimen trees in
the 90's, is undergoing restoration
and development with exciting
new planting. Well planted shrub/
herbaceous borders around Castle.
Unusual and rare trees planted over
a period of 25 years by Anthony
Barbour now at their best (Autumn
colour in October). Regret no
wheelchair access.

11 BOLLIN HOUSE

Hollies Lane, Wilmslow,
SK9 2BW. Angela Ferguson &
Gerry Lemon, 07828 207492,
fergusonang@doctors.org.uk.
*From Wilmslow past Station &
proceed to T-junction. Turn L onto
Adlington Rd. Proceed for 1/2 m,
then turn R into Hollies Lane(just
after One Oak Lane). Drive to the
end of Hollies Lane and follow
yellow signage. Park on Hollies L,
or Browns L(other side Adlington
Rd).* **Visits by arrangement May
to July for groups of 10 to 30. Up
to 6 cars can be parked at the
premises. Refreshments/tailored
to group. Adm £5, chd free. Light
refreshments. Tea and cake or
scones at £4, drinks only £1-£2.**
There are 2 parts to the garden, a
formal garden and the wild flower
meadow. The garden has deep
herbaceous borders, (think hollyhocks
and roses), and an orchard. A new
landscaped area has just been added
with a central water feature. The
meadow with it's annual and perennial
wild flower areas (with mown
pathways and benches) attracts lots
of butterflies and humming insects
on a sunny day. Bollin House is in
an idyllic location with the garden,
orchard and meadow flowing into
the Bollin Valley. The meadow is a
combination of perennial and annual
wild flowers areas. Ramps to gravel
lined paths to most of the garden.
Some narrow paths through borders.
Mown pathways in the meadow.

12 BOWMERE COTTAGE

5 Bowmere Road, Tarporley,
CW6 0BS. Romy & Tom
Holmes, 01829 732053,
romy@bowmerecottage.co.uk.
*10m E of Chester. From Tarporley
High St (old A49) take Eaton Rd
signed Eaton. After 100 metres take
R fork into Bowmere Rd, Garden 100
metres on LH-side.* **Sun 21 June (1-
5.30). Adm £4.50, chd free. Visits
also by arrangement June & July.**

A colourful and relaxing one acre country style garden around a Grade II listed house. The lawns are surrounded by three well stocked herbaceous and shrub borders and rose covered pergolas. There are two plant filled courtyard gardens and a small vegetable garden. Shrub and rambling roses, clematis, hardy geraniums and a wide range of mostly hardy plants make this a very traditional English garden.

⓭ BRIARFIELD
The Rake, Burton, Neston, CH64 5TL. Liz Carter, 0151 336 2304, carter.burton@btinternet.com. *9m NW of Chester. Turn off A540 at Willaston-Burton Xrds T-lights & follow rd for 1m to Burton village centre.* **Sat 22, Sun 23 Feb (1-4). Adm £4, chd free. Sun 19 Apr (1-5). Adm £5, chd free. Home-made teas in St Nicholas Church, just along the lane. No refreshments in February, only main garden open. 2021: Sat 20, Sun 21 Feb. Opening with Burton Village Gardens on**

Sun 28 June (11-5). Visits also by arrangement Apr to Sept.
Tucked under the S-facing side of Burton Wood the garden is home to many specialist and unusual plants, some available in plant sale. This 2 acre garden is on two sites, a couple of minutes along an unmade lane. Shrubs, colourful herbaceous, bulbs, alpines and water features compete for attention as you wander through four distinctly different gardens. Always changing, Liz can't resist a new plant! Rare and unusual plants sold (70% to NGS) in Neston Market most Fridays.

⓮ NEW BROOK FARM
Newcastle Road, Astbury, Congleton, CW12 4RL. Mrs Emma Ingham. *Follow the A34 until you reach Astbury Garden Centre, Watery Lane is opposite & we are opposite the small red post box around 100 metres down the lane.* **Sun 31 May (11-4.30). Adm £4, chd free. Home-made teas.**
Established country gardens set in over an acre of lawns and borders

packed with all seasonal plants. With large pond and stream running through the property.

⓯ BROOKE COTTAGE
Church Road, Handforth, SK9 3LT. Barry & Melanie Davy. *1m N of Wilmslow. Centre of Handforth, behind Health Centre. Turn off Wilmslow Rd at St Chads, follow Church Rd round to R. Garden last on L. Parking in Health Centre car park.* **Sat 2, Sun 3 May (11-5). Adm £4, chd free. Home-made teas.**
A chance to see this plant-filled garden in Spring. Shady woodland area of ferns, azaleas, rhododendrons, camellias, magnolia, erythroniums, trilliums, arisaema and blue poppies. Patio with hostas, daylilies, small pond. Borders with grasses, perennials, euphorbia, alliums and tulips. Anthriscus, aquilegia, persicaria and astrantia create meadow effect popular with insects. Featured in RHS magazine.

Brooke Cottage

16 BROOKLANDS
Smithy Lane, Mouldsworth, CH3 8AR. Barbara & Brian Russell-Moore, 01928 740413, wbrm1@netscape.co.uk. *1½m N of Tarvin. 5½m S of Frodsham. Smithy Lane is off B5393 via A54 Tarvin/Kelsall rd or the A56 Frodsham/Helsby rd.* **Visits by arrangement May to Aug for groups of 10 to 30. Adm £4, chd free. Home-made teas. and cakes using eggs from our own hens.**
A lovely country style, ¾ acre garden with backdrop of mature trees and shrubs. The planting is based around azaleas, rhododendrons, mixed shrub and herbaceous borders. There is a small vegetable garden, supported by a greenhouse and hens providing eggs for all the afternoon tea cakes!! Repeat visitors will notice significant changes following damage and tree loss caused by 'Storm Doris.'.

17 BUCKLOW FARM
Pinfold Lane, Plumley, Knutsford, WA16 9RP. Dawn & Peter Freeman. *2m S of Knutsford. M6 J19, A556 Chester. L at 2nd set of T-lights. In 1¼m, L at concealed Xrds. 1st R. From Knutsford A5033, L at Sudlow Lane. becomes Pinfold Lane.* **Sun 23 Feb (12.30-4). Adm £3.50, chd free. Light refreshments. Sun 14 June (2-5). Adm £4.50, chd free. Cream teas. Mulled Wine in February. Cream teas in June. 2021: Sun 28 Feb. Donation to Knutsford First Responders.**
Country garden with shrubs, perennial borders, rambling roses, herb garden, vegetable patch, wildlife pond/water feature and alpines. Landscaped and planted over the last 30yrs with recorded changes. Free range hens. Carpet of snowdrops and spring bulbs. Leaf, stem and berries to show colour in autumn and winter. Featured in Cheshire Life. Cobbled yard from car park, but wheelchairs can be dropped off near gate.

GROUP OPENING

18 BURTON VILLAGE GARDENS
Burton, Neston, CH64 5SJ. *9m NW of Chester. Turn off A540 at Willaston-Burton Xrds T-lights & follow rd for 1m to Burton. Maps given to visitors. Buy your ticket at first garden.* **Sun 28 June (11-5). Combined adm £5, chd free. Home-made teas in the Sports and Social Club behind the village hall. Drinks and biscuits in Burton Manor Glasshouse.**

BRIARFIELD
Liz Carter.
(See separate entry)

♦ BURTON MANOR WALLED GARDEN
Burton Manor Gardens Ltd, 0151 336 6154, www.burtonmanorgardens.org.uk.

TRUSTWOOD
Peter & Lin Friend, lin@trustwoodbnb.uk, , www.trustwoodbnb.uk.
Visits also by arrangement June & July for groups of up to 20.

Burton is a medieval village built on sandstone overlooking the Dee estuary. Three gardens are open. Trustwood is a country wildlife garden with fruit, flowers and vegetables in raised beds at the front; at the back a more formal garden blends into the wood where the hens live. Briarfield's sheltered site, on the south side of Burton Wood (NT), is home to many specialist and unusual plants, some available in the plant sale at the house. The 1½ acre main garden invites exploration not only for its huge variety of plants but also for the imaginative use of ceramic sculptures. Period planting with a splendid vegetable garden surrounds the restored Edwardian glasshouse in Burton Manor's walled garden. Plants for sale at two gardens. Well signed free car parks. Maps available. All within walking distance. Limited disabled parking at each garden. Briarfield is unsuitable for wheelchairs.

Burton Manor Walled Garden

Ashton Grange

SAT NAV SY14 8ET. **For NGS: Thur 7 May (11-5). Adm £8.50, chd £4. Light refreshments. For other opening times and information, please phone, email or visit garden website.**
70 acres of romantically landscaped gardens with fine views and eye-catching water features, which still manages to retain its intimacy. Beautiful mature trees form a background to millions of spring bulbs and superb plant collections including magnolias, rhododendrons, camellias and more, particularly *Davidia involucrata* which will be in flower in late May. Magnificent magnolias. One of the finest features of the gardens are its trees, many of which are rare and unusual, Cholmondeley Gardens is home to over 40 county champion trees. 100m long double mixed herbaceous border and extended Rose Garden with 250 roses. Light lunches and home-made teas available in Tea Room located in the heart of the Gardens. Partial wheelchair access.

&. 🐕 🚐 ☕ 🍷

22 CLEMLEY HOUSE
Well Lane, Duddon Common, Tarporley, CW6 0HG. Sue & Tom Makin. *8m SE of Chester, 3m W of Tarporley. A51 from Chester towards Tarporley. 1m after Tarvin turn off, at bus shelter, turn L into Willington Rd. After community centre, 2nd L into Well Lane.* **Sat 30 May (12-4). Adm £6, chd free. Home-made teas. Home grown organic fruits used in jams & cakes. Vegan & gluten free available.**
2 acre organic, wildlife friendly, gold award winning cottage garden. Orchard, 3 wildlife ponds, perennial wild flower meadow, fruit and vegetable areas, badger sett, rose pergola & verandah, gazebo, shepherd's hut, summer house, barn owl and many other nest and bat boxes. Drought tolerant gravel garden and shade garden. New wild areas. Year round interest. 'Frogwatch' charity volunteers transport migrating amphibians to the safety of these ponds when they are found on the roads in early spring. Butterflies, bees and more unusual insects are plentiful in their season. The garden is a clear example of how an oasis for wildlife can stil be beautiful. Gravel paths may be difficult to use but most areas are flat and comprise grass paths or lawn.

&. 🐕 🌸 ☕

19 64 CARR WOOD
Hale Barns, Altrincham, WA15 0EP. Mrs John Booth & Mr David Booth. *10m S of Manchester city centre. 2m from J6 M56: Take A538 to Hale Barns. L at 'triangle' by church into Wicker Lane & L at mini r'about into Chapel Lane & 1st R into Carr Wood.* **Sat 9 May (2-6). Adm £5, chd free. Home-made teas.**
Two-thirds acre landscaped, S-facing garden overlooking Bollin Valley laid out in 1959 by Clibrans of Altrincham, royal warrant holders. Gently sloping lawn, woodland walk, seating areas and terrace, extensive mixed shrub and plant borders. Partial wheelchair access and ample parking on Carr Wood. Wheelchair access to terrace overlooking main garden.

 &. 🌸 ☕

20 CHERITON
34 Congleton Road, Alderley Edge, SK9 7AB. David & Jo Mottershead. *400yds S of Alderley Edge on R of Congleton Road. Park on rd.* **Sat 20, Sun 21 June (11-5). Adm £6, chd £2. Light refreshments. Selection of teas, coffee, wine, biscuits and cakes.**

SW-facing, 1-acre garden with views on a fine day to the Clwydian Range. Garden of mature rhododendron, magnolias and wisteria with early clematis, hellebores and a range of unusual herbaceous plants and young specimen trees. The third year of the new and previously open garden with significant and exciting changes made. Large free-standing Wisteria. Interesting planted flowing water feature with ponds. Front garden now planted as a stunning winter garden, with white barked birches underplanted with heuchera and hellebore. Wheelchair access to rear garden only via a short flight (4) of low steps. No WC facilities for wheelchair users.

☕

21 ♦ CHOLMONDELEY CASTLE GARDENS
Cholmondeley, nr Malpas, SY14 8AH. The Cholmondeley Gardens Trust, 01829 720383, office@cholmondeleycastle.co.uk, www.cholmondeleycastle.com. *4m NE of Malpas Sat Nav SY14 8ET. Signed from A41 Chester-Whitchurch rd & A49 Whitchurch-Tarporley rd*

23 5 COBBS LANE

Hough, Crewe, CW2 5JN. David & Linda Race. *4m S of Crewe. add directions in CRM.* **Thur 9, Sat 11 July (11-5). Adm £5, chd free. Home-made teas at Village Hall 300m up Cobbs Lane.**
A plant person's ²/₃ acre garden with island beds, wide cottage style herbaceous borders with bark paths. A large variety of hardy and some unusual perennials. Interesting features, shrubs, grasses and trees, with places to sit and enjoy the surroundings. A water feature runs to a small pond, wildlife friendly garden containing a woodland area. Finalists in Daily Mail Garden Competition.

24 DRAKE CARR

Mudhurst Lane, Higher Disley, SK12 2AN. Alan & Joan Morris. *8m SE of Stockport, 12m NE of Macclesfield. From A6 in Disley centre turn into Buxton Old Rd, go up hill 1m & turn R into Mudhurst Lane. After ⅓m park on lay-by or grass verge. No parking at garden. Approx 150 metre walk.* **Sat 6, Sun 7 June (11-5). Adm £4, chd free. Home-made teas. Home-made gluten-free cakes available.**
½ acre cottage garden in beautiful rural setting with natural stream running into large wildlife pond containing many native species. Surrounding C17 stone cottage, the garden, containing herbaceous borders, shrubs and veg plot, is on several levels divided by grassed areas, slopes and steps. This blends into boarded walk through bog garden and mature wooded area. Not suitable for wheelchairs.

25 THE FIRS

Old Chester Road, Barbridge, Nantwich, CW5 6AY. Richard & Valerie Goodyear, 07775 924929, Goodyear.Pickford@btinternet. com. *3m N of Nantwich on A51. After entering Barbridge turn R at Xrds after 100 metres. The Firs is 2nd house on L.* **Sun 26 July, Sun 2 Aug (1-5). Adm £4.50, chd free. Home-made teas. Visits also by arrangement June to Aug for groups of 10+.**
Canalside garden set idyllically by a wide section of the Shropshire Union Canal with long frontage. Long garden alongside canal with varied trees, shrubs and herbaceous beds, with some wild areas. All leading

down to an observatory at the end of the garden. There is wheelchair access to some or all of the garden. The extent of access depends on the type of wheelchair wheels.

26 FRAMLEY

Hadlow Road, Willaston, Neston, CH64 2US. Mrs Sally Reader, 07496 015259, sllyreader@yahoo.co.uk. *½m S of Willaston village centre. From Willaston Green, proceed along Hadlow Rd, crossing the Wirral Way. Framley is the next house on R.* **Visits by arrangement Apr to June for groups of up to 20. Adm £4, chd free. Home-made teas.**
This 5 acre garden holds many hidden gems. Comprising extensive mature wooded areas, underplanted with a variety of interesting and unusual woodland plants - all at their very best in spring. A selection of deep seasonal borders surround a mystical sunken garden, planted to suit its challenging conditions. Wide lawns and sandstone paths invite you to discover what lies around every corner. Please phone ahead for parking instructions for wheelchair users - access around much of the garden although the woodland paths may be challenging.

27 HALL LANE FARM

Hall Lane, Daresbury, Warrington, WA4 4AF. Sir Michael & Lady Beverley Bibby. *1m from J11 of*

M56. *Leave M56 at J11, head towards Warrington take 2nd R turn into Daresbury village go around sharp bend then take L into Daresbury Lane. Entrance on L after 100 yds.* **Sun 31 May (1-5). Adm £5, chd free. Home-made teas.**
The 2 acres of private formal garden originally designed by Arabella Lennox-Boyd are arranged in a 'gardens within gardens' style to create a series of enclosed spaces each with their own character and style. The gardens also include a vegetable garden, orchard, Koi pond, as well as lawns and a tree house.

28 NEW 213 HIGHER LANE

Higher Lane, Lymm, WA13 0RN. Mark Stevenson, 07470 715007, mjs.stevenson@btinternet.com. *From M56 use J7 follow the signs for Lymm A56 the garden is approx 300 yards from the Jolly Thresher pub towards Lymm on R.* **Visits by arrangement May to Sept for groups of 10 to 20. Adm £4, chd free.**
Half an acre, segregated into various plant themes. Herbaceous borders, specimen rhododendrons, hydrangeas, ferns and grasses, gingers and subtropical plants. A water feature surrounded by Japanese acers with far reaching views across fields and woodland. Many rare and unusual plants and shrubs.

10 Statham Avenue

29 18 HIGHFIELD ROAD

Bollington, Macclesfield, SK10 5LR. Mrs Melita Turner. *3m N of Macclesfield. A523 to Stockport. Turn R at B5090 r'about signed Bollington. Pass under viaduct. Take next R (by Library) up Hurst Lane. Turn R into Highfield Rd. Property on L. Park on wider road just past it.* **Sat 20, Sun 21 June (10-4.30). Adm £4, chd free. Home-made teas.** This small terraced garden packed with plants was designed by Melita and has evolved over the past 12yrs. This plantswoman is a plantaholic and RHS Certificate holder. An attempt has been made to combine formality through structural planting with a more casual look influenced by the style of Christopher LLoyd. Refreshments by East Cheshire Hospice. Steep step on to top tier at front. Steps up to higher tiers at rear.

30 73 HILL TOP AVENUE

Cheadle Hulme, Stockport, SK8 7HZ. Mrs Elaine Land, 0161 486 0055. *4m S of Stockport. Leave A34 (new bypass) at r'about signed Cheadle Hulme (B5094). 2nd turn L into Gillbent Rd signed Cheadle Hulme Sports Centre. At end, small r'about, R into Church Rd. Garden 2nd rd on L. From Stockport or Bramhall turn R/L into Church Rd by Church Inn. Garden 1st rd on R.* **Sun 24 May, Sun 2 Aug (2-6). Adm £3.50, chd free. Tea. Visits also by arrangement May to Aug for groups of 5+.** ⅙ acre plantswoman's garden. Well stocked with a wide range of sun-loving herbaceous plants, shrub and climbing roses, many clematis varieties, pond and damp area, shade-loving woodland plants and some unusual trees and shrubs, in an originally designed, long narrow garden.

31 HILLTOP

Flash Lane, Prestbury, SK10 4ED. Martin Gardner, 07768 337525, hughmartingardner@gmail.com, www.yourhilltopwedding.com. *2m N of Macclesfield. A523 to Stockport. Turn R at B5090 r'about signed Bollington, after ½ m turn L at Cock & Pheasant Pub into Flash Lane. At bottom of lane turn R into cul de sac. Hilltop Country House signed on R.* **Visits by arrangement May to Aug for groups of 10 to 20. Adm £6, chd free. Light refreshments.**

Interesting country garden of approx 4 acres. Woodland walk, parterre, herb garden, herbaceous borders, dry stone walled terracing, lily ponds with waterfall. Wisteria clad 1693 house (not open). Mature trees, orchard, magnificent views to Pennines and to West. Partial wheelchair access, disabled WC, easy parking.

32 THE HOMESTEAD

2 Fanners Lane, High Legh, Knutsford, WA16 0RZ. Janet Bashforth, 01925 349895, janbash43@sky.com. *J20 M6/J9 M56 at Lymm interchange take A50 for Knutsford, after 1m turn R into Heath Lane then 1st R into Fanners Lane. Follow parking signs.* **Sun 7 June, Sun 12 July (11-4.30). Adm £4, chd free. Home-made teas. Visits also by arrangement May to Aug for groups of 10 to 20.** Nestled in the Cheshire countryside this compact gem of a garden has been created over the last 4 years by a keen gardener and plants woman. Enter past groups of Liquidamber and White Stemmed Birch, visit shaded nooks with their own distinctive planting. Past topiary nestled in grasses, enjoy the exuberant colours of the hot area. Greenhouse and a small pond. Further on there is a small pond with water lilies and Iris. Many types of roses and clematis adorn the fencing along the paths and into the trees. The garden will be featured in the June 2020 edition of Garden Answers.

33 INGLEWOOD

4 Birchmere, Heswall, CH60 6TN. Colin & Sandra Fairclough, www. inglewood-birchmere.blogspot. co.uk. *6m S of Birkenhead. From A540 Devon Doorway/Clegg Arms r'about go through Heswall. ¼ m after Tesco, R into Quarry Rd East, 2nd L into Tower Rd North & L into Birchmere.* **Sat 16, Sun 17 May (1.30-4.30). Adm £4, chd free.** Beautiful ½ acre garden with stream, large koi pond, 'beach' with grasses, wildlife pond and bog area. Brimming with shrubs, bulbs, acers, conifers, rhododendrons, herbaceous plants and new hosta border. Interesting features including hand cart, antique mangle, wood carvings, bug hotel and Indian dog gates leading to a secret garden. Lots of seating to enjoy refreshments. Live music may be available.

34 60 KENNEDY AVENUE

Macclesfield, SK10 3DE. Bill North. *5min NW of Macclesfield Town Centre. Take A537 Cumberland St, 3rd r'bout (West Park) take B5087 Prestbury Rd. Take 5th turn on L into Kennedy Ave, last house on L before Brampton Ave opp Belong Care Home.* **Sun 14 June (12.30-4.30). Adm £4, chd free. Home-made teas. Catering provided by East Cheshire Hospice.** Small suburban garden which featured in 2017 August edition of Amateur Gardening magazine, designed to provide Al Fresco dining and relaxed entertaining, also providing relaxing Cottage Garden tranquillity which for 2020 new planting features and 65 hanging baskets.The garden also features a fabulous collection of Northern Marsh Orchids. This garden has so much to offer and is well worth a visit. Teas and cakes provided by The East Cheshire Hospice. Wheelchair access will require a carer to guide up the drive and will only provide access to part of the garden.

35 ♦ LANE END COTTAGE GARDENS

Old Cherry Lane, Lymm, WA13 0TA. Imogen & Richard Sawyer, 01925 752618, imogen@ laneendcottagegardens.co.uk, www.laneendcottagegardens .co.uk. *1m SW of Lymm. J20 M6/ J9 M56/A50 Lymm interchange. Take B5158 signed Lymm. Turn R 100 metres into Cherry Corner, turn immed R into Old Cherry Lane.* **Sat 9, Sun 10 May, Sat 12, Sun 13 Sept (10-5). Adm £4, chd free. Home-made teas.** Formerly a nursery, this 1 acre cottage garden is densely planted for all year round colour with many unusual plants. Features include deep mixed borders, scented shrub roses, ponds, herb garden, walled orchard with trained fruit, shady woodland walk, sunny formal courtyard, vegetable garden and chickens. Teas served in large greenhouse. Plants for sale. For other opening times see garden website. Wheelchair accessible WC.

36 LASKEY FARM

Laskey Lane, Thelwall, Warrington, WA4 2TF. Howard & Wendy Platt, 07740 804825, wendy.platt1@gmail.com, www.laskeyfarm.com. *2m From M6/M56. From M56/M6 follow directions to Lymm. At T-junction turn L onto the A56 in Warrington direction. Turn R onto Lymm Rd. Turn R onto Laskey Lane.* **Sat 8, Sun 9 Aug (11-5). Adm £5, chd free. Home-made teas. Visits also by arrangement June to Aug for groups of 10+. Refreshment options. Can open in conjunction with 10 Statham Avenue.**

1½ acre garden packed with late summer colour including herbaceous and rose borders and a maze showcasing sculptures set among grasses and prairie style planting. Interconnected pools for wildlife, fish and terrapins form an unusual water garden and there is also a treehouse to explore. A new area for chickens is planned for 2020. Live music and an art exhibition will take place over the weekend. Exhibition of the work of Lymm Artists both days. Live music between 1pm and 4pm both days. Sculpures by Jo Risley. Quiz for children. Most areas of the garden may be accessed by wheelchair.

37 LONG ACRE

Wyche Lane, Bunbury, CW6 9PS. Margaret & Michael Bourne, 01829 260944, mjbourne249@tiscali.co.uk. *3½ m SE of Tarporley. In Bunbury village, turn into Wyche Lane by Nags Head Pub car park, garden 400yds on L.* **Sun 19 Apr, Sun 21 June (2-5). Adm £5, chd free. Home-made teas. Visits also by arrangement Apr to June for groups of 10+.** Donation to St Boniface Church Flower Fund and Bunbury Village Hall.

Plantswoman's garden of approx 1 acre with unusual and rare plants and trees including Kentucky Coffee Tree, Scadiopitys, Kalapanax Picta and others, pool garden, exotic conservatory with bananas, anthuriums and medinilla, herbaceous, greenhouses with Clivia in Spring and Disa Orchids in Summer. Spring garden with camellias, magnolias, bulbs; roses and lilies in summer.

38 ◆ THE LOVELL QUINTA ARBORETUM

Swettenham, CW12 2LD. Tatton Garden Society, 01565 831981, admin@tattongardensociety.org.uk, www.lovellquintaarboretum.co.uk. *4m NW of Congleton. Turn off A54 N 2m W of Congleton or turn E off A535 at Twemlow Green, NE of Holmes Chapel. Follow signs to Swettenham. Park at Swettenham Arms. Do not follow Sat Nav.* **For NGS: Sun 11 Oct (1-4). Adm £5, chd free. For other opening times and information, please phone, email or visit garden website.**

The 28-acre arboretum has been established since 1960s and contains around 2,500 trees and shrubs, some very rare. Incl National Collections of Pinus and Fraxinus, large collection of oak, a collection of hebes and autumn

Bluebell Cottage Gardens

© Fiona Lea

flowering, fruiting and colouring trees and shrubs. A lake and way-marked walks. Autumn colour, winter walk and spring bulbs. Refreshments at the Swettenham Arms during licenced hours or by arrangement. Care required but wheelchairs can access much of the arboretum on the mown paths.

39 MANLEY KNOLL
Manley Road, Manley, WA6 9DX. Mr & Mrs James Timpson, 07854 661989, Thomas.leese@hotmail.co.uk, www.manleyknoll.com. *3m N of Tarvin. On B5393, via Ashton & Mouldsworth. 3m S of Frodsham, via Alvanley.* **Sun 3, Sun 24 May (12-5). Adm £5, chd free. Home-made teas. Visits also by arrangement Apr to June for groups of 10 to 30.**
Arts and Crafts garden created early 1900s. Covering 6 acres, divided into different rooms encompassing parterres, clipped yew hedging, ornamental ponds and herbaceous borders. Banks of rhododendron and azaleas frame a far-reaching view of the Cheshire Plain. Also a magical quarry/folly garden with waterfall and woodland walks.

40 MAYFIELD HOUSE
Moss Lane, Bunbury Heath, Tarporley, CW6 9SY. Mr & Mrs J France Hayhurst, jeanniefh@me.com. *Mayfield House is off the A49 on Tarporley/ Whitchurch Rd. Moss Lane is opposite School Lane which leads to Bunbury village . There's a yellow speed camera (30 mph) across the road from the house.* **Sun 31 May, Sun 14 June (2-5). Adm £5, chd free. Home-made teas. Visits also by arrangement June & July for groups of 10 to 30.**
A thoroughly English mature garden with a wealth of colour and variety throughout the year. A background of fine trees, defined areas bordered by mixed hedging, masses of rhododendrons, azaleas, camellias,hydrangeas and colourful shrubs. Clematis and wisteria festoon the walls in early Summer. Easy access and random seating areas. Small lake with an island and broad lawns with glades of foxgloves. Garden statuary, large pond with fish, swimming pool, close to pretty villages and very good gastro-pubs and some beautiful gardens nearby.

Gravel drive. Very wide wrought iron gates lead to the garden and it is entirely navigable.

41 NEW MILFORD HOUSE FARM
Long Lane, Wettenhall, Winsford, CW7 4DN. Chris & Heather Pope, 07887 760930, hclp@btinternet.com. *3m Et of Tarporley. From A51 at Alpraham turn into Long Lane. Proceed for 2½m to St David's Church on L. Milford House Farm is 150 metres further on L Park at Church. Limited mobility park at house.* **Sat 20 June, Sat 5 Sept (12-5). Adm £4, chd free. Home-made teas at St. David's Church 150 metres from garden on flat lane. Visits also by arrangement May to Sept for groups of 5 to 20. Parking at garden for all groups. Refreshments by arrangement.**
A large country garden created over 18 years with lawn, herbaceous borders, trees, perennials and annuals. Modern walled garden for vegetables, fruit, greenhouse, flowers, shrubs and various pots. Orchard with fruit, native and ornamental trees, large wildlife pond with toads and newts. Gardened on organic lines to increase biodiversity and attract wildlife. All areas are flat. Parking. Good views over borders, lawn, orchard. Teas in aid of St David's Church 20 June, MS Society 5 Aug. Walled garden has gravel and flags. Church fully accessible for refreshments/ WC.

42 ◆ MOUNT PLEASANT
Yeld Lane, Kelsall, CW6 0TB. Dave Darlington & Louise Worthington, 01829 751592, louisedarlington@btinternet.com, www.mountpleasantgardens. co.uk. *8m E of Chester. Off A54 at T-lights into Kelsall. Turn into Yeld Lane opp Farmers Arms Pub, 200yds on L. Do not follow SatNav directions.* **For NGS: Sat 2, Sun 3 May, Sat 5, Sun 6 Sept (12-5). Adm £6, chd £2.50. Cream teas. For other opening times and information, please phone, email or visit garden website.**
10 acres of landscaped garden and woodland started in 1994 with impressive views over the Cheshire countryside. Steeply terraced in places. Specimen trees, rhododendrons, azaleas, conifers,

mixed and herbaceous borders; 4 ponds, formal and wildlife. Vegetable garden, stumpery with tree ferns, sculptures, wild flower meadow and Japanese garden. Bog garden, tropical garden. Sculpture trail. Sculpture Exhibition. Please ring prior to visit for wheelchair access.

43 ◆ NESS BOTANIC GARDENS
Neston Road, Ness, Neston, CH64 4AY. The University of Liverpool, 0151 795 6300, nessgdns@liverpool.ac.uk, www. liverpool.ac.uk/ness-gardens. *10m NW of Chester. Off A540. M53 J4, follow signs M56 & A5117 (signed N Wales). Turn onto A540 follow signs for Hoylake. Ness Gardens is signed locally.* **For NGS: Sat 25 Apr (10-5). Adm £7.50, chd £3.50. For other opening times and information, please phone, email or visit garden website.**
Looking out over the dramatic Dee Estuary from a lofty perch of the Wirral peninsula, Ness Botanic Gardens boasts 64 spectacular acres of landscaped and natural gardens overflowing with horticultural treasures. With a delightfully peaceful atmosphere, a wide array of events taking place, plus a cafe and gorgeous open spaces it's a great fun-filled day out for all. National Collection of Sorbus. Herbaceous borders, Rock Garden, Mediterranean Bank, Potager and conservation area. Wheelchairs are available free to hire [donations gratefully accepted] but advance booking is highly recommended.

44 NEW **NORLEY BANK FARM**
Cow Lane, Norley, Frodsham,
WA6 8PJ. Margaret & Neil Holding.
*From the Tigers Head pub in the
centre of Norley village keep the pub
on L, carry straight on through the
village for approx 300 metres. Cow
Lane is on the R.* Sun 19 July (11-
5). Adm £4.50, chd free. Home-
made teas.
A garden well stocked perennials,
annuals and shrubs that wraps
around this very traditional Cheshire
farmhouse. The garden is split into
smaller areas with a variety of planting
styles to suit the location. There is
an enclosed vegetable garden and
greenhouse set within an orchard.
And a walk across a field to a large
wildlife pond. All set in about 2
acres. Free range hens, donkeys and
Coloured Ryeland sheep. Access in
the main is available for wheelchairs
although not the toilet. There are
some stone steps and a small
number of narrow paths.

45 **OAKFIELD VILLA**
Nantwich Road, Wrenbury,
Nantwich, CW5 8EL. Carolyn &
Jack Kennedy, 01270 781106. *6m
S of Nantwich & 6m N of Whitchurch.
Garden on main rd through village
next to Dairy Farm. Limited parking
outside house. Parking available
in Community Centre 2 minutes
walk away.* Visits by arrangement
in June for groups of 15 to 30.
Combined with Wren's Nest adm
£8, chd free, single adm £4, chd
free. Adm £4, chd free. Light
refreshments.
Romantic S-facing garden of densely
planted borders and creative planting
in containers, incl climbing roses,
clematis and hydrangeas. Divided
by screens into 'rooms'. Pergola
clothed in beautiful climbers provides
relaxed sheltered seating area and
there is a small water feature. Small
front garden, mainly hydrangeas and
clematis. Refreshments in Café at
Community Centre and 2 pubs in the
village. Some gravelled areas and
small lawn area.

46 **24 OLD GREASBY ROAD**
Upton, Wirral, CH49 6LT. Lesley
Whorton & Jon Price, 07905 775
750, wlesley@hotmail.co.uk.
*Approx 1m from J2A M53 (Upton
Bypass). M53 J2; follow Upton sign.
At r'about (J2A) straight on to Upton
Bypass. At 2nd r'about, turn L by*

Upton Cricket Club. 24 Old Greasby
Rd on L. Sun 14 June (11-4). Adm
£4, chd free. Home-made teas.
Visits also by arrangement June &
July for groups of 10 to 30.
A multi-interest and surprising
suburban garden. Both front and
rear gardens incorporate innovative
features designed for climbing and
rambling roses, clematis, underplanted with cottage garden plants
with a very productive kitchen
garden. Unfortunately, due to narrow
access and gravel paths, there is no
wheelchair access.

47 **THE OLD PARSONAGE**
Arley Green, Northwich, CW9 6LZ.
The Hon Rowland & Mrs Flower,
www.arleyhallandgardens.com.
*5m NNE of Northwich. 3m NNE of
Great Budworth. M6 J19 & 20 &
M56 J10. Follow signs to Arley Hall
& Gardens. From Arley Hall notices
to Old Parsonage which lies across
park at Arley Green (approx 1m).* Sat
16, Sun 17 May (2-5). Adm £5, chd
free. Home-made teas.
2-acre garden in attractive and
secretive rural setting in secluded
part of Arley Estate, with ancient
yew hedges, herbaceous and mixed
borders, shrub roses, climbers,
leading to woodland garden and
unfenced pond with gunnera and
water plants. Rhododendrons,
azaleas, meconopsis, cardiocrinum,
some interesting and unusual trees.
Wheelchair access over mown grass,
some slopes and bumps and rougher
grass further away from the house.
& 🐕 ✿ ☕

48 **39 OSBORNE STREET**
Bredbury, Stockport, SK6 2DA.
Geoff & Heather Hoyle, www.
youtube.com/user/Dahliaholic.
*1½m E of Stockport, just off B6104.
Follow signs for Lower Bredbury/
Bredbury Hall. Leave M60 J27 (from
S & W) or J25 (from N & E). Osborne
St is adjacent to pelican crossing
on B6104.* Sat 5, Sun 6 Sept
(1-4.30). Adm £4, chd free. Light
refreshments. Teas, coffees, and
cakes.
This dahliaholic's garden contains
over 400 dahlias in 150+ varieties,
many of exhibition standard. Shapely
lawns are surrounded by deep flower
beds that are crammed with dahlias
of all shapes, sizes and colours,
and complemented by climbers,
soft perennials and bedding plants.
An absolute riot of early autumn

colour. The garden comprises two
separate areas, both crammed with
very colourful flowers. The dahlias
range in height from 18 inches to
8 feet tall, and are in a wide variety
of shapes and colours. They are
interspersed with salvias, fuchsias,
argyranthemums, and bedding plants.
The garden is on YouTube: search for
Dahliaholic.
☕

49 **15 PARK CRESCENT**
Appleton, Warrington, WA4 5JJ.
Linda & Mark Enderby, 07949 496
747, lmaenderby@outlook.com.
*2½m S of Warrington. From M56
J10 take A49 towards Warrington
for 1½m. At 2nd set of lights turn
R into Lyons Lane , then 1st R
into Park Crescent. No.15 is last
house on R.* Sun 19 July (11.30-
5). Adm £4, chd free. Light
refreshments. Prosecco will be
available by donation. Visits also
by arrangement June to Aug for
groups of 10 to 30.
An abundant garden containing
many unusual plants, trees and a
mini orchard. A cascade, ponds and
planting encourage wildlife. There are
also vegetable and herb plots and
many roses in various forms. The
garden has been split into distinct
areas on different levels each with
their own vista drawing one through
the garden. A Chinese model railway
will also be on show.
🐕 ✿ ☕

50 **PARM PLACE**
High Street, Great Budworth,
CW9 6HF. Peter & Jane
Fairclough, 01606 891131,
janefair@btinternet.com. *3m N of
Northwich. Great Budworth on E
side of A559 between Northwich &
Warrington, 4m from J10 M56, also
4m from J19 M6. Parm Place is W
of village on S side of High St.* Visits
by arrangement Mar to Aug for
groups of 10 to 30. Adm £4, chd
free. Home-made teas. Donation
to Great Ormond Street Hospital.
Well-stocked ½ acre plantswoman's
garden with stunning views towards
S Cheshire. Curving lawns, parterre,
shrubs, colour co-ordinated
herbaceous borders, roses, water
features, rockery, gravel bed with
some grasses. Fruit and vegetable
plots. In spring large collection
of bulbs and flowers, camellias,
hellebores and blossom.

51 ◆ PEOVER HALL GARDENS

Over Peover, Knutsford, WA16 9HW. Randle Brooks, 07836219128, bookings@peoverhall.com, www.peoverhall.com. *4m S of Knutsford. Do not rely on SATNAV. From A50/Holmes Chapel Rd at Whipping Stocks Pub turn onto Stocks Lane. Follow - R onto Grotto Ln ¼m turn R onto Goostrey Ln. Main entrance on R on bend - through white gates.* **For NGS: Sat 6, Sun 7 June (2-5). Adm £5, chd free. Light refreshments in the Park House Tea Room. For other opening times and information, please phone, email or visit garden website.**

The extensive formal gardens to Peover Hall feature a series of 'garden rooms' filled with clipped box, water garden, Romanesque loggia, warm brick walls, unusual doors, secret passageways, beautiful topiary work and walled gardens, C19 dell and rockery, rhododendrons and pleached limes. With Peover Hall a Grade 2* listed Elizabethan family house dating from 1585 providing a fine backdrop. The Grade I listed Carolean Stables which are of significant architectural importance will be open to view. Partial wheelchair access to garden - wheelchair users please ask the car-park attendant for parking on hard standing rather than on the grass.

52 17 POPLAR GROVE

Sale, M33 3AX. Mr Gordon Cooke, www.gordoncooke.co.uk. *3m N of Altrincham. From the A6144 at Brooklands Stn turn into Hope Rd. Poplar Grove 3rd on R.* **Sat 27, Sun 28 June (2-5). Adm £4.50, chd free. Home-made teas.**

This S-facing suburban garden is on many levels. Its strongly diagonal design features a pebble mosaic 'cave', topiary, sculpture garden, living roof and exotic planting. A mix of formality and dense planting in the contemporary 'English' style. Reopening this year after a break to make changes which include a viewing platform and bug hotel screen with ceramic lights. Exhibition of Garden Ceramics. The garden is not suitable for wheel chairs.

Stoneyford Cottage

Clemley House

53 POULTON HALL
Poulton Lancelyn, Bebington, Wirral, CH63 9LN. The Poulton Hall Estate Trust & Poulton Hall Walled Garden Charitable Trust, 07836-590875, info@poultonhall.co.uk, www.poultonhall.co.uk. *2m S of Bebington. From M53, J4 towards Bebington; at T-lights R along Poulton Rd; house 1m on R.* **Sat 11, Sun 12 Apr (2-5). Adm £5, chd free. Home-made teas. Visits also by arrangement for groups of 20+.**
3 acres; lawns fronting house, wild flower meadow. Surprise approach to walled garden, with reminders of Roger Lancelyn Green's retellings, Excalibur, Robin Hood and Jabberwocky. Scented sundial garden for the visually impaired. Memorial sculpture for Richard Lancelyn Green by Sue Sharples. Rose, nursery rhyme, witch, herb and oriental gardens and new Memories Reading room. There are often choirs or orchestral music in the garden. Childrens toys and play house. Afternoon teas are served by a separate charity, usually St Johns Hospice, with any surplus going to their funds. Level gravel paths. Separate wheelchair access (not across parking field). Disabled toilet.

54 ◆ RODE HALL
Church Lane, Scholar Green, ST7 3QP. Randle & Amanda Baker Wilbraham, 01270 873237, enquiries@rodehall.co.uk, www.rodehall.co.uk. *5m SW of Congleton. Between Scholar Green (A34) & Rode Heath (A50).* **For opening times and information, please phone, email or visit garden website.**
Nesfield's terrace and rose garden with view over Humphry Repton's landscape is a feature of Rode, as is the woodland garden with terraced rock garden and grotto. Other attractions incl the walk to the lake with a view of Birthday Island complete with heronry, restored ice house, working two-acre walled kitchen garden and Italian garden. Fine display of snowdrops in Feb and Bluebells in May. Snowdrop Walks: 2 Feb - 3 March, 11-4, Tues - Sat (Closed Mons). Bluebell Walks: 27 Apr - 8 May daily. Summer: Weds and Bank Hol Mons until end of Sep, 11-5. Stables Tearooms offering wide variety of refreshments. Partial wheelchair access, some steep areas with gravel and woodchip paths, access to WC, kitchen garden and tearooms.

55 ROSEWOOD
Old Hall Lane, Puddington, Neston, CH64 5SP. Mr & Mrs C E J Brabin, 0151 353 1193, angela.brabin@btinternet.com. *8m N of Chester. From A540 turn down Puddington Lane, 1½m. Park by village green. Walk 30yds to Old Hall Lane, turn L through archway into garden.* **Visits by arrangement. Adm £3, chd free. Tea.**
All yr garden; thousands of snowdrops in Feb, Camellias in autumn, winter and spring. Rhododendrons in April/May and unusual flowering trees from March to June. Autumn Cyclamen in quantity from Aug to Nov. Perhaps the greatest delight to owners are two large Cornus capitata, flowering in June. Bees kept in the garden. Honey sometimes available.

56 ROWLEY HOUSE
Forty Acre Lane, Kermincham, Holmes Chapel, CW4 8DX. Tim & Juliet Foden. *3m ENE from Holmes Chapel. J18 M6 to Holmes Chapel, from Holmes Chapel take A535 (Macclesfield). Take R turn in Twemlow (Swettenham) at Yellow Broom restaurant. Rowley House ½m on L.* **Sun 24 May, Sun 12 July (11-4.30). Adm £5, chd free. Home-made teas. and cakes.**
Our aim is to give nature a home and create a place of beauty. There is a formal courtyard garden and informal gardens featuring rare trees, and herbaceous borders, a pond with swamp cypress and woodland walk with maples, rhododendrons, ferns and shade-loving plants. Beyond the garden there are wild flower meadows, natural ponds and a wood with ancient oaks. Also wood sculptures by Andy Burgess. Many unusual plants and trees.

57 SANDYMERE
Middlewich Road, Cotebrook, CW6 9EH. Sir John Timpson, 07900 567944, rme2000@aol.com. *5m N of Tarporley. On A54 approx 300yds W of T-lights at Xrds of A49/A54.* **Sun 31 May (12-5). Adm £7, chd free. Home-made teas. Visits also by arrangement June & July for groups of 10+.**
16 landscaped acres of beautiful Cheshire countryside with terraces, walled garden, extensive woodland walks and an amazing hosta garden. Turn each corner and you find

another gem with lots of different water features including a new rill built in 2014, which links the main lawn to the hostas. Partial wheelchair access.

 ♿ ✱ 🚌 ☕

58 21 SCAFELL CLOSE
High Lane, Stockport, SK6 8JA. Lesley & Dean Stafford, 01663 763015, lesley.stafford@live.co.uk. *High Lane is on A6 SE of Stockport towards Buxton. From A6 take Russell Ave then Kirkfell Drive. Scafell Close on R.* **Sat 1, Sun 2 Aug (1-4.30). Adm £4, chd free. Light refreshments. tea/coffee and cakes. Visits also by arrangement July & Aug for groups of 10+.**
⅓ acre landscaped suburban garden. Colour themed annuals border the lawn featuring the Kinder Ram statue in a heather garden, passing into vegetables, soft fruits and fruit trees. Returning perennial pathway leads to the fishpond and secret terraced garden with modern water feature and patio planting. Finally visit the blue front garden. Refreshments in aid of Cancer Research UK. Partial wheelchair access.

 ♿ 🐕 ☕

59 68 SOUTH OAK LANE
Wilmslow, SK9 6AT. Caroline Melliar-Smith, 01625 528147, caroline.ms@btinternet.com. *¾ m SW of Wilmslow. From M56 (J6) take A538 (Wilmslow) R into Buckingham Rd. From centre of Wilmslow turn R onto B5086, 1st R into Gravel Lane, 4th R into South Oak Lane.* **Visits by arrangement May to July for groups of up to 20. Adm £5, chd free.**
With year-round colour, scent and interest, this attractive, narrow, hedged cottage garden has evolved over the years into 5 natural 'rooms'. These Hardy Plant Society members passion for plants, is reflected in the variety of shrubs, trees, flower borders and pond, creating havens for wildlife. Share this garden with its' varied history from the 1890's. Some rare and unusual hardy, herbaceous and shade loving plants and shrubs.

60 34 STANLEY MOUNT
Sale, M33 4AE. Debbie & Steve Bedford. *1m from J7 M60 heading S on A56 (Washway Rd.) towards Altrincham. From A56 Altrincham N towards Sale (Washway Rd) Turning for Stanley Mount off Washway Rd, no.34 on R.* **Sun 24 May (1-5). Adm**

£4, chd free. Home-made teas. Informal small suburban garden designed and created from scratch. Mature trees, hedges, shrubs and climbers provide the framework. Colour and contrasting foliage are key. Planted areas feature herbaceous perennials, grasses bulbs, clematis, hostas, ferns and groundcover. Seated areas, creative pots, productive greenhouse, cacti, alpines and a shed hotel.

✱ ☕

61 10 STATHAM AVENUE
Lymm, WA13 9NH. Mike & Gail Porter, 01925 753488, porters@mikeandgailporter.co.uk. *Approx 1m from J20 M6 /M56 interchange. From M/way follow B5158 to Lymm. Take A56 Booth's Hill Rd, L towards Warrington, turn R on to Barsbank Lane, pass under Bridgewater canal, after 50 metres turn R on to Statham Ave. No 10 is 100 metres on R.* **Sat 30, Sun 31 May (12-5). Adm £5, chd free. Home-made teas. Enjoy home-made cakes or try Gail's famous meringues with fresh fruit and cream. Visits also by arrangement May to July for groups of 10+. Can also open in conjunction with nearby Laskey Farm. Refreshment options.**
Peaceful, pastel shades in early summer. Beautifully structured ¼ acre south facing garden carefully terraced and planted rising to the Bridgewater towpath. Hazel arch opens to clay paved courtyard with peach trees. Rose pillars lead to varied herbaceous beds and quiet shaded areas bordered by fuchsias, azaleas and rhododendrons. Wide variety of plants and shrubs. Interesting garden buildings. A treasure hunt / quiz to keep the children occupied. Delicious refreshments to satisfy the grown ups. Short gravel driveway and some steps to access the rear garden.The rear garden is sloping.

 ♿ 🐕 ✱ 🚌 ☕

62 ◆ STONYFORD COTTAGE
Stonyford Lane, Oakmere, CW8 2TF. Janet & Tony Overland, 01606 888970, info@stonyfordcottagegardens.co.uk, www.stonyfordcottagegardens.co.uk. *5m SW of Northwich. From Northwich take A556 towards Chester. ¾ m past A49 junction turn R into Stonyford Lane. Entrance ½ m on L.* **For NGS: Sun 10 May (11-4).**

Adm £4.50, chd free. Home-made teas. Lunches and cream teas available. **For other opening times and information, please phone, email or visit garden website.**
Set around a tranquil pool this Monet style landscape has a wealth of moisture loving plants, incl iris and candelabra primulas. Drier areas feature unusual perennials and rarer trees and shrubs. Woodland paths meander through shade and bog plantings, along boarded walks, across wild natural areas with views over the pool to the cottage gardens. Unusual plants available at the adjacent nursery. Open Tues - Sat & BH Mons Apr - Oct 10-5pm. Cottage Tea Room. Plant Nursery. Some gravel paths.

 ♿ 🐕 ✱ 🚌 ☕

63 STRETTON OLD HALL
Stretton, Tilston, Malpas, SY14 7JA. Stephen Gore Head Gardener, 07800602225, stegore244@hotmail.com. *5m N of Malpas. From Chester follow A41, Broxton r'about follow signs for Stretton Water Mill, turn L at Cock o Barton. 2m on L.* **Sat 18, Sun 19 July (11-5). Adm £6, chd free. Home-made teas. Visits also by arrangement Mar to Oct for groups of 20+.**
5 acre Cheshire countryside garden with a planting style best described as controlled exuberance with a definite emphasis upon perennials, colour, form and scale. Divided into several discrete and individual gardens incl stunning herbaceous borders, scree garden, walled kitchen garden and glass house. Wild flower meadows, wildlife walk around the lake with breathtaking vistas in every direction. Gravel paths.

 ♿ 🚌 ☕

We help ordinary people open the gates to their extraordinary private gardens to raise impressive amounts of money through admissions, teas and slices of cake!

64 TATTENHALL HALL

High Street, Tattenhall, Chester, CH3 9PX. Jen & Nick Benefield, Chris Evered & Jannie Hollins, 01829 770654, janniehollins@gmail.com. *8m S of Chester on A41. Turn L to Tattenhall, through village, turn R at Letters pub, past war memorial on L through Sandstone pillared gates. Park on rd or in village car park.* **Sun 24 May (2-5.30). Adm £5, chd free. Home-made teas. Visits also by arrangement. We are happy to show groups round the garden.**
Plant enthusiasts' garden around Jacobean house (not open). 4½ acres, wild flower meadows, interesting trees,large pond, stream, walled garden, colour themed borders, succession planting, spinney walk with shade plants, yew terrace overlooking meadow, views to hills. Glasshouse and vegetable garden. Wildlife friendly sometimes untidy garden, interest throughout the year, continuing to develop. Partial wheelchair access due to gravel paths, cobbles and some steps.

♿ 🐕 ❄ ☕

65 ♦ TATTON PARK

Knutsford, WA16 6QN. National Trust, leased to Cheshire East Council, 01625 374400, tatton@cheshireeast.gov.uk, www.tattonpark.org.uk. *2½ m N of Knutsford. Well signed on M56 J7 & from M6 J19.* **For NGS: Wed 13 May, Wed 10 June (10-6). Adm £7, chd £5. For other opening times and information, please phone, email or visit garden website.**
Features incl orangery by Wyatt, fernery by Paxton, restored Japanese garden, Italian and rose gardens. Greek monument and African hut. Hybrid azaleas and rhododendrons; swamp cypresses, tree ferns, tall redwoods, bamboos and pines. Fully restored productive walled gardens. Wheelchair access apart from rose garden and Japanese garden.

♿ ❄ 🚗 🚌 ☕

66 THORNCAR

Windmill Lane, Appleton, Warrington, WA4 5JN. Mrs Kath Carey, 01925 267633, john.carey516@btinternet.com. *South Warrington. From M56 J10 take A49 towards Warrington for 1½ m. At 2nd set of T-lights turn L into Quarry Lane, as the rd swings R it becomes Windmill Lane. Thorncar is 4th house on R.* **Sat 1 Aug**
(12.30-4.30). Adm £4, chd free. Home-made teas. Visits also by arrangement Mar to Sept for groups of 5 to 20.
One third acre plantwoman's suburban garden planted since 2011 within the framework of part of an older garden to provide year round interest. In August the hydrangeas, fuchsias, Eucryphia 'Nymansay' and in the in the face yellow of a hardy Calceolaria bring colour following on from daffodils in April, self seeded perfoliate alexandras in early May, peonies in June and day lilies in July. Refreshments provided by WI. Plants for St Josephs Family Centre, Warrington.

♿ ❄ ☕

67 NEW TIRESFORD

Tarporley, CW6 9LY. Miss Susanna Posnett. *Tiresford is on the A49 Tarporley Bypass. It is adjacent to the farm on the R leaving Tarporley in the direction of Four Lane Ends T-lights.* **Sun 12 July (2-5.30). Adm £6, chd free. Home-made teas. Ice-Cream.**
Established garden from the 1930's undergoing a major regeneration project to reinstate it to its former glory. Overlooking both Beeston and Peckforton Castles, it was last opened for the National Garden Scheme 25 years ago. Work has focused on hard landscaping but planting has begun on the herbaceous borders, the rhododendron woodland walk and the sunken garden. This is a work in progress. The House has been transformed into a stylish 6 Bedroom B&B. There is parking for wheelchair users next to the house. There is a disabled loo in the house which wheelchair users will have access to.

♿ 🐕 ❄ ☕

68 TIRLEY GARTH GARDENS

Mallows Way, Willington, Tarporley, CW6 0RQ. Tirley Garth. *2m N of Tarporley. 2m S of Kelsall. Entrance 500yds from village of Utkinton. At N of Tarporley take Utkinton rd.* **Sun 3, Sun 17, Sun 31 May (1-5). Adm £5, chd free. Home-made teas.**
40-acre garden, terraced and landscaped, designed by Thomas Mawson (considered the leading exponent of garden design in early C20), it is the only Grade II* Arts and Crafts garden in Cheshire that remains complete and in excellent condition. The gardens are an
important example of an early C20 garden laid out in both formal and informal styles. By early May the garden is bursting into flower with almost 3000 Rhododendron and Azalea many 100 years old. Art Exhibition by local Artists. Wheelchair access to tea rooms, only partial access in gardens.

♿ ☕

69 TWIN GATES

3 Earle Drive, Parkgate, Neston, CH64 6RY. John Hinde & Lilian Baker. *Approx ½ m N of Neston town centre. From Neston (Tesco/ Brown Horse PH), N towards Methodist Church. At church (Brewers Arms on L), take L fork into Park St, becomes Leighton Rd. Continue for approx ½ m, L into Earle Drive.* **Evening opening Fri 19 June (6-9.30). Adm £6, chd free. Wine.**
Garden developed over last decade and now looking mature. Mixed herbaceous and shrub borders, with some choice small trees all set in fully stocked sinuous borders. In June, peonies and roses come to the fore, but there are plenty of other genus, too. This year's Friday evening opening will include a glass of wine or soft drink.

♿ 🐕 ☕

70 NEW 26 WARWICK DRIVE

Hale, Altrincham, WA15 9DY. Mr Adrian & Mrs Sara Apps. *Go through Hale village on Ashley Road. Turn L after St Peter's church into Harrop Road. After 50 yds turn R onto Bower Road. After 250 yds turn R into Warwick Drive. No 26 is 1st house on L.* **Sat 18, Sun 19 July (1-5). Adm £4, chd free. Light refreshments.**
Densely planted, the garden is full of colour, especially in summer. There is some deep shade and a small boggy area. Many of our plants are raised in the greenhouse.

❄ ☕

71 8A WARWICK DRIVE

Hale, Altrincham, WA15 9EA. Gill & Chris Turner, 01619 803258, gillandchris_turner@hotmail.com. *M56 J6, take A538 to Altrincham. Turn L at 2nd T-lights into Park Rd. Take 2nd R into Bower Rd & turn L immed into Warwick Drive. Garden is 200yds on L, on corner of Lindop Rd.* **Sat 4, Sun 5 July (1-5). Adm £4, chd free. Home-made teas**

at 21 Warwick Drive. **Visits also by arrangement May to Aug for groups of 20 to 30.**
This is a small suburban garden which is constantly evolving. Recent changes include replacing an old mixed hedge with yew, making room for more planting areas, more sunlight and, of course, more plants! We design and maintain the garden ourselves for all year round interest but the front herbaceous border provides an explosion of colour in July. The highlight in July is still the front herbaceous border, designed by a plantaholic flower arranger to provide glorious colour from Apr-Oct.

72 THE WELL HOUSE
Wet Lane, Tilston, Malpas, SY14 7DP. Mrs S H French-Greenslade, 01829 250332. *3m NW of Malpas. On A41, 1st R after Broxton r'about, L on Malpas Rd through Tilston. House on L.* **Visits by arrangement Feb to Oct for groups of 5+. Adm £5, chd free. Pre-booked refreshments for small groups only.**
1-acre cottage garden, bridge over natural stream, spring bulbs, perennials, herbs and shrubs. Triple ponds. Adjoining ¾-acre field made into wild flower meadow; first seeding late 2003. Large bog area of kingcups and ragged robin. February for snowdrop walk. Victorian parlour and collector's items on show only. Not suitable for wheelchairs. Dogs on leads only.

GROUP OPENING

73 WEST DRIVE GARDENS
6, 9 West Drive, Gatley, Cheadle, SK8 4JJ. David & Ann Gane, Thelma Bishop & John Needham, 01614 280204, Davidjgane@btinternet.com. *4m N of Wilmslow on B5166. 4 m N of Wilmslow on B5166. From J5 (M56) drive past airport. to B5166 (Styal Rd).L to Gatley. Go over T-lights at Heald Green. West Drive is last turn on R before Gatley(approx.1½ m from T-lights).* **Sun 16 Feb (12-3). Combined adm £4, chd free. Light refreshments. Sun 7 June (11-5). Combined adm £6, chd free. Home-made teas. and WC at No 6. Visits also by arrangement Feb to Sept for groups of up to 30.**
Here are two gardens of very different

character, reflecting their owner's gardening style. Although suburban , they are surrounded by mature trees and have a secluded feel. Rich variety of planting including ferns, hostas with clematis, roses, astrantia at their best. Wild life pond at no.6 and other water features.Ceramics and containers with alpines complete the picture. Home-made teas, no.6. Opening in February for displays of hellebores and snowdrops as well as June. Access to top of gardens giving general overview, with shallow step leading onto gravel at no.6 and several steps and narrow paths at no.9.

74 WILLASTON GRANGE
Hadlow Road, Willaston, Neston, CH64 2UN. Mr & Mrs M Mitchell. *Willaston. On the A540 (Chester High Rd) take the B5151 into Willaston. From the Village Green in the centre of Willaston turn onto Hadlow Rd, Willaston Grange is ½ m on your L.* **Sat 6 June (11.30-5). Adm £5, chd free. Home-made teas.**
Willaston Grange returns after a break last year. The gardens extend to almost 6 acres with a small lake, wide range of mature and rare trees, herbaceous borders, woodland and vegetable gardens, orchard and magical tree house. The fully restored Arts and Crafts house provides the perfect backdrop, along with afternoon tea and live music. Most areas accessible by wheelchair.

75 WIRRAL HOSPICE ST JOHN'S
Mount Road, Higher Bebington, Wirral, CH63 6JE. Wirral Hospice St John's, www.wirralhospice.org. *Easy access from J4 M53. Follow signs for Clatterbridge Hospital, enter Clatterbridge Hospital site & take 1st L at mini r'about. Free parking on site.* **Sat 18, Sun 19 July (12-4). Adm £4, chd free. Home-made cakes & Pimm's.**
The garden underwent a significant makeover in 2019, featuring bright annual bedding, perennials, shrubs, and vegetables. It also benefited from the donation of BBC North West Tonight's Sunshine Garden in memory of Dianne Oxberry. The gardens are maintained by volunteers, patients, families, and the support of the local community. Refreshments, live music,

stalls, small animals, family-friendly. Access to disabled toilets, and all amenities.

76 WOOD END COTTAGE
Grange Lane, Whitegate, Northwich, CW8 2BQ. Mr & Mrs M R Everett, 01606 888236, woodendct@supanet.com. *4m SW of Northwich. Turn S off A556 (Northwich bypass) at Sandiway T-lights; after 1¾ m, turn L to Whitegate village; opp school follow Grange Lane for 300yds.* **Visits by arrangement May to Aug. Adm £4, chd free. Tea, Coffee, Cakes.**
Plantsman's ½ acre garden in attractive setting, sloping to a natural stream bordered by shade and moisture-loving plants. Background of mature trees. Well stocked herbaceous borders, trellis with roses and clematis, magnificent delphiniums, many phlox, meconopsis and choice perennials. Interesting shrubs and flowering trees. Vegetable garden.

77 WREN'S NEST
Wrenbury Heath Road, Wrenbury, Nantwich, CW5 8EQ. Sue & Dave Clarke, 01270 780704, wrenburysue@gmail.com. *12m from Nantwich signs for A530 to Whitchurch, reaching Sound school turn 1st R Wrenbury Heath Rd, across the Xrds & bungalow is on L, telegraph pole outside Open by arrangement with Oakfield Villa.* **Visits by arrangement in June for groups of 15 to 30. Combined with Oakfield Villa adm £8. Single adm £4, chd free.**
Set in a semi-rural area, this bungalow has a Cottage Garden Style of lush planting and is 80ft x 45ft. The garden is packed with unusual and traditional perennials and shrubs incl over 100 hardy geraniums, campanulas, crocosmias, iris and alpine troughs. Plants for sale. Proceeds from this garden will be for the NGS. National collection of Hardy Geranium sylvaticum and renardii. Plant Heritage National Collection of Hardy Geraniums sylvaticum and renardii.

Cornwall has some of the most beautiful natural landscapes to be found anywhere in the world.

Here, you will discover some of the country's most extraordinary gardens, a spectacular coastline, internationally famous surfing beaches, windswept moors and countless historic sites. Cornish gardens reflect this huge variety of environments particularly well.

A host of National Collections of magnolias, camellias, rhododendrons and azaleas, as well as exotic Mediterranean semitropical plants and an abundance of other plants flourish in our acid soils and mild climate.

Surrounded by the warm currents of the Gulf Stream, with our warm damp air in summer and mild moist winters, germination continues all year.

Cornwall boasts an impressive variety of beautiful gardens. These range from coastal-protected positions to exposed cliff-top sites, moorland water gardens, Japanese gardens and the world famous tropical biomes of the Eden Project.

Volunteers

County Organiser
Christopher Harvey Clark
01872 530165
suffree2012@gmail.com

County Treasurer
Peter Hyde 01208 872048
peter.hyde@ngs.org.uk

Publicity
Sara Gadd 07814 885141
sara@gartendesign.co.uk

Emma Skilton 07772 542143
emma24nyrorganic@gmail.com

Booklet Co-ordinator
Peter Stanley 01326 565868
stanley.m2@sky.com

Photographer
Lucie Averill 01736 711971
lucieaverill@ymail.com

Assistant County Organisers
Charlie Barrie 01208 841284
charlie.blossom.cc@gmail.com

Ginnie Clotworthy 01208 872612
ginnieclotworthy@hotmail.co.uk

Sarah Gordon 01579 362076
sar.gordon@talktalk.net

Alison O'Connor 01726 882460
tregoose@tregoose.co.uk

Marion Stanley 01326 565868
stanley.m2@sky.com

[f] @CornwallNGS
[o] @ngs_cornwall

Right: Arundell

OPENING DATES

All entries subject to change. For latest information check www.ngs.org.uk

Extended openings are shown at the beginning of the month.

Map locator numbers are shown to the right of each garden name.

February

Snowdrop Festival

Sunday 2nd
Tregoose   40

Sunday 16th
Tregoose   40

April

Daily from Wednesday 1st to Wednesday 15th
Waye Cottage   46

Sunday 5th
Meudon Hotel   23
◆ Trewidden Garden   45

Monday 6th
◆ Pencarrow   27

Saturday 25th
Ash Barn   4
◆ Chygurno   12

Sunday 26th
Ash Barn   4
Bodwannick Manor
  Farm   6
◆ Chygurno   12
Ethnevas Cottage   17

Tuesday 28th
Pinsla Garden   31

Wednesday 29th
Pinsla Garden   31

May

Sunday 3rd
◆ Boconnoc   5
Navas Hill House   25

Friday 8th
East Down Barn   15
◆ Moyclare   24
Penmilder   29

Sunday 10th
Anvil Cottage   2
◆ The Japanese
  Garden   20
South Lea   36
Windmills   47

Monday 11th
◆ The Japanese
  Garden   20

Tuesday 12th
Pinsla Garden   31

Wednesday 13th
Pinsla Garden   31
South Bosent   35

Thursday 14th
South Bosent   35

Sunday 17th
Alverton Cottage   1
Trebartha Estate
  Garden   37

Sunday 24th
Bokelly   7

Tuesday 26th
Pinsla Garden   31

Wednesday 27th
Gardens Cottage   19
Pinsla Garden   31

June

Wednesday 3rd
Kestle Barton   21

Sunday 7th
Caervallack   10

Tuesday 9th
Pinsla Garden   31

Wednesday 10th
Kestle Barton   21
Pinsla Garden   31

Sunday 14th
Bodwannick Manor
  Farm   6

Wednesday 17th
Kestle Barton   21
South Bosent   35

Thursday 18th
South Bosent   35

Sunday 21st
Arundell   3
Crugsillick Manor   13
◆ St Michael's Mount   34
Trenarth   41

Tuesday 23rd
Pinsla Garden   31

Wednesday 24th
Gardens Cottage   19
Kestle Barton   21
Pinsla Garden   31

Friday 26th
Dye Cottage   14

Saturday 27th
Dye Cottage   14

Sunday 28th
Dye Cottage   14
South Lea   36

July

Wednesday 1st
Kestle Barton   21

Sunday 5th
Trethew   44

Tuesday 7th
Pinsla Garden   31

Wednesday 8th
Kestle Barton   21
Pinsla Garden   31
South Bosent   35

Thursday 9th
South Bosent   35

Sunday 12th
Parkhenver   26

Wednesday 15th
Kestle Barton   21

Saturday 18th
◆ Chygurno   12

Sunday 19th
Anvil Cottage   2
◆ Chygurno   12
NEW Treprenn Vean   42
Windmills   47

Tuesday 21st
Pinsla Garden   31

Wednesday 22nd
Kestle Barton   21
Pinsla Garden   31

Sunday 26th
Byeways   9

Wednesday 29th
Gardens Cottage   19
Kestle Barton   21

August

Sunday 2nd
Tregonning   39

Wednesday 5th
Kestle Barton   21
South Bosent   35

Thursday 6th
South Bosent   35

Tuesday 11th
◆ Bonython Manor   8

Wednesday 12th
Kestle Barton   21

Wednesday 19th
Kestle Barton   21

Wednesday 26th
Gardens Cottage   19
Kestle Barton   21

We open the gates to the nation's best gardens, offering a relaxing, memorable and affordable day out. A perfect experience to share with friends and family.

September

Daily from Tuesday 1st to Tuesday 15th
Waye Cottage　　　46

Wednesday 2nd
Kestle Barton　　　21
South Bosent　　　35

Thursday 3rd
South Bosent　　　35

Saturday 5th
◆ Roseland House　　33

Sunday 6th
◆ Roseland House　　33

Wednesday 9th
Kestle Barton　　　21

Sunday 13th
Tregonhayne　　　38

Wednesday 16th
Kestle Barton　　　21

Wednesday 23rd
Kestle Barton　　　21

Wednesday 30th
Kestle Barton　　　21

October

Sunday 11th
Trebartha Estate
Garden　　　37

By Arrangement

Arrange a personalised garden visit with your club, or group of friends, on a date to suit you. See individual garden entries for full details.

Anvil Cottage　　　2
Arundell　　　3
Caervallack　　　10
Carminowe Valley
　Garden　　　11
Crugsillick Manor　　13
Dye Cottage　　　14
East Down Barn　　15
Ethnevas Cottage　　17
Garden Cottage　　18
Gardens Cottage　　19
Pendower House　　28
Penwarne　　　30
South Bosent　　　35
South Lea　　　36
Tregonning　　　39
Trenarth　　　41
Trereife　　　43
Waye Cottage　　　46
Windmills　　　47

THE GARDENS

1 ALVERTON COTTAGE
Alverton Road, Penzance, TR18 4TG. David & Lizzie Puddifoot. *Next door to YMCA. About 600 metres from Penlee car park travelling towards A30. Morrab Gardens are also close to car park.* **Sun 17 May (2-5). Adm £4, chd free. Home-made teas.**
Alverton Cottage is a grade 2 listed Regency house. The garden is modest in size though large for a Penzance garden, S-facing and sheltered by mature trees incl elms. Very large monkey-puzzle tree and holm oak. Laid out in 1860s, we have added a succulent area, fernery and barefoot walk. In nearby Morrab Sub-tropical Gardens the 'Friends' will also welcome visitors. Off road disabled parking but wheelchair access is limited to garden terrace.

2 ANVIL COTTAGE
South Hill, PL17 7LP. Geoff & Barbara Clemerson, 01579 362623, gcclemerson@gmail.com. *3m NW of Callington. Head N on A388 from Callington centre. After ½ m L onto South Hill Rd (signed South Hill), straight on for 3m. Gardens on R just before St Sampson's Church.* **Sun 10 May, Sun 19 July (1-5). Combined adm with Windmills £5, chd free. Home-made teas. Gluten free refreshments available. Visits also by arrangement for groups of up** to 30 from 10 May to 31 May and 1 July to 19 July. Donation to local charities.
Essentially a plantsman's garden, with new features added each year. Winding paths take you through a series of themed rooms with familiar, rare and unusual plants. Paths lead up steps to a raised viewpoint with spectacular views of Caradon Hill and Bodmin Moor, and then into a formal rose garden, and on to a wildlife friendly area with trees and shrubs. Regret no dogs, please. Only partial wheelchair access due to steps.

3 ARUNDELL
West Pentire, Crantock, TR8 5SE. Brenda & David Eyles, 01637 831916, david@davideyles.com. *1m W of Crantock. From A3075 take signs to Crantock. At junction in village keep straight on to West Pentire (1m). Park in field (signed) or public car parks at W Pentire.* **Sun 21 June (1-5). Adm £5, chd free. Cream teas & home-made biscuits. Visits also by arrangement May to Aug for groups of up to 20 (not Fridays).**
A garden where no garden should be! - on windswept NT headland between 2 fantastic beaches. 1 acre packed with design and plant interest round old farm cottage. Front: cottage garden. Side: Mediterranean courtyard. Rear: rockery and shrubbery leading to stumpery and fernery and on to stream and pond, Cornish Corner, herbaceous borders, Beth Chatto dry garden, and exotic garden. Wheelchair access from public car park with entrance via rear gate. 14 shallow steps in centre of garden useable with care.

4 ASH BARN
Callington, PL17 8BP. Mary Martin. *3m E of Callington. Leaving Callington on A390 (Tavistock direction) take 1st R signed Harrowbarrow. Turn R at T junction in village then 1m down hill to Glamorgan Mill parking on L.* **Sat 25, Sun 26 Apr (10-5). Adm £5, chd free. Tea.**
Terraced 3 acre woodland garden, full of magnolias, camellias and fruit trees, under-planted with old roses, shrubs and Tamar Valley narcissi. Intensive herbaceous planting provides interest for most of the year, and contrasts with box and holly topiary. Narrow, uneven paths and steps reflect the wild wood atmosphere. There is also a quarry edge, so no dogs or unsupervised children. Regret no wheelchair access.

5 ◆ BOCONNOC
Lostwithiel, PL22 0RG. Elizabeth Fortescue, 01208 872507, office@boconnoc.com, www.boconnoc.com. *Off A390 between Liskeard & Lostwithiel. From East Taphouse follow signs to Boconnoc. (SatNav does not work well in this area).* **For NGS: Sun 3 May (2-5). Adm £5, chd free. For other opening times and information, please phone, email or visit garden website.**
20 acres surrounded by parkland and woods with magnificent trees,

flowering shrubs and stunning views. The gardens are set amongst mature trees which provide the backcloth for exotic spring flowering shrubs, woodland plants, with newly-planted magnolias and a fine collection of hydrangeas. Bathhouse built in 1804, woodland gardens, obelisk built in 1771, house dating from Domesday, deer park, C15 church.

Navas Hill House

🚫 🐂 🍴 🚗 🛏 ☕

6 BODWANNICK MANOR FARM

Nanstallon, Bodmin, PL30 5LN. Gaia Trust, www.gaiatrust.org.uk/bodwannick. *From A30, take A389 signed to Lanivet and Bodmin. 1m after Lanivet turn L (signed to Nanstallon). From Bodmin, take A389 signed for A30. After 1½m turn R at Jim's hardware store.* **Sun 26 Apr, Sun 14 June (10.30-3.30). Adm by donation.** 1½-acre plantsman's garden with fern-rich rockery, water garden and new terraced garden in the making, daffodils, roses and shrubs. Remarkable for its aura of peace and tranquillity, but its air of antiquity is deceptive as it was the lifetime creation of Martin Appleton and his family. Now in the care of the Gaia Trust, it has particular features of note and yr-round interest. Wheelchair access possible to much but not all of garden.

🚫 🐂 ❀ ☕

7 BOKELLY

St Kew, Bodmin, PL30 3DY. Toby & Henrietta Courtauld. *Follow road to Trelill from St Kew Highway, leaving Red Lion pub on L. Garden on L after approx 1m.* **Sun 24 May (1.30-5.30). Adm £5, chd free. Cream teas.**
The 7-acre garden surrounds a beautiful C15 barn and lichened stone outbuildings. It has been expanded and rejuvenated with new plantings to suit the varied levels and soil types, incl woodland planting, herbaceous border, little orchard and vegetable plot, and cut flower beds (a particular passion of garden designer Henrietta).
☕

8 ◆ BONYTHON MANOR

Cury Cross Lanes, Helston, TR12 7BA. Mr & Mrs Richard Nathan, 01326 240550, sbonython@gmail.com, www.bonythonmanor.co.uk. *5m S of Helston. On main A3083 Helston to Lizard Rd. Turn L at Cury Cross*

Lanes (Wheel Inn). Entrance 300yds on R. **For NGS: Tue 11 Aug (2-4.30). Adm £9, chd £2. For other opening times and information, please phone, email or visit garden website.**
Magnificent 20 acre colour garden incl sweeping hydrangea drive to Georgian manor (not open). Herbaceous walled garden, potager with vegetables and picking flowers; 3 lakes in valley planted with ornamental grasses, perennials and South African flowers. A 'must see' for all seasons colour.

🚫 🐂 ❀ 🚗 🛏 ☕

9 BYEWAYS

Dunheved Road, Launceston, PL15 9JE. Tony Reddicliffe. *Launceston town centre. 100yds from multi-storey car park past offices of Cornish & Devon Post into Dunheved Rd, 3rd bungalow on R.* **Sun 26 July (1-5). Adm £5, chd free. Light refreshments.**
Small town garden developed over 10yrs by enthusiastic amateur gardeners. Herbaceous borders, rockery. Tropicals incl bananas, gingers and senecio. Stream and water features. Roof garden. Japanese inspired tea house and courtyard with bridge. Fig tree and Pawlonia flank area giving secluded seating. Living pergola. Wild flower planting.

🐂 ❀ ☕

10 CAERVALLACK

St Martin, Helston, TR12 6DF. Matt Robinson & Louise McClary, 01326 221339, mat@build-art.co.uk. *5m SE of Helston. Go through Mawgan village, over 2 bridges, past Gear Farm shop; go past turning on L, garden next farmhouse on L.* **Sun 7 June (1.30-4.30). Adm £5, chd free. Tea & home-made cakes; scones, clotted cream & jam. Visits also by arrangement Apr to Sept for groups of 5 to 30. We welcome groups by appointment - ideally we would like 3 weeks notice.**
Romantic garden arranged into rooms, the collaboration between an artist and an architect. Colour and form of plants against architectural experiments in cob, concrete and shaped hedges and topiary. Grade II listed farmhouse and orchard. Roses and wisteria a speciality. 25 years in the making. Heroic 54ft pedestrian footbridge, 5 sided meditation studio, cast concrete pond and amphitheatre; coppice and wild flower meadow; mature orchard and veg plot. Partial wheelchair access but if you can negotiate the opening 2 steps, some of front garden will be accessible. Brick, grass and gravel paths.

❀ 🚗 🛏 ☕

◻1 CARMINOWE VALLEY GARDEN

Tangies, Gunwalloe, TR12 7PU. Mr & Mrs Peter Stanley, 01326 565868, stanley.m2@sky.com, www.carminowevalleygarden. co.uk. *3m SW of Helston. A3083 Helston-Lizard rd. R opp main gate to Culdrose. 1m downhill, garden on R.* **Visits by arrangement May & June. Adm £5, chd free.**
Overlooking the beautiful Carminowe Valley towards Loe Pool this abundant garden combines native oak woodland, babbling brook and large natural pond with more formal areas. Wild flowers, mown pathways, shrubberies, orchard. Enclosed cottage garden, spring colours and roses early summer provide huge contrast. Gravel paths, slopes.

◻2 ◆ CHYGURNO

Lamorna, TR19 6XH. Dr & Mrs Robert Moule, 01736 732153, rmoule010@btinternet.com. *4m S of Penzance. Off B3315. Follow signs for The Lamorna Cove Hotel. Garden is at top of hill, past Hotel on L.* **For NGS: Sat 25, Sun 26 Apr, Sat 18, Sun 19 July (2-5). Adm £5, chd free. For other opening times and information, please phone or email.**
Beautiful, unique, 3 acre cliffside garden overlooking Lamorna Cove. Planting started in 1998, mainly S-hemisphere shrubs and exotics with hydrangeas, camellias and rhododendrons. Woodland area with tree ferns set against large granite outcrops. Garden terraced with steep steps and paths. Plenty of benches so you can take a rest and enjoy the wonderful views.

◻3 CRUGSILLICK MANOR

Ruan High Lanes, Truro, TR2 5LJ. Dr Alison Agnew & Mr Brian Yule, 01872 501972, alisonagnew@icloud.com. *On Roseland Peninsula. Turn off A390 Truro-St Austell rd onto A3078 towards St Mawes. Approx 5m after Tregony turn 1st L after Ruan High Lanes towards Veryan, garden is 200yds on R.* **Sun 21 June (11-5). Adm £5, chd free. Pasties and light lunches available, also teas, coffee, soft drinks and cakes. Visits also by arrangement Apr to Sept for groups of 10+. Home-made teas £3.00 per head.**
2 acre garden, substantially re-landscaped and planted, mostly over last 7 yrs. To the side of the C17/C18 house, a wooded bank drops down to walled kitchen garden and hot garden. In front, sweeping yew hedges and paths define oval lawns and broad mixed borders. On a lower terrace, the focus is a large pond and the planting is predominantly exotic flowering trees and shrubs. Partial wheelchair access. Garden is on several levels connected by fairly steep sloping gravel paths.

◻4 DYE COTTAGE

St Neot, PL14 6NG. Sue & Brian Williams, 01579 321394, dyecottage@googlemail.com. *Opp The London Inn in centre of St Neot village. Turn off A38 to St Neot. Street parking.* **Fri 26, Sat 27, Sun 28 June (2-5). Adm £4, chd free. Home-made teas. Visits also by arrangement May to Sept for groups of 10 to 30.**
1/3 acre cottage garden, designed and completely maintained by the owners over the past 27 yrs. Many seating areas - down by the river, in courtyard garden, fire pit corner, and on rose terrace. Wisteria walk, potting shed, greenhouse, summerhouse, office (once the tree house!), mature borders, and roses everywhere. Regret no disabled access due to steps from road to cottage.

◻5 EAST DOWN BARN

Menheniot, Liskeard, PL14 3QU. David & Shelley Lockett, 07803 159662. *S side of village near cricket ground. Turn off A38 at Hayloft restaurant/railway station junction and head towards Menheniot village. Follow NGS signs from sharp L hand bend as you enter village.* **Fri 8 May (1-4.30). Adm £3, chd free. Home-made teas. Visits also by arrangement Apr to July for groups of 20+.**
Garden laid down between 1986-1991 with the conversion of the barn into a home and covers almost 1/2 acre of East sloping land with stream running North - South acting as the Easterly boundary. 3 terraces before garden starts to level out at stream. Garden won awards in the early years under the stewardship of the original owners. Steep slopes.

◻6 ◆ EDEN PROJECT

Bodelva, PL24 2SG. The Eden Trust, 01726 811911, www.edenproject.com. *4m E of St Austell. Brown signs from A30 & A390.* **For opening times and information, please phone or visit garden website.**
Described as 8th wonder of the world, the Eden Project is a global garden for the C21. Discover the story of plants that have changed the world and which could change your future. The Eden Project is an exciting attraction where you can explore your relationship with nature, learn new things and get inspiration

Crugsillick Manor

© Rosalind Simon

about the world around you. Yr-round programme of talks, events and workshops. Wheelchairs available - booking of powered wheelchairs is essential; please call 01726 818895 in advance.

17 ETHNEVAS COTTAGE
Constantine, Falmouth, TR11 5PY. Lyn Watson & Ray Chun, 01326 340076. *6m SW of Falmouth. Nearest main rds A39, A394. Follow signs for Constantine. At lower village sign, at bottom of winding hill, turn off on private lane. Garden ¾m up hill.* **Sun 26 Apr (1-4.30). Adm £5, chd free. Home-made teas. Visits also by arrangement Apr to Aug.**
Isolated granite cottage in 2 acres. Intimate flower and vegetable garden. Bridge over stream to large pond and primrose path through semi-wild bog area. Hillside with grass paths among native and exotic trees. Many camellias and rhododendrons. Mixed shrubs and herbaceous beds, wild flower glade, spring bulbs. A garden of discovery of hidden delights.

18 GARDEN COTTAGE
Gunwalloe, Helston, TR12 7QB. Dan & Beth Tarling, 01326 241906, beth@gunwalloe.com, www.gunwalloecottages.co.uk. *Just beyond Halzephron Inn at Gunwalloe. Cream cottage with green windows.* **Visits by arrangement Apr to Sept for groups of up to 20. Adm £4.**
Coastal cottage garden. Small garden with traditional cottage flowers, vegetable garden, greenhouse and meadow with far reaching views. Instagram: seaview_gunwalloe. Featured in Country Living magazine. Gravel paths and a few steps.

19 GARDENS COTTAGE
Prideaux, St Blazey, PL24 2SS. Sue & Roger Paine, 07786 367610, sue.newton@btinternet.com. *1m from railway Xing on A390 in St Blazey. Turn into Prideaux Rd opp Gulf petrol station on A390 in St Blazey (signed Luxulyan). Proceed ½m. Turn R (signed Luxulyan Valley and Prideaux) and follow signs.* **Wed 27 May, Wed 24 June, Wed 29 July, Wed 26 Aug (11-5). Adm £4, chd free. Home-made teas. Visits also by arrangement June to Aug**

for groups of up to 30.
Set in tranquil location on edge of Luxulyan Valley, work commenced on creating a one and a half acre garden from scratch in winter 2015. The aim has been to create a garden that's sympathetic to its surrounding landscape, has yr-round interest with lots of colour, is productive and simply feels good to be in. Although there is still lots to do that aim has been achieved in just 5 short years. Check our Facebook page for special events - @gardenscottageprideaux.

20 ◆ THE JAPANESE GARDEN
St Mawgan, TR8 4ET. Natalie Hore & Stuart Ellison, 01637 860116, info@japanesegarden.co.uk, www.japanesegarden.co.uk. *6m East of Newquay. St Mawgan village is directly below Newquay Airport. Follow brown and white road signs on A3059 and B3276.* **For NGS: Sun 10, Mon 11 May (10-6). Adm £5, chd £2.50. Refreshments available in village 2-3 min walk from garden. For other opening times and information, please phone, email or visit garden website.**
Discover an oasis of tranquillity in a Japanese-style Cornish garden, set in approx 1 acre. Spectacular Japanese maples and azaleas, symbolic teahouse, koi pond, bamboo grove, stroll woodland, zen and moss gardens. A place created for contemplation and meditation. Adm free to gift shop, bonsai and plant areas. Featured in BBC2 Big Dreams Small Spaces. 90% wheelchair accessible, gravel paths.

21 KESTLE BARTON
Manaccan, Helston, TR12 6HU. Karen Townsend, 01326 231811, info@kestlebarton.co.uk, www.kestlebarton.co.uk. *A3083 Helston - Lizard, 2m L B3293 for St Keverne. 2m L Helford, Newtown St Martin, R then L for Helford. 1m L at Xrds to Kestle Barton, R after several hundred yds, follow signs.* **Every Wed 3 June to 30 Sept (10.30-5). Adm by donation. Tea.**
A delightful garden near Frenchmans Creek, on the Lizard, which is the setting for Kestle Barton Gallery; wild flower meadow, Cornish orchard with named varieties and a formal garden with prairie planting in blocks by James Alexander Sinclair. It is a riot of colour in summer and continues

to delight well into late summer. Parking, honesty box tea hut. Art Gallery. Good wheelchair access and reasonably accessible loo. Dogs on leads welcome. Large coaches cannot reach Kestle Barton.

22 ◆ THE LOST GARDENS OF HELIGAN
Pentewan, St Austell, PL26 6EN. Heligan Gardens Ltd, 01726 845100, info@heligan.com, www.heligan.com. *5m S of St Austell. From St Austell take B3273 signed Mevagissey, follow signs.* **For opening times and information, please phone, email or visit garden website.**
Lose yourself in the mysterious world of The Lost Gardens where an exotic sub-tropical jungle, atmospheric Victorian pleasure grounds, an interactive wildlife project and the finest productive gardens in Britain all await your discovery. Wheelchair access to Northern gardens. Armchair tour shows video of unreachable areas. Wheelchairs available at reception free of charge.

23 MEUDON HOTEL
Maenporth Road, Mawnan Smith, Falmouth, TR11 5HT. Tessa Rabett, 01326 250541, wecare@meudon.co.uk, www.meudon.co.uk. *Follow signs for Mabe, then Mawnan Smith.* **Sun 5 Apr (12-5). Adm £7, chd free. At hotel, bar drinks, snacks, cream teas are available.**
Meudon has 9 acres of sub-tropical valley garden created by the Fox family in 1800. Wealthy Quakers and shipping agents, their Packet ships provided transport for Meudon's wonderful collection of rare and exotic trees and shrubs from around the world. Terraces, pathways, meander down to Bream Cove (private beach). Formal garden, herbaceous borders, indigenous plants, and sunken pond area. Brazilian Gunnera manicata, Japanese banana trees Musa basjoo, Wollemia pine, Dicksonia antarctica, rhodendendrons, camellias, magnolia, azaleas,Trachycarpus fortunei, Drimys winteri, Monterey cypress, bamboo, agapanthus, Cornus kousa, myrtle. Wheelchair access limited to upper terrace and ponds (although they take a little longer to get to).

24 ◆ MOYCLARE

Lodge Hill, Liskeard, PL14 4EH. Elizabeth & Philip Henslowe, 01579 343114, elizabethhenslowe@btinternet.com, www.moyclare.co.uk. *1m S of Liskeard centre. Approx 300yds S of Liskeard railway stn on St Keyne-Duloe rd (B3254).* **For NGS: Fri 8 May (11-5). Combined adm with Penmilder £7, chd free. Home-made teas. For other opening times and information, please phone, email or visit garden website.**

Gardened by one family for over 90yrs; mature trees, shrubs and plants (many unusual, many variegated). Once most televised Cornish garden. Now revived and rejuvenated and still a plantsman's delight, full of character. Camellia, brachyglottis and astrantia (all Moira Reid) and cytisus Moyclare Pink originated here. Meandering paths through fascinating shrubberies, herbacious borders and sunny corners. Well stocked pond. Wildlife habitat area. Over 70 named camellias. Rare and unusual plants and ferns. Quite a lot of the garden can be enjoyed by wheelchair users.

 ♿ ✿ 🚍 ☕

25 NAVAS HILL HOUSE

Bosanath Valley, Mawnan Smith, Falmouth, TR11 5LL. Aline & Richard Turner. *1½ m from Trebah & Glendurgan Gdns. Head for Mawnan Smith, pass Trebah and Glendurgan Gdns then follow yellow signs. Don't follow SatNav which suggests you turn R before Mawnan Smith - congestion alert!* **Sun 3 May (2-5). Adm £5, chd free. Home-made teas. 'All you can eat' £4.00.**

8½ -acre elevated valley garden with paddocks, woodland, kitchen garden and ornamental areas. The ornamental garden consists of 2 plantsman areas with specialist trees and shrubs, walled rose garden, water features and rockery. Young and established wooded areas with bluebells, camellia walks and young large leafed rhododendrons. Seating areas with views across wooded valley. Partial wheelchair access, some gravel and grass paths.

 ♿ 🐕 ☕

26 PARKHENVER

Penventon, Redruth, TR15 3AA. Dr & Mrs David Quill Smart. *Important: To enter gardens, please use main entrance of Roman Catholic Church - about 100m to town end of our main gate (white balustrading). Leave by Exit lane.* **Sun 12 July (12.30-6). Adm £5, chd free. Light refreshments on lawn in marquee. Wine available.**

The Parkhenver Estate gardens were created in about 1850. We are in the midst of a complete restoration project to return them to their original glory. The greenhouses and walled garden have already been restored. Two fascinating woodland walks have also been found and restored. The fountain and other flower beds are in the process of restoration. Access to some gravelled areas may be difficult.

 ♿ 🐕 ✿ ☕

27 ◆ PENCARROW

Washaway, Bodmin, PL30 3AG. Molesworth-St Aubyn family, 01208 841369, info@pencarrow.co.uk, www.pencarrow.co.uk. *4m NW of Bodmin. Signed off A389 & B3266. Free parking.* **For NGS: Mon 6 Apr (10-5.30). Adm £6.75, chd free. Cream teas. For other opening times and information, please phone, email or visit garden website.**

50 acres of tranquil, family-owned Grade II* listed gardens. Superb specimen conifers, azaleas, magnolias and camellias galore. 700 varieties of rhododendron give a blaze of spring colour; blue hydrangeas line the mile-long carriage drive throughout the summer. Discover the Iron Age hill fort, lake, Italian gardens and granite rockery. Dogs welcome, café and children's play area. Gravel paths, some steep slopes.

 ♿ 🐕 ✿ 🚍 ☕

28 PENDOWER HOUSE

Lanteglos-by-Fowey, PL23 1NJ. Mr Roger Lamb, 01726 870884, rl@rogerlamb.com. *Near Polruan off the B3359 towards Bodinnick. 2m from Fowey using the Bodinnick ferry. Please ask for directions when arranging to visit the garden. Do not use SatNav.* **Visits by arrangement May to July for groups of up to 20. Adm £4.50, chd free. Home-made teas. Other refreshments available by prior arrangement.**

Set in the heart of Daphne du Maurier country in its own valley this established garden surrounding a Georgian Rectory is now undergoing a revival having been wild and neglected for some years. It has formal herbaceous terraces, a cottage garden, orchard, ponds, streams and a C19 shrub garden with a fine collection of azaleas, camellias and rhododendrons plus rare mature specimen trees. House and garden available for filming and photography. Sadly difficult wheelchair access to much of this garden.

 ✿ ☕

29 PENMILDER

Lodge Hill, Liskeard, PL14 4EL. Chris & Mandy Deegan. *1m S of Liskeard town centre. On 3254 (Duloe road). Entrance on L directly opp 'Santa Trees'.* **Fri 8 May (11-5). Combined adm with Moyclare £7, chd free. Light refreshments.**

This is a gently sloping, S-facing garden of approx 2½ acres. Lawns with mature borders and a lily pond with plenty of wild life. There are also natural wooded areas and an apple orchard which is particularly pretty in spring with daffodils, bluebells and primroses. Sadly it is not suitable for wheelchair users due to gravel paths.

 ☕

30 PENWARNE

Mawnan Smith, Falmouth, TR11 5PH. Mrs R Sawyer, penwarnegarden@gmail.com. *1m outside Mawnan Smith.* **Visits by arrangement Feb to May for groups of 5 to 20. Adm £5, chd free.**

Originally planted in the late C19, this 12 acre garden incl extensive plantings of camellias, rhododendrons and azaleas. Special features incl large magnolias and a number of fine mature trees incl copper beech, handkerchief tree and Himalayan cedar. The walled garden, believed to be the site of a medieval chapel, houses herbaceous planting, climbing roses and fruit trees.

31 PINSLA GARDEN

Glynn, Nr. Cardinham, Bodmin, PL30 4AY. Mark & Claire Woodbine, www.pinslagarden.net. *3½ m E of Bodmin. From A30 or Bodmin take A38 towards Plymouth, 1st L to Cardinham & Fletchers Bridge, 2m on R.* **Tue 28, Wed 29 Apr, Tue 12, Wed 13, Tue 26, Wed 27 May, Tue 9, Wed 10, Tue 23, Wed 24 June, Tue 7, Wed 8, Tue 21, Wed 22 July (9-4). Adm £4, chd free. For other opening times and information, please phone, email or visit garden website.**

Surround yourself with deep nature.

Pinsla is a tranquil cottage garden buzzing with insects enjoying the sheltered sunny edge of a wild wood. Lose yourself in a colourful tapestry of naturalistic planting. There are lots of unusual planting combinations, cloud pruning, intricate paths, garden art and a stone circle. Sorry, no teas but you are welcome to bring your own thermos. Partial wheelchair access as some paths are narrow and bumpy.

♿ 🐕

32 ◆ POTAGER GARDEN
High Cross, Constantine, Falmouth, TR11 5RF. Mr Mark Harris, 01326 341258, enquiries@potagergarden.org, www.potagergarden.org. *5m SW of Falmouth. From Falmouth, follow signs to Constantine. From Helston, drive through Constantine and continue towards Famouth.* **For opening times and information, please phone, email or visit garden website.**
Potager has emerged from the bramble choked wilderness of an abandoned plant nursery. With mature trees which were once nursery stock and lush herbaceous planting interspersed with fruit and vegetables Potager Garden aims to demonstrate the beauty of productive organic gardening. There are games to play, hammocks to laze in and boule and badminton to enjoy.

♿ 🐕 ❀ ☕

33 ◆ ROSELAND HOUSE
Chacewater, TR4 8QB. Mr & Mrs Pridham, 01872 560451, charlie@roselandhouse.co.uk, www.roselandhouse.co.uk. *4m W of Truro. At Truro end of main st. Park in village car park (100yds) or on surrounding rds.* **For NGS: Sat 5, Sun 6 Sept (1-5). Adm £4, chd free. Home-made teas.** **For other opening times and information, please phone, email or visit garden website.**
The 1-acre garden is home to the National collection of Lapageria rosea which will be in flower for this opening plus much other late summer interest such as salvia, mandevilla, abutilon and passiflora. Some slopes.

♿ 🐕 ❀ NPC ☕

34 ◆ ST MICHAEL'S MOUNT
Marazion, TR17 0HS. James & Mary St Levan, 01736 710507, mail@stmichaelsmount.co.uk, www.stmichaelsmount.co.uk.

2½m E of Penzance. ½m from shore at Marazion by Causeway; otherwise by motor boat. **For NGS: Sun 21 June (10.30-5). Adm £8.50, chd £4. For other opening times and information, please phone, email or visit garden website.**
Infuse your senses with colour and scent in the unique sub-tropical gardens basking in the mild climate and salty breeze. Clinging to granite slopes the terraced beds tier steeply to the ocean's edge, boasting tender exotics from places such as Mexico, the Canary Islands and South Africa. Laundry lawn, mackerel bank, pill box, gun emplacement, tiered terraces, well, tortoise lawn. Walled gardens, seagull seat. The garden lawn can be accessed with wheelchairs although further exploration is limited due to steps and steepness.

❀ 🚗 ☕

35 SOUTH BOSENT
Liskeard, PL14 4LX. Adrienne Lloyd & Trish Wilson, 01579 320753, lloydadj@btinternet.com. *2½m W of Liskeard. From r'about at junction of A390 and A38 take turning to Dobwalls. At mini-r'about R to Duloe, after 1m at X-rds turn R. Garden on L after ¼m.* **Wed 13, Thur 14 May, Wed 17, Thur 18 June, Wed 8, Thur 9 July, Wed 5, Thur 6 Aug, Wed 2, Thur 3 Sept (2-5). Adm £5, chd free. Home-made teas. Visits also by arrangement May to Sept for groups of up to 30.**
This garden is an example of work in progress currently being developed from farmland. The aim is to create

a combination of interesting plants coupled with habitat for wildlife over a total of 9.5 acres. There are several garden areas, woodland gardens, a meadow, ponds of varying sizes, incl new rill this year and waterfall. In spring, the bluebell wood trail runs alongside the stream. Regret no wheelchair access to bluebell wood due to steps.

♿ 🐕 ❀ ☕

36 SOUTH LEA
Pillaton, Saltash, PL12 6QS. Viv & Tony Laurillard, 01579 350629, tony@laurillard.eclipse.co.uk. *Pillaton, opp Weary Friar PH. 4m S of Callington. Signed from r'abouts on A388 at St Mellion and Hatt, and on A38 at Landrake. Roadside parking. Please do not park in PH car park.* **Sun 10 May, Sun 28 June (1-5). Adm £5, chd free. Home-made teas. Visits also by arrangement May to July for groups of 10+.**
In the front a path winds through interesting landscaping with a small pond. Tropical beds by front door with palms, cannas, etc. The back garden, with views over the valley, is a pretty picture in May with spring bulbs and clematis, whilst in June the herbaceous borders are a riot of colour. Lawns are separated by a fair sized fish pond and the small woodland area is enchanting in spring. Plenty of seating. Due to steps, wheelchair access is limited to front dry garden and rear terrace, from which much of garden can be viewed.

♿ 🐕 🚗 ☕

Tregonhayne

Your visits help change lives – since 1927, we've donated over £60 million to nursing and caring charities

37 TREBARTHA ESTATE GARDEN

Trebartha, nr Launceston, PL15 7PD. The Latham Family. *6m SW of Launceston. North Hill, SW of Launceston nr junction of B3254 & B3257. No coaches.* **Sun 17 May, Sun 11 Oct (2-5). Adm £6, chd free. Home-made teas.**
Historic landscape gardens featuring ponds, streams, cascades, rocks and woodlands, incl fine trees, bluebells in spring, ornamental walled garden and private modern country garden at Lemarne. Ongoing development of C19 American Garden. Allow at least 1 hour for a circular walk. Some steep and rough paths, which can be slippery when wet. Stout footwear advised. October opening for autumn colour.

38 TREGONHAYNE

Tregony, Truro, TR2 5SE. Ms Gillian Burnett. *A390 in easterly direction, then A3078 to Tregony. Drive through the village and park at the Roseland Academy School; the Roseland Community bus will bring visitors to the garden from the school.* **Sun 13 Sept (1.30-4.30). Adm £4, chd free. Home-made teas. Refreshments will be provided by and in support of Cats Protection.**
The garden has 3 distinct areas; hot courtyard garden featuring some New Zealand plants; shade garden with a sculpture of a horse's head as a focal point; the third area, started in 2000, is the autumn star performer and features a sculpture installation. Some unusual plants such as ehretia and the red hop bush should give good autumn colour. Regret no toilet facilities. Due to steps, regret not suitable for wheelchairs.

39 TREGONNING

Carleen, Breage, Helston, TR13 9QU. Andrew & Kathryn Eaton, 01736 761840, **alfeaton@aol.com, Tregonninggarden.co.uk.** *1m S of Godolphin Cross. From Xrds in centre of Godolphin Cross head S towards Carleen. In ½m at fork signed Breage 1¼ turn R up narrow lane marked no through road. After ½m parking on L opp Tregonning Farm.* **Sun 2 Aug (11-4.30). Adm £5, chd free. Home-made teas. Visits also by arrangement May to Sept for groups of up to 20.**
Located 300ft up NE side of Tregonning Hill this small (1¼ acre) maturing garden will hopefully inspire those thinking of making a garden from nothing more than a pond and copse of trees (in 2009). With the ever present challenge of storm force winds, garden offers yr-round interest and a self-sufficient vegetable and soft fruit paddock. Sculpted grass meadow, with panoramic views from Carn Brea to Helston. A section of the garden is designed in the form of a plant (incorporating a deck, leaf shaped beds, stream and large pond). Front cottage garden, spring garden, Mediterranean patio. Carp pond/fernery. Packed vegetable garden. Spring garden not accessible to wheelchairs. See us on Facebook - Tregonninggarden.

40 TREGOOSE

Grampound, TR2 4DB. Mr & Mrs Anthony O'Connor, 01726 882460, **tregoose@tregoose.co.uk.** *7m E of Truro, 1m W of Grampound. Off A390. Lane entrance is 100yds W of New Stables Xrds and ½m E of Trewithen r'about. Half way between Probus and Grampound.* **Sun 2, Sun 16 Feb (1-4.30). Adm £5, chd free. Home-made teas.**
2-acre garden. Woodland area with early spring shrubs underplanted with snowdrops, erythroniums, hellebores and small narcissus cultivars. Summer and autumn flowering areas incl walled garden overtopped by Acacia baileyana purpurea, scarlet blue and yellow border and potager full of herbs and cutting beds with arches covered with gourds, roses and honeysuckle. Snowdrop collection. Most of the summer flowering area can take a wheelchair.

41 TRENARTH

High Cross, Constantine, Falmouth, TR11 5JN. Lucie Nottingham, 01326 340444, **lmnottingham@btinternet.com, www.trenarthgardens.com.** *6m SW of Falmouth. Main rd A39/A394 Truro to Helston, follow Constantine signs. High X garage turn L for Mawnan, 30yds on R down dead end lane, Trenarth is ½m at end of lane.* **Sun 21 June (2-5). Adm £5, chd free. Cream teas. Great teas provided by local committee. Visits also by arrangement. Easy parking, tours with refreshments with prior notice.**
4 acres round C17 farmhouse in peaceful pastoral setting. Yr-round interest. Emphasis on tender, unusual plants, structure and form. C16 courtyard, listed garden walls, yew rooms, vegetable garden, traditional potting shed, orchard, woodland area with children's interest, palm and gravel garden. Circular walk down ancient green lane via animal pond to Trenarth Bridge, returning through woods. Abundant wildlife. Bees in tree bole, lesser horseshoe bat colony, swallows, wild flowers and butterflies. Family friendly, children's play area, the Wolery, and plenty of room to run, jump and climb.

42 NEW TREPRENN VEAN

Pednavounder, Coverack, Helston, TR12 6SE. Mike & Jill Newell. *Pednavounder near Coverack. Head out of Helston on A3083 towards Lizard and take B3293 to Coverack and St Keverne. After about 7m turn R at Zoar Garage and follow the road for about 2m.* **Sun 19 July (1-5). Adm £5, chd free. Home-made teas in neighbour's garden through a linking gate.**
The ⅓rd of an acre garden has been created by the owners since late 2014. Rural setting about ½m from the sea. Large pond with bridge over it which forms the major axis of the garden. To the right the planting is more tropical, to the left more cottage garden. Productive veg growing area and fruit cage with other fruit trees. The garden is flat, only one step up onto bridge but there are alternative routes to see all of the garden.

43 TREREIFE

Penzance, TR20 8TJ. Mr & Mrs T Le Grice, 01736 362750, trereifepark@btconnect.com, www.trereifepark.co.uk. *2m W of Penzance on A30 on Lands End rd. Garden and house signed R through estate gates.* **Visits by arrangement Mar to Sept. Adm £10, chd free.**
Mature gardens undergoing restoration in the historic setting of Trereife Established specimen camellia, rhododendron, azalea walk under mature beech trees. Modern parterre, sculptural yew hedge, S-facing walled terrace with wisteria and magnolia. New hot border with unusual Mediterranean planting. Medlar collection around events lawn and old kitchen garden awaiting restoration.

44 TRETHEW

Lanlivery, Nr Bodmin, PL30 5BZ. Ginnie & Giles Clotworthy. *3 m W of Lostwithiel. On rd between Lanlivery and Luxulyan. Signed from both villages and A390. Do not use Satnav.* **Sun 5 July (12-6). Adm £5, chd free. Home-made teas.**
Series of profusely planted and colourful areas surrounding an ancient Cornish farmhouse. Features incl terracing with pergola, gazebo and herbaceous borders within yew hedges, all overlooking orchard with roses and pond beyond. Magnificent views.

45 ◆ TREWIDDEN GARDEN

Buryas Bridge, Penzance, TR20 8TT. Mr Alverne Bolitho - Richard Morton, Head Gardener, 01736 364275/363021, contact@trewiddengarden.co.uk, www.trewiddengarden.co.uk. *2m W of Penzance. Entry on A30 just before Buryas Bridge. SatNav TR19 6AU.* **For NGS: Sun 5 Apr (10.30-4.30). Adm £7, chd free. For other opening times and information, please phone, email or visit garden website.**
Historic Victorian garden with magnolias, camellias and magnificent tree ferns planted within ancient tin workings. Tender, rare and unusual exotic plantings create a riot of colour thoughout the season. Water features, specimen trees and artefacts from Cornwall's tin industry provide a wide range of interest for all.

46 WAYE COTTAGE

Lerryn, nr Lostwithiel, PL22 0QQ. Malcolm & Jennifer Bell, 01208 872119, lerrynbells@gmail.com. *4m S of Lostwithiel along north river bank. Parking usually available at property or in village car park. Garden 10 minute level stroll along riverbank/ stepping stones.* **Daily Wed 1 Apr to Wed 15 Apr (10-5), daily Tue 1 Sept to Tue 15 Sept (10-5) but do ring first - best after 6pm. Adm £5, chd free. Light refreshments. Visits also by arrangement Apr to Sept for groups of up to 24.**
An enchanting cottage garden on the footprint of an old market garden - many interesting plants, enticing paths, secluded seats and stunning river views. New grass garden. 'Magical! The perfect place for a botanical recharge and horticultural inspiration.' Reproduced courtesy of Cornwall Life magazine. Garden groups very welcome. Sadly the garden is steep with too many steps for disabled access.

47 WINDMILLS

South Hill, Callington, PL17 7LP. Mr & Mrs Peter Tunnicliffe, tunnicliffesue@gmail.com. *3m NW of Callington. Head N from Callington A388, after about ½m turn L onto South Hill Rd (signed South Hill). Straight on for 3m, gardens on R just before church.* **Sun 10 May, Sun 19 July (1-5). Combined adm with Anvil Cottage £5, chd free. Home-made teas. Gluten free cakes available. Visits also by arrangement May to July for groups of 10 to 20. Donation to local charities.**
Next to medieval church and on the site of an old rectory and there are still signs in places of that long gone building. A garden full of surprises, formal paths and steps lead up from the flower beds to extensive vegetable and soft fruit area. More paths lead to a pond, past a pergola, and down into large lawns with trees and shrubs and chickens. Partial wheelchair access.

Trethew

OPENING DATES

All entries subject to change. For latest information check www.ngs.org.uk

Extended openings are shown at the beginning of the month.

Map locator numbers are shown to the right of each garden name.

February

Snowdrop Festival

Daily from Monday 17th
◆ Swarthmoor Hall 46

Saturday 8th
◆ Holker Hall Gardens 22

Sunday 9th
◆ Holker Hall Gardens 22

Saturday 15th
Summerdale House 45

Sunday 16th
Summerdale House 45

Friday 21st
Summerdale House 45

Saturday 22nd
Summerdale House 45

March

Every Friday and Saturday
Summerdale House 45

Daily to Sunday 8th
◆ Swarthmoor Hall 46

Sunday 22nd
◆ Dora's Field 12
◆ High Close Estate & Arboretum 20
◆ Holehird Gardens 21
◆ Rydal Hall 41

April

Every Friday and Saturday to Saturday 11th
Summerdale House 45

Sunday 26th
Summerdale House 45

May

Sunday 3rd
Chapelside 6

Sunday 10th
Deer Rudding 11
Low Fell West 32
◆ Rydal Hall 41

Monday 11th
Low Fell West 32

Sunday 17th
Chapelside 6
Cherry Cottage 7
Matson Ground 33

Wednesday 20th
Church View 8

Saturday 23rd
Armathwaite Gardens 2
Langholme Mill 29

Sunday 24th
Armathwaite Gardens 2
Langholme Mill 29
The Ryebeck Hotel 42

Monday 25th
Langholme Mill 29

Saturday 30th
Galesyke 15

Sunday 31st
Chapelside 6
Galesyke 15
Grange over Sands Hidden Gardens 17
NEW Lea Cottage 31

June

Every Saturday
Beckside Farm 4

Every Friday and Saturday from Saturday 6th
Summerdale House 45

Saturday 6th
Deer Rudding 11

Sunday 7th
Hayton Village Gardens 19
◆ Hutton-In-The-Forest 25
Park House 36
◆ Rydal Hall 41
Tithe Barn 47

Friday 12th
◆ Swarthmoor Hall 46

Saturday 13th
◆ Swarthmoor Hall 46
NEW Whetstone Croft & Cottage 49

Sunday 14th
Chapelside 6
NEW 5 Primrose Bank 38
◆ Swarthmoor Hall 46
NEW Whetstone Croft & Cottage 49

Thursday 18th
Haverthwaite Lodge 18
Lakeside Hotel 28

Sunday 21st
Askham Hall 3
Ivy House 26
8 Oxenholme Road 35
Summerdale House 45

Saturday 27th
Deer Rudding 11

Sunday 28th
Chapelside 6
Park House 36
Ulverston Gardens 48

July

Every Saturday
Beckside Farm 4

Every Friday and Saturday to Saturday 11th
Summerdale House 45

Saturday 4th
NEW Keerside 27

Sunday 5th
Abi and Tom's Garden Plants 1
NEW Beulah 5
NEW Keerside 27
Yewbarrow House 53

Thursday 9th
◆ Holehird Gardens 21
Larch Cottage Nurseries 30

Sunday 12th
Chapelside 6
Holme Meadow 23
Winton Park 51

Saturday 18th
Armathwaite Gardens 2
NEW Keerside 27

Sunday 19th
Armathwaite Gardens 2
NEW Crumble Cottages 10
NEW Keerside 27
◆ Rydal Hall 41

Wednesday 22nd
The Ryebeck Hotel 42

August

Every Saturday
Beckside Farm 4

Sunday 2nd
Fell Yeat 13
Yewbarrow House 53

Sunday 9th
HPB Merlewood 24

Thursday 13th
Larch Cottage Nurseries 30

Sunday 16th
Fell Yeat 13

Thursday 27th
Haverthwaite Lodge 18
Lakeside Hotel 28

September

Every Saturday to Saturday 12th
Beckside Farm 4

Sunday 6th
Yewbarrow House 53

Monday 7th
◆ Sizergh Castle 43

Sunday 13th
Woodend House 52

Wednesday 16th
Church View 8

Thursday 17th
Larch Cottage Nurseries 30

THE GARDENS

1 ABI AND TOM'S GARDEN PLANTS

Halecat, Witherslack, Grange-Over-Sands, LA11 6RT. Abi & Tom Attwood, www.abiandtom.co.uk. *20 mins from Kendal. From A590 turn N to Witherslack. Follow brown tourist signs to Halecat. Rail Grange-over-sands 5m, Bus X6 2m, NCR 70.* **Sun 5 July (10-5). Adm £3.50, chd free. Home-made teas.**

The 1 acre nursery garden is a fusion of traditional horticultural values with modern approaches to the display, growing and use of plant material. Our full range of perennials can be seen growing alongside one another in themed borders be they shady damp corners or south facing hot spots. The propagating areas, stock beds and family garden, normally closed to visitors, will be open on the NGS day. More than 1,000 different herbaceous perennials are grown on the nursery, many that are excellent for wildlife. For other opening times and information please phone, e-mail or visit our website. Sloping site that has no steps but steep inclines in places.

& ⛟ ✻ 🚗 ☕ ▣

> Your visits help change lives – we've donated over £17 million to Macmillan Cancer Support since 1984

GROUP OPENING

2 ARMATHWAITE GARDENS

Armathwaite, Carlisle, CA4 9PG. *Turn off A6 just S of High Hesket signed Armathwaite, after 2m Coombe House is on R & Hazel Cottage is at the junction. Turn R at junction to Armathwaite - 2 The Faulds is in the village.* **Sat 23, Sun 24 May, Sat 18, Sun 19 July (12-5). Combined adm £5, chd free. Home-made teas at Hazel Cottage. Home-made cakes produced by Armathwaite village hall ladies group.**

COOMBE EDEN
Belinda & Mike.

HAZEL COTTAGE
Mr D Ryland & Mr J Thexton.

Coombe Eden is approx 1 acre Victorian garden renovation project of traditional and contemporary beds. Steeply banked to a Japanese style bridge over the stream to a woodland area. Contemporary mixed beds, large rhododendrons give a breathtaking display in May. Hazel Cottage is a flower arranger's and plantsman's garden extending to 5 acres. Mature herbaceous borders with many unusual plants. Planted for a ll seasons. Wheelchair: only partial access for Hazel Cottage and Coombe Eden as they are on gentle slopes.

& ✻ ▣

3 ASKHAM HALL

Askham, Penrith, CA10 2PF. Charles Lowther, 01931 712350, enquiries@askhamhall.co.uk, www.askhamhall.co.uk. *5m S of Penrith. Turn off A6 for Lowther & Askham.* **Sun 21 June (11-6). Adm £3, chd free. Light refreshments.**

Donation to Askham and Lowther Churches.

Askham Hall is a Pele Tower incorporating C14, C16 and early C18 elements in a courtyard plan. Opened in 2013 with luxury accommodation, a restaurant, cafe and wedding barn. Splendid formal garden with terraces of herbaceous borders and topiary, dating back to C17. Meadow area with trees and pond, kitchen gardens and animal trails. Combined with Summer Fair. Cafe serving tea, coffee, light lunches, cake. Wood-fired pizza oven. BBQ and bar in the courtyard. Partial wheelchair access but not all areas due to steps.

 ⛟ ✻ 🚗 🚌 ▣

4 BECKSIDE FARM

Little Urswick, Cumbria, nr Ulverston, LA12 0PY. Anna Thomason, 01229 869151, anna@becksidefarm.eclipse.co.uk. *On outskirts of village - good off road parking. A590 towards Barrow. S off A590 to Urswick. Go through Great Urswick & Little Urswick. Park at T-junction. Rail Ulverston 4m, NCR 70 & 700 ½m.* **Every Sat 6 June to 12 Sept (12-5). Adm £3.50, chd free. Light refreshments. Visits also by arrangement June to Sept for groups of up to 30.**

Organic cottage garden with raised beds, herbaceous borders. Many unusual\new varieties of tender perennials and annuals, raised from seed and cuttings each year. Several interesting patio/seating areas. Productive greenhouse, again with unusual varieties. Ferns and summer flowering bulbs in pots.

& ⛟ ✻ ☕ ▣

Swarthmoor Hall

are at the heart of the design. With self-contained vistas and maximum use of planting space, the garden photographs very well and has been a subject for many local and national publications and photographers over the last decade. Partial wheelchair, main garden is on a sloping site with gravel paths.

⑨ CROOKDAKE FARM
Aspatria, Wigton, CA7 3SH. Kirk & Alannah Rylands, 016973 20413, alannah.rylands@me.com. *3m NE of Aspatria. Between A595 & A596. From A595 take B5299 at Mealsgate signed Aspatria. After 2m turn sharp R in Watch Hill signed Crookdake. House 1m on L.* **Visits by arrangement June & July for groups of 10+. Adm £4, chd free. Home-made teas.**
Windswept informal farmhouse (not open) garden with a careful colour combination of interesting planting sympathetic to the landscape incl various different areas with densely planted herbaceous borders, fenced vegetable patch, wild meadow and large pond area home to moisture-loving plants, hens, ducks and moorhens.

5 NEW ▸ BEULAH
Pooley Bridge, Penrith, CA10 2NG. Mr & Mrs M Macinnes. *½m outside the village of Pooley Bridge on Ullswater. From M6 (J40), A66 W onto A592 to Ullswater. At the lake, turn L into Pooley Bridge; through village towards Tirril. Parking signed at 1st L turn.* **Sun 5 July (1-5). Adm £4, chd free. Light refreshments.**
Beech hedged country garden with ha-ha giving stunning views towards Ullswater and the fells. Mixed perennial borders; formal box edged parterre with flowers, herbs, fruits and vegetables. Small rose garden. Orchard and shrubbery. Interesting shrubs and trees. Varied garden sculptures.

⑥ CHAPELSIDE
Mungrisdale, Penrith, CA11 0XR. Tricia & Robin Acland, 017687 79672. *12m W of Penrith. On A66 take minor rd N signed Mungrisdale. After 2m, sharp bends, garden on L immed after tiny church on R. Park at foot of our short drive. On C2C Reivers 71, 10 cycle routes.* **Sun 3, Sun 17, Sun 31 May, Sun 14, Sun 28 June, Sun 12 July (1-5). Adm £4, chd free. Visits also by arrangement May to July. Group refreshments also by arrangement.**
1 acre windy garden below fell round C18 farmhouse and outbuildings. Fine views. Tiny stream, large pond. Herbaceous, gravel, alpine, damp and shade areas, bulbs in grass. Wide range of plants, many unusual. Relaxed planting regime. Run on organic lines. Art constructions in and out, local stone used creatively. Featured in leading magazines and several books.

⑦ CHERRY COTTAGE
Crosby Moor, Crosby-On-Eden, Carlisle, CA6 4QX. Mr & Mrs John & Lesley Connolly, 01228 573614, jtlaconnolly@aol.com. *Off A689 midway between Carlisle & Brampton. Take turn signed 'Wallhead'. Cherry Cottage is on the corner of junction on R. Park in the lane.* **Sun 17 May (11-5). Adm £4, chd free. Light refreshments. Visits also by arrangement Apr to Sept for groups of 5 to 20.**
Relaxed country garden surrounding an C18 cottage on an approx. ⅓ acre site. It has a wide range of habitats incl herbaceous borders, wildlife pond, bog garden, shady woodland, productive fruit and vegetable area, 2 greenhouses and summer house. Various seating areas connected by grass and gravel paths. Not suitable for wheelchairs. Refreshment and plant sales proceeds to Epilepsy Action.

⑧ CHURCH VIEW
Bongate, Appleby-in-Westmorland, CA16 6UN. Mrs H Holmes, 017683 51397, engcougars@btinternet.com, www.sites.google.com/site/engcougars/church-view. *0.4m SE of Appleby town centre. A66 W take B6542 for 2m St Michael's Church on L garden opp. A66 E take B6542 & continue to Royal Oak Inn, garden next door, opp church.* **Wed 20 May, Wed 16 Sept (1-4). Adm £4, chd free. Visits also by arrangement May to Sept.**
It's all about the plants! Less than ½ acre of garden but with layers of texture, colour and interest in abundance, this is a garden for plantaholics. Plant combinations

10 NEW ▸ CRUMBLE COTTAGES
Beckside, Cartmel, Grange-Over-Sands, LA11 7SP. Sarah Byrne and Stewart Cowe, 015395 34405, sarah@crumblecottages.co.uk, www.crumblecottages.co.uk. *http://crumblecottages.co.uk/contact-us/. Car sat nav brings you directly here however mobile phone sat navs take you up the wrong lane.* **Sun 19 July (10-5). Adm £4, chd £1. Home-made teas. Visits also by arrangement May to Oct for groups of 10 to 30. No coaches Limited parking 6 spaces.**
1½ acre water garden built just over 4 years ago to improve the biodiversity of the area. Grade 2 listed wall with 7 beeboles. Walled kitchen garden. Ornamental cottage style planting around the house with yew hedges, topiary, and box hedging. Wild flower meadow. Cut flower borders for cottages. Beehives. Wheelchair access ornamental areas by house and outlying areas of garden are accessible but only by a wheelchair that can cope with uneven ground.

11 DEER RUDDING

Hesket Newmarket, Wigton, CA7 8HU. **Mrs Lynne Carruthers, deerrudding.garden.** *Located off the road from Millhouse to Haltcliff Bridge, not in Hesket Newmarket. From Penrith J41 M6 take B5305 6.8m, L to Hesket Newmarket 2.2m, at Millhouse L to Haltcliffe Bridge by village hall, continue 1m, R over cattle grid.* **Sun 10 May, Sat 6, Sat 27 June (11-5). Adm £5, chd free. Light refreshments at Millhouse Village Hall by Friends of Fellview school (May), Fellview Nursery (6 June) and Castle Sowerby Church (27 June).**
Set in the lee of the Northern Fells on the bank of the Caldew and enjoying views into the wider landscape, notably Carrock Fell. The garden extends to 8 acres and surrounds a former Cumbrian farmhouse and outbuildings. Mixed shrub and perennial borders; woodland and meadow grass areas; extensive rockery and stone walls built by Cumbrian champion waller, Steve Allen of Tebay. The rockery and meadow areas are very attractive in May and June. There are a number of gravel pathways.

12 ◆ DORA'S FIELD

Rydal, Ambleside, LA22 9LX. **National Trust, www.nationaltrust.org.uk.** *1½m N of Ambleside. Follow A591 from Ambleside to Rydal. Dora's Field is next to St Mary's Church.* **For NGS: Sun 22 Mar (11-4). Adm by donation. Also open High Close Estate and Arboretum. For other opening times and information, please visit garden website.**
Named for Dora, the daughter of the poet William Wordsworth. Wordsworth planned to build a house on the land but, after her early death, he planted the area with daffodils in her memory. Now known as Dora's field the area is renowned for its spring display of daffodils and bluebells. 22 March; Wordsworth's Daffodil Legacy. Old School Tea Room Cafe located at neighbouring Rydal Hall.

13 FELL YEAT

Casterton, Kirkby Lonsdale, LA6 2JW. **Mrs A E Benson, 01524 271340.** *1m E of Casterton Village. On the rd to Bull Pot. Leave A65 at Devils Bridge, follow A683 for 1m, take the R fork to High Casterton at golf course, straight across at two sets of Xrds, house on L, ¼m from no-through-rd sign.* **Sun 2, Sun 16 Aug (1-5). Adm £4, chd free. Home-made teas. Visits also by arrangement May to Sept for groups of 10 to 30.**
1 acre country garden with mixed planting, incl unusual trees, shrubs and some topiary. Small woodland garden and wooded glades. 2 ponds which encourage wildlife, including newts and dragonflies. Explore the fernery and maturing stumpery and new grotto house with rocks and ferns. Large collection of hydrangeas. A garden to explore, with several arbours where you can sit and relax. Adjoining nursery specialising in ferns, hostas, hydrangeas and many unusual plants. Gravel paths and some slopes.

14 FERNHILL COACH HOUSE

Bleacragg Road,, Witherslack, Grange-Over-Sands, LA11 6RX. **Adele & Mike Walford, 015395 52102, mwandaj@btinternet.com.** *Country road, ½m beyond Halecat & Abi and Tom's Garden Plants. From A590 turn N to Witherslack. Follow brown signs to Halecat, continue on lane for ½m. Fernhill on L. Rail; Grange-over-sands; 5m, bus X6. 2m walk, NCR 70. Roads & parking are not suitable for coaches.* **Visits by arrangement May to Sept for groups of up to 20. Adm £5, chd free. Home-made teas.**
Approx one acre garden - a riot of chaotic exuberance. From a stable yard, old tip and remnants of an orchard, 10 years of hard work have resulted in a cottage garden. Mixed borders, lots of vegetables, greenhouse, polytunnel, orchard, ponds and lots of roses. We propagate cottage garden plants and grow heritage and northern fruit trees. Witherslack Orchard Group apple juice, damson and apple juice. Numerous apple trees for sale. Plant sale. Sale of refreshments supports

our community shop which is managed largely by volunteers and is a registered charity. Wheelchair access is limited to the flower garden only. Paths are uneven and on sloping ground.

15 GALESYKE

Wasdale, CA20 1ET. **Christine & Mike McKinley, 01946 726267, mckinley2112@sky.com.** *From Gosforth, follow signs to Nether Wasdale & then to Lake, approx 5m. From Santon Bridge follow signs to Wasdale then to Lake, approx 2¼m.* **Sat 30, Sun 31 May (10.30-5). Adm £5, chd free. Cream teas. Visits also by arrangement May to Sept.**
4 acre woodland garden with spectacular views of the Wasdale fells.The R Irt runs through the garden and both banks are landscaped, you can cross over the river via a picturesque, mini, suspension bridge. The garden has an impressive collection of rhododendrons and azaleas that light up the woodlands in springtime.

ALLOTMENTS

16 GRANGE FELL ALLOTMENTS

Fell Road, Grange-Over-Sands, LA11 6HB. **Mr Bruno Gouillon, 01539 532317, brunog45@hotmail.com.** *Opposite Grange Fell Golf Club. Rail 1.3 m, Bus 1m X6, NCR 70.* **Visits by arrangement Apr to Sept for groups of up to 30. Car Park at site for small buses. Adm £4, chd free.**
The allotments are managed by Grange Town Council. Opened in 2010, 30 plots are now rented out and offer a wide selection of gardening styles and techniques. The majority of plots grow a mixture of vegetables, fruit trees and flowers. There are a few communal areas where local fruit tree varieties have been donated by plot holders with herbaceous borders and annuals.

GROUP OPENING

17 GRANGE OVER SANDS HIDDEN GARDENS

Grange-Over-Sands, LA11 7AF. Off Kents Bank Road, 3 gardens on Cart Lane then 1 garden up Carter Road for Shrublands Rail 1.4m; Bus X6; NCR 70. Sun 31 May (11.30-4.30). Combined adm £5, chd free. Light refreshments.

21 CART LANE
Veronica Cameron.

ELDER COTTAGE
Bruno Gouillon & Andrew Fairey, 01539 532317, brunog45@hotmail.com.
Visits also by arrangement Mar to Oct.

SHRUBLANDS
Jon & Avril Trevorrow.

WHISTLING GEM
Joan & Peter Lawton.

4 very different gardens hidden down narrow lanes off the road south out of Grange. Off Kents Bank Road, 3 gardens on Cart Lane all back onto the railway embankment, providing shelter from the wind but also creating a frost pocket. 21 is a series of rooms designed to create an element of surprise with fruit and vegetables in raised beds. Elder cottage is an organised riot of fruit trees, vegetables, shrubby perennials and herbaceous plants. Productive and peaceful. Whistling Gem has been redesigned and replanted over the last 4 years to create a garden with colour and interest. Up the hill on Carter Road for Shrublands, a ³/₄ acre garden situated on a hillside overlooking Morecambe Bay.

18 HAVERTHWAITE LODGE

Haverthwaite, LA12 8AJ. David Snowdon. *100yds off A590 at Haverthwaite. Turn S off A590 opp Haverthwaite railway stn. Bus 6, NCR 70.* Thur 18 June, Thur 27 Aug (11-4). Combined adm with Lakeside Hotel & Rocky Bank £6, chd free. Light refreshments at Lakeside Hotel. Single adm £4. Refreshments - 20% discount from Lakeside Hotel Conservatory Menu on the Open Day.

Traditional Lake District garden that has been redesigned and replanted. A wonderful display of hellebores and spring flowers. Gardens on a series of terraces leading down to the R Leven and incl: rose garden, cutting garden, dell area, rock terrace, herbaceous borders and many interesting mature shrubs. In a stunning setting the garden is surrounded by oak woodland and was once a place of C18 and C19 industry.

GROUP OPENING

19 HAYTON VILLAGE GARDENS

Hayton, Brampton, CA8 9HR. *5m E of M6 J43 at Carlisle, 1/2 mile S of A69. 3m W of Brampton. signed to Hayton off A69. Narrow roads: Please park courteously 1 side only. If able park less centrally leaving space for less able nr pub. Tickets sold in east(Townhead), west end & middle with Map. Map will go on Facebook.* Sun 7 June (11-6). Combined adm £5, chd free. Home-made teas at Hayton Village Primary School with live music, and also in one of the gardens - outside if suitable. Donation to Hayton Village Primary School.

ARNWOOD
Joanne Reeves-Brown.

ASH TREE FARM
Mr & Mrs J Dowling.

BECK COTTAGE
Fiona Cox.

CHESTNUT COTTAGE
Mr Barry Brian.

CURLEW COTTAGE
Frances & David Scales.

HAYTON C OF E PRIMARY SCHOOL
Hayton C of E Primary School, www.hayton.cumbria.sch.uk.

KINRARA
Tim & Alison Brown, 01228 670067 (Ashton Design), tim@tjbgallery.com.
Visits also by arrangement May to Sept for groups of up to 10. Teas may be possible if booked in advance.

MILLBROOK
Monica & John Carruthers.

THE PADDOCK
Phil & Louise Jones.

TOWNHEAD COTTAGE
Chris & Pam Haynes.

WEST GARTH COTTAGE
Debbie Jenkins, www.westgarth-cottage-gardens.co.uk.

A valley of gardens of varied size and styles all within ¹/₂ m, mostly of old stone cottages. Smaller and larger cottage gardens, courtyards and containers, steep wooded slopes, lawns, exuberant borders, frogs, pools, colour and texture throughout. Home-made teas and live music at the school where the children annually create gardens within the main school garden. Other refreshments usually in a garden and outside if suitable. Gardens additional to those listed also generally open or visible. Popular Scarecrow Trail also open over the same route this year. Facebook: Hayton Open Gardens. Two of the gardens: Westgarth Cottage and Kinrara are designed by artist/s and an architect with multiple garden design experience. Access from full to none. If mobility an issue note that gardens are spread out & some walking needed to see all. Come early/late for easier parking.

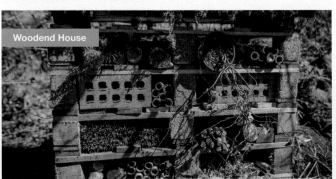
Woodend House

20 ◆ HIGH CLOSE ESTATE & ARBORETUM

Loughrigg, Ambleside, LA22 9HH. National Trust, 015394 37623, neil.winder@nationaltrust.org. uk, www.nationaltrust.org.uk. *10 min NW from Ambleside. Ambleside (A593) to Skelwith Bridge signed for High Close, turn R & head up hill until you see a white painted stone sign to 'Langdale', turn L, High Close on L.* For NGS: Sun 22 Mar (11-4). Adm by donation. Also open Dora's Field. For other opening times and information, please phone, email or visit garden website.

Originally planted in 1866 by Edward Wheatley-Balme, High Close was designed in the fashion of the day using many of the recently discovered 'exotic' conifers and evergreen shrubs coming into Britain from America. Today the garden works in partnership with the Royal Botanic Gardens Edinburgh and International Conifer Conservation Programme, preserving endangered Conifers species. Guided walk at 11am, tree trail and chat to our volunteers. Small cafe in house part of the YHA (please check with YHA for opening times).

21 ◆ HOLEHIRD GARDENS

Patterdale Road, Windermere, LA23 1NP. Lakeland Horticultural Society, 015394 46008, enquiries@holehirdgardens.org.uk, www.holehirdgardens.org.uk. *1m N of Windermere. On A592, Windermere to Patterdale rd.* For NGS: Sun 22 Mar, Thur 9 July (10-5). Adm £5, chd free. Self-service hot drinks available. For other opening times and information, please phone, email or visit garden website.

Run by volunteers of the Lakeland Horticultural Society to promote knowledge of gardening in Lakeland conditions. On fellside overlooking Windermere, the 12 acres provide interest year round. 4 National Collections (*astilbe*, daboecia, *polystichum*, meconopsis). Lakeland Collection of hydrangeas. Walled garden has colourful mixed borders and island beds. Alpine beds and display houses. Many interesting trees and shrubs. Wheelchair access limited to walled garden and beds accessible from drive.

22 ◆ HOLKER HALL GARDENS

Cark-in-Cartmel, Grange-over-Sands, LA11 7PL. The Cavendish Family, 015395 58328, info@holker.co.uk, www.holker.co.uk. *4m W of Grange-over-Sands. 12m W of M6 (J36) Follow brown tourist signs. Rail 1m, NCR 700 ½ m.* For NGS: Sat 8, Sun 9 Feb (10.30-5). Adm by donation. Cream teas. NGS will receive all donations made from guided tours and the garden entrance income on this weekend. For other opening times and information, please phone, email or visit garden website.

25 acres of romantic gardens, with peaceful arboretum, inspirational formal gardens, flowering meadow and Labyrinth. Summer brings voluptuous mixed borders and bedding. Discover unusually large rhododendrons, magnolias and azaleas, and the National Collection of Styracaceae. Discover our latest garden feature - The Pagan Grove, designed by Kim Wilkie. Guided tour of the gardens with our experienced guide. Donation to NGS required.

23 HOLME MEADOW

1 Holme Meadow, Cumwhinton, Carlisle, CA4 8DR. John & Anne Mallinson, 01228 560330, jwai.mallinson@btopenworld.com. *2m S of Carlisle. From M6 J42 take B6263 to Cumwhinton, in village take 1st L then bear R at Lowther Arms, Holme Meadow is immed on R.* Sun 12 July (11-4). Adm £3, chd free. Light refreshments. Visits also by arrangement June to Aug for groups of 10 to 30.

Village garden developed and landscaped from scratch by owners. Incl shrubbery, perennial beds supplemented by annuals; gazebo, pergola and trellis with climbers, slate beds and water feature, ornamental copse, pond, wild flower meadow and kitchen garden. Designed, planted and maintained to be wildlife friendly.

24 HPB MERLEWOOD

Windermere Road, Grange-Over-Sands, LA11 6JT. Marion St Quinton Site Manager. *Merlewood is on B5271 between Grange over Sands & Lindale. Rail 1m; Bus X6, NCR 70 (1m).* Sun 9 Aug (10.30-3.30). Adm £5, chd free. Home-made teas.

Extensive and varied gardens with a dramatic view to Morecambe Bay from the terrace. Newly planted formal and terraced gardens surround the house. A woodland including a nature trail for children. The wood on the limestone crags contain a variety of tree species many of which are from the original Victorian planting. The rockery is work in progress! Some areas are not accessible due to steps.

25 ◆ HUTTON-IN-THE-FOREST

Penrith, CA11 9TH. Lord & Lady Inglewood, 017684 84449, info@hutton-in-the-forest.co.uk, www.hutton-in-the-forest.co.uk. *6m NW of Penrith. On B5305, 3m from exit 41 of M6 towards Wigton.* For NGS: Sun 7 June (10-5). Adm £6.50, chd free. Light refreshments. For other opening times and information, please phone, email or visit garden website.

Hutton-in-the-Forest is surrounded on two sides by distinctive yew topiary and grass terraces -, which to the S lead to C18 lake and cascade. 1730s walled garden is full of old fruit trees, tulips in spring, roses and an extensive collection of herbaceous plants in summer.

26 IVY HOUSE

Cumwhitton, Brampton, CA8 9EX. Martin Johns & Ian Forrest, 01228 561851, martinjohns193@btinternet.com. *6m E of Carlisle. At the bridge at Warwick Bridge on A69 take turning to Great Corby & Cumwhitton. Through Great Corby & woodland until you reach a T-junction Turn R.* Sun 21 June (1-5). Adm £4, chd free. Home-made teas in Cumwhitton village hall. Visits also by arrangement Apr to Aug.

Approx 2 acres of sloping fell-side garden with meandering paths leading to a series of 'rooms': pond, fern garden, gravel garden with assorted grasses, vegetable and herb garden. Copse with meadow leading down to beck. Trees, shrubs, ferns, bamboos and herbaceous perennials planted with emphasis on variety of texture and colour. WC available. Steep slopes.

Tithe Barn

27 NEW KEERSIDE

Arkholme, Carnforth, LA6 1AP.
Geoffrey Ford. *7m from J35 or J36 of M6. From Burton in Kendal take Dalton Lane at southern end of village. After approx 3m turn R signed Arkholme & Docker. Continue for approx 1m. Garden is on R.* **Sat 4, Sun 5, Sat 18, Sun 19 July (10-4). Adm £4, chd free. Home-made teas.**
This ½ acre rural garden is constantly evolving, after 7 years' hard work. An abundance of roses ramble over trees and an unusual pergola is clad in more roses and honeysuckle. A new bog garden adds to the recent stumpery and an area of bog oak planted with ferns and hostas. Herbaceous borders; well-mown lawns; and a vista which follows the R Keer towards Morecambe Bay complete the picture.
♿ ❀ ☕

28 LAKESIDE HOTEL

Lake Windermere, Newby Bridge, Ulverston, LA12 8AT.
Sheena, 015395 39841, sheena. taylforth@lakesidehotel.co.uk, www.lakesidehotel.co.uk. *1m N of Newby Bridge. Turn N off A590 across R Leven at Newby Bridge along W side of Windermere.* **Thur 18 June, Thur 27 Aug (11-4). Combined adm with Haverthwaite Lodge £6, chd free. Light refreshments. Single adm £4. Refreshments - 20% discount from Hotel Conservatory menu on the Open Day.**
On the shores of Lake Windermere, Lakeside has been created for year round interest, packed with choice plants, incl some unusual varieties. Main garden area with herbaceous borders and foliage shrubs, scented and winter interest plants and seasonal bedding. Roof garden with lawn, espaliered local heritage apple varieties and culinary herbs.
♿ 🚗 🛏 ☕

29 LANGHOLME MILL

Woodgate, Lowick Green, LA12 8ES. Judith & Graham Sanderson, 01229 885215, judith@themill.biz. *7m NW of Ulverston. West on A590. At Greenodd, North on A5902 towards Broughton. Langholme Mill is approx 3m along this rd on L as road divides on the hill.* **Sat 23, Sun 24, Mon 25 May (11-5). Adm £4, chd free. Home-made teas. Visits also by**

arrangement Apr to Oct for groups of up to 30.
Approx 1 acre of mature woodland garden with meandering lakeland slate paths surrounding the mill race stream which can be crossed by a variety of bridges. The garden hosts well established bamboo, rhododendrons, hostas, acers and astilbes and a large variety of country flowers. There is a surprise round every corner! Home-made teas £3.00, large variety of delicious home-made scones, cakes, tea and coffee. A side gate entrance from the road side.

30 LARCH COTTAGE NURSERIES

Melkinthorpe, Penrith, CA10 2DR. Peter Stott, www.larchcottage.co.uk. *From N leave M6 J40 take A6 S. From S leave M6 J39 take A6 N signed off A6.* Thur 9 July, Thur 13 Aug, Thur 17 Sept (1-4). Adm £4, chd free.
For 3 days only Larch Cottage Nurseries are opening the new lower gardens and chapel for NGS visitors. The gardens include lawns, flowing perennial borders, rare and unusual shrubs, trees, small orchard and a kitchen garden. A natural stream runs into a small lake - a haven for wildlife and birds. At the head of the lake stands a chapel, designed and built by Peter for family use only. Larch Cottage has a Japanese Dry garden, ponds and Italianesque columned garden specifically for shade plants, the Italianesque tumbled down walls are draped in greenery acting as a backdrop for the borders filled with stock plants. Newly designed and constructed lower gardens and chapel. The gardens are accessible to wheelchair users although the paths are rocky in places.

31 NEW LEA COTTAGE

Red Bank Road, Grasmere, Ambleside, LA22 9PY. Tony and Marie Reynolds. *1m W of Grasmere village on Red Bank Road. Park in Grasmere village public car parks. There is NO visitor parking at Lea Cottage. Visitors wishing to see the garden must park in Grasmere near the garden centre and walk the 1m to the cottage along Red Bank Road in a West direction.* Sun 31 May (2-5). Adm £4, chd free.
Intimate and secluded Arts & Crafts garden, subdivided into 'rooms' by yew hedges, stone walls & gabions

using stone from garden. Inspired by its location in Wordsworth's 'loveliest spot that man hath found'. Designed to be both productive & beautiful by its architect owner. Steep steps, hidden behind a high wall, and restricted parking, so best combined with a walk from Grasmere village 1m. away. No wheelchair access to garden. Stone, potentially slippery, steps within garden at level changes.

32 LOW FELL WEST

Crosthwaite, Kendal, LA8 8JG. Barbie & John Handley, 015395 68297, barbie@handleyfamily.co.uk. *4½m S of Bowness. Off A5074, turn W just S of Damson Dene Hotel. Follow lane for ½m.* Sun 10 May (2-5). Home-made teas. Mon 11 May (10-1); Sun 18 Oct (1-4). Light refreshments. Adm £4.50, chd free. Visits also by arrangement for groups of up to 30.
This 2 acre woodland garden in the tranquil Winster Valley has extensive views to the Pennines. The four season garden, restored since 2003, incl expanses of rock planted sympathetically with grasses, unusual trees and shrubs, climaxing for autumn colour. There are native hedges and areas of plant rich meadows. A woodland area houses a gypsy caravan and there is direct access to Cumbria Wildlife Trust's Barkbooth Reserve of Oak woodland, blue bells and open fellside. Wheelchair access to much of the garden, but some rough paths, steep slopes.

33 MATSON GROUND

Windermere, LA23 2NH. Matson Ground Estate Co Ltd, 07831 831918, sam@matsonground.co.uk. *⅔m E of Bowness. Turn N off B5284 signed Heathwaite. From E 100yds after Windermere Golf Club, from W 400yds after Windy Hall Rd. Rail 2½m; Bus 1m, 6, 599, 755, 800; NCR 6 (1m).* Sun 17 May (1-5). Adm £4.50, chd free. Home-made teas. Visits also by arrangement for groups of 5+.
2 acres of mature, south facing gardens. A good mix of formal and informal planting including topiary features, herbaceous and shrub borders, wild flower areas, stream leading to a large pond and developing arboretum. Rose garden,

rockery, topiary terrace borders, ha-ha. Productive, walled kitchen garden c 1862, a wide assortment of fruit, vegetables, cut flowers, cobnuts and herbs. Greenhouse.

34 ORCHARD COTTAGE

Hutton Lane, Levens, Kendal, LA8 8PB. Shirley & Chris Band, 015395 61005, chrisband67@gmail.com. *6m S of Kendal. Turn N off A590 signed Levens. From Xrds by Methodist Church, 300 metres down Hutton Lane. Park near this Xrds. Garden access via 'The Orchard'.* Visits by arrangement Mar to Sept for groups of up to 30. Adm £4, chd free.
¾ acre sloping garden in old orchard. Plantsperson's paradise. Winding paths, diverse habitats, secret vistas. All yr interest and colour. Collections of ferns (100+ varieties), hellebores (70+), grasses, cottage plants, geraniums, Acers (36) Hostas. Auricula theatres, 'imaginary' stream, bog garden. Trees support clematis, roses and honeysuckle. Wildlife friendly.

35 8 OXENHOLME ROAD

Kendal, LA9 7NJ. Mr & Mrs John & Frances Davenport, 01539 720934, frandav8@btinternet.com. *SE Kendal. From A65 (Burton Rd, Kendal/Kirkby Lonsdale) take B6254 (Oxenholme Rd). No.8 is 1st house on L beyond red post box.* Sun 21 June (10-5). Adm £4, chd free. Home-made teas. Visits also by arrangement Apr to Sept for groups of 5 to 30.
Artist and potters garden of approx ½ acre of mixed planting designed for year-round interest, incl two linked small ponds. Roses, grasses and colour themed borders surround the house, with a gravel garden at the front, as well as a number of woodland plant areas, vegetable and fruit areas and sitting spaces. John is a ceramic artist and Frances is a painter. Paintings and pots are a feature of the garden display. Garden essentially level, but access to WC is up steps.

36 PARK HOUSE

Barbon, Kirkby Lonsdale, LA6 2LG. Mr & Mrs P Pattison. *2½ m N of Kirkby Lonsdale. Off A683 Kirkby Lonsdale to Sedburgh rd. Follow signs into Barbon Village.* **Sun 7, Sun 28 June (10.30-4). Adm £5, chd free. Cream teas.** Romantic Manor House (not open). Extensive vistas. Formal tranquil pond encased in yew hedging. Meadow with meandering pathways, water garden filled with bulbs and ferns. Formal lawn, gravel pathways, cottage borders with hues of soft pinks and purples, shady border, kitchen garden. An evolving garden to follow.

37 PEAR TREE COTTAGE

Dalton, Burton-in-Kendal, LA6 1NN. Linda & Alec Greening, 01524 781624, greening@ngs.org.uk. *5m from J35 & J36 of M6. From northern end of Burton-in-Kendal (A6070) turn E into Vicarage Lane & continue approx 1m.* **Visits by arrangement June & July for groups of 10+. Adm £4.50, chd free. Home-made teas. Refreshments by prior arrangement.**
⅓ acre cottage garden in a delightful rural setting. A peaceful and relaxing garden, harmonising with its environment and incorporating many different planting areas, from packed herbaceous borders and rambling roses, to wildlife pond, bog garden, rock garden and gravel garden. A plantsperson's delight, incl over 200 different ferns, and many other rare and unusual plants.

38 NEW 5 PRIMROSE BANK

Crosby-On-Eden, Carlisle, CA6 4QT. Cate Bowman. *3m NE of Carlisle off A689. From M6 J44 take A689 towards Hexham. At the next r'about take the 1st turn towards Brampton/Hexham. Take the 2nd turn on R to Crosby on Eden. Park at the village hall.* **Sun 14 June (1-5). Adm £4, chd free. Home-made teas at Crosby on Eden Village Hall.**
A surprise garden in a modern housing development, making use of reclaimed scrubland next to the Hadrian's Wall Path and close to the River Eden. Mixed productive and flower garden, featuring extensive vegetable garden with poly tunnel, small orchard, cut flower garden, ornamental pond, rose border and wide mixed borders. Rose clad pergola. Gravel paths unsuitable for wheelchairs.

39 QUARRY HILL HOUSE

Boltongate, Mealsgate, Wigton, CA7 1AE. Mr Charles Woodhouse & Mrs Philippa Irving, 01697 371225/07887 844351, cfwoodhouse@btinternet.com. *½ m W of Boltongate, 6m SSW of Wigton, 13m NW of Keswick, 10m E Cockermouth. M6 J41, direction Wigton, through Hesket Newmarket, Caldbeck, & Boltongate on B5299, entrance gates Quarry Hill House drive on L. On A595 Carlisle to Cockermouth turn L for Boltongate, Ireby.* **Visits by arrangement June & July. Adm by donation. Tea. Donation to Cumbria Community Foundation--Quarry Hill Grassroots Fund.**
3 acre parkland setting country house (not open) woodland garden with marvellous views of Skiddaw, Binsey and the Northern Fells and also the Solway and Scotland. Herbaceous borders, trees, shrubs, potager vegetable garden.

40 ROSE CROFT

Levens, Kendal, LA8 8PH. Enid Fraser, 07976 977018, enidfraser123@btinternet.com. *Approx 4m from J36. M6 J36 take A590 toward Barrow. R turn Levens, L at pub, follow rd to garden on L. From A6, into Levens, past shop, bear L, over Xrds, downhill. L turn signed 'PV Dobson'. Garden on R after Dobsons.* **Visits by arrangement June to Sept for groups of up to 30. Adm £4, chd free. Light refreshments.**
Gardening on a steep slope with wildlife in mind. Naturalistic plantings, perennials and grasses pouring away from the top terrace, shrubs, rose arches and silver birches for supporting structure. August sees the peak of this colourful drama: set against the views that dominate the westerly scene beyond the summer house, past the sown wild flowers and lawn which fold into the garden-bounding stream. Refreshments at Hare and Hounds pub approx 6 min walk, 1 min drive. Sizergh Castle less than 10 mins drive.

41 ◆ RYDAL HALL

Ambleside, LA22 9LX. Diocese of Carlisle, 01539 432050, gardens@rydalhall.org, www.rydalhall.org. *2m N of Ambleside. E from A591 at Rydal signed Rydal Hall. Bus 555, 599, X8, X55; NCR 6.* **For NGS: Sun 22 Mar, Sun 10 May, Sun 7 June, Sun 19 July (9-4). Adm by donation. Light refreshments in tea shop on site.** For other opening times and information, please phone, email or visit garden website.
Forty acres of Park, Woodland and Gardens to explore. The Formal Thomas Mawson Garden has fine examples of herbaceous planting, seasonal displays and magnificent views of the Lakeland Fells. Enjoy the peaceful atmosphere created in the Quiet Garden with informal planting around the pond 'and stunning views of the waterfalls from The Grot, the UK's first viewing station.'. Partial Wheelchair access, top terrace only.

42 THE RYEBECK HOTEL

Lyth Valley Road, Bowness-on-Windermere, Windermere, LA23 3JP. Helena Adamson - General Manager. *From the A590 at Newby Bridge take A592 lakeside rd, turn R at the B5360. Follow up to T-junction turning L, the hotel is on L. From A591 drive towards Bowness-on-Windermere. In Bowness with lake on R take A5074 Kendal Rd on L & follow for 2/3 mins. Hotel signed on R.* **Sun 24 May, Wed 22 July, Sun 25 Oct (10-4). Adm £5, chd free. Light refreshments.** Donation to Cumbria Wildlife Trust.
This 5 acre garden, which was originally set out in the Edwardian period, encompasses a variety of interesting areas including, to the front, formal lawns flanked by flower beds, rockeries and specimen trees and shrubs. To the rear of the hotel are terraced borders containing year round interest and colour, with flowering perennials and shrubs. The greater garden descends into a wide vista of grass and wild flower meadows set against a glorious backdrop of Lake Windermere, and include also a newly planted holly walk and a wild rose garden, all of which have been planted to encourage wildlife into the garden. Unfortunately, due to the presence of steps and the sloping nature of some parts of the garden, there is no wheelchair access. Dogs are

welcome on a lead. No coaches, but a minibus would be acceptable with up to 24 seats.

43 ◆ SIZERGH CASTLE
Sizergh, Kendal, LA8 8DZ. National Trust, 015395 60951, sizergh@nationaltrust.org.uk, www.nationaltrust.org.uk. *3m S of Kendal. Approach rd leaves A590 close to & S of A590/A591 interchange.* **For NGS: Mon 7 Sept (10-5). Adm £8, chd £4. Light refreshments. For other opening times and information, please phone, email or visit garden website.**
$2/3$ acre limestone rock garden, largest owned by National Trust; Wild flower areas, hot wall and herbaceous borders, productive ornamental kitchen garden and fruit orchard with spring bulbs. Holders of the National Collections of Asplenium scolopendrium, Cystopteris, Dryopteris and Osmunda. Stumpery garden built 2016. National Trust members are admitted free with an opportunity to donate to the good causes the NGS supports. Non National Trust members entrance fees are donated to the NGS. Featured in The Times in their 20 best Great British gardens to visit in summer.

44 SPRINT MILL
Burneside, LA8 9AQ. Edward & Romola Acland, 01539 725168, mail@sprintmill.uk. *2m N of Kendal. From Burneside follow signs towards Skelsmergh for ½m, then L into drive of Sprint Mill. Or from A6, about 1m N of Kendal follow signs towards Burneside, then R into drive.* **Visits by arrangement. Open most days Apr to Oct but courtesy phone call or email helpful. Adm £4, chd free. Light refreshments always available.**
Unorthodox organically run garden,the wild and natural alongside provision of owners' fruit, vegetables and firewood. Idyllic riverside setting, 5 acres to explore including wooded riverbank with hand-crafted seats. Large vegetable and soft fruit area, following no-dig and permaculture principles. Hand-tools prevail. Historic water mill with original turbine.The 3-storey building houses owner's art studio and personal museum, incl collection of old hand tools associated with rural crafts. Goats, hens, ducks, rope swing, very

family-friendly. Short walk to our flower-rich hay meadows. Access for wheelchairs to some parts of both garden and mill.

45 SUMMERDALE HOUSE
Nook, Lupton, LA6 1PE. David & Gail Sheals, www. summerdalegardenplants.co.uk. *7m S of Kendal, 5m W of Kirkby Lonsdale. From J36 M6 take A65 towards Kirkby Lonsdale, at Nook take R turn Farleton. Location not signed on highway. Detailed directions available on our website.* **Sat 15, Sun 16 Feb (11-4.30). Home-made teas. Fri 21, Sat 22 Feb (11-4.30). Every Fri and Sat 6 Mar to 28 Mar (11-4.30). Every Fri and Sat 3 Apr to 11 Apr (11-4.30).**

Sun 26 Apr (11-4.30). Home-made teas. Every Fri and Sat 6 June to 27 June (11-4.30). Sun 21 June (11-4.30). Home-made teas. Every Fri and Sat 3 July to 11 July (11-4.30). Adm £5, chd free. Home-made soups, bread, cakes (Feb 15/16 and April 26).
$1½$ acre part-walled country garden set around C18 former vicarage. Several defined areas have been created by hedges, each with its own theme and linked by intricate cobbled pathways. Relaxed natural planting in a formal structure. Rural setting with fine views across to Farleton Fell. Large collections of auricula, primulas and snowdrops. Adjoining RHS Gold Medal winning nursery. Not suitable for wheelchairs, many steps.

Hamilton Grove

46 ◆ SWARTHMOOR HALL

Swarthmoor Hall Lane, Ulverston, LA12 0JQ. Belinda Smith, 01229 583204, info@swarthmoorhall.co.uk, www.swarthmoorhall.co.uk. *1½ m SW of Ulverston. A590 to Ulverston. Turn off to Ulverston railway stn. Follow Brown tourist signs to Hall. Rail 0.9m. NCR70 & 700 (1m).* **For NGS: Daily Mon 17 Feb to Sun 8 Mar (10.30-4.30). Fri 12, Sat 13, Sun 14 June (10.30-4.30). Adm £3, chd free. For other opening times and information, please phone, email or visit garden website.**

Formal gardens and wild flower meadow. Wild purple crocus meadow in early spring: late February or early March depending on weather, earlier if mild winter later if cold and frosty. Also, good displays of snowdrops, daffodils and tulips in spring. Barn Cafe serves wonderful local food and recaptures the Hall's reputation for hospitality: delicious cakes and light lunches. Our historic house is also open for visitors 10.30-4.30 daily.

   ✿ 🛏 ☕

47 TITHE BARN

Laversdale, Irthington, Carlisle, CA6 4PJ. Mr & Mrs Gordon & Christine Davidson, +4401228573090, christinedavidson7@sky.com. *8m N E of Carlisle. Laversdale, N. Cumbria, ½ m from Carlisle Lake District Airport. From 6071 turn for Laversdale, from M6 J44 follow A689 Hexham. Follow NGS signs.* **Sun 7 June (1-5). Adm £4, chd free. Home-made teas. Visits also by arrangement May to July for groups of up to 30.**

Set on a slight incline, the thatched property has stunning views of the Lake District, Pennines and Scottish Border hills. Planting follows the cottage garden style, the surrounding walls, arches, grottos and quirky features have all been designed and created by the owners. There is a peaceful sitting glade beside a rill and pond. Wheelchairs unable to view the sloped South boundary area down steep steps.

   ✿ 🚐 🛏 ☕

48 ULVERSTON GARDENS

Ulverston, LA12 7LA. *LA12 9JR/9NY, LA12 7BE. A590 to Ulverston. 3 gardens near Booths Supermarket. Rail Ulverston; Bus 6, 6X; NCR 70. Gardens located as a 3, 2 & 1 with a car needed to travel between them. Maps available at each garden.* **Sun 28 June (10-4). Combined adm £5, chd free. Light refreshments available at several of the gardens.**

NEW 5 APPLETREE ROAD
Rachel & John Tarr.

104 BIRCHWOOD DRIVE
Jane Parker.

51 DALTONGATE
Ian & Angela Hutt.

HAMILTON GROVE
Helen & Martin Cooper.

11 OUBAS HILL
David & Janet Parratt.

14 OUBAS HILL
Pat & Barry Bentley.

6 very varied gardens in and around a historic market town, with its canal and lighthouse monument to Sir John Barrow. 'Every garden a surprise'. Hamilton Grove garden slopes down from a large terrace to the, now dry, canal feeder via beds of annuals and perennials. There is a large collection of scented leaf pelargoniums. The two houses on Oubas Hill rise up towards the lighthouse and are busy and varied with unconventional features. Handmade pottery products at No 11 (partial income to NGS). 51 Daltongate is medium sized and wildlife friendly with a lovely wild flower area. 104 Birchwood makes the most of a small corner plot with roadside vegetables, formal front garden and delightful secret back garden. 5 Appletree Road will surprise - a large family garden with mature trees, herbaceous borders, vegetable plot and patio area. Regrettably only 5 Appletree Road has wheelchair access the others being on slopes or with narrow access. Regrettably only 5 Appletree Road has wheelchair access, due to others being on slopes or with narrow access.

🐕 ✿ ☕

Armathwaite Gardens

49 NEW WHETSTONE CROFT & COTTAGE

Woodland, Broughton-In-Furness, LA20 6AE. John & Elaine Hudson, Rob Wilson & Iain Speak. *On the A593, approx 2m N of Broughton-in-Furness. Follow NGS signs through yard to park.* **Sat 13, Sun 14 June (12-4). Adm £5, chd free. Home-made teas.**

Two different, tranquil, south-facing cottage gardens overlooking the Woodland valley. Herbaceous borders bursting with cottage-garden favourites, mature flowering shrubs, azaleas, herb beds, stoop garden, courtyard and shrubbery surrounding C18 farmhouse and barns. Easy access to ten acres of renowned traditional hay meadows including eyebright, orchids, yellow rattle and oxeye-daisies. Restricted access due to gravel, slate and bark paths and some steep steps.

Grange over sands Hidden Gardens

50 WINDY HALL

Crook Road, Windermere, LA23 3JA. Diane Hewitt & David Kinsman, 015394 46238, dhewitt.kinsman@gmail.com, windy-hall.co.uk. *½m S of Bowness-on-Windermere. On western end of B5284, pink house up Linthwaite House Hotel driveway. Rail 2.6m; Bus 1m, 6, 599, 755, 800; NCR 6 (1m).* **Visits by arrangement Apr to Aug for groups of up to 30. Adm £5, chd free. Light refreshments.**

"Paradise". "I was bowled over by the ecologically intelligent approach you and Diane take and the exquisitely planted back garden or hill with rare species and subspecies so elegantly placed where they will flourish. It was truly superb." "The garden left a lasting impression on all. It is beautiful, exciting and charming. It nestles so comfortably in its landscape and totally belongs there.". Plant Heritage Aruncus collection. Mosses & Ferns, rare Hebridean sheep, exotic waterfowl and pheasants. We can provide Teas and home-made cake (ad lib) for any size group and Light Lunches for groups of 8+.

51 WINTON PARK

Appleby Road, Kirkby Stephen, CA17 4PG. Mr Anthony Kilvington, www.wintonparkgardens.co.uk. *2m N of Kirkby Stephen. On A685 turn L signed Gt Musgrave/Warcop*

(B6259). After approx 1m turn L as signed. **Sun 12 July (11-5). Adm £6, chd free. Light refreshments.**

5 acre country garden bordered by the banks of the R Eden with stunning views. Many fine conifers, acers and rhododendrons, herbaceous borders, hostas, ferns, grasses, heathers and several hundred roses. Four formal ponds plus rock pool. Partial wheelchair access.

52 WOODEND HOUSE

Woodend, Egremont, CA22 2TA. Grainne & Richard Jakobson, 019468 13017, gmjakobson22@gmail.com. *2m S of Whitehaven. Take the A595 from Whitehaven towards Egremont. On leaving Bigrigg take 1st turn L. Go down hill, garden at bottom on R opp Woodend Farm.* **Sun 13 Sept (11-4.30). Adm £4, chd free. Home-made teas. Visits also by arrangement May to Sept for groups of up to 20.**

An interesting garden tucked away in a small hamlet. Meandering gravel paths lead around the garden with imaginative, colourful planting. Take a look around a productive, organic potager, wildlife pond, mini spring and summer meadows and a pretty summer house. Designed to be beautiful throughout the year and wildlife friendly. Plant sale, home-made teas, mini-quiz for children. Live

Blues and Jazz in the garden. The gravel drive and paths are difficult for wheelchairs but more mobile visitors can access the main seating areas in the rear garden.

53 YEWBARROW HOUSE

Hampsfell Road, Grange-over-Sands, LA11 6BE. Jonathan & Margaret Denby, 015395 32469, jonathan@bestlakesbreaks.co.uk, www.yewbarrowhouse.co.uk. *¼m from town centre. Proceed along Hampsfell Rd passing a house called Yewbarrow to brow of hill then turn L onto a lane signed 'Charney Wood/ Yewbarrow Wood' & sharp L again. Rail 0.7m, Bus X6, NCR 70.* **Sun 5 July, Sun 2 Aug, Sun 6 Sept (11-4). Adm £5, chd free. Cream teas. Visits also by arrangement Apr to Oct for groups of 10+.**

'More Cornwall than Cumbria' according to Country Life, a colourful 4 acre garden filled with exotic and rare plants, with dramatic views over the Morecambe Bay. Outstanding features include the Orangery; the Japanese garden with infinity pool, the Italian terraces and the restored Victorian kitchen garden. Dahlias, cannas and colourful exotica are a speciality. Find us on youTube. Ltd wheelchair access owing to the number of steps.

OPENING DATES

All entries subject to change. For latest information check www.ngs.org.uk

Map locator numbers are shown to the right of each garden name.

February

Snowdrop Festival

Saturday 15th
The Dower House 21

Sunday 16th
The Dower House 21

Saturday 22nd
The Old Vicarage 50

Sunday 23rd
10 Chestnut Way 12
The Old Vicarage 50

March

Sunday 15th
◆ Cascades Gardens 11

Saturday 28th
Chevin Brae 13

April

Monday 13th
◆ The Burrows Gardens 7

Sunday 19th
334 Belper Road 4
◆ Cascades Gardens 11

Sunday 26th
◆ Old English Walled Garden, Elvaston Castle Country Park 48
The Paddock 52

May

Sunday 3rd
Moorfields 45
12 Water Lane 67

Monday 4th
12 Water Lane 67

Friday 8th
Barlborough Gardens 3

Sunday 10th
NEW 26 Stiles Road 60

Wednesday 13th
◆ Bluebell Arboretum and Nursery 5

Saturday 16th
Treetops Hospice Care 64

Sunday 17th
Broomfield Hall 6
Fir Croft 23
27 Wash Green 66

Tuesday 19th
◆ Thornbridge Hall Gardens 61

Sunday 24th
12 Ansell Road 1
334 Belper Road 4
Gamesley Fold Cottage 24
Higher Crossings 26
NEW Littleover Lane Allotments 37
Rectory House 53

Monday 25th
12 Ansell Road 1
◆ The Burrows Gardens 7
Tilford House 62

Sunday 31st
◆ Cascades Gardens 11
13 Chiltern Drive 14
Fir Croft 23
Repton NGS Village Gardens 55

June

Saturday 6th
The Dower House 21
The Holly Tree 33

Sunday 7th
The Dower House 21
Fir Croft 23
Highfield House 27
The Holly Tree 33
Walton Cottage 65

Wednesday 10th
◆ Bluebell Arboretum and Nursery 5

Friday 12th
The Smithy 57

Sunday 14th
Hollies Farm Plant Centre 32
◆ Meynell Langley Trials Garden 44
24 Wheeldon Avenue 71
26 Wheeldon Avenue 72
Whitwell Open Gardens 73

Friday 19th
330 Old Road 49

Saturday 20th
12 Ansell Road 1
Holmlea 34
◆ Melbourne Hall Gardens 43
330 Old Road 49

Sunday 21st
12 Ansell Road 1
◆ The Burrows Gardens 7
Hill Cottage 29
58A Main Street 41
◆ Melbourne Hall Gardens 43
13 Westfield Road 68
NEW 18a Wood Lane 77

Saturday 27th
◆ Calke Abbey 9
Elmton Gardens 22

Sunday 28th
Barlborough Gardens 3
◆ Cascades Gardens 11
Elmton Gardens 22
High Roost 25
Highfields House 28
7 Main Street - Old Shoulder of Mutton 40

July

Saturday 4th
12 Ansell Road 1
The Smithy 57
Smithy House 58

Sunday 5th
12 Ansell Road 1
◆ The Burrows Gardens 7
NEW Candlemas Cottage 10
The Lilies 36
58A Main Street 41
Moorfields 45

Monday 6th
The Smithy 57

Saturday 11th
New Mills School 46
Otterwood 51

Sunday 12th
8 Curzon Lane 17
New Mills School 46
Wild in the Country 74

Wednesday 15th
◆ Bluebell Arboretum and Nursery 5
Tilford House 62

Saturday 18th
108 Macclesfield Road 38
Repton NGS Village Gardens 55

Sunday 19th
◆ Cascades Gardens 11
8 Curzon Lane 17
108 Macclesfield Road 38
◆ Meynell Langley Trials Garden 44
Otterwood 51
15 Windmill Lane 75

Saturday 25th
12 Ansell Road 1
Byways 8
Stanton in Peak Gardens 59

Sunday 26th
12 Ansell Road 1
Byways 8
The Paddock 52
Stanton in Peak Gardens 59

August

Saturday 1st
9 Main Street 39

Sunday 2nd
NEW Candlemas Cottage 10
8 Curzon Lane 17
Hollies Farm Plant Centre 32
9 Main Street 39
13 Westfield Road 68

Saturday 8th
26 Windmill Rise 76

Sunday 9th
◆ Cascades Gardens 11
◆ Old English Walled Garden, Elvaston Castle Country Park 48

Byways

THE GARDENS

1 12 ANSELL ROAD

Ecclesall, Sheffield, S11 7PE.
Dave Darwent, 01142 665881,
dave@poptasticdave.co.uk,
www.poptasticdave.co.uk. *Approx
3m SW of City Centre. Travel to
Ringinglow Rd (88 bus), then Edale
Rd (opp Ecclesall C of E Primary
School). 3rd R - Ansell Rd. No 12
on L ¾ way down, solar panel on
roof.* Sun 24, Mon 25 May, Sat 20,
Sun 21 June, Sat 4, Sun 5, Sat 25,
Sun 26 July (11.30-6). Adm £3.50,
chd free. Light refreshments.
Savoury and gluten free available.
Visits also by arrangement Apr
to Aug for groups of 5 to 20. By
Arrangement admission fee incl
cakes & unlimited tea & coffee.
Now in its 92nd year since being
created by my grandparents, this is
a suburban mixed productive and
flower garden retaining many original
plants and features as well as the
original layout. A book documenting
the history of the garden has been
published and is on sale to raise
further funds for charity. Original
rustic pergola with 90+ year old
roses. Then and now pictures of
the garden in 1929 and 1950's vs
present. Map of landmarks up to
55m away which can be seen from
garden. 7 water features. Wide variety
of unique-recipe homemade cakes
with take-away service available. New
winter garden.
✿ ☕

2 ASKEW COTTAGE

23 Milton Road, Repton,
Derby, DE65 6FZ. Louise
Hardwick, 07970411748,
louise.hardwick@hotmail.co.uk,
www.hardwickgardendesign
.co.uk. *6m S of Derby. From A38/
A50 junction S of Derby. Follow signs
to Willington then Repton on B5008.
In Repton turn 1st L then bear sharp
R into Milton Rd.* Sun 18 Oct (11-4).
Adm £3.50, chd free. Also open
10 Chestnut Way. Opening with
Repton NGS Village Gardens on
Sun 31 May, Sat 18 July (1.30-
5.30). Visits also by arrangement
Apr to Oct for groups of 5 to 20.
The owner, a professional garden
designer, has used curved paths
and structural beech, box and yew
hedges to make several different
areas, each with a distinct feel. The

planting within the borders changes
as areas are altered and new
combinations tried. Features include
a circle of meadow grass set within a
cloud box hedge, trained apple trees
and a small wildlife pool.
🐕 D ☕

GROUP OPENING

3 BARLBOROUGH GARDENS

Chesterfield Road, Barlborough,
Chesterfield, S43 4TR. Christine
Sanderson, 07956 203184,
christine.r.sanderson@uwclub.
net, www.facebook.com/
barlboroughgardens. *7m NE of
Chesterfield. Off A619 midway
between Chesterfield & Worksop.
½m E M1, J30. Follow signs for
Barlborough then yellow NGS signs.
Parking available in village.* Fri 8
May (2-6). Combined adm £4, chd
free. Sun 28 June (1-6). Combined
adm £6, chd free. Refreshments
available at 'The Hollies' on all
dates listed plus chefs canapes &
cool drinks at 'Raiswells House'
at the June opening.

CLARENDON
Neil & Lorraine Jones.
Open on Fri 8 May

GOOSE COTTAGE
Mick & Barbara Housley.
Open on Sun 28 June

THE HOLLIES
Vernon & Christine Sanderson.
Open on all dates
(See separate entry)

LINDWAY
Thomas & Margaret Pettinger.
Open on all dates

RAISWELLS HOUSE
Mr & Mrs Andrew and Rosie Dale.
Open on Sun 28 June

NEW 19 WEST VIEW
Mrs Pat Cunningham.
Open on Sun 28 June

Barlborough is an attractive historic
village and a range of interesting
buildings can be seen all around
the village centre. The village is
situated close to Renishaw Hall for
possible combined visit. Map detailing
location of all the gardens is issued
with admission ticket, which can be
purchased at any of the gardens
listed. For more information visit our
Facebook page - see details above.
The Hollies incl an area influenced by
the Majorelle Garden in Marrakech.
This recent makeover was achieved

using upcycled items together with
appropriate planting. This garden
project was featured on the recent
series of "Love Your Garden". Partial
wheelchair access at The Hollies.
♿ 🐕 ✿ 🚗 ☕

4 334 BELPER ROAD

Stanley Common, DE7 6FY. Gill
& Colin Hancock, 01159 301061,
gillandcolin@tiscali.co.uk. *7m
N of Derby. 3m W of Ilkeston. On
A609, ¾m from Rose & Crown Xrds
(A608). Please park in field up farm
drive or Working Men's Club rear car
park if wet.* Sun 19 Apr (12-4.30).
Light refreshments. Sun 24 May
(12-4.30). Home-made teas. Adm
£4, chd free. Home-made soup
available in February and April.
Visits also by arrangement Feb to
June for groups of 10+.
Beautiful country garden with many
attractive features incl a laburnum
tunnel, rose and wisteria domes,
old workmen's hut, wild life pond
and much more. Take a scenic walk
through the ten acres of woodland
and glades to a ½ acre lake and
see Snowdrops and Hellebores in
February, cowslips in April and wild
orchids in May. Plenty of seating to
enjoy delicious home-made cakes.
Children welcome with plenty of
activities to keep them entertained.
Paths round wood and lake not
suitable for wheelchairs.
♿ 🐕 ✿ 🚗 ☕

Your visits help
change lives –
your generosity
has supported
unpaid carers
through donations
to Carers Trust
totalling over £4
million since 1996

Water Lane

5 ◆ BLUEBELL ARBORETUM AND NURSERY
Annwell Lane, Smisby, Ashby de la Zouch, LE65 2TA. Robert & Suzette Vernon, 01530 413700, sales@bluebellnursery.com, www.bluebellnursery.com. *1m NW of Ashby-de-la-Zouch. Arboretum is clearly signed in Annwell Lane (follow brown signs), ¼ m S, through village of Smisby off B5006, between Ticknall & Ashby-de-la-Zouch. Free parking.* **For NGS: Wed 13 May, Wed 10 June, Wed 15 July, Wed 12 Aug, Wed 16 Sept (9-5). Adm £5, chd free. Tea/coffee available on request at office. For other opening times and information, please phone, email or visit garden website.**
Beautiful 9 acre woodland garden with a large collection of rare trees and shrubs. Interest throughout the yr with spring flowers, cool leafy areas in summer and sensational autumn colour. Many information posters describing the more obscure plants. Adjacent specialist tree and shrub nursery. Please be aware this is not a wood full of bluebells, despite the name. The woodland garden is fully labelled and the staff can answer questions or talk at length about any of the trees or shrubs on display. Rare trees and shrubs. Educational signs. Woodland. Arboretum. Please wear sturdy, waterproof footwear during or after wet weather! Full wheelchair access in dry, warm weather however grass paths can become wet and inaccessible in snow or after rain.
♿ ✿ ☕

6 BROOMFIELD HALL
Morley, Ilkeston, Ilkeston, DE7 6DN. Derby College, www.facebook.com/BroomfieldPlantCentre. *4m N of Derby. 6m S of Heanor on A608.* **Sun 17 May, Sun 20 Sept (10-4). Adm £4, chd free. Light refreshments in a pop-up volunteer-run cafe.**
25 acres of constantly developing educational Victorian gardens/woodlands maintained by volunteers and students. Trees, herbaceous borders, walled garden, themed gardens, rose garden, rhododendrons, prairie plantings, Japanese tea garden, tropical garden, winter garden, garden tours, plant centre, light entertainment, arts and crafts stalls, bonsai demonstrations, cacti and plant specialists. Most of garden is accessible to wheelchair users and we are all on hand to help.
♿ 🐕 ✿ 🚌 ☕

7 ◆ THE BURROWS GARDENS
Burrows Lane, Brailsford, Ashbourne, DE6 3BU. Mrs N M Dalton, 01335 360745, enquiries@burrowsgardens.com, www.burrowsgardens.com. *5m SE of Ashbourne; 5m NW of Derby. A52 from Derby: turn L opp sign for Wild Park Leisure 1m before village of Brailsford. ¼ m & at grass triangle head straight over through wrought iron gates.* **For NGS: Mon 13 Apr, Mon 25 May, Sun 21 June, Sun 5 July, Mon 31 Aug (11-4). Adm £5, chd free. Home-made teas. For other opening times and information, please phone, email or visit garden website.**
5 acres of stunning garden set in beautiful countryside where immaculate lawns show off exotic rare plants and trees, mixing with old favourites in this outstanding garden. A huge variety of styles from temple to Cornish, Italian and English, gloriously designed and displayed. This is a must see garden. Visit our website for more information. Most of garden accessible to wheelchairs.
♿ ✿ 🚌 ☕

8 BYWAYS
7A Brookfield Avenue, Brookside, Chesterfield, S40 3NX. Terry & Eileen Kelly, 07414827813, telkel1@aol.com. *1½m W of Chesterfield. Follow A619 from Chesterfield towards Baslow. Brookfield Ave is 2nd R after Brookfield School. Please park on Chatsworth Rd (A619).* **Sat 25, Sun 26 July (12.30-4.30). Adm £3.50, chd free. Home-made teas. Visits also by arrangement July & Aug for groups of 10 to 30.** Donation to Ashgate Hospice.
Previous winners of the Best Back Garden over 80sqm, Best Front Garden, Best Container Garden and Best Hanging Basket in Chesterfield in Bloom. Well established perennial borders incl helenium, monardas, phlox, penstenom, grasses, acers, giving a very colourful display. Rockery and many planters containing acers, pelargoniums, hostas, fuchsias and roses. 6 seating areas.
✿ ☕

9 ◆ CALKE ABBEY
Ticknall, DE73 7LE. National Trust, 01332 863822, calkeabbey@nationaltrust.org.uk, www.nationaltrust.org.uk/calke. *10m S of Derby. On A514 at Ticknall between Swadlincote & Melbourne. For Sat Nav use DE73 7JF.* **For NGS: Sat 27 June, Sat 12 Sept (10-5). Adm £5, chd £2.50. Light refreshments at the main visitor facilities. For other opening times and information, please phone, email or visit garden website.**
With peeling paintwork and overgrown courtyards, Calke Abbey tells the story of the dramatic decline of a country-house estate. The large kitchen garden, impressive collection of glasshouses, garden buildings and tunnels hint at the work of past gardeners, while today the flower garden, herbaceous borders and unique auricula theatre providing stunning displays all year. Restaurant at main visitor facilities for light refreshments and locally sourced food. House is also open by timed ticket only. Electric buggy available for those with mobility problems.
♿ ✿ 🚌 ☕

10 NEW CANDLEMAS COTTAGE
Alport Lane, Youlgrave, Bakewell, DE45 1WN. Jane Ide. *3½m S of Bakewell. From A6: pass playing fields on L, then Youlgrave Garage on R. From A515: through village & straight on at church/George pub Xrds. Blue house directly opp Youlgrave Primary School.* **Sun 5 July, Sun 2 Aug (1.30-5). Adm £3.50, chd free. Home-made teas.**
A newly established plantswoman's contemporary cottage garden in the heart of the Peak National Park, featuring rose beds and wisteria arch, winter garden, green garden, long mixed border, specimen trees, kitchen garden and pollinator's patch. Gardened to maximise benefits to wildlife and humans, with carefully sited seating areas in shade and sunshine.
🐕 ✿ ☕

11 ◆ CASCADES GARDENS
Clatterway, Bonsall, Matlock, DE4 2AH. Alan & Alesia Clements, 01629 822813, cascadesgardens@gmail.com, www.cascadesgardens.com. *5m SW of Matlock. From Cromford A6 T-lights turn towards Wirksworth. Turn R along Via Gellia, signed Buxton & Bonsall. After 1m turn*

R up hill towards Bonsall. Garden entrance at top of hill. Park in village car park. **For NGS: Sun 15 Mar, Sun 19 Apr, Sun 31 May, Sun 28 June, Sun 19 July, Sun 9 Aug (12-4). Adm £7, chd free. Home-made teas. For other opening times and information, please phone, email or visit garden website.**

The Meditation Garden. Fascinating 4 acre peaceful garden in spectacular natural surroundings with woodland, cliffs, stream, pond and ruined corn mill. Inspired by Japanese gardens and Buddhist philosophy, secluded garden rooms for relaxation and reflection. Beautiful landscape with a wide collection of unusual perennials, conifers, shrubs and trees. Nursery. Plants for sale. Hellebore month in March. Mostly wheelchair accessible. Gravel paths, some steep slopes.

& ⚘ ✿ 🚗 🛏 ☕

12 10 CHESTNUT WAY

Repton, DE65 6FQ. Robert & Pauline Little, 01283 702267, rlittleq@gmail.com, www.littlegarden.org.uk. 6m S of Derby. From A38/A50, S of Derby, follow signs to Willington, then Repton. In Repton turn R at r'about. Chestnut Way is ¼ m up hill, on L. **Sun 23 Feb (11-3). Sun 18 Oct (11-4), also open Askew Cottage. Adm £4, chd free. Home-made soup (Feb). Home-made teas (all dates). Opening with Repton NGS Village Gardens on Sun 31 May, Sat 18 July (1.30-5.30). Visits also by arrangement Feb to Oct for groups of 10+. Admission includes private tour and refreshments.**

A large garden full of interesting and unusual plants designed to have colour and interest throughout the year. The recent felling of some large trees has given the opportunity for some new planting. Many benches to sit and soak up the atmosphere enjoying our renowned tea and cake and unusual sculptures. Overflowing borders and a surprise round every corner. Excellent plant stall, best in Spring. Special interest in viticella clematis, organic vegetables and composting. Level garden, good solid paths to main areas. Some grass/ bark paths.

& ⚘ ✿ 🚗 ☕

13 CHEVIN BRAE

Milford, Belper, DE56 0QH. Dr David Moreton, 07778004374, davidmoretonchevinbrae@gmail. com. 1½ m S of Belper. Coming from S on A6 turn L at Strutt Arms & cont up Chevin Rd. Park on Chevin Rd. After 300 yds follow arrow to L up Morrells Lane. After 300 yds Chevin Brae on L with silver garage. **Sat 28 Mar, Sat 22 Aug (1-5). Adm £3, chd free. Visits also by arrangement Mar to Oct for groups of up to 30.**

A large garden, with swathes of daffodils in the orchard a spring feature. Extensive wild flower planting along edge of wood features aconites, snowdrops, wood anemones, fritillaries and dog tooth violets. Other parts of garden will have hellebores and early camelias. During the summer the extensive flower borders and rose trellises give much colour. Large kitchen garden and fruit cages. Tea and home-made pastries, many of which feature fruit and jam from the garden, served from the summer house in the middle of the orchard.

⚘ ✿ ☕

14 13 CHILTERN DRIVE

West Hallam, Ilkeston, DE7 6PA. Jacqueline & Keith Holness. Approx 7m NE of Derby. From A609, 2m W of Ilkeston, nr The Bottle Kiln, take St Wilfreds Rd. Take 1st R onto Derbyshire Av, Chiltern Drive is 3rd turning on L. **Sun 31 May (11.30-4.30). Adm £3, chd free. Home-made teas. Gluten free options also available.**

A plant lover's garden that's as pretty as a picture. A secret walled suburban garden, every corner brimming with plants, many rare and unusual. Paris, podophyllum, beesia, schefflera to name but a few and more than 30 varieties of hosta. A pretty summerhouse, two small ponds and fernery, together with over 60 different acers and some well hidden lizards!

✿ ☕

15 COXBENCH HALL

Alfreton Road, Coxbench, Derby, DE21 5BB. Mr Brian Ballin, 01332 880200, office@coxbench-hall.co.uk, www.coxbench-hall.co.uk. 4m N of Derby close to A38. After passing thru Little Eaton, turn L onto Alfreton Rd for 1m, Coxbench Hall is on L next to Fox & Hounds PH between

Little Eaton & Holbrook. From A38, take Kilburn turn & go towards Little Eaton. **Sun 6 Sept (2.30-4.30). Adm £5, chd free. Light refreshments. incl diabetic and gluten free cakes. Visits also by arrangement Mar to Oct for groups of up to 20. By arrangement admission fee incl refreshments.**

Formerly the ancestral home of the Meynell family, the gardens reflect the Georgian house standing in 4½ acres of grounds most of which is accessible and wheelchair friendly. The garden has 2 fishponds connected by a stream, a sensory garden for the sight impaired, a short woodland walk through shrubbery, rockery, raised vegetable beds, an orchard and seasonal displays in the mainly lawned areas. As a Residential Home for the Elderly, our Gardens are developed to inspire our residents from a number of sensory perspectives - different colours, textures and fragrances of plants, growing vegetables next to the C18 potting shed. There is also a veteran (500 - 800 yr old) Yew tree. Most of garden is lawned or block paved incl a block paved path around the edges of the main lawn. Regret no wheelchair access to woodland area.

& ⚘ ☕

16 CRAIGSIDE

Reservoir Road, Whaley Bridge, SK23 7BW. Jane & Gerard Lennox, 07939 012634, jane@lennoxonline.net, www.craigside.info. 11m SE of Stockport. 11m NNW of Buxton. Turn off A6 onto A5004 to Whaley Bridge. Turn R at train station 1st L under railway bridge onto Reservoir Rd. Park on roadside or in village. Garden ½ m from village. **Visits by arrangement June to Aug. Admission price incl homemade cake & tea/coffee. Adm £7, chd free. Gluten free cakes are available.**

1 acre garden rising steeply from the reservoir giving magnificent views across Todbrook reservoir into Peak District. Gravel paths, stone steps with stopping places. Many mature trees incl 500+yr old oak. Spring bulbs, herbaceous borders, alpine bed, steep mature rockery many heucheras and hydrangeas. Herbs, vegetables and fruit trees. Refreshments also available for 4 legged visitors with a selection of home-made dog biscuits!

 ⚘ ☕

17 8 CURZON LANE

Alvaston, Derby, DE24 8QS. John & Marian Gray, 01332 601596, maz@curzongarden.com, www.curzongarden.com. *2m SE of Derby city centre. From city centre take A6 (London Rd) towards Alvaston. Curzon Lane on L, approx ½ m before Alvaston shops.* **Sun 12, Sun 19 July, Sun 2 Aug (12-5). Adm £3, chd free. Light refreshments. Visits also by arrangement July & Aug for groups of 10 to 30.**
Mature garden with lawns, borders packed full with perennials, shrubs and small trees, tropical planting and hot border. Ornamental and wildlife ponds, greenhouse with different varieties of tomato, cucumber, peppers and chillies. Well stocked vegetable plot. Gravel area and large patio with container planting.

18 DAM STEAD

3 Crowhole, Barlow, Dronfield, S18 7TJ. Derek & Barbara Saveall, 01142 890802, barbarasaveall@hotmail.co.uk. *Chesterfield B6051 to Barlow. Tickled Trout Pub on L. Springfield Rd on L, then R on unnamed rd round the bend. Last cottage on R.* **Visits by arrangement. Adm £3, chd free. Light refreshments.**

Approx one acre with stream, weir, fragrant garden, rose tunnel, orchard garden and dam with an island. Long woodland path, alpine troughs, rockeries and mixed planting. A natural wildlife garden, large summerhouse with seating inside and out. 3 village well dressings and carnival over one week mid August. Parking is within the village at owners discretion so please park with due care and consideration. Also, we do not have pathways so strong/ waterproof footwear is required.

19 NEW DEWSNAPS

Chinley, High Peak, SK23 6AW. Sally Williams, 01663 751175, williams.sally@live.co.uk. *1½ m from Chapel-en-le-Frith. From A624, turn up by the side of the Crown & Mitre Apartments. veer L, then R to travel on single lane rd into countryside for ¼ m. At Xrds, turn L up private lane (Sandy Lane).* **Visits by arrangement Mar to Oct for groups of up to 20. Adm £4, chd free. Tea.** Donation to Plant Heritage. Garden arranged as a series of garden rooms and terraces with views south over Combs Moss and Eccles Pike. Different theme to each of the rooms, such as summer garden, spring garden, topiary avenue. National Plant Collection of Peperomia cvs.

20 NEW DOVECOTE COTTAGE

Stony Houghton, Mansfield, NG19 8TR. Rachel Hayes, 01623 811472, rachelhayes_@hotmail.com. *Between Rotherham Rd & Water Lane opp the phone box.* **Visits by arrangement Apr to Sept for groups of up to 10. Adm £6, chd free. Home-made teas.**
Wildlife friendly, mature garden set in a rural location. A variety of evergreens, foliage plants and cottage garden favourites with Spring and Autumn highlights. The garden is on different levels with steps and slopes and is not suitable for wheelchairs. Dogs welcome. Limited parking.

21 THE DOWER HOUSE

Church Square, Melbourne, DE73 8JH. William & Griselda Kerr, 01332 864756, griseldakerr@btinternet.com. *6m S of Derby. 5m W of exit 23A M1. 4m N of exit 13 M42. When in Church Square, turn R just before the church by a blue sign giving church service times. Gates are then 50 yds ahead.* **Sat 15, Sun 16 Feb (10-3.30). Adm £4, chd free. Sat 6, Sun 7 June (10-5). Adm £5, chd free. Light refreshments. Visits also by arrangement Feb to Sept for groups of 20+. Refreshment is**

The Old Vicarage

provided in the dining room for a maximum of 26.
Beautiful view of Melbourne Pool from balustraded terrace running length of 1829 house. Garden drops steeply by paths and steps to lawn with herbaceous borders and bank of shrubs. Numerous paths lead to different areas of intimacy or openness providing a variety of planting opportunities - a bog garden, glade, shrubbery, grasses, herb and vegetable garden, rose tunnel, orchard and small woodland. Children enjoy the garden as it is full of hidden paths and different areas worth exploring. They can also be set to find various animals such as a bronze crocodile and stone dragon. Wheelchair access to top half of the garden only. Shoes with a good grip are highly recommended as slopes are steep. No parking within 50 yards.

GROUP OPENING

22 ELMTON GARDENS
Elmton, Worksop, S80 4LS. *2m from Creswell, 3m from Clowne, 5m from J30, M1. From M1 J30 take A616 to Newark. Follow approx 4m. Turn R at Elmton signpost. At junction turn R, the village centre is in ½ m.* **Sat 27, Sun 28 June (1-5). Combined adm £5, chd free. Cream teas at the Old Schoolroom next to the church. Food also available all day at the Elm Tree Inn.**

ELM TREE COTTAGE
Mark and Linda Hopkinson.

ELM TREE FARM
Angie & Tim Caulton.

PEAR TREE COTTAGE
Geoff & Janet Cutts.

PINFOLD
Nikki Kirsop, Barry Davies.

Elmton is a lovely little village situated on a stretch of rare unimproved Magnesian limestone grassland with quaking grass, bee orchids and harebells all set in the middle of attractive, rolling farm land. It has a pub, a church and a village green with award winning wildlife conservation area and newly restored Pinfold. Garden opening coincides with Elmton Festival and Well Dressing celebrations (three well dressings on display). There are two exhibitions to view, both with a local theme. Other attractions incl a brass band at Elm Tree Farm and cream teas in the old School Room. The four very colourful but different open gardens have wonderful views. They show a range of gardening styles, themed beds and have a commitment to fruit and vegetable growing. Elmton received a gold award and was voted best small village for the 7th time and best wildlife and conservation area in the East Midlands in Bloom competition in 2019.

23 FIR CROFT
Froggatt Road, Calver, S32 3ZD. Dr S B Furness, www.alpineplantcentre.co.uk. *4m N of Bakewell. At junction of B6001 with A625 (formerly B6054), adjacent to Froggat Edge Garage.* **Sun 17, Sun 31 May, Sun 7 June (2-5). Adm by donation.**
Massive scree with many varieties. Plantsman's garden; rockeries; water garden and nursery; extensive collection (over 3000 varieties) of alpines; conifers; over 800 sempervivums, 500 saxifrages and 350 primulas. Many new varieties not seen anywhere else in the UK. Huge new tufa wall planted with many rare Alpines and sempervivums.

24 GAMESLEY FOLD COTTAGE
Gamesley Fold, Glossop, SK13 6JJ. Mrs G M Carr, 01457 867856, gcarr@gamesleyfold.co.uk, www.gamesleyfold.co.uk. *2m W of Glossop. Off A626 Glossop/Marple Rd nr Charlesworth. Turn down lane directly opp St. Margaret's School, white cottage at the bottom. Car parking in the adjacent field if weather is dry.* **Sun 24 May (1-4). Adm £3, chd free. Home-made teas. Visits also by arrangement May & June.**
Old fashioned cottage garden with rhododendrons, herbaceous borders with candelabra primulas, cottage garden perennial flowers and herbs also a plant nursery selling a wide variety of these plus wild flowers. Small ornamental fish pond and an orchard. Lovely views of the surrounding countryside and plenty of seats available to relax and enjoy tea and cakes. Garden planted to be in keeping with the great age of the house, 1650. Gravel & grass, not very good wheelchair access.

25 HIGH ROOST
27 Storthmeadow Road, Simmondley, Glossop, SK13 6UZ. Peter & Christina Harris, 01457 863888, harrispeter448@gmail.com. *¾ m SW of Glossop. From Glossop A57 to M/CL at 2nd r'about, up Simmondley Ln nr top R turn. From Marple A626 to Glossop, in Chworth R up Town Ln past Hare & Hound PH 2nd L.* **Sun 28 June (12-4). Adm £3, chd free. Light refreshments. Visits also by arrangement May to July. Donation to Donkey Sanctuary.**
Garden on terraced slopes, views over fields and hills. Winding paths, archways and steps explore different garden rooms packed with plants, designed to attract wildlife. Alpine bed, gravel gardens; vegetable garden, water features, statuary, troughs and planters. A garden which needs exploring to discover its secrets tucked away in hidden corners. Craft stall, children's garden quiz and lucky dip.

26 HIGHER CROSSINGS
Crossings Road, Chapel-en-le-Frith, High Peak, SK23 9RX. Malcolm & Christine Hoskins, 01298 812970, malcolm275@btinternet.com. *Turn off B5470 N from Chapel-en-le-Frith on Crossings Rd signed Whitehough/ Chinley. Higher Crossings is 2nd house on R beyond 1st Xrds. Park best before crossroads on Crossings Rd or L on Eccles Rd.* **Sun 24 May (2-5). Adm £4, chd free. Light refreshments. Tea and home-made cakes. Visits also by arrangement May to July for groups of 10+.**
Nearly 2 acres of formal terraced country garden, sweeping lawns and magnificent Peak District views. Rhododendrons, acers, azaleas, hostas, herbaceous borders, Zen garden. Mature specimen trees and shrubs leading through a dell. Beautiful stone terrace and sitting areas. Garden gate leading into meadow.

27 HIGHFIELD HOUSE
Wingfield Road, Oakerthorpe, Alfreton, DE55 7AP. Paul & Ruth Peat and Janet & Brian Costall, 01773 521342, highfieldhouseopengardens@hotmail.co.uk, www.highfieldhouse.weebly.com. *Rear of Alfreton Golf Club. A615 Alfreton-Matlock Rd.* **Sun 7 June** (10.30-5). Adm £3, chd free. Home-made teas. Visits also by arrangement Feb to July for groups of 10+. £8 incl entry & home made cream teas.
Lovely country garden of approx 1 acre, incorporating a shady garden, woodland, pond, laburnum tunnel, orchard, herbaceous borders and vegetable garden. Fabulous AGA baked cakes and lunches. Groups welcome by appointment - (incl 16th -24th February for Snowdrops with afternoon tea or lunch inside by the fire). Lovely walk to Derbyshire Wildlife Trust nature reserve to see Orchids in June. Some steps, slopes and gravel areas.

28 HIGHFIELDS HOUSE
Shields Lane, Roston, Ashbourne, DE6 2EF. Sarah Pennell. *6m SW of Ashbourne. From Ashbourne: Follow A515 S, after 3m turn R onto B5033. After 2m turn L at grass triangle with blue flower container and follow signs. Turn L at Roston Inn and follow signs.* **Sun 28 June, Sun 6 Sept** (1-5). Adm £3, chd free. Home-made teas.
A countryside garden with extensive views. Colourful mixed borders and alpine garden, patio, small pond, greenhouse and veg plot with fruit trees. Enjoy sitting in the summerhouse area watching the butterflies on the replanted wildlife bank. Art in the garden and a short walk through field to the brook and willow area. Partial wheelchair access. Garden crafts. Some gravel paths.

29 HILL COTTAGE
Ashover Road, Littlemoor, Ashover nr Chesterfield, S45 0BL. Jane Tomlinson and Tim Walls. *Littlemoor. 1.8m from Ashover village, 6.3m from Chesterfield and 6.1m from Matlock. Hill Cottage is on Ashover Rd (also known as Stubben Edge Lane). Opp the end of Eastwood Lane.* **Sun 21 June** (11-5). Adm £3.50, chd free. Home-made teas.

Hill Cottage is a lovely example of an English country cottage garden. Whilst small, the garden has full, colourful and fragrant mixed borders with hostas and roses in pots along with a heart shaped lawn. A greenhouse full of chillies and scented pelargoniums and a small veg patch. Views over a pastoral landscape on Ogston reservoir. There are several steps.

30 HILLSIDE
286 Handley Road, New Whittington, Chesterfield, S43 2ET. Mr E J Lee, 01246 454960, eric.lee5@btinternet.com. *3m N of Chesterfield. Between B6056 & B6052.* **Visits by arrangement Apr to Sept. Adm £4, chd free. Light refreshments.**
Part of the $\frac{1}{3}$ of an acre site, slopes steeply but there are handrails for all the steps. New items are a Japanese feature showcasing Japanese plants and a tree trail with 60 named trees, both small and large.There is a Himalayan bed with 40 species grown from wild collected seeds and an Asian area with bamboos, acers and a Chinese border. Other attractions are pools, streams and bog gardens.

31 THE HOLLIES
87 Clowne Road, Barlborough, Chesterfield, S43 4EH. Vernon & Christine Sanderson, wwwfacebook.com/barlboroughgardens. *7m NE of Chesterfield. Off A619 midway between Chesterfield & Worksop. $\frac{1}{2}$m E M1, J30. Follow signs for Barlborough then yellow NGS signs. Parking available along Clowne Road.* **Sun 13 Sept** (2-6). Adm £3, chd free. The 'Cool Café' cake menu will include a number of Autumnal home-made cakes reflecting the change in season plus a selection of hot & cold drinks. Opening with Barlborough Gardens on Fri 8 May (2-6), Sun 28 June (1-6).
The Hollies maximises the unusual garden layout and includes a shade area, patio garden with a Moroccan corner, cottage border plus a fruit and vegetable plot. A wide selection of home-made cakes on offer including gluten free and vegan options, plus tea, coffee and cold drinks. Home-made tombola stall. Extensive view across arable farmland. The garden includes an area influenced by the Majorelle Garden in Marrakech. This recent makeover was achieved

using upcycled items together with appropriate planting. This garden project was featured on the recent series of "Love Your Garden". Partial wheelchair access.

32 HOLLIES FARM PLANT CENTRE
Uppertown, Bonsall, Matlock, DE4 2AW. Robert & Linda Wells, www.holliesfarmplantcentre.co.uk. *From Cromford turn R off A5012 up The Clatterway. Keep R past Fountain Tearoom to village cross, take L up High St, then 2nd L onto Abel Lane. Garden straight ahead.* **Sun 14 June, Sun 2 Aug** (11-3). Adm £3.50, chd free. Home-made teas.
The best selection in Derbyshire with advice and personal attention from Robert and Linda Wells at their family run business. Enjoy a visit to remember in our beautiful display garden - set within glorious Peak District countryside. Huge variety of hardy perennials incl the rare and unusual. Vast selection of traditional garden favourites. Award winning hanging baskets. Ponds, herbaceous borders and glorious views. Plenty of parking available.

33 THE HOLLY TREE
21 Hackney Road, Hackney, Matlock, DE4 2PX. Carl Hodgkinson. *$\frac{1}{2}$m NW of Matlock, off A6. Take A6 NW past bus stn & 1st R up Dimple Rd. At T-junction, turn R & immed L, for Farley & Hackney. Take 1st L onto Hackney Rd. Continue $\frac{3}{4}$m.* **Sat 6, Sun 7 June** (11-4.30). Adm £3, chd free. Light refreshments.
The garden is in excess of 1½ acres and set on a steeply sloping S-facing site, sheltering behind a high retaining wall and incl a small arboretum, bog garden, herbaceous borders, pond, vegetables, fruits, apiary and chickens. Extensively terraced with many paths and steps. Spectacular views across the Derwent valley to Snitterton and Oker.

34 HOLMLEA
Derby Road, Ambergate, Belper, DE56 2EJ. Bill & Tracy Reid. *On the A6 in Ambergate - between Belper and Matlock. Bungalow set slightly back from the road between petrol station and St Anne's Church. Additional parking at The Hurt Arms overflow car park.* **Sat 20 June, Sat**

12 Sept (11-4.30). Adm £4, chd free. Light refreshments.
A garden with something for everyone to enjoy. Set beside the River Derwent the garden comprises a formal garden, a large vegetable plot, fruit trees, greenhouses, herbaceous borders, and a gravel garden. A path from the vegetable garden leads you to a dramatic wooden arch down steps to the stunning riverside walk. Partial wheelchair access. Most of the garden is level and easy to access, except the lower garden and riverside walk. Some grass paths.

35 ◆ LEA GARDENS
Lea, Matlock, DE4 5GH. Mr & Mrs J Tye, 01629 534380, www.leagarden.co.uk. *5m SE of Matlock. Off A6 & A615.* **For opening times and information, please phone or visit garden website.**
Rare collection of rhododendrons, azaleas, kalmias, alpines and conifers in delightful woodland setting. Gardens are sited on remains of medieval quarry and cover about 4 acres. Specialised plant nursery of rhododendrons and azaleas on site. Plant sales by appointment out of season. Visitors welcome throughout the yr. Coffee shop noted for home baked cakes and light refreshments. Gravel paths, steep slopes. Free access for wheelchair users.

36 THE LILIES
Griffe Grange Valley, Grange Mill, Matlock, DE4 4BW. Chris & Bridget Sheppard, www.thelilies.com. *On A5012 Via Gellia Rd 4m N Cromford. 1st house on R after junction with B5023 to Middleton. From Grange Mill, 1st house on L after IKO Grangemill (Formerly Prospect Quarry).* **Sun 5 July, Sun 16 Aug (11.30-4.30). Adm £4, chd free. Home-made teas. Light Lunches served 11.30 to 3.00. Home-made teas all day.**
One acre garden gradually restored over the past 14yrs situated at the top of a wooded valley, surrounded by wildflower meadow and ash woodland. Area adjacent to house with seasonal planting and containers. Mixed shrubs and perennial borders many raised from seed. 3 ponds, vegetable plot, barn conversion with separate cottage garden. Natural garden with stream developed from old mill pond. Walks in large wildflower meadow and ash woodland both

SSSI's. Handspinning demonstration and natural dyeing display using materials from the garden and wool from sheep in the meadow. Locally made crafts for sale. Partial wheelchair access. Steep slope from car park, limestone chippings at entrance, some boggy areas if wet.

37 NEW LITTLEOVER LANE ALLOTMENTS
19 Littleover Lane, Normanton, Derby, DE23 6JF. Mr David Kenyon, 07745227230, davidkenyon@tinyworld.co.uk, littleoverlaneallotments.org.uk. *On Littleover Lane, opp the junction with Foremark Avenue. Just off the Derby Outer Ring Road (A5111). At the Normanton Park r'about turn into Stenson Rd then R into Littleover Lane. The Main Gates are on the L as you travel down the rd.* **Sun 24 May, Sun 16 Aug, Sun 6 Sept (11-5). Adm £5, chd free. Light refreshments. Visits also by arrangement Apr to Oct for groups of 10 to 30. Evenings only Mon to Fri 6pm to 9pm.**
A large private allotment site in SW Derby. About 170 plots, many cultivated to a high standard. If you are interested in growing your own you should find help, advice and inspiration. Many plot holders practice organic methods and some cultivate unusual and heritage vegetables. On site disabled parking available. All avenues have been stoned but site is on a slope and extensive (12 acres) so some areas may not be accessible.

38 108 MACCLESFIELD ROAD
Whaley Bridge, High Peak, SK23 7DH. John Taylor & Peter Holden. *500 metres from Horwich End T-lights on B5470 towards Macclesfield. The New Mills to Macclesfield bus stops 50 metres from the house. There is on-street parking on the opp side of the rd to the house.* **Sat 18, Sun 19 July (11-5). Adm £3, chd free. Home-made teas.**
Taking inspiration from many an hour visiting gardens large and small we have begun our garden refurbishment; having dug over the old lawn it now forms our main herbaceous border. The garden is a collection of our favourite plants crammed into every nook and cranny. We have adopted a cottage garden style approach, with shrubs, perennials, fruit and vegetables

mixing with colourful annuals. The garden is on several levels with narrow paths, and unfortunately there is no step-free access.

39 9 MAIN STREET
Horsley Woodhouse, DE7 6AU. Ms Alison Napier, 01332 881629, ibhillib@btinternet.com. *3m SW of Heanor. 6m N of Derby. Turn off A608 Derby to Heanor Rd at Smalley, towards Belper, (A609). Garden on A609, 1m from Smalley turning.* **Sat 1, Sun 2 Aug (1.30-4.30). Adm £3.50, chd free. Tea. Visits also by arrangement Apr to Sept.**
⅓ acre hilltop garden overlooking lovely farmland view. Terracing, borders, lawns and pergola create space for an informal layout with planting for colour effect. Features incl large wildlife pond with water lilies, bog garden and small formal pool. Emphasis on carefully selected herbaceous perennials mixed with shrubs and old fashioned roses. Gravel garden for sun loving plants and scree garden, both developed from former drive. Please ensure you bring your own carrier bags for the plant stall. Wide collection of home grown plants for sale. All parts of the garden accessible to wheelchairs. Wheelchair adapted WC.

40 7 MAIN STREET - OLD SHOULDER OF MUTTON
Walton on Trent, DE12 8LY. Sarah & Mark Smith, mark_and_sarah@live.co.uk. *Off the A38 at the Barton/Walton junction. Parking available at The White Swan pub. Garden 2 min walk from there.* **Sun 28 June (11-5). Adm £4, chd free. Light refreshments. Visits also by arrangement in July for groups of 5 to 20. Thursdays to Sundays only.**
Delightful herbaceous borders fill this former pub garden, transformed in 5 yrs from a neglected space to a cottage garden idyll. From the courtyard, climb the steps to the large garden with hens, pond and wild flower area. Lush foliage fills the deep shade border whilst delphiniums tower over the colourful herbaceous borders. Take a moment to sit and enjoy the scents and colours of the garden. Only the Courtyard is accessible to wheelchairs as access to the main garden is via 7 steps.

41 58A MAIN STREET
Rosliston, Swadlincote, DE12 8JW.
Paul Marbrow, 01283 761011,
paulmarbrow@hotmail.co.uk.
*Rosliston. if exiting the M42, J11
onto the A444 to Overseal follow
signs Linton then Rosliston. From
A38, exit to Walton on Trent, then
follow Rosliston signs.* **Sun 21 June,
Sun 5 July (12-5). Adm £4, chd
free. Light refreshments. Visits
also by arrangement in June for
groups of 5 to 30.**
Large ½ acre garden formed from
a once open field over the last few
years. The garden has developed
into themed areas and is ongoing
changing and maturing. Japanese,
arid beach, bamboo grove with ferns
etc. The one hundred square metre
indoor garden for cacti, exotic and
tender plants, are now becoming
established as a mini Eden. There
are also vegetable and fruit gardens.
Areas are easily accessible, although
some are only for the sure of foot.

42 NEW MEADOW COTTAGE
1 Russell Square, Hulland
Ward, Ashbourne, DE6 3EA.
Michael Halls, 01335 372064,
mvaehalls@gmail.com. *5m Et of
Ashbourne. There is a lane between
and on the same side as the two
garages in Hulland Ward. Meadow
Cottage is just down the lane to the
R.* **Visits by arrangement Feb to
Sept. Adm £6, chd free. Home-
made teas.**
This garden was created from a field
from 1995. It faces south and is on a
sloping site. There is a wooded area,
a wild flower orchard, herbaceous
and vegetable areas. The soil is heavy
clay so roses do well here. At 750'
above sea level, growing seasons are
later and shorter. The lawns are all
original meadow. There are bees and
hens too. The access to the garden
is over a gravel area and the slope is
significant down the garden but can
be mastered with care.

43 ◆ MELBOURNE HALL
GARDENS
Church Square, Melbourne,
Derby, DE73 8EN. Melbourne
Gardens Charity, 01332 862502,
info@melbournehall.com,
www.melbournehallgardens.com.
*6m S of Derby. At Melbourne
Market Place turn into Church St,
go down to Church Sq. Garden
entrance across visitor centre*
next to Melbourne Hall tea room.
**For NGS: Sat 20, Sun 21 June
(1.30-5.30). Adm £6, chd £5. Light
refreshments in Melbourne Hall
Tearooms and locally. For other
opening times and information,
please phone, email or visit garden
website.**
A 17 acre historic garden with an
abundance of rare trees and shrubs.
Woodland and waterside planting
with extensive herbaceous borders.
Meconopsis, candelabra primulas,
various Styrax and Cornus kousa.
Other garden features incl Bakewells
wrought iron arbour, a yew tunnel and
fine C18 statuary and water features.
300yr old trees, waterside planting,
feature hedges and herbaceous
borders. Fine statuary and stonework.
Gravel paths, uneven surface in
places, some steep slopes.

44 ◆ MEYNELL LANGLEY
TRIALS GARDEN
Lodge Lane (off Flagshaw
Lane), Kirk Langley, Ashbourne,
DE6 4NT. Robert & Karen Walker,
01332 824358, enquiries@meynell-
langley-gardens.co.uk, www.
meynell-langley-gardens.co.uk.
*4m W of Derby, nr Kedleston Hall.
Head W out of Derby on A52. At
Kirk Langley turn R onto Flagshaw
Lane (signed to Kedleston Hall) then
R onto Lodge Lane. Follow Meynell
Langley Gardens signs.* **For NGS:
Sun 14 June, Sun 19 July, Sun
16 Aug, Sun 20 Sept, Sun 11 Oct
(10-4). Adm £5, chd free. For other
opening times and information,
please phone, email or visit garden
website.**
Formal ¾ acre Victorian style
garden established over 25 years,
displaying and trialling new and
existing varieties of bedding plants,
herbaceous perennials and vegetable
plants grown at the adjacent nursery.
Over 180 hanging baskets and
floral displays, plus apple, pear and
other fruit. Summer fruit pruning
demonstrations on July NGS day.
Adjacent tea rooms serving lunches
and refreshments daily. Level ground
and firm grass.

45 MOORFIELDS
257/261 Chesterfield Road,
Temple Normanton, Chesterfield,
S42 5DE. Peter, Janet & Stephen
Wright. *4m SE of Chesterfield.
From Chesterfield take A617 for 2m,
turn on to B6039 through Temple*
Normanton, taking R fork signed
Tibshelf, B6039. Garden ¼m on R.
Limited parking. **Sun 3 May, Sun 5
July (1-5). Adm £3.50, chd free.
Light refreshments.**
Two adjoining gardens each planted
for seasonal colour. The larger one
has mature, mixed island beds and
borders, a gravel garden to the
front, a small wild flower area, large
wildlife pond, orchard and soft fruit,
vegetable garden. Show of late
flowering tulips. The smaller gardens
of No. 257 feature herbaceous
borders and shrubs. Extensive views
across to mid Derbyshire.

46 NEW MILLS SCHOOL
Church Lane, New Mills, High
Peak, SK22 4NR. Mr Craig
Pickering, 07833 373593,
cpickering@newmillsschool.co.uk,
www.newmillsschool.co.uk. *12m
NNW of Buxton. From A6 take
A6105 signed New Mills, Hayfield.
At C of E Church turn L onto Church
Lane. School on L. Parking on site.*
**Sat 11 July (12-5); Sun 12 July
(2-5). Adm £4, chd free. Visits also
by arrangement June to Aug for
groups of 10+.**
Mixed herbaceous perennials/shrub
borders, with mature trees and lawns
and gravel border situated in the
semi rural setting of the High Peak
incl a Grade II listed building with
4 themed quads. The school was
awarded highly commended in the
School Garden 2019 RHS Tatton
Show and won the Best High School
Garden and the People's Choice
Award. Come and see exhibits from
this. Hot and Cold Beverages and a
selection of sandwiches, cream teas
and home-made cakes are available.
Ramps allow wheelchair access to
most of outside, flower beds and into
Grade II listed building and library.

47 9 NEWFIELD CRESCENT
Dore, Sheffield, S17 3DE.
Mike Jackson, 01142 366198,
mandnjackson@googlemail.com.
*Dore - SW Sheffield. Turn off
Causeway Head Rd on Heather Lea
Av. 2nd L into Newfield Crescent.
Parking on roadside.* **Sat 26, Sun
27 Sept (2-5). Adm £4, chd free.
Light refreshments. Visits also by
arrangement Mar to Oct.**
Mature, wildlife friendly garden
planted to provide all yr interest,
particularly in Autumn and Winter.
Upper terrace with alpines in troughs

and bowls. Lower terrace featuring pond with cascade and connecting stream to second pond. Bog garden, rock gardens, lawn alpine bed, wilder areas, mixed borders with trees, shrubs and perennials. Featuring azaleas, rhododendrons, camellias, primulas. Wheelchair access without steps to top terrace offering full view of garden.

48 ◆ OLD ENGLISH WALLED GARDEN, ELVASTON CASTLE COUNTRY PARK

Borrowash Road, Elvaston, Derby, DE72 3EP. Derbyshire County Council, 01629 533870, www.derbyshire.gov.uk/elvaston. *4m E of Derby. Signed from A52 & A50. Car parking charge applies.* **For NGS: Sun 26 Apr, Sun 9 Aug (12-4). Adm £2.50, chd free. Homemade teas. For other opening times and information, please phone or visit garden website.** Come and discover the beauty of the Old English walled garden at Elvaston Castle. Take in the peaceful atmosphere and enjoy the scents and colours of all the varieties of trees, shrubs and plants. Summer bedding and large herbaceous borders. After your visit to the walled garden take time to walk around the wider estate featuring romantic topiary gardens, lake, woodland and nature reserve. Estate gardeners on hand during the day. Delicious home-made cakes available.

49 330 OLD ROAD

Brampton, Chesterfield, S40 3QH. Christine Stubbs & Julia Stubbs, 07919217559, julia.stubbs@aecom.com. *Approx 1½ m from town centre. 50 yds from junc with Storrs Rd. 1st house next to grazing field; on-road parking available adjacent to tree-lined roadside stone wall.* **Fri 19, Sat 20 June (10.30-5). Adm £3, chd free. Home-made teas. Visits also by arrangement June to Aug.** Deceptive ⅓ acre plot of mature trees, landscaped lawns, orchard and cottage style planting. Unusual perennials, species groups such as astrantia, lychnis, thalictrum, heuchera and 40+ clematis. Acers, actea, hosta, ferns and acanthus lie within this interesting garden. Through a hidden gate, another smaller plot of similar planting, with delphinium, helenium, Echinacea, acers and

hosta. Winner Chesterfield in Bloom Best Large Garden 2017. Wheelchair access on terrace area only, for views and refreshments - all welcome. Steps with handrail down to main garden. WC available.

50 THE OLD VICARAGE

The Fields, Middleton by Wirksworth, Matlock, DE4 4NH. Jane Irwing, 01629 825010, irwingjane@gmail.com. *Garden located behind church on Main St & nr school. Travelling N on A6 from Derby turn L at Cromford, at top of hill turn R onto Porter Ln, at T-lights, turn R onto Main St. Park in Village Hall. Walk through churchyard. No parking at house.* **Sat 22, Sun 23 Feb (11-4). Adm £3.50, chd free. Light refreshments. For Snowdrops opening, home-made soup will be served in the kitchen. Visits also by arrangement Feb to Oct for groups of 5 to 30.** Glorious garden with mixed flowering borders and mature trees in gentle valley with fantastic views overlooking Black Rocks. To the side a courtyard garden where acid loving plants such as camellias and rhododendrons are

grown in pots and, in the fernery, tender ferns and exotic plants. Beyond is the orchard, fruit garden, vegetable patch and greenhouse, the home of honey bees, doves and hens. Enchanting garden with fantastic views. Spectacular Rambling Rector rose over front of house in late June early July. All season interest. Cakes, tea and coffee and cold drinks served in the garden or in fernery if wet (limited space). Path through Churchyard ends in some steep steps leading onto the lane and into the garden gate. Once in the garden much can be seen from the terrace.

Barlborough Gardens

Your visits help change lives – we are Hospice UK's largest charitable funder donating more than £5.5 million to support hospices in local communities since 1996

51 OTTERWOOD

88 St Johns Road, Buxton, SK17 6TP. Ms Simone Harch & Mr Gary Mellor, simoneharch@hotmail.co.uk. *Parking on St Johns Rd & Gadley Lane.* **Sat 11, Sun 19 July (12-5). Adm £4, chd free. Visits also by arrangement in July for groups of 10+. Refreshments can be arranged for private groups.**
This is a romantic, peaceful garden featuring summer borders, kitchen garden, natural pond with viewing pontoon and a newly planted wildflower garden. A haven for wildlife, the garden is organically managed.

52 THE PADDOCK

12 Manknell Rd, Whittington Moor, Chesterfield, S41 8LZ. Mel & Wendy Taylor, 01246 451001, debijt9276@gmail.com. *2m N of Chesterfield. Whittington Moor just off A61 between Sheffield & Chesterfield. Parking available at Victoria Working Mens Club, garden signed from here.* **Sun 26 Apr, Sun 26 July (11-5). Adm £3.50, chd free. Cream teas. Visits also by arrangement.**
½ acre garden incorporating small formal garden, stream and koi filled pond. Stone path over bridge, up some steps, past small copse, across the stream at the top and back down again. Past herbaceous border towards a pergola where cream teas can be enjoyed.
ᕼ 🐏 ✿ ☕

53 RECTORY HOUSE

Kedleston, Derby, DE22 5JJ. Helene Viscountess Scarsdale. *5m NW Derby. A52 from Derby turn R Kedleston sign. Drive to village turn R. Brick house standing back from rd on sharp corner.* **Sun 24 May (2-5). Adm £5, chd free. Home-made teas.**
The garden is next to Kedleston Park and is of C18 origin. Many established rare trees and shrubs also rhododendrons, azaleas and unusual roses. Large natural pond with amusing frog fountain. Primulas, gunneras, darmeras and lots of moisture loving plants. The winding paths go through trees and past wild flowers and grasses. New woodland with rare plants. An atmospheric garden. A sphere of Cumbrian slate built by Jo Smith, Kirkcudbrightshire. Lily fountain in tea courtyard area. Uneven paths.
✿ ☕

54 ♦ RENISHAW HALL & GARDENS

Renishaw, Sheffield, S21 3WB. Alexandra Hayward, 01246 432310, enquiries@renishaw-hall.co.uk, www.renishaw-hall.co.uk. *10m from Sheffield city centre. By car: Renishaw Hall only 3m from J30 on M1, well signed from junction r'about.* **For NGS: Tue 8 Sept (10.30-4.30). Adm £7, chd £3. Light refreshments at The Cafe. For other opening times and information, please phone, email or visit garden website.**
Renishaw Hall and Gardens boasts 7 acres of stunning gardens created by Sir George Sitwell in 1885. The Italianate gardens feature various rooms with extravagant herbaceous borders. Rose gardens, rare trees and shrubs, National Collection of Yuccas, sculptures, woodland walks and lakes create a magical and engaging garden experience. The Cafe will be open for light meals, hot and cold drinks and cakes. Wheelchair route around garden.
ᕼ 🐏 ✿ 🚗 NPC ☕

GROUP OPENING

55 REPTON NGS VILLAGE GARDENS

Repton, Derby, DE65 6FQ. *6m S of Derby. From A38/A50, S of Derby, follow signs to Willington, then Repton, then R at r'about towards Newton Solney to reach 10 Chestnut Way, other gardens signposted from the r'about.* **Sun 31 May, Sat 18 July (1.30-5.30). Combined adm £6, chd free. Home-made teas at 10 Chestnut Way (for NGS) & Woodend Cottage (for St. Wystan's Church).**

ASKEW COTTAGE
Louise Hardwick.
(See separate entry)

10 CHESTNUT WAY
Robert & Pauline Little.
(See separate entry)

22 PINFOLD CLOSE
DE65 6FR. Mr & Mrs O Jowett.

REPTON ALLOTMENTS
DE65 6FX. Mr A Topping.

WOODEND COTTAGE
DE65 6FB. Wendy & Stephen Longden, 01283 703259, wendylongden@btinternet.com. **Visits also by arrangement June to Aug for groups of 10 to 30.**

Repton is a thriving village dating back to Anglo Saxon times. The village gardens are all very different, ranging from the very small to very large, several of them have new features for 2020. Askew Cottage is a professionally designed garden and has many structural features linked together by curving paths. 10 Chestnut Way is a plantaholic's garden often likened to a tardis - be prepared to be surprised. 22 Pinfold Close is a small garden but is packed full with a special interest in tropical plants. Repton Allotments is a small set of allotments currently undergoing a revival with community area, new polytunnel and attractive views across Derbyshire. Woodend Cottage is an organic garden with stunning views, a grass labyrinth and rose pergola. All gardens have plenty of seats. Some gardens have grass or gravel paths but most areas wheelchair accessible.
ᕼ ✿ 🚗 ☕

56 NEW 40 ST OSWALD'S CRESCENT

Ashbourne, DE6 1FS. Anne McSkimming, 01335 342235, anneofashbourne@hotmail.com. *From centre of Ashbourne, Shaw Croft car park, go along Park St. L into Park Ave then 2nd R into St Oswald's Crescent. Follow rd til you see signs. Park on rd.* **Visits by arrangement May to July for groups of up to 10. Guided Tour. Adm £4, chd free. Light refreshments. £1 for tea/coffee and biscuits.**
Small enclosed town garden, developed by a plantswoman, from scratch 9 years ago. Trees, lots of shrubs, perennials, climbers. Some unusual specimens. Wide and narrow beds. Plenty of colour and interest throughout the season. A few steps lead up to a level garden. Can be slippery in places. Maximum group size 8.
🐏 ✿ ☕

57 THE SMITHY

Church Street, Buxton, SK17 6HD. Roddie & Kate MacLean. *350 metres S of Buxton Market Place, in Higher Buxton. Located on access-only Church St, which cuts corner between B5059 & A515. Walk S from Buxton Market Place car park. Take slight R off A515, between Scriveners Bookshop & The Swan Inn.* **Fri 12 June (2-8). Wine. Sat 4 July (11-5). Mon 6 July (2-8).**

Wine. **Adm £3, chd free.**
Architect-designed small oasis of calm in the town centre, subliminally inspired by Geoff Hamilton. Created from a sloping lawn into terraces, following the party walls of former houses on the site, demolished into themselves in 1930s - hence the garden is elevated above Church St. Herbaceous borders, wildlife pond, octagonal greenhouse, raised vegetable beds. Alliums in June; sweet peas in July. Garden with many levels; steps at entrance and around the garden.

58 SMITHY HOUSE
Mansfield Road, Heath, Chesterfield, S44 5SB. Christine & Michael Hasty, 01246850361, c.hasty@sky.com. *5m SE of Chesterfield and 1m from J29 M1. From Chesterfield take A617 for 2m, take B6039 through Temple Normanton & follow signs for Heath. From M1 take A6175 signed Clay Cross. After 400 metres turn R into Heath.* **Sat 4 July (11-5). Adm £4, chd free. Cream teas. Visits also by arrangement June to Aug for groups of 10+.**
Set among mature trees is a one acre cottage garden. A broad gravel path takes you past a formal herb garden, patio, koi pond and pergola, before sweeping lawns lead you through colour themed herbaceous borders past a large wildlife pond overlooked by a deck and summerhouse to a vegetable parterre. Seating areas allow you to enjoy colourful containers, scented rose arbour and the sound of water.

GROUP OPENING

59 STANTON IN PEAK GARDENS
Stanton-In-The-Peak, Matlock, DE4 2LR. *At the top of the hill in Stanton in Peak, on the rd to Birchover. Stanton in Peak is 5m south of Bakewell. Turn off the A6 at Rowsley, or at the B5056 & follow signs up the hill.* **Sat 25, Sun 26 July (1-5). Combined adm £4.50, chd free. Home-made teas at 2 Haddon View. At Woodend a pop-up pub serves real ale from the barrel.**

2 HADDON VIEW
Steve Tompkins.

HARE HATCH COTTAGE
Bill Chandler.

WOODEND COTTAGE
Will Chandler.

Stanton in Peak is a hillside, stone village with glorious views, and is a Conservation Area in the Peak District National Park. Three gardens are open. Steve's garden at 2 Haddon View is at the top of the village and is 1/10th acre crammed with plants. Follow the winding path up the garden with a few steps. There are cacti flowering in the greenhouse, lots of patio pots, herbaceous borders, three wildlife ponds with red, pink and white water lilies, a koi pond, rhododendrons and a summerhouse. Tea and home-made cakes served. Just down the hill is Woodend where Will has constructed charming roadside follies on a strip of raised land along the road. The hidden, rear garden has diverse planting, and an extended vegetable plot. All with breath-taking views. A pop-up 'pub' will have draught beer from a local brewery. Nearby is Hare Hatch where Bill's garden wraps around the cottage. This is carefully designed to get the best of every planting opportunity, with a little bit of everything!

60 NEW 26 STILES ROAD
Alvaston, Derby, DE24 0PG. Mr Colin Summerfield. *Off A6. 2m SE of Derby city centre. From city take A6 (London Rd) towards Alvaston. At Blue Peter Island take L into Beech Ave 1st R into Kelmore Rd and 1st L into Stiles Rd.* **Sun 10 May (1-5). Adm £3, chd free. Home-made teas.**
Small town garden with lawn and paved areas, fish and wild life ponds, stream, fruit and veg area, summerhouse, seating areas, woodland walk. Clematis, Azaleas, Alliums and mixed borders. Aubretia wall in front garden. Most of garden visible from patio.

61 ♦ THORNBRIDGE HALL GARDENS
Ashford in the Water, DE45 1NZ. Jim & Emma Harrison, 07500 698795, gardeners@thornbridgehall.co.uk, www.thornbridgehall.co.uk. *2m NW of Bakewell. From Bakewell*

take A6, signed Buxton. After 2m, R onto A6020. ½m turn L, signed Thornbridge Hall. For NGS: **Tue 19 May (9-5). Adm £7, chd free. Light refreshments.** For other opening times and information, please phone, email or visit garden website.
A stunning C19, 12 acre garden, set in the heart of the Peak District overlooking rolling Derbyshire countryside. Designed to create a vision of 1000 shades of green, the garden has many distinct areas. These incl koi lake and water garden, Italian garden with statuary, grottos and temples, 100ft herbaceous border, kitchen garden, scented terrace, hot border and refurbished glasshouses. Contains statuary from Clumber Park, Sydnope Hall and Chatsworth. Tea, coffee, sandwiches and cakes available. Gravel paths, steep slopes, steps.

62 TILFORD HOUSE
Hognaston, Ashbourne, DE6 1PW. Mr & Mrs P R Gardner. *5m NE of Ashbourne. A517 Belper to Ashbourne. At Hulland Ward follow signs to Hognaston. Downhill (2m) to bridge. Roadside parking 100 metres.* **Mon 25 May, Wed 15 July (1-5). Adm £4, chd free. Home-made teas.**
A 1½ acre streamside English country garden. Woodland, wildlife areas, alpine beds and ponds lie alongside colourful seasonal planting. Fruit cage and raised beds for vegetables. New beds and borders continually under development in this plantsman's garden. Sit and relax with tea and cake whilst listening to the continuous sounds of the birds.

63 ◆ TISSINGTON HALL

Tissington, Ashbourne, DE6 1RA. Sir Richard & Lady FitzHerbert, 01335 352200, tisshall@dircon.co.uk, www.tissingtonhall.co.uk. *4m N of Ashbourne. E of A515 on Ashbourne to Buxton Rd in centre of the beautiful Estate Village of Tissington.* **For NGS: Mon 24, Mon 31 Aug (12-3). Adm £6, chd free. Cream teas at Herbert's Fine English Tearooms. For other opening times and information, please phone, email or visit garden website.**
Large garden celebrating over 80yrs in the NGS, with stunning rose garden on west terrace, herbaceous borders and 5 acres of grounds. Refreshments available at the award winning Herberts Fine English Tearooms in village (Tel 01335 350501). Wheelchair access advice from ticket seller. Please seek staff and we shall park you nearer the gardens.

64 TREETOPS HOSPICE CARE

Derby Road, Risley, Derby, DE72 3SS. Treetops Hospice Care, www.treetopshospice.org.uk. *On main rd, B5010 in centre of Risley village. From J25 M1 take rd signed to Risley. Turn L at T-lights, Treetops Hospice Care on L approx ½m through village. From Borrowash direction Treetops is on R just after church.* **Sat 16 May (11-3). Adm £3, chd free. Home-made teas.**
The 12 acre site of began as a Spring garden over 10 years ago following an appeal for daffodil bulbs. Today a team of volunteers help to create all-year round colour with woodland planting, hebaceous/perennial boarders, rose garden, wildlife pond and small fruit orchard. Raised wheelchair walkways allow access through some woodland areas and 15 mins circular walk along bark chipped paths. There is a plants and homemade preserves stall.

Wheelchair access is limited through some of the woodland areas.

65 WALTON COTTAGE

Matlock Road, Walton, Chesterfield, S42 7LG. Neil & Julie Brown, 07968 128313, jmbrown.waltoncottage@gmail.com. *3m from Chesterfield. 6½m from Matlock. On A632 Matlock to Chesterfield main rd. From Chesterfield 1m after junction nr garage with T-lights. From Matlock 1m after B5057 junction.* **Sun 7 June (11-4). Adm £4, chd free. Light refreshments. Visits also by arrangement June & July.**
A large garden that has both formal and informal areas, incl woodland, orchard, kitchen garden and sweeping lawns with views over Chesterfield.

Coxbench Hall

66 27 WASH GREEN
Wirksworth, Matlock,
DE4 4FD. Mr & Mrs Paul &
Kathy Harvey, 01629822218,
pandkharvey@btinternet.com.
*⅓m E of Wirksworth centre. From
Wirksworth centre, follow B5035
towards Whatstandwell. Cauldwell
St leads over railway bridge to Wash
Green, 200 metres up steep hill on
L. Park in town or uphill from garden
entry.* **Sun 17 May (1-5). Adm
£3.50, chd free. Home-made teas.
Visits also by arrangement Apr
to Oct.**
Secluded 1 acre garden, with
outstanding views over Wirksworth
and the Ecclesbourne valley. Inner
enclosed area has formal knot
garden, pergola and lawn surrounded
by mixed borders, with paved seating
area. The larger part of the garden
has an open sweep of grass, large
borders, beds, areas of woodland
and orchard. Roughly ¼ is a
productive fruit and vegetable garden
with polytunnel. Drop off at property
entry for wheelchair access. The inner
garden has flat paths with good views
of whole garden.
&. ⋔ ✿ ☕

67 12 WATER LANE
Middleton, Matlock,
DE4 4LY. Hildegard
Wiesehofer, 07809 883393,
wiesehofer@btinternet.com.
*Approx 2½m SW of Matlock. 1½m
NW of Wirksworth. From Derby: at
A6 & B5023 intersection take rd to
Wirksworth. R to Middleton. Follow
NGS signs. From Ashbourne take
Matlock rd & follow signs. Park on
main rd. Limited parking in Water
Ln.* **Sun 3, Mon 4 May (11-5). Adm
£3.50, chd free. Home-made
teas. Visits also by arrangement
May to Aug for groups of 10 to 20.
Groups will be required to pay for
admissions in advance of the visit.**
Small, eclectic hillside garden on
different levels, created as a series of
rooms. Each room has been designed
to capture the stunning views over
Derbyshire and Nottinghamshire
and incl a woodland walk, ponds,
eastern and infinity garden. Emphasis
is on holistic and organic principles.
Featured in Derbyshire Life, Practical
Gardener. Glorious views and short
distance from High Peak Trail,
Middleton Top and Engine House.
Very rare specimen of a limestone
vaulted ceiling, so we are told.
⋔ ⊟ ☕

68 13 WESTFIELD ROAD
Swadlincote, DE11 0BG. Val
& Dave Booth, 01283 221167
or 07891 436632,
valerie.booth@sky.com. *5m E of
Burton-on-Trent, off A511. Take
A511 from Burton-on-Trent. Follow
signs for Swadlincote. Turn R into
Springfield Rd, take 3rd R into
Westfield Rd.* **Sun 21 June, Sun 2
Aug (1-5). Adm £3.50, chd free.
Home-made teas. Visits also
by arrangement May to Aug for
groups of 10 to 30.**
A deceptive country-style garden in
Swadlincote, a real gem. The garden
is on 2 levels of approx ½ acre.
Packed herbaceous borders designed
for colour. Shrubs, baskets and
tubs. Lots of roses. Greenhouses,
raised-bed vegetable area, fruit trees
and 2 ponds. Free range chicken
area. Plenty of seating to relax and
take in the wonderful planting from 2
passionate gardeners. WC.
⋔ ✿ ☕

69 WESTGATE
Combs Road, Combs, Chapel-
en-le-Frith, High Peak, SK23 9UP.
Maurice & Chris Lomas,
07854 680170, ca-lomas@sky.com.
*N of Chapel-en-le-Frith off B5470.
Turn L immed before Hanging Gate
PH, signed Combs Village. ¾m
on L by railway bridge.* **Visits by
arrangement May to July for
groups of 10+. Adm £3, chd free.
Tea.**
Large sloping garden in quiet village
with beautiful views. Features incl
mixed borders and beds containing
many perenials, hosta and heuchera.
Large rockery. Fruit beds. Wild flower
area, grasses and fernery. Natural
pond and stream with bog area. 3
formal ponds. Chicken area. Lots of
places to sit and enjoy the views.
☕

70 WHARFEDALE
34 Broadway, Duffield,
Belper, DE56 4BU. Roger &
Sue Roberts, 01332 841905,
rogerroberts34@outlook.com,
www.garden34.co.uk. *4m N
of Derby. Turn onto B5023 to
Wirksworth (Broadway) off A6 at
T-lights midway between Belper &
Derby.* **Visits by arrangement June
to Aug for groups of up to 30.
Adm £4, chd free. Home-made
teas.**
Garden design and plant enthusiast
with over 500 varieties and rare
specimens. Eclectic yet replicateable.

12 distinct areas incl naturalistic,
choice shrub and single colour
borders. Italian walled garden.
Woodland with pond and walkway.
Japanese landscape with stream,
moon gate and pavilion. Front cottage
garden with winter shrubs. Stone,
wire and wood sculptures. Fully
labelled. Comfortable seating around
the garden. Close to Kedleston Hall
and Derwent Valley World Heritage
Site.
✿ ⊟ ☕

71 24 WHEELDON AVENUE
Derby, DE22 1HN. Laura
Burnett, 01332 384893,
lauraburnett@outlook.com. *1m N
Derby city centre. Off Kedleston Rd.
Limited on street parking. Local bus
stop nearby.* **Sun 14 June (2-5).
Combined adm with 26 Wheeldon
Avenue £5, chd free. Home-made
teas at 24 Wheeldon Avenue.
Visits also by arrangement June
& July fr groups of up to 10.
Combined with 26 Wheeldon
Avenue.**
Small Victorian garden, with original
walling supporting many shrubs and
climbers with contrasting colour
and texture. Small lawn surrounded
by herbaceous border with main
colour scheme of blue, purple, black,
yellow and orange tones. This leads
to a new re-modelled area, mostly
naturalistic, with a Japanese influence
and a green palette, designed to be a
calming area to sit in and planted
accordingly, incl the use of tall mirror
to give impression of the garden being
extended beyond the wall. Wheelchair
access to side of property.
&. ⋔ ✿ ☕

Your visits help
change lives – we
are the largest
single funder
of the Queen's
Nursing Institute

72 26 WHEELDON AVENUE

Derby, DE22 1HN. Ian Griffiths, 01332 342204, idhgriffiths@gmail.com. *1m N of Derby. 1m from city centre & approached directly off Kedleston Rd or from A6 Duffield Rd via West Bank Ave. Limited on street parking.* **Sun 14 June (2-5). Combined adm with 24 Wheeldon Avenue £5, chd free. Home-made teas at 24 Wheeldon Avenue. Visits also by arrangement June & July for groups of up to 10. Combined with 24 Wheeldon Avenue.**

Tiny Victorian walled garden near to city centre. Lawn and herbaceous borders with newly expanded old rose collection, lupins, delphiniums and foxgloves. Small terrace with topiary, herb garden and lion fountain. Rose collection Open for the final time this year after twenty years of NGS opening due to owner relocating to another NGS garden in Cornwall. Garden on one level, lawn may be soft if wet.

GROUP OPENING

73 WHITWELL OPEN GARDENS

Ashbarn, 9a Hight Street, Whitwell, Worksop, S80 4QZ. Lynn and Keith Basford. *Whitwell is off A619 Barlborough to Worksop. 4m from M1 J30 at Barlborough or A57 Worksop or A60 from Mansfield. Parking is opp the Co-op S80 4QR plus street parking around the village.* **Sun 14 June (2-5). Combined adm £5, chd free. Home-made teas at 1 Manor Farm Court.**

NEW **ASHBARN**
Lynn Basford.

NEW **THE CHESTNUTS,**
Mr & Mrs Stuart & Jane Riddell.

NEW **THE COTTAGE,**
Mrs Geraldine Pearce.

GREENWELL COTTAGE
Ruth & Jack Denston.

NEW **1 MANOR FARM COURT**
Mrs Victoria & Martin Glossop.

2 MANOR FARM COURT
Denise Watts.

4 MANOR FARM COURT
Kate & John Taylor.

NEW **SHEPHERDS COTTAGE**
Dr Tim Bristow.

THE STABLES
Victoria & Neil Truman.

Whitwell - an ancient village sandwiched between the woods with Special Scientific and Archelogical Interest and the prehistoric caves of Creswell Crags. Gardens on view vary both in size and style, including small and quirky, a pot puree of rare plants plus grassland beautifully maintained by a busy robot. Five new gardens showcase composite ways in which gardens have been orchestrated to fit into an ancient landscape. Partial access to some gardens.

74 WILD IN THE COUNTRY

Hawkhill Road, Eyam, Hope Valley, S32 5QQ. Mrs Gill Bagshawe, www.wildinthecountryflowers. co.uk. *In Eyam, follow signs to public car park. Located next to Eyam Museum & opp public car park on Hawkhill Rd.* **Sun 12 July (11-4). Adm £2.50, chd free.**

A rectangular plot devoted totally to growing flowers and foliage for cutting. Sweet pea, rose, larkspur, cornflower, nigella, ammi. All the florist's favourites can be found here. There is a tea room, a village pub and several cafes in the village to enjoy refreshments.

75 15 WINDMILL LANE

Ashbourne, DE6 1EY. Jean Ross & Chris Duncan. *Take A515 (Buxton Rd) from the market place and at the top of the hill turn R into Windmill Lane; house by 4th tree on L.* **Sun 19 July (1-5). Adm £3, chd free.**

Landscaped and densely-planted town garden providing ideas others may wish to develop. Using a limited palette (mainly white, pink, mauve & burgundy) and emphasising leaf shape and colour, the key aims in establishing this garden were all-year interest; low maintenance; no grass; attraction of pollinators; and growing some soft fruit, peas & beans. Extensive views. A few steps.

76 26 WINDMILL RISE

Belper, DE56 1GQ. Kathy Fairweather. *From Belper Market Place take Chesterfield Rd towards Heage. Top of hill, 1st R Marsh Lane, 1st R Windmill Lane, 1st R Windmill Rise - limited parking on Windmill Rise - disabled mainly.* **Sat 8, Sun 9 Aug (11.30-4.30). Adm £3.50, chd free. Light refreshments. Gluten free options available.**

Behind a deceptively ordinary façade, lies a real surprise. A lush oasis, much larger than expected, with an amazing collection of rare and unusual plants. A truly plant lovers' organic garden divided into sections: woodland, Japanese, secret garden, cottage, edible, ponds and small stream. Many seating areas, incl a new summer house in which to enjoy a variety of refreshments. Live music, delicious home baking and light lunches available.

77 NEW 18A WOOD LANE

Horsley Woodhouse, Ilkeston, DE7 6BN. Martin Gallimore, 01332 902437, martingallimore@hotmail.com. *NE of Derby on A608. From Derby on the A609 at the Xrds with the Rose & Crown pub turn L onto Woodside. Continue past the turning for Smalley Mill Rd on the L, the garden can be found on the R.* **Sun 21 June (2-5). Adm £3.50, chd free. Light refreshments. Visits also by arrangement June to Sept for groups of up to 20. Light refreshments incl in entry price for group bookings.**

Quirky ⅓ acre garden full of interest and creative flair. Inspiration can be found around every corner along with fabulous countryside views. Large trees give a feeling of maturity to this relatively young, developing garden.

Chevin Brae

DEVON

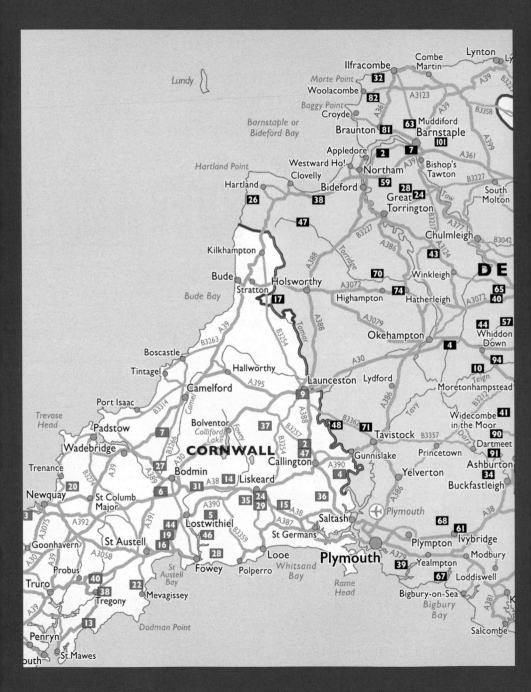

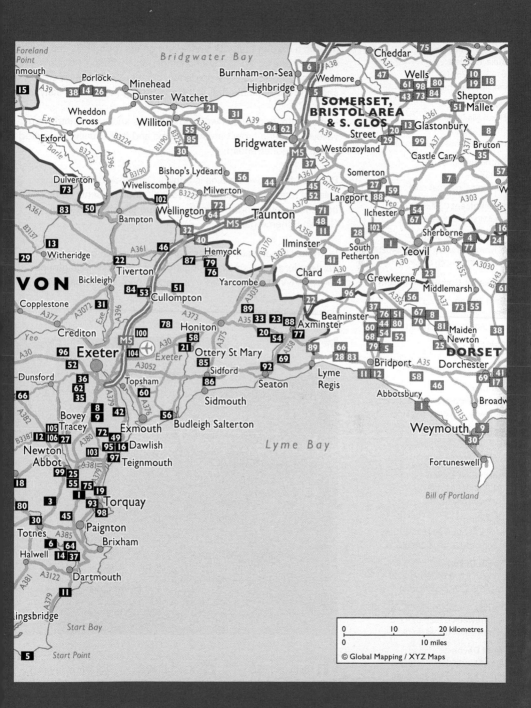

Volunteers

**County Organisers
& Central Devon**
Edward & Miranda Allhusen
01647 440296
Miranda@allhusen.co.uk

County Treasurer
Julia Tremlett
01392 832671
jandjtremlett@hotmail.com

Publicity
Brian Mackness
01626 356004
brianmackness@clara.co.uk

Cath Pettyfer
01837 89024
cathpettyfer@gmail.com

Paul Vincent 01803 722227
paul.vincent@ngs.org.uk

Booklet Co-ordinator
Edward Allhusen 01647 440296
edward@allhusen.co.uk

Assistant County Organisers

East Devon
Peter Wadeley 01297 631210
wadeley@btinternet.com

Exeter
Jenny Phillips 01392 254076
jennypips25@hotmail.co.uk

Exmoor
Anna Whinney 01598 760217
annawhinney@yahoo.co.uk

North Devon
Jo Hynes 01805 804265
hynesjo@gmail.com

North East Devon
Jill Hall 01884 38812
jill22hall@gmail.com

Plymouth
Maria Ashurst 01752 351396
maria.ashurst@ngs.org.uk

South Devon
Sally Vincent 01803 722227
sallyvincent14@gmail.com

Torbay
Gill Treweek 01626 879313
gilltreweek@hotmail.co.uk

West Devon
Alex Meads 01822 615558
ameads2015@outlook.com

Devon is a county of great contrasts in geography and climate, and therefore also in gardening.

The rugged north coast has terraces clinging precariously to hillsides so steep that the faint-hearted would never contemplate making a garden there. But here, and on the rolling hills and deep valleys of Exmoor, despite a constant battle with the elements, National Garden Scheme gardeners create remarkable results by choosing hardy plants that withstand the high winds and salty air.

In the south, in peaceful wooded estuaries and tucked into warm valleys, gardens grow bananas, palms and fruit usually associated with the Mediterranean.

Between these two terrains is a third: Dartmoor, 365 square miles of rugged moorland rising to 2000 feet, presents its own horticultural demands. Typically, here too are many National Garden Scheme gardens.

In idyllic villages scattered throughout this very large county, in gardens large and small, in single manors and in village groups within thriving communities – gardeners pursue their passion.

Below: Silver Street Farm

OPENING DATES

All entries subject to change. For latest information check www.ngs.org.uk

Extended openings are shown at the beginning of the month.

Map locator numbers are shown to the right of each garden name.

February

Snowdrop Festival

Friday 7th
Higher Cherubeer — 43

Friday 14th
Higher Cherubeer — 43

Saturday 15th
The Mount, Delamore — 68
Summers Place — 96

Sunday 16th
Bickham House — 9
The Mount, Delamore — 68

Saturday 22nd
Higher Cherubeer — 43

March

Sunday 1st
East Worlington House — 29

Sunday 8th
East Worlington House — 29

Saturday 21st
Haldon Grange — 35
Holbrook Garden — 46

Sunday 22nd
Bickham House — 9
Haldon Grange — 35
Holbrook Garden — 46

Monday 23rd
NEW Houndspool — 49

Tuesday 24th
NEW Houndspool — 49

Saturday 28th
Haldon Grange — 35
Monkscroft — 65
Samlingstead — 82

Sunday 29th
Haldon Grange — 35
Heathercombe — 41
Monkscroft — 65
Summers Place — 96

April

Saturday 4th
Haldon Grange — 35

Sunday 5th
Haldon Grange — 35
High Garden — 42
Upper Gorwell House — 101

Thursday 9th
Holbrook Garden — 46

Friday 10th
Greatcombe — 34
Holbrook Garden — 46

Saturday 11th
Greatcombe — 34
Haldon Grange — 35
Holbrook Garden — 46
Sidmouth Gardens — 86

Sunday 12th
Andrew's Corner — 4
Greatcombe — 34
Haldon Grange — 35
Holbrook Garden — 46
Kia-Ora Farm & Gardens — 53
Sidmouth Gardens — 86

Monday 13th
Andrew's Corner — 4
Greatcombe — 34
Haldon Grange — 35
Kia-Ora Farm & Gardens — 53
Sidmouth Gardens — 86

Wednesday 15th
Haldon Grange — 35

Saturday 18th
Haldon Grange — 35

Sunday 19th
Bickham House — 9
Haldon Grange — 35
St Merryn — 81
Summers Place — 96

Friday 24th
Holbrook Garden — 46
Sidbury Manor — 85

Saturday 25th
Haldon Grange — 35
Holbrook Garden — 46

Sunday 26th
Haldon Grange — 35
◆ Hotel Endsleigh — 48
Kia-Ora Farm & Gardens — 53
Shapcott Barton Knowstone Estate — 83
Sidbury Manor — 85

Monday 27th
NEW Houndspool — 49

Tuesday 28th
NEW Houndspool — 49

May

Saturday 2nd
Haldon Grange — 35

Sunday 3rd
Chevithorne Barton — 22
Haldon Grange — 35
High Garden — 42
Mothecombe House — 67
South Wood Farm — 89

Wednesday 6th
Haldon Grange — 35

Thursday 7th
Holbrook Garden — 46

Friday 8th
Greatcombe — 34
Haldon Grange — 35
Holbrook Garden — 46
Torview — 99

Saturday 9th
Andrew's Corner — 4
NEW Bradford Tracey House — 13
East Woodlands Farmhouse — 28
Greatcombe — 34
Haldon Grange — 35
Holbrook Garden — 46
Musbury Barton — 69
Spitchwick Manor — 91
Torview — 99

Sunday 10th
Andrew's Corner — 4
Bickham House — 9
NEW Bradford Tracey House — 13
East Woodlands Farmhouse — 28
Greatcombe — 34
Haldon Grange — 35
Heathercombe — 41
Holbrook Garden — 46

Kia-Ora Farm & Gardens — 53
Musbury Barton — 69
Spitchwick Manor — 91
Torview — 99

Friday 15th
Moretonhampstead Gardens — 66

Saturday 16th
Haldon Grange — 35
Kentlands — 52
Kilmington (Shute Road) Gardens — 54
Moretonhampstead Gardens — 66
The Old Vicarage — 73

Sunday 17th
Haldon Grange — 35
Heathercombe — 41
Kentlands — 52
Kilmington (Shute Road) Gardens — 54
Moretonhampstead Gardens — 66
The Old Vicarage — 73
St Merryn — 81
Upper Gorwell House — 101

Wednesday 20th
Haldon Grange — 35

Saturday 23rd
◆ Cadhay — 21
Greatcombe — 34
Haldon Grange — 35
Lewis Cottage — 57
Springfield House — 92

Sunday 24th
Andrew's Corner — 4
◆ Cadhay — 21
Greatcombe — 34
Haldon Grange — 35
Heathercombe — 41
Kia-Ora Farm & Gardens — 53
Lewis Cottage — 57

Monday 25th
Andrew's Corner — 4
◆ Cadhay — 21
Greatcombe — 34
Haldon Grange — 35
NEW Houndspool — 49
Kia-Ora Farm & Gardens — 53
Lewis Cottage — 57

Tuesday 26th
Heathercombe — 41
NEW Houndspool — 49

Wednesday 27th
Heathercombe 41

Thursday 28th
Heathercombe 41

Friday 29th
Heathercombe 41
Little Ash Bungalow 58

Saturday 30th
Goren Farm 33
Haldon Grange 35
Heathercombe 41
Higher Orchard
Cottage 45

Sunday 31st
Blackaton 10
The Bridge Mill 17
Goren Farm 33
Haldon Grange 35
Heathercombe 41
Higher Orchard
Cottage 45

June

Every evening
Goren Farm 33

Tuesday 2nd
Heathercombe 41
Holbrook Garden 46

Wednesday 3rd
Heathercombe 41
Holbrook Garden 46

Thursday 4th
Heathercombe 41
Holbrook Garden 46

Friday 5th
Bridge House 16
Heathercombe 41

Saturday 6th
Abbotskerswell
Gardens 1
Brendon Gardens 15
Dunley House 27
Goren Farm 33
Haldon Grange 35
Heathercombe 41
Riverford Field Kitchen
Garden 80
NEW Silver Street Farm 87
Treetops 100

Sunday 7th
Abbotskerswell
Gardens 1
Brendon Gardens 15

Dunley House 27
Goren Farm 33
Haldon Grange 35
Hayne 40
Heathercombe 41
Higher Cherubeer 43
Kia-Ora Farm &
Gardens 53
NEW Silver Street Farm 87
Treetops 100

Wednesday 10th
Bickham House 9
◆ Fursdon 31

Friday 12th
Bramble Torre 14
Marshall Farm 62
◆ Marwood Hill
Garden 63

Saturday 13th
Bramble Torre 14
Goren Farm 33
Haldon Grange 35
NEW Pounds 76
Regency House 79
Southcombe Barn 90
NEW West Clyst
Barnyard Gardens 104

Sunday 14th
Bramble Torre 14
◆ Docton Mill 26
Goren Farm 33
Haldon Grange 35
Heathercombe 41
Marshall Farm 62
Regency House 79
Southcombe Barn 90
Upper Gorwell
House 101
NEW West Clyst
Barnyard Gardens 104

Monday 15th
NEW Houndspool 49
NEW Pounds 76
Regency House 79

Tuesday 16th
Heathercombe 41
NEW Houndspool 49

Wednesday 17th
Bickham House 9
Heathercombe 41

Thursday 18th
Heathercombe 41

Friday 19th
Greatcombe 34
Heathercombe 41

Saturday 20th
Bovey Tracey Gardens 12
Greatcombe 34
Harbour Lights 38
Heathercombe 41
Lewis Cottage 57
NEW Littlefield 60

Sunday 21st
NEW Barnstaple World
Gardens 7
Bovey Tracey Gardens 12
The Croft 24
Greatcombe 34
Harbour Lights 38
Heathercombe 41
Kia-Ora Farm &
Gardens 53
Lewis Cottage 57
NEW Littlefield 60
St Merryn 81

Tuesday 23rd
Heathercombe 41

Wednesday 24th
Heathercombe 41

Thursday 25th
NEW Brunel Manor 19
Heathercombe 41

Friday 26th
NEW Brunel Manor 19
Heathercombe 41
Socks Orchard 88

Saturday 27th
NEW Decoy Allotment
Field 25
Halscombe Farm 36
Heathercombe 41
NEW 37 Kingskerswell
Rd 55
Socks Orchard 88
Springfield House 92
Teignmouth Gardens 97
NEW Torquay Gardens 98

Sunday 28th
Chevithorne Barton 22
NEW Decoy Allotment
Field 25
Halscombe Farm 36
Heathercombe 41
NEW 37 Kingskerswell
Rd 55
Socks Orchard 88
Teignmouth Gardens 97
NEW Torquay Gardens 98

Tuesday 30th
Heathercombe 41

July

**Every evening from
Tuesday 7th to
Friday 31st**
Goren Farm 33

Wednesday 1st
Goren Farm 33
Heathercombe 41

Thursday 2nd
Heathercombe 41

Friday 3rd
Heathercombe 41

Saturday 4th
East Woodlands
Farmhouse 28
Heathercombe 41
Kentisbeare House 51
Musbury Barton 69
NEW Pangkor House 74

Sunday 5th
East Woodlands
Farmhouse 28
Heathercombe 41
High Garden 42
Kentisbeare House 51
Kia-Ora Farm &
Gardens 53
Musbury Barton 69
NEW Pangkor House 74
NEW Ratclyffe House 78

Thursday 9th
Holbrook Garden 46

Friday 10th
Holbrook Garden 46

Saturday 11th
Cleave Hill 23
Holbrook Garden 46
Shutelake 84

Sunday 12th
Cleave Hill 23
Holbrook Garden 46
◆ Hotel Endsleigh 48
NEW Ratclyffe House 78
Shutelake 84

Wednesday 15th
Bickham House 9

Saturday 18th
Am Brook Meadow 3
The Old Vicarage 73
Squirrels 93

Sunday 19th
Am Brook Meadow 3
The Croft 24

Moretonhampstead Gardens

Halscombe Farm

THE GARDENS

GROUP OPENING

🏠 ABBOTSKERSWELL GARDENS

Abbotskerswell, TQ12 5PN. *2m SW of Newton Abbot town centre. A381 Newton Abbot/Totnes rd. Sharp L turn from NA, R from Totnes. Field parking at Fairfield. Maps available at all gardens and at Church House.* **Sat 6, Sun 7 June (1-5). Combined adm £6, chd free. Home-made teas at Church House. Teas available from 2pm. Maps and tickets from 1pm.**

ABBOTSFORD
Wendy & Phil Grierson.

ABBOTSKERSWELL ALLOTMENTS
Tasha Mundy.

1 ABBOTSWELL COTTAGES
Jane Taylor.

BRIAR COTTAGE
Peggy & David Munden.

FAIRFIELD
Brian Mackness.

4 LABURNUM TERRACE
Ms Mary Down.

10 WILTON WAY
Mrs Margaret Crompton.

16 WILTON WAY
Katy & Chris Yates.

For 2020, Abbotskerswell offers 7 gardens plus the village allotments, ranging from very small to large they offer a wide range of planting styles and innovative landscaping. Cottage gardens, terracing, wild flower areas, a wild garden and specialist plants. Changes to some gardens from 2019. Ideas for every type and size of garden. Visitors are welcome to picnic in the field or arboretum at Fairfield. Sales of plants, garden produce, jams and chutneys and other creative crafts. Disabled access to 3 gardens.

🏠 32 ALLENSTYLE DRIVE

Yelland, Barnstaple, EX31 3DZ. Steve & Dawn Morgan, 01271 861433, fourhungrycats@aol.com, www. devonsubtropicalgarden.co.uk. *5m W of Barnstaple. From Barnstaple take B3233 towards Instow. Through Bickington & Fremington. L at Yelland sign into Allenstyle Rd. 1st R into Allenstyle Dr. Light blue bungalow. From Bideford go past Instow on B3233.* **Sun 30 Aug, Sun 13 Sept (12-5). Adm £4, chd free. Light refreshments. Visits also by arrangement Aug & Sept for groups of up to 30.**

Wander through prairie and South African/Mediterranean inspired plantings to find the gorgeous scents, huge leaves and exotic flowers of the jungle areas and greenhouses. Our 50 x 100 ft garden focuses on ginger lilies, big leaved monsters, brugmansias, bananas and passion flowers (from the hardy to the very tender and scented). Partial wheelchair access due to narrow paths and gravelled areas.

🏠 AM BROOK MEADOW

Torbryan, Ipplepen, Newton Abbot, TQ12 5UP. Jennie and Jethro Marles. *5m from Newton Abbot on A381. Leaving A381 at Causeway Cross go through Ipplepen village, heading towards Broadhempston. Stay on Orley Rd for 3/4 m. At Poole Cross Turn L signed Totnes, then 1st L into Am Brook Meadow.* **Sat 18, Sun 19 July (2-6.30). Adm £5, chd free. Home-made teas.**

Country garden developed over past 12 years to encourage wildlife. Perennial native wildflower meadows, large ponds with ducks and swans, streams and wild areas covering 10 acres are accessible by gravel and grass pathways. Formal courtyard garden with water features and herbaceous borders and prairie-style planting together with poultry and bees close by. Wheelchair access to most gravel path areas is good, but grass pathways in larger wildflower meadow are weather dependent.

🏠 ANDREW'S CORNER

Skaigh Lane, Belstone, EX20 1RD. Robin & Edwina Hill, 01837 840332, edwinarobinhill@outlook.com, www.andrewscorner.garden. *3m E of Okehampton. Signed to Belstone from A30. In village turn L, signed Skaigh. Follow NGS signs. Garden approx 1/2 m on R. Visitors may be dropped off at house, parking in nearby field.* **Sun 12, Mon 13 Apr, Sat 9, Sun 10, Sun 24, Mon 25 May (2-5). Adm £5, chd free.**

Home-made teas. Visits also by arrangement Feb to Oct.
Well established, wildlife friendly, well labelled plantsman's garden in stunning high moorland setting. Variety of garden habitats incl woodland areas and pond; wide range of unusual trees, shrubs, herbaceous plants for yr-round effect with blue poppies, rhododendrons, bulbs and maples; spectacular autumn colour. Family friendly, with quiz sheet, fairy doors, playhouse, fruit, vegetables and chickens. Wheelchair access difficult when wet.

🏠 ASH PARK

East Prawle, Kingsbridge, TQ7 2BX. Chris & Cathryn Vanderspar. *Ash Park, East Prawle South Devon. Take A379 Kingsbridge to Dartmouth, at Frogmore after PH R to East Prawle, after 1.1m L, in 1.4m at Cousins Cross bear R (middle of 3 rds). In village head to Prawle Point.* **Sat 5, Sun 6 Sept (11-5). Adm £5, chd free. Home-made teas.**

In a stunning location, with 180° view of the sea, Ash Park nestles at the foot of the escarpment, with 3½ acres of sub-tropical gardens, paths to explore, woodland glades, ponds and hidden seating areas. In Sept; cannas, hydrangeas, ginger lilies, salvias and dahlias should be at their best. Partial access for wheelchairs. Access is possible up a drive to the teas, but the garden itself has no hard paths and the lawns are sloping.

🏠 AVENUE COTTAGE

Ashprington, Totnes, TQ9 7UT. Mr Richard Pitts & Mr David Sykes, 01803 732769, richard.pitts@btinternet.com, www.avenuecottage.com. *.3m SW of Totnes. A381 Totnes to Kingsbridge for 1m; L for Ashprington, into village then L by PH. Garden 1/4 m on R after Sharpham Estate sign.* **Visits by arrangement for groups of up to 20. Adm £4, chd free. Home-made teas by arrangement.**

11 acres of mature and young trees and shrubs. Once part of an C18 landscape, the neglected garden has been cleared and replanted over the last 30 yrs. Good views of Sharpham House and R Dart. Azaleas and hydrangeas are a feature.

GROUP OPENING

7 NEW BARNSTAPLE WORLD GARDENS

Anne Crescent, Barnstaple, EX31 3AF. Gavin Hendry. *31 Anne Cres L off Old Torrington Rd into Phillips Ave then follow signs: 21 Becklake Close from A3125 turn into Roundswell on Westermoor Way then signs: 25 Elmfield Rd from B3233 L at Bickington PO.* **Sun 21 June (1-5). Combined adm £5, chd free. Cream teas. Japanese snacks.**

NEW 31 ANNE CRESCENT

Mr Gavin Hendry, 07879 614511, gavhendry9676@hotmail.co.uk. **Visits also by arrangement May to Oct for groups of up to 10.**

NEW 21 BECKLAKE CLOSE

Karen & Steve Moss, 07795 201249, karenthedancer@icloud.com. **Visits also by arrangement June to Dec.**

NEW 25 ELMFIELD ROAD

Nigel & Carol Oates.

Explore three very different spaces, one focusing on everything Japanese, one on tropical plants, and one to interest the plantsman. 31 Anne Crescent: North Devon's Elche. Small urban L-shaped tropical garden complete with wide variety of palms, agaves, bananas, cacti, tree ferns and delightful koi pond loaded with a wide variety of colourful koi. 21 Becklake Close: All things Japanese. 25 Elmfield Road: Front: mixed borders and gravel area containing hardy palms and Mount Etna Broom. Rear: L shaped patio leading to lawn edged by mixed borders of unusual plants. The overall impression is of a colourful but calm place, enhanced by the sound of the stream trickling past the end of the garden. A garden to attract those interested in plants with a difference.

🌸 ☕

---

8 BICKHAM COTTAGE

Kenn, Exeter, EX6 7XL. Steve Eyre, 01392 833964, bickham@live.co.uk. *6m S of Exeter. 1m off A38. Leave A38 at Kennford Services, follow signs to Kenn. 1st R in village, follow lane for 3/4m to end of no through rd.* **Sun 4 Oct (2-5). Home-made teas. Visits also by arrangement Sept to Nov.**
Small cottage garden divided into separate areas by old stone walls and hedge banks. Front garden with mainly South African bulbs and plants. Lawn surrounded by borders with agapanthus, eucomis, crocosmia, diorama etc. Stream garden with primulas. Pond with large Koi carp. Glasshouses with National Collection of Nerine sarniensis and cultivars, 3500 pots in excess of 450 varieties. Visitors are also welcome to wander around Bickham House gardens.

♿ 🌸 🚻 NPC ☕

9 BICKHAM HOUSE

Kenn, Exeter, EX6 7XL. Julia Tremlett, 01392 832671, jandjtremlett@hotmail.com. *6m S of Exeter, 1m off A38. Leave A38 at Kennford Services, follow signs to Kenn, 1st R in village, follow lane for 3/4m to end of no through rd.* **Sun 16 Feb, Sun 22 Mar, Sun 19 Apr, Sun 10 May, Wed 10, Wed 17 June, Wed 15, Wed 22 July, Sun 9 Aug, Sat 5, Sun 6 Sept (2-5). Adm £6, chd free. Home-made teas. Visits also by arrangement Apr to Sept.**
8 acres with borders, mature trees. Hellebores and snowdrops, small named collection of snowdrops at Bickham Cottage. Formal parterre with lily pond. Walled garden with colourful profusion of vegetables and flowers. Palm tree avenue leading to millennium summerhouse. Late summer colour with dahlias, crocosmia, agapanthus etc. Cactus and succulent greenhouse. Pelargonium collection. Lakeside walk. WC, disabled access.

♿ 🐕 🌸 🚻 ☕

10 BLACKATON

Chagford, Newton Abbot, TQ13 8HW. Anthony and Kit Newsome. *From Whiddon Down take A382 S; after 1 1/2m R to Gidleigh, after 3/4m R at white farmhouse, over staggered Xrd and straight on to bottom of hill. From Chagford follow signs to Thowleigh.* **Sun 31 May (1.30-5). Adm £5, chd free. Home-made teas.**
6 acre garden lying in a high wooded valley below Providence. Moorland trout and salmon stream flows over weir and beneath Monet bridge as it tumbles down beside sloping lawns. Borders at top of garden, mature rhododendrons and azaleas provide a swathe of colour. Mixed shrubs and perennials below 2 terraces. Through the orchard, a vegetable garden and small Japanese Zen garden. Partially surrounded by Woodland Trust land creating an extension to the existing garden. Very rural. Gravel drive and level paths for disabled access. Well behaved dogs on leads welcome.

♿ 🐕 ☕

Stone Lane Gardens

◆ **BLACKPOOL GARDENS**
Dartmouth, TQ6 0RG. Sir
Geoffrey Newman, 01803 771801,
beach@blackpoolsands.co.uk,
www.blackpoolsands.co.uk. *3m
SW of Dartmouth. From Dartmouth
follow brown signs to Blackpool
Sands on A379. Entry tickets,
parking, toilets and refreshments
available at Blackpool Sands. Sorry,
no dogs permitted.*
Carefully restored C19 subtropical
plantsman's garden with collection
of mature and newly planted tender
and unusual trees, shrubs and carpet
of spring flowers. Paths and steps
lead gradually uphill and above the
Captain's seat offering fine coastal
views. Recent plantings follow the S
hemisphere theme with callistemons,
pittosporums, acacias and buddlejas.
Gardens open 1st Apr - 30th Sept
(10-4pm) weather permitting.
Admission: adult £4, children free.
Group visits by arrangement.

Bickham House

GROUP OPENING

BOVEY TRACEY GARDENS
Bovey Tracey, TQ13 9NA. *6m
N of Newton Abbot. Gateway to
Dartmoor. Take A382 to Bovey
Tracey. Car parking at town car parks
and on some roads for 3 near-central
gardens, on roads for 3 towards
Brimley.* **Sat 20, Sun 21 June (1.30-
5.30). Combined adm £6, chd
free. Home-made teas at Gleam
Tor. Wine at Ashwell.**

ASHWELL
TQ13 9EJ. Jeanette Pearce.
 **FOOTLANDS**
TQ13 9JX. Jon & Helen Elliott.
GLEAM TOR
TQ13 9DH. Gillian & Colin Liddy.
PARKE VIEW
TQ13 9AD. Peter & Judy Hall.
2 REDWOODS
TQ13 9YG. Mrs Julia Mooney.
23 STORRS CLOSE
TQ13 9HR. Roger Clark & Chie
Nakatani.

Bovey Tracey is a pretty cob
and granite built town nestling in
Dartmoor foothills. Ashwell: large,
steeply sloping 1840s stone walled
garden (some steps but lovely views)
with vineyard, orchard, soft fruit,
vegetables, colourful mixed borders
and wild flower areas. Footlands:
newly redesigned round established,
unusual and colourful shrubs and
conifers, with perennials, grasses
and young trees. Gleam Tor: lots
to see - long colourful herbaceous
border, white garden, wild flower
meadow, prairie planting, interesting
'memory patio' (and Colin's legendary
cakes and cream teas). Parke View:
romantic 1 acre town centre garden.
Meandering old stone walls lead to
separate planted areas and colour
themed herbaceous borders. 2
Redwoods: mature trees, Dartmoor
leat, unusual fernery, sunny gravel
garden and acid loving spring and
summer shrubs. 23 Storrs Close:
plantsman's small garden full of
uncommon trees, shrubs, herbaceous
and bulbous plants, many rare
examples from China and Japan.
Partial wheelchair access, none at
Ashwell and Storrs Close.

We open the gates
to the nation's best
gardens, offering a
relaxing, memorable
and affordable
day out. A perfect
experience to share
with friends and
family.

🔟3️⃣ NEW BRADFORD TRACEY HOUSE

Witheridge, Tiverton, EX16 8QG. Elizabeth Wilkinson. *20 minutes from Tiverton. Postcode will get you to thatched lodge at bottom of drive which has 2 bouncing hares on the top.* **Sat 9, Sun 10 May (1.30-5.30). Adm £5, chd free. Home-made cakes including gluten free and low sugar served in lovely coach house with lashings of top notch tea! Cakes and cookie boxes to take away.**

A pleasure garden set around a Regency hunting lodge combining flowers with grasses, shrubs and huge trees in a natural and joyful space. It is planted for productivity and sustainability giving harvests of wonderful flowers, fruits, herbs and vegetables (and weeds!). There are beautiful views over the lake, forest walks, deep blowsy borders, an ancient wisteria and an oriental treehouse garden. Mostly grass, gravel and stepping stones so not suitable for wheelchairs but disabled parking up at the house.

🔟4️⃣ BRAMBLE TORRE

Dittisham, nr Dartmouth, TQ6 0HZ. Paul & Sally Vincent, www.rainingsideways.com. *³⁄₄ m from Dittisham. Leave A3122 at Sportsman's Arms. Drop down into village, at Red Lion turn L to Cornworthy. Continue ³⁄₄ m, Bramble Torre straight ahead. Follow signs to Car Park.* **Fri 12, Sat 13, Sun 14 June (2-6). Adm £5, chd free. Cream teas.**

Set in 30 acres of farmland, the 3 acre garden follows a rambling stream through a steep valley: lily pond, herbaceous borders, roses, camellias, lawns & shrubs, a formal herb and vegetable garden. All are dominated by a huge embothrium glowing scarlet in late spring against a sometimes blue sky! Well behaved dogs on leads welcome. Partial wheelchair access, parts of garden very steep and uneven. Tea area with wheelchair access and excellent garden view.

GROUP OPENING

🔟5️⃣ BRENDON GARDENS

Brendon, Lynton, EX35 6PU. 01598 741343, lalindevon@yahoo.co.uk. *1m S of A39 North Devon coast rd between Porlock and Lynton.* **Sat 6, Sun 7 June, Sat 29, Sun 30 Aug (12-5). Combined adm £5, chd free. Light refreshments. Higher Tippacott Farm serves light lunches, home-made cakes & cream teas. W.C. Visits also by arrangement May to Sept.**

BRENDON HOUSE
Pat Young & Martin Longhurst, patbrendonhouse@ outlook.com. **Visits also by arrangement May to Sept.**

1 DEERCOMBE COTTAGES
Valerie & Stephen Exley, Valerie.exley@btinternet.com. **Visits also by arrangement May to Sept.**

HALL FARM
Karen & Nick Wall, kwall741604@btinternet.com. **Visits also by arrangement May to Sept.**

HIGHER TIPPACOTT FARM
Angela & Malcolm Percival, 01598 741343, lalindevon@yahoo.co.uk. **Visits also by arrangement May to Sept.**

NEW LOWER WILSHAM COTTAGE
Jane Glover, janeglover17@icloud.com. **Visits also by arrangement May to Sept.**

Stunning part of Exmoor National Park. All gardens have lovely views. Excellent walking along river and between gardens; map online. Brendon Hse: C18 in idyllic village location. Established front garden, kitchen garden and greenhouse. Emphasis on recycling and gardening in harmony with wildlife. 1 Deercombe Cottages: delightful small garden in steeply wooded valley overlooking river, ditched stone walls providing a variety of levels to display planting rich in contrasting foliage and variety of perennials. Hall Farm:(please check online for availability, thankyou)C16 longhouse set in 2 acres of tranquil mature gardens, with lake and wild area beyond. Rheas, chickens, rare-

breed cattle & black bees. H. Tippacott Farm: 950ft alt. on moor, overlooking own idyllic valley with stream and pond. Sunny levels of planting and lawns. Organic. L.Wilsham Cottage: Medium-sized cottage garden, small fernery, ponds and raised flower beds with wide variety of interesting and unusual plants. Plants, produce, books and bric-a-brac for sale.

🐕 ❋ ☕

🔟6️⃣ BRIDGE HOUSE

2 Church Street, Dawlish, EX7 9AU. Annette Everett. *From A379 through Dawlish follow signs to Hospital, with Hosp on L carry on to T junction, turn R, Bridge House on corner of Church St opp Swan pub.* **Fri 5 June (10-2). Adm £4, chd free. Home-made teas.**

Bridge House enjoys a quiet secluded 3 acre garden at the edge of Dawlish. The beautifully landscaped garden has wide lawns and deep colourful herbaceous borders on one side of the trout stream which runs through the grounds into Dawlish Water. An ornate bridge takes visitors to the other side where many mature trees and secluded seating areas can be found. Wheelchair access to most areas.

& ❋ ☕

🔟7️⃣ THE BRIDGE MILL

Mill Rd, Bridgerule, Holsworthy, EX22 7EL. Rosie & Alan Beat, www.thebridgemill.org.uk. *In Bridgerule village on R Tamar between Bude and Holsworthy. Between the chapel by river bridge and church at top of hill. Garden is at bottom of hill opp Short and Abbott agricultural engineers. See website for detailed directions.* **Sun 31 May (11-5). Adm £4, chd free. Home-made teas. Refreshments in garden if fine or in stable if wet! Plenty of dry seating.**

1-acre organic gardens around mill house and restored working water mill. Small cottage garden; herb garden with medicinal and dye plants; productive fruit and vegetable garden, and wild woodland and water garden by mill. 16 acre smallholding: lake and riverside walks, wildflower meadows, friendly livestock, local crafts. Exhibition of embroideries by Linda Chilton. The historic water mill was restored to working order in April 2012 and in 2017 was awarded a plaque by the Society for the Protection of Ancient Buildings. For

Sutton Mead

other opening times and information, please see website. Wheelchair access to some of gardens. WC with access for wheelchairs.

& ✿ ⊟ ☕

18 BROCTON COTTAGE
Pear Tree, Ashburton, Newton Abbot, TQ13 7QZ. Mrs Naomi Hindley. *¼ m from A38. From A38 take Ashburton Peartree junction. Turn R towards Princetown, then 1st L towards Buckfastleigh. Park on road or at Dartmoor Lodge Hotel (lunches and refreshments available). Short walk to garden entrance.* **Sat 12, Sun 13 Sept (2-5). Adm £4, chd free. Home-made teas.**
1.3 acres recovered from neglect, combining established planting with newly developed areas. New orchard, woodland, ponds and productive area linked to established herbaceous borders and shrubberies.

The woodland area being developed was inspired by the winter garden at Anglesea Abbey. Latest project is a new cutting garden. Views over Devon countryside. Dogs on leads only please. Gravelled drive but there is wheelchair access to patio area. Garden can be explored without using steps.

& 🐕 ✿ ☕

19 NEW BRUNEL MANOR
Teignmouth Road, Torquay, TQ1 4SF. Woodlands House of Prayer, 01803 329333, info@brunelmanor.com, www.brunelmanor.com. *satnav postcode TQ1 4SB north outskirts of Torquay, on A379. No. 22 bus Torquay/Teignmouth.* **Thur 25, Fri 26 June (11-4). Adm £4, chd free. Tea Room: fairtrade, speciality teas and coffees, delicious home-made cakes,**

cream teas, light lunches. Visits also by arrangement Mar to Sept for groups of 5+. Guided tour available.
Explore Brunel's hidden kingdom - 9 acres of gardens and woodland, created in 1850s by Victorian Engineer Isambard Kingdom Brunel. Wander through the woods to see Brunel's original exotic trees and garden features, potter around colourful herbaceous borders, take time to be still in the prayer garden, or relax on the terrace with a cuppa and enjoy the extensive views across Torbay. Dogs on leads welcome. Also - children's adventure play area, Brunel's Hidden Kingdom indoor exhibition and guided tours. Sloping site with steps and steep paths, ramped access to upper parts of woodland and gardens. Disabled toilets and parking available.

& 🐕 ⊟ 🚌 ☕

20 ◆ BURROW FARM GARDENS

Dalwood, Axminster, EX13 7ET. Mary & John Benger, 01404 831285, enquiries@burrowfarmgardens.co.uk, www.burrowfarmgardens.co.uk. *3½ m W of Axminster. From A35 turn N at Taunton Xrds then follow brown signs.*

Beautiful 13 acre garden with unusual trees, shrubs and herbaceous plants. Traditional summerhouse looks towards lake and ancient oak woodland with rhododendrons and azaleas. Early spring interest and superb autumn colour. The more formal Millennium garden features a rill. Anniversary garden featuring late summer perennials and grasses. A photographer's dream. Open 1st April – 31 Oct (10 – 6). Adm £8. Café and gift shop. Various events incl spring and summer plant fair and open air theatre held at garden each yr. Visit events page on Burrow Farm Gardens website for more details.

21 ◆ CADHAY

Ottery St Mary, EX11 1QT. Rupert Thistlethwayte, 01404 813511, jayne@cadhay.org.uk, www.cadhay.org.uk. *1m NW of Ottery St Mary. On B3176 between Ottery St Mary and Fairmile. From E exit A30 at Iron Bridge. From W exit A30 at Patteson's Cross, follow brown signs for Cadhay.* **For NGS: Sat 23, Sun 24, Mon 25 May, Sun 30, Mon 31 Aug (2-5). Adm £5, chd £1. Our tea room serves a range of home-made cakes and cream teas. For other opening times and information, please phone, email or visit garden website.**

Tranquil 2 acre setting for Tudor manor house. 2 medieval fish ponds surrounded by rhododendrons, gunnera, hostas and flag iris. Roses, clematis, lilies and hellebores surround walled water garden. 120ft herbaceous border walk informally planted with cottage garden perennials and annuals. Walled kitchen gardens have been turned into allotments and old apple store is now tea room. Gravel paths.

22 CHEVITHORNE BARTON

Chevithorne, Tiverton, EX16 7QB. Chris McDonald (Head Gardener), chevithornebarton.co.uk. *3m NE of Tiverton. Follow yellow signs from A361, A396 or Sampford Peverell.* **Sun 3 May, Sun 28 June, Sun 2, Sun 30 Aug (2-5.30). Adm £5, chd free. Cream teas. Home-made cakes. Tea area undercover.**

Newly planted areas complement walled garden, summer borders and woodland of rare trees and shrubs. In spring, garden features a large collection of magnolias, camellias, and rhododendrons. Home to National Collection of Quercus (Oaks) comprising over 440 different taxa. From time to time within the gardens are a flock of Jacob sheep and rare breed woodland pigs.

NPC

23 CLEAVE HILL

Membury, Axminster, EX13 7AJ. Andy & Penny Pritchard, 01404 881437, penny@tonybenger.com. *4m NW of Axminster. From Membury Village, follow rd down valley. 1st R after Lea Hill B&B, last house on drive, approx 1m.* **Sat 11, Sun 12 July (11-5). Adm £4, chd free. Light lunches, cream teas and cakes. Visits also by arrangement for groups of 5+.**

Artistic garden in pretty village situated on edge of Blackdown Hills. Cottage style garden, planted to provide all season structure, texture and colour. Designed around pretty thatched house and old stone barns. Wonderful views, attractive vegetable garden and orchard, wild flower meadow.

Regency House

24 THE CROFT

Yarnscombe, Barnstaple,
EX31 3LW. Sam & Margaret Jewell,
01769 560535. *8m S of Barnstaple,
10m SE of Bideford, 12m W of
South Molton, 4m NE of Torrington.
From A377, turn W opp Chapelton
railway stn. Follow Yarnscombe
signs for 3m. From B3232, ¼ m N
of Huntshaw Cross TV mast, turn
E and follow Yarnscombe signs
for 2m. Parking in village hall car
park.* **Sun 21 June, Sun 19 July,
Sun 16 Aug (2-6). Adm £4, chd
free. Cream teas. Home-made
sponges and meringues. Visits
also by arrangement June to Aug
for groups of 5+. Donation to North
Devon Animal Ambulance.**
1 acre plantswoman's garden
featuring exotic Japanese garden
with tea house, koi carp pond and
cascading stream, tropical garden
with exotic shrubs and perennials,
herbaceous borders with unusual
plants and shrubs, bog garden with
collection of irises, astilbes and
moisture-loving plants, duck pond.
Exotic borders, new beds around
duck pond and bog area, large
collection of rare and unusual plants.
2019 was our 30th year of opening
for the NGS. Not all areas wheelchair
accessible.
占 ⽝ ❀ 🚌 ☕

25 NEW DECOY ALLOTMENT FIELD

Bladon Close, Newton Abbot,
TQ12 1WA. Newton Abbot Town
Council, nadcaa.org.uk/. *From
Sainsburys at Penn Inn go past
Keyberry Hotel, next L into Bladon
Close, an iron gate entrance to
allotment field at top of the cul-de-
sac, which is next to Decoy Primary
School.* **Sat 27, Sun 28 June
(1-4). Combined adm with 37
Kingskerswell Rd £5, chd free.**
Within 2 acres are hundreds of
allotments, each of them individual to
their owners. Beautiful wildlife areas,
unusual plants, diverse habitats for
flora and fauna and a shop with
garden plants and honey from local
bees. Many different nationalities
and people with different abilities are
involved in working on the allotments.
Also open is the nearby garden of
one of our allotment holders. Some
of the paths are uneven on the field
with steep inclines in places. The
other garden nearby does not have
wheelchair access.
占 ⽝ ❀ ☕

26 ◆ DOCTON MILL

Lymebridge, Hartland,
EX39 6EA. Lana & John
Borrett, 01237 441369,
docton.mill@btconnect.com,
www.doctonmill.co.uk. *8m W of
Clovelly. Follow brown tourist signs
on A39 nr Clovelly.* **For NGS: Sun 14
June (10-5). Adm £4.50, chd free.
Light refreshments. Cream teas
and light lunches available all
day. For other opening times and
information, please phone, email or
visit garden website.**
Situated in stunning valley location.
Garden surrounds original mill
pond and the microclimate created
within the wooded valley enables
tender species to flourish. Recent
planting of herbaceous, stream and
summer garden give variety through
the season. Regret not suitable for
wheelchairs.
⽝ ❀ ☕

27 DUNLEY HOUSE

Bovey Tracey, Newton Abbot,
TQ13 9PW. Mr & Mrs F Gilbert. *2m
E of Bovey Tracey on rd to Hennock.
From A38 going W turn off slip
rd R towards Chudleigh Knighton
on B3344, in village follow yellow
signs to Dunley House. From A38
eastwards turn off on Chudleigh K
slip rd L and follow signs.* **Sat 6, Sun
7 June (2-5). Adm £5, chd free.
Home-made teas.**
9 acre garden set among mature
oaks, sequoiadendrons and a huge
liquidambar started from a wilderness
in mid eighties. Rhododendrons,
camellias and over 40 different
magnolias. Arboretum, walled garden
with borders and fruit and vegetables,
rose garden and new enclosed
garden with lily pond. Large pond
renovated 2016 with new plantings.
Woodland walk around perimeter of
property.
占 ⽝ ❀ ☕

28 EAST WOODLANDS FARMHOUSE

Alverdiscott, Newton Tracey,
Barnstaple, EX31 3PP. Ed &
Heather Holt, 07342 632211,
heatherholtexmoor@gmail.com.
*5m NE of Great Torrington, 5m S of
Barnstaple, off B3232. From Great
Torrington turn R into single track
rd before Alverdiscott; and from
Barnstaple turn L after Alverdiscott.
1m down rd R fork at Y-junction.*
**Sat 9, Sun 10 May, Sat 4, Sun
5 July (2-5). Adm £5, chd free.**

Home-made teas. Gluten free
cakes available. Visits also by
arrangement May to Aug for
groups of 10+.
East Woodlands is a beautiful RHS
inspired and designed garden full of
rooms packed with plants, shrubs
and trees. Enjoy the spectacular
bamboos, flowing grasses, colourful
roses and Mediterranean, cottage and
bog gardens (unfenced pond), all set
in an acre looking out over N Devon
countryside. Occasional live music.
Lots of seating areas and vintage
crockery teas served. Plants for sale.
Partial wheelchair access.
占 ❀ ☕

29 EAST WORLINGTON HOUSE

East Worlington, Witheridge,
Crediton, EX17 4TS. Barnabas
& Campie Hurst-Bannister. *In
centre of East Worlington, 2m W of
Witheridge. From Witheridge Square
R to East Worlington. After 1½ m R
at T-junction in Drayford, then L to
Worlington. After ½ m L at T-junction.
200 yds on L. Parking nearby,
disabled parking at house.* **Sun 1,
Sun 8 Mar (1.30-5). Adm £4, chd
free. Cream teas in thatched
parish hall next to house.**
Thousands of crocuses. In 2 acre
garden, set in lovely position with
views down valley to Little Dart river,
these spectacular crocuses have
spread over many years through the
garden and into the neighbouring
churchyard. Dogs on leads please.
占 ⽝ ❀ ☕

30 FOXHOLE COMMUNITY GARDEN

Dartington, Totnes,
TQ9 6EB. Zoe Jong, www.
foxholecommunitygarden.org.uk.
*On the Dartington Estate near the
Foxhole Centre at Old School Farm.*
**Sun 19 July (10-4). Adm £4, chd
free. Home-made teas.**
Beautiful community garden and
orchard on the Dartington Estate.
Since 2016 it has been developed
to provide a garden space for all
abilities. Nature trail and garden crafts
for children, talks and walks run on
organic, no-dig low maintenance
principles. Raised veg beds, orchard,
herb, wildlife, wildflower, cutting flower,
pond and potager planting areas. Full
of colour, produce and wildlife. Parking
directly outside the garden, main area
of the garden accessible by wheelchair
as is the toilet.
占 ⽝ ❀ ☕

31 ◆ FURSDON

Cadbury, Thorverton, Exeter, EX5 5JS. Oliver and Emily Fursdon, 01392 860860, admin@fursdon.co.uk, www.fursdon.co.uk. *2m N of Thorverton. From Tiverton S on A396. Take A3072 at Bickleigh towards Crediton. L after 2½ m signed to Fursdon. From Exeter N on A396. L to Thorverton and R in centre of village opp Thorverton Arms.* **For NGS: Wed 10 June, Wed 26 Aug (2-5). Adm £4.50, chd free. Cream teas in the Coach Hall from 2pm, also home-made cakes. Tea proceeds not for NGS. For other opening times and information, please phone, email or visit garden website.**

Beautiful gardens surround Fursdon House, home of the Fursdon family for 7 centuries. A lovely hillside setting, with extensive views S over parkland and beyond. Sheltered by house, hedges and cob walls, there are terraces of fragrant roses, herbs and perennials in mixed traditional and contemporary planting. Woodland walk, seasonal wild flowers and pond in meadow garden. Fursdon House open for guided tours on NGS days (separate entrance fee not for NGS). Some steep slopes, grass and gravel paths.

🐕 🚐 🛏 ☕ 🌿

32 THE GATE HOUSE

Lee, EX34 8LR. Mrs H Booker, 01271 862409. *3m W of Ilfracombe. Park in Lee village car park. Take lane alongside The Grampus PH. Garden approx 30 mtres past inn buildings. Not open in school holidays open most days wise check via booker@ loveleebay the day before.* **Visits by arrangement Apr to Sept for groups of up to 20. No children under 7. Adm by donation.**

Described by many visitors as a peaceful paradise, this streamside garden incl National Collection of over 100 rodgersia (at their best end of June), interesting herbaceous areas, patio gardens with semi-hardy exotics, many unusual mature trees and shrubs and large organic vegetable garden. If you are making a special journey check I'm open. Level gravel paths.

♿ 🐕 NPC ☕

33 GOREN FARM

Broadhayes, Stockland, Honiton, EX14 9EN. Julian Pady, 07770 694646, gorenfarm@hotmail.com, www.goren.co.uk. *6m E of Honiton, 6m W of Axminster. Go to the Stockland television mast. Head 100 metres North signed from Ridge Cross.* **Every Sat and Sun 30 May to 14 June (10-6). Light refreshments. Evening openings Sat 30 May to Wed 1 July (6-10). Evening openings Tue 7 July to Fri 31 July (6-10). Adm £5, chd free. Teas on farmhouse lawn. Home-made cakes and light lunches on open weekends made with local produce from the farm. Visits also by arrangement May to July.**

Wander through 50 acres of natural species rich wild flower meadows. Easy access foot paths cut as well as signs. Dozens of varieties of wild flowers and grasses. Thousands of orchids from early June and butterflies July. Stunning views of Blackdown Hills. Georgian house and walled gardens, guided walks 10.30 and 2.30 on open weekends. Species information signs and picnic tables around the fields. Farm café and shop selling seeds and home grown produce and some hot food. Partial wheelchair access to meadows. Dogs welcome on a lead only, please clean up after your pet.

♿ 🐕 ☕

34 GREATCOMBE

Holne, Newton Abbot, TQ13 7SP. Robbie & Sarah Richardson. *Michelcombe, Holne, TQ13 7SP. 4m NW Ashburton via Holne Bridge and Holne Village. 4m NE Buckfastleigh via Scorriton. Narrow lanes. Large car park adjacent to garden.* **Fri 10, Sat 11, Sun 12, Mon 13 Apr, Fri 8, Sat 9, Sun 10, Sat 23, Sun 24, Mon 25 May, Fri 19, Sat 20, Sun 21 June, Fri 31 July, Sat 1, Sun 2 Aug (1-5). Adm £4, chd free. Home-made teas.**

We thought we'd let our visitors describe the garden. "A truly beautiful, tranquil garden with unusual plants and exciting use of colour. A garden to visit again and again! Fantastic Cream Tea by the stream!", "Enchanting, magical place. One of our favourites which has given us much inspiration. A real asset to the NGS. Fabulous home-made cake and scones too!" Artist's Studio featuring brightly coloured acrylic paintings,

prints and cards all available to purchase along with ornamental metal plant supports in all sizes and shapes and 'Made by Robbie' metal artefacts. Regret only partial wheelchair access.

🐕 ❄ ☕ 🌿

35 HALDON GRANGE

Dunchideock, Exeter, EX6 7YE. Ted Phythian, 01392 832349. *5m SW of Exeter. From A30 through Ide Village to Dunchideock 5m. L to Lord Haldon, Haldon Grange is next L. From A38 (S) turn L on top of Haldon Hill follow Dunchideock signs, R at village centre to Lord Haldon.* **Sat 21, Sun 22, Sat 28, Sun 29 Mar, Sat 4, Sun 5, Sat 11, Sun 12, Mon 13, Wed 15, Sat 18, Sun 19, Sat 25, Sun 26 Apr, Sat 2, Sun 3, Wed 6, Fri 8, Sat 9, Sun 10, Sat 16, Sun 17, Wed 20, Sat 23, Sun 24, Mon 25, Sat 30, Sun 31 May, Sat 6, Sun 7, Sat 13, Sun 14 June (1-5). Adm £5, chd free. Home-made teas. Visits also by arrangement Apr to June for groups of 10+.**

Peaceful, well established 12 acre garden some dating back to 1770's. This hidden gem boasts one of the largest collections of rhododendrons, azaleas, magnolias and camellias. Interspersed with mature and rare trees and complimented by a lake and cascading ponds. 5 acre arboretum, large lilac circle, wisteria pergola with views over Exeter and Woodbury complete this family run treasure. Wheelchair access to main parts of garden.

♿ ❄ ☕ 🌿

36 HALSCOMBE FARM

Halscombe Lane, Ide, Exeter, EX2 9TQ. Prof J Rawlings. *From Exeter go through Ide to mini r'about take 2nd exit and continue to L turn into Halscombe Lane.* **Sat 27, Sun 28 June (2-5). Adm £4, chd free. Home-made teas. Donation to The Friends of Exeter Cathedral.**

Farmhouse garden created over last 7 yrs. Large collection of old roses and peonies, long and colourful mixed borders, knot garden, productive fruit cage and vegetable garden all set within a wonderful borrowed landscape.

🐕 ❄ ☕ 🌿

37 HAMBLYN'S COOMBE

Dittisham, Dartmouth, TQ6 0HE. Bridget McCrum, 01803 722228, mccrum.sculpt@waitrose.com, www.bridgetmccrum.com. *3m N of Dartmouth. From A3122 L to Dittisham. In village R at Red Lion, The Level, then Rectory Lane, past River Farm to Hamblyn's Coombe.* **Visits by arrangement Mar to Sept for groups of up to 20. Adm £5, chd free.**

7 acre garden with stunning views across the river to Greenway House and sloping steeply to R Dart at bottom of garden. Extensive planting of trees and shrubs with unusual design features accompanying Bridget McCrum's stone carvings and bronzes. Wild flower meadow and woods. Good rhododendrons and camellias, ferns and bamboos, acers and hydrangeas. Exceptional autumn colour. No wheelchair access.

38 HARBOUR LIGHTS

Horns Cross, Bideford, EX39 5DW. Brian & Faith Butler, 01237 451627, brian.nfu@gmail.com. *7m W of Bideford, 3m E of Clovelly. On main A39, so easy to find and access, between Bideford and Clovelly, halfway between Hoops Inn and Bucks Cross.* **Sat 20, Sun 21 June (11-6). Adm £4, chd free. Home-made teas. Light lunches, home-made cakes and cream teas, or perhaps a glass of wine. Visits also by arrangement June to Aug for groups of 10+. If you want something different to a 'normal' garden, then come here!**

½ acre colourful garden with Lundy views. A garden of wit, humour, unusual ideas, artwork, volcano and many surprises. Water features, shrubs, foliage area, grasses in an unusual setting, fernery, bonsai and polytunnel, time saving ideas. You will never have seen a garden like this! Superb conservatory for cream teas. Free leaflet. We like our visitors to leave with a smile! Child friendly. A 'must visit' interactive garden. Intriguing artwork of various kinds, original plantings and ideas.

39 THE HAVEN

Wembury Road, Hollacombe, Wembury, South Hams, PL9 0DQ. Mrs S Norton & Mr J Norton, 01752 862149, suenorton1@hotmail.co.uk. *20mins from Plymouth city centre. Use A379 Plymouth to Kingsbridge Rd. At Elburton r'about follow signs to Wembury. Parking on roadside. Bus stop nearby on Wembury Rd. Route 48 from Plymouth.* **Visits by arrangement Mar to May for groups of 5 to 20.**

½ acre sloping plantsman's garden in South Hams AONB. Tearoom and seating areas. 2 ponds. Substantial collection of large flowering Asiatic and hybrid tree magnolias. Large collection of camellias including camellia reticulata. Rare dwarf, weeping and slow growing conifers. Daphnes, early azaleas and rhododendrons, spring bulbs and hellebores. Wheelchair access to top part of garden.

Fursdon

40 HAYNE

Zeal Monachorum, Crediton, EX17 6DE. Tim & Milla Herniman, www.haynedevon.co.uk. *Located ½m S of Zeal Monachorum. From Zeal Monachorum, keeping church on L, drive through village. Continue on this road for ⅓m, garden drive is 1st entrance on R.* **Sun 7 June (2-6). Adm £4, chd free. Home-made teas.**
Hayne has a magical walled garden brimming with mature trees, shrubs, roses and borders. Highlights incl beautiful tree peonies, mature wisteria in both purple and white and rambling wild roses in combination with a more modern Piet Oudolf style perennial planting which surrounds the recently renovated grade II* farm buildings. Magic, mystery and soul by the spadeful! Live jazz band. Disabled WC. Wheelchair access to walled garden through orchard.

41 HEATHERCOMBE

Manaton, Nr Bovey Tracey, TQ13 9XE. Claude & Margaret Pike Woodlands Trust, 01626 354404, gardens@pike.me.uk, www.heathercombe.com. *7m NW of Bovey Tracey. From Bovey Tracey take scenic B3387 to Haytor/Widecombe. 1.7m past Haytor Rocks (before Widecombe hill) turn R to Hound Tor and Manaton. 1.4m past Hound Tor turn L at Heatree Cross to Heathercombe.* **Sun 29 Mar, Sun 10, Sun 17, Sun 24 May (1.30-5.30). Daily Tue 26 May to Sun 31 May (1.30-5.30). Daily Tue 2 June to Sun 7 June (1.30-5.30). Sun 14 June (11-5.30). Daily Tue 16 June to Sun 21 June (11-5.30). Daily Tue 23 June to Sun 28 June (11-5.30). Daily Tue 30 June to Sun 5 July (11-5.30). Adm £5, chd free. Home-made teas in pretty cottage garden or conservatory if wet. Visits also by arrangement Apr to Oct.** Donation to Rowcroft Hospice.
Tranquil secluded valley with streams running through woods, ponds and lake - 30 acres of spring/summer interest with many sculptures and new developments - daffodils, extensive bluebells, large displays of rhododendrons, many unusual specimen trees, cottage gardens, orchard, orchid/wild flower meadow, bog/fern/woodland gardens and woodland walks. 2 miles of mainly level sandy paths with many benches. Disabled reserved parking close to tea room & toilet.

42 HIGH GARDEN

Chiverstone Lane, Kenton, EX6 8NJ. Chris & Sharon Britton, www.highgardennurserykenton.wordpress.com. *5m S of Exeter on A379 Dawlish Rd. Leaving Kenton towards Exeter, L into Chiverstone Lane, 50yds along lane. Entrance clearly marked at High Garden. Phone for directions 01626 899106.* **Sun 5 Apr, Sun 3 May, Sun 5 July, Sun 2 Aug (12-5). Adm £4, chd free. Delicious home-made cakes and usually cream teas are available in tearoom.**
Stunning garden of over 4 acres. Huge range of trees, shrubs, perennials, grasses, climbers and exotics planted over the past 13 yrs. Great use of foliage to give texture and substance as well as offset the floral display. 70 metre summer herbaceous border. Over 40 individual mixed beds surrounded by meandering grass walkways. Exciting new formal plantings anticipated for 2020. Teas not for NGS charities. Selection of interesting plants available at attached nursery. 10% of plant sales to NGS. For other opening times and information please phone, email or visit the garden website. Slightly sloping site but the few steps can be avoided.

43 HIGHER CHERUBEER

Dolton, Winkleigh, EX19 8PP. Jo & Tom Hynes, 01805 804265, hynesjo@gmail.com, www.sites.google.com/site/cherubeergardens/the-gardens. *2m E of Dolton. From A3124 turn S towards Stafford Moor Fisheries, take 1st R, garden 500m on L.* **Fri 7, Fri 14, Sat 22 Feb (2-5); Sun 7 June (2.30-6). Adm £5, chd free. Home-made teas. 2021: Fri 5, Fri 12, Sat 20 Feb. Visits also by arrangement Feb to Oct for groups of 10+ (not August).**
1¾ acre country garden with gravelled courtyard and paths, raised beds, alpine house, lawns, herbaceous borders, woodland beds with naturalised cyclamen and snowdrops, potager style kitchen garden with large greenhouse and orchard. Winter openings for National Collection of cyclamen species, hellebores and over 400 snowdrop varieties.

NPC

44 HIGHER CULLAFORD

Spreyton, Crediton, EX17 5AX. Dr & Mrs Kennerley, 01837 840974, kenntoad@yahoo.com. *Approx ¾m from centre of Spreyton, 20m W of Exeter, 10 E of Okehampton. From A30 at Whiddon Down follow signs to Spreyton. Yellow signs from A3124, centre of village and Spreyton parish church.* **Visits by arrangement for groups of up to 20. Adm £4, chd free.**
Traditional cottage style garden developed over past 12yrs from steep field and farmyard on northern edge of Dartmoor National Park. Mixed borders of herbaceous plants, roses and shrubs. 30ft pergola covered with seagull rose and many varieties of clematis. Wildlife pond. Newly planted pleached hornbeam hedge. Additional vegetable garden with polytunnel, fruit cage and fruit trees. Partial wheelchair access but can drive in to garden on request.

Foxhole Community Garden

45 HIGHER ORCHARD COTTAGE

Aptor, Marldon, Paignton, TQ3 1SQ. Mrs Jenny Saunders, 01803 551221. *1m SW of Marldon. A380 Torquay to Paignton. At Churscombe Cross r'about R for Marldon, L towards Berry Pomeroy, take 2nd R into Farthing Lane. Follow for exactly 1m. Turn R at NGS sign for parking at Aptor Farm.* **Sat 30, Sun 31 May (11-5). Adm £4, chd free. Home-made teas. Open air teas available from 2pm to 4pm if weather permits. Visits also by arrangement Apr to Sept for groups of up to 10. Larger groups may be possible please telephone to check.**

2 acre garden with generous colourful herbaceous borders, wildlife pond, productive vegetable beds and grass path walks through wild flower meadows in lovely countryside. Sculpture and art installations by local artists add excitement at every turn. Home-made cakes and teas supplied by Marldon Gardening Club. Each year the garden is a showcase for local artists. Often the featured artists are in residence at the garden ready to chat to visitors about their work. Only area immediately at house is accessible for wheelchairs. All paths through garden are on gently sloping grass.

46 HOLBROOK GARDEN

Sampford Shrubs, Sampford Peverell, EX16 7EN. Martin Hughes-Jones & Susan Proud. *1m NW from M5 J27. From M5 J27 follow signs to Tiverton Parkway. At top of slip rd off A361 follow brown sign to Holbrook Garden 07741 192915.* **For NGS: Sat 21, Sun 22 Mar, Thur 9, Fri 10, Sat 11, Sun 12, Fri 24, Sat 25 Apr, Thur 7, Fri 8, Sat 9, Sun 10 May, Tue 2, Wed 3, Thur 4 June, Thur 9, Fri 10, Sat 11, Sun 12 July, Thur 27, Fri 28, Sat 29, Sun 30 Aug, Thur 10, Fri 11, Sat 12 Sept (11-5). Adm £5, chd free. Tea/coffee & home-made cakes in new summerhouse.**

Ask our visitors - "Heaven for bumble bees", "sun shining through layers of plants", "an immersive experience", "inspiring", "exciting plants", "magical, artistic, free flowing paradise", "cleverly planted but looks so natural". Productive vegetable garden and polytunnel. 2 acres of respite for people and wildlife alike

but if you like 'neat and tidy' then this garden may not be for you. Coaches by arrangement only, see holbrookgarden.com. Donation to MSF UK (Medecin sans Frontieres). Partial access for wheelchairs and buggies.

47 HOLE FARM

Woolsery, Bideford, EX39 5RF. Heather Alford. *11m SW of Bideford. Follow directions for Woolfardisworthy, signed from A39 at Bucks Cross. From village follow NGS signs from school for approx 2m.* **Sun 19 July, Sun 13 Sept (2-6). Adm £5, chd free. Home-made teas in converted barn. Room to sit and have a cup of tea even if its raining!**

3 acres of exciting gardens with established waterfall, ponds, vegetable and bog garden. Terraces and features incl round house have all been created using natural stone from original farm quarry. Peaceful walks through Culm grassland and water meadows border R Torridge and host a range of wildlife. Home to a herd of pedigree native Devon cattle.

48 ◆ HOTEL ENDSLEIGH

Milton Abbot, Tavistock, PL19 0PQ. Olga Polizzi, 01822 870000, mail@hotelendsleigh.com, www.hotelendsleigh.com/garden. *7m NW of Tavistock, midway between Tavistock and Launceston. From Tavistock, take B3362 to Launceston. 7m to Milton Abbot then 1st L, opp school. From Launceston & A30, B3362 to Tavistock. At Milton Abbot turn R opp school.* **For NGS: Sun 26 Apr, Sun 12 July (11-4). Adm £5.50, chd free. For other opening times and information, please phone, email or visit garden website.**

200 year old Repton-designed garden in 3 parts; formal garden around house, picturesque dell with pleasure dairy and rockery and arboretum. Gardens were laid out in 1814 and have been carefully renovated over last 14yrs. Bordering River Tamar, it is a hidden oasis of plants and views. Hotel was built in 1810 by Sir Jeffry Wyattville for the 6th Duchess of Bedford in the romantic cottage Orné style. Plant Nursery adjoins hotel's 108 acres. Partial wheelchair access.

49 NEW HOUNDSPOOL

Ashcombe Road, Dawlish, EX7 0QP. Mr and Mrs Edward Bourne. *Situated 3m from Dawlish centre or between 3m and 4m from A380. From A380 exit at Ashcombe Cross (dist. 2.8m) or Great Haldon Café (dist. 3.8m), follow signs to Ashcombe. Garden is adjacent to Whetman Plants International nursery.* **Mon 23, Tue 24 Mar, Mon 27, Tue 28 Apr, Mon 25, Tue 26 May, Mon 15, Tue 16 June, Sat 1, Sun 2 Aug (2-5). Adm £4, chd free. Self service: light refreshments, cold and hot drinks, biscuits, cakes. Donations appreciated.**

Formerly a market garden, now a private pleasure garden developed over past 40 yrs. The garden is very much a work in progress, the owners aiming to make it as labour saving as possible indulging in their love of trees, shrubs, herbaceous, water, vegetables/flowers and fruit, to provide interest all yr round. Dogs on leads. Children welcome. Gravel paths may cause a little difficulty for some wheelchairs but motorised wheelchairs should have no problem accessing most of the garden.

50 HUTSWELL FARM

Blackaller Lane, Oakford, Tiverton, EX16 9JE. Paul & Jean Marcus, 01398 351241, barvanjack@aol.com. *1½m NNW of Oakford. Signed narrow lane off B3227. Turn L 12m E of S Molton. 2½m NW of Black Cat junction turn R. Signs to Hutswell.* **Visits by arrangement May to Sept for groups of 10 to 20. Adm £5, chd free. Light refreshments.**

Delightful 8 acre S-facing country garden around old farmhouse. Ponds, bog garden, shrubaceous borders, prairie planting, maturing arboretum with Pyrus calleryana Chanticleer avenue, serpentine hornbeam walk, vegetable garden and orchard with local apple varieties. Walks through ancient wet woodland and plantation of over 11,000 native trees to viewpoints. Variety and interest all yr round.

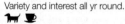

Your visits help change lives - since 1927, we've donated over £60 million to nursing and caring charities

51 KENTISBEARE HOUSE
Kentisbeare, Cullompton, EX15 2BR. Nicholas & Sarah Allan. *2m E of M5 J28 (Cullompton). Turn off A373 at Post Cross signed Kentisbeare. After ½m past cricket field and main drive on R, entrance to carpark is through next gate on R.* Sat 4 July (2-5); Sun 5 July (11-5). Adm £5, chd free. Home-made teas.
Surrounding the listed former Kentisbeare rectory, the gardens have been redesigned and planted by the present owners in recent years with various planting themes that complement the surrounding countryside. Formal beds, lake walk, kitchen garden and glasshouse, recently established wildflower meadow, orchard. Diverse and interesting collection of trees, shrubs and woodland plants.
&. ✿ D ☕

52 KENTLANDS
Whitestone, Exeter, EX4 2JR. David & Gill Oakey. *NW of Exeter mid way between Exwick and Tedburn St Mary. Follow NGS signs from centre of Whitestone village.* Sat 16, Sun 17 May, Sun 26 July (11-5); Sun 13 Sept (11-4). Adm £4, chd free. Home-made teas.
Our 2 acre tucked away garden is S-facing with distant views across Exeter towards W Devon and Sidmouth. Garden was started in 2010 and is still developing. Planting is mainly perennials with some shrubs, large salvia collection, orchids and alpines, productive vegetable garden with polytunnel, fruit cage and fruit trees. Sloping garden.
&. 🐾 ✿ ☕

53 KIA-ORA FARM & GARDENS
Knowle Lane, Cullompton, EX15 1PZ. Mrs M B Disney, www.kia-orafarm.co.uk. *On W side of Cullompton and 6m SE of Tiverton. M5 J28, through town centre to r'about, 3rd exit R, top of Swallow Way turn L into Knowle Lane, garden beside Cullompton Rugby Club.* Sun 12, Mon 13, Sun 26 Apr, Sun 10, Sun 24, Mon 25 May, Sun 7, Sun 21 June, Sun 5, Sun 19 July, Sun 2, Sun 16, Sun 30, Mon 31 Aug, Sun 13 Sept (2-5.30). Adm £3.50, chd free. Home-made teas at Kia-ora, inside or outside depending on personal preference and the weather! Teas and sales not for NGS charities.
Charming, peaceful 10 acre garden with lawns, lakes and ponds. Water features with swans, ducks and other wildlife. Mature trees, shrubs, rhododendrons, azaleas, heathers, roses, herbaceous borders and rockeries. Nursery avenue, novelty crazy golf. Stroll leisurely around and finish by sitting back, enjoying a traditional home-made Devonshire cream tea or choose from the wide selection of cakes!
&. ✿ 🚗 ☕

GROUP OPENING

54 KILMINGTON (SHUTE ROAD) GARDENS
Kilmington, Axminster, EX13 7ST. www.Kilmingtonvillage.com. *1½ m W of Axminster. Signed off A35.* Sat 16, Sun 17 May (1.30-5). Combined adm £6, chd free. Home-made teas at Breach.

BETTY'S GROUND
Michael & Mary-Anne Driscoll.

BREACH
Judith Chapman & BJ Lewis, 01297 35159, jachapman16@btinternet.com. Visits also by arrangement for groups of 10 to 30.

SPINNEY TWO
Paul & Celia Dunsford.

Set in rural E Devon in AONB yet easily accessed from A35. 3 gardens just under 1 mile apart. Spinney Two: ½ acre garden planted for yr-round colour, foliage and texture. Mature oaks and beech. Spring bulbs, hellebores, shrubs; azaleas, camellias, cornus, pieris, skimmias, viburnums. Roses, acers, flowering trees, clematis and other climbers. Vegetable patch. Breach: 3+ acres with woodland, partially underplanted with rhododendrons, camellia and hydrangea; rose bed, variety of trees and shrubs, wild flower area, colourful borders, vegetable garden and fruit trees. Two ponds, one in bog garden, which was extended in 2018/19. Betty's Ground, Haddon Corner: 1½ acres, a third of which was designed and replanted 4 yrs ago. Remaining two thirds has been restored, replanted in places and continues to evolve. Good selection of mature trees incl beautiful Wisteria walk. Beds both formal and relaxed incl woodland area all united by repeated perennial planting.
&. 🐾 ✿ ☕

55 NEW 37 KINGSKERSWELL RD
Kingskerswell Road, Newton Abbot, TQ12 1DQ. Ferai Akyol & Heather Mather. *Entrance via rear of 37 Kingskerswell Rd. One minute's walk from Decoy allotments. A small garden, open in conjunction with the allotments as it is very close by.* Sat 27, Sun 28 June (1-4). Combined adm with Decoy Allotment Field £5, chd free.
Small town garden created for peace and relaxation. It's a garden for entertaining family and friends as well as bringing nature to your home. Not suitable for wheelchair access.

56 LEE FORD
Knowle Village, Budleigh Salterton, EX9 7AJ. Mr & Mrs N Lindsay-Fynn, 01395 445894, crescent@leeford.co.uk, www.leeford.co.uk/. *3½m E of Exmouth. For SatNav use postcode EX9 6AL.* Visits by arrangement Apr to Sept for groups of 10+. Adm £6, chd free. Cream teas. Numbers and special dietary requests must be pre-booked. Donation to Lindsay-Fynn Trust.
Extensive, formal and woodland garden, largely developed in 1950s, but recently much extended with mass displays of camellias, rhododendrons and azaleas, incl many rare varieties. Traditional walled garden filled with fruit and vegetables, herb garden, bog garden, rose garden, hydrangea collection, greenhouses. Ornamental conservatory with collection of pot plants. Lee Ford has direct access to the Pedestrian route and National Cycle Network route 2 which follows the old railway line that linked Exmouth to Budleigh Salterton. Garden is ideal destination for cycle clubs or rambling groups. Formal gardens are lawn with gravel paths. Moderately steep slope to woodland garden on tarmac with gravel paths in woodland.
&. 🚗 ☕

57 LEWIS COTTAGE
Spreyton, nr Crediton, EX17 5AA. Mr & Mrs M Pell and Mr R Orton, 07773 785939, rworton@mac.com, www.lewiscottageplants.co.uk. *5m NE of Spreyton, 8m W of Crediton. From Hillerton X, keep Stone X to your R. Drive approx 1½m, Lewis Cottage on L, drive down farm track. From Crediton follow A377 North. Turn L at Barnstaple X junction,*

Shutelake

then 2m from Colebroke church.
**Sat 23, Sun 24, Mon 25 May, Sat
20, Sun 21 June, Sat 25, Sun 26
July, Sun 30, Mon 31 Aug (11-5).
Adm £4.50, chd free. Home-made
cakes, sweet & savoury tarts,
tea & coffee available. Visits also
by arrangement May to Sept for
groups of 10 to 30. Maximum
coach size is 27 seater by prior
arrangement.**
4 acre garden located on SW-
facing slope in rural Mid Devon.
Evolved primarily over last 27 yrs,
harnessing and working with the
natural landscape. Using informal
planting and natural formal structures
to create a garden that reflects the
souls of those who garden in it, it
is an incredibly personal space that
is a joy to share. Spring camassia
cricket pitch, rose garden, large
natural dew pond, woodland walks,
bog garden, hornbeam rondel, winter
garden, hot and cool herbaceous
borders, fruit and veg garden, picking
garden, outdoor poetry reading
room and plant nursery selling
plants propagated from garden.
Wheelchairs/motorised buggies not
advised due to garden being on a
slope (though many have successfully
tried!).

58 LITTLE ASH BUNGALOW
**Fenny Bridges, Honiton,
EX14 3BL. Helen & Brian
Brown, www.facebook.com/
littleashgarden.** *3m W of Honiton.
Leave A30 at Iron Bridge from
Honiton 1m, Patteson's Cross from
Exeter ½ m and follow NGS signs.*
**Fri 29 May, Sat 15 Aug (1-5). Adm
£4, chd free. Light refreshments.**
Country garden of 1½ acres,
packed with different and unusual
herbaceous perennials, trees,
shrubs and bamboos. Designed for
yr-round interest, wildlife and owners'
pleasure. Naturalistic planting in
colour coordinated mixed borders,
highlighted by metal sculptures,
provides foreground to the view.
Natural stream, pond and damp
woodland area, mini wildlife meadows
and raised gravel/alpine garden.
Grass paths.

59 LITTLE WEBBERY

Webbery, Bideford, EX39 4PS. Mr & Mrs J A Yewdall, 01271 858206, jyewdall1@gmail.com. *2m E of Bideford. From Bideford (East the Water) along Alverdiscott Rd, or from Barnstaple to Torrington on B3232. Take rd to Bideford at Alverdiscott, pass through Stoney Cross.* **Visits by arrangement for groups of up to 30.**
Approx 3 acres in valley setting with pond, lake, mature trees, 2 ha-has and large mature raised border. Large walled kitchen garden with yew and box hedging incl rose garden, lawns with shrubs and rose and clematis trellises. Vegetables and greenhouse and adj traditional cottage garden. Partial wheelchair access.

60 NEW LITTLEFIELD

Parsonage Way, Woodbury, Exeter, EX5 1HY. Bruno Dalbiez & Caryn Vanstone. *Please park cars in Woodbury village and follow signs to narrow driveway shared with Summer Lodge. Access to driveway from Parsonage Way, opp the stone cross on junction with Pound Lane.* **Sat 20, Sun 21 June (12.30-5). Adm £4, chd £1. Light refreshments.**
½ acre eco-garden. Rescued from derelict land in 2009/10, only 13m wide, 150m long, divided into herbaceous, shrub and tree planting, with large veg area, fruit and orchard with chickens. Plantsperson's garden - stocked with large range of varieties, in colourful combinations. Sculptures, unusual ironwork, wildlife pond all add charm and interest. Managed using permaculture techniques. The entire garden can be accessed in a wheelchair, but be aware that most paths are gravel and can be soft.

61 ◆ LUKESLAND

Harford, Ivybridge, PL21 0JF. Mrs R Howell and Mr & Mrs J Howell, 01752 691749, lorna.lukesland@gmail.com, www.lukesland.co.uk. *10m E of Plymouth. Turn off A38 at Ivybridge. 1½ m N on Harford rd, E side of Erme valley.*
24 acres of flowering shrubs, wild flowers and rare trees with pinetum in Dartmoor National Park. Beautiful setting of small valley around Addicombe Brook with lakes, numerous waterfalls and pools. Extensive and impressive collections of camellias, rhododendrons, azaleas and acers; also spectacular Magnolia campbellii and huge Davidia involucrata. Superb spring and autumn colour. Children's trail. Open Suns, Weds and BH (11-5) 22 March - 10 June and 11 Oct - 15 November. Adm £6, under 16s free. Group discount for parties of 20+. Group tours available by appointment. Partial wheelchair access in garden. Accessible café and WC.

62 MARSHALL FARM

Ide, nr Exeter, EX2 9TN. Jenny Tuckett. *Between Ide and Dunchideock. Drive through Ide to top of village r'about, straight on for 1½ m. Turn R onto concrete drive, parking in farmyard at rear of property.* **Fri 12, Sun 14 June (1-5). Adm £4, chd free. Home-made teas.** Donation to Spinal Injuries Association.
Garden approached along lane lined with home grown lime, oak and chestnut trees. A country garden created approx 1967. One acre featuring wild flower gardens, gravel beds, pond, parterre garden and a vegetable and cutting garden. New for 2020 wildlife ponds set in old orchard. Stunning views of Woodbury, Sidmouth gap and Haldon. Partial wheelchair access.

63 ◆ MARWOOD HILL GARDEN

Marwood, EX31 4EB. Dr J A Snowdon, 01271 342528, info@marwoodhillgarden.co.uk, www.marwoodhillgarden.co.uk. *4m N of Barnstaple. Signed from A361 & B3230. Look out for brown signs. See website for map and directions. www.marwoodhillgarden. co.uk.* **Coach & Car park. For NGS: Fri 12 June (10-4.30). Adm £7, chd £3.50. Garden Tea Room offers selection of light refreshments throughout the day, all home-made or locally sourced delicious food to suit most tastes. For other opening times and information, please phone, email or visit garden website.**
Marwood Hill is a very special private garden covering an area of 20

Bradford Tracy House

acres with lakes and set in a valley tucked away in N Devon. From early spring snowdrops through to late autumn there is always a colourful surprise around every turn. National Collections of astilbe, iris ensata and tulbaghia, large collections of camellia, rhododendron and magnolia. Winner of MacLaren Cup at rhododendron and camellia show RHS Rosemoor. Partial wheelchair access.

64 MIDDLE WELL

Waddeton Road, Stoke Gabriel, Totnes, TQ9 6RL. Neil & Pamela Millward, 01803 782981, neilandpamela@talktalk.net. *A385 Totnes towards Paignton. R at Riviera Motors (light traffic only), straight on for 1m to Four Cross. Straight across. From A380, R at A385 toward Totnes, L in 400m, L at Four Cross.* **Sun 6 Sept (11-5). Adm £5, chd free. Home-made teas. Morning tea/coffee. Visits also by arrangement Apr to Oct. Large coaches must park 300 yards away.**
Tranquil 2 acre garden plus woodland and streams contain a wealth of interesting plants chosen for colour, form and long season of interest. Many seating places from which to enjoy the vistas. Interesting structural features (rill, summerhouse, pergola, cobbling, slate bridge). Heady mix of exciting perennials, shrubs, bulbs, climbers and specimen trees. Vegetable garden. Child friendly. Teas, produce and books in aid of Stoke Gabriel Primary School. Mostly accessible by wheelchair.

65 MONKSCROFT

Zeal Monachorum, Crediton, EX17 6DG. Mr & Mrs Ken and Jane Hogg. *Lane opp Church.* **Sat 28, Sun 29 Mar (12-5). Adm £3.50, chd free. Home-made teas.**
Pretty, medium sized garden of oldest cottage in village. Packed with spring colours, primroses, daffodils, tulips, magnolias and camellias. Views to far hills. New exotic garden. Parking in farmyard. Also tranquil fishing lake with daffodils and wild flowers in beautiful setting, home to resident kingfisher. Steep walk to lake approx 20mins, or 5mins by car. Dogs on leads welcome. WC at lake.

GROUP OPENING

66 MORETONHAMPSTEAD GARDENS

Moretonhampstead, TQ13 8PW. *12m W of Exeter, 12m N of Newton Abbot. Signs from the Xrd of A382 and B3212. On E slopes of Dartmoor National Park. Parking at both gardens.* **Fri 15, Sat 16, Sun 17 May, Sat 5, Sun 6 Sept (2-6). Combined adm £6, chd free. Home-made teas at both gardens.**

MARDON
Graham & Mary Wilson.

SUTTON MEAD
Edward & Miranda Allhusen, 01647 440296, miranda@allhusen.co.uk. **Visits also by arrangement Apr to Sept. Guided tours.**

2 large gardens on edge of moorland town. One in a wooded valley, the other higher up with magnificent views of Dartmoor. Both have mature orchards and yr-round vegetable gardens. Substantial rhododendron, azalea and tree planting, croquet lawns, summer colour and woodland walks through hydrangeas and acers. Mardon: 4 acres based on its original Edwardian design. Long herbaceous border and formal granite terraces supporting 2 borders of agapanthus. Fernery and colourful bog garden beside stream fed pond with its thatched boathouse. Arboretum. Sutton Mead: also 4 acres, shrub lined drive. Lawns surrounding granite lined pond with seat at water's edge. Unusual planting, dahlias, grasses, bog garden, rill fed round pond, secluded seating and gothic concrete greenhouse. Sedum roofed summer house. Enjoy the views as you wander through the woods. Dogs on leads welcome, plant sale. Teas are a must. Partial wheelchair access.

67 MOTHECOMBE HOUSE

Mothecombe, Holbeton, Plymouth, PL8 1LA. Mr & Mrs J Mildmay-White, www.flete.co.uk. *12m E of Plymouth. From A379 between Yealmpton and Modbury turn S for Holbeton. Continue 2m to Mothecombe.* **Sun 3 May (11-5). Adm £5, chd free. Home-made teas. Lunches at The Schoolhouse, Mothecombe village.**
Queen Anne house (not open) with Lutyens additions and terraces set in private estate hamlet. Walled pleasure gardens, borders and Lutyens courtyard. Orchard with spring bulbs, unusual shrubs and trees, camellia walk. Autumn garden, streams, bog garden and pond. Bluebell woods. Yr-round interest. Sandy beach at bottom of garden, unusual shaped large liriodendron tulipifera. Gravel paths, two slopes.

68 THE MOUNT, DELAMORE

Cornwood, Ivybridge, PL21 9QP. Mr & Mrs Gavin Dollard. *Delamore Park PL21 9QP. Please park in car park for Delamore Park Offices not in village. From Ivybridge turn L at Xrds in Cornwood village keep PH on L, follow wall on R to sharp R bend, turn R.* **Sat 15, Sun 16 Feb (10.30-3.30). Adm £4.50, chd free.**
Welcome one of the first signs of spring by wandering through swathes of thousands of snowdrops in this lovely wood. Closer to the village than to Delamore gardens (open only in May for the Sculpture and Art Exhibition), paths meander through a sea of these lovely plants, some of which are unique to Delamore and which were sold as posies to Covent Garden market as late as 2002. Main house and garden open for sculpture exhibition every day in May. Mainly rough paths/woodland tracks so difficult wheelchair access.

69 MUSBURY BARTON

Musbury, Axminster, EX13 8BB. Lt Col Anthony Drake. *3m S of Axminster off A358. Turn E into village, follow yellow arrows. Garden next to church, parking for 12 cars, otherwise park on road in village.* **Sat 9, Sun 10 May, Sat 4, Sun 5 July (1.30-5). Adm £5, chd free. Tea. Tea proceeds to Musbury Church.**
6 acres. Extensive areas of well established trees and shrubs, many rare or unusual. Over 2000 roses spread round the garden. Stream. Pond. Lots of steps and bridges. Always interesting never perfect.

Your visits help change lives – we've donated over £17 million to Macmillan Cancer Support since 1984

70 MUSSELBROOK COTTAGE GARDEN

Sheepwash, Beaworthy, EX21 5PE.
Richard Coward, 01409 231677,
coward.richard@sky.com. *1.3
miles N of Sheepwash. A3072
to Highampton. Take rd through
Sheepwash. L on track signed Lake
Farm. A386 S of Merton take rd to
Petrockstow. Up hill opp then L. After
350 yards turn R down track signed
Lake Farm.* **Visits by arrangement
Apr to Sept for groups of up to
30. Parking for 8 cars (possibly
a few more). Guided tours £25.
Adm £4.50, chd free. Tea, coffee,
cakes.**
1 acre naturalistic/wildlife/plantsman's
garden. All season interest. Rare/
unusual plts on sloping site. 10 ponds
(koi, orfe, lilies). Stream, Japanese
gdn, oriental features, Mediterranean
gdn, wildflower meadow, clock golf,
1000s of bulbs. Ericaceous incl
magnolias, rhododendrons, acers,
hydrangeas. Dierama, crocosmia,
grasses, miscanthus. Superb autumn
colour. Aquatic nursery incl waterlilies.
Planting extremely labour intensive
- ground is full of rocks. A mattock
soon became my indispensable tool,
even for planting bulbs.

❀ ☕

71 OAKWOOD

Orchard Court, Lamerton,
Tavistock, PL19 8SF. Karen
& Rod Dreher, 07813 435987,
k.dreher@hotmail.co.uk.
*Lamerton. At Blacksmith's Arms
PH in Lamerton on Tavistock to
Launceston Road, turn into village,
follow road for 1/4 m cross bridge,
turn L into lane, follow NGS signs.*
**Visits by arrangement Mar to
July for groups of up to 20. Not
suitable for coaches; limited on
site parking. Adm £5, chd free.
Home-made teas. Please request
when booking if required.**
Created in 2008, garden provides
all yr round interest with winding
paths through well stocked borders
and sloping beds, water features,
laburnum and wisteria tunnel, mature
specimen trees, intimate garden
rooms taking advantage of the
landscape. Soft fruit and vegetable
areas and small potting shed; wilder
area of lawn and trees with spring
bulbs. Wheelchair access to around
60% of flower garden; some steps:
Grassland area sloping.

 ❀ ☕

72 NEW THE OLD SCHOOL HOUSE

Ashcombe, Dawlish, EX7 0QB.
Vanessa Hurley. *From A38 at
Kennford take A380 towards
Torquay. Turn off onto B3192 signed
to Teignmouth, take 1st exit off
r'about follow windy road for 1 1/2 m
1st R after church and follow signs.*
**Sat 1, Sun 2 Aug (1-5). Adm £4,
chd free. Cream teas.**
The Old School House is part of
Ashcombe Estate. Created by
Queen's Nurse Vanessa and husband
Chaz. It is an artistic palette of colour
with a hint of the theatrical. Set in over
half an acre there is a variety of plants
shrubs, vines, banana's and trees
attracting insects and wildlife plus an
interesting array of quirky recycled
materials. Dawlish water stream
circles around the pretty garden.
There are gravelled areas to entrances
and some uneven ground. Some
disabled parking outside house.

🚻 🐕 ❀ ☕

73 THE OLD VICARAGE

West Anstey, South Molton,
EX36 3PE. Tuck & Juliet
Moss, 01398 341604,
julietm@onetel.com. *9m E of South
Molton. From S Molton go E on
B3227 to Jubilee Inn. From Tiverton
r'about take A396 7m to B3227 then
L to Jubilee Inn. Follow NGS signs to
garden.* **Sat 16, Sun 17 May, Sat 18
July (12-5); Sun 19 July (12-5.30).
Adm £4.50, chd free. Cream teas.
Visits also by arrangement May to
Sept for groups of up to 30.**
Croquet lawn leads to multi-level
garden overlooking 3 large ponds
with winding paths, climbing roses
and overviews. Brook with waterfall
flows through garden past fascinating
summerhouse built by owner.
Benched deck overhangs first pond.
Features rhododendrons, azaleas and
primulas in spring and large collection
of wonderful hydrangeas in Aug. A wall
fountain is mounted on handsome,
traditional dry wall above house.
Access by path through kitchen
garden. A number of smaller standing
stones echoing local Devon tradition.

🐕 🚗 ☕

74 NEW PANGKOR HOUSE

Runnon Moor Lane, Hatherleigh,
Okehampton, EX20 3PL. Sally
& John Ingram. *8m NW of
Okehampton. Follow Runnon Moor
Lane for the whole length (approx
1 mile). At fork at end turn R onto*
unmade track (follow Pangkor House
sign). Pangkor House is 1/4 m uphill on
R. **Sat 4, Sun 5 July (1.30-5). Adm
£5, chd free. Home-made teas.**
4 acre naturalistic garden with
spectacular views over Dartmoor. A
freeform lawn with a series of grass
paths with lovely vista views. Quirky
and highly personal with sculptures
and random artefacts hidden within
the borders. Incl wildflower meadow,
wild garden, Zen garden, courtyard
garden and pond area with a
waterfall. Access to much of garden is
via mown grass paths with a medium
slope, i.e. accessible if the ground is
reasonably firm and dry.

🚻 🐕 ☕

75 ♦ PLANT WORLD

St Marychurch Road,
Newton Abbot, TQ12 4SE.
Ray Brown, 01803 872939,
info@plant-world-seeds.com,
www.plant-world-gardens.co.uk.
*2m SE of Newton Abbot. 1 1/2 m from
Penn Inn turn-off on A380. Follow
brown tourist signs at end of A380
dual carriageway from Exeter.*
The 4 acres of landscape gardens
with fabulous views have been
called Devon's 'Little Outdoor
Eden'. Representing each of the five
continents, they offer an extensive
collection of rare and exotic plants
from around the world. Superb mature
cottage garden and Mediterranean
garden will delight the visitor. Attractive
viewpoint café, picnic area and shop.
Open April 1st to end of Sept (9.30-
5.00). Wheelchair access to café and
nursery only.

🐕 ❀ 🚗 ☕

76 NEW POUNDS

Hemyock, Cullompton, EX15 3QS.
Diana Elliott, 01823 680802,
shillingscottage@yahoo.co.uk,
www.poundsfarm.co.uk. *8m N
of Honiton. M5 J26. From ornate
village pump, near pub and church,
turn up rd signed Dunkeswell Abbey.
Entrance 1/2 m on R. Park in field.
Short walk up to garden on R.* **Sat
13, Mon 15 June (2-5.30). Adm £5,
chd free. Light refreshments. Also
open Regency House. Home-
made elderflower cordial and
apple juice. Teas also available at
Regency House.**
Cottage garden of lawns, colourful
borders and roses, set within low
flint walls with distant views. Slate
paths lead through an acer grove
to a swimming pool, amid scented
borders. Beyond lies a traditional

ridge and furrow orchard, with a rose hedge, where apple, pear, plum and cherries grow among ornamental trees. Further on, an area of raised beds combine vegetables with flowers for cutting. Some steps, but most of the garden accessible via sloping grass, concrete, slate or gravel paths.

77 PROSPECT HOUSE

Lyme Road, Axminster, EX13 5BH. Peter Wadeley, 07814 693856, wadeley@btinternet.com. ½ m uphill from centre of Axminster. Just before service station. Fri 4, Sat 5, Sun 6 Sept (1-5). Adm £4.50, chd free. Home-made teas. Visits also by arrangement June to Sept for groups of 10+.

1 acre plantsman's garden hidden behind high stone walls with Axe Valley views. Well stocked borders with rare shrubs, many reckoned to be borderline tender. 200 varieties of salvia, and other late summer perennials incl rudbeckia, helenium, echinacea, helianthus, crocosmia and grasses creating a riot of colour. A gem, not to be missed. Artist Zee Jones will be showing and selling her work. Zee uses mixed media to produce contemporary colourful semi abstract paintings. In her own words, Zee tries to portray her intuitive understanding of the way colours work together and how they can affect emotion.

78 NEW RATCLYFFE HOUSE

Aunk Cross, Clyst Hydon, Cullompton, EX15 2NQ. Alison Beresford. 6m SE of Cullompton, 9m SW of Honiton. A30 follow Escot signs. R at Fairmile past Escot to Talaton. From M5 J28 Cullompton B3181 S. After 2m L at Merry Harriers PH. Follow signs to Clyst Hydon. 1½ m to Aunk Cross. Sun 5, Sun 12 July (2-5.30). Adm £4.50, chd free. Home-made teas.

5 acres of lawn, oaks and a few borders to stroll around, incl a short 'broadwalk' of David Austen Roses. Walled garden of shrubs, cypress trees and central putting green. Sports field with croquet lawn; newly planted trees and shrubs; natural pond. Wild woodland path. Work in progress! Low fencing protects shrubs/trees from rabbits. All shrubs and young trees planted by Alison since 2007. Wheelchair access to walled garden, path around house and terrace only.

79 REGENCY HOUSE

Hemyock, EX15 3RQ. Mrs Jenny Parsons, 01823 680238, jenny.parsons@btinternet.com, www.regencyhousehemyock. co.uk. 8m N of Honiton. M5 J26. From Catherine Wheel pub and church in Hemyock take Dunkeswell-Honiton Rd. Entrance ½ m on R. Disabled parking (only) at house. Sat 13 June (2-5.30), also open Pounds. Sun 14 June (2-5.30). Mon 15 June (2-5.30), also open Pounds. Sun 18 Oct (2-5.30). Adm £5, chd free. Home-made teas. Visits also by arrangement June to Oct for groups of up to 30.

5 acre plantsman's garden approached across private ford. Many interesting and unusual trees and shrubs. Visitors can try their hand at identifying plants with the plant list or have a game of croquet. Plenty of space to eat your own picnic. Walled vegetable and fruit garden, lake, ponds, bog plantings and sweeping lawns. Horses, Dexter cattle and Jacob sheep. Gently sloping gravel paths give wheelchair access to the walled garden, lawns, borders and terrace, where teas are served.

80 RIVERFORD FIELD KITCHEN GARDEN

Wash Farm, Buckfastleigh, TQ11 0JU. Riverford Farm, www. theriverfordfieldkitchen.co.uk. Take A384 between Totnes and Buckfastleigh. Take turning for Riverford Organic (not the Farm Shop) and follow yellow NGS signs. Sat 6 June, Sat 5 Sept (11-5). Adm £4, chd free. Home-made teas. Hot and cold drinks and freshly made veg-inspired cakes! Booking essential if you want to eat in the restaurant for lunch – 01803 762074.

An impressive 5yr old, organic kitchen garden and huge polytunnel. Planted up with an inspiring range of organic vegetables, herbs and flowers which are used daily in the farm restaurant, the award-winning Riverford Field Kitchen. Come and be inspired to grow your own! Practical demos throughout the day, guided tours of our polytunnels, plenty of fun for the kids. Mini tutorials and demo's with Penny in the polytunnel and garden. Play tractor and swings for little ones.

81 ST MERRYN

Higher Park Road, Braunton, EX33 2LG. Dr W & Mrs Ros Bradford, 01271 813805, ros@st-merryn.co.uk. 5m W of Barnstaple. On A361, R at 30mph sign, then at mini r'about, R into Lower Park Rd, then L into Seven Acre Lane, at top of lane R into Higher Park Rd. Pink house 200 yds on R. Sun 19 Apr, Sun 17 May, Sun 21 June (2-5.30). Adm £4, chd free. Cream teas. Visits also by arrangement Apr to Aug for groups of up to 20.

Very sheltered, peaceful, gently sloping, S-facing, artist's garden, emphasis on shape, colour, scent and yr-round interest. A garden for pleasure with swimming pool. Thatched summerhouse leading down to herbaceous borders. Winding crazy-paving paths, many seating areas. Shrubs, mature trees, fish ponds, grassy knoll, gravel areas, hens. Many environmental features. Open gallery (arts & crafts).

82 SAMLINGSTEAD

Near Roadway Corner, Woolacombe, EX34 7HL. Roland & Marion Grzybek, 01271 870886, roland135@msn.com. 1m outside Woolacombe. Stay on A361 road all the way to Woolacombe. Passing through town head up Chalacombe Hill, L at T-junction, garden 150metres on L. Sat 28 Mar, Sat 25 July (10-4). Adm £4, chd free. Cream teas in 'The Swallows' a purpose built out-building. Cream teas (£3), home-made hot sausage rolls (50p), hot and cold drinks (£1). Visits also by arrangement Mar to Oct.

Garden is within 2 mins of N Devon coastline and Woolacombe AONB. 6 distinct areas; cottage garden at front, patio garden to one side, swallows garden at rear, meadow garden, orchard and field (500m walk with newly planted hedgerow). Slightly sloping ground so whilst wheelchair access is available to most parts of garden certain areas may require assistance.

83 SHAPCOTT BARTON KNOWSTONE ESTATE

(East Knowstone Manor), East Knowstone, South Molton, EX36 4EE. **Anita Allen, 01398 341664.** *13m NW of Tiverton. J27 M5 take Tiverton exit. 6½m to r'about take exit South Molton 10m on A361. Turn R signed Knowstone. Leave A361 travel ¼m to Roachhill through hamlet turn L at Wiston Cross, entrance on L ¼m.* **Sun 26 Apr, Sun 26 July (10.30-4.30). Adm £5, chd free. Visits also by arrangement Apr to Aug. Donation to Cats Protection.**
Large, ever developing garden of 200 acre estate around ancient historic manor house. Wildlife garden. Restored old fish ponds, stream and woodland rich in bird life. Unusual fruit orchard. Scented historic narcissi bulbs in Apr, roses in June, astilbes and phlox early July. Flowering burst July/Aug of National Plant Collections Leucanthemum superbum (shasta daisies) and buddleja davidii. Hydrangeas in late summer. Very limited wheelchair access, steep slopes.

84 SHUTELAKE

Butterleigh, Cullompton, EX15 1PG. **Jill & Nigel Hall, 01884 38812, jill22hall@gmail.com.** *3m W of Cullompton; 3m S of Tiverton. Between Tiverton & Cullompton, Follow signs for Silverton from Butterleigh village. Take L fork 100yds after entrance to Pound Farm. Car park sign on L after 150yds.* **Sat 11, Sun 12 July (11.30-5). Adm £5, chd free. Light refreshments in Studio Barn if weather inclement. Snack lunches 12 to 1.30 pm and 'free-from' cakes for allergy visitors. Visits also by arrangement June to Aug for groups of 10 to 20.**
Bridge over stream brings you to garden terraced into hillside. From a natural pond full of wildlife, and woodland walk, climb up to an herbaceous border of reds and oranges, and up again to discover a cobbled courtyard, sculptures, rockery, orchard and lawns surrounding 300 yr old house. Sit awhile under the pagoda and look out across Devon farmland. A place of serenity.

85 SIDBURY MANOR

Sidmouth, EX10 0QE. **Lady Cave, www.sidburymanor.co.uk.** *1m NW of Sidbury. Sidbury village is on A375, S of Honiton, N of Sidmouth.* **Fri 24, Sun 26 Apr (2-5). Adm £5, chd free. Cream teas.**
Built in 1870s this Victorian manor house built by owner's family and set within E Devon AONB comes complete with 20 acres of garden incl substantial walled gardens, extensive arboretum containing many fine trees and shrubs, a number of champion trees, and areas devoted to magnolias, rhododendrons and camellias. Partial wheelchair access.

GROUP OPENING

86 SIDMOUTH GARDENS

Coulsdon Road, Sidmouth, EX10 9JP. *From Exeter on A3052 10m. R at Woolbrook Rd. In ½m R at St Francis Church. 2 gardens will be open in April and 3 gardens in August.* **Sat 11, Sun 12, Mon 13 Apr, Sat 29, Sun 30, Mon 31 Aug (2-5.30). Combined adm £5, chd free. Home-made teas at all gardens. Cream teas at Fairpark. Gluten free, lactose free cakes available.**

BYES REACH

26 Coulsdon Road, Sidmouth, EX10 9JP. Lynette Talbot & Peter Endersby, 01395 578081, latalbot01@gmail.com.
Open on all dates
Visits also by arrangement Apr to Aug for groups of 5 to 20. Coaches can park in street.

FAIRPARK

Knowle Drive, Sidmouth, EX10 8HP. Helen & Ian Crackston. Open on Sat 29, Sun 30, Mon 31 Aug

ROWAN BANK

44 Woolbrook Park, Sidmouth, EX10 9DX. Barbara Mence. Open on all dates

Situated on Jurassic Coast World Heritage Site, Sidmouth has fine beaches, beautiful gardens and magnificent coastal views. 3 contrasting ¼ acre gardens 1m apart. Byes Reach: Potager style vegetable garden, colour-themed herbaceous borders, rill, ferns, rockery, hostas. Spring colour of fruit blossom, spring bulbs - tulips, erythroniums and alliums. 20m arched walkway. Seating in secluded niches

each with views of garden. Front hot border. Fairpark lies behind a 12ft red brick wall, terraces, rockery, impressionist palette of colour, texture, many acers, small woodland and greenhouse, grasses, raised beds and willow sculptures. Seating areas to enjoy home-made treats. Rowan Bank is NW facing, sloping, generously planted with trees, shrubs, perennials, bulbs. Steps lead to wide zigzag path leading to woodland and Mexican pine, Seats and summerhouse. No wheelchair access at Rowan Bank and Fairpark.

87 NEW SILVER STREET FARM

Prescott, Uffculme, Cullompton, EX15 3BA. **Alasdair Cameron, www.camerongardens.co.uk.** *Devon. Signs will guide you from A38 between M5 and Wellington.* **Sat 6, Sun 7 June, Sat 12, Sun 13 Sept (1-5). Adm £5, chd free. Tea and cakes available.**
Formerly a dairy farm, the gardens embrace the surrounding agricultural landscape. The front planting of grasses, herbs, roses and perennials create a secret garden. The back garden includes a large 3m wide herbaceous border filled with perennials and shrubs, a woodland border, kitchen garden, tree houses and large lawn perfect for football, rugby, croquet or simply relaxing.

88 SOCKS ORCHARD

Smallridge, Axminster, EX13 7JN. **Michael & Hilary Pritchard, 01297 33693, michael.j.pritchard@btinternet.com.** *2m from Axminster. From Axminster on A358 L at Weycroft Mill T-lights. Pass Ridgeway Hotel on L. Continue on lane for ½m. Park in field opp.* **Fri 26, Sat 27, Sun 28 June (1.30-5.30). Adm £4.50, chd free. Home-made teas. Visits also by arrangement Apr to Aug for groups of 10 to 30.**
1 acre plus plantaholic's garden designed for yr-round structure and colour. Many specimen trees, large collection of herbaceous plants, over 200 roses, woodland shrubs, dahlias, gravel and grass borders, small orchard, vegetable patch, small pond. Steep bank inset with shrubs underplanted with wild flowers with view point at top. Alpine troughs and alpine house. Relaxing, species rich. Chickens. Wheelchair access to most of garden.

89 SOUTH WOOD FARM
Cotleigh, Honiton, EX14 9HU. Professor Clive Potter, williamjamessmithson@gmail.com. *3m NE of Honiton. From Honiton head N on A30, take 1st R past Otter Dairy layby. Follow for 1m. Go straight over Xrds and take first L. Entrance after 1m on R.* **Sun 3 May (2-5). Adm £10, chd free. Pre-booking essential at www.ngs.org.uk/events. Sat 19, Sun 20 Sept (2-5). Adm £6, chd free. Home-made teas. Visits also by arrangement May to Sept for groups of 10 to 30. Fully booked for 2020, now booking for 2021.** Designed by renowned Arne Maynard around C17 thatched farmhouse, country garden exemplifying how contemporary design can be integrated into a traditional setting. Herbaceous borders, roses, yew topiary, knot garden, wildflower meadows, orchards, lean-to greenhouses and a mouthwatering kitchen garden create an unforgettable sense of place. Rare opportunity to visit spring garden in all its glory. In May: 5000 bulbs incl 2500 tulips and hundreds of camassias in flower meadow. Regional Finalist, The English Garden's The Nation's Favourite Gardens 2019. Gravel pathways, cobbles and steps.

90 SOUTHCOMBE BARN
Southcombe Barn, Widecombe-in-the-Moor, Newton Abbot, TQ13 7TU. Tom Dixon. *6m W of Bovey Tracey. B3387 from Bovey Tracey after village church take rd SW for 400yds then sharp R signed Southcombe, after 200yds pass C17 farmhouse and park on L.* **Sat 13, Sun 14 June (2-5). Adm £5, chd free. Home-made teas. Cream teas.** New owners are enjoying the challenge of a Dartmoor garden. 2 tea lawn terraces with a super colourful rockery between 3 acre garden of crazy colourful flower meadow and flowering trees with mown grass paths running through and around and alongside the stream. Wildlife. If it is a very hardy wheelchair it can bump it's way as far as the tea terraces.

91 SPITCHWICK MANOR
Poundsgate, Newton Abbot, TQ13 7PB. Mr & Mrs P Simpson. *4m NW of Ashburton. Princetown rd from Ashburton through Poundsgate, 1st R at Lodge. From Princetown L at Poundsgate sign. Past Lodge. Park after 300yds at Xrds.* **Sat 9, Sun 10 May (11-4.30). Adm £5, chd free. Home-made teas.** 6½-acre garden with extensive beautiful views. Mature garden undergoing refreshment. A variety of different areas; lower walled garden with glasshouses, formal rose garden with fountain, camellia walk with small leat and secret garden with Lady Ashburton's plunge pool built 1763. 2.6 acre vegetable garden sheltered by high granite walls housing 9 allotments and lily pond. Mostly wheelchair access.

92 SPRINGFIELD HOUSE
Seaton Road, Colyford, EX24 6QW. Wendy Pountney. *Colyford. Starting on A3052 coast rd, at Colyford PO take Seaton Rd. House 500m on R. Ample parking in field.* **Sat 23 May, Sat 27 June, Sat 1 Aug (10.30-5). Adm £4, chd free. Tea and cake/coffee/cream teas.** 1 acre garden of mainly fairly new planting. Numerous beds, majority of plants from cuttings and seed keeping cost to minimum, full of colour spring to autumn. Vegetable garden, fruit cage and orchard with ducks and chicken. New large formal pond. Wonderful views over R Axe and bird sanctuary, which is well worth a visit, path leads from the garden. Featured in Amateur Gardening magazine.

Chevithorne Barton

93 SQUIRRELS

98 Barton Road, Torquay, TQ2 7NS. Graham & Carol Starkie, 01803 329241, calgra@talktalk.net. *5m S of Newton Abbot. From Newton Abbot take A380 to Torquay. After ASDA store on L, turn L at T-lights up Old Woods Hill. 1st L into Barton Rd. Bungalow 200yds on L. Also could turn by B&Q. Parking nearby.* **Sat 18 July (2-5). Light refreshments. Sun 19 July (2-5). Adm £5, chd free. Visits also by arrangement in July.**

Plantsman's small town environmental garden, landscaped with small ponds and 7ft waterfall. Interlinked through abutilons to Japanese, Italianate, Spanish, tropical areas. Specialising in fruit incl peaches, figs, kiwi. Tender plants incl bananas, tree fern, brugmansia, lantanas, oleanders. Collection of fuchsia, dahlias, abutilons, bougainvillea. Enviromental and Superclass Winners. 27 cleverly hidden rain water storage containers. Advice on free electric from solar panels and solar hot water heating and fruit pruning. 3 sculptures. Many topiary birds, and balls. Huge 20ft Torbay palm. 9ft geranium. 15ft abutilons. New Moroccan and Spanish courtyard with tender succulents etc. Regret no wheelchair access. Conservatory for shelter and seating.

94 ✦ STONE LANE GARDENS

Stone Farm, Chagford, TQ13 8JU. Stone Lane Gardens Charitable Trust, 01647 231311, admin@stonelanegardens.com, www.stonelanegardens.com. *Halfway between Chagford and Whiddon Down, close to A382. 2.3m from Chagford, 1.5m from Castle Drogo, 2.5m from A30 Whiddon Down via Long Lane.* **For NGS: Sat 19, Sat 26 Sept (10-6). Adm £6, chd £2.50. Light refreshments. For other opening times and information, please phone, email or visit garden website.**

Outstanding and unusual 5-acre arboretum and water garden on edge of Dartmoor National Park. Our birch have lovely colourful peeling bark, from dark brown, reds, orange, pink and white. Interesting under-planting. Near by: NT Castle Drogo and garden. Stone Lane Gardens is a Royal Horticultural Society Partner Garden and a National Collection of Birch and Alder. The Gardens have a Gallery Barn and converted barn Tea Room. Partial wheelchair access. WC.

95 STONELANDS HOUSE

Stonelands Bridge, Dawlish, EX7 9BL. Mr Kerim Derhalli (Owner) Mr Saul Walker (Head Gardener), 07815 807832, saulwalkerstonelands@outlook.com. *Outskirts of NW Dawlish. From A380 take junction for B3192 and follow signs for Teignmouth, after 2m L at Xrds onto Luscombe Hill, further 2m main gate on L.* **Visits by arrangement Apr to July for groups of 10 to 20. Adm £7, chd free.**

Beautiful 12 acre pleasure garden surrounding late C18 property designed by John Nash. Mature specimen trees, shrubs and rhododendrons, large formal lawn, recently landscaped herbaceous beds, vegetable garden, woodland garden, orchard with wild-flower meadow and river walk. An atmospheric and delightful horticultural secret! Featured on BBC Radio Devon and in Devon Life magazine. Wheelchair access limited to lower area of gardens, paths through woodland, meadow and riverside walk may be unsuitable.

96 SUMMERS PLACE

Little Bowlish, Whitestone, EX4 2HS. Mr & Mrs Stafford Charles, 01647 61786. *6m NW of Exeter. From M5, A30 Okehampton. After 7m R to Tedburn St Mary R at r'about past golf course 1st L after ½m signed Whitestone straight ahead at Xrds follow signs. From Exeter on Whitestone rd 1m beyond Whitestone, follow sign from Heath Cross. From Crediton follow Whitestone rd through Fordton. Due to recent wet conditions, parking on nearby concrete yard.* **Sat 15 Feb, Sun 29 Mar, Sun 19 Apr (1.30-5). Adm £5, chd free. Home-made teas. £5 includes cup of tea. Hot soup on snowdrop day. Visits also by arrangement Mar to Sept for groups of 10 to 20.**

Rambling rustic paths and steps (some steep) lead down a shaded woodland garden; unusual trees and shrubs (profusion of spring bulbs) and roses galore in June to ornamental orchard (berries, fruit, hip, autumn colour) with follies, sculpture, stream and ponds. Conservation as important as horticulture (wild areas) Special opening for snowdrops - over 60 varieties. Further details of garden on website. Intimate gardens round house, recently revamped new vistas. Animal sculptures and water features. Further new amusing features. Children and dogs love gardens. Garden related experts usually attend with sales tables.

GROUP OPENING

97 TEIGNMOUTH GARDENS

Cliff Road, Teignmouth, TQ14 8TW. *½m from Teignmouth town centre. 5m E of Newton Abbot. 11m S of Exeter. Purchase ticket for all gardens at first garden visited, a map will be provided showing location of gardens and parking.* **Sat 27, Sun 28 June (1-5). Combined adm £6, chd free. Home-made teas at High Tor, Cliff Road.**

BERRY COTTAGE
Alan & Irene Ward.

7 COOMBE AVENUE
Stewart & Pat Henchie.

GROSVENOR GREEN GARDENS
Michelle & Neal Fairley, www.grosvenorgreengardens.co.uk.

26 HAZELDOWN ROAD
Mrs Ann Sadler.

HIGH TOR
Gill Treweek.

LOWER COOMBE COTTAGE
Tim & Tracy Armstrong.

THE ORANGERY
Teignmouth Council.

NEW **SEA VISTA**
Mrs S.A. Williams.

NEW **21 WOODLAND AVENUE**
Larissa Letwyn.

NEW **14 WOODWAY ROAD**
Ann & Sam.

6 YANNON TERRACE
Stuart Barker & Grahame Flynn, No6yannon.co.uk.

Popular coastal town Teignmouth has 3 new gardens joining the group this yr and visitors can view the Orangery, a beautifully restored glasshouse built in 1842. 21 Woodland Ave: large exotic clifftop garden overlooking sea with pond, palm trees and subtropical plants incl echiums, agaves, puyas and ginger lilies. Sea Vista: stunning

Middle Well

sea views with Mediterranean court yard and Asian inspired planting. 14 Woodway Rd: cottage style garden with feature pond, Gros Green Gdns: ⅓ acre with fruit, veg and large greenhouse. 6 Yannon Terrace: shrubs and perennials for yr round interest incl summer hot bed. Lower Coombe Cottage: country garden with Bitton Brook running through. 26 Hazeldown Rd: manicured garden with clipped topiary and large koi carp pond. 7 Coombe Ave: plantsman's garden with exotic plants. Berry Cott: planted to provide a haven for wildlife. High Tor: home-made teas served overlooking sea in ½ acre bee and butterfly friendly garden. Limited wheelchair access at some gardens. Partial wheelchair access at some gardens.

GROUP OPENING

98 NEW TORQUAY GARDENS
Middle Warberry Road, Torquay, TQ1 1RS. *Take A379 Babbacombe Road from Torquay harbour. Turn opp St Matthias church, then follow NGS signs.* **Sat 27, Sun 28 June (1-5). Combined adm £5, chd free.**

Light refreshments. Cakes, Teas, Coffee.

NEW CROFT LODGE
Jacquie Felix - Mitchell, 07753 231132, jacquiefelix@gmail.com, www.windchimeshayloft.com.

NEW LANGUARD PLACE
Alison & Steve Dockray.

Languard Place: Plantsman's delight.180ft long S-facing garden packed with unusual plants and shrubs. Beautiful sunny garden with a hint of Piet Oudolf, who is well known among garden lovers for prairie style planting. Plants incl clematis, roses, foxgloves, specimen trees and grasses. Curved lawn area flanked by deep borders filled with gorgeous planting. Hidden area with Monet style pond and bridge, with magical seating area from which to view the gardens. Completely organic garden. The garden at Croft Lodge, owned by a garden designer, can be described as 'English Country, with Tropical overtones.' Walled S-facing garden with yr round interest and strong architectural themes. Mixed borders complimented by informal lawn with seating areas. Not suitable for wheelchair users.

99 TORVIEW
44 Highweek Village, Newton Abbot, TQ12 1QQ. Ms Penny Hammond. *On N of Newton Abbot accessed via A38. From Plymouth: A38 to Goodstone, A383 past Hele Park, L onto Mile End Rd. From Exeter: A38 to Drumbridges then A382 past Forches X, R signed Highweek. R at top of hill. Locally take Highweek signs.* **Fri 8, Sat 9, Sun 10 May (12-5). Adm £4.50, chd free. Home-made teas.**
Run by two semi-retired horticulturalists: Mediterranean formal front garden with wisteria-clad Georgian house, small alpine house. Rear courtyard with tree ferns, pots/ troughs, lean-to 7m conservatory with tender plants and climbers. Steps to 30x20m walled garden - flowers, vegetables and trained fruit. Shade tunnel of woodlanders. Many rare/ unusual plants. Rear garden up 7 steps, pebble areas in front garden.

Higher Orchard Cottage

100 TREETOPS

Broadclyst, Exeter, EX5 3DT.
Geoffrey & Margaret Gould. *From Exeter direction on B3181 drive through Broadclyst past school, next turn R. Follow signs.* **Sat 6, Sun 7 June (1-5). Adm £4, chd free. Home-made teas.**
Previously an orchard this 1-acre cottage garden, which is still evolving, is bordered by a forest and set within a beautiful borrowed landscape. Incorporating an avenue of Olivia Austin roses and an old restored brick path surrounded by borders featuring traditional and unusual cottage garden plants and pond.

101 UPPER GORWELL HOUSE

Goodleigh Rd, Barnstaple, EX32 7JP. Dr J A Marston, www.gorwellhousegarden.co.uk. *³/₄ m E of Barnstaple centre on Bratton Fleming rd. Drive entrance between 2 lodges on L coming uphill (Bear Street) approx ³/₄ m from Barnstaple centre. Take R fork at end of long drive. New garden entrance to R of house up steep slope.* **Sun 5 Apr, Sun 17 May, Sun 14 June, Sun 19 July, Sun 4 Oct (2-6). Adm £5, chd free. Cream teas by Goodleigh WI.**
Created mostly since 1979, this 4 acre garden overlooking the Taw estuary has a benign microclimate which allows many rare and tender plants to grow and thrive, both in the open and in walled garden. Several strategically placed follies complement the enclosures and vistas within the garden. Mostly wheelchair access but some very steep slopes to get into garden.

102 VENN CROSS ENGINE HOUSE

Venn Cross, Waterrow, Taunton, TA4 2BE. Kevin & Samantha Anning, 01398 361392, venncross@btinternet.com. *Devon/Somerset border. Use main B3227 between Bampton and Wiveliscombe.* **Visits by arrangement May to Sept. Adm £5, chd free. Home-made teas. Gluten-free cakes also available.**
Former GWR goods yard. 4 acres of formal and less formal gardens of interest to gardeners and railway buffs alike. An acre of orchid rich wild flower meadow. Areas of mass-planted candelabra primulas start the summer with many large sweeping herbaceous borders bursting into colour as the season progresses. Sculptures, streams, ponds, vegetable beds and woodland walk, railway relics and historic pictures. Wheelchair access to main areas.

103 THE WALLED GARDEN, LINDRIDGE

Humber, Teignmouth, TQ14 9TE. William & Surya Patterson, 01626 870548, wspatterson@btinternet.com. *12m S of Exeter. From B3192 turn alongside Teignmouth golf course to Gipsy Corner then follow signs for Bishopsteignton. After 1m, at Rowden Cross, turn R to Lindridge. Garden 0.7m further on L.* **Visits by arrangement May to Sept for groups of 10 to 30, 1st Friday of each month. No Coaches. Adm £5, chd free. Home-made teas.**
1 acre historical walled former kitchen garden of the Lindridge Park Estate, fallow for over 50 years. Now half way through a 10-yr renovation plan, the garden has a geometric layout, lawns, mixed borders, juvenile hedges, trained fruit trees, wild flower meadow, ponds, woodland area, set in attractive countryside with far reaching views. Managed on an organic basis to provide a haven for wildlife. Wildlife friendly planting and ponds. Sloping site with gravel paths. Some steps. Limited accessible parking.

GROUP OPENING

104 NEW WEST CLYST BARNYARD GARDENS

West Clyst, Exeter, EX1 3TR. Malcolm & Ethel Hillier. *From Pinhoe take B3181 towards Broadclyst. At Westclyst T-lights continue straight past speed camera 1st R onto Private Road over M5 bridge, R into West Clyst Barnyard.* **Sat 13, Sun 14 June (1-5). Combined adm £5, chd free. Home-made teas.**

NEW 2 WEST CLYST BARNYARD
Mark & Gill McIlroy.

NEW 3 WEST CLYST BARNYARD
Adam & Sarah Hemmings.

NEW 6 WEST CLYST BARNYARD
Alan & Toni Coulson.

7 WEST CLYST BARNYARD
Malcolm & Ethel Hillier.

These gardens have been planted in farmland around a converted barnyard of a medieval farm There are 4 gardens with a wild flower meadow, wild life ponds, bog garden, David Austin roses, magnolias and many trees and shrubs. Cars may be driven to the gate of No 7 for disabled access to the gardens but then please park in the car park.

105 WHITSTONE FARM

Whitstone Lane, Bovey Tracey, TQ13 9NA. Katie & Alan Bunn, 01626 832258, katie@whitstonefarm.co.uk. *½ m N of Bovey Tracey. From A382 turn towards hospital (sign opp golf range), after ⅓ m L at swinging sign 'Private road leading to Whitstone'. Follow NGS signs.* **Visits by arrangement Jan to Sept for groups of up to 30. Please phone to check on latest flowerings. Adm £5, chd free. Tea and home-made cakes, gluten free option.**
Nearly 4 acres of steep hillside garden with stunning views of Haytor and Dartmoor. Snowdrops start in January followed by bluebells throughout the garden. Arboretum planted 40 yrs ago, over 200 trees from all over the world incl magnolias, camellias, acers, alders, betula, davidias and sorbus. Always colour in the garden and wonderful tree bark. Major plantings of rhododendrons and cornus. Late flowering eucryphia and hydrangeas. National Collection of Eucryphia. Display of architectural and metal sculptures and ornaments. Limited access to lower terraces for wheelchair users.

Your visits help change lives – your generosity has supported unpaid carers through donations to Carers Trust totalling over £4 million since 1996

DORSET

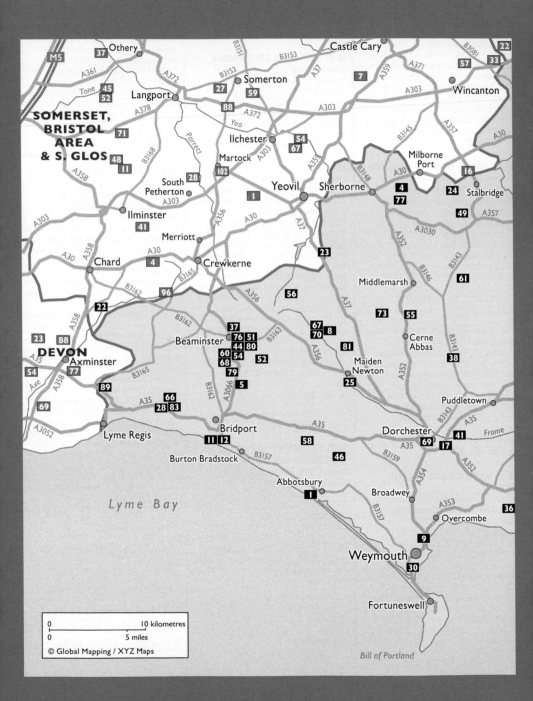

Othery
37
M5
A361
Tone
45
52
Langport
A378
A372
Parrett

SOMERSET,
BRISTOL
AREA
& S. GLOS
71
48
11
B3168
A358

South
Petherton
28
A303
Ilminster
41
Merriott
A30
Chard
4
A358
B3165
96
22
A358
B3162
23
88
DEVON
A35
Axminster
54
77
Axe
A358
89
69
A3052
Lyme Regis

Castle Cary
B3081
22
B3151
B3153
33
57
Somerton
7
A37
A359
A371
Wincanton
27
59
A372
A303
A303
88
Yeo
A357
A30
Ilchester
54
67
B3145
Milborne
Port
16
Martock
102
A303
A353
B3148
A30
4
24
Stalbridge
Yeovil
Sherborne
77
49
A357
1
A37
A352
A3030
23
A356
A30
B3146
Middlemarsh
B3143
61
56
A356
73
55
37
76
51
B3163
67
70
8
Cerne
Abbas
B3143
44
80
60
54
52
81
38
68
Maiden
Newton
A352
79
25
5
66
Puddletown
28
83
A35
A3066
B3162
A35
Dorchester
41
11
12
58
A35
69
17
Bridport
46
A354
A352
Burton Bradstock
B3157
A35
A353
36
Abbotsbury
Broadway
1
B3157
Overcombe
9
Weymouth
30

Lyme Bay

Fortuneswell

0   10 kilometres
0   5 miles
© Global Mapping / XYZ Maps

Bill of Portland

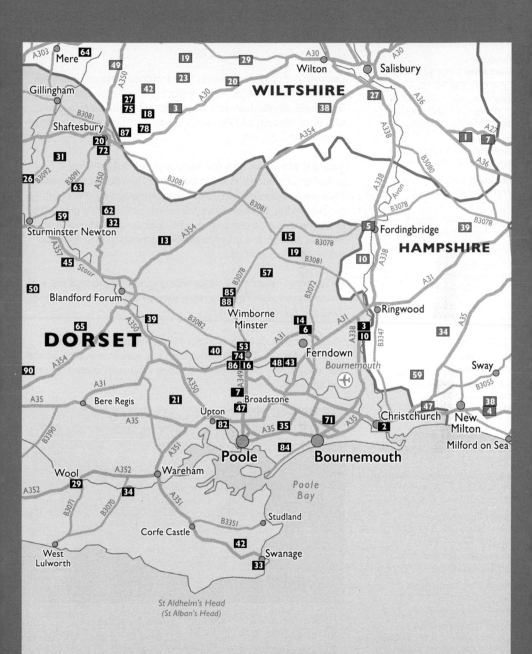

A303
Mere **64**
49
Gillingham
19
29
Wilton
Salisbury
A30
A30
A30
WILTSHIRE
23
20
A350
A36
A338
27
42
A30
A354
B3080
A27
Shaftesbury
27
75
18
3
38
1
7
B3081
A36
87
78
A26
20
72
31
A338
A36
B3092
B3091
A350
B3081
A354
B3081
A338
B3078
5 Fordingbridge
39
26
63
B3078
HAMPSHIRE
59
62
32
Sturminster Newton
15
A338
A354
13
19
B3081
10
A31
A357
Stour
45
B3078
57
B3072
Ringwood
50
85
88
Blandford Forum
39
Wimborne
Minster
B3082
14
6
A31
A338
3
10
B3347
34
A35
65
DORSET
A350
A354
40
53
74
A31
Ferndown
Bournemouth
90
A31
86 16
48 43
59
Sway
A35
Bere Regis
21
A350
7
Broadstone
A349
B3055
Upton
47
38
4
A35
82
47
New
29
Wool
A352
Wareham
35
71
A35
2
Christchurch
Milton
Milford on Sea
A351
Poole
84
Bournemouth
B3390
B3071
B3070
34
A351
Poole
Bay
A352
Studland
Corfe Castle
B3351
West
Lulworth
42
Swanage
33
St Aldhelm's Head
(St Alban's Head)

Volunteers

County Organiser
Alison Wright 01935 83652
alison.wright@ngs.org.uk

County Treasurer
Richard Smedley 01202 528286
richard@carter-coley.co.uk

Publicity
Clare Arber 07939 071806
clare.arber@ngs.org.uk

Social Media
Di Reeds 07973 241028
digardengate@hotmail.co.uk

Booklet Editor
Judith Hussey 01258 474673
judithhussey@hotmail.com

Booklet Distributor
Alison Wright (as above)

Photographer
Jane Terry 07968 800075
darwineurope@aol.com

Assistant County Organisers

Central East
Trish Neale 01425 403565
trish.neale@ngs.org.uk

North East
Alexandra Davies 01747 860351
alex@theparishhouse.co.uk

North East Central
Caroline Renner 01747 811140
croftfarm12@gmail.com

**North East/Ferndown/
Christchurch**
Mary Angus 01202 872789
mary@gladestock.co.uk

North West & Central
Annie Dove 01300 345450
anniedove1@btinternet.com

South East/Poole/Bournemouth
Position vacant. For details please
contact Alison Wright (as above)

South Central/East
Helen Hardy 01929 471379
helen.hardy@ngs.org.uk

South Central/West
Di Reeds (as above)

South West/Lyme Regis
Debbie Bell 01297 444833
debbie@debbiebell.co.uk

South West/Beaminster
Christine Corson 01308 863923
christine.corson@ngs.org.uk

West Central
Alison Wright (as above)

Dorset is not on the way to anywhere. We have no cathedral and no motorways. The county has been inhabited forever and the constantly varying landscape is dotted with prehistoric earthworks and ancient monuments, bordered to the south by the magnificent Jurassic Coast.

Discover our cosy villages with their thatched cottages, churches and pubs. Small historic towns including Dorchester, Blandford, Sherborne, Shaftesbury and Weymouth are scattered throughout, with Bournemouth and Poole to the east being the main centres of population.

Amongst all this, we offer the visitor a wonderfully diverse collection of gardens, found in both towns and deep countryside. They are well planted and vary in size, topography and content. In between the larger ones are the tiniest, all beautifully presented by the generous garden owners who open for the National Garden Scheme. Most of the county's loveliest gardens in their romantic settings also support us.

Each garden rewards the visitor with originality and brings joy, even on the rainiest day! They are never very far away from an excellent meal and comfortable bed.

So do come, discover and explore what the gardens of Dorset have to offer with the added bonus of that welcome cup of tea and that irresistible slice of cake, or a scone laden with clotted cream and strawberry jam!

Above: The Mill House

f @NGS.Dorset

🐦 @DorsetNGS

📷 @dorset_national_garden_scheme

OPENING DATES

All entries subject to change. For latest information check www.ngs.org.uk

Extended openings are shown at the beginning of the month.

Map locator numbers are shown to the right of each garden name.

February

Snowdrop Festival

Saturday 8th
The Old Vicarage 63

Sunday 16th
Herons Mead 29
Lawsbrook 45

Saturday 22nd
Manor Farm,
   Hampreston 48

Sunday 23rd
Lawsbrook 45
Manor Farm,
   Hampreston 48

March

Sunday 15th
Frankham Farm 23
22 Holt Road 35
The Old Vicarage 63

Sunday 22nd
Herons Mead 29
Ivy House Garden 38

Sunday 29th
Ivy House Garden 38

April

Saturday 4th
◆ Cranborne Manor
   Garden 15

Wednesday 8th
◆ Edmondsham
   House 19

Friday 10th
Knitson Old
   Farmhouse 42

Saturday 11th
Knitson Old
   Farmhouse 42

Sunday 12th
22 Holt Road 35
Ivy House Garden 38
Knitson Old
   Farmhouse 42

Monday 13th
◆ Edmondsham
   House 19
Ivy House Garden 38
Knitson Old
   Farmhouse 42

Wednesday 15th
◆ Edmondsham
   House 19

Sunday 19th
Broomhill 8
Herons Mead 29

Wednesday 22nd
◆ Edmondsham
   House 19
Horn Park 37

Sunday 26th
NEW Dorchester
   Gardens 17
Frankham Farm 23
Ivy House Garden 38
The Old Vicarage 63

Wednesday 29th
◆ Edmondsham
   House 19

May

Sunday 3rd
The Manor House,
   Beaminster 51
The Old Rectory,
   Litton Cheney 58

Monday 4th
The Manor House,
   Beaminster 51

Wednesday 6th
The Old Rectory, Litton
   Cheney 58

Friday 8th
Mayfield 53

Saturday 9th
Ivy House Garden 38
NEW Knowle Cottage 44
The Secret Garden 73

Sunday 10th
22 Avon Avenue 3
NEW Falconers 21
Herons Mead 29
Holworth Farmhouse 36
Ivy House Garden 38
The Old Rectory,
   Pulham 61
The Secret Garden 73
Wolverhollow 89

Monday 11th
Wolverhollow 89

Wednesday 13th
Deans Court 16
Wincombe Park 87

Thursday 14th
The Old Rectory,
   Pulham 61

Saturday 16th
Edwardstowe 20
Pilsdon View 66
NEW Rosebank 72
Well Cottage 83

Sunday 17th
Broomhill 8
NEW Dorchester
   Gardens 17
Edwardstowe 20
NEW Falconers 21
22 Holt Road 35
The Mill House 54
Pilsdon View 66
2 Pyes Plot 68
NEW Rosebank 72
Slape Manor 79
Well Cottage 83
Wincombe Park 87

Monday 18th
Pilsdon View 66
Well Cottage 83

Friday 22nd
Knitson Old
   Farmhouse 42

Saturday 23rd
Knitson Old
   Farmhouse 42
NEW Shute Farm 78

Sunday 24th
Harcombe House 28
Holworth Farmhouse 36
Knitson Old
   Farmhouse 42
The Manor House,
   Beaminster 51
Mayfield 53

The Parish House 64
NEW Shute Farm 78

Monday 25th
Harcombe House 28
Holworth Farmhouse 36
Knitson Old
   Farmhouse 42
The Manor House,
   Beaminster 51
Mayfield 53
The Parish House 64

Saturday 30th
NEW Manor Farm,
   Stourton Caundle 49
Old Down House 57

Sunday 31st
Annalal's Gallery 2
Lawsbrook 45
NEW Manor Farm,
   Stourton Caundle 49
Mayfield 53
Old Down House 57
The Old Vicarage 63

June

Tuesday 2nd
◆ Keyneston Mill 39

Wednesday 3rd
Old Down House 57

Friday 5th
24 Carlton Road North 9

Saturday 6th
24 Carlton Road North 9
The Grange 26
NEW Witchampton
   Gardens 88

Sunday 7th
Annalal's Gallery 2
24 Carlton Road North 9
Frankham Farm 23
The Grange 26
NEW Witchampton
   Gardens 88

Monday 8th
24 Carlton Road North 9

Saturday 13th
NEW Philipston House 65

Sunday 14th
22 Avon Avenue 3
Holworth Farmhouse 36
Manor Farm,
   Hampreston 48
Manor House Farm 50
Mayfield 53

The Old Rectory, Litton
 Cheney   58
The Old School House 62

Wednesday 17th
NEW Frome Vauchurch
 Farm   25
The Old School House 62
Stable Court   81

Saturday 20th
The Hollow, Blandford
 Forum   32
NEW Philipston House 65

Sunday 21st
NEW Dorchester
 Gardens   17
NEW East End Farm   18
The Hollow, Blandford
 Forum   32
22 Holt Road   35
Manor House Farm   50
The Manor House,
 Beaminster   51
25 Richmond Park
 Avenue   71
Stable Court   81
Western Gardens   84

Tuesday 23rd
◆ Littlebredy Walled
 Gardens   46

Wednesday 24th
Deans Court   16
The Hollow, Blandford
 Forum   32
Horn Park   37

Friday 26th
◆ Knoll Gardens   43

Saturday 27th
NEW Yardes Cottage   90

Sunday 28th
Annalal's Gallery   2
Black Shed   4
Cliff Cottage   11
Cliff Lodge   12
NEW Grove House   27
Rampisham Gardens   70
NEW Semley Grange   75
NEW Yardes Cottage   90

Tuesday 30th
◆ Littlebredy Walled
 Gardens   46

July

Every Wednesday
The Hollow, Swanage   33

Saturday 4th
◆ Cranborne Manor
 Garden   15

Sunday 5th
Holworth Farmhouse   36
25 Richmond Park
 Avenue   71

Tuesday 7th
NEW ◆ Holme for
 Gardens   34

Saturday 11th
NEW 16 Chapel Rise   10
NEW Knowle Cottage   44

Sunday 12th
22 Avon Avenue   3
NEW 16 Chapel Rise   10
NEW 6 Hillcrest Road   30
The Secret Garden
 and Serles House   74
NEW White House   85

Monday 13th
NEW White House   85

Thursday 16th
The Secret Garden
 and Serles House   74

Sunday 19th
Cottesmore Farm   14
NEW 6 Hillcrest Road   30
Hilltop   31
22 Holt Road   35
The Secret Garden
 and Serles House   74

Saturday 25th
10 Brookdale Close   7

Sunday 26th
Annalal's Gallery   2
10 Brookdale Close   7
Cottesmore Farm   14
Hilltop   31
Manor Farm,
 Hampreston   48
25 Richmond Park
 Avenue   71
The Secret Garden
 and Serles House   74

Thursday 30th
The Secret Garden
 and Serles House   74

August

Every Wednesday
The Hollow, Swanage   33

Saturday 1st
Harcombe House   28
44 Lower Blandford
 Road   47

Sunday 2nd
Harcombe House   28
Hilltop   31
44 Lower Blandford
 Road   47
The Old Rectory,
 Pulham   61
The Secret Garden
 and Serles House   74
Western Gardens   84
Wolverhollow   89

Monday 3rd
Wolverhollow   89

Tuesday 4th
Harcombe House   28

Wednesday 5th
Manor Farm,
 Hampreston   48

Thursday 6th
The Old Rectory,
 Pulham   61

Saturday 8th
10 Brookdale Close   7

Sunday 9th
Annalal's Gallery   2
10 Brookdale Close   7
Cottesmore Farm   14
Hilltop   31
Manor Farm,
 Hampreston   48

Thursday 13th
Broomhill   8

Saturday 15th
Edwardstowe   20

Sunday 16th
22 Avon Avenue   3
Edwardstowe   20
NEW Grove House   27
Hilltop   31
22 Holt Road   35
The Secret Garden
 and Serles House   74

Thursday 20th
The Secret Garden
 and Serles House   74

Sunday 23rd
The Secret Garden
 and Serles House   74

Saturday 29th
44 Lower Blandford
 Road   47

Sunday 30th
Black Shed   4
44 Lower Blandford
 Road   47
The Secret Garden
 and Serles House   74

Monday 31st
The Secret Garden
 and Serles House   74

September

Wednesday 2nd
Brook View Care Home 6

Thursday 3rd
The Secret Garden
 and Serles House   74

Saturday 5th
The Secret Garden
 and Serles House   74

Sunday 6th
Brook View Care Home 6
The Secret Garden
 and Serles House   74

Thursday 10th
The Secret Garden
 and Serles House   74

Sunday 13th
Annalal's Gallery   2
22 Avon Avenue   3
The Secret Garden
 and Serles House   74

Tuesday 15th
◆ Keyneston Mill   39

Sunday 20th
Herons Mead   29

Friday 25th
◆ Knoll Gardens   43

October

Wednesday 7th
◆ Edmondsham
 House   19

Wednesday 14th
◆ Edmondsham
 House   19

THE GARDENS

1 ◆ ABBOTSBURY GARDENS
Abbotsbury, Weymouth, DT3 4LA.
Ilchester Estates, 01305 871387,
info@abbotsbury-tourism.co.uk,
www.abbotsburygardens.co.uk.
*8m W of Weymouth. From B3157
Weymouth-Bridport, 200yds W of
Abbotsbury village.* **For opening times
and information, please phone, email
or visit garden website.**
30 acres, started in 1760 and
considerably extended in C19. Much
recent replanting. The maritime
micro-climate enables Mediterranean
and southern hemisphere garden to
grow rare and tender plants. National
collection of Hoherias (flowering Aug
in NZ garden). Woodland valley with
ponds, stream and hillside walk to
view the Jurassic Coast. Open all yr
except Christmas week. Featured in
Country Life and on Countrywise and
Gardeners' World. Partial wheelchair
access, some very steep paths and
rolled gravel but we have a selected
wheelchair route with sections of
tarmac hard surface.

2 ANNALAL'S GALLERY
25 Millhams Street,
Christchurch, BH23 1DN. Anna
& Lal Sims, 01202 567585,
anna.sims@ntlworld.com,
www.annasims.co.uk. *Town centre.
Park in Saxon Square PCP - exit
to Millhams St via alley at side of
church.* **Sun 31 May, Sun 7, Sun
28 June, Sun 26 July, Sun 9 Aug,
Sun 13 Sept, Sun 6, Sun 13 Dec
(2-4). Adm £3, chd free. Visits also
by arrangement May to Dec for
groups of 10+.**
Enchanting 150 yr-old cottage, home
of two Royal Academy artists. 32ft
x 12½ ft garden on 3 patio levels.
Pencil gate leads to colourful scented
Victorian walled garden. Sculptures
and paintings hide among the
flowers and shrubs. Unusual studio
and garden room. Not suitable for
wheelchairs; not suitable for dogs.

3 22 AVON AVENUE
Ringwood, BH24 2BH. Terry &
Dawn Heaver, 01425 473970,
terry@avongas.com. *Past
Ringwood from east A31 turn L after
garage, L again into Matchams Ln,
Avon Castle 1m on L. A31 from
west turn R into Boundary Ln, then
L into Matchams Ln, Avon Ave ½ m
on R.* **Sun 10 May, Sun 14 June,
Sun 12 July, Sun 16 Aug, Sun 13
Sept (12-5). Adm £5, chd free.
Home-made teas. Visits also by
arrangement May to Sept.**
Japanese themed water garden
featuring granite sculptures, ponds,
waterfalls, azaleas, rhododendrons
cloud topiary and a collection of large
koi carp. Regret, no wheelchair access
due to narrow gravel path. Children
only under parental supervision, due to
large, deep water pond.

4 BLACK SHED
Blackmarsh Farm, Dodds
Cross, Sherborne, DT9 4JX.
Paul & Helen Stickland,
blackshedflowers.blogspot.com/.
*On A30 just E of Sherborne. From
Sherborne, follow A30 towards
Shaftesbury. Black Shed approx 1m
E at Blackmarsh Farm, on L, next to
The Toy Barn. Large Car Park shared
with The Toy Barn.* **Sun 28 June,
Sun 30 Aug (1-5). Adm £5, chd
free. Light refreshments.**
Over 200 colourful and productive
flower beds growing a sophisticated
selection of cut flowers and foliage
to supply florists and the public, for
weddings, events and occasions
throughout the seasons. Traditional
garden favourites, delphiniums,
larkspur, foxgloves, scabious and
dahlias alongside more unusual
perennials, foliage plants and
grasses, creating a stunning and
unique display. A warm welcome and
generous advice on creating your
own cut flower garden is offered. Easy
access from gravel car park. Wide
grass pathways enabling access for
wheelchairs. Gently sloping site.

5 BRADDOCKS

Oxbridge, Bridport, DT6 3TZ. Dr & Mrs Roger Newton, 01308 488441, rogernewton329@btinternet.com, www.braddocksgarden.co.uk. *3m N of Bridport. From Bridport, A3066 to Beaminster 3m, just before Melplash, L into Camesworth Lane signed Oxbridge. Single track rd, down steep hill. Garden signed.* **Visits by arrangement Apr to June for groups of 5 to 30. Adm £5.50, chd free.**
3 acres of plant-packed sloping gardens, conceived, planted and looked after by owner. 'A feast of a garden at all times of the year'. Wild flower meadows and water. Herbaceous, underplanted shrubs and roses of all types and hues. Shady woodland garden and fine mature specimen trees. Steep slopes and gravel paths make the garden unsuitable for wheelchairs.

6 BROOK VIEW CARE HOME

Riverside Road, West Moors, Ferndown, BH22 0LQ. Charles Hubberstey, www.brookviewcare.co.uk. *Past village shops, L into Riverside Road, Brook View Care Home is on R after 100 metres. Parking onsite or nearby roads.* **Wed 2, Sun 6 Sept (11-5). Adm £3.50, chd free. Home-made teas. Teas in morning. Cream teas in afternoon. Payment by donation.**
Our colourful and vibrant garden is spread over two main areas, one warm and sunny, the other cooler and shadier. A cool fountain area, games lawn and mixed borders, then walking past our greenhouse leads to the fruit and vegetable gardens. Produce is eagerly used by the kitchen, and residents will help out with the production of the bedding plants, all expertly managed by our gardener.

7 10 BROOKDALE CLOSE

Broadstone, BH18 9AA. Michael & Sylvia Cooper, 01202 693280, Michaelcooper6744@hotmail .co.uk. *Located just 100yds from centre of Broadstone, Brookdale Close is on Higher Blandford Rd, with additional parking in next road, Fairview Cres.* **Sat 25, Sun 26 July, Sat 8, Sun 9 Aug (2-5). Adm £4, chd free. Home-made teas. Visits also by arrangement in Aug.**
Described as a 'little piece of paradise', with the 'WOW' factor, our

70ft x 50ft garden is centred around a wildlife pond and tumbling waterfall. A rich kaleidoscope of colour combining both tropical and cottage garden, with tree ferns, bananas, grasses, beautiful perennials and stunning dahlia display, with a different view at every turn. Very limited wheelchair access.

8 BROOMHILL

Rampisham, Dorchester, DT2 0PU. Mr & Mrs D Parry, 01935 83266, carol.parry2@btopenworld.com. *11m NW of Dorchester. From Dorchester A37 Yeovil, 9m L Evershot. From Yeovil A37 Dorchester, 7m R Evershot. From Crewkerne A356, 1½m after Rampisham Garage L Rampisham. Follow signs.* **Sun 19 Apr, Sun 17 May, Thur 13 Aug (2-5). Adm £5, chd free. Home-made teas. Opening with Rampisham Gardens on Sun 28 June (1.30-5.30). Visits also by arrangement May to Aug for groups of 10+. Lunch or tea can be arranged with advance notice.**
Once a farmyard now a delightful, tranquil garden set in 1½ acres. Island beds and borders are planted with shrubs, roses, masses of unusual perennials and choice annuals to give vibrancy and colour into the autumn. Lawns and paths lead to less formal area with large wildlife pond, meadow, shaded areas, bog garden and late summer border. Gravel entrance, the rest is grass, some gentle slopes.

9 24 CARLTON ROAD NORTH

Weymouth, DT4 7PY. Anne & Rob Tracey, 01305 786121, mellie_52@hotmail.com. *8m S of Dorchester. A354 from Dorchester, R into Carlton Rd North. From Town Centre follow esplanade towards A354 Dorchester and L into C Rd N.* **Fri 5, Sat 6, Sun 7, Mon 8 June (2-5). Adm £3, chd free. Home-made teas. Visits also by arrangement Mar to Sept for groups of up to 15.**
Long garden on several levels. Steps and narrow sloping paths lead to beds and borders filled with trees, shrubs and herbaceous plants incl many unusual varieties. A garden which continues to evolve and reflect an interest in texture, shape and colour. Wildlife is encouraged. Raised beds in the front garden create a space for vegetable growing.

10 NEW 16 CHAPEL RISE

Ringwood, BH24 2BL. Angela Ward. *Avon Castle. From East A31, past Ringwood L after garage, immediate L Hurn Ln, 1½m L Avon Ave, R to Egmont Drv, R Chapel Rise. A31 from West turn R into Boundary Ln then L Matchams Ln Avon Ave ½m R.* **Sat 11, Sun 12 July (12-5). Adm £4, chd free. Home-made teas.**
Garden of ¾ acre set to lawn with shrubs and herbaceous borders surrounded by yew hedge. Water feature, bamboos and various wooden and stone sculptures by owner's late husband. Steep short drive to garden. Thereafter only grass paths.

11 CLIFF COTTAGE

West Cliff, West Bay, Bridport, DT6 4HS. Mr Asit Acharya. *Across harbour bridge in West Bay, 2nd exit at r'about, along Forty Foot Way and uphill to very top of West Walks.* **Sun 28 June (1-5). Combined adm with Cliff Lodge £5, chd free. Home-made teas.**
One acre cottage garden, originally 3 small workers' dwellings built around 1750 and set on top of West Cliff. The garden was overgrown when the present owner moved in 6 yrs ago and is still a work in progress. Some mature borders, new areas of planting, small orchard. Relaxed, informal planting. Shepherds hut and viewing deck with views towards East Cliff and Portland.

12 CLIFF LODGE

West Cliff, West Bay, Bridport, DT6 4HS. Mrs Dawn Gibson. *At top of West Cliff private estate in West Bay. See directions on Cliff Cottage.* **Sun 28 June (1-5). Combined adm with Cliff Cottage £5, chd free.**
⅓ acre mature garden with good rural views. Mature camellias, hydrangeas, silver birch, old bramley apple tree with rambling fragrant roses planted through, fruit cage, geraniums, roses, lavenders, grasses, thatched summerhouse.

13 COTTAGE ROW

School Lane, Tarrant
Gunville, nr Blandford Forum,
DT11 8JJ. Carolyn & Michael
Pawson, 01258 830212,
michaelpawson637@btinternet
.com. *6m NE of Blandford Forum.
From Blandford take A354
towards Salisbury, L at Tarrant
Hinton. After 1½m R in Tarrant
Gunville into School Lane.* Visits
by arrangement Apr to Sept
for groups of 5 to 30. Adm £5,
chd free. Refreshments by
arrangement for groups.
Maturing ½ acre partly walled
garden. Formal and informal areas
separated by yew hedges. Pergola,
arbours, brick paths, tree house,
kitchen garden and the sound of
water; bees and butterflies abound in
this tranquil spot. This sophisticated
cottage garden reflects the owners'
love of unusual plants, structure and
an artist's eye for sympathetic colour.

14 COTTESMORE FARM

Newmans Lane, West Moors,
Ferndown, BH22 0LW. Paul &
Valerie Guppy, 07413 925372,
paulguppy@googlemail.com.
*1m N of West Moors. Off B3072
Bournemouth to Verwood rd. Car
parking in owner's field.* Sun 19, Sun
26 July, Sun 9 Aug (2-5). Adm £5,
chd free. Home-made teas. Visits
also by arrangement July & Aug
for groups of 10 to 20.
Gardens of over an acre, created from
scratch over 20 yrs. Wander through
a plantsman's tropical paradise of
giant gunneras, bananas, towering
bamboos and over 100 palm trees,
into a floral extravaganza. Large
borders and sweeping island beds
overflowing with phlox, heliopsis,
helenium and much more combine
to drown you in scent and colour.
Wheelchair access to garden to avoid
2 lots of steps, please ask on arrival
to make use of level route through
main drive gate.

15 ◆ CRANBORNE MANOR
GARDEN

Cranborne, BH21 5PP. Viscount
Cranborne, 01725 517289,
info@cranborne.co.uk,
www.cranborne.co.uk. *10m N
of Wimborne on B3078. Enter
garden via Cranborne Garden
Centre, on L as you enter top of
village of Cranborne.* For NGS:
Sat 4 Apr, Sat 4 July (9-5). Adm

£6, chd £1. Cream teas in Café,
Cranborne Garden Centre www.
cranbornegardencentre.co.uk.
Breakfast, hot & cold lunches,
afternoon tea. For other opening
times and information, please
phone, email or visit garden
website.
Beautiful and historic garden laid
out in C17 by John Tradescant and
enlarged in C20, featuring several
gardens surrounded by walls and
yew hedges: blue and white garden,
cottage style and mount gardens,
water and wild garden. Many
interesting plants, with fine trees and
avenues. Mostly wheelchair access.

16 DEANS COURT

Deans Court Lane, Wimborne
Minster, BH21 1EE. Sir William
Hanham, 01202 849314,
info@deanscourt.org,
www.deanscourt.org. *Pedestrian
Entrance (no parking) - Deans Court
Lane, Wimborne (BH21 1EE). Vehicle
Entrance (free parking) on A349,
Poole Road, Wimborne (BH21 1QF).*
Wed 13 May, Wed 24 June (11-
5). Adm £5, chd free. Morning
coffee, lunches, and teas.
Donation to Friends of Victoria
Hospital, Wimborne.
13 acres of peaceful, partly wild
gardens in ancient monastic setting
with mature specimen trees, Saxon
fish pond, herb garden, orchard
and apiary beside R Allen close to
town centre. First Soil Association
accredited garden, within C18
serpentine walls. The Permaculture
system has recently been introduced
here with chemical free produce
supplying the Deans Court café
nearby where light lunches and teas
are available. Tours of house available
on National Garden Scheme open
days 13 May and 24 June (2020) £5
at 12pm and 2pm, book upon arrival.
For disabled access, follow signs
within grounds for parking closer
to the gardens. Some paths have
deeper gravel.

Knowle Cottage

GROUP OPENING

17 NEW DORCHESTER GARDENS

Fordington, Dorchester, DT1 1ED. *3 town gardens in vicinity of Salisbury Fields, St Georges Church and Fordington Green. They are accessed by a lane leading to the large park, Salisbury Fields, between nos 10 & 12 South Walks Road.* **Sun 26 Apr, Sun 17 May, Sun 21 June (2-5). Combined adm £4, chd free. Refreshments at commercial café near to the gardens.**

NEW 6 SOUTH WALKS ROAD
Paul Cairnes.

NEW 8 SOUTH WALKS ROAD
Mrs Margaret Somerville.

NEW 18 SOUTH WALKS ROAD
Sally James.

18 South Walks Road: tiny Victorian front garden with olive trees and bulbs. Back garden: a corridor of stunning Japanese Acers and exotic trees leading into the park. 6 South Walks Rd: large mid 20th Century walled garden with ongoing restoration. Peonies, magnolias, climbing and shrub roses. Wisteria sinensis and spring bulbs. 8 South Walks Road: small sheltered garden. Upper level Heptacodium miconoides. Lower courtyard garden with mature climbers including Hydrangea seemanii.

18 NEW EAST END FARM
Barkers Hill, Semley, Shaftesbury, SP7 9BJ. Celia & Piers Petrie. *Semley. From A350 take exit to Semley and continue to Church. Take turning next to church towards Tisbury then 1st R to Barkers Hill. Continue along lane (1m) continue up hill East End Farm on R.* **Sun 21 June (2-5). Adm £4, chd free. Home-made teas. Gluten free.** Exquisite wildflower meadow started 20 yrs ago. 2 acres on spectacular site overlooking Pyt House. Orchids, yellow rattle, grass vetchling, ragged robin, agrimony, meadow cranesbill, various vetches, amongst many other species. Very pretty and relaxed garden with wild areas. Wheelchair access to garden only but views from garden to wildflower meadow.

19 ◆ EDMONDSHAM HOUSE
Edmondsham, Wimborne, BH21 5RE. Mrs Julia Smith, 01725 517207, julia.edmondsham@homeuser.net. *9m NE of Wimborne. 9m W of Ringwood. Between Cranborne & Verwood. Edmondsham off B3081. Wheelchair access and disabled parking at West front door.* **For NGS: Every Wed 8 Apr to 29 Apr (2-5). Mon 13 Apr (2-5). Every Wed 7 Oct to 28 Oct (2-5). Adm £2.50, chd £0.50. Light refreshments. Tea, coffee, cake and soft drinks 3.30-4pm in Edmondsham House Weds only. Donation to Prama Care. For other opening times and information, please phone or email.** 6 acres of mature gardens, grounds, views, trees, rare shrubs, spring bulbs and shaped hedges surrounding C16/C18 house, giving much to explore incl C12 church adjacent to garden. Large Victorian walled garden is productive and managed organically (since 1984) using 'no dig' vegetable beds. Wide herbaceous borders planted for seasonal colour. Traditional potting shed, cob wall, sunken greenhouse. House also open on NGS days. Coaches by appointment only. Some grass and gravel paths.

20 EDWARDSTOWE
50-52 Bimport, Shaftesbury, SP7 8BA. Mike & Louise Madgwick. *Park in town's main car park. Walk along Bimport (B3091) 500mts, Edwardstowe last house on L.* **Sat 16, Sun 17 May, Sat 15, Sun 16 Aug (10.30-4.30). Adm £3.50, chd free.** Parts of the garden have been extensively remodelled during 2018, a new greenhouse and potting shed have been added, along with changing pathways and the vegetable garden layout. Long borders have been replanted in places with trees managed letting in more light.

21 NEW FALCONERS
89 High Street, Lytchett Matravers, Poole, BH16 6BJ. Hazel & David Dent. *6m W from Poole. Garden is past Village Hall at end of High Street, on L.* **Sun 10, Sun 17 May (11-4). Adm £3.50, chd free. Home-made teas.** Behind the gate of 150 year old Falconers Cottage lies a 1/4 acre mature garden with some interesting plants. The characterful cottage and

garden have been cared for and enhanced by the current custodians. As you wander round the many aspects, which include a pond, herbaceous bed, climbers and vegetable plot you will find restful areas to sit and enjoy this garden in spring. Regret unsuitable for wheelchairs.

22 ◆ FORDE ABBEY GARDENS
Forde Abbey, Chard, TA20 4LU. Mr & Mrs Julian Kennard, 01460 221290, info@fordeabbey.co.uk, www.fordeabbey.co.uk. *4m SE of Chard. Signed off A30 Chard-Crewkerne and A358 Chard-Axminster. Also from Broadwindsor B3164.* **For opening times and information, please phone, email or visit garden website.** 30 acres of fine shrubs, magnificent specimen trees, ponds, herbaceous borders, rockery, bog garden containing superb collection of Asiatic primulas, Ionic temple, working walled kitchen garden supplying the tearoom. Centenary fountain, England's highest powered fountain. Gardens open daily (10am-5.30pm, last adm 4.30pm), house open from 2 April Tues to Fri incl, Suns & BH Mons. Please ask at reception for best wheelchair route. Wheelchairs available to borrow/hire, advance booking advised.

23 FRANKHAM FARM
Ryme Intrinseca, Sherborne, DT9 6JT. Susan Ross, 07594 427365, neilandsusanross@gmail.com. *3m S of Yeovil. A37 Yeovil-Dorchester; turn E; 1/4 m; drive is on L.* **Sun 15 Mar, Sun 26 Apr, Sun 7 June (11.30-5); Sun 18 Oct (11.30-5.30). Adm £6, chd free. Home-made teas in tea room up a flight of steps. Home produced lunch 12-2.30 sausage in a roll, vegetarian soup, vegan falafels.** 3 1/2 acre garden, created since 1960 by the late Jo Earle for yr-round interest. This large and lovely garden is filled with a wide variety of well grown plants, roses, unusual labelled shrubs and trees. Productive vegetable garden. Clematis and other climbers. Spring bulbs through to autumn colour, particularly oaks. Modern toilets incl disabled. Sorry, no dogs. Contactless payment available in tearoom.

24 FRITH HOUSE

Stalbridge, DT10 2SD. Mr & Mrs Patrick Sclater, 01963 250809, rosalynsclater@btinternet.com. *5m E of Sherborne. Between Milborne Port and Stalbridge. From A30 1m, follow sign to Stalbridge. From Stalbridge 2m and turn W by PO.* **Visits by arrangement Apr to July for groups of 10+. Adm £5, chd free. Home-made teas.**
Approached down long drive with fine views. 4 acres of garden around Edwardian house and self-contained hamlet. Range of mature trees, lakes and flower borders. House terrace edged by rose border and featuring Lutyensesque wall fountain and game larder. Well stocked kitchen gardens.

25 NEW FROME VAUCHURCH FARM

Frome Vauchurch, Dorchester, DT2 0DY. Mrs Alison Blazeby. *Across the River Frome from Maiden Newton. ½m from Maiden Newton on Back Lane between Cruxton and Tollerford.* **Wed 17 June (12-5). Adm £4.50, chd free. Tea/coffee and home-made cakes.**
Mature gardens surround mid C19 farmhouse and yard with central threshing barn where teas may be served under cover on rainy days. Paths lead to beds and borders filled with trees, shrubs and herbaceous plants, small wildlife pond, woodland walk, and other areas under development. Very slopey and quite rough - sadly unsuitable for wheelchairs.

26 THE GRANGE

Burton Street, Marnhull, Sturminster Newton, DT10 1PS. Francesca Pratt. *Marnhull. 8m SW from Shaftesbury take A30 and B3092, to Marnhull turn R into Sodom lane. From south B3092 to Marnhull turn L into Church St - follow NGS signs to Grange.* **Sat 6, Sun 7 June (2-5). Adm £4.50, chd free. Home-made teas.**
Large village garden created 4-5 yrs ago. Large terrace with integrated colourful borders. Main lawn leading to 2 herbaceous borders planted in hot colours onto fastigiated hornbeam avenue. Woodland garden with shade loving shrubs and ground cover, magnificent treehouse, leading onto a wildflower meadow. Swimming pool garden with pool house. Scented courtyard at front and herb garden at rear. Wheelchair access to lawn and woodland garden - 6 steps down to terrace.

27 NEW GROVE HOUSE

Semley, Shaftesbury, SP7 9AP. Judy and Peter Williamson. *A350 turn to Semley. Grove House approx ½m on L just before railway bridge. From Semley village leave pub on R go under railway bridge (approx ⅓m) Grove House 2nd on R.* **Sun 28 June (2-5), also open Semley Grange. Sun 16 Aug (2-5). Adm £5, chd free. Home-made teas. Gluten free cakes.**
Classic English garden divided into rooms. Yew hedges and topiary. Rose garden. Large herbaceous border. Late summer hot garden with grasses. Lawns. Mown walks.

28 HARCOMBE HOUSE

Pitmans Lane, Morcombelake, Bridport, DT6 6EB. Jan & Martin Dixon, 01297 489229, harcombe@hotmail.co.uk. *4m W of Bridport - do not follow SatNav. A35 from Bridport: R to Whitchurch just past The Artwave Gallery. Immed R, bear L into Pitmans Lane. Approx 800m, park in paddock on L.* **Sun 24, Mon 25 May, Sat 1, Sun 2, Tue 4 Aug (11-5). Adm £5, chd free. Home-made teas. All cakes home-made by Jan, sausage rolls home-made by Martin. Visits also by arrangement Apr to Sept for groups of up to 30. Groups welcome but lane is too narrow for coaches.**
Landscaped into hillside 500ft above the Char Valley with spectacular views across Charmouth and Lyme Bay. Steeply sloping site comprises ¾ acre formal garden and ½ acre wild garden. The beautiful ¾ acre garden has been rediscovered, restored and replanted in natural and relaxed style over last 14 yrs with an abundance of shrubs and perennials, many unusual and visually stunning. Majestic rhododendrons and azaleas complement spring bulbs and bluebells in a blaze of colour in May/June and in Aug the beautiful Eucryphia is the star of the garden. Challenging for the less mobile visitor and definitely unsuitable for wheelchairs and buggies. Very steep paths and steps to/in garden.

29 HERONS MEAD

East Burton Road, East Burton, Wool, BH20 6HF. Ron & Angela Millington. *6m W of Wareham on A352. Approaching Wool from Wareham, turn R just before level crossing into East Burton Rd. Herons Mead ¾m on L.* **Sun 16 Feb, Sun 22 Mar, Sun 19 Apr, Sun 10 May, Sun 20 Sept (2-5). Adm £3.50, chd free. Home-made teas.**
½ acre plantlover's garden full of interest from spring (bulbs, many hellebores, pulmonaria, fritillaries) through abundant summer perennials, old roses scrambling through trees and late seasonal exuberant plants amongst swathes of tall grasses. Wildlife pond and plants to attract bees, butterflies, etc. Tiny woodland. Cacti. Small wheelchairs can gain partial access - as far as the tea house!

30 NEW 6 HILLCREST ROAD

Weymouth, DT4 9JP. Helen & Michael Toft. *6 Hillcrest Road. Via Weymouth take A345 towards Portland, L at Rylands Lane, last L at bottom of hill 3rd Bungalow on R. Via Bridport take B13156 to W'mth follow signs to Portland, L at A345, R at Rylands Lane.* **Sun 12, Sun 19 July (2-5.30). Adm £4, chd £1. Home-made cakes and drinks.**
Typical suburban garden with the sea at the end, allows the cultivation of some exotic plants inc strelizia, banana and Cobaea scandens. Fish Pond, mature fruit trees, veg patch and soft fruit. Hot bed nearest the house is balanced by white bed at bottom of lawn. A mixed border of perennials and annuals runs down one side. Long grass area completes the mix of habitats.

Your visits help change lives - we are Hospice UK's largest charitable funder donating more than £5.5 million to support hospices in local communities since 1996

31 HILLTOP

Woodville, Stour Provost, Gillingham, SP8 5LY. Josse & Brian Emerson, www.hilltopgarden.co.uk. *7m N of Sturminster Newton, 5m W of Shaftesbury. On B3092 turn E at Stour Provost Xrds, signed Woodville. After 1¼m thatched cottage on R. On A30, 4m W of Shaftesbury, turn S opp Kings Arms. 2nd turning on R signed Woodville, 100 yds on L.* **Every Sun 19 July to 16 Aug (2-6). Adm £3.50, chd free. Home-made teas.**

Summer at Hilltop is a gorgeous riot of colour and scent, the old thatched cottage barely visible amongst the flowers. Unusual annuals and perennials grow alongside the traditional and familiar, boldly combining to make a spectacular display, which attracts an abundance of wildlife. Always something new, the unique, gothic garden loo a great success.

32 THE HOLLOW, BLANDFORD FORUM

Tower Hill, Iwerne Minster, Blandford Forum, DT11 8NJ. Sue Le Prevost. *Between Blandford and Shaftesbury. Follow signs on A350 to Iwerne Minster. Turn off at Talbot Inn, continue straight to The Chalk, bear R along Watery Lane for parking in Parish Field on R. 5 min uphill walk*

to house. **Sat 20, Sun 21, Wed 24 June (2-5). Adm £3.50, chd free. Cream teas. Home-made cakes and gluten-free available.**

Hillside cottage garden built on chalk, about ⅓ acre with an interesting variety of plants in borders that line the numerous sloping pathways. Water features for wildlife and well placed seating areas to sit back and enjoy the views. Productive fruit and vegetable garden in converted paddock with raised beds and greenhouses. A high maintenance garden which is constantly evolving. Slopes, narrow gravel paths and steep steps so sadly not suitable for wheelchairs or limited mobility.

33 THE HOLLOW, SWANAGE

25 Newton Road, Swanage, BH19 2EA. Stuart & Suzanne Nutbeem, 01929 423662, gdnsuzanne@gmail.com. *½m S of Swanage town centre. From town follow signs to Durlston Country Park. At top of hill turn R at red postbox into Bon Accord Rd. 4th turn R into Newton Rd.* **Every Wed 1 July to 26 Aug (2-5.30). Adm £3, chd free. Visits also by arrangement July & Aug.**

Come and wander round a dramatic sunken former stone quarry, a surprising garden at the top of a hill above the seaside town of Swanage. Stone terraces with many unusual shrubs and grasses, showing the

owners' passion for plants, form a beautiful pattern of colour and foliage attracting happy butterflies and bees. Pieces of mediaeval London Bridge lurk in the walls. Steps have elegant handrails. WC available. Exceptionally wide range of plants including cacti and airplants.

34 NEW ◆ HOLME FOR GARDENS

West Holme Farm, Wareham, BH20 6AQ. Simon Goldsack, 01929 554716, simon@holmefg.co.uk, www.holmefg.co.uk. *Easy to find on the B3070 road to Lulworth 2m out of Wareham.* **For NGS: Tue 7 July (10-4.30). Adm £4, chd free. The Orchard Café serves breakfast, lunch and cream teas with both indoor and outdoor pondside seating. For other opening times and information, please phone, email or visit garden website.**

Extensive formal and informal gardens strongly influenced by Hidcote Manor and The Laskett and the garden is made up of distinct rooms separated by hedges and taller planting. Extensive collection of trees, shrubs, perennials and annuals sourced from across the UK. Grass amphitheatre, Holme henge heather garden, lavender avenue, cutting garden, pear tunnel, annual flower field, hot borders, white borders, ornamental grasses, unusual

The Old Rectory, Netherbury

trees and shrubs. Grass paths are kept in good order and soil is well drained so wheelchair access is reasonable except immediately after heavy rain.

♿ 🐑 ✿ 🚗 ☕

35 22 HOLT ROAD
Branksome, Poole, BH12 1JQ. Alan & Sylvia Lloyd, 01202 387509, alan.lloyd22@ntlworld.com. *2½ m W of Bournemouth Square, 3m E of Poole Civic Centre. From Alder Rd turn into Winston Ave, 3rd R into Guest Ave, 2nd R into Holt Rd, at end of cul de sac. Park in Holt Rd or in Guest Ave.* **Sun 15 Mar, Sun 12 Apr, Sun 17 May, Sun 21 June, Sun 19 July, Sun 16 Aug (2-5). Adm £3.50, chd free. Home-made teas. Visits also by arrangement Mar to Sept for groups of 10+.**
¾ acre walled garden for all seasons. Garden seating throughout the diverse planting areas, incl Mediterranean courtyard garden and wisteria pergola. Walk up slope beside rill and bog garden to raised bed vegetable garden. Return through shrubbery and rockery back to waterfall cascading into a pebble beach. Partial wheelchair access.

♿ 🐑 ✿ 🚗 ☕

36 HOLWORTH FARMHOUSE
Holworth, Dorchester, DT2 8NH. Anthony & Philippa Bush, 01305 852242, bushinarcadia@yahoo.co.uk. *7m E of Dorchester. 1m S of A352. Follow signs to Holworth. Through farmyard with duckpond on R. 1st L after 200yds of rough track. Ignore No Access signs.* **Sun 10, Sun 24, Mon 25 May, Sun 14 June, Sun 5 July (2-5). Adm £5, chd free. Home-made teas. Visits also by arrangement May to Sept. We are a working garden with no extra help so are not always perfect!**
Escape briefly from the cares and pressures of the world. Visit this unusual garden tucked away in an area of extraordinary peace and tranquility chosen by the Monks of Milton Abbey. The garden was created 35 years ago and is constantly evolving. New projects every year. Many mature and unusual trees and shrubs, numerous borders with seats to ponder and reflect. Vegetables, water and wild spaces. Beautiful unspoilt views. Many birds and butterflies. Very limited wheelchair access.

🐑 ✿ ☕

37 HORN PARK
Tunnel Rd, Beaminster, DT8 3HB. Mr & Mrs David Ashcroft, 01308 862212, angieashcroft@btinternet.com. *1½ m N of Beaminster. On A3066 from Beaminster, L before tunnel (see signs).* **Wed 22 Apr, Wed 24 June (2-5). Adm £4.50, chd free. Home-made teas. Visits also by arrangement Apr to Oct for groups of up to 30.**
Large plantsman's garden with magnificent views over Dorset countryside towards the sea. Many rare and mature plants and shrubs in terrraced, herbaceous, rock and water gardens. Woodland garden and walks in bluebell woods. Good amount of spring interest with magnolia, rhododendron and bulbs which are followed by roses and herbaceous planting, Wild flower meadow with 164 varieties incl orchids. Very limited access for wheelchair users, gravel paths and some steep slopes.

🐑 🚗 ☕

38 IVY HOUSE GARDEN
Piddletrenthide, DT2 7QF. Bridget Bowen, 07586 377675, beepeebee66@icloud.com. *9m N of Dorchester. On B3143. In middle of Piddletrenthide village, opp Village Stores near Piddle Inn.* **Sun 22, Sun 29 Mar, Sun 12, Mon 13, Sun 26 Apr, Sat 9, Sun 10 May (2-5). Adm £5, chd free. Home-made teas. Visits also by arrangement Mar to May for groups of 10+.**
Unusual and challenging ½ acre garden set on steep hillside with fine views. Wildlife friendly garden with mixed borders, ponds, propagating area, vegetable garden, fruit cage, greenhouses and polytunnel, chickens and bees, nearby allotment. Daffodils, tulips and hellebores in quantity for spring openings. Come prepared for steep terrain and a warm welcome! We hope to hold a special Live Music event in the garden sometime during the last w/e. Run on organic lines with plants to attract birds, bees and other insects. Insect-friendly plants usually for sale. Honey and hive products available and, weather permitting, observation hive of honey bees in courtyard. Beekeeper present to answer queries!

✿ ☕

39 ◆ KEYNESTON MILL
Tarrant Keyneston, Blandford Forum, DT11 9HZ. Julia & David Bridger, 01258 456831, events@keynestonmill.com, www.keynestonmill.com. *From Blandford or Wimborne take the B3082. Turn into Tarrant Keyneston village and continue right through to Xrds, we are straight ahead.* **For NGS: Tue 2 June, Tue 15 Sept (2-5). Adm £5, chd free. Home-made teas. Tea and home-made cake on NGS days. For other opening times and information, please phone, email or visit garden website.**
Keyneston Mill is the creative home of Parterre Fragrances - a 50 acre estate dedicated to fragrant and aromatic plants. Enjoy the Collection Gardens, each compartment featuring plants from a different perfume family eg. floral, fern, spice. Walk through the crop fields where we grow the ingredients for our perfumes, visit the exhibition and distillery. Open all yr, please see above website for details. Compacted gravel paths in floral garden, lawns elsewhere. Wheelchair access to bistro-café and WCs. Dogs on leads allowed.

♿ 🐑 ✿ ☕

40 ◆ KINGSTON LACY
Wimborne Minster, BH21 4EA. National Trust, 01202 883402, kingstonlacy@nationaltrust.org.uk, www.nationaltrust.org.uk/kingston-lacy. *2½ m W of Wimborne Minster. On Wimborne-Blandford rd B3082.* **For opening times and information, please phone, email or visit garden website.**
35 acres of formal garden, incorporating parterre and sunk garden planted with Edwardian schemes during spring and summer. 5 acre kitchen garden and allotments. Victorian fernery containing over 35 varieties. Rose garden, mixed herbaceous borders, vast formal lawns and Japanese garden restored to Henrietta Bankes' creation of 1910. 2 National Collections: Convallaria and Anemone nemorosa. Snowdrops, blossom, bluebells, autumn colour and Christmas light display. Deep gravel on some paths but lawns suitable for wheelchairs. Slope to visitor reception and South lawn. Dogs allowed in some areas of woodland.

♿ ✿ 🚗 NPC ☕

41 ◆ KINGSTON MAURWARD GARDENS AND ANIMAL PARK
Kingston Maurward, Dorchester, DT2 8PY. Kingston Maurward College, 01305 215003, events@kmc.ac.uk, www.morekmc.com. *1m E of Dorchester. Off A35. Follow brown Tourist Information signs.* **For opening times and information, please phone, email or visit garden website.**
Stepping into the grounds you will be greeted with 35 impressive acres of formal gardens. During the late spring and summer months, our National Collection of penstemons and salvias display a lustrous rainbow of purples, pinks, blues and whites, leading you on through the ample hedges and stonework balustrades. An added treat is the Elizabethan walled garden, offering a new vision of enchantment. Open early Jan to mid Dec. Hours will vary in winter depending on conditions - check garden website or call before visiting. Partial wheelchair access only, gravel paths, steps and steep slopes. Map provided at entry, highlighting the most suitable routes.

&. 🚗 🍵

42 KNITSON OLD FARMHOUSE
Corfe Castle, Wareham, BH20 5JB. Rachel Helfer, 01929 421681, rjehelfer@gmail.com. *2m NW of Swanage. 3m E of Corfe Castle. Signed L off A351 to Knitson. Very narrow rds for 1m. Ample parking in yard or in adjacent field.* **Fri 10, Sat 11, Sun 12, Mon 13 Apr, Fri 22, Sat 23, Sun 24, Mon 25 May (2-5). Adm £4, chd free. Home-made cakes, gluten free cakes, cream teas. Visits also by arrangement Mar to Oct for groups of up to 30.**
Mature cottage garden nestled at base of chalk downland. Herbaceous borders, rockeries, climbers and shrubs, evolved and designed over 50yrs for yr-round colour and interest. Large wildlife friendly kitchen garden for self sufficiency. Rachel is delighted to welcome visitors, discuss all aspects of sustainable gardening, soil health and the benefits of gardening for mental and physical wellbeing. We have used a lot of local stone in the design and have interesting old stones and stone baths around the garden. The garden is on a slope, the main lawn and tea area is level. But there are uneven, sloping paths.

&. 🐕 ❀ 🍵

43 ◆ KNOLL GARDENS
Hampreston, Wimborne, BH21 7ND. Mr Neil Lucas, 01202 873931, enquiries@knollgardens.co.uk, www.knollgardens.co.uk. *2½ m W of Ferndown. ETB brown signs from all directions approaching Wimborne. Large car park.* **For NGS: Fri 26 June, Fri 25 Sept (10-5). Adm £6.95, chd £4.50. Light refreshments. Self catering drinks and pre-wrapped cakes. For other opening times and information, please phone, email or visit garden website.**
A stunning naturalistic garden, its renowned ornamental grasses steal the show whilst also providing a fabulous foil for thousands of flowering perennials. A mini-arboretum of unusual trees and shrubs adds height, interest and a further habitat for wildlife. Practical planting ideas abound, with plants from the onsite nursery taking the starring role in this inspirational garden. Year round event programme includes grass masterclasses, naturalistic design workshops and creative courses. Events are bookable online at knollgardens.co.uk The garden's charity the Knoll Gardens Foundation researches and promotes sustainable, wildlife friendly gardening: knollgardensfoundation.org. Some slopes. Various surfaces incl gravel, paving, grass and bark.

&. ❀ 🍴 NPC 🍵

44 NEW KNOWLE COTTAGE
Shorts Lane, Beaminster, DT8 3BD. Claire Fender. *Park in main square of Beaminster or in Main Town Car Park and walk down Church lane to single track Shorts lane, where there is no parking. Entry through gates on L.* **Sat 9 May, Sat 11 July (11-3.30). Adm £4.50, chd £2.50. Light refreshments. Limited outside seating available.**
Large one and half acre garden with 35m long S-facing herbaceous border with yr round colour. Formal rose garden within a circular floral planting is bound on 3 sides by lavender. Small orchard and vegetable with raised beds in adjacent walled area, with whole garden leading to small stream, and bridge to pasture. Beds accessed from level grass, slope not suitable for wheelchairs. No dogs.

&. 🍵

45 LAWSBROOK
Brodham Way, Shillingstone, DT11 0TE. Clive Nelson, 01258 860148, cne70bl@aol.com, www.facebook.com/Lawsbrook. *5m NW of Blandford. To Shillingstone on A357. Turn up Gunn Lane - up lane (past Wessex Avenue on L & Everetts Lane on R) then turn R at next opportunity as road bends to L. Lawsbrook 250m on R.* **Sun 16, Sun 23 Feb, Sun 31 May, Sun 8, Sun 15 Nov (10-5). Adm £3.50, chd free. Home-made teas. Visits also by arrangement Feb to Nov. Lunches by arrangement.**
Open for over 10 yrs for NGS. Garden incl over 130 different tree species spread over 6 acres. Native species and many unusual specimens incl Dawn redwood, Damyio oak and Wollemi pine. Large borders, raised bed vegetable and flower garden. Wildlife, stream and meadow. You can be assured of a relaxed and friendly day out. Children's activities, all day teas/cakes and dogs are very welcome. Large scale snowdrop days in Feb, wonderful all summer garden and intense autumn hues in Nov. Enough space and interest for everyone. Gravel path at entrance, grass paths over whole garden.

&. 🐕 ❀ 🚗 🍵

46 ◆ LITTLEBREDY WALLED GARDENS
Littlebredy, DT2 9HL. The Walled Garden Workshop, 01305 898055, secretary@wgw.org.uk, www.littlebredy.com. *8m W of Dorchester. 10m E of Bridport. 1½ m S of A35. NGS days: park on village green then walk 300yds. For the less mobile (and on normal open days) use gardens car park.* **For NGS: Tue 23, Tue 30 June (2-6). Adm £5, chd free. Home-made teas. For other opening times and information, please phone, email or visit garden website.**
1 acre walled garden on S-facing slopes of Bride River Valley. Herbaceous borders, riverside rose walk, lavender beds and potager vegetable and cut flower gardens. Original Victorian glasshouses, one under renovation. Partial wheelchair access, some steep grass slopes. For disabled parking please follow signs to main entrance.

&. 🐕 ❀ 🍵

47 44 LOWER BLANDFORD ROAD
Broadstone Poole, BH18 8NY.
Mike & Tina Clifford. *Take Lower
Blandford Rd leading up to
Broadstone centre approaching
from Derbys Corner r'about. Take
1st turning on R. (Fontmell Rd) then
sharp L. Extra parking in Fontmell
Rd.* **Sat 1, Sun 2, Sat 29, Sun 30
Aug (11-4). Adm £4, chd free.
Home-made teas.**
Exotic garden full of bananas, palms
and lush tropical planting, the garden
is filled to the brim with unusual
and rare plants, many seldom seen
in British gardens. Paths lead you
through to the greenhouses and
an Abbotsbury inspired colonial
summerhouse and water feature
surrounded by tree ferns and shade
loving plants. A true plantaholic's
paradise!

**48 MANOR FARM,
HAMPRESTON**
Wimborne, BH21 7LX. **Guy &
Anne Trehane, 01202 574223,
anne.trehane@live.co.uk.** *2½ m E
of Wimborne, 2½ m W of Ferndown.
From Canford Bottom r'about on
A31, take exit B3073 Ham Lane.
½ m turn R at Hampreston Xrds.
House at bottom of village.* **Sat 22
Feb (10-1); Sun 23 Feb (12-4);
Sun 14 June, Sun 26 July, Wed
5, Sun 9 Aug (1-5). Adm £4, chd
free. Home-made teas. Soup also
available at Feb openings. Visits
also by arrangement Feb to Aug
for groups of 10+.**
Traditional farmhouse garden
designed and cared for by 3
generations of the Trehane family
through over 100yrs of farming and
gardening at Hampreston. Garden
is noted for its herbaceous borders
and rose beds within box and yew
hedges. Mature shrubbery, water and
bog garden. Open for hellebores and

snowdrops in Feb. Dorset Hardy Plant
Society sales at openings. Hellebores
for sale in Feb.

**49 NEW MANOR FARM,
STOURTON CAUNDLE**
Stourton Caundle, DT10 2JW.
Mr & Mrs O S L Simon. *6m E of
Sherborne, 4 m W of Sturminster
Newton. From Sherborne take
A3030. At Bishops Caundle, L
signed Stourton Caundle. After
1½ m, L opp Trooper Inn in middle
of village.* **Sat 30, Sun 31 May
(2-5.30). Adm £6, chd free. Home-
made teas.**
C17 farmhouse and barns with walled
garden in middle of village. Mature
trees, shrubberies, herbaceous
borders, lakes and vegetable garden.
Lovingly created over last 50 yrs by
current owners. Wheelchair access
to lower areas of garden, steps to top
areas of garden.

Manor Farm, Stourton Caundle

50 MANOR HOUSE FARM

Ibberton, Blandford Forum, DT11 0EN. Fiona Closier, www.instagram.com/ thefloristwithin/?hl=en. *Off A357 between Blandford Forum and Sturminster Newton. From A357 at Shillingstone take road to Okeford Fitzpaine. Follow signs for Belchalwell and Ibberton. Continue through Belchalwell to Ibberton.* Sun 14, Sun 21 June (2-5). Adm £5, chd free. Home-made teas.
Set in the lee of Bulbarrow Hill, this 1½ acre partially terraced garden has formal yew and beech hedging interspersed with topiary, lawn, and many abundantly filled herbaceous borders. Native trees, 2 spring-fed ponds attracting wildlife, and walled kitchen garden also give many areas of interest. Orchard area left to meadow with spring bulbs. Partial wheelchair access due to steps and steep grass areas. No ground floor level disabled toilet.

51 THE MANOR HOUSE, BEAMINSTER

North St, Beaminster, DT8 3DZ. Christine Wood. *200yds N of town square. Park in the square or public car park, 5 mins walk along North St from the Square. Limited disabled parking on site.* Sun 3, Mon 4 May (11-5, sorry, no teas). Sun 24, Mon 25 May, Sun 21 June (11-5). Home-made teas in Coach House Garden or bring a picnic. Adm £5, chd free.
Set in heart of Beaminster, 16½ acres of stunning parkland with mature specimen trees, lake and waterfall, The Manor House looks forward to welcoming visitors after a 2 year break from opening the grounds. A peaceful garden with woodland walk, wild flower meadow and walled garden "serendipity", designed and lovingly planted over last 10 yrs. Ornamental ducks, black swans, pigmy goats, chickens and guinea pigs. Partial wheelchair access.

52 ◆ MAPPERTON GARDENS

Mapperton, Beaminster, DT8 3NR. The Earl & Countess of Sandwich, 01308 862645, office@mapperton.com, www.mapperton.com. *6m N of Bridport. Off A356/A3066. 2m SE of Beaminster off B3163.* For opening times and information, please phone, email or visit garden website.
Terraced valley gardens surrounding Tudor/Jacobean manor house. On upper levels, walled croquet lawn, orangery and Italianate formal garden with fountains, topiary and grottoes. Below, C17 summerhouse and fishponds. Lower garden with shrubs and rare trees, leading to woodland and spring gardens. Garden & Café open 8 Mar to 29 Oct (except Fri/Sat) (10-5); house open 8 Mar to 29 Oct (except Fri/Sat) guided tours only at 12, 1, 2 and 3pm (booking advisable). Snowdrop Sundays 2, 9 & 16 Feb 2020. Partial wheelchair access (lawn and upper levels).

53 MAYFIELD

4 Walford Close, Wimborne Minster, BH21 1PH. Mr & Mrs Terry Wheeler, 01202 849838, terpau@talktalk.net. *½m N of Wimborne Town Centre. B3078 out of Wimborne, R into Burts Hill, 1st L into Walford Close.* Fri 8, Sun 24, Mon 25, Sun 31 May, Sun 14 June (2-5). Adm £3.50, chd free. Home-made teas. Visits also by arrangement May & June for groups of 5 to 30.
Town garden of approx ¼ acre. Front: formal hard landscaping planted with drought-resistant shrubs and perennials. Back garden contrasts with a seductive series of garden rooms containing herbaceous perennial beds separated by winding grass paths and rustic arches. Pond, vegetable beds and greenhouses containing succulents and vines. Garden access is across a pea-shingle drive. If this is manageable, wheelchairs can access the back garden provided they are no wider than 65cms.

54 THE MILL HOUSE

Crook Hill, Netherbury, DT6 5LX. Mike & Shirley Bennett. *1m S of Beaminster. Turn R off A3066 Beaminster to Bridport rd signed Netherbury. Car park at Xrds at bottom of hill.* Sun 17 May (11-4.30). Adm £6, chd £1. Light refreshments.
6½ acres of garden next to R Brit, incl mill house, mill stream and pond. Extensive garden with formal beds, lawns, terraced areas, stunning walled garden and vegetable patch. Explore the paddock and orchard, planted with rare and interesting trees including magnolias, conifers, eucalyptus and fruit trees. The Mill House garden is a haven for wildlife - you may be lucky to see a kingfisher or two. Children to be supervised at all times due to river and mill pond. Partial wheelchair access due to some steps.

55 ◆ MINTERNE GARDEN

Minterne House, Minterne Magna, Dorchester, DT2 7AU. Lord & Lady Digby, 01300 341370, enquiries@minterne.co.uk, www.minterne.co.uk. *2m N of Cerne Abbas. On A352 Dorchester-Sherborne rd.* For opening times and information, please phone, email or visit garden website.
As seen on BBC Gardeners' World and voted one of the 10 prettiest gardens in England by The Times. Famed for their display of rhododendrons, azaleas, Japanese cherries and magnolias in April/May. Small lakes, streams and cascades offer new vistas at each turn around the 1m horseshoe shaped gardens covering 23 acres. The season ends with spectacular autumn colour. Snowdrops in Feb. Spring bulbs, blossom and bluebells in April. Garden at its peak in April/May with historic rhododendron collection, magnolias and azaleas. Over 200 acers provide spectacular autumn colour in Sept/Oct. Regret unsuitable for wheelchairs.

56 NORWOOD HOUSE GARDENS & WALKS

Corscombe, Dorchester, DT2 0PD. Mr & Mrs Jonathan Lewis, 07836 600185, jonathan.lewis@livegroup.co.uk. *Equidistant between Halstock and Corscombe. 1m from Fox Inn towards Halstock. 1m from national speed limit sign leaving Halstock towards Corscombe. Access for medium sized coaches only. Parking for private cars* Visits by arrangement Thursdays mid-June to mid-July for groups of 20+. Adm £6, chd £3. Home-made teas in large garage in very poor weather. Light canapes and wine for early evening bookings.
Our garden is hidden away in a stunning West Dorset Valley surrounded by our small family estate. We started our landscaping adventure from scratch in 2011. Today the glorious purple, pink and white borders surround the house and lawns. Many varieties of geranium

Abbey House, Witchampton Gardens

and other perennials, grasses, shrubs and rockery. Lake, woodland and wild flower walks thoroughly recommended, weather permitting. We can organise a special double garden visit locally which makes for an excellent day out to view 2 entirely different gardens. Catering can be provided at both. We can assist wheelchair users to access the gardens only some parts of which are inaccessible.

57 OLD DOWN HOUSE
Horton, Wimborne,
BH21 7HL. Dr & Mrs Colin
Davidson, 07765 404248,
pipdavidson59@gmail.com.
7½ m N of Wimborne. Horton Inn at junction of B3078 with Horton Rd, pick up yellow signs leading up through North Farm. No garden access from Matterley Drove. 5min walk to garden down farm track. **Sat 30, Sun 31 May, Wed 3 June (2-5). Adm £3.50, chd free. Home-made teas in comfortable garden room if weather inclement.**
Nestled down a farm track, this ¾ acre garden on chalk surrounds C18 farmhouse. Stunning views over Horton Tower and farmland. Cottage garden planting with formal elements.

Climbing roses clothe pergola and house walls along with stunning wisteria sinensis and banksia rose. Part walled potager, well stocked. Chickens. Hardy Plant Society plant stall. Not suitable for wheelchairs.

58 THE OLD RECTORY, LITTON CHENEY
Litton Cheney, Dorchester,
DT2 9AH. Richard & Emily
Cave, 01308 482266,
emilycave@rosacheney.com. *9m W of Dorchester. 1m S of A35, 6m E of Bridport. Small village in the beautiful Bride Valley. Park in village and follow signs.* **Sun 3, Wed 6 May, Sun 14 June (2-5). Adm £6, chd free. Home-made teas. Visits also by arrangement.**
Steep paths lead to beguiling 4 acres of natural woodland with many springs, streams, 2 pools one a natural swimming pool planted with native plants. Front garden with pleached crabtree border, topiary and soft planting incl tulips, peonies, roses and verbascums. Walled garden with informal planting, kitchen garden, orchard and 350 rose bushes for a cut flower business. Formal front garden designed by Arne Maynard.

Not suitable for wheelchairs.

59 THE OLD RECTORY, MANSTON
Manston, Sturminster Newton,
DT10 1EX. Andrew & Judith
Hussey, 01258 474673,
judithhussey@hotmail.com.
6m S of Shaftesbury, 2½ m N of Sturminster Newton. From Shaftesbury, take B3091. On reaching Manston, past Plough Inn, L for Child Okeford on R-hand bend. Old Rectory last house on L. **Visits by arrangement May to Sept for groups of 5+. Adm £5, chd free. Home-made teas.**
Beautifully restored 5 acre garden. S-facing wall with 120ft herbaceous border edged by old brick path. Enclosed yew hedge flower garden. Wildflower meadow marked with mown paths and young plantation of mixed hardwoods. Well maintained walled Victorian kitchen garden with new picking flower section. Large new greenhouse also installed. Knot garden now well established.

60 THE OLD RECTORY, NETHERBURY

Beaminster, DT6 5NB.
Simon & Amanda Mehigan,
mehigansimon@gmail.com, , www.
oldrectorynetherbury.tumblr.com.
2m SW of Beaminster. Please park considerably in village as directed bearing in mind that large tractors need to be able to pass. Parking for the less mobile available at house. **Visits by arrangement Apr to June. We will be open on 3 specific dates only. Please email for further details. Home-made teas.**
5 acre garden designed and maintained by present owners over last 25 yrs. Formal areas with topiary near house, large drifts of naturalistic planting elsewhere. Spring bulbs incl species tulips and erythroniums are a speciality. Extensive bog garden with pond and stream, large collection of candelabra primulas and other moisture lovers. Hornbeam walk. Wild flower areas and orchards. Decorative kitchen/cutting garden. Regional Finalist, The English Garden's The Nation's Favourite Gardens 2019. Unsuitable for wheelchairs due to steps and steep slopes.

61 THE OLD RECTORY, PULHAM

Dorchester, DT2 7EA. Mr & Mrs N Elliott, 01258 817595, gilly.elliott@hotmail.com. *13m N of Dorchester. 8m SE of Sherborne. On B3143 turn E at Xrds in Pulham. Signed Cannings Court.* **Sun 10, Thur 14 May, Sun 2, Thur 6 Aug (2-5). Adm £6, chd free. Home-made teas. Visits also by arrangement May to Sept for groups of 5+.**
4 acres formal and informal gardens surround C18 rectory, splendid views. Yew pyramid allées and hedges, circular herbaceous borders with late summer colour. Exuberantly planted terrace, purple and white beds. Box parterres, mature trees, pond, fernery, ha-ha, pleached hornbeam circle. 10 acres woodland walks. Flourishing extended bog garden with islands; awash with primulas and irises in May. Interesting plants for sale. Mostly wheelchair access.

62 THE OLD SCHOOL HOUSE

The Street, Sutton Waldron, Blandford Forum, DT11 8NZ.
David Milanes. *Turn into Sutton Waldron from A350, continue for 300 yds, 1st house on L in The Street. Entrance past house through gates in wall.* **Sun 14, Wed 17 June (2-5). Adm £3.50, chd free. Home-made cakes and gluten free.**
Small village garden laid out in last 6 yrs with planting of hedges into rooms incl orchard, secret garden and pergola walkway. Strong framework of existing large trees, beds are mostly planted with roses and herbaceous plants. Pleached hornbeam screen. A designer's garden with interesting semi-tender plants close to house. Level lawns.

63 THE OLD VICARAGE

East Orchard, Shaftesbury, SP7 0BA. Miss Tina Wright, 01747 811744, tina_lon@msn.com. *4½m S of Shaftesbury, 3½m N of Sturminster Newton. Between 90 degree bend and lay-bye with old red phone box. Parking is on opp corner towards Hartgrove.* **Sat 8 Feb (2-4.30); Sun 15 Mar, Sun 26 Apr, Sun 31 May (2-5). Adm £4, chd free. Home-made teas will be inside if raining, with wood stove if cold. Visits also by arrangement Feb to Nov.**
A 1.7 wildlife garden with lots of different snowdrops and other winter flowering shrubs. Followed by other bulbs including hundreds of narcissi and tulips, followed by camassias and alliums. A wonderful stream meanders down to a pond and there are lovely reflections from the swimming pond. Tree viewing platform allows you to look over garden and to the wider area. Grotto, lots of ponds, old Victorian man pushing his lawn mower his owner purchased brand new in 1866. Not suitable for wheelchairs if very wet.

64 THE PARISH HOUSE

West Knoyle, Warminster, BA12 6AJ. Philip & Alex Davies. *Nr Mere Wiltshire. From east on A303 take signpost to West Knoyle at petrol station. Continue down hill and past church, take first R signposted Charnage, continue 1m to end of lane. Parking in field on L.* **Sun 24, Mon 25 May (2-5). Adm £4, chd free. Home-made teas. Gluten free.**
The garden at The Parish House is small and S-facing surrounded by hedges protecting it from the exposure of a high wide open landscape beyond. The garden is laid out with gravel to encourage a self-seeding natural look but there are also roses and herbaceous perennials as well. The look is held together with topiary. Beyond this garden there is a larger area of lawn, trees and developing bulb cover (Camassias in May). Large conservatory greenhouse containing mature Muscat grapevine, Passiflora exoniensis and pelargoniums. Small vegetable garden recently added. Level but gravel surfaces, some lawn.

65 NEW PHILIPSTON HOUSE

Winterborne Clenston, Blandford Forum, DT11 0NR. Mark & Ana Hudson. *Off road between Winterborne Whitechurch and Winterborne Stickland. 2m N of Winterborne Whitechurch and 1 km S of Crown Inn in Winterborne Stickland. Park in signed track/field off road, near Bourne Farm Cottage. Enter garden from field.* **Sat 13, Sat 20 June (2-6). Adm £4, chd free. Cream teas and cakes, tea and coffee on terrace and/or main lawn.**
Charming 2 acre garden with lovely views in the Clenston Valley. Many unusual trees, rambling roses, wisteria, mixed borders and shrubs. Rose parterre, walled garden, swimming pool garden, vegetable garden. Winterbourne stream with bridge over to wooded shady area with cedar-wood pavilion. Orchard with mown paths planted with spring bulbs. Wheelchair access good providing it is dry. Plants for sale on at least one of the open days.

66 PILSDON VIEW

Junction Butts Lane and Pitman's Lane, Ryall, Bridport, DT6 6EH. D Lloyd. *5m W of Bridport, through Chideok. From E through Morecombelake A35. Take the Ryall turning opp Felicity's farm shop on A35. Garden ¾m on L at junction Butts Lane/Pitmans Lane. High hedge with PO box in wall.* **Sat 16, Sun 17, Mon 18 May (1-5.30). Combined adm with Well Cottage £6, chd free. Teas at Well Cottage.**
Started over 25 yrs ago, the hard landscaping provides different levels

with breathtaking views over the Marshwood Vale towards Pilson Pen. Mature copper beech and evolving garden gives all yr round interest. Water features with wildlife add to the essence of the garden. We have now added a rose garden. Winner of the Melplash Show (West Dorset) large and overall garden contest 2012 and 2nd in the large garden contest 2019. Partial wheelchair access.

67 PUGIN HALL

Rampisham, nr Dorchester, DT2 0PR. Mr & Mrs Tim Wright, 01935 83652, wright.alison68@yahoo.com. *Near centre of village. NW of Dorchester. From Dorchester A37 Yeovil, 9m L Evershot, follow signs. From Crewkerne A356, take 1st L to Rampisham, Pugin Hall is on L after ½ m.* **Visits by arrangement May to Aug. Adm £6, chd £3. Home-made teas at Pugin Hall refreshments such as canapes and early evening wine can be provided if required. A special double garden visit can be organised.**
Pugin Hall was once Rampisham Rectory, designed in 1847 by Augustus Pugin, who also helped to design the interior of the Houses of Parliament. A grade 1 listed building, it is surrounded by 4½ acres of garden, including a large front lawn with rhododendrons and perennial borders, a walled vegetable, fruit and cut flower garden, orchard and beyond the river Frome a woodland walk. Partial wheelchair access, gravel driveway and steps to terraced lawns.

68 2 PYES PLOT

St. James Road, Netherbury, Bridport, DT6 5LP. Sarah Porter Martyn Lock. *2m SW of Beaminster. Turn off A3066. Go over R Brit into centre of village. L into St James Rd, signed to Waytown, R corner Hingsdon Lane.* **Sun 17 May (11-4.30). Adm £4, chd free. Also open The Mill House.**
Small but perfectly formed front and back courtyard garden, created from new in 2007. Cream walls and black paintwork make a striking framework for softer planting. Climbing plants, foliage and running water feature enhance the tranquil feel to this space, which uses every inch creatively. Home-made teas at Slape Manor.

69 Q

113 Bridport Road, Dorchester, DT1 2NH. Heather & Chris Robinson, 01305 263088, hmrobinson45@gmail.com. *Approx 300m W of Dorset County Hospital. From Top o' Town r'about head W towards Dorset County Hospital, Q 300 metres further on from Hospital on R.* **Visits by arrangement Mar to July for groups of 10 to 30. Adm £3.50, chd free. Home-made teas. Can provide light refreshment if requested early.**
Q is essentially all things to all men, a modern cottage town garden, divided into rooms, with many facets, jam packed with shrubs, trees, climbers and herbaceous plants. Gazebo, statutes, water, bonsai and topiary. Planting reflects the owners' many and varied interest incl over 100 clematis. In spring the garden flourishes with different types and varieties of bulbs, planted yearly, from early snowdrops, herbaceous plants incl hellebores, clematis, daphne. Vegetable garden and fruit trees dotted around the garden. Small number of paths available for wheelchair users.

GROUP OPENING

70 RAMPISHAM GARDENS

Rampisham, DT2 0PR. *11m NW of Dorchester. From Dorchester A37 Yeovil, 4m L A356 to Crewkerne, 6m R to Rampisham. From Yeovil A37 Dorchester, 7m R Evershot. From Crewkerne A356, 1½ m after Rampisham Garage L Rampisham. Follow signs.* **Sun 28 June (1.30-5.30). Combined adm £8, chd free. Home-made teas at Broomhill.**

BROOMHILL
Mr & Mrs D Parry.
(See separate entry)

THE CURATAGE
Mr & Mrs Tim Hill.

ROSEMARY COTTAGE
Lady Ford.

This beautiful historic village hosts a wide variety of gardens with 3 hidden gems. A delightful, tranquil garden set in 1½ acres. Island beds and borders are planted with shrubs, roses, masses of unusual perennials and choice annuals to give vibrancy and colour. Lawns and paths lead to less formal area with large wildlife pond, meadow, shaded areas, bog garden and late summer

border. A small cottage style garden, growing flowers, fruit and vegetables, with eating area, small pond, wild grass circle, and Wendy house! An informal, 1½ acre, country garden, with stream, pond, and bog garden. Borders of shrub roses and perennials give way to an area of wild flowers and grasses. Since allowing the wild areas to flourish many flowers are returning, including orchids, and insect life is thriving. C15 church with modifications in the 1840s by Pugin. At Rosemary Cottage grassy slopes and stone steps make wheelchair access to most of the garden difficult.

71 25 RICHMOND PARK AVENUE

Bournemouth, BH8 9DL. Barbara Hutchinson & Mike Roberts, 01202 531072, barbarahutchinson@tiscali.co.uk. *2½ m NE Bournemouth Town Centre. From T-lights at junction with Alma Rd and Richmond Park Rd, head N on B3063 Charminster Rd, 2nd turning on R into Richmond Park Ave.* **Sun 21 June, Sun 5, Sun 26 July (2-5). Adm £4, chd free. Home-made teas. Visits also by arrangement June to Aug for groups of 10 to 30.**
Beautifully designed town garden with pergola leading to ivy canopy over raised decking. Cascading waterfall connects 2 wildlife ponds enhanced with domed acers. Circular lawn with colourful herbaceous border planted to attract bees and butterflies. Fragrant S-facing courtyard garden at front, sparkling with vibrant colour and Mediterranean planting. As featured in Amateur Gardening & Garden News. VOICE community choir will be singing in the garden at 3pm on Sunday 26th. July. Partial wheelchair access.

Holme For Gardens

72 NEW ▸ **ROSEBANK**
8 Love Lane, Shaftesbury, SP7 8BG.
Nigel and Shouanna Hawkins.
*Shaftesbury. Park in town's main car
park. Walk along Bimport Take 3rd
L opp hospital sign into Magdalene
Lane, continue past hospital into Love
Lane. Reserved disabled parking in
drive.* Sat 16, Sun 17 May (10.30-
4.30). Adm £3, chd free. Also open
Edwardstowe.
Delightful small garden living up to
its name, 106 rose plants have been
bedded in during the last three years,
transforming the front garden into
box-edged flower beds with peonies,
rose arches and pergolas. The back
garden is in cottage style, planted
with many varieties of herbaceous
perennials and T-roses. Entrance
slope and access around garden.
&

73 THE SECRET GARDEN
The Friary, Hilfield, Dorchester,
DT2 7BE. The Society of
St Francis, 01300 341345,
hilfieldssf@franciscans.org.uk,
www.hilfieldfriary.org.uk. *10m N
of Dorchester, on A352 between
Sherborne & Dorchester. 1st L after
Minterne Magna, 1st turning on
R signed The Friary. From Yeovil
turn off A37 signed Batcombe,
3rd turning on L.* Sat 9, Sun 10
May (2-5). Adm £5, chd free.
Home-made cakes and teas.
Visits also by arrangement May
to Oct for groups of 5 to 30.
Light refreshments available for a
further donation.
A beautiful array of diverse plants
and trees. Empty wine bottles as
suggested by the RHS now line the
pathway to the Secret Garden. In time
the metal guideposts will be blue and
the bridges painted red. New plantings
of viburnums and further planting from
Crug Farm Plants. The £5 entry fee
does not include tea and cakes for
which a further donation is suggested.
Friary grounds open where meadows,
woods and livestock can be viewed.
Friary Shop selling a variety of gifts.
Wheelchair access along our private
road and main areas.
& 🐄 🚐 🛏 ☕ 🌳

74 THE SECRET GARDEN AND
SERLES HOUSE
47 Victoria Road, Wimborne,
BH21 1EN. Ian Willis. *Centre of
Wimborne. On B3082 W of town,
very near hospital, Westfield car park
300yds. Off-road parking close by.*
Sun 12, Thur 16 July, Sun 19, Sun
26 July, Thur 30 July, Sun 2 Aug.
Sun 16, Thur 20, Sun 23, Sun 30,
Mon 31 Aug. Thur 3, Sat 5, Sun 6,
Thur 10, Sun 13 Sept (2-5). Adm
£3.50, chd free. Home-made teas.
Donation to Wimborne Civic Society
and The Arts' Society.
Alan Titchmarsh described this
amusingly creative garden as 'one
of the best 10 private gardens in
Britain'. The ingenious use of unusual
plants complements the imaginative
treasure trove of garden objects
d'art. The enchanting house is also
open. A feeling of a bygone age
accompanies your tour as you step
into a world of whimsical fantasy that
is theatrical and unique. 'Deliciously
bonkers'. Antiques and bric-a-brac
on sale. On 12th July, an Auctioneer/
Valuer from Duke's of Dorchester

will be in attendance to appraise/value items visitors choose to bring along. Voluntary donations to NGS. Period Victorian House also open with Gothic Conservatory. Oriental Summer House and Indian Summer Room to view. High summer garden with dahlias at their best late August/early September. Wheelchair access to garden only. Narrow steps may prohibit wide wheelchairs.

🔥 ✿ 🚐 ☕

75 NEW SEMLEY GRANGE
Semley, Shaftesbury, SP7 9AP. Mr & Mrs Reid Scott. *From A350 take turning to Semley continue along road and under railway bridge. Take 1st R up Sem Hill. Semley Grange is first on L - parking on green.* **Sun 28 June (2-5). Adm £5, chd free. Home-made teas. Also open Grove House. Gluten free cakes.** Large garden recreated in the last 10 years. Herbaceous border, lawn and wild flower meadow intersected by paths and planted with numerous bulbs. The garden has been greatly expanded by introducing many standard weeping roses, new mixed borders, pergolas and raised beds for dahlias, underplanted with alliums. Numerous fruit and ornamental trees introduced over last 10 yrs.

🔥 ☕

76 SHADRACK HOUSE
Shadrack Street, Beaminster, DT8 3BE. Mr & Mrs Hugh Lindsay, 01308 863923, christine.corson@ngs.org.uk. *Centre of Beaminster. Combined with 21A the Square, Beaminster DT8 3AU, Shadrack St is within 5 mins walk.* **Visits by arrangement May to Sept for groups of 5 to 10. Adm £5, chd free.** Delightful small mature garden, hidden behind high walls, with abundance of roses, clematis, shrubs, and climbers galore. Entrance through garden gates below the house. Beaminster Festival end of June, beginning of July. Sadly not very wheelchair friendly, steepish steps to enter.

✿ ☕

77 ◆ SHERBORNE CASTLE
New Rd, Sherborne, DT9 5NR. Mr E Wingfield Digby, www.sherbornecastle.com. *½m E of Sherborne. On New Rd B3145. Follow brown signs from A30 & A352.* **For opening times and**

information, please visit garden website.
40+ acres. Grade I Capability Brown garden with magnificent vistas across surrounding landscape, incl lake and views to ruined castle. Herbaceous planting, notable trees, mixed ornamental planting and managed wilderness are linked together with lawn and pathways. Dry grounds walk. Partial wheelchair access, gravel paths, steep slopes, steps.

🔥 🐕 🚐 ☕

78 NEW SHUTE FARM
Donhead St Mary, SP7 9DG. John and Caroline David. *5m E of Shaftesbury. Take A350 towards Warminster from Shaftesbury. Turn R at 1st turning outside of Shaftesbury, signed Wincombe & Donhead St Mary. At Donhead St Mary, turn R at T-junction. 1st house on L opp tel box.* **Sat 23, Sun 24 May (2-5). Adm £5, chd free. Tea.** Charming cottage garden around thatched house. Plenty to see and explore. Small stream, pond, kitchen garden and wild flower area. Neat and tidy flower beds change to a wild garden as they join the fields. Magnificent views over the Donheads.

🐕 🚐 ☕

79 SLAPE MANOR
Netherbury, DT6 5LH. Mr & Mrs Antony Hichens. *1m S of Beaminster. Turn W off A3066 to Netherbury. House ½m S of Netherbury on back rd to Bridport signed Waytown.* **Sun 17 May (2-5). Adm £5, chd free. Home-made teas.** River valley garden with spacious lawns and primula fringed streams down to lake. Walk over the stream with magnificent hostas, gunneras and horizontal Cryptomeria japonica Elegans, and around the lake. Admire the mature wellingtonias, ancient wisterias, rhododendrons and planting around the house. Mostly flat with some sloping paths and steps.

🔥 🐕 ✿ ☕

Your visits help change lives – we are the largest single funder of the Queen's Nursing Institute

80 NEW 21A THE SQUARE
Beaminster, DT8 3AU. Christine Corson, 01308 863923, christine.corson@ngs.org.uk. *The Square Beaminster. 6m N of Bridport. 6m S of Crewkerne on B3162. Both gdns 5 mins walk from Public Car Park.* **Visits by arrangement May to Sept for groups of 5 to 10. Several cafés nearby for lunch or tea. Adm £5, chd free.** Together with 4 Shadrack St, 2 town gardens, within walking distance of each other, one 4 yrs old, started from scratch, the other well established, both with lovely views and both quite large for town gardens. 21A is a plantaholic and flower arranger's garden which says all! There is something to pick all yr round. Wide collection of shrubs, trees, roses and borders. 3rd prize at Melplash Show in 2019 for medium gardens. Very wheelchair friendly, house and garden flat, and ramp from house into garden.

☕

81 STABLE COURT
Chalmington, Dorchester, DT2 0HB. Jenny & James Shanahan, 01300 321345, jennyshanahan8@gmail.com. *From A37 travel towards Cattistock & Chalmington for 1½m turn R at triangle to Chalmington. ½m house on R red letter box at gate. From Cattistock take first turn R then next L at triangle.* **Wed 17, Sun 21 June (2-5.30). Adm £5, chd free. Home-made teas. There is a covered area with seating for teas. Visits also by arrangement May to Sept for groups of up to 20.** This exuberant garden was begun in 2010. Extending to about 1½ acres, it is naturalistic in style with a shrubbery, gravel garden, wild garden and pond where many trees have been planted. Overflowing with roses scrambling up trees, over hedges and walls. More formal garden closer to house with lawns and herbaceous borders. Lovely views over Dorset countryside. Exhibition of paintings in studio. Gravel path partway around garden, otherwise the paths are grass, not suitable for wheelchairs in wet weather.

🔥 🐕 ✿ ☕

82 ◆ UPTON COUNTRY PARK

Upton, Poole, BH17 7BJ.
Borough of Poole, 01202 262753,
uptoncountrypark@poole.gov.uk,
www.uptoncountrypark.com. *3m
W of Poole town centre. On S side
of A35/A3049. Follow brown signs.*
**For opening times and information,
please phone, email or visit garden
website.**
Over 130 acres of award winning
parkland incl formal gardens, walled
garden, woodland and shoreline.
Maritime micro-climate offers a
wonderful collection of unusual trees,
vintage camellias and stunning roses.
Home to Upton House, Grade II*
listed Georgian mansion. Regular
special events. Plant centre, art
gallery and tea rooms. Car parking
pay + display (cash or card), free entry
to the park. Open 8am - 6pm (winter)
and 8am - 9pm (summer). www.
facebook.com/uptoncountrypark.
Surfaced paths throughout site,
allowing easy access for wheelchair
users.

83 WELL COTTAGE

Ryall, Bridport, DT6 6EJ. John
& Heather Coley, 01297 489066,
jfrcoley@btinternet.com. *Less than
1m N of A35 from Morcombelake.
From E: R by farm shop in
Morcombelake. Garden 0.9m on R.
From W: L entering Morcombelake,
immed R by village hall and L on
Pitmans Lane to T junc. Turn R,
Well Cott on L. Parking on site
and nearby.* **Sat 16, Sun 17, Mon
18 May (1-5.30). Combined
adm with Pilsdon View £6, chd
free. Home-made teas. Visits
also by arrangement Apr to
Sept for groups of up to 30. By
arrangement visiting for Well
Cottage only.**
1-acre garden brought back to life
since 2012. There is now much more
light after some trees were taken
down and new areas have been
cultivated. The planting is intended
to be natural and the emphasis is
very much on colour. A number of
distinct areas, some quite surprising
but most still enjoy wonderful views
over Marshwood Vale. Heather's
textile art studio will be open to view.
Wheelchair access possible but there
are a few hard surface paths, slopes
and steps.

84 WESTERN GARDENS

24A Western Ave, Branksome
Park, Poole, BH13 7AN. Mr
Peter Jackson, 01202 708388,
pjbranpark@gmail.com. *3m W of
Bournemouth. From S end Wessex
Way (A338) at gyratory take The
Avenue, 2nd exit. At T-lights turn R
into Western Rd then at bottom of
hill L. At church turn R into Western
Ave.* **Sun 21 June, Sun 2 Aug
(2-5). Adm £4.50, chd free. Tea
and delicious home-made cakes.
Visits also by arrangement Apr to
Sept for groups of 20+.**
'This secluded and magical 1-acre
garden captures the spirit of warmer
climes and begs for repeated visits'
(Gardening Which?). Created over
40 yrs it offers enormous variety
with rose, Mediterranean courtyard
and woodland gardens, herbaceous
borders and cherry tree and camellia
walk. Lush foliage and vibrant flowers
give yr-round colour and interest
enhanced by sculpture and topiary.
Home-made jams and chutneys
for sale. Wheelchair access to ¾
garden.

85 NEW WHITE HOUSE

Newtown, Witchampton,
Wimborne, BH21 5AU. Mr
Tim Read, 01258 840438,
tim.read@catralex.com. *5 miles
N of Wimborne off B3078. Travel
through village of Witchampton
towards Newtown for 800m. Pass
Crichel House's castellated gates
on L. White House is a modern
house sitting back from road on L
after further 300m.* **Sun 12, Mon
13 July (11.30-4.30). Adm £4, chd
free. Home-made teas. Visits also
by arrangement June to Aug for
groups of 10 to 30.**
1½ acre garden set on different
levels, with a Mediterranean feel,
planted to encourage wildlife and
pollinators. Wild flower border, pond
surrounded by moisture loving
plants, prairie planting of grasses
and perennials. orchard. Reasonable
wheelchair access to all but the top
level of the garden.

86 ◆ WIMBORNE MODEL TOWN & GARDENS

King Street, Wimborne, BH21 1DY.
Wimborne Minster Model
Town Ltd Registered Charity
No 298116, 01202 881924,
info@wimborne-modeltown.com,
www.wimborne-modeltown.com.
*2 mins walk from Wimborne Town
Centre & the Minster Church.
Follow Wimborne signs from A31;
from Poole/Bournemouth follow
Wimborne signs on A341; from
N follow Wimborne signs B3082/
B3078. Public parking opp in King
Street Car Park.* **For opening times
and information, please phone,
email or visit garden website.**
Attractive garden surrounding
intriguing model town buildings, incl
original 1950s miniature buildings
of Wimborne. Herbaceous borders,
rockery, perennials, shrubs and rare
trees. Miniature river system incl bog
garden and other water features.
Sensory area incorporates vegetable
garden, grasses, a seasonally fragrant
and colourful border, wind and water
elements. Plentiful seating. Open 28
March - 1 November (10am - 5pm).
Seniors discount; groups welcome.
For admission charges see website.
Tea room, shop, miniature dolls'
house collection and digital model
railway. Gardens, model town and
facilities are wheelchair accessible. 2
wheelchairs available on site.

87 WINCOMBE PARK

Shaftesbury, SP7 9AB. John &
Phoebe Fortescue, 01747 852161,
pacfortescue@gmail.com,
www.wincombepark.com. *2m N
of Shaftesbury. A350 Shaftesbury
to Warminster, past Wincombe
Business Park, 1st R signed
Wincombe & Donhead St Mary. ¾m
on R.* **Wed 13, Sun 17 May (2-5).
Adm £5, chd free. Home-made
scones, cakes and biscuits, tea,
coffee, squash. Dairy and gluten
free available. Visits also by
arrangement Apr & May for groups
of 10+. Coaches welcome. £10
including refreshments.**
Extensive mature garden with
sweeping panoramic views from lawn
over parkland to lake and enchanting
woods through which you can
wander amongst bluebells. Garden is
a riot of colour in spring with azaleas,
camellias and rhododendrons in
flower amongst shrubs and unusual
trees. Beautiful walled kitchen garden.
Partial wheelchair access only, slopes
and gravel paths.

GROUP OPENING

88 NEW WITCHAMPTON GARDENS
Witchampton, BH21 5AG. *Approx 3½ m N of Wimborne. From B3078 take Witchampton turning. Follow signs into village. Parking available. Garden guide/admission at any of gardens.* Sat 6, Sun 7 June (2-6). Combined adm £6, chd free. Home-made teas in Village Hall.

ABBEY COTTAGE
Ms Helen de Mattos.

NEW ABBEY HOUSE
Mr Stephen Hodges.

NEW SWISS COTTAGE
Mr Simon Meyrick-Jones.

These three different gardens in picturesque Witchampton involve a short and interesting walk through the village - passing the church with its attractive lychgate and Ivy house built 1580, now a club, village shop and café. The gardens consist of Swiss Cottage a delightful, densely planted, mature cottage garden borrowing elements from larger and more formal gardens; Abbey House, with several acres of garden running down to the River Allen, and including the ruins of a C13 manor house and meadow walk; and Abbey Cottage, a small garden with herbaceous borders, trees, roses, koi pond and views of the Manor House ruins.

89 WOLVERHOLLOW
Elsdons Lane, Monkton Wyld, DT6 6DA. Mr & Mrs D Wiscombe, 01297 560610. *4m N of Lyme Regis. 4m NW of Charmouth. Monkton Wyld is signed from A35 approx 4m NW of Charmouth off dual carriageway. Wolverhollow next to church.* Sun 10, Mon 11 May, Sun 2, Mon 3 Aug (11.30-4.30). Adm £4, chd free. Home-made teas. Visits also by arrangement Apr to Oct.
Over 1 acre of informal mature garden on different levels. Lawns lead past borders and rockeries down to a shady lower garden. Numerous paths take you past a variety of uncommon shrubs and plants. A managed meadow has an abundance of primulas growing close to stream. A garden not to be missed! Cabin in meadow area from which vintage, retro and other lovely things can be purchased.

90 NEW YARDES COTTAGE
Dewlish, Dorchester, DT2 7LT. Christine & Ross Robertson. *9m NE of Dorchester. From A35 Puddletown/A354 junction, take B3142 and immediately turn R onto Long Lane. From here, follow yellow NGS signs which will take you to Dewlish.* Sat 27, Sun 28 June (2-5). Adm £5, chd free. Home-made teas. Refreshments in aid of All Saints Parish Church, Dewlish.
Country cottage garden of 1½ acres bordering the Devil's Brook, having a wealth of different planting areas including woodland, stream, small lake, extensive lawns fringed with formal herbaceous borders, vegetable and soft fruit areas. Much of the planting encourages insect life and supports our bees and chickens. Wheelchair access: from lower parking area there is access only to upper sections of garden around house.

Rosemary Cottage, Rampisham Gardens

ESSEX

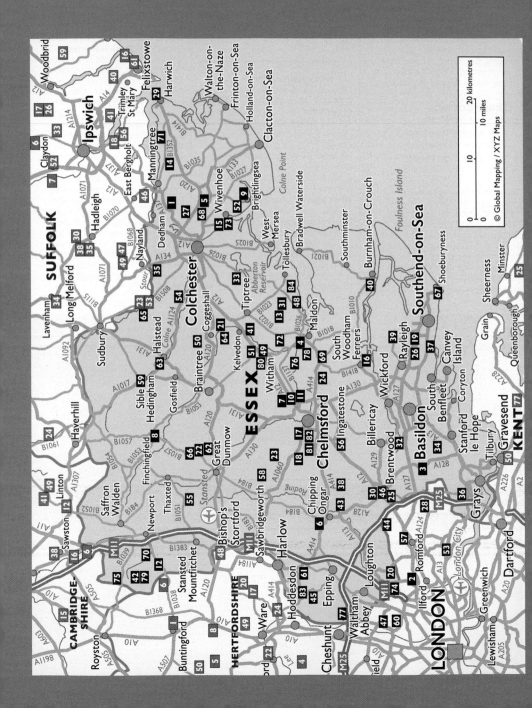

© Global Mapping / XYZ Maps

20 kilometres

10 miles

Close to London but with its own unique character, Essex is perhaps England's best kept secret - with a beautiful coastline, rolling countryside and exquisite villages. It is a little known fact that over seventy per cent of Essex is rural. There are wide horizons, ancient woodlands and hamlets pierced by flint church spires.

A perfect mix of villages, small towns, coast line and riverside settings enables Essex to provide some of the most varied garden styles in the country.

Despite its proximity to London, Essex is a largely rural county, its rich, fertile soil and long hours of sunshine make it possible to grow a wide variety of plants and our garden owners make the most of this opportunity. We have some grand country estates, small town gardens and much in between.

Our year starts with snowdrop gardens in February, runs through tulip gardens in the spring and makes the most of the high summer months with gardens full of roses and colourful perennials. Our visiting season extends into late summer when many gardens feature more exotic and tropical planting schemes making September a good time to explore.

Whether you wish to visit as part of a group or club, with family, friends or on your own, you will be sure of a warm welcome. Our garden owners are usually on hand to talk about their garden to ensure you leave with a little more knowledge and lots of inspiration.

We look forward to sharing our gardens with you.

Volunteers

County Organiser
Susan Copeland
01799 550553
susan.copeland@ngs.org.uk

County Treasurer
Richard Steers
07392 426490
steers123@aol.com

Publicity & Social Media Coordinator
Debbie Thomson 01279 600241
debbie.thomson@ngs.org.uk

Booklet Co-ordinator and Publicity Assistant
Doug Copeland
01799 550553
doug.copeland@ngs.org.uk

Assistant County Organisers
Tricia Brett 01255 870415
tricia.brett@ngs.org.uk

Avril & Roger Cole-Jones
01245 225726
randacj@gmail.com

David Cox 01245 222165
david.cox@ngs.org.uk

Lesley Gamblin 07801 445299
lesley.gamblin@ngs.org.uk

Linda & Frank Jewson
01992 714047
linda.jewson@ngs.org.uk

Talks
Ed Fairey 07780 685634
ed@faireyassociates.co.uk

County Photographer
Caroline Cassell 07973 551196
caroline.cassell@ngs.org.uk

Left: Ulting Wick

 @EssexNGS   @EssexNGS   @essexngs

OPENING DATES

All entries subject to change. For latest information check www.ngs.org.uk

Extended openings are shown at the beginning of the month.

Map locator numbers are shown to the right of each garden name.

February

Snowdrop Festival

Wednesday 12th
Dragons   18

Saturday 22nd
Horkesley Hall   35

March

Saturday 14th
◆ Beth Chatto's Plants
& Gardens   5

Sunday 22nd
NEW Heath House   33

Every Thursday from Thursday 9th
Barnards Farm   3

Every Thursday and Friday
Feeringbury Manor   21

Friday 3rd
Wycke Farm   84

Sunday 5th
Wycke Farm   84

Sunday 12th
Tudor Roost   73

Monday 13th
Tudor Roost   73

Friday 24th
◆ Beeleigh Abbey
Gardens   4

Sunday 26th
South Shoebury Hall   67
Ulting Wick   76
Wickets   79

Wednesday 29th
Furzelea   24
Writtle University
College   82

Thursday 30th
NEW Scrips House   64

May

Every Thursday
Barnards Farm   3

Every Thursday and Friday
Feeringbury Manor   21

Friday 1st
NEW Tsuru   72
Ulting Wick   76

Saturday 2nd
Brookfield   10

Sunday 3rd
Brookfield   10
Furzelea   24
◆ Green Island   27
Wickets   79

Saturday 16th
Ardleigh Gardens   1
NEW 14 Clifton Terrace   15

Sunday 17th
Ardleigh Gardens   1
NEW 14 Clifton Terrace   15
Longyard Cottage   45
79 Royston Avenue,
E4   60
1 Whitehouse
Cottages   78

Wednesday 20th
The Punchbowl   58

Sunday 24th
Fairfield   19
Tudor Roost   73

Monday 25th
Fairwinds   20
Rookwoods   59
Tudor Roost   73

Friday 29th
8 Dene Court   17
Dragons   18

Saturday 30th
Moverons   52

Sunday 31st
Chippins   14
NEW The Gates   25
Moverons   52

June

Every Thursday
Barnards Farm   3

Every Thursday and Friday
Feeringbury Manor   21

Tuesday 2nd
Caynton Cottage   11

Wednesday 3rd
NEW Oak Farm   54

Friday 5th
Haytor   32
NEW 56 Maldon Road   48

Saturday 6th
Boreham Gardens   7
NEW Isabella's Garden   37
NEW 56 Maldon Road   48

Sunday 7th
Blake Hall   6
Boreham Gardens   7
Chestnut Cottage   12
Furzelea   24
Haytor   32
Horkesley Hall   35
NEW Isabella's Garden   37
NEW 56 Maldon Road   48
Waltham Abbey Group
Gardens   77
1 Whitehouse
Cottages   78

Tuesday 9th
8 Dene Court   17

Wednesday 10th
Long House Plants   44

Thursday 11th
Caynton Cottage   11

Friday 12th
NEW Heath House   33

Sunday 14th
NEW Heath House   33
Miraflores   51
NEW Stocksmead   70
37 Turpins Lane   74
Writtle Gardens   81

Friday 19th
8 Dene Court   17

Sunday 21st
Fudlers Hall   23
Two Cottages   75

Saturday 27th
Keeway   40
18 Pettits Boulevard,
RM1   57
Spring Cottage   68

Sunday 28th
Barnards Farm   3
Chippins   14
Havendell   31
Langley Village
Gardens   42
18 Pettits Boulevard,
RM1   57
Spring Cottage   68
Wychwood   83

Tuesday 30th
8 Dene Court   17

July

Every Thursday
Barnards Farm   3

Every Thursday and Friday
Feeringbury Manor   21

Wednesday 1st
Keeway   40

Thursday 2nd
NEW Scrips House   64

Friday 3rd
NEW Chilterns   13
Ulting Wick   76

Saturday 4th
NEW Brick House   8
16 Maida Way, E4   47
NEW Witham Town
Gardens   80

Sunday 5th
NEW Chilterns   13
Field Cottage   22
Fudlers Hall   23
Halfway Haley's   28
262 Hatch Road   30
Hilldrop   34
Little Myles   43
9 Malyon Road   49
NEW The Old Vicarage   55
Two Cottages   75

Wednesday 8th
Long House Plants   44

Friday 10th
8 Dene Court   17

Saturday 11th
69 Rundells - The Secret
Garden   61

Colville

THE GARDENS

GROUP OPENING

1 ARDLEIGH GARDENS

Colchester, CO7 7LZ. $3\frac{1}{2}$ m
NE of Colchester. From Ardleigh
village centre continue on A137 to
Manningtree. 3rd R Tile Barn Lane.
R again Hungerdown Lane. 500yds
gardens on R. As narrow lane
please follow this clockwise route to
the gardens. **Sat 16, Sun 17 May
(11-4). Combined adm £8.50,
chd free. Home-made teas at
Mayfield Farm.**

CHARITY FARM
Jacqueline & Arthur Cork.

NEW HUNGERDOWNS
Sarah Vermont.

MAYFIELD FARM
Ed Fairey & Jennifer
Hughes, 07780 685634,
ed@faireyassociates.co.uk.
**Visits also by arrangement in
May for groups of 10+.**

Three lovely, large country gardens
set in the beautiful setting of nearby
Constable country of north east
Essex. Refreshments, and parking in
paddock at Mayfield Farm. Mayfield
Farm a 3 acre garden which only a
few years ago was largely a field with
a huge glass house and poly tunnels.
Now planted with long borders, a
secret garden and yew hedging for
topiary. Over 200,000 bulbs have
been planted in the last 4 years to
create a wonderful spring display.
Shepherds Hut and new potting shed.
Charity Farm is a $4\frac{1}{2}$ acre garden
created from an open and empty site
since 2001. Woodland walks and 2
avenues of trees create vistas. A large
lake surrounded with natural planting
and contains lots of pool frogs which
sing loudly in early summer. Parts of
the garden are delineated with beech
and yew hedging, and the latest
planting is a birch grove containing
12 different kinds of birch trees. NEW
Hungerdowns a garden of $1\frac{1}{2}$ acres,
formally laid out around the house.
Box hedges, topiary, a white garden,
pond, orchard. Well planted and will
provide plenty of interest. There is a
yew maze and a 6 acre woodland.
Guided tours of Mayfield Farm.
♿ ☕

2 254 ASHURST DRIVE

Barkingside, IG6 1EW. Maureen
Keating, 0208 550 0934. *2m S of
Chigwell. Nearest tube: Barkingside
on Central Line approx 8 mins walk.
Bus: 150 stops outside Tesco's on
Cranbrook Rd. go round R side of
Tescos car park. Keep R, alleyway
leads to Ashurst Drive.* **Visits by
arrangement June to Sept for
groups of 5 to 20. Adm £3.50,
chd free.**
Bird friendly colour filled town garden
with interesting nooks and crannies
each telling a story. Contains 7 water
features, 6 seating areas, waterfall,
pond and stream, miniature railway,
model village and vibrant planting all
in 40 ft square area! Regret, garden
unsuitable for children.

3 BARNARDS FARM

Brentwood Road, West Horndon,
Brentwood, CM13 3LX. Bernard &
Sylvia Holmes & The Christabella
Charitable Trust, 01268 454075,
vanessa@barnardsfarm.eu,
www.barnardsfarm.eu. *5m S of
Brentwood. On A128 $1\frac{1}{2}$ m S of
A127 Halfway House flyover. From
Junction continue on A128 under the
railway bridge. Garden on R just past
bridge.* **Every Thur 9 Apr to 27 Aug
(11-4.30). Adm £7.50, chd free.
Sun 28 June, Sun 30 Aug (1-5).
Adm £10, chd free. Home-made
teas. On Thurs Vanessa and her
team serve home-made sandwich
based light lunches. On Suns it's
all cake served from both the
Barn and our Tented area. Visits
also by arrangement for groups of
30+.** Donation to St Francis Church.
So much to explore! Climb the
Belvedere for the wider view and take
the train for a woodland adventure.
Spring bulbs and blossom, summer
beds and borders, ponds, lakes
and streams, walled vegetable plot.
'Japanese garden', sculptures grand
and quirky enhance and delight.
Barnards Miniature Railway rides
(BMR) :Separate charges apply.
Sunday extras: Bernard's Sculpture
tour 2.30pm Car collection. 1920s
Cycle shop. Archery. Model T Ford
Rides. Collect loyalty points on
Thur visits and earn a free Sun or
Thur entry. Season Tickets available
Aviators welcome (PPO). Wheelchair
accessible WC Golf Buggy tours
available.
♿ ✿ 🚐 NPC ☕

4 ◆ BEELEIGH ABBEY GARDENS

Abbey Turning, Beeleigh, Maldon,
CM9 6LL. Christopher & Catherine
Foyle, 07506 867122, www.
visitmaldon.co.uk/beeleigh-abbey.
*1m NW of Maldon. Leaving Maldon
via London Road take 1st R after
Cemetery into Abbey Turning.* **For
NGS: Fri 24 Apr (10.30-4.30).
Adm £6, chd £2.50. Cream teas.**
**For other opening times and
information, please phone or visit
garden website.**
3 acres of secluded gardens in rural
historic setting. Mature trees surround
variety of planting and water features,
woodland walks under planted with
bulbs leading to tidal river, cottage
garden, kitchen garden, orchard, wild
flower meadow, rose garden, wisteria
walk, magnolia trees, lawn with 85yd
long herbaceous border. Scenic
backdrop of remains of C12 abbey
incorporated into private house (not
open). Refreshments including Hot
and Cold Drinks, Cakes, Rolls and
Quiche Salads. Gravel paths, some
gentle slopes and some steps. Large
WC with ramp and handlebars.
♿ ✿ ☕ ⚖

5 ◆ BETH CHATTO'S PLANTS & GARDENS

Elmstead Market, Colchester,
CO7 7DB. Beth Chatto's Plants
& Gardens, 01206822007,
info@bethchatto.co.uk,
www.bethchatto.co.uk. *$\frac{1}{4}$ m
E of Elmstead Market. On A133
Colchester to Clacton Rd in village of
Elmstead Market.* **For NGS: Sat 14
Mar (10-5). Adm £6.95, chd free.
Sun 27 Sept (10-5). Adm £8.45,
chd free. For other opening times
and information, please phone,
email or visit garden website.**
Internationally famous gardens,
including dry, damp, shade, reservoir
and woodland areas. The result
of over 50 years of hard work and
application of the huge body of
plant knowledge possessed by Beth
Chatto and her husband Andrew.
Visitors cannot fail to be affected by
the peace and beauty of the garden.
The Reservoir Garden was opened by
Beth in 2017: a wonderful area, and
a must-visit for those who haven't
seen it yet. Large plant nursery. Gift
Shop. Free parking. Garden courses
and events held all year. Venue hire
for celebrations, funeral receptions
and corporate events. Open all year
round. Large, fully licensed Tearoom
overlooking the Gravel Garden

and Nursery, offering homemade breakfasts, lunches and teas. Disabled WC & parking. Wheelchair access around all of the gardens - on gravel or grass (concrete in Nursery, Giftshop and Tearoom areas).

6 BLAKE HALL
Bobbingworth, CM5 0DG.
Mr & Mrs H Capel Cure,
www.blakehall.co.uk. *10m W of Chelmsford. Just off A414 between Four Wantz r'about in Ongar & Talbot r'about in North Weald. Signed on A414.* **Sun 7 June (11-4). Adm £5, chd free. Home-made teas in C17 barn.**

25 acres of mature gardens within the historic setting of Blake Hall (not open). Arboretum with broad variety of specimen trees. Spectacular rambling roses clamber up ancient trees. Traditional formal rose garden and herbaceous border. Sweeping lawns. Teas served from Essex Barn. Some gravel paths.

GROUP OPENING

7 BOREHAM GARDENS
Boreham, Chelmsford, CM3 3EF.
4m NE Chelmsford. Take B1137 Boreham Village, turn into Church Rd at Lion Inn. Caynton Cottage is 50mtrs on L. the other gardens are within walking distance. Map available. Limited parking at school Juniper Rd. **Sat 6, Sun 7 June (1-5). Combined adm £7, chd free. Home-made teas.**

CAYNTON COTTAGE
Les & Lynn Mann.
(See separate entry)

NEW 4 CHURCH COTTAGES
Justine and Patrick Atterbury.

NEW 38 JUNIPER ROAD
Sharon Rose.

Three stunning, inspirational and different gardens in the lovely village of Boreham. The garden at Caynton Cottage has been designed and planted from a neglected plot with a C15 thatched cottage. A plants woman's garden. It is planted with a selection of shrubs and perennials for maximum all year interest, with a small wildlife pond and dry stream. 4 Church Cottages, is a beautiful cottage garden overlooking St Andrew's Church. Perennials, roses and a touch of the exotic intermingled with trees and hedging. Simply succulents and cacti in quirky recycled planters provide a twist to the cottage planting scheme. Relax and enjoy the ambience or just pop in to meet the chickens. 38 Juniper Road, is an end of terrace in the heart of the village. Three distinct gardens in one, with the colours ranging from hot reds and oranges to softer pinks and lilacs with a little bit of the jungle thrown in to spice things up. Built on a budget with lots of recycling ideas from waterfalls to sundials. Caynton Cottage, gravel paths, 4 Church Cottages has wheelchair access and 38, Juniper Road has partial access.

Brick House

8 NEW BRICK HOUSE

The Green, Finchingfield, Braintree, CM7 4JS. Mr & Mrs Graham and Susan Tobbell. *9m NW of Braintree. Brick House in the centre of the picturesque village of Finchingfield, which is at the Xrds of the B1053 & B1057 in rural north-west Essex.* Sat 4 July, Fri 4 Sept (1-5). Adm £6. Home-made teas. This recently renovated period property and garden covers 1½ acres, with a brook running through the middle. The garden features contemporary sculptures, and several distinct planting styles; most notably a hidden scented cottage-style garden, a crinkle-crankle walled area with an oriental feel and some rather glorious late-summer herbaceous borders inspired by the New Perennial Movement. Modern marble sculptures by Paul Vanstone add drama and contrast to the soft landscaping. Garden is professionally designed to be a calming space. There is wheelchair access to the property from where the garden can be viewed but there is limited wheelchair access to the garden itself.

GROUP OPENING

9 BRIGHTLINGSEA GARDENS

Brightlingsea, Colchester, CO7 0JF. *Approx 10m SE of Colchester. Go to Thorrington on B1027 & head S for approx 3m towards Brightlingsea on B1029. Group gardens are either side of Church Rd. 100yds beyond Autosmith Garage.* Sun 19 July (10-4.30). Combined adm £7, chd free. Home-made teas. Refreshments at 44 Church Road.

44 CHURCH ROAD
Mandy Livingstone & Steven Nicholson.

77 CHURCH ROAD
Mr & Mrs Mick & Gill Tokley.

SANDY HOOK
Mr & Mrs Peter & Elaine Sedwell.

Three very interesting and contrasting gardens to enjoy in the unique and ancient maritime town of Brightlingsea. Sandy Hook has traditional borders, a raised rose bed, dahlias, penstemons and salvias, with a small woodland stream and a sheltered "White Garden". 44 Church Road has a traditional country garden, with gentle colours, mature trees, evergreen shrubs, a water feature and a wisteria covered pergola. The garden offers various places to relax and contemplate the different features of this quintessentially English garden. At 77 Church Road we have a colourful garden with an eclectic mix of trees, shrubs and perennials in borders alongside a range of hard landscaping. The garden is filled with plants and features and you can wander through pathways to hidden corners offering peaceful and tranquil seating. At Brightlingsea the spectacular award winning floral displays adorning the centre are not to be missed. There is much to see along the harbour, the marina with bracing walks along the promenade. Brightlingsea is blessed with plenty of watering holes and places to eat. Access to main border garden only at Sandy Hook. At No 77 the side passage is partially obstructed by a gas meter.

10 BROOKFIELD

Church Road, Boreham, Chelmsford, CM3 3EB. Bob & Linda Taylor. *4m NE Chelmsford. Take B1137 Boreham village, turn R into Church Road at Lion Inn. In approx ¼ m turning on R after The Chase marked 58-76 Church Road. Pedestrians & disabled access only.* Sat 2, Sun 3 May (1-5). Adm £5, chd free. Home-made teas. Warm cheese scones and hot sausage rolls, together with other savouries also available. Open in spring for the first time a large garden with perennial island beds and borders, enhanced with tulips and various spring bulbs, a vegetable garden with raised beds, lawns and pond. The main feature at this time of year is a woodland walk where camellias, rhododendrons and bluebells bloom while a wide variety of deciduous trees are bursting into life around the meadow. Wheelchair access to main part of garden. Partial access to meadow.

11 CAYNTON COTTAGE

Church Road, Boreham, Chelmsford, CM3 3EF. Les & Lynn Mann, 01245 463490, mannlynn15@gmail.com. *4m NE Chelmsford. Take B1137 Boreham Village, turn into Church Rd at the Lion Inn. 50mtrs on L.* Tue 2, Thur 11 June (1-5). Adm £3.50, chd free. Home-made teas. Opening with Boreham Gardens on Sat 6, Sun 7 June. Visits also by arrangement in June for groups of up to 20. A traditional cottage garden designed and planted by the owners since 2013 from a neglected and overgrown plot surrounding a C15th thatched cottage (not open). Planted with a good selection of shrubs and perennials for maximum all year interest with a small wildlife pond and dry stream. It is ever changing as the plants grow and mature to fill the space, with new features added each season. Gravel paths throughout.

12 CHESTNUT COTTAGE

Middle Street, Clavering, Saffron Walden, CB11 4QL. Carol & Mike Wilkinson. *At the bottom of Middle Street, Chestnut Cottage faces you across the ford (River Stort) - walk across the footbridge. Parking in Middle Street.* Sun 7 June (2-5). Adm £4, chd free. Home-made teas. Cottage garden with sweeping lawns and wide flower borders, opposite Clavering Ford. Lots of pathways and seats to sit and contemplate. Stunning views over the medieval heart of the village. Come and see 'The Little House', (open), built in 1760 and reputedly the smallest thatched cottage in England.

13 NEW CHILTERNS

Chelmer Close, Little Totham, Nr. Maldon, CM9 8JN. Mrs Jane Kynaston. *3m S of Tiptree. From A12 take Rivenall/Silverend junction towards Braxted/Tiptree. At T junction turn R then immediately L signed Little Totham. At The Swan pub turn R onto Post Office Lane 100yds Chelmer Close on L.* Fri 3, Sun 5 July (11-4). Adm £3.50, chd free. Home-made teas. including cream teas. Chilterns has always been a family garden, now with a 'grown up' feel that has a friendly welcoming atmosphere, full of plants that give something special to the visitor. Plants are here for their beauty, their perfume, their pollen and nectar for our bee hive. Learning which plants work where seems to have now created a serendipitous, restful and reflective space. Informal cottage style garden where ex battery hens roam free. Informal cottage style garden. Small exhibition of arts, crafts, cards and paintings for sale. Mediterranean gravel area, please check with owner re wheelchair access 07743 906788.

14 CHIPPINS

Heath Road, Bradfield, CO11 2UZ. Kit & Ceri Leese, 01255 870730, ceriandkit1@btinternet.com. *3m E of Manningtree. Take A137 from Manningtree Station, turn L opp garage. Take 1st R towards Clacton. At Radio Mast turn L into Bradfield continue through village. Bungalow is opp primary school.* **Sun 31 May, Sun 28 June (11-4.30). Adm £4, chd free. Home-made teas. Delicious home-made cakes!. Visits also by arrangement May to July for groups of 5 to 30. Art societies welcome.**
Artist's garden and plantaholics' paradise packed with interest. Springtime heralds irises, hostas and alliums. Stream, with wildlife pond and Horace the Huge! Summer hosts an explosion of colour with daylilies and rambling roses. Front garden with tubs, hanging baskets and exotic border with cannas, banana and cacti. Studio in conservatory with paintings and etching press. Kit is a landscape artist and printmaker, pictures always on display. Afternoon tea with delicious homemade cakes is also available for small parties (minimum of 5) on specific days if booked in advance.

15 NEW 14 CLIFTON TERRACE

Wivenhoe, Colchester, CO7 9DY. Mr & Mrs Michael and Liz Taylor Jones. *Clifton Terrace ends in our front garden situated just above the station platform. Clifton Terrace is a turning on R off Wivenhoe High St opp Greyhound Pub, beside Concord estate agents. On R of Clifton Terrace is the public car park and WC.* **Sat 16, Sun 17 May (11-4). Adm £3.50, chd free. Tea.**
A very long, narrow garden alongside the railway station. Near house: herbaceous border, shrubs, lawn and roses. Slope down to station

footpath: ground cover shrubs. Beyond the lawn: vegetable garden and small orchard, tree house in walnut tree and swing. Continue to part of old coppiced Wivenhoe Woods. Beyond a wildlife pond, natural woodland continues to rhododendrons, bamboos and a second pond.

16 NEW 10 COLNE CLOSE

South Woodham Ferrers, Chelmsford, CM3 5XW. Ms Zoe Abel. *At the Shaw Farm r'about turn R onto Ferrers Road, straight across the 2nd r'about. L at the 3rd onto Inchbonnie Rd. Take 4th turn on R to public car park. Walk up Leighlands Rd to Colne Close.* **Sat 18 July (12-5). Adm £4, chd free. Home-made teas.**
A small north facing town garden. An interesting use of space mixing old and new. The lush green foliage and clusters of pots and containers give this compact garden an urban feel. Small seating areas placed throughout the garden make full use of the space, capturing the sun as it moves across the garden, creating new vistas and restful places to sit and ponder.

17 8 DENE COURT

Chignall Road, Chelmsford, CM1 2JQ. Mrs Sheila Chapman, 01245 266156. *W of Chelmsford (Parkway). Take A1060 Roxwell Rd for 1m. Turn R at T-lights into Chignall Rd. Dene Court 3rd exit on R. Parking in Chignall Rd.* **Fri 29 May (2-5), also open Dragons. Tue 9, Fri 19, Tue 30 June, Fri 10 July (2-5). Tue 21 July (2-5), also open Dragons. Fri 31 July (2-5). Sun 9, Tue 18 Aug (2-5), also open Dragons. Fri 28 Aug, Sun 6 Sept (2-5). Adm £3.50, chd free. Visits also by arrangement May to Sept for groups of 10+. Max size 50.**
Beautifully maintained and designed compact garden (250sq yds). Owner is well-known RHS gold medal-winning exhibitor (now retired). Circular lawn, long pergola and walls festooned with roses and climbers. Large selection of unusual clematis. Densely-planted colour coordinated perennials add interest from May to Sept in this immaculate garden.

Feeringbury Manor

18 DRAGONS
Boyton Cross, Chelmsford,
CM1 4LS. Mrs Margot
Grice, 01245 248651,
mandmdragons@tiscali.co.uk. *3m
W of Chelmsford. On A1060. ½ m
W of The Hare Pub.* **Wed 12 Feb
(12-3). Light refreshments. Fri 29
May, Tue 21 July, Sun 9, Tue 18
Aug (2-5). Home-made teas. Also
open 8 Dene Court. Thur 10, Wed
23 Sept (2-5). Home-made teas.
Adm £4, chd free. Visits also by
arrangement Feb to Oct for groups
of 10+.**
A plantswoman's ¾ acre garden,
planted to encourage wildlife.
Sumptuous colour-themed borders
with striking plant combinations,
featuring specimen plants, fernery,
clematis and grasses. Meandering
paths lead to ponds, patio, scree
garden and small vegetable garden.
Two summerhouses, one overlooking
stream and farmland.

19 FAIRFIELD
5 Fairfield Road, Leigh-On-Sea,
SS9 5RZ. Rob & Gwen Evison,
gwenevison@yahoo.co.uk.
*Follow A127 towards Southend
past Rayleigh Weir. At Progress
Rd T-lights turn L. At the end turn
R at the T-lights along Rayleigh Rd
A1015. Fairfield Road is approx 1m
on the L.* **Sun 24 May (12-5). Adm
£4, chd free. Light refreshments.
Visits also by arrangement June &
July for groups of 10 to 20. Cream
teas available by arrangement.**
A lovingly kept garden divided into
different areas. Koi pond surrounded
by climbing plants and topiary. Well
tended lawn with numerous beds
filled with roses, alliums, irises and
peonies. Rose covered arch leads
to a secluded woodland area,
young birch and maple trees and
many woodland plants including
camellias and rhododendrons. Living
evergreen arches lead to a magical
secret garden. Most of the garden is
wheelchair accessible. There are a
few shallow steps.

Stocksmead

20 FAIRWINDS
Chapel Lane, Chigwell Row, IG7 6JJ. Sue & David Coates, 07731 796467, scoates@forest.org.uk. *2m SE of Chigwell. Grange Hill Tube, turn R at exit, 10 mins walk uphill. Car: Nr M25 J26 & N Circular Waterworks r'about. Follow signs for Chigwell. Fork R for Manor/Lambourne Rd. Park in Lodge Close Car Park.* **Mon 25 May (2-5). Adm £4, chd free. Home-made teas. Free refills of tea/coffee Soya milk available. Some green/ fruit teas and decaf on request. Visits also by arrangement May to Oct for groups of 5 to 20.**
Gravelled front garden and three differently styled back garden spaces with planting changes every year. Meander, sit, relax and enjoy. NEW this year: Wildflower meadow seeded autumn 2019, extension to Long Border and fresh planting in woodland. Beyond the rustic fence, lies the wildlife pond and vegetable plot. Planting influenced by Beth Chatto, Penelope Hobhouse and Christopher Lloyd. Happy hens. Happy insects in bee house, bug house, log piles and sampling the spring pollen. Newts in pond. There be dragons a plenty!! Space for 2 disabled cars to park by the house. Wood chip paths in woodland area may require assistance.

21 FEERINGBURY MANOR
Coggeshall Road, Feering, Colchester, CO5 9RB. Mr & Mrs Giles Coode-Adams, 01376 561946, seca@btinternet.com, www.ngs.org.uk. *Between Feering & Coggeshall on Coggeshall Rd, 1m from Feering village.* **Every Thur and Fri 2 Apr to 31 July (9-4). Every Thur and Fri 3 Sept to 9 Oct (9-4). Adm £5, chd free. Visits also by arrangement.** Donation to Feering Church.
There is always plenty to see in this peaceful 10 acre garden with two ponds and river Blackwater. Jewelled lawn in early April then spectacular tulips and blossom lead on to a huge number of different and colourful plants, many unusual, culminating in a purple explosion of michaelmas daisies in late Sept. Wonderful sculpture by Ben Coode-Adams. No wheelchair access to arboretum, steep slope.

22 FIELD COTTAGE
Pound Gate, Stebbing, nr Great Dunmow, CM6 3RH. Wal & Jenny Hudgell, 01371 856406, jenny_hudgell@yahoo.co.uk. *3m E of Great Dunmow. Leave Gt Dunmow on B1256. Take first L to Stebbing. At the War Memorial junction turn L, down hill to High Street. Take 2nd R past the School, signed to Garden Fields.* **Sun 5 July (12-5). Adm £4, chd free. Light refreshments. Visits also by arrangement June & July for groups of 10 to 30.**
$\frac{1}{3}$ acre garden with countryside views reinvented in 2010 and still evolving. Borders packed with perennials and shrubs for all year round interest including iris, hemerocallis, hostas, roses, ferns and grasses. Many new trees planted around the garden to provide height and shade to a very flat site. Summer house and arbour to relax in and enjoy a cuppa. A medium size vegetable garden. The garden is fully accessible to wheelchairs.

23 FUDLERS HALL
Fox Road, Mashbury, Chelmsford, CM1 4TJ. Mr & Mrs A J Meacock, 01245 231335. *7m NW of Chelmsford. Chelmsford take A1060, R into Chignal Rd. ½ m L to Chignal St James approx 5m, 2nd R into Fox Rd signed Gt Waltham. Fudlers FROM GT WALTHAM. Take Barrack Lane for 3m.* **Sun 21 June, Sun 5 July (2-5). Adm £6, chd free. Cream teas. Visits also by arrangement June & July.**
An award winning, romantic 2 acre garden surrounding C17 farmhouse with lovely pastoral views, across the Chelmer Valley. Old walls divide garden into many rooms, each having a different character, featuring long herbaceous borders, ropes and pergolas festooned with rambling old fashioned roses. Enjoy the vibrant hot border in late summer. Yew hedged kitchen garden. Ample seating. Wonderful views across Chelmer Valley. 2 new flower beds, many roses. 500year old yew tree. gravel farmyard and 30foot path to gardens, all of which is level lawn.

24 FURZELEA
Bicknacre Road, Danbury, CM3 4JR. Avril & Roger Cole-Jones, 01245 225726, randacj@gmail.com. *4m E of Chelmsford, 4m W of Maldon A414 to Danbury. At village centre S into Mayes Lane. Then 1st R. Go past Cricketers Pub, L on to Bicknacre Rd Use NT carpark immed on L Garden 50m on R. Extra parking 200 m past on L. Use NT Common paths from carparks.* **Wed 29 Apr (2-5); Sun 3 May, Sun 7 June, Sun 12 July, Sun 13 Sept (11-5); Wed 16 Sept (2-5). Adm £5, chd free. Home-made teas. Visits also by arrangement Apr to Oct. For groups of 15+.**
The garden surrounding this late C19 house was designed, created and is maintained solely by the owners for year round interest. Coordination of plant colour is important. Grasses, climbers and perennials are used to enhance this throughout. Topiary gives added dimension April starts with thousands of tulips, by June Roses are blooming, July is Hemerocallis showtime. Autumn is a spectacular display. A Black & White garden plus exotics and many unusual plants add to the Visitors interest. International garden tour visitors voted us the best garden in their recent tours of East Anglia. Opp Danbury Common (NT), short walk to Danbury Country Park and Lakes and short drive to RHS Hyde Hall. Very limited wheelchair access, with some steps and gravel paths and drive.

25 NEW THE GATES
London Road Cemetery, London Road, Brentwood, CM14 4QW. Ms Mary Yiannoullou, www.frontlinepartnership.org. *At the rear of the cemetery. Enter the Cemetery (opp Tesco Express). Drive to the rear of the cemetery where you will see our site to your L. There is limited parking within but plenty in the surrounding rds.* **Sun 31 May, Sun 30 Aug (12-4.30). Adm £3.50, chd free. Home-made teas.**
'The Gates' horticultural project offers local citizens, including vulnerable adults, an opportunity to develop new skills within a horticultural setting. Greenhouses and allotments for raising bedding plants, educational workshops and growing fruit and vegetables. Walks through the Woodland Dell and Sensory area. Refreshments in the Tea House. Large variety of plants and produce for sale. Enjoy the mosaic garden, visit the apiary and relax in the various seating areas around the site. All areas are accessed via slopes and ramps.

26 30 GLENWOOD AVENUE

Leigh-On-Sea, SS9 5EB.
Joan Squibb, 07543 031772,
squibb44@gmail.com. *Follow A127
towards Southend. Past Rayleigh
Weir. At Progress Rd T-lights turn L.
At next T-lights turn L down Rayleigh
Rd A1015. Past shops turn 2nd L
into Glenwood Ave. Garden halfway
down on R.* **Visits by arrangement
for groups of 10 to 20. Home-
made teas.**

Nestled next to the busy A127 lies a
beautifully transformed town garden.
Home-made raised beds with tulips
in spring, dahlias and roses in the
summer. From a corridor, you emerge
into an open garden giving a vista
of colour, inspiration and peaceful
harmony, with many different scents
to savour. Hanging baskets bloom in
the fruit trees and along the fences.
A paved area allows one to enjoy the
view of the garden as does a deck
at the back where herbs and some
vegetables live alongside the flowers.
A peaceful vista, to sit in and restore
the batteries. Vegetables are also
grown in raised beds.

27 ◆ GREEN ISLAND

Park Road, Ardleigh,
Colchester, CO7 7SP. Fiona
Edmond, 01206 230455,
greenislandgardens@gmail.com,
www.greenislandgardens.co.uk.
*3m NE of Colchester. From Ardleigh
village centre, take B1029 towards
Great Bromley. Park Rd is 2nd on
R after level Xing. Garden is last on
L.* **For NGS: Sun 3 May, Sat 10
Oct (10-5). Adm £8, chd £2.50.
Light refreshments. Home-made
cakes, scones, sandwiches and
baguettes, Cream teas or full
afternoon teas to order. 2021: Sun
24 Jan. For other opening times
and information, please phone,
email or visit garden website.**

A garden for all seasons, highlights:
bluebells, azaleas, autumn colour,
winter hamamelis and snowdrops.
A plantsman's paradise. Carved
within 20 acre mature woodland are
huge island beds, Japanese garden,
terrace, gravel, seaside and water
gardens, all packed with rare and
unusual plants. Bluebells Bazaar W/E
2/3 May. Aut colour W/E 10 October,
Snowdrops Jan 24 2021 for NGS.
National collections of Hamamelis cvs
and Camellias (autumn and winter
flowering). January-Hamamelis,
February-snowdrops, May-bluebells,
azaleas, acers and rhododendrons.

Summer-water gardens, island beds
and tree lilies. Oct/Nov-Stunning
autumn colour. Light lunches, home-
made cakes and cream teas. Flat and
easy walking /pushing wheelchairs.
Ramps at entrance and tearoom.
Disabled parking and WC.

28 HALFWAY HALEY'S

26 Courtenay Gardens, Upminster,
RM14 1DD. Mr & Mrs Jan & Eddie
Haley. *From Upminster Station
main entrance turn R, Take1st R into
Deyncourt Gardens. Take 1st rd on
L which is Courtenay Gardens. The
garden is aprox 5 mins walk from
Upminster Station.* **Sun 5 July, Sun
23 Aug (12.30-5.30). Adm £4, chd
free. Light refreshments.**

This is a long and narrow secluded
garden split into 4 rooms the last
being a secret garden. There are 3
mature ornamental cherry trees plus
shrubs and climbing plants. There is a
Hosta bed, Dahlia bed, lots of Fuchsia
plants, a medium well stocked pond,
Pergola and Arbours, Willow Wigwam
and plenty of seating. Although
there are flower beds and borders
the garden is informal and natural.
Garden not suitable for wheelchairs.

GROUP OPENING

29 HARWICH AND RAMSEY GARDENS

St Helens Green, Harwich,
CO12 3NH. *Centre of Old Harwich
& Ramsey village, A120 to Harwich
and onto The Quay. Continue to car
park on Wellington Rd, CO12 3DT
within 50 metres of St Helens Green.
Colville from A120 take Ramsey
r'about B1352. Parking at Church
Hill Memorial Hall.* **Sun 26 July (12-
4). Combined adm £5, chd free.
Home-made teas at 8 St Helens
Green. Soup and rolls available
between 12 and 1.**

63 CHURCH STREET
Sue & Richard Watts.

NEW **COLVILLE**
Mr & Mrs Colin & Brenda Knight.

NEW **3 MARKET STREET**
Mrs Jackie Denton.

QUAYSIDE COURT
Brendan & Rachel Boreham.

8 ST HELENS GREEN
Frances Vincent.

Five different gardens. Four within
walking distance in the historical
town of Harwich. 8 St Helens Green,
just 100m from the sea. A small
town garden, with an abundance of
dahlias, and hydrangeas mixed with
perennials. 63 Church Street (access
via Cow Lane/Kings Head Street)
is a long, narrow walled courtyard
with shrubs, climbers, perennials
and veg packed into the garden
and architectural features including
an Elizabethan window with original
glass. 3 Market Street is a hidden
garden behind houses bordered by
high walls with lawn, trees, borders
and lots of potted plants. Quayside
Court unusually boasts a sunken
garden hidden from view at the end
of the car park which features a
pond, veg patch, roses and climbers.
Colville an enchanting small garden in
the village of Ramsey with a surprising
variety of traditional and specimen
exotic perennials and shrubs.

30 262 HATCH ROAD

Pilgrims Hatch, Brentwood,
CM15 9QR. Mike & Liz Thomas.
*2m N of Brentwood town centre. On
A128 N toward Ongar turn R onto
Doddinghurst Rd at mini-r'about
(to Brentwood Centre) After the
Centre turn next L into Hatch Rd.
Garden 4th on R.* **Sun 5, Sun 19
July (11.30-4.30). Adm £5, chd
free. Tea.**

A formal frontage with lavender. An
eclectic rear garden of around an
acre divided into 'rooms' with themed
borders, several ponds, three green
houses, fruit and vegetable plots and
oriental garden. There is also a secret
white garden, spring and summer
wild flower meadows,Yin and Yang
borders, a folly and an exotic area.
There is plenty of seating to enjoy the
views and a cup of tea and cake.

31 HAVENDELL

Beckingham Street, Tolleshunt
Major, Maldon, CM9 8LJ. Malcolm
& Val. *5m E of Maldon 3m W of
Tiptree. From B1022 take Loamy
Hill rd. At the Xrds L into Witham
Rd. Follow NGS signs.* **Sun 28
June (11-4.30). Adm £4, chd free.
Home-made teas.**

This beautiful and tranquil garden will
amaze and inspire you as you walk
among the herbaceous and shrub
borders, allowing all of your senses
to be aroused. Meandering paths

and seating areas entice you to take time out in a garden that surrounds you with nature in all its splendour. The many scented roses allowing all of your senses to be aroused. Exotic sub- tropical plants and over 50 hostas. WC available.

32 HAYTOR
Rectory Road, Little Burstead, Billericay, CM12 9TR. Carol & Roger Savage, 01268 416520, cas21savage@gmail.com. *From Billericay: B1007, R A176, Little Burstead, L onto Rectory Rd, Haytor is on LHS. Or A176 to Billericay, L Wash Rd 1st R, Dunton Rd.1st R, Rectory Rd, Haytor is on RHS.* Fri 5, Sun 7 June (11-4). Adm £4, chd free. Home-made teas. Visits also by arrangement June & July for groups of 5 to 10.
Lovingly cultivated over the past 30 years, its original one acre grass field is now an eclectic mix of gardeners' delights, with the lower area left to allow natural growth. There are ponds, lovely mature trees, mixed shrubs and herbaceous borders. This garden invites you to take in nature's beauty and there are many seating areas, with wild flowers and even a 'Monet' style bridge.

33 NEW HEATH HOUSE
Crayes Green, Layer Breton, Colchester, CO2 0PN. Geoff & Julia Russell Grant. *7m SW of Colchester off B1022. Going S ½m after Heckfordbridge go L to Birch, past school & church spire, after 0.7m go L. Garden 50 metres, next but one to Hare & Hounds.* Sun 22 Mar (2-4). Adm £3, chd free. Tea. Evening opening Fri 12 June (6-8). Adm £10. Wine. Sun 14 June (12-5). Adm £5, chd free. Home-made teas. Evening adm incl glass of wine.
2 acre spring and summer garden of surprises. Some areas ablaze, others calming. Formal ponds with box, yew, lavender, nepeta, and many different hostas, leading gently into lyrical colour-co-ordinated beds, rambling roses and fragrant Philadelphus. On to lawns bordered by stunning imaginative planting, expanding to an oak-bordered perennial wild flower meadow with a large pond; a wildlife haven.

34 HILLDROP
Laindon Road (B1007), Horndon-On-The-Hill, Stanford-le-Hope, SS17 8QB. John Little & Fiona Crummay, 07967 733720, grassroofcompany@gmail.com, www.grassroofcompany.co.uk. *Just N of Horndon on the Hill. 80m E of junction B1007 & Lower Dunton Rd.* Sun 5 July (2-7). Adm £5, chd free. Home-made teas. Tea, coffee, Pimms, Elderflower Champagne, home-made cakes. Vegetarian savoury snacks. Visits also by arrangement May to Aug for groups of 10 to 20.
Since building our turf roof house in 1995 we have trialled waste materials in our 4 acre garden to mimic brownfield habitat, one of the most undervalued places for wildlife. These are now our most beautiful and diverse habitats for plants and insects. Several green roofs and lots of ideas to create biodiverse habitats, especially for solitary bees. Views across the Thames Estuary to Kent. The 4 acre garden features a self build timber house with green roof, 6 other green roofs, 3 ponds, brownfield landscapes to create plant diversity and solitary bee habitats. New area created this year, using local sand and gravel from A13 widening work to trial climate change plant species. Some wheelchair friendly paths and grass paths that may be accessible depending on rabbit damage. Garden is on a slight slope.

The Old Vicarage

35 HORKESLEY HALL

Little Horkesley, Colchester, CO6 4DB. Mr & Mrs Johnny Eddis, 07808 599290, pollyeddis@hotmail.com, www.airbnb.co.uk/rooms/ 10354093. *6m N of Colchester City Centre. 2m W of A134, 10 mins from A12. At the grass triangle with tree in middle, turn into Little Horkesley Church car park to the very far end - access is via low double black gates at the far end.* Sat 22 Feb (1-4); Sun 7 June (11-5); Sun 13 Sept (12.30-4). Adm £6, chd free. Home-made teas. Visits also by arrangement Feb to Oct. Excellent parking, tours, teas & light lunches for groups.

Magical setting with 8 acres of romantic garden surrounding classical house. Mature parkland setting with major sculpture of balancing stones. Many unusual, ancient, vast trees inc largest Gingko outside Kew. New planting of over 50 varieties of Iris. Walled garden, snowdrops, many hellebores & Feb interest, wild flower garden, glorious hydrangeas, lakeside jungle walk, roses, dahlias, charming enclosed swimming pool garden to relax with teas. Excellent Plant Stall. Soups, teas, cream teas, cakes, meringues, ice creams available depending on the season. Partial wheelchair access to some areas, gravel paths and slopes but easy access to tea area with lovely views over lake and garden.

 ❧ 🐄 ✿ ☂ 🛏 ☕

We help ordinary people open the gates to their extraordinary private gardens to raise impressive amounts of money through admissions, teas and slices of cake!

36 61 HUMBER AVENUE

South Ockendon, RM15 5JW. Mr & Mrs Kasia & Greg Purton-Dmowski, 07711 721629, kasia.purtondmowski@gmail.com. *M25 - J30/31 or A13 - exit to Lakeside. J31/M25 to Thurrock Services, or Grays from A13, at the r'about take exit onto Ship Ln to Aveley, turn R and then 2nd exit at the r'about onto Stifford Rd/ B1335, take Foyle Dr to Humber Ave.* Sun 19 July (12-6); Sun 13 Sept (12-5). Adm £3.50, chd free. Home-made teas. Gluten Free refreshments available. Visits also by arrangement Apr to Oct for groups of 10+.

A suburban garden close to Nature Reserve, 30m x 14m space featuring an old cherry tree from the orchard of the famous Belhus Mansion. The garden features abundant large borders planted heavily with herbaceous plants, small trees, roses, lilies, and ornamental grasses with oriental senses mixed with a traditional English feel with shady areas with hostas, tree ferns and Japanese style plants. The owners are interested in design and are members of Sogetsu International School, original arrangements will be on display during open day.

 ❧ 🐄 ✿ ☕

37 NEW ISABELLA'S GARDEN

42 Theobalds Road, Leigh-On-Sea, SS9 2NE. Mrs Elizabeth Isabella Ling-Locke, 01702714424, ling_locke@yahoo.co.uk. *Take A13 towards Southend on Sea As you pass welcome to Leigh-on-Sea sign, turn R at T-lights onto Thames Drive then L onto Western Road, carry on 0.6 miles then R onto Theobalds Rd.* Sat 6, Sun 7 June, Sat 18, Sun 19 July (11.30-5). Adm £4, chd free. Light refreshments. Visits also by arrangement May to Sept. Not available in August.

This enchanting town garden is bursting with a profusion of colour from early Spring through to the Autumn months. Roses, clematis, agapanthus, herbaceous plants, alpines and pots with unusual succulents fill every corner of this garden. There is a wildlife pond. Lilies and water features as well as other garden ornaments which are to be found hiding within the shrubbery and throughout the garden. This garden is situated in the town of Leigh on Sea, and just a 5 min walk from the cockle sheds of old Leigh and Leigh railway

station. Selection of delicious home-made cakes incl cream teas and gluten free cakes. Cakes made by Broadway Belles, the local WI. Most of the garden is accessible, there are steps near to the house.

 ❧ ☕

38 JERICHO COTTAGE (MEGARRY'S ANTIQUES & TEASHOP)

The Green, Blackmore, Ingatestone, CM4 0RR. Judi Wood, 01277 822170, megarrys@yahoo.co.uk, www.antique-teashop.co.uk. *4m E of Chipping Ongar 4m N of Brentwood. At centre of Blackmore village head for village green. Turn by the war memorial into Blacksmith Alley. Jericho Cottage straight ahead.* Visits by arrangement Mar to Oct for groups of 5 to 20. Weekdays up to 20. Weekends only 10 max. Mon & Tues 15 plus. Adm £3. Cream teas.

Small walled wildlife & woodland garden with mature trees, shrubs, bamboos, palms and ponds. Historic Romany Vardo and Victorian Glasshouse. Primroses, bluebells, camellias, rhododendrons and later hydrangeas, euphorbias and geraniums clothe the ground, while a canopy of wisteria, rambling roses, honeysuckle and kiwi vine shade the patio and pergola. The garden is an untamed hidden oasis. Antique shop. Megarry's Teashop scones with Rodda's clotted cream. Home-made cakes. A gentle paved path leads to the pergola and patio where there is access to the garden through a wrought iron gate onto the lawn.

 ❧ 🐄 ✿ ☕

39 KAMALA

262 Main Road, Hawkwell, Hockley, SS5 4NW. Karen Mann, 07976 272999, karenmann10@hotmail.com. *3m NE of Rayleigh. From A127 at Rayleigh Weir take B1013 towards Hockley. Garden on L after White Hart Pub & village green.* Sun 2, Sun 23 Aug (12.30-5.30). Adm £4, chd free. Home-made teas. Visits also by arrangement in Aug for groups of 10+.

Come and enjoy spectacular herbaceous borders which sing with colour as displays of salvia are surpassed by Dahlia drifts. Gingers, brugmansia, various bananas, bamboos and canna add an exotic note. Grasses sway above the blooms, giving movement. Rest awhile in the rose clad pergola while listening to the two Amazon Parrots in the aviary. The garden also features a completely new, RHS accredited Dahlia named "Jake Mann". Trees and shrubs include Acers, Catalpa aurea, Cercis 'Forest Pansy' and a large unusual Sinocalycanthus (Chinese Allspice) a stunning, rare plant with fantastic flowers.

&. ❁ ☕

40 KEEWAY

Ferry Road, Creeksea, nr Burnham-on-Crouch, CM0 8PL. John & Sue Ketteley, 01621 782083, sueketteley@hotmail.com. *2m W of Burnham-on-Crouch. B1010 to Burnham on Crouch. At town sign take 1st R into Ferry Rd signed Creeksea & Burnham Golf Club & follow NGS signs.* Sat 27 June, Wed 1 July (2-5). Adm £4, chd free. Home-made teas. Visits also by arrangement June & July for groups of 10 to 30.
Large, mature country garden with stunning views over the R Crouch. Formal terraces surround the house with steps leading to sweeping lawns, mixed borders packed full of bulbs and perennials, formal rose and herb garden with interesting water feature. Further afield there are wilder areas, paddocks and lake. A productive greenhouse, vegetable and cutting gardens complete the picture.

&. ❁ ☕

41 KELVEDON HALL

Kelvedon, Colchester, CO5 9BN. Mr & Mrs Jack Inglis, 07973 795955, v_inglis@btinternet.com. *Take Maldon Rd direction Great Braxted from Kelvedon High St. Go over R Blackwater bridge & bridge over A12 At T-junction turn R onto Kelvedon Rd. Take 1st L, single gravel road, oak tree on corner.* Visits by arrangement May & June for groups of 20+. Adm £7.50, chd free. Home-made teas in the Courtyard Garden by the house or for larger numbers in the Pool House Walled Garden, weather permitting. Teas, coffees and cakes.
Varied 6 acre garden surrounding a gorgeous C18 house. A blend of formal and informal spaces interspersed with modern sculpture. Pleached hornbeam and yew and box topiary provide structure. A courtyard

walled garden juxtaposes a modern walled pool garden, both providing season long displays. Herbaceous borders offset an abundance of roses around the house. Lily covered ponds with a wet garden. Topiary, sculpture, tulips and roses. Wheelchair access not ideal as there is a lot of gravel.

❁ D ☕

GROUP OPENING

42 LANGLEY VILLAGE GARDENS

Langley Upper Green, Saffron Walden, CB11 4RY. *7m W of Saffron Walden 10m N of Bishops Stortford. At Newport take B1038. After 3m turn R at Clavering, signed Langley. Upper Green is 3m further on.* Sun 28 June (11-5). Combined adm £7, chd free. Light refreshments at Village Hall on Langley Village Green. Light lunches & home-made teas.

APRIL COTTAGE
Anne & Neil Harris.

1 SPARROWS
Kevin and Gill Shepherd.

WICKETS
Susan & Doug Copeland.
(See separate entry)

April Cottage, at Sheepcote Green, just 2m from Langley, is a charming thatched cottage. It boasts well established, colourful garden with many unusual plants: old fashioned roses, clematis and herbaceous perennials galore. Ornamental ponds. Viewing platform offers wonderful views. Damp garden, hosta collection. I Sparrows is a compact garden with fruit trees, raised vegetable beds and greenhouse. Lawn edged with buxus. Shrubs and climbers. Small water feature and wildlife friendly. A collection of Heuchera and Heucherella. Wickets is 3 acres & has wide, beautiful mixed borders featuring hundreds of roses. There are two landscaped meadows, a large lily pond, with Monet Style bridge & Griffin glasshouse nearby. Espalier apples surround parterre. Secluded dry garden. New Mediterranean courtyard. Rural village with views over rolling Essex countryside. April Cottage is in the tiny hamlet of Sheepcote Green 5min drive from Langley. Gravel drives at Wickets.

&. 🐕 ❁ 🚗 ☕

43 LITTLE MYLES

Ongar Road, Stondon Massey, Brentwood, CM15 0LD. Judy & Adrian Cowan. *1½m SE of Chipping Ongar. Off A128 at Stag Pub, Marden Ash, towards Stondon Massey. Over bridge, 1st house on R after 'S' bend. 400yds Ongar side of Stondon Church.* Sun 5 July (11-4). Adm £5, chd free. Home-made teas. Seating in Tea Room, also under trees and on main lawn.
A romantic, naturalistic garden full of hidden features, set in 3 acres. Evolving experimental flower meadow. Full borders, meandering paths to Beach Garden, Perennial Prairie border, Exotic Jungle with elephant, monkeys and giraffe. Fountains, sculptures and tranquil benches. Hidden Asian garden, Slate garden, hornbeam pergola natural pond. Herb garden that inspired Little Myles herbal cosmetics. Hand painted jungle mural. Crafts and handmade herbal cosmetics for sale. Explorers sheet and map for children. New flower meadow in the making. Gravel paths. No disabled WC available.

&. ❁ ☕

44 LONG HOUSE PLANTS

Church Road, Noak Hill, Romford, RM4 1LD. Tim Carter, 01708 371719, tim@thelonghouse.net, www.longhouse-plants.co.uk. *3½m NW of J28 M25. J28 M25 take A1023 Brentwood. At 1st T-lights, turn L to South Weald after 0.8m turn L at T junction. After 1.6m turn L, over M25 after ½m turn R into Church Rd, nursery opp church.* Wed 10 June, Wed 8 July, Wed 5 Aug, Wed 9 Sept (11-4). Adm £5, chd £3. Home-made teas. Visits also by arrangement June to Oct for groups of 30+.
A beautiful garden - yes, but one with a purpose. Long House Plants has been producing home grown plants for more than 10 years - here is a chance to see where it all begins! With wide paths and plenty of seats carefully placed to enjoy the plants and views. It has been thoughtfully designed so that the collections of plants look great together through all seasons. Disabled Car Parking. Paths are suitable for wheelchairs and mobility scooters. Disabled toilet in nursery. Two small cobbled areas not suitable.

&. ❁ 🚗 ☕

45 LONGYARD COTTAGE

Betts Lane, Nazeing, Essex, EN9 2DA. Jackie & John Copping, 07780 802863, Nigella11@btopenworld.com. *Opposite red telephone box.* **Sun 17 May (11-4). Adm £4, chd free. Home-made teas. Visits also by arrangement Feb to Oct for groups of 5 to 30.**
Longyard Cottage is an interesting ³/₄ of an acre garden situated within yards of an SSSI site, a C11 Church, a myriad of footpaths and a fine display of snowdrops and spring bulbs. This conceptual garden is based on a 'journey' and depicted through the use of paths which take you through 3 distinct areas each with its own characteristics. It's a tactile garden with which you can engage or simply sit and relax.

46 LOXLEY HOUSE

49 Robin Hood Road, Brentwood, CM15 9EL. Robert & Helen Smith. *1m N of Brentwood town centre. On A128 N towards Ongar turn R onto Doddinghurst Rd at mini r'about. Take the 1st rd on L into Robin Hood Rd. 2 houses before the bend on L.* **Sat 18, Sun 19 July (11-3). Adm £4, chd free. Home-made teas.**
On entering the rear garden you will be surprised and delighted by this town garden. A colourful patio with pots and containers. Steps up onto a circular lawn surrounded by hedges, herbaceous borders, trees and climbers. 2 water features, one a Japanese theme and another with ferns in a quiet seating area. The garden is planted to offer colour throughout the seasons.

47 16 MAIDA WAY

Chingford, E4 7JL. Clare & Steve Francis. *1m from Chingford town centre off Kings Head Hill. Maida Way is a cul-de-sac off Maida Avenue that can be accessed via Kings Head Hill or Sewardstone Rd.* **Evening opening Sat 4 July (4-7.30). Adm £7.50, chd free. Wine. Adm incl a glass of wine and selection of canapes.**
There are three distinct areas to the garden. A walled patio with raised beds of ferns, climbers, hostas and planters. Steps up to middle garden with a large koi pond, seating area, with acers, shrubs, herbaceous plants, grasses and grapevine. Numerous retro artefacts creatively upcycled. The third area is a kitchen garden with raised beds of fruit trees and bushes, herbs and vegetables.

48 NEW 56 MALDON ROAD

Goldhanger, Maldon, CM9 8BG. Mr & Mrs Peter and Chris French. *On main road between Heybridge & Tolleshunt Darcy.* **Fri 5, Sat 6, Sun 7 June (10-4). Adm £4, chd free. Light refreshments.**
A variety of garden rooms including the walled vegetable, cottage and courtyard gardens, shrubbery and oriental arbour. Take a seat in the teahouse to enjoy the tree fountain and the sculptures, or relax in the gazebo. Visit the vegetable garden with its greenhouse and covered fruit garden. From the courtyard you can see the substantial 'work in progress' to complete our project.

49 9 MALYON ROAD

Witham, CM8 1DF. Maureen & Stephen Hicks. *Car park at bottom of High St opp Swan Pub, 5 min walk from car park cross High St by pedestrian crossing onto River Walk, follow path, take 1st R turn into Luard Way, Malyon Rd straight ahead.* **Sun 5 July (10.30-5). Adm £4. Home-made teas. Opening with Witham Town Gardens on Sat 4 July (11-4.30).**
Large town garden with mature trees and shrubs made up of a series of garden rooms. Flower beds, pond,

Kelvedon Hall

summerhouse and greenhouse giving all year interest. Plenty of places to sit and relax with paths that take you on a tour of the garden. A quiet hidden place not expected in a busy town. Our garden is a hidden oasis, where you can escape from the hustle and bustle of busy life. On the edge of town, close to the Witham's Rambling Town River Walk. Wheelchair access, but there is a step down into part of the garden.

50 ◆ MARKS HALL GARDENS & ARBORETUM

Coggeshall, CO6 1TG. Marks Hall Estate, 01376 563796, enquiries@markshall.org.uk, www.markshall.org.uk. *1½ m N of Coggeshall. Follow brown & white tourism signs from A120 Coggeshall bypass.* **For opening times and information, please phone, email or visit garden website.**
Marks Hall Gardens and Arboretum features a tree collection from all the temperate areas of the world set in more than 200 acres of historic landscape providing interest and enjoyment throughout the year. Highlights include: the Millennium Walk designed for structure, colour and scent on the shortest days of the year; the largest planting in Europe of Wollemi pine and the inspired combination of traditional and contemporary planting in the C18 Walled Garden. Spring snowdrop and autumn colour displays are annual highlights. Tea room serving homemade cakes, hot and cold beverages, light lunches including homemade soup and daily specials. See website for opening times. Hard paths lead to all key areas of interest. Wheelchairs or staff-driven buggy available for visitors with mobility issues (booking essential).

51 MIRAFLORES

Witham, CM8 2LJ. Yvonne & Danny Owen, 07976 603863, danny@dannyowen.co.uk. *Please DO NOT go via Rowan Way, go to Forest Rd as there is rear access only to garden. Access is ONLY by rear gate at the top The Spinney, off of FOREST RD, CM8 2TP. Please follow yellow signs. PLEASE do not park in The Spinney as this is a private parking area.* **Sun 14 June (1-5). Adm £4, chd free. Home-made teas. Visits also by arrangement May & June for** groups of 10 to 30.
An award-winning, medium-sized garden described as a "Little Bit of Heaven'. A blaze of colour with roses, clematis, pergola, rose arch, triple fountain with box hedging and deep herbaceous borders. See our 'Folly', exuberant and cascading hanging baskets.find our Secret Door. Featured in Garden Answers, Amateur Gardening and Essex Life. Tranquil seating areas. Cakes (incl gluten free), savouries, teas, coffee, soft drinks, herbal teas are available. No access for wheelchair users as step up to garden.

We open the gates to the nation's best gardens, offering a relaxing, memorable and affordable day out. A perfect experience to share with friends and family.

52 MOVERONS

Brightlingsea, CO7 0SB. Lesley & Payne Gunfield, lesleyorrock@me.com, , www.moverons.co.uk. *7m SE of Colchester. At old church turn R signed Moverons Farm. Follow lane & garden signs for approx 1m. Beware some SatNavs take you the wrong side of the river.* **Open garden with Sculpture Exhibition. Sat 30, Sun 31 May (10.30-5). Adm £5, chd free. Home-made teas. Visits also by arrangement May to July for groups of 10+.**
Tranquil 4 acre garden in touch with its surroundings and enjoying stunning estuary views. A wide variety of planting in mixed borders to suit different growing conditions and provide all year colour. Courtyard, large natural ponds, sculptures and barn for rainy day teas! We're busy redeveloping the reflection pool area. Magnificent trees some over 300yrs old give this garden real presence. Most of the garden is accessible by wheelchair via grass and gravel paths, There are some steps and bark paths.

53 23 NEW ROAD

Dagenham, RM10 9NH. John Seaman, 07504 712818, jseaman@talktalk.net. *Leave A13 at the junction signed for A1306 - Dagenham & Hornchurch. Go around the r'about following it off at the 4th exit. Then follow the 2nd r'about straight onwards.* **Sat 22, Sun 23 Aug (12-5). Adm £4, chd free. Visits also by arrangement July to Sept for groups of 5 to 20.**
This is an exotic garden, themed on the foothills of the Himalayas in India. This garden will be like no other you may have seen before despite its modest size. It is filled with exquisite tropical plants including Canna, Gingers and Bananas. A feast for the eyes filled with good ideas for vertical space. An extravaganza of plants in all shapes, colour and form.

54 NEW OAK FARM

Vernons Road, Wakes Colne, Colchester, CO6 2AH. Ann and Peter Chillingworth. *Vernons Road is just off A1124 between Ford Street & Chappel. Oak Farm is 200 metres up lane on R.* **Wed 3 June, Thur 16 July, Wed 12 Aug (2-5). Adm £4, chd free. Home-made teas.**
Farmhouse garden of about 1 acre on an exposed site with extensive views south and west across the Colne Valley. Shrubberies, lawned borders and shady secret spots where people can enjoy refreshments. Although there are some steps in places, access can be gained to most of the garden.

55 NEW THE OLD VICARAGE

Church End, Broxted, Dunmow, CM6 2BU. Ruth & Adam Tidball. *3m S of Thaxted. From Thaxted on the B1051, take Broxted turning. Just before next junction, turn R into field for parking.* **Sun 5 July (1-5). Adm £5, chd free. Light refreshments.**
Victorian former vicarage surrounded by three acres of formal gardens, one-acre woodland garden and seven-acre hay meadow. Deep mixed borders. Rose garden with recently added perennial underplanting. Many rare and special plants and trees. Wild flower meadow, alpine rockery, series of ponds providing habitat for ornamental goldfish and native wildlife. Views across the meadow to church and beyond.

Green Island

Found in the village centre next to the church, this garden offers a mixture of mature shrubs and trees and coloured themed herbaceous borders. Lawns and paths lead through entertainment spaces littered with animal sculptures. With a small pond and plenty of seating the garden is accessible to wheelchairs.

&. 🐕 ✳ 🚐 ☕

59 ROOKWOODS
Yeldham Road, Sible Hedingham, CO9 3QG. Peter & Sandra Robinson, 07770 957111, sandy1989@btinternet.com, www.rookwoodsgarden.com. *8m NW of Halstead. Entering Sible Hedingham from the direction of Haverhill on A1017 take 1st R just after 30mph sign. Coming through SH from the Braintree direction turn left just before the 40mph leaving the village.* **Mon 25 May (10.30-5). Adm £5, chd free. Home-made teas. Visits also by arrangement May to Sept for groups of 10 to 30.**
Rookwoods is a tranquil garden in which you can enjoy a variety of mature trees; herbaceous borders; a shrubbery; pleached hornbeam rooms; a work-in-progress wild flower bed; a buttercup meadow, and an ancient oak wood. There is no need to walk far, you can come and linger over tea, under a dreamy wisteria canopy while enjoying views across the garden. Bee hive. Wild flower garden. Meadow to walk through leading to Ancient Oak Wood. Mature Foxglove tree. Terrace with views across garden. Gravel drive.

&. ✳ 🚐 ☕

60 79 ROYSTON AVENUE
Chingford, E4 9DE. Paul & Christine Lidbury. *From A406 Crooked Billet r'about take A112 towards Chingford. Continue ½m, across T-lights (Morrison's), Royston Ave is 3rd turn on R. Bus 97, 158, 215, 357 (Leonard Rd or Ainslie Wood Rd stops).* **Sun 17 May (12-5). Adm £3.50, chd £1. Home-made teas.**
A 55 x 19ft urban garden with over 600 different varieties of plants - a great many in containers, including collections of Hostas, Acers, and Sempervivums. An oasis for local birds and wildlife with two small ponds and insect habitats with further interest provided by ornaments, sculptures and artwork, where words of gardening wisdom abound. Not suitable for young children. Tea/

56 PEACOCKS
Main Road, Margaretting, CM4 9HY. Phil Torr, 07802 472382, phil.torr@btinternet.com. *Margaretting Village Centre. From village Xrds go 75yds in the direction of Ingatestone, entrance gates will be found on L set back 50 feet from the road frontage.* **Visits by arrangement Mar to June for groups of 20+. Smaller groups may be accommodated if the organiser is flexible on dates. Adm £10, chd free. Home-made teas. Tea/coffee and cake served. Donation to St Francis Hospice.**
5-acre garden with mature native and specimen trees. Restored horticultural buildings. Series of garden rooms including Paradise Garden, Garden of Reconciliation, Alhambra fusion. Long herbaceous/mixed border. Temple of Antheia on the banks of a lily lake. Large areas for wildlife incl woodland walk, a nuttery and orchard. Traditionally managed wild flower meadow. Sunken dell with waterfall. Display of old Margaretting postcards. Small art exhibition. Garden sculpture. Wild flower meadow in traditional orchard. Most of garden wheelchair accessible.

&. 🚐 ☕

57 18 PETTITS BOULEVARD,
Rise Park, Romford, RM1 4PL. Peter & Lynn Nutley. *From M25 take A12 towards London, turn R at Pettits Lane junction then R again into Pettits Blvd or Romford Stn then 103 or 499 bus to Romford Fire Stn and follow NGS signs.* **Sat 27 June (1-5). Home-made teas. Sun 28 June (1-5). Sun 13 Sept (1-5). Home-made teas. Adm £3.50, chd free.**
The garden is 80ft x 23ft on three levels with an ornamental pond, patio area with shrubs and perennials, many in pots. Large eucalyptus tree leads to a woodland themed area with many ferns and hostas. There are agricultural implements and garden ornaments giving a unique and quirky feel to the garden. There are also tranquil seating areas situated throughout.

&. 🐕 ☕

58 THE PUNCHBOWL
The Street, High Easter, Chelmsford, CM1 4QW. Penny Kelsey. *Centre of High Easter. Next to the church.* **Wed 20 May (2.30-5). Adm £5, chd free. Home-made teas.**

coffee and home-made cakes. Quality home-brewed beer tastings available.

61 69 RUNDELLS - THE SECRET GARDEN

Harlow, CM18 7HD. Mr & Mrs K Naunton, 01279 303471, k_naunton@hotmail.com. *3m from J7 M11. A414 exit T-lights take L exit Southern Way, mini r'about 1st exit Trotters Rd leading into Commonside Rd, take 2nd L into Rundells.* **Sat 11 July (1-5). Adm £3, chd free. Home-made teas. Visits also by arrangement Mar to Oct for groups of 5 to 30. The garden is relatively small.**

As featured on Alan Tichmarsh's first 'Love Your Garden' series ('The Secret Garden') 69, Rundells is a very colourful, small town garden packed with a wide variety of shrubs, perennials, herbaceous and bedding plants in over 200 assorted containers. Hard landscaping on different levels incl's summer house, various seating areas and water features. Steep steps. Access to adjacent allotment open to view. Various small secluded seating areas. A small fairy garden has been added to give interest for younger visitors. The garden is next to a large allotment and this is open to view with lots of interesting features including a bee apiary. Honey and other produce for sale (conditions permitting). Cakes, tea, coffee and soft drinks available.

62 ST HELENS

High Street, Stebbing, CM6 3SE. Stephen & Joan Bazlinton, 01371 856495, jbazlinton@gmail.com. *3m E of Great Dunmow. Leave Gt Dunmow on B1256. Take 1st L to Stebbing, at T-junction turn L into High St, garden 2nd on R.* **Visits by arrangement Apr to July. Admission price includes teas. Adm £8, chd free. Home-made teas. Donation to Dentaid.**

A garden established over 40 years from a bog-ridden, cricket-bat plantation into a gently sloping woodland garden. Springs and ponds divide the garden into different areas with various shrubs and perennial planting. Partial wheelchair access.

63 SANDY LODGE

Howe Drive, Hedingham Road, Halstead, CO9 2QL. Emma & Rick Rengasamy. *8m NE of Braintree. Turn off Hedingham Rd into Ashlong Grove. Howe Drive is on L. Please park in Ashlong Grove & walk up Howe Drive.* **Sun 13 Sept (11-5). Adm £4.50, chd free. Home-made teas.**

A stunning garden, with amazing views over Halstead, there is something to see every day. $\frac{3}{4}$ acre created over the last 5 years, enter to our gravel Bee Border, wander in our Winter Wedding border and the Woodlands Walk. Across the lawn you find double borders with flowing prairie planting. Lots of seating and viewing spots. Featured in the Garden Gate is Open https://thegardengateisopen.blog/. Wheelchair access restricted due to large amount of gravel.

64 NEW SCRIPS HOUSE

Cut Hedge Lane, Coggeshall, Colchester, CO6 1RL. Mr & Mrs James and Sophie Bardrick. *From A12 N/S take Kelvedon/Feering exit. Turn L/R passed Kelvedon stn. Continue for 2m turn L into Scrips Rd. From A120 take Coggeshall exit. Drive through village towards Kelvedon. Turn R up Scrips Rd.* **Thur 30 Apr, Thur 2 July (1-4). Adm £7, chd free. Home-made teas.**

A large garden with further paddocks. Includes a mature woodland with a memorial avenue of fastigiate oaks. The garden is divided into smaller areas including a walled pool garden and a Spring garden. A pleached lime

walk leads to a white garden flanked by two 30m herbaceous borders. There is an ornamental pond with ducks, an ample vegetable garden and fruit cage, an orchard and a chicken run. Most areas accessible with a fairly strong wheelchair pusher.

65 SHRUBS FARM

Lamarsh, Bures, CO8 5EA. Mr & Mrs Robert Erith, 01787 227520, bob@shrubsfarm.co.uk, www.shrubsfarm.co.uk. *1¼m from Bures. On rd to Lamarsh, the drive is signed to Shrubs Farm.* **Visits by arrangement May to Sept for groups of 5+. Adm £8, chd free. Home-made teas. £6.00 per head. Wine & canapes by arrangement.**

2 acres with shrub borders, lawns, roses and trees. 50 acres parkland with wild flower paths and woodland trails. Over 60 species of oak. Superb 10m views over Stour valley. Ancient coppice and pollards incl largest goat (pussy) willow (*Salix caprea*) in England. Wollemi and Norfolk pines, and banana trees. Full size black rhinoceros. Display of Bronze Age burial urns. Large grass maze. Guided Tour to incl garden, park and ancient woodland, historic items including Bronze Age Burial Urns and painting of the Stour valley 200 years ago. Restored C18 Essex barn is available for refreshment by prior arrangement. Tea proceeds to Lamarsh Church. Some ground may be boggy in wet weather.

66 SNARES HILL COTTAGE

Duck End, Stebbing, CM6 3RY. Pete & Liz Stabler, 01371 856565, petestabler@gmail.com. *Between Dunmow & Bardfield. On B1057 from Great Dunmow to Great Bardfield, ½m after Bran End on L.* **Visits by arrangement Apr to Sept for groups of 5+. Adm £5, chd free. Home-made teas.**

A 'quintessential English Garden' - Gardeners World. Our quirky 1½ acre garden has surprises round every corner and many interesting sculptures. A natural swimming pool is bordered by romantic flower beds, herb garden and Victorian folly. A bog garden borders woods and leads to silver birch copse, beach garden and 'Roman' temple. Natural Swimming Pond. Classic cars. Sculptures. Not wheelchair friendly as it is a hilly garden with some steep slopes.

67 SOUTH SHOEBURY HALL

Church Road, Shoeburyness, SS3 9DN. Mr & Mrs M Dedman, 07881954733, michael@shoeburyhall.co.uk. *4m E of Southend-on-Sea. Enter Southend on A127 to Eastern Ave A1159 signed Shoebury. R at r'about to join A13. Proceed S to Ness Rd. R into Church Rd. Garden on L 50 metres.* **Sun 26 Apr, Sun 26 July (2-5). Adm £4, chd free. Home-made teas. cakes, tea/coffee and cold drinks. Visits also by arrangement Apr to Aug for groups of 10+.**
Delightful, 1-acre established walled garden surrounding Grade II listed house (not open) and bee house. Charming agapanthus and hydrangea beds. April is ablaze with 3000 tulips and fritillaria. July shows 200+ varieties of agapanthus incl 'Queen Mum' and 'Black Magic'. Unusual trees, shrubs, rose borders, with 50yr old plus geraniums, Mediterranean and Southern Hemisphere planting in dry garden. C11 St Andrews Church open to visitors (by arrangement). Garden close to sea. Bumper agapanthus sale at both open days.
&. 🐄 ❀ 🚗 ☕ ❦

68 SPRING COTTAGE

Chapel Lane, Elmstead Market, Colchester, CO7 7AG. Mr & Mrs Roger & Sharon Sciachettano. *3m from Colchester. Overlooking village green North of A133 through Elmstead Market. Parking limited adjacent to cottage, village car park nearby on South side of A133.* **Sat 27, Sun 28 June (2-4.30). Adm £3.50, chd free. Home-made teas.**
From Acteas to Zauschenerias and Aressima to Zebra grass we hope our large variety of plants will please. Our award winning garden features a range of styles and habitats e.g. woodland dell, stumpery, Mediterranean area, perennial borders and pond. Our C17 thatched cottage and garden show case a number of plants found at the world famous Beth Chatto gardens ½ m down the road. In early June our 17 rose varieties take centre stage and several clematis will be at their best. We can promise colour and scent to delight the senses and a range of unusual species to please the plant enthusiast. Refreshments provided by the WI served on the village green in front of Spring Cottage.
❀ ☕

69 NEW 2 SPRING COTTAGES

Conduit Lane, Woodham Mortimer, Maldon, CM9 6SZ. Sharon & Michael Cox, 07841867908, coxmichael1958@gmail.com. *From Danbury continue on A414 towards Maldon for 1½m until you come to Oak Corner r'about, 1st L continuing on A414. 200 yards take 1st R into Conduit Lane.* **Fri 17, Sun 19 July (10-5). Adm £4, chd free. Cream teas. and home-made cakes available. Visits also by arrangement in July for groups of up to 20. Please note terraced garden with many steps.**
A small pretty terraced cottage garden, featuring many different levels, each area exhibiting good use of space and varied planting. Plenty of seating in a relaxed quiet setting. The garden has been developed to encourage wildlife, with an abundance of bee, butterfly, bird houses and water feature.
☕

70 NEW STOCKSMEAD

Wicken Road, Arkesden, Saffron Walden, CB11 4EY. Mr & Mrs Paul and Louise Kimberley. *5m W of Saffron Walden. 3m W from Newport via B1038 through Wicken Bonhunt. Enter Wicken Road from the village we are the last house on R. Conversely if you enter Wicken Road from Wicken Bonhunt we are the 1st house on L as you enter the village.* **Sun 14 June (11-4). Adm £5, chd free. Home-made teas.**
A beautiful country garden in North Essex with open views to the distant landscape.The garden is split into three distinct areas. A dry gravel garden featuring Mediterranean plants, a traditional herbaceous garden full of colour and a more structured garden with topiary interplanted with grasses and more structural herbaceous plants.
D ☕

71 STRANDLANDS

off Rectory Road, Wrabness, Manningtree, CO11 2TX. Jenny & David Edmunds, 01255 886260, strandlands@outlook.com. *1km along farm track from the corner of Rectory Rd. If using a SatNav, the post code will leave you at the corner of Rectory Rd. Turn onto a farm track, signed to Woodcutters Cottage & Strandlands, & continue for 1km.* **Visits by arrangement May & June for groups of 10 to 20. Adm £5, chd free. Tea, coffee & a slice of home-made cake.**
Cottage surrounded by 4 acres of land bordering beautiful and unspoilt Stour Estuary. One acre of decorative garden: formal courtyard with yew, box and perovskia hedges, lily pond, summerhouse and greenhouse; 2 large island beds, secret 'moon garden', madly and vividly planted 'Madison' garden, 3 acres of wildlife meadows with groups of native trees, large wildlife pond, also riverside bird hide. View the Stour Estuary from our own bird hide. Grayson Perry's 'A House for Essex' can be seen just one field away from Strandlands. Mostly accessible and flat although parking area is gravelled.
&. ❀ ☕

72 NEW TSURU

Back Lane, Wickham Bishops, Witham, CM8 3LU. Ina Siddall & Liz Wager. *3m from A12 Witham exit towards Maldon. Over bridge, up Blue Mills hill via Witham Road into The Street. R opp Mulberry Tree into School Road, L into Back Lane parking in Library car park.* **Fri 1 May, Fri 11 Sept (12-4). Adm £4.50, chd free. Home-made teas. Soup will be available between 12 - 2pm.**
3/4 acre, Tsuru an established garden with mature shrubs underplanted with bulbs and hardy perennials. Well stocked front garden. Side gate through alley into rear garden. 4 distinct areas. Rockery planted with alpines and bulbs. Section between 2 arches with large acer, mature shrubs and grasses. Opening out to wider lawn and sweeping borders. Woodland section with rare Cut Beech tree.
&. ❀ 🚗 ☕

73 TUDOR ROOST

18 Frere Way, Fingringhoe, Colchester, CO5 7BP. Chris & Linda Pegden. *5m S of Colchester. In Fingringhoe by Whalebone PH*

follow sign to Ballast Quay, after ½ m turn R into Brook Hall Rd, then 1st L into Frere Way. **Sun 12, Mon 13 Apr, Sun 24, Mon 25 May, Sat 25, Sun 26 July (2-5). Adm £4, chd free. Home-made teas. Large conservatory to sit in if inclement weather.**
An unexpected hidden colourful ¼-acre garden. Well manicured grassy paths wind round island beds and ponds. Densely planted subtropical area with architectural and exotic plants - cannas, bananas, palms, agapanthus, agaves and tree ferns surround a colourful gazebo. Garden planted to provide yr-round colour and encourage wildlife. Many peaceful seating areas. Within 1m of Fingringhoe Wick Nature Reserve. PLEASE CONFIRM OPENING DATES ON NGS WEBSITE OR TELEPHONE.

74 37 TURPINS LANE
Chigwell, IG8 8AZ. Fabrice Aru & Martin Thurston, 0208 5050 739, martin.thurston@talktalk.net. *Between Woodford & Epping. Tube: Chigwell, 2m from North Circular Rd at Woodford, follow the signs for Chigwell (A113) through Woodford Bridge into Manor Rd & turn L, Bus 275 & W14.* **Sun 14 June (11-6). Adm £4, chd free. Visits also by arrangement May to Oct for groups of up to 10.**
An unexpected hidden, magical, part-walled garden showing how much can be achieved in a small space. An oasis of calm with densely planted rich, lush foliage, tree ferns, hostas, topiary and an abundance of well maintained shrubs complemented by a small pond and 3 water features designed for yr round interest. Featured on BBC Gardeners' World and ITV Good Morning Britain.

75 TWO COTTAGES
Church Road, Chrishall, Saffron Walden, SG8 8QT. Michelle Thomas, 07581 745130, mrsdthomas@btinternet.com. *7m W of Saffron Walden. Continue on B1039, take R turn to Chrishall. Bury Lane leading into Church Rd. You will find Two Cottages on your 1st L with an old planted boat on the bank.* **Sun 21 June, Sun 5 July (12-4). Adm £5, chd free. Home-made teas. Visits also by arrangement May to Sept for groups of up to 30.**
Magic lurks within this charming 1½ acre garden, evolved over 30 yrs.

Many treasures hidden amongst a variety of planting. Over 215 roses showcased in island borders. Meandering lawn paths lead through wisteria walkway to find two miniature Shetland ponies keen to show off to guests. Tranquil seating areas, teas, cakes and gifts for sale in 'The Shed' shop. The perfect place to buy unusual gifts. Large smoking dragon, once on display at Hampton Court garden show. Superb views over countryside to village church. Fragrance and colour that only Mother Nature can create. Garden featured on BBC Gardeners' World in which I commented, "I love my roses and they love me back."

76 ULTING WICK
Crouchmans Farm Road, Maldon, CM9 6QX. Mr & Mrs B Burrough, 01245 380216, philippa.burrough@btinternet.com, www.ultingwickgarden.co.uk. *3m NW of Maldon. Take R turning to Ulting off B1019 as you exit Hatfield Peverel by a green. Garden on R after 2 M.* **Sun 26 Apr (11-5). Light refreshments. Fri 1 May,** Fri 3 July, Mon 31 Aug, Fri 4 Sept (2-5). Home-made teas. **Adm £6, chd free. Home-made soup using ingredients from the garden, filled rolls and home-made teas on 26 April. Visits also by arrangement Mar to Sept. For groups of 15+. Refreshments by prior arrangement. Donation to All Saints Ulting Church.**
Listed black barns provide backdrop for vibrant and exuberant planting in 8 acres. Thousands of colourful tulips, flowing innovative spring planting, herbaceous borders, pond, mature weeping willows, kitchen garden, dramatic late summer beds with zingy, tender, exotic plant combinations. Drought tolerant perennial and mini annual wild flower meadows. Woodland. Many plants propagated in-house. Lots of unusual plants for sale. All Saints Church Ulting will be open in conjunction with the garden for talks on its history. Beautiful dog walks along the R Chelmer from the garden. Some gravel around the house but main areas of interest are accessible for wheelchairs.

Fudlers Hall

GROUP OPENING

77 WALTHAM ABBEY GROUP GARDENS

Waltham Abbey,
EN9 1LG. 01992 714047,
frank.jewson@btconnect.com.
M25, J26 to Waltham Abbey. At T-lights by McD turn R to r'about. Take 2nd exit to next r'about. Take 3rd exit (A112) to T-lights. L to Monkswood Av. **Sun 7 June, Sun 6 Sept (12-5.30). Combined adm £6, chd free. Home-made teas at Silver Birches, Quendon Drive. Visits also by arrangement May to Oct for groups of 10 to 20.**

62 EASTBROOK ROAD
Caroline Cassell.

39 HALFHIDES
Chris Hamer.

76 MONKSWOOD AVENUE
Cathy & Dan Gallagher.

SILVER BIRCHES
Linda & Frank Jewson.

Come and visit our four gardens in the historic town of Waltham Abbey. Silver Birches lawns are surrounded by mixed borders with mature shrubs and trees. The pond is covered in water lilies and is home to much wildlife. Take a short stroll in the hidden woodland walk before enjoying tea and home-made cake. 39 Halfhides the owner has evolved her garden over 50 years. Deep perennial borders and a small pond which leads to a stream and a larger pond in the secluded shade garden. There is an opportunity to purchase many of the plants used in this garden. 76 Monkswood - a plantswomans garden with mixed borders, greenhouse and wildlife pond. You may also be tempted to purchase one of the many Victorian chimney pots which are on sale from the wildlife friendly front garden. 62 Eastbrook Road - winner of 'Gardeners' World magazine 'Best Small Space' and 'Judges' choice 2017' and described as a 'circular seclusion' (please note limited parking and approx. 7 mins walk from other gardens). 62 Eastbrook Rd and Halfhides are not suitable for wheelchairs and parts of Silver Birches.

78 1 WHITEHOUSE COTTAGES

Blue Mill Lane, Woodham Walter,
Maldon, CM9 6LR. Mrs Shelley
Rand. *In between Maldon & Danbury, short drive from A12. From A414 Danbury, turn L at The Anchor & continue into the village. Directly after the white village gates at the far end of the village, turn R into Blue Mill Lane.* **Sun 17 May, Sun 7 June, Sun 12 July (11-4). Adm £3.50, chd free. Home-made teas.**
Nestled betwixt farmland in rural Essex, is our small secret garden, that has a wonderful charm and serenity to it. Set in 3½ acres, mostly paddocks, a little plot of loveliness wraps around our Victorian cottage, and roses smother the porch in June. A meandering lawn takes you through beds and borders softly planted with a cottage feel, a haven for wildlife and people alike. Dean Harris a local blacksmith will have a pop-up forge on-site making and selling metal plant accessories on the day of your visit. Parking available a short walk up the lane near The Cats pub. Unsuitable for wheelchairs unless you're intrepid.

79 WICKETS

Langley Upper Green,
CB11 4RY. Susan & Doug
Copeland, 01799 550553,
susan.copeland@ngs.org.uk. *7m W of Saffron Walden, 10m N of Bishops Stortford. At Newport take B1038 After 3m turn R at Clavering, signed Langley. Upper Green is 3m further on. At cricket green turn R. House 200m on R.* **Sun 26 Apr, Sun 3 May (2-5). Adm £6, chd free. Home-made teas. Opening with Langley Village Gardens on Sun 28 June (11-5). Visits also by arrangement May & June for groups of 20+. Refreshments by arrangement.**
Rejuvenate your spirits in this wonderfully floral garden. A froth of billowing borders. Narcissus and tulips, roses and summer colour. Wild flower meadow with shepherd's hut and orchard. Lily pond and Monet style bridge sheltered by silver birch. Griffin Glasshouse. Espalier apples enclose an informal parterre. New Mediterranean courtyard. Secluded Dry Garden and Pergola, perfect places to rest awhile. Auricula theatre. Lots of places to sit and enjoy the rural views. Perhaps the ultimate romantic garden? Gravel drive.

GROUP OPENING

80 NEW WITHAM TOWN GARDENS

Witham, CM8 1NB. 01376 514931
whitechat@sky. com. *Witham is on the B1038 approx 8 miles from Chelmsford and 10 miles from Colchester. A map will be available at all gardens with locations and parking details.* **Sat 4 July (11-4.30). Combined adm £6, chd free. Home-made teas.**

9 MALYON ROAD
Maureen & Stephen Hicks.
(See separate entry)

NEW 5 OUSE CHASE
CM8 1TX. Charlotte & Simon Boddy.

NEW 13 STEVENS ROAD
CM8 1NB. Robin & Isobel Norton.

A warm welcome awaits you at our three contrasting town gardens in Witham. 13 Stevens Road is an established garden full of plants including many Salvia, Sanguisorba and Thalictrum. From the lawn the garden slopes down to a secluded shaded area and stream. The paved patio is a welcoming area to sit and enjoy home-made cakes, tea and soft drinks as well as an opportunity to purchase home-made jam. The garden at Ouse Chase is only three years old but already has lots of character. Enter through the cottage style front garden to the small rear garden where young trees are mixed with an abundance of plants that enjoy full sun and partial shade. The patio area is packed with tropical plants in a variety of pots and containers. Malyon Road is a large town garden with mature trees and shrubs laid out in a series of garden rooms. Flower beds, pond and summerhouse give year round interest. Plenty of places to sit and relax with paths taking you on a tour of the garden. Partial wheelchair access at Stevens Road and Malyon Road. Well-behaved dogs welcome at Ouse Chase. Plant Sales at Malyon Road and Ouse Chase.

GROUP OPENING

81 WRITTLE GARDENS
Chelmsford, CM1 3NA. *Writtle can be approached from 3 directions. From the A1060, A1016 and A414 follow the yellow signs to Writtle Village.* Sun 14 June (1-6). Combined adm £6, chd free.

8 THE GREEN
CM1 3DU. Andrea Johnson.

53 LONG BRANDOCKS
CM1 3JL. Roger & Margaret Barker.

65 ONGAR ROAD
CM1 3NA. Doug & Jean Pinkney.

40 ST JOHNS ROAD
CM1 3EB. Catherine Eubanks.

Four contrasting, colourful and interesting gardens to enjoy in the delightful village of Writtle. 8 The Green offers creatively planted borders and a tapestry of colour, texture and form, with perennials, shrubs, ornamental trees, annuals and alpines, and a south-facing summerhouse. The garden at 65 Ongar Road will transport visitors to tropical destinations, with its colour and "summer living" features. 40 St Johns Road is a relatively new garden, now in its 5th year and beginning to mature. The front is designed to echo the country hedgerows of the local area and the back is a tranquil haven in a modern Italian style. 53 Long Brandocks is a plantsman's garden with a wealth of unusual shrubs, clematis, daylilies, and some exotic herbaceous plants. There is also a selection of trees including catalpas and acers. No refreshments are offered at these gardens, but Writtle offers a number of pubs and cafes, including the renowned Tiptree Tea Room in Lordship Rd. The ancient and traditional village of Writtle, with its delightful Norman church, village green and pond, dates back to pre-Roman times, and was featured in the Doomsday Book.

82 WRITTLE UNIVERSITY COLLEGE
Writtle, CM1 3RR. Writtle University College, www.writtle.ac.uk. *4m W of Chelmsford. On A414, nr Writtle village.* Wed 29 Apr (11-4). Adm £5, chd free.

15 acres; informal lawns with naturalised bulbs and wild flowers. Large tree collection, mixed shrubs, herbaceous borders. Landscaped gardens designed and built by students. Landscaped glasshouses and wide range of seasonal bedding displays. New Dry/Mediterranean garden designed and built by staff and students on our RHS courses. Herbaceous perennial borders. Extended naturalised bulb areas on front campus lawns. Renovated Rockery Open Day is coordinated by Level 3 Horticultural Students who are on hand to assist visitors. Some gravel, however majority of areas accessible to all.

83 WYCHWOOD
Epping Road, Roydon, Harlow, CM19 5DW. Mrs Madeleine Paine. *At Tylers Cross r'about head in the direction of Roydon. Garden on R approx 400 metres from the r'about. Parking is available in Redrick's nursery next to garden.* Sun 28 June (12-5.30). Adm £4, chd free. Home-made teas.
A garden approx. 3/4 acre with a large pond, attracting much wildlife, as well as the owners resident ducks. Free ranging chickens roam in the shrubbery and budgerigar aviary. There are numerous features incl, vegetable and fruit plot, mixed shrub and herbaceous borders, 1920's summer house and Scandinavian cabin. English roses are a particular feature of the garden. Lake fully stocked with fish and inhabited by resident ducks. Sit in the Norwegian hut and enjoy your refreshments.

84 WYCKE FARM
Pages Lane, Tolleshunt D'Arcy, Maldon, CM9 8AB. Nancy & Anthony Seabrook. *5m E of Maldon, 10m SW of Colchester. B1023 from Tolleshunt D'Arcy 1m towards Tollesbury. Turn R into Pages Lane. Follow for 1m to Wycke Farm.* Fri 3, Sun 5 Apr (11-5). Adm £5, chd free. Home-made teas.
Large cottage style farmhouse garden situated in the peaceful Essex countryside with mature trees, mixed borders, vegetables, greenhouses and a small flock of sheep. Developed from a neglected state over 12 years ago with a fine view of the Blackwater Estuary. Walk to estuary, 1200 metres. Some gravel and grass paths.

Heath House

GLOUCESTERSHIRE

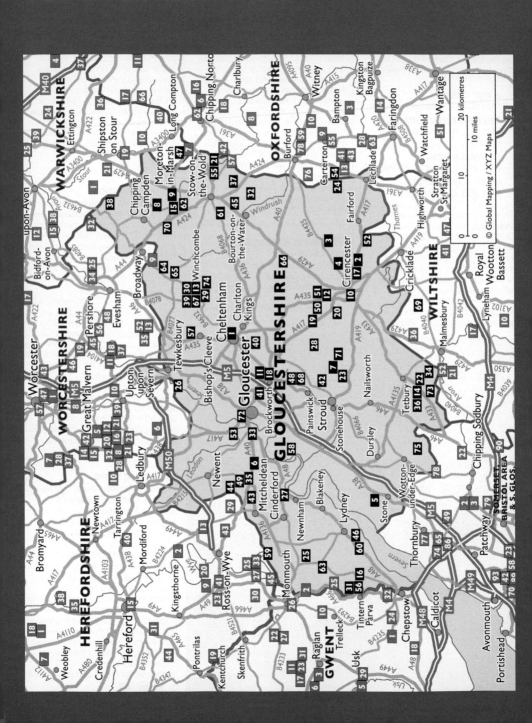

Gloucestershire is one of the most beautiful counties in England, spanning as it does a large part of the area known as the Cotswolds as well as the Forest of Dean and Wye and Severn Valleys.

The Cotswolds is an expanse of gently sloping green hills, wooded valleys and ancient, picturesque towns and villages; it is designated as an area of Outstanding Natural Beauty, and its quintessentially English charm attracts many visitors.

Like the county itself many of the gardens that open for the National Garden Scheme are simply quite outstanding. There are significant gardens which open for the public as well, such as Kiftsgate and Bourton House. There are also some large private gardens which only open for us, such as Highnam Court and Stowell Park.

There are however many more modest private gardens whose doors only open on the National Garden Scheme open day, such as Bowling Green Road in Cirencester with over 300 varieties of Hemerocallis. This tiny garden has now opened for over 35 years. The National collection of Rambling Roses is held at Moor Wood and that of Juglans and Pterocarya at Upton Wold.

Several very attractive Cotswold villages also open their gardens and a wonderful day can be had strolling from cottage to house marvelling at both the standard of the gardens and the beauty of the wonderful buildings, only to pause for the obligatory tea and cake!

Volunteers

County Organiser
Vanessa Berridge
01242 609535
vanessa.berridge@ngs.org.uk

County Treasurer
Pam Sissons
01242 573942
pam.sissons@ngs.org.uk

Social Media
Mandy Bradshaw
01242 512491
mandy.bradshaw@ngs.org.uk

Publicity
Ruth Chivers 01452 542493
ruth.chivers@ngs.org.uk

Booklet Coordinator
Nick Kane
07768 478668
nick.kane@ngs.org.uk

Assistant County Organisers
Valerie Kent
01993 823294
valerie.kent@ngs.org.uk

Colin & Verena Olle
01452 863750
colin.olle@ngs.org.uk

Rose Parrott 07853 164924
rosemary.parrott@ngs.org.uk

Heather Stopher
01453 882576
heather.stopher@ngs.org.uk

Gareth & Sarah Williams
01531 821654
dgwilliams84@hotmail.com

f @gloucestershirengs

@Glosngs

Left: Monastery Garden at Prinknash Abbey

OPENING DATES

All entries subject to change. For latest information check www.ngs.org.uk
Map locator numbers are shown to the right of each garden name.

Monks Spout Cottage

THE GARDENS

1 NEW 1 ALBERT ROAD

Cheltenham, GL52 2QY. Linda Marsh, 07813 851815. *Close to Pittville Park and Cheltenham Racecourse. 1st house on R after Pittville Circus r'about towards Racecourse. Parking 4 hrs free in Albert Road. Cheltenham N bus stops directly outside.* **Sat 18 July (2-5). Adm £3, chd free. Teas in Pittville Park at café 2 mins walk away. Visits also by arrangement July to Sept with home-made teas.** Town garden enclosed by walls and yew hedges showcasing what one can achieve in a small space. Two distinct garden areas and styles of planting from shady tree ferns and Roscoes to an exuberant exotic summer garden in the Christopher Lloyd style. Retired garden designer who has previously designed a garden for Hampton Court Flower Show and the HPS exhibit in the Main Marquee at Chelsea Flower Show 2017.

2 AMPNEY BROOK HOUSE

School Lane, Ampney Crucis, Cirencester, GL7 5RT. Allan Hirst, 01285 851098, allan.hirst@clmail.co.uk. *From Cirencester go E on A417 toward Fairford. After passing the Crown of Crucis take 1st L and also immed L again onto School Lane and L again into the gated (open automatically) drive.* **Visits by arrangement Mar to Oct. Refreshments by arrangement. Adm £5, chd free.** Striking Grade II Cotswold country house on 4.3 acres fronting Ampney Brook. The gardens are a haven for wildlife with fun and stimulating spaces yr-round. Incl woodland, kitchen garden, herbaceous borders, meadows, newly planted arbour. Ample areas and lawns for picnicking (encouraged). No wheelchair access to kitchen garden/greenhouse.

3 AWKWARD HILL COTTAGE

Awkward Hill, Bibury, GL7 5NH. Mrs Victoria Summerley, v.summerley@hotmail.com, , www.awkwardhill.co.uk. *Bibury, Gloucestershire. No parking at property, best to park in village and walk past Arlington Row up Awkward Hill, or up Hawkers Hill from Catherine Wheel pub.* **Sun 5 July (2-6). Adm £4, chd free. Home-made teas. Evening opening Sun 30 Aug (6-8). Adm £5, chd free. Wine. Visits also by arrangement June to Sept for groups of 20 to 30. Admission price incl tea and cake. No children please.** An ever-evolving country garden in one of the most beautiful villages in the Cotswolds, designed to reflect the local landscape and encourage wildlife. Planting is both formal and informal, contributing yr-round interest with lots of colour and texture. Pond and waterfall, beehives, and lots of seating areas. Wonderful views over neighbouring meadow and woodland, small pond jetty, 2 sunny terraces and plenty of places to sit and relax.

4 BARNSLEY HOUSE

Barnsley, Cirencester, GL7 5EE. Calcot Health & Leisure Ltd, 01285 740000, reception@barnsleyhouse.com, www.barnsleyhouse.com. *4m NE of Cirencester. From Cirencester, take B4425 to Barnsley. House entrance on R as you enter village.* **Tue 14 Apr (10-4). Adm £5, chd free. Tea.** The beautiful garden at Barnsley House, created by Rosemary Verey, is one of England's finest and most famous gardens incl knot garden, potager garden and mixed borders in Rosemary Verey's successional planting style. The house also has an extensive kitchen garden which will be open with plants and vegetables available for purchase. Narrow paths mean restricted wheelchair access but happy to provide assistance.

Daglingworth House

5 BERKELEY CASTLE

Berkeley, GL13 9PJ.
Mrs RJG Berkeley,
www.berkeley-castle.com. *Half-way between Bristol & Gloucester, 10mins from J13 &14 of M5. Follow signs to Berkeley from A38 & B4066. Visitors' entrance is on L of Canonbury St, just before town centre.* **Mon 8 June (10.30-5). Adm £6, chd £3. Light refreshments in Yurt restaurant, next to ticket office/gift shop. Delicious home-made cakes, light lunches and locally-sourced items available.** Unique historic garden of a keen plantsman, with far-reaching views across the River Severn. Gardens contain many rare plants which thrive in the warm micro-climate against the stone walls of this medieval castle. Woodland, historic trees and stunning terraced borders. Butterfly house with free-flying tropical butterflies. Difficult for wheelchairs due to terraced nature of gardens.

6 BERRYS PLACE FARM

Bulley Lane, Churcham, Gloucester, GL2 8AS. Anne Thomas, 07950 808022, gary.j.thomas1953@gmail.com. *6m W of Gloucester. A40 towards Ross. Turning R into Bulley Lane at Birdwood.* **Sat 20, Sun 21, Wed 24, Thur 25 June (11-5). Adm £4, chd free. Home-made teas. Ploughmans lunches, cream teas.** Country garden, approx 2 acres, surrounded by farmland and old orchards. Lawns and large sweeping mixed herbaceous borders with over 100 roses. Formal kitchen garden and beautiful rose arbour leading to lake and summerhouse with a variety of water lilies and carp. All shared with ducks.

GROUP OPENING

7 BISLEY GARDENS

Wells Road, Bisley, Stroud, GL6 7AG. *Gardens & car park well signed in Bisley village. Gardens on S edge of village at head of Toadsmoor Valley, N of A419 Stroud to Cirencester road.* **Sun 21 June (2-6). Combined adm £5, chd free. Home-made teas at Paulmead.**

PAULMEAD

Judy & Philip Howard and Tom & Emma Howard.

PAX

Mr David Holden & Mr Ramesh Mootoo.

WELLS COTTAGE

Mr & Mrs Michael Flint, 01452 770289, bisleyflints@bisleyflints.plus.com.

3 beautiful gardens with differing styles. Paulmead: 1 acre landscaped garden constructed in stages over last 25yrs. Terraced in 3 main levels. Natural stream garden, herbaceous and shrub borders, formal vegetable garden, summerhouse overlooking pond. Unusual tree house. Development of new garden around hen house, incl ha ha. Pax: Small very well kept cottage garden, in a hidden away location, with box hedging and topiary. Great views. Wells Cottage: Just under 1 acre. Terraced on several levels with beautiful views over valley. Much informal planting of trees and shrubs to give colour and texture. Lawns and herbaceous borders. Collection of grasses. Formal pond area. Rambling roses on rope pergola. Vegetable garden with raised beds.

GROUP OPENING

8 BLOCKLEY GARDENS

Blockley, GL56 9DB. *3m NW of Moreton-in-Marsh. Just off the Morton-in-Marsh to Evesham Rd A44.* **Sun 19 Apr, Sun 7 June (2-6). Combined adm £6, chd free. Home-made teas at St George's Hall on April 19, at Colebrook House & The Manor House on June 7.**

BLOCKLEY ALLOTMENTS

Blockley and District Allotment Association.
Open on Sun 7 June

CHURCH GATES

Mrs Brenda Salmon.
Open on all dates

COLEBROOK HOUSE

Mr & Mrs G Apsion.
Open on all dates

NEW ELM HOUSE

Chris & Val Scragg.
Open on all dates

THE MANOR HOUSE

George & Zoe Thompson.
Open on all dates

♦ MILL DENE GARDEN

Mrs B S Dare, 01386 700457, info@milldenegarden.co.uk, www.milldenegarden.co.uk.
Open on all dates

MILL GARDEN HOUSE

Andrew & Celia Goodrick-Clarke.
Open on Sun 7 June

PEAR TREES

Cliff & Jo Murphy.
Open on all dates

PORCH HOUSE

Mr & Mrs Johnson.
Open on Sun 19 Apr

SNUGBOROUGH MILL

Rupert & Mandy Williams-Ellis, 01386 701310, rupert.williams-ellis@talk21.com.
Open on Sun 7 June

WOODRUFF

Paul & Maggie Adams.
Open on all dates

This popular historic hillside village has a great variety of high quality, well-stocked gardens - large and small, old and new. Blockley Brook, an attractive stream which flows right through the village, graces some of the gardens; these incl gardens of former water mills, with millponds attached. From some gardens there are wonderful rural views. Children welcome but close supervision is essential. Access to some gardens quite steep and allowances should be made.

9 ♦ BOURTON HOUSE GARDEN

Bourton-on-the-Hill, GL56 9AE. Mr & Mrs R Quintus, 01386 700754, info@bourtonhouse.com, www.bourtonhouse.com. *2m W of Moreton-in-Marsh. On A44.* **For NGS: Sun 16 Aug (10-5). Adm £8, chd free. Light refreshments & home-made cakes in Grade I Listed C16 Tithe Barn. For other opening times and information, please phone, email or visit garden website.** Award winning 3 acre garden featuring imaginative topiary, wide herbaceous borders with many rare, unusual and exotic plants, water features, unique shade house and many creatively planted pots. Fabulous at any time of year but magnificent in summer months and early autumn. Walk in 7 acre pasture with free printed guide to specimen trees available to garden visitors. 70% access for wheelchairs. Disabled toilet.

10 25 BOWLING GREEN ROAD

Cirencester, GL7 2HD. Mrs
Sue Beck, 01285 653778,
zen155198@zen.co.uk. *On NW
edge of Cirencester. Take A435 to
Spitalgate/Whiteway T-lights, turn
into The Whiteway (Chedworth turn),
then 1st L into Bowling Green Rd,
garden in bend in rd between Nos
23 & 27.* **Sun 5 July (2-5); Mon 6
July (11-4); Sun 12 July (2-5); Mon
13 July (11-4). Adm £3.50, chd
free. Visits also by arrangement
June to Sept for groups of up to
30. Tea/coffee/biscuits etc. can
be provided for small groups by
arrangement.**
Welcome to this naturalistic
garden, increasingly designed by
plants themselves, where you can
wander at will in a mini-jungle of
curvaceous clematis, gorgeous
grasses, romantic roses, heavenly
hemerocallis and plentiful perennials,
glimpsing a graceful giraffe and
friendly frogs, rated by visitors as
an amazing hidden gem with a
unique atmosphere. See: The Chatty
Gardener, July 10 2019, https://
wp.me/p6LDlk-2Dv - posting on
Growing Hemerocallis and that the
garden owner had a daylily cultivar
registered by a UK Hybridizer to
mark her 40th Anniversary of opening
for the NGS. Sadly, not suitable for
wheelchair access.

🐕 ✳ ☕

11 BROCKWORTH COURT

Court Road, Brockworth,
GL3 4QU. Tim & Bridget
Wiltshire, 01452 862938,
timwiltshire@hotmail.co.uk. *6m E
of Gloucester. 6m W of Cheltenham.
Adj St Georges Church on Court Rd.
From A46 turn into Mill Lane, turn
R, L, R at T junctions. From Ermin
St, turn into Ermin Park, then R at
r'about then L at next r'about.* **Wed
13 May (2.30-5.30). Adm £6, chd
free. Home-made teas in tithe
barn. Visits also by arrangement
Apr to Oct for groups of 10+.
House tours max 18.**
This intense yet informal tapestry
style garden beautifully complements
the period manor house which it
surrounds. Organic, naturalistic,
with informal cottage-style planting
areas that seamlessly blend together.
Natural fish pond, with Monet
bridge leading to small island with
thatched Fiji house. Kitchen garden
once cultivated by monks. Views
to Crickley and Coopers Hill. Adj
Norman Church (open). Historic tithe
barn, historic manor house visited by
Henry VIII and Anne Boleyn in 1535.
Partial wheelchair access.

🚿 ✳ 🛏 ☕

12 ◆ CERNEY HOUSE GARDENS

North Cerney, Cirencester,
GL7 7BX. Mr N W Angus &
Dr J Angus, 01285 831300,
janet@cerneygardens.com,
www.cerneygardens.com. *4m NW
of Cirencester. On A435 Cheltenham
rd turn L opp Bathurst Arms, follow
rd past church up hill, then go
straight towards pillared gates on R
(signed Cerney House).* **For NGS:
Sat 13 June (1-5). Adm £5, chd
£1. For other opening times and
information, please phone, email or
visit garden website.**
Romantic walled garden filled with old-
fashioned roses and long herbaceous
borders. Knot garden filled with
spring tulip display and dahlias later
in the year. Working kitchen garden
with heritage vegetables, scented
garden and lavender walk. Drifts of
naturalised snowdrops end Jan/Feb.
Large collection of hellebores and
woodland bluebell walk. Herb garden
(in development), koi carp pond,
woodland and nature walk. Dogs
welcome. Partial wheelchair access.

🚿 🐕 ✳ 🛏 ☕

13 CHARINGWORTH COURT

Broadway Road, Winchcombe,
GL54 5JN. Susan & Richard
Wakeford, 01242 603033,
susanwakeford@gmail.com,
www.charingworthcourtcotswolds
garden.com. *8m NE of Cheltenham.
400 metres N of Winchcombe
town centre. Limited parking along
Broadway Rd. Town car parks in
Bull Lane (short stay) and all day
parking (£1) in Back Lane. Map on
our website.* **Sat 16, Sun 17 May
(11.30-6). Adm £5, chd free.
Home-made teas. Visits also
by arrangement May & June for
groups of 10 to 30.**
Artistically and lovingly created 1½
acre garden surrounding restored
Georgian/Tudor house (not open).
Relaxed country style with Japanese
influences, large pond and walled
vegetable/flower garden, created
over 24 years from a blank canvas.
Mature copper beech trees, Cedar
of Lebanon and Wellingtonia; and
younger trees replacing an earlier
excess of Cupressus leylandii. Once
again the garden will showcase a
range of sculpture, most for sale with a

percentage going to NGS charities. The
garden website shows photographs
of all the previous 8 exhibitions. Most
paths gravelled which can make them
challenging but several areas accessible
without steps. Limited disabled parking
next to house.

🚿 🐕 ☕

14 CHARLTON DOWN HOUSE

Charlton Down, Tetbury, GL8 8TZ.
Neil & Julie Record. *2m SW of
Tetbury, Glos. From Tetbury, take
A433 towards Bath for 1½m; turn
R (north) just before the Hare and
Hounds, then R again after 200yds
into Hookshouse Lane. Charlton
Down House is 600yds on R.* **Sun 26
Apr, Sun 14 June (11-5). Adm £6,
chd free. Teas and home-made
cakes in the barn.**
Extensive country house gardens in
180 acre equestrian estate. Formal
terraces, perennial borders, walled
topiary garden, enclosed cut flower
garden and large glasshouse. Newly
planted copse. Rescue animals.
Ample parking. Picnickers welcome.
Largely flat terrain; most garden areas
accessible.

🚿 🐕 🚗 ☕

15 THE CHASE

Bourton on the Hill, Moreton-
In-Marsh, GL56 9AL. Mr & Mrs
J Stoker, Kate Burtonwood
- 07949 448483,
info@cultivatedgardener.co.uk.
*2m W of Moreton-in-Marsh.
From Moreton, take A44 towards
Evesham. Pass through Bourton
on the Hill, take first L signed
Longborough. Garden 2nd property
on R.* **Visits by arrangement May
to Sept for groups of 5 to 30
weekdays except Tuesday. Adm
£5, chd free.**
5-acre private garden undergoing
extensive renovation, recently
opened. The Chase offers areas
of natural planting, with a focus on
making space for wildlife. The main
garden area is a disused quarry
which gives challenges of access,
shade and water, with areas of
woodland, ponds, a new glasshouse
used for propagation and tropical
plants. Unfortunately not suitable for
wheelchairs or pushchairs.

16 CLOUDS REST

Brockweir, Chepstow, NP16 7NW.
Mrs Jan Basford. *In the Wye Valley,
6.7m N of Chepstow and 10.6m
S of Monmouth, off A466, across
Brockweir Bridge.* **Sun 13 Sept**

(12.30-5). Combined adm with The Patch £7, chd free. Home-made teas.

The garden at Clouds Rest was started in 2012 from a south-westerly facing, stony paddock, with views across the Wye Valley. Its many gravel pathways meander through herbaceous beds with a mixture of roses, then later a wide selection of Michaelmas daisies in September. Easy parking in our paddock. New additions incl woodland area. Partial wheelchair access.

17 ◆ THE COACH HOUSE GARDEN
Church Lane, Ampney Crucis, Cirencester, GL7 5RY. Mr & Mrs Nicholas Tanner, 01285 850256, mel@thegenerousgardener.co.uk, www.thegenerousgardener.co.uk. *3m E of Cirencester. Turn into village from A417, immed before Crown of Crucis Inn. Over hump-back bridge, parking to R on cricket field (weather permitting) or signed nearby field. Disabled parking near house.* **For NGS: Sun 10 May (2-5). Adm £5, chd free. Coffee/tea home-made cakes and cream teas available for visiting groups and NGS opening. For other opening times and information, please phone, email or visit garden website.** Approx 1½ acres, full of structure and design. Garden is divided into rooms incl rill garden, gravel garden, rose garden, herbaceous borders, green garden with pleached lime allee and potager. Created over last 30yrs by present owners and constantly evolving. New potting shed and greenhouse added in 2018. Visitors welcome during mid March - mid July (groups of 15+), please see above website. Rare plant sales (in aid of James Hopkins Trust) and Garden Lecture Days. Partial wheelchair access. Ramp available to enable access to main body of garden, steps to other areas.

GROUP OPENING

18 NEW ▶ COTSWOLD CHASE GARDENS
Spinners Road, Brockworth, Gloucester, GL3 4LR. *4m E Gloucester, 7m SW Cheltenham. Follow signs off Ermin Street.* **Sun 5 July (2-5). Combined adm £5, chd free. Tea and cake at MidGlos Bowls Club.**

A group of small gardens all recently created on a new development. A wide range of designs, planting and imaginative ideas that show what can be achieved in a short space of time. The Chase is rich in open spaces which have been beautifully landscaped, with many foot/cycle paths, a sports field (football and cricket), children's play areas and three wildlife friendly balancing ponds. Lots of places to walk, take in the open vistas (e.g. Coopers Hill) and view some new gardens. Parking, tickets, maps and toilets at MidGlos Bowls Club.

19 COTSWOLD FARM
Duntisbourne Abbots, Cirencester, GL7 7JS. Mrs Mark Birchall, www.cotswoldfarmgardens.org.uk. *5m NW of Cirencester off old A417. From Cirencester L signed Duntisbourne Abbots Services, R and R underpass. Drive ahead. From Gloucester L signed Duntisbourne Abbots Services. Pass Services. Drive L.* **Sat 13, Sun 14 June (2-5). Adm £7.50, chd free. Home-made teas by WI. Donation to A Rocha.** Arts and Crafts garden in lovely position overlooking quiet valley on descending levels with terrace designed by Norman Jewson in 1930s. Snowdrops named and naturalised, aconites in Feb. Winter garden. Bog garden best in May, white border overflowing with texture and scent. Shrubs, trees, shrub roses. 8 native orchids, hundreds of wild flowers and Roman snails. Family day out. Rare orchid walks. Picnics welcome. Wheelchair access to main terrace.

20 DAGLINGWORTH HOUSE
Daglingworth, nr Cirencester, GL7 7AG. David & Henrietta Howard, 01285 885626, ettajhoward@gmail.com. *3m N of Cirencester off A417/419. House with blue gate beside church in centre of Daglingworth, at end of No Through Road.* **Visits by arrangement for groups of 10 to 30 from 1 May to 5 Sept. Tea and cake by arrangement. Adm £7, chd free.** Walled garden, temple, grotto, and pools. Classical garden of 2.5 acres, with humorous contemporary twist. Hedges, topiary shapes, herbaceous borders. Pergolas, grass garden, meadow, woodland, cascade and mirror canal. New sunken garden 2019. Pretty Cotswold village setting beside church. Visitor comment: 'It breaks every rule of gardening - but it's wonderful!' Limited wheelchair access. Very limited access due to steps and level changes - narrow gates.

21 DAYLESFORD HOUSE
Daylesford, GL56 0YG. Lord & Lady Bamford. *5m W of Chipping Norton. Off A436. Between Stow-on-the-Wold & Chipping Norton.* **Wed 25 Mar (1-4). Adm £6, chd free. Home-made teas.** Magnificent C18 landscape grounds created 1790 for Warren Hastings, greatly restored and enhanced by present owners under organic regime. Lakeside and woodland walks within natural wild flower meadows. Large formal walled garden, centred around orchid, peach and working glasshouses. Trellised rose garden. Collection of citrus within period orangery. Secret garden, pavilion formal pools. Very large garden with substantial distances. Partial wheelchair access.

Hawkley Cottage, Eastcombe and Bussage Gardens

22 NEW DOUGHTON MANOR

Doughton, Tetbury, GL8 8TG. Mrs Andrea Moore. *One mile west of Tetbury on Bath Road (A433) opp Highgrove. The drive nearest Tetbury will be to enter and the drive nearer to Westonbirt will be to exit.* **Sat 30 May (11-4). Adm £5, chd free.** Elizabethan manor house with three walled gardens which have been slowly restored in last 15 yrs after many years of sporadic upkeep. Ancient peonies, forget-me-nots, perennials, 30 yr old orchard, roses; old and new, walk ways lined with lavender are some highlights of the garden. The house and garden are survivors after the owners lived at Highgrove and let Doughton Manor to tenant farmers. The garden is all on one level. Some gravel paths and stone paths adequate for wheelchairs.

GROUP OPENING

23 EASTCOMBE AND BUSSAGE GARDENS

Eastcombe, Stroud, GL6 7EB. *3m E of Stroud. Tickets and maps are available on the day from Eastcombe Village Hall, GL6 7EB and also from Redwood, nr Bussage Village Hall, GL6 8AZ. On street parking only.* **Sat 2, Sun 3 May (2-6). Combined adm £8, chd free.** Home-made teas in Eastcombe Village Hall. Cold drinks & ice creams available at some gardens. Donation to Gloucestershire Wildlife Trust, Stroud District Ring and Ride.

BREWERS COTTAGE
Jackie & Nick Topman.

CADSONBURY
Natalie & Glen Beswetherick.

NEW **17 FARMCOTE CLOSE**
John & Sheila Coyle.

20 FARMCOTE CLOSE
Ian & Dawn Sim.

21 FARMCOTE CLOSE
Mr & Mrs Robert Bryant.

HAMPTON VIEW
Geraldine & Mike Carter.

HAWKLEY COTTAGE
Helen & Gerwin Westendorp.

12 HIDCOTE CLOSE
Mr K Walker.

HIGHLANDS
Helen & Bob Watkinson.

1 THE LAURELS
Andrew & Ruth Fraser.

MARYFIELD AND MARYFIELD COTTAGE
Mrs M Brown.

MOUNT PLEASANT
Mr & Mrs R Peyton.

REDWOOD
Heather Collins.

50 STONECOTE RIDGE
Julie & Robin Marsland.

VALLEY VIEW
Mrs Rebecca Benneyworth.

YEW TREE COTTAGE
Andy & Sue Green.

Medium and small gardens in a variety of styles and settings within this picturesque, hilltop village location with its spectacular views of the Toadsmoor Valley. In addition, there is one large garden located in the bottom of this valley, approachable only by foot as are some of the other gardens. The 2 mile long trail has, however, a courtesy minibus to join the two extremities and a few points in between, for which donations are invited. Full descriptions of each garden can be found on NGS website. No dogs at 1 The Laurels, 20 Farmcote Close, Yew Tree Cottage. Plants for sale at Eastcombe Village Hall and some gardens. Wheelchair access to some gardens - check which ones on NGS website.

24 EASTLEACH HOUSE

Eastleach Martin, Cirencester, GL7 3NW. Mrs David Richards, garden@eastleachhouse.com, www.eastleachhouse.com. *5m NE of Fairford, 6m S of Burford. Entrance opp church gates in Eastleach Martin. Lodge at gate, gravel driveway is quite steep and curves up to house.* **Visits by arrangement May to July. Adm £10, chd free.** Large traditional all-yr-round garden. Wooded hilltop position with long views S and W. New parkland, lime avenue and arboretum. Wild flower walks, wildlife pond, lawns, walled and rill gardens, with mixed borders, yew and box hedges, iris and paeony borders, lily ponds, formal herb garden and topiary. Rambling roses into trees. Partial wheelchair access. Steep entrance drive. Gravel paths.

25 20 FORSDENE WALK

Coalway, Coleford, GL16 7JZ. Pamela Buckland, 01594 837179. *From Coleford take Lydney/ Chepstow Rd at T-lights. L after police station ½m up hill turn L at Xrds then 2nd R (Old Road) straight on at minor Xrds then L into Forsdene Walk.* **Sun 17 May, Sun 21 June, Sun 19 July (2-6). Adm £3, chd free.**

3 Church Road, Longhope Gardens

Visits also by arrangement May to Sept for groups of up to 20. Corner garden filled with interest and design ideas to maximise smaller spaces. A series of interlinking colour themed rooms, some on different levels. Packed with perennials, grasses, ferns and bamboos. A pergola, small man-made stream, fruit and vegetables and pots in abundance on gravelled areas. Featured in Amateur Gardening.

26 FORTHAMPTON COURT
Forthampton, Tewkesbury, GL19 4RD. Alan & Anabel Mackinnon. *W of Tewkesbury. From Tewkesbury A438 to Ledbury. After 2m turn L to Forthampton. At Xrds go L towards Chaceley. Go 1m turn L at Xrds.* **Sun 31 May (12.30-4.30). Adm £6, chd free. Home-made teas.**
Charming and varied garden surrounding north Gloucestershire medieval manor house (not open) within sight of Tewkesbury Abbey. Incl borders, lawns, roses and magnificent Victorian vegetable garden.

27 THE GABLES
Riverside Lane, Broadoak, Newnham on Severn, GL14 1JE. Bryan & Christine Bamber, 01594 516323, bryanbamber@sky.com. *1m NE of Newnham on Severn. Park in White Hart PH overspill car park, to R of PH when facing river. Please follow signs to car park. Walk, turning R along rd towards Gloucester for approx 250yds. Access through marked gate.* **Sun 14 June, Sun 16 Aug (11-5). Adm £4, chd free. Home-made teas. Visits also by arrangement May to Aug for groups of 10+.**
Large flat ¾ acre garden with formal lawns, colourful herbaceous borders from May - September, rose beds, shrubberies, hidden long border, mini stumpery with hostas, bamboos, grasses, wild flower meadow with soft fruits and fruit trees, allotment size productive potager vegetable plot with herbaceous borders, greenhouse and composting bin area. Disabled parking information available at entrance. Partial wheelchair access but all areas of garden visible.

28 ◆ THE GARDEN AT MISERDEN
Miserden, Nr Stroud, GL6 7JA. Mr Nicholas Wills, 01285 821303, estate.office@miserden.org, www.miserden.org. *6m NW of Cirencester. Leave A417 at Birdlip, drive through Whiteway and follow signs for Miserden.* **For NGS: Fri 15 May (10-5). Adm £7.50, chd free. Light refreshments in The Garden Café in Nursery. For other opening times and information, please phone, email or visit garden website.**
Winner of Historic Houses Garden of the Year 2018, the Garden at Miserden is a lovely, timeless walled garden with amazing views over a deer park and rolling Cotswold hills beyond. The garden was designed in C17 and still retains a wonderful sense of peace and tranquillity, especially with its spectacular 92m long mixed borders. Stunning gardens. 20% Donated to St Andrews Church & Miserden Primary School. Partial wheelchair access.

29 THE GATE
80 North Street, Winchcombe, GL54 5PS. Vanessa Berridge & Chris Evans, 01242 609535, vanessa.berridge@sky.com. *Winchcombe is on B4632 mid-way between Cheltenham and Broadway. Parking behind Library in Back Lane, 50 yds from The Gate.* **Visits by arrangement Apr to Sept. Groups of 10 to 20. Adm £7, chd free. Home-made teas included in admission.**
Cottage-style garden planted with bulbs in spring, and with summer perennials, annuals, climbers and herbs in the walled courtyard of C17 former coaching Inn. Also a separate, productive, walled kitchen garden with espaliers and other fruit trees.

30 NEW GREEN BOUGH
Market Lane, Greet, Winchcombe, GL54 5BL. Mary & Barry Roberts, 07966 528646, barryandmary@gmail.com. *1¼m N of Winchcombe. From Winchcombe take B4078. After railway bridge, R into Becketts Lane, immediately L into Market Lane. Garden on R at Mill Lane junction.* **Visits by arrangement Mar to June for groups of 5 to 20. Combined opening with La Borie. Adm £5, chd free. Home-made teas.**
Small informal country garden

developed over 6 yrs, planted for all seasons starting in early spring with massed bulbs and flowers surrounding the house, including the grass verge. Most of the plants are either grown from seed or propagated from cuttings by the owner, to give generous drifts of colour.

31 GREENFIELDS, BROCKWEIR COMMON
Brockweir, NP16 7NU. Jackie Healy, 07747 186302, greenfieldsgarden@icloud.com, www.greenfields.garden. *Located in Wye valley - midway between Chepstow and Monmouth. A446: from M'mouth: Thru Llandogo. L to Brockweir, (from Chepstow, thru Tintern. R to B'weir) over bridge, pass PH up hill, 1st L, follow lane to fork, L at fork. 1st property on R. No coaches.* **Sun 24 May (12.30-5.30). Combined adm with The Patch £7, chd free. Home-made teas. Visits also by arrangement May to Sept for groups of up to 30.**
1½ acre plant person's gem of a garden set in the beautiful Wye Valley. Many mature trees and numerous unusual plants and shrubs, all planted as discrete gardens within a garden. Greenfields is the passion and work of head gardener Jackie who has a long interest in the propagation of plants. Featured in Garden Answers magazine. Mostly wheelchair access.

32 GREENFIELDS, LITTLE RISSINGTON
Cheltenham, GL54 2NA. Mrs Diana MacKenzie-Charrington, 01451 821851, dcharrington@btinternet.com. *On Rissington Road between Bourton-on-the-Water and Little Rissington, opp turn to Great Rissington (Leasow Lane). SatNav using postcode does not take you to house.* **Sun 28 June (2-6). Adm £5, chd free. Home-made teas. Visits also by arrangement June to Aug for groups of 5 to 20.**
The honey coloured Georgian Cotswold stone house sits in 2 acres of garden, created by current owners over last 20 yrs. Lawns are edged with borders full of flowers and flowering bulbs. A small pond and stream overlook fields. Bantams roam freely. Mature apple trees in wild garden, greenhouse in working vegetable garden. Sorry no dogs. Partial wheelchair access.

Colebrook House, Blockley Gardens

33 HIGHNAM COURT
Highnam, Gloucester,
GL2 8DP. Mr & Mrs R J Head,
mike.highnamcourt@gmail.com,
www.HighnamCourt.co.uk. *2m
W of Gloucester. On A40/A48
junction from Gloucester to Ross
or Chepstow. At this r'about take
exit at 3 o'clock if coming from
Gloucester direction. Do NOT go into
Highnam village.* **Sun 5 Apr, Sun 3
May, Sun 7 June, Sun 5 July, Sun
2 Aug, Sun 6 Sept (11-5). Adm
£5, chd free. Tea, coffee from
11.00am. Sandwiches available
until 1.30pm. Cream teas served
from 1.30 to 5pm. Visits also by
arrangement Apr to Sept.**
40 acres of Victorian landscaped
gardens surrounding magnificent
Grade I house (not open), set out by
artist Thomas Gambier Parry. Lakes,
shrubberies and listed Pulhamite
water gardens with grottos and
fernery. Exciting ornamental lakes,
and woodland areas. Extensive 1
acre rose garden and many features,
incl numerous wood carvings.

Contact: Mike Bennett, Events &
Visits Manager, 01684 292875, email
above. *Some gravel paths and steps
into refreshment area. Disabled WC
outside.*

34 HODGES BARN
Shipton Moyne, Tetbury,
GL8 8PR. Mr & Mrs N Hornby,
www.hodgesbarn.com. *3m S of
Tetbury. On Malmesbury side of
village.* **Sun 7, Mon 8 June (2-6).
Adm £6, chd free. Home-made
teas at the Pool House.**
Very unusual C15 dovecote converted
into family home. Cotswold stone
walls host climbing and rambling
roses, clematis, vines, hydrangeas
and together with yew, rose and
tapestry hedges create formality
around house. Mixed shrub and
herbaceous borders, shrub roses,
water garden, woodland garden
planted with cherries and magnolias.

35 HOME FARM
Newent Lane, Huntley, GL19 3HQ.
Mrs T Freeman, 01452 830210,
torillfreeman@gmail.com. *4m S of
Newent. On B4216 ½m off A40 in
Huntley travelling towards Newent.*
**Sun 26 Jan, Sun 9 Feb (11-3); Sun
8 Mar, Sun 5, Sun 26 Apr (11-4).
Adm £3.50, chd free. 2021: Sun
31 Jan, Sun 14 Feb. Visits also
by arrangement Jan to May for
groups of up to 30.**
Set in elevated position with
exceptional views. 1m walk through
woods and fields to show carpets of
spring flowers. Enclosed garden with
fern border, sundial and heather bed.
White and mixed shrub borders. Stout
footwear advisable in winter. Two
delightful cafés within a mile.

36 HOOKSHOUSE POTTERY
Hookshouse Lane, Tetbury, GL8 8TZ. Lise & Christopher White, www.hookshousepottery.co.uk. *2½ m SW of Tetbury. Follow signs from A433 at Hare and Hounds Hotel, Westonbirt. Alternatively take A4135 out of Tetbury towards Dursley and follow signs after ½ m on L.* **Daily Sat 23 May to Sun 31 May (11-5.30). Adm £4, chd free. Home-made teas.**
Garden offers a combination of dramatic perspectives and intimate corners. Planting incl wide variety of perennials, with emphasis on colour interest throughout the seasons. Herbaceous borders, new woodland garden and flower meadow, water garden containing treatment ponds (unfenced) and flowform cascades. Kitchen garden with raised beds, orchard. Sculptural features. Run on organic principles. Pottery showroom with hand thrown wood-fired pots incl frostproof garden pots. Art & Craft exhibition incl garden furniture and sculptures. Garden games and tree house. Mostly wheelchair accessible.

GROUP OPENING

37 ICOMB GARDENS
Icomb, Stow-on-the-Wold, GL54 1JL. *3m S of Stow-on-the-Wold. Take Icomb Rd off A424 Burford-Stow Rd. After 1m turn R signed Icomb. Parking near gardens as directed by stewards. No parking on street.* **Sun 14 June (1.30-5). Combined adm £5, chd free. Home-made teas in the village hall.**

> ### NEW ASHLAR
> Joanne & Eric Shepley.

> ### NEW BEALE COTTAGE
> Veronica & Leigh Roberts.

> ### HOME FARM
> Miss Ellen Fisher.

> ### ICOMB BANK
> David & Susie Dugdale.

> ### LITTLE DORMERS
> Vanessa & Jonathan Curry.

> ### NEW OLD RECTORY
> Isabel Bickmore.

> ### 1 ORCHARD ROW
> John & Janet Bausor.

> ### NEW 4 ORCHARD ROW
> Sarah & Paul Bennett.

> ### 2 PARK VIEW COTTAGES
> David Cowdery.

> ### PARK VIEW HOUSE
> Ros & Steve Watson.

> ### NEW THE VINE HOUSE
> Rosie & Nick Clark.

> ### NEW YEW TREE COTTAGE
> David & Susie Dugdale.

Beautiful hillside village with pretty cottages, glorious views and early C13 church. A selection of small to medium inspirational and well stocked gardens ranging from sweeping herbaceous borders and productive fruit and veg plots to tranquil country estate grounds and stone-walled courtyard rear gardens. 2 Park View Cottages & Little Dormers have no wheelchair access. Dogs on leads welcome in all gardens.

38 ◆ KIFTSGATE COURT
Chipping Campden, GL55 6LN. Mr & Mrs J G Chambers, 01386 438777, info@kiftsgate.co.uk, www.kiftsgate.co.uk. *4m NE of Chipping Campden. Adj to Hidcote NT Garden.* **For NGS: Wed 15 Apr, Mon 10 Aug (2-6). Adm £9, chd £3. Cream teas. For other opening times and information, please phone, email or visit garden website.**
Magnificent situation and views, many unusual plants and shrubs, tree peonies, hydrangeas, abutilons, species and old-fashioned roses incl largest rose in England, Rosa filipes Kiftsgate. Steep slopes and uneven surfaces.

39 NEW LA BORIE
Littleworth, Winchcombe, Cheltenham, GL54 5BT. Jean Jones, 07966 528646, barryandmary@gmail.com. *1½ m N of Winchcombe. From M5 J9 take A46/B4077 towards Stow for 6m. Turn R onto B4087 signed Winchcombe for 1½ m.* **Visits by arrangement Mar to June for groups of 5 to 20. Combined with Green Bough. Parking limited. Adm £5, chd free. Home-made teas at Green Bough.**
La Borie is an acre with three differing parts. Closest to the house is a gardener's garden with patios, pergola and informal cottage garden style borders. Furthest from the house

is the wilderness with plants that want to grow there, and where insects and animals can thrive. Between these two extremes is a transitional grassland where spring bulbs flourish under the mature trees.

40 LECKHAMPTON COURT HOSPICE
Church Road, Leckhampton, Cheltenham, GL53 0QJ. Sue Ryder Leckhampton Court Hospice, www.sueryder.org/care-centres/hospices/leckhampton-court-hospice. *2m SW of Cheltenham. From Church Rd take driveway by Church signed Sue Ryder Leckhampton Court Hospice and follow parking signs.* **Sat 4 July (10.30-4). Adm £5, chd free. Light refreshments.**
Set within this Grade 2* listed medieval estate, the informal gardens at Leckhampton Court Hospice surround the buildings combining lawns and planted beds. Feature garden designed by Peter Dowle, RHS Chelsea gold medal winner. Highlights incl woodland walk around lake and into woodland, numerous protected mature trees and a terrace from where to see views across Cheltenham towards Malvern. Wheelchair access in some areas: from back of reception to Sir Charles Irving terrace; woodland walk; main courtyard.

41 NEW **78 LILLESFIELD AVENUE**
Lilliesfield Avenue,
Barnwood, Gloucester,
GL3 3AH. Roger Le Couteur,
Roger.lecouteur@hotmail.com. *3m E of Gloucester. Barnwood Road turn R into North Upton Lane then 1st L and follow signs or from Brockworth turn L into Brookfield Road by Lloyd's Pharmacy and follow signs.* **Visits by arrangement May to Aug for groups of 10 to 20. Admission incl home-made teas. Adm £6, chd free.**
Semi-detached house with a well stocked front garden and a small enclosed garden at the rear. The front has acers, palms and hydrangeas and other perennials. The rear garden is very well stocked with palms, acers, bamboo, hydrangeas and pines. Ornamental grasses, other perennials and fish pond. The close planting gives a jungle feel. Not suitable for wheelchairs, children or dogs.

42 NEW **LITTLE ORCHARD**
Slad, Stroud, GL6 7QD.
Mr & Mrs Terry & Rod Clifford, 01452 813944,
terryclifford.tlc@gmail.com. *2m from Stroud, 10 m from Cheltenham. Last property on L in Slad village before leaving 30mph speed limit travelling from Stroud to Birdlip on B4070. Sat Nav may not bring you directly to property. Parking on verge opp.* **Sun 31 May (10.30-5). Adm £4, chd free. Home-made teas. Cider tasting available. Visits also by arrangement June & July for groups of 10 to 30.**
Steeply sloping, terraced acre plot using many reclaimed materials, stonework and statuary. Enhanced with different styles of planting to complement the natural surroundings, varied areas include Apple Orchard, Mediterranean Courtyard, Vegetable Parterre and Children's Play Area. Stunning views of the Slad Valley. Access into adjoining Nature Reserve. Local craft on sale. Children's Trail. Wheelchair access possible but challenging due to the severity of slopes and steps. Please phone for further details.

&

GROUP OPENING

43 **LONGHOPE GARDENS**
Longhope, GL17 0NA.
01452 830406,
sally.j.gibson@btinternet.com. *10m W of Gloucester. 7m E of Ross on Wye. A40 take Longhope turn off to Church Rd. From A4136 follow Longhope signs and turn onto Church Rd. Parking available on Church Rd.* **Sat 23 May (1-5); Sun 24 May (2-5.30); Sat 6 June (1-5); Sun 7 June (2-5.30). Combined adm £5, chd free. Home-made teas. Visits also by arrangement May & June for groups of 10+.**

3 CHURCH ROAD
Rev Clive & Mrs Linda Edmonds.

SPRINGFIELD HOUSE
Sally & Martin Gibson.

WOODBINE COTTAGE
Mrs Lucille Roughley.

Three stunning gardens set in the valley of Longhope. Each garden has its own style and sweeping views which take in the valley, May Hill and the Forest of Dean. Wander through the long garden at 3 Church Road, visiting each room, and enjoy the large collection of hardy geraniums. Delight in the rich planting throughout the large enclosed garden at Springfield House, framing the terraced lawns with large herbaceous borders and a wildlife pond in a woodland setting. Woodbine Cottage garden offers a tranquil and soothing refuge, a beautiful hornbeam arbour, a natural pond and individual planting. Home-made cakes, refreshments and plant sales available. Keep up to date with Longhope Gardens on our Facebook page. 3 Church Road and Springfield House featured in Amateur Gardening magazine. Springfield House also appeared in Austrian TV special Classic English Gardens. Wheelchair access at Springfield House and Woodbine Cottage but not at 3 Church Road.

&

44 **LOWER FARM HOUSE**
Cliffords Mesne, Newent,
GL18 1JT. Gareth & Sarah Williams. *2m S of Newent. From Newent, follow signs to Cliffords Mesne and Birds of Prey Centre (1½ m). Approx ½ m beyond Centre, turn L at Xrds (before church).* **Sat**

23 May (2-6). Adm £5, chd free. Home-made teas.
2½ acre garden, incl woodland, stream and large natural lily pond with rockery and bog garden. Herbaceous borders, pergola walk, terrace with ornamental fishpond, kitchen and herb garden; collections of irises, hostas and paeonies. Many interesting and unusual trees and shrubs incl magnolias and cornus. Some gravel paths.

&

45 **LOWER SLAUGHTER**
Cheltenham, GL54 2HP.
Jane Moore, George Leonte, 01451 820456,
info@slaughtersmanor.co.uk,
www.slaughtersmanor.co.uk/. *1m NE of Bourton on the Water.* **Thur 23 Apr (2-5). Adm £3.50, chd free. Home-made teas.**
2 individual gardens filled with spring bulbs, flowering cherries and sparkling water features. Managed by the same team of gardeners and subject to ongoing development and investment. The C17 Slaughters Manor House is set within beautiful grounds while across the road lies The Slaughters Country Inn on the banks of the River Eye with its wildlife friendly feel. Gravel paths and lawns.

&

46 ♦ **LYDNEY PARK SPRING GARDEN**
Lydney Park Estate, GL15 6BT. The Viscount Bledisloe, 01594 842844,
accounts@lydneyparkestate.co.uk,
www.lydneyparkestate.co.uk. *½ m SW of Lydney. On A48 Gloucester to Chepstow rd between Lydney & Aylburton. Drive is directly off A48.* **For NGS: Wed 13 May (10-5). Light refreshments. Light lunches. For other opening times and information, please phone, email or visit garden website.**
Spring garden in 8 acre woodland valley with lakes, profusion of rhododendrons, azaleas and other flowering shrubs. Formal garden; magnolias and daffodils (April). Picnics in deer park which has fine trees. Important Roman Temple site and museum. Not suitable for wheelchairs due to rough pathway through garden and steps to WC.

47 THE MANOR

Little Compton, Moreton-In-Marsh, GL56 0RZ. Reed Foundation (Charity), www.reedbusinessschool.co.uk/. *Next to church in Little Compton. ½ m from A44 or 2m from A3400. Follow signs to Little Compton, then yellow NGS signs.* **Sun 28 June, Sun 23 Aug (2-5). Adm £6, chd free. Home-made teas.**
Extensive Arts and Crafts garden with meadow and arboreta. Footpaths around our fields, playground between car park and garden. Croquet, and tennis free to play. Children and dogs welcome! We occasionally donate 15% of ticket proceeds to a charity of our choice. One ramp in main part of the garden. Rock garden, tennis court lawn and meadow not accessible by wheelchair. Disabled drop-off at entrance.

48 NEW MONASTERY GARDEN AT PRINKNASH ABBEY

Cranham, Gloucester, GL4 8EX. Prinknash Abbey Trustees. *The Prinknash Abbey Estate is located on the A46 between Painswick and Brockworth. Park in main car park and walk down past Café. Entrance to walled garden is below.* **Wed 9 Sept (11-5). Adm £4, chd free. Light refreshments in the Café/Gift Shop. Home-made lunches, teas and cakes. Donation to Stroud Valleys Project and Butterfly Conservation.**
An unusual, circular walled garden undergoing restoration and now managed mainly by volunteers from Stroud Valleys Project. Features incl vegetable garden, orchard with mature mulberry trees, apple and pear arches, lily pond, beehives and uncultivated areas to attract wildlife. Butterfly nectar garden with colourful herbaceous borders and wildflower areas managed by Butterfly Conservation. Partial wheelchair access; a sloping site with some level areas and some quite steep paths. Disabled parking close to garden entrance.

49 NEW MONKS SPOUT COTTAGE

Glasshouse Hill, May Hill, Longhope, GL17 0NN. Nigel & Jane Jackson, 07767 858295, monksspout@icloud.com. *1m from National Trust May Hill, in the hamlet of Glasshouse. access via lane (which is also a public footpath called the Wysis Way) immediately adjacent to Glasshouse Inn. Very limited disabled parking at the cottage. Parking signed.* **Sun 31 May (1-6). Adm £5, chd free. Home-made teas. Visits also by arrangement Apr to Sept for groups of up to 30. £7.50 incl tea and cake.**
The ⅔ acre garden is adjacent to Castle Wood which is the backdrop for a mix of herbaceous borders, lawns and ponds, with greenhouse, stream and large display of insectivorous plants, mostly planted outside but some in the greenhouse. With several mature trees and recently planted acers, there is a mix of shade and sun creating both damp and dry planting opportunities. Insectivorous plants, both outdoor and hot house. Garden sculptures. Adjacent public footpaths through the wood (not part of the garden) where visitors can see the remains of a moat and bailey castle dating from C12. Wheelchair access is not practical.

50 MOOR WOOD

Woodmancote, GL7 7EB. Mr & Mrs Henry Robinson, www.moorwoodroses.co.uk. *3½ m NW of Cirencester. Turn L off A435 to Cheltenham at North Cerney, signed Woodmancote 1¼ m; entrance in village on L beside lodge with white gates.* **Sun 28 June (2-6). Adm £5, chd free. Home-made teas.**
2 acres of shrub, orchard and wild flower gardens in beautiful isolated valley setting. Holder of National Collection of Rambler Roses. Not recommended for wheelchairs.

NPC

Your visits help change lives – your generosity has supported unpaid carers through donations to Carers Trust totalling over £4 million since 1996

51 NEW NORTH CERNEY VILLAGE GARDENS

North Cerney, Cirencester, GL7 7BZ. North Cerney Village. *Parking available off A435 (opp Bathurst Arms pub), which will be signed. Please access the village from Cirencester or Cheltenham using A435, not through the village itself.* **Sat 13 June (1-5). Combined adm £5, chd free. Home-made teas.**
Enjoy a range of gardens in this quintessential Cotswold village for our inaugural open gardens event.

52 THE OLD RECTORY, QUENINGTON

Church Rd, Quenington, Cirencester, GL7 5BN. Mr & Mrs David Abel Smith, www.freshairsculpture.com. *Opp St Swithins Church at bottom of village. 8m NE of Cirencester. Garden well signed once in village.* **Sun 28 June (2-5.30). Adm £5, chd free. Home-made teas.**
On the banks of the mill race and the River Coln, this is an organic garden of great variety. Mature trees, large vegetable garden, herbaceous borders, shade garden, pool and bog gardens. Permanent sculpture collection in the gardens. The majority of the garden is accessible by wheelchair.

53 THE OLD VICARAGE

Murrells End, Hartpury, GL19 3DF. Mrs Carol Huckvale. *5m NW of Gloucester. From Over r'about on A40 N Gloucester bypass, take A417 NW to Hartpury (Ledbury Road). After Maisemore, turn L at signs for Hartpury College. House 1m on R. Follow signs for parking.* **Sun 17 May (2-5). Adm £5, chd free. Cream teas.**
Tranquil garden of about 2 acres, with yew oval, mature trees, steps to croquet lawn, mixed borders around main lawn, potager, fruit trees. Work in progress developing wildflower meadow area and dry, shady woodland walk. Spring bulbs and wild flowers. Partial wheelchair access, disabled parking at house; gravel drive and path.

54 ◆ OXLEAZE FARM

Between Eastleach & Filkins, Lechlade, GL7 3RB. Mr & Mrs Charles Mann, 01367 850216, chipps@oxleaze.co.uk, www.oxleazebarn.co.uk. *5m S of Burford, 3m N of Lechlade off A361 to W (signed Barringtons). Take 2nd L then follow signs.* **For NGS: Wed 17 June (2-6). Adm £6, chd free. Home-made teas. For other opening times and information, please phone, email or visit garden website.**
Set amongst beautiful traditional farm buildings, plantsperson's good size garden combining formality and informality. Yr round interest; mixed borders, vegetable potager, decorative fruit cage, pond and bog garden, bees, potting shed, wild meadow, and topiary for structure when the flowers fade. Garden rooms off central lawn with reflective corners in which to enjoy this Cotswold garden. Mostly wheelchair access.

55 PASTURE FARM

Upper Oddington, Moreton-In-Marsh, GL56 0XG. Mr & Mrs John LLoyd. *3m W of Stow-on-the-Wold. Just off A436, mid-way between Upper & Lower Oddington.* **Sun 24, Mon 25 May (11-6); Sat 6 June (11-5). Adm £6, chd free. Home-made teas.**
Informal country garden developed over 30 yrs by current owners. Mixed borders, topiary, orchard and many species of trees. Gravel garden in 'the ruins', concrete garden and wild flower area leads to vegetable patch. Big spring-fed pond with ducks. Also bantams, chickens and 1 Kunekune pig. Large plant sale 24/25 May with proceeds to Kate's Home Nursing. Public footpath across 2 small fields arrives at C11 church, St Nicholas, with doom paintings, set in ancient woodlands. Truly worth a visit. See Simon Jenkins' Book of Churches.

Your visits help change lives – we are Hospice UK's largest charitable funder donating more than £5.5 million to support hospices in local communities since 1996

56 THE PATCH

Hollywell Lane, Brockweir, Chepstow, NP16 7PJ. Mrs Immy Lee. *In the Wye Valley, 6.7m N of Chepstow and 10.6m S of Monmouth, off A466, across Brockweir Bridge.* **Sun 24 May (12.30-5.30). Combined adm with Greenfields, Brockweir Common £7, chd free. Sun 13 Sept (12.30-5). Combined adm with Clouds Rest £7, chd free. Home-made teas.**
Restructured over the last few years, this is a well designed garden with fine borders containing a collection of 60+ repeat flowering roses and a variety of shrubs and perennials, providing colour and interest throughout the year. Partial wheelchair access.

57 PEAR TREE COTTAGE

58 Malleson Road, Gotherington, GL52 9EX. Mr & Mrs E Manders-Trett, 01242 674592, mmanderstrett@gmail.com. *4m N of Cheltenham. From A435, travelling N, turn R into Gotherington 1m after end of Bishop's Cleeve bypass at garage. Garden on L approx 100yds past Shutter Inn.* **Sun 19 Apr (2-5). Adm £5, chd free. Light refreshments. Visits also by arrangement Mar to June for groups of up to 30.**
Mainly informal country garden of approx ½ acre with pond and gravel garden. Herbaceous borders, trees and shrubs surround lawns and seating areas. Wild garden and orchard lead to greenhouses, vegetable garden and beehives. Spring bulbs, early summer perennials and shrubs particularly colourful. Gravel drive and several shallow steps can be overcome for wheelchair users with prior notice.

58 PERRYWOOD HOUSE

Longney, Gloucester, GL2 3SN. Gill & Mike Farmer. *7m SW of Gloucester, 4m W of Quedgeley. From N: R off B4008 at Tesco Quedgeley r'about. R at end then R at 2nd mini r'about, then signed. From S: L off A38 at Moreton Valence to Epney/Longney, over canal bridge, R at T junction then signed.* **Sat 27, Sun 28 June (11-5). Adm £4, chd free. Home-made teas.**
1 acre plant lover's garden in the Severn Vale surrounded by open farmland. Established over 20 years,

an informal country garden with mature trees and shrubs, colourful herbaceous borders and containers. Plenty of places to sit and enjoy the garden and your tea. Lots of interesting plants for sale. All areas accessible with level lawns and gravel drives. Disabled parking available.

59 NEW RADNORS

Wheatstone Lane, Lydbrook, GL17 9DP. Mrs Mary Wood, 01594 861690, mary.wood37@btinternet.com. *Lower Lydbrook in the Wye Valley. From Lydbrook, go through the village. At the T junction turn L into Stowfield Rd. Wheatstone Lane (300m) is the first turning L, a small lane after the white cottages. Radnors is the last house.* **Visits by arrangement May to Sept for groups of up to 10. Adm £4, chd free. Light refreshments. Tea, coffee and cake available, by arrangement.**
5 acre hillside garden in AONB on bank above the River Wye. Focus on wildlife with naturalistic planting and weeds, some left for specific insects/birds. It has many paths, a wooded area, wildflower area, flower beds and borders, lawns, stumpery, fernery, veg beds and white garden. Of particular interest are the path along a disused railway line, and the summer dahlias. The garden has many narrow and uneven paths and steps and is not accessible to wheelchair users or those with mobility difficulties.

60 RAMBLERS

Lower Common, Aylburton, Lydney, GL15 6DS. Jane & Leslie Hale. *1½m W of Lydney. Off A48 Gloucester to Chepstow Rd. From Lydney through Aylburton, out of de-limit turn R signed Aylburton Common, ¾m along lane.* **Sun 3 May (1.30-5). Adm £4, chd free. Home-made teas.**
Peaceful medium sized country garden with informal cottage planting, herbaceous borders and small pond looking through hedge windows onto wild flower meadow and mature apple orchard. Some shade loving plants and topiary. Large productive vegetable garden. Past winner of The English Garden magazine's Britain's Best Gardener's Garden competition.

61 ROCKCLIFFE
Upper Slaughter, Cheltenham, GL54 2JW. Mr & Mrs Simon Keswick, www.rockcliffegarden.co.uk. *2m from Stow-on-the-Wold. 1½m from Lower Swell on B4068 towards Cheltenham. Leave Stow on the Wold on B4068 through Lower Swell. Continue on B4068 for 1½m. Rockcliffe is well signed on R.* **Wed 3 June, Wed 1 July (10-5). Adm £7, chd free. Home-made teas.** Donation to Kate's Home Nursing.
Large traditional English garden of 8 acres incl pink garden, white and blue garden, herbaceous borders, rose terrace, large walled kitchen garden and orchard. Greenhouses and pathway of topiary birds leading up through orchard to stone dovecot. 2 wide stone steps through gate, otherwise good wheelchair access. Sorry no dogs.

62 ◆ SEZINCOTE
Moreton-in-Marsh, GL56 9AW. Mrs D Peake, 01386 700444, enquiries@sezincote.com, www.sezincote.co.uk. *3m SW of Moreton-in-Marsh. From Moreton-in-Marsh turn W along A44 towards Evesham; in 1½m (just before Bourton-on-the-Hill) turn L, by stone lodge with white gate.* **For NGS: Sun 7 June (2-6). Adm £5, chd free. Home-made teas. Teas provided by and in aid of Longborough School. For other opening times and information, please phone, email or visit garden website.**
Exotic oriental water garden by Repton and Daniell with lake, pools and meandering stream, banked with massed perennials. Large semi-circular orangery, formal Indian garden, fountain, temple and unusual trees of vast size in lawn and wooded park setting. House in Indian manner designed by Samuel Pepys Cockerell. Garden on slope with gravel paths, so not all areas wheelchair accessible.

63 SOUTH LODGE
Church Road, Clearwell, Coleford, GL16 8LG. Andrew & Jane MacBean, 01594 837769, southlodgegarden@btinternet.com, www.southlodgegarden.co.uk. *2m S of Coleford. Off B4228. Follow signs to Clearwell. Garden on L of castle driveway. Please park on rd in front of church or in village. No parking on castle drive.* **Sat 28 Mar, Sat 2 May, Sat 13 June (1-5). Adm £4, chd free. Home-made teas. Visits also by arrangement Apr to June for groups of 20+.**
Peaceful country garden in 2 acres with stunning views of surrounding countryside. High walls provide a backdrop for rambling roses, clematis, and honeysuckles. Organic garden with large variety of perennials, annuals, shrubs and specimen trees with yr-round colour. Vegetable garden, wildlife and formal ponds. Rustic pergola planted with English climbing roses and willow arbour in gravel garden. Gravel paths and steep grassy slopes. Assistance dogs only.

GROUP OPENING

64 STANTON VILLAGE GARDENS
Stanton, nr Broadway, WR12 7NE. *3m S of Broadway. Off B4632, between Broadway (3m) and Winchcombe (6m).* **Sun 14 June (2-6). Combined adm £7.50, chd free. Home-made teas in Burland Hall in village centre and several gardens. Ice cream trike in village.** Donation to Village charities.
A selection of gardens open in this picturesque, unspoilt Cotswold village. Many houses border the street with long gardens hidden behind. Gardens vary, from houses with colourful herbaceous borders, established trees, shrubs and vegetable gardens to tiny cottage gardens. Some also have attractive, natural water features fed by the stream which runs through the village. Plants for sale and book stall. Delicious teas and cakes in various locations. Free parking. An NGS visit not to be missed. A gem of a Cotswold village. Church also open. The Mount Inn open for lunches. Very few gardens suitable for wheelchair users, due to gravel drives.

The Patch

65 ◆ STANWAY FOUNTAIN & WATER GARDEN

Stanway, Cheltenham, GL54 5PQ. The Earl of Wemyss & March, 01386 584528, office@stanwayhouse.co.uk, www.stanwayfountain.co.uk. *9m NE of Cheltenham. 1m E of B4632 Cheltenham to Broadway rd on B4077 Toddington to Stow-on-the-Wold rd.* **For NGS: Sun 17 May, Sun 16 Aug (2-5). Adm £6, chd free. Home-made teas in Stanway Tea Room. For other opening times and information, please phone, email or visit garden website.**

20 acres of planted landscape in early C18 formal setting. The restored canal, upper pond and fountain have re-created one of the most interesting Baroque water gardens in Britain. Striking C16 manor with gatehouse, tithe barn and church. Britain's highest fountain at 300ft, the world's highest gravity fountain which runs at 2.45 and 4.00pm for 30 mins each time. Partial wheelchair access in garden, some flat areas, able to view fountain and some of garden. House is not wheelchair suitable.

66 STOWELL PARK

Northleach, Cheltenham, GL54 3LE. The Lord & Lady Vestey, www.stowellpark.co.uk. *8m NE of Cirencester. Off Fosseway A429 2m SW of Northleach.* **Sun 17 May, Sun 21 June (2-5). Adm £6, chd free. Donation to another charity.**

Magnificent lawned terraces with stunning views over Coln Valley. Fine collection of old-fashioned roses and herbaceous plants, pleached lime approach to C14 house (not open). 2 large walled gardens containing vegetables, fruit, cut flowers and range of greenhouses incl vinery, peach and orchid houses. Long rose pergola and wide, plant filled borders. Fountain garden and water features. Open continuously for over 50yrs. Plants for sale June opening only. Church open. Wheelchair access to walled gardens, terraces and teas. Limited access on some pathways.

♿ ✿ ☕ ▶

67 TREE HILL

76 Gretton Road, Winchcombe, Cheltenham, GL54 5EL. Mark Caswell. *½m N of Winchcombe. Leave Winchcombe via North St, straight ahead onto Gretton Rd for*

½m. From M5 J9, take A46 towards Evesham, at r'about take B4077 to Stow, then R to Gretton. **Sun 9 Aug (11-5). Combined adm with Woodlands Farm £8, chd free.**

Stepping into this garden is akin to stepping into another world. As one visitor remarked 'this is unlike any English garden I have ever seen.' On this modest plot one finds huge leaves, tall exotic plants jostling for light with the small and the delicate. Built by one man with a passion for the exotic landscapes of the Caribbean which was borne during a visit to Barbados at the age of 24. Two stone steps down to the garden.

♿

68 TRENCH HILL

Sheepscombe, GL6 6TZ. Celia & Dave Hargrave, 01452 814306, celia.hargrave@btconnect.com. *1½m E of Painswick. From Cheltenham A46 take 1st turn signed Sheepscombe. Follow lane (1¼m) to bottom of hill, continue uphill towards Sheepscombe. Garden on L. SatNav leads to neighbouring garden, follow NGS signs.* **Sun 9, Sun 16 Feb, Sun 15 Mar (11-5); Sun 12, Mon 13 Apr, Sun 3 May (11-6). Every Wed 10 June to 24 June (2-6). Sun 19 July, Sun 30 Aug, Sun 13 Sept (11-6). Adm £5, chd free. Home-made teas. 2021: Sun 7, Sun 14 Feb. Visits also by arrangement Feb to Oct. Any use of coaches must be agreed with the owner.**

Approx 3 acres set in small woodland with panoramic views. Variety of herbaceous and mixed borders, rose garden, extensive vegetable plots, wild flower areas, plantings of spring bulbs with thousands of snowdrops and hellebores, woodland walk, 2 small ponds, waterfall and larger conservation pond. Interesting wooden sculptures, many within the garden. Run on organic principles. Children's play area, wooden sculptures. Mostly wheelchair access but some steps and slopes.

♿ ✿ 🚗 ☕ ▶

GROUP OPENING

69 UPPER MINETY OPEN GARDENS AND PLANT FAIR

Upper Minety, Malmesbury, SN16 9PY. Mr & Mrs C Gallop, 01666 860286, katiegallop@btinternet.com. *7m SE of Cirencester. Follow signs from A429 (Cotswold Water Park) or alternatively from B4040 to Minety Church. Ample parking.* **Sun 28 June (11-5). Combined adm £6, chd free. Home-made teas.**

South Lodge

Welcome to the 5th anniversary of Upper Minety Open Gardens, which takes its name from the wild mint plant found growing in and around the village. A collection of village gardens from sweeping herbaceous borders, cottage gardens, productive fruit/veg plots, tranquil nature reserve and arboretum, meadow walk with St Leonard's Church floral arrangements. Specialist plant nurseries and imaginative stalls offering accessories for your home and garden together with a display of vintage and classic cars will be hosted at Oakwood Farm with teas on the farm lawn and where garden maps can be obtained. Some gravel, mostly grass. Disabled parking available. Coaches by arrangement only.

70 UPTON WOLD

Moreton-in-Marsh, GL56 9TR. Mr & Mrs I R S Bond, www.uptonwold.co.uk. *4½m W of Moreton-in-Marsh. From Moreton/Stow on A44 1.1m past A424 junction at Troopers Lodge Garage turn R at stone posts. From Evesham/Broadway ½m beyond B4081 Chipping Campden Xrds turn L at stone posts.* **Sun 26 Apr (11-5). Adm £12, chd free.**
Garden of ongoing development, architecturally laid out around C17 house (not open) with commanding views. Yew hedges, herbaceous walk, some unusual plants and trees, vegetables, pond and woodland gardens, labyrinth. National Collections of Juglans and Pterocarya. 2 Star award from GGG.

71 WATERLANE HOUSE

Waterlane, Oakridge, Stroud, GL6 7PN. Mr & Mrs Hall. *2m S of Bisley, turn L out of Bisley and follow rd. From Cirencester on A419 turn R towards Sapperton, through Sapperton, turn L opp Daneway pub, follow single track rd to Waterlane.* **Thur 25 June (11-4). Adm £4, chd free. Home-made teas.**
Private estate with 4 acre garden with a variety of gardening interest ranging from herbaceous borders, white garden, kitchen garden, wild flower meadows, orchard and fine lawns. The estate is set in the idyllic countryside hamlet of Waterlane. Partial wheelchair access, a lot of gravel paths and lawns. Some steps.

72 WEIR REACH

The Rudge, Maisemore, Gloucester, GL2 8HY. Sheila & Mark Wardle. *3m NW of Gloucester. Turn into The Rudge by White Hart Pub. Field parking 100m from garden.* **Sun 14, Wed 17 June (11-5). Adm £4, chd free. Home-made teas.**
Country garden by R Severn. Approx 2 acres, half cultivated with herbaceous beds and mixed borders plus fruit and vegetable cages. Clematis and acers, stone ornaments, small sculptures, Bonsai collection. Planted rockery with waterfall and stream connect 2 ponds. Large specimen koi pond borders patio. Meadow with specimen and fruit trees and bamboo collection leading to river and country views.

73 ♦ WESTONBIRT SCHOOL GARDENS

Tetbury, GL8 8QG. Holfords of Westonbirt Trust, 01666 881373, jbaker@holfordtrust.com, www.holfordtrust.com. *3m SW of Tetbury. On A433 opp Westonbirt Arboretum. Please enter using main wrought iron school gates.* **For NGS: Sun 19 July (10.30-5). Adm £5, chd free. Tea, coffee & cake available to purchase. For other opening times and information, please phone, email or visit garden website.**
28 acres. Former private garden of Robert Holford, founder of Westonbirt Arboretum. Formal Victorian gardens incl walled Italian garden now restored with early herbaceous borders and exotic border. Rustic walks, lake, statuary and grotto. Rare, exotic trees and shrubs. Beautiful views of Westonbirt House open with guided tours to see fascinating Victorian interior on designated days of the year. Afternoon tea with sandwiches and scones available for pre-booked private tours, groups of 20-60. Only some parts of garden accessible to wheelchairs. Ramps and lift allow access to house.

74 WOODLANDS FARM

Rushley Lane, Winchcombe, GL54 5JE. Mrs Morag Dobbin, 01242 604261, mdobbin@btinternet.com. *6m NE of Cheltenham. Take Rushley Lane turn off B4632 N through Winchcombe, at Footbridge. Gate is 50yd up lane, behind*
Stancombe Lane sign. Park in field next to garden. **Sun 9 Aug (11-5). Combined adm with Tree Hill £8, chd free. Home-made teas. Visits also by arrangement May to Aug for groups of 10 to 20.**
1½ acre garden with generously sized garden rooms. The planting and landscaping are both thoughtful and tranquil. Generous borders throughout with colourful and harmonious planting schemes. Tall hornbeam hedge creates dramatic vista to stone monolith. Long contemporary pond. New prairie style border. Cottage borders. Wheelchair assistance needed with one steepish slope to access garden.

75 WORTLEY HOUSE

Wortley, Wotton-Under-Edge, GL12 7QP. Simon & Jessica Dickinson. *1m from Wotton-under-Edge. Full directions will be provided with ticket.* **Tue 16 June (2-5). Adm £15, chd free. Pre-booking essential, booking fees may apply. Please visit www.ngs.org.uk/events for information & booking. Home-made teas included.**
This diverse garden of over 20 acres has been created during the last 30 yrs by the current owners and includes walled garden, pleached lime avenues, nut walk, potager, ponds, Italian garden, shrubberies and wild flower meadows. Strategically placed follies, urns and statues enhance extraordinary vistas throughout, and the garden is filled with plants, arbours, roses through trees and up walls, and herbaceous borders. The stunning surrounding countryside is incorporated into the garden with views up the steep valley that are such a feature in this part of Gloucestershire. Wheelchair access to most areas, golf buggy also available.

Your visits help change lives - your generosity helps Marie Curie fund nurses to care for people night and day in their homes, with donations of more than £9 million

HAMPSHIRE

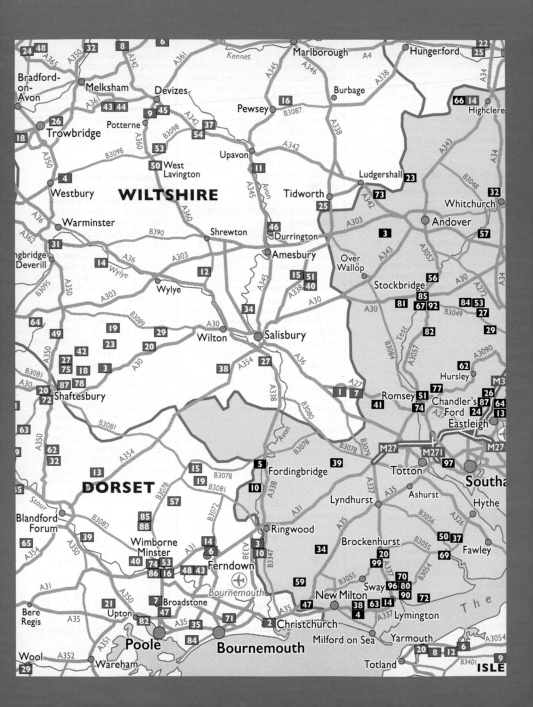

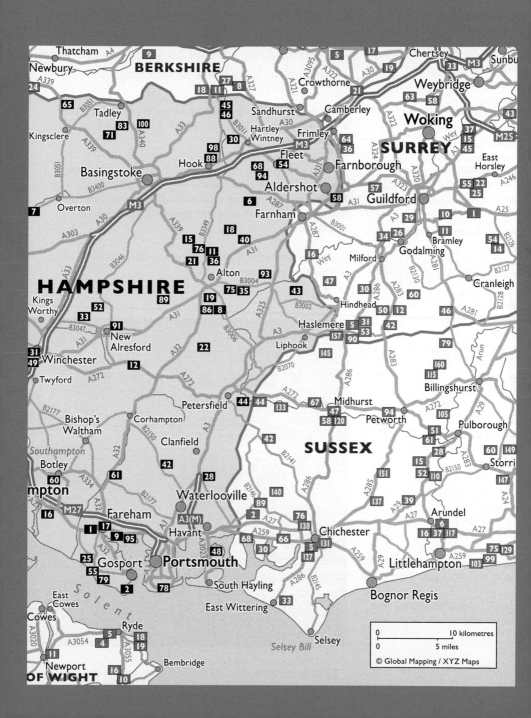

Volunteers

County Organiser
Mark Porter 01962 791054
markstephenporter@gmail.com

County Treasurer
Fred Fratter 01962 776243
fred@fratter.co.uk

Publicity
Pat Beagley 01256 764772
pat.beagley@ngs.org.uk

Social Media
Neil & Kerry Littleales
07727 657246
littleales@ngs.org.uk

Booklet Co-ordinator
Mark Porter (as above)

Assistant County Organisers

Central
Sue Cox 01962 732043
suealex13@gmail.com

Central West
Kate Cann 01794 389105
kategcann@gmail.com

East
Linda Smith 01329 833253
linda.ngs@btinternet.com

North
Cynthia Oldale 01420 520438
c.k.oldale@btinternet.com

North East
Lizzie Powell 01420 23185
lizzie.powell@btconnect.com

North West
Adam Vetere 01635 268267
adam.vetere@ngs.org.uk

South
Barbara Sykes 02380 254521
barandhugh@aol.com

South West
Elizabeth Walker 01590 677415
elizabethwalker13@gmail.com

West
Jane Wingate-Saul 01725 519414
jane.wingatesaul@ngs.org.uk

Hampshire is a large, diverse county. The landscape ranges from clay/gravel heath and woodland in the New Forest National Park in the south west, across famous trout rivers – the Test and Itchen – to chalk downland in the east, where you will find the South Downs National Park.

Our open gardens are spread right across the county and offer a very diverse range of interest for both the keen gardener and the casual visitor.

We have a large number of gardens with rivers running through them such as those in Longstock, Bere Mill, Dipley Mill and Weir House; gardens with large vegetable kitchen gardens such as Bramdean House; and eight new gardens will open for the very first time.

You will be assured of a warm welcome by all our garden owners and we hope you enjoy your visits.

Below: 5 Oakfields

 @HampshireNGS   @HantsNGS @hantsngs

OPENING DATES

All entries subject to change. For latest information check www.ngs.org.uk

Extended openings are shown at the beginning of the month.

Map locator numbers are shown to the right of each garden name.

February

Snowdrop Festival

Sunday 9th
Bramdean House 12

Sunday 16th
The Down House 33
Little Court 53

Monday 17th
Little Court 53

Sunday 23rd
◆ Chawton House 19
Little Court 53

Monday 24th
Little Court 53

March

Sunday 22nd
Bere Mill 7
Little Court 53

Saturday 28th
Pilley Hill Cottage 70

Sunday 29th
Beechenwood Farm 6
Pilley Hill Cottage 70

April

Sunday 5th
Bramdean House 12

Friday 10th
Crawley Gardens 27

Sunday 12th
Pylewell Park 72
Southsea Gardens 78
Twin Oaks 87

Monday 13th
Crawley Gardens 27
Twin Oaks 87

Saturday 18th
The Island 51
Pilley Hill Cottage 70

Sunday 19th
Durmast House 34
The Island 51
Pilley Hill Cottage 70
NEW Woodpeckers
Care Home 99

Friday 24th
Bluebell Wood 11

Saturday 25th
Bluebell Wood 11

Sunday 26th
◆ Spinners Garden 80
Terstan 85

May

Saturday 2nd
The Cottage 24

Sunday 3rd
The Cottage 24
NEW Tadley Place 83
Walhampton 90

Thursday 7th
Appleyards 5

Friday 8th
Appleyards 5
The Cottage 24

Saturday 9th
Appleyards 5

Sunday 10th
Appleyards 5
Brick Kiln Cottage 15
The Cottage 24
The House in the
Wood 50

Thursday 14th
Tanglefoot 84

Friday 15th
◆ Alverstoke Crescent
Garden 2

Saturday 16th
146 Bridge Road 16
21 Chestnut Road 20
Selborne 75

Sunday 17th
146 Bridge Road 16
21 Chestnut Road 20

Hinton Admiral 47
Selborne 75
Tanglefoot 84
Tylney Hall Hotel 88

Monday 18th
Selborne 75

Wednesday 20th
NEW Heckfield Place 45

Saturday 23rd
Little Court 53

Sunday 24th
Bere Mill 7
Berry Cottage 8
Little Court 53
Pylewell Park 72
Romsey Gardens 74
The Thatched Cottage 86
Twin Oaks 87

Monday 25th
Beechenwood Farm 6
Bere Mill 7
Romsey Gardens 74
Twin Oaks 87

Saturday 30th
Ferns Lodge 38

Sunday 31st
Amport & Monxton
Gardens 3
Dipley Mill 30
Ferns Lodge 38
Meon Orchard 61

June

Monday 1st
Amport & Monxton
Gardens 3

Wednesday 3rd
NEW Heckfield Place 45
NEW 6 Wimpson
Gardens 97

Thursday 4th
NEW 6 Wimpson
Gardens 97

Saturday 6th
Froyle Gardens 40
Oak Tree Cottage 63
NEW 1 Povey's
Cottage 71
Spitfire House 81

Sunday 7th
Froyle Gardens 40
108 Heath Road 44
Little Court 53
Oak Tree Cottage 63

Old Thatch & The
Millennium Barn 68
NEW 1 Povey's
Cottage 71
Southsea Gardens 78
Weir House 91

Monday 8th
Little Court 53

Thursday 11th
Appleyards 5
Lake House 52
Stockbridge Gardens 82

Friday 12th
Appleyards 5

Saturday 13th
Appleyards 5
21 Chestnut Road 20

Sunday 14th
Appleyards 5
Bramdean House 12
21 Chestnut Road 20
Cranbury Park 26
Dipley Mill 30
Fritham Lodge 39
Lake House 52
Little Owls 55
Shalden Park House 76
Stockbridge Gardens 82
Tylney Hall Hotel 88

Tuesday 16th
◆ Apple Court
Garden & Nursery 4

Thursday 18th
Tanglefoot 84

Friday 19th
Walden 89

Saturday 20th
5 Oakfields 64

Sunday 21st
Berry Cottage 8
Conholt Park 23
Durmast House 34
Longstock Park 56
5 Oakfields 64
Tanglefoot 84
The Thatched Cottage 86
Walden 89

Tuesday 23rd
Colemore House
Gardens 22

Wednesday 24th
Colemore House
Gardens 22

Saturday 27th
NEW Briar Patch 14

East Worldham Manor 35
26 Lower Newport
  Road 58
Selborne 75

Sunday 28th
NEW Briar Patch 14
61 Cottes Way 25
The Dower House 31
East Worldham Manor 35
Little Owls 55
26 Lower Newport
  Road 58
Selborne 75
Terstan 85
Wicor Primary School
  Community Garden 95

Monday 29th
61 Cottes Way 25
East Worldham Manor 35
Selborne 75

July

Every Tuesday
Old Swan House 67

Thursday 2nd
Crawley Gardens 27

Saturday 4th
15 Bruce Close 17
The Island 51
Manor Lodge 60
NEW 1 Povey's
  Cottage 71

Sunday 5th
Bleak Hill Nursery &
  Garden 10
15 Bruce Close 17
Bumpers 18
Crawley Gardens 27
The Island 51
Manor Lodge 60
NEW 1 Povey's
  Cottage 71
Spindles 79

Monday 6th
Bleak Hill Nursery &
  Garden 10

Thursday 9th
Appleyards 5

Friday 10th
Appleyards 5

Saturday 11th
Appleyards 5

Sunday 12th
Appleyards 5
Berry Cottage 8
Bramdean House 12
◆ The Hospital of St
  Cross 49
Little Owls 55
The Thatched Cottage 86
Tylney Hall Hotel 88
1 Wogsbarne
  Cottages 98

Monday 13th
1 Wogsbarne
  Cottages 98

Wednesday 15th
Wychwood 100

Thursday 16th
Tanglefoot 84

Saturday 18th
21 Chestnut Road 20
Fairweather's Nursery 37

Sunday 19th
Bleak Hill Nursery &
  Garden 10
21 Chestnut Road 20
Dipley Mill 30

Fairweather's Nursery 37
Tanglefoot 84
Whispers 94

Monday 20th
Bleak Hill Nursery &
  Garden 10

Wednesday 22nd
Wychwood 100

Saturday 25th
8 Birdwood Grove 9
Twin Oaks 87

Sunday 26th
Meon Orchard 61
Terstan 85
Twin Oaks 87

August

Saturday 1st
Old Camps 65
Selborne 75

Sunday 2nd
Bleak Hill Nursery &
  Garden 10
Dipley Mill 30
Old Camps 65

Merdon Manor

© Leigh Clapp

By Arrangement

Arrange a personalised garden visit with your club, or group of friends, on a date to suit you. See individual garden entries for full details.

THE GARDENS

1 80 ABBEY ROAD
Fareham, PO15 5HW. Brian & Vivienne Garford, 01329 843939, vgarford@aol.com. *From M27 J9 take A27 E to Fareham for approx 2m. At top of hill, turn L at lights into Highlands Rd. Turn 4th R into Blackbrook Rd. Abbey Rd is 4th L.* **Visits by arrangement Apr to Aug for groups of up to 30. Light refreshments.**
A small garden, designed to use all the available space. Many unusual plants, including a large collection of herbs and native wild flowers. Interesting use of containers and other ideas for the smaller garden. Two ponds and tiny meadow help attract a wide range of wildlife. Living willow seat, summerhouse and trained grapevine. There will be new planting to offset damage by Box Moth Caterpillar.
❀ ➔ ☕ ♿

2 ◆ ALVERSTOKE CRESCENT GARDEN
Crescent Road, Gosport, PO12 2DH. Gosport Borough Council, www. alverstokecrescentgarden.co.uk. *1m S of Gosport. From A32 & Gosport follow signs for Stokes Bay. Continue alongside bay to small r'about, turn L into Anglesey Rd. Crescent Garden signed 50yds on R.* **For NGS: Fri 15 May (10-4).** **Adm by donation. Home-made teas. For other opening times and information, please visit garden website.**
Restored Regency ornamental garden, designed to enhance fine crescent (Thomas Ellis Owen 1828). Trees, walks and flowers lovingly maintained by community and council partnership. A garden of considerable local historic interest highlighted by impressive restoration and creative planting. Adjacent to St Mark's churchyard, worth seeing together. Heritage, history and horticulture, a fascinating package. Plant sale. Green Flag Award.
♿ 🐕 ❀ ☕ ♿

GROUP OPENING

❸ AMPORT & MONXTON GARDENS

Amport and Monxton, SP11 8AY. *3m SW of Andover. Turn off the A303 signed East Cholderton from the E or Thruxton village from the W. Follow signs to Amport. Car parking in a field next to Amport village green. Please drive between the two villages.* **Sun 31 May, Mon 1 June (2-5.30). Combined adm £6, chd free. Cream teas at village hall, Monxton.**

BRIDGE COTTAGE
John & Jenny Van de Pette.

SANDLEFORD HOUSE
Michael & Valerie Taylor.

WHITE GABLES
David & Coral Eaglesham.

Monxton and Amport are two pretty villages linked by Pill Hill Brook. Visitors have three gardens to enjoy. Bridge Cottage a 2 acre haven for wildlife with the banks of the trout stream and lake planted informally with drifts of colour, a large vegetable garden, fruit cage, small mixed orchard and arboretum with specimen trees. White Gables a cottage style garden with a collection of trees, along with old roses and herbaceous plants. The garden at Sandleford House was created from a plot attached to The Bothy next door, which was basically meadow grass on a sloping site. It is now 8-9 yrs in the making and consists of a level, sunken lawn surrounded by perennial flower beds and brick and flint walls on three sides. There are two terraces and an arched pergola running the length of the west side of the garden. Amport has a lovely village green, come early and bring a picnic to enjoy the views of the thatched cottages, before the gardens open. No wheelchair access to White Gables.

❹ ✦ APPLE COURT GARDEN & NURSERY

Hordle Lane, Hordle, Lymington, SO41 0HU. Mrs Emma Taylor, 07388 562749, applecourtgarden@icloud.com, www.applecourtgarden.co.uk. *4m W of Lymington. From A337 between Lymington & New Milton, follow the brown signs by turning into Hordle Lane, opp the Royal Oak at Downton Xrds.* **For NGS: Tue 16 June (10-2). Adm £5, chd free. Home-made teas. For other opening times and information, please phone, email or visit garden website.**

1 acre, exuberantly planted, sheltered walled garden, designed and planted by world-renowned horticulturists, as a series of garden rooms to provide interest throughout the seasons. Theatrical white garden, ornamental grasses, new and established subtropical borders, and many unusual specimens. Display garden of 200 varieties of daylilies and Japanese style garden with koi pond. Well stocked nursery with interesting varieties. The garden is mostly flat. WC is not accessible to wheelchair users.

❺ APPLEYARDS

Bowerwood Road, Fordingbridge, SP6 3BP. Mr & Mrs Bob & Jean Carr. *½m from Fordingbridge on B3078. After church & houses, 400yds on L as road climbs after bridge. Parking for 8 cars only. No parking on narrow road. Coaches welcome (drop-off & pick-up only).* **Thur 7, Fri 8, Sat 9, Sun 10 May, Thur 11, Fri 12, Sat 13, Sun 14 June, Thur 9, Fri 10, Sat 11, Sun 12 July (1-5). Adm £4, chd free. Home-made teas. Pre-booking essential, please phone 01425 657613 or email bob.carr.rtd@gmail.com to reserve car park space (8 only).**

2 acre, sloping, s-facing garden, newly restored, overlooking pasture. 100+ trees, sloping lawns, and paths though wooded sections with massed daffodils and bluebells in spring. Herbaceous beds, two rose beds, shrubberies, two wildlife ponds, orchard, sloping rockery beds, soft fruit cages, and greenhouse. Large patio looking down over garden for home-made teas (unable to cater for special dietary requirements).

❻ BEECHENWOOD FARM

Hillside, Odiham, Hook, RG29 1JA. Mr & Mrs M Heber-Percy, 01256 702300, beechenwood@totalise.co.uk. *5m SE of Hook. Turn S into King St from Odiham High St. Turn L after cricket ground for Hillside. Take 2nd R after 1½m, modern house ½m.* **Sun 29 Mar, Mon 25 May (2-5). Adm £4, chd free. Home-made teas. Visits also by arrangement Mar to June. No coaches due to narrow lane.**

2 acre garden in many parts. Lawn meandering through woodland with drifts of spring bulbs. Rose pergola with steps, pots with spring bulbs and later aeoniums. Fritillary and cowslip meadow. Walled herb garden with pool and exuberant planting. Orchard incl white garden and hot border. Greenhouse and vegetable garden. Rock garden extending to grasses, ferns and bamboos. Shady walk to belvedere. 8 acre copse of native species with grassed rides. Assistance available with gravel drive and avoidable shallow steps.

❼ BERE MILL

London Road, Whitchurch, RG28 7NH. Rupert & Elizabeth Nabarro, 01256 892210, rupertnab@gmail.com, www.beremillfarm.com. *9m E of Andover, 12m N of Winchester. In centre of Whitchurch, take London Rd at r'about. Uphill 1m, turn R 50yds beyond The Bell on R. Drop-off point for the disabled at garden.* **Sun 22 Mar, Sun 24, Mon 25 May, Sun 20 Sept (1.30-5). Adm £7, chd free. Home-made teas. Visits also by arrangement Feb to Nov. Fixed fee of £400 per private visit, plus £2.50 per person for tea & cake. Donation to Smile Train.**

On the Upper Test with water meadows and wooded valleys, this garden offers herbaceous borders, bog and Mediterranean plants, as well as a replanted orchard and two small arboretums. Features incl early bulbs, species tulips, Japanese prunus, peonies, wisteria, irises, roses, and semi-tropical planting. At heart it aims to complement the natural beauty of the site and to incorporate elements of oriental garden design and practice. The working mill was where Portals first made paper for the Bank of England in 1716. Unfenced and unguarded rivers and streams. Wheelchair access unless very wet.

8 BERRY COTTAGE

Church Road, Upper Farringdon, Alton, GU34 3EG. Mrs P Watts, 01420 588318. *3m S of Alton off A32. Turn L at Xrds, 1st L into Church Rd. Follow road past Massey's Folly, 2nd house on R, opp church.* **Suns 24 May, 21 June, 12 July, 9 Aug, 6 Sept (2-5.30). Combined adm with The Thatched Cottage £8, chd free. Home-made teas. Visits also by arrangement May to Sept for groups of 10+.**

Small organic cottage garden with yr-round interest, designed and maintained by owner, surrounding C16 house (not open). Spring bulbs, roses, clematis and herbaceous borders. The borders are colour themed and contain many unusual plants. Pond, bog garden and shrubbery. Close to Massey's Folly built by the Victorian rector incl 80ft tower with unique handmade floral bricks, C11 church and some of the oldest yew trees in the county. Partial wheelchair access.

9 8 BIRDWOOD GROVE

Downend, Fareham, PO16 8AF. Jayne & Eddie McBride, 01329 280838, jayne.mcbride@ntlworld.com. *M27 J11, L lane slip to Delme r'about, L on A27 to Portchester over 2 T-lights, completely around small r'about, Birdwood Grove 1st L.* **Sat 25 July (1-5). Adm £3, chd free. Home-made teas. Visits also by arrangement July & Aug for groups of up to 20.**

The subtropics in Fareham! This small garden is influenced by the flora of Australia and New Zealand and incl many indigenous species and plants that are widely grown down under. The 4 climate zones; arid, temperate, lush fertile and a shady fernery, are all densely planted to make the most of dramatic foliage, from huge bananas to towering cordylines. Fareham in Bloom Gold Award, Small Plantsman's Back Garden and presentation of special Community Award in recognition of services to In Bloom. Wheelchair access with short gravel path, not suitable for mobility scooters.

10 BLEAK HILL NURSERY & GARDEN

Braemoor, Bleak Hill, Harbridge, Ringwood, BH24 3PX. Tracy & John Netherway, www.bleakhillplants.co.uk. *2½m S of Fordingbridge. Turn off A338 at Ibsley. Go through Harbridge village to T-junction at top of hill, turn R for ¼m.* **Sun 5, Mon 6, Sun 19, Mon 20 July, Sun 2, Mon 3 Aug (2-5). Adm £4, chd free. Home-made teas on Sundays only.**

Through the moongate and concealed from view are billowing borders contrasting against a seaside scene with painted beach huts and a boat on the gravel. Herbaceous borders fill the garden with colour wrapping around a pond and small stream. Greenhouses with cacti and sarracenias. Vegetable patch and bantam chickens. Small adjacent nursery.

11 BLUEBELL WOOD

Stancombe Lane, Bavins, New Odiham Road, Alton, GU34 5SX. Mrs Jennifer Ospici, www.bavins.co.uk. *On the corner of Stancombe Lane & the B3349 2½m N of Alton.* **Fri 24, Sat 25 Apr (11-4). Adm £5, chd free. Light refreshments.**

Unique 100 acre ancient bluebell woodland. If you are a keen walker you will have much to explore on the long meandering paths and rides dotted with secluded seats. Those who enjoy a more leisurely pace will experience the perfume of the carpet of blue, listen to the birdsong and watch the contrasting light through the trees nearer to the entrance of the woods. Refreshments will be served in an original rustic building and include soups using natural woodland ingredients.

Shalden Park House

© Leigh Clapp

🔟 BRAMDEAN HOUSE
**Bramdean, Alresford, SO24 0JU.
Mr & Mrs E Wakefield,
office@bramdeanhouse.com.**
*4m S of Alresford; 9m E of
Winchester; 9m W of Petersfield. In
centre of village on A272. Entrance
opp sign to the church. Parking
is usually immed across the road
from entrance.* **Suns 9 Feb, 5 Apr,
14 June, 12 July, 9 Aug, 13 Sept
(2-4). Adm £5, chd free. Home-
made teas.**
Beautiful 5 acre garden best known
for its mirror image herbaceous
borders. Also carpets of spring bulbs,
especially snowdrops and a large
and unusual collection of plants and
shrubs giving yr-round interest. 1
acre walled garden featuring prize-
winning vegetables, fruit and flowers.
Small arboretum. Many hardy Nerine
cultivars. Features incl a wildflower
meadow, boxwood castle, a large
collection of old fashioned sweet
peas. Home of the nation's tallest
sunflower 'Giraffe'. Flowering cherries
recently imported from Japan. Private
visits Mar to Sept for groups of 5+
(non-NGS).
♿ ✿ 🚌 ☕

🔟 6 BREAMORE CLOSE
**Boyatt Wood, Eastleigh,
SO50 4QB. Mr & Mrs R
Trenchard, 02380 611230,
dawndavina6@yahoo.co.uk.** *1m
N of Eastleigh. M3 J12, follow
signs to Eastleigh. Turn R at r'about
into Woodside Ave, then 1st L
into Broadlands Ave (park here).
Breamore Close 3rd on L.* **Visits
by arrangement May & June for
groups of 10+. Adm £4, chd free.
Home-made teas.**
Delightful plant lover's garden with
coloured foliage and unusual plants,
giving a tapestry effect of texture and
colour. Many hostas displayed in
pots and in May a wonderful wisteria
scrambles over a pergola. The garden
is laid out in distinctive planting
themes with seating areas to sit and
contemplate. In June many clematis
scramble through roses and there are
many varieties of phlox. Wheelchair
access with small gravel areas.
♿ ✿ 🚌 ☕

🔟 NEW BRIAR PATCH
**Northover Road, Pennington,
Lymington, SO41 8GU. Annette
Eales.** *2m NW of Lymington. From
N off A337, turn into Sway Rd, follow
for 1½m to the Wheel Inn. Turn L,
into Ramley Rd & follow the signs;*
*Northover Rd is the 1st turning on
the L.* **Sat 27, Sun 28 June (2-5).
Adm £3, chd free. Cream teas &
gluten free option.**
Meander through this luscious
cottage garden 140ft by 40ft with
extended views over farmland. A
glorious palette of pinks, blues,
purples and burgundy excite the
senses. A long central pergola divides
the garden into numerous areas;
woodland planting, a cutting garden,
a shade and wildflower hedgerow.
Herbaceous borders interspersed
with salvaged vintage tables
displaying plant collections.
✿ ☕

🔟 BRICK KILN COTTAGE
**The Avenue, Herriard, Nr
Alton, RG25 2PR. Barbara
Jeremiah, 01256 381301,
barbara@klca.co.uk.** *4m NE of
Alton. A339 Basingstoke to Alton,
7m out of Basingstoke turn L along
The Avenue, past Lasham Gliding
Club on R, then past Back Lane on L
& take next track on L, one field later.*
**Sun 10 May (12-4). Adm £4.50,
chd free. Home-made teas. Visits
also by arrangement May & June.**
Bluebell woodland garden with 2
acres with a perimeter woodland
path incl treehouse, pebble garden,
billabong, stumpery, ferny hollow, bug
palace, waterpool, shepherd's hut and
a traditional cottage garden filled with
herbs. The garden is maintained using
eco-friendly methods as a haven for
wild animals, butterflies, birds, bees
and English bluebells. Wildlife friendly
garden in a former brick works. A
haven in the trees. Excellent cream
teas, home-made cakes and endless
pots of tea. Wheelchair access to
some parts of the garden.
 🐐 ✿ ☕

🔟 146 BRIDGE ROAD
**Sarisbury Green, Southampton,
SO31 7EJ. Audrey & Jonathan
Crutchfield.** *4m W of Fareham. On
A27 between Chapel Rd & Glen Rd.
Free car parking by kind permission
of the United Reformed Church on
Chapel Rd.* **Sat 16, Sun 17 May
(12-5). Adm £3.50, chd free. Light
refreshments.**
A rambling, deceptively large and
tranquil cottage garden that is
accessed from a side gate and
unexpectedly removed from the
sometimes bustling A27. Creatively
divided with rooms, richly filled
borders, patios and lawns giving
intense variety. These are interspersed
with nooks, arbours, mirrors, statues
and unexpected resting spots that
offer promise, privacy and the chance
to unwind and reflect.
♿ ✿ ☕

🔟 15 BRUCE CLOSE
**Fareham, PO16 7QJ. Teresa &
John Greenwood, 07545 242654,
tgreenwood@ntlworld.com.** *M27
W leave J10 under M27 bridge
RH-lane, do a U-turn. At r'about 3rd
exit, across T-lights. Ist R Miller Drive,
2nd R Somervell Drive. 1st R Bruce
Close. Free parking at Fareham
Leisure Centre.* **Sat 4, Sun 5 July,
Sat 15, Sun 16 Aug (11-5). Adm
£3.50, chd free. Home-made teas,
cream teas & savoury scones.
Visits also by arrangement July
& Aug for groups of 5 to 20.
Weekends only.**
Step into a garden 88ft x 42ft with
a number of secluded areas, each
with their own character including a
Mediterranean garden, decking with
raised beds and a seating area with
a living wall. An arched folly leads
to a fireplace and summerhouse.
There are a wide range of colourful
plants, hanging baskets annuals and
a lower patio with planted gazebo.
It is ideal for entertaining and is low
maintenance. Fareham in Bloom Gold
Awards for large floral back garden,
large floral front garden, floral display,
containers and hanging baskets.
Overall winner for large floral front
garden for the 4th year running.
✿ ☕

🔟 BUMPERS
**Sutton Common, Long Sutton,
Hook, RG29 1SJ. Stella
Wildsmith, 07766 754993,
sfw@staxgroup.com.** *From village
of Long Sutton, turn up Copse Lane,
immed opp duck pond. Follow lane
for 1½m to top of steep hill, house
on L.* **Sun 5 July (2-6). Adm £5,
chd free. Home-made teas. Visits
also by arrangement Apr to Oct for
groups of 10+.**
Large country garden with beautiful
views spread over 2 acres, mixed
herbaceous and shrub borders and
laid out in a series of individual areas.
Some interesting sculptures and water
features with informal paths through
the grounds and a number of places
to sit and enjoy the views. Wheelchair
users, please park at front of house.
♿ ✿ ☕

19 ◆ CHAWTON HOUSE

Chawton, Alton, GU34 1SJ. Anthony Hughes-Onslow, 01420 541010, info@chawtonhouse.org, www.chawtonhouse.org. *2m S of Alton. Take the road opp Jane Austen's House museum towards St. Nicholas Church. Property is at the end of this road on the L.* **For NGS: Sun 23 Feb (11-4). Adm £5, chd free. Light refreshments. For other opening times and information, please phone, email or visit garden website.**

Snowdrops are scattered through this 14 acre listed English landscape garden which is being restored. Sweeping lawns, ha-ha, wilderness, terraces, fernery and shrubbery walk surround the Elizabethan manor house. The walled garden designed by Edward Knight now includes rose garden, cutting beds, orchard and 'Elizabeth Blackwell' herb garden based on her book 'A Curious Herbal' of 1737-39. Refreshments are available in our tea room, in the old kitchen, serving hot and cold drinks, wine, light lunches, cream teas, home-made cakes and local ice creams. Due to slopes and gravel paths, we regret this garden is not suitable for wheelchairs.

🐕🦮☕️🏵️

20 21 CHESTNUT ROAD

Brockenhurst, SO42 7RF. Iain & Mary Hayter, 01590 622009, maryiain.hayter@gmail.com, www.21-chestnut-rdgardens.co.uk. *New Forest, 4m S of Lyndhurst. At Brockenhurst turn R, B3055 Grigg Lane. Limited parking, village car park nearby. Leave M27 J2, follow Heavy Lorry Route. Mainline station less than 10 mins walk.* **Sat 16 May (11-5); Sun 17 May (1-5); Sat 13 June (11-5); Sun 14 June (1-5); Sat 18 July (11-5); Sun 19 July (1-5); Sat 15 Aug (11-5); Sun 16 Aug (1-5). Adm £4, chd free. Home-made teas & gluten free option. Visits also by arrangement Apr to Aug for groups of 10+.**

A mature ever evolving plant lovers dream and labour of love, this garden holds a surprise around every corner. Wildlife friendly with packed borders, vegetables, ponds, pergolas and arches, each season offers a wealth of ideas and inspiration. All this in the heart of the New Forest. Statues, fairies, arches and water used creatively in the garden.

🐕🦮🏵️🦮☕️🏵️

21 CLOVER FARM

Shalden Lane, Shalden, Alton, GU34 4DU. Tom & Sarah Floyd, 01420 86294. *Approx 3m N of Alton in the village of Shalden. Take A339 out of Alton. After approx 2m turn R up Shalden Lane. At top, turn sharp R next to church sign.* **Visits by arrangement June to Sept for groups of 20+. Adm £7, chd free. Light refreshments.**

3 acre garden with far reaching views. Herbaceous borders and sloping lawns down to reflection pond, wildflower meadow, lime avenue, rose and kitchen garden and ornamental grass area.

22 COLEMORE HOUSE GARDENS

Colemore, Alton, GU34 3RX. Mr & Mrs Simon de Zoete, 01420 588202, simondezoete@gmail.com. *4m S of Alton (off A32). Approach from N on A32, turn L (Shell Lane), ¼m S of East Tisted. Go under bridge, keep L until you see Colemore Church. Park on verge of church.* **Tue 23, Wed 24 June (2-6). Adm £5, chd free. Home-made teas. Visits also by arrangement May to July for groups of 5+.**

4 acres in lovely unspoilt countryside, featuring rooms containing many unusual plants and different aspects. A spectacular arched rose walk, water rill, mirror pond, herbaceous and shrub borders and a new woodland walk. Many admire the lawns, new grass gardens and thatched pavilion (built by students from the Prince's Trust). A small arboretum is being planted. Every year the owners seek improvement and the introduction of new, interesting and rare plants. We propagate and sell plants, many of which can be found in the garden. Some are unusual and not readily available elsewhere. For private visits, we endeavour to give a conducted tour and try to explain our future plans, rationale and objectives.

🏵️☕️

23 CONHOLT PARK

Hungerford Lane, Andover, SP11 9HA. Conholt Park Estate Ltd. *7m N of Andover. Turn N off A342 at Weyhill Church, 5m N through Clanville. L at T-junction, Conholt ½m on R, opp Chute Causeway. A343, Hurstbourne Tarrant, turning for Upton/Vernham Dean 3½m L signed Conholt.* **Sun 21 June (11-5). Adm £6, chd free. Home-made teas.**

Enjoy the peace and tranquility of Conholt Park, nestled in rural Wiltshire. It is 10 acres spread over rolling hills surrounding a Regency House (not open). The garden has varied styles and lawns with mature cedars. Highlights include the walled garden with its fantastic range of plants and the extended arboretum. Don't miss the stunning glasshouses and the laurel maze. Deep gravel and steps, not suitable for wheelchairs.

🐕🏵️🦮☕️🏵️

24 THE COTTAGE

16 Lakewood Road, Chandler's Ford, Eastleigh, SO53 1ES. Hugh & Barbara Sykes, 02380 254521, barandhugh@aol.com. *Leave M3 J12, follow signs to Chandler's Ford. At King Rufus on Winchester Rd, turn R into Merdon Ave, then 3rd road on L.* **Sat 2, Sun 3, Fri 8, Sun 10 May (2-6). Adm £4, chd free. Home-made teas. Visits also by arrangement Apr & May.**

The house was built in 1905 but the ¾ acre garden has been designed, planted and cared for since 1950 by 2 keen garden loving families. Azaleas, camellias, trilliums and erythroniums under old oaks and pines. Herbaceous cottage style borders with many unusual plants for yr-round interest. Bog garden, ponds, kitchen garden. Bantams, bees and birdsong with over 30 bird species noted. Wildlife areas. NGS sundial for opening for 30yrs. Childrens' quiz. 'A lovely tranquil garden', Anne Swithinbank. Hampshire Wildlife Trust Wildlife Garden Award. Honey from our garden hives for sale.

🏵️🦮☕️🏵️

Your visits help change lives – we are the largest single funder of the Queen's Nursing Institute

25 61 COTTES WAY

Hill Head, Fareham,
PO14 3NL. Norma Matthews
& Alan Stamps, 01329 282932,
norma_matthews@live.com. *4½m
S of Fareham. From Fareham follow
signs to Stubbington, then Hill Head.
Turn R into Bells Lane, L bend to
Crofton Lane, R opp shops into
Carisbrooke Ave, L into Cottes Way.*
**Sun 28, Mon 29 June (11-4). Adm
£3, chd free. Light refreshments.
Visits also by arrangement June &
July for groups of up to 20.**
33ft x 33ft garden, designed by owner
in 2015, a fine example of a low
maintenance, spacious and relaxing
outdoor living room. Colourful with
a wide variety of shrubs, perennials
and climbers. Water features and
patterned natural stone patio. Many
pots and containers incl chimney
pots and champagne bottles create
a blaze of colour. Small vegetable
patch. Two Fareham in Bloom Gold
Awards for small back garden and
front garden.

 ♿ 🐕 ❀ ☕

26 CRANBURY PARK

Otterbourne, nr Winchester,
SO21 2HL. Mrs Chamberlayne-
Macdonald. *3m NW of Eastleigh.
Main entrance on old A33 at top
of Otterbourne Hill by Bus Stop;.
Entrances also in Hocombe Rd,
(opp Nichol Rd), Chandlers Ford &
next to Otterbourne Church.* **Sun
14 June (2-6). Adm £5, chd free.
Home-made teas. Donation to St
Matthew's Church, Otterbourne.**
Extensive pleasure grounds laid
out in late C18 and early C19 by
Papworth; fountains, rose garden,
specimen trees and pinetum, lakeside
walk and fern walk. Family carriages
and collection of prams will be on
view, also photos of King George
VI, Eisenhower and Montgomery
reviewing Canadian troops at
Cranbury before D-Day. Disabled WC.
All dogs on leads please.

 ♿ 🐕 ❀ ☕

GROUP OPENING

27 CRAWLEY GARDENS

Crawley, Winchester, SO21 2PR.
F J Fratter, 01962 776243,
fred@fratter.co.uk. *5m NW of
Winchester. Between B3049
(Winchester - Stockbridge) & A272
(Winchester - Andover). Parking
throughout village & in field at
Tanglefoot.* **Fri 10, Mon 13 Apr,
Thur 2, Sun 5 July (2-5.30).
Combined adm £7.50, chd free.
Home-made teas in the village
hall.**

BAY TREE HOUSE
Julia & Charles Whiteaway.
Open on all dates
🅓

LITTLE COURT
Mrs A R Elkington.
Open on Fri 10, Mon 13 Apr
(See separate entry)

PAIGE COTTAGE
Mr & Mrs T W Parker.
Open on all dates

Pilley Hill Cottage

TANGLEFOOT
Mr & Mrs F J Fratter.
Open on Thur 2, Sun 5 July
(See separate entry)

Crawley is an exceptionally pretty period village nestling in chalk downland with thatched houses, C14 church and village pond with ducks. The spring gardens are Bay Tree House, Little Court and Paige Cottage; the summer gardens are Bay Tree House, Paige Cottage and Tanglefoot; providing seasonal interest of varied character, and with traditional and contemporary approaches to landscape and planting. Most of the gardens have beautiful country views and there are other good gardens to be seen from the road. Bay Tree House has bulbs, wild flowers, a Mediterranean garden, pleached limes, a rill and contemporary borders of perennials and grasses. Little Court is a 3 acre traditional English country garden with carpets of spring bulbs and a large meadow. Paige Cottage is a 1 acre traditional English country garden surrounding a period thatched cottage (not open) with bulbs and wild flowers in spring, and old climbing roses in summer. Tanglefoot has colour themed borders, herb wheel, exceptional kitchen garden, traditional Victorian boundary wall supporting trained fruit including apricots; and a large wildflower meadow. Plants from the garden for sale at Little Court and Tanglefoot.

28 CROOKLEY POOL
Blendworth Lane, Horndean, PO8 0AB. Mr & Mrs Simon Privett, 02392 592662, jennyprivett@icloud.com. *5m S of Petersfield, 2m E of Waterlooville, off the A3. From Horndean up Blendworth Lane between bakery & hairdresser. Parking 200yds before church on L with white railings.* Visits by arrangement May to Sept.
Here the plants decide where to grow. Californian tree poppies elbow valerian aside to crowd round the pool. Evening primroses obstruct the way to the door and the steps to wisteria shaded terraces. Hellebores bloom under the trees. Salvias, Pandorea jasminoides, Justicia, Pachystachys lutea and passion flowers riot quietly with tomatoes in the greenhouse. Not a garden for the neat or tidy minded, although this is

a plantsman's garden full of unusual plants and a lot of tender perennials. Bantams stroll throughout. Oil and watercolour paintings of flowers found in the garden will be on display and for sale in the studio.

29 THE DEANE HOUSE
Sparsholt, Winchester, SO21 2LR. Mr & Mrs Richard Morse, 07774 863004, chrissiemorse7@gmail.com. *3½m NW of Winchester. Off A3049 Stockbridge Rd, onto Woodman Lane, signed Sparsholt. Turn L at 1st cottage on L, white with blue gables, at top of drive.* **Visits by arrangement Feb to Oct for groups of 10+. Adm £10, chd free. Tea, coffee & cake included. Wine & canapés provided for evening visitors.**
Flowering cherry trees, statuesque copper beech and tulip trees grace the sweeping lawns at The Deane House (not open), leading the eye to the landscape beyond. This spacious garden entices you to meander from one level to another. The walled garden is best in June when the heady perfume of roses fills the air. Stained glass and modern water features abound. Modern naturalist planting. Water sculpture formerly seen at the Chelsea Flower Show. Sorry No Dogs. Although the garden is on the side of a hill there is always a path to avoid steps.

30 DIPLEY MILL
Dipley Road, Hartley Wintney, Hook, RG27 8JP. Miss Rose McMonigall, www.dipley-mill.co.uk. *2m NE of Hook. Turn E off B3349 at Mattingley (1½m N of Hook) signed Hartley Wintney, West Green & Dipley. Dipley Mill ½m on L just over bridge.* **Suns 31 May, 14 June, 19 July, 2 Aug; 6, 27 Sept (2-5.30). Adm £6, chd free. Cream teas.** Donation to St Michael's Hospice.
A romantic adventure awaits as you wander by the meandering streams surrounding this Domesday Book listed mill! Explore many magical areas, such as the rust garden, the pill box grotto and the ornamental courtyard, or just escape into wild meadows. Alpacas. 'One of the most beautiful gardens in Hampshire' according to Alan Titchmarsh in his TV programme Love Your Garden. Featured on BBC TV and other press

coverage as a result of a show garden at Hampton Court for Turismo De Galicia and the Spanish Tourist Office. Regret, no dogs.

31 THE DOWER HOUSE
Springvale Road, Headbourne Worthy, Winchester, SO23 7LD. Mrs Judith Lywood, 01962 882848, hannahlomax@ thedowerhousewinchester.co.uk, www.thedowerhousewinchester. co.uk. *2m N of Winchester. Entrance is directly opp watercress beds in Springvale Rd & near Cobbs Farm Shop & Kitchen. Parking at main entrance to house, following path to garden.* **Sun 28 June (2.30-5). Adm £4.50, chd free. Home-made teas. Visits also by arrangement May to Sept for groups of 10 to 30.**
The Dower House is set within 5½ acres of gardens with meandering paths allowing easy access around the grounds. There are plenty of places to sit, relax and enjoy the surroundings. Areas of interest incl a scented border, iris bed, geranium bed, shrubbery, a pond populated with fish and water lilies, bog garden, bluebell wood and secret courtyard garden.

32 DOWN FARM HOUSE
Whitchurch, RG28 7FB. Pat & Steve Jones, 01256 892490, patthehound@gmail.com. *1½m from the centre of Whitchurch. From the centre of Whitchurch take the Newbury road up the hill, over railway bridge & after approx 1m turn L over the A34, after 300 metres turn L along bridleway.* **Visits by arrangement Mar to Sept for groups of 10+. Space for small coaches only. Adm £5, chd free. Home-made teas.**
Step back in time in this 2 acre garden, created from an old walled farmyard and the surrounding land. Many of the original features are used as hard landscaping, incl organic vegetables, succulents, alpine bed created from the old concrete capped well, informal and naturalistic planting, wooded area and orchard. The garden has been created slowly over the last 36 yrs. New small stumpery in 2019. Wheelchair access by gravel drive onto lawn.

33 THE DOWN HOUSE

Itchen Abbas, SO21 1AX. Jackie & Mark Porter, 01962 791054, markstephenporter@gmail.com, www.thedownhouse.co.uk. *5m E of Winchester on B3047. 5th house on R after the Itchen Abbas village sign if coming on B3047 from Kings Worthy. 400yds on L after Plough Pub if coming on B3047 from Alresford.* **Sun 16 Feb (1-4). Adm £5, chd free. Home-made teas. Visits also by arrangement in Feb for groups of 20+. Pre-payment is required for groups.**

A 2 acre garden laid out in rooms overlooking the Itchen Valley, adjoining the Pilgrim's Way with walks to the river. In February come and see the snowdrops, winter aconites and crocus, plus borders of coloured dogwoods, willow stems and white birches. A garden of structure with pleached hornbeams, a rope-lined fountain garden and yew lined avenues, plus a pruned vineyard and a warm tea room!

34 DURMAST HOUSE

Bennetts Lane, Burley, BH24 4AT. Mr & Mrs P E G Daubeney, 01425 402132, philip@daubeney.co.uk, www.durmasthouse.co.uk. *5m SE of Ringwood. Off Burley to Lyndhurst Rd, near White Buck Hotel, C10 road.* **Sun 19 Apr, Sun 21 June (2-5). Adm £5, chd free. Cream teas. Visits also by arrangement Apr to Sept. Talk, tour & tea included in admission.** Donation to Delhi Commonwealth Women's Association Medical Clinic.

Designed by Gertrude Jekyll, Durmast has contrasting hot and cool colour borders, formal rose garden edged with lavender and a long herbaceous border. Many old trees, Victorian rockery and orchard with beautiful spring bulbs. Rare azaleas; Fama, Princeps and Gloria Mundi from Ghent. Features incl new rose bowers with rare French roses; Eleanor Berkeley, Psyche and Reine Olga de Wurtemberg. New Jekyll border with a blue, yellow and white scheme. Many old trees incl Monterey Pine, about 150 yrs old. Wheelchair access on stone and gravel paths.

35 EAST WORLDHAM MANOR

Worldham Hill, East Worldham, Alton, GU34 3AX. Hermione Wood, www.worldham.org. *2m SE of*

Alton on B3004 in East Worldham. Coming from Alton, turn R by village hall, signed car park. **Sat 27, Sun 28, Mon 29 June (2-5). Combined adm with Selborne £6, chd free. Home-made teas.**

A rambling double-walled garden laid out in the 1870s with far-reaching views to the South Downs. Illustrates a substantial Victorian garden with fruit, vegetables and flower borders, rose garden, many shrubs, herbaceous plants, apple and pear orchard and large productive greenhouses. Gravel paths, some naturalised with white foxgloves and campanulas, wind through many parts of the garden. WC at village hall.

36 FAIRBANK

Old Odiham Road, Alton, GU34 4BU. Jane & Robin Lees, 01420 86665, j.lees558@btinternet.com. *1½m N of Alton. From S, past Sixth*

Form College, then 1½m beyond road junction on R. From N, turn L at Golden Pot & then 50yds turn R. Garden 1m on L before road junction. **Visits by arrangement May to Aug for groups of up to 30. Adm £4, chd free. Home-made teas.**

The planting in this large garden reflects our interest in trees, shrubs, fruit and vegetables. A wide variety of herbaceous plants provide colour and are placed in sweeping mixed borders that carry the eye down the long garden to the orchard and beyond. Near the house (not open), there are rose beds and herbaceous borders, as well as a small formal pond. There is a range of acers, ferns and unusual shrubs and 60 different varieties of fruit, along with a large vegetable garden. Wheelchair access with uneven ground in some areas.

Old Swan House

37 FAIRWEATHER'S NURSERY

Hilltop, Beaulieu, SO42 7YR. Patrick Fairweather, 01590 612113, info@fairweathers.co.uk, www.fairweathers.co.uk. *1½ m NE of Beaulieu village. Signed Hilltop Nursery on B3054 between Heath r'about (A326) & Beaulieu village.* Sat 18, Sun 19 July (10-4). Adm £3.50, chd free. Cream teas in Aline Fairweather's garden.

Fairweather's hold a specialist collection of over 400 agapanthus grown in pots and display beds, incl AGM award-winning agapanthus trialled by the RHS. Features incl guided tours of the nursery at 11am and 2pm and demonstrations of how to get the best from agapanthus and companion planting. Agapanthus and a range of other traditional and new perennials for sale. Aline Fairweather's garden (adjacent to the nursery) will also be open, with mixed shrub and perennial borders containing many unusual plants. Also open Patrick's Patch at Fairweather's Garden Centre.

& 🐄 ✳ 🚗 ☕

38 FERNS LODGE

Cottagers Lane, Hordle, Lymington, SO41 0FE. Sue Grant, www.fernslodge.co.uk. *Approx 5½ m W of Lymington. From Silver St turn into Woodcock Lane, 100 metres to Cottagers Lane, parking in field ½ m on L. From A337 turn into Everton Rd & drive approx 1½ m, Cottagers Lane on R.* Sat 30, Sun 31 May (2-5). Adm £3.50, chd free. Home-made teas. Visits also by arrangement Apr to Aug for groups of up to 10.

½ acre of atmospheric cottage garden that wraps itself around a pretty Victorian lodge house (not open) providing a riot of colour and scent. A happy jumble of azalea, lupin, camellia, hydrangea and many foxgloves. Gravelled areas to a terrace, to brick beds, to a gazebo covered with clematis and honeysuckle via winding brick paths, to the 3½ acre Victorian garden in restoration (wellies are a must), started winter 2019. Wildlife abounds! We love our guests to enjoy the many peaceful seating areas around the garden and enjoy our amazing home-made cakes. Wheelchair access to some areas.

& 🐄 ✳ ☕

39 FRITHAM LODGE

Fritham, SO43 7HH. Sir Chris & Lady Powell. *6m N of Lyndhurst. 3m NW of M27 J1 (Cadnam). Follow signs to Fritham.* Sun 14 June (2-4). Adm £4, chd free. Home-made teas.

A walled garden of 1 acre in the heart of the New Forest, set within 18 acres surrounding a house that was originally a Charles 1 hunting lodge (not open). Herbaceous and blue and white mixed borders, pergolas and ponds. A box hedge enclosed parterre of roses, fruit and vegetables. Visitors will enjoy the ponies, donkeys, sheep and old breed hens on their meadow walk to the woodland and stream.

& 🐄 ✳ 🚗 ☕

GROUP OPENING

40 FROYLE GARDENS

Lower Froyle, Froyle, GU34 4LG. www.froyle.com/ngs. *5m NE of Alton. Access to Lower Froyle from A31 between Alton & Farnham at Bentley, or via Upper Froyle at Hen & Chicken Pub, or via B3349 & Golden Pot Pub. Park at recreation ground in Lower Froyle. Map provided.* Sat 6, Sun 7 June (2-6). Combined adm £7.50, chd free. Home-made teas at Froyle Village Hall.

ALDERSEY HOUSE
Nigel & Julie Southern.

NEW 3 BURNHAM SQUARE
Bernie & Vonny Wilks.

DAY COTTAGE
Nick & Corinna Whines, www.daycottage.co.uk.

MANOR COTTAGE
Russell Pearn & Victoria Spearing.

OLD BREWERY HOUSE
Vivienne & John Sexton.

WARREN COTTAGE
Gillian & Jonathan Pickering.

WELL LANE CORNER
Mark & Sue Lelliott.

You will certainly receive a warm welcome as Froyle Gardens open their gates this year, enabling visitors to enjoy a wide variety of gardens, which have undergone development since last year and will be looking splendid. Froyle is a beautiful village with many old and interesting buildings, our gardens harmonise well with the surrounding landscape and most have spectacular views. The gardens themselves are diverse with rich planting. You will see greenhouses, water features, vegetables, roses, clematis and wildflower meadows, as well as a gem of a courtyard garden. Lots of ideas to take away with you, along with plants for sale. The delicious teas served in the village hall are famous and there is also a plant stall. Close by there is a children's playground with a zip wire and climbing frame where younger visitors can let off steam. The main parking area is at the recreation ground, close to the village hall in Lower Froyle. Additional signed parking in Upper Froyle. In conjunction with Froyle Open Gardens there is an exhibition of richly decorated historic vestments to be held in St Mary's Church, Upper Froyle GU34 4LB (separate donation). Parking by the church (Sun only). No wheelchair access to Day Cottage and Manor Cottage. Gravel area at Warren Cottage with access on request.

& 🐄 ✳ 🚗 ☕

41 GILBERTS DAHLIA FIELD

Gilberts Nursery, Dandysford Lane, Sherfield English, nr Romsey, SO51 6DT. Nick & Helen Gilbert, www.gilbertsdahlias.co.uk. *Midway between Romsey & Whiteparish on A27, in Sherfield English Village. From Romsey 4th turn on L, just before small petrol station on R, visible from main road.* Sun 30 Aug (10-4). Adm £3, chd free. Light refreshments.

This may not be a garden, but do come and be amazed by the sight of over 300 varieties of dahlias in our dedicated 1½ acre field. Prize-winning blooms are in all colours, shapes and sizes and can be closely inspected from wheelchair friendly hard grass paths. An inspiration for all gardeners.

& 🐄 ✳ ☕

We help ordinary people open the gates to their extraordinary private gardens to raise impressive amounts of money through admissions, teas and slices of cake!

42 HAMBLEDON HOUSE

East Street, Hambledon,
PO7 4RX. Capt & Mrs David
Hart Dyke, 02392 632380,
dianahartdyke@gmail.com. *8m SW
of Petersfield, 5m NW of Waterlooville.
In village centre, driveway leading
to house in East St. Do not go up
Speltham Hill even if advised by
SatNav.* **Visits by arrangement Apr
to Oct for groups of 5+.**
3 acre partly walled plantsman's
garden for all seasons. Large
borders filled with a wide variety
of unusual shrubs and perennials
with imaginative plant combinations
culminating in a profusion of colour
in late summer. Hidden, secluded
areas reveal surprise views of garden
and village rooftops. Planting a large
central area, which started in 2011,
has given the garden an exciting new
dimension. Partial wheelchair access
as garden is on several levels.

43 HANGING HOSTA GARDEN

Narra, Frensham Lane, Lindford,
Bordon, GU35 0QJ. June Colley
& John Baker, 01420 489186,
hanginghostas@btinternet.com.
*Approx 1m E of Bordon. From the
A325 at Bordon take the B3002,
then B3004 to Lindford. Turn L into
Frensham Lane, 3rd house on L.*
**Visits by arrangement Mon 29
June to Sun 5 July for groups of
up to 20. Adm £3.50, chd free.**
This garden is packed with almost
2000 plants. The collection of
over 1700 hosta cultivars is one
of the largest in England. Hostas
are displayed at eye level to give a
wonderful tapestry of foliage and
colour. Islamic garden, waterfall and
stream garden, cottage garden. Talks
given to garden clubs.

44 108 HEATH ROAD

Petersfield, GU31 4EL. Mrs
Karen Llewelyn, 01730 269541,
k.llewelyn@btinternet.com. *A3 N & S
take A272 exit signed Midhurst. Take
1st exit from r'about, 1st R into Pullens
Lane (B2199) & then the 6th road on
R into Heath Rd.* **Sun 7 June, Sun 13
Sept (2-5.30). Adm £3.50, chd free.
Home-made teas. Visits also by
arrangement June to Sept.**
²⁄₃ acre garden close to town centre
and Heath Pond. Greenhouse and
succulent collection. Tropical plants,
acers, small woodland walk. 30 metre
long border with shade loving plants
including many hostas and ferns. Patio

garden, seasonal pots and late summer
herbaceous border. Newly planted
driveway borders. Wheelchair access
after a 5 metre sloping gravel drive.

45 NEW HECKFIELD PLACE

Heckfield, RG27 0LD. Heckfield
Management Ltd, 01189 326868,
enquiries@heckfieldplace.com,
www.heckfieldplace.com. *9m S
of Reading. 4½m NW of Hartley
Wintney on B3011. Two car parks,
signed on the day.* **Wed 20 May,
Wed 3 June (2-5.30). Adm £8,
chd under 12 free. Pre-booking
essential, please visit www.ngs.
org.uk/events for information &
booking. Home-made teas in the
sun house of the walled garden.**
Heckfield Place is a hotel on a
438 acre estate with an original
1927 NGS garden, now reopening
with walled garden and pleasure
grounds, including two lakes and
arboretum. Both tamed and gently
wild, the garden was created by Head
Gardener William Walker Wildsmith
in the C19 and has been lovingly
restored through yrs of diligent work.
To book optional 30 min tour of
the walled garden at 2pm or 3pm
(30 tickets per tour), go to 'Events'
page at www.ngs.org.uk (additional
charge). Home-made teas including
dairy, nut and gluten free options £4
(cash on the day only). Wheelchair
access to the upper walled garden on
gravel pathway. No dogs please.

46 NEW HECKFIELD PLACE - THE MARKET GARDEN

Hook, RG27 0LD. Heckfield
Management Ltd, 01189 326868,
enquiries@heckfieldplace.com,
www.heckfieldplace.com. *Please
use the postcode RG27 0LA for the
Market Garden; which is approached
from Bramshill Road, near Heckfield
Place. Parking in field, signed on the
day.* **Sat 5 Sept (2-5.30). Adm £8,
chd under 12 free. Pre-booking
essential, please visit www.ngs.
org.uk/events for information &
booking. Home-made teas.**
Heckfield Home Farm is a living
landscape, a part of Heckfield Place
estate and provides the produce
for the hotel and restaurants. The
5 acre Market Garden is farmed
following bio-dynamic principles and
incl extensive vegetable and flower
beds, glasshouses and polytunnels.
There is also an orchard with 500 fruit
trees, incl quince and apple, and is

surrounded by cattle, sheep, chicken
and bees. To book optional 30 min
tour at 2pm or 3pm (30 tickets per
tour), go to 'Events' page at www.ngs.
org.uk (additional charge). Home-
made teas including dairy, nut and
gluten free options £4 (cash on the day
only). Partial wheelchair access with
gravel path around the market garden
and glasshouses. No dogs please.

47 HINTON ADMIRAL

Lyndhurst Road, Hinton,
Christchurch, BH23 7DY. Sir
George & Lady Meyrick. *4m NE
of Christchurch. On N side of A35,
¾m E of Cat & Fiddle Pub.* **Sun 17
May (1-4.30). Adm £7, chd free.
Donation to Julia's House Childrens
Hospice.**
Magnificent 20 acre garden within
a much larger estate, now being
restored and developed. Mature
plantings of deciduous azaleas
and rhododendrons amidst a sea
of bluebells. Wandering paths lead
through rockeries and beside ponds
and a stream with many cascades.
Orchids appear in the large lawns.
The two walled gardens are devoted
to herbs and wild flowers and a very
large greenhouse. The terrace and
rock garden were designed by Harold
Peto. Wheelchair access over gravel
paths and some steps.

48 THE HOMESTEAD

Northney Road, Hayling
Island, PO11 0NF. Stan &
Mary Pike, 02392 464888,
jhomestead@aol.com,
www.homesteadhayling.co.uk.
*3m S of Havant. From A27 Havant &
Hayling Island r'about, travel S over
Langstone Bridge & turn immed L
into Northney Rd. Car park entrance
on R after Langstone Hotel.* **Sun 9
Aug (2-5.30). Adm £4, chd free.
Home-made teas. Visits also by
arrangement June to Sept for
groups of 10+.**
1¼ acre garden surrounded by working
farmland with views to Butser Hill and
boats in Chichester Harbour. Trees,
shrubs, colourful herbaceous borders
and small walled garden with herbs,
vegetables and trained fruit trees. Large
pond and woodland walk with shade-
loving plants. A quiet and peaceful
atmosphere with plenty of seats to
enjoy the vistas within the garden and
beyond. New planting where shrubs
have become overgrown and tired, have
enabled us to experiment with new

plant combinations. We have recently constructed a look-out platform to provide different views of the garden. Wheelchair access with some gravel paths.

 ♿ 🐕 🌼 🚐 ☕

49 ◆ THE HOSPITAL OF ST CROSS

St Cross Road, Winchester, SO23 9SD. The Hospital of St Cross & Almshouse of Noble Poverty, 01962 851375, porter@hospitalofstcross.co.uk, www.hospitalofstcross.co.uk. ½ m S of Winchester. From city centre take B3335 (Southgate St & St Cross Rd) S. Turn L immed before The Bell Pub. If on foot follow riverside path S from Cathedral & College, approx 20 mins. **For NGS: Sun 12 July (2-5). Adm £4, chd free. Home-made teas in the Hundred Men's Hall in the Outer Quadrangle. For other opening times and information, please phone, email or visit garden website.**
The Medieval Hospital of St Cross nestles in water meadows beside the River Itchen and is one of England's oldest almshouses. The tranquil, walled Master's Garden, created in the late C17 by Bishop Compton, now contains colourful herbaceous borders, old fashioned roses, interesting trees and a large fish pond. The Compton Garden has unusual plants of the type he imported when Bishop of London. Wheelchair access, but surfaces are uneven in places.

 ♿ 🌼 ☕

50 THE HOUSE IN THE WOOD

Beaulieu, SO42 7YN. Victoria Roberts. New Forest. 8m NE of Lymington. Leaving the entrance to Beaulieu Motor Museum on R (B3056), take next R signed Ipley Cross. Take 2nd gravel drive on RH-bend, approx ½ m. **Sun 10 May (2-5). Adm £5, chd free. Cream teas.**
Peaceful 12 acre woodland garden with continuing progress and improvement. Very much a spring garden with tall mature azaleas and rhododendrons interspersed with acers and other woodland wonders. A magical garden to get lost in with many twisting paths leading downhill to a pond and a more formal layout of lawns around the house (not open). Used in the war to train the Special Operations Executive. Partial wheelchair access.

 🐕 🚐 ☕

51 THE ISLAND

Greatbridge, Romsey, SO51 0HP. Mr & Mrs Christopher Saunders-Davies. 1m N of Romsey on A3057. Entrance alongside Greatbridge (1st bridge Xing the River Test), flanked by row of cottages on roadside. **Sat 18, Sun 19 Apr, Sat 4, Sun 5 July (2-5). Adm £5, chd free. Home-made teas.**
6 acres either side of the River Test. Fine display of paeonies, wisteria and spring flowering trees. Main garden has herbaceous and annual borders, fruit trees, rose pergola, lavender walk and extensive lawns. An arboretum planted in the 1930s by Sir Harold Hillier contains trees and shrubs providing interest throughout the yr. Please Note: No Dogs Allowed.

 ♿ 🌼 ☕

52 LAKE HOUSE

Northington, SO24 9TG. Lord Ashburton, 07795 364539, lake.house.gardenvisits@gmail.com. 4m N of Alresford. Off B3046. Follow English Heritage signs to The Grange, and then to Lake House. **Thur 11, Sun 14 June (12.30-5). Adm £5, chd free. Home-made teas. Visits also by arrangement May to Oct for groups of 10+.**
Two large lakes in Candover Valley set off by mature woodland with waterfalls, abundant birdlife, long landscaped vistas and folly. 1½ acre walled garden with rose parterre, mixed borders, long herbaceous border, rose pergola leading to moongate. Flowering pots, conservatory and greenhouses. Picnicking by lakes. Grass paths and slopes to some areas of the garden.

 ♿ 🐕 🌼 🚐 ☕

53 LITTLE COURT

Crawley, Winchester, SO21 2PU. Mrs A R Elkington, 01962 776365, elkslc@btinternet.com. 5m NW of Winchester. Between B3049 (Winchester - Stockbridge) & A272 (Winchester - Andover) 400yds from either pond or church. **Sun 16, Mon 17, Sun 23, Mon 24 Feb (2-5); Sun 22 Mar, Sat 23, Sun 24 May, Sun 7, Mon 8 June (2-5.30). Adm £5, chd free. Home-made teas in Crawley Village Hall. 2021: Sun 14, Mon 15, Sun 21, Mon 22 Feb. Opening with Crawley Gardens on Fri 10, Mon 13 Apr. Visits also by arrangement Feb to Aug. Coaches park by church please.**
This walled sheltered garden has naturalised crocuses in the apple

orchard, large and small herbaceous borders in harmonious colours and unusual plants with touches of humour. There is a traditional kitchen garden, colourful bantams running free, a tree house and a south facing natural wildlife field. Many seats with good views both within the garden and to the surrounding farmland. A garden for all seasons and ages. Regional Finalist, The English Garden's The Nation's Favourite Gardens 2019.

 ♿ 🌼 🚐 ☕

54 LITTLE CROFT

Church Grove, Fleet, GU51 4LA. Graham & Pauline Bowyer, graham.bowyer@me.com. Less than ½ m from Fleet town centre. When entering Fleet from M3 J4A, turn R into Church Rd. Where the road bends to the L, turn L into Church Grove. Little Croft is the 2nd house on the L. **Visits by arrangement from 15 April to 13 May only for groups of 10 to 30. Adm £4, chd free.**
A garden with features inspired by Japanese garden design principles. There are 3 main Japanese style features; a pond and stream garden, a tea garden with stepping stone pathway leading to an arbour and a dry stone garden. Home-made teas £3 per person by prior request.

☕

55 LITTLE OWLS

27 Russell Road, Lee-on-the-Solent, PO13 9HR. Kerry & Neil Littleales, 07727 657246, kerrylittleales@outlook.com. 4½ m S of Fareham. From Fareham on B3385 follow signs for Lee-on-the-Solent. Continue S past The Bun Penny Pub on L. Turn L after pub into Grove Rd & L again into Russell Rd. **Sun 14, Sun 28 June, Sun 12 July (11-4). Adm £3, chd free. Home-made teas & gluten free cake. Visits also by arrangement June & July for groups of 5 to 30. Weekdays & evenings only.**
Come and see unusual plants, exuberant colour, newts in the pond, driftwood from our beach, chimney pots full of hostas, the piano dining table, a naturally styled bonsai collection and new for this year, our rose walk ending in a newly planted shabby shack area. And all this fits into a suburban 40ft garden! There are quirky recycled pieces created by the owners and unique craft items on display for viewing and sale. NGS quilt on display.

🌼 ☕

56 LONGSTOCK PARK

Leckford, Stockbridge, SO20 6EH. Leckford Estate Ltd, part of John Lewis Partnership, www.leckfordestate.co.uk. *4m S of Andover. From Leckford village on A3057 towards Andover, cross the river bridge & take 1st turning to the L signed Longstock.* **Sun 21 June (1-4). Adm £7, chd £2.**
Famous water garden with extensive collection of aquatic and bog plants set in 7 acres of woodland with rhododendrons and azaleas. A walk through the park leads to National Collections of *Buddleja* and *Clematis viticella*; arboretum and herbaceous border at Longstock Park Nursery. Refreshments at Longstock Park Farm Shop and Nursery (last orders at 3.30pm). Assistance dogs only. Regret no card facilities at water garden.

57 LOWER MILL

Mill Lane, Longparish, Andover, SP11 6PS. Mrs K-M Dinesen. *Off A303 from the W signed Longparish B3048 & from the E signed Barton Stacey, then Longparish.* **Sun 13 Sept (1-5). Adm £5, chd free. Home-made teas.**
Set in 15 acres of informally planted gardens, magnificent trees and water are but two features of this widely anticipated re-opening. Stunning late summer and winter beds complement the existing array of grasses, perennials and shrubs leading to a captivating lake surrounded by wild flowers. A hidden sunken garden, tranquil riverside walks, a delightful water garden and much more, await your discovery. Limited wheelchair access.

58 26 LOWER NEWPORT ROAD

Aldershot, GU12 4QD. Mr & Mrs P Myles. *From the A331 coming off at the Aldershot junction, head towards Aldershot. Take the 1st R turn at the T-lights next to McDonalds into North Lane & then 1st L into Lower Newport Rd.* **Sat 27, Sun 28 June (11-4). Adm £3, chd free. Light refreshments.**
A 'T' shaped small town garden full of ideas, split into four distinct sections; a semi-enclosed patio area with pots and water feature; a free-form lawn with a tree fern, perennials, bulbs and shrubs and 130 varieties of hosta; secret garden with a 20ft x 6ft raised pond, exotic planting backdrop and

African carvings; and a potager garden with a selection of vegetable, roses and plant storage.

59 ◆ MACPENNYS WOODLAND GARDEN & NURSERIES

Burley Road, Bransgore, Christchurch, BH23 8DB. Mr & Mrs T M Lowndes, 01425 672348, office@macpennys.co.uk, www.macpennys.co.uk. *6m S of Ringwood, 5m NE of Christchurch. From Crown Pub Xrds in Bransgore take Burley Rd, following sign for Thorney Hill & Burley. Entrance ¼m on R.* **For opening times and information, please phone, email or visit garden website.**
4 acre woodland garden originating from worked out gravel pits in the 1950s, offering interest yr-round, but particularly in spring and autumn. Attached to a large nursery that offers for sale a wide selection of home-grown trees, shrubs, conifers, perennials, hedging plants, fruit trees and bushes. Tearoom offering home-made cakes, afternoon tea (pre-booking required) and light lunches using locally sourced produce wherever possible. Nursery closed Christmas through to the New Year. Partial wheelchair access on grass and gravel paths which can be bumpy with tree roots and muddy in winter.

60 MANOR LODGE

Brook Lane, Botley, Southampton, SO30 2ER. Gary & Janine Stone. *6m E of Southampton. From A334 to the W of Botley village centre, turn into Brook Lane. Manor Lodge is ½m on the R. Limited disabled parking. Continue past Manor Lodge to parking (signed).* **Sat 4, Sun 5 July (2-5). Adm £3.50, chd free. Home-made teas.**
Close to Manor Farm Country Park, this mid-Victorian house (not open), set in over 1½ acres is the garden of an enthusiastic plantswoman. A garden in evolution with established areas and new projects, a mixture of informal and formal planting, woodland and wildflower meadow areas. There are large established and new specimen trees, common and exotic perennials, planting combinations for extended seasonal interest. Largely flat with hard paving, but some gravel and grass to access all areas.

61 MEON ORCHARD

Kingsmead, North of Wickham, PO17 5AU. Doug & Linda Smith, 01329 833253, meonorchard@btinternet.com. *5m N of Fareham. From Wickham take A32 N for 1½m. Turn L at Roebuck Inn. Garden in ½m. Park on verge or in field N of property.* **Sun 31 May, Sun 26 July, Sun 6 Sept (2-6). Adm £6, chd free. Home-made teas.**
2 acre garden designed and constructed by current owners. An exceptional range of rare, unusual and architectural plants incl National Collection of Eucalyptus. Dramatic foliage plants from around the world, see plants you have never seen before! Flowering shrubs in May and June; perennials in July; bananas, tree ferns, cannas, gingers, palms dominate in Sept; and streams and ponds, plus an extensive range of planters complete the display. Visitors are welcome to explore the 20 acre meadow and ½m of Meon River frontage attached to the garden. Extra big plant sale of the exotic and rare on Sun 6 Sept. Garden fully accessible by wheelchair, reserved parking.

62 MERDON MANOR

Merdon Castle Lane, Hursley, Winchester, SO21 2JJ. Mr & Mrs J C Smith, 01962 775215, vronk@fastmail.com. *5m SW of Winchester. From A3090 Winchester to Romsey road, turn R at Standon, onto Merdon Castle Lane. Proceed for 1¼m. Entrance on R between 2 curving brick walls.* **Visits by arrangement May to Sept for groups of up to 30. Adm £6, chd free. Home-made teas.**
5 acre country garden surrounded by panoramic views; pond with ducks, damsel flies, dragonflies and water lilies; large wisteria, roses, fruit-bearing lemon trees, extensive lawns, impressive yew hedges and small secret walled garden with fountains. Black Hebridean sheep (St. Kildas). Very tranquil and quiet. Wheelchairs have to go down a drive to reach the sunken garden.

63 OAK TREE COTTAGE

Upper Common Road, Pennington, Lymington, SO41 8LD. Sue Kent, Sue.kent9@btinternet.com. *2m NW of Lymington. From N off A337, turn into Sway Rd, 1½m to Wheel Inn.*

Weir House

© Leigh Clapp

Turn L into Ramley Rd & follow signs. Leave M27 J2 & follow Heavy Lorry Route to avoid traffic in Lyndhurst. **Sat 6, Sun 7 June (2-5). Adm £4, chd free. Home-made teas. Visits also by arrangement May to July for groups of 20 to 30.**
As it matures this 1½ acre garden has a wealth of surprises round every corner, but with continuity. Using a limited palette of plants with repetition of blue and silver, it flows from one secluded space to another. Designed with a gentle variation of levels and using many silver birch trees, contrasting foliage and flowers, one can become delightfully lost.

64 5 OAKFIELDS
Boyatt Wood, Eastleigh, SO50 4RP. Martin & Margaret Ward. *M3 J12, follow signs to Eastleigh. 3rd exit at r'about into Woodside Ave, 2nd R into Bosville, 2nd R onto Boyatt Lane, 1st R to Porchester Rise & 1st L into Oakfields.* **Sat 20, Sun 21 June (2-5). Adm £3.50, chd free. Home-made teas.**
A ⅓ acre garden full of interesting and unusual plants with predominately woodland beds of rhododendrons, various species of foxgloves and aquilegia. A pond with rockery, water cascade and flower beds formed from the intermittent winter streams, accommodate

moisture loving plants. Mixed herbaceous border and a collection of shrub and pillar roses with a backdrop of impressive ramblers in the trees. Wheelchair access over hard paths and some gravel.

65 OLD CAMPS
Newbury Road, Headley, Thatcham, RG19 8LG. Mr & Mrs Adam & Heidi Vetere, 07720 449702, gardens@oldcamps.co.uk, www.oldcamps.co.uk. *Directions for Open Weekend only: Turn off the A339 into Galley Lane & after 100yds turn L into Plumtrees Farm. Follow the concrete road to the car park (signed). Walk 400yds to garden.* **Sat 1, Sun 2 Aug (10-5). Adm £7, chd free. Home-made teas. BBQ cooked burgers are served from 11-2 (weather permitting). Visits also by arrangement June to Sept for groups of 20+. For parking details and directions see garden website.**
As featured on Gardeners' World, a breathtaking garden set over an acre, which benefits from panoramic views of Watership Down. Surprises await, ranging from traditional herbaceous borders through desert/prairie planting, an enchanted knot garden, potager to exuberant subtropical schemes; featuring bananas, cannas, hedychiums and more. New additions

include the Ravine Garden and Orto. The garden is built on the site of a Roman Camp and Bath House. Partial wheelchair access. Non-disabled WC, though there is enough room for a wheelchair.

66 THE OLD RECTORY
East Woodhay, Newbury, RG20 0AL. David & Victoria Wormsley, 07801 418976, victoria@wormsley.net. *6m SW of Newbury. Turn off A343 between Newbury & Highclere to Woolton Hill. Turn L to East End, continue ¾m beyond East End. Turn R, garden opp St Martin's Church.* **Visits by arrangement for groups of 20+. Adm £10, chd free. Home-made teas.**
A classic English country garden of about 2 acres surrounding a Regency former rectory (not open). Formal lawns and terrace provide tranquil views over parkland. A large walled garden with grass paths, full of interesting herbaceous plants including topiary, roses and unusual perennials. A Mediterranean pool garden, wildflower meadow and fruit garden. Explore and enjoy.

67 OLD SWAN HOUSE
High Street, Stockbridge, SO20 6EU. Mr Herry Lawford. *9m W of Winchester on the A30. The garden is accessed from Recreation Ground Lane which runs off the eastern end of the High St, next to the Framing Shop.* **Every Tue 7 July to 28 July (1.30-5). Adm £4, chd free. Home-made teas. Opening with Stockbridge Gardens on Thur 11, Sun 14 June.**
This town garden is designed around seven areas defined by the sun at different times of the day. Planting is modern perennial with euphorbias, rosemary and box used extensively. Particular interest is provided by a grass and gravel garden and a small wildflower meadow. There is an ancient hazel under a brick and flint wall, a loggia hung with creeper, an orchard and a pond.

& 🐕 ☕

GROUP OPENING

68 OLD THATCH & THE MILLENNIUM BARN
Sprats Hatch Lane, Winchfield, Hook, RG27 8DD. *3m W of Fleet. 1½m E of Winchfield Station, follow NGS signs. Sprats Hatch Lane is opp the Barley Mow Pub. Public car park at Barley Mow slipway is ½m from garden. Parking in field next to Old Thatch, if dry, disabled on-site. Park info: www.old-thatch.co.uk.* **Sun 7 June, Sun 6 Sept (2-6). Combined adm £4.50, chd free. Home-made teas. Pimms if hot & mulled wine if cool.**

THE MILLENNIUM BARN
Mr & Mrs G Carter.

OLD THATCH
Jill Ede, www.old-thatch.co.uk.

Who could resist visiting Old Thatch, a chocolate box thatched cottage (not open), featured on film and TV, a smallholding with a 5 acre garden and woodland alongside the Basingstoke Canal (unfenced). A succession of spring bulbs, a profusion of wild flowers, perennials and homegrown annuals pollinated by our own bees and fertilised by the donkeys, who await your visit. Over 30 named clematis and rose cultivars. Children enjoy our garden quiz, adults enjoy tea and home-made cakes. Arrive by narrow boat! Trips on 'John Pinkerton' may stop at Old Thatch on NGS days www.basingstoke-canal.org.uk. Also Accessible Boating shuttle available from Barley Mow wharf, approx every 45 mins. Signed parking for Blue Badge holders: please use entrance by the red telephone box. Paved paths and grass slopes give access to the whole garden.

& 🐕 ❀ ☕

69 ♦ PATRICK'S PATCH
Fairweather's Garden Centre, High Street, Beaulieu, SO42 7YB. Patrick Fairweather, 01590 612307, info@fairweathers.co.uk, www.fairweathers.co.uk. *SE of New Forest at head of Beaulieu River. Leave M27 at J2 & follow signs for Beaulieu Motor Museum. Go up High St & park in Fairweather's on LH-side.* **For opening times and information, please phone, email or visit garden website.**
Model kitchen garden with a full range of vegetables, trained top and soft fruit and herbs. Salads in succession used as an educational project for all ages. Maintained by volunteers, primary school children and a head gardener. We run a series of fun educational gardening sessions for children as well as informal workshops for adults. Open daily by donation from dawn to dusk. Wheelchair access on gravelled site.

& ❀ ☕

Warren Cottage, Froyle Gardens

70 PILLEY HILL COTTAGE
Pilley Hill, Pilley, Lymington, SO41 5QF. **Steph & Sandy Glen, 01590 677844, stephglen@hotmail.co.uk.** *New Forest. 2m N of Lymington off A337. To avoid traffic delays in Lyndhurst leave M27 at J2 & follow Heavy Lorry Route.* Sat 28, Sun 29 Mar, Sat 18, Sun 19 Apr (2-5). Adm £3, chd free. Cream teas. **Visits also by arrangement Mar & Apr.**
Pilley Hill Cottage garden changes constantly through the seasons. Entering through the creeper covered lych gate, the garden reveals itself via winding pathways with surprises around every corner. Dogwood, cornus and ghost bramble supply spring structure. Gnarled fruit trees provide shelter for bulbs and wild flowers are making a welcome debut. Steph will be giving a demonstration of spring bulb propagation at 3pm on each open day, a particular interest to those who may wish to increase their stock of snowdrops. Some slippery slopes. Visitors with wheelchairs have managed our garden, so please phone to discuss.

71 NEW 1 POVEY'S COTTAGE
Stoney Heath, Baughurst, Tadley, RG26 5SN. **Jonathan & Sheila Richards.** *Between villages of Ramsdell & Baughurst, 10 mins drive from Basingstoke. Take A339 out of Basingstoke, direction Newbury. Turn R off A339 towards Ramsdell, then 4m to Stoneyheath. Pass under overhead power cables, take next turn L into unmade road. Povey's 1st R.* Sat 6, Sun 7 June, Sat 4, Sun 5 July (11-5). Adm £4, chd free. Home-made teas.
Herbaceous borders, wild flowers, trees and shrubs and a small orchard, greenhouses, fruit cage and a vegetable garden. Beehives in one corner of the garden and chickens in another corner. A feature of the garden is an unusual natural swimming pond. Mostly wheelchair friendly, across flat grassed areas, but no hard pathways. WC available.

72 PYLEWELL PARK
South Baddesley, Lymington, SO41 5SJ. **Lord Teynham.** *Coast road 2m E of Lymington. From Lymington follow signs for Car Ferry to Isle of Wight, continue for 2m to South Baddesley.* Sun 12 Apr, Sun 24 May (2-5). Adm £5, chd free.
A large parkland garden laid out in 1890.

Enjoy a walk along the extensive informal grass and moss paths, bordered by fine rhododendron, magnolia and azalea. Wild daffodils bloom at Easter and bluebells in May. Large lakes are bordered by giant gunnera. Magnificent swans! Distant views of the Isle of Wight across the Solent. Lovely for families and dogs. Bring your own tea or picnic and wellingtons! Old glasshouses and other out buildings are not open to visitors. Wear suitable footwear for muddy areas.

73 REDENHAM PARK HOUSE
Redenham Park, Andover, SP11 9AQ. **Lady Olivia Clark, 01264 772511, oliviaclark@redenhampark.co.uk.** *Approx 1½m from Weyhill on the A342 Andover to Ludgershall road.* Wed 16, Thur 17 Sept (2.30-4.30). Adm £6, chd free. Home-made teas in the thatched pool house. **Visits also by arrangement June to mid-July and mid-Sept to mid-Oct only for groups of 10 to 30.**
Redenham Park built in 1784. The garden sits behind the house (not open). The formal rose garden is planted with white flowered roses. Steps lead up to the main herbaceous borders which peak in late summer. A calm green interlude, a gate opens into gardens with espaliered pears, apples, mass of scented roses, shrubs and perennial planting surrounds the swimming pool. A door opens onto a kitchen garden.

GROUP OPENING

74 ROMSEY GARDENS
Town Centre, Romsey, SO51 8LD. *All gardens are within walking distance of each other & are clearly signed. Use Lortemore Place public car park (SO51 8LD), free on Sundays & BH.* Sun 24, Mon 25 May (10.30-4). Combined adm £6, chd free.

KING JOHN'S GARDEN
Friends of King John's Garden & Test Valley Borough, www.facebook.com/ KingJohnsGarden/.

4 MILL LANE
Miss J Flindall, 01794 513926. **Visits also by arrangement May to Sept. Combined with Old Thatched Cottage.**

THE NELSON COTTAGE
Margaret Prosser.

OLD THATCHED COTTAGE
Genevieve & Derek Langford, derek.langford33@ googlemail.com. **Visits also by arrangement May to Sept. Combined opening with 4 Mill Lane.**

Romsey is a small, unspoilt, historic market town with the majestic C12 Norman Abbey as a backdrop to 4 Mill Lane, a garden described by Joe Swift as 'the best solution for a long thin garden with a view'. King John's Garden with its fascinating listed C13 house (not open Sun), has all period plants that were available before 1700; it also has an award-winning Victorian garden with a courtyard (no dogs, please). The C15 Old Thatched Cottage (not open) has a cottage garden with hollyhocks, wisteria and roses; it features a variety of shrubs, vegetable patch, fruit cordons, rockery, water features and gazebo. The Nelson Cottage was formally a pub; the ½ acre garden has a variety of perennial plants and shrubs with a wild grass meadow bringing the countryside into the town. No wheelchair access at 4 Mill Lane.

75 SELBORNE
Caker Lane, East Worldham, Alton, GU34 3AE. **Brian & Mary Jones, www.worldham.org.** *2m SE of Alton. On B3004 at Alton end of the village of East Worldham, near The Three Horseshoes Pub. Please note: 'Selborne' is the name of the house, it is not in the village of Selborne. Parking signed.* Sat 16, Sun 17, Mon 18 May (2-5). Adm £4, chd free. Sat 27, Sun 28, Mon 29 June (2-5). Combined adm with East Worldham Manor £6, chd free. Sat 1, Sun 2, Mon 3 Aug (2-5). Adm £4, chd free. Home-made teas in the orchard with plenty of seating.
This much-loved ½ acre mature cottage-style garden provides visitors with surprises around every corner. Views across farmland. Productive 60 yr old orchard of named varieties, densely-planted borders, shrubs and climbers, especially clematis. Metal and stone sculptures enhance the borders. Bug mansion. Enjoy tea in the shade of the orchard. Summerhouses and conservatory provide shelter. Book stall, garden quizzes for children and a sandpit for small children. Wheelchair access with some gravel paths.

76 SHALDEN PARK HOUSE
The Avenue, Shalden, Alton,
GU34 4DS. Mr & Mrs Michael
Campbell. 4½m NW of Alton.
B3349 from Alton or M3 J5 onto
B3349. Turn W at Golden Pot Pub
marked Herriard, Lasham, Shalden.
Entrance ¼m on L. Disabled parking
on entry. **Sun 14 June (2-5). Adm
£4.50, chd free. Home-made teas.**
Large 4 acre garden to stroll around with
beautiful views. Herbaceous borders incl
kitchen walk and rose garden, all with
large-scale planting and foliage interest.
Pond, arboretum, perfect kitchen
garden and garden statuary.

**77 ♦ SIR HAROLD HILLIER
GARDENS**
Jermyns Lane, Ampfield,
Romsey, SO51 0QA. Hampshire
County Council, 01794 369318,
info.hilliers@hants.gov.uk,
www.hants.gov.uk/hilliergardens.
2m NE of Romsey. Follow brown
tourist signs off M3 J11, or off M27
J2, or A3057 Romsey to Andover.
Disabled parking available. **For
opening times and information,
please phone, email or visit garden
website.**
Established by the plantsman Sir
Harold Hillier, this 180 acre garden
holds a unique collection of 12,000
different hardy plants from across
the world. It incl the famous Winter
Garden, Magnolia Avenue, Centenary
Border, Himalayan Valley, Gurkha
Memorial Garden, Magnolia Avenue,
spring woodlands, Hydrangea Walk,
fabulous autumn colour, 14 National
Collections and over 600 champion
trees. The Centenary Border is one
of the longest double mixed border
in the country, a feast from early
summer to autumn. Celebrated
Winter Garden is one of the largest in
Europe. Electric scooters are available
for hire (please pre-book). Disabled
WC. Guide and hearing dogs only.

GROUP OPENING

78 SOUTHSEA GARDENS
Southsea, Portsmouth, PO4 0PR.
Ian & Liz Craig, 07415 889648,
ian.craig1@mac.com. St Ronan's
Rd can be found off Albert Rd,
Southsea. Follow signs from Albert
Rd or Canoe Lake on seafront.
Parking in Craneswater School.
**Sun 12 Apr, Sun 7 June (2-6).
Combined adm £4.50, chd**

free. **Home-made teas at 28 St
Ronan's Avenue. Visits also by
arrangement Apr to July.**

NEW 67 GAINS ROAD
Lynne & Ian Payne.

28 ST RONAN'S AVENUE
Ian & Liz Craig,
www.28stronansavenue.co.uk.

Two town gardens in adjacent roads
within easy walking distance, off St
Ronan's Road. Victorian houses (not
open) where the owners have created
peaceful green spaces about 700
metres from Southsea promenade.
67 Gains Road is a small garden
designed with artistic flair to create
a haven where art and horticulture
meet. The creative gardener has made
the very most of the limited space
with a good range of sculptures and
plants including bamboos, ferns and
succulents. The front garden has
sculpted box and interesting planters.
28 St Ronan's Avenue (145ft by 25ft)
is divided into different areas including
a wildflower meadow and pond.
Agaves and echeverias grow in drier
sandy parts. Some unusual trees and
a pleached hornbeam screen at the
end of the garden to give structure.
Planting is a mixture of traditional and
tender plants including proteas, puyas
and echiums, along with tree ferns.
Tulips feature in April and alliums in
May and June. Recycled items are
used to create sculptures.

79 SPINDLES
24 Wootton Road, Lee-on-
the-Solent, Portsmouth,
PO13 9HB. Peter & Angela
Arnold, 02393 115181,
angelliana62@gmail.com. 6m S
of Fareham. Exit A27, turn L onto
Gosport Rd A32. At r'about take 2nd
exit Newgate Lane B3385. Through
3 r'abouts, turn L into Marine Parade
B3333 onto Wootton Rd. **Sun 5
July (12-5.30). Adm £3, chd free.
Home-made teas. Visits also
by arrangement June to Aug for
groups of 5 to 30. Day & eve visits.
Art groups welcome.**
Visit this small gold award-winning
garden where cottage style planting
merges with tropical and the exotic.
Over 50 roses vie for your attention as
you meander under clematis covered
arches towards a small wildlife pond,
tree ferns and bamboo. Interest to
new and experienced gardeners. Just
3 mins from the sea, why not make a

day of it, you won't be disappointed!
Winner of Best Back Garden, Gosport
and Lee on The Solent in Bloom
2019. Wheelchair access very limited
due to narrow paths.

80 ♦ SPINNERS GARDEN
School Lane, Pilley, Lymington,
SO41 5QE. Andrew & Vicky
Roberts, 07545 432090,
info@spinnersgarden.co.uk,
www.spinnersgarden.co.uk.
1½m N of Lymington. Follow sign
to Boldre off the A337 between
Brockenhurst & Lymington. At top
of Pilley Hill turn R into School Lane.
Spinners Garden is at the end of a
row of houses on the R. **For NGS:
Sun 26 Apr (2-5). Adm £5, chd
free. Cream teas on the patio.
For other opening times and
information, please phone, email or
visit garden website.**
Peaceful woodland garden overlooking
the Lymington valley with many rare
and unusual plants. The garden
continues to be developed with new
plants added to the collections and the
layout changed to enhance the views.
The house was rebuilt in 2014 to reflect
its garden setting. Andy will take groups
of 15 on tours of the hillside with its
woodland wonders and draw attention
to the treats at their feet; trilliums, wood
anemones and erythroniums! Partial
wheelchair access.

81 SPITFIRE HOUSE
Chattis Hill, Stockbridge,
SO20 6JS. Tessa & Clive
Redshaw, 07711 547543,
tessa@redshaw.co.uk. 2m from
Stockbridge. Follow the A30 W from
Stockbridge for 2m. Go past the
Broughton/Chattis Hill Xrds & take
the next R towards the Wallops, then
next R up private drive to Spitfire
House. **Sat 6 June (2-5). Adm £4,
chd free. Home-made teas. Visits
also by arrangement June & July
for groups of 10 to 30.**
A country garden situated high on
chalk downland. On the site of a
WW11 Spitfire assembly factory with
Spitfire tethering rings still visible. This
garden has wildlife at its heart and
includes fruit and vegetables, a small
orchard, wildlife pond, woodland
planting and large areas of wildflower
meadow. Wander across the downs
to be rewarded with extensive views.
Wheelchair access with areas of gravel
and a slope up to wildflower meadow.

GROUP OPENING

82 STOCKBRIDGE GARDENS
Stockbridge, SO20 6EX. *9m W of Winchester. On A30, at the junction of A3057 & B3049. Parking on High St. All gardens on High St.* Thur 11, Sun 14 June (1.30-5). Combined adm £7, chd free.

LITTLE WYKE
Mrs Mary Matthews.

THE OLD RECTORY
Robin Colenso & Chrissie Quayle.

OLD SWAN HOUSE
Mr Herry Lawford.
(See separate entry)

SHEPHERDS HOUSE
Kim & Frances Candler.

TROUT COTTAGE
Mrs Sally Milligan.

Five gardens will open this year in Stockbridge, offering a variety of styles and character. Little Wyke, next to the Town Hall has a long mature town garden with mixed borders and fruit trees. Trout Cottage is a small walled garden, which will inspire those with small spaces and little time to achieve tranquillity and beauty. Full of approx 180 plants flowering for almost 10 mths of the year, all set around a rectangular lawn. The Old Rectory has a partially walled garden with formal pond, fountain and planting near the house (not open) with a stream-side walk under trees, many climbing and shrub roses and a woodland area. Old Swan House, at the east end of the High St has modern mixed planting. There is a gravel grass garden and an orchard, as well as a pond. Shepherds House on Winton Hill with herbaceous borders and a new kitchen garden with a belvedere overlooking the pond. Gravel path at Shepherds House.
⛿ 🚗 ☕

83 NEW TADLEY PLACE
Church Lane, Baughurst, Tadley, RG26 5LA. Lyn & Ronald Duncan. *10 mins drive from Basingstoke, near Tadley.* Sun 3 May (2-5). Adm £5, chd free. Cream teas.
Tadley Place is a Tudor manor house dating from the C15. The gardens surround the house (not open) and include formal areas, a large kitchen garden and access to a bluebell wood with a pond. Wheelchair access to the majority of the garden on slightly uneven lawn.
⛿ ☕

84 TANGLEFOOT
Crawley, Winchester, SO21 2QB. Mr & Mrs F J Fratter, 01962 776243, fred@fratter.co.uk. *5m NW of Winchester. Between B3049 (Winchester - Stockbridge) & A272 (Winchester - Andover). Lane beside Crawley Court (Arqiva). Parking in adjacent mown field.* Thur 14, Sun 17 May, Thur 18, Sun 21 June, Thur 16, Sun 19 July (2-5.30). Adm £5, chd free. Drinks & biscuits included. Opening with Crawley Gardens on Thur 2, Sun 5 July. Visits also by arrangement May to July.
Developed by owners since 1976, Tanglefoot's ½ acre garden is a blend of influences, from Monet-inspired rose arch and small wildlife pond to Victorian boundary wall with trained fruit trees. Highlights include a raised lily pond, herbaceous bed (a riot of colour later in the summer), herb wheel, large productive kitchen garden and unusual flowering plants. In contrast to the garden, a 2 acre field with views over the Hampshire countryside has recently been converted into spring and summer wildflower meadows with mostly native trees and shrubs; it has delighted visitors in recent summers. Plants from the garden for sale. Wheelchair access with narrow paths in vegetable area.
⛿ ☕ 🚗 ☕

85 TERSTAN
Longstock, Stockbridge, SO20 6DW. Alexander & Penny Burnfield, paburnfield@gmail.com, www.pennyburnfield.wordpress.com. *¾ N of Stockbridge. From Stockbridge (A30) turn N to Longstock at bridge. Garden ¾ m on R.* Suns 26 Apr, 28 June, 26 July, 13 Sept (2-5). Adm £5, chd free. Home-made teas. Visits also by arrangement Apr to Sept for groups of 20+.
A garden for all seasons, developed over 50 yrs into a profusely planted, contemporary cottage garden in peaceful surroundings. There is a constantly changing display in pots, starting with tulips and continuing with many unusual plants. Gravel garden, water features, cutting garden and Showman's Caravan. Art Groups welcome. Live music for NGS openings. Wheelchair access with some gravel paths and steps.
⛿ ⚘ 🚗 ☕

86 THE THATCHED COTTAGE
Church Road, Upper Farringdon, Alton, GU34 3EG. Mr David & Mrs Cally Horton, 01420 587922, dwhorton@btinternet.com. *3m S of Alton off A32. From the A32, take the road to Upper Farringdon. At the top of the hill turn L into Church Rd, follow round corner, past Masseys Folly & we are the 1st house on the R.* Suns 24 May, 21 June, 12 July, 9 Aug, 6 Sept (2-5.30). Combined adm with Berry Cottage £8, chd free. Visits also by arrangement May to Sept for groups of 10+. Donation to Jubilee Sailing Trust.
A 1½ acre garden hidden behind a C16 thatched cottage (not open). Borders burst with cottage garden plants and a pond provides the soothing sound of water. A pergola of roses, clematis and honeysuckle leads to chickens and ducks under a walnut, one of several specimen trees. A productive garden with fruit trees, fruit cage and raised vegetable beds. Enjoy the wild flower area and gypsy caravan. Fully accessible by wheelchair after a short gravel drive.
⛿ 🐄 ⚘ 🚗 ☕

Little Wyke, Stockbridge Gardens

87 TWIN OAKS

13 Oakwood Road, Chandler's Ford, Eastleigh, SO53 1LW. Syd & Sue Hutchinson, 02380 907517, syd@sydh.co.uk. *Leave M3 J12. Follow signs to Chandlers Ford onto Winchester Rd. After ½m turn R into Hiltingbury Rd. After approx ½m turn L into Oakwood Rd.* **Sun 12, Mon 13 Apr, Sun 24, Mon 25 May, Sat 25, Sun 26 July (1-5). Adm £3.50, chd free. Home-made teas. Visits also by arrangement Apr to Aug for groups of up to 20.**
Continually evolving ⅓ acre suburban woodland water garden, designed and planted by owners, bordered by mature oak beech and birch trees. Enjoy spring colour from azaleas, rhododendrons and bulbs. The lawn meanders between informal beds and ponds and bridges lead to a tranquil pergola seating area overlooking a wildlife pond. Rockery skirted by a stream with a waterfall into a lily pond. Aviary.

🐕 ❀ ☕

88 TYLNEY HALL HOTEL

Ridge Lane, Rotherwick, RG27 9AZ. Elite Hotels, 01256 764881, sales@tylneyhall.com, www.tylneyhall.co.uk. *3m NW of Hook. From M3 J5 via A287 & Newnham, M4 J11 via B3349 & Rotherwick.* **Sun 17 May, Sun 14 June, Sun 12 July (10-4). Adm £5, chd free. Light refreshments in the Chestnut Suite from 12pm.**
Large garden of 66 acres with extensive woodlands and beautiful vista. Fine avenues of wellingtonias; rhododendrons and azaleas, Italian garden, lakes, large water and rock garden, dry stone walls originally designed with assistance of Gertrude Jekyll. Partial wheelchair access.

♿ 🐕 ❀ 🛏 ☕

89 WALDEN

Common Hill, Medstead, Alton, GU34 5LZ. Terri & Neil Burman. *5m S of Alton. From N on A31 turn R into Boyneswood Rd signed Medstead. At small Xrds go R into Roedowns Rd. At T-junction at village green turn L. After church, Common Hill is 1st turning on L.* **Fri 19, Sun 21 June (1-5). Adm £3.50, chd free. Home-made teas.**
2 acre sloping garden on chalk, designed by the owners with panoramic views towards Winchester. Restored 60ft rockery with many alpine species. Early summer colour with hardy perennials, peonies,

roses, mature shrubs and fruit trees. Interesting sculptures enhance the garden whilst recycled objects add interest and humour. Parking for disabled visitors in front of house on paved driveway. The garden is mainly grass with some slopes. Assistance required.

♿ 🐕 ❀ ☕

90 WALHAMPTON

Beaulieu Road, Walhampton, Lymington, SO41 5ZG. Walhampton School Trust Ltd, 07928 385694, d.hill@walhampton.com. *1m E of Lymington. From Lymington follow signs to Beaulieu (B3054) for 1m & turn R into main entrance at 1st school sign, 200yds after top of hill.* **Sun 3 May (2-6). Adm £5, chd free. Home-made teas in school dining room (2-4.30). Visits also by arrangement May to July for groups of 5 to 20. Donation to St John's Church, Boldre.**
Glorious walks through large C18 landscape garden surrounding magnificent mansion (not open). Visitors will discover three lakes, serpentine canal, climbable prospect mount, period former banana house and orangery, fascinating shell grotto, plantsman's glade and Italian terrace by Peto (c1907), drives and colonnade by Mawson (c1914) with magnificent views to the Isle of Wight. Exedrae and sunken garden, rockery, Roman arch, fountain and seating. Guided garden history tours available on the day. Wheelchair access with gravel paths and some slopes.

♿ ☕

91 WEIR HOUSE

Abbotstone Road, Old Alresford, SO24 9DG. Mr & Mrs G Hollingbery, 07767 606729, jhollingbery@me.com. *½m N of Alresford. From New Alresford down Broad St (B3046), past Globe Pub, take 1st L signed Abbotstone. Weir House is 1st drive on L. Park in signed field.* **Sun 7 June, Sun 6 Sept (2-5). Adm £5, chd free. Home-made teas. Visits also by arrangement Apr to Oct for groups of 10+.**
Spectacular riverside garden with sweeping lawn backed by old walls, yew buttresses and mixed perennial beds. Over 3 acres of garden including contemporary vegetable garden at its height in Sept, a contemporary garden around pool area, bog garden at its best in May/

June and wilder walkways through wooded areas. Children and dogs welcome. Wheelchair access to most of the garden.

♿ 🐕 ❀ ☕

92 WEST VIEW

Old London Road, Stockbridge, SO20 6EL. Rebecca & Matthew Ferris. *Old London Rd is directly opp The White Hart Pub at the E end of Stockbridge High St. West View is 300yds on R, at the opp end of the road from the primary school.* **Sun 2 Aug (10-4); Wed 5 Aug (1-4). Adm £4, chd free. Home-made teas on 5 Aug only.**
½ acre garden designed and constructed by the current owners, built into the natural chalk cliff on levels. 60 steep steps take you up through a series of small garden rooms from pool area to sun deck, copper garden and white garden. The garden opens up as you get higher, culminating in a field with wildlife pond, shepherds hut, wild flower area, orchard and spectacular views of the Test Valley. On 2 Aug Food Festival in Stockbridge.

☕

93 WHEATLEY HOUSE

Wheatley Lane, between Binsted & Kingsley, Bordon, GU35 9PA. Mr & Mrs Michael Adlington, 01420 23113, adlingtons36@gmail.com. *4m E of Alton, 5m SW of Farnham. Take A31 to Bentley, follow sign to Bordon. After 2m, R at Jolly Farmer Pub towards Binsted, 1m L & follow signs to Wheatley.* **Sat 22, Sun 23 Aug (1.30-5.30). Adm £5, chd free. Home-made teas. Visits also by arrangement May to Oct for groups of 10+.**
Situated on a rural hilltop with panoramic views over Alice Holt Forest and the South Downs. The owner admits to being much more of an artist than a plantswoman, but has had great fun creating this 1½ acre garden full of interesting and unusual planting combinations. The sweeping mixed borders and shrubs are spectacular with colour throughout the season, particularly in late summer. The black and white border, now with bright red accents, is very popular with visitors. Local variety of craft, produce and home-made teas in Old Barn. Wheelchair access with care on lawns, good views of garden and beyond from terrace.

♿ ❀ 🚗 ☕

94 WHISPERS

Chatter Alley, Dogmersfield, Hook, RG27 8SS. Mr & Mrs John Selfe. *3m W of Fleet. Turn N to Dogmersfield off A287 Odiham to Farnham Rd. Turn L by Queen's Head Pub.* **Sun 19 July (12.30-5). Adm £6, chd free. Home-made teas.**

Come and discover new plants in this 2 acre garden of manicured lawns surrounded by large borders of colourful shrubs, trees and long flowering perennials. Wild flower area, water storage system, greenhouse, kitchen garden and living sculptures. Spectacular waterfall cascades over large rock slabs and magically disappears below the terrace. A garden not to be missed. Wheelchair access with gravel entrance.

 ♿ ❄ 🚐 ☕

95 WICOR PRIMARY SCHOOL COMMUNITY GARDEN

Portchester, Fareham, PO16 9DL. Louise Moreton, www.wicor.hants.sch.uk. *Halfway between Portsmouth & Fareham on A27. Turn S at Seagull Pub r'about into Cornaway Lane, 1st R into Hatherley Drive. Entrance to school is almost opp. Parking on-site, pay at main gate.* **Sun 28 June (12-4). Adm £3.50, chd free. Home-made teas.**

As shown on Gardeners' World in 2017. Beautiful school gardens tended by pupils, staff and community gardeners. Wander along Darwin's path to see the new coastal garden, Jurassic garden, orchard, tropical bed, wildlife areas, allotment and apiary, plus one of the few camera obscuras in the south of England. Wheelchair access to all areas, flat ground.

 ♿ 🐄 ❄ ☕

96 WILLOWS

Pilley Hill, Boldre, Lymington, SO41 5QF. Elizabeth & Martin Walker, 01590 677415, elizabethwalker13@gmail.com, www.willowsgarden.co.uk. *New Forest. 2m N Lymington off A337. To avoid traffic in Lyndhurst, leave M27 at J2 & follow Heavy Lorry Route. Disabled parking at gate.* **Sat 8, Sun 9 Aug (2-5). Adm £4, chd free. Cream teas. Visits also by arrangement July & Aug for groups of 20+.**

Front borders overflow with colourful dahlias, cannas, crocosmias and swathes of heleniums. Exciting exotics contrast with a jungly mix of gunneras, ferns and giant hostas around the tranquil pond and lower bog garden. Here the ginger lilies may be in flower! Sunny upper borders have interesting topiary, a border of wonderful blue hydrangeas, another of dark leaved dahlias and billowing grasses. Willows will hold Dahlia and Hydrangea Demo Days on each open day at 3pm. Elizabeth will demonstrate how to take cuttings, plant seeds, grow on and plant out. Also, how to over winter mature plants in the ground (or dig them up and store dahlia tubers indoors) and feed and protect all plants from slugs. Wheelchairs usually manage to access all parts of garden.

 ♿ 🐄 ❄ 🚐 ☕

97 NEW 6 WIMPSON GARDENS

Southampton, SO16 9ES. Kevin Liles, 02380 777590, www.gardenatendhouse.com. *Exit M27 J1, take road to Lordshill at 2nd r'about, turn R into Romsey Rd to Shirley. After ½m turn R at Xrds into Wimpson Lane, 3rd on R Crabwood Rd (additional parking). Wimpson Gardens 4th on R.* **Wed 3, Thur 4 June (12-4). Adm £3.50, chd free. Home-made teas. Visits also by arrangement May & June for groups of 5 to 20.**

Surprising award-winning urban oasis of linked garden areas including small secret garden. Best in spring and summer months, but rich year round plant interest including tree ferns, palms, acers and wisteria. Deep herbaceous borders including hostas, grasses, agapanthus, alstroemerias. Significant sculpture and gallery quality ceramic collection. Winner of Southampton in Bloom, Best Private Garden.

 ☕

We open the gates to the nation's best gardens, offering a relaxing, memorable and affordable day out. A perfect experience to share with friends and family.

98 1 WOGSBARNE COTTAGES

Rotherwick, RG27 9BL. Miss S & Mr R Whistler. *2½m N of Hook. M3 J5, M4 J11, A30 or A33 via B3349.* **Sun 12, Mon 13 July (2-5). Adm £3, chd free. Home-made teas.**

Small traditional cottage garden with a roses around the door look, much photographed for calendars, jigsaws and magazines. Mixed flower beds and borders. Vegetables grown in abundance. Ornamental pond and alpine garden. Views over open countryside to be enjoyed whilst you take afternoon tea on the lawn. The garden has been open for the NGS for more than 30 yrs. Wheelchair access with some gravel paths.

 ♿ ❄ ☕

99 NEW WOODPECKERS CARE HOME

Sway Road, Brockenhurst, SO42 7RX. Mr Charles Hubberstey. *New Forest. Sway Road from village centre. Past petrol station, then school, Woodpeckers on R.* **Sun 19 Apr, Sun 23, Wed 26 Aug (11-5). Adm £3.50, chd free. Home-made teas.**

A vibrant and colourful garden surrounds our nursing home. We have active involvement from our residents who enjoy the wide paths, whether in a wheelchair or strolling on foot. The peaceful courtyard area, small orchard, and allotments all look particularly beautiful in spring with views through neighbouring fields. You may see deer to the west and ponies to the east and do spot the Bug House!

 ♿ 🐄 ❄ ☕

100 WYCHWOOD

Silchester Road, Little London, Tadley, RG26 5EP. Jenny Inwood. *Please do not park in The Plough car park. Access to Wychwood garden is by rear access with limited parking. Follow the signs opp Beach's Crescent.* **Wed 15, Wed 22 July (2-5). Adm £3.50, chd free. Light refreshments.**

A joyful garden comprising a stunning water feature with statuary and countless containers brimming with annuals. A tranquil and peaceful atmosphere invites you to sit and enjoy the many seating areas, amidst shrubs, roses and trees. The garden offers gentle access to different levels and habitats and extends into a natural wooded area with views over the fields beyond. Wheelchair access may be difficult on gravel path and through the woods.

 ♿ ❄ ☕

HEREFORDSHIRE

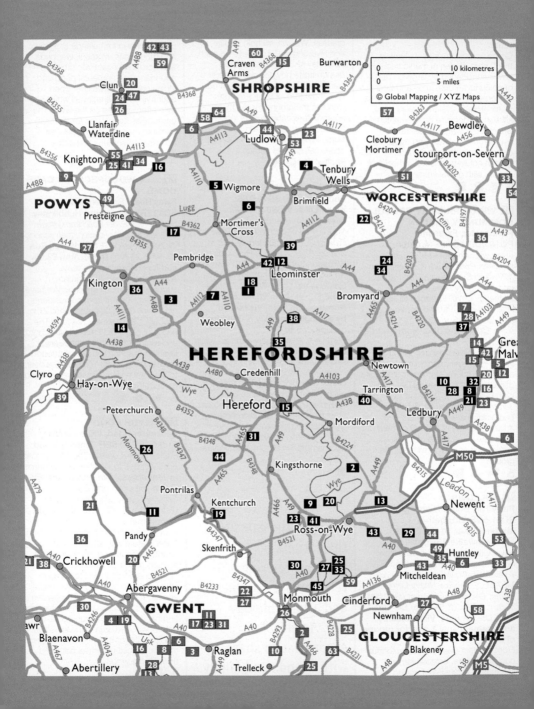

Craven Arms
Burwarton
SHROPSHIRE
Clun
Llanfair Waterdine
Knighton
POWYS
Presteigne
Ludlow
Wigmore
Mortimer's Cross
Brimfield
Cleobury Mortimer
Tenbury Wells
Bewdley
Stourport-on-Severn
WORCESTERSHIRE
Pembridge
Leominster
Kington
Weobley
Bromyard
HEREFORDSHIRE
Clyro
Hay-on-Wye
Peterchurch
Credenhill
Hereford
Newtown
Tarrington
Ledbury
Great Malv
Mordiford
Kingsthorne
Newent
Pontrilas
Kentchurch
Pandy
Crickhowell
Abergavenny
Skenfrith
Ross-on-Wye
Huntley
Mitcheldean
Cinderford
Newnham
GWENT
Blaenavon
Abertillery
Raglan
Trelleck
Monmouth
GLOUCESTERSHIRE
Blakeney

0   10 kilometres
0   5 miles
© Global Mapping / XYZ Maps

Herefordshire is essentially an agricultural county, characterised by small market towns, black and white villages, fruit and hop orchards, meandering rivers, wonderful wildlife and spectacular, and often remote, countryside (a must for keen walkers).

As a major region in the Welsh Marches, Herefordshire has a long and diverse history, as indicated by the numerous prehistoric hill forts, medieval castles and ancient battle sites. Exploring the quiet country lanes can lead to many delightful surprises.

For garden enthusiasts the National Garden Scheme offers a range of charming and interesting gardens ranging from informal cottage plots to those of grand houses with parterres, terraces and parkland. Widely contrasting in design and plantings they offer inspiration and innovative ideas.

National collections of Asters and Siberian Iris can be found at The Picton Garden and Aulden Farm, respectively; and, for Galanthophiles, Ivycroft will not disappoint. The numerous specialist nurseries offer tempting collections of rare and unusual plants.

You can always be sure of a warm welcome at a National Garden Scheme open garden.

Volunteers

County Organiser
Lavinia Sole
07880 550235
lavinia.sole@ngs.org.uk

County Treasurer
Angela Mainwaring
01981 251331
angela.mainwaring@ngs.org.uk

Booklet Coordinator
Chris Meakins
01544 370215
christine.meakins@btinternet.com

Booklet Distribution
Graham Sole
01568 797522
grahamsole3@gmail.com

Assistant County Organisers
David Hodgson
01531 640622
dhodgson363@btinternet.com

Sue Londesborough
01981 510148
slondesborough138@btinternet.com

Gill Mullin
01989 750593
gill@longorchard.plus.com

Penny Usher
01568 611688
pennyusher@btinternet.com

@NGSHerefordshire
@HerefordNGS

Left: Michaelchurch Court

OPENING DATES

All entries subject to change. For latest information check www.ngs.org.uk

Extended openings are shown at the beginning of the month.

Map locator numbers are shown to the right of each garden name.

February

Snowdrop Festival

Every Thursday
Ivy Croft 18

Friday 14th
◆ The Picton Garden 32

Friday 21st
Coddington Vineyard 10

Sunday 23rd
The Old Corn Mill 29

Saturday 29th
◆ The Picton Garden 32

March

Saturday 14th
◆ The Picton Garden 32
◆ Ralph Court Gardens 34

Sunday 15th
◆ Ralph Court Gardens 34

Sunday 29th
The Old Corn Mill 29
Whitfield 44

April

Wednesday 1st
◆ Stockton Bury Gardens 39

Saturday 4th
◆ The Picton Garden 32
NEW Wainfield 41

Sunday 5th
Lower Hope

Monday 13th
◆ Moors Meadow Gardens 24
◆ The Picton Garden 32

Sunday 19th
Hill House Farm 16
Woodview 45

Saturday 25th
Shuttifield Cottage 37

Sunday 26th
Coddington Vineyard 10
The Old Corn Mill 29

May

Every Tuesday and Wednesday from Tuesday 26th
Church Cottage 9

Sunday 3rd
Aulden Farm 1
Ivy Croft 18
Lower House Farm 22
◆ The Picton Garden 32

Monday 4th
Aulden Farm 1
Ivy Croft 18
◆ The Picton Garden 32

Saturday 9th
Revilo 35
Shuttifield Cottage 37

Sunday 10th
Coddington Vineyard 10
Revilo 35
Shuttifield Cottage 37

Monday 11th
◆ Moors Meadow Gardens 24

Sunday 17th
Hill House Farm 16
Lower Hope

Friday 22nd
NEW Wainfield 41

Saturday 23rd
Shuttifield Cottage 37
NEW Wainfield 41

Sunday 24th
Kentchurch Court 19
Southbourne & Pine Lodge 38

Monday 25th
◆ The Picton Garden 32
Southbourne & Pine Lodge 38

Sunday 31st
◆ Caves Folly Nurseries 8
Longacre 21
Mulberry House 25
Old Colwall House Sheepcote 28
The Old Corn Mill 29

June

Every Tuesday and Wednesday
Church Cottage 9

Saturday 6th
◆ Ralph Court Gardens 34

Sunday 7th
NEW The Nutshell 27
◆ The Picton Garden 32
◆ Ralph Court Gardens 34

Monday 8th
◆ Moors Meadow Gardens 24

Sunday 14th
NEW Grange Court 12
Hill House Farm 16
Lower House Farm 22
Revilo 35

Friday 19th
◆ Hereford Cathedral Gardens 15

Saturday 20th
Newton St Margarets Gardens 26

Sunday 21st
NEW Grange Court 12
NEW Michaelchurch Court 23
Newton St Margarets Gardens 26
◆ The Picton Garden 32
Whitfield 44

Tuesday 23rd
Hillcroft 17

Wednesday 24th
Hillcroft 17

Thursday 25th
Hillcroft 17

Saturday 27th
Byecroft 6
Castle Moat House 7
◆ The Garden of the Wind at Middle Hunt House 11

Sunday 28th
Broxwood Court 3
◆ The Garden of the Wind at Middle Hunt House 11
Rhodds Farm 36
The Vine 40

Hillcroft

July

Every Tuesday and Wednesday
Church Cottage   9

Sunday 5th
Lower Hope
NEW 22 Westfield Walk 42
Woodview   45

Monday 6th
◆ Moors Meadow
   Gardens   24

Saturday 11th
NEW Wainfield   41

Sunday 12th
Kentchurch Court   19

Thursday 16th
◆ The Picton Garden   32

Friday 17th
Herbfarmacy   14

Saturday 18th
Aulden Farm   1
Herbfarmacy   14
Ivy Croft   18
Shuttifield Cottage   37

Sunday 19th
Aulden Farm   1
Burnt House Farm   4
Hill House Farm   16
Ivy Croft   18
Woodview   45

Thursday 23rd
Herbfarmacy   14

Friday 24th
Herbfarmacy   14

Sunday 26th
Burnt House Farm   4

August

Every Tuesday and Wednesday to Wednesday 12th
Church Cottage   9

Monday 3rd
◆ Moors Meadow
   Gardens   24

Sunday 16th
Hill House Farm   16
◆ The Picton Garden   32

Saturday 22nd
Shuttifield Cottage   37

Saturday 29th
◆ The Garden of the
   Wind at Middle Hunt
   House   11

Sunday 30th
◆ The Garden of the
   Wind at Middle Hunt
   House   11
Mulberry House   25

Monday 31st
◆ The Picton Garden   32

September

Sunday 6th
Brockhampton Cottage 2
Grendon Court   13
Lower Hope
Old Grove   30
NEW 22 Westfield Walk 42

Saturday 12th
Southbourne & Pine
   Lodge   38

Sunday 13th
Hill House Farm   16
Southbourne & Pine
   Lodge   38

Wednesday 16th
◆ The Picton Garden   32

October

Saturday 10th
◆ Ralph Court Gardens
   34

Sunday 11th
◆ Ralph Court Gardens
   34

Tuesday 20th
◆ The Picton Garden   32

November

Saturday 14th
◆ Ralph Court
   Gardens   34

Sunday 15th
◆ Ralph Court
   Gardens   34

By Arrangement

Arrange a personalised garden visit with your club, or group of friends, on a date to suit you. See individual garden entries for full details.

Aulden Farm   1
Brighton House, Newton
   St Margarets
   Gardens   26
Bury Court Farmhouse   5
Byecroft   6
Church Cottage   9
Coddington Vineyard   10
Hillcroft   17
Ivy Croft   18
Lawless Hill   20
Mulberry House   25
The Old Corn Mill   29
The Old Rectory   31
Poole Cottage   33
Revilo   35
Shuttifield Cottage   37
Weston Hall   43
Whitfield   44
Woodview   45

The Old Rectory

© Ellen Rooney

THE GARDENS

1 AULDEN FARM

Aulden, Leominster, HR6 0JT. Alun & Jill Whitehead, 01568 720129, web@auldenfarm.co.uk, www.auldenfarm.co.uk. *4m SW of Leominster. From Leominster take Ivington/Upper Hill rd, ³/₄ m after Ivington church turn R signed Aulden. From A4110 signed Ivington, take 2nd R signed Aulden.* **Sun 3, Mon 4 May, Sat 18, Sun 19 July (2-5.30). Combined adm with Ivy Croft £7, chd free. Home-made teas. Single garden opening £4. Home-made teas and ice cream. Visits also by arrangement Apr to Sept. Prior booking for teas please.**
Informal country garden, thankfully never at its Sunday best! 3 acres planted with wildlife in mind. Emphasis on structure and form, with a hint of quirkiness, a garden to explore with eclectic planting. Irises thrive around a natural pond, shady beds and open borders, seats abound, feels mature but ever evolving. Our own ice cream and home-burnt cakes, Lemon Chisel a speciality! National Collection of Siberian Iris and plant nursery.

2 BROCKHAMPTON COTTAGE

Brockhampton, HR1 4TQ. Peter Clay. *8m SW of Hereford. 5m N of Ross-on-Wye on B4224. In Brockhampton take rd signed to B Crt nursing home, pass N Home after ³/₄ m, go down hill and turn L. 'Drop-off' at gate, car park 500yds downhill on L in orchard.* **Sun 6 Sept (1-4). Combined adm with Grendon Court £10, chd free. Single garden adm £6. Teas at Grendon Court.**
Created from scratch in 1999 by the owner and Tom Stuart-Smith, this beautiful hilltop garden looks S and W over miles of unspoilt countryside. On one side a woodland garden and 5 acre wild flower meadow, on the other side a Perry pear orchard and in valley below: lake, stream and arboretum. The extensive borders are planted with drifts of perennials in the modern romantic style. Allow 1hr 30 mins. Picnic parties welcome by the lake . Visit Grendon Court (2 - 5.30) after your visit to us.

3 BROXWOOD COURT

Broxwood, nr Pembridge, Leominster, HR6 9JJ. Richard Snead-Cox & Mike & Anne Allen. *From Leominster follow signs to Brecon A44/A4112. After approx 8m, just past Weobley turn off, go R to Broxwood/Pembridge. After 2m straight over Xrds to Lyonshall. 500yds on L over cattle grid.* **Sun 28 June (2-5.30). Adm £5, chd free. Home-made teas. Also open Rhodds Farm.**
Stunning 29 acre garden and arboretum, designed in 1859 by W. Nesfield for great-grandfather of present owner. Magnificent yew hedges and km long avenue of cedars and Scots pines. Spectacular view of Black Mountains, sweeping lawns, rhododendrons, gentle walks to summer house, chapel and ponds. Rose garden, mixed borders, rill, gazebo and fountain. Peacocks and white doves. Some gravel, but mostly lawn. Gentle slopes. Disabled WC.

4 BURNT HOUSE FARM

Ashford Carbonel, Ludlow, SY8 4LD. Julie Alviti. *3m SE Ludlow. Turn L off A49 (Ludlow - Leominster) at Xrds 0.25m past B4361 signed Ashford Carbonel, over 2 bridges, over 1st Xrds, R at 2nd Xrds signed Little Hereford, Tenbury. Large white FM house on L in 0.75m.* **Sun 19, Sun 26 July (2-6). Adm £5, chd free. Home-made teas. indoor tearoom.**
³/₄ acre farmhouse garden developed over 35 years by current owners. Lawn with mixed borders, patio, fire pit and gazebo. Garden rooms including vegetable garden with raised beds, cut flower garden, parterre and gravel garden. Extensively planted stream and pond, orchard, cottage garden with traditional potting shed and vintage tools. Unusual plants, 60+ clematis. Many seating areas. Some deep water. Indoor tearoom. Some steps.

Poole Cottage

5 BURY COURT FARMHOUSE

Ford Street, Wigmore, Leominster, HR6 9UP. **Margaret & Les Barclay, 01568 770618, l.barclay@zoho.com.** *10m from Leominster, 10m from Knighton, 8m from Ludlow. On A4110 for Leominster, at Wigmore turn R just after shop & garage. Follow signs to parking and garden.* **Visits by arrangement Feb to Oct for groups of up to 30. Adm £4, chd free. Home-made teas.**

¾ acre garden, 'rescued' since 1997, surrounds the 1820's stone farmhouse (not open). The courtyard contains a pond, mixed borders, fruit trees and shrubs, with steps up to a terrace which leads to lawn and vegetable plot. The main garden (semi-walled) is on two levels with mixed borders, greenhouse, pond, mini-orchard , many spring flowers, and wildlife areas. Year-round colour. Mostly accessible for wheelchairs by arrangement.

🐄 ✾ ⛄ ☕

6 BYECROFT

Welshman's Lane, Bircher, Leominster, HR6 0BP. **Sue & Peter Russell, 01568 780559, peterandsuerussell@btinternet. com, www.byecroft.weebly.com.** *6m N of Leominster. From Leominster take B4361. Turn L at T-junction with B4362. ¼m beyond Bircher village turn R at war memorial into Welshman's Lane, signed Bircher Common.* **Sat 27 June (12.30-5). Adm £4, chd free. Home-made teas. Visits also by arrangement May & June for groups of 10+.**

Developed almost from scratch over 12 yrs, Byecroft is a compact garden stuffed full of interesting plants, many grown from seed. Herbaceous borders, pergola with old roses, formal pond, lots of pots, vegetable garden, wild flower orchard, soft fruit area. Sue and Peter take particular pride in their plant sales table. Most areas accessible with assistance. Some small steps.

♿ ✾ ⛄ ☕

7 CASTLE MOAT HOUSE

Dilwyn, Hereford, HR4 8HZ. **Mr & Mrs T Voogd.** *6m W of Leominster. A44, after 4m take A4112 to Dilwyn. Garden by the village green.* **Sat 27 June (11-4). Adm £4, chd free. Light refreshments. and Light lunches.**

A 2 acre plot consisting of a more formal cottage garden that wraps around the house. The remaining area is a tranquil wild garden which includes paths to a Medieval Castle Motte, part filled Moat and Medieval fish and fowl ponds. A haven for wildlife and people alike. The garden contains some steep banks and deep water, with limited access to Motte, Moat and ponds.

⛄

8 ♦ CAVES FOLLY NURSERIES

Evendine Lane, Colwall, WR13 6DX. **Wil Leaper & Bridget Evans, 01684 540631, bridget@cavesfolly.com, www.cavesfolly.com.** *1¼m NE of Ledbury. B4218. Between Malvern & Ledbury. Evendine Lane, off Colwall Green.* **For NGS: Sun 31 May (2-5). Combined adm with Longacre £7, chd free. Home-made teas. Single garden adm £3.50. For other opening times and information, please phone, email or visit garden website.**

Organic nursery and display gardens. Specialist growers of cottage garden plants herbs and alpines. All plants are grown in peat free organic compost. This is not a manicured garden! It is full of drifts of colour and wild flowers and a haven for wildlife.

♿ 🐄 ✾ ⛄ 🛏 ☕

9 CHURCH COTTAGE

Hentland, Ross-on-Wye, HR9 6LP. **Sue Emms & Pete Weller, 01989 730222, sue.emms@mac.com, www.wyegardensbydesign.com.** *6m from Ross-on-Wye. A49 from Ross. R turn Hentland/Kynaston. Sharp R to St Dubricius, narrow lane few passing places for ½m. Park at Church 150 metres to garden, can drop off at gate. Lane unsuitable for motor homes.* **Every Tue and Wed 26 May to 12 Aug (2-5.30). Adm £3.50, chd free. Home-made teas. Visits also by arrangement May to Aug for groups of up to 30.**

Garden designer & plantswoman's ½ acre garden - feels much larger than it is! Series of garden rooms melting seamlessly into one another. Huge variety of plants, many of which are for sale, unusual varieties mixed with old favourites, providing interest over a long period. Wildlife pond, rose garden, potager, mixed borders, white terrace. Interesting plant combinations and design ideas to inspire.

✾ ☕

10 CODDINGTON VINEYARD

Coddington, HR8 1JJ. **Sharon & Peter Maiden, 01531 641817, sgmaiden@yahoo.co.uk, www.coddingtonvineyard.co.uk.** *4m NE of Ledbury. From Ledbury to Malvern A449, follow brown signs to Coddington Vineyard.* **Fri 21 Feb (11-2.30); Sun 26 Apr (11.30-3.30); Sun 10 May (12-4). Adm £3.50, chd free. Home-made teas. Wine. Visits also by arrangement Feb to Sept for groups of 10+. Light lunches by arrangement.**

5 acres incl 2 acre vineyard, listed farmhouse, threshing barn and cider mill. Garden with terraces, wild flower meadow, woodland with massed spring bulbs, large pond with wildlife, stream garden with masses of primula and hosta. Hellebores and snowdrops, hamamelis and parottia. Azaleas followed by roses and perennials. Lots to see all year. In spring, the gardens are a mass of bulbs. Wine, home-made ice cream and our own apple juice available.

♿ 🐄 ✾ ⛄ 🛏 ☕

11 ♦ THE GARDEN OF THE WIND AT MIDDLE HUNT HOUSE

Middle Hunt House, Walterstone, Hereford, HR2 0DY. **Rupert & Antoinetta Otten, 077770234889, gardenofthewind@gmail.com, www.gardenofthewind.co.uk.** *4m W of Pandy, 17m S of Hereford, 10m N of Abergavenny. A465 to Pandy, West towards Longtown, turn R at Clodock Church, 1m on R. Disabled parking available. Sat Nav may take you via a different route but indicates arrival at adjacent farm.* **For NGS: Sat 27, Sun 28 June, Sat 29, Sun 30 Aug (2-5). Adm £5, chd free. Home-made teas. For other opening times and information, please phone, email or visit garden website.**

A modern garden using swathes of herbaceous plants and grasses, surrounding stone built farmhouse and barns with stunning views of the Black Mountains. Special features: rose border, hornbeam alley, formal parterre and water rill and fountains, William Pye water feature, architecturally designed greenhouse and RIBA bridge, vegetable gardens. Carved lettering and sculpture throughout, garden covering about 4 acres. Garden seating throughout the site on stone, wood and metal benches including some with carved lettering. Partial wheelchair access. Disabled WC facilities not easily accessible for wheelchair users due to gravel.

♿ 🐄 ✾ ⛄ ☕

12 NEW GRANGE COURT
Pinsley Road, Leominster, HR6 8NL. Leominster Area Regeneration Company, www.grangecourt.org. *Grange Court in the centre of Leominster is accessible by car via Church St but not from Pinsley Rd via Etnam St. Short walk from Broad St & Etnam St car parks.* **Sun 14, Sun 21 June (10-5). Adm £5, chd free. Light refreshments.**
Set in the beautiful, tranquil Grange, Leominster's C17 market hall, Grange Court, has an ornate knot garden edged by the Saverne roses from our twin in France and the woodland garden to the front. Behind is the beautiful walled garden planted with a variety of roses, climbers and herbaceous flowers in the informal style of Marjory Fish. The Victorian Folly adds a little bit of kitsch! There will be a display of beautiful garden sculptures from the Metalsmiths, Claudia Petley and Paul Shepherd. The Court will be open for visitors to see the various displays and the extraordinary exhibition of the history of Leominster in embroidery by Leominster in Stitches. The gardens and building are fully accessible. We have accessible toilets, baby-changing facilities and a walk-in shower available.

13 GRENDON COURT
Upton Bishop, Ross on Wye, HR9 7QP. Mark & Kate Edwards.
3m NE of Ross-on-Wye. M50, J3 . Hereford B4224 Moody Cow PH, 1m open gate on R. From Ross. A40, B449, Xrds R Upton Bishop. 100yds on L by cream cottage. **Sun 6 Sept (2-5.30). Combined adm with Brockhampton Cottage £10, chd free. Home-made teas in the barn. Single garden adm £5.**
A contemporary garden designed by Tom Stuart-Smith. Planted on 2 levels, a clever collection of mass-planted perennials and grasses of different heights, textures and colour give all-yr interest. The upper walled garden with a sea of flowering grasses makes a highlight. Views of the new pond and valley walk. Visit Brockhampton Cottage (1-4) before you visit us (picnic in parking field). Please note that Grendon Court garden does not open until 2pm. Wheelchair access possible but some gravel.

14 HERBFARMACY
The Field, Eardisley, Hereford, HR3 6NB. Paul Richards, www.herbfarmacy.com. *11m NW of Hereford. Take A438 from Hereford, turn onto A4112 to Leominster, then A4111 to Eardisley. In Eardisley turn L off A4111 by Tram Inn & turn R 3 times. Farm is at end of No Through Road on L.* **Fri 17, Sat 18, Thur 23, Fri 24 July (10-4). Adm £5, chd free. Home-made teas.**
A 4 acre organic herb farm overlooking the Wye valley with views to the Black Mountains. Featured on BBC Countryfile, crops are grown for use in herbal skincare and medicinal products. Colourful plots of Echinacea, Marshmallow, Mullein (Verbascum) and Calendula will be on show as well as displays on making products. Refreshments will be available along with a shop selling Herbfarmacy products. Wheelchair Access possible when dry with assistance but some ground rough and some slopes.

15 ◆ HEREFORD CATHEDRAL GARDENS
Hereford, HR1 2NG. Dean of Hereford Cathedral, 01432 374202, Peter.Challenger@ herefordcathedral.org, www. herefordcathedral.org/garden-tours. *Centre of Hereford. Approach rds to the Cathedral are signed. Tours leave from information desk in the cathedral building or as directed.* **For NGS: Fri 19 June (10-4). Adm £5, chd free. Refreshments in the Cathedral Cafe. For other opening times and information, please phone, email or visit garden website.**
A guided tour of late 15th century historic award-winning gardens. Tours include colourful courtyard garden, an atmospheric cloisters garden enclosed by C15 buildings, the Vicars Choral garden, with plants with ecclesiastical connections and roses, the private Dean's Garden and the Bishop's Garden with fine trees and an outdoor chapel for meditation in ancient surroundings. Collection of plants with ecclesiastical connections in College Garden. Open every Wed & Sat 1 May to 30 Sept, guided tours 2.30. Please see website for other dates and information on booked and guided tours. Partial wheelchair access. Tours can be adapted to suit individual needs. For more information please visit www.herefordcathedral. org/accessibility.

16 HILL HOUSE FARM
Knighton, LD7 1NA. Caroline Gourlay, www.hillhousefarmgarden.com. *4m SE of Knighton. S of A4113 via Knighton (Llanshay Lane, 4m) or Bucknell (Reeves Lane, 3m).* **Sun 19 Apr, Sun 17 May, Sun 14 June, Sun 19 July, Sun 16 Aug, Sun 13 Sept (2-5). Adm £5, chd free. Light refreshments. Self service teas, coffee and soft drinks.**
5 acre south facing garden developed over 50 years, set in magnificent hilly countryside. Some herbaceous and extensive lawns around the house. Mown paths lead through shrubs, roses and specimen trees down to the half acre Oak Pool 200ft below. There are 11 sculptures and as many sitting places scattered around this very peaceful garden. Good range of snack bars and biscuits. Suggested contributions into an honesty box. Surrounded by pastureland with distant views of the Black Mountains.

17 HILLCROFT
Coombes Moor, Presteigne, LD8 2HY. Liz O'Rourke & Michael Clarke, 01544 262795, lorconsulting@hotmail.co.uk. *North Herefordshire. 10m from Leominster. Coombes Moor is under Wapley Hill on the B4362, between Shobdon & Presteigne. The house is on R just beyond Byton Cross when heading west.* **Tue 23, Wed 24, Thur 25 June (11-5). Adm £4, chd free. Home-made teas. Visits also by arrangement June & July. No access for coaches.**
The garden is part of a 5 acre site on the lower slopes of Wapley Hill in the beautiful Lugg Valley. The highlight in mid summer is the romantic Rose Walk, combining sixty roses with mixed herbaceous planting set in an old cider apple orchard. In addition to the garden area around the house, there is a secret garden, wild flower meadow and a vegetable and fruit area. Tea, coffee and cold drinks along with delicious home-made cakes can be enjoyed in the garden or the conservatory.

18 IVY CROFT

Ivington Green, Leominster, HR6 0JN. Roger Norman, 01568 720344, ivycroft@homecall.co.uk, www.ivycroftgarden.co.uk. *3m SW of Leominster. From Leominster take Ryelands Rd to Ivington. Turn R at church, garden ¾ m on R. From A4110 signed Ivington, garden 1¾ m on L.* **Every Thur 6 Feb to 27 Feb (9-4.30). Adm £4, chd free. Sun 3, Mon 4 May, Sat 18, Sun 19 July (2-5.30). Combined adm with Aulden Farm £7, chd free. Home-made teas. Single garden adm £4. Visits also by arrangement.**
A maturing rural garden with areas of meadow, wood and orchard, blending with countryside and providing habitat for wildlife. The cottage is surrounded by borders, raised beds, trained pears and containers giving all year interest. Paths lead to the wider garden including herbaceous borders, vegetable garden framed with espalier apples and seasonal pond with willows, ferns and grasses. Snowdrops. Partial wheelchair access.

&♿ ❀ 🚗 ☕

19 KENTCHURCH COURT

Pontrilas, HR2 0DB. Mrs Jan Lucas-Scudamore, 01981 240228, jan@kentchurchcourt.co.uk, www.kentchurchcourt.co.uk. *12m SW of Hereford. From Hereford A465 towards Abergavanny, at Pontrilas turn L signed Kentchurch. After 2m fork L, after Bridge Inn. Garden opp church.* **Sun 24 May, Sun 12 July (11-5). Adm £5, chd free. Home-made teas.**
Kentchurch Court is sited close to the Welsh border. The large stately home dates to C11 and has been in the Scudamore family for over 1000yrs The deer-park surrounding the house dates back to the Knights Hospitallers of Dinmore and lies at the heart of an estate of over 5000 acres. Historical characters associated with the house incl Welsh hero Owain Glendower, whose daughter married Sir John Scudamore. The house was modernised by John Nash in 1795. First opened for NGS in 1927. Formal rose garden, traditional vegetable garden redesigned with colour, scent and easy access. Walled garden and herbaceous borders, rhododendrons and wild flower walk. Deer-park and ancient woodland. Extensive collection of mature trees and shrubs. Stream with habitat for spawning trout. Some slopes, shallow gravel.

&♿ 🐕 ❀ 🚗 🚌 ☕

20 LAWLESS HILL

Sellack, Ross on Wye, HR9 6QP. Katalin & Keith Meehan, 07595 678837, Lawlesshill@gmail.com, www. facebook.com/Lawless-Hill-315093135189525. *4m NW of Ross-on-Wye. 4m NW of Ross on Wye, Western end of M50. On A49 to Hereford, take 2nd R signed Sellack. After 2m, turn R by white house to Sellack church. At next church sign turn L. and follow signs.* **Visits by arrangement Mar to Oct for groups of up to 30. Adm £5, chd free. Light refreshments. On request for extra charge.**
Modernist Japanese-influenced garden with dramatic views over R Wye. Collection of 'rooms' sculpted from the steep hillside using network of natural stone walls and huge rocks. Among exotic and unusual plantings, natural ponds are held within the terracing, forming waterfalls between them. Due to steep steps and stepping stones by open water, the garden is unsuitable for the less mobile and young children. - magical views overlooking waterfall and the river Wye - infinity pond offers great photographic opportunities - cloud shaped pines and taxus trees from Japan - zen meditation/gravel garden - dry river garden - sophisticated stone walls- exquisite engineering works.

☕

Grange Court

21 LONGACRE

Evendine Lane, Colwall Green,
WR13 6DT. Mr & Mrs C Hellowell.
*3m S of Malvern. Off Colwall Green.
Off B4218. Car parking at Caves
Folly Nursery.* **Sun 31 May (2-5).
Combined adm with Caves Folly
Nurseries £7, chd free. Single
garden adm £4.50.**
2-acre garden-cum-arboretum
developed since 1970. Island
beds of trees and shrubs, some
underplanted with bulbs and
herbaceous perennials, present a
sequence of contrasting pictures
and views through the seasons.
There are no 'rooms' - rather
long vistas lead the eye and feet,
while the feeling of spaciousness
is enhanced by glimpses caught
between trunks and through gaps in
the planting. Over 50 types of conifer
provide the background to maples,
rhododendrons, azaleas, dogwoods,
eucryphias etc. over gravel paths and
lawns.

LOWER HOPE

Lower Hope Estate, Ullingswick,
Hereford HR1 3JF. Mr & Mrs
Clive Richards, 01432 820557,
cliverichards@crco.co.uk
www.lowerhopegardens.co.uk.
*5m S of Bromyard. A465 N from
Hereford, after 6m turn L at Burley
Gate on A417 towards Leominster.
After approx 2m turn R to Lower
Hope. After ½ m garden on L.
Disabled parking available.*

**Sun 5 Apr, Sun 17 May, Sun 5
July, Sun 13 Sept (2-5). Adm
£6, chd £1. Light refreshments.**
Tea and cakes. Visits also by
arrangement Apr to Sept for
groups of 20+.
Outstanding 5 acre garden with
wonderful seasonal variations.
Impeccable lawns with herbaceous
borders, rose gardens, white garden,
Mediterranean, Italian and Japanese
gardens. Natural streams, man-made
waterfalls, bog gardens. Woodland
with azaleas and rhododendrons
with lime avenue to lake with wild
flowers and bulbs. Glasshouses with
exotic plants and breeding butterflies.
Prizewinning Hereford cattle and
Suffolk sheep. Wheelchair access to
most areas.

22 LOWER HOUSE FARM

Vine Lane, Sutton, Tenbury
Wells, WR15 8RL. Mrs Anne
Durston Smith, 01885 410233,
www.kyre-equestrian.co.uk. *3m
SE of Tenbury Wells; 8m NW of
Bromyard. From Tenbury take A4214
to Bromyard. After approx 3m turn R
into Vine Lane, then R fork to Lower
House Farm.* **Sun 3 May, Sun 14
June (2-6). Adm £5, chd free.
Home-made teas.**
Award-winning country garden
surrounding C16 farm-house (not
open) on working farm. Herbaceous
borders, roses, box-parterre,
productive kitchen and cutting
garden, spring garden, ha-ha allowing

wonderful views. Wildlife pond and
children's activities in adjoining
field. Walkers and dogs can enjoy
numerous footpaths across the farm
land. Home to Kyre Equestrian Centre
with access to safe rides and riding
events.

23 NEW MICHAELCHURCH COURT

St Owens Cross, HR2 8LD. John
Handby. *7m N of Ross-on-Wye.
On A4137 Hereford/Monmouth rd,
coming from St Owen's Cross, take
small, unmarked lane 200 yds on L,
garden 1m on L.* **Sun 21 June (11-
4). Adm £5, chd free. Home-made
teas.**
Early C17 house (not open), in open
countryside near Norman church.
Approx 2 acres incl large pond,
stream with flower borders. Old-
fashioned roses and herbaceous
borders set amongst lawns, one long
border backed by high wall covered
with climbing roses, honeysuckle.
Long pergola covered with roses,
honeysuckle, clematis and wisteria
leads to sunken garden with water
feature and seating area. Climbing
roses and hydrangeas over 20ft
high cover house. Small arboretum.
Small exhibition of the history of the
property from its origins as a mill to
becoming the centre of a farming
community in the C19.

☕

The Garden of the Wind at Middle Hunt House

24 ✦ MOORS MEADOW GARDENS

Collington, Bromyard, HR7 4LZ. Ros Bissell, 01885 410318/07812 041179, moorsmeadow@hotmail.co.uk, www.moorsmeadow.co.uk. *4m N of Bromyard, on B4214. ½m up lane follow yellow arrows.* **For NGS: Mon 13 Apr, Mon 11 May, Mon 8 June, Mon 6 July, Mon 3 Aug (11-5). Adm £6.50, chd £1.50. For other opening times and information, please phone, email or visit garden website.**
7-acre organic hillside garden brimming with rarely seen plant species, an emphasis on working with nature to create a wildlife haven. With intriguing features and sculptures it is an inspiration to the garden novice as well as the serious plantsman. Wander through fernery, grass garden, extensive shrubberies, herbaceous beds, meadow, dingle, pools and kitchen garden. Resident Blacksmith. Huge range of unusual and rarely seen plants from around the world. Unique home-crafted sculptures.

25 MULBERRY HOUSE

Knapp Close, Goodrich, Ross-on-Wye, HR9 6JW. Tina & Adrian Barber, 01600 891372 & 07825 835300, tinaabarber@hotmail.co.uk. *Centre of Goodrich. 5m from Ross on Wye 7m from Monmouth. Close to Goodrich Castle in Wye Valley AONB. Goodrich signed from A40 or take B4234 from Ross on Wye. Park in village & follow signs to the garden.* **Sun 31 May, Sun 30 Aug (11-5.30). Adm £5, chd free. Visits also by arrangement May to Sept.**
Mulberry House: a beautiful, peaceful and inspiring half acre garden created from scratch 13 years ago. Imaginatively planted and nurtured by a professional gardener. Winding paths lead you to themed herbaceous borders, areas of shrub planting including clipped box and ornamental grasses all providing a long season of interest with views out to beautiful listed buildings.

GROUP OPENING

26 NEWTON ST MARGARETS GARDENS

Newton St. Margarets, Hereford, HR2 0JU. Sue Londesborough. *17m SW of Hereford, 9m SE of Hay-on-Wye. A465 S from Hereford,* R onto B4348, then L to Vowchurch & Michaelchurch Escley. After approx. 3m take either 1st or 3rd L turns. Follow yellow signs. From Hay B4348, R to Vowchurch, then as above. **Sat 20, Sun 21 June (2-6). Combined adm £7, chd free. Home-made teas at Court Y Pella not open for NGS.**

BRIGHTON HOUSE
Sue & Richard Londesborough, 01981 510148, slondesborough138@btinternet.com.
Visits also by arrangement June to Sept.

OLD FARM COTTAGE
Jane Wake & Alan McCardle.
Two country gardens with very different styles in the picturesque Herefordshire Golden valley. Brighton House: a plantswoman's garden of just over an acre, divided into several distinct areas crammed with many unusual and interesting plants. Herbaceous borders, ornamental and fruit trees, kitchen garden, two small ponds. The garden is planted to encourage wildlife. Views to the Black Mountains. Children's garden trail and play area. Plants for sale propagated from the garden. Old Farm Cottage: cottage garden, with herbaceous borders, shrubs, vegetable garden and greenhouse. Rill and bog garden. Brook side walk with wild flowers and mature oak trees. Secluded seating areas with views to the Black Mountains. Garden not suitable for wheelchairs due to steep access and gravel. Plants for sale at Brighton House and teas at Court Y Pella.

Lawless Hill

Your visits help change lives – since 1927, we've donated over £60 million to nursing and caring charities

27 NEW ▶ THE NUTSHELL
Goodrich, Ross-On-Wye,
HR9 6HG. Louise Short. *The
garden is half way between Ross on
Wye & Monmouth, close to the A40
& the Cross Keys pub.* **Sun 7 June
(9.30-4). Adm £5, chd free. Home-
made teas. Bacon rolls available
from 9.30 until 12 noon.**
The Nutshell is a cottage garden in
approx half an acre, created from
scratch over the last twenty years.
The garden is made up of different
areas separated by herbaceous
borders and rose arches.There is
a lovely selection of plants used
incl many peonys and an extensive
collection of hostas .The owner has
a keen interest in propagation with
two poly tunnels of plants available to
purchase.

28 OLD COLWALL HOUSE
Old Colwall, Malvern, WR13 6HF.
Mr & Mrs Roland Trafford-Roberts.
*3m NE of Ledbury. From Ledbury,
turn L off A449 to Malvern towards
Coddington. Signed from 2½m
along lane. Signed from Colwall &
Bosbury. Visitors will need to walk
from car park to garden.* **Sun 31
May (2-5). Adm £5, chd free.
Home-made teas.**
Early C18 garden on a site owned by
the Church till Henry VIII. Walled lawns
and terraces on various levels. The
heart is the yew walk, a rare survival
from the 1700s: 100 yds long, 30ft
high, cloud clipped, and with a church
aisle-like quality inside. Later centuries
have brought a summer house, water
garden, and rock gardens. Fine trees,
incl enormous veteran yew; fine
views. Steep in places. C18 yew walk.

29 THE OLD CORN MILL
Aston Crews, Ross-on-
Wye, HR9 7LW. Mrs Jill
Hunter, 01989 750059,
www.theoldcornmillgarden.com.
*5m E of Ross-on-Wye. A40 Ross
to Gloucester. Turn L at T-lights
at Lea Xrds onto B4222 signed
Newent, Garden ½m on L. Parking
for disabled down drive. DO NOT
USE THE ABOVE POSTCODE IN
YOUR SATNAV - try HR9 7LA.* **Sun
23 Feb, Sun 29 Mar, Sun 26 Apr,
Sun 31 May (1-5). Adm £5, chd
free. Home-made teas. incl in
adm. Visits also by arrangement
Feb to Oct.**
Snowdrops in February, Daffodils in

March, Tulips in April, Orchids in May.
Do come and enjoy the calm of this
very natural valley garden. Pretty good
cakes too. Prize winning conversion
of a ruined 18th century mill.

30 OLD GROVE
Llangrove, Ross-On-Wye,
HR9 6HA. Ken & Lynette Knowles.
*Between Ross & Monmouth. 2m off
A40 at Whitchurch. Disabled parking
at house otherwise follow signs for
parking in nearby field.* **Sun 6 Sept
(2-6). Adm £4, chd free. Home-
made teas.**
1 ½ acre garden plus two fields.
SW facing with unspoilt views. Lots
of mixed beds with plenty of late
summer colour and many unusual
plants. Large collection of dahlias and
salvias; wild life pond; formal herb
garden; masses of pots; interesting
trees. Seating throughout. Gentle
slopes, some steps but accessible.

31 THE OLD RECTORY
Thruxton, Hereford, HR2 9AX.
Mr & Mrs Andrew Hallett,
01981 570401 & 07774
129690, ar.hallett@gmail.com,
www.thruxtonrectory.co.uk. *6m
SW of Hereford. A465 to Allensmore.
At Locks (Shell) garage take B4348
towards Hay-on-Wye. After 1½m
turn L towards Abbey Dore &
Cockyard. Car park 150yds on L.*
**Visits by arrangement May to
Sept for groups of 10+. Min adm
£70 if less than 14 people. Adm
£5, chd free. Home-made teas.**
Constantly changing plantsman's
garden stocked with unusual
perennials and roses, woodland
borders, gazebo, vegetable parterre
and glasshouse. Mown paths
meander through interesting collection
of specimen trees and shrubs to
the wildlife pond. This four acre
garden, with breathtaking views over
Herefordshire countryside has been
created since 2007. Many places to
sit. Most plants labelled. Mainly level
with some gravel paths.

32 ◆ THE PICTON GARDEN
Old Court Nurseries, Walwyn
Road, Colwall, WR13 6QE. Mr &
Mrs Paul Picton, 01684 540416,
oldcourtnurseries@btinternet.com,
www.autumnasters.co.uk. *3m W of
Malvern. On B4218 (Walwyn Rd) N
of Colwall Stone. Turn off A449 from*

Ledbury or Malvern onto the B4218
for Colwall. **For NGS: Fri 14, Sat
29 Feb, Sat 14 Mar, Sat 4, Mon
13 Apr, Sun 3, Mon 4, Mon 25
May, Sun 7, Sun 21 June, Thur 16
July, Sun 16, Mon 31 Aug, Wed 16
Sept, Tue 20 Oct (11-5). Adm £4,
chd free. For other opening times
and information, please phone,
email or visit garden website.**
1½ acres W of Malvern Hills. Bulbs
and a multitude of woodland plants
in spring. Interesting perennials
and shrubs in Aug. In late Sept and
early Oct colourful borders display
the National Plant Collection of
Michaelmas daisies, backed by
autumn colouring trees and shrubs.
Many unusual plants to be seen, incl
bamboos, more than 100 different
ferns and acers. Features raised
beds and silver garden. National
Plant Collection of autumn-flowering
asters and an extensive nursery that
has been growing them since 1906.
Wheelchair access gravel paths but
all fairly level, no steps.

33 POOLE COTTAGE
Coppett Hill, Goodrich, Ross on
Wye, HR9 6JH. Jo Ward-Ellison
& Roy Smith, 01600 890148,
jo@ward-ellison.com, www.
herefordshiregarden.wordpress.
com. *5m from Ross on Wye, 7m
from Monmouth. Above Goodrich
Castle in Wye Valley AONB.
Goodrich signed from A40 or
take B4234 from Ross.* **Visits by
arrangement June to Aug for
groups of up to 20. Parking for
up to 5 cars. Regret no coaches.
Adm £4, chd free. Home-made
teas.**
A modern country garden in
keeping with the local natural
landscape. Home to designer Jo
Ward-Ellison the 2-acre garden is
predominately naturalistic in style with
a contemporary feel. A long season
of interest with grasses and later
flowering perennials. Some steep
slopes, steps and uneven paths.
Features include a small orchard, a
pond loved by wildlife and kitchen
garden with fabulous views.

34 ◆ RALPH COURT GARDENS
Edwyn Ralph, Bromyard,
Hereford, HR7 4LU. Mr &
Mrs Morgan, 01885 483225,
ralphcourtgardens@aol.com,
www.ralphcourtgardens.co.uk.
From Bromyard follow the Tenbury

rd for approx 1m. On entering the village of Edwyn Ralph take 1st turning on R towards the church. **For NGS: Sat 14, Sun 15 Mar, Sat 6, Sun 7 June, Sat 10, Sun 11 Oct, Sat 14, Sun 15 Nov (10-5). Adm £9, chd £6. Light refreshments. For other opening times and information, please phone, email or visit garden website.**
12 amazing gardens set in the grounds of a gothic rectory. A family orientated garden with a twist, incorporating an Italian Piazza, an African Jungle, Dragon Pool, Alice in Wonderland and the elves in their conifer forest and our new section 'The Monet Garden'. These are just a few of the themes within this stunning garden. Overlooking the Malvern Hills 120 seater Licenced Restaurant. Offering a good selection of daily specials, delicious Sunday roasts, Afternoon tea and our scrumptious homemade cakes. All areas ramped for wheelchair and pushchair access. Some grass areas, without help can be challenging during wet periods.

&. ✳ 🚗 ☕

35 REVILO
Wellington, Hereford, HR4 8AZ.
Mrs Shirley Edgar, 01432 830189, Shirleyskinner@btinternet.com. *6m N of Hereford. On A49 from Hereford turn L into Wellington village, pass church on R. Then just after barn on L, turn L up driveway in front of The Harbour, to furthest bungalow.* **Sat 9, Sun 10 May, Sun 14 June (1-5). Adm £3.50, chd free. Home-made teas. Visits also by arrangement Apr to Sept for groups of 5 to 30.**
Third of an acre garden surrounding bungalow includes mixed borders, meadow and woodland areas, scented garden, late summer bed, gravelled herb garden and vegetable/fruit garden. Flower arranger's garden. Wheelchair access to all central areas of the garden from the garage side.

&. 🐕 ✳ ☕

Your visits help change lives – we've donated over £17 million to Macmillan Cancer Support since 1984

Rhodds Farm

36 RHODDS FARM

Lyonshall, HR5 3LW. Richard & Cary Goode, 01544 340120, cary.goode@russianaeros.com, www.rhoddsfarm.co.uk. *1m E of Kington. From A44 take small turning S just E of Penrhos Farm, 1m E of Kington. Continue 1m, garden straight ahead.* Sun 28 June (11-5). Adm £5, chd free. Home-made teas. Also open Broxwood Court. Tea and cake available for guests to help themselves in return for a donation.
Created by the owner, a garden designer, over the past 14 years, the garden contains an extensive range of interesting plants. Formal garden with dovecote housing 50 white doves, mixed borders, double herbaceous borders of hot colours, large gravel garden, several ponds, arboretum, wild flower meadow and 13 acres of woodland. A natural garden that fits the setting with magnificent views. Interesting and unusual trees, shrubs and perennials. Magnificent views. A natural garden on a challenging site. A number of sculptures by different artists. No pesticides used. Not suitable for wheelchairs.

SHEEPCOTE

Putley, Ledbury HR8 2RD. Tim & Julie Beaumont, 01531 670801, tim.beaumont@btinternet.com. *5m W of Ledbury off the A438 Hereford to Ledbury Rd. Passenger drop off; parking 200 yards.* Sun 31 May (1-5.30). Adm £5, chd free. Light refreshment. Visits also by arrangement June to Aug for groups of 10 to 20.
1/3 acre garden taken in hand from 2011 retaining many quality plants, shrubs and trees from earlier gardeners. Topiary holly, box, hawthorn, privet and yew formalise the varied plantings around the croquet lawn and gravel garden; beds with heathers, azaleas, lavender surrounded by herbaceous perennials and bulbs; small ponds; kitchen garden with raised beds. Not suitable for wheelchairs.

37 SHUTTIFIELD COTTAGE

Birchwood, Storridge, WR13 5HA. Mr & Mrs David Judge, 01886 884243, judge.shutti@btinternet.com. *15m E of Hereford. Turn L off A4103 at Storridg opp the Church to Birchwood. After 1¼m L down steep tarmac drive. Please park on roadside at the top of the drive but drive down if walking is difficult (150 yards).* Sat 25 Apr, Sat 9, Sun 10, Sat 23 May, Sat 18 July, Sat 22 Aug (1.30-5). Adm £5, chd free. Home-made teas. Visits also by arrangement Apr to Sept.
Superb position and views. Unexpected 3-acre plantsman's garden, extensive herbaceous borders, primula and stump bed, many unusual trees, shrubs, perennials, colour-themed for all-yr interest. Anemones, bluebells, rhododendrons and azaleas are a particular spring feature. Large old rose garden with many spectacular climbers. Small deer park, vegetable garden. Wildlife ponds, wild flowers and walks in 20 acres of ancient woodland. Some sloping lawns and steep paths and steps.

38 SOUTHBOURNE & PINE LODGE

Dinmore, Hereford, HR1 3JR. Lavinia Sole & Frank Ryding. *8m N of Hereford; 8m S of Leominster. From Hereford on A49, turn R at bottom of Dinmore Hill towards Bodenham, gardens 1m on L. From Leominster on A49, L onto A417, 2m turn R & through Bodenham, following NGS signs to garden.* Sun 24, Mon 25 May, Sat 12, Sun 13 Sept (11-4.30). Adm £5, chd free. Home-made teas. Tea/coffee and home-made cakes in both gardens.
2 south facing linked gardens totalling 4½ acres with panoramic views over Bodenham Lakes to the Black Mountains and Malvern Hills. Southbourne: Steep access to 2 acres of terraced lawns, herbaceous beds, shrubs, pond and ornamental woodland. Pine Lodge: Goblin Wood is 2½ acres featuring most of Britain's native trees plus unusual oaks with the emphasis on tree history and folklore. Not suitable for wheelchair access.

39 ◆ STOCKTON BURY GARDENS

Kimbolton, HR6 0HA. Raymond G Treasure, 07880 712649, twstocktonbury@outlook.com, www.stocktonbury.co.uk. *2m NE of Leominster. From Leominster to Ludlow on A49 turn R onto A4112. Gardens 300yds on R.* For NGS: Wed 1 Apr (11-5). Adm £7.50, chd £3. Home-made teas in Tithe Barn. For other opening times and information, please phone, email or visit garden website.
Superb, sheltered 4-acre garden with colour and interest from April until the end of September. Extensive collection of plants, many rare and unusual set amongst medieval buildings. Features pigeon house, tithe barn, grotto, cider press, auricula theatre, pools, secret garden, garden museum and rill, all surrounded by unspoilt countryside. We pride ourselves in offering plant and gardening advice to our visitors. Café serves coffee, tea, homemade cakes and lunches made from local and seasonal produce open 11- 4.30. Last lunches served 2.45pm. Stockton Bury has a small garden school - all classes to be found at www. stocktonbury.co.uk. Partial wheelchair access. If the weather has been very wet it is wise to call first to check suitability.

40 THE VINE

Tarrington, HR1 4EX. Richard and Tonya Price. *Between Hereford & Ledbury on A438. Follow signs from A438 in Tarrington. Park as directed. Disabled parking only at house.* Sun 28 June (2-6). Adm £5, chd free. Home-made teas.
Mature, traditional garden in peaceful setting with stunning views of the surrounding countryside. Consisting of various rooms with mixed and herbaceous borders. Secret garden in blue/yellow/white, croquet lawn with C18 summer house, temple garden with ponds, herb and nosegay garden, vegetable/cutting/soft fruit garden around greenhouse on the paddock. Cornus avenues with obelisk and willow bower.

Your visits help change lives – your generosity has supported unpaid carers through donations to Carers Trust totalling over £4 million since 1996

41 NEW WAINFIELD

Peterstow, Ross-On-Wye, HR9 6LJ. Nick & Sue Helme. *From the A49 between Ross-on-Wye & Hereford. Take the B4521 to Skenfrith/Abergavenny. Wainfeild is 50yrds on R.* **Sat 4 Apr, Fri 22, Sat 23 May, Sat 11 July (10-4). Adm £5, chd free. Home-made teas.**
3 acre informal, wildlife garden including rose garden, fruit trees, climbing roses and clematis. Delightful pond with waterfall. Climbing roses, many different clematis and honeysuckle. In spring, tulips, bluebells, crocuses and grasses followed by lush summer planting. Fruit walk with naturalised cowslips all set in an open area of interesting, unusual mature trees and sculptures. Wheelchair access on uneven grass.
♿ ☕

42 NEW 22 WESTFIELD WALK

Leominster, HR6 8HD. Mr & Mrs Vic & Sue Hamer. *Westfield Walk can be accessed from both Bargates Road & Ryelands Road.* **Sun 5 July, Sun 6 Sept (2-5). Adm £4, chd free. Home-made teas.**
A flower arranger's haven amongst the bustling town, this terraced garden is full of many unusual plants in various mixed borders and boasts a wildlife pond and large working vegetable and fruit area. All year round colour is ensured with such a variety of flora and fauna on show. Plants for sale. Partial wheelchair access. Some steps and steeper slopes. Partial wheelchair access to lower level only.
✿ ☕

43 WESTON HALL

Weston-under-Penyard, Ross-on-Wye, HR9 7NS. Mr P & Miss L Aldrich-Blake, 01989 562597, aldrichblake@btinternet.com. *1m E of Ross-on-Wye. on A40 towards Gloucester.* **Visits by arrangement Apr to Sept for groups of 5+. Light refreshments by request (small cost). Adm £5, chd free.**
6 acres surrounding Elizabethan house (not open). Large walled garden with herbaceous borders, vegetables and fruit, overlooked by Millennium folly. Lawns and mature and recently planted trees and shrubs, with many unusual varieties. Orchard, ornamental ponds and lake. 4 generations in the family, but still evolving year on year. Wheelchair access to walled garden only.
♿ ☕

44 WHITFIELD

Wormbridge, HR2 9BA. Mr & Mrs Edward Clive, 01981 570202, tclive@whitfield-hereford.com, www.whitfield-hereford.com. *8m SW of Hereford. The entrance gates are off the A465 Hereford to Abergavenny rd, 1/2 m N of Wormbridge.* **Sun 29 Mar, Sun 21 June (2-5). Adm £5, chd free. Home-made teas. Visits also by arrangement Mar to Oct for groups of 10 to 30.**
Parkland, wild flowers, ponds, walled garden, many flowering magnolias (species and hybrids), 1780 ginkgo tree, 1 1/2 m woodland walk with 1851 grove of coastal redwood trees. Picnic parties welcome. Dogs on leads welcome. Delicious teas. Partial access to wheelchair users, some gravel paths and steep slopes.
♿ 🐎 ✿ 🚐 ☕

45 WOODVIEW

Great Doward, Whitchurch, Ross-on-Wye, HR9 6DZ. Janet & Clive Townsend, 01600 890477, clive.townsend5@homecall.co.uk. *6m SW of Ross-on-Wye, 4m NE of Monmouth. A40 Ross/Mon At Whitchurch follow signs to Symonds Yat west, then to Doward Park campsite. Take forestry rd 1st L garden 2nd L - follow NGS signs. (Don't rely on satnav).* **Sun 19 Apr, Sun 5, Sun 19 July (1-6). Adm £5, chd free. Home-made teas. Visits also by arrangement Apr to Sept.**
Formal and informal gardens approx 4 acres in woodland setting. Herbaceous borders, hosta collection, mature trees, shrubs and seasonal bedding. Gently sloping lawns. Statuary and found sculpture, local limestone, rockwork and pools. Woodland garden, wild flower meadow and indigenous orchids. Collection of vintage tools and memorabilia. Croquet, clock golf and garden games.
♿ 🐕 ✿ ☕

Grendon Court

© Ellen Rooney

OPENING DATES

All entries subject to change. For latest information check www.ngs.org.uk

Extended openings are shown at the beginning of the month.

Map locator numbers are shown to the right of each garden name.

February

Snowdrop Festival

Saturday 8th
Walkern Hall — 50

Sunday 9th
Walkern Hall — 50

Saturday 15th
Old Church Cottage — 35

Sunday 16th
Old Church Cottage — 35

Friday 21st
1 Elia Cottage — 17

Sunday 23rd
1 Elia Cottage — 17

March

Saturday 21st
Walkern Hall — 50

Sunday 22nd
Walkern Hall — 50

Saturday 28th
◆ Hatfield House West Garden — 23

Sunday 29th
◆ Hatfield House West Garden — 23
◆ St Paul's Walden Bury — 42

April

Monday 13th
10 Cross Street — 13

Sunday 19th
Amwell Cottage — 2

Sunday 26th
Alswick Hall — 1
Hill House — 24
Serendi — 44

May

Friday 1st
Rustling End Cottage — 41

Sunday 3rd
Patchwork — 36
Pie Corner — 38
◆ St Paul's Walden Bury — 42

Monday 4th
Rustling End Cottage — 41

Sunday 10th
NEW Brockholds Manor — 8

Sunday 17th
NEW 28 Dale Avenue — 15
The Manor House, Ayot St Lawrence — 32
◆ Pembroke Farm — 37

Saturday 23rd
The White Cottage — 54

Monday 25th
43 Mardley Hill — 33

Friday 29th
Mackerye End House — 31

Sunday 31st
The Cherry Tree — 11
15 Gade Valley Cottages — 21

June

Friday 5th
NEW 77 Warren Way — 51
NEW Welwyn Village Gardens — 53

Saturday 6th
Brent Pelham Hall — 6

Sunday 7th
Brent Pelham Hall — 6
NEW The Kennels — 27
◆ St Paul's Walden Bury — 42
Thundridge Hill House — 49
NEW 77 Warren Way — 51
NEW Welwyn Village Gardens — 53

Friday 12th
Foxglove Cottage — 20

Saturday 13th
Cunningham Hill Road Gardens — 14

Sunday 14th
◆ Ashridge House — 3
Cunningham Hill Road Gardens — 14
Mackerye End House — 31
Serge Hill Gardens — 45

Saturday 20th
NEW 71 Stansted Road — 48

Sunday 21st
Bayford Musical Gardens Day — 4
NEW Brockholds Manor — 8

Friday 26th
28 Fishpool Street — 19

Saturday 27th
NEW 71 Stansted Road — 48

Sunday 28th
◆ Benington Lordship — 5
28 Fishpool Street — 19
St Stephens Avenue Gardens — 43

July

Friday 3rd
Railway Cottage — 39

Saturday 4th
Kearns & Meiring Physic Garden — 26
NEW 71 Stansted Road — 48

Sunday 5th
Kearns & Meiring Physic Garden — 26
Railway Cottage — 39

Saturday 11th
42 Falconer Road — 18
NEW 71 Stansted Road — 48

Sunday 12th
42 Falconer Road — 18

Friday 17th
102 Cambridge Road — 9

Saturday 18th
Kearns & Meiring Physic Garden — 26

Sunday 19th
102 Cambridge Road — 9
42 Falconer Road — 18
15 Gade Valley Cottages — 21

Kearns & Meiring Physic Garden — 26
South Harpenden Gardens — 46

Sunday 26th
35 Digswell Road — 16

Friday 31st
44 Broadwater Avenue — 7

August

Sunday 2nd
44 Broadwater Avenue — 7
NEW 12 Longmans Close — 30

Friday 7th
8 Kingcroft Road — 28

Sunday 9th
NEW Southdown Gardens — 47

Friday 14th
NEW 12 Longmans Close — 30

Sunday 16th
NEW 12 Longmans Close — 30

Friday 21st
8 Gosselin Road — 22

Sunday 23rd
8 Gosselin Road — 22
Patchwork — 36

Sunday 30th
Reveley Lodge — 40

September

Daily from Saturday 5th to Sunday 13th
◆ The Celebration Garden — 10

Sunday 6th
◆ Pembroke Farm — 37
St Stephens Avenue Gardens — 43

Sunday 13th
102 Cambridge Road — 9
Huntsmoor — 25

November

Sunday 1st
42 Falconer Road — 18

Your visits help change lives – we are the largest single funder of the Queen's Nursing Institute

THE GARDENS

Waterend House

1 ALSWICK HALL

Hare Street Road, Buntingford, SG9 0AA. Mike & Annie Johnson, www.alswickhall.co.uk/gardens. *1m from Buntingford on B1038. From the S take A10 to Buntingford, drive into town & take B1038 E towards Hare Street Village. Alswick Hall is 1m on R.* **Sun 26 Apr (12-4.30). Adm £5, chd free. Home-made teas.**

Listed Tudor House with 5 acres of landscaped gardens set in unspoiled farmland. Two well established natural ponds with rockeries. Herbaceous borders, shrubs, woodland walk and wild flower meadow with a fantastic selection of daffodils, tulips, camassias and crown imperial. Spring blossom, formal beds, orchard and glasshouses. Licensed Bar, Hog Roast, Teas, delicious home-made cakes, plant stall and various other trade stands, children's entertainment. Good access for disabled with lawns and wood chip paths. Slight undulations.

2 AMWELL COTTAGE

Amwell Lane, Wheathampstead, AL4 8EA. Colin & Kate Birss. *½m S of Wheathampstead. From St Helen's Church, Wheathampstead turn up Brewhouse Hill. At top L fork (Amwell Lane), 300yds down lane, park in field opp.* **Sun 19 Apr (2-5). Adm £4, chd free. Home-made teas.**

Informal garden of approx 2½ acres around C17 cottage. Large orchard of mature apples, plums and pear laid out with paths. Extensive lawns with borders, framed by tall yew hedges and old brick walls. A large variety of roses, stone seats with views, woodland pond, greenhouse, vegetable garden with raised beds and fire-pit area. Gravel drive.

3 ◆ ASHRIDGE HOUSE
Berkhamsted, HP4 1NS.
Ashridge (Bonar Law
Memorial) Trust, 01442 843491,
events@ashridge.hult.edu,
www.ashridgehouse.org.uk. *3m
N of Berkhamsted. A4251, 1m S of
Little Gaddesden.* **For NGS: Sun
14 June (11-5). Adm £4.50, chd
£2.50. Home-made teas. For other
opening times and information,
please phone, email or visit garden
website.**
The gardens cover 190 acres forming
part of the Grade II Registered
Landscape of Ashridge Park. Based
on designs by Humphry Repton in
1813 modified by Jeffry Wyatville.
Small secluded gardens, as well as
a large lawn area leading to avenues
of trees. 2013 marked the 200th
anniversary of Repton presenting
Ashridge with the Red Book, detailing
his designs for the estate. In 2020
Ashridge House will be holding a plant
sale on the same day as the National
Garden Scheme Open Day. Plants
are all provided by local growers
and gardens and will be reasonably
priced.

GROUP OPENING

4 BAYFORD MUSICAL GARDENS DAY
Bayford, SG13 8PX.
www.bayfordgardensday.org. *3m
S of Hertford. Off B158 between
Hatfield & Hertford. Free car parking.*
**Sun 21 June (11.30-5). Entry
to all gardens £10, chd free.
Refreshments in gardens, village
school and village hall.**
A popular biennial event held for
over 30yrs. A variety of gardens
from large, long established formal
layouts to pretty cottage gardens.
Live bands incl jazz, steel and brass
add a festive backdrop, while visitors
can enjoy a variety of ploughman's
lunches, cream teas, BBQs and
licensed bars. Stalls sell plants, local
produce, cakes and ice-cream.
Complementary transport around the
village is also provided and there is
ample free car parking. Bayford itself
remains an oasis of countryside even
though it is just 3m S of Hertford,
and 10mins from Potters Bar. The
village has a station which is on
the Stevenage to Moorgate line.
Mentioned in the Doomsday book of
1086 as Begesford, the village today
is fortunate to retain much of its old

world charm, incl a fine church with
C15 font. Please see website for more
details. All proceeds are for charitable
causes. People return year after year
and many regard it as a great day
out in the countryside. Wheelchairs
are of course welcome but we would
ask people to remember that garden
surfaces can be difficult.

5 ◆ BENINGTON LORDSHIP
Stevenage, SG2 7BS. Mr &
Mrs R Bott, 01438 869668,
garden@beningtonlordship.co.uk,
www.beningtonlordship.co.uk. *4m
E of Stevenage. In Benington Village,
next to church. Signs off A602.* **For
NGS: Sun 28 June (12-5). Adm £5,
chd free. Light refreshments at
Benington parish hall, next door
to garden entrance. For other
opening times and information,
please phone, email or visit garden
website.**
7 acre garden incl historic buildings,
kitchen garden, lakes. Spectacular
herbaceous borders, unspoilt
panoramic views. As garden is on
a steep slope there is only partial
wheelchair access. Accessible WC
available in parish hall.

6 BRENT PELHAM HALL
Brent Pelham, Buntingford,
SG9 0HF. Alex & Mike Carrell. *From
Buntingford take the B1038 E for
5m. From Clavering take the B1038
W for 3m.* **Sat 6, Sun 7 June (2-5).
Adm £5, chd free. Home-made
teas in the Estate Office.**
Surrounding a beautiful grade 1
listed property, the gardens consist
of 12 acres of formal gardens,
redesigned 10 years ago by the
renowned landscaper Kim Wilkie.
They include two walled gardens,
potager, walled kitchen garden,
greenhouses, an orchard and a new
double herbaceous border. The
further 14 acres of parkland include
wild flower meadows and two lakes.
It is all gardened organically. Access
by wheelchair to most areas of the
garden, including paths of paving,
gravel and grass.

7 44 BROADWATER AVENUE
Letchworth Garden City, SG6 3HJ.
Karen & Ian Smith. *½m SW
Letchworth town centre. A1(M) J9
signed Letchworth. Straight on at
1st three r'abouts, 4th r'about take
4th exit then R into Broadwater Ave.*
**Evening opening Fri 31 July (6-9).
Wine. Sun 2 Aug (1-5). Home-
made teas. Adm £4.50, chd free.**

Rustling End Cottage

© Rosalind Simon

Town garden in the Letchworth Garden City conservation area that successfully combines a family garden with a plantswoman's garden. Out of the ordinary, unusual herbaceous plants and shrubs. Constantly evolving to include lots of colour and texture. Topiary underpins the whole garden. Attractive front garden designed for year- round interest.

8 NEW BROCKHOLDS MANOR
Old Hall Green, Ware, SG11 1HE. Richard & Juliet Penn Clark, 07931520152, juliet@julietdesign.co.uk. *8m north of Ware 5 mins from A10. Once on Stockalls Lane, drive for about half a mile and look out for a tree-lined driveway/track on the right. Drive to the very bottom, past the pond and Barn conversions.* **Sun 10 May, Sun 21 June (1.30-5.30). Adm £4, chd £2. Home-made teas. Visits also by arrangement Apr to July for groups of 5 to 20.**
A new garden of 4 acres, surrounding a C15 farmhouse. The site of Brockholds dates from the C13. Small woodland walk in spring, an orchard planted 2 years ago with spring bulbs, remains of the original moat, New garden rooms with Yew and Beech hedges, 50 varieties of Old and English Roses, 20 varieties of peonies all planted since 2017. New Potager and Cuttings garden. Some wheelchair access.

9 102 CAMBRIDGE ROAD
St Albans, AL1 5LG. Anastasia & Keith, arezanova@gmail.com. *Nr Ashley Road end of Cambridge Road in The Camp neighbourhood on east side of city. S of the A1057 (Hatfield Rd). Take the A1057 from the A1(M) J3. Take the A1081 from M25 J22.* **Evening opening Fri 17 July (5-8.30). Wine. Sun 19 July, Sun 13 Sept (2-6). Home-made teas. Adm £4, chd free. Friday: Wines and authentic home-made samosas. Sunday: Selection of teas, barista/coffee-shop coffee, home-made cakes. Visits also by arrangement May to Oct for groups of up to 20. Cakes/ samosas on request. Video presentation as part of visit. Donation to Alzheimer's Society.**
Contemporary space sympathetically redesigned in 2017 to keep as much of the existing plants, trees and shrubs in a 1930s semi's garden.

Modern take on the classic garden in two halves: ornamental and vegetable. All-year interest gabion borders packed with perennials and annuals, central bed featuring a pond and a mature Japanese maple. All vegetables, annuals, and some perennials, grown from seed. 'Count the Frog' activity for children and young-at-heart. The garden features steps - there is no wheelchair access.

10 ◆ THE CELEBRATION GARDEN
North Orbital Road, St Albans, AL2 1DH. Aylett Nurseries Ltd, 01727 822255, info@aylettnurseries.co.uk, www.aylettnurseries.co.uk. *The Celebration Garden is adjacent to the Garden Centre. Aylett Nurseries is situated on the eastbound carriageway of the A414 S of St Albans, between the Park Street r'about & London Colney r'about. Drive through green gates at end of car park.* **For NGS: Daily Sat 5 Sept to Sun 13 Sept (9-4.30). Adm by donation. Home-made teas. For other opening times and information, please phone, email or visit garden website.**
The Celebration Garden is sited next to our famous Dahlia Field. Dahlias are planted amongst other herbaceous plants and shrubs. We also have a wild flower border complete with insect hotel. The garden is open all year to visit, during the garden centre opening hours, but it is especially spectacular from July to early autumn when the Dahlias are in flower. Annual Autumn Festival held in September. Refreshments available in the Dahlia Coffee House open all year round. Grass paths.

11 THE CHERRY TREE
Stevenage Road, Little Wymondley, Hitchin, SG4 7HY. Patrick Woollard & Jane Woollard. *½m W of J8 off A1M. Follow sign to Little Wymondley; under railway bridge & house is R at central island flower bed opp Bucks Head Pub. Parking in adjacent rds.* **Sun 31 May (1-5). Adm £4, chd free. Home-made teas.**
The Cherry Tree is a small, secluded garden on several levels containing shrubs, trees and climbers, many of them perfumed. Much of the planting, including exotics, is in containers that are cycled in various positions

throughout the seasons. A heated greenhouse and summerhouse maintain tender plants in winter. The garden has been designed to be a journey of discovery as you ascend.

12 CHURCH BARN
Church Road, Puttenham, Tring, HP23 4PR. R Barker, 07908 719607, bec.barker@btinternet.com, digwithdorris.wordpress.com. *Set in the heart of Puttenham, this is one of the 51 Thankful Villages of England and Wales. From A41 take B4009 Tring/ Wendover exit. Take 1st exit on to Tring Hill towards Aston Clinton. At r'about exit to Lower Icknield Way. After 0.9m turn L. Follow signs from here.* **Visits by arrangement May & June for groups of 5 to 30. Adm £5, chd free. Home-made teas. Apple juice from the garden apples.**
Started from scratch in 2014, rural crafts and bee-friendly plants have been chosen to blend the garden within its rural setting. Willow stock fencing, woven in situ, a shelter crafted in locally grown sweet chestnut, hedges of Hornbeam give structure to tall, wild, colourful borders. Later flowering perennials and grasses self-seed amongst roses, annuals and dahlias. Mainly flat with lawn and stone path.

13 10 CROSS STREET
Letchworth Garden City, SG6 4UD. Renata & Colin Hume, www.cyclamengardens.com. *Nr town centre. From A1(M) J9 signed Letchworth, across 2 r'abouts, R at 3rd, across next 3 r'abouts L into Nevells Rd, 1st R into Cross St.* **Mon 13 Apr (2-5). Adm £4.50, chd free. Home-made teas.**
A garden with mature fruit trees is planted for interest throughout the year. The structure of the garden evolved around three circular lawns, one of which has been turned into a wildlife pond. Borders connect the different levels of the garden. There is also a large pond near the house. Featured in the 2017 Chelsea Special Edition of 'Garden Answers' and 'The English Garden' in Nov 2019. Not suitable for wheelchairs.

GROUP OPENING

14 CUNNINGHAM HILL ROAD GARDENS

St Albans, AL1 5BX. *1m S of St Albans City Centre. At A414 London Colney r'about turn onto London Road (City Centre). Turn R at sign 30mph.* **Sat 13, Sun 14 June (2-5.30). Combined adm £6, chd free. Home-made teas in garden of no 25. Gluten free cakes, home-made elderflower cordial and lemonade.**

25 CUNNINGHAM HILL ROAD
David & Anne Myles.

28 CUNNINGHAM HILL ROAD
Rosemarie & Steve Frost.

Set on opposite sides of a tree lined road, these two ½ acre gardens have a similar mature backdrop, but differ in their aspects and design. No. 25 has been developed by the owner for more than 25 years to include ponds and a rock/ bog garden, large lawns, double herbaceous borders, a wild meadow area, and a rose trellis concealing a sizeable fruit, vegetable and nursery garden with seating. No. 28 while retaining many of the mature planting from its origins in the thirties, has mainly been planted in the last 6 years, by an established garden designer, to provide a peaceful haven of lawns, flanked by mixed borders, leading to a mature wooded area. Not all of no 28 is wheelchair accessible.

  よ ❀ ☕

---

15 NEW 28 DALE AVENUE

Wheathampstead, St Albans, AL4 8LS. Judy Shardlow, www.heartwoodgardendesign. co.uk. *Up Lamer Lane (B651) through Lower Gustard Wood, past Mid Herts Golf Course. Turn R onto The Slype, continuing then take L onto The Broadway & 1st R into Dale Avenue.* **Sun 17 May (1.30-5). Adm £5, chd £2. Light refreshments.**
A large country garden designed by Heartwood Garden Design, with sweeping central lawn and deep mixed borders with evergreen and perennial plants and grasses. It includes a large island bed with a stepping stone path to a lawned border beneath a large Silver Birch. The border includes herbs, salvias, irises, agapanthus, lavender, eryngiums and many varieties of Harkness and David Austin roses.

  D ☕

---

16 35 DIGSWELL ROAD

Welwyn Garden City, AL8 7PB. Adrian & Clare de Baat, 01707 324074, adrian.debaat@ntlworld.com, www.adriansgarden.org. *½ m N of Welwyn Garden City centre. From the Campus r'about in city centre take N exit just past the Public Library into Digswell Rd. Over the White Bridge, 200yds on L.* **Sun 26 July (2-5.30). Adm £4, chd free. Home-made teas. Visits also by arrangement July to Oct for groups of up to 20. Adm incl tea or coffee and home-made cakes.**
Town garden of around a third of an acre with naturalistic planting inspired by the Dutch garden designer, Piet Oudolf. The garden has perennial borders plus a small meadow packed with herbaceous plants and grasses. The contemporary planting gives way to the exotic, incl a succulent bed and under mature trees, a lush jungle garden incl bamboos, bananas, palms and tree ferns. Daisy Roots Nursery will be selling plants. Grass paths and gentle slopes to all areas of the garden.

  よ ❀ ☕

---

17 1 ELIA COTTAGE

Nether Street, Widford, Ware, SG12 8TH. Margaret & Hugh O'Reilly, hughoreilly56@yahoo.co.uk. *B1004 from Ware, Wareside to Widford past Green Man pub into dip at Xrd take R Nether St. 8m W of Bishop's Stortford on B1004 through Much Hadham at Widford sign turn L. B180 from Stanstead Abbots.* **Fri 21, Sun 23 Feb (12.30-4.30). Adm £3.50, chd free. Light refreshments. Visits also by arrangement May to Sept for groups of 5 to 20.**
A third of an acre garden reflecting the seasons. Snowdrops are our first welcome visitors combined with crocus tommasinianus and hellebores. There is a stream with Monet-style bridge, pond and cascade plus water features. Plenty of seats and two summerhouses. Warm baguettes and tea and cake available. Garden quiz. Steep nature of garden means we are sorry no wheelchair access.

  ☕

---

18 42 FALCONER ROAD

Bushey, Watford, WD23 3AD. Mrs Suzette Fuller, 077142 94170, suzettesdesign@btconnect.com. *M1 J5 follow signs for Bushey. From London A40 via Stanmore towards Watford. From Watford via Bushey Arches, through to Bushey High St, turn L into Falconer Rd, opp St James church.* **Sat 11, Sun 12, Sun 19 July (12-6). Home-made teas. Evening opening Sun 1 Nov (6-8). Wine. Adm £3.50, chd free. Mulled Wine on 1st November. Visits also by arrangement May to Sept for groups of up to 20.**
Enchanting magical unusual Victorian style space. Children so very welcome. Winter viewing for fairyland lighting, for all ages, bring a torch. Bird cages and chimneys a feature, plus a walk through conservatory with orchids.

  よ 🚐 ☕

---

19 28 FISHPOOL STREET

St Albans, AL3 4RT. Jenny & Antony Jay. *A5183 to St Albans city centre. Turn into George St. onto Romeland then Fishpool St. At The Lower Red Lion pub walk through archway to the end of the pub car park.* **Evening opening Fri 26 June (6-8). Wine. Sun 28 June (2-5). Home-made teas. Adm £5, chd free.**
Sculpted box and yew hedging and a C17 Tripe House feature strongly in this tranquil oasis set in the vicinity of St Albans Cathedral. Gravel paths lead to a lawn surrounded by late flowering sustainable herbaceous perennial borders and a relaxed woodland retreat. Imaginative planting in these areas offer unique perspectives. Not suitable for wheelchairs due to differing levels.

  ❀ ☕

---

20 FOXGLOVE COTTAGE

Perry Green, Much Hadham, SG10 6EF. Jennifer & John Flexton, 07778 037044, jenniferflexton@hotmail.com. *6m SW of Bishops Stortford. Follow brown signs to Henry Moore Foundation. Foxglove is 4 mins walk from Hoops Inn Pub & Henry Moore Foundation Satnav postcode SG10 6EE Free Parking at Hoops Inn Pub.* **Evening opening Fri 12 June (6-8). Adm £4, chd free. Wine. Visits also by arrangement June to Aug for groups of 10+.**
A beautiful thatched cottage in an idyllic setting on ⅔ of an acre, the epitome of English country charm. Colourful abundant successional planting and classic cottage garden plants fill the overflowing herbaceous

St Stephens Avenue Gardens

borders. A hardworking greenhouse is bordered by organic vegetables, herbs and rose garden. Vibrant blooms attract bees, butterflies and bird boxes abound. Foxgloves pop up everywhere!

21 15 GADE VALLEY COTTAGES

Dagnall Road, Great Gaddesden, Hemel Hempstead, HP1 3BW. Bryan Trueman. *3m N of Hemel Hempstead. Follow B440 N from Hemel Hempstead. Past Water End. Go past turning for Great Gaddesden. Gade Valley Cottages on R. Park in village hall car park.* **Sun 31 May, Sun 19 July (1.30-5). Adm £4, chd free. Home-made teas.**
Medium sized sloping rural garden. Patio, lawn, borders and pond. Paths lead through a woodland area emerging by wildlife pond and sunny border. A choice of seating offers views across the beautiful Gade valley or quiet shady contemplation with sounds of rustling bamboos and bubbling water.

22 8 GOSSELIN ROAD

Bengeo, Hertford, SG14 3LG. Annie Godfrey & Steve Machin, www.daisyroots.com. *Take B158 from Hertford signed to Bengeo. Gosselin Rd 2nd R after White Lion Pub.* **Evening opening Fri 21 Aug (6-8). Sun 23 Aug (12-5). Adm £4, chd free.**
Owners of Daisy Roots nursery, garden acts as trial ground and show case for perennials and ornamental

grasses grown there. Lawn replaced in 2010 by a wide gravel path, flanked by deep borders packed with perennials and grasses. Sunken area surrounded by plants chosen for scent. Small front garden with lots of foliage interest. Regret no dogs.

23 ◆ HATFIELD HOUSE WEST GARDEN

Hatfield, AL9 5HX. The Marquess of Salisbury, 01707 287010, r.ravera@hatfield-house.co.uk, www.hatfield-house.co.uk. *Pedestrian Entrance to Hatfield House is opp Hatfield Railway Stn, from here you can obtain directions to the gardens. Free parking is available, please use AL9 5HX with a sat nav.* **For NGS: Sat 28, Sun 29 Mar (11-4). Adm £6, chd free. For other opening times and information, please phone, email or visit garden website. Donation to another charity.**
Visitors can enjoy the spring bulbs in the lime walk, sundial garden and view the famous Old Palace garden, childhood home of Queen Elizabeth I. The adjoining woodland garden is at its best in spring with masses of naturalised daffodils and bluebells. Beautifully designed gifts, jewellery, toys and much more can be found in the Stable Yard shops. Visitors can also enjoy relaxing at the River Cottage Restaurant which serves a variety of delicious foods throughout the day. There is a good route for wheelchairs around the West garden and a plan can be picked up at the garden kiosk.

24 HILL HOUSE

Stanstead Abbotts, Ware, SG12 8BX. Mr & Mrs J M Pilkington, johnniepilk@hotmail.com. *nr Stanstead Abbotts from A10 turn E on to A414; then B181 for Stanstead Abbotts; L at end of High St, garden 1st R past Church.* **Sun 26 Apr (11-5). Adm £5, chd free. Light refreshments.**
9 acres incl wood; species roses, herbaceous border, water garden, conservatory, woodland walks. Lovely view over Lea Valley. Gravel paths and steep contours do not make it easy.

25 HUNTSMOOR

Stoney Lane, Bovingdon, Hemel Hempstead, HP3 0DP. Mr & Mrs Brian & Jane Bradnock, 01442 832014, b.bradnock@btinternet.com. *Between Bovingdon & Hemel Hempstead. Do not follow SatNav directions along Stoney Lane. Huge pot holes & ruts in lane. Approach from Bushfield Rd. Huntsmoor is facing you at the end of Bushfield Road.* **Sun 13 Sept (2-5). Adm £7, chd free. Home-made teas. Gluten free provided. Visits also by arrangement Aug & Sept for groups of 10+.**
Rose garden, rhododendron border, arboretum, Koi pond, nature pond, shrub and herbaceous borders. Also has a 'cave', and lots of places to sit. Full access to garden including easy access to WC.

26 KEARNS & MEIRING PHYSIC GARDEN

89 Mildred Avenue, Watford, WD18 7DU. Victoria Kearns & Pieter Meiring, www.kmherbalists.co.uk. *Metered parking is available at top of Mildred Ave (opp church) & limited free parking is available on Shepherds Rd (opp Watford Grammar School for Boys) or at Cassiobury Park.* **Sat 4, Sun 5, Sat 18, Sun 19 July (11-4). Adm by donation. Home-made teas. a selection of herbal teas and home-made cakes.**

The Kearns & Meiring Physic Garden – an impressive display of medicinal herbs from Europe and beyond by practising herbalists Victoria Kearns & Pieter Meiring, based in Watford. The garden is divided into medicinal plants by body system and features 70+ different herbs. Talks about the medicinal plants in the garden with teas and cakes. Wheelchair access is available through the side passage. Contact us for parking arrangements.

27 NEW THE KENNELS

Old Common Road, Chorleywood, Rickmansworth, WD3 5LW. Gena Sallis. *½ m from J18 M25. Turn L off A404 at T-lights onto Common Road. Follow road to car park at golf club. Walk back to turning by Rose & Crown pub into Old Common Road and walk down gravel track.* **Sun 7 June (1.30-5). Adm £4, chd free. Home-made teas.**

Set on Chorleywood Common, a character garden on two levels. Traditional structure and planting including roses, herbaceous plants, alpines, and a long established wisteria. A keen focus on maintaining the garden to attract wildlife. Enjoy views of surrounding trees from the terrace and a walk through the wild garden.

28 8 KINGCROFT ROAD

Southdown, Harpenden, AL5 1EJ. Zia Allaway, www.ziaallaway.com. *1½ m S of Harpenden town centre. From Harpenden take the St Albans Rd A1081 S. At 1st r'about turn L onto Southdown Rd. Continue straight over 3 r'abouts to Grove Rd. Take the 3rd turning on R to Coleswood Rd. Take 1st turning on L.* **Evening opening Fri 7 Aug (5-8). Adm £3.50, chd free. Wine. Opening with Southdown Gardens on Sun 9 Aug (2-5.30).**

Beautiful mature town garden designed by garden writer and designer in a contemporary informal style, with small pond and pebbled beach area, gravel garden, a wide range of summer bulbs, herbaceous perennials and shrubs, mature trees, shady borders, greenhouse, and inspirational container displays. A small courtyard features flower-filled window boxes and fruit and vegetables in raised beds.

29 ◆ KNEBWORTH HOUSE GARDENS

Knebworth, SG1 2AX. The Hon Henry Lytton Cobbold, 01438 812661, info@knebworthhouse.com, www.knebworthhouse.com. *nr Stevenage. Direct access from A1(M) J7 at Stevenage.* **For opening times and information, please phone, email or visit garden website.**

The present layout of Knebworth House's delightful Formal Gardens dates largely from the Edwardian era. Sir Edwin Lutyens' garden rooms and pollarded lime walks, Gertrude Jekyll's herb garden, the restored maze, yew hedges, roses and herbaceous borders are key features of the formal gardens with peaceful woodland walks beyond. The Garden Terrace Tea Room is available for visitors to the Park and Gardens, offering a selection of snacks and locally produced hot and cold lunches. The Gift Shop stocks a wide range of affordable gifts and souvenirs, seasonal plants and concert memorabilia, much of which is unique to Knebworth. For more details please see the website.

30 NEW 12 LONGMANS CLOSE

Byewaters, Watford, WD18 8WP. Mark Lammin, 07966 625559, markjango@msn.com. *Byewaters, Croxley Green. Leave M25 at J18 (A404) & follow signs for Rickmansworth/Croxley Green/Watford then follow A412 towards Watford & follow signs for Watford & Croxley Business Parks then follow the NGS signs.* **Sun 2 Aug (1-5). Home-made teas. Evening opening Fri 14 Aug (7-10). Wine. Sun 16 Aug (1-5). Home-made teas. Adm £3.50, chd £1. Visits also by arrangement July & Aug for groups of up to 10.**

Hertfordshire's Tiny Tropical Garden. See how dazzling colour, scent,

lush tropical foliage, trickling water and clever use of pots in a densely planted small garden can transport you to the tropics. Stately bananas and canna rub shoulders with delicate lily and roses amongst a large variety of begonia, hibiscus, ferns and houseplants in a tropical theme more often associated with warmer climes.

31 MACKERYE END HOUSE

Mackerye End, Harpenden, AL5 5DR. Mr & Mrs G Penn. *3m E of Harpenden. A1 J4 follow signs Wheathampstead, then turn R Marshalls Heath Lane. M1 J10 follow Lower Luton Road B653. Turn L Marshalls Heath Lane. Follow signs.* **Evening opening Fri 29 May (6-9). Wine. Sun 14 June (12-5). Home-made teas. Adm £6, chd free. Friday evening wine with canapés.**

C16 (Grade 1 listed) Manor House (not open) set in 15 acres of formal gardens, parkland and woodland, front garden set in framework of formal yew hedges. Victorian walled garden with extensive box hedging and box maze, cutting garden, kitchen garden and lily pond. Courtyard garden with extensive yew and box borders. West garden enclosed by pergola walk of old English roses. All proceeds from the refreshments will be donated to the Isabel Hospice. Walled garden access by gravel paths.

32 THE MANOR HOUSE, AYOT ST LAWRENCE

Welwyn, AL6 9BP. Rob & Sara Lucas. *4m W of Welwyn. 20 mins J4 A1M. Take B653 Wheathampstead. Turn into Codicote Rd follow signs to Shaws Corner. Parking in field, short walk to garden. A disabled drop-off point is available at the end of the drive.* **Sun 17 May (11-5). Adm £5, chd free. Home-made teas.**

A 6-acre garden set in mature landscape around Elizabethan Manor House (not open). 1-acre walled garden incl glasshouses, fruit and vegetables, double herbaceous borders, rose and herb beds. Herbaceous perennial island beds, topiary specimens. Parterre and temple pond garden surround the house. Gates and water features by Arc Angel. Garden designed by Julie Toll. Home-made cakes and tea/coffee and produce for sale.

33 43 MARDLEY HILL

Welwyn, AL6 0TT. Kerrie & Pete, www.agardenlessordinary. blogspot.co.uk. *5m N of Welwyn Garden City. On B197 between Welwyn & Woolmer Green, on crest of Mardley Hill by bus stop for Arriva 300/301.* **Mon 25 May (1-5). Adm £4, chd free. Home-made teas.**
An unexpected garden created by plantaholics and packed with unusual plants. Focus on foliage and long season of interest. Constantly being developed and new plants sourced. Various areas: alpine bed; sunny border; deep shade; white-stemmed birches and woodland planting; naturalistic stream, pond and bog; chicken house and potted vegetables; potted exotics. Seating areas on different levels. Featured in Garden News and Garden Answers.

34 MORNING LIGHT

7 Armitage Close, Loudwater, Rickmansworth, WD3 4HL. Roger & Patt Trigg, 01923 774293, roger@triggmail.org.uk. *From M25 J18 take A404 towards Rickmansworth, after ¾m turn L into Loudwater Lane, follow bends, then turn R at T-junction & R again into Armitage Close.* **Visits by arrangement Apr to Sept for groups of up to 30. Adm £4, chd free. Home-made teas.**
Compact, south-facing plantsman's garden, densely planted with mainly hardy and tender perennials and shrubs in shady environment. Features include island beds, pond, chipped cedar paths and raised deck. Tall perennials can be viewed advantageously from the deck. Large conservatory (450 sq ft) stocked with sub-tropicals.

Your visits help change lives – we are Hospice UK's largest charitable funder donating more than £5.5 million to support hospices in local communities since 1996

43 Mardley Hill

35 OLD CHURCH COTTAGE

Chapel Lane, Long Marston, Tring, HP23 4QT. Dr John & Margaret Noakes. *A41 to Aylesbury take Tring exit. On outskirts of Tring take B488 towards Ivinghoe. At 1st r'about go on to Long Marston. Park in village - accessible parking & drop off only at house.* **Sat 15, Sun 16 Feb (11.30-3). Adm £5, chd free. Wine. Mulled wine and shortbreads served, incl in the adm.**
Small garden around a 400yr old thatched cottage adjoining a disused churchyard with ancient yews and Norman tower being the remnant of a Chapel of Ease. Garden laid out with raised beds with many species and varieties of snowdrops together with cyclamen, crocuses, irises and other early spring bulbs. Garden is at the end of a very narrow country lane, hence request to park in village. Ancient listed buildings in a conservation zone. Garden laid out with raised beds with many unusual snowdrops. Difficult for wheelchairs but we can help.

36 PATCHWORK

22 Hall Park Gate, Berkhamsted, HP4 2NJ. Jean & Peter Block, 01442 864731, patchwork2@btinternet.com. *3m W of Hemel Hempstead. Entering E side of Berkhamsted on A4251, turn L 200yds after 40mph sign.* **Sun 3 May, Sun 23 Aug (2-5). Adm £4, chd free. Light refreshments. Visits also by arrangement Feb to Oct for groups of 10 to 30.**
¼-acre garden with lots of year-round colour, interest and perfume, particularly on opening days. Sloping site containing rockeries, 2 small ponds, herbaceous border, island beds with bulbs in Spring and dahlias in Summer, roses, fuchsias, hostas, begonias, patio pots and tubs galore - all set against a background of trees and shrubs of varying colours. Seating and cover from the elements. Not suitable for wheelchairs, as side entrance is narrow, and there are many steps and levels.

37 ◆ PEMBROKE FARM
Slip End, Ashwell, Baldock, SG7 6SQ. Krysia Selwyn-Gotha, 01462 743102, Pembrokefarmgarden@gmail.com, www.pembrokefarmgarden.co.uk. ½m S of Ashwell. Turn off A505 (The Ashwell turn opp the Wallington & Rushden junction.) Go under railway bridge & past a cottage on R, after 200 yards enter the white farm gates on R. Car park close to garden entry. **For NGS: Sun 17 May, Sun 6 Sept (12-5). Adm £5, chd free. Home-made teas in the courtyard. For other opening times and information, please phone, email or visit garden website.**
A country house garden in a bosquet setting, with formal gardens intermingled with nature. You are invited to meander through changing spaces creating a palimpsest of nature and structure. Wheelchair access is available through the blue door off the car-park entering the garden through the potager.

& 🐕 ✿ 🛏 ☕

38 PIE CORNER
Millhouse Lane, Bedmond, WD5 0SG. Bella & Jeremy Stuart-Smith, piebella1@gmail.com. Between Watford & Hemel Hempstead. 1½m from J21 M25. 3m from J8 of M1. Go to the centre of Bedmond. Millhouse Lane is opp the shops. Entrance is 50m down Millhouse Lane. **Sun 3 May (2-5). Adm £5, chd free. Home-made teas. Visits also by arrangement**

May to Sept for groups of 10+.
A garden designed to complement the modern classical house. Formal areas near the house, with views down the valley, include lawns and a formal pool. The garden becomes more informal towards the woodland edge. A dry garden leads through new meadow planting to the vegetable garden. Enjoy blossom, bulbs, wild garlic, bluebells and rhododendrons in late spring. Wheelchair access to all areas on grass or gravel paths except the formal pond where there are steps.

& ✿ ☕

39 RAILWAY COTTAGE
16 Sandpit Lane, St Albans, AL1 4HW. Siobhan & Barry Brindley. ½m N of St Albans city centre. J21a M25, follow St Albans A5183. Through town centre on A1081. Please use on-street parking in Battlefield, Lancaster, & Gurney Court Roads. **Evening opening Fri 3 July (5-8). Wine. Sun 5 July (2-5). Home-made teas. Adm £4.50, chd free.**
Sandwiched between a main road and railway line, this urban cottage garden is a hidden gem. Little paths are bordered by plants and flowers of all descriptions creating a mass of colour and a haven for insects and birds. There is seating throughout the garden with an eclectic collection of reclaimed items old and new. Raised bed vegetable plot with greenhouse, summerhouses and water features.

✿ ☕

40 REVELEY LODGE
88 Elstree Road, Bushey Heath, WD23 4GL. Reveley Lodge Trust, www.reveleylodge.org. 3½m E of Watford & 1½m E of Bushey Village. From A41 take A411 signed Bushey & Harrow. At mini-r'about 2nd exit into Elstree Rd. Garden ½m on L. Disabled parking only onsite. **Sun 30 Aug (2-6). Adm £5, chd free. Home-made teas.**
2½-acre garden surrounding a Victorian house bequeathed to Bushey Museum in 2003 and in process of re-planting and renovation. Featuring colourful annual, tender perennial and medicinal planting in beds surrounding a mulberry tree. Conservatory, lean-to greenhouse, rose garden, vegetable garden and beehives. Analemmatic (human) sundial constructed in stone believed unique to Hertfordshire. Live music by Guitar n Brass: guitar/ vocals and trombone / vocals performing a mix of happy jazz and smooth and mellow jazz. Partial wheelchair access.

& 🐕 ✿ ☕

41 RUSTLING END COTTAGE
Rustling End, Codicote, SG4 8TD. Julie & Tim Wise, www.rustlingend.com. 1m N of Codicote. From B656 turn L into '3 Houses Lane' then R to Rustling End. House 2nd on L. **Evening opening Fri 1 May (4-8). Wine. Mon 4 May (1-5). Home-made teas. Adm £5, chd free.**
Meander through our wild flower meadow to a cottage garden with

Cunningham Hill Road

contemporary planting. Behind lumpy hedges explore borders of abundant planting featuring bulbs early in the season. A rewilding project with small newly planted orchard provides an environment for many wild birds and small mammals. Our terrace features drought tolerant low maintenance simplistic planting. An abundant flowery vegetable garden provides produce for the summer. Hens in residence.

Your visits help change lives – your generosity helps Marie Curie fund nurses to care for people night and day in their homes, with donations of more than £9 million

42 ◆ ST PAUL'S WALDEN BURY
Whitwell, Hitchin, SG4 8BP.
The Bowes Lyon family,
stpaulswalden@gmail.com, ,
www.stpaulswaldenbury.co.uk.
5m S of Hitchin. On B651; ½ m N of Whitwell village. From London leave A1(M) J6 for Welwyn (not Welwyn Garden City). Pick up signs to Codicote, then Whitwell. **For NGS: Sun 29 Mar, Sun 3 May, Sun 7 June (2-7). Adm £5, chd £1. Home-made teas. Cakes, cream scones, sandwiches. For other opening times and information, please email or visit garden website.** Donation to St Paul's Walden Charity.
Spectacular formal woodland garden, Grade 1 listed, laid out 1720, covering over 50 acres. Long rides lined with clipped beech hedges lead to temples, statues, lake and a terraced theatre. Seasonal displays of snowdrops, daffodils, cowslips, irises, magnolias, rhododendrons, lilies. Wild flowers are encouraged. This was the childhood home of the late Queen Mother. Children welcome. 7 June, Open Garden combined with Open Farm Sunday with free tours of the farm. Wheelchair access to part of the garden. Steep grass slopes in places.

GROUP OPENING

43 ST STEPHENS AVENUE GARDENS
St Albans, AL3 4AD. *1m S of St Albans City Centre. From A414 take A5183 Watling St. At mini-r'about by St Stephens Church/King Harry Pub take B4630 Watford Rd. St Stephens Ave is 1st R.* **Sun 28 June, Sun 6 Sept (2.30-5.30). Combined adm £5, chd free. Home-made teas at No 20. Gluten free cake available, WC.**

20 ST STEPHENS AVENUE
Heather & Peter Osborne.

30 ST STEPHENS AVENUE
Carol & Roger Harlow.

Two gardens of similar size and the same aspect, developed in totally different ways. Dense planting at number 20 makes it impossible to see from one end to the other, enticing visitors to explore, and is designed to blur the boundaries of a long and narrow plot (53 x 12m). Paths meander through and behind the colour coordinated borders, giving access to all parts of the garden. Specimen trees, and fences clothed with climbers contribute to the peaceful seclusion. Varied plant habitats include cool shade, hot dry gravel and lush pondside displays. Seating is in both sun and shade, a large conservatory provides shelter. Number 30 has a southwest facing gravelled front garden that has a Mediterranean feel. Herbaceous plants, such as sea hollies and achilleas, thrive in the poor, dry soil. Clipped box, beech and hornbeam in the back garden provide a cool backdrop for the strong colours of the herbaceous planting. A gate beneath a beech arch frames the view to the park beyond. Plants for sale at June opening only. Compost making demonstrations.

44 SERENDI
22 Hitchin Road, Letchworth Garden City, SG6 3LT. Valerie. *1m from city centre. A1(M) J9 signed Letchworth on A505. At 2nd r'about take 1st exit Hitchin A505. Straight over T-lights. Garden 1m on R.* **Sun 26 Apr (11-5). Adm £5, chd free. Home-made teas.**
A well designed plants woman's garden. A mass of Spring bulbs,

a silver birch grove, a 'dribble of stones', contemporary knot garden, and dry planted area with alliums. Later in the year an abundance of roses climbing 5 pillars, perennials and grasses. A greenhouse for over wintering and a Griffin glass house with Brugmansia and Plumbago to list a few of the features. Regional Finalist, The English Garden's The Nation's Favourite Gardens 2019. Gravel entrance driveway and paths, can be difficult. Plenty of lawns.

GROUP OPENING

45 SERGE HILL GARDENS
Serge Hill Lane, Bedmond, WD5 0RT. *½ m E of Bedmond. Go to Bedmond & take Serge Hill Lane, where you will be directed past the lodge & down the drive.* **Sun 14 June (2-5). Combined adm £8, chd free. Home-made teas at Serge Hill.**

THE BARN
Sue & Tom Stuart-Smith.
Ⓓ

SERGE HILL
Kate Stuart-Smith.

Two very diverse gardens. At its entrance the Barn has an enclosed courtyard, with tanks of water, herbaceous perennials and shrubs tolerant of generally dry conditions. To the N there are views over the 5-acre wild flower meadow, and the West Garden is a series of different gardens overflowing with bulbs, herbaceous perennials and shrubs. The house at Serge Hill results principally from the work of Charles Augustin Busby (1786-1817), an architect and engineer perhaps most renowned for a development west of Brighton christened Brunswick Town and for his 1808 publication: A series of designs for villas and country houses. In 1811 Busby exhibited his designs for Serge Hill House at the Royal Academy. It has wonderful views over the ha-ha to the park; a walled vegetable garden with a large greenhouse, roses, shrubs and perennials leading to a long mixed border. At the front of the house there is an outside stage used for family plays, and a ship.

GROUP OPENING

46 SOUTH HARPENDEN GARDENS

Harpenden, AL5 2AN. *1m S of Harpenden on A1081, after 1m turn R into Beesonend Lane,. bear R into Burywick to T junction follow signs. 40 West Common: back to A1081 & turn L towards Harpenden. Cross the r'about junction with B497 & after 200yds turn L into West Common & follow signs.* **Sun 19 July (2-5.30). Combined adm £6, chd free. Home-made teas at 2 & 7 Barlings Rd.**

2 BARLINGS ROAD
Liz & Jim Machin.

7 BARLINGS ROAD
Chris Berendt.
D

NEW 40 WEST COMMON
Maggie Cartmell.

Three gardens all reflecting their owner's individual interests and needs. 2 Barlings Road is packed with perennials, shrubs and climbers and a formal pond to provide yr-round structure and privacy. A courtyard suntrap and shade garden provide extra interest. 7 Barlings Road is a professionally landscaped garden designed for minimal maintenance and maximum impact with mature trees, climbers, water feature, children's play area, pagoda and plant filled borders. 40 West Common (new for 2020) is essentially a wildlife garden filled with insect-friendly wild and cultivated plants enclosed by a mixed boundary hedge. An informal pond attracts frogs, newts and dragonflies. Fruit trees, soft fruit, vegetables and an active beehive and roaming bumblebees complete the picture. Plants for sale at No.2. Wheelchair access to Barlings Road, level gardens accessed via side paths. No access to 40 West Common.
&. ✿ ☕

Foxglove Cottage

GROUP OPENING

47 NEW SOUTHDOWN GARDENS

Harpenden, AL5 1EL. *Exit M1 J9 & turn R onto A5183 heading towards Redbourn; turn L at r'about towards Harpenden on B487; pass the White Horse Pub on the L; take 2nd exit at r'about onto Walkers Road.* **Sun 9 Aug (2-5.30). Combined adm £6, chd free. Home-made teas.**

NEW 4 COLESWOOD ROAD
Mrs Linzi Claridge.

NEW 5 COLESWOOD ROAD
Marilyn Couldridge.

8 KINGCROFT ROAD
Zia Allaway.
(See separate entry)

Three exquisite town gardens. Two gardens on opposite sides of Coleswood Road. Neither have a lawn; instead an abundance of mixed planting to make the most of each garden space. There is structure, height, loose planting, pots, water features. These gardens will show you what can be achieved within 2 years. The third, in Kingcroft Road, is a beautiful mature town garden designed in a contemporary informal style, with small pond and pebbled beach area, gravel garden, summer bulbs, herbaceous perennials and shrubs, mature trees, shady borders, greenhouse, and inspirational container displays.
☕

48 NEW 71 STANSTED ROAD

Bishop's Stortford, CM23 2DT. **Jill & Nigel Kerby.** *E of town centre. 2½ m W from J8 M11 - take A120 to 2nd r'about, then L onto Stansted Rd. Or 9m E from A10 - take A120 to 2nd r'about, R onto Stansted Rd.* **Every Sat 20 June to 11 July (11-2, 2-5). Adm £10, chd free. Ticket includes guided tour and refreshments. Pre-booking essential, please contact jill. kerby@icloud.com or 07931 255812 for information and booking.**
An intriguing wildlife garden, set in ⅔ acre in the heart of town. Designed by the Butterfly Brothers to encourage wildlife, with a wild flower meadow, three ponds and an extensive woodland border. Formal areas feature a romantic garden with

many herbaceous plants chosen to encourage insects. Open to a limited number of visitors by pre-booking only. Featured on Gardeners World magazine July 2019.

❀ ☕

49 THUNDRIDGE HILL HOUSE
Cold Christmas Lane, Ware, SG12 0UE. Christopher & Susie Melluish, 01920 462500, c.melluish@btopenworld.com. *2m NE of Ware. ¾ m from Maltons off the A10 down Cold Christmas Lane, crossing bypass.* **Sun 7 June (2-5.30). Adm £5, chd free. Cream teas. Visits also by arrangement Apr to Sept for groups of 10+.** Well-established garden of approx 2½ acres; good variety of plants, shrubs and roses, attractive hedges. Visitors often ask for the unusual yellow-only bed. Several delightful places to sit. Wonderful views in and out of the garden especially down to the Rib Valley to Youngsbury, visited briefly by Lancelot 'Capability' Brown. 'A most popular garden to visit'. Fine views down to Thundridge Old Church.

& 🐕 ☕

50 WALKERN HALL
Walkern, Stevenage, SG2 7JA. Mrs Kate de Boinville. *4m E of Stevenage. Turn L at War Memorial as you leave Walkern, heading for Benington (immed after small bridge). Garden 1m up hill on R.* **Sat 8, Sun 9 Feb (12-4); Sat 21, Sun 22 Mar (12-5). Adm £5, chd free. Home-made teas. Warming home-made soup and cakes.** Walkern Hall is essentially a winter woodland garden. Set in 8 acres, the carpet of snowdrops and aconites is a constant source of wonder in Jan/Feb. This medieval hunting park is known more for its established trees such as the tulip trees and a magnificent London plane tree which dominates the garden. Following on in March and April is a stunning display of daffodils. and other spring bulbs. There is wheelchair access but quite a lot of gravel. No disabled WC.

& ❀ 🚐 ☕

51 NEW 77 WARREN WAY
Digswell, Welwyn, AL6 0DL. Caroline Goodchild. *Close to Welwyn North Station, Digswell. 2m N of Welwyn Garden City. 1m from J6 A1 (M). Approaching from the B1000 take the exit at the mini*

r'about into Station Rd. Turn L into Warren Way. Continue to the top LH corner of Warren Way. **Evening opening Fri 5 June (6-8). Wine. Sun 7 June (2-5). Home-made teas. Adm £3.50, chd free. Also open Welwyn Village Gardens.** Family garden with access to surrounding woodland. Children welcome. Medium sized multi purpose family garden with an eclectic mix of planting. A variety of bulbs, perennial borders and mixed shrubs provide all year round interest and colour. Foxgloves, alliums and hellebores throughout the many beds.

& ❀ ☕

52 WATEREND HOUSE
Waterend Lane, Wheathampstead, St Albans, AL4 8EP. Mr & Mrs J Nall-Cain, 07736 880810, sj@nallcain.com. *2m E of Wheathampstead. Approx 10 mins from J4 of A1M. Take B653 to Wheathampstead, past Crooked Chimney Pub, after ½ m turn R into Waterend Lane. Cross river, house is immed. on R.* **Visits by arrangement Mar to June for groups of 20 to 30. Home-made teas.** A hidden garden of 4 acres sets off an elegant Jacobean Manor House (not open). Steep grass slopes and fine views of glorious countryside. Formal flint-walled garden. Snowdrops and bulbs in the spring. Formal beds and lots of colour throughout most of the year. Mature specimen trees, new pond, formal vegetable garden, bantams and Indian runner ducks. Hilly garden. Wheelchair access to lower gardens only. No accessible WC.

& ☕

We help ordinary people open the gates to their extraordinary private gardens to raise impressive amounts of money through admissions, teas and slices of cake!

GROUP OPENING

53 NEW WELWYN VILLAGE GARDENS
Welwyn, AL6 9EU. *J6 A1M approx ⅓ m to gardens, follow yellow signs to Welwyn village.* **Evening opening Fri 5 June (5-8.30). Wine. Sun 7 June (2-5.30). Home-made teas at Mill House. Combined adm £6, chd free. Also open 77 Warren Way.**

THE MILL HOUSE
Sarah & Ian.

NEW 44 MILL LANE
Bryan & Ann Parkes.

NEW 6 ROMAN WAY
Harry & Hilary Ward.

A group of very different but lovely gardens all located in Welwyn village. Ranging from, a romantic riverside mill house setting, with deep herbaceous borders, a parterre, potager and secret paths leading to a riverside seat, to the second, being a show case for a sculptor's work, in a tranquil and mature setting with water features to the third being a compact, lusciously planted and quirky garden, full of surprises with an eclectic mix of architectural, Mediterranean and traditional plants. 6 Roman Way is an eight minute walk or a short car journey with ample parking. Wheelchair access to all three, but there are some gravel and uneven paths.

& ❀ ☕

---

54 THE WHITE COTTAGE
Waterend Lane, Wheathampstead, St Albans, AL4 8EP. Sally Trendell, 07775 897713, 01582 834617, sallytrendell@me.com. *2m E of Wheathampstead. Approx 10 mins from J5 A1M Take B653 to Wheathampstead. Soon after Crooked Chimney pub turn R into Waterend Lane, garden 300yds on L. Parking in field opp.* **Evening opening Sat 23 May (5-9). Adm £5, chd free. Wine. Picnickers are welcome. Visits also by arrangement Apr to Oct.** An idyllic and atmospheric setting. A riverside retreat of over an acre in rural position adjacent to a ford. The River Lea widens and forms the boundary to this wildlife haven which could be a setting for 'Wind in the Willows'. Sally's cottage garden reflects her unique eclectic style.

& 🐕 🛏

OPENING DATES

All entries subject to change. For latest information check www.ngs.org.uk

Map locator numbers are shown to the right of each garden name.

April

Sunday 5th
Northcourt Manor Gardens   15

May

Sunday 3rd
Morton Manor   10

Saturday 16th
NEW April Cottage   1

Sunday 17th
NEW April Cottage   1

Saturday 30th
NEW Copsefield Gardens   5

Sunday 31st
NEW Copsefield Gardens   5
NEW Goldings   8
Meadowsweet   9
Red Cross Cottage   18
Salterns Cottage   19
Thorley Manor   20

June

Sunday 7th
The Old Rectory   17

Saturday 13th
Niton Gardens   13

Sunday 14th
Niton Gardens   13
◆ Nunwell House   16

Saturday 20th
Carpe Diem   4

Sunday 21st
Carpe Diem   4

Saturday 27th
Ashknowle House   2

Sunday 28th
Ashknowle House   2

July

Sunday 5th
North Grounds Farm   14

Saturday 11th
NEW Mountbatten Gardens   11

Sunday 12th
The Beeches   3
NEW Mountbatten Gardens   11

Saturday 18th
NEW East Dene   7

Sunday 19th
NEW East Dene   7

September

Sunday 6th
Morton Manor   10

By Arrangement

Arrange a personalised garden visit with your club, or group of friends, on a date to suit you. See individual garden entries for full details.

NEW April Cottage   1
Crab Cottage   6
Morton Manor   10
Ningwood Manor   12
Northcourt Manor Gardens   15
The Old Rectory   17

THE GARDENS

1 NEW APRIL COTTAGE

Headon Hall Estate, Alum Bay, PO39 0JD. Ms Melody Dean, 01983 756771, theneedlesview@gmail.com. *Under Headon Warren, heather clad side of the Chine. Follow signs to The Needles Park, turn R 100 metre before their r'about, park along lane, if no space follow on into gated estate.* Sat 16 May (2-6); Sun 17 May (10-6). Adm £4, chd free. Light refreshments. Visits also by arrangement May to Dec for groups of 30+.

'A cottage is no cottage without a wild cottage garden' my Gran would say. 8 yrs old, no straight lines, only curves and islands of flowers in the lawn, mine is now taken shape. Foxgloves rule May, growing where they desire as herbs, annuals and perennials fight for their spot. Agapanthus flowers stand tall in all gales and migrating birds pop in for water and rest in this little oasis at Alum Bay. Stunning views to The Needles, Tennyson monument and heather clad Headon Hill. Historic 152 yr old intact Victorian Stable in the Coach House, which will be open for the first time to the public, under private ownership.

✿ 🚗 🛏 ☕

2 ASHKNOWLE HOUSE

Ashknowle Lane, Whitwell, Ventnor, PO38 2PP. Mr & Mrs K Fradgley. *4m W of Ventnor. Take the Whitwell Rd from Ventnor or Godshill. Turn into unmade lane next to Old Rectory. Field parking. Disabled parking at house.* Sat 27, Sun 28 June (12-4). Adm £4.50, chd free. Home-made teas.

A variety of features to explore in the grounds of this Victorian house (not open). Woodland walks, wildlife and fish ponds, many colourful beds and borders. The large, well maintained, kitchen garden is highly productive and boasts a wide range of fruit and vegetables grown in cages, tunnels, glasshouses and raised beds. Diversely planted and highly productive orchard incl protected cropping of strawberries, peaches and apricots.

🐕 ✿ ☕

3 THE BEECHES

Chale Street, Chale, Ventnor, PO38 2HE. Mr Andrew Davidson, 01983 551876, andrewdavidson06@btinternet.com. *Turn off A3055 at Chale onto B3399. Entrance between Old Rectory & bus stop, in gap in stone wall.* Sun 12 July (10-5). Adm £3, chd free. Home-made teas.

The garden is laid out mainly to shrubs and border plants designed for colour and texture. A haven of peace with extensive 270 degree views of the countryside incl the south west coast of the island down to The Needles and Dorset beyond. Features incl a wildflower meadow and a deep pond home to fish and wildlife (children to be supervised because of deep water). Come and see how the new wildflower meadow is settling in. Due to gravel driveway and some steps, wheelchair access is not easy, however we can accommodate with prior arrangement.

♿ 🐕 ✿ ☕

4 CARPE DIEM

75 Newnham Road, Binstead, Ryde, PO33 3TE. Tim & Tracy Welstead. *From the A3045 Newport to Ryde road, at Binstead Hill r'about, turn into Newnham Rd.* Sat 20, Sun 21 June (10-4). Adm £3.50, chd free. Home-made teas.

This organic principled ¼ acre

garden has evolved over 16 yrs. It is divided into different themed planting areas and contains 2 wildlife ponds, vegetable and fruit areas. The garden can be wet in winter and dry in summer, the planting is chosen to meet these needs. The garden has now reached a happy balance where pests are dealt with by our wildlife friends, which are all welcomed in.

GROUP OPENING

5 NEW **COPSEFIELD GARDENS**
Copsefield Drive, Ryde, PO33 3AR. *At the bottom of Copsefield Drive, off Spencer Rd to the R when coming from Ryde.* Sat 30, Sun 31 May (10-6). Combined adm £5, chd free. Light refreshments.

NEW **COPSEFIELD HOUSE**
Andrew Wilson-Jenner & Stephen Baum Webb.

NEW **COPSEFIELD LODGE**
Mark Ager & Wendy Newman.

NEW **COPSEFIELD WEST**
Fergus Smith & Kate Freeman.

A group of three gardens all very different, clustered around the historic Copsefield House, situated on the west side of Ryde, rolling down to

the sea. The house was once owned by Queen Victoria's physician and the Queen planted two trees in the garden, one of which stands as the tallest tree on the island. There are a number of mature trees and oaks in the grounds that form the start of the wood between Ryde and Fishbourne. Each garden has its own personality, from the traditional to the wild with multiple places to sit and enjoy the planting, the woods, wildlife and the sea views. The garden is open during the Round the Island Sailing Race weekend and provides a perfect place to watch this spectacle in the Solent. Uneven ground and gravel drive. No steps to view main features.

---

6 **CRAB COTTAGE**
Mill Road, Shalfleet, PO30 4NE. Mr & Mrs Peter Scott, 07768 065756, mencia@btinternet.com. *4½ m E of Yarmouth. At New Inn, Shalfleet, turn into Mill Rd. Continue 400yds, drive through open NT gates. After 100yds pass Crab Cottage on L, turn L into gate. Limited parking in gravel drive.* **Visits by arrangement May to Sept. Adm £4, chd free. Home-made teas.**
1¼ acres on gravelly soil. Part glorious views across croquet lawn over Newtown Creek and Solent, leading through wildflower meadow to

hidden water lily pond and woodland walk. Part walled garden protected from westerlies with mixed borders, leading to terraced sunken garden with ornamental pool and pavilion, planted with exotics, tender shrubs and herbaceous perennials. Croquet, plant sales and excellent teas £1.50, or with cakes £3 on request. Wheelchair access over gravel and uneven grass paths.

7 NEW **EAST DENE**
Atherfield Green, Ventnor, PO38 2LF. Marc & Lisa Morgan-Huws. *From the A3055 Military Rd, turn into Southdown. At the end of the road turn L on to Atherfield Rd & the garden is ahead on the R.* Sat 18, Sun 19 July (11-5). Adm £4, chd free. Light refreshments. Planted from 2 acres of farmland in the 1970s, the garden is structured around a variety of mature trees. Taken over by brambles and nettles prior to our arrival 4 yrs ago, the garden is slowly being rediscovered and restored, whilst still being a haven for wildlife. Occupying a windswept coastal location with areas of woodland, fruit trees, mature pond and informal planting. Alpacas. Although the garden has level access, the ground is unmade.

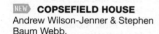

Morton Manor

© Heather Edwards

8 NEW GOLDINGS

Main Road, Thorley, Yarmouth, PO41 0SN. John & Dee Sichel. *E of Yarmouth. Follow directions for Thorley from Yarmouth/Newport road or from Wilmington Lane. Then follow NGS signs. Parking shared with Thorley Manor.* **Sun 31 May (2-5). Combined adm with Thorley Manor £4, chd free. Home-made teas at Thorley Manor.**

A country garden with many focuses of interest. A newly planted orchard already producing cider apples in large amounts. A small but productive vegetable garden and a well maintained lawn with shrub borders and roses. A micro-climate has been created by the adjustment of levels to create a series of terraced areas for planting.

9 MEADOWSWEET

5 Great Park Cottages, off Betty-Haunt Lane, Carisbrooke, PO30 4HR. Gunda Cross. *4m SW of Newport. From A3054 Newport/ Yarmouth road, turn L at Xrd Porchfield/Calbourne, over bridge into 1st lane on R. Parking along one side, on grass verge & past house.* **Sun 31 May (11.30-4.30). Adm £4, chd free. Home-made teas.**

From windswept, barren 2 acre cattle field to developing tranquil country garden. Natural, mainly native planting and wild flowers. Cottagey front garden, herb garden, orchard, fruit cage and large pond. The good life and a haven for wildlife! Creative planting, wildlife pond and woodland. Very popular and unusual plants for sale. Wheelchair access over flat level garden with grass paths.

10 MORTON MANOR

Morton Manor Road, Brading, Sandown, PO36 0EP. Mr & Mrs G Godliman, 07768 605900, patricia.godliman@yahoo.co.uk. *Off A3055 5m S of Ryde, just out of Brading. At Yarbridge T-lights turn into The Mall. Take next L into Morton Manor Rd.* **Sun 3 May, Sun 6 Sept (11-4). Adm £4, chd free. Home-made teas. Visits also by arrangement Apr to Oct.**

A colourful garden of great plant variety. Mature trees incl many acers with a wide variety of leaf colour. Early in the season a display of rhododendrons, azaleas and camellias and later hydrangeas and hibiscus. Ponds, sweeping lawns, roses set on a sunny terrace and much more to see in this extensive garden surrounding a picturesque C16 manor house (not open). Wheelchair access with gravel driveway.

11 NEW MOUNTBATTEN GARDENS

Halberry Lane, Newport, PO30 2ER. *5 mins from Newport. Halberry Lane is off the A3054 Fairle Rd from either Newport or Ryde. Or from Staplers Rd take Cross Lane to Halberry Lane. Bus 9 from Ryde or Newport. Bus 5 from East Cowes.* **Sat 11, Sun 12 July (10-4). Adm by donation. Light refreshments.**

A garden of tranquility with a variety of interesting planted areas. Trees, shrubs, herbaceous, grasses, water feature and decking are just a few of the delights and the wildlife catered for too. Wander from area to area and admire the interesting plantings, or sit and reflect in a quiet corner or take refreshment in our lovely café serving cream teas, cakes and light refreshments.

12 NINGWOOD MANOR

Station Road, Ningwood, Nr Newport, PO30 4NJ. Nicholas & Claire Oulton, 07738 737482, claireoulton@gmail.com. *Nr Shalfleet. From Newport, turn L opp the Horse & Groom Pub. Ningwood Manor is 300-400yds on the L. Please use 2nd set of gates.* **Visits by arrangement May to Sept for groups of up to 30. Adm £5, chd free. Light refreshments.**

A 3 acre, landscape designed country garden divided into several rooms; a walled courtyard, croquet lawn, white garden and kitchen garden. They flow into each other, each with their own gentle colour schemes, the exception to this is the croquet lawn garden which is a riot of colour, mixing oranges, reds, yellows and pinks. Much new planting has taken place over the last few yrs. The owners have several new projects underway, so the garden is a work in progress. Features incl a vegetable garden with raised beds and a small summerhouse, part of which is alleged to be Georgian.

GROUP OPENING

13 NITON GARDENS

Niton, PO38 2AZ. *5m W of Ventnor. Parking at football ground (Blackgang Rd), in village & Allotment Rd car park. Tickets & maps from the library in the heart of the village on Niton Gardens open days only.* **Sat 13, Sun 14 June (11-4). Combined adm £5, chd free. Home-made teas at selected gardens on route.**

NEW 8 CHATFIELD ROAD
Mr John Etherton.

CROSSWAYS
Barry & Mary Howes.

NEW 12 GREENLYDD CLOSE
Gaye Rolfe.

KINGS MANOR FARM
Ian & Catherine Hoare.

NEW PINE RIDGE
Mr Martin Ward.

PUCKASTER CORNER
Mr & Mrs Ian McCallum.

SPRING COTTAGE
Mr & Mrs Neil White.

TALSA
Frances Pritchard.

TILLINGTON VILLA
Paul & Catherine Miller.

WINFRITH
Mrs Janet Tedman.

Niton is a delightful village with a busy community spirit, blessed with lovely churches, two pubs (one of which was renowned for smuggling), PO and shops, lovely walks and bridleways, school, football and cricket pitches and recreation ground. The gardens of this walk are very varied in both style and size and are full of colour, fragrance and interest; from cottage and country gardens to vegetable plot and havens for wildlife. The gardens are situated both in the heart of the village and the undercliff. We do hope you will enjoy them all.

14 NORTH GROUNDS FARM

Appleford Road, Chale Green, Ventnor, PO38 2AP. Michael & Miranda Acland. *From the E we are opp the Chale Green village sign as you approach the village. From the W go through Chale Green, past the village shop & the farm is ½m further*

on the L. Parking in field. **Sun 5 July (2-6). Adm £4, chd free. Home-made teas.**
Stunning landscaped garden with mature borders and a wide range of unusual plants, currently being restored by new owners. Ornamental garden, cottage garden, spring garden, orchard, greenhouses, vegetable and herb garden, rose pergola, gazebo and meadow. Small lake with boathouse and duckhouse, planted with willows, lilies and shrubs. Barns, old piggery, woodland and sheep. Wheelchair access to garden is over rough grass and parts are only accessible via steps.

15 NORTHCOURT MANOR GARDENS
Main Road, Shorwell, Newport, PO30 3JG. Mr & Mrs J Harrison, 01983 740415, john@northcourt.info, www.northcourt.info. *4m SW of Newport. On entering Shorwell from Newport, entrance at bottom of hill on R. If entering from other directions head through village in direction of Newport. Garden on the L, on bend after passing the church.* **Sun 5 Apr (12-4). Adm £5, chd free. Tea. Visits also by arrangement for groups of 5+. Introduction & teas or light lunches for large groups only.**
15 acre garden surrounding large C17 manor house (not open). Boardwalk along jungle garden. A large variety of plants enjoying the different microclimates. Large collection of camellias and magnolias. Kitchen garden might not be open. Woodland walks. Tree collection. Picturesque wooded valley around the house. Bathhouse and snail mount leading to terraces. 1 acre walled garden. The house celebrated its 404th yr anniversary. A plantsman' garden. Wheelchair access on main paths only, some paths are uneven and the terraces are hilly.

16 ❖ NUNWELL HOUSE
Coach Lane, Brading, PO36 0JQ. Mr & Mrs S Bonsey, 01983 407240, info@nunwellhouse.co.uk, www.nunwellhouse.co.uk. *3m S of Ryde. Signed off A3055 as you arrive at Brading from Ryde & turn into Coach Lane.* **For NGS: Sun 14 June (1-4). Adm £5, chd free. Home-made teas. For other opening times and information, please phone, email or visit garden website.**

6 acres of tranquil and beautifully set formal and shrub gardens and old fashioned shrub roses prominent. Exceptional Solent views over historic parkland and Brading Haven from the terraces. Small arboretum and walled garden with herbaceous borders. House developed over 5 centuries and full of architectural interest.

17 THE OLD RECTORY
Kingston Road, Kingston, PO38 2JZ. Derek & Louise Ness, louiseness@gmail.com, www.theoldrectorykingston.co.uk. *8m S of Newport. Entering Shorwell from Carisbrooke, take L turn at mini-r'about towards Chale (B3399). Follow road, house 2nd on L, after Kingston sign. Park in adjacent field.* **Sun 7 June (2-5). Adm £4, chd free. Home-made teas. Visits also by arrangement in June for groups of up to 30.**
Constantly evolving romantic country garden surrounding the late Georgian Rectory (not open). Areas of interest incl the walled kitchen garden, orchard, formal and wildlife ponds, a wonderfully scented collection of old and English roses and two perennial wildflower meadows. Partial wheelchair access, some gravel and grass paths.

> We open the gates to the nation's best gardens, offering a relaxing, memorable and affordable day out. A perfect experience to share with friends and family.

18 RED CROSS COTTAGE
Salterns Road, Seaview, PO34 5AG. Mr & Mrs Stephen Jones. *Enter Seaview from Springvale. Take signs for the Duver.* **Sun 31 May (11-5). Combined adm with Salterns Cottage £4, chd free. Home-made teas at Salterns Cottage. Also open Meadowsweet.**
A great variety of plantings for colour and form. Much perennial colour enriched by seasonal plantings.

19 SALTERNS COTTAGE
Salterns Road, Seaview, PO34 5AH. Susan & Noël Dobbs. *Enter Seaview from W via Springvale, Salterns Rd links the Duver Rd with Bluett Ave.* **Sun 31 May (11-5). Combined adm with Red Cross Cottage £4, chd free. Home-made teas.**
A glasshouse, a potager, exotic borders and fruit trees are some of the many attractions in this 40 metre x 10 metre plot. Salterns Cottage is a listed building built in 1640 and was bought in 1927 by Noel's grandmother Florence, married to Bram Stoker the author of Dracula. The garden was created by Susan in 2005 when she sold her school. Flooding and sandy soil poses a constant challenge to the planting. The greenhouse and potager all raised to cope with floods. A flood step makes it difficult for wheelchair access.

20 THORLEY MANOR
Thorley, Yarmouth, PO41 0SJ. Mr & Mrs Anthony Blest. *1m E of Yarmouth. From Bouldnor take Wilmingham Lane, house ½ m on L.* **Sun 31 May (2-5). Combined adm with Goldings £4, chd free. Home-made teas.**
Mature informal gardens of over 3 acres surrounding manor house (not open). Garden set out in a number of walled rooms incl herb garden, perennial and colourful self-seeding borders, shrub borders, lawns, large old trees and an unusual island croquet lawn, all seamlessly blending in to the surrounding farmland.

KENT

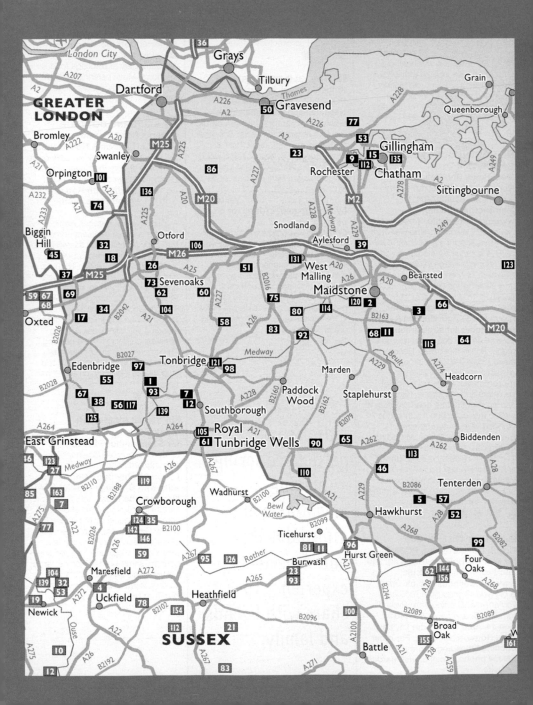

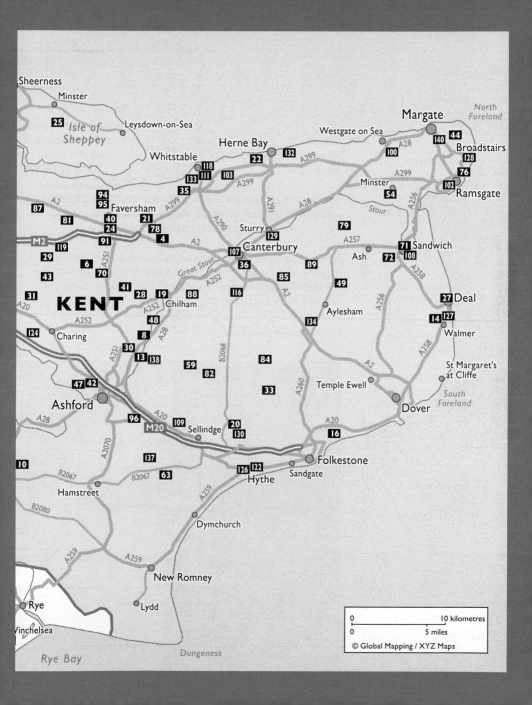

Sheerness

Minster

25 Isle of
Sheppey

Leysdown-on-Sea

North
Foreland

Margate

Westgate on Sea

140 44

Broadstairs

Herne Bay

22 132

100

128

Whitstable

A299

A28

76

118

A299

Minster

102

Ramsgate

133 111 103

54

A299

35

A2

94

A2

Stour

95

Faversham

A29

87

Sturry

79

81

40

21

129

A257

71

Sandwich

119

24

78

Canterbury

Ash

72

108

M2

91

4

A2

107

A258

29

A251

6

36

89

6

70

85

49

27

Deal

43

41

28

19

88

116

14

127

31

KENT

Chilham

A2

Walmer

A20

48

A252

A258

124

Charing

8

A28

Aylesham

St Margaret's
at Cliffe

30

134

A256

13 138

59

84

A2

South
Foreland

82

33

A260

Temple Ewell

47 42

Dover

Ashford

96

109

A20

16

A28

M20

Sellindge

20

A2070

130

137

126 122

Folkestone

10

B2067

63

Hythe

Sandgate

B2067

A259

Hamstreet

B2080

Dymchurch

A259

A259

New Romney

Rye

Lydd

inchelsea

Rye Bay

Dungeness

0   10 kilometres

0   5 miles

© Global Mapping / XYZ Maps

Volunteers

County Organiser
Jane Streatfeild 01342 850362
janestreatfeild@btinternet.com

County Treasurer
Andrew McClintock 01732 838605
andrew.mcclintock@ngs.org.uk

Publicity
Jane Streatfeild (as above)

Booklet Advertising
Nicola Denoon-Duncan
01233 758600
nicoladd@sky.com

Booklet Co-ordinator
Ingrid Morgan Hitchcock
01892 528341
ingrid@morganhitchcock.co.uk

Booklet Distribution
Diana Morrish 01892 723905
diana.morrish@ngs.org.uk

Group Tours
Sue Robinson 01622 729568
suerobinson.timbers@gmail.com

Assistant County Organisers
Jacqueline Anthony 01892 518879
jacqueline.anthony@ngs.org.uk

Marylyn Bacon 01797 270300
ngsbacon@ramsdenfarm.co.uk

Clare Barham 01580 241386
clarebarham@holepark.com

Mary Bruce 01795 531124
mary.bruce@churchmans.co.uk

Bridget Langstaff 01634 842721
bridget.langstaff@btinternet.com

Virginia Latham 01303 862881
lathamvj@gmail.com

Andrew Montgomery 01843 822971
andrew.montgomery2012@btinternet.
com

Diana Morrish (as above)

Sue Robinson (as above)

Nicola Talbot 01342 850526
nicola@falconhurst.co.uk

 @KentNGS

 @NGSKent

 @nationalgardenschemekent

Famously known as 'The Garden of England', Kent is a county full of natural beauty, special landscapes and historical interest.

Being England's oldest county, Kent unsurprisingly boasts an impressive collection of castles and historic sites, notably the spectacular Canterbury Cathedral, and the medieval Ightham Mote.

Twenty eight per cent of the county forms two Areas of Outstanding Natural Beauty: the Kent Downs and the High Weald. The landscapes of Kent are varied and breathtaking, and include haunting marshes, rolling downs, ancient woodlands and iconic white cliffs.

The gardens of Kent are well worth a visit too, ranging from the landscaped grounds of historic stately homes and castles, to romantic cottage gardens and interesting back gardens.

Never has a county been so close to London and yet feels so far away, so why not escape to the peace of a Kent garden? The variety of the gardens and the warmth of the garden owners will ensure a memorable and enjoyable day out.

Below: Brewery Farmhouse

OPENING DATES

All entries subject to change. For latest information check www.ngs.org.uk

Map locator numbers are shown to the right of each garden name.

January

Sunday 26th
Copton Ash 24
Spring Platt 115

Wednesday 29th
Spring Platt 115
Yew Tree Cottage 139

February

Snowdrop Festival

Saturday 1st
Spring Platt 115

Sunday 2nd
Spring Platt 115

Wednesday 5th
Spring Platt 115

Saturday 8th
Knowle Hill Farm 64

Sunday 9th
Knowle Hill Farm 64
Mere House 75

Monday 10th
Knowle Hill Farm 64

Tuesday 11th
Spring Platt 115

Wednesday 12th
Hoath House 56
Yew Tree Cottage 139

Sunday 16th
Copton Ash 24
Mere House 75

Sunday 23rd
◆ Doddington Place 29
◆ Goodnestone Park
Gardens 49

Every day from Monday 24th to Friday 28th
Hoath House 56

Wednesday 26th
Yew Tree Cottage 139

By Arrangement
The Old Rectory 86

March

Wednesday 11th
Yew Tree Cottage 139

Sunday 15th
Copton Ash 24
◆ Godinton House &
Gardens 47
Stonewall Park 117

Sunday 22nd
Haven 54

Wednesday 25th
◆ The Salutation
Garden 108
Yew Tree Cottage 139

Sunday 29th
Godmersham Park 48
◆ Great Comp Garden 51
Mere House 75
◆ Mount Ephraim
Gardens 78
The Old Barn 83

April

Wednesday 1st
Great Maytham Hall 52

Saturday 4th
Parsonage Oasts 92

Sunday 5th
Balmoral Cottage 5
◆ Hole Park 57
Mere House 75

Wednesday 8th
Yew Tree Cottage 139

Friday 10th
Oak Cottage and
Swallowfields Nursery 82

Saturday 11th
Oak Cottage and
Swallowfields Nursery 82

Sunday 12th
Copton Ash 24
Eaglewood 31
Frith Old Farmhouse 43
Haven 54

Monday 13th
Haven 54

Thursday 16th
◆ Ightham Mote 60

Sunday 19th
Bilting House 8
◆ Doddington Place 29
Ladham House 65

Tuesday 21st
◆ Hever Castle &
Gardens 55

Wednesday 22nd
Yew Tree Cottage 139

Saturday 25th
Bishopscourt 9
Watergate House 129

Sunday 26th
Eaglewood 31
Frith Old Farmhouse 43
NEW The Knoll Farm 63
May Cottage 73
Potmans Heath
House 99

Tuesday 28th
◆ Riverhill Himalayan
Gardens 104

May

Sunday 3rd
14 Anglesey Avenue 2
Stonewall Park 117

Monday 4th
14 Anglesey Avenue 2

Wednesday 6th
Yew Tree Cottage 139

Friday 8th
Haven 54
NEW Pilgrims Hospice,
Ashford 96

Saturday 9th
Avalon 4
Copton Ash 24
NEW Pilgrims Hospice,
Ashford 96

Sunday 10th
Avalon 4
◆ Boughton
Monchelsea Place 11
Eaglewood 31
Frith Old Farmhouse 43

Wednesday 13th
Balmoral Cottage 5
Great Maytham Hall 52
◆ Hole Park 57
◆ Scotney Castle 110

Saturday 16th
Little Gables 69

Sunday 17th
Bilting House 8
Elgin House 32
◆ Godinton House &
Gardens 47
Little Gables 69
The Orangery 88
Sandown 109
Torry Hill 123

Wednesday 20th
Yew Tree Cottage 139

Saturday 23rd
Copton Ash 24
Denne Manor Farm 28
18 Royal Chase 105

Sunday 24th
The Coach House 21
Denne Manor Farm 28
Haven 54
18 Royal Chase 105

Monday 25th
The Coach House 21
Falconhurst 38
Haven 54

Friday 29th
Oak Cottage and
Swallowfields
Nursery 82

Saturday 30th
Brompton Village
Gardens 15
Copton Ash 24
Oak Cottage and
Swallowfields
Nursery 82
Orchard End 90

Sunday 31st
Brompton Village
Gardens 15
Chevening 18
NEW Linton Park 68
Nettlestead Place 80
Old Bladbean Stud 84
Orchard End 90
3 Post Office
Cottages 97
43 The Ridings 103
Tram Hatch 124

June

Wednesday 3rd
The Postern 98
Yew Tree Cottage 139

Doddington Place

THE GARDENS

1 NEW ALDERWOOD
Penshurst Road, Penshurst, Tonbridge, TN11 8HY. Jon Little. *From Leigh B2176 towards Penshurst. Approx 1.2m on R. Through stone pillars - See NGS yellow signs. From Penshurst B2176 towards Leigh, approx 0.9m turn L just after post box on L.* **Fri 19, Sat 20, Fri 26, Sat 27 June (10.30-4.30). Adm £10 per adult or £20 per car, chd free. Light refreshments. Refreshments incl gluten free option.**
14 acres of recently restored formal gardens, parkland, woodland and large walled garden. Originally part of The Redleaf estate, the gardens were featured in JC Loudon's Garden Magazine in 1833. Sumptuous planting, incl delphiniums, nepeta, artichokes and roses, surrounds a formal pond. The 18th C walled garden incl a wild flower meadow, fruit and vegetables, pergolas and vibrant planting. We have tarmac and 'tar and chip' paths in much of the garden allowing access to the major areas - except the woodland and rockery.
&. ❀ ☕ ♥

2 14 ANGLESEY AVENUE
Maidstone, ME15 9SH. Mike & Hazel Brett, 01622 299932, mandh.brett@tiscali.co.uk. *2m S of Maidstone. From Maidstone take A229 (bus routes 5 & 89) & after Swan pub take 1st R into Anglesey Avenue. Limited street parking.* **Sun 3, Mon 4 May (11-4). Adm £3, chd free. Light refreshments. Visits also by arrangement Apr to June for groups of up to 20.**
Plantsman's 120ft x 30ft garden with many unusual plants. Raised beds, rockeries and troughs accommodating alpine/rock garden plants. Herbaceous and shrub borders plus a shady woodland area at the end of the garden with hellebores, erythroniums, trilliums, anemones etc.
&. ❀ ☕ ♥

3 NEW ARNOLD YOKE
Back Street, Leeds, Maidstone, ME17 1TF. Richard and Patricia Stileman. *5m E of Maidstone. From M20 J8 take A20 Lenham R onto B2163 to Leeds. Through Leeds village R into Horseshoes La, 1st R into Back St. House ¾ m on L. From A274 follow B2163 to Langley L into Horseshoes La 1st R Back St.* **Sun 7 June (2-6). Adm £5, chd free. Home-made teas.**
½ acre garden redesigned and planted since 2012 and adjacent to 15thC Wealden Hall House. Balance of formal structure of box and yew embracing long mixed border with full and ebullient planting, and centrally placed 'paradise garden' with water feature. Other borders and special trees incl Albizia and Myrtus Luma. Wheelchair access from the car park and around most parts of the garden.
&. ☕

4 AVALON
57 Stoney Road, Dunkirk, ME13 9TN. Mrs Croll, hernhillopengardens@gmail.com. *4m E of Faversham, 5m W of Canterbury, 2.5m W of J7 M2. M2 J7 or A2 W of Faversham take A299, first L, Staplestreet, then L, R past Mt Ephraim, turn L, R. From A2 Canterbury, turn off Dunkirk, bottom hill turn R, Staplestreet then R, R. Park in side roads.* **Sat 9, Sun 10 May (11-5). Sat 6 June (11-5), also open Tankerton Gardens. Sat 4 July (11-5). Adm £4, chd free. Visits also by arrangement May to Sept for groups of 10 to 20. Applications by letter or email please.**
½ acre sheltered woodland garden planted for all seasons on a NW

Boughton Monchelsea Place

slope with views of Thames estuary. Collections of roses, hostas and ferns plus rhododendrons, shrubs, trees, vegetables, fruit, unusual plants and cut flowers for local shows. It is planted by feeling, making it a reflective space and a plant lovers' garden. Plenty of seating for taking in the garden and resting from lots of steps.

☑ BALMORAL COTTAGE
The Green, Benenden, Cranbrook, TN17 4DL. Charlotte Molesworth, thepottingshedholidaylet@gmail. com. *Few 100 yds down unmade track to W of St George's Church, Benenden.* Sun 5 Apr, Wed 13 May, Sun 11 Oct (12-6). Adm £6, chd £2.50. Refreshments available at Hole Park (separate additional price).

An owner created and maintained garden now 33yrs mature. Varied, romantic and extensive topiary form the backbone for mixed borders. Vegetable garden, organically managed. Particular attention to the needs of nesting birds and small mammals lend this artistic plantswoman's garden a rare and unusual quality. No hot borders or dazzling dahlias here, where autumn exemplifies the 'season of mists and mellow fruitfulness'.

☑ ◆ BELMONT
Belmont Park, Throwley, Faversham, ME13 0HH. Harris (Belmont) Charity, 01795 890202, administrator@belmont-house.org, www.belmont-house.org. *4½ m SW of Faversham. A251 Faversham-Ashford. At Badlesmere, brown tourist signs to Belmont.* For NGS: Sat 4, Sun 5 July (12-5). Adm £5, chd free. Home-made teas. For other opening times and information, please phone, email or visit garden website.

Belmont House is surrounded by large formal lawns that are landscaped with fine specimen trees, a pinetum and a walled garden containing long borders, wisteria and large rose border. There is a second walled kitchen garden, restored in 2000 (to a design by Arabella Lennox Boyd), featuring lawns, hop arbours, pleached fruit, vegetables and flowers. During the season (April- Sept) the tea room is open on Wednesdays from 12pm for light lunches and afternoon teas. At the

---

weekend tea and home-made cake available between 1-5pm. Out of season the tea room is open on a self service basis and welcomes visitors.

GROUP OPENING

☑ BIDBOROUGH GARDENS
Bidborough, Tunbridge Wells, TN4 0XB. *3m N of Tunbridge Wells, between Tonbridge & Tunbridge Wells W off A26. Take B2176 Bidborough Ridge signed to Penshurst. Take 1st L into Darnley Drive, then 1st R into St Lawrence Ave, no. 2.* Sun 5 July (1-5). Combined adm £5, chd free. Home-made teas. Gluten and dairy free cake available. Donation to Hospice in the Weald.

The Bidborough gardens (collect garden list from Boundes End, 2 St Lawrence Avenue) are in a small village at the heart of which are The Kentish Hare pub (book in advance), the church, village store and primary school. It is a thriving community with many clubs incl a very active Garden Association! In the surrounding countryside there are several local walks. The gardens are owner designed. Enjoy a variety of formal and informal features in front and main gardens, raised beds, a pebble bed, terraces and pergolas. There are specimen trees, interesting plants and plenty of places to sit and enjoy the peaceful surroundings. Partial wheelchair access, some gardens have steps.

☑ BILTING HOUSE
nr Ashford, TN25 4HA. Mr John Erle-Drax, 07764 580011, erle-drax@marlboroughgallery.com. *5m NE of Ashford. A28, 9m S from Canterbury. Wye 1½m.* Sun 19 Apr, Sun 17 May (2-6). Adm £5, chd free. Home-made teas. Visits also by arrangement May to July for groups of 10+.

6 acre garden with ha-ha set in beautiful part of Stour Valley. Wide variety of rhododendrons, azaleas and ornamental shrubs. Woodland walk with spring bulbs. Mature arboretum with recent planting of specimen trees. Rose garden and herbaceous borders. Conservatory.

☑ BISHOPSCOURT
24 St Margaret's Street, Rochester, ME1 1TS. Mrs Bridget Langstaff. *Central Rochester, nr castle & cathedral. On St Margaret's St at junction with Vines Lane. Rochester train stn 7 mins walk. Disabled parking only at garden but many car parks within 5-7 mins walk.* Sat 25 Apr (11-3). Sat 13, Sun 14 June (1-5), also open Sir John Hawkins Hospital. Adm £5, chd free. Home-made teas.

The residence of the Bishop of Rochester, this 1 acre historic walled garden is a peaceful oasis in the heart of Rochester with views of the castle from a raised lookout. Mature trees, lawns, yew hedges, rose garden, sculptures, fountain, wild flowers and mixed herbaceous borders with perennials. Greenhouse and small vegetable garden. Child friendly garden. Cashless payments accepted. WC incl disabled.

☑ BOLDSHAVES
Woodchurch, nr Ashford Kent, TN26 3RA. Mr & Mrs Peregrine Massey, 01233 860283, masseypd@hotmail.co.uk, www.boldshaves.co.uk. *Between Woodchurch & High Halden off Redbrook St. From centre of Woodchurch, with church on L and Bonny Cravat/Six Bells PH on R, 2nd L down Susan's Hill, then 1st R after ½ mile before L after a few 100 yards to Boldshaves. P as indicated.* Sun 5 July (2-6). Adm £7.50, chd free. Home-made teas in Cliff Tea House or 17C Barn (weather-dependent). Donation to Kent Minds.

7-acre garden developed over past 25 years, partly terraced, S-facing, with wide range of ornamental trees and shrubs, walled garden, Italian garden, Diamond Jubilee garden, camellia dell, herbaceous borders (incl flame bed, red borders and rainbow border), vegetable garden, bluebell walks in April, woodland and ponds. For details of other opening times see garden website www.boldshaves. co.uk Home of the Wealden Literary Festival. Grass paths.

◆ BOUGHTON MONCHELSEA PLACE
Church Hill, Boughton Monchelsea, Maidstone, ME17 4BU. Mr & Mrs Dominic Kendrick, 01622 743120, mk@boughtonplace.co.uk, www.boughtonplace.co.uk. *4m SE of Maidstone. From Maidstone follow A229 (Hastings Rd) S for 3½m to major T-lights at Linton Xrds, turn L onto B2163, house 1m on R; or take J8 off M20 & follow Leeds Castle signs to B2163, house 5½m on L.* **For NGS: Sun 10 May, Sun 14 June (2-5). Adm £5, chd £1. Home-made teas. For other opening times and information, please phone, email or visit garden website.**
150 acre estate mainly park & woodland, spectacular views over own deer park & the Weald. Grade I manor house (not open). Courtyard herb garden, intimate walled gardens, box hedges, herbaceous borders, orchard. Planting is romantic rather than manicured. Terrace with panoramic views, bluebell woods, wisteria tunnel, David Austin roses, traditional greenhouse & kitchen garden. Visit St. Peter's Church next door to see the huge stained glass Millennium Window designed by renowned local artist Graham Clark & the tranquil rose garden overlooking the deer park of Boughton Place. Regrettably, steep steps and narrow paths render the garden difficult for disabled visitors and unsuitable for wheelchairs.

BOUNDES END
2 St Lawrence Avenue, Bidborough, Tunbridge Wells, TN4 0XB. Carole & Mike Marks, 01892 542233, carole.marks@btinternet.com, www.boundesendgarden.co.uk. *Between Tonbridge & Tunbridge Wells off A26. Take B2176 Bidborough Ridge signed to Penshurst. Take 1st L into Darnley Drive, then 1st R into St Lawrence Ave.* **Visits by arrangement June to Aug for groups of up to 20. Adm £8, chd free. Home-made teas incl in adm. Gluten and dairy free options available. Donation to Hospice in the Weald.**
Garden, designed by owners, on an unusually shaped ⅓ acre plot formed from 2 triangles of land. Front garden features raised beds, and the main garden divided into a formal area with terrace, pebble bed and 2 pergolas, an informal area in woodland setting with interesting features and specimen trees. Plenty of places to sit and enjoy the garden. Some uneven ground in lower garden.

3 BRAMBLE CLOSE
Wye, TN25 5QA. Dr M Copland. *two min walk from Wye Station car park. Bramble Close is off Bramble Lane, nearly opp Wye Motors and close to Wye Stn where parking is available.* **Sun 19 July (2-6). Adm £3, chd free. Opening with Wye Gardens on Sun 14 June.**
A very wild, experimental garden sown from seed 1987-89. Wild flower meadow, pond and ditches, mown paths, native copse and hedges buzzing with wildlife - a unique experience. Demonstrating how plants manipulate diseases, insects and other animals to establish and maintain their natural population density. A completely wild meadow cut each year in September but supporting a large populations of butterflies, moths and other insects, amphibians, reptiles, birds, mammals including bats. Some soft ground with some uneven pathways.

NEW BREWERY FARMHOUSE
Great Mongeham, Deal, CT14 9LR. Mr & Mrs David and Maureen Royston-Lee. *on the corner of Mongeham Rd and Northbourne Rd. From Deal take the A258 via London Rd From A2 - Whitfield r'about, 1st exit onto Sandwich Rd, turn L onto A256, next r'about 3rd exit, then turn L onto Willows Wood Road for 3m.* **Sun 21 June (11-4.30). Adm £6, chd free. Light refreshments at the village hall.**
An established country walled garden divided into a series of 'rooms'. Roses, clematis, poppies abound in herbaceous borders and against walls and trellises. With water features, fruit tree pergola and a chinese pagoda. There is a gravel drive and one step up into the garden.

GROUP OPENING

BROMPTON VILLAGE GARDENS
Garden Street and Prospect Row, Brompton, Gillingham, ME7 5AL. Jennifer Jones. *Brompton is between Chatham & Gillingham A231 - Dock Rd next to Historic Dockyard. At r'about take A231 Wood St, opp. RSME Barracks enter Mansion Row, 1st L Garden St. Road parking in village.* **Sat 30, Sun 31 May (2-5). Combined adm £6, chd free. Home-made teas at 17 Prospect Row and Mansion Row.**

NEW 6 GARDEN STREET
Mr & Mrs John and Diane Brice.

26 GARDEN STREET
Mrs Lissie Larkin.

7 PROSPECT ROW
Ms Elaine Fowler.

14 PROSPECT ROW
Ms Audrey Iles.

16 PROSPECT ROW
Jennifer Jones.

20 PROSPECT ROW
Clive and Karen Perry.

In Brompton, the 'village in the Towns' on the Saxon Shore Way, and a stone's throw from the Historic Dockyard and other historic attractions, there are 6 town gardens in two adjacent streets showing different ideas for small plots. Most of these have been re-designed in recent years, and form a combination of formal and informal designs giving alternative views about how to make interesting use of small spaces. These ideas incl a garden made entirely of containers (20 Prospect Row), differing approaches to planting schemes and hard landscaping. The gardens range from low maintenance (20 Prospect Row), creative use of pots and containers (6 Garden St), Italianate style garden (20 Prospect Row),sunny courtyard with summer house (26 Garden St) and a more established garden with mature trees and all year colour attracting wildlife (14 Prospect Row), a plantswoman garden with unusual plants (16 Prospect Row) to a recently re-designed garden where plants are still establishing themselves, (7 Prospect Row).

NEW 69 CAPEL STREET
Capel-Le-Ferne, Folkestone, CT18 7LY. John & Jenny Carter. *Capel-le-Ferne. Take B2011 from Folkestone towards Dover. Past Battle of Britain Memorial on R and then take first L into Capel Street. 69 is 400yds on L.* **Sat 6, Sun 7 June (11-4.30). Adm £3, chd free. Light refreshments. Also open Topgallant.**
A contemporary urban cottage

garden. A clever use of traditional and modern planting providing colour throughout the seasons. A rectangular garden where straight lines have been diffused by angles and planting. Space is provided for vegetables. A quiet location occasionally amplified by a passing Spitfire. Walking distance to the famous Battle of Britain Memorial and pleasant walks along the White Cliffs of Dover. Garden access can be achieved via the garage.

🚻 🐄 💷

17 ♦ CHARTWELL
Mapleton Road, Westerham, TN16 1PS. National Trust, 01732 868381, chartwell@nationaltrust.org.uk, www.nationaltrust.org.uk/ chartwell. *4m N of Edenbridge, 2m S of Westerham. Fork L off B2026 after 1½ m.* **For NGS: Wed 23 Sept (10-5). Adm £11, chd £5.50. For other opening times and information, please phone, email or visit garden website.**
Informal gardens on hillside with glorious views over Weald of Kent. Water features and lakes together with red brick wall built by Sir Winston Churchill, former owner of Chartwell. Lady Churchill's rose garden. Avenue of golden roses runs down the centre of a must see productive kitchen garden. Hard paths to Lady Churchill's rose garden and the terrace. Some steep slopes and steps.

🚻 🐄 ❀ 🚗 💷

18 CHEVENING
Nr Sevenoaks, TN14 6HG. The Board of Trustees of the Chevening Estate, www.cheveninghouse.com. *4m NW of Sevenoaks. Turn N off A25 at Sundridge T-lights on to B2211; at Chevening Xrds 1½ m turn L.* **Sun 31 May (2-5). Adm £7, chd £1. Home-made teas. Local ice cream available.**
The pleasure grounds of the Earls Stanhope at Chevening House are today characterised by lawns and wooded walks around an ornamental lake. First laid out between 1690 and 1720 in the French formal style, in the 1770s a more informal English design was introduced. In early C19 lawns, parterres and a maze were established and many specimen trees planted to shade woodland walks. A new cascade, modelled on a 1718 predecessor, commemorates 250 years of the Stanhope family's

ownership of Chevening and 50 years stewardship by the Board of Trustees. Group guided tours of park and gardens can sometimes be arranged with the Estate Office when the house is unoccupied. Gentle slopes, gravel paths throughout.

🚻 🐄 ❀ 💷

19 ♦ CHILHAM CASTLE
Canterbury, CT4 8DB. Mr Stuart Wheeler, 01227 733100, enquiries@chilham-castle.co.uk, www.chilham-castle.co.uk. *6m SW of Canterbury, 7m NE of Ashford, centre of Chilham Village. Follow NGS signs from A28 or A252 up to Chilham village square & through main gates of Chilham Castle.* **For NGS: Sat 15 Aug (10-4). Adm £5, chd free. Light refreshments. For other opening times and information, please phone, email or visit garden website.**
The garden surrounds Jacobean house 1616 (not open). C17 terraces with herbaceous borders. Topiary frames the magnificent views with lake walk below. Extensive kitchen and cutting garden beyond spring bulb filled quiet garden. Established trees and ha-ha lead onto park. Check website for other events and attractions. Partial wheelchair access.

🚻 🐄 ❀ 💷

20 CHURCHFIELD
Pilgrims Way, Postling, Hythe, CT21 4EY. Chris and Nikki Clark, 01303 863558, coulclark@hotmail.com. *2m NW of Hythe. From M20 J11 turn S onto A20. 1st L after ½ m on bend take rd signed Lyminge. 1st L into Postling.* **Visits by arrangement Apr to July for groups up to 30. Churchfield opens in conjunction with West Court Lodge. Adm £6, chd free. Home-made teas at Churchfield.**
At the base of the Downs, springs rising in this garden form the source of the East Stour. Two large ponds are home to wildfowl and fish and the banks have been planted with drifts of primula, large leaved herbaceous bamboo and ferns. The rest of the 5 acre garden is a Kent cobnut platt and vegetable garden, large grass areas and naturally planted borders and woodland. Postling Church open for visitors. Areas around water may be slippery. Children must be carefully supervised.

🐄 ❀ 🚗 💷

21 THE COACH HOUSE
Kemsdale Road, Hernhill, Faversham, ME13 9JP. Alison & Philip West, 07801 824867, alison.west@kemsdale.plus.com. *3m E of Faversham. At J7 of M2 take A299, signed Margate. After 600 metres take 1st exit signed Hernhill, take 1st L over dual carriageway to T-junction, turn R & follow yellow NGS signs.* **Sun 24, Mon 25 May (11-6). Adm £4, chd free. Cream teas. Visits also by arrangement May to July. Refreshments can be provided with prior arrangements.**
The ¾ acre garden has views over surrounding fruit-producing farmland. Sloping terraced site and island beds with yr-round interest, a pond room, herbaceous borders containing bulbs, shrubs, perennials and a tropical bed. The different areas are connected by flowing curved paths. Unusual planting on light sandy soil where wildlife is encouraged. Kent Wild for Wildlife gold award winner 2019. Most of garden accessible to wheelchairs. Seating available in all areas.

🚻 🐄 ❀ 🚗 💷

22 NEW 52 COBBLERS BRIDGE ROAD
Herne Bay, CT6 8NT. Mercy Morris, 0786 0537664, mercy@home-plants.com, www.home-plants.com. *10 mins walk from centre of Herne Bay. Exit the A299 to Herne Bay. Cobblers Bridge Rd can be accessed from Sea St or Eddington Lane. Street parking can be scarce at weekends.* **Visits by arrangement Mar to Nov for groups of up to 6. Small groups encouraged as all the plants are in a small home. Adm £4. Light refreshments.**
As you walk through the house to the garden, admire around 150 houseplants in a 1.5 bedroom house; from tiny airplants to philodendrons and monsteras. A range of cacti, succulents, tillandsia, tropical and half-hardy plants. A further selection of house plants are on view in the greenhouse outside. Collection of indoor plants suitable for most homes.

❀ 💷

32 ELGIN HOUSE

Main Road, Knockholt, Sevenoaks, TN14 7LH. Mrs Avril Bromley. *Off A21 between Sevenoaks/Orpington at Pratts Bottom r'about, rd signed Knockholt (Rushmore Hill) 3m on R, follow yellow NGS signs. Main Rd is continuation of Rushmore Hill.* **Sun 17 May (12-5). Adm £5, chd free. Home-made teas.**
Victorian family house surrounded by a garden which has evolved over the last 50 years rhododendrons, azaleas, wisteria, camellias, magnolias, mature trees, incl a magnificent cedar tree and spacious lawns. This garden is on the top of the North Downs.

GROUP OPENING

33 ELHAM GARDENS

Elham, CT4 6TU. *10m S of Canterbury, 6m N of Hythe. Enter Elham from Lyminge (off A20) or Barham (off A2). Car parking in various locations as signposted incl the Village Hall & weather permitting, the Primary School Grounds in New Rd.* **Sat 13, Sun 14 June (12-4.30). Combined adm £7.50, chd free. Light refreshments in St Mary's Church for Ploughman's lunches 12-2pm, and home-made teas 2.00-4.30 in the Old Vicarage garden.**
Elham has a thriving community of amateur gardeners, many of whom will open their gardens in this idyllic setting. The wide range of styles of garden are all within easy walking distance of each other and owners will be on hand to ensure you make the most of your visit. This picturesque village with its beautiful Grade 1 listed St Mary's church at its centre, is situated in glorious countryside within the Elham Valley Area of Outstanding Natural Beauty. The Elham Food & Craft Festival will be in The Square and St Mary's Church between 11am - 2pm on Sunday 14 June with the declaration of the winners of the Elham Scarecrow competition. There will be a plant stall in the Vicarage Garden (proceeds to Elham Gardening Society).

34 ♦ EMMETTS GARDEN

Ide Hill, Sevenoaks, TN14 6BA. National Trust, 01732 751507, emmetts@nationaltrust.org.uk, www.nationaltrust.org.uk/emmetts-garden. *5m SW of Sevenoaks. 1½m S of A25 on Sundridge-Ide Hill Rd. 1½m N of Ide Hill off B2042.* **For NGS: Wed 23 Sept (10-5). Adm £12.10, chd £6.05. For other opening times and information, please phone, email or visit garden website.**
5 acre hillside garden, with the highest tree top in Kent, noted for its fine collection of rare trees and flowering shrubs. The garden is particularly fine in spring, while a rose garden, rock garden and extensive planting of acers for autumn colour extend the interest throughout the season. Hard paths to the Old Stables for light refreshments and WC. Some steep slopes. Volunteer driven buggy available for lifts up steepest hill.

35 ENCHANTED GARDENS

Sonoma House, Pilgrims Lane, Seasalter, Whitstable, CT5 3AP. Mrs Donna Richardson, 07967917161, donna@enchantedgardenskent.co.ukwww.enchantedgardens kent.co.uk. *2m from Whitstable Town. Whitstable: At r'about, take exit onto A290 Canterbury. At r'about, take 3rd exit onto A299 ramp London/Faversham Merge onto A299. Take slip rd offered on L, turn R for Pilgrims Lane.* **Sat 6 June (10-5), also open Avalon. Sun 7 June, Sat 26, Sun 27 Sept (10-5). Adm £5, chd free. Home-made teas. Open by arrangement Sat 4, Sun 5 April, Sat 12, Sun 13 September. Contact garden owner to book.**
It has taken 25 years to create Enchanted Gardens from open farmland to the traditional cottage style garden it is today. I am passionate about the loss of our pollinating insects and am organic. I have collections of roses, shrubs and perennials in herbaceous borders for all garden situations to provide colour and interest from February to December. Over 100 roses, 40+ peony, established natural habitats, pond, bog garden, mature trees.

36 [NEW] 16 ETHELBERT ROAD

Canterbury, CT1 3NE. Mr & Mrs Stephanie & Nicholas Fairbank. *Off Old Dover Rd. Less than 1m/20 min walk from Canterbury centre. Travel up Old Dover Rd away from Canterbury. Ethelbert Rd is on the R, signed for K & C Hospital. No16 is half way up on the L. Park on the rd (no time limit at weekends).* **Sat 20, Sun 21 June (2-5.30). Adm £5, chd free. Home-made teas. Cakes by bakedhandmade.co.uk.**
Established walled city garden being brought back to life after a decade 'resting'. Approximately ⅓ acre, highlights incl colourful herbaceous borders, established rose gardens, acer and grass section, small orchard, vegetable plot, "Zen Corner", patio area with potted plants and some stunning feature trees (incl two magnificent magnolias) and a variety of shrubs. Wheelchair access into the garden and on to the patio area but the paths are not suitable for wheelchairs.

37 EUREKA

Buckhurst Road, Westerham Hill, TN16 2HR. Gordon & Suzanne Wright. *Off A233, 1½m N of Westerham, 1m S from centre of Biggin Hill. 5m from J5 & J6 of M25 Parking at Westerham Heights Garden Centre at top of Westerham Hill on A233, 300yds from garden. Satnav: use TN16 2HW. Parking at house for those with walking difficulties.* **Sat 27, Sun 28 June, Sat 18, Sun 19 July, Sat 8, Sun 9 Aug (11-4). Adm £5, chd free. Home-made teas.**
Approx 1 acre garden with a blaze of colourful displays in perennial borders and the 8 cartwheel centre beds. Hundreds of annuals in tubs, troughs and hanging baskets. Sculptures, garden art, chickens, lots of seating and stairs to a viewing platform. Many quirky surprises at every turn. Great fun for children incl a free Treasure Trail with prizes for all, bubbles & small watering cans. Garden art incl 12ft dragon, a horse's head carved out of a 200yr old yew tree stump and a 10ft dragonfly on a reed. 2 'Secret' paths through rhododendrons & bamboos and a 'Spooky' walk inside the 20ft high Laurel hedge. Wheelchair access to most of the garden.

38 FALCONHURST

Cowden Pound Road, Markbeech, Edenbridge, TN8 5NR. Mr & Mrs Charles Talbot, 01342 850526, nicola@falconhurst.co.uk, www.falconhurst.co.uk. *3m SE of Edenbridge. B2026 at Queens Arms pub turn E to Markbeech. 2nd drive on R before Markbeech village.* **Mon 25 May, Sun 14 June, Mon 31 Aug (1.30-5). Adm £6, chd free. Home-made teas. Visits also by arrangement May to Sept for groups of 20+.**

4 acre garden with fabulous views devised and cared for by the same family for 160yrs. Deep mixed borders with old roses, peonies, shrubs and a wide variety of herbaceous and annual plants; ruin garden; walled garden; interesting mature trees and shrubs; kitchen garden; wildflower meadows with woodland and pond walks. Woodland pigs; orchard chickens; lambs in the paddocks.

39 THE FARMHOUSE GARDEN AT TYLAND BARN

Chatham Road, Sandling, Maidstone, ME14 3BD. Kent Wildlife Trust, www.kentwildlifetrust.org.uk/nature-reserves/tyland-barn. *2½ m N of Maidstone. From M20 J6 take A229 to Chatham. Take 2nd L signposted Tyland Barn, R at Lower Bell Pub. Go under A229, R back onto A229 towards Maidstone. L at Esso Garage & follow Tyland Barn sign & Yellow Signs.* **Sat 6 June (10-3). Adm £4, chd free. Light refreshments in the Visitor Centre Cafe.**

Encouraging wildlife into The Farmhouse Garden is the number one priority. No manicured lawns or use of chemicals but relaxed borders containing pollinator friendly flowers throughout the season. Wildflower banks, bee hotels, log piles, small wildlife pond. Stepover apples, small fruit area. Plenty of ideas to make your garden wildlife friendly. Plants labelled. Wild Orchids. Look out for solitary bees, dragonflies & butterflies. Garden normally closed to the public. In Nature Park many native plants and wildflower meadows. Large pond. Tours with Head Gardener around the Nature park & gardeners on hand to answer questions. Parking for blue badge users. Wheelchair access to the Farmhouse Garden is possible but with care. Wheelchair accessible path around Nature park.

GROUP OPENING

40 FAVERSHAM GARDENS

Faversham, ME13 8QN. *On edge of town, short distance from A2 & train stn. From M2 J6 take A251, L into A2, R into The Mall. Combined tickets & maps from No. 58.* **Sat 13 June (10-5). Combined adm £5, chd free. Teas widely available in Faversham.**

54 ATHELSTAN ROAD
Sarah Langton-Lockton OBE.

NEW **58 THE MALL**
Jane Beedle.

19 NEWTON ROAD
Posy Gentles, www.posygentles.co.uk.

17 NORMAN ROAD
Mary & John Cousins.

4 distinctive walled gardens in historic Faversham. Start at 58 The Mall. A contemporary garden packed with pollinators, created in 2018, with materials reused in wire gabions to create raised beds and a wildlife haven. On to 54 Athelstan Road, a maturing garden on a once-neglected site. Ornamental vegetable beds take centre stage. Climbing roses, clematis, thalictrums, Regale lilies, sibirica irises and unusual shrubs, sheltered by old walls. Next, 17 Norman Road, an established town garden offering privacy and delight. A large apple tree gives dappled shade, wisteria and clematis clothe the walls. Small ponds teem with wildlife. Perennials interwoven with mature shrubs throughout. 19 Newton Road, a long, thin town garden, where the plant loving owner has used billowing roses, shrubs, climbers and perennials to blur boundaries. The judicious planting of trees, and curving paths, veil rather than conceal the garden as you move through it. Teas widely available in Faversham. Level access to 54 Athelstan Road.

Alderwood

41 NEW FISHER STREET OAST
Badlesmere, Faversham, ME13 0LB. Group Captain & Mrs Robert Perry. *4m from Faversham. Off A251 at Sheldwich Lees; follow Lees Court Rd & bear L into Fisher Street Rd.* Sun 21 June (11-5). Adm £6, chd free. Home-made teas. Donation to St James' Church, Sheldwich.

This 2 acre garden surrounds a pretty flint Oast & restored barn. Designed by the owners over 20 years, the garden has a distinctive structure with flint and brick walls, mature trees and topiary. Mixed planting in soft hues attracts wildlife in an Italian style garden room with fountain. Newly created pond; sculptures and vegetable / nursery garden. Extensive views over farmland and Perry Wood. There are a few single, shallow steps in various parts of the garden but these can be avoided.

42 31 FOREST AVENUE
Orchard Heights, Ashford, TN25 4GB. Tony and Wendy Green. *From Drovers Island Ashford take A20 Maidstone L @ 1st r'about Orchard Heights, R @ next r'about cont. to next r'about L into Forest Ave follow NGS signs.* Sun 14 June, Sun 5 July, Sun 6 Sept (11-4). Adm £4, chd free. Home-made teas. Also open Sandown.

Small suburban garden evolved since May 2017 containing unusual and rare trees, shrubs and plants e.g. Multi-stemmed Ginkgo Biloba, Japanese Redwood, Wolemi Pine and a collection of Salvias. There is a sunken garden with an exotic section and a Japanese style area. Wheelchair access to a small part of the garden.

43 FRITH OLD FARMHOUSE
Frith Road, Otterden, Faversham, ME13 0DD. Drs Gillian & Peter Regan, 01795 890556, peter.regan@cantab.net. *½m off Lenham to Faversham rd. From A20 E of Lenham turn N up Hubbards Hill, follow signs Eastling; after 4m turn L into Frith Rd. From A2 in Faversham turn S (Brogdale Rd); continue 7m (thro' Eastling), turn R into Frith Rd.* Sun 12, Sun 26 Apr, Sun 10 May (11-5), also open Eagleswood. Sun 19 July (11-5). Adm £5, chd free. Home-made teas. Visits also by arrangement Apr to Sept. Please contact owners in advance.

A riot of plants growing together as if in the wild, developed over 40 yrs. No neat edges or formal beds, but several hundred interesting (& some very unusual) plants. Trees and shrubs chosen for year-round appeal. Special interest in bulbs and woodland plants. Visitor comments - 'one of the best we have seen, natural & full of treasures', 'a plethora of plants', 'inspirational', 'a hidden gem'. Altered habitat areas to increase the range of plants grown. Areas for wildlife.

44 THE GARDEN GATE
Northdown Park, Northdown Park Road, Margate, Kent, CT9 3TP. The Garden Gate Project Ltd, 07714742456, info@thegardengateproject.co.uk, www.thegardengateproject.co.uk. *Located within Northdown Park, opp Friends Corner on Northdown Park Rd B2052 between Margate and Broadstairs, nr Northdown House.* Sat 13 June (11.30-3). Adm £3, chd free. Light refreshments. Wood fired pizzas with toppings from the garden will be on sale. Visits also by arrangement.

The Garden Gate is a community garden based in Northdown Park, growing a mixture of plants, flowers and vegetables using organic methods. We also have a wildlife pond, two polytunnels, a shade house, some coppiced woodland and a green roof on one of our buildings. The garden is flat and on one level with grass or wood chip paths.

45 GARDENVIEW
6 Edward Road, Biggin Hill, Westerham, TN16 3HL. Freda Davis, 07958534074, fredagdavis@aol.com, www.fredasgarden.co.uk. *Off A233, 7½m S of Bromley, 3½m N of Westerham. Edward Rd is located at the southern end of Main Rd, Biggin Hill by the pedestrian crossing. Parking available on rd. Buses 246 (Village Green Way stop) and 320 (Lebanon Gardens stop).* Sun 9 Aug (12-4). Adm £5, chd free. teas and light refreshments. Visits also by arrangement May to Aug for groups of 10+.

Full of interest with a wide variety of shrubs, small orchard, veg beds and tranquil seating areas with carefully situated statuary, this garden has been transformed into an oasis, where live music is performed with an art exhibition in the studio. Various musicians will entertain visitors during the main opening. Just a 4 inch step.

46 GODDARDS GREEN
Angley Road, Cranbrook, TN17 3LR. John & Linde Wotton, 01580 715507, jpwotton@gmail.com, www.goddardsgreen.btck.co.uk. *½m SW of Cranbrook. On W of Angley Rd. (A229) at junction with High St, opp War Memorial.* Sun 5 July (12.30-4.30). Adm £5, chd free. Home-made teas. We request prior notice by groups of dietary requirements. Visits also by arrangement May to Sept for groups of 10+. Coaches need to drop and pick up visitors in the road.

Gardens of about 5 acres, surrounding beautiful 500+yr old clothier's hall (not open), laid out in 1920s and redesigned since 1992 to combine traditional and modern planting schemes. Fountain and rill, water garden, fern garden, mixed borders of bulbs, perennials, shrubs, trees and exotics; birch grove, grass border, pond, kitchen garden, meadows, arboretum and mature orchard. We hope to have an art exhibition coinciding with our NGS Open Garden on 5 July 2020. Some slopes and steps, but most areas (though not the toilets) are wheelchair accessible. Disabled parking is reserved near the house.

47 ♦ GODINTON HOUSE & GARDENS
Godinton Lane, Ashford, TN23 3BP. The Godinton House Preservation Trust, 01233 643854, info@godintonhouse.co.uk, www.godintonhouse.co.uk. *1½m W of Ashford. M20 J9 to Ashford. Take A20 towards Charing & Lenham, then follow brown tourist signs.* For NGS: Sun 15 Mar, Sun 17 May, Fri 19 June (1-6). Adm £7, chd free. Home-made teas. For other opening times and information, please phone, email or visit garden website.

12 acres complement the magnificent Jacobean house. Terraced lawns lead through herbaceous borders, rose garden and formal lily pond to intimate Italian garden and large walled garden with delphiniums, potager, cut flowers and iris border. March/April the 3 acre wild garden is a mass of daffodils,

fritillaries, primroses and other spring flowers. Delphinium Festival (12 June - 21 June). Garden workshops and courses throughout the yr. Partial wheelchair access to ground floor of house and most of gardens.

   ᕕ ✿ ☕

48 GODMERSHAM PARK
Godmersham, CT4 7DT. Mrs
Fiona Sunley, 01227 730293,
ben@godmershampark.com. *5m
NE of Ashford. Off A28, midway
between Canterbury & Ashford.*
**Sun 29 Mar, Sun 14 June (1-5).
Adm £5, chd free. Home-made
teas in The Mansion Orangery.
Visits also by arrangement Mar to
Sept for groups of 5+.** Donation to
Godmersham Church.
24 acres of restored wilderness
and formal gardens set around C18
mansion (not open). Topiary, rose
garden, herbaceous borders, walled
kitchen garden and recently restored
Italian & swimming pool gardens.
Superb daffodils in spring and roses
in June. Historical association with
Jane Austen. Also visit the Heritage
Centre. Deep gravel paths.

   ᕕ 🐎 🚗 ☕

**49 ◆ GOODNESTONE PARK
GARDENS**
Wingham, Canterbury,
CT3 1PL. Francis Plumptre,
01304 840107, enquiries@
goodnestoneparkgardens.co.uk,
www.goodnestoneparkgardens.
co.uk. *6m SE of Canterbury. Village
lies S of B2046 from A2 to Wingham.
Brown tourist signs off B2046.* **For
NGS: Sun 23 Feb (12-4). Home-
made teas. Sun 21 June (11-5).
Also open Brewery Farmhouse.
Adm £7, chd £2. Light lunches are
available at June opening. Only
tea & homemade cake at Feb
opening. For other opening times
and information, please phone,
email or visit garden website.**
One of Kent's outstanding gardens
and the favourite of many visitors.
14 acres around C18 house (not
open) and with views over cricket
ground and parkland. Something
special yr-round from snowdrops and
spring bulbs to the famous walled
garden with old fashioned roses and
kitchen garden. Outstanding trees
and woodland garden with cornus
collection and hydrangeas later. 2
arboretums, a contemporary gravel
garden. Picnics welcome.

   ᕕ ✿ 🚗 ☕

GROUP OPENING

**50 GRAVESEND GARDENS
GROUP**
Gravesend, DA12 1JZ. *Approx ½ m
from Gravesend town centre. From
A2 take A227 towards Gravesend. At
T-lights with Cross Lane turn R then
L at next T-lights following yellow
NGS signs. Park in Sandy Bank Rd
or Leith Park Rd.* **Sat 18, Sun 19
July (12-5). Combined adm £5,
chd free. Cream teas.**

58A PARROCK ROAD
Mr Barry Bowen.

68 SOUTH HILL ROAD
Judith Hathrill, 07810 550991,
judith.hathrill@live.com.
**Visits to 68 South Hill Rd also
by arrangement for groups up
to 20, Sunday afternoons,
May and June.**

Enjoy two lovely gardens, very
different in character, close to
Windmill Hill which has extensive
views over the Thames estuary. 58A
Parrock Road is a beautiful, well
established town garden, approx
120ft x 40ft, nurtured by owner for
57yrs. There is a stream running
down to a pond, luscious planting
along the rocky banks, fascinating
water features, mature trees and
shrubs, magnificent display of hostas
and succulents. 68 South Hill Road
is an award winning wildlife garden,
showing that wildlife friendly gardens
need not be wild. Flowers, herbs
and vegetables in the raised beds.
Perennials, ferns, grasses, shrubs and
annuals in the borders all grown with
wildlife in mind. Fruit and vegetables
grown in containers on the terraces.
Two wildlife ponds surrounded by
grasses and wild flowers. Quiet
corners to sit and watch the bees and
butterflies. New front terraced garden.
Jazz Trio at 58A Parrock Road.

   ✿ ☕

51 ◆ GREAT COMP GARDEN
Comp Lane, Platt, nr Borough
Green, Sevenoaks, TN15 8QS.
Great Comp Charitable
Trust, 01732 885094,
office@greatcompgarden.co.uk,
www.greatcompgarden.co.uk. *7m
E of Sevenoaks. 2m from Borough
Green Station. Accessible from M20
& M26 motorways. A20 at Wrotham
Heath, take Seven Mile Lane, B2016;*

at 1st Xrds turn R; garden on L ½ m.
**For NGS: Sun 29 Mar, Sun 25
Oct (11-5). Adm £8.50. For other
opening times and information,
please phone, email or visit garden
website.**
Skilfully designed 7 acre garden of
exceptional beauty. Spacious setting
of well maintained lawns and paths
lead visitors through plantsman's
collection of trees, shrubs, heathers
and herbaceous plants. Early
C17 house (not open). Magnolias,
hellebores and snowflakes (leucojum),
hamamellis and winter flowering
heathers are a great feature in the
spring. A great variety of perennials
in summer incl salvias, dahlias and
crocosmias. Tearoom open daily for
morning coffee, home-made lunches
and afternoon teas. Most of garden
accessible to wheelchair users.
Disabled WC.

   ᕕ ✿ 🚗 ☕

52 GREAT MAYTHAM HALL
Maytham Road, Rolvenden,
Tenterden, TN17 4NE. The Sunley
Group. *3m from Tenterden. Maytham
Rd off A28 at Rolvenden Church,
½ m from village on R. Designated
parking for visitors.* **Wed 1 Apr, Wed
13 May, Wed 10 June, Wed 1 July
(1-4). Adm £7, chd free.**
Lutyens designed gardens famous
for having inspired Frances Hodgson
Burnett to write The Secret Garden
(pre Lutyens). Parkland, woodland
with bluebells. Walled garden with
herbaceous beds and rose pergola.
Pond garden with mixed shrubbery
and herbaceous borders. Interesting
specimen trees. Large lawned area,
rose terrace with far reaching views.

   🚗

64 KNOWLE HILL FARM

Ulcombe, Maidstone,
ME17 1ES. The Hon Andrew
& Mrs Cairns, 01622 850240,
elizabeth@knowlehillfarm.co.uk,
www.knowlehillfarmgarden.co.uk.
*7m SE of Maidstone. From M20
J8 follow A20 towards Lenham
for 2m. Turn R to Ulcombe. After
1½m, L at Xrds, after ½m 2nd R
into Windmill Hill. Past Pepper Box
PH, ½m 1st L to Knowle Hill.* Sat 8,
Sun 9, Mon 10 Feb (11-3). Light
refreshments. Sun 19, Mon 20
July (2-5.30). Home-made teas.
Adm £5, chd free. Hot food in
February. 2021: Sat 6, Sun 7, Mon
8 Feb. Visits also by arrangement
Feb to Sept for groups of up to 30.
Access only possible for 35 seater
coaches.
2 acre garden created over 35yrs
on S-facing slope of N Downs.
Spectacular views. Snowdrops and
hellebores, many tender plants, china
roses, agapanthus, verbenas, salvias
and grasses flourish on light soil.
Topiary continues to evolve with birds
at last emerging. Lavender ribbons
hum with bees. Pool enclosed in small
walled white garden. A green garden
completed 2018. Some steep slopes.

65 LADHAM HOUSE

Ladham Road, Goudhurst,
TN17 1DB. Guy & Nicola Johnson.
*8m E of Tunbridge Wells. On NE of
village, off A262. Through village
towards Cranbrook, turn L at The
Goudhurst Inn. 2nd R into Ladham
Rd, main gates approx 500yds on
L.* Sun 19 Apr (2-5). Adm £5, chd
free. Home-made teas.
Ten acres of garden with many
interesting plants, trees and shrubs,
incl rhododendrons, camellias,
azaleas and magnolias. A beautiful
rose garden, arboretum, an
Edwardian sunken rockery, ponds,
a vegetable garden & a woodland
walk leading to bluebell woods.
There is also a spectacular 60 meter
twin border designed by Chelsea
Flower Show Gold Medal winner, Jo
Thompson. Small Classic Car Display.

66 ◆ LEEDS CASTLE

Maidstone, ME17 1PL. Leeds
Castle Trustees, 01622 765400,
enquiries@leeds-castle.co.uk,
www.leeds-castle.com/gardens.
Off J8 of M20. For NGS: Evening
opening Wed 1 July (6-8). Adm
£12.50 when booked in advance,
£15 if bought at main gate, chd
free. Pre-booking advisable,
please visit www.ngs.org.
uk/events for information &
booking. Light refreshments.
Refreshments available before
Garden Tour. For other opening
times and information, please
phone, email or visit garden
website.
Visitors to the 'loveliest castle in the
world' are often surprised by the
glorious gardens which surround the
magnificent moated Castle. Natural
woodland walks in the Princess
Alexandra Gardens, the Culpeper
Garden - a quintessential English
cottage garden, the Mediterranean
style terraced garden overlooking the
Great Water - are complemented by
the beautiful surrounding parkland.
Within the grounds of Leeds Castle
there are additional attractions
including a splendid yew maze
created by internationally renown
designer Adrian Fisher; and for
youngsters there's the Knight's
Stronghold playground and Adventure
Golf. Pre-booking advised. Fully
wheelchair accessible with smooth
paths through gardens, disabled WC
and mobility bus.

67 LEYDENS

Hartfield Road, Edenbridge,
TN8 5NH. Roger Platts,
www.rogerplatts.com. *1m S of
Edenbridge. On B2026 towards
Hartfield (use Nursery entrance & car
park).* Sun 21 June (12-5). Adm £5,
chd free.
Private garden of garden designer,
nursery owner and author who created
NGS Garden at Chelsea in 2002,
winning Gold and Best in Show, and
in 2010 Gold and People's Choice for
the M&G Garden and Gold in 2013.
A wide range of roses, shrubs and
perennials adjoining wild flower hay
meadow and plant nursery. Kitchen
garden and orchard. Plants clearly
labelled and fact sheet available.

68 NEW LINTON PARK

Linton, Maidstone,
ME17 4AB. Linton Park Plc,
www.camellia.plc.uk. *Surrounding
the main house on the estate. ME17
4AJ is the post code for North Lodge
at the top of drive on the main rd.
Visitors need to come down the
drive for around ¼m to reach the
main house & garden.* Sun 31 May
(10.30-4). Adm £10, chd free.
Home-made teas.
Overlooking the Weald of Kent this
south facing, hillside garden is set in
450 acres of parkland. Re-imagined
over the last 35 years, using original
J C Loudon plans and historic
maps, it boasts wonderful mature
tree specimens of, amongst others,
Copper Beech, Cedars, Limes and
Oaks crowned by a magnificent
avenue of Wellingtonia planted in the
mid 19th century. The paths around
the garden are mostly flat, gently
undulating with a gravel surface. Most
stairs can be avoided by taking a
different signed route.

69 LITTLE GABLES

Holcombe Close, Westerham,
TN16 1HA. Mrs Elizabeth James.
*Centre of Westerham. Off E side of
London Rd A233, 200yds from The
Green. Please park in public car
park. No parking available at house.*
Sat 16, Sun 17 May, Sat 6, Sun
7 June (2-5). Adm £4, chd free.
Home-made teas.
¾ acre plant lover's garden
extensively planted with a wide range
of trees, shrubs, perennials etc, incl
many rare ones. Collection of climbing
and bush roses. Large pond with fish,
water lilies and bog garden. Fruit and
vegetable garden. Large greenhouse.

70 LORDS

Sheldwich, Faversham,
ME13 0NJ. John Sell CBE &
Barbara Rutter, 01795 536900,
john@sellwade.co.uk. *On A251
4m S of Faversham & 3½m N of
Challock Xrds. From A2 or M2 take
A251 towards Ashford. ½m S of
Sheldwich church find entrance
lane on R adjacent to wood.* Sun
28 June (2-5). Adm £5, chd free.
Home-made teas. Visits also
by arrangement Mar to July for
groups of 10 to 30. £100 min
payment for groups - refreshments
incl if required.
C18 walled garden and greenhouse.
Mediterranean terrace and citrus
standing. Flowery mead beneath
fruit trees incl medlars and quinces.
Across a grass tennis court a cherry
orchard grazed by Jacob sheep.
Pleached hornbeams, clipped yew
hedges and topiary, lawns, ponds and
wild area. Fine old sweet chestnuts,
planes, copper beech and 120ft tulip
tree. Some gravel paths.

71 MANWOOD HOUSE
Strand Street, Sandwich, CT13 9HX. Mr & Mrs Philip & Rebecca Croall. *Access to the garden is through white gates in Paradise Row, which is a small lane off Strand St.* **Sat 6 June (2-5). Adm £6, chd free. Home-made teas.** The abundantly planted gardens of Manwood House (not open) built in 1564 as the first home of the free school founded by Sir Roger Manwood, a favourite of Elizabeth 1. The gardens extend to the side and rear of the property and are bounded by flint walls. They feature a remarkable and ancient robinia tree, an ornamental pond and luxuriantly planted borders, extensively replanted in 2015. Sandstone paths into and through large parts of the garden, though narrow in places. A small number of shallow steps to access certain areas.

&. ⚞ D ☕

72 MARSHBOROUGH FARMHOUSE
Farm Lane, Marshborough, Sandwich, CT13 0PJ. David & Sarah Ash, 01304 813679. *1½m W of Sandwich, ½m S of Ash. From Ash take R fork to Woodnesborough. After 1m Marshborough sign. L into Farm Lane at white thatched cottage, garden 100yds on L. Coaches must phone for access information.* **Visits by arrangement for groups of 5+; May 25-June 6, June 27-July 10. Adm £5, chd free. Home-made teas.** Interesting 2½ acre plantsman's garden, developed enthusiastically over 20yrs by the owners. Paths and lawns lead to many unusual shrubs, trees and perennials in island beds, borders, rockery and raised dry garden creating yr-round colour and interest. Tender pot plants, succulents in glass house, pond and water features. Over 70 varieties of Salvia both hardy and tender.

&. ⚘ ☕

73 MAY COTTAGE
52, St Botolphs Road, Sevenoaks, TN13 3AG. Graham & Maggie Moat. *Central Sevenoaks, close to the historic Vine cricket ground & Knole Park. Easy walking distance from mainline railway station with trains direct from London & the Coast. 2m from J5 M25, on the B2020. Park for free on either side of the rd, where there is plenty of room.* **Sun 26 Apr (11-4). Adm £5, chd free. Light refreshments.**

A ⅓ of an acre urban family spring garden, comprising mature shrubs and specimen plants, with spring bulbs, cowslips, vegetable patch and local trees that shield the garden. Blue, white and pink bluebells spread amongst many shrubs featuring wire-netting bush (Corokia cotoneaster), Enkianthus campanulatus, Azalea April Showers, Japanese maples together with apple blossom on a mature tree.

&. ☕

74 12 THE MEADOWS
Chelsfield, Orpington, BR6 6HS. Mr Roger & Mrs Jean Pemberton. *3m from J4 on M25. 10 mins walk from Chelsfield station. Exit M25 at J4. At r'about 1st exit for A224, next r'about 3rd exit - A224, ½m, take 2nd L, Warren Rd. Bear L into Windsor Drive. 1st L The Meadway, follow signs to garden.* **Sun 7 June (11-5). Adm £5, chd free. Home-made teas.** Front garden Mediterranean style gravel with sun loving plants. Rear ¾ acre garden in 2 parts. Semi-formal Japanese style area with tea house, two ponds, one Koi and one natural (lots of spring interest). Acers, grasses, huge bamboos etc and semi wooded area, children's path with 13ft high giraffe, Sumatran tigers and lots of points of interest. Children and well behaved dogs more than welcome. Designated children's area. Adults only admitted if accompanied by responsible child! Silver award for garden with the LGS. Winner of first prize for our back garden from Bromley in Bloom. Wheelchair access to all parts except small stepped area at very bottom of garden.

&. ⚞ ❊ ☕

75 MERE HOUSE
Mereworth, ME18 5NB. Mr & Mrs Andrew Wells, www.mere-house.co.uk. *7m E of Tonbridge. From A26 turn N on to B2016 & then R into Mereworth village. 3½m S of M20/M26 junction, take A20, then B2016 to Mereworth.* **Sun 9, Sun 16 Feb, Sun 29 Mar, Sun 5 Apr (2-5). Adm £5, chd free. Home-made teas.** C18 landscape surrounding 6 acre garden, completely replanted since 1958, bounded to the south by lake created 1780 and park to west. Increasing areas of snowdrops and daffodils in spring. Extensive lawns set off herbaceous borders, ornamental shrubs and trees with yr-round foliage contrast. Major tree

planting since 1987 storm; woodland, park and lake walks can be enjoyed beyond the garden.

&. ⚞ ❊ ☕

76 5 MONTEFIORE AVENUE
Ramsgate, CT11 8BD. Pauline and Mike Ashley. *Opp Thanet Bowls Club. A255 Hereson Rd from Ramsgate to Broadstairs. Turn R (L if from Broadstairs) at Garden Centre into Montefiore Av. Cross Dumpton Pk Dr into continuation of Montefiore Av. House on R.* **Sat 1, Sun 2 Aug (12-5). Adm £4, chd free. Home-made teas. Also open The Watch House.** An Edwardian walled garden densely planted with a variety of herbaceous and tropical plants. A courtyard with over 100 pots features acers, hostas, agaves, aeoniums and more. Through an arch, a lawned area with gazebo, borders, large koi pond, waterfall and two small wildlife ponds. A pergola leads to a vegetable garden and treehouse garden with a mix of roses, mediterranean and tropical plants. A highlight of the garden is the Koi pond, with a mix of large fish, and the wide variety of plants, both Mediterranean and tropical.The garden is situated in a cul-de-sac with an entrance to King George VI park where the famous Italianate Greenhouse is located. Gravel paths.

&. ⚞ ❊ ☕

77 THE MOUNT
Haven Street, Wainscott, Rochester, ME3 8BL. Marc Beney & Susie Challen. *3½m N of Rochester. At M2 J1, take A289 twds Grain. At r'bout, R into Wainscott. Co-op ahead, turn R into Higham Rd. R into Islingham Farm Rd, parking in field on corner of Woodfield Way. House 7min walk up slight hill.* **Sat 18, Sun 19 July (11-4). Adm £5, chd free. Home-made teas. Also open Hammond Place.** Previously neglected 2-acres now has a renovated walled kitchen garden with fruit trees, roses, veg beds & colourful herbaceous border. Old grass tennis court with mown labyrinth & small nuttery around new pond at one end. White & yellow terrace garden above a pleached lime path, lined with iris and lavender. Remains of Victorian glasshouses below. Lovely countryside views. Mature specimen trees. Gravel drive, uneven paths and steps.

⚞ ❊ ☕

68 South Hill Road

90 ORCHARD END

Cock Lane, Spelmonden Road, Horsmonden, TN12 8EQ. Mr Hugh Nye, 01892 723118, hughnye@aol.com. *8m E of Tunbridge Wells. From A21 going S turn L at r'bout onto B2162 to Horsmonden. After 2m turn R onto Spelmonden Rd. After ½m turn R into Cock Lane. Garden on R.* **Sat 30, Sun 31 May, Sat 25, Sun 26 July (11-5). Adm £5, chd free. Home-made teas. Visits also by arrangement May to July.** Donation to The UCL Amyloidosis Research Fund.

Contemporary Arts and Crafts garden within a 4 acre site. Made over 25yrs by resident landscape designer. Divided into rooms with linking vistas. Incl hot borders, white garden, exotics, oak and glass summerhouse amongst magnolias and huge perennials. Dramatic changes in level. Formal pool with damp garden, ornamental vegetable potager. Yew and box topiary. Wildlife orchards and woodland walks. Whilst we welcome all, wheelchair access to some areas is limited due to level changes. Refreshments/dry garden accessible.

&. 🐕 ☕ 🌿

91 OUDEN

Brogdale Road, Ospringe, Faversham, ME13 8XY. Frances & Paul Moskovits. *Close to Faversham. From A2 in Faversham turn S along Brogdale Rd for ¾m, Ouden is on R. Parking on roadside or at Brogdale Farm 100 yds before property.* **Sat 11, Sun 12 July (11-4). Adm £4, chd free. Light refreshments. Limited teas at Ouden. Courtyard Restaurant at Brogdale serving lunches and teas.**

A variety of mature shrubs and trees form the backbone of this ¼ acre garden. The front garden features a shrubbery and cottage planting. The rear garden has a well stocked colourful long border leading to two working greenhouses. Exotic planting intermingles with traditional garden favourites. Small paths allow time for a closer look. Situated close to National Fruit Collection at Brogdale Farm, Belmont House and gardens and market town of Faversham.

❀ ☕ 🌿

92 PARSONAGE OASTS

Hampstead Lane, Yalding, ME18 6HG. Edward & Jennifer Raikes, 01622 814272, jmraikes@parsonageoasts.plus.com. *6m SW of Maidstone. On B2162 between Yalding village & stn, turn off at Boathouse PH. over lifting bridge, cont 100 yds up lane. House and car park on L.* **Sat 4 Apr (2-5.30). Adm £6, chd free. Cream teas. Visits also by arrangement Apr to Sept for groups of 10 to 30. Adm price incl cream tea.**

Our garden has a lovely position on the bank of the R Medway. Typical Oast House (not open) often featured on calendars and picture books of Kent. 70yr old garden now looked after by grandchildren of its creator.

¾ acre garden with walls, daffodils, crown imperials, shrubs, clipped box and a spectacular magnolia. Small woodland on river bank. Best in spring, but always something to see. Unfenced river bank. Gravel paths.

&. ☕ 🌿

93 ♦ PENSHURST PLACE & GARDENS

Penshurst, TN11 8DG. Lord & Lady De L'Isle, 01892 870307, contactus@penshurstplace.com, www.penshurstplace.com. *6m NW of Tunbridge Wells. SW of Tonbridge on B2176, signed from A26 N of Tunbridge Wells.* **For NGS: Wed 9 Sept (10.30-6). Adm £10, chd £6. For other opening times and information, please phone, email or visit garden website.**

11 acres of garden dating back to C14. The garden is divided into a series of rooms by over a mile of yew hedge. Profusion of spring bulbs, formal rose garden and famous peony border. Woodland trail and arboretum. Yr-round interest. Toy museum. Some paths not paved and uneven in places; own assistance will be required. 2 wheelchairs available for hire.

&. ❀ ♿ ☕ 🌿

94 PHEASANT BARN

Church Road, Oare, ME13 0QB. Paul & Su Vaight, 07843 739301, paul.vaight@btinternet.com. *2m NW of Faversham. Entering Oare from Faversham, turn R at*

Three Mariners PH towards Harty Ferry. Garden 400yds on R, before church. Parking on roadside. **Visits by arrangement May to July for groups of up to 30. Adm £5, chd free. Refreshments by prior arrangement only.** Series of smallish gardens around award-winning converted farm buildings in beautiful situation overlooking Oare Creek. Main area is nectar-rich planting in formal design with a contemporary twist inspired by local landscape. Also vegetable garden, dry garden, water features, wild flower meadow and labyrinth. July optimum for wild flowers. Kent Wildlife Trust Oare Marshes Bird Reserve within 1m. Two village inns serving lunches/dinners.

95 PHEASANT FARM
Church Road, Oare, Faversham, ME13 0QB. Jonathan & Lucie Neame, 01795 535366, pheasantfarm2019@gmail.com. *2m NW of Faversham. Enter Oare from Western Link Road. L at T-junction. R at Three Mariners PH into Church Rd. Garden 450yds on R, beyond Pheasant Barn, before church. Parking on roadside & as directed.* **Visits by arrangement Apr to June for groups of 10+. Adm £10, chd free. Home-made teas. Entry price incl cream tea and cakes.** A walled garden surrounding C17 farmhouse with outstanding views over Oare marshes and creek. Main garden with shrubs and herbaceous plants. Circular walk through orchard and adjoining churchyard. Two local public houses serving lunches. Wheelchair access in main garden only.

96 NEW PILGRIMS HOSPICE, ASHFORD
Hythe Road, Willesborough, Ashford, TN24 0NE. Pilgrims Hospices, www.pilgrimshospices.org. *Pilgrims Hospice, Ashford. Pilgrims Hospices.* **Fri 8, Sat 9 May (9.30-5). Adm £3, chd free. Cream teas.** Pilgrims Hospice Ashford invites you to visit our vibrant hospice gardens tenderly cared for by our skilful volunteer gardening team. We are opening up our garden as part of our 'Beyond the Hospice Walls' strategy. Pilgrims work began with the vision to make a difference for the people of our community. Today,

Pilgrims' supports more than 850 people per month when they need us most. Sensory garden, roses, waterfall fountain pond, woodland walk, wildflower meadow and memory path. There will be a vintage style tea available with sumptuous cakes, delicious goodies and drinks. The hospice garden is wheelchair accessible (although in poor weather some parts may not be accessible during open days).

97 3 POST OFFICE COTTAGES
Chiddingstone Causeway, Tonbridge, TN11 8JP. Julie & Graham Jones-Ellis. *Approx 6m W of Tonbridge & approx 6m E of Edenbridge. On B2027 Clinton Lane into Chiddingstone Causeway same side as shop/PO, garden is end of terrace cottage with hedge & small gravel driveway.* **Sun 31 May (11-5.30). Adm £3.50, chd free. Home-made teas.** Small, but charming cottage garden, showing good use of space. With large selection of clematis and over 30 varieties of roses. Herbaceous borders filled with colour in May. Several seating areas and small water features.

98 THE POSTERN
Postern Lane, Tonbridge, TN11 0QU. Mr & Mrs David Tennant, 07807229414. *Postern Lane runs E of Tonbridge off B2017, between Tonbridge & Tudeley.* **Wed 3 June (1.30-5.30). Adm £5, chd free. Light refreshments. Visits also by arrangement May & June.** 4 acres with lawns, flowering shrubs, old and new shrub borders; apple and pear orchards. Georgian house (not open). Garden designed by Anthony du Gard Pasley. Wheelchair users could be dropped off in the main drive.

99 POTMANS HEATH HOUSE
Wittersham, TN30 7PU. Dr Alan & Dr Wilma Lloyd Smith. *1½m W of Wittersham. Between Wittersham & Rolvenden, 1m from junction with B2082. 200yds E of bridge over Potmans Heath Channel.* **Sun 26 Apr, Sun 21 June (2-6). Adm £5, chd free. Home-made teas.** Large country garden divided into compartments each with a different style. Daffodils, tulips and many

blossoming ornamental cherry and apple trees in Spring, often spectacular. Many and varied rose species; climbers a speciality. Early summer beds and borders. Orchards, some unusual trees, lawns, vegetable garden, 2 greenhouses. Some awkward slopes but generally accessible.

100 ◆ QUEX GARDENS
Quex Park, Birchington, CT7 0BH. Powell-Cotton Museum, 01843 842168, enquiries@quexmuseum.org, www.quexpark.co.uk/museum/ quex-gardens. *3m W of Margate. Follow signs for Quex Park on approach from A299 then A28 towards Margate, turn R into B2048 Park Lane. Quex Park is on L.* **For NGS: Sun 19 July (10-5). Adm £4.95, chd £3.50. Light refreshments in Mama Feelgoods Café and Quex Barn. For other opening times and information, please phone, email or visit garden website.** 10 acres of woodland and gardens with fine specimen trees unusual in Thanet, spring bulbs, wisteria, shrub borders, old figs and mulberries, herbaceous borders. Victorian walled garden with cucumber house, long glasshouses, cactus house, fruiting trees. Peacocks, dovecote, woodland walk, wildlife pond, children's maze, croquet lawn, picnic grove, lawns and fountains. Head Gardener will be available on NGS day to give tours & answer questions. Mama Feelgood's Boutique Café serving morning coffee, lunch or afternoon tea. Quex Barn farmers market selling local produce and serving breakfasts to evening meals. Picnic sites available. Garden almost entirely flat with tarmac paths. Sunken garden has sloping lawns to the central pond.

Your visits help change lives – we've donated over £17 million to Macmillan Cancer Support since 1984

GROUP OPENING

102 NEW **RAMSGATE GARDENS**
Grange Road, Ramsgate,
CT11 9PX. Anne-Marie Nixey.
Enter Ramsgate on A299, continue on A255. At r'about take 2nd exit London Rd. Continue for less than 1m to the r'about and turn L onto Grange Rd. **Sun 7 June (12-5). Combined adm £5, chd free. Home-made teas.**

> NEW **6 EDITH ROAD**
> Nicolette McKenzie.

> NEW **104 GRANGE ROAD**
> Anne-Marie Nixey.

> NEW **106 GRANGE ROAD**
> Mrs Sally Smart.

> NEW **108 GRANGE ROAD**
> Mrs Barbara Warner.

Four evolving medium sized gardens in the beautiful, yet windy coastal town of Ramsgate. Showing off the creativeness of having similar sized plots, making unique gardens out of them, yet each being in harmony with the architecture and surrounding area. Varied planting from traditional roses and bedding plants, to a range of fruit trees, as well as subsistence techniques and incorporating areas used by families. Wheelchairs can access all, or part of 6 Edith Road, 104 Grange Road and 106 Grange Road,.

♿ ❀ ☕

Your visits help change lives – your generosity has supported unpaid carers through donations to Carers Trust totalling over £4 million since 1996

103 **43 THE RIDINGS**
Chestfield, Whitstable,
CT5 3QE. David & Sylvie Buat-Menard, 01227 500775,
sylviebuat-menard@hotmail.com.
Nr Whitstable. From M2 heading E cont onto A299. In 3m take A2990. From r'about on A2990 at Chestfield, turn onto Chestfield Rd, 5th turning on L onto Polo Way which leads into The Ridings. **Sun 31 May (10-4). Sat 6 June (10-4), also open Avalon. Adm £4, chd free. Home-made teas. Visits also by arrangement May to Aug for groups of 5 to 20.**
Delightful small garden brimming with interesting plants both in the front and behind the house. Many different areas. Dry gravel garden in front, raised beds with alpines and bulbs and borders with many unusual perennials and shrubs. The garden ornaments are a source of interest for visitors. The water feature will be of interest for those with a tiny garden as planted with carnivorous plants. Many alpine troughs & raised beds as well as dry shade & mixed borders all in a small space.

♿ ❀ 🚌 ☕

104 ♦ **RIVERHILL HIMALAYAN GARDENS**
Riverhill, Sevenoaks, TN15 0RR.
The Rogers Family, 01732 459777,
info@riverhillgardens.co.uk,
www.riverhillgardens.co.uk. *2m S of Sevenoaks on A225. Leave A21 at A225 & follow signs for Riverhill Himalayan Gardens.* **For NGS: Tue 28 Apr, Wed 10 June (10.30-5). Adm £9.25, chd £6.50. Light refreshments in the Riverhill Café. For other opening times and information, please phone, email or visit garden website.**
Beautiful hillside garden, privately owned by the Rogers family since 1840. Extensive views across the Weald of Kent. Spectacular rhododendrons, azaleas and fine specimen trees. Bluebell and woodland walks. Rose garden. Walled garden with planting, terracing and water feature. Children's adventure playground, den building trail, hedge maze and Yeti spotting. Our Edwardian Rock Garden is now open. Café serving freshly-ground coffee, speciality teas, light lunches, home-made cream teas, cakes. Quirky shed shop selling beautiful gifts & garden ornaments as well as a good selection of plants. Disabled parking. Wheelchair access to Walled Garden,

Rock Garden. Easy access to café, shop and tea terrace (no disabled WC).

♿ ♿ ❀ 🚌 ☕

105 **18 ROYAL CHASE**
Tunbridge Wells, TN4 8AY. Eithne Hudson. *Situated at the top of Mount Ephraim & The Common. Leave A21 at Southborough, follow signs for Tunbridge Wells. After St John's Rd take R turn at junction on Common & sharp R again. From South, follow A26 through town up over Common. Last turn on L.* **Sat 23, Sun 24 May (1-5). Adm £4, chd free. Home-made teas.**
Town garden of a $\frac{1}{4}$ of acre on sandy soil which was originally Common and woodland. Lovely in late Spring with camellias, acers, rhododendrons and alliums. Large lawn with island beds planted with roses and herbaceous perennials and a small pond with lilies and goldfish.The owner is a florist and has planted shrubs and annuals specifically with flower arranging in mind. Access through right hand side gate.

♿ ♿ ☕

106 **ST CLERE**
Kemsing, Sevenoaks, TN15 6NL.
Mr & Mrs Simon & Eliza Ecclestone, www.stclere.com. *6m NE of Sevenoaks. 1m E of Seal on A25, turn L signed Heaverham. In Heaverham turn R signed Wrotham. In 75yds straight ahead marked Private Rd; 1st L to house.* **Sun 7 June (2-5). Adm £5, chd free. Home-made teas in The Garden Room.**
4 acre garden, full of interest. Formal terraces surrounding C17 mansion (not open), with beautiful views of the Kent countryside. Herbaceous and shrub borders, productive kitchen and herb gardens, lawns and rare trees. Garden tour with Head Gardener at 3pm (£1 per person). Some gravel paths and small steps.

♿ 🚌 ☕

GROUP OPENING

107 NEW **ST DUNSTAN'S CANTERBURY**
Orchard Street, Canterbury,
CT2 8AP. Frances Gerth. *From St Dunstan's St turn into Orchard St, if coming from Canterbury 1st L after the level crossing. 5 mins walk from Canterbury West Station.* **Sun 14 June (2-5). Combined adm £5,**

chd free. Home-made teas in garden at 44 Orchard Street.

NEW 6 ORCHARD STREET
Sarah Carter.

NEW 35 ORCHARD STREET
Eddy Koukkides.

NEW 44 ORCHARD STREET
Frances Gerth.

NEW 14 ST DUNSTAN'S TERRACE
Diana Holbrook.

NEW 18 ST DUNSTAN'S TERRACE
Jan Pahl.

Five hidden walled gardens of great charm and elegance in a particularly historic part of Canterbury within a few minutes stroll of each other. Five mins walk from Canterbury West Station. Buy a ticket in any garden. 6 Orchard Street: enter through the house to a well planted garden bursting with interest and colour, fruit trees and a summer house. 35 Orchard Street; entry through the house to a paved area full of container plants, colourful planting and well stocked living roofs. 44 Orchard Street: a spacious walled garden full of roses, fruit trees and herbaceous plants. 14 St Dunstan's Terrace: entrance via garage from New Street to a joyfully exhuberant garden full of climbers. 18 St Dunstan's Terrace: entrance via garage in New Street to an elegant town garden with flowers, fruit trees and a rose arbour. Free parking in surrounding streets. The Westgate Gardens with award winning planting along the banks of the river Stour are five mins away. A fine collection of trees in nearby Canterbury cemetery. The historic church of St Dunstan's was a last stop for pilgrims before entering the city and its famous cathedral. With many steps and entrance through houses there is wheelchair access to 44 Orchard Street only, which has one step in to the garden.

108 ◆ THE SALUTATION GARDEN
Knightrider Street, Sandwich, CT13 9EW. Mr J Fothergill, 01304 619919, enquiries@the-salutation.com, www.the-salutation.com. *In the heart of Sandwich. Turn L at Bell Hotel & into Quayside car park. Entrance in far R corner of car park.* For NGS: Wed 25 Mar, Wed 23 Sept (10-5). Adm £8.50, chd free.

Restaurant and tea room on site, see The Salutation website. For other opening times and information, please phone, email or visit garden website.
3½ acres of ornamental and formal gardens designed by Sir Edwin Lutyens in 1911 surrounding Grade I listed house. Designated historic park and garden. White, yellow, spring, and exotic gardens. Herbaceous borders and vegetable garden. Designed to provide yr-round changing colour. Regional Finalist, The English Garden's The Nation's Favourite Gardens 2019. Unusual plants for sale.

109 SANDOWN
Plain Road, Smeeth, nr Ashford, TN25 6QX. Pamela Woodcock, 01303813478, pmwoodcock078@gmail.com. *4m SE of Ashford. Exit J10 onto A20, take 2nd L signed Smeeth, turn R Woolpack Hill, past garage on L, past next L, garden on L. From A20 in Sellindge at Church, turn R carry on 1m. Park in layby on hill.* Sun 17 May, Sun 14 June, Sun 5 July, Sun 6 Sept (11-4), also open 31 Forest Avenue. Adm £5, chd free. Light refreshments. Visits also by arrangement May to Sept for groups of 10 to 20.
My small compact Japanese style garden and pond has visitor book comments such as: inspirational, just like Japan, a stunning hidden gem. There is a Japanese arbour, tea house/veranda, waterfall and stream. Acers, bamboos, ginkgo, fatsia japonica, clerodendrum trichotomum, pinus mugos, wisterias, hostas and mind your own business for ground cover. WC available. Regret no small children owing to deep pond. Wheelchair access to top section of garden only.

110 ◆ SCOTNEY CASTLE
Lamberhurst, TN3 8JN. National Trust, 01892 893820, scotneycastle@nationaltrust.org.uk, www.nationaltrust.org.uk/scotneycastle. *6m SE of Tunbridge Wells. On A21 London - Hastings, brown tourist signs. Bus: (Mon to Sat) Tunbridge Wells - Wadhurst, alight Lamberhurst Green.* For NGS: Wed 13 May (10-5). Adm £14.90, chd £7.45. Light refreshments.
For other opening times and information, please phone, email or visit garden website.
The medieval moated Old Scotney

Castle lies in a peaceful wooded valley. In C19 its owner Edward Hussey III set about building a new house, partially demolishing the Old Castle to create a romantic folly, the centrepiece of his picturesque landscape. From the terraces of the new house, sweeps of rhododendron and azaleas cascade down the slope in summer, mirrored in the moat. In the house three generations have made their mark, adding possessions and character to the homely Victorian mansion which enjoys far reaching views out across the estate. Wheelchairs available for loan.

111 NEW 45 SEYMOUR AVENUE
Whitstable, CT5 1SA. Kevin Tooher, sirplantalot@outlook.com. *Near the centre of Whitstable town and 400yrds from Whitstable station. Take Thanet Way off A299 towards Whitstable. 2nd r'about, l into Millstrood Rd, bottom of hill R into Old Bridge Rd, Station car park on L & Seymour Ave on R.* Sat 19, Sun 20 Sept (11-4). Adm £5, chd free. Home-made teas. Visits also by arrangement Sept & Oct for groups of 10 to 20.
Larger than usual town centre garden - about ¼ acre with wide range of unusual plants grown on heavy wet clay with lots of exotics growing in containers, troughs and pots.

112 NEW SIR JOHN HAWKINS HOSPITAL
High Street, Chatham, ME4 4EW. Susan Fairlamb, www.hawkinshospital.org. *On the N side of Chatham High St, R on the border between Rochester & Chatham. Leave A2 at J1 & follow signs to Rochester. Pass Rochester Station & turn L at main junction T-lights, travelling E towards Chatham.* Sat 13, Sun 14 June (11-5). Adm £3, chd free. Cream teas. Also open Bishopscourt.
Built on the site of Kettle Hard - part of Bishop Gundulph's Hospital of St Bartholomew, the Almshouse is a square of Georgian houses dating from the 1790s. A delightful small secluded garden overlooks the River Medway, full of vibrant and colourful planting. A lawn with cottage style borders leads to the riverside and a miniature gnome village captivates small children and adults alike. Disabled access via stairlift, wheelchair to be carried separately.

113 ◆ SISSINGHURST CASTLE GARDEN

Biddenden Road, Sissinghurst, Cranbrook, TN17 2AB.
National Trust, 01580 710700, sissinghurst@nationaltrust.org.uk, www.nationaltrust.org.uk/sissinghurst-castle-garden. *2m NE of Cranbrook, 1m E of Sissinghurst on Biddenden Rd (A262), see our website for more information.* **For NGS: Tue 29 Sept (11-5.30). Adm £13.80, chd £6.90. Cream teas in Coffee Shop or Restaurant at Sissinghurst Castle Garden. For other opening times and information, please phone, email or visit garden website.**
Historic, poetic, iconic; a refuge dedicated to beauty. Vita Sackville-West and Harold Nicolson fell in love with Sissinghurst Castle and created a world renowned garden. More than a garden, visitors can also find Elizabethan and Tudor buildings, find out about our history as a Prisoner of War Camp and see changing exhibitions. Free welcome talks and estate walks leaflets. Café, restaurant, gift, secondhand book and plant shops are open from 10am-5.30pm. Some areas unsuitable for wheelchair access due to narrow paths and steps.

114 SMITHS HALL

Lower Road, West Farleigh, ME15 0PE. Mr S Norman, www.smithshall.com. *3m W of Maidstone. A26 towards Tonbridge, turn L into Teston Lane B2163. At T-junction turn R onto Lower Rd B2010. Opp Tickled Trout PH.* **Sun 28 June (11-5). Adm £5, chd free. Light refreshments.** Donation to Heart of Kent Hospice.
Delightful 3 acre gardens surrounding a beautiful 1719 Queen Anne House (not open). Lose yourself in numerous themed rooms: sunken garden, iris beds, scented old fashioned rose walk, formal rose garden, intense wild flowers, peonies, deep herbaceous borders and specimen trees. Walk 9 acres of park and woodland with great variety of young native and American trees and fine views of the Medway valley. Cakes available. Gravel paths.

115 SPRING PLATT

Boyton Court Road, Sutton Valence, Maidstone, ME17 3BY. Mr & Mrs John Millen, 01622 843383, carolyn.millen1@gmail.com, www.kentsnowdrops.com. *5m SE of Maidstone. From A274 nr Sutton Valence follow yellow NGS signs.* **Sun 26, Wed 29 Jan, Sat 1, Sun 2, Wed 5, Tue 11 Feb (10.30-3). Adm £5, chd free. Light refreshments. Home made bread and soup. Limited parking. Please ring to book an appointment for the dates shown, 01622 843383.**
One acre garden under continual development with panoramic views of the Weald. Over 700 varieties of snowdrop grown in tiered display beds with spring flowers in borders. An extensive collection of alpine plants in a large greenhouse. Vegetable garden and natural spring fed water feature. Home-made soup, home-made bread, tea/coffee and cake. Garden on a steep slope and many steps.

116 NEW STABLE HOUSE, HEPPINGTON

Street End, Canterbury, CT4 7AN. Charlie & Lucy Markes. *Stable House, Heppington, CT4 7AN. 2m S of Canterbury, off B2068. 1st R after Bridge Rd if coming from Canterbury, 400m after Granville pub on the L if coming towards Canterbury.* **Sat 27, Sun 28 June (1.30-5.30). Adm £4, chd free. Home-made teas.**
Approx 2 acres of relaxed, informal interlinked gardens surrounding converted Edwardian stable block in lovely setting with views towards the North Downs. Mixed borders with mature shrubs and perennials. Climbing roses, honeysuckle and clematis. Gravel garden, veg garden and walkthrough garden room beneath clocktower. Adjoining 5 acre wildflower meadow and 15 acre vineyard. Disabled parking by arrangement close to garden. Not all areas wheelchair accessible.

117 STONEWALL PARK

Chiddingstone Hoath, nr Edenbridge, TN8 7DG. Mr & Mrs Fleming. *4m SE of Edenbridge. Via B2026. ½ way between Markbeech & Penshurst.* **Sun 15 Mar, Sun 3 May (2-5). Adm £5, chd free. Home-made teas in the conservatory.** Donation to Sarah Matheson Trust & St Mary's Church, Chiddingstone.
Even from the driveway you can see a vast amount of self seeded daffodils, leading down to a romantic woodland garden in historic setting featuring species such as rhododendrons, magnolias, azaleas, bluebells and a range of interesting trees and shrubs, sandstone outcrops, wandering paths and lakes. Historic parkland with cricket ground.

GROUP OPENING

118 TANKERTON GARDENS

Tankerton, CT5 2EP. *The gardens are in a triangle, either on Northwood Road or directly off it, or parallel to it.* **Sat 6 June (10-5). Combined adm £5, chd free. Tea at 16 Northwood Road. Also open 43 The Ridings. Local cafes are available in Tankerton High Street, Tower Parade and the Sea Front.**

17A BADDLESMERE ROAD
Mr Derek Scoones.

NEW 14 NORTHWOOD ROAD
Philippa Langton.

16 NORTHWOOD ROAD
Mr Simon Courage.

12 STRANGFORD ROAD
Sarah Yallop.

NEW 18 STRANGFORD ROAD
Mia Young.

Five very different gardens within a mile of the sea, enjoying a mild climate. Baddlesmere, densely planted for colour all year round, Strangford a more traditional garden and Northwood Road, a very contemporary garden space. Two new gardens for 2020 also in Northwood Road and Strangford Road, one with raised beds and one traditionally planted. Stepped access in three gardens (12 and 18 Strangford Road and 17a Baddlesmere Road).

119 TAWNYHILL KENNELS

Homestall Road, Doddington, Sittingbourne, ME9 0HF. Jean Price. *Junction 6 off M2 - A2 towards Sittingbourne. L into Faversham Rd. Under motorway bridge, first R into Straight Hill. Junction 8 off M20 - A20 to Lenham. L into Faversham Rd. Drive for nearly 7m.* **Sun 7, Mon 8 June (11-6). Adm £5, chd free. Light refreshments.**
The garden started off as an overgrown orchard in 2002. ⅓ of an acre and is all on one level. The soil

is Faversham brick earth. The garden consists of two man made ponds linked by a stream. A lawn area with flower borders, a herb border, 6 raised vegetable beds, a rose garden at the front of the bungalow, 2 greenhouses. Cutting garden. Plant lover's wildlife garden. Ploughmans lunches served from midday. £7.00 per meal. Access to most of the garden by wheelchair. Disabled parking near to house.

&. ✻ ☕

120 TIMBERS
Dean Street, East Farleigh, nr Maidstone, ME15 0HS. Mrs Sue Robinson, 07905281764, suerobinson.timbers@gmail.com, www.timbersgardenkent.co.uk. *2m S of Maidstone. From Maidstone take B2010 to East Farleigh. After Tesco's on R follow Dean St for ½ m. Timbers on L behind 8ft beech hedge. Parking through gates.* **Visits by arrangement Apr to June for groups of 20+. Adm £6, chd free. Cream teas.**
Beautiful 5 acre garden surrounding house built in Arts & Crafts' style. Unusual perennials, annuals, dahlias, roses and shrubs. Plant House. Partly walled garden, parterre, arbour, pergola, island beds, lawns and mature specimen trees plus 100yr old Kentish cobnut plat. Wildflower meadows. Wild orchids. Some woodland. Rock pool with waterfalls. Plant List. Tea room. Colour co-ordinated borders. Tulips in Spring. Roman archaeological site. Most of garden is flat, some steep slopes to rear.

&. ✻ 🚗 ☕

121 NEW ▶ TONBRIDGE SCHOOL
High Street, Tonbridge, TN9 1JP. The Governors. *Various gardens around the school. Maps and guides for visitors. At N end of Tonbridge High St. Parking signed off London Rd (B245 Tonbridge-Sevenoaks).* **Sat 1, Sun 2 Aug (11-5). Adm £5, chd £1. Home-made teas.**
In front of and behind Tonbridge School you will find the five main gardens that you can visit: Front of School Garden, The Garden of Remembrance, Smythe Library and Skinners Library Garden as well as the newly created Barton Science Centre Garden. As well as these you can visit Ferox Hall and view our magnificent Cedar of Lebanon. Tea/coffee and cake available. Head Gardener available to chat. Toilets on

site. All gardens can be accessed via wheelchair and gardeners will be on hand to help and guide.

&. ✻ 🚗 ☕

122 TOPGALLANT
5 North Road, Hythe, CT21 5UF. Mary Sampson. *M20 exit 11, take A259 to Hythe, then going towards Folkestone at r'about, take 2nd L up narrow hill signed to Saltwood. L at junction with North Rd. House on L. See 'Vergers'.* **Sat 6, Sun 7 June (2-5). Combined adm with Vergers £6, chd free. Cream teas at Vergers, Church Road, Hythe. CT21 5DP.**

Also open 69 Capel Street. Opening with Vergers, two very different hillside gardens, both terraced and developed to cope with the prevailing winds and the slope. Top Gallant is a secluded Sculptors' garden, with mature trees and shrubs, a wildlife pond. Decking and grass paths wind down through the garden giving glimpses of the sea. Relaxed planting for year round interest and to encourage wildlife. Ceramics studio open. Sloping hillside garden with many steps.

✻ ☕

Hurst House

123 TORRY HILL
Frinsted/Milstead, Sittingbourne, ME9 0SP. Lady Kingsdown, 01795 830258, lady.kingsdown@btinternet.com. *5m S of Sittingbourne. From M20 J8 take A20 (Lenham). At r'about by Mercure Hotel turn L Hollingbourne (B2163). Turn R at Xrds at top of hill (Ringlestone Rd). Thereafter Frinsted-Doddington (not suitable for coaches), then Torry Hill/NGS signs. From M2 J5 take A249 towards Maidstone, then 1st L (Bredgar), Lagain (follow Bredgar signs), R at War Memorial, 1st L (Milstead), Torry Hill/NGS signs from Milstead. For disabled parking please follow the disabled signs.* **Sun 17 May, Sun 14 June, Sun 19 July (2-5). Adm £5, chd free. Home-made teas. Visits also by arrangement May to Sept for groups of 10 to 30. Discuss refreshments prior to booking. Donation to St. Dunstan's Church, Frinsted and Sounding Out, Saturday Music Centre c/o The** King's School.

8 acres; large lawns, specimen trees, flowering cherries, rhododendrons, azaleas and naturalised daffodils; walled gardens with lawns, shrubs, herbaceous borders, rose garden incl shrub roses, wild flower areas and vegetables. Extensive views to Medway and Thames estuaries. Some shallow steps. No wheelchair access to rose garden due to very uneven surface but can be viewed from pathway.

124 TRAM HATCH
Charing Heath, Ashford, TN27 0BN. Mrs P Scrivens, www.tramhatchgardens.co.uk. *10m NW of Ashford. A20 turn towards Charing Railway Stn on Pluckley Rd, over motorway then 1st R signed Barnfield to end, turn L carry on past Barnfield, Tram Hatch ahead.* **Sun 31 May, Sun 5 July, Sun 9 Aug (12-5). Adm £5. Home-made teas.**

Meander your way off the beaten track to a mature, extensive garden changing through the seasons. You will enjoy a garden laid out in rooms - what surprises are round the corner? Large selection of trees, vegetable, rose and gravel gardens, colourful containers. The River Stour and the Angel of the South enhance your visit. Please come and enjoy, then relax in our lovely garden room for tea. Water features and statuary. The garden is totally flat, apart from a very small area which can be viewed from the lane.

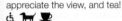

125 UPPER PRYORS
Butterwell Hill, Cowden, TN8 7HB. Mr & Mrs S G Smith. *4½m SE of Edenbridge. From B2026 Edenbridge-Hartfield, turn R at Cowden Xrds & take 1st drive on R.* **Wed 17 June (11-5). Adm £5, chd free. Home-made teas.**
10 acres of English country garden surrounding C16 house - a garden of many parts; colourful profusion, interesting planting arrangements, immaculate lawns, mature woodland, water and a terrace on which to appreciate the view, and tea!

126 VERGERS
Church Road, Hythe, CT21 5DP. Nettie & John Wren. *Hythe 6 mins walk from Topgallant. M20 Exit 11, take A259 to Hythe. Take directions as for Topgallant. L at junc into North Rd, then 1st L into Church Rd, Vergers is next door to St Leonards Church. Parking in Church car park.* **Sat 6, Sun 7 June (2-5). Combined adm with Topgallant £6, chd free. Cream teas at Vergers. Also open 69 Capel Street.**
South facing hillside garden which has been reclaimed and developed over the past five years by the present owners. Steps from car park lead up to the garden terrace, goldfish pond and lawn. Winding paths slope up to many seating areas with spectacular views of the town and Channel. Kitchen garden, wildlife area and pond, bug hotels, mixed planting for year round interest. Church and Ossuary open.

Cobham Hall

© Leigh Clapp

GROUP OPENING

127 NEW WALMER GARDENS
Walmer, Deal, CT14 7SQ. *Yellow signs from A258. Dover Rd.* Sat 13 June (2-5.30); Sun 14 June (2-5). Combined adm £6. Home-made teas at Sunnybank, 12 Herschell Rd East.

196 DOWNS ROAD
Sue Turner.

NEW 31 HERSCHELL SQUARE
Kay Valentine & Johnny Morris.

OLD CHURCH HOUSE
Christine Symons.

SUNNYBANK
Mr & Mrs James & Flora Cockburn.

169 Downs Rd: long garden through wisteria arch, fruit trees, delphiniums, penstemon, agapanthus grown from seed. 31 Herschell Sq: has zonal plantings with silver birch, fig, flowers and shrubs, herbs, white themed front garden, fruit and veg. Sunnybank: long borders flank lawn, roses on obelisks, salvias, shrubs, annuals. Rosa Albertine climbs old crabapple. Old Church House: packed with wide variety of interesting plants on different levels divided by pergola, paths and steps. With bamboos, palms, ponds and hydrangeas.

128 THE WATCH HOUSE
7 Thanet Road, Broadstairs, CT10 1LF. Dan Cooper, www.frustratedgardener.com. *Town Centre Location. Off Broadstairs High St on narrow side rd. At Broadstairs station, cont along High St (A255) towards sea front. Turn L at Terence Painter Estate Agent then immed turn R.* Sat 1, Sun 2 Aug (12-4). Adm £4.50, chd free. Home-made teas. Also open 5 Montefiore Avenue.
Adjoining an historic fishermen's cottage, two small courtyard gardens shelter an astonishing array of unusual plants. Thanks to a unique microclimate, the east-facing garden is home to a growing collection of exotics, chosen principally for exuberant, colourful, jungly foliage. In the west-facing courtyard a garden room leads onto a terrace where flowering plants jostle for space. Within a few mins walk of Viking Bay, The Dickens Museum and Bleak House.

129 WATERGATE HOUSE
King Street, Fordwich, Canterbury, CT2 0DB. Fiona Cadwallader, www.cadwallader.co.uk. *2m E of Canterbury. From Canterbury A257 direction, Sandwich, 1m L to Fordwich. 1m L on Moat Lane, direct to Watergate House bottom of High St. Follow parking instructions.* Sat 25 Apr, Sat 13 June (2-6). Adm £4.50, chd free. Home-made teas.
Magical walled garden by the River Stour: defined areas of formal, spring, woodland, vegetable and secret garden reveal themselves in a naturally harmonious flow, each with its own colour combinations. Ancient walls provide the garden's basic structure, while a green oak pergola echoes a monastic cloister. The garden is mainly on one level with one raised walkway under pergola.

130 WEST COURT LODGE
Postling Court, The Street, Postling, nr Hythe, CT21 4EX. Mr & Mrs John Pattrick, 01303 863285, pattrickmalliet@gmail.com. *2m NW of Hythe. From M20 J11 turn S onto A20. Immed 1st L. After ½ m on bend take rd signed Lyminge. 1st L into Postling.* Visits by arrangement Apr to July for groups of 5 to 30. Visits together with Churchfield. Adm £6, chd free. Home-made teas in Village Hall or garden.
S-facing one acre walled garden at the foot of the N Downs, designed in 2 parts: main lawn with large sunny borders and a romantic woodland glade planted with shadow loving plants and spring bulbs, small wildlife pond. Lovely C11 church will be open next to the gardens.

GROUP OPENING

131 WEST MALLING EARLY SUMMER GARDENS
West Malling, ME19 6LW. *On A20, nr J4 of M20. Park (Ryarsh Lane and Station) in West Malling. Maps and directions to 1&2 New Barns Cottages (parking) are available from gardens in town.* Sun 7 June (12-5). Combined adm £8, chd free. Home-made teas at New Barns Cottages. Donation to St Mary's Church, West Malling.

ABBEY BREWERY COTTAGE
Dr & Mrs David and Lynda Nunn.

BROME HOUSE
John Pfeil & Shirley Briggs.

LUCKNOW, 119 HIGH STREET
Ms Jocelyn Granville.

NEW BARNS COTTAGES
Mr & Mrs Anthony Drake.

TOWN HILL COTTAGE
Mr & Mrs P Cosier.

WENT HOUSE
Alan & Mary Gibbins.

West Malling is an attractive small market town with some fine buildings. Enjoy six lovely gardens that are entirely different from each other and cannot be seen from the road. Brome House and Went House have large gardens with specimen trees, old roses, mixed borders, attractive kitchen gardens and garden features incl a coach house, Roman temple, fountain and parterre. Lucknow and Town Hill Cottage are walled town gardens with mature and interesting planting. Abbey Brewery Cottage is a recent jewel-like example of garden restoration and development. New Barns Cottages has serpentine paths leading through woodland to roomed gardens: tea and cakes in the courtyard garden of the cottages. Town Hill Cottage garden, Abbey Brewery Cottage and New Barns Cottages are more difficult to access but the other gardens have wheelchair access.

132 NEW WHITE HORSES
Conyngham Road, Herne Bay, CT6 6PT. Dr Tim Waltham. *No parking in Conyngham Rd, but there is unrestricted parking close by in surrounding rds. There's also a free car park about 5 mins walk away (via the seafront/downs path) in Reculver Dr.* Sun 30 Aug (12-6). Adm £4, chd free.
Front and back garden replanted in the last five years with shrubs, perennials and grasses. Situated in a dry and windy position, many of the plants are drought tolerant and selected for a long period of interest or winter structure. The front lawn was replaced with an open bed and border which peaks in late summer. Many unusual and choice plants combined to very good effect. A collection of unusual ivies throughout the garden.

GROUP OPENING

133 WHITSTABLE GARDENS
Whitstable, CT5 4LT. *Off A299, or
A290. Down Borstal Hill, L by garage
into Joy Lane to collect map of
participating gardens (also available
at other gardens). Parking at Joy
Lane School and Gorrell Tank.* **Sun
14 June (10-5). Combined adm
£6, chd free. Home-made teas at
Stream Walk Community Gardens
and at the Umbrella Centre Cafe.**

87 ALBERT STREET
Paul Carey & Phil Gomm.

6 ALEXANDRA ROAD
Andrew Mawson & Sarah Rees.

NEW **8 ALEXANDRA ROAD**
Henry Kernighan.

NEW **21 ALEXANDRA ROAD**
Sarah Morgan.

56 ARGYLE ROAD
Emma Burnham & Mel Green.

NEW **42 CANTERBURY ROAD**
Elspeth Dougall.

NEW **76 CANTERBURY ROAD**
Deborah & Gary Parks.

5 CLARE ROAD
Janet Maxwell & Philip Adam.

**THE GUINEA, 31 ISLAND
WALL**
Sheila Wyver.

NEW **15 JOY LANE**
Mr & Mrs Clare Godley.

19 JOY LANE
Francine Raymond,
www.kitchen-garden-hens
.co.uk.

**67A JOY LANE, JUPITER
HOUSE**
Ed Lamb, Shelagh O'Riordan.

96 JOY LANE
Vernon & Terrie Brown.

OCEAN COTTAGE
Katherine Pickering.

ST MARY'S TOWN GARDEN
Whitstable Umbrella Community
Centre.

NEW **STARLINGS**
Mr & Mrs David & Pat Roberts.

STREAM WALK TRUST
Stream Walk Community
Gardens.

NEW **10 WARWICK ROAD**
Lizzie Simpson.

NEW **WAYPOST HOUSE**
Zinnia Slade.

NEW **40 WEST CLIFF**
Lisa Feurtado,
www.fuchsiagreen.com.

30A WESTGATE TERRACE
Graeme Jenkins and Jane
Davidson.

Enjoy a day of eclectic gardens by the
sea. 22 people are showing off their
gardens, 10 of them for the first time,
with 3 favourites returning, but others
marked with yellow balloons, are
there to admire from the street. From
fishermen's yards to formal gardens,
the residents of Whitstable are
making the most of the mild climate.
Choose a few from our leaflet, drop in
and admire contemporary gardens,
seaside gardens, rose gardens, gravel
gardens, designers' gardens and
wildlife friendly plots, both large and
small and some with fabulous views.
Stream Walk and the Umbrella Centre
are at the heart of our community, ideal
for those without gardening space of
their own. We toil on heavy clay soils
and are prone to northerly winds. By
opening, we're hoping to encourage
those new to gardening with our
ingenuity and style, rather than rolling
acres. To find out more see Whitstable
Gardens on Facebook. Combined
adm £6 per adult or £10 for 2. Plant
stalls at 19 Joy Lane, Stream Walk and
the Umbrella Centre.
✿ ☕ 🍷

GROUP OPENING

134 WOMENSWOLD GARDENS
Womenswold, Canterbury,
CT4 6HE. **Mrs Maggie McKenzie,
maggiemckenzie@vfast.co.uk.** *6m
S of Canterbury, midway between
Canterbury & Dover. Take B2046
for Wingham at Barham Xover. Turn
1st R, following signs.* **Sat 27, Sun
28 June (11-5). Combined adm
£5, chd free. Home-made teas at
Brambles, Womenswold. Visits
also by arrangement June & July
for groups of 10+. Check when
booking which gardens will be
open.**
A diverse variety of cottage gardens
in an idyllic situation in an unspoilt
hamlet, mostly surrounding C13
Church. Cottage garden with variety of
old climbing & shrub roses, clematis,
vegetable bed & beehives; a garden in
a setting of a traditional C17 thatched
cottage; colourful garden with ponds,
waterfalls, tropical area with many
rare plants and a large collection of
agapanthus; a garden with a large

display of perennials, kniphofias &
hemerocallis; a 2 acre plantsman's
garden partially created in old chalk
quarry-with vegetables, orchard,
alpines, poly-tunnel with tender fruit .
A very picturesque terraced cottage
garden, with unusual plants, feature
pond with lovely views of the church.
Teas in lovely garden setting. Easy
walking distance between gardens.
North Downs Way runs through village.
Many unusual plants for sale. Teas in
lovely restful garden with home-made
cakes. Produce stall; Church open.
Additional parking in village with minibus running regularly for garden lying
outside main village. Most gardens
have good wheelchair access although
some areas may be inaccessible.
&♿ 🐏 ✿ 🚗 ☕ 🍷

**135 WOODLANDS ROAD
ALLOTMENTS**
47 Tangmere Close, Gillingham,
ME7 2TN. Medway Council,
www.gillinghamhs.co.uk. *From
A2 by Gillingham Golf Club onto
Woodlands Rd, after railway bridge,
1st R onto Hazelmere Dr, 1st R onto
Tangmere Cl.* **Sat 25, Sun 26 July
(12-4). Adm £4, chd free. Home-
made teas.**
162 individual allotments on the
site include topiary, espalier fruits,
many plots of unusual fruit and
vegetables, as well as floral and
wildlife areas. Access is via a level
concrete roadway. There will be
ample opportunity to chat to many
friendly allotmenteers, followed by
home-made cakes and tea with an
opportunity to purchase plants or
produce, making for a very worth-
while visit. Beehives, local wildlife,
and a plot imaginatively using many
up-cycled materials. Concrete level
path round much of the site.
&♿ 🐏 ✿ ☕ 🍷

**136 ♦ THE WORLD GARDEN AT
LULLINGSTONE CASTLE**
Eynsford, DA4 0JA. Mrs Guy
Hart Dyke, 01322 862114,
info@lullingstonecastle.co.uk,
www.lullingstonecastle.co.uk. *1m
from Eynsford. Over Ford Bridge
in Eynsford Village. Follow signs
to Roman Villa. Keep Roman Villa
immed on R then follow Private Rd to
Gatehouse.* **For NGS: Sun 21 June
(12-5). Adm £9, chd £4.50. Light
refreshments. For other opening
times and information, please
phone, email or visit
garden website.**

The World Garden is located within a two-acre, 18th-century Walled Garden in the stunning grounds of Lullingstone Castle, where heritage meets cutting-edge horticulture. The garden is laid out in the shape of a miniature map of the world. Thousands of species are represented, all planted out in their respective beds. The World Garden Nursery offers a host of horticultural and homegrown delights, to reflect the unusual and varied planting of the garden. To celebrate our 15th garden anniversary, we are opening a new cactus attraction, adding a new pergola structure and new planting in our arboretum. Wheelchairs available upon request.

137 WYCKHURST

Mill Road, Aldington, Ashford, TN25 7AJ. Mr & Mrs Chris Older, 01233 720395, cdo@rmfarms.co.uk. *4m SE of Ashford. From M20 J10 take A20 2m E to Aldington turning; turn R at Xrds & proceed 1½m to Aldington Village Hall. Turn R & immed L by Walnut Tree Inn down Forge Hill. After ¼m turn R into Mill Rd.* **Sat 6, Sun 7, Sat 13, Sun 14 June (12-5). Adm £5, chd free. Cream teas on the Sun Terrace. Visits also by arrangement in June for groups of 5 to 20.**
Delightful C16 Kent Cottage (not open) nestles in romantic seclusion at the end of a drive. This enchanting 1 acre garden is a mixture of small mixed herbaceous borders, roses and much unusual topiary incl a wildflower meadow. There is plenty of seating round the lawns to enjoy the garden and teas with extensive views over the Kent countryside across to the Romney Marsh and on towards the sea. There is a dell with a small water feature and in the wildflower meadow is a shepherd's hut to enjoy rest after a stroll. The garden is under continuous redesign and development with fresh plantings each year to provide changing interest for every visitor. Home made cakes & scones. A gentle slope which limits wheelchair access in a small area.

GROUP OPENING

138 WYE GARDENS

Churchfield Way, Wye, TN25 5BP. *3m NE of Ashford. From A28 take turning signed Wye.* **Sun 14 June (2-6). Combined adm £5, chd free. Home-made teas at Wye Church.**

3 BRAMBLE CLOSE
Dr M Copland.
(See separate entry)

MIDDLEFIELD HOUSE
TN25 5EP. Kathy and Steve Bloom.

3 ORCHARD DRIVE
TN25 5AU. Liz Coulson.

32 OXENTURN ROAD
TN25 5BE. Rosemary Fitzpatrick.

SPRING GROVE FARM HOUSE
TN25 5EY. Heather Van den Bergh.

The gardens open in the Historic Market Town of Wye are all very different in character. 3 Bramble Close: a very wild experimental garden buzzing with wildlife demonstrates how plants maintain their natural population density. Middlefield House: a half-acre plot with sweeping views over open fields, woodland, borders, wildlife meadow, raised vegetable beds, sculpture and huge wildlife photographs peering through foliage. 3 Orchard Drive: a relatively new garden packed with plants and features (rose arches, benches, raised beds), a great example of what can be achieved in a modest plot. 32 Oxenturn Road: a wildlife garden featuring a wild flower meadow, a green-roofed shed and worm composting as well as shrubs, flowers and raised vegetable beds. Spring Grove Farm House: a large country garden full of colour and many interesting features including a lake, pond and a gravel garden. Wheelchair access to 32 Oxenturn Rd & Spring Grove Farm House only.

139 YEW TREE COTTAGE

Penshurst, TN11 8AD. Mrs Pam Tuppen, 01892 870689. *4m SW of Tonbridge. From A26 Tonbridge to Tunbridge Wells, join B2176 Bidborough to Penshurst Rd. 2m W of Bidborough, 1m before Penshurst. Unsuitable for coaches.* **Wed 29 Jan, Wed 12, Wed 26 Feb, Wed 11, Wed 25 Mar, Wed 8, Wed 22**

Apr, Wed 6, Wed 20 May, Wed 3, Wed 17 June, Wed 1 July (12-5). Adm £3, chd free. Light refreshments.
Small, romantic cottage garden with steep hillside entrance. Lots of seats and secret corners, many unusual plants - hellebores, spring bulbs, old roses, many special perennials. Small pond; something to see in all seasons. Created and maintained by owner, a natural garden full of plants.

140 YOAKLEY HOUSE

Drapers Close, Margate, CT9 4AH. Michael Yoakley's Charity, www.yoakleycare.co.uk. *Drapers Close, Margate. Near Margate QEQM Hospital, Drapers Cl is a cul de sac turning off St Peters Rd. At the end of Drapers Cl is access to the Yoakley car park, through the hedge.* **Sun 19 July (2.30-4.30), also open Quex Gardens. Sun 6 Sept (2.30-4.30). Adm £5, chd £2.50. Light refreshments in Yoakley House Care Home on site.**
Set in 2½ acres of grounds, cultivated the old fashioned way to complement the ancient almshouses it serves. Well-manicured lawns with extensive borders and densely planted display beds: summer bedding, carpet bedding, specimen trees, shrubs and rockery plants, herbaceous planting, shrub rose beds with standard roses. Magnificent hanging baskets. Accessible pathways from the main car park throughout the grounds.

Your visits help change lives – we are Hospice UK's largest charitable funder donating more than £5.5 million to support hospices in local communities since 1996

LANCASHIRE
Merseyside, Greater Manchester

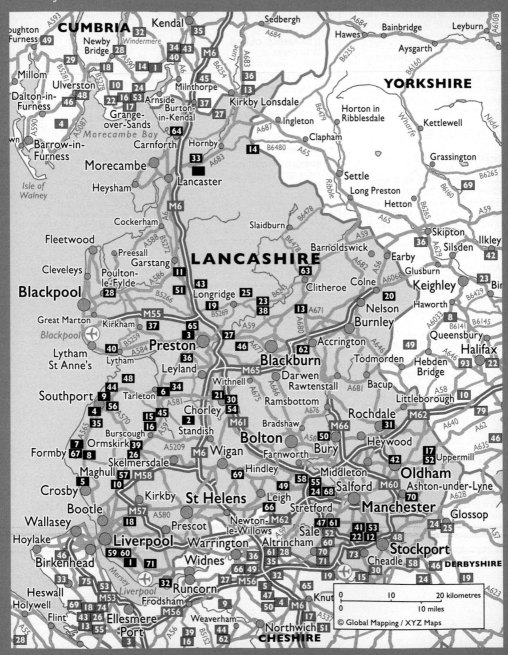

CUMBRIA

YORKSHIRE

LANCASHIRE

CHESHIRE

DERBYSHIRE

0   10   20 kilometres
0   10 miles

© Global Mapping / XYZ Maps

The gardens of the Red Rose County of Lancashire offer a wide range of horticultural excellence and inspiration.

Hidden behind walls, hedges and fences lie some of the most exquisite private gardens in the country; a range of expertly tended plots full of colour, innovation and seasonal interest. There is something here to inspire all the family, whether it be allotments, wildlife sanctuaries, rows of back to back terrace gardens, inner city sanctuaries with water features or rolling acres with lakes.

So, whatever size your own patch, why not visit some of our stunning gardens and maybe take away a few brilliant ideas to copy at home- all with the added pleasure of home- made cakes and tea, and often plants for sale too.

Our gardeners look forward to welcoming you!

Below: Sefton Villa

Volunteers

County Organiser
Margaret Fletcher
01704 567742
margaret.fletcher@ngs.org.uk

County Treasurer
Geoff Fletcher
01704 567742
geoffwfletcher@hotmail.co.uk

Publicity
Barbara & Richard Farbon
01772 600750
barbaraandrichard.farbon@ngs.org.uk

Christine Ruth
01517 274877
caruthchris@aol.com

Social Media
Carole Ann & Stephen Powers
01254 824903
chows3@icloud.com

Booklet Co-ordinator
Brenda Doldon
01704 834253
doldon@btinternet.com

Assistant County Organisers
Anne & Jim Britt
01614 458100
annebritt@btinternet.com

Peter & Sandra Curl
01704 893713
peter.curl@btinternet.com

Deborah Jackson
debs136@icloud.com

John & Jennifer Mawdsley
01704 564708

Eric & Sharon Rawcliffe
01253 883275
ericrawk@talktalk.net

Claire Spendlove
01524 727770
claire@lavenderandlime.co.uk

 @Lancsngs

@lancsngs

OPENING DATES

All entries subject to change. For latest information check www.ngs.org.uk

Extended openings are shown at the beginning of the month.

Map locator numbers are shown to the right of each garden name.

February

Snowdrop Festival

Sunday 16th
Weeping Ash Garden 66

Sunday 23rd
Weeping Ash Garden 66

April

Saturday 25th
Dale House Gardens 19

Sunday 26th
Dale House Gardens 19

May

Sunday 10th
NEW Derian House
Children's Hospice 21
◆ The Ridges 54
Sefton Park May
Gardens 59

Saturday 16th
NEW Halton Park House 33
Matshead Lodge 43

Sunday 17th
79 Crabtree Lane 16
NEW Halton Park House 33
◆ Hazelwood 34
Hillside Gardens 35

Saturday 23rd
NEW Willow Wood
Hospice Gardens 70

Sunday 24th
Bretherton Gardens 6
◆ Clearbeck House 14
Parkers Lodge 50

Monday 25th
◆ Clearbeck House 14

Saturday 30th
Dent Hall 20

Sunday 31st
Birkdale Gardens 4
Blundell Gardens 5
Dent Hall 20
Waddow Lodge
Garden 63

June

Saturday 6th
136 Buckingham
Road 10
NEW Calder House
Lane Gardens 11
Hale Village Gardens 32

Sunday 7th
136 Buckingham Road 10
NEW Calder House Lane
Gardens 11
45 Grey Heights View 30
Hale Village Gardens 32
Kington Cottage 37
6 Menivale Close 44
Meresands Kennels &
Cattery 45
120 Roe Lane 56
NEW St Thomas Primary
School 57

Saturday 13th
35 Ellesmere Road 24
Giles Farm 25
Mill Barn 46
NEW Old Hollows Farm 48
The Old Vicarage 49
NEW 8 Water Head 65
11 Westminster Road 68

Sunday 14th
8 Andertons Mill 2
31 Cousins Lane 15
79 Crabtree Lane 16
Didsbury Village
Gardens 22
Giles Farm 25
Green Farm Cottage 28
◆ Hazelwood 34
Mill Barn 46
NEW Old Hollows Farm 48
The Old Vicarage 49
The Secret Garden 58
NEW 8 Water Head 65

Saturday 20th
5 Crib Lane 17

Dale House Gardens 19
Mill Barn 46
11 Platt Lane 52

Sunday 21st
5 Crib Lane 17
Dale House Gardens 19
Mill Barn 46
11 Platt Lane 52

Sunday 28th
Bridge Inn Community
Farm 8
Dutton Hall 23

July

Saturday 4th
Kington Cottage 37
NEW 4 Roe Green 55
Warton Gardens 64

Sunday 5th
Bretherton Gardens 6
33 Brewery Lane 7
6 Cannock Drive 12
◆ Clearbeck House 14
Hutton Gardens 36
Kington Cottage 37
Parkers Lodge 50
NEW 36 Queens Drive 53
Warton Gardens 64
6 West Lane 67

Sunday 12th
Birkdale Gardens 4
NEW Gorse Hill Nature
Reserve 26
45 Grey Heights View 30
◆ Hazelwood 34
72 Ludlow Drive 39
Waddow Lodge
Garden 63

Saturday 18th
NEW Willow Wood
Hospice Gardens 70

Sunday 19th
Hillside Gardens 35
Maggie's, Oldham 42
Southlands 61
Wigan & Leigh
Hospice 69
Woolton Village
Gardens 71

Sunday 26th
NEW Allerton & Mossley
Hill Gardens 1
Lytham Hall 40
Maggie's Manchester 41
Moss Park Allotments 47

August

Saturday 1st
Lower Dutton Farm 38

Sunday 2nd
45 Grey Heights View 30
Kington Cottage 37
Lower Dutton Farm 38

Saturday 8th
The Growth Project 31

Sunday 9th
NEW Derian House
Children's Hospice 21
Weeping Ash Garden 66

Sunday 16th
Plant World 51

Saturday 22nd
Stanhill Exotic Garden 62

Sunday 23rd
Stanhill Exotic Garden 62

Saturday 29th
NEW Ashton Walled
Community Gardens 3

Sunday 30th
Bretherton Gardens 6
◆ Croxteth Park Walled
Garden 18

Monday 31st
◆ The Ridges 54

September

Saturday 5th
NEW Grange Community
Garden 27

Sunday 13th
Sefton Park September
Gardens 60
Weeping Ash Garden 66

October

Sunday 25th
Weeping Ash Garden 66

By Arrangement

Arrange a personalised garden visit with your club, or group of friends, on a date to suit you. See individual garden entries for full details.

8 Andertons Mill 2

THE GARDENS

GROUP OPENING

1 NEW ALLERTON & MOSSLEY HILL GARDENS

Liverpool, L18 7JQ. *3m S of end of M62. From L lane at end of M62 follow Ring Road A5058 (S). Follow A5058 through 1st island. Keep to L lane through 2nd island then take B5180 for about ½ m to signage.* Sun 26 July (12-5). Combined adm £5, chd free. Light refreshments. at 30 Ballantrae Road.

NEW 30 BALLANTRAE ROAD
L18 6JQ. Mrs Caroline Williams.

NEW 33 GREENHILL ROAD
L18 6JJ. Tony Rose, 07867 504995, tonyrose@blueyonder.co.uk. Visits also by arrangement Aug & Sept for groups of up to 10.

NEW 146 MATHER AVENUE
L18 7HB. Barbara Peers.

NEW 128 PITVILLE AVENUE
L18 7JQ. Paul & Theresa Jevons.

A lawned garden awaits at Ballantrae Rd. Deep borders are planted with a wide variety of herbaceous perennials and shrubs. A very pretty waterfall and pond is surrounded by dense planting. There is a lovely octagonal greenhouse and arbour. At Greenhill Rd you will find a splendid collection of exotic and architectural plants, both containerised and ground-planted. The garden is mainly paved. Paths wend around a raised pond fed by a cobble-bedded stream, which provides a central focal point. The Mather Ave garden has a very informal feel with an emphasis on providing for wildlife. There is a fishpond, wildlife pond and a woodpile for insects. The borders include perennials in mostly pinks

and blues, a corner of hot colours and self-seeding wildflowers. The garden on Pitville Ave is an example of what can be achieved in very small space. It has well laid out paths, herbaceous borders, a pergola, arch and arbour seat. It also includes a small water feature and stonework adornments.

2 8 ANDERTONS MILL

Mawdesley, Ormskirk, L40 3TW. Mr & Mrs R Mercer, 01257 450636, margaret.mercer6@btinternet.com. *9m E of Ormskirk. M6 J27 A5209 over Parbold Hill, R Lancaster Lane/Chorley Rd, L after Farmers Arms to Bentley Lane/Andertons Mill. Garden 500yds on R. From Burscough A59, A5209 towards Parbold, L Lancaster Lane.* Sun 14 June (12.30-5). Adm £3.50, chd free. Home-made teas. Visits also by arrangement June & July for groups of 10 to 30.
This ½ acre cottage garden started in 2010, has many colourful borders of perennials, shrubs, and roses. A patio with raised beds, secluded potted plant area, Vegetable and cut flower gardens. Rose and clematis covered

arches and many wrought iron features made by Bob. An extensive bed of scented roses and a wonderful view of Harrock Hill.

🐎 ❀ ☕ 🍽

3 NEW ASHTON WALLED COMMUNITY GARDENS

Pedders Lane, Ashton-On-Ribble, Preston, PR2 1HL. Annie Wynn, www.letsgrowpreston.org. *W of Preston. From M6 J30 head towards Preston turn R onto Blackpool Rd. Follow Blackpool Rd for 3.4m turn L onto Pedders Lane & next R onto the park. Entrance to walled garden is 50 metres on your L.* Sat 29 Aug (10-3). Adm £4, chd free. Cream teas. Formal raised beds within a walled garden, a peace garden and an edible garden. The formal part of the garden uses plants predominantly from just 3 families, rose, geranium and aster. It is punctuated by grasses and has been designed to demonstrate how diverse and varied plants can be from just the one family. Live musical entertainment Formal and informal gardens workspace and plant sales edible garden.

♿ 🐎 ❀ ☕ 🍽

Lower Dutton Farm

© Fiona Lea

GROUP OPENING

4 BIRKDALE GARDENS
Birkdale, Southport, PR8 2AX.
1m S of Southport. Gardens signed from A565 Southport to Liverpool rd & A5267 S through Birkdale Village. Maps available at each location. **Sun 31 May, Sun 12 July (11-5). Combined adm £5, chd free. Home-made teas at Saxon Rd & Westbourne Gdns, ice cream at Meadow Ave. Bacon sandwiches at Hartley Cres.**

22 HARTLEY CRESCENT
PR8 4SG. Sandra & Keith Birks.

10 MEADOW AVENUE,
PR8 5HF. John & Jenny Smith.

14 SAXON ROAD
PR8 2AX. Margaret & Geoff
Fletcher, 01704 567742,
margaret.fletcher@ngs.org.uk.
Visits also by arrangement May to Aug for groups of 10+.
NEW **1 WESTBOURNE GARDENS**
PR8 2EZ. Ken & Rita Carlin.

An established group of gardens surrounding the bustling Victorian village of Birkdale, reached by a short car journey. Gardens feature a delightful plants woman's L shaped garden with a very special secret garden, a walled garden with an array of tender plants amongst informal island beds and a family garden full of surprises with imaginative use of reclaimed materials. A new garden joining the group which

has been transformed over 4 years into a delight for the senses. Wheelchair access to some gardens.

GROUP OPENING

5 BLUNDELL GARDENS
Blundell Road, Hightown,
Liverpool, L38 9EF. *11m N of Liverpool, 11m S of Southport. M57/58-Switch Island; A5758 to Southport; join A565; L onto B5193, T-junction turn R Moss Lane, L onto Alt Rd, R onto Kerslake Way, over r'bout into Thornbeck, L onto Village Way, R onto Blundell Rd.* **Sun 31 May (1-5). Combined adm £5, chd free. Home-made teas at 11 Blundell Rd.**

5 BLUNDELL AVENUE
Denise & Dave Ball.

11 BLUNDELL AVENUE
Karen Rimmer.

NEW **11 BLUNDELL ROAD**
Mrs Joyce Batey.

75 BLUNDELL ROAD
Shirley & Phil Roberts.

A varied group of gardens in Hightown Village. Featuring a quaint courtyard full of curiosities, a quirky garden full of surprises and a wide variety of plants and a wildlife-friendly garden with pond, pergola and fairy glen. New this year a large mature garden with wooded terraced area planted with azaleas, gravel path

leading to Zen garden on upper level, views back to house, mature monkey puzzle tree. Wheelchair access to lower part of 11 Blundell Rd.

GROUP OPENING

6 BRETHERTON GARDENS
South Road, Bretherton, Leyland,
PR26 9AS. *8m SW of Preston. Between Southport & Preston, from A59, take B5247 towards Chorley for 1m. Gardens signed from South Rd (B5247).* **Sun 24 May, Sun 5 July, Sun 30 Aug (12-5). Combined adm £6, chd free. Home-made teas at Bretherton Congregational Church on all dates, also light lunches 5 July.**

GLYNWOOD HOUSE
PR26 9AS. Terry & Sue Riding.

HAZEL COTTAGE
PR26 9AN. John & Kris
Jolley, 01772 600896,
jolley@johnjolley.plus.com.
Visits also by arrangement May to Oct for groups of 10+.

OWL BARN
PR26 9AD. Richard & Barbara
Farbon, 01772 600750,
farbons@btinternet.com.
Visits also by arrangement May to Aug for groups of up to 20.

PEAR TREE COTTAGE
PR26 9AS.
John & Gwenifer Jackson,
gweniferjackson@gmail.com.
Visits also by arrangement June to Aug for groups of 20+.

Four contrasting gardens spaced across attractive village with conservation area. Glynwood House a finalist in the 2019 Nation's Favourite Garden Competition is a ¾ acre garden of mixed borders, pond with drystone-wall water feature, woodland walk, patio garden with pergola and raised beds, all in a peaceful location with spectacular open aspects. Pear Tree Cottage garden blends seamlessly into its rural setting with informal displays of ornamental and edible crops, water and mature trees, against a backdrop of open views to the West Pennine Moors. Owl Barn has herbaceous borders with cottage garden and hardy plants, a productive kitchen garden providing fruit, vegetables and cut flowers, and two ponds with fountains which complement the C18 converted barn (not open). Hazel Cottage garden has

22 Hartley Crescent

evolved from a Victorian subsistence plot to encompass a series of themed spaces packed with plants to engage the senses and the mind. Live music at Glynwood. Home-made preserves for sale at Pear Tree Cottage. Narrow or uneven paths in some parts of all the gardens. Partial wheelchair access at Hazel Cottage.

7 33 BREWERY LANE

Formby, Liverpool, L37 7DY. **Sue and Dave Hughes.** *7m S of Southport. S on Formby by-pass A565 past RAF Woodvale R at r'about to Southport Rd , R to Green Ln continues to Massams Ln, first R into West Ln continues to Brewery Ln.* **Sun 5 July (11-4). Combined adm with 6 West Lane £3.50, chd free. Home-made teas.** We started planting up the garden in 2015 with perennials, shrubs and climbers. There are colour themed raised beds with lawns and a paved terrace. Seating throughout the garden. Productive area with raised beds of vegetables and cut flowers raised from seed in the greenhouse.

8 BRIDGE INN COMMUNITY FARM

Moss Side, Formby, Liverpool, L37 0AF. Bridge Inn Community Farm, 01704 830303, bridgeinnfarm@talktalk.net, www. bridgeinncommunityfarm.co.uk. *7m S of Southport. Formby by-pass A565, L onto Moss Side.* **Sun 28 June (10-4). Adm £3.50, chd free. Light refreshments. Visits also by arrangement.** Bridge Inn Community Farm was established in 2010 in response to a community need. Our farm sits on a beautiful 4 acre small holding with views looking out over the countryside. We provide a quality service of training in a real life work environment and experience in horticulture, conservation and animal welfare.

9 4 BROCKLEBANK ROAD

Southport PR9 9LP. **Heather Sidebotham,** 01704 543389, alansidebotham@yahoo.co.uk. *1¼ m N of Southport. Off A565 Southport to Preston Rd, opp North entrance to Hesketh Park.* **Visits**

---

by arrangement May to Aug for groups of 10+. A walled garden incorporating a church folly. Landscaped with reclaimed materials from historic sites in the Southport area. There are several water features, an extensive herbaceous border and areas of differing planting, thus creating a garden with much interest. Described by Matthew Wilson of Gardeners Question Time as a lovely garden with beautiful vistas at every turn.

10 136 BUCKINGHAM ROAD

Maghull, L31 7DR. **Debbie & Mark Jackson.** *7m N of Liverpool. End M57/M58, take A59 towards Ormskirk. Turn L after car superstore onto Liverpool Rd Sth, cont' on past Meadows pub, 3rd R into Sandringham Rd, L into Buckingham Rd.* **Sat 6 June (12-5). Adm £3, chd free. Sun 7 June (12-5). Combined adm with St Thomas Primary School £3.50, chd free. Home-made teas. Donation to Headway.** A profusion of plants within a small suburban garden, cottage style planting, shrubs, climbers, perennials and containers brimming with hostas, acers and much more. Rose bed, wisteria covered pergola and water features . The garden is planted to attract butterflies and bees. Plenty of seating.

GROUP OPENING

11 NEW CALDER HOUSE LANE GARDENS

Calder House Lane, Bowgreave, Preston, PR3 1ZE. **Mrs Margaret Richardson.** *7m N of M6 J32. 7m S of M6 J33. Turn R on to B6340 1m. Follow A6 for 7m turn L onto Cock Robin Lane, Catterall turn L at the end, B6340. ½m turn R into Calder House Lane.* **Sat 6 June (10.30-5); Sun 7 June (12-5). Combined adm £5, chd free. Home-made teas at the Friends Meeting House.**

NEW CALDER COACH HOUSE Lila Thomas.

NEW CALDER COTTAGE Lynn Jones, 01995 604121, marg254@btinternet.com. **Visits also by arrangement June & July.**

NEW 1 CALDER HOUSE COTTAGE Paul Hafren & Gaynor Gee, 01995 604121, marg254@btinternet.com. **Visits also by arrangement June & July.**

NEW 2 CALDER HOUSE COTTAGE Phil & Sarah Schofield, 01995 604121, marg254@btinternet.com. **Visits also by arrangement June & July.**

NEW 3 CALDER HOUSE COTTAGE Margaret & Mick Richardson, 01995 604121, marg254@btinternet.com. **Visits also by arrangement June & July.**

The gardens range from a small satellite to a large (relatively new) garden featuring over 100 Hosta varieties. Mainly cottage gardens in style, each having its own features and interest. 1,2,3 Cottages have small front gardens with 3 very different designs. The Coach House a large cobbled yard with horse mounting steps and beds at the front, steps and herb terrace access the main lawn area at the rear. Calder Cottage a small cottage garden packed with interesting perennials, roses. No 1 the satellite garden at the top of the track, small but beautiful use of the space, making a tranquil haven. No 2 divided in to 3 rooms, cottage garden, a secluded seating area and finally a greenhouse, veg & fruit. No 3 the large garden planted with perennials, trees, roses, hostas and shrubs. With a separate fruit and cut flower garden and greenhouse. All rear gardens apart from No1 have a step from the patio areas onto the main garden.

Your visits help change lives – your generosity helps Marie Curie fund nurses to care for people night and day in their homes, with donations of more than £9 million

12 6 CANNOCK DRIVE
Heaton Mersey, Stockport,
SK4 3JB. Andrea & Stefan
Schumacher. *5m S of Manchester.
A 5154 (Didsbury Rd). The rd takes
a slight ascent & you need to turn in
Lodge Court, then next L is Cannock
Drive.* **Sun 5 July (12-5). Combined
adm with 36 Queens Drive £6, chd
free. Light refreshments. Wine.**
A large atmospheric woodland garden
containing an idyllic lake, sweeping
lawns and well stocked borders
planted according to principles of
colour energy. Snaking path to the
central circular seating area, through
a wooded area and alongside the
waters edge. Summerhouse, fire pit
and historic former glasshouse wall
are some of the other features of this
surprising and secluded garden.

  🐕 ✤ ☕

13 CASA LAGO
1 Woodlands Park, Whalley,
BB7 9UG. Carole Ann &
Stephen Powers, 01254 824903,
chows3@icloud.com. *2½ m S of
Clitheroe. From M6 J31, take A59
to Clitheroe. 9m take 2nd exit at
r'about for Whalley. After 2m reach
village & follow yellow signs. Parking
in village car parks or nearby.* **Visits
by arrangement June to Aug for
groups of 5 to 30. Adm £4.50, chd
free. Home-made teas.**
Traverse the globe in a micro
climate location enabling hints of
The Far East, Italy and England…
Bonsai Trees, Koi / Wildlife Ponds,
Succulents, Hostas, Bamboos,
grasses, black limestone wall, oak
pergolas, elevated glass areas,
Coniston slate path and the furry
'Bear' Chow Chows! Consistent
2019 visitor comments: "Inspirational,
so much exotic stuff, fascinating
planting, a credit to you both!

  ✤ ☕

14 ◆ CLEARBECK HOUSE
Mewith Lane, Higher Tatham
via Lancaster, LA2 8PJ. Peter &
Bronwen Osborne, 01524 261029,
bronwenmo@gmail.com,
www.clearbeckgarden.org.uk.
*13m NE of Lancaster. Signed from
Wray (M6 J34, A683, B6480) & Low
Bentham.* **For NGS: Sun 24, Mon
25 May, Sun 5 July (11-5). Adm
£4, chd free. Light refreshments.
For other opening times and
information, please phone, email or
visit garden website.**
It is our 31st. year with NGS 'A
surprise round every corner' say

visitors. They can enjoy streams,
ponds, sculptures, boathouses and
follies: Rapunzel's tower, temple,
turf maze, giant fish made of CDs,
walk-through pyramid. 2 acre
wildlife lake attracts many species
of insects and birds. Planting incl
herbaceous borders, grasses, bog
plants and many roses. Vegetable
and fruit garden. Painting studio
open. Children- friendly incl quiz.
Artists and photographers welcome
by arrangement. Wheelchair access
-many grass paths, some sloped.

  🐕 ✤ ☕

15 31 COUSINS LANE
Rufford, Ormskirk, L40 1TN.
Brenda & Roy Caslake. *From M6
J27, follow signs for Parbold then
Rufford. Turn L onto the A59. Turn
R at Hesketh Arms Pub. 4th turn.*
**Sun 14 June (10.30-4). Adm £3.50,
chd free. take time to re-energise
with a glass of prosecco, a cream
tea whilst enjoying the best of
English pastimes.**
The village cricket ground provides a
backcloth to the garden with an open
aspect to the north & west. Bordered
by a stream flower beds run along
three sides of the house and are
populated in a cottage garden style.
The subtle planting is enhanced by a
design which provides discrete areas
to come and enjoy.

  ✤ ☕

16 79 CRABTREE LANE
Burscough, L40 0RW. Sandra
& Peter Curl, 01704 893713,
peter.curl@btinternet.com,
www.youtube.com/
watch?v=Tqpx W7_8HT4. *3m NE
of Ormskirk. A59 Preston - Liverpool
Rd. From N before bridge R into
Redcat Lane signed for Martin
Mere. From S over 2nd bridge L
into Redcat Lane after ¾ m L into
Crabtree Lane.* **Sun 17 May, Sun
14 June (11-4). Adm £4, chd free.
Home-made teas. Visits also by
arrangement May to July. Short
talk on how the garden developed.**
¾ acre all year round plants person's
garden with many rare and unusual
plants. Herbaceous borders and
colour themed island beds leading
to a pond and rockery, rose garden,
spring area and autumn hot bed.
Many stone features built with
reclaimed materials. Shrubs and
rhododendrons, Koi pond with
waterfall, hosta and fern walk. Gravel
garden with Mediterranean plants.
Patio, surrounded by shrubs and

raised alpine bed. Trees giving areas
for shade loving plants. Flat grass and
bark paths.

  🐕 🌳 ✤ 🚗 ☕

17 5 CRIB LANE
Dobcross, Oldham, OL3 5AF.
Helen Campbell. *5m E of Oldham.
From Dobcross village-head towards
Delph on Platt Lane, Crib Lane
opp Dobcross Band Club - about
100 metres up, limited parking for
disabled visitors only opp double
green garage door, signed NGS.* **Sat
20, Sun 21 June (1-4). Combined
adm with 11 Platt Lane £3.50, chd
free. Home-made teas.**
Open with 11 Platt Lane -a well
loved and well used family garden
- challenging as on a high terraced
hillside and visited by deer, hares
and the odd cow! Additional
interests are wildlife ponds,wildflower
areas,vegetable garden, a poly tunnel,
four bee hives and an art gallery and
garden sculptures. Areas re thought
annually, dug up and changed
depending on time and aged bodies
aches and pains! Art gallery and stone
sculptures in the garden. Four bee
hives and local honey for sale.

  ✤ ☕

**18 ◆ CROXTETH PARK
WALLED GARDEN**
Liverpool, L11 1EH. Liverpool
City Council. Dina Younis,
croxtethcountrypark@
liverpool.gov.uk, ,
www.liverpoolcityhalls.co.uk. *6m
NE of Liverpool. From M57 Exit J4
take A580 towards Liverpool. Look
for brown tourist signs directing L.
Main car park off Muirhead Ave East.*
**Sun 30 Aug (11.30-5). Adm £3.50,
chd free. Home-made teas.**
The two acre Victorian Walled Garden
at Croxteth Hall was built around
1850. It produced a year round supply
of fresh fruit, vegetable and cut flowers
for the Hall until the last Earl died in
1972. Bedding display, herbaceous
and mixed borders, trained espalier
and goblet fruit trees, herb garden,
wild flower maze, peach house, rose
beds, cut flower beds, soft fruits and a
Fuchsia collection. The garden houses
part of Liverpool's historic botanical
collection under glass. The estate
offers ample opportunities for walking.
There is disabled permit parking
available near to the Hall and Garden –
use the service entrance from Croxteth
Hall Lane (Satnav postcode L12 0HB).

  🐕 🌳 ✤ 🚗 NPC ☕

19 DALE HOUSE GARDENS
off Church Lane, Goosnargh,
Preston, PR3 2BE. Caroline
& Tom Luke, 01772 862464,
tomlukebudgerigars@hotmail.com.
*2½ m E of Broughton. M6 J32
signed Garstang Broughton, T-lights
R at Whittingham Lane, 2½ m to
Whittingham at PO turn L into Church
Lane garden between nos 17 & 19.*
Sat 25, Sun 26 Apr, Sat 20, Sun 21
June (10-4). Adm £3.50, chd free.
Home-made teas. Visits also by
arrangement Mar to July. Donation
to St Francis School, Goosnargh.
½ acre tastefully landscaped gardens
comprising of limestone rockeries, well
stocked herbaceous borders, raised
alpine beds, well stocked koi pond,
lawn areas, greenhouse and polytunnel,
patio areas, specialising in alpines
rare shrubs and trees, large collection
unusual bulbs. All year round interest.
Large indoor budgerigar aviary. 300+
budgies. New for 2020 a secret garden.
Gravel path, lawn areas.

20 DENT HALL
Colne Road, Trawden,
Colne, BB8 8NX. Mr Chris
Whitaker-Webb & Miss
Joanne Smith, 01282 861892,
denthall@tiscali.co.uk. *Turn L at
end of M65. Follow A6068 for 2m;
just after 3rd r'about turn R down
B6250. After 1½ m, in front of
church, turn R, signed Carry Bridge.
Keep R, follow road up hill, garden
on R after 300yds.* Sat 30, Sun 31
May (12-5). Adm £3.50, chd free.
Home-made teas. Visits also by
arrangement June to Sept for
groups of 10+. Donation to MIND.
Nestled in the oldest part of Trawden
villlage and rolling Lancashire
countryside, this mature and evolving
country garden surrounds a 400 year
old grade II listed hall (not open);
featuring a parterre, lawns, herbaceous
borders, shrubbery, wildlife pond with
bridge to seating area and a hidden
summerhouse in a woodland area.
Plentiful seating throughout. Some
uneven paths and gradients.
❀ ☕

**21 NEW DERIAN HOUSE
CHILDREN'S HOSPICE**
Chancery Road, Chorley, PR7 1DH.
Gareth Elliot. *2m from Chorley town
centre From B5252 pass Chorley
Hospital on L at r'about 1st exit to
Chancery Lane Hospice on L after 0.4
m where parking around the building
available & on the road. Sat Nav*

directions not always accurate Sun
10 May, Sun 9 Aug (11-5). Adm £3,
chd free. Light refreshments.
The gardens play a large part in
creating an atmosphere of relaxation,
tranquillity and joy. Distinct areas
include the Smile Park, the Memorial,
and Seaside Gardens. The gardens
are an on going project, with two
new areas being created this winter
– an "enchanted" fairy garden and
"Jurassic" dinosaur garden - both
designed by the children in a shady
corner offering a magical place to play
♿ ❀ ☕ ♿

GROUP OPENING

22 DIDSBURY VILLAGE GARDENS
Tickets: Any Village Garden, or
68 Brooklawn Drive M20 3GZ
or Moor Cottage, Grange Lane,
Didsbury, Manchester, M20 6RW.
*5m S of Manchester. From M60 J5
follow signs to Northenden. Turn
R at T-lights onto Barlow Moor
Rd to Didsbury. From M56 follow
A34 to Didsbury.* Sun 14 June
(12-5). Combined adm £6, chd
free. Home-made teas at Moor
Cottage & 68 Brooklawn Drive.

68 BROOKLAWN DRIVE
M20 3GZ. Anne & Jim Britt,
www.thefruitygardener.com.
3 THE DRIVE
M20 6HZ.
Peter Clare & Sarah Keedy,
www.theshadegarden.com.
MOOR COTTAGE, M20 6RW
M20 6RW. William Godfrey,
0161 448 8372,
info@manlangschool.co.uk.
Visits also by arrangement Apr
to Oct for groups of 10+.
NEW 1 OSBORNE STREET
M20 2QZ. Richard & Teresa
Pearce-Regan.
2 PARKFIELD ROAD SOUTH
M20 6DA. Conrad & Kate
Jacobson, Mary Butterworth.
38 WILLOUGHBY AVENUE
M20 6AS. Simon Hickey.

Didsbury is an attractive South
Manchester suburb which retains
its village atmosphere. There
are interesting shops, cafes and
restaurants, well worth a visit in
themselves! This year we have 6
gardens demonstrating a variety of
beautiful spaces- new for this year is
a stylish contemporary garden with
porcelain paving, two water features

and fabulous planting. We also have a
large walled family garden surrounding
a Georgian cottage, divided into
several enchanting areas with towering
Echiums and free range chickens.
Another is an expertly planted shade
garden with many choice rarities,
whilst another reflects the charm
of the cottage garden ethos with
rose covered pergola, old fashioned
perennials and tranquil raised pool.
Our smaller gardens show beautifully
how suburban plots, with limited
space, can be packed full of interesting
features and a range of planting styles.
Dogs allowed at some gardens.
Wheelchair access to some gardens.
♿ 🐕 ❀ ☕

23 DUTTON HALL
Gallows Lane, Ribchester,
PR3 3XX. Mr & Mrs A H Penny,
www.duttonhall.co.uk. *2m NE of
Ribchester. Signed from B6243 &
B6245 also directions on website.*
Sun 28 June (1-5). Adm £5, chd
free. Home-made teas. Donation
to Plant Heritage.
An increasing range of interesting
trees and shrubs have been added to
the existing collection of old fashioned
roses, including rare and unusual
varieties and Plant Heritage National
Collection of Pemberton Hybrid
Musk roses. Formal garden at front
with backdrop of C17 house (not
open). A range of other features and
extensive views over the Ribble Valley.
Analemmatic Sundial, pond, meadow
areas all with extensive views over
Ribble Valley. Teas provided by St
John's Church. Plant Heritage Plant
Stall with unusual varieties for sale.
Disabled access difficult due to
different levels and steps.
❀ NPC ☕

Your visits help
change lives – we
are the largest
single funder
of the Queen's
Nursing Institute

24 35 ELLESMERE ROAD

Eccles, Salford, Manchester, M30 9FE. Enid Noronha. *3m W of Salford, 4m W of Manchester. From M60 exit at M602 for Salford. Take A576 for Trafford Park & Eccles, stay on A576. Turn L onto Half Edge Lane, keep L to Monton on Half Edge Lane. Turn R onto Stafford Rd & L onto Ellesmere Rd.* **Sat 13 June (12-5). Combined adm with 11 Westminster Road £5, chd free. Home-made teas.**

Amidst the busy urban environment of Eccles in Salford, lies a hidden pocket of grand houses with wide roads, and these two havens of tranquillity. 35 Ellesmere Rd is a peaceful country garden with deep herbaceous borders filled with shrubs, scented roses, and perennials. A climber covered pergola leads to a productive vegetable garden where raised beds and fruit trees add to the feeling of abundance.

25 GILES FARM

Four Acre Lane, Thornley, Preston, PR3 2TD. Kirsten & Phil Brown, 07925 603246, phil.brown32@aol.co.uk. *3m NE of Longridge. From J31A or J32 of M6 follow signs for Longridge. Pass through Longridge & follow signs for Chipping. Pass the Derby Arms on the L & then turn R at the old school for 1m. Parking at the farm.* **Sat 13, Sun 14 June (12-5). Adm £4, chd free. Light refreshments. A selection of sandwiches & home baked cakes. Visits also by arrangement May to July. Adm incls refreshments.**

Nestled high on the side of Longridge fell, with beautiful long-reaching views across the Ribble Valley, the gardens surround the old farmhouse and buildings. The gardens are ever evolving and include an acre of perennial wildflower meadows, wildlife pond, woodland areas and cottage gardens. There are plentiful areas to sit and take in the views. There are steps and uneven surfaces in the gardens. Disabled access difficult due to different levels, surface areas and steps.

26 NEW GORSE HILL NATURE RESERVE

Holly Lane, Aughton, Ormskirk, L39 7HB. Jonathan Atkins (Reserve Manager), www.nwecotrust.org.uk. *1½ m S of Ormskirk. A59 from L'pool past Royal Oak pub take 1st L Gaw Hill Lane turn R Holly Lane. From Preston follow A59 across T-lights at A570 J & at r'about. After Xing lights turn R Gaw Hill Lane turn R Holly Lane.* **Sun 12 July (11-4). Combined adm with 72 Ludlow Drive £5, chd free. Home-made teas.**

Situated on a sandstone ridge offering spectacular views across the Lancashire Plain, our wildflower meadow in summer is brimming with a wide variety of wildflowers and grasses. The meadow wildlife pond is patrolled by dragonflies and damselflies and the air is full of butterflies and bees. Mown grassy paths take you through the meadow to enable close views of the flowers and insects. The woodland walk leading to the wild flower meadow has wheelchair accessible paths although access is limited in the meadow to mown grass paths.

27 NEW GRANGE COMMUNITY GARDEN

opposite 79 Fir Trees Avenue, Ribbleton, Preston, PR2 6PQ. Annie Wynn, www.letsgrowpreston.org. *4m NE of Preston. From J30 of M6 head towards Preston. Turn R at r'about, take R at 2nd T-lights onto Ribbleton Lane B6243. After 2m turn R onto Grange Lane. R at Xrds. Turn R opposite 79.* **Sat 5 Sept (12-4). Adm £4, chd free. Light refreshments. Pizzas.**

An oasis of a community garden with large polytunnels, vegetable and herbacious beds as well as an orchard, outdoor kitchen, pond and various willow structures. Willow chair, willow tepees and igloos. Pizza oven will be firing and you will have the chance to make your own pizza for a small donation Mud kitchen for children. There are disabled WCs on site and a main path and paved area to access visibility to all areas.

Warton Gardens

28 GREEN FARM COTTAGE

42 Lower Green, Poulton-le-Fylde, FY6 7EJ. Eric & Sharon Rawcliffe. *500yds from Poulton-le-Fylde Village. M55 J3 follow A585 Fleetwood. T- lights turn L. Next lights bear L A586. Poulton 2nd set of lights turn R Lower Green. Cottage on L.* Sun 14 June (10-5). Adm £4, chd free. Home-made teas.

½ acre well established formal cottage gardens. Feature koi pond, paths leading to different areas. Lots of climbers and rose beds. Packed with plants of all kinds. Many shrubs and trees. Well laid out lawns. Collections of unusual plants. A surprise round every corner. Said by visitors to be 'a real hidden jewel'.

30 45 GREY HEIGHTS VIEW

Off Eaves Lane, Chorley, PR6 0TN. Barbara Ashworth, 07941339702. *1m from Chorley Hospital. From Wigan/Coppull B5251. At (town centre) Xrds straight across . At r'about across to Lyons Ln and follow NGS signs. From M61, J8 follow signs A6 Town Centre to Lyons Ln signed from here.* Sun 7 June, Sun 12 July, Sun 2 Aug (10-5). Adm £3, chd free. Cream teas. Visits also by arrangement for groups of 10 to 30.

A small suburban garden with cottage garden style planting including fruit trees. Heavily planted with a profusion of perennials, roses and clematis. No repeat planting. Including a greenhouse, small vegetable and fruit area. An abundance of recycling and space saving ideas. Back drop of Healey Nab, and a stones throw from the Leeds - Liverpool Canal. Craft items for sale.

31 THE GROWTH PROJECT

Kellett Street Allotments, Rochdale, OL16 2JU. Karen Hayday, 01706 810245, k.hayday@hourglass.org.uk, www.rochdalemind.org.uk/growth-project. *From A627M. R A58 L Entwistle Rd R Kellett St.* Sat 8 Aug (11.30-3.30). Adm £3.50, chd free. Home-made teas. Home-made lunches. Visits also by arrangement June to Sept. Best day to visit Weds or Thurs, though others are possible. Donation to The Growth Project.

The project is set on over an acre and incl a huge variety of organic veg,

wildlife pond, insect hotels, formal flower and wild flower borders, potager and enchanted woodland garden. See the mock Elizabethan straw bale build and station, stroll down the pergola walk to the wild flower meadow and orchard. Afternoon tea served in the Victorian style ornate 'Woodland Green' woodworking station. Jams and cakes to buy. The new attraction this year is the wild flower meadow and orchard The Growth Project is a partnership between Hourglass and Rochdale and District mind. Providing cut flowers, veg, preserves and gifts plus guides to give horticultural advice and show you round. No disabled WC, ground can be uneven.

GROUP OPENING

32 HALE VILLAGE GARDENS

Liverpool, L24 4BA. *6m S of M62 J6. Take A5300, A562 towards L'pool, then A561, L for Hale opp the old RSPCA. From S L'pool head for the airport then L sign for Hale. The 500 bus from Widnes/Runcorn to Liverpool stops in the village.* Sat 6, Sun 7 June (1-5). Combined adm £5, chd free. Home-made teas at 66 Church Rd.

NEW 4 CHURCH ROAD
Mr & Mrs Chesters.

54 CHURCH ROAD
Norma & Ray Roe.

66 CHURCH ROAD
Liz Kelly-Hines & David Hines.

The delightful village of Hale, is set in rural S Merseyside between Widnes and Liverpool Airport. It is home to the cottage, sculpture and grave of the famous giant known as the Childe of Hale. Gardens of various sizes have been developed by their present owners and this year are all in Church Road which leads to the old lighthouse at Hale Point. They have either woodland backdrop or wonderful views over the river Mersey and the distant Welsh Hills. A wildlife pond and mixed planting for year round structure, colour and fragrance, along with a substantial allotment, all feature. Plants at 66 Church Rd.

33 NEW HALTON PARK HOUSE

Halton Park, Halton, Lancaster, LA2 6PD. Mr & Mrs Duncan Bowring. *7min drive from both J34 & 35 M6. On Park Lane, approx. 1½m from Halton or Caton. Park Lane accessed either from Low Rd or High Rd out of Halton. From Low Rd turn into Park Lane through pillars over cattle grid.* Sat 16, Sun 17 May (10-4). Adm £4, chd free. Home-made teas.

Approx 6 acres of garden, with gravel paths leading through large mixed herbaceous borders, terraces, orchard, terraced vegetable beds. Wildlife pond and woodland walk in dell area, extensive lawns, greenhouse. Cream teas and home made cakes. Gravel paths (some sloping) access viewing points over the majority of the garden. Hard standing around the house.

34 ♦ HAZELWOOD

North Road, Bretherton, Leyland, PR26 9AY. Jacqueline Iddon & Thompson Dagnall, 01772 601433, jacquelineiddon@gmail.com, www.jacquelineiddon.co.uk. *8m SW of Preston. Between Southport & Preston, from A59, take B5247 for 1m then L onto (B5248) Garden signed from North Rd.* For NGS: Sun 17 May, Sun 14 June, Sun 12 July (1-5). Adm £3.50, chd free. Home-made teas. Vegan and gluten free options. For other opening times and information, please phone, email or visit garden website.

New for 2020 cutting and vegetable garden. 1½ acre garden and hardy plant nursery, gravel garden with pots and seating area bottle wall and folly, shrubs, herbaceous borders, stream-fed pond with woodland walk, Victorian fern house. Oak-framed, summerhouse, log cabin Sculpture gallery fronted by cottage garden beds. Sculpture demonstration at 2 pm, Beach area. Teas in Coach house in aid of Queenscourt Hospice. Extensive sculpture collection, the work of Thompson Dagnall. Majority of the garden is accessible to wheelchairs.

GROUP OPENING

35 HILLSIDE GARDENS
Clovelly Drive, Southport,
PR8 3AJ. *3m S of Southport.
Gardens signed from A565 Waterloo
Rd & A5267 Liverpool Rd.* **Sun 17
May (11-5). Combined adm £3.50,
chd free. Light refreshments at
23 Ashton Road, 339 Liverpool
Rd & 18 Clovelly Drive Wine. Sun
19 July (11-5). Combined adm £5,
chd free. Home-made teas at 23
Ashton Road, 339 Liverpool Rd &
18 Clovelly Drive Wine.**

23 ASHTON ROAD
PR8 4QE.
John & Jennifer Mawdsley.
Open on all dates

33 CLOVELLY DRIVE
PR8 3AJ.
Bob & Eunice Drummond.
Open on all dates

LINKS VIEW, 18 CLOVELLY DRIVE
PR8 3AJ.
Christine & Dave McGarry.
Open on Sun 19 July

339 LIVERPOOL ROAD
PR8 3DE. Ian & Sue Dexter.
Open on Sun 19 July

The gardens of Hillside are full of
variety and interest, each having
ponds or water features which create a
relaxed atmosphere. 23 Ashton Road
is separated into three rooms with
interesting shrubs, herbaceous plants
and a vegetable plot. 18 Clovelly Drive
is a developing garden with a patio.
Glass features around the perimeter
fencing add a different dimension,
with chain saw carvings interspersed
amongst plants. Whimsical features.
At 33 Clovelly Drive mature trees and
shrubs set off the circular lawn with
sweeping colour-themed herbaceous
borders. Rhododendrons and azaleas
give colour in spring. Liverpool Road
was a neglected landscape garden
full of beautiful and unusual trees and
shrubs. It is now being brought back
to life and developed with herbaceous
planting and grasses. Excellent spring
colour. WC facilities available. Partial
wheelchair access to 3 gardens, fully
accessible to 1.

& ⚑ ✿ ☕ ☕

GROUP OPENING

36 HUTTON GARDENS
Tolsey Drive, Hutton, Preston,
PR4 5SH. Heather & John Lund.
*2m SW of Preston. Take A59
towards Southport, at the r'about
head towards Longton on Liverpool
Rd. Tolsey Dr is 100 yds on the L.
Signed from A59 r'about.* **Sun 5
July (11.30-4.30). Combined adm
£4, chd free. Home-made teas
at 10 Tolsey Drive. At 2 Tolsey
Drive home-made sausage rolls,
cheese and onion rolls and
home-made rhubarb gin.**

2 TOLSEY DRIVE
Vicki & Alex Cullen.

5 TOLSEY DRIVE
Marilyn & James Woods.

10 TOLSEY DRIVE
Heather & John Lund.

Hutton is a small village on the
outskirts of Preston. There are 3 long,
fairly narrow gardens which vary in
style. 2 Tolsey Drive has an open
aspect with sweeping lawns tapering
to a point, mature trees, shrubs and
developing flower beds. 5 Tolsey
Drive is an informal garden with mixed
planting of vegetables and herbs within
abundant flower beds. A wild life pond,
with hedgerow and trees, peaceful
places to sit and contemplate. James
and Marilyn helped to design and
build a garden for the NGS display at
Southport Flower Show 2019 which
won a Large Gold Medal. 10 Tolsey
Drive is an eclectic garden divided
into three rooms. There is a formal
lawn with large herbaceous borders
with some unusual plants, a working
section with various greenhouses
growing vegetables and exotic plants
and a quiet, shady secret garden.
As featured in Lancashire Life as the
Recycled Garden with Wonky Wall,
water feature and planters made from
recycled materials from the house
renovations. Wheelchair access to
patio area only in all gardens.

✿ ☕ ☕

37 KINGTON COTTAGE
Kirkham Road, Treales, Preston,
PR4 3SD. Mrs Linda Kidd,
01772 683005. *M55 J3. Take A585
to Kirkham, exit Preston St, L into
Carr Lane to Treales Village. Cottage
on L in front of Derby Arms parking
here by kind permission of owner.*

**Sun 7 June, Sat 4, Sun 5 July,
Sun 2 Aug (10-5). Adm £3.50, chd
free. Home-made teas. Visits also
by arrangement June to Aug for
groups of 10+.**
Nestling in the beautiful village
of Treales this generously sized
Japanese garden has many authentic
and unique Japanese features, along
side its 2 ponds linked by a river. The
stroll garden leads down to the tea
house garden. The planting and the
meandering pathway blend together
to create a tranquil meditative garden
in which to relax. Runner up in Daily
Mail Best Kept Garden Competition.
Wheelchair access to some areas,
uneven paths.

& ⚑ ✿ ☕ ☕

38 LOWER DUTTON FARM
Gallows Lane, Ribchester,
PR3 3XX. Mr R
Robinson, 01254 878405,
rrobinson2019@outlook.com.
*1½ m NE of Ribchester. Leave M6
J31. Take A59 towards Clitheroe,
turn L at T-lights towards Ribchester.
Signed from B6243 & B6245. Ample
car parking in adjacent field.* **Sat
1, Sun 2 Aug (1-5). Adm £4, chd
free. Light refreshments. Visits
also by arrangement June to Aug
for groups of 10 to 30.**
Traditional long Lancashire farmhouse
and barn, with 2 acre gardens.
Formal gardens nr house with mixed
herbaceous beds and shrubs.
Sweeping lawns lead down past
island beds to wildlife area and
established large pond with small
woodland. Small orchard at rear of
house with mix of fruit-trees and
shrubs. Several seating areas. Lawns
may be difficult in very wet weather.

& ⚑ ✿ ☕ ☕

39 72 LUDLOW DRIVE
Ormskirk, L39 1LF. Marian &
Brian Jones, 01695 574628,
72ludlow@gmail.com. *½ m W
of Ormskirk on A570. From M58
J3 follow A570 to Ormskirk town
centre. Continue on A570 towards
Southport. At A570 junction with
A59 cross T-lights after ½ m turn R
at Spar garage onto Heskin Lane
then R Ludlow Drive.* **Sun 12 July
(11-4). Combined adm with Gorse
Hill Nature Reserve £5, chd free.
Home-made teas. Gluten free and
vegan cake also provided. Visits
also by arrangement June & July
for groups of 10 to 30.**
A beautiful town garden overflowing
with a wide variety of bee friendly

planting. Developed over the last 14 years it includes a gravel garden, herbaceous and shrub borders including a newly developed Jewel garden. The back garden has raised shade and rose borders with roses and many clematis, also an attractive raised pond, alpine troughs, succulents and greenhouse. Wheelchair access to front garden but only partial access to rear garden.

🕭 ❀ ☕

40 LYTHAM HALL
Ballam Rd, Lytham, Lytham St. Annes, FY8 4JX. Paul Lomax. *Follow the brown tourist signs for Lytham Hall Sat Nav users use postcode FY8 4TQ.* **Sun 26 July (10-4.30). Adm £4, chd free. Light refreshments. There are picnic tables on the East Lawn.**
Lytham Hall is a C18 Georgian house set in 78 acres of historic woodlands, with a parterre, herbaceous border, south prospect garden, a lake and two wildlife ponds. A mount, that can be climbed with views over the parkland and 4km of paths. There is a RHS Gold award winning vegetable garden and potager. 1m drive from the main gates to the Hall. There is a separate designated path for pedestrians past fields and through woodland. An outside catering vehicle will be available for hot drinks and snacks in addition to the cafe. Wheelchair access available to most areas. Gravel paths in woodland. Coaches by appointment only.

🕭 🐎 ❀ 🚐 ☕

41 MAGGIE'S MANCHESTER
Kinnaird Road, Manchester, M20 4QL. Jemma Halman. *At the end of Kinnaird Rd which is off Wilmslow Rd opposite the Christie Hospital.* **Sun 26 July (12-4). Adm £3, chd free. Light refreshments.**
The architecture of Maggie's Manchester, designed by world-renowned architect Lord Foster, is complemented by gardens designed by Dan Pearson, Best in Show winner at Chelsea Flower Show. Combining a rich mix of spaces, including the working glass house and vegetable garden, the garden provides a place for both activity and contemplation. The colours and sensory experience of nature becomes part of the Centre through micro gardens and internal courtyards, which relate to the different spaces within the building. Wheelchair access to most of the garden from the front entrance.

🕭 🐎 ☕

42 MAGGIE'S, OLDHAM
The Royal Oldham Hospital, Rochdale Road, Oldham, OL1 2JH. Maggie's Centres, 0161 989 0550, oldham@maggiescentres.org, www.maggiescentres.org/oldham. *Maggie's in the grounds of the Royal Oldham Hospital, next door to A&E. It's the wooden building on stilts & the garden lies underneath the building.* **Sun 19 July (11-3). Adm £5, chd free. Home-made teas. Visits also by arrangement Mar to Oct.**
The garden is framed by enclosing walls. The building 'floating' aloft is like a drop curtain to the scene, creating a picture window effect. The trees soar upwards filling the volume of space. A woodland understorey weaves between the structure of the numerous white birch and crispy bark of the pine trunks. The garden could be described as an ornamental woodland. Please introduce yourself to a member of the team on arrival who will guide you to the wheelchair entrance to the garden.

🕭 🐎 🚐 ☕

43 MATSHEAD LODGE
Brock Side, Bilsborrow, Preston, PR3 0GL. Sheila & Nick Baines. *2m N of Bilsborrow. Parking at Barton Grange Garden Centre on A6 (permission granted), cross A6 to. car sales yard follow public footpath over railway bridge along river & foot*

bridge to NGS signage. Parking in lay-bys on Lydiate Lane & Claughton, 5 mins walk away. **Sat 16 May (10-4.30). Adm £3.50, chd free. Light refreshments.**
Set in approx 2 acres, a garden of mixed herbaceous borders, with shrubs, orchard and loose stone paths.Hidden away on the banks of river Brock featuring Japanese area, walled vegetable garden and pond, The walk from Barton Grange to the garden takes approx 10mins after crossing A6. Disabled parking for 6 cars at garden address only.

☕

44 6 MENIVALE CLOSE
Southport, PR9 9RY. Ann-Marie Hutson. *4m N of Southport. A565 from Preston. 2nd exit at Plough r'bout. At BP garage turn R. Then 3rd R. At T junction turn R, then 1st L. A565 from Southport at BP garage turn L. Then 3rd R. At T junction turn R. then 1st L.* **Sun 7 June (10-5). Combined adm with 120 Roe Lane £3.50, chd free. Light refreshments.**
The house having been built in the 1970's, the garden follows a cottage garden style with brick edged island beds, each bed having a seasonal focus. Surrounded by neighbouring trees, the garden is sheltered from the NW winds. Partial access for wheelchairs.

❀ ☕

Maggies Manchester

54 ◆ THE RIDGES
Weavers Brow (cont. of Cowling Rd), Limbrick, Chorley, PR6 9EB. Mr & Mrs J M Barlow, 01257 279981, barbara@barlowridges.co.uk, www.bedbreakfast-gardenvisits.com. *2m SE of Chorley town centre. From M6 J27. From M61 J8. Follow signs for Chorley A6 then signs for Cowling & Rivington. Passing Morrison's up Brook St, mini r'about 2nd exit, Cowling Brow. Pass Spinners Arms on L. Garden on R.* For NGS: Sun 10 May, Mon 31 Aug (11-5). Adm £5, chd free. Home-made teas. by ladies of St James Church. **For other opening times and information, please phone, email or visit garden website.**
3 acres, incl old walled orchard garden, cottage-style herbaceous borders, with perfumed rambling roses and clematis thru fruit trees. Arch leads to formal lawn, surrounded by natural woodland, shrub borders and specimen trees with contrasting foliage. Woodland walks and dell. Natural looking stream, wildlife ponds. Walled water feature with Italian influence, and walled herb garden. Classical music played. Wheelchair access some gravel paths and woodland walks not accessible.

55 NEW 4 ROE GREEN
Worsley, Manchester, M28 2JB. Geoff & Pauline Ogden. *5m W of Manchester. Roe Green is adjacent to J14 of the M60 motorway. Please park on Old Clough Lane.* Sat 4 July (12-5). Adm £5, chd free. Home-made teas.
A 300 year old cottage located on the edge of the village green in the picturesque conservation area of Roe Green. This is a plantswoman's quintessential Cottage Garden, packed with many unusual perennials and mixed wild flowers that thrive in this sheltered walled space. In addition to a woodland area, there is an old bothy which adds to the delightful atmosphere of this garden.

56 120 ROE LANE
Southport, PR9 7PJ. Mrs Mavis Standing. *2m N Southport. A565 N on Lord St at r'about 3rd exit to Manchester Rd continue to Roe Lane.* Sun 7 June (10-5). Combined adm with 6 Menivale Close £3.50, chd free. Home-made teas.
Mature garden encouraged to develop over 25 years and includes trees, shrubs, succulents and perennials. Diverse corners and wildlife.

57 NEW ST THOMAS PRIMARY SCHOOL
Kenyons Lane, Lydiate, Liverpool, L31 0BP. Mr Mark Ward. *8m N of Liverpool. From end of M57/58 take A59 towards Ormskirk From end of M57/58 take A59 to Ormskirk after 2.3m turn L into Lydiate Lane.* Sun 7 June (12-5). Combined adm with 136 Buckingham Road £3.50, chd free. Home-made teas.
A collection of gardens planted and cared for by the children and school gardener, which features our 'Bookshelf Beach', blissful prayer garden, bog garden and tranquil wildlife garden with colourful bee friendly planting. The gardens provide a place for both activity and contemplation and year-round colour and interest. There are picnic tables and an adventure playground at the rear.

58 ◆ THE SECRET GARDEN
Walkden, Worsley, M28 3LU. Sally Berry, www.thesecretvalley.com. *7m from Manchester. 3m from J13 M60, Walkden train stn 1m. No Parking on The Reach or Hopefold Drive, disabled visitor drop off only. Please park on Manchester Rd and only 2min walk to the garden.* Sun 14 June (10.30-4). Adm £5, chd free. Tea.
As featured on gardeners world. Large 2 acre water garden created from derelict site over last 10 years. With ponds, streams, islands and lake. A variety of trees, plants and climbers. It is a haven for waterfowl and local wildlife. 2 acre natural garden with lake, ponds, streams, fountain, statues, wild swans and ducks, lots of seating and areas to relax. Sorry but paths are mainly woodchip surface and difficult to access with a wheelchair particularly when wet.

GROUP OPENING

59 SEFTON PARK MAY GARDENS
Sefton Drive, Sefton Park, Liverpool, L8 3SD. 0151 281 3687. *1m S of Liverpool city centre. From end of M62 take A5058 Queens Drive ring rd S through Allerton to Sefton Park. Parking roadside in Sefton Drive.* Sun 10 May (12-5). Combined adm £5, chd free. Home-made teas at 17 Sydenham Ave, the Community Orchard and Wildlife Garden in Arundel Avenue and at the Winter Garden in Cairns St.

THE COMMUNITY ORCHARD AND WILDLIFE GARDEN
L17 2AT. The Society of Friends, www.tann.org.uk.

SEFTON VILLA
L8 3SD. Patricia Williams, 0151 281 3687, seftonvilla@live.co.uk.

17 SYDENHAM AVENUE
L17 3AU. Fatima Aabbar-Marshall.

NEW 18 SYDENHAM AVENUE
L17 3AX. Michael Davies.

THAT BLOOMIN' GREEN TRIANGLE, DUCIE ST
L8 2XA. Mrs Helen Hebden.

This is a fascinatingly varied group of Liverpool gardens. In That Bloomin' Green Triangle, the most recent project has been the creation of a delightful indoor Winter Garden in what were two derelict houses. It was the guerrilla gardening by residents which led to the area's regeneration. And now the entire length of one back alley has become a garden. The Community Orchard in Arundel Avenue is a quiet haven with glorious planting in at the former Quaker Burial Ground. An new garden in Sydenham Avenue joins this year, demonstrating how an extremely shady back garden can be beautified. And two exquisitely planted gardens in Sydenham Avenue and Sefton Drive complete this varied group. Tours of the Bloomin' Green Triangle at 1 and 3 pm starting from the Winter Garden in Cairns Street.

GROUP OPENING

60 SEFTON PARK SEPTEMBER GARDENS

Sefton Drive, Sefton Park, Liverpool, L8 3SD. *From end of M62, take A5058 Queens Drive ring road S through Allerton to Sefton Park & follow the yellow signs. Parking roadside in Sefton Park.* **Sun 13 Sept (12-5). Combined adm £5, chd free. Home-made teas at all venues.**

FERN GROVE COMMUNITY GARDEN
L8 0RX. Liverpool City Council.

PARKMOUNT
L17 3BP. Jeremy Nicholls.

37 PRINCE ALFRED ROAD
L15 8HH. Jane Hammett.

SEFTON PARK ALLOTMENTS
L17 1AS. Sefton Park Allotments Society.

Two beautiful gardens planted for late summer colour and interest, nearly 100 allotments full of abundant produce and flowers. and children's activities and beekeeping demonstration at Fern Grove Community. The secret garden at 37 Prince Alfred Road is so hidden away, you'd never guess it was there. And inside the sandstone walled space is glorious planting, a lovely greenhouse, summerhouse and bothy. The long borders at Park Mount reach their peak in late summer, with a flaming hot colour scheme, and hidden woodland paths. At the allotments, vegetable production will be at its peak, and many of the gardeners have lovely dahlia displays. No wheelchair access at 37 Prince Alfred Road. Disabled WC at Sefton Park allotments.

&♿ ❀ 🚐 ☕

61 SOUTHLANDS

12 Sandy Lane, Stretford, M32 9DA. Maureen Sawyer & Duncan Watmough, www.southlands12.com. *3m S of Manchester. Sandy Lane (B5213) is situated off A5181 (A56) ¼m from M60 J7.* **Sun 19 July (12-5.30). Adm £4, chd free. Home-made teas. Cake-away service (take a slice of your favourite cake home) Home-made Ice-cream.** Described by visitors as 'totally inspirational', this artists' multi-award winning garden unfolds into a series of beautiful spaces including Mediterranean, Ornamental and

Woodland gardens. Organic kitchen garden with large glasshouse containing vines. Recently redesigned herbaceous borders, hanging baskets and stunning container plantings throughout the garden, 2 ponds and a water feature. 20th year opening celebrations. Artist's work on display.

❀ 🚐 ☕

62 STANHILL EXOTIC GARDEN

19 Stanhill Street, Oswaldtwistle, Accrington, BB5 4QE. Tez Donnelly, www.facebook.com/stanhillgarden. *From M65 J5 take A6077 towards Shadsworth, first R to B623. 2.3m, L at Black Dog Pub, 0.2m R into Thwaites Rd for parking. Then cross Rd to Stanhill St on foot. Garden at rear.* **Sat 22, Sun 23 Aug (1-4). Adm £4, chd free. Light refreshments.** Behind a row of terraced houses lies a hidden gem. A lush exotic style garden containing palms, tree ferns, bananas, and many other unusual plants. A mixture of paving and bark chipping paths takes you on a journey round the tropical garden, encountering a pond and an aviary along the way.

🐕 ❀ ☕

63 WADDOW LODGE GARDEN

Clitheroe Road, Waddington, Clitheroe, BB7 3HQ. Liz & Peter Foley, www.gardentalks.co.uk. *1½m N of Clitheroe. From M6 J31 take A59 (Preston-Skipton). A671 to Clitheroe then B6478. 1st house on L in village. Parking available on rd before entering village; blue badges in drive parking area on gravel.* **Sun 31 May, Sun 12 July (1-5). Adm £4, chd free. Home-made teas.** Inspirational 2-acre organic garden for all seasons surrounding Georgian house (not open) with views to Pendle and Bowland. An enthusiast's collection of many unusual plants with herbaceous borders, large island beds, shrubs, heathers, rhododendrons, small mature wooded area, old fashioned and hybrid roses. Extensive kitchen garden of vegetables and soft fruit, interesting heritage apple orchard, herbs, alpines and greenhouse, wildlife meadow and bog garden. Colourful containers. Circa 500 year old Yew Tree. Some gravel/bark paths, otherwise level surfaces.

&♿ ❀ ☕

Green Farm Cottage

GROUP OPENING

64 WARTON GARDENS

Warton, LA5 9PJ. *1½m N of Carnforth. From M6 J35 take A601M NW for 1m, then N on A6 for 0.7m turn L signed Warton Old Rectory. Warton Village 1m down Borwick Lane. From Carnforth pass train stn & follow signs Warton & Silverdale.* **Sat 4, Sun 5 July (11-4.30). Combined adm £5, chd free. Home-made teas at 109/111 Main Street.**

BRIAR COTTAGE

LA5 9PT. Mr Bendall.

2 CHURCH HILL AVENUE

LA5 9NU. Mr & Mrs J Street.

NEW 107 MAIN STREET

Becky Hindley.

111 MAIN STREET

LA5 9PJ. Mr & Mrs J Spendlove, 01524 727 770, claire@lavenderandlime.co.uk.

NEW WARTON ALLOTMENT HOLDERS

LA5 9QU. Mrs Jill Slaughter.

The gardens and allotments are spread across the village and offer a wide variety of planting and design ideas. Our group offers a contemporary garden on limestone pavement, flower picking garden, unusual herbaceous and vegetable garden, 21 allotments and a large more formal garden. Parking at the bottom of village (LA5 9NU) or the public car park, next to Old School Brewery (LA5 9PL). Warton has 2 Pubs . It is the birthplace of the medieval ancestors of George Washington, of which the family coat of arms can be seen in St Oswald's Church. The ruins of the Old Rectory (English Heritage) is the oldest surviving building in the village. Ascent of Warton Crag (AONB), provides panoramic views across Morecambe Bay to the Lakeland hills beyond. All gardens have steps and uneven surfaces unsuitable for wheelchair access.

65 NEW 8 WATER HEAD

Fulwood, Preston, PR2 3TU. Phil Parkinson, philinterfaith@gmail.com. *3m N of Preston. 2m from M6 J32 follow A6 Preston r at Black Bull Lane at 2nd r'about 2nd exit to B5411 to signage from here. Parking in Hollins Grove.* **Sat 13 June (11-5); Sun 14 June (1-4.30). Adm £3.50. Home-made teas. Refreshments: Sat 12 - 4, Sun 2 - 4. Visits also by arrangement May to Sept.**

A medium sized, rigorously structured, suburban garden in 5 rooms with a canal bank for extras. Over 70 roses, entirely crimson and white in the first room, a large fernery, a Germanica iris collection, some rare ferns and trees, Langdale slate paving, and an imaginative use of levels and height, the whole being suffused with a contemplative, centred energy.

Croxteth Walled Park Gardens

66 WEEPING ASH GARDEN

Bents Garden & Home, Warrington Road, Glazebury, WA3 5NS. John Bent, www.bents.co.uk. *15m W of Manchester. Located next to Bents Garden & Home, just off the A580 East Lancs Rd at Greyhound r'about near Leigh. Follow brown 'Garden Centre' signs.* **Sun 16, Sun 23 Feb, Sun 9 Aug, Sun 13 Sept, Sun 25 Oct (10.30-4). Adm £5, chd free. Light refreshments at Bents Garden & Home.**

Created by retired nurseryman and photographer John Bent, Weeping Ash is a garden of all-year interest with a beautiful display of early snowdrops. Broad sweeps of colour lend elegance to this stunning garden which is much larger than it initially seems with hidden paths and wooded areas creating a sense of natural growth. Bents offers a choice of six dining destinations from including The Fresh Approach Restaurant, Caffe nel Verde and its Mediterranean style Tapas Bar. Partial wheelchair access and weather dependent.

67 6 WEST LANE

Formby, Liverpool, L37 7BA. Laurie & Sue Lissett. *7m S of Southport. From Formby By-pass turn into Southport Rd (Esso at junction). Proceed to mini r'about and turn R into Green Ln (Grapes pub on corner). Follow road to West Lane which is 2nd on R.* **Sun 5 July (10-4). Combined adm with 33 Brewery Lane £3.50, chd free. Home-made teas.**

Suburban garden on sandy soil near to NT Nature Reserve home to red squirrels and Formby Sand Dunes. Garden with pergola and arches with mixed planting to rockeries and borders. Features sunny and shaded areas and colourful rose and hydrangea displays. Small water feature and greenhouse. Large selection of baskets and containers with decking and patio areas.

68 11 WESTMINSTER ROAD

Eccles, Manchester, M30 9HF. George & Lynne Meakin. *3m W of Salford, 4m W of Manchester. 1st exit M602 Manchester direction 1st exit (r'about) 2nd T-lights turn L. After Xing turn R, Victoria Rd 2nd R (Westminster Rd) no.11 on L.* **Sat 13 June (12-5). Combined adm with 35 Ellesmere Road £5, chd**

free. Wine. Home-made teas at Ellesmere Rd. Wine & nibbles at 11 Westminster Rd.

There is pretty front garden with topiary chickens and well stocked with perennials, mature trees, and box hedging. The garden is divided by a trellis and rose arch which separates the flower beds and lawn from the fruit growing area, and there are a large number of fuchsias grown in pots. A coach house to the rear of the garden where wine/nibbles will be served. The garden is on the flat except for a small area in the front garden, care will need to be taken in case the path is slippy.

69 WIGAN & LEIGH HOSPICE

Kildare Street, Hindley, Wigan, WN2 3HZ. Wigan & Leigh Hospice, thehospicegardener.com. *1½m SW of Wigan. From Wigan on A577 Leigh/Manchester Rd. In Hindley turn R at St Peter's Church onto Liverpool Rd A58. After 250 metres turn R into Kildare St.* **Sun 19 July (11-4). Adm £3.50, chd free. Light refreshments.**

Large attractive gardens surround the Hospice creating a place of tranquillity. At the front are beautiful raised beds and a new courtyard garden, at the rear 3 large ponds. Outside patients' rooms are colourful tubs and flower beds. A memorial daisy garden. A wildflower garden has been created - 'The Amberswood Garden'. The gardens are a haven for wildlife. Garden awarded 'Gold' in NW in Bloom. Fully accessible, including WC.

70 NEW WILLOW WOOD HOSPICE GARDENS

Willow Wood Close, Mellor Road, Ashton-Under-Lyne, OL6 6SL. Willow Wood Hospice, www.willowwood.info/www. teaselgardens.co.uk. *3mins from J23 M60. Exit onto A6140 towards Ashton-u-Lyne turn R onto Manchester Rd/A635 then slight R onto Park Parade/A635 keep R, stay on A635 turn L onto Mellor Rd L onto Willow Wood Close.* **Sat 23 May, Sat 18 July (11-5). Adm £5, chd free. Refreshments cream teas, cakes, light snacks, hot and cold beverages, Pimms, wine and cocktails.**

The sensory gardens, redesigned and maintained by two former National Trust gardeners and a wonderful team of volunteers comprise of

a series of formal and informal gardens. These spaces contain lush, romantic planting design, filled with scent, texture, studies in colour combinations and sculptural form, water features, a kitchen garden, wildlife friendly planting and two woodland areas. The Sensory and Tranquil gardens are wheelchair accessible, we hope get funding within the next 12 months to create full access to the upper garden.

GROUP OPENING

71 WOOLTON VILLAGE GARDENS

Woolton, Liverpool, L25 8QF. *7m S of Liverpool. Woolton Rd B5171 or Menlove Ave A562 follow signs for Woolton.* **Sun 19 July (12-5). Combined adm £4, chd free. Light refreshments. at 23 Hillside Drive & Speke Rd.**

23 HILLSIDE DRIVE
L25 5NR. Bruce & Fiona Pennie.

71 MANOR ROAD
L25 8QF. John & Maureen Davies.

231 SPEKE ROAD
L25 0LA. Paul & Helen Ekoku, 07765 379967, iekoku@yahoo.co.uk.

A group of gardens surrounding the NW and Britain in Bloom award winning Woolton Village, all within a short walk or drive. The contrasting gardens show what can be achieved in a suburban garden all different and reflecting their owners gardening styles A family garden with raised patio and decked area planted with roses, clematis and passion flowers, wildlife pond with hostas, ferns, trees and shrubs. A garden with unusual veg, well stocked borders and domed seating area. Another interesting garden with mature trees, fruit and beautiful flowers. Wheelchair access to some gardens.

We help ordinary people open the gates to their extraordinary private gardens to raise impressive amounts of money through admissions, teas and slices of cake!

OPENING DATES

All entries subject to change. For latest information check www.ngs.org.uk

Extended openings are shown at the beginning of the month.

Map locator numbers are shown to the right of each garden name.

February

Snowdrop Festival

Sunday 16th
NEW Oak Cottage 37

Sunday 23rd
The Acers 1
Mary's Garden 32

Saturday 29th
Hedgehog Hall 25
Westview 58

March

Sunday 1st
Hedgehog Hall 25
Westview 58

Sunday 22nd
Gunthorpe Hall 20

April

Sunday 26th
Tresillian House 54

May

Sunday 3rd
Westview 58

Saturday 9th
Hedgehog Hall 25

Sunday 10th
Burrough Hall 9
Hedgehog Hall 25
Westbrooke House 57

Saturday 16th
Grimston Gardens 19

Sunday 17th
1 The Dairy, Hurst
Court 12
Grimston Gardens 19
Mill House 33
The Old Vicarage,
Burley 42
◆ Whatton House 59

Wednesday 20th
Thorpe Lubenham
Hall 53

Sunday 24th
The Old Vicarage,
Whissendine 43

Monday 25th
Newtown Linford
Gardens 36

Saturday 30th
10 Brook Road 6
109 Brook Street 7
88 Brook Street 8
Goadby Marwood Hall 17

Sunday 31st
13 Bantlam Lane 4
10 Brook Road 6
109 Brook Street 7
88 Brook Street 8
Nevill Holt Hall 35
47 Parklands Drive 46

June

Every Wednesday
Stoke Albany House 52

Friday 5th
Redhill Lodge 49

Saturday 6th
28 Gladstone Street 16
13 Highcroft Avenue 28
NEW Snowdrop Ridge 51

Sunday 7th
Exton Hall 14
28 Gladstone Street 16
13 Highcroft Avenue 28
4 Packman Green 44
NEW Silver Birches 50
NEW Snowdrop Ridge 51
Uppingham Gardens 55

Wednesday 10th
NEW Snowdrop Ridge 51

Saturday 13th
The Paddocks 45

Sunday 14th
Crossfell House 10
NEW 12 Hastings
Close 24
The Paddocks 45
Wing Gardens 63

Saturday 20th
Oak Tree House 38

Sunday 21st
Dairy Cottage 11
Oak Tree House 38
Quaintree Hall 47

Wednesday 24th
The Old Vicarage,
Burley 42

Saturday 27th
NEW The Old Barn 39

Sunday 28th
Market Bosworth
Gardens 31
NEW The Old Barn 39
NEW The Old Vicarage,
Harringworth 41
4 Packman Green 44
15 The Woodcroft 64

July

Every Wednesday
Stoke Albany House 52

Saturday 4th
28 Gladstone Street 16
Tresillian House 54
Wigston Gardens 61

Sunday 5th
28 Gladstone Street 16
The Old Hall 40
NEW The Old Vicarage,
Harringworth 41
Westbrooke House 57
Wigston Gardens 61

Sunday 12th
NEW 28 Ashby Road 3
Empingham Gardens 13
Green Wicket Farm 18
Mill House 33
Willoughby Gardens 62

Wednesday 15th
Green Wicket Farm 18

Saturday 18th
Mountain Ash 34

Sunday 19th
Mountain Ash 34

August

Sunday 2nd
Honeytrees Tropical
Garden 29

Sunday 9th
The Firs 15
NEW Harborough
Allotments, Stevens
Street 23
Honeytrees Tropical
Garden 29

Sunday 16th
NEW Harborough
Allotments,
Northampton Road 22

Sunday 23rd
NEW 12 Hastings
Close 24
Honeytrees Tropical
Garden 29

Sunday 30th
Honeytrees Tropical
Garden 29
Tresillian House 54

September

Sunday 6th
Washbrook Allotments 56
Westview 58

October

Sunday 11th
Hammond Arboretum 21

Sunday 25th
Tresillian House 54

February 2021

Saturday 27th
Westview 58

Sunday 28th
Westview 58

By Arrangement

Arrange a personalised garden visit with your club, or group of friends, on a date to suit you. See individual garden entries for full details.

THE GARDENS

❶ THE ACERS
10 The Rills, Hinckley, LE10 1NA. Mr Dave Baggott, 07983639683, davebaggott18@hotmail.com. *Off B4668 out of Hinckley. Turn into Dean Rd then 1st on the R.* **Sun 23 Feb (11-4). Combined adm with Mary's Garden £5, chd free. Home-made teas. Visits also by arrangement Sept to Nov for groups of 5 to 30.**
Medium sized garden, with a Japanese theme incl a zen garden, Japanese tea house, koi pond, more than 20 different varieties of Acers, many choice alpines, Trilliums, Cyclamen, Erythroniums, Cornus, Hamamelis and dwarf conifers. Over 150 different varieties of Snowdrops in spring. Large greenhouse.
&♿ 🐄 ❀ ☕

❷ AQUEDUCT COTTAGE
Gelsmoor Road, Coleorton, Coalville, LE67 8JF. Jayne Wright, 07713 624595, jaynewright38@yahoo.co.uk. *Nr Ashby de la Zouch. Corner of Gelsmoor Rd and Aqueduct Rd. Access is via gate on Aqueduct Rd.* **Visits by arrangement in June. Refreshments incl in adm. Adm £6.50, chd free. Home-made teas.**
Mature, classic English garden, in excess of 3 acres. It is flanked by a disused (1836) railway line which is wooded and boasts a large variety of specimen trees. There are formal perennial beds and specimen rose beds with a lot of roses! A small classic fish pond in the formal part of the garden and a 30m open pond in a wildlife friendly setting. Please advise if dietary requirements are needed at time of booking an appointment.
&♿ ☕

❸ NEW 28 ASHBY ROAD
Hinckley, LE10 1SL. Stan & Carol Crow. *Hinckley is SW of Leicester with easy access off the M69 or A5. Ashby Rd is on the A447 running N from Hinckley to Ibstock. Easy parking in rd.* **Sun 12 July (11-5). Adm £3.50, chd free. Home-made teas.**
Behind the post war house lies a garden packed full of colour and interesting planting combinations. Approximately 150 feet long. Natural sculptures and pots abound. Wildlife area with pond and wildflowers to attract bees and butterflies into the garden. Plenty of hideaway seating to view the garden at your leisure. Vegetable garden with cut flower area. Eco friendly as much as possible.
🐕 ❀ ☕

❹ 13 BANTLAM LANE
Enderby, Leicester, LE19 4NB. Clive and Helen Biggs. *Turn R from the B4114 at the Foxhunter r'about towards Enderby. Follow the signs for the Leisure Centre. Turn into Bantlam Lane on the L by the Cricket Ground.* **Sun 31 May (11.30-5). Adm £2.50, chd free. Home-made teas.**
A pretty cottage garden packed full of flowering shrubs and herbaceous perennials. There are many areas of interest with ornaments and water features. A small courtyard garden opens into a wisteria covered pergola lined with a fern filled bog garden and large potted acers. This leads to a wildlife pond and additional paved seating areas surrounded with fragrant roses. Not suitable for wheelchairs. (some steps and narrow bark chip paths).
❀ ☕

❺ BARRACCA
Ivydene Close, Earl Shilton, LE9 7NR. Mr & Mrs John & Sue Osborn, 01455 842609, susan.osborn1@btinternet.com, www.barraccagardens.com. *10m W of Leicester. From A47 after entering Earl Shilton, Ivydene Close is 4th on L from Leicester side of A47.* **Visits by arrangement Feb to July for groups of 10+. Price incl tea & cakes, other refreshments available on request. Adm £8, chd free. Home-made teas.**
1 acre garden with lots of different areas, silver birch walk, wildlife pond with seating, apple tree garden, Mediterranean planted area and lawns surrounded with herbaceous plants and shrubs. Patio area with climbing roses and wisteria. There is also a utility garden with greenhouse, vegetables in beds, herbs and perennial flower beds, lawn and fruit cage. Part of the old gardens owned by the Cotton family who used to open approx 9 acres to the public in the 1920's. Partial wheelchair access.
&♿ 🐄 🚌 ☕

❻ 10 BROOK ROAD
Woodhouse Eaves, Loughborough, LE12 8RS. Geoff & Carol Fowle. *4m south of Loughborough, opp Bulls Head PH. Parking at pub.* **Sat 30, Sun 31 May (12-5.30). Adm £4, chd free. Light refreshments.**
1 acre mature country garden with different and interesting areas incl a stream & clay lined pond, lawn areas with island beds containing roses, rhododendrons, azaleas & Japanese maples, created by the owners over 20 yrs from a neglected Victorian garden. Many ornaments and recycled quirky materials made into garden features with a traditional summer house for you to enjoy your refreshments. Partial wheelchair access.
&♿ 🐄 ❀ ☕

Oak Tree House

7 109 BROOK STREET
Wymeswold, LE12 6TT. Maggie
& Steve Johnson, 07973692931,
steve@brookend.org,
www.brookend.org. *4m NE of
Loughborough. From A6006
Wymeswold turn S onto Stockwell,
then E along Brook St. Roadside
parking along Brook St. Steep drive
with limited disabled parking at
house.* **Sat 30, Sun 31 May (2-5).
Combined adm with 88 Brook
Street £5, chd free. Home-made
teas. Gluten free option available.
Visits also by arrangement May &
June for groups of 10 to 30.**
South facing, ¾ acre, gently sloping
garden with views to open country.
Modern garden with mature features.
Patio with roses and clematis, wildlife
and fish ponds, mixed borders,
vegetable garden, orchard, hot garden
and woodland garden. Something for
everyone! Optional tour of rain water
harvesting. Some gravel paths.
&. 🐕 ❀ 🍵

8 88 BROOK STREET
Wymeswold, LE12 6TU. Adrian
& Ita Cooke, 01509 880155,
itacooke@btinternet.com. *4m
NE of Loughborough. From A6006
Wymeswold turn S by church onto
Stockwell, then E along Brook St.
Roadside parking on Brook St.* **Sat
30, Sun 31 May (2-5). Combined
adm with 109 Brook Street £5,
chd free. Home-made teas at
109 Brook Street. Visits also
by arrangement May & June for
groups of 10 to 30. Admission to
88 Brook Street only will be £3, or
£5 including tea and cakes.**
The ½ acre garden is set on a hillside,
which provides lovely views across the
village, and comprises 3 distinct areas:
firstly, a cottage style garden; then a
series of water features incl a stream
and a 'champagne' pond; and finally
at the top there is a vegetable plot,
small orchard and wildflower meadow.
The ponds attract great crested and
common newts, frogs, toads and
grass snakes.
🐕 🚗 🍵

9 BURROUGH HALL
Burrough on the Hill, LE14 2QZ.
Richard & Alice Cunningham.
*Somerby Rd, Burrough on the Hill.
Close to B6047. 10 mins from A606.
20 mins from Melton Mowbray.* **Sun
10 May (2-5). Adm £4, chd free.
Home-made teas.**
Burrough Hall was built in 1867
as a classic Leicestershire hunting

lodge. The garden, framed by mature trees and shrubs, was extensively redesigned by garden designer George Carter in 2007. The garden continues to develop. This family garden designed for all generations to enjoy is surrounded by magnificent views across High Leicestershire. In addition to the garden there will be a small collection of vintage and classic cars on display. Gravel paths and lawn.

&. ✿ ☕

10 CROSSFELL HOUSE
4d Nether End, Great Dalby, Melton Mowbray, LE14 2EY. Jane & Ian West. *3m S of Melton Mowbray on B6047. On entering Great Dalby from Melton Mowbray remain on B6047. Crossfell House is on L approx 300 yrds from village 30mph sign. From the N or E, continue towards Melton Crossfell House on R.* **Sun 14 June (11-5). Adm £4, chd free. Home-made teas.**
A formal garden consisting of a terraced herbaceous border and rockery, flanked by a border of shrubs, two small areas of lawn and a sweeping path leading to a two acre meadow with wild grasses, flowers and a recently created wildlife pond. Paths criss-cross the meadows, culminating in spectacular countryside views from our Shepherd's Hut and picnic area. Far reaching views. Wheelchair access to patio and garden area, only partial wheelchair access to meadow.

&. ☕

11 DAIRY COTTAGE
15 Sharnford Road, Sapcote, LE9 4JN. Mrs Norah Robinson-Smith, 01455 272398, nrobinsons@yahoo.co.uk. *9m SW of Leicester. Sharnford Rd joins Leicester Rd in Sapcote to B4114 Coventry Rd. Follow NGS signs at both ends.* **Sun 21 June (1-5). Adm £3.50, chd free. Home-made teas. Tea & cakes £2.00. Visits also by arrangement May to July for groups of 10+.**
From a walled garden with colourful mixed borders to a potager approached along a woodland path, this mature cottage garden combines extensive perennial planting with many unusual shrubs and specimen trees. More than 90 clematis and 30 climbing roses are trained up pergolas, arches and into trees – so don't forget to look up! Also

a Hornbeam hedge covered with varieties of viticella clematis.

&. ☕

12 1 THE DAIRY, HURST COURT

Netherseal Road, Chilcote, Swadlincote, DE12 8DU. Alison Dockray, alisondockray56@gmail.com. *3m from J11 of the M42. 10m from Tamworth & Ashby de la Zouch. Hurst Court is situated on Netherseal Rd but sat navs show it as Church Rd. Due to limited parking it is advisable to park on Netherseal Rd.* **Sun 17 May (1-5). Adm £4, chd free. Light refreshments. Visits also by arrangement May to Aug.**
Developed over the last 11 years from a muddy ¼ acre patch attached to a barn conversion, the garden now contains a large Japanese Koi Carp pond, goldfish pond and a stream with planting having a Japanese connection viewed from winding paths. With many rhododendrons, camellias and azaleas combined with cloud pruning and a variety of other plants, an air of peace pervades the garden.

☕

GROUP OPENING

13 EMPINGHAM GARDENS
Empingham, LE15 8PS. *Empingham Village. 5m E of Oakham, 5m W of Stamford on A606.* **Sun 12 July (1-5.30). Combined adm £6, chd free. Home-made teas at Prebendal House.**

HONEYLEA
Mr & Mrs Barry & Janet Chalmers-Stevens.

LAVANDER COTTAGE
Virginia Todd.

PREBENDAL HOUSE
Matthew & Rebecca Eatough.

3 very different gardens in a lovely village. Park and start your visit at Prebendal House, next door to the Church and standing in four acres of garden with open parkland views to the River Gwash. Incl extensive herbaceous borders, topiary and a sunken water garden. The tiny garden of Lavander Cottage in Nook Lane has been developed over 10yrs into a series of rooms linked by rose and honeysuckle arches and packed with climbing, shrub and

standard roses, richly underplanted with lavender, alliums and clematis and full of colour & scent. Honeylea, opposite, is an 'Enabled Garden'. The owner is registered disabled and has designed it for maximum accessibility & relaxation with yr round interest. Wheelchair access only at Prebendal House and Honeylea.

&. 🐾 ✿ ☕

14 EXTON HALL
Cottesmore Road, Exton, LE15 8AN. Viscount & Viscountess Campden, www.extonpark.co.uk. *Exton, Rutland. 5m E of Oakham. 8m from Stamford off A1 (A606 turning).* **Sun 7 June (11-4). Adm £5, chd free. Home-made teas.**
Extensive park, lawns, specimen trees and shrubs, lake, private chapel and C19 house (not open). Pinetum, woodland walks, lakes, ruins, dovecote and formal herbaceous garden. Whilst there is wheelchair access, areas of the garden are accessible along grass or gravel paths which, weather dependent, may make access difficult.

&. ✿ Ⓓ ☕

15 THE FIRS
Main Street, Bruntingthorpe, LE17 5QF. Howard & Carmel Grant, 07968131711, thefirsgarden@gmail.com. *5m NE of Lutterworth. Exit J20 M1 to Lutterworth A426.Turn R to Gilmorton & Bruntingthorpe opp petrol station. From Leicester A5199 to Arnesby. Turn R & follow rd 2m to T-junction. Turn L to Bruntingthorpe.* **Sun 9 Aug (11-5). Adm £4, chd free. Home-made teas. Visits also by arrangement July & Aug for groups of 10+.**
A tranquil garden of 1½ acres with views over open countryside. The front garden features terraced borders and paving. The main rear garden has large areas of sweeping lawn and grass walkways around many flowing borders. There is a large variety of themed coloured planting, shrubs and trees. In amongst the borders can be found many unusual design features, artefacts and seating areas. Large sequoia tree at the front of the property was damaged by a bomber returning from a night training flight during the WWII. Some shelter available if the weather is not so good. Short gravel drive, some paving, rest grass.

✿ ☕

16 28 GLADSTONE STREET

Wigston Magna, LE18 1AE. Chris & Janet Huscroft. *4m S of Leicester. Off Wigston by-pass (A5199) follow signs off McDonalds r'about.* **Sat 6, Sun 7 June (11-5). Combined adm with 13 Highcroft Avenue £4.50, chd free. Home-made teas. Sat 4, Sun 5 July (11-5). Combined adm with Wigston Gardens £5, chd free.**
Our mature 70'x15' town garden is divided into rooms and bisected by a pond with a bridge. It is brimming with unusual hardy perennials, incl collections of ferns and hostas. David Austin roses chosen for their scent feature throughout, incl a 30' rose arch. A shade house with unusual hardy plants. Regular changes to planting, new in 2019, a Hosta Theatre. Framework Knitters Museum and garden nearby - open Sunday afternoons 2-5.

17 GOADBY MARWOOD HALL

Goadby Marwood, LE14 4LN. Mr & Mrs Westropp, 01664 464202. *4m NW of Melton Mowbray. Between Waltham-on-the-Wolds & Eastwell, 8m S of Grantham. Plenty of parking space available.* **Sat 30 May (10.30-5). Adm £5, chd £3.50. Home-made teas in Village Hall. Visits also by arrangement.**
Redesigned in 2000 by the owner based on C18 plans. A chain of 5 lakes (covering 10 acres) and several ironstone walled gardens all interconnected. Lakeside woodland walk. Planting for yr-round interest. Landscaper trained under plantswoman Rosemary Verey at Barnsley House. Beautiful C13 church open. Gravel paths and lawns.

18 GREEN WICKET FARM

Ullesthorpe Road, Bitteswell, Lutterworth, LE17 4LR. Mrs Anna Smith, 01455 552646, greenfarmbitt@hotmail.com. *2m NW of Lutterworth J20 M1. From Lutterworth follow signs through Bitteswell towards Ullesthorpe. Garden situated behind Bitteswell Cricket Club. Use this as a landmark rather than relying totally on satnav.* **Sun 12, Wed 15 July (2.30-5.30). Adm £4, chd free. Home-made teas. Visits also by arrangement June to Sept for groups of 10 to 30.**
Created in 2008 on a working farm with clay soil and a very exposed site.

Many unusual hardy plants along with a lot of old favourites have been used to provide a long season of colour and interest. Anemone nemorosa, Pacific coast iris and Salvias are of particular interest. Formal pond and water features. Some gravel paths.

GROUP OPENING

19 GRIMSTON GARDENS

Main Street, Grimston, Melton Mowbray, LE14 3BZ. Brian & Monica Ravenscroft. *5m NW Melton Mowbray. Follow Yellow NGS signs. The gardens are situated either side of the Church on Main Street/Perkins Lane.* **Sat 16, Sun 17 May (10-5). Combined adm £5, chd free. Home-made teas in Grimston Village Hall.**

FOURWINDS
Monica and Brian Ravenscroft.

THE YEWS FARM
Tony and Claire Moore.

Grimston is a small village with a c13 church restored in 1856. The village green has a large stone and stocks set under a mature Chestnut. Fourwinds is approx. 1 acre, with mature trees and shrubs, extensive flower beds, vegetable garden and long stretches of lawns. The Yews Farm is thought to be the oldest house in the village and the garden of approx 1 acre contains 2 notable Yew trees considered to be 500+ years old. The peaceful garden has mixed borders, fruit trees and a productive vegetable garden as well as a glorious wisteria on the house. The adjoining paddock boasts extensive views over the countryside as well as an ancient 'holloway'. Fourwinds has a gravel drive with a rather sharp slope. The Yews Farm has gravel drive and uneven lawn.

20 GUNTHORPE HALL

Gunthorpe, Nr Oakham, LE15 8BE. Tim Haywood, 01572 737514 ask for lettings. *A6003 between Oakham & Uppingham; 1m from Oakham, up drive between lodges. Proceed over railway bridge, look for sign to gardens, which are 600 yds ahead. Please follow the signs for parking.* **Sun 22 Mar (2-5). Adm £5, chd free. Home-made teas.**
Large garden in a country setting

with extensive views across the Rutland landscape with the carpets of daffodils being a key seasonal feature. The Stable Yard has been transformed into a series of parterres. The kitchen garden and borders have all been rejuvenated over the last five years. Gravel path allows steps to be avoided.

21 HAMMOND ARBORETUM

Burnmill Road, Market Harborough, LE16 7JG. The Robert Smyth Academy, www.hammondarboretum.org.uk. *15m S of Leicester on A6. From High St, follow signs to The Robert Smyth Academy via Bowden Lane to Burnmill Rd. Park in 1st entrance on L.* **Sun 11 Oct (2-4.30). Adm £4, chd free. Home-made teas. Provided by the Academy Parents Association.**
A site of just under 2½ acres containing an unusual collection of trees and shrubs, many from Francis Hammond's original planting dating from 1913 to 1936 whilst headmaster of the school. Species from America, China and Japan with malus and philadelphus walks and a moat. Proud owners of 3 champion trees identified by national specialist. Walk plans available. Some steep slopes.

22 NEW HARBOROUGH ALLOTMENTS, NORTHAMPTON ROAD

Northampton Road, Market Harborough, LE16 9HF. Mr John Howell. *½m S of town on A508, opposite petrol station.* **Sun 16 Aug (11-3). Adm £3, chd free. Home-made teas.**
Site has variety of full, half & quarter plots growing a wide selection of vegetables, fruit & fowers. A communal polytunnel extends the range of produce to view. Conservation & recycling are featured round the site. Wild flower area under development for 2020. Site has good access with main paths suitable for wheelchairs. Extensive parking adjacent to venue.

23 NEW HARBOROUGH ALLOTMENTS, STEVENS STREET

Stevens Street, Market Harborough, LE16 9BB. Mr John Howell. *Off Logan St, accessed from*

Coventry Rd, follow yellow signs.
**Sun 9 Aug (11-3). Adm £3, chd
free. Home-made teas.**
Site has over 130 full, half or starter
plots, growing fruit, vegetables
& flowers. 2 small orchards with
heritage trees & wildlife areas incl
ponds. Dedicated site composting
area (demos on the day). Good
access with main paths suitable for
wheelchairs.

24 **NEW** **12 HASTINGS CLOSE**
Breedon-On-The-Hill, Derby,
DE73 8BN. Mrs Rosie Winship. *5m
N from Ashby de la Zouch. Follow
NGS signs in the Village. Parking
around the Village Green.* **Sun 14
June, Sun 23 Aug (1-5). Adm £3,
chd free.**
A medium sized prairie garden,
organically managed and planted
in the Piet Oldolf style. Also many
roses and a wide range of perennials.
The back garden has a small 'white'
garden with box hedging and a more
colourful style perennial borders. The
garden has narrow paths and steps
so is not suitable for wheelchairs. The
garden is open for Breedon on the Hill
village open garden day.

25 **HEDGEHOG HALL**
Loddington Road, Tilton on
the Hill, LE7 9DE. Janet &
Andrew Rowe, 01162597339.
*8m W of Oakham. 2m N of A47 on
B6047 between Melton & Market
Harborough. Follow yellow NGS
signs in Tilton towards Loddington.*
**Sat 29 Feb, Sun 1 Mar (11-4).
Light refreshments. Sat 9, Sun
10 May (11-4). Home-made teas.
Adm £4, chd free. Visits also by
arrangement in May for groups of
20+. Adm £7 incl refreshments.**
½ acre organically managed plant
lover's garden. Steps leading to three
stone walled terraced borders filled
with shrubs, perennials, bulbs and a
patio over looking the valley. Lavender
walk, herb border, beautiful spring
garden, colour themed herbaceous
borders. Courtyard with collection of
hostas and acers and terrace planted
for yr-round interest with topiary and
perennials. Snowdrop collection.
Homemade soup and a roll February
opening. Cake, tea or coffee May
opening. Regret, no wheelchair
access to terraced borders. Disabled
parking in the road outside the White
House.

26 **134 HERRICK ROAD**
Loughborough, LE11 2BU.
Janet Currie, 01509 212191,
janet.currie@me.com,
www.thesecateur.com. *1m SW of
Loughborough centre. From M1 J23
take A512 Ashby Rd to L'boro. At
r'about R onto A6004 Epinal Way.
At Beacon Rd r'about L, Herrick Rd
1st on R.* **Visits by arrangement
June & July for groups of up
to 20. Adm £2, chd £1. Home-
made teas. Dietary requirements
catered for, please phone to
discuss.**
A small garden brimming with
texture, colour and creative flair.
Trees, shrubs and climbers give
structure. A sitting area surrounded
by lilies, raised staging for herbs and
alpines. A lawn flanked with deeply
curving and gracefully planted beds
of perennials growing through willow
structures made by Janet. A shaded
area under the Bramley apple tree,
raised vegetable beds and potting
area. Janet makes attractive willow
plant supports to her own designs,
and to order for equally enthusiastic
gardeners!

27 **94 HERRICK ROAD**
Loughborough, LE11 2BT.
Marion Smith, 01509 554927,
marion_smith@ntlworld.com.
*1m SW of Loughborough. From
M1 J23 take A512 Ashby Rd to
Loughborough. At r'about R onto
A6004 Epinal Way. At Beacon Rd
r'about L, Herrick Road 1st on R.*
**Visits by arrangement June &
July for groups of 5 to 20. Adm
£2, chd £1. Tea.**
Traditional old-fashioned English
medium sized garden at rear of
Victorian house. Mainly perennial
planting with interest in hardy
geraniums and Heucheras. Small
pond and three active beehives.
Wormery, composting and green
cone to use all household waste. This
peaceful walled garden also has a
Coach House. Ramp onto lawn, no
steps otherwise.

Hedgehog Hall

28 13 HIGHCROFT AVENUE

Oadby, Leicester, LE2 5UH. Sharon Maher & Mike Costall. *Just off A6, 5m S Leicester & 9m N Market Harborough. Follow NGS yellow arrows.* **Sat 6, Sun 7 June (11-5). Combined adm with 28 Gladstone Street £4.50, chd free. Home-made teas.**
Our garden continues to evolve and develop. It is approx 22m x 14m. We have a bed of David Austin roses, a herbaceous border, a wildlife area, alpine bed, patio planters and a small wildlife pond. There are four raised beds for vegetables which is supplemented by a small greenhouse. We also have a herb area. There's plenty of room on the patio to sit and enjoy the tea and cake too!

29 HONEYTREES TROPICAL GARDEN

85 Grantham Road, Bottesford, NG13 0EG. Julia Madgwick & Mike Ford, 01949 842120, Julia_madgwick@hotmail.com. *7m E of Bingham on A52. Turn into village. Garden is on L on slip road behind hedge going out of village towards Grantham. Parking on grass opp property.* **Sun 2, Sun 9, Sun 23, Sun 30 Aug (11-4). Adm £4, chd free. Home-made teas. Visits also by arrangement July & Aug for groups of 10+.**
Tropical and exotic with a hint of jungle! Raised borders with different themes from lush foliage to arid cacti. Exotic planting as you enter the garden gives way on a gentle incline to surprises to incl glass houses dedicated to various climatic zones interspersed with more exotic planting, ponds and a stream. A representation of in excess of 20 years plant hunting. There are steps and some gravel but plenty to view and enjoy from a wheelchair.

30 KNIGHTON SENSORY

Knighton Park, Leicester, LE2 3YQ. Debby Orange, 0116 2102425, kpgc@hotmail.co.uk, www.knightonparkgardeningclub.com. *Off A563 (Outer Ring Rd) S of Leicester. From Palmerston Blvd, turn into South Kingsmead Rd then 1st L into Woodbank Rd. Park entrance at end of rd. Enter park, follow path to R, garden on R.* **Visits by arrangement May to Aug for groups of 10 to 20. Tea and cake available at £2 per person. Adm £3, chd free. Tea.**
This ¼ acre community garden stands in a secluded corner of Knighton Park away from the bustle of the city. It is a feast for all the senses incl shrubs, some traditional bedding, herbaceous borders, bog garden with bridge, dry riverbed, wildflower meadow and wildlife area, Separate area contains raised beds for edibles. Awarded outstanding by the It's Your Neighbourhood Scheme.

GROUP OPENING

31 MARKET BOSWORTH GARDENS

Market Bosworth, CV13 0LE. *13m W of Leicester; 8m N of Hinckley. 1m off A447 Coalville to Hinckley Rd, 3m off A444. Burton to Nuneaton Rd.* **Sun 28 June (1-6). Combined adm £6, chd free. Light refreshments at 13 Spinney Hill. Donation to Bosworth in Bloom.**

GLEBE FARM HOUSE
Mr Peter Ellis & Ms Ginny Broad.

4 LANCASTER AVENUE
Mr Peter Bailiss.

26 NORTHUMBERLAND AVENUE
Mrs Kathy Boot.

30 PARK STREET
Lesley Best.

4 PRIORY ROAD
Mrs Margaret Barrett, 01455 290112, info@margaretbarrett.co.uk. **Visits also by arrangement May to Aug for groups of 5 to 30.**

5 PRIORY ROAD
David & Linda Chevell.

RAINBOW COTTAGE
Mr David Harrison.

13 SPINNEY HILL
Mrs J Buckell.

Market Bosworth is an attractive market town, with an enviable record for the quality of its regular entry in the annual East Midlands in Bloom competition. There are a number of gardens open, all within walking distance of the Market Square. The gardens show various planting styles and different approaches to small and intimate spaces in the historic town centre, as well as larger plots in more recent developments. Tickets and descriptive maps obtainable in the Market Place, with refreshments available there and at some of the gardens. Plants will be on sale at a number of gardens. A proportion of the proceeds from the Gardens Open Day will be used to support Bosworth in Bloom, the voluntary group responsible for the town's floral displays; see www.bosworthinbloom.co.uk. Farmers' Market in town centre (9-2) local produce, hot and cold food.

The Dairy, Hurst Court

32 MARY'S GARDEN

7 Hall Road Burbage, Hinckley, LE10 2LU. Don Baker, 014556356167, donmary7@tiscali.co.uk. *Sketchley Manor Estate. From M69 J1, take B4109 signed Hinckley. At 2nd r'about follow NGS yellow arrows.* **Sun 23 Feb (11-4). Combined adm with The Acers £5, chd free. Light refreshments. Visits also by arrangement Feb to June for groups of 10 to 20.**
Medium sized garden with a good mix of shrubs, large selection snowdrops, erythroniums, spring bulbs and hellebores. Partial wheelchair access.

33 MILL HOUSE

118 Welford Road, Wigston, LE18 3SN. Mr & Mrs P Measures, 01162 885409, petemeasures@hotmail.co.uk. *4m S of Leicester. From Leicester to Wigston Magna follow A5199 Welford Rd S towards Kilby, up hill past Mercers Newsagents, 100yds on L.* **Sun 17 May, Sun 12 July (12-5). Adm £2.50, chd free. Home-made teas. Visits also by arrangement May to July for groups of up to 20.**
Walled town garden with an extensive plant variety, many rare and unusual. A plant lovers garden, with interesting designs incorporated in the borders, rockery and scree. It is full of surprises with memorabilia and bygones as reminders of our past. Good variety of reasonably priced plants on sale both open days.

34 MOUNTAIN ASH

140 Ulverscroft Lane, Newtown Linford, LE6 0AJ. Mike & Liz Newcombe, 01530 242178, mjnew12@gmail.com. *7m SW of Loughborough, 7m NW of Leicester, 1m NW of Newtown Linford. Head ½m N along Main St towards Sharpley Hill, fork L into Ulverscroft Lane and Mountain Ash, is about ½m along on the L. Parking is along the opp verge.* **Sat 18, Sun 19 July (11-5). Adm £5, chd free. Home-made teas. Visits also by arrangement Apr to Aug for groups of 20+.**
2 acre garden with stunning views across Charnwood countryside. Nr the house are patios, lawns, water feature, flower & shrub beds, fruit trees, soft fruit cage, greenhouses & vegetable plots. Lawns slope down to a gravel garden, large wildlife pond and small areas of woodland with walks through many species of trees. Many statues and ornaments. Several places to sit and relax around the garden. Only the top part of the garden around the house is reasonably accessible by wheelchair.

35 NEVILL HOLT HALL

Drayton Road, Nevill Holt, Market Harborough, LE16 8EG. Mr David Ross. *5m NE of Market Haborough. Signed off B664 at Medbourne.* **Sun 31 May (12-4). Adm £5, chd free. Light refreshments.**
The gardens are at their peak in late May/early June. Whilst the walled kitchen garden shows signs of a harvest to come, our two other walled gardens and adjoining cedar lawn garden are full of colour and texture, all working together to create a summer scene that feels warm and summery, even on the dullest days. Please do join us for tea and cake – we would love to share our garden with you. Nevill Holt Opera Event partner with the RHS.

GROUP OPENING

36 NEWTOWN LINFORD GARDENS

Main Street, Newtown Linford, Leicester, LE6 0AD. *6m NW Leicester. 2½m from M1 J22. The gardens are along Main St between Markfield Lane & Ulvercroft Lane.* **Mon 25 May (11-5). Combined adm £5, chd free. Home-made teas at The Old Vicarage, Bradgate Rd, LE6 0HB.**

APPLETREE COTTAGE
Katherine Duffy Anthony.

BANK COTTAGE
Jan Croft.

DINGLE HOUSE
Mr & Mrs R Howard.

PILGRIM COTTAGE
Mr & Mrs S Salter.

WOODLANDS
Mary Husseini.

Newtown Linford is a historic village bordering Bradgate Park with the River Lin flowing through it and is part of the Charnwood Forest. Two of the gardens opening have river banks from where you can see brown trout and the occasional kingfisher. The gardens opening are each quite different. Appletree Cottage has a charming enclosed garden surrounding a C17 thatched cottage with interesting paths leading to lawns, borders, sun terrace and small lily pond. Bank Cottage, Pilgrim Cottage and Dingle House have cottage gardens set on different levels that provide year-round colour but are prettiest in spring. The River Lin runs through Woodlands, a 1 acre garden where many varied shrubs and spring flowers grow around mature trees. Come and enjoy your day with us!

37 NEW OAK COTTAGE

Well Lane, Blackfordby, Swadlincote, DE11 8AG. Colin and Jenny Carr. *Blackfordby, just over a mile from (and between) Ashby-de-la-Zouch or Swadlincote. From Ashby-de-la-Zouch take Moira Rd, turn R on Blackfordby Lane. As you enter the village, turn L to Butt Lane and quickly R to Strawberry Lane. Park then 2 min walk to Well Lane entrance.* **Sun 16 Feb (11-4). Adm £4, chd free. Home-made teas.**
½ acre garden set around Blackfordby's "hidden" listed thatched cottage, which itself is more than 300 years old. In total there are 3.4 acres of paddocks, front and rear gardens to explore with extensive displays of snowdrops, crocuses, hellebores and snakes heads in the Spring. The lower paddock has been planted with 425 native trees as part of the National Forest Freewoods scheme, with a large pond created at its base. The central swathe is being developed with wildflowers. At the top of the garden there is a chicken run, old and new orchards and a peach house. Garden is heavily sloped in parts.

We open the gates to the nation's best gardens, offering a relaxing, memorable and affordable day out. A perfect experience to share with friends and family.

The Old Vicarage, Harringworth

38 OAK TREE HOUSE

North Road, South Kilworth, LE17 6DU. Pam & Martin Shave. *15m S of Leicester. From M1 J20, take A4304 towards Market Harborough. At North Kilworth turn R, signed South Kilworth. Garden on L after approx 1m.* **Sat 20 June (1-5); Sun 21 June (11-4). Adm £4, chd free. Home-made teas.**
2/3 acre beautiful country garden full of colour, formal design, softened by cottage style planting. Modern sculptures. Large herbaceous borders, vegetable plots, pond, greenhouse, shady area, colour-themed borders. Extensive collections in pots, incl pelargoniums and hostas. Trees with attractive bark. Many clematis and roses. Dramatic arched pergola. Constantly changing garden as borders enlarge. Access to patio and greenhouse via steps.

39 NEW THE OLD BARN

Rectory Lane, Stretton-En-Le-Field, Swadlincote, DE12 8AF. Gregg and Claire Mayles. *On A444, 1½m from M42/A42 J11. Rectory Lane is a concealed turn off the A444, surrounded by trees. Look out for brown 'church' signs. Postcode in Sat Nav very useful.* **Sat 27, Sun 28 June (11-4). Adm £4, chd free. Home-made teas.**

2 acres in leafy hamlet, lots of interest. Main garden has lawns, many colourful shrubs and tree-lined cobbled paths. Walled garden with fishpond, pergola with climbers and cottage garden planting. Orchard, meadow with paths and open views. Lots of wildlife, incl our Peafowl. Plenty of drinks, cakes and seats to enjoy them! Redundant medieval church close, open to visitors. Main garden fully wheelchair accessible. Walled garden partial access due to gravel. Orchard and meadow is accessible, but uneven.

40 THE OLD HALL

Main Street, Market Overton, LE15 7PL. Mr & Mrs Timothy Hart. *6m N of Oakham. Beyond Cottesmore, 6m N of Oakham; 5m from A1 via Thistleton. 10m E from Melton Mowbray via Wymondham.* **Sun 5 July (2-6). Adm £5, chd free. Home-made teas. incl Hambleton Bakery cakes.**
Set on a southerly ridge overlooking Catmose Vale. Stone walls and yew hedges divide the garden into enclosed areas with herbaceous borders, shrubs, and young and mature trees. In 2006 the lower part of garden was planted with new shrubs to create a walk with mown paths. There are interesting plants

flowering most of the time. Partial wheelchair access. Gravel and mown paths. Return to house is steep. It is, however, possible to just sit on the terrace.

41 NEW THE OLD VICARAGE, HARRINGWORTH

Seaton Road, Harringworth, Corby, NN17 3AF. Mr & Mrs Alan Wordie, 07719658569. *5m SE of Uppingham, 9m SW of Stamford and 10m west of A1/A47 junction near Peterborough. Next to Harringworth church.* **Sun 28 June, Sun 5 July (11-5). Adm £5, chd free. Light refreshments. Visits also by arrangement June to Aug.**
An established and romantic country garden of rooms, which incl a 'quiet garden' leading into the adjacent church, bee garden, mixed long border, nuttery, orchard, kitchen garden, paddock with wild flower areas and paths stretching to the River Welland. Working bee hives and mischievous guinea fowl. Home-made teas, plant stall and honey. Bring a picnic if you wish and watch the kingfishers. Ploughmans lunches available. Partial wheelchair access.

42 THE OLD VICARAGE, BURLEY

Church Road, Burley, Nr Oakham, LE15 7SU. Jonathan & Sandra Blaza, 01572 770588, sandra.blaza@btinternet.com, www.theoldvicarageburley.com. *1m NE of Oakham. In Burley just off B668 between Oakham & Cottesmore. Church Rd is opp village green.* **Sun 17 May (11-5). Home-made teas. Evening opening Wed 24 June (6-9). Light refreshments. Adm £5, chd free. Visits also by arrangement May & June for groups of 10+.**
The Old Vicarage is a relaxed country garden, planted for year round interest and colour. There are lawns and borders, a lime walk, rose gardens and a sunken rill garden with an avenue of standard wisteria. The walled garden produces fruit, herbs, vegetables and cut flowers. There two orchards and areas planted for wildlife incl woodland, a meadow and a pond. Some gravel and steps between terraces. Regional Finalist, The English Garden's The Nation's Favourite Gardens 2019.

43 THE OLD VICARAGE, WHISSENDINE

2 Station Road, Whissendine, LE15 7HG. Prof Peter & Dr Sarah Furness, www.pathology.plus.com/Garden. *Garden situated up hill from St Andrew's church in Whissendine. 1st gate on L in Station Rd.* **Sun 24 May (2-5). Adm £5, chd free. Home-made teas in St Andrew's Church, Whissendine.**
2/3 acre packed with variety. Terrace with topiary, a formal fountain courtyard and raised beds backed by gothic orangery. Herbaceous borders surround main lawn. Wisteria tunnel leads to raised vegetable beds and large ornate greenhouse, four beehives, Gothic hen house plus rare breed hens. Hidden white walk, unusual plants. New Victorian style garden room. Featured on BBC Gardener's World in 2019. Teas served in the Lady Chapel of the Church and outside if clement. Access to the church can be gained directly from the garden or from Main Street.

44 4 PACKMAN GREEN

Countesthorpe, Leicester, LE8 5WS. Roger Whitmore & Shirley Jackson. *Countesthorpe. 5m S of Leicester. Garden is close to village centre pass bank of shops off Scotland way.* **Sun 7, Sun 28 June (11-5). Adm £2, chd free. Tea.**
A small town house garden packed with hardy perennials surrounded by climbing roses and clematis. A pond and rose arch complete the picture to make it an enclosed peaceful haven filled with colour and scent. Lots of inexpensive plants for sale besides a refreshing cuppa and slice of cake.

45 THE PADDOCKS

Main Street, Hungarton, LE7 9JY. Helen Martin, 01162 595230, Michael.c.martin@talk21.com. *8m E of Leicester. Follow NGS signs in village.* **Sat 13, Sun 14 June (11-5). Adm £4, chd free. Home-made teas. Visits also by arrangement May to Sept for groups of 20+.**
2 acre garden with mature and specimen trees, rhododendrons, azaleas, magnolia grandiflora, wisterias. Two lily ponds and stream. Three lawn areas surrounded by herbaceous and shrub borders. Woodland walk. Pergola with clematis and roses, hosta collection and two rockeries, fern bed. Large well established semi permanent plant stall in aid of local charities. Huge magnolia grandiflora & hydrangea petiolaris. Rhododendrum spinney. Partial wheelchair access due to steep slopes at rear of garden. Flat terrace by main lawn provides good viewing area.

46 47 PARKLANDS DRIVE

Loughborough, LE11 2SZ. Lynda & Alan Burton. *5m from M1 J23. From A6004 (Epinal Way) to Park Rd. First R after Tesco Car Park.* **Sun 31 May (10.30-4.30). Adm £3, chd free. Light refreshments.**
NW facing 30's semi garden 90m x7m. Step down from the sunny patio onto gravel paths that meander round the rest of the garden. Mixed borders with a wide variety of shrubs, herbaceous perennials and bulbs, planted to attract and support wildlife and be an attractive place to sit and relax. There is a fishpond and a wildlife pond as well as raised vegetable beds, greenhouse and fruit areas.

47 QUAINTREE HALL

Braunston, LE15 8QS. Mrs Caroline Lomas. *Braunston, nr Oakham. 2m W of Oakham, in the centre of the village of Braunston in Rutland on High St.* **Sun 21 June (12.30-5). Adm £5, chd free. Home-made teas.**
An established garden surrounding the medieval hall house (not open) incl a formal box parterre to the front of the house, a woodland walk, formal walled garden with yew hedges, a small picking garden and terraced courtyard garden with conservatory. A wide selection of interesting plants can be enjoyed, each carefully selected for its specific site by the knowledgeable garden owner.

48 RAVENSTONE HALL

Ashby Road, Ravenstone, Coalville, LE67 2AA. Jemima Wade, 07976 302260, jemimawade@hotmail.com. *Ravenstone village is situated off the A511 between Ashby de la Zouch and Coalville. The house is 1st on the L if approached from Ashby.* **Visits by arrangement Mar to Sept for groups of up to 20. Adm £6, chd free. Home-made teas. Tea and cake £4.**
The garden was transformed in 2009 when the new owners moved to the house and planting and development has been on-going since that time. Azaleas and rhododendrons are planted on the bank of the drive. Beech trees and a beech hedge line the main front lawn. There is a woodland walk planted with bluebells. The main garden comprises a sunken garden, a rose garden, gravel path with herbaceous planting one side and iris and tulip on the other, a vegetable garden, an orchard, and a koi pond situated in a courtyard with white flowering plants and mixed foliage. Bluebell walk for groups from mid April, please call for details.

Your visits help change lives – since 1927, we've donated over £60 million to nursing and caring charities

Westview

are full of interesting trees, shrubs, bulbs and perennials. Robin Hill has recently had a major makeover and is in the course of re-development. Return to church, cross main road at lights into High Street West past school buildings. Stop to take in the lovely school gardens on L with their new planting. Continue straight into Stockerston Road, diagonally opposite Science Centre on L is Hillside, a 1 acre S facing garden with terraces, patio, new rose planting, orchard, vegetable garden and woodland walk with spring fed pond. Wheelchair access is available at Hillside but garden is on steep slope in parts.

♿ 🐄 ✻ ☕

---

56 WASHBROOK ALLOTMENTS
Welford Road, Leicester, LE2 6FP.
Sharon Maher. *Approx 2½ m S of Leicester, 1½ m N of Wigston. Regret no onsite parking. Welford Rd difficult to park on. Please use nearby side rds & Pendlebury Drive (LE2 6GY).* **Sun 6 Sept (11-3). Adm £3, chd free. Home-made teas.**
Our allotment gardens are a hidden oasis off the main Welford Road. There are over 100 whole, half and quarter plots growing a wide variety of fruit, vegetables and flowers. We have a wildflower meadow, and other wildlife friendly areas and a composting toilet! Look out for the remains of Anderson Shelters, and other 'Heath Robinson' constructions. Circular route around the site is uneven in places but is suitable for wheelchairs.

♿ 🐄 ✻ ☕

57 WESTBROOKE HOUSE
52 Scotland Road, Little Bowden, Market Harborough, LE16 8AX. Bryan & Joanne Drew, 07872 316153, Jwsd1980@hotmail.co.uk. *½ m S Market Harborough. From Northampton Rd follow NGS arrows.* **Sun 10 May, Sun 5 July (11-5). Adm £5, chd free. Cream teas. Visits also by arrangement May & June for groups of 20+.**
Westbrooke House is a late Victorian property built in 1887. The gardens comprise 6 acres in total and are approached through a tree lined driveway of mature limes and giant redwoods. Key features are walled flower garden, walled kitchen garden, lower garden, pond area, spring garden, lawns, woodland paths and a meadow with a wild flower area, ha-ha and hornbeam avenue.

✻ Ⓓ ☕

58 WESTVIEW
1 St Thomas's Road, Great Glen, Leicester, LE8 9EH. Gill & John Hadland, 01162592170, gillhadland1@gmail.com. *7m S of Leicester. Take either r'about from A6 into village centre then follow NGS signs. Please park in Oaks Rd.* **Sat 29 Feb, Sun 1 Mar (12-4); Sun 3 May, Sun 6 Sept (12-5). Adm £3, chd free. Home-made teas. Hot soup and home-made bread rolls also available in Feb/March. 2021: Sat 27, Sun 28 Feb. Visits also by arrangement Feb to Sept for groups of 5 to 20.**
Organically managed small walled cottage garden with year-round interest. Rare and unusual plants, many grown from seed. Formal box parterre herb garden, courtyard garden, herbaceous borders,

woodland garden, small wildlife pond, greenhouse, vegetable and fruit garden. Display of alpines. Collection of Galanthus (Snowdrops.) Recycled materials used to make quirky garden ornaments. Restored Victorian outhouse functions as a garden office and houses a collection of old garden tools and ephemera.

✻ ☕

59 ◆ WHATTON HOUSE
Long Whatton, Loughborough, LE12 5BG. Crawshaw Family, 01509 431193, hello@whattonhouse.co.uk, www.whattonhouse.co.uk. *4m NE of Loughborough. On A6 between Hathern & Kegworth; 2½m SE of M1J24.* **For NGS: Sun 17 May (9.30-5). Adm £5, chd free. Home-made teas. For other opening times and information, please phone, email or visit garden website.**
Come explore our tranquil gardens. Often described by visitors as a hidden gem, this 15 acre C19 Country House garden is a relaxing experience for all the family. Listen to the birds, and enjoy walking through the many fine trees, spring bulbs and shrubs, large herbaceous border, traditional rose garden, ornamental ponds and lawns. We are available for group bookings and hope to have a new tea room up and running during the 2020 season, which will be a wonderful events venue. Gravel paths.

♿ 🐄 ✻ 🚗 ☕

60 THE WHITE HOUSE FARM
Ingarsby, nr Houghton-on-the-Hill, LE7 9JD. Pam & Richard Smith, 0116 259 5448, Pamsmithtwhf@aol.com. *7m E of Leicester. 12m W of Uppingham. Take A47 from Leicester through Houghton-on-the-Hill towards Uppingham. 1m after Houghton, turn L (signed Tilton). After 1m turn L (signed Ingarsby), garden is 1m further on.* **Visits by arrangement May to Sept for groups of 20+. Adm £5, chd free. Home-made teas.**

Former Georgian farm in 2 acres of country garden. Beautiful views. Box, yew & beech hedges divide a cottage garden of gaily coloured perennials and roses; a formal herb garden; a pergola draped with climbing plants; an old courtyard with roses, shrubs & trees. Herbaceous borders lead to pools with water lilies & informal cascade. Orchard, wild garden and lake. Home for lots of wildlife.

GROUP OPENING
61 WIGSTON GARDENS
Wigston, LE18. Zoe Lewin. *Just south of Leicester off A5199.* **Sat 4, Sun 5 July (11-5). Combined adm with 28 Gladstone Street £5, chd free. Home-made teas at 7 Little Dale and 40 Rolleston Road.**

NEW 2A HOMESTEAD DRIVE
Mrs Sheila Bolton.

7 LITTLE DALE
Zoe Lewin & Neil Garner, www.facebook.com/zoes opengarden.

40 ROLLESTON ROAD
Jenni & Glen Proudman, www.facebook.com/Rolleston-Road-Garden-2302334216523185/.

Wigston Gardens consists of 4 relatively small gardens all within a 2 mile radius of each other. There is something different to see at each garden from traditional and formal to a taste of the exotic via wildflowers, upcycling and interesting artefacts! A couple of the gardens are within walking distance of one another but you will need to travel by car to visit all of the gardens in the group or it will make for quite a long walk and you'll need your comfy shoes.

GROUP OPENING
62 WILLOUGHBY GARDENS
Willoughby Waterleys, LE8 6UD. *9m S of Leicester. From A426 heading N turn R at Dunton Bassett lights. Follow signs to Willoughby. From Blaby follow signs to Countesthorpe. 2m S to Willoughby.* **Sun 12 July (11-5). Combined adm £5, chd free. Light refreshments in the Village Hall.**

2 CHURCH FARM LANE
Valerie & Peter Connelly.

FARMWAY
Eileen Spencer, 01162 478321, eileenfarmway9@msn.com. **Visits also by arrangement June to Aug for groups of up to 20. Please book at least 7 days in advance.**

HIGH MEADOW
Phil & Eva Day.

JOHN'S WOOD
John & Jill Harris.

KAPALUA
Richard & Linda Love.

3 ORCHARD ROAD
Diane Brearley.

NEW 3 YEW TREE CLOSE
Emma Clanfield.

Willoughby Waterleys lies in the South Leicestershire countryside. The Norman Church will be open, hosting a film of the local bird population filmed by a local resident. 7 gardens will be open. John's Wood is a 1½ acre nature reserve planted to encourage wildlife. 2 Church Farm Lane has been professionally designed with many interesting features. Farmway is a plant lovers garden with many unusual plants in colour themed borders. High Meadow has been evolving over 10yrs. Incl mixed planting and ornamental vegetable garden. 3 Orchard Road is a small garden packed with interest. Kapalua has an interesting planting design incorporating views of open countryside. 3 Yew Tree Close is a wrap around garden that naturally creates a series of rooms with cottage garden style borders. Willoughby embroidery on display in village hall. 30mins film of local wildlife in the church.

GROUP OPENING
63 WING GARDENS
Wing, Oakham, LE15 8SA. *2m S of Rutland Water. Off A6003 between Oakham & Uppingham.* **Sun 14 June (11-5). Combined adm £5, chd free. Home-made teas in Wing Village Hall.**

16 CHURCH STREET
Mr & Mrs Mick & Mary Rodgers.

DOVE COTTAGE
Mr & Mrs David & Alison Seviour.

STONECROP HOUSE
Mr & Mrs Matthew & Nicky Lyttelton, nicky@lytt.myzen.co.uk. **Visits also by arrangement.**

TOWNSEND HOUSE
David & Jeffy Wood.

Four very different gardens in pretty stone village of Wing with medieval church and turf maze. For map and directions start visit at Townsend House opp Village Hall. Each planted in traditional cottage garden style but with the distinctive touch of their individual owners, the larger with mature trees and lawns, and all with mixed borders of shrubs, perennials and grasses, roses, fruit trees and vegetable and herb gardens. Sizes range from the largest, Stonecrop House (with stunning wildflower meadow), cottage gardens at Dove Cottage and Townsend House, to the very small at 16 Church Street. The latter, with panoramic views over the Rutland countryside from sitting areas, along with Dove Cottage both have Open Studios displaying work by the garden owners. Partial wheelchair access to some gardens.

64 15 THE WOODCROFT
Diseworth, Derby, DE74 2QT. Nick & Sue Hollick. *The Woodcroft is off The Green, parking on The Woodcroft.* **Sun 28 June (11-5). Adm £4, chd free. Home-made teas.**

⅓ acre garden developed over 39 years with mature choice trees and shrubs, old and modern shrub roses, ferns, wildlife area and mixed herbaceous borders, planted with a garden designers eye with plantsmans passion.

OPENING DATES

All entries subject to change. For latest information check www.ngs.org.uk
Map locator numbers are shown to the right of each garden name.

February

Snowdrop Festival

Sunday 16th
Sedgebrook Manor 40

Sunday 23rd
Ashfield House 1

April

Saturday 4th
◆ Burghley House Private South Gardens 5

Sunday 5th
◆ Burghley House Private South Gardens 5
Woodlands 52

Thursday 9th
◆ Grimsthorpe Castle 15

Friday 10th
◆ Easton Walled Gardens 9

Monday 13th
Firsby Manor 10

Saturday 18th
NEW Springfields Festival Gardens 44

Sunday 19th
The Old Rectory 32
NEW Springfields Festival Gardens 44

Saturday 25th
Marigold Cottage 28

Sunday 26th
◆ Goltho House 13
Marigold Cottage 28

May

Sunday 3rd
Dunholme Lodge 8
Woodlands 52

Sunday 10th
Cantello Cottage 6
NEW Fydell House 12
66 Spilsby Road 42

Saturday 16th
The Poplars 36
Willoughby Road Allotments 50

Sunday 17th
The Old Rectory 32

Saturday 23rd
Marigold Cottage 28
Oasis Garden - Your Place 31

Sunday 24th
Marigold Cottage 28
Oasis Garden - Your Place 31
Pottertons Nursery 37

Monday 25th
Firsby Manor 10

June

Saturday 6th
NEW Kings Hill Lodge 22

Sunday 7th
Ludney House Farm 26
Manor Farm 27
The Old Vicarage 33
Old White House 34
Springfield 43
Woodlands 52

Wednesday 10th
◆ Grimsthorpe Castle 15

Sunday 14th
Auburn Hall 3
Inner Lodge 21
Little Ponton Hall 23
West Syke 45
NEW White House Farm 48

Saturday 20th
Marigold Cottage 28

Sunday 21st
Little Ponton Hall 23
Marigold Cottage 28
Shangrila 41

Sunday 28th
Aswarby Park 2
Dunholme Lodge 8
Gosberton Gardens 14
Ludney House Farm 26
NEW Wildwood 49

July

Sunday 5th
NEW Home Farm 19
◆ Mill Farm 30
Woodlands 52

Sunday 12th
Ludney House Farm 26

Saturday 18th
Marigold Cottage 28

Sunday 19th
Ballygarth 4
Inner Lodge 21
Marigold Cottage 28

Sunday 26th
School House 38
The Secret Garden of Louth 39
NEW 6 Westgate 46
Yew Tree Farm 53

August

Every Sunday
The Secret Garden of Louth 39

Sunday 2nd
◆ Gunby Hall and Gardens 16
Woodlands 52

Sunday 9th
Cantello Cottage 6
19 Low Street 25
NEW 21 Low Street 24

Sunday 23rd
Inner Lodge 21
Willoughby Road Allotments 50

Saturday 29th
Marigold Cottage 28

Sunday 30th
Marigold Cottage 28

September

Sunday 6th
Fotherby Gardens 11
◆ Hall Farm 17

Sunday 13th
Cantello Cottage 6
NEW White House Farm 48

Wednesday 16th
◆ Doddington Hall Gardens 7

Saturday 19th
Inley Drove Farm 20

Sunday 20th
Inley Drove Farm 20

Sunday 27th
◆ Goltho House 13

October

Sunday 4th
Woodlands 52

By Arrangement

Arrange a personalised garden visit with your club, or group of friends, on a date to suit you. See individual garden entries for full details.

Ashfield House 1
Aswarby Park 2
Auburn Hall 3
Ballygarth 4
23 Handley Street 18
Inley Drove Farm 20
Little Ponton Hall 23
Ludney House Farm 26
Manor Farm 27
Marigold Cottage 28
Mere House 29
The Old Rectory 32
The Old Vicarage 33
Overbeck 35
School House 38
The Secret Garden of Louth 39
West Syke 45
NEW 6 Westgate 46
NEW Westholme 47
NEW White House Farm 48
Willow Cottage 51
Woodlands 52

THE GARDENS

❶ ASHFIELD HOUSE

Lincoln Road, Branston, Lincoln, LN4 1NS. John & Judi Tinsley, 07977 505682, john@tinsleyfarms.co.uk. *3m S of Lincoln on B1188. Northern outskirts of Branston on B1188 Lincoln Rd. Signed 'Tinsley Farms - Ashfield'. Near bus stop, follow signs down drive.* **Sun 23 Feb (10.30-3). Adm £4, chd free. Home-made teas. Visits also by arrangement Feb to Oct for groups of 10 to 30.**
10 acre garden with sweeping lawns constructed around a planting of trees and shrubs. The main feature in the spring is the collection of some 110 flowering cherries of 40 different varieties along with massed plantings of spring flowering bulbs. We recently planted a magnolia collection in a newly constructed woodland garden. In the autumn the colours can be amazing. Fairly level garden. Grass paths.

The Secret Garden of Louth

❷ ASWARBY PARK

Aswarby, Sleaford, NG34 8SD. Mr & Mrs George Playne, 01529 455222/07770 721646, cgp@playne.co.uk, www.aswarbyestate.co.uk. *5m S of Sleaford on A15. Take signs to Aswarby. Entrance is straight ahead by Church through black gates.* **Sun 28 June (1-4). Adm £5, chd free. Home-made teas at Aswarby Park. Visits also by arrangement Apr to Sept for groups of 10 to 30.**
Formal and woodland garden in a parkland setting of approx 20 acres. Yew Trees form a backdrop to borders and lawns surrounding the house which is a converted stable block. Walled garden contains a greenhouse with a Muscat vine, which is over 300 years old. Large display of daffodils, snowdrops and climbing roses in season. Partial wheelchair access on gravel paths and drives.

❸ AUBOURN HALL

Harmston Road, Aubourn, Lincoln, LN5 9DZ. Mr & Mrs Christopher Nevile, 01522 788224, becky@aubournhall.co.uk, www.aubournhall.co.uk. *7m SW of Lincoln. Signed off A607 at Harmston & off A46 at Thorpe on the Hill.* **Sun 14 June (10-**

5). **Adm £5.50, chd free. Light refreshments. Visits also by arrangement Apr to Oct.**
Approx 9 acres. Lawns, mature trees, shrubs, roses, mixed borders, rose garden, large prairie and topiary garden, spring bulbs, woodland walk and ponds. C11 church adjoining. Access to garden is fairly flat and smooth. Depending on weather some areas may be inaccessible to wheelchairs. Parking in field not on tarmac.

❹ BALLYGARTH

Post Office Lane, Whitton, Scunthorpe, DN15 9LF. Joanne & Adrian Davey, 07871 882339, joanne.davey1971@gmail.com. *From Scunthorpe on A1077 follow signs to West Halton. Through West Halton approx 3m to Whitton. Follow signs for parking at Village Hall.* **Sun 19 July (11-4). Adm £3.50, chd free. Visits also by arrangement June to Aug for groups of 5 to 20.**
Set in the rural village of Whitton our end terraced house has approx ⅓ acre garden with large herbaceous and grass borders and two water features. Seating areas overlooking the garden, countryside. Many home-made garden artifacts using recycled

materials incl a small folly. Everything in wood, brick and metal has been made by us. Drop off for those with limited mobility but parking is at village hall.

❺ ◆ BURGHLEY HOUSE PRIVATE SOUTH GARDENS

Stamford, PE9 3JY. Burghley House Preservation Trust, 01780 752451, burghley@burghley.co.uk, www.burghley.co.uk. *1m E of Stamford. From Stamford follow signs to Burghley via B1443.* **For NGS: Sat 4, Sun 5 Apr (11-3.30). Adm £5, chd £3. For other opening times and information, please phone, email or visit garden website.**
On 4 and 5 April the Private South Gardens at Burghley House will open for the NGS with spectacular spring bulbs in park like setting with magnificent trees and the opportunity to enjoy Capability Brown's famous lake and summerhouse. Entry to the Private South Gardens via Orangery. The Garden of Surprises, Sculpture Garden and House are open as normal. (Regular adm prices apply). Fine Food Market. Gravel paths.

Woodlands

6 CANTELLO COTTAGE

56 High Street, Heighington, Lincoln, LN4 1JS. Robert & Gillian How. *4m SE of Lincoln. From Lincoln take B1188 to Branston. At furthest end of village turn L onto Moor Lane, L at x-roads, 3rd L in Heighington.* **Sun 10 May, Sun 9 Aug, Sun 13 Sept (10.30-4.30). Adm £3, chd free. Home-made teas.**
C18 Grade II listed cottage. Garden developed from a blank canvas. Twenty-one foot original stone-lined well with wrought iron cover. Yew tree cut in heart shape. Mixed perennials. Pergolas with clematis, roses and other climbers. Seating areas for refreshments. Craft garden room open with plants for sale. Gravel paths and some steps.

7 ◆ DODDINGTON HALL GARDENS

Doddington, Lincoln, LN6 4RU. Claire & James Birch, 01522 694308, info@doddingtonhall.com, www.doddingtonhall.com. *5m W of Lincoln on B1190. Signed from the A46 Newark to Lincoln Rd. Also from the A57 between the A1 & Lincoln. Use postcode LN6 4RU for sat nav.* **For NGS: Wed 16 Sept (11-4.30). Adm £7.50, chd £3.50. Light refreshments. For other opening times and information, please phone, email or visit garden website.**
5 acres of romantic walled and wild gardens. Naturalised autumn crocus and colchicums, cyclamen, shrubs, grasses, roses and late flowering perennials. Turf maze and ancient chestnut trees. Fully productive working walled kitchen garden with pleached, espaliered and fan-trained fruit trees, dahlias, herbs and plants for butterflies and bees. Doddington Cafe, Restaurant & Coffee Shop, serving hot and cold drinks, cream teas and lunch. Wheelchair access possible via gravel paths. Ramps also in use. Access map available from the Gatehouse.

8 DUNHOLME LODGE

Dunholme, Lincoln, LN2 3QA. Hugh & Lesley Wykes. *4m NE of Lincoln. Turn off A46 towards Welton at hand car wash garage. After ½m turn L up long private road. Garden at top.* **Sun 3 May (11-5). Light refreshments. Sun 28 June (11-5). Home-made teas. Adm £4, chd free.**
3 acre garden. Spring bulb area, shrub borders, fern garden, natural pond, wild flower area, orchard and vegetable garden. RAF Dunholme Lodge Museum and War Memorial in the grounds Lincoln Ukulele Band performances on both open days. Most areas wheelchair accessible but some loose stone and gravel.

9 ◆ EASTON WALLED GARDENS

Easton, NG33 5AP. Sir Fred & Lady Cholmeley, 01476 530063, info@eastonwalledgardens.co.uk, www.visiteaston.co.uk. *7m S of Grantham. 1m from A1, off B6403.* **For NGS: Fri 10 Apr (11-4). Adm £7.70, chd £3.50. Light refreshments & lunches. For other opening times and information, please phone, email or visit garden website.**
A 400-year-old, restored, 12 acre garden set in the heart of Lincolnshire. Home to snowdrops, sweet peas, roses and meadows. The tearoom serves delicious light lunches and cream teas and there is a well-stocked gift shop and plants for sale. Other highlights include a turf maze, swing, yew tunnel and bird hide. Regional Finalist, The English Garden's The Nation's Favourite Gardens 2019. Regret no wheelchair access to lower gardens but tearoom, shop and upper gardens all accessible.

10 FIRSBY MANOR

Firsby, Spilsby, PE23 5QJ. David & Gill Boldy. *5m E of Spilsby. From Spilsby take B1195 to Wainfleet all Saints. In Firsby, turn R into Fendyke Rd. Firsby Manor is 0.8m along lane on L.* **Mon 13 Apr, Mon 25 May (1-4.30). Adm £3, chd free. Home-made teas.**

Firsby Manor is a lovely garden which has been developed to provide peace and pleasure for humans as well as a restful haven for wildlife. Snowdrops appear in February, followed by over a hundred daffodil cultivars in April. By June the garden is full of cottage garden perennials. Partial wheelchair access due to large areas of shingle and uneven ground and no toilet access.

GROUP OPENING

⑪ FOTHERBY GARDENS
Peppin Lane, Fotherby, Louth, LN11 0UW. *2m N of Louth on A16 signed Fotherby. Limited parking on Peppin Lane where signed. Further space in village but please park considerately. Ltd space for B Badge holders at each site. Free taxi service between Woodlands & Nut Tree Farm.* Sun 6 Sept (11-5). Combined adm £5, chd free. Home-made teas at Woodlands.

NUT TREE FARM
Tim & Judith Hunter.

SHEPHERDS HEY
Barbara Chester.

WOODLANDS
Ann & Bob Armstrong.
(See separate entry)

Start your visit at Shepherds Hey, a small garden packed with unusual and interesting perennials. Its open frontage gives a warm welcome, with a small pond, terraced border and steep bank side to a stream. The rear garden, with colour themed borders, takes advantage of the panoramic views over open countryside. 350yds along Peppin Lane is Woodlands, a lovely mature woodland garden with many unusual plants set against a backdrop of an ever changing tapestry of greenery. A peaceful garden where wildlife thrives. The front garden is a crevice area of sand for alpine plants. There is a Plant Heritage collection of Codonopsis and the nursery, featured in RHS Plantfinder, gives visitors the opportunity to purchase plants seen in the garden. An award winning professional artist's studio/gallery is also open. Complete your visit at Nut Tree Farm. The garden, established in 2007, is over an acre and enjoys stunning views of Lincolnshire Wolds. A sweeping herbaceous border frames the lawn and a double wall,

planted with seasonal annuals, surrounds the house. From the raised terrace a rill runs to the large pond. There is also a raised brick edged vegetable garden. Surrounding the garden are fields with a flock of pedigree Hampshire Down sheep and a small herd of Lincoln Red cattle. Local honey (Nut Tree Farm produced) for sale. Partial access at each garden.

⑫ NEW FYDELL HOUSE
South Square, Boston, PE21 6HU. Boston Preservation Trust, www.bostonpreservationtrust.com/fydell-garden.html. *Central Boston down South Street. Through the Market Square, past Boots the Chemist. One way street. by Guildhall There are three car parks within 200 yards of the house. Disabled parking in council car park opposite the house.* Sun 10 May (1.30-5). Adm £3.50, chd free. Cream teas.
Within three original red brick walls a formal garden has been created in 1995. Yew buttresses, arbours and four parterres use dutch themes. The borders contain herbaceous plants and shrubs. The north facing border holds shade loving plants. There is a mulberry and walnut tree The astrolabe was installed in 1997. A Victorian rockery is built from slag from ironworks in Boston. Walled garden Astrolabe Parterres formal borders topiary of box and yew. Wheelchair access is along the south alleyway from the front to the back garden.

Your visits help change lives – we've donated over £17 million to Macmillan Cancer Support since 1984

---

⑬ ◆ GOLTHO HOUSE
Lincoln Road, Goltho, Wragby, Market Rasen, LN8 5NF. Mr & Mrs S Hollingworth, 01673 857768, bookings@golthogardens.com, www.golthogardens.com. *10m E of Lincoln. On A158, 1m before Wragby. Garden on L (not in Goltho Village).* For NGS: Sun 26 Apr, Sun 27 Sept (10-4). Adm £5, chd free. Light refreshments. For other opening times and information, please phone, email or visit garden website.
4½ acre garden started in 1998 but looking established with long grass walk flanked by abundantly planted herbaceous borders forming a focal point. Paths and walkway span out to other features incl nut walk, prairie border, wild flower meadow, rose garden and large pond area. Snowdrops, hellebores and shrubs for winter interest.

GROUP OPENING

⑭ GOSBERTON GARDENS
Gosberton, Spalding, PE11 4NQ. *Entering Gosberton on A152, from Spalding , Salem St on L & Mill Lane on R opp the War Memorial.* Sun 28 June (12-5). Combined adm £5, chd free. Home-made teas at Salem Street

MILLSTONE HOUSE
Mrs J Chatterton.

4 SALEM STREET
Roley and Tricia Hogben.

The village of Gosberton welcomes visitors to 2 private houses to view their gardens. We hope that everyone will find interesting features during their tour and enjoy the 2 locations. Millstone House. Colourful herbaceous borders are hidden by a privet hedge. Dappled shade creates a feeling of relaxation at the rear of the house. 4 Salem Street. Delightful secluded garden. Mixed borders including a small water feature lead to a productive vegetable plot. Cream Teas and home-made cakes. Tea, Coffee and cold drinks also available. Partial wheelchair access.

15 ◆ GRIMSTHORPE CASTLE

Grimsthorpe, Bourne, PE10 0LZ. Grimsthorpe & Drummond Castle Trust, 01778 591205, ray@grimsthorpe.co.uk, www.grimsthorpe.co.uk. *3m NW of Bourne. 8m E of A1 on A151 from Colsterworth junction. Main entrance gates indicated by brown tourist sign.* **For NGS: Thur 9 Apr, Wed 10 June (10.30-6). Adm £7, chd £3. Light refreshments at Coach House Tearoom. For other opening times and information, please phone, email or visit garden website.**

The Grade I listed gardens encompass nearly 70 acres and incl large formal lawns, fine topiary and formal hedges, ornamental and productive kitchen garden, large herbaceous borders, rose parterre and woodland walks with spring bulb displays. Visitors can explore the surrounding 3000 acre estate that encompasses a Capability Brown landscape, in addition to the tranquil and relaxing gardens. Home-made lunches, afternoon tea and cakes, open 10.30-5 Lunches 12-2.30. Gift shop, adventure playground, historic house and park trails. Gravel paths.

  ♿ 🐕 ☕

16 ◆ GUNBY HALL AND GARDENS

Spilsby, PE23 5SS. National Trust, 01754 890102, gunbyhall@nationaltrust.org.uk, www.nationaltrust.org.uk/gunby-hall. *2½m NW of Burgh-le-Marsh. 7m W of Skegness. On A158. Signed off Gunby r'about.* **For NGS: Sun 2 Aug (11-5). Adm £7, chd £4. Light refreshments in Gunby tea-room. For other opening times and information, please phone, email or visit garden website.**

Eight acres of formal and walled gardens. Old roses, herbaceous borders, herb garden and kitchen garden with fruit trees and vegetables. Greenhouses, carp pond and sweeping lawns. Tennyson's Haunt of Ancient Peace. House built by Sir William Massingberd in 1700. There will be plant sales, trade and craft stalls and free guided garden walks throughout the day. Wheelchair access in gardens and with Gunby's dedicated wheelchair on ground floor of house.

♿ 🐕 ❀ 🛏 ☕

17 ◆ HALL FARM

Harpswell, Gainsborough, DN21 5UU. Pam & Mark Tatam, 01427 668412, pam.tatam@gmail.com, www.hall-farm.co.uk. *7m E of Gainsborough. On A631, 1½m W of Caenby Corner.* **For NGS: Sun 6 Sept (1-5). Adm £4, chd free. Light refreshments. For other opening times and information, please phone, email or visit garden website.**

The 3 acre garden encompasses formal and informal areas, a sunken garden, a courtyard with rill, a walled Mediterranean garden, double herbaceous borders for late summer, lawns, bog garden, giant chess set, and a flower and grass meadow. It is a short walk to the medieval moat, which surrounds over an acre of wild semi-woodland garden with picnic table, benches and 'beach'. Free seed collecting on Sun 6th Sept. Most of garden suitable for wheelchairs.

♿ 🦮 🐕 ❀ 🚗 ☕

18 23 HANDLEY STREET

Heckington, nr Sleaford, NG34 9RZ. Stephen & Hazel Donnison, 01529 460097, donno5260@gmail.com. *A17 from Sleaford, turn R into Heckington. Follow rd to the Green. L, follow rd past Church, R into Cameron St. At end of this rd L into Handley St.* **Visits by arrangement June to Aug for groups of up to 20. Adm £3, chd free. Home-made teas.**

Compact, quirky garden, large fish pond. Further 5 small wildlife ponds. Small wooded area and Jurassic style garden with Tree ferns. Densely planted flower borders featuring Penstemons. Large patio with seating.

❀ ☕

Your visits help change lives – your generosity has supported unpaid carers through donations to Carers Trust totalling over £4 million since 1996

19 **NEW** HOME FARM

Little Casterton Road, Ryhall, Stamford, PE9 4HA. Steve & Karen Bourne. *1½m N of Stamford. Off A6121 at mini r'about, towards Little Casterton.* **Sun 5 July (11-4). Adm £4, chd free. Home-made teas.**

Nine acres including formal garden with herbaceous, rose and shrub borders. Recent additions include a Mediterranean border and a Rugosa rose hedge interspersed with striking Tibetan cherry trees. Raised vegetable beds, asparagus and rhubarb beds in front of the ha-ha. Fruit cage with soft fruit, orchard of old local varieties of top fruit. Woodland walk.

❀ ☕

20 INLEY DROVE FARM

Inley Drove, Sutton St James, Spalding, PE12 0LX. Francis & Maisie Pryor, 01406 540088, maisietaylor7@gmail.com, www.pryorfrancis.wordpress.com. *Just off rd from Sutton St James to Sutton St Edmund. 2m S of Sutton St James. Look for yellow NGS signs on double bend.* **Sat 19, Sun 20 Sept (11-4). Adm £4.50, chd free. Home-made teas. Visits also by arrangement Apr to July for groups of 10 to 30. Restricted parking.**

Over 3 acres of Fenland garden and meadow plus 6½ acre wood developed over 20yrs. Garden planted for colour, scent and wildlife. Double mixed borders and less formal flower gardens all framed by hornbeam hedges. Unusual shrubs and trees, incl fine stand of Black Poplars, vegetable garden, woodland walks and orchard. Disabled WC outside. Some gravel and a few steps but mostly flat grass.

♿ ❀ ☕

21 INNER LODGE

Somerby, Gainsborough, DN21 3HG. Paul & Karen Graves. *On A631 Gainsborough to Grimsby rd. From Gainsborough, track on R at Very end of the dual carriageway, follow ½m track to find marked parking areas in small woodland glades.* **Sun 14 June, Sun 19 July, Sun 23 Aug (11-4). Adm £3, chd free. Home-made teas. Home-made cakes by Karen (Chocolate Cake a must) Hot & Cold Drinks.**

Set in woodland our colourful cottage garden of approx 1 acre was started in 2013 and is still developing. We have mixed borders, shrubs, fernery, several quirky features, and small secret garden. Plenty of seating around the garden but regret it is not suitable for wheelchairs. Plants and Craft sales on all the days.

22 NEW KINGS HILL LODGE
Gorse Hill Lane, Caythorpe, Grantham, NG32 3DY. Tim & Carol Almond. *Off the A607 approx 10m from Grantham towards Lincoln. From S turn L into Church Lane (R from N) at Xrds. Pass church on R, after 100m turn R onto Waterloo Road. Then sharp L, drive 150m then L into Gorse Hill Lane with Lodge on R.* Sat 6 June (12.30-5). Adm £4, chd free. Home-made teas.
A new garden of about 1000 sq metres developed over 6 years from 800 sq metres of neglected lawn and 200 sq metres overgrown, boggy shrubbery. Now consists of 250 sq metres of managed lawn with the remainder put to over 20 mixed herbaceous beds, 7 large raised vegetable beds, cedar greenhouse, 4 sitting out areas, water feature with 15 different climbing roses around the house. There is a circular path around the house which is wide enough for a wheelchair with care. Wide-wheeled chairs would be able to use the lawn.

23 LITTLE PONTON HALL
Grantham, NG33 5BS. Bianca & George McCorquodale, 01476 530216, george@ stokerochfordestate.co.uk, www. littlepontonhallgardens.org.uk. *2m S of Grantham. ½m E of A1 at S end of Grantham bypass. Disabled parking.* Sun 14, Sun 21 June (11-4). Adm £5, chd free. Home-made teas. Visits also by arrangement in June. (15 to 19 June only).
3 to 4 acre garden. River walk. Spacious lawns with cedar tree over 200 years old. Formal walled kitchen garden and listed dovecote, with herb garden. Victorian greenhouses with many plants from exotic locations. Wheelchair access on hard surfaces, unsuitable on grass. Disabled WC.

24 NEW 21 LOW STREET
Winterton, Scunthorpe, DN15 9RT. Brian Dale & Nigel Bradford. *Garden is in the centre of the village & parking is limited. A short walk from the parking area near*

Mill Farm

the church & Coop. Sun 9 Aug (11-5). Combined adm with 19 Low Street £5, chd free. Light refreshments at the Church.
The garden is approximately half an acre and when we moved into the house, five years ago, it mainly consisted of shrubs that had been allowed free rein. We have enlarged the existing beds and created new beds and borders which are now mostly planted with herbaceous perennials. There is a large area given over to vegetables and soft fruits which is now producing successfully. Wheelchair access to the first area of the garden approximately 150sq metres.

25 19 LOW STREET
Winterton, DN15 9RT. Jane & Allan Scorer. *Winterton is on A1077 4m N of Scunthorpe & 7m S of the Humber Bridge. Garden signed from A1077. Parking on Low Street & nearby Market Place (2 mins walk from Low Street).* Sun 9 Aug (11-5). Combined adm with 21 Low Street £5, chd free. Light refreshments at All Saints Church, Churchside, Winterton. Max 5 min walk to church.
A half acre garden with an emphasis on dense sub tropical planting,

although there are other distinct areas too, including an arid bed, greenhouses, an extensive variety of pots and planters, ornamental pond, wildlife pond set in informal area, soft fruit, cut flower garden and seating areas. Wheelchair is difficult but not impossible as areas of the garden have bark or gravel paths.

26 LUDNEY HOUSE FARM
Ludney, Louth, LN11 7JU. Jayne Bullas, 07733 018710, jayne@theoldgatehouse.com. *Between Grainthorpe & Conisholme.* Sun 7, Sun 28 June, Sun 12 July (1.30-4). Adm £6.50, chd free. Home-made teas. incl in adm. Visits also by arrangement Apr to July for groups of 5 to 30.
A beautiful landscaped garden of several defined spaces containing formal and informal areas. There is an excellent mix of trees, shrubs, perennials ,rose garden and wild flower area which is home to the bee hives. In spring there is a nice selection of bulbs and spring flowers. There is also a new pond area , There are plenty of seats positioned around to sit and enjoy a cuppa and piece of cake! Wheelchair access to most parts.

27 MANOR FARM
Horkstow Road, South
Ferriby, Barton-upon-
Humber, DN18 6HS. Geoff &
Angela Wells, 01652 635214,
wells.farming@btinternet.com.
*3m from Barton-upon-Humber on
A1077, turn L onto B1204, opp
Village Hall.* **Sun 7 June (11-5).
Combined adm with Springfield
£5, chd free. Home-made teas.
Visits also by arrangement for
groups of 10+.**
A garden which is much praised by
visitors. Set within approx 1 acre
with mature shrubberies, herbaceous
borders, gravel garden and pergola
walk. Rose bed, white garden
and fernery. Many old trees with
preservation orders. Wildlife pond set
within a paddock.

28 MARIGOLD COTTAGE
Hotchin Road, Sutton-on-Sea,
LN12 2NP. Stephanie Lee &
John Raby, 01507 442151,
marigoldlee@btinternet.com,
www.rabylee.uk/marigold/. *16m N
of Skegness on A52. 7m E of Alford
on A1111. 3m S of Mablethorpe
on A52. Turn off A52 on High St at
Cornerhouse Cafe. Follow rd past
playing field on R. Rd turns away
from the dunes. House 2nd on L.*
**Sat 25, Sun 26 Apr, Sat 23, Sun
24 May, Sat 20, Sun 21 June,
Sat 18, Sun 19 July, Sat 29, Sun
30 Aug (2-5). Adm £3, chd free.
Home-made teas. Visits also
by arrangement May to Sept for
groups of 10+.**
Slide open the Japanese gate to
find secret paths, lanterns, a circular
window in a curved wall, water
lilies in pots and a gravel garden,
vegetable garden and propagation
area. Take the long drive to see the
sea. Back in the garden, find a seat,
enjoy the birds and bees. We face
the challenges of heavy clay and salt
ladened winds but look for unusual
plants not the humdrum for these
conditions. Most of garden accessible
to wheelchairs along flat, paved
paths.

29 MERE HOUSE
Stow Road, Sturton by Stow,
Lincoln, LN1 2BZ. Nigel &
Alice Gray, 07932 442349,
alice@merehome.uk. *10m NW of
Lincoln between Sturton & Stow.
1m from centre of Sturton village
heading to Stow, house on L.*

*NB: Postcode will not bring you far
enough out of Sturton village.* **Visits
by arrangement Apr to Sept for
groups of up to 30. Adm £6, chd
free. Home-made teas. Adm incl
tea/coffee and home-made cakes.**
Approx 1½ acres of established
garden planted for the first time in
1975, redesigned in 1996. Renovated
over the last 7yrs to incl new beds
with drift planting but still incl the
formal parterre. Spring bulbs and late
summer colour are highlights. There
is also a cutting garden, pleached
hedges, vegetable garden and
orchard. Work in progress incl a new
garden project and long herbaceous
border. There is the highly acclaimed
Cross Keys pub in Stow Village that
does a very good lunch. The garden
is wheelchair accessible on grass.

30 ♦ MILL FARM
Caistor Road, Grasby, Caistor,
DN38 6AQ. Mike & Helen
Boothman, 01652 628424,
boothmanhelen@gmail.com,
www.millfarmgarden.co.uk. *3m
NW of Caistor on A1084. Between
Brigg & Caistor. From Cross Keys
pub towards Caistor for approx
200yds. Do not go into Grasby
village.* **For NGS: Sun 5 July (11-4).
Adm £4, chd free. Home-made
teas. For other opening times and
information, please phone, email or
visit garden website.**
A much loved garden by visitors,
which continues to be developed
and maintained to a high standard by
the owners. Over 3 acres of garden
with many diverse areas. Formal
frontage with shrubs and trees. The
rear is a plantsman haven with a
peony and rose garden, specimen
trees, vegetable area, old windmill
adapted into a fernery, alpine house
and shade house with a variety of
shade loving plants. Herbaceous
beds with different grasses and hardy
perennials. Small nursery on site with
home grown plants available. Open
by arrangement for groups. Mainly
grass, but with some gravelled areas.

Kings Hill Lodge

31 OASIS GARDEN - YOUR PLACE

Wellington Street, Grimsby, DN32 7JP. Grimsby Neighbourhood Church, www.yourplacegrimsby.com. *Enter Grimsby (M180) over flyover, along Cleethorpes Rd. Turn R into Victor St, Turn L into Wellington St. Your Place is on the R on junction of Wellington St & Weelsby St.* **Sat 23, Sun 24 May (11-3). Adm £3, chd free. Light refreshments.**
The multi award winning Oasis Garden, Your Place, recently described by the RHS as the 'Most inspirational garden in the six counties of the East Midlands', is approximately 1½ acres and nestles in the heart of Great Grimsby's East Marsh Community. A working garden producing 15k plants per year, grown by local volunteers of all ages and abilities. Lawns, fruit, vegetable, perennial and annual beds.

32 THE OLD RECTORY

Church Lane, East Keal, Spilsby, PE23 4AT. Mrs Ruth Ward, 01790 752477, rfjward@btinternet.com. *2m SW of Spilsby. Off A16. Turn into Church Lane by PO.* **Sun 19 Apr, Sun 17 May (2-4.30). Adm £3.50, chd free. Home-made teas. Visits also by arrangement Mar to Oct.**
Beautifully situated, with fine views, rambling cottage garden on different levels falling naturally into separate areas, with changing effects and atmosphere. Steps, paths and vistas to lead you on, seats well placed for appreciating special views or relaxing and enjoying the peace. Dry border, vegetable garden, orchard, woodland walk, wild flower meadow. Yr-round interest. Welcoming to wildlife. Parial wheelchair access

33 THE OLD VICARAGE

Low Road, Holbeach Hurn, PE12 8JN. Mrs Liz Dixon-Spain, 01406 424148, lizdixonspain@gmail.com. *2m NE of Holbeach. Turn off A17 N to Holbeach Hurn, past post box in middle of village, 1st R at war memorial into Low Rd. Old Vicarage is on R approx 400yds Parking in grass paddock.* **Sun 7 June (1-5). Combined adm with Old White House £5, chd free. Home-made teas at Old White House. Visits also by arrangement Apr to Sept**
for groups of up to 30.
2 acres of garden with 150yr old tulip, plane and beech trees: borders of shrubs, roses, herbaceous plants. Shrub roses and herb garden in old paddock area, surrounded by informal areas with pond and bog garden, wild flowers, grasses and bulbs. Small fruit and vegetable gardens. Kids love exploring winding paths through the wilder areas. Garden is managed environmentally. Fun for kids! Gravel drive, some paths, mostly grass access.

34 OLD WHITE HOUSE

Baileys Lane, Holbeach Hurn, PE12 8JP. Mrs A Worth. *2m N of Holbeach. Turn off A17 N to Holbeach Hurn, follow signs to village, cont through, turn R after Rose & Crown pub at Baileys Lane.* **Sun 7 June (12-5). Combined adm with The Old Vicarage £5, chd free.**
1½ acres of mature garden, featuring herbaceous borders, roses, patterned garden, herb garden and walled kitchen garden. Large catalpa, tulip tree that flowers, ginko and other specimen trees. Flat surfaces, some steps, wheelchair access to all areas without using steps.

35 OVERBECK

46 Main Street, Scothern, LN2 2UW. John & Joyce Good, 01673 862200, jandjgood@btinternet.com. *4m E of Lincoln. Scothern signed from A46 at Dunholme & A158 at Sudbrooke. Overbeck is E end of Main St.* **Visits by arrangement May to July for groups of 10+. Adm £4, chd free. Light refreshments.**
Situated in an attractive village this approx ⅔ acre garden is a haven for wildlife. Long herbaceous borders and colour themed island beds with some unusual perennials. Hosta border, gravel bed with grasses, fernery, interesting range of trees, numerous shrubs, small stumpery, climbers including roses and clematis, recently developed parterre and large prolific vegetable and fruit area.

36 THE POPLARS

Church Lane, Frithville, Boston, PE22 7ET. James & Zoe Mitchell. *3m N of Boston. 1m S of Frithville. Unclassified rd. On W side of West Fen Drain. Marked on good maps.*
Sat 16 May (1-5). Adm £4, chd free. Light refreshments. Tea, coffee & cake.
Previously used as paddock and later as a pig farm, our garden has had a variety of uses over the years. Work on the garden in its current form began in 2010 after the site was completely cleared of rubbish, and the main house renovated. The garden today has a mix of formal spaces and semi-mature borders, and features a large ornamental pond with a rock waterfall and reed bed.

37 POTTERTONS NURSERY

Moortown Road, Nettleton, Caistor, LN7 6HX. Rob & Jackie Potterton, www.pottertons.co.uk. *1m W of Nettleton. From A46 at Nettleton turn onto B1205 (Moortown). Nursery 1¼m, turn by edge of wood.* **Sun 24 May (9-5). Adm £3, chd free. Cream teas. We will be offering excellent cream teas and home-made light refreshments & drinks.**
5 acre garden of alpine rockeries, stream and waterfall, raised beds, troughs, tufa bed, crevice garden, woodland beds, extensively planted with alpines, bulbs and woodland plants, which will be at their flowering peak. On the day we have invited Plant Hunters Fairs to the garden, with 10 specialist nurseries offering a range incl Acers, shrubs, alpines, rare perennials and cottage garden plants. Access mostly on mixed grass surfaces.

38 SCHOOL HOUSE

Market Rasen Road, Holton-le-Moor, Market Rasen, LN7 6AE. Chris & Rosemary Brown, 01673 828657, 67chris.47holton@gmail.com. *15m N of Lincoln. A46 towards Caistor, take B1434 to Holton le Moor. School House on R next to village (Moot) hall.* **Sun 26 July (1-5). Adm £4, chd free. Light refreshments. Adm incl tea/coffee and biscuits. Visits also by arrangement June to Aug for groups of 5 to 20.**
An all around the house garden, ranging from shaded early area to summer and autumn flowering areas. Central gravel garden with alliums followed by agapanthus and supplemented with grasses. Designed and built by Chris Brown a now retired garden designer.

47 NEW **WESTHOLME**
Millgate, Whaplode,
Spalding, PE12 6RT. Nicola
& Mark Hill, 01406 373694,
nicolawestholme@gmail.com.
*From A151 turn down Churchgate
beside JR Cycles in village of
Whaplode. Garden on R approx
½ m down this road which becomes
Millgate as you exit the village.* **Visits
by arrangement May & June for
groups of up to 20. Home-made
teas.**
2.5 acre site of which approximately 1
acre is gardened. The rest is paddock
leading via mown paths to a small
wood. The garden wraps around the
house and includes mixed borders,
a formal pond, hidden, small wildlife
pond, shade border, orchard and
vegetable garden in which both
vegetables and cut flowers are grown.
The garden is cared for with wildlife
in mind. Access is over granite chip
driveway and lawn/grass paths. The
site is flat. Some paths are narrow.

48 NEW **WHITE HOUSE FARM**
Metheringham Fen, Lincoln,
LN4 3AW. Bruce & Lisa
Spencer-Knott, 07775 904174,
Bruceysk@me.com. *From
Metheringham turn on to Fen Lane
opposite the Fire Station & proceed
for approx 4m to our property on
the L.* **Sun 14 June, Sun 13 Sept
(11-5). Adm £5, chd free. Light
refreshments. Visits also by
arrangement June to Sept.**
White House Farm is a stunning
Georgian manor and idyllic focal point
for the Spencer-Knott's beautiful
English garden. A sensitive fusion of
French renaissance and quintessential
English naturalistic garden design
inspired this elegant, serene and
restorative space. Teas, coffees,
home-made cakes and soft drinks.
Posies of cut flowers. Mixture of hard
paving and lawn.

The Poplars

49 NEW **WILDWOOD**
Aisby, Grantham, NG32 3NE.
Paul & Joy King. *Halfway between
Grantham and Sleaford. Off A52 for
Dembelby or Oasby. Follow signs to
Aisby. In the village take a track with
a footpath sign on the west side of
the green opposite the village hall.
There is plenty of parking on site.*
**Sun 28 June (11-5). Adm £4, chd
free. Home-made teas.**
Created over 9 yrs from fields and
existing hard landscaping. Windbreaks
protect the garden which is heavy clay,
wet in winter, dry in summer. There
are many borders (some sloping)
planted with unusual and rare trees,
shrubs, climbers, perennials, bulbs
and alpines. This is a wildlife-friendly
garden with a bee orchid patch and
fruit and vegetable areas. Grass,
gravel and paving provide access. A
modern glass Huf Haus, the only one
in Lincolnshire, and possibly the only
one in the country open as part of the
NGS scheme. There are over 250 Huf
Haus in the UK, most in the south.
Most paths are grass or gravel.

ALLOTMENTS

50 **WILLOUGHBY ROAD
ALLOTMENTS**
Willoughby Road, Boston,
PE21 9HN. Willoughby Road
Allotments Association,
willoughbyroadallotments.org.uk.
*Entrance is adjacent to 109
Willoughby Road. Street Parking
only.* **Sat 16 May, Sun 23 Aug
(10.30-4). Adm £3.50, chd free.
Light refreshments.**
Set in 5 acres the allotments comprise
60 plots growing fine vegetables, fruit,

flowers and herbs. There is a small
orchard and wild flower area and a
community space adjacent. Grass paths
run along the site. Several plots will be
open to walk round. There will be a seed
and plant stall. Light refreshments are
available. Small orchard and wild flower
beds Community area with kitchen and
disabled WC. Large Polytunnel with
raised beds inside and out. Accessible
for all abilities.

51 **WILLOW COTTAGE**
Gravel Pit Lane, Burgh le
Marsh, Lincs, PE24 5DW. Bob
& Karen Ward, 01754 811450,
ward86842@gmail.com,
www.Birdsongtouringpark.com.
*6m W of Skegness. S of Gunby
r'about on A158, take 1st R signed
Bratoft & Burgh-le-Marsh. 1st
R again onto Bratoft Lane. L at
T-junction, parking on R 25yds.*
**Visits by arrangement in June
for groups of 20+. Adm £4, chd
free. Home-made teas on terrace.
Sumptuous home-made cakes,
tea in china pots.**
Amidst the hustle n bustle that
surrounds us everyday, to find a place
of peace, search indeed we may. An
oasis of calm, tranquility, nature at its
best, wildlife and fauna, altogether
here at rest. So much to discover, the
hours simply do fly by, to uplift and
refresh you, inspire you we will try! So
get a group of friends visit us and see,
you'll be delighted by ALL you'll find,
even the cake and tea. Woodland walk
and Victorian glasshouse, new prairie
border and caravan site pond walk now
open. Partial wheelchair access. For
assistance please phone ahead of visit.

**Your visits help change
lives – we are Hospice UK's
largest charitable funder
donating more than £5.5
million to support hospices
in local communities
since 1996**

Little Ponton Hall Gardens

52 WOODLANDS

Peppin Lane, Fotherby, Louth, LN11 0UW. Ann & Bob Armstrong, 01507 603586, annbobarmstrong@btinternet.com, www.woodlandsplants.co.uk. *2m N of Louth off A16 signed Fotherby. Please park on R verge opp allotments & walk approx 350 yds to garden. If full please park considerately elsewhere in the village. No parking at garden. Please do not drive beyond designated area.* **Sun 5 Apr, Sun 3 May, Sun 7 June, Sun 5 July, Sun 2 Aug (11-5); Sun 4 Oct (11-4). Adm £3, chd free. Home-made teas. Opening with Fotherby Gardens on Sun 6 Sept.** Visits also by arrangement Mar to Nov.

A lovely mature woodland garden where a multitude of unusual plants are the stars, many of which are available from the well stocked RHS listed nursery. The two new areas completed recently have developed well and this year there will be a new shrub border. Award winning professional artist's studio/gallery open to visitors. Specialist collection of Codonopsis for which Plant Heritage status has been granted. Possible to access most areas with care. We leave space for parking at the house for those who cannot manage the walk from the car park.

53 YEW TREE FARM

Westhorpe Road, Gosberton, Spalding, PE11 4EP. Robert & Claire Bailey-Scott. *Nr Spalding. Enter the village of Gosberton. Turn into Westhorpe Rd, opp The Bell Inn, cont for approx. 1½ m. Property is 3rd on R after bridge.* **Sun 26 July (11-5). Adm £4, chd free. Home-made teas.**

A lovely country garden, 1½ acres. Large herbaceous and mixed borders surround the well kept lawns. Wildlife pond with two bog gardens, woodland garden and shaded borders containing many unusual plants. A Mulberry tree forms the centre piece of one lawn. Orchard, wild flower meadows and large vegetable plot. Winner of the Daily Mail National Garden Competition 2019. Gravel driveway, some gravel paths.

Volunteers

County Organiser
Penny Snell
01932 864532
pennysnellflowers@btinternet.com

County Treasurer
John McNicholas
07785 701770
john.mcnicholas@ngs.org.uk

Publicity
Penny Snell (as above)

Booklet Co-ordinator
Sue Phipps
07771 767196
sue@suephipps.com

Booklet Distributor
Joey Clover
020 8870 8740
joey.clover@ngs.org.uk

Social Media
Sue Phipps (as above)

Alex Redfern 07976849344
alex.redfern@ngs.org.uk

Assistant County Organisers

Central London
Eveline Carn
07831 136069
evelinecbcarn@icloud.com

Clapham & surrounding area
Sue Phipps (as above)

Croydon & outer South London
Ben & Peckham Carroll
0208 777 9012
b.j.carroll@btinternet.com

Dulwich & surrounding area
Clive Pankhurst
07941 536934
alternative.ramblings@gmail.com

E London
Teresa Farnham
07761 476651
farnhamz@yahoo.co.uk

Finchley & Barnet
Debra Craighead 07415 166617
dcraighead@icloud.com

Hackney
Philip Lightowlers
020 8533 0052
plighto@gmail.com

Hampstead
Joan Arnold
020 8444 8752
joan.arnold40@gmail.com

Hampstead Garden Suburb
Caroline Broome
020 8444 2329
carosgarden@virginmedia.com

Islington
Penelope Darby Brown
020 7226 6880
penelope.darbybrown@ngs.org.uk

Gill Evansky
020 7359 2484
gevansky@gmail.com

Northwood, Pinner, Ruislip & Harefield
Hasruty Patel
07815 110050
hasruty@gmail.com

NW London
Susan Bennett & Earl Hyde
020 8883 8540
suebearlh@yahoo.co.uk

Outer NW London
James Duncan Mattoon
020 8830 7410
jamesmattoon@msn.com

Outer W London
Julia Hickman
020 8339 0931
julia.hickman@virgin.net

SE London
Janine Wookey
07711 279636
j.wookey@btinternet.com

SW London
Joey Clover (as above)

Tower Hamlets
Vivien Taylor 07903 933881
vivien.taylor@ngs.org.uk

W London, Barnes & Chiswick
Siobhan McCammon
07952 889866
siobhan.mccammon@gmail.com

f @LondonNGS

🐦 @LondonNGS

📷 @londonngs

From the tiniest to the largest, London gardens offer exceptional diversity. Hidden behind historic houses in Spitalfields are exquisite tiny gardens, while on Kingston Hill there are 9 acres of landscaped Japanese gardens.

The oldest private garden in London boasts 5 acres, while the many other historic gardens within these pages are smaller – some so tiny there is only room for a few visitors at a time – but nonetheless full of innovation, colour and horticultural excellence.

London allotments have attracted television cameras to film their productive acres, where exotic Cape gooseberries, figs, prizewinning roses and even bees all thrive thanks to the skill and enthusiasm of city gardeners.

The traditional sit comfortably with the contemporary in London – offering a feast of elegant borders, pleached hedges, topiary, gravel gardens and the cooling sound of water – while to excite the adventurous there are gardens on barges and green roofs to explore.

The season stretches from April to October, so there is nearly always a garden to visit somewhere in London. Our gardens opening this year are the beating heart of the capital just waiting to be visited and enjoyed.

LONDON GARDENS LISTED BY POSTCODE

Inner London Postcodes

E and EC London

Spitalfields Gardens E1
Lower Clapton Gardens E5
84 Lavender Grove E8
Mapledene Gardens E8
17 Greenstone Mews E11
37 Harold Road E11
Flat 2, 333 Victoria Road E9
Aldersbrook Gardens E12
12 Western Road E13
87 St Johns Road E17
46 Cheyne Avenue E18
25 Mulberry Way E18
83 Cowslip Road E18
The Charterhouse EC1
The Inner and Middle Temple Gardens EC4

N and NW London

Arlington Square Gardens N1
Barnsbury Group N1
4 Canonbury Place N1
De Beauvoir Gardens N1
91 Englefield Road N1
King Henry's Walk Garden N1
2 Lonsdale Square N1
19 St Peter's Street N1
Malvern Terrace Gardens N1
5 Northampton Park N1
131 Southgate Road N1
66 Abbots Gardens N2
12 Lauradale Road N2
24 Twyford Avenue N2
31 Hendon Avenue N3
79 Church Lane N2
7 Deansway N2
18 Park Crescent N3
7 The Grove N6
3 The Park N6
32 Highbury Place N5
19 Cholmeley Park N6
Southwood Lodge N6
5 Blackthorn Av Apartment 5 N7
9 View Road N6
33 Huddleston Road N7
1a Hungerford Road N7

20 Furlong Road N7
60 & 62 Hungerford Road N7
23 & 24b Penn Road N7
19 Coolhurst Road N8
12 Fairfield Road N8
11 Park Avenue North N8
35 Weston Park N8
12 Warner Road N8
Princes Avenue Gardens N10
55 Dukes Avenue N10
5 St Regis Close N10
25 Springfield Avenue N10
33 Wood Vale N10
9 Churston Gardens N11
Golf Course Allotments N11
9 Shortgate N12
70 Farleigh Road N16
53 Manor Road N16
15 Norcott Road N16
21 Gospatrick Road N17
36 Ashley Road N19
21 Oakleigh Park South N20
30 Mercers Road N19
24 Langton Avenue N20
20 Hillcrest N21
5 Harwood's Yard N21
1 Wades Grove N21
10 York Road N21
Railway Cottages N22
Garden of Medicinal Plants NW1
The Gable End Gardens NW1
69 Gloucester Crescent NW1
70 Gloucester Crescent NW1
The Holme NW1
98 Parkway NW1
93 Tanfield Avenue NW2
Fenton House NW3
Marie Curie Hospice Hampstead NW3
Highwood Ash NW7
48 Erskine Hill NW11
74 Willifield Way NW11
10 Wordsworth Walk NW11

SE and SW London

Garden Barge Square at Downings Roads Moorings SE1
The Garden Museum SE1
Lambeth Palace SE1
Camberwell Grove Gardens SE5
24 Grove Park SE5
226 Conisborough Crescent SE6
41 Southbrook Road SE12

Blackheath Gardens SE13
Choumert Square SE15
Lyndhurst Square Group SE15
4 Becondale Road SE19
103 and 105 Dulwich Village SE21
4 Cornflower Terrace SE22
Gardens of Court Lane SE21
38 Lovelace Road SE21
58 Cranston Road SE23
Forest Hill Gardens Group SE23
5 Burbage Road SE24
28 Ferndene Road SE24
South London Botanical Institute SE24
Cadogan Place South Garden SW1
Stoney Hill House SE26
7 Norwood Park Road SE27
Eccleston Square SW1
Chelsea Physic Garden SW3
Spencer House SW1
Brixton Water Lane Gardens SW2
31 Trelawn Road SW2
51 The Chase SW4
Royal Trinity Hospice SW4
The Hurlingham Club SW6
97 Arthur Road SW19
36 Melrose Road SW18
61 Arthur Road SW19
Paddock Allotments & Leisure Gardens SW20

W and WC London

Rooftopvegplot W1
Hyde Park Estate Gardens W2
41 Mill Hill Road W3
65 Mill Hill Road W3
Zen Garden at Japanese Buddhist Centre W3
Chiswick Mall Gardens W4
Park Road Gardens W4
10 Loris Road W6
Maggie's West London W6
27 St Peters Square W6
White Cottage W7
1 York Close W7
Edwardes Square W8
57 St Quintin Avenue W10
Arundel & Elgin Gardens W11
Arundel & Ladbroke Gardens W11
12 Lansdowne Road W11
49 Loftus Road W12

Outer London Postcodes

209 Worsley Bridge Road BR3
81 Baston Road BR2
14 Lovelace Avenue BR2
40 Greenways BR3
1 Spring Park Avenue CR0
45 Cotswold Way EN2
Oak Farm/Homestead EN2
West Lodge Park EN4
190 Barnet Road EN5
26 Normandy Avenue EN5
36 Potters Lane EN5
31 Arlington Drive HA4
4 Manningtree Road HA4
12 Haywood Close HA5
470 Pinner Road HA5
4 Ormonde Road HA6
74 Glengall Road IG8
The Watergardens KT2
7 Woodbines Avenue KT1
The Circle Garden KT3
Hampton Court Palace KT8
Berrylands Gardens KT5
15 Catherine Road KT6
Church Walk Gardens KT7
3 Elmbridge Lodge KT7
5 Pemberton Road KT8
61 Wolsey Road KT8
40 Ember Lane KT10
9 Imber Park Road KT10
40 The Crescent SM2
7 St George's Road TW1
Maggie's SM2
20 Beechwood Avenue TW9
Kew Green Gardens TW9
Trumpeters House & Sarah's Garden TW9
31 West Park Road TW9
Ormeley Lodge TW10
Petersham House TW10
Stokes House TW10
16 Links View Road TW12
Dragon's Dream UB8
Wensleydale Road Gardens, Hampton TW12
Church Gardens UB9
Swakleys Cottage 2 The Avenue UB10

OPENING DATES

All entries subject to change. For latest information check www.ngs.org.uk

February

Snowdrop Festival

Sunday 9th
7 The Grove, N6

April

Wednesday 1st
◆ Chelsea Physic Garden, SW3

Sunday 5th
Edwardes Square, W8
74 Glengall Road, IG8
7 The Grove, N6

Sunday 12th
Royal Trinity Hospice, SW4

Saturday 18th
Hyde Park Estate Gardens, W2

Sunday 19th
4 Canonbury Place, N1
20 Hillcrest, N21
Petersham House, TW10
South London Botanical Institute, SE24

Thursday 23rd
◆ Hampton Court Palace, KT8

Saturday 25th
NEW Maggie's, SM2
Maggie's West London, W6

Sunday 26th
NEW 19 Cholmeley Park, N6
19 Coolhurst Road, N8
27 St Peters Square, W6

Thursday 30th
51 The Chase, SW4

May

Sunday 3rd
51 The Chase, SW4
Malvern Terrace Gardens, N1
21 Oakleigh Park South, N20
5 St Regis Close, N10
Southwood Lodge, N6
The Watergardens, KT2
33 Wood Vale, N10

Thursday 7th
12 Lansdowne Road, W11

Friday 8th
King Henry's Walk Garden, N1

Sunday 10th
NEW 7 Deansway, N2
Eccleston Square, SW1
West Lodge Park, EN4

Saturday 16th
The Circle Garden, KT3
The Hurlingham Club, SW6
NEW Maggie's, SM2

Sunday 17th
Arundel & Elgin Gardens, W11
Arundel & Ladbroke Gardens, W11
Forest Hill Gardens Group, SE23
3 The Park, N6
Princes Avenue Gardens, N10

Monday 18th
Lambeth Palace, SE1

Saturday 23rd
Cadogan Place South Garden, SW1
16 Links View Road, TW12

Sunday 24th
61 Arthur Road, SW19
36 Ashley Road, N19
The Circle Garden, KT3
55 Dukes Avenue, N10
91 Englefield Road, N1
Kew Green Gardens, TW9
16 Links View Road, TW12
53 Manor Road, N16
36 Potters Lane, EN5

Stoney Hill House, SE26

Monday 25th
36 Ashley Road, N19

Sunday 31st
5 Burbage Road, SE24
NEW Church Walk Gardens, KT7
Dragon's Dream, UB8
12 Fairfield Road, N8
NEW 20 Furlong Road, N7
Garden Barge Square at Downings Roads Moorings, SE1
31 Hendon Avenue, N3
Kew Green Gardens, TW9
4 Ormonde Road, HA6
Royal Trinity Hospice, SW4
41 Southbrook Road, SE12
12 Warner Road, N8
12 Western Road, E13

June

Saturday 6th
Chiswick Mall Gardens, W4
Zen Garden at Japanese Buddhist Centre, W3

Sunday 7th
66 Abbots Gardens, N2
31 Arlington Drive, HA4
190 Barnet Road, EN5
Barnsbury Group, N1
Berrylands Gardens, KT5
Brixton Water Lane Gardens, SW2
Chiswick Mall Gardens, W4
Choumert Square, SE15
4 Cornflower Terrace, SE22
48 Erskine Hill, NW11
21 Gospatric Road, N17
7 The Grove, N6
1a Hungerford Road, N7
60 & 62 Hungerford Road, N7
NEW 24 Langton Avenue, N20
2 Lonsdale Square, N1
10 Loris Road, W6
Lower Clapton Gardens, E5
Mapledene Gardens, E8

Marie Curie Hospice, Hampstead, NW3
23 & 24b Penn Road, N7
7 St George's Road, TW1
Stokes House, TW10
31 Trelawn Road, SW2
NEW 333 Victoria Park Road, Flat 2, E9
31 West Park Road, TW9
White Cottage, W7
10 Wordsworth Walk, NW11
Zen Garden at Japanese Buddhist Centre, W3

Tuesday 9th
◆ Fenton House, NW3

Saturday 13th
Spitalfields Gardens, E1

Sunday 14th
Arlington Square Gardens, N1
97 Arthur Road, SW19
Blackheath Gardens, SE13
79 Church Lane, N2
40 The Crescent, SM2
De Beauvoir Gardens, N1
37 Harold Road, E11
12 Haywood Close, HA5
49 Loftus Road, W12
Lyndhurst Square Garden Group, SE15
36 Melrose Road, SW18
5 Pemberton Road, KT8
19 St Peter's Street, N1
NEW 9 View Road, N6
White Cottage, W7
61 Wolsey Road, KT8

Wednesday 17th
The Inner and Middle Temple Gardens, EC4

Saturday 20th
NEW Maggie's, SM2
NEW Wensleydale Road Gardens, Hampton, TW12
Zen Garden at Japanese Buddhist Centre, W3

Sunday 21st
20 Beechwood Avenue, TW9
103 and 105 Dulwich Village, SE21
32 Highbury Place, N5
Highwood Ash, NW7
84 Lavender Grove, E8
Ormeley Lodge, TW10

18 Park Crescent, N3
25 Springfield Avenue, N10
74 Willifield Way, NW11
Zen Garden at Japanese Buddhist Centre, W3

Wednesday 24th
The Charterhouse, EC1

Saturday 27th
The Holme, NW1
5 Northampton Park, N1
Paddock Allotments & Leisure Gardens, SW20
Rooftopvegplot, W1
Trumpeters' House & Sarah's Garden, TW9
1 York Close, W7

Sunday 28th
5 Blackthorn Av, Apartment 5, N7
40 Ember Lane, KT10
70 Farleigh Road, N16
NEW The Gable End Gardens, NW1
Garden of Medicinal Plants, Royal College of Physicians, NW1
Gardens of Court Lane, SE21
69 Gloucester Crescent, NW1
70 Gloucester Crescent, NW1
40 Greenways, BR3
The Holme, NW1
9 Imber Park Road, KT10
26 Normandy Avenue, EN5
Oak Farm/Homestead, EN2
NEW 36 Park Village East, NW1
98 Parkway, NW1
Rooftopvegplot, W1
5 St Regis Close, N10
1 York Close, W7
10 York Road, N21

July

Saturday 4th
NEW Maggie's, SM2

Sunday 5th
NEW Aldersbrook Gardens, E12
Camberwell Grove Gardens, SE5

51 The Chase, SW4
46 Cheyne Avenue, E18
NEW 5 Harwood's Yard, N21
33 Huddleston Road, N7
NEW 14 Lovelace Avenue, BR2
30 Mercers Road, N19
11 Park Avenue North, N8
Railway Cottages, N22
57 St Quintin Avenue, W10
NEW 9 Shortgate, N12
131 Southgate Road, N1
Swakeleys Cottage, 2 The Avenue, UB10
1 Wades Grove, N21

Saturday 11th
226 Conisborough Crescent, SE6

Sunday 12th
226 Conisborough Crescent, SE6
83 Cowslip Road, E18
38 Lovelace Road, SE21
25 Mulberry Way, E18
NEW 1 Spring Park Avenue, CR0
24 Twyford Avenue, N2

Thursday 16th
◆ Hampton Court Palace, KT8

Friday 17th
41 Mill Hill Road, W3
65 Mill Hill Road, W3

Sunday 19th
81 Baston Road, BR2
NEW 15 Catherine Road, KT6
45 Cotswold Way, EN2
NEW 28 Ferndene Road, SE24
20 Hillcrest, N21
15 Norcott Road, N16
NEW 7 Norwood Park Road, SE27
18 Park Crescent, N3
Park Road Gardens, W4
57 St Quintin Avenue, W10
93 Tanfield Avenue, NW2
7 Woodbines Avenue, KT1

Sunday 26th
4 Manningtree Road, HA4

87 St Johns Road, E17
5 St Regis Close, N10
35 Weston Park, N8

Monday 27th
87 St Johns Road, E17

August

Saturday 1st
The Holme, NW1

Sunday 2nd
69 Gloucester Crescent, NW1
70 Gloucester Crescent, NW1
The Holme, NW1

Sunday 16th
4 Becondale Road, SE19
36 Melrose Road, SW18
31 West Park Road, TW9

Sunday 23rd
41 Mill Hill Road, W3
65 Mill Hill Road, W3

Monday 31st
Church Gardens, UB9

September

Sunday 6th
9 Churston Gardens, N11
NEW 58 Cranston Road, SE23
Golf Course Allotements, N11
24 Grove Park, SE5
12 Lauradale Road, N2
2 Littlebury Road, SW4
Royal Trinity Hospice, SW4

Saturday 12th
◆ The Garden Museum, SE1

Sunday 27th
470 Pinner Road, HA5

October

Sunday 18th
The Watergardens, KT2

Sunday 25th
51 The Chase, SW4
West Lodge Park, EN4

By Arrangement

Arrange a personalised garden visit with your club, or group of friends, on a date to suit you. See individual garden entries for full details.

8 Almack Road, Lower Clapton Gardens, E5
36 Ashley Road, N19
20 Beechwood Avenue, TW9
5 Burbage Road, SE24
51 The Chase, SW4
NEW 7 Deansway, N2
NEW 3 Elmbridge Lodge, KT7
48 Erskine Hill, NW11
69 Gloucester Crescent, NW1
70 Gloucester Crescent, NW1
21 Gospatrick Road, N17
17 Greenstone Mews, E11
7 The Grove, N6
12 Haywood Close, HA5
1a Hungerford Road, N7
69 Kew Green, Kew Green Gardens, TW9
71 Kew Green, Kew Green Gardens, TW9
84 Lavender Grove, E8
2 Littlebury Road, SW4
49 Loftus Road, W12
41 Mill Hill Road, W3
65 Mill Hill Road, W3
NEW 7 Norwood Park Road, SE27
3 The Park, N6
7 St George's Road, TW1
27 St Peters Square, W6
57 St Quintin Avenue, W10
5 St Regis Close, N10
Southwood Lodge, N6
Stokes House, TW10
NEW 333 Victoria Park Road, Flat 2, E9
61 Wolsey Road, KT8
33 Wood Vale, N10
7 Woodbines Avenue, KT1

THE GARDENS

66 ABBOTS GARDENS, N2
East Finchley, N2 0JH. Stephen & Ruth Kersley. *8 mins walk from rear exit East Finchley tube on Causeway to East End Rd. 2nd L into Abbots Gardens. 143 stops at Abbots Gardens on East End Rd. 102, 263 & 234 all go to East Finchley High Rd.* Sun 7 June (2-6). Adm £4, chd free. Home-made teas.
Combination of grass & glass: designed for year round interest with calm yet dramatic environment via plant form, texture, asymmetrical geometry, water features & restricted colour palette. Stephen studied Garden design at Capel, Ruth is a glass artist. Glass amphorae, mosaics catch the eye amongst grasses, ornamental shrubs & perennials; rose bedecked archway to quiet space with vegetable plot, silver birch, 2nd water feature.

GROUP OPENING

NEW ALDERSBROOK GARDENS, E12
Wanstead, E12 5ES. *Empress Avenue is a turning off Aldersbrook Road. 101 bus from Manor Park or Wanstead Stns. From Manor Park Stn take the 3rd R off Aldersbrook Rd, from Wanstead, drive past St Gabriel's Church, take the sixth turning on L.* Sun 5 July (12-5). Combined adm £7, chd free. Light refreshments at Empress Avenue, Clavering Rd and Park Rd.

NEW **1 CLAVERING ROAD**
Theresa Harrison.

NEW **4 EMPRESS AVENUE**
Ruth Martin.

NEW **21 PARK ROAD**
Theresa & Barry O'Driscoll & Reeves.

NEW **47 ST MARGARETS ROAD**
Jane Karavasili.

Four different gardens situated on the Aldersbrook Estate - between Wanstead Park and Wanstead Flats. Park Rd is a colour themed garden with evergreen shrubs for year round structure and a vine covered pergola leading to a vegetable area. The St Margaret's Road garden has a small

front south facing garden where as well as off street parking, tomatoes and chillies grow, the back garden is designed with a theme of circles and curves with closely planted borders. 1 Clavering Rd is an end of terrace garden where incremental space to the side has been adapted to create a kitchen garden and chicken coop - excess produce is eagerly received by 5 resident hens. Borders and beds contain variety of planting. At 4 Empress Avenue a largish garden is divided in two with a vegetable growing area, areas to attract more wildlife incl pond, 2 mixed borders 1 with hot colours and 1 with white planting.

31 ARLINGTON DRIVE, HA4
Ruislip, HA4 7RJ. John & Yasuko O'Gorman. *Tube: Ruislip. Then bus H13 to Arlington Drive, or 15 mins walk up Bury St. Arlington Drive is opp Millar & Carter Steakhouse on Bury St.* Sun 7 June (2-5.30). Adm £3.50, chd free. Home-made teas.
Cottage garden at heart with a wonderful oriental influence. Traditional cottage garden favourites have been combined with Japanese plants - a reflection of Yasuko's passion for plants and trees of her native Japan. Acers, paeonies, rhododendrons and flowering cherries underplanted with hostas, ferns and hellebores, create a lush exotic scheme. Emphasis on structure and texture.

Your visits help change lives – your generosity helps Marie Curie fund nurses to care for people night and day in their homes, with donations of more than £9 million

GROUP OPENING

ARLINGTON SQUARE GARDENS, N1
N1 7DP.
www.arlingtonassociation.org.uk. *South Islington. Off New North Rd via Arlington Ave or Linton St. Buses: 21, 76, 141, 271.* Sun 14 June (2-5.30). Combined adm £8, chd free. Home-made teas at St James' Vicarage, 1A Arlington Square. Also open 19 St Peter's Street.

26 ARLINGTON AVENUE
Thomas Blaikie.

21 ARLINGTON SQUARE
Alison Rice.

25 ARLINGTON SQUARE
Michael Foley.

30 ARLINGTON SQUARE
James & Maria Hewson.

5 REES STREET
Gordon McArthur & Paul Thompson-McArthur.

ST JAMES' VICARAGE, 1A ARLINGTON SQUARE
John & Maria Burniston.

Behind the early Victorian facades of Arlington Square and Arlington Avenue are 6 contrasting town gardens; 5 plantsmen's gardens and a delightful spacious garden at the Vicarage with an impressive herbaceous border created over the last few years, and mature London Plane trees. The group reflects the diverse tastes and interests of each garden owner, who know each other through the community gardening of Arlington Square. It is hard to believe you are minutes from the bustle of the City of London. Live music at St James' Vicarage, 1A Arlington Square.

61 ARTHUR ROAD, SW19
Wimbledon, SW19 7DN. Daniela McBride. *Tube: Wimbledon Park, then 8 mins walk. Mainline: Wimbledon, 18 mins walk.* Sun 24 May (2-6). Adm £5, chd free. Home-made teas.
This steeply sloping garden comprises woodland walks, filled with flowering shrubs and ferns. Azaleas, Rhododendrons and Acers bring early season colour; in early summer the focus is the many roses grown

around the garden. Partial wheelchair access to top lawn and terrace only, steep slopes elsewhere.

97 ARTHUR ROAD, SW19

Wimbledon, SW19 7DP. Tony & Bella Covill. *Wimbledon Park tube, then 200yds up hill on R.* Sun 14 June (2-6). Adm £5, chd free. Light refreshments. Wine, beer, soft drinks, biscuits etc.
½ acre garden of an Edwardian house. Garden est. for more than 25yrs, constantly evolving with a large variety of plants and shrubs. It has grown up around several lawns with ponds and fountains, encouraging an abundance of wildlife and a bird haven. A beautiful place with much colour, foliage and texture. New gravel garden, planting to attract butterflies. Wild meadow.

ARUNDEL & ELGIN GARDENS, W11

Kensington Park Road, Notting Hill, W11 2JD. Residents of Arundel Gardens & Elgin Crescent, www.arundelandelgingardens.org. *Entrance opp 174 Kensington Park Rd. Nearest tube within walking distance: Ladbroke Grove (3mins) or Notting Hill (8mins). Buses: 52, 452, 23, 228 all stop opp garden entrance.* Sun 17 May (12-5). Adm £4, chd free. Tea. Also open Arundel & Ladbroke Gardens.
A friendly and informal garden square with mature and rare trees, plants and shrubs laid out according to the original Victorian design of 1862, one of the best preserved gardens of the Ladbroke estate. The central hedged garden area is an oasis of tranquillity with extensive and colourful herbaceous borders. The garden incl several topiary hedges, a rare Mulberry tree, a pergola and benches from which the vistas can be enjoyed. Gardeners Chris Jelston & Anna Park. Play areas for young children.

ARUNDEL & LADBROKE GARDENS, W11

Kensington Park Road, Notting Hill, W11 2EP. Arundel & Ladbroke Gardens Committee, www.arundelladbrokegardens.co.uk. *Entrance on Kensington Park Rd, between Ladbroke & Arundel Gardens. Tube: Notting Hill Gate or Ladbroke Grove. Buses: 23, 52, 228, 452. Alight at stop for Portobello*

Market/Arundel Gardens. Sun 17 May (2-6). Adm £4, chd free. Home-made teas. Also open Arundel & Elgin Gardens.
This private communal garden is one of the few that retains its attractive mid Victorian design of lawns and winding paths. A woodland garden at its peak in spring, with rhododendrons, flowering dogwoods, early roses, bulbs, ferns and rare exotics. Live music on the lawn during tea. Playground for small children. A few steps and gravel paths to negotiate.

36 ASHLEY ROAD, N19

N19 3AF. Alan Swann & Ahmed Farooqui, swann.alan@googlemail.com. *Between Stroud Green & Crouch End. Underground: Archway or Finsbury Park. Overground: Crouch Hill. Buses: 210 or 41 from Archway to Hornsey Rise. W7 from Finsbury Park to Heathville Road. Car: Free parking in Ashley Road at weekends.*

Sun 24, Mon 25 May (2-6). Adm £3.50, chd free. Home-made teas. A good selection of home-made cakes with vegan & gluten free options, and home-brewed ginger beer. **Visits also by arrangement May to Sept. Guided tour and short talk on the garden.**
A lush town garden rich in textures, colour and forms. At its best in late spring as Japanese maple cultivars display great variety of shape and colour whilst ferns unfurl fresh, vibrant fronds over a tumbling stream and alpines and clematis burst into flower on the rockeries and pergola. The garden has a number of micro habitats incl ferneries, bog garden, stream and pond plantings, rockeries, alpines and shade plantings. Young ferns and plants propagated from specimens in the garden for sale. Pop-up tearoom with indoor seating and views over the garden. Entrance to the garden is down a flight of 7 steps.

6 Church Walk

190 BARNET ROAD, EN5

Arkley, Barnet, EN5 3LF. Hilde & Lionel Wainstein. *1m S of A1, 2m N of High Barnet tube. Garden located on corner of A411 Barnet Rd & Meadowbanks cul-de-sac. Nearest tube: High Barnet, then 107 bus, Glebe Lane stop. Ample unrestricted roadside parking.* Sun 7 June (2-6). Adm £4, chd free. Home-made teas.

The Upcycled garden. Garden designer's walled garden, 90ft x 36ft. Modern, idiosyncratic design, year round interest. Flowing herbaceous drifts around a central pond. Upcycled containers, recycled objects and home-made sculptures. Copper trellis divides space into contrasting areas. Garden continues to evolve as planted areas are expanded. Rusty tin can 'Derek Jarman' garden. Selection of home-made cakes worthy of Mary Berry! The favourite at our last opening was raspberry and white chocolate layer cake. Gluten free cakes also available. Wide range of interesting plants for sale, all propagated from the garden. Single steps within garden.

GROUP OPENING

BARNSBURY GROUP, N1

Islington, N1 1DB. *Barnsbury, London N1. Tube: King's Cross, Caledonian Rd or Angel. Overground: Caledonian Rd & Barnsbury. Buses: 17, 91, 259 to Caledonian Rd.* Sun 7 June (2-6). Combined adm £8, chd free. Home-made teas at 57 Huntingdon Street N1 1BX. Also open 2 Lonsdale Square.

◆ **BARNSBURY WOOD**
London Borough of Islington, ecologycentre@islington.gov.uk.

44 HEMINGFORD ROAD
Peter Willis & Haremi Kudo.

57 HUNTINGDON STREET
Julian Williams.

36 THORNHILL SQUARE
Anna & Christopher McKane.

Within Barnsbury's historic Georgian squares and terraces, discover these four contrasting spaces. Barnsbury Wood is London's smallest nature reserve, a hidden secret and Islington's only site of mature woodland, a tranquil oasis of wild flowers and massive trees just minutes from Caledonian Road. Wildlife info available. The gardens have extensive collections of unusual plants; 57 Huntingdon St is a secluded garden room - an understorey of silver birch and hazel, ferns, native perennials and grasses and two container ponds to encourage wildlife. 44 Hemingford Road is a small, dense composition of trees (some unusual), shrubs, perennials and lawns – and a small pond. 36 Thornhill Square, a 120 ft garden with a country atmosphere, filled with old and new roses and many herbaceous perennials. A bonsai collection will astound! These gardens have evolved over many years and show what can be achieved in differing spaces with the right plants growing in the right conditions, surmounting the difficulties of dry walls and shade. Plants for sale at 36 Thornhill Square.

81 BASTON ROAD, BR2

Hayes, Bromley, BR2 7BS. Jill & Charles Wimble. *On B265, 2m S of Bromley. 10 mins walk from Hayes, Kent Rail stn, 146 & 353 bus-stop outside property. Opp Hayes Secondary School. Free on-site parking.* Sun 19 July (2-5.30). Adm £4, chd free. Home-made teas.

A generous ½ acre plot converted by the owners into a colourful, plant-filled garden, with many features of interest. A gravel garden influenced in style by Beth Chatto greets visitors. Detailed paving and brick work give a structure to the garden and divide areas of interest incl exotics, vegetable garden, water features and fabulous pebble mosaic. Mainly level with grass and paved paths. A few steps and slopes.

4 BECONDALE ROAD, SE19

Gipsy Hill, Norwood, SE19 1QJ. Christopher & Wendy Spink. *Off Gipsy Hill. Nearest stn Gipsy Hill. Buses 3 & 322. Some parking on Becondale rd.* Sun 16 Aug (1-5). Adm £3.50, chd free. Home-made teas.

This garden takes vertical planting to new heights - but is not for those who are afraid to walk a gangplank. It is packed with a mass of exotic and rich planting with a Mediterranean feel from Bougainvillea to bananas and palms to plumbago. Steeply sloping, it maximises every bit of height with plants cascading over high rise balconies and dropping down to a theatrically styled well of a garden. Mediterranean planting on four levels. Regret, with narrow paths and very steep steps, garden not suitable for small children or mobility challenged.

20 BEECHWOOD AVENUE, TW9

Kew, Richmond, TW9 4DE. Dr Laura de Beden, 02083921969, lauradebeden@hotmail.com, www.lauradebeden.co.uk. *Within walking distance of Kew Gardens Tube Station on E side exit.* Evening opening Sun 21 June (5-7.30). Adm £5.50, chd free. Wine. Visits also by arrangement May & June for groups of 5 to 10.

Delightful town garden minutes away from Royal Botanic Gardens and Kew Retail Park. Minimalist layout by the designer owner offsets exquisite favourite plant combinations. Writing shed holds pride of place as safe refuge & main idea production centre. Topiary, pots, sculpture, surprises (the latest in the new small fernery) and good humour are all on offer for an inspiring innovative visit.

GROUP OPENING

BERRYLANDS GARDENS, KT5

Berrylands, Surbiton, KT5 9AF. Andy Hutchings. *2m S of Kingston-upon-Thames. From A3 take A240 joining Ewell Rd. Take Hollyfield Rd on R, cross King Charles Rd into Alexandra Drive. Map to other gardens from here.* Sun 7 June (12-5). Combined adm £5, chd free. Home-made teas at 1 The Crest.

68 ALEXANDRA DRIVE
Andy Hutchings.

1 THE CREST
Robert & Julia Humphries.

64 PINE GARDENS
Barbara Hutchings.

A selection of three gardens all within 10 mins walk of each other, all owned by different members of the same family. The gardens are all very varied ; country cottage, chicken run, hidden garden, giants head, even a shed made out of reclaimed materials Have an enjoyable afternoon being nosey, buying plants and sampling my sister's fantastic cakes. We look forward to seeing you.

GROUP OPENING

BLACKHEATH GARDENS, SE13
Lewisham, SE13 7EA. *Gardens sit between Lewisham, Lee & Blackheath stns. DLR: Buses 54, 89, 108, 202,122,178, 261, 321, 621 Free parking on Sundays but space limited.* Sun 14 June (2-5). Combined adm £6, chd free. Home-made teas at Lee Rd, Michael's Cl & Southbrook Rd.

49 LEE ROAD
Jane Glynn & Colin Kingsnorth.

1 MICHAEL'S CLOSE
Jeffrey Warren.

41 SOUTHBROOK ROAD, SE12
Barbara & Marek Polanski.
(See separate entry)

Grouped together are three lovely gardens, set among the gentle hills and winding roads of Blackheath area. A love of roses is a common thread. In Michael's Cl, a magnificent Rambling Rector rose blankets a hawthorn hedge of this enclosed garden wrapped round three sides of a modern flat with densely planted borders defined by paths, steps and low retaining walls. There is a generous oasis of calm in Lee Rd. Benches are set beneath rambling roses overlooking sweeps of formal lawns with flowerbeds. Paths through silver birches and grasses reveal a treehouse clad with roses and clematis. The prolific vegetable garden is a sight to see! A little further lies a well bedded-in garden in Southbrook Rd with an abundance of big rambling roses. An abundance of everything, in fact, from Indian pergolas to lily ponds, box parterres and ancient pear trees & everywhere elegant seating. Plants for sale at Lee Road and Michael's Close. See NGS website for trail map.

Spitalfields Gardens

© Julie Skelton

5 BLACKTHORN AV, APARTMENT 5, N7

N7 8AQ. Juan Carlos Cure Hazzi. *Barnsbury. 5 min walk from Highbury & Islington Stn. Building is on S side of Arundel Sq.* Sun 28 June (11-5). Adm £5. Pre-booking essential, please visit www.ngs.org.uk/ events for information & booking. Light refreshments.

Small patio garden with beautiful connection with the house, with plenty of colour, texture and year-round interest with lush tropical, sub-tropical and temperate plants. Has been featured in BBC Gardeners' World magazine and program, The Garden, The English Garden and Garden Answers magazines, The Evening Standard and was a finalist in the BBC's Small Space category competition.

GROUP OPENING

BRIXTON WATER LANE GARDENS, SW2

Brixton, SW2 1QB. *Tube: Brixton. Mainline: Herne Hill, both 10 mins. Buses: 3, 37, 196 or 2, 415, 432 along Tulse Hill.* Sun 7 June (2-5). Combined adm £5, chd free. Home-made teas. Also open 31 Trelawn Road.

60 BRIXTON WATER LANE
Caddy & Chris Sitwell.

62 BRIXTON WATER LANE
Daisy Garnett & Nicholas Pearson.

Two 90ft gardens backing onto Brockwell Park with original apple trees from the old orchard. No 60 has a large garden with floral borders and a mature wisteria covering the house. Strong colour comes from laburnum and lilac under which teas will be served. Number 62 is a country garden with exuberant borders of soft colours, a productive greenhouse and a mass of pots on the terrace. Plenty of colour from old fashioned roses, peonies and other perennials.

5 BURBAGE ROAD, SE24

Herne Hill, SE24 9HJ. Crawford & Rosemary Lindsay, 020 7274 5610, rl@rosemarylindsay.com, www.rosemarylindsay.com. *Nr junction with Half Moon Lane. Herne Hill & N Dulwich mainline stns, 5 mins walk. Buses: 3, 37, 40, 68, 196, 468.* Sun 31 May (2-5). Adm £4, chd free. Home-made teas. Visits also by arrangement Mar to July.

The garden of a member of The Society of Botanical Artists and regular writer for Hortus magazine. 150ft x 40ft with large and varied range of plants- many unusual. Herb garden, packed herbaceous borders for sun and shade, climbing plants, pots, terraces, lawns. Immaculate topiary. Gravel areas to reduce watering. All the box has been removed because of attack by blight and moth, and replaced with suitable alternatives to give a similar look. A garden that delights from spring through summer. See our website for what the papers say. Incl in The London Garden Book A-Z. Plants for sale. Elegant topiary.

CADOGAN PLACE SOUTH GARDEN, SW1

Sloane Street, Chelsea, SW1X 9PE. The Cadogan Estate, www.cadogan.co.uk. *Entrance to garden opp 97 Sloane St.* Sat 23 May (10-4). Adm £5, chd free. Light refreshments.

Many surprises, unusual trees and shrubs are hidden behind the railings of this large London square. The first square to be developed by architect Henry Holland for Lord Cadogan at the end of C18, it was then called the London Botanic Garden. Mulberry trees planted for silk production at end of C17. Cherry trees, magnolias and bulbs are outstanding in spring. Beautiful 300 year old Black Mulberry Tree (originally planted to produce silk, but incorrect variety!). This was once the home of the Royal Botanic Garden. Now featuring a Bug Hotel & Children's Playground.

Conisborough Crescent

GROUP OPENING

CAMBERWELL GROVE GARDENS, SE5

Camberwell, SE5 8JE. *10 mins from Denmark Hill mainline & overgound stn. Buses: 12, 36, 68, 148, 171, 176, 185, 436. Entrance through garden rooms at rear.* **Sun 5 July (2-6). Combined adm £5, chd free. Home-made teas. Wine available by donation.**

131 Southgate Road

81 CAMBERWELL GROVE
Jane & Alex Maitland Hudson.

83 CAMBERWELL GROVE
Robert Hirschhorn & John Hall.

These neighbouring walled gardens behind C18 houses in this beautiful tree lined street open in July. At No. 81 a tall Trachycarpus Palm and magnolia grandiflora shade York stone paving and borders filled with herbaceous perennials and shade loving ground cover. There is a pond and bog garden. Pots of all sizes line the steps to the kitchen door and the terrace outside the garden room and greenhouse. No. 83 is a mature garden, with abundant, unusual planting within a structure of box hedging, providing varied and interesting areas of peace and privacy. As trees mature the nature of the garden is changing, and more shade tolerant perennials are being introduced. Contemporary garden room, gravel and York stone paths and seating areas, calming pool and lovely views of parish church. Come and celebrate our 10th and final NGS garden opening with home-made cakes and tea at No. 81 and sparkling wine at No. 83.

4 CANONBURY PLACE, N1

N1 2NQ. Mr & Mrs Jeffrey **Tobias.** *Highbury & Islington Tube & Overground. Buses: 271 to Canonbury Square. Located in old part of Canonbury Place, off Alwyne Villas, in a cul de sac.* **Sun 19 Apr (2-5.30). Adm £3.50, chd free. Home-made teas.**
Come and enjoy the romance of early Spring, in our historic, secluded 100ft London garden, where daffodils, tulips and bluebells abound. Many architectural features incl. a superb Indian statue and ancient hidden fountain, echoing the 1780 house. Spectacular mature trees. Mostly pots

and interesting shrubs and climbers. Featured in 'Garden Answers' magazine. Artisan pastries and sourdough bread from the legendary Dusty Knuckle Bakery also on sale - as supplied to Fortnum & Masons, Ottolenghi etc.

NEW 15 CATHERINE ROAD, KT6
Surbiton, KT6 4HA. Malcolm Simpson & Stefan Gross. *15 Catherine Road, KT6 4HA. 5-10 min walk from Surbiton Station.* **Sun 19 July (12-6). Combined adm with 7 Woodbines Avenue £7, chd free. Home-made teas at 7 Woodbines Avenue.**
A well loved town garden approx 40 ft by 70 ft with ancient tall trees, deep borders of shrubs and perennial planting and with sculptures and a walled area. This is our first showing so we are looking forward to sharing our tranquil space with you.

THE CHARTERHOUSE, EC1

Charterhouse Square, EC1M 6AN. The Governors of Sutton's Hospital, www.thecharterhouse.org. *Buses: 4, 55. Tube: Barbican. Turn L out of stn, L into Carthusian St & into square. Entrance around or through Charterhouse Square.* **Evening opening Wed 24 June (5.30-8.30). Adm £5, chd free. Evening to incl Bar & BBQ.**
Enclosed courtyard gardens within the grounds of historic Charterhouse, which dates back to 1347. English country garden style featuring roses, herbaceous borders, ancient mulberry trees and small pond. Various garden

herbs found here are still used in the kitchen today. In addition, two other areas are being opened for the NGS. Pensioners Court, which is partly maintained by the private tenants and Master's Garden, the old burial ground which now consists of lawns, borders and wildlife garden planted to camouflage a war time air raid shelter. A private garden for the Brothers of Charterhouse, not usually open to the public. (Buildings not open).

51 THE CHASE, SW4

SW4 0NP. Mr Charles Rutherfoord & Mr Rupert Tyler, 02076270182, www.charlesrutherfoord.net. *Off Clapham Common. Tube: Clapham Common. Buses: 136, 452, 77, 87.* **Evening opening Tues 28 April (5.30-8). Sun 3 May (12-5). Sun 5 July (12-5). Sun 25 Oct (12-4). Adm £4.50, chd free. Light refreshments. Visits also by arrangement Apr to Sept for groups of 10 to 20.**
Member of the Society of Garden Designers Charles has created a garden over the last 35 years A remarkably well established plantsman's garden front and back surrounded by mature trees. Year round colour - most notably from spectacular display of 2500 tulips in the Spring - followed by tree peonies delphiniums iris peonies dahlias echiums. Significant number of unusual trees shrubs and bushes. Rupert's Geodetic dome brings on seedlings succulent and subtropicals The garden has been televised and widely published.

◆ CHELSEA PHYSIC GARDEN, SW3

66 Royal Hospital Road, SW3 4HS. Chelsea Physic Garden Company, 020 7352 5646, www.chelseaphysicgarden.co.uk. *Tube: Sloane Square (15 mins). Bus: 170. Parking: Battersea Park (charged). Entrance in Swan Walk off Royal Hospital Rd.* **For NGS: Wed 1 Apr (11-5). Adm £13.50, chd £9.50. Brunches, lunch and afternoon tea at The Physic Garden Café. For other opening times and information, please phone or visit garden website.** Explore London's oldest botanic garden situated in the heart of Chelsea for 350 years. With a unique living collection of around 5000 plants, this walled garden is a celebration of the importance of plants and their beauty. Highlights incl Europe's oldest pond rockery, the Garden of Edible and Useful Plants, the Garden of Medicinal Plants and the World Woodland Garden. Free tours available, led by knowledgeable guides. Walks, Talks and Workshops. Café, Shop, Toilets. Wheelchair access is via 66 Royal Hospital Rd.

46 CHEYNE AVENUE, E18

South Woodford, Essex, E18 2DR. Helen Auty. *Nearest tube S Woodford. Short walk. From station take Clarendon Rd. Cross High Rd into Broadwalk, 3rd on L Bushey Ave. 1st R Cheyne Ave.* **Sun 5 July (12-4). Adm £4, chd free. Home-made teas.** On site of Lord Cheyne's original market garden, typical suburban garden with lawn and borders of shrubs, climbers and perennials - greenhouse and productive fruit and vegetable garden.

GROUP OPENING

CHISWICK MALL GARDENS, W4

Chiswick, W4 2PR. *Car: Towards Hogarth r'about, A4 (W) turn Eyot Grds S. Tube: Stamford Brook or Turnham Green. Buses: 27, 190, 267 & 391 to Young's Corner. From Chiswick High Rd or Kings St S under A4 to river.* **Evening opening Sat 6 June (6-8). Combined adm £12.50, chd free. Sun 7 June (12-4). Combined adm £8, chd free. Saturday: wine at Swan House & Field House. Sunday: Teas at Eyot Grdns (2pm - 5pm).**

16 EYOT GARDENS
Dianne Farris.
Open on all dates

FIELD HOUSE
Rupert King,
www.fieldhousegarden.co.uk.
Open on all dates

LONGMEADOW
Charlotte Fraser.
Open on all dates

ST PETERS WHARF
Barbara Brown.
Open on Sun 7 June

SWAN HOUSE
Mr & Mrs George Nissen.
Open on all dates

Five gardens on or nr the River Thames: An exotic water garden, featured in the RHS 'Garden' magazine and in Gardener's World, a riverside garden in an artists' complex, a town house garden with an extensive vegetable garden, a large walled garden with the emphasis on foliage and shade-loving plants, and a small walled garden demonstrating the clever use of restricted space.

NEW 19 CHOLMELEY PARK, N6
Highgate, HIGHGATE, N6 5EL. Rhian and Andrew Bliss. *Accessed from Causton Rd. From Highgate High St L down Cholmeley Park at Channing school. From Highgate Tube Stn either Highgate Ave to Peacock Walk or Archway Rd to Causton Rd.* **Sun 26 Apr (2-5). Adm £4, chd free. Home-made teas.** A lived-in and constantly evolving family garden. Situated on a corner site, the plot is very varied as are the uses to which space has been put - from climbing frame to rose bower and from goal to apple tree border. Recently updated to make space for a green house, potting shed and raised beds. Planting influenced by family's experiences (e.g. of living in Japan) as well as horticultural merit.

CHOUMERT SQUARE, SE15
Peckham, SE15 4RE. The Residents. *Off Choumert Grove. Trains from London Victoria, London Bridge, London Blackfriars, Clapham Junction to Peckham Rye; buses (12, 36, 37, 63, 78, 171, 312, 345). Free Car park (1 min) in Choumert Grove.* **Sun 7 June (1-6). Adm £4, chd free. We will be serving afternoon teas, a variety of home-made cakes & Pimms. Donation to St Christopher's Hospice.** About 46 mini gardens with maxi planting in Shangri-la situation that the media has described as a Floral Canyon, which leads to small communal secret gardens. The day is primarily about gardens and sharing with others our residents' love of this little corner of the inner city; but it is also renowned for its demonstrable community spirit. Stalls in the style of a village fete and Live Music. The popular open gardens will combine this year with our own take on a village fete with home produce stalls, arts, crafts and music. No steps within the Square just a tiny step to a raised paved space in the communal garden area.

CHURCH GARDENS, UB9
Church Hill, Harefield, Uxbridge, UB9 6DU. Patrick & Kay McHugh, www.churchgardens.co.uk/. *From Harefield Village, continue for ¼ m down Church Hill. From A40 Uxbridge junction, follow signs to Harefield. Turn of Church Hill towards St Mary's Church.* **Mon 31 Aug (2-5). Adm £5, chd £2. Home-made teas.** Harefield's own 'secret garden'. C17 Renaissance walled gardens on the outskirts of Harefield, incl a traditional organic kitchen garden, consisting of 56 geometrically arranged raised beds, 60m long herbaceous borders, trained fruit trees, alpines, herb garden and an orchard with rare arcaded wall, dating back to the early 1600's. Unique opportunity to view ongoing restoration project.

We help ordinary people open the gates to their extraordinary private gardens to raise impressive amounts of money through admissions, teas and slices of cake!

79 CHURCH LANE, N2
N2 0TH. Caro & David Broome.
*Tube: E Finchley, then East End Rd
for ³/₄ m, R into Church Lane. Buses:
143 to Five Bells PH, 3 min walk;
263 to E Finchley Library, 5 min walk.*
Sun 14 June (2-6). Adm £5, chd
free. Home-made teas. Gluten
free cakes available.
Explore new paths, rose arbour, water
features, trees & perennial colour
schemes throughout this award-
winning garden. Contemporary front
garden leads to plant filled Catio,
featuring metal hanging buckets
crammed with exotic floral delights.
Step into a garden full of voluptuous
mixed borders, leading to secluded
fernery, secret hideaway with beach
hut summer house & prairie roof
terrace. Children's Treasure Hunt.

GROUP OPENING

 **CHURCH WALK GARDENS,
KT7**
Thames Ditton, KT7 0NW. Lesley
& Keith Evetts. *CHURCH WALK
THAMES DITTON KT7 0NW.
From Thames Ditton Stn 100m
along Speer Rd, Church Walk R.
From Ashley Rd car park KT7 0NJ
Church Walk at end of rd. Tickets
& facilities at Guide Hut opposite
no 40 Church Walk.* Sun 31 May
(2-6). Combined adm £5, chd free.
Light refreshments at Guide Hut
opposite No 40 Church Walk. Tea,
cake.

[NEW] **6 CHURCH WALK**
Lesley & Keith Evetts.
[NEW] **52 CHURCH WALK**
Jill & Charlie Poole.

Church Walk is a delightful ancient
path. Cottagers find different ways
of coping with baking sunshine and
unlit shade within small gardens.
Visitors will enjoy several front
gardens without entering. Two with
notable gardens front and rear are
open. No 52 is an exuberant cottage
garden making ingenious use of small
spaces. There's a lovely collection
of small acers around a little pond,
and lusty hydrangeas, weigela
and nandina behind a pittosporum
hedge. No 6 celebrates a love of
plants, some recondite. Foliage is
as important as flowers. Formal
fishpond; some twenty varieties of
ferns and clematis; hostas, bamboos,
hardy geraniums, roses, grasses,
heucheras and succulents and a
very old apple tree. At the Guide
Hut (tickets, toilets, refreshments;
entrance opp. No 40) discerning
visitors will see what can be conjured
from a thin strip of poor soil either
side of a long six-foot high fence.
Local volunteers keep the nearby train
station gardens which have an NGS
award. Idyllic Church Walk leads to a
church dating from 1125, complete
with a garden of remembrance,
yards from an Italian restaurant (Ditto
- formerly Red Lion) and a riverside
inn (The Swan, C16) for visitors who
want to combine lunch with garden
viewing.

Fenton House

9 CHURSTON GARDENS, N11
Bounds Green, N11 2NJ. Pauline Hamilton. *Tube Bounds Green or Overground Bowes Park both 10 mins walk. Buses 102, 184, 299 and 221 look for NGS arrows.* Sun 6 Sept (2-5.30). Adm £4, chd free. Home-made teas. Also open Golf Course Allotments.
A charming garden created by the owner who studied garden design at Capel Manor. This garden combines elegant & contemporary hard landscaping with informal pretty planting. Structure is provided by several specimen trees, evergreens and grasses. These are interspersed with bulbs, roses, clematis and herbaceous perennials in a palette of strong pinks, plums and purples with splashes of orange.

THE CIRCLE GARDEN, KT3
33 Cambridge Avenue, New Malden, KT3 4LD. Vincent & Heidi Johnson-Paul-McDonnell, www.thecirclegarden.com. *1¼ m N of A3 Malden junction. Bus: 213. 10 mins walk from New Malden train stn; A3 signposted for Kingston; 213 bus stop located a short distance from end of rd; our house is pink!* Sat 16, Sun 24 May (2-6). Adm £3.50, chd free. Home-made teas.
You are welcomed by a traditional cottage front garden. Hidden to the right is a side garden gate that guides you into a world of the unexpected and unknown. Do you head down the swirly hand laid path to the Japanese Garden or do you venture to the circle garden where opportunity and enjoyment abound? Whatever your choice, visionary and sensory rewards await.

226 CONISBOROUGH CRESCENT, SE6
Catford, SE6 2SF. Alex Redfern & Joe Shannon, www.thegardeningguys.co.uk. *Off A21Bromley Rd, Bellingham. Rail: Bellingham (10 mins) or Catford (15 mins). Approach via Bellingham Rd or Daneswood Ave, short walk from A21. Parking in nearby streets.* Sat 11, Sun 12 July (10.30-5.30). Adm £4, chd free. Home-made teas.
Award winning Garden, hidden behind this terraced house in South London lies an unexpected tropical oasis. Towering bamboos, bananas, cannas, palms and other lush exotic planting transport you to the tropics.

The garden reveals a hidden spa area as you venture through. In contrast the front garden is overflowing with colour from an interesting mix of annuals, perennials and collection of Dahlias. Lush tropical planting.

19 COOLHURST ROAD, N8
Hornsey, N8 8EP. Jane Muirhead. *Exit tube at Highgate onto Priory Gardens, L on Shepherd's Hill, R on Stanhope Rd, L on Hurst Ave, R on Coolhurst Rd (15mins) W7 from Finsbury Park to Crouch End & 5min walk 41 & 91 busses nearby.* Sun 26 Apr (2-6). Adm £4, chd free. Home-made teas.
Evolving, organic and wildlife garden with dappled sunlight, bees, birds and butterflies. Informal woodland planting under magnificent deciduous trees with interesting shrubs, box shapes and perennials. Small vegetable patch and wild flower garden where knapweed, campion, honesty, wild carrot and sweet rocket have naturalised. Large lawn with seating. Some steps and uneven surfaces.

4 CORNFLOWER TERRACE, SE22
East Dulwich, SE22 0HH. Clare Dryhurst. *5 mins walk from 363 & 63 bus stop at bottom of Forest Hill Rd. Turn into Dunstans Rd, then 2nd on L. Stn: Peckham Rye or Honor Oak Park.* Sun 7 June (2-5). Adm £3.50, chd free. Tea.
Come here for ideas on greening really tiny spaces and the confidence to bring biodiversity and beauty to long suffering front gardens, all adding to the beauty and oxygen levels of our streets. The little back garden is a calm retreat. Surrounding this terraced cottage are climbing roses, lavender, star jasmine, heuchera and annuals with a tiny solar fountain, seating and beautiful sculptures.

45 COTSWOLD WAY, EN2
Oakwood, Enfield, EN2 7HD. Ian Brownhill & Michael Hirschl. *Short bus ride from either Oakwood tube stn or Enfield Chase train stn. Use buses 121 or 307 and alight at Cotswold Way.* Sun 19 July (2-6.30). Adm £4.50, chd free. Home-made teas. Selection of home-made cakes and biscuits served with tea or coffee.
Designed and created in 2016 this contemporary, sunny, medium sized

garden looks out over London's Green Belt. The garden contains a number of features incl an imposing outdoor fireplace with dining area, raised Koi pond and large deck. These provide a backdrop to the overflowing, densely planted borders featuring a wide range of trees, grasses, perennials and annuals.

83 COWSLIP ROAD, E18
South Woodford, E18 1JN. Fiona Grant. *5 minute walk from Central Line tube. Close to exit for A406.* Sun 12 July (1-5). Combined adm with 25 Mulberry Way £5, chd free. Home-made teas.
80 ft long wildlife-friendly garden. On two levels at rear of Victorian semi. Patio has a selection of containers with a step down to the lawn past a pond full of wildlife. Flowerbeds stuffed with an eclectic mix of perennials. Planting includes unusual white flowering Leycesteria formosa. Ample seating on patio and under an ancient pear tree. Wheelchair access through side of house to patio. Steps down to main garden and into kitchen for homemade teas.

NEW 58 CRANSTON ROAD, SE23
Forest Hill, SE23 2HB. Mr Sam Jarvis amd Mr Andres Sampedro. *12-min walk from nearest Overground stns Forest Hill or Honor Oak. Nearest bus stops: Stanstead Rd / Colfe Rd (185, 122), Kilmorie Rd (185, 171) or Brockley Rise / Cranston Rd (122, 171).* Sun 6 Sept (12-6). Adm £3.50, chd free. Teas, cakes and tortilla.
This exotic-style plant-lover's garden features a modern landscaped path and carefully curated subtropical planting. Vivid evergreens – including palms, cordylines, loquat and cycad – provide structure and year-round interest. Tree ferns, bananas and tetrapanax add to the striking foliage, whilst cannas, dahlias and agapanthus provide vibrant pops of colour against the black-painted boundaries.

40 THE CRESCENT, SM2
Belmont, Sutton, SM2 6BJ. Mrs Barbara Welch. *Off B2230 Brighton Road, Belmont. Train: 5 min walk from Belmont Stn, from Sutton Stn take Bus 280 to Belmont. Over bridge into Station Rd, 1st L into The*

Crescent. No 40 ½ way up on L. Street parking. **Sun 14 June (1-5). Adm £4, chd free. Home-made teas.**

The structured layout of this rectangular suburban garden, 80' x 50', contains beds and island borders surrounded by clipped box hedges with box and yew topiary, many different shrubs incl philadelphus, deutzias, weigela, lilacs, and borders filled with cottage-style planting. Small paths dissect the borders and central lawn leading to various enclosed areas, some with seating, incl a circular tree seat, a water feature and a rose-covered pergola. Terrace with second water feature, many pots for ericaceous-loving plants, fuchsias and seasonal planting.

GROUP OPENING

DE BEAUVOIR GARDENS, N1

N1 4HU. *Highbury & Islington tube then 30 bus; Angel tube then 38, 56 or 73 bus; Bank tube then 21, 76 or 141 bus. 10 mins walk from Dalston Overground Stns. Street parking available.* **Sun 14 June (12-4). Combined adm £8, chd free. Home-made teas at 158 Culford Road.**

158 CULFORD ROAD
Gillian Blachford.

NEW ✿ **100 DOWNHAM ROAD**
Ms Cecilia Darker.

64 LAWFORD ROAD

21 NORTHCHURCH TERRACE
Nancy Korman.

Four gardens to explore in De Beauvoir, a leafy enclave of Victorian villas near to Islington and Dalston. The area boasts some of Hackney's keenest gardeners and a thriving garden club. New this year is 100 Downham Rd which features garden sculpture, giant echiums and two green roofs. The walled garden at 21 Northchurch Terrace has a formal feel, with deep herbaceous borders, pond, fruit trees, pergola, patio pots and herb beds. 64 Lawford Road is a small cottage style garden with old fashioned roses, espaliered apples and scented plants. 158 Culford Road is a long narrow garden with a path winding through full borders with shrubs, small trees, perennials and many unusual plants.

NEW ▶ **7 DEANSWAY, N2**
East Finchley, N2 0NF. Joan Arnold & Tom Heinersdorff, 07850 764543, joan.arnold40@gmail.com. *From East Finchley Tube Stn exit along the Causeway to East End Rd then L down Deansway. From Bishops Ave head North up Deansway towards East End Rd close to the top.* **Sun 10 May (2-6). Adm £5, chd free. Home-made teas. Visits also by arrangement Apr to Sept for groups of 10 to 30. Tea/coffee and cake included for day visit. Glass wine for evening visit.**

A garden of stories, statues, shapes and structures surrounded by trees and hedges. Bird friendly, cottage style with scented roses, clematis, mature shrubs, a weeping mulberry and abundant planting. Containers, Spring bulbs and grape vine provide all-year colour. Developing secret shady woodland area with ferns and hostas. Easy access through the side passage to the patio but there is one shallow step on to the lawn and main garden which would need assistance.

DRAGON'S DREAM, UB8
Grove Lane, Uxbridge, UB8 3RG. Chris & Meng Pocock. *Garden is in a small lane that is very close to Hillingdon Hospital. Parking is available in nearby Royal Lane. Buses from Uxbridge Tube Station: U1,U3,U4,U5,U7. Buses from West Drayton : U1, U3.* **Sun 31 May (2-5). Adm £4, chd free. Home-made teas. Malaysian curry puffs also available.**

This is an unusual and secluded garden with two contrasting sections divided by a brick shed that has been completely covered by a rampant wisteria and a climbing hydrangea and rose. Other highlights include rare dawn redwood tree, large yucca and a huge gunnera manicata . More features include a romneya poppy, ferns, rose and herb beds, tree peonies, acers and pond.

55 DUKES AVENUE, N10
Muswell Hill, N10 2PY. Jo de Banzie & Duncan Lampard, www.jodebanzie.com. *W3 Bus (Alexandra Palace Garden Centre stop) or W7 Bus (Muswell Hill stop). Free on-street parking available on Dukes Av.* **Sun 24 May (2-6). Adm £4, chd free.**

A photographer's small town garden uses curves and spheres to add shape and interest to a pretty, shady space. Gravel, paving, decking and a planting platform in an old apple tree create structure, whilst black bamboo, ferns and box provide the backdrop for a gentle palette of white and purple planting. Exhibition of Botanica Photographs. Unfortunately not suitable for wheelchairs due to access via stairs through house.

GROUP OPENING

103 AND 105 DULWICH VILLAGE, SE21

SE21 7BJ. Mr and Mrs N Annesley,Mr & Mrs A Rutherford. *Rail: N Dulwich or W Dulwich then 10 -15 mins walk. Tube: Brixton then P4 bus, alight Dulwich Picture Gallery stop. Street parking.* **Sun 21 June (2-5). Combined adm £8, chd free. Home-made teas at 103 Dulwich Village.** Donation to Macmillan Cancer Care.

103 DULWICH VILLAGE
Mr & Mrs N Annesley.

105 DULWICH VILLAGE
Mr & Mrs A Rutherford.

2 Georgian houses with large gardens, 3 mins walk from Dulwich Picture Gallery and Dulwich Park. 103 Dulwich Village is a country garden in London with a long herbaceous border, lawn, pond, roses and fruit and vegetable gardens. 105 Dulwich Village is a very pretty garden with many unusual plants, lots of old fashioned roses, fish pond and water garden. Wind band also performing! Amazing collection of plants for sale from both gardens. Please bring your own bags for plants.

We open the gates to the nation's best gardens, offering a relaxing, memorable and affordable day out. A perfect experience to share with friends and family.

ECCLESTON SQUARE, SW1

SW1V 1NP. Roger Phillips & the Residents. *London. Off Belgrave Rd nr Victoria Stn, parking allowed on Suns.* Sun 10 May (2-5). Adm £5, chd free. Home-made teas.
Planned by Cubitt in 1828, the 3 acre square is subdivided into mini gardens with camellias, iris, ferns and containers. Dramatic collection of tender climbing roses and 20 different forms of tree peonies. National Collection of ceanothus incl more than 70 species and cultivars. Notable important additions of tender plants being grown and tested. World collection of ceanothus, tea roses and tree peonies.

&. ❀ NPC ☕

EDWARDES SQUARE, W8

South Edwardes Square, Kensington, W8 6HL. Edwardes Square Garden Committee. *South Edwardes Square. Tube: Kensington High St & Earls Court. Buses: 9, 10, 27, 28, 31, 49 & 74 to Odeon Cinema. Entrance in South Edwardes Square.* Sun 5 Apr (11-5.30). Adm £5, chd free. Light refreshments.
One of London's prettiest secluded garden squares. 3½ acres laid out differently from other squares, with serpentine paths by Agostino Agliothe, Italian artist and decorator who lived at No.15 from 1814-1820, and a beautiful Grecian temple which is traditionally the home of the head gardener. Romantic rose tunnel winds through the middle of the garden. Good displays of bulbs and blossom. Pimms available if sunny. Children's play area. WC. Wheelchair access through Main Gate, South Edwardes Square.

&. ☕

Your visits help change lives – since 1927, we've donated over £60 million to nursing and caring charities.

NEW 3 ELMBRIDGE LODGE, KT7

Weston Green Road, Thames Ditton, KT7 0HY. Mrs Julia Hickman, 020 8339 0931, julia.hickman@virgin.net. *House opposite Esher College on Weston Green Rd and 5 minutes walk from Thames Ditton station.* Visits by arrangement May to Sept for groups of 10 to 30.
Mature garden 70' x 35' designed by Cleve West four years ago. From a sunny terrace steps lead through two oak pergolas festooned with climbing plants. Gravelled areas feature unusual and drought tolerant plants. Decorative greenhouse. Generous perennial border brims with a kaleidoscope of plants. Beyond is a productive vegetable area opposite a catalpa with wild flowers beneath.

🚌 D

40 EMBER LANE, KT10

Esher, KT10 8EP. Sarah & Franck Corvi. *½ m from centre of Esher. From the A307, turn into Station Rd which becomes Ember Lane.* Sun 28 June (1-5). Combined adm with 9 Imber Park Road £6, chd free. Home-made teas.
A contemporary family garden designed and maintained by the owners with distinct areas for outdoor living. A 70ft East facing plot with some unusual planting and several ornamental trees. Home-made teas can be enjoyed outside or in the large, airy kitchen. Wide steps lead down to tour the garden.

❀ ☕

91 ENGLEFIELD ROAD, N1

N1 3LJ. Antoinette and Michael. *East Canonbury. Highbury & Islington tube or Canonbury Overground stn; 30 bus to Southgate Rd stop, 5 min wk. Angel tube; 38, 56 or 73 bus to Ockendon Rd, 5 min wk.* Sun 24 May (2-6). Adm £3.50, chd free. Light refreshments.
This garden surprises. South facing yet shaded by a 40ft magnolia and a mature apple tree, a hammock slung between, making a sublime place to relax and read. The philosophy is 'if you like a plant you can find a space', so dense and varied planting, more at home in a country garden, creates an eclectic mix and it works! A patio crammed with pots and hanging baskets seeks to entertain. Garden is approached via steep steps at side of house.

☕

48 ERSKINE HILL, NW11

Hampstead Garden Suburb, NW11 6HG. Marjorie & David Harris, 020 8455 6507, marjorieharris@btinternet.com. *Hampstead Garden Suburb. Nr A406 & A1. Tube: Golders Green. H2 Hail & Ride bus from Golders Green to garden, or 13, 102 or 460 buses to Temple Fortune (10 mins walk).* Sun 7 June (2-6). Adm £4.50, chd free. Home-made teas. Also open 10 Wordsworth Walk. Limited supply of dairy-free/gluten free cakes also available. Visits also by arrangement May to Sept for groups of up to 20.
Restful organic cottage garden. Copious perennials, pots, roses, clematis and trees, with containerised veg plot and greenhouse. Nest box. Organic and pesticide free. Quirky water feature. Some single steps and narrow paths. Handrail/step to lawn.

&. ❀ 🚌 ☕

12 FAIRFIELD ROAD, N8

Hornsey, N8 9HG. Christine Lane. *Tube: Finsbury Park & then W3 (Weston Park stop) or W7 (Crouch End Broadway), alternatively Archway & then 41 bus (Crouch End Broadway) it's then a short walk.* Sun 31 May (2-5.30). Adm £4, chd free. Home-made teas.
A tranquil garden created on 2 levels with a lawn, a cobbled zen garden and a patio on the lower level and a secluded woodland garden with sculptures on the higher level. There is a variety of trees, shrubs and flowers, as well as succulents, palms and bamboos all of which creates different atmospheres and plants in pots give height and interest. Seating provides places to contemplate and enjoy.

❀ ☕

70 FARLEIGH ROAD, N16

Stoke Newington, N16 7TQ. Mr Graham Hollick. *Short walk from junction of Stoke Newington High St & Amhurst Rd.* Sun 28 June (11-6). Adm £3.50, chd free. Home-made teas.
A diverse garden in a Victorian terrace with an eclectic mix of plants, many in vintage pots reflecting the owner's interests. A small courtyard leads onto a patio surrounded by pots followed by a lawn flanked by curving borders. At the rear is a paved area with raised beds containing vegetables.

❀ ☕

71 Kew Green

◆ **FENTON HOUSE, NW3**
Hampstead Grove, Hampstead, NW3 6SP. National Trust, www.nationaltrust.org.uk. *300yds from Hampstead tube. Entrances: Top of Holly Hill & Hampstead Grove.* For NGS: Evening opening Tue 9 June (6.30-7.30). Adm £20. Pre-booking essential, please visit www.ngs.org.uk/events for information & booking. Wine. For other opening times and information, please visit garden website.

Join the Gardener-in-Charge for a special evening tour. Andrew Darragh, who brings over ten years experience from Kew to Fenton House, will explore this timeless 1½ acre walled garden. Laid out over three levels and featuring formal areas, a small sunken rose garden, a 300 year old orchard and kitchen garden, Andrew will present the garden and the changes he has made over the past seven years.

 28 FERNDENE ROAD, SE24
Herne Hill, SE24 0AB. Mr & Mrs David & Lynn Whyte. *Overlooking Ruskin Park. Buses 68, 468, 42. A 5 min walk from Denmark Hill. Train sts: Herne Hill, Denmark Hill, Loughborough Junction. All 15 min walk. House overlooks Ruskin Park. Free parking.* Sun 19 July (1-5.30). Adm £3.50, chd free. Home-made teas. Home-made cakes and scones with garden produce jam.
It's all about structure and careful planting in this dramatically sloping S.S.E. facing garden, 30m long x 18m. A lively blend of perennials and shrubs show definite Kiwi influences. The kitchen garden with raised beds and soft fruits is wonderfully secluded. Lower level planting has a coastal feel. Upper level has a 'hot colour' border. Borrowed views of mature trees and big skies set it off. The garden office/Summer house was constructed from sustainable sources materials, has a rubble roof to attenuate water runoff. Upper levels not suitaable for wheelchairs.

GROUP OPENING

FOREST HILL GARDENS GROUP, SE23
Forest Hill, SE23 3BP. *Off S Circular (A205) behind Horniman Museum & Gardens. Station: Forest Hill,*
10 mins walk. Buses: 176, 185, 197, 356, , P4 - alight for this bus' Horniman Drive'. Buses: 176, 185, , P4. 197 & 356 buses stop at Horniman Museum. Sun 17 May (1-6). Combined adm £8, chd free. Home-made teas at 53 Ringmore Rise. Donation to St Christopher's Hospice and Marsha Phoenix Trust.

7 CANONBIE ROAD
June Wismayer.

THE COACH HOUSE, 3 THE HERMITAGE
Pat Rae.

HILLTOP, 28 HORNIMAN DRIVE
Frankie Locke.

27 HORNIMAN DRIVE
Rose Agnew.

53 RINGMORE RISE
Valerie Ward.

25 WESTWOOD PARK
Beth & Steph Falkingham-Blackwell.

Six character-packed gardens on the highest hill in SE London, nr Horniman Museum, with spectacular views over London and North Downs. All within a short walk of each other. For those with mobility problems, lifts available between gardens for small donation. Enjoy the intricate combinations and zonal planting of a plantswoman's urban garden, with a dry, prairie planting contrasting with a watery fern garden. Admire the tiered, bee and butterfly-enticing organic garden. Wander in a country-style garden with a

cutting garden, meadow, assorted chicken breeds, and an ever-popular children's story trail. Relax in a haven of peace and harmony amid an embroidery of vibrant colours and enjoy breathtaking views. Watch for tame robins in the walled courtyard of an artist's 18thC coach house with sculptures, fountain, birdbath and decorative pots for interest all year. Unwind with delicious cakes and listen to music while looking out over the London skyline. Plants for sale: 27 Horniman Dr and 7 Canonbie Rd. Garden ceramics and sculptures for sale at the Coach House. Teas and music: 53 Ringmore Rise. Gardens have slopes/steps

 20 FURLONG ROAD, N7
N7 8LS. Mr Simon Toms. *Close to Highbury & Islington Tube/ Overground. Tube & Overground: Highbury & Islington, 3 mins walk along Holloway Rd, 2nd L. Furlong Rd joins Holloway Rd & Liverpool Rd. Buses: 43, 271, 393.* Sun 31 May (12-4). Adm £5, chd free. Light refreshments.
A mature garden hidden away from the busy streets of Islington. The garden draws from planting to be found in Cornish spring gardens, incl rhododendrons, magnolias, cherry and cercis trees. There is a degree of formality with topiary, pleached magnolias and lawn mixed with a touch of fun in the form of banana trees, palms and cannas. The rhododendrons will be in bloom.

NEW THE GABLE END GARDENS, NW1
52 Hawley Road, Camden Town, NW1 8RG. Magda Segal. *Set back off Chalk Farm Rd opp the Stables Market. On the L approx. 600yds down from Chalk Farm tube station. The nearest bus stop is served by the 31, 24, 168 & 88 Buses.* Sun 28 June (2-6). Adm £5, chd free. Home-made teas. Also open 70 Gloucester Crescent.
The Gable End Gardens consist of a series of planted areas that together create a wildlife haven in the heart of Camden Town, within them can be found a colony of sparrows, beehives and ponds. The planting, based around rescued and donated plants, is dominated by a mature fig tree at the front of the property and a willow in the rear garden, providing forage for the bees and cover for the birds. A must-see example of what can be achieved to help wildlife in urban environments. Plus prize winning tree pits. Home baking incl. real Scottish tea cake and shortbread! Only the rear garden is not wheelchair accessible, the rest can be enjoyed with comparative ease.

GARDEN BARGE SQUARE AT DOWNINGS ROADS MOORINGS, SE1
31 Mill Street, SE1 2AX. Mr Nick Lacey. *5 mins walk from Tower Bridge. Mill St off Jamaica Rd, between London Bridge & Bermondsey Stns, Tower Hill also nearby. Buses: 47, 188, 381, RV1.* Sun 31 May (2-5). Adm £5, chd free. Home-made teas. Donation to RNLI.
Series of seven floating barge gardens connected by walkways and bridges. Gardens have an eclectic range of plants for yr-round seasonal interest. Marine environment: suitable shoes and care needed. Small children must be closely supervised.

◆ THE GARDEN MUSEUM, SE1
5 Lambeth Palace Road, SE1 7LB. The Garden Museum, www.gardenmuseum.org.uk. *Lambeth side of Lambeth Bridge. Tube: Lambeth North, Vauxhall, Waterloo. Buses: 507 Red Arrow from Victoria or Waterloo mainline & tube stns, also 3, 77, 344.* For NGS: Sat 12 Sept (10.30-4). Adm £6.50, chd free. Light refreshments in the Garden Cafe. For other

opening times and information, please visit garden website.
At the heart of the Garden Museum is the Sackler Garden. Designed by Dan Pearson as an 'Eden' of rare plants, the garden is inspired by John Tradescant's journeys as a plant collector. Taking advantage of the sheltered, warm space, Dan has created a green retreat in response to the bronze and glass architecture, conjuring up a calm, reflective atmosphere. Visitors will also see a permanent display of paintings, tools, ephemera and historic artefacts: a glimpse into the uniquely British love affair with gardens. The Garden Cafe is an award-winning lunch venue that is considered one of the best Museum restaurants in the country. The Museum is accessible for wheelchair users via ramps and access lift.

♿ ❀ D ☕ ♨

GARDEN OF MEDICINAL PLANTS, ROYAL COLLEGE OF PHYSICIANS, NW1
11 St Andrews Place, Regents Park, NW1 4LE. Royal College of Physicians of London, www.garden.rcplondon.ac.uk. *Tubes: Great Portland St & Regent's Park. Garden is one block N of stn exits, on Outer Circle opp SE corner of Regent's Park.* Sun 28 June (2-5.30). Adm £5, chd free. Also open 36 Park Village East.
One of several individual and distinctive gardens opening in NW1. Here are 1,100 different plants used in medicines around the world and throughout history: plants named after physicians; plants which make modern medicines and plants used by herbalists. Unique beds with the plants used medicinally in the College's Pharmacopoeia of 1618. Guided tours by physicians explaining the uses of the plants, their histories and stories about them. Books about the plants in the medicinal garden will be on sale. The entry to the garden is at far end of St Andrews Place. Wheelchair ramps at steps. Wheelchair lift for lavatories. No parking on site.

♿

GROUP OPENING

GARDENS OF COURT LANE, SE21
Dulwich Village, SE21 7EA. Jean & Charles Cary-Elwes. *Court Lane, Dulwich. Buses P4, 12, 40, 176, 185 (to Dulwich Library) 37. Mainline; North Dulwich then 12 mins walk. Ample free parking.* Sun 28 June (2-5.30). Combined adm £8, chd free. Home-made teas.

122 COURT LANE, SE21
Jean & Charles Cary-Elwes.
125 COURT LANE, SE21
Stephen Henden & Neil Ellis.
NEW 148 COURT LANE
Mr & Mrs Sue and Anthony Wadsworth.
164 COURT LANE
James & Katie Dawes.
Visits also by arrangement Jan to Sept.

164 was recently redesigned to create a more personal and intimate space with several specific zones. A modern terrace and seating area leads onto a lawn with abundant borders and a beautiful mature oak. A rose arch leads to the vegetable beds and greenhouse. At 125, winding paths weave between the lawn and colourful herbaceous borders of vibrant interest. Hidden at the bottom of the garden is a secretive Druid Chair. Renowned teas and cakes. 122 has a countryside feel, backing onto Dulwich Park with colourful herbaceous borders, live Jazz on the terrace, a children's trail, plant sales and a wormery demonstration. 148, a spacious garden, developed over 20 years backs on to Dulwich Park. From the wide sunny terrace surrounded by tall, golden bamboos and fan palms, step down into a garden designed with an artist's eye for colour, form, texture and flow, creating intimate spaces beneath mature trees and shrubs, with colourful perennials. Jazz, children's trail, wormery demonstration at 125. Savoury refreshments at 164. Refreshments and plant sale at 148.

74 GLENGALL ROAD, IG8
Woodford Green, IG8 0DL. Mr & Mrs J Woolliams. *0208 504 1709, email jgmwoolliams@outlook.com, 5 mins walk from Woodford Central*

line, off Snakes Lane West. Buses nearby incl 275,179,W13 & 20. No parking restrictions on Suns. **Sun 5 Apr (2-5). Adm £4, chd free.**
A secluded S-facing cottage style garden, developed over 25 years for yr-round interest. Areas incl 2 lawns, a rock garden, small wildlife pond with bog garden, shade borders and a gravel garden, linked by several paths. Throughout are mixtures of trees shrubs perennials bulbs bamboos grasses and climbers, including many spring bulbs. Some steps but mostly wheelchair accessible.

69 GLOUCESTER CRESCENT, NW1

Camden, NW1 7EG. Sandra Clapham, 020 7485 5764, set69@gloscres.com. *Between Regent's Park & Camden Town tube station. Tube: Camden Town 2 mins, Mornington Crescent 10 mins. Metered parking in Oval Rd.* **Sun 28 June (2-5.30), also open 98 Parkway. Sun 2 Aug (2-5.30), also open The Holme. Combined adm with 70 Gloucester Crescent £6, chd free. Visits also by arrangement Apr to Oct for groups of up to 30.**
Delightful little cottage front garden, opening jointly with No. 70 next door. It shows what can be done with a front garden as an attractive alternative to a paved parking space. Ursula Vaughan Williams lived here and the very old iceberg rose at the front, the yellow roses, the border of London pride and the Crinum powellii Rosea lily in a pot are all inherited from her. Many plants have been added since, incl a bed of tomatoes and a delicious 23yr-old grape vine, trained up and along the balcony, that produces generous amounts of grape jelly! One of several local gardens opening for the National Garden Scheme in NW1.

70 GLOUCESTER CRESCENT, NW1

NW1 7EG. Lucy Gent, 07531 828752 (texts please), gent.lucy@gmail.com. *Between Regent's Park & Camden Town tube station. Tube: Camden Town 2 mins, Mornington Crescent 10 mins. Metered parking in Oval Rd.* **Sun 28 June (2-5.30), also open 36 Park Village East. Sun 2 Aug (2-5.30), also open The Holme. Combined adm with 69 Gloucester Crescent**

£6, chd free. Visits also by arrangement Apr to Oct for groups of up to 30.
Here is an oasis in Camden's urban density, where resourceful planting outflanks challenges of space and shade and Mrs Dickens, who once lived here, is an amiable ghost. June open day occurs alongside other distinctive local gardens while an August opening shows how wonderful the month can be in a town garden. Other unexpected times of the year also worth another visit, especially September.

GOLF COURSE ALLOTMENTS, N11

Winton Avenue, N11 2AR. GCAA Haringey, www.golfcourseallotments.co.uk. *Junction of Winton Av & Blake Rd. Tube: Bounds Green. Buses: 102, 184, 299 to Sunshine Garden Centre, Durnsford Rd. Through park to Bidwell Gdns. Straight on up Winton Ave. No cars on site.* **Sun 6 Sept (1-4.30). Adm £4, chd free. Home-made teas. Also open 9 Churston Gardens. Light lunches also available.**
Large, long established allotment with over 200 plots, some organic. Maintained by culturally diverse community growing wide variety of fruit, vegetables and flowers enjoyed by the bees. Picturesque corners and quirky sheds - a visit feels like being in the countryside. Autumn Flower and Produce Show features prize winning horticultural and domestic exhibits and beehives. Tours of best plots. Fresh allotment produce, chutneys, jams, honey, cakes and light refreshments for sale. Wheelchair access to main paths only. Gravel and some uneven surfaces. WC incl disabled.

21 GOSPATRICK ROAD, N17

Tottenham, N17 7EH. Matthew Bradby, 020 8352 2354, mattbradby@hotmail.com. *London Zone 3. Nearest underground stn Turnpike Lane or Wood Green, overland stn Bruce Grove. Bus routes 144, 217, 231, 444 to Gospatrick Rd, or 123, 243 to Waltheof Ave, or 318 to Gt Cambridge Rd.* **Sun 7 June (2-5.30). Adm £4, chd free. Light refreshments. Home-made wine: tea, cake and cheese nibbles. Visits also by arrangement May to**

Sept for groups of up to 10.
Diverse 40 metre plot with lawn dominated by large weeping willow, giving dappled shade over fan palms, grasses, ferns and climbers. Fruit and vegetable garden with large Japanese banana, grapevine, olive and bay trees, climbing roses, greenhouse and pond. Patio with exotics in pots. Mainly organic and managed for nature, this is a very tranquil and welcoming garden.

17 GREENSTONE MEWS, E11

Wanstead, E11 2RS. Mrs T Farnham, 07761 476651, farnhamz@yahoo.co.uk. *Wanstead. Tube: Snaresbrook or Wanstead, 5 mins walk. Bus: 101, 308, W12, W14 to Wanstead High St. Greenstone Mews is accessed via Voluntary Place which is off Spratt Hall Road.* **Visits by arrangement Apr to Sept for groups of 5 to 10. Adm £5, chd free. Light refreshments. Adm incl tea or coffee.**
Coloured Slate paved garden (20ft x 17ft). Height provided by a mature strawberry tree. Sunken reused bath now a fishpond surrounded by climbers clothing fences underplanted with herbs, vegetables, shrubs and perennials grown from cuttings. Ideas aplenty for small space gardening. Regret garden unsuitable for children. Wheelchair access through garage. Limited turning space.

40 GREENWAYS, BR3

Beckenham, BR3 3NQ. N Dooley and C Murray. *S of Beckenham High St. Nearest station Beckenham Jnt 10min walk Village Way to Uplands. Bus route 194 to War Memorial High St. Garden is located on the corner of Greenways & Uplands, close to the triangular green.* **Sun 28 June (2-5.30). Adm £4, chd free. Home-made teas.**
Two contrasting garden spaces. The tapering 70ft rear garden, redesigned in 2015 gives all year interest and is wildlife friendly. Features incl a Mediterranean planted bed, olive trees, grasses, thyme bed, insect hotels/screens, alpine roof garden, pond and sculptures and areas to relax. The front garden has fruit trees and small meadow surrounded by newly replanted borders in coloured 'rooms'.

7 THE GROVE, N6

Highgate Village, N6 6JU. Mr Thomas Lyttelton, 07713 638161. *Between Highgate West Hill & Hampstead Lane. Tube: Archway or Highgate. Buses: 143, 210, 214 and 271.* **Sun 9 Feb (11-3). Light refreshments. Sun 5 Apr, Sun 7 June (2-6). Home-made teas. Adm £5, chd free. Visits also by arrangement Feb to Dec for groups of up to 30.** Donation to The Harington Scheme.

½ acre garden designed for yr round interest in shades of green and gold. A wild garden with mature trees giving a woodland feel, much improved by removal of box. Large lawn, perfect for teas. Water garden, paths and views galore. Brilliant for hide & seek, Pooh-sticks and young explorers. Snowdrops in Feb. Exceptional camellias and magnolia in spring, 'hidden' cyclamen in early autumn. Hot soup incl with entry for Snowdrop opening. Cup of tea incl with entry for Spring/Summer openings.

24 GROVE PARK, SE5

Camberwell, SE5 8LH. Clive Pankhurst, www.alternative-planting.blogspot.com. *Chadwick Rd end of Grove Park. Stns: Peckham Rye or Denmark Hill, both 10 mins walk. Good street parking.* **Sun 6 Sept (2-5.30). Adm £4.50, chd free. Home-made teas.**

An inspiring exotic jungle of lush big leafed plants and Southeast Asian influences. Towering exotica transport you to the tropics. Huge hidden garden created from the bottom halves of two neighbouring gardens gives the 'wow' factor and unexpected size. Lawn and lots of hidden corners give spaces to sit and enjoy. Renowned for delicious home-made cake.

♦ HAMPTON COURT PALACE, KT8

East Molesey, KT8 9AU. Historic Royal Palaces, www.hrp.org.uk. *Follow brown tourist signs on all major routes. Junction of A308 with A309 at foot of Hampton Court Bridge.* **For NGS: Evening opening Thur 23 Apr, Thur 16 July (6-8). Adm £12. Pre-booking essential, please visit www.ngs.org.uk/events for information & booking. Wine. For other opening times and information, please visit garden website.**

Take the opportunity to join 2 special NGS private tours, after the wonderful historic gardens have closed to the public. Spring Walk in April and Mid-Summer abundance in July in the wonderful gardens of Hampton Court Palace. Some un-bound gravel paths.

37 HAROLD ROAD, E11

Leytonstone, E11 4QX. Dr Matthew Jones Chesters. *Tube: Leytonstone exit L subway 5 mins walk. Overground: Leytonstone High Rd 5 mins walk. Buses: 257 & W14. Parking at station or limited on street.* **Sun 14 June (1-5). Adm £4, chd free. Home-made teas.**

50ft x 60ft pretty corner garden arranged around 7 fruit trees. Fragrant climbers, woodland plants and shade-tolerant fruit along north wall. Fastigiate trees protect raised vegetable beds and herb rockery. Long lawn bordered by roses and perennials on one side; prairie plants on the other. Patio with raised pond, palms and rhubarb. Planting designed to produce fruit, fragrance and lovely memories. Plant list and garden plan available.

NEW 5 HARWOOD'S YARD, N21

Winchmore, N21 1BJ. Mr Matthew Eccleston. *Tube Southgate then W9 to Winchmore Hill Green short walk. Train Winchmore Hill and short walk via Wades Hill. Look for big arrows.* **Sun 5 July (2-6). Adm £4, chd free. Also open 1 Wades Grove.**

Set in a secret cul de sac two contrasting spaces. The front has English country village feel with cottage style borders, traditional flowers, roses and lawn The rear, considering his health issues Matthew created an Islamic inspired meditative space with seating arranged to enjoy all aspects, scents and the calming sound of water. The planting complements the design. An inspiration. Wheelchair access to FRONT garden only. There are steps and shingle in the rear garden.

12 HAYWOOD CLOSE, HA5

Pinner, HA5 3LQ. Brenda & Roy Jakes, 020 886 86638, royjakes@gmail.com. *Approx ½ m from Pinner Met Line Stn. off Elm Park Rd. From Northwood, Stanmore, Harrow & Watford head towards Pinner Green & look for signs. Park in Elm Park Rd as*

Haywood Close has limited parking. **Sun 14 June (2-5). Adm £4.50, chd free. Light refreshments. Tea, Coffee, soft drinks and cakes including gluten free cakes. Visits also by arrangement in June for groups of 20 to 30.**

A beautiful suburban garden created by enthusiastic, plantaholic owners. Herbaceous borders containing many interesting species surround the lawn. The garden contains over 100 varieties of roses and clematis, a rose walk, rose covered gazebo, water features, sink garden, pleached hornbeam trees with box collars, fruit and vegetable plot. There are seating areas and summerhouse to sit and relax. Most of garden wheelchair accessible.

31 HENDON AVENUE, N3

Finchley, N3 1UJ. Sandra Tomaszewska Day. *Finchley Central. 15 mins walk from Finchley Central Tube. Buses: 326 & 143. Car: 5 mins from A1 via Hendon Ln. No parking restrictions on Sun.* **Sun 31 May (2-6). Adm £4, chd free. Home-made teas.**

An extensive garden with mature trees, shrubs and perennials divided into areas. Herbaceous beds in semi shade, a raised triangular bed with lavender, agapanthus and roses. Two arches, draped with grapevines, wisteria, kiwi and clematis, guide you into a tranquil, white garden and a wildlife pond, lead to tropical and Mediterranean beds with olive, bean Albizia julibrissin Rosa trees and palms. Refreshments served from the pool house; relax by the pool in the tropical garden. Partial wheelchair access.

32 HIGHBURY PLACE, N5

N5 1QP. Michael & Caroline Kuhn. *Highbury Fields. Highbury & Islington Tube; Overground & National Rail. Buses: 4, 19, 30, 43, 271, 393 to Highbury Corner. 3 mins walk up Highbury Place which is opp stn.* **Sun 21 June (2-6). Adm £4, chd free. Home-made teas.**

This 80ft long garden lies behind a C18 terrace house. An upper York stone terrace leads down to a larger terrace surrounded by overfilled beds of cottage garden style planting. Further steps lead to a lawn by a rill and an end terrace. A large willow tree dominates the garden which also has amelanchiers and fruit trees as well as dwarf acers, winter flowering cherry, lemon trees and magnolia.

HIGHWOOD ASH, NW7
Highwood Hill, Mill Hill, NW7 4EX. Mr & Mrs R Gluckstein. *Totteridge & Whetstone on Northern line, then bus 251 stops outside - Rising Sun/ Mill Hill stop. By car: A5109 from Apex Corner to Whetstone. Garden located opp The Rising Sun PH.* Sun 21 June (2-6). Adm £5, chd free. Home-made teas.
Created over the last 50yrs, this 3¼ acre garden features rolling lawns, two large interconnecting ponds with koi, herbaceous and shrub borders and a modern gravel garden. A garden for all seasons with many interesting plants and sculptures. A country garden in London. Partial access for wheelchairs, lowest parts too steep.

20 HILLCREST, N21
Winchmore Hill, N21 1AT. Gwyneth & Ian Williams. *Tube: Southgate then W9 to Winchmore Hill Green followed by a short walk via Wades Hill. Train: Winchmore Hill, turn R towards the Green, then short walk via Wades Hill.* Sun 19 Apr (12.30-4.30). Light refreshments. Sun 19 July (2-6). Home-made teas. Adm £4, chd free.
A beautiful NW facing hillside garden offers a panoramic horizon and afternoon sun. A terrace has seating in an iron-work gazebo. Wide stone steps descend to a pretty, evergreen pergola, water feature and oasis of dappled sunlight. Mature borders with lawn, perennials, rockery and meandering path reach a cozy summer house with alpine borders and a new miniature wildlife pond. Steep Steps!

THE HOLME, NW1
Inner Circle, Regents Park, NW1 4NT. Lessee of The Crown Commission. *In centre of Regents Park on The Inner Circle. Within 15 mins walk from Great Portland St or Baker St Underground Stations, opp Regents Park Rose Garden Cafe.* Sat 27, Sun 28 June, Sat 1, Sun 2 Aug (2.30-5.30). Adm £5, chd free.
4 acre garden filled with interesting and unusual plants. Sweeping lakeside lawns intersected by islands of herbaceous beds. Extensive rock garden with waterfall, stream and

pool. Formal flower garden with unusual annual and half hardy plants, sunken lawn, fountain pool and arbour. Gravel paths and some steps which gardeners will help wheelchair users to negotiate.

&

33 HUDDLESTON ROAD, N7
N7 0AD. Gilly Hatch & Tom Gretton. *5 mins from Tufnell Park Tube. Tube: Tufnell Park. Buses: 4, 134, 390 to Tufnell Park. Follow Tufnell Park Rd to 3rd rd on R.* Sun 5 July (2-6). Adm £3.50, chd free. Home-made teas. Also open 30 Mercers Road.
The rambunctious front garden weaves together perennials, grasses and ferns, while the back garden makes a big impression in a small space. After 40+yrs, the lawn is now a wide curving path, a deep sunny bed on one side; mixing shrubs and perennials in an ever changing blaze of colour, on the other; a screen of varied greens and textures. This flowery passage leads to a secluded area.

1A HUNGERFORD ROAD, N7
N7 9LA. David Matzdorf, davidmatzdorf@blueyonder.co.uk, www.growingontheedge.net. *Between Camden Town & Holloway. Tube: Caledonian Rd. Buses: 17, 29, 91, 253, 259, 274, 390 & 393. Parking free on Sundays.* Sun 7 June (1-6). Adm £3, chd free. Also open 60 & 62 Hungerford Road. Visits also by arrangement Apr to

Oct for groups of up to 10.
Unique eco house with walled, lush front garden in modern exotic style, densely planted with palms, acacia, bamboo, ginger lilies, bananas, ferns, yuccas, abutilons and unusual understorey plants. Floriferous and ambitious green roof resembling Mediterranean or Mexican hillside, planted with yuccas, dasylirions, agaves, aloes, flowering shrubs, euphorbias, grasses, alpines, sedums and aromatic herbs. Sole access to roof is via built in ladder. Garden and roof each 50ft x 18ft.

60 & 62 HUNGERFORD ROAD, N7
N7 9LP. John Gilbert, Lynne Berry & Frances Pine. *Between Camden Town & Holloway. Tube: Caledonian Rd, 6 mins walk. Buses: 29 & 253 to Hillmarton Rd stop in Camden Rd. Also 17, 91, 259, 393 to Hillmarton Rd. 10 to York Way.* Sun 7 June (2-6). Adm £5, chd free. Tea. Also open 23 & 24b Penn Road.
Two contrasting gardens behind a Victorian terrace. No. 62 is densely planted and mature, designed to maximise space for planting and create several different sitting areas, views and moods. Professional garden designer's own garden. No 60 is a family garden with large lawn and a good range of shrubs, flowering perennials and trees. Together they form an inspiring oasis, connected by a secret door.

38 Lovelace Road

THE HURLINGHAM CLUB, SW6
Ranelagh Gardens, SW6 3PR. The
Members of the Hurlingham Club,
www.hurlinghamclub.org.uk. *Main
gate at E end of Ranelagh Gardens.
Tube: Putney Bridge (110yds). NB:
No onsite parking. Meter parking
on local streets & restricted parking
on Sats (9-5).* Sat 16 May (10-
4.30). Adm £5, chd free. Light
refreshments in the Napier
Servery in the East Wing.
Rare opportunity to visit this 42 acre
jewel with many mature trees, 2 acre
lake with water fowl, expansive lawns
and a river walk. Capability Brown
and Humphry Repton were involved
with landscaping. The gardens are
renowned for their roses, herbaceous
and lakeside borders, shrubberies
and stunning bedding displays. The
riverbank is a haven for wildlife with
native trees, shrubs and wild flowers.
Garden Tours at 11am and 2pm -
tickets available at entrance.

GROUP OPENING

**HYDE PARK ESTATE GARDENS,
W2**
Kendal Street, W2 2AN. Church
Commissioners for England,
www.hydeparkestate.com. *The
Hyde Park Estate is bordered by
Sussex Gardens, Bayswater Rd and
Edgware Rd. Nearest tube stations
incl. Marble Arch, Paddington and
Edgware Rd.* Sat 18 Apr (11-4).
Combined adm £5, chd free.
Pre-booking preferred, please
visit www.ngs.org.uk/events
for information & booking, but
tickets are available on the day
from Coniston Court Garden.

CONISTON COURT
Church Commissioners
for England,
www.hydeparkestate.com.

DEVONPORT
Church Commissioners for
England.

THE QUADRANGLE
Church Commissioners for
England.

THE WATER GARDENS
Church Commissioners for
England.

Four gardens only open to the public
through the National Garden Scheme.
Each garden planted sympathetically
to reflect the surroundings. Uniquely

The Water Gardens feature vast
expanses of open water and was
fully refurbished in 2019. The
gardens on the Hyde Park Estate are
owned and managed by the Church
Commissioners for England and play
a key part in the environmental and
ecological strategy on the Hyde Park
Estate. In 2018 we met the target we
had set of ensuring that 10% of the
Estate was 'green' - not only with
the garden spaces but by installing
planters on unused paved areas,
green roofs on new developments
and olive trees throughout Connaught
Village. Most of the gardens can be
accessed by wheelchairs. There are
some steps at The Water Gardens for
the upper levels.

9 IMBER PARK ROAD, KT10
Esher, KT10 8JB. Jane & John
McNicholas. *½m from centre of
Esher. From the A307, turn into
Station Rd which becomes Ember
Lane. Go past Esher train station on
R. Take 3rd rd on R into Imber Park
Rd.* Sun 28 June (1-5). Combined
adm with 40 Ember Lane £6, chd
free. Home-made teas.
An established cottage style
garden, always evolving, and
designed and maintained by the
owners who are passionate about
gardening and collecting plants.
The garden is S-facing, with well
stocked, large, colourful herbaceous
borders containing a wide variety of

Your visits help
change lives -
we've donated
over £17 million
to Macmillan
Cancer Support
since 1984

perennials, evergreen and deciduous
shrubs, a winding lawn area and a
small garden retreat. There is a short
gravel path at the side of the house.

**THE INNER AND MIDDLE
TEMPLE GARDENS, EC4**
Crown Office Row, Inner Temple,
EC4Y 7HL. The Honourable
Societies of the Inner and Middle
Temples, www.innertemple.org.
uk/www.middletemple.org.uk.
*London. Entrance: Main Garden
Gate on Crown Office Row, access
via Tudor Street gate or Middle
Temple Lane gate.* Wed 17 June
(10.30-3). Adm £50. Pre-booking
essential, please visit www.ngs.
org.uk/events for information &
booking. Light refreshments.
Inner Temple Garden is a haven of
tranquillity and beauty with sweeping
lawns, unusual trees and charming
woodland areas. The well known
herbaceous border shows off inspiring
plant combinations from early spring
through to autumn. The award
winning gardens of Middle Temple are
comprised of a series of courtyards
and one larger formal garden. **Adm
incl conducted tour of the gardens
by Head Gardeners. Light lunch
in Middle Temple Hall, one of the
finest examples of an Elizabethan
hall in the country.** Please advise
in advance if wheelchair access is
required.

GROUP OPENING

KEW GREEN GARDENS, TW9
Kew, TW9 3AH. *NW side of Kew
Green. Tube: Kew Gardens. Mainline
Stn: Kew Bridge. Buses: 65, 391.
Entrance via riverside.* Sun 24 May
(2-5). Combined adm £6, chd free.
Evening opening Sun 31 May
(6-8). Combined adm £8, chd free.
Wine. Teas at St Anne's Church
(24 May). Wine (31May).

65 KEW GREEN
Giles & Angela Dixon.

67 KEW GREEN
Lynne & Patrick Lynch.

69 KEW GREEN
John & Virginia Godfrey,
virginiagodfrey69@gmail.com
Visits also by arrangement in
June.

71 KEW GREEN
Mr & Mrs Jan Pethick,
linda@bpethick.co.uk.
Visits also by arrangement in June.

73 KEW GREEN
Sir Donald & Lady Elizabeth
Insall.

These five adjacent long gardens
run for 100 yds from the back of
historic houses on Kew Green down
to the Thames towpath. Together
they cover nearly 1½ acres, and in
addition to the style and structure of
the individual gardens they can be
seen as one large space, exceptional
in London. The borders between
the gardens are mostly relatively
low and the trees and large shrubs
in each contribute to viewing the
whole, while roses and clematis climb
between gardens giving colour to two
adjacent gardens at the same time.
On open days we try to have music
as the sound carries through the five
gardens. South East Regional Winner,
The English Garden's The Nation's
Favourite Gardens 2019. Difficult for
wheelchairs.

**KING HENRY'S WALK GARDEN,
N1**
11c King Henry's Walk, N1 4NX.
**Friends of King Henry's Walk
Garden, www.khwgarden.org.uk.**
*Buses incl: 21, 30, 38, 56, 141, 277.
Behind adventure playground on
KHW, off Balls Pond Rd.* Fri 8 May
(2-4.30). Adm £4, chd free. Home-
made teas. Donation to Friends of
KHW Garden.
Vibrant ornamental planting welcomes
the visitor to this hidden oasis and
leads you into a verdant community
garden with secluded woodland area,
bee hives, wildlife pond, wall trained
fruit trees, and plots used by local
residents to grow their own fruit and
vegetables. Disabled WC.

LAMBETH PALACE, SE1
Lambeth Palace Rd, SE1 7JU.
**The Church Commissioners,
www.archbishopofcanterbury.org.**
*Entrance via Main Gatehouse facing
Lambeth Bridge. Station: Waterloo.
Tube: Westminster, Vauxhall all
10 mins walk. Buses: 3, C10, 77,
344, 507.* Evening opening Mon
18 May (5-8). Adm £6, chd free.
Wine.
Lambeth Palace has one of the

oldest and largest private gardens
in London. It has been occupied by
Archbishops of Canterbury since
1197. Formal courtyard boasts
historic White Marseilles fig planted
in 1556. Parkland style garden
features mature trees, woodland
and native planting. There is a
formal rose terrace, summer gravel
border, scented chapel garden and
active beehives. Garden Tours will
be available. Ramped path to rose
terrace, disabled WC.

NEW **24 LANGTON AVENUE, N20**
Whetstone, N20 9DA. Quentin &
Xihomara Zentner. *Tube: Totteridge:
Buses 263:125:234. 10 mins walk
from Whetstone High St. M&S on R.
Turn R at Buckingham Ave. House
behind conifers corner Langton &
Buckingham. Parking in side road.*
Sun 7 June (2-6). Adm £4. Home-
made teas. Light refreshments,
home-made cakes.
Contemporary front and rear garden
with a big heart. Designed by Chelsea
winner Jilayne Rickards as part of
house renovation. With naturalistic
planting, it reflects the lives of its
owners incorporating Corten steel
screens (Arabic motifs), water feature,
fire pit and ample covered seating
area. The garden is transformed by
lighting into an intimate space at
night. Corten steel hoop sculpture.
Winner of a prestigious BALI award.
Not suitable for wheelchairs. Access
steps with care. Help can be
provided.

12 LANSDOWNE ROAD, W11
W11 3LW. The Lady Amabel
Lindsay. *Tube: Holland Park.
Buses: 12, 88, 94, 148, GL711,
715 to Holland Park, 4 mins walk up
Lansdowne Rd.* Thur 7 May (2.30-
6.30). Adm £5, chd free. Light
refreshments.
A country garden in the heart of
London. An old mulberry tree,
billowing borders, rambling Rosa
banksiae, and a greenhouse of
climbing pelargoniums. Partial
wheelchair access to level paved
surfaces.

12 LAURADALE ROAD, N2
Fortis Green, N2 9LU. David
Gilbert and Mary Medyckyj,
www.sites.google.com/site/
davidgilbertportfolio/garden.
300 metres from 102 & 234 bus

*stops. 500 metres from 43 & 134
bus stops. 10 min walk from East
Finchley Underground Stn Look for
arrows.* Sun 6 Sept (1-6). Adm £4,
chd free. Home-made teas.
Exotic, huge, recently-designed
garden, featuring tropical/
Mediterranean-zone plants. Dramatic,
architectural planting incl bananas,
large tree ferns and rare palms,
weave along curving stone paths,
culminating in a paradise garden. A
modern take on the rockery embeds
glacial boulders amid dry zone
plants, incl many succulents. New
developments this year. Sculptures by
artist owner.

84 LAVENDER GROVE, E8
Hackney, E8 3LS. Anne Pauleau,
a.pauleau@hotmail.co.uk. *Short
walk from Haggerston or London
Fields overground stations.* Sun 21
June (2-5). Adm £3.50, chd free.
**Visits also by arrangement Apr to
Nov for groups of up to 20.**
Two gardens for the price of one!
Country meets town in the heart
of Hackney. Courtyard garden with
tropical backdrop of bamboos and
palms, foil to clipped shrubs leading
to wilder area, the cottage garden
mingling roses, lilies, alliums, grasses,
clematis, poppies, star jasmine and
jasmine. A very highly scented garden
with rampant ramblers and billowing
vegetation enchanting all senses.
Children's quiz offered with prize on
completion.

16 LINKS VIEW ROAD, TW12
Hampton Hill, TW12 1LA. Guy &
Virginia Lewis. *5 mins walk from
Fulwell station. On 281,267,285 and
R70 bus routes.* Sat 23, Sun 24
May (2-5.30). Adm £4, chd free.
Home-made teas. An exciting
selection of home-made cakes
incl gluten free. Cream teas and
herbal teas.
A surprising garden featuring acers,
hostas and fern collection and
other unusual shade loving plants.
Many climbing roses, clematis and
herbaceous border. Rockery and folly
with waterfall, bog garden and small
pond, with grotto. A formal pond. A
mini meadow with chickens. Raised
vegetable and fruit plot. Summer
house and Greenhouse with tender
pelargonium collection. A verandah
with planted pots. Wheelchair access
with help.

2 LITTLEBURY ROAD, SW4

Clapham, SW4 6DN. Jack Wallington, Christopher Anderson & Rosanna Falconer, contact@jackwallington.com, , www.jackwallington.com. *2 mins from Clapham High St station, 4 mins walk from Clapham N & Clapham Common. From main High St, head down Clapham Manor St, turn R down Voltaire Rd past leisure centre. Take 1st L on Littlebury Rd, house on R.* Sun 6 Sept (1-5). Adm £4.50, chd free. Home-made teas.
Visits also by arrangement July to Oct for groups of up to 30.
Small garden, creatively packed with bright colours and interesting plants. Features a collection of 50 different ferns, a micro-pond, unusual tropical plants and quirky indoor plants. September opening sees Dahlias in triumphant, unmissable glory plus canna, persicaria, salvia, clematis and many exotics. Owned by a garden designer/writer who uses his garden as a trial ground for new ideas. Plants in every part of the house, from the front, through rooms and out to the garden. Cut flowers from Jack's allotment.

49 LOFTUS ROAD, W12

W12 7EH. Emma Plunket, emma@plunketgardens.com, www.plunketgardens.com. *Shepherds Bush or Shepherds Bush Market tube, train or bus to Uxbridge Rd. Free street parking.* Sun 14 June (3-6.30). Adm £5, chd free. Wine. **Visits also by arrangement June to Aug for groups of 5 to 10.**
Professional garden designer, Emma Plunket, opens her acclaimed walled garden. Richly planted, it is the ultimate hard working city garden with all year structure and colour incorporating fruit and herbs. Set against a backdrop of trees, this city haven is unexpectedly open and peaceful. Garden plan, plant list and advice available.

2 LONSDALE SQUARE, N1

N1 1EN. Jenny Kingsley, www.artisticmiscellany.com. *Barnsbury. Tube: Highbury & Islington or Angel. Along Liverpool Rd, walk up Richmond Ave. 1st R, entrance via passageway on R.* Sun 7 June (2-6). Adm £2.50, chd free. **Also open Barnsbury Group.**
One could describe our garden as a person: small and unpretentious.

Attractively formed by yew and box hedges and beds with hellebores, fatsia, hydrangeas, arum lily and lively climbing roses, star jasmine and solanum. Planters with olive trees, lavender and pansies are fine companions, mauve, white and emerald favoured colours. She walks delicately on cobblestones, a fountain calms her soul.

10 LORIS ROAD, W6

Hammersmith, W6 7QA. Mrs Cordelia Fraser Trueger. *Loris Rd is a cul-de-sac off Lena Gardens, located behind Shepherds Bush Rd, midway between Hammersmith Underground & Shepherds Bush Underground stations.* Evening opening Sun 7 June (5-7.30). Adm £5, chd free. Light refreshments. Home-made pizza.
Long narrow garden designed by award winning Jo Thompson. This garden is separated into four distinct rooms by clever use of 3D hardscaping, so as to obscure surrounding houses. Espaliered apple trees, steel-framed pergolas, seating areas & a mix of ground textures together with a working pizza oven. Host to more than 20 different roses and 15 clematis as well as many perennials.

NEW 14 LOVELACE AVENUE, BR2

Bromley, BR2 8DQ. Mr Alan Bridger. *3m E of Bromley. Bus 208 from Bromley South Stn to Oxhawth Crescent, or 10min walk from Petts Wood St. Car A21 turn into Magpie Hall Lane to Southborough Lane & then Oxhawth Crescent. Parking in nearby streets.* Sun 5 July (1-5). Adm £4, chd free. Home-made teas.
Hidden behind this terrace house lies a small and exotic garden. Owner has transformed garden of 4m x 22m in just over a year to a tropical oasis filled with colour and towering plants. Room found for a sunny terrace, greenhouse and staggering range of specimen plants, many grown from seed. Wandering path takes you past palms, bananas, cannas, aloes, agaves, yuccas and bright perennials. Terrific example of a tropical garden in a smaller space. Unfortunately not suitable for wheelchair access.

38 LOVELACE ROAD, SE21

Dulwich, SE21 8JX. José & Deepti

Ramos Turnes. *Midway between West Dulwich & Tulse Hill stations.* Buses: 2, 3 & 68. Sun 12 July (1-6). Adm £4, chd free. Home-made teas.
This gem of a garden has an all-white front and a family friendly back. The garden slopes gently upwards with curving borders, packed with an informal mix of roses, perennials and annuals. The garden is designed to be an easy to maintain oasis of calm at the end of a busy day. There are several smile-inducing features e.g. a dragon, the Cheshire cat and a stream. Lots of seating and delicious cake. Here you'll find: a brook with stepping stones and wild-life ponds, wide curving borders packed with colourful perennials - plants for shade, some that love full sun and several that thrive on neglect, two magnificent 40 year old acers, raised vegetable beds & fruit trees and a children's play area.

GROUP OPENING

LOWER CLAPTON GARDENS, E5

Hackney, E5 0RL. *12 mins walk from Hackney Central, Hackney Downs or Homerton stns. Buses 38, 55, 106, 242, 253, 254 or 425, alight Lower Clapton Rd or Powerscroft Rd.* Sun 7 June (2-6). Combined adm £7, chd free. Home-made teas at 77 Rushmore Rd and 75 Mayola Road.

8 ALMACK ROAD
Philip Lightowlers, 07910 850276, plighto@gmail.com.
Visits also by arrangement May to July for groups of up to 20.

NEW 51 GLENARM ROAD
Ms Alice Chadwick.

NEW ✿ 75 MAYOLA ROAD
Ms Christine Taylor.

77 RUSHMORE ROAD
Penny Edwards.

Lower Clapton is an area of mid Victorian terraces sloping down to the River Lea. These gardens reflect their owner's tastes and interests. Two new gardens this year: 15 Glenarm Rd features lush, English gardening with Mediterranean overtones plus a miniature allotment, and 75 Mayola Rd which has a woodland walk and Caribbean style shed. 77 Rushmore Rd has a fruit and vegetable garden and wildlife pond. 8 Almack Rd is a long thin garden with two rooms, one cool and peaceful the other with hot colours and tropical foliage.

GROUP OPENING

LYNDHURST SQUARE GARDEN GROUP, SE15
Lyndhurst Square, SE15 5AR. Group Gardens. *Rail and overground services to Peckham Rye Station or by bus.* Sun 14 June (1.30-5). Combined adm £8, chd free. Home-made teas at number 4. Teas, coffee and soft drinks with delicious home-made cakes. Donation to MIND, Mental Health Charity.

3 LYNDHURST SQUARE
Susan Spindler.

4 LYNDHURST SQUARE
Amelia Thorpe & Adam Russell.

5 LYNDHURST SQUARE
Martin Lawlor & Paul Ward.

7 LYNDHURST SQUARE
Pernille Ahlström & Barry Joseph.

Four very attractive gardens open in this small, elegant square of 1840s listed villas located in Peckham SE London. Each approx 90ft x 50ft has its own shape and style as the Square curves in a U shape. Number 3 traditional English garden. Number 4 family garden serving refreshments. Number 5, the design combines Italianate and Gothic themes with unusual herbaceous plant and towering Echiums. Plants for sale. Number 7 Simplicity, Swedish style, is key with roses and raised beds, framed by yew hedges. Regret no wheelchair access due to narrow paths and uneven surfaces.

NEW MAGGIE'S, SM2
17 Cotswold Road, Sutton, SM2 5NG. Lydia Spencer. *Maggie's at The Royal Marsden is located on the corner of Cotswold Road via the staff entrance to The Royal Marsden NHS Foundation Trust.* Sat 25 Apr, Sat 16 May, Sat 20 June, Sat 4 July (10-5). Adm £5, chd £1. Light refreshments.
The garden surrounding the centre has been designed by world-famous Dutch Landscape Architect Piet Oudolf. The garden has many different zones, some enjoying full

sun and others in dappled shade, whilst the pathway from the hospital meanders under mature trees. Plant communities are carefully chosen, including 14 different grasses, a palette of 6 hardy ferns and more than 50 different perennials.

MAGGIE'S WEST LONDON, W6
Charing Cross Hospital, Fulham Palace Road, Hammersmith, W6 8RF. Miss Anna Wall-Budden. *Follow Fulham Palace Rd from the station towards Charing Cross Hospital. The centre is on the corner of St Dunstan's Rd & is painted tomato-orange so is very visible.* Sat 25 Apr (10-2). Adm £4, chd free. Tea.
The garden at Maggie's West London was designed by Dan Pearson in 2008. It is now a well-established space offering therapy and peace to those affected by cancer each year. The gardens surround the vivid orange walls of the centre. The path leading to the centre meanders through scented beds and mature trees. Visitors have access to various courtyards with a wonderful array of flora including fig trees, grape vines and even a mature pink silk mimosa. Wheelchair access ground floor gardens and courtyards are accessible. Roof gardens not accessible.

GROUP OPENING

MALVERN TERRACE GARDENS, N1
Malvern Terrace, N1 1HR. *Barnsbury, Islington. Malvern Terrace is off Thornhill Rd (nr The Albion PH) between Hemingford Rd & Liverpool Rd.* Sun 3 May (2-5.30). Combined adm £4, chd free. Home-made teas.
Front gardens in this pretty cobbled cul-de-sac of terraced houses, overlooking Thornhill Road Gardens in the heart of Barnsbury. In early May wisteria and roses contribute to the picturesque street. Delicious home-made teas and music add a sense of festivity enjoyed by neighbours and visitors from further afield. One of Islington's hidden gems - an oasis of peace in the city. Live music. There is access but cobbles are hard going for wheelchairs.

4 MANNINGTREE ROAD, HA4
Ruislip, HA4 0ES. Costas Lambropoulos & Roberto Haddon. *Manningtree Rd is just off Victoria Rd, 10-15 mins walk from South Ruislip tube station.* Sun 26 July (2-6). Adm £5, chd free. Home-made teas. Cakes and savouries. Home-made jams and biscuits also for sale.
Compact garden with an exotic feel that combines hardy architectural plants with more tender ones. A feeling of a small oasis incl plants like Musa Basjoo, Ensette Montbelliardii, tree ferns, black bamboo etc. Potted mediterranean plants on the patio incl a fig tree and two olive trees.

53 MANOR ROAD, N16
Stoke Newington, N16 5BH. Jonathan Trustram. *Nr Stoke Newington station & Heathland Rd 106 bus stop.* Sun 24 May (2-6.30). Adm £4, chd free. Home-made teas. Also jams and chutneys for sale.
Big garden for London, thickly enclosed by ivy, roses and jasmine, crowded with plants, many unusual: eryngiums, thalictrums, salvias, pelargoniums, eucomis, inulas, lilies, indigofera, azara, myrtle. Small sculptural rock garden. Soft fruit. Lots of poorly policed self-seeders. Organic credentials finally lost in 30 years war against slugs. Popular plant sale.

GROUP OPENING

MAPLEDENE GARDENS, E8
Mapledene Road, Hackney,
E8 3JW. *7 mins walk from 67, 149, 242, 243 bus stop Middleton Rd, 10 mins from 30, 38, 55 stops on Dalston Lane. 7 mins from Haggerston Overground or 10 mins walk through London Fields from Mare St buses.* **Sun 7 June (2-5.30). Combined adm £6, chd free. Home-made teas at 59 Mapledene Road.**

53 MAPLEDENE ROAD
Tigger Cullinan.

55 MAPLEDENE ROAD
Amanda & Tony Mott.

NEW ✣ **59 MAPLEDENE ROAD**
Sam & Alex Sarginson.

63 MAPLEDENE ROAD
Helen Hunsperger & Simon Mathews.

With much the same space, these 4 long, N-facing and strongly contrasting neighbouring gardens have very different design intentions and styles. No. 53 is an established plantaholic's garden, divided into 4 areas with jewel-like planting. No. 55 is a garden with Moorish influenced terrace leading to a wildlife garden planted to attract birds, butterflies and bees. No. 59's thickly enclosed terraced garden with richly planted mixed border between decking and paving is framed at its entrance by a modern glass extension. and 63 has a romantic feel with repeat planting of roses, hydrangeas and box balls.

MARIE CURIE HOSPICE, HAMPSTEAD, NW3
Lyndhurst Gardens, NW3 5NS. Tracy Annunziato. *In the heart of Hampstead. Nearest tube: Belsize Park. Buses: 46, 268 & C11 all stop nr the Hospice.* **Sun 7 June (2.30-5). Adm £3.50, chd free. Cream teas. In addition to Cream Teas there will also be a range of other refreshments available.**
This peaceful and secluded two part garden surrounds the Marie Curie Hospice, Hampstead. A garden, tended by dedicated volunteers, makes for a wonderful space for patients to enjoy the shrubs and seasonal colourful flowers. The garden has seating areas for

relaxation either in the shade or in the sunshine with great views of the garden and in company with squirrels running through the trees. Step free access to garden and WC.

36 MELROSE ROAD, SW18
SW18 1NE. John Tyrwhitt. *¼ m E of A3 Wandsworth. Entrance behind wooden gates is on Viewfield Rd (on corner of Melrose Rd).* **Sun 14 June, Sun 16 Aug (2-6). Adm £4.50, chd free. Tea. Cake and wine also available.**
Unusual walled and paved garden with different compartments on 2 levels, substantially restructured since previous opening in 2008. Created to provide colour from May through September and year-round interest. Exotic late summer border. Densely planted with roses, architectural plants, shrubs, climbers, and pots. Private and not overlooked.

🍵

30 MERCERS ROAD, N19
N19 4PJ. Ms Joanne Bernstein, www.joannebernstein-gardendesign.com. *Tube: Tufnell Park. Tube: Tufnell Park then 10 mins walk. Holloway Rd, then 5 min Bus 43, 271 to Manor Gardens stop.* **Sun 5 July (2-6). Adm £5, chd free. Home-made teas. Also open 33 Huddleston Road.**
Created by the garden designer owner, strong geometry complements the contemporary architecture of the house extension, softened by billowing prairie style planting in the sunny area and shade tolerant shrubs and perennials in the woodland. There is openness and seclusion and light and shade, all linked by the planting and simple landscaping.

41 MILL HILL ROAD, W3
W3 8JE. Marcia Hurst, 020 8992 2632/07989 581940, marcia.hurst@sudbury-house.co.uk. *Tube: Acton Town, cross zebra crossing, turn R, Mill Hill Rd 2nd R off Gunnersbury Lane. Many local Buses & Overground.* **Evening opening Fri 17 July (7-9). Combined adm with 65 Mill Hill Road £6, chd free. Wine. Sun 23 Aug (2-6). Combined adm with 65 Mill Hill Road £5, chd free. Home-made teas. Visits also by arrangement June to Aug for groups of up to 20.**

Large S-facing garden terrace with pots, lawn bordered by lavender hedge & box topiary. Border incl. salvias, clematis & annuals looking best in July & Aug. In 2019 the owner acquired a large adjoining plot doubling the size of the garden, creating a meadow, gravel garden & pond, mature trees & native hedges for a wildlife garden. Lots of space to sit & enjoy the garden. Good selection of the plants growing in the garden are for sale in pots with planting and growing advice from the knowledgeable owner.

65 MILL HILL ROAD, W3
W3 8JF. Anna Dargavel, 07802 241965, annadargavel@mac.com. *Tube: Acton Town, turn R, Mill Hill Rd on R off Gunnersbury Lane.* **Evening opening Fri 17 July (7-9). Combined adm with 41 Mill Hill Road £6, chd free. Wine. Sun 23 Aug (2-6). Combined adm with 41 Mill Hill Road £5, chd free. Home-made teas. Visits also by arrangement June to Aug for groups of up to 20.**
Garden designer's own garden. A secluded and tranquil space, paved, with changes of level and borders. Sunny areas, topiary, a greenhouse and interesting planting combine to provide a wildlife haven. A pond and organic principles are used to promote a green environment and give a stylish walk to a studio at the end of the garden.

25 MULBERRY WAY, E18
South Woodford, E18 1EB. Mrs Laura Piercy-Farley. *100 metres from South Woodford tube station. ¼ m M11 JW. Public transport central line to South Woodford use westbound exit. Cross the pedestrian crossing & turn L. Garden is 100 meters on the R opp public car park.* **Sun 12 July (1-5). Combined adm with 83 Cowslip Road £5, chd free. Tea.**
A pretty Victorian terraced London house with a dog friendly Italian patio style garden. The garden has a tranquil white theme with a preference for white hydrangeas. The garden has all year interest with box hedges, bay trees evergreen shrubs and climbers. There are places to sit, lounge, eat and relax.

15 NORCOTT ROAD, N16

Stoke Newington, N16 7BJ.
Amanda & John Welch. *Buses: 67, 73, 76, 106, 149, 243, 393, 476, 488. Clapton & Rectory Rd overground stns. One way system: by car approach from Brooke Rd which crosses Norcott Rd, garden in S half of Norcott Rd.* Sun 19 July (2-6). Adm £3.50, chd free. Home-made teas.
A large walled garden developed by the present owners over the last 40 years with pond, aged fruit trees and an abundance of herbaceous plants, many available in our plant sale. We enjoy opening at different times of the year, last year May, this year July - a very different experience. We have plenty of room for people to sit about in the garden enjoying their tea.

26 NORMANDY AVENUE, EN5

Barnet, EN5 2JA. Derek Epstein & Jo Vargas. *Tube: High Barnet then 5 mins walk. Buses: 34, 184, 84,107, 307, 263, 326, 234. Ample parking. Normandy Ave is opp QE Girls School with Old Court House on corner.* Sun 28 June (2-6). Adm £4, chd free. Home-made teas.
120ft garden with three water features, two lawns, two 1920s garden buildings, two terraces, 40 pots, woodland walk, a veggie patch, sculptures and ornaments. A host of plants incl roses, hydrangeas, begonias, shrubs. Some of owners' sculpture and pottery will be on display. Sit on one of the terraces, in the lovely summerhouse, or by the pond while you enjoy tea and delicious cakes.

5 NORTHAMPTON PARK, N1

N1 2PP. Andrew Bernhardt & Anne Brogan. *Backing on to St Paul's Shrubbery, Islington. 5 mins walk from Canonbury stn, 10 mins from Highbury & Islington Tube (Victoria Line) Bus: 30, 277, 341, 476.* Sat 27 June (2-6). Adm £4, chd free. Wine. Refreshments.
Early Victorian S-facing walled garden, (1840's) saved from neglect and developed over the last 25yrs. Cool North European blues, whites and greys moving to splashes of red/orange Mediterranean influence. The contrast of the cool garden shielded by a small park creates a sense of seclusion from its inner London setting.

7 NORWOOD PARK ROAD, SE27

West Norwood, SE27 9UB.
Miss Victoria Twyman & Mr M McKown, 07771543490, victoriatwyman@hotmail.com. *Down the driveway garden to the rear of property on the L. Off Elder Rd. Nearest stn West Norwood. Bus 432 or 10 min walk from West Norwood train station. Some parking on Norwood Park Rd.* Sun 19 July (2-6). Adm £3.50, chd free. Home-made teas. **Visits also by arrangement May to July for groups of up to 10.**
The skills of two artists created this pretty cottage style garden in a suburban setting. Victoria does the planting and Mark created the structures to this 100ft garden divided into three areas. The plants are vibrant, and the star of the summer show is an eye-catching plum tree which in July hangs heavy with luscious fruits. Artists studio doubles up as a relaxing spot for evening sundowners. Homemade cakes and tea for sale incl homemade Plum jam and Elderflower cordial from the garden.

OAK FARM/HOMESTEAD, EN2

Cattlegate Road, Crews Hill, Enfield, EN2 9DS. Genine & Martin Newport. *5 mins. from M25 J24 & J25. Follow yellow signs. Few mins walk from Crews Hill station. Opposite Warmadams. Entrance in Homestead.* Sun 28 June (12-4). Adm £5, chd free. Tea. and cakes in the barn.
In the heart of Crews Hill is our 3 acre garden & meadow. It has been reclaimed over 30 years from pig farm to relaxed planting, a haven for wildlife. Walled garden leads to veg plot, greenhouse, chickens and orchard. Romantic woodland walk, lawns and stone ornaments Martin built the house, the brick walls and metal work The barn will have a exhibition of quilts made by local group that use the barn for charity.

21 OAKLEIGH PARK SOUTH, N20

N20 9JS. Carol and Robin Tullo. *Totteridge and Whetstone tube on N. Line (15 min walk or 251 bus) & Oakleigh Park station (10 mins). Also 34 and 125 from High Rd. Plenty of street parking.* Sun 3 May (2-6). Adm £4, chd free. Home-made teas.

A Spring opening for our second year. A mature 200ft garden framed by a magnificent 100 year old ash tree. Path leads to a pond area fed by a natural spring within landscaped terraced paving. Beyond is a herb and vegetable area, orchard with bulbs and wild flowers and the working part of the garden. A mix of sunny borders, pond marginals and woodland shade areas with seating. Level access to terrace and lawn. Path up to pond area but raised levels beyond.

ORMELEY LODGE, TW10

Ham Gate Avenue, Richmond, TW10 5HB. Lady Annabel Goldsmith. *From Richmond Park exit at Ham Gate into Ham Gate Ave, 1st house on R. From Richmond A307, after 1 1/2 m, past New Inn on R. At T-lights turn L into Ham Gate Ave.* Sun 21 June (3-6). Adm £5, chd free. Home-made teas.
Large walled garden in delightful rural setting on Ham Common. Wide herbaceous borders and box hedges. Walk through to orchard with wild flowers. Vegetable garden, knot garden, aviary and chickens. Trellised tennis court with roses and climbers. A number of historic stone family dog memorials. Dogs not permitted.

4 ORMONDE ROAD, HA6

Moor Park, Northwood, HA6 2EL. Hasruty & Yogesh Patel. *Approx 5m from J17 & 18, M25; 6 1/2 m from J5, M1. From Batchworth Lane take Wolsey Rd exit at mini r'about. Ormonde Rd is 2nd turning on L. Ample parking on Ormonde Rd & surrounding rds.* Sun 31 May (2-5). Adm £5, chd free. Home-made teas.
Beautifully planted frontage entices visitors to a large rear garden. A calm oasis enclosed by mature hedging. A rare variegated flowering tulip tree provides dappled shade alongside rhododendrons, peonies, magnolias and diverse acers. Lavender hues of phlox foam along the raised patio. Much interest throughout the whole garden due to attention paid to successional planting. New lily pond.

PADDOCK ALLOTMENTS & LEISURE GARDENS, SW20

51 Heath Drive, Raynes Park, SW20 9BE. Paddock Horticultural Society. *Bus: 57, 131, 200 to Raynes Pk station then 10 min walk or bus 163. 152 to Bushey Rd 7 min walk; 413, 5 min walk from Cannon Hill Lane. Street parking.* Sat 27 June (12-5). Adm £4, chd free. Light refreshments.

An allotment site not to be missed, over 150 plots set in 5½ acres. Our tenants come from diverse communities growing a wide range of flowers, fruits and vegetables, some plots are purely organic others resemble English country gardens. Winner of London in Bloom Best Allotment on four occasions. Plants, jams and produce for sale. Ploughman's Lunch available. Display of arts and crafts by members of the Paddock Hobby Club. Paved and grass paths, mainly level.

11 PARK AVENUE NORTH, N8

Crouch End, N8 7RU. Mr Steven Buckley & Ms Liz Roberts. *Tube: Finsbury Park or Turnpike Lane, nearest bus stop W3, 144, W7.* Sun 5 July (11.30-5.30). Adm £4, chd free. Home-made teas. Also open Railway Cottages.

An exotic 250ft garden. Dramatic, mainly spiky, foliage dominates, with the focus on palms, agaves, dasylirions, aeoniums, tree ferns, nolinas, cycads, bamboos, yuccas, bananas, cacti and many succulents. Aloes are a highlight. Trees include peach, Cussonia spicata and Szechuan pepper. Rocks and terracotta pots lend a Mediterranean accent. Vegetables grow in oak raised beds and a glasshouse.

18 PARK CRESCENT, N3

Finchley, N3 2NJ. Rosie Daniels. *Tube: Finchley Central. Buses: 13 to Victoria Park, also 125, 460, 626, 683. Walk from Ballards Lane into Etchingham Pk Rd, 2nd L Park Crescent.* Sun 21 June, Sun 19 July (2-6). Adm £4.50, chd free. Home-made teas.

This charming constantly evolving "Secret Garden" is designed and densely planted by the owner. Tumbling roses & clematis in June, lots of salvias and more clematis in July. Two very small ponds, tub water features, bird haven. Stepped terrace with lots of pots. New glass

installations and sculptures by owner. Hidden seating with view through garden. Children's treasure hunt. Extensive collection of clematis and salvias. London Gardens Society: Silver Gilt Award.

GROUP OPENING

PARK ROAD GARDENS, W4

W4 3HH. *Arrive by overground train at Chiswick Stn, follow Park Rd (opp the stn, N side) for approx ½m north.* Sun 19 July (2.30-6.30). Combined adm £5.50, chd free. Tea. Wine will be served for a donation.

34 PARK ROAD
Simon Lockett.

36 PARK ROAD
Meyrick & Louise Chapman.

56 PARK ROAD
Richard Treganowan.

Three gardens, each with a distinct aesthetic. One emphases the mediterranean planting in a modern, architectural setting. A second offers a more formal interpretation of a modern design, with overt reference to historic elements of nearby Chiswick House Gardens. The third, 56, offers an exciting interpretation of exotic planting created over many years by Richard Treganowan and his late wife, Diane. Within its own microclimate it showcases exotics and foliage over flowers. The garden also features a mature stumpery. Each garden is an exercise in scale and appropriate planting resulting in entirely different personalities within just 100 meters of a suburban London Street. Partial wheelchair access.

NEW 36 PARK VILLAGE EAST, NW1

Camden Town, NW1 7PZ. Christy Rogers. *Tube: Mornington Crescent or Camden Town 7 mins. Opp railway just S of Mornington Street Bridge. Free parking all weekend.* Sun 28 June (2-6). Adm £5, chd free. Home-made teas. Also open 70 Gloucester Crescent.

A large peaceful garden behind a sympathetically modernised John Nash house. Re-landscaped in 2014, retaining the original mature

sycamores and adding hornbeam hedges dividing a woodland area and orchard from a central large lawn, mixed herbaceous border and rose bank. Children enjoy an artificial grass slide. Musical entertainment is provided by young local musicians. Grass ramp down from driveway to main garden, however, much steeper than stipulated by wheelchair regulations.

3 THE PARK, N6

off Southwood Lane, N6 4EU. Mr & Mrs G Schrager, 020 8348 3314, buntyschrager@gmail.com. *3 mins from Highgate tube, up Southwood Lane. The Park is 1st on R. Buses: 43, 134, 143, 263.* Sun 17 May (2.30-5.30). Adm £4, chd free. Home-made teas. Visits also by arrangement Apr to June for groups of 5 to 20.

Established large garden with informal planting for colour, scent and bees. Pond with fish, frogs and tadpoles. Tree peonies, Crinodendron hookerianum and Paulownia. Plants, tea and home-made jam for sale. Children particularly welcome - a treasure hunt with prizes!

98 PARKWAY, NW1

Camden Town, NW1 7AN. Fanny Calder. *A short walk from Camden Tube Station - the entrance is at basement level, next door to the Rock and Roll Charity Shop.* Sun 28 June (2-5.30). Adm £3, chd free. Home-made teas. Also open 70 Gloucester Crescent.

A small, walled townhouse garden hidden away unexpectedly behind a busy street of shops and cafes in Camden. The garden is predominantly a very diverse collection of white flowering plants in several raised beds and large pots - roses, allium, iris, peonies, clematis, aquilegia, geraniums, dicentra and more. Accessed by steep steps so not suitable for people with mobility problems.

5 PEMBERTON ROAD, KT8

East Molesey, KT8 9LG. Armi Maddison. *Please enter the garden down the side path to the RHS of the house.* Sun 14 June (2-5). Adm £4.50, chd free. Light refreshments.

An artist's sheltered and secluded gravel garden designed alongside our new build in 2015. Many grasses, pink blue and white planting with occasional 'pops' of bright colour, a galvanised drinking trough with bullrushes and water lilies, a large mature central acer tree combine with several sitting areas to extend our living space into fabulous outdoor room.

23 & 24B PENN ROAD, N7

Lower Holloway, N7 9RD. Pierre Delarue & Mark Atkinson. *Between Camden Town & Holloway. Buses: 29 or 253 to Hillmarton Rd or 91 to Camden Rd stops. Tube: Caledonian Road on Piccadilly line, 6 mins walk.* Sun 7 June (1.30-5.30). Adm £5, chd free. Home-made teas. Also open 60 & 62 Hungerford Road. 2 neighbouring gardens famous for their planting as well as delicious teas & home-made cakes. Access through a leafy passage at No.23, fronted with prairie wilderness. The main 25x70ft back garden presents a mixture of old-fashioned roses & Mediterranean plants to achieve an exotic feel. Specimen plants incl a Red Barked Arbutus, a Santa Cruz Ironwood, an Orange Barked Myrtle & a tall 'stripped' Trachycarpus. A neoclassic studio with patio and newly installed water feature act as focal point. The 25X46ft 'pleasure garden' at 24b is now accessible through a gate & features three contrasting borders: dry, woodland & roses. A selection of refreshments will be served inside the Garden Studio alongside a wide range of delicious homemade Bundt cakes in a variety of interesting flavours, now integral to the NGS experience at 23 Penn Road.

PETERSHAM HOUSE, TW10

Petersham Road, Petersham, Richmond, TW10 7AA. Francesco & Gael Boglione, www.petershamhouse.com. *Stn: Richmond, Bus 65 to Dysart. Entry to garden off Petersham Rd, through nursery. Parking very limited on Church Lane.* Sun 19 Apr (11-5). Adm £5, chd free. Light refreshments in the nursery. Broad lawn with large topiary, generously planted double borders. Productive vegetable garden with chickens. Adjoins Petersham Nurseries with extensive plant sales, shop and café serving lunch, tea and cake.

3 Elmbridge Lodge

470 PINNER ROAD, HA5

Pinner, HA5 5RR. Nitty Chamcheon. *N Harrow Station, L to T-lights, L at next T-lights, cross to be on Pinner Rd. L - 3rd house from T-lights. Parking: Pinner Rd & George V Av - yellow lines stop after 15 yds.* Sun 27 Sept (2-5). Adm £4, chd free. Home-made teas. Once (20 yrs ago) a back yard with just a lawn in the first half and the second half a jungle with a very mature apple and pear tree; now a beautiful garden. A path passing through fruit and vegetable garden to the secret log cabin after a bridge over the pond with waterfall in front of a tree house in the pear tree. An attempt has been made to extend the season as far as possible.

36 POTTERS LANE, EN5

Barnet, EN5 5BE. Roderick Muir & Laurence Little. *New Barnet. High Barnet tube 15 min walk down Meadway. R into King Edward Rd and 2nd R into Potters Lane. Buses: from N get off opp BP garage. From S Everyman cinema. 7min walk up Potters Lane.* Sun 24 May (1-6). Adm £5, chd free. Home-made teas.

Our garden has evolved, and is still evolving, over the 31 years that we have been working on it. The garden is unusually long (325 ft) for a suburban garden and is on a gentle slope away from the house. It is divided into different areas, a formal garden, a working garden, a less formal area leading to a gate through a purple beech hedge into a secret garden and wildlife pond.

Your visits help change lives – we are Hospice UK's largest charitable funder donating more than £5.5 million to support hospices in local communities since 1996

GROUP OPENING

PRINCES AVENUE GARDENS, N10

Muswell Hill, N10 3LS. Buses: 43 & 134 from Highgate tube; also W7, 102, 144, 234, 299. Princes Ave opp M&S in Muswell Hill Broadway, or John Baird PH in Fortis Green. Sun 17 May (2-6). Combined adm £5, chd free. Home-made teas.

17 PRINCES AVENUE
Patsy Bailey & John Rance.

28 PRINCES AVENUE
Ian & Viv Roberts.

In a beautiful Edwardian avenue in the heart of Muswell Hill Conservation Area, two very different gardens reflect the diverse life styles of their owners. The charming garden at No 17 is designed for relaxing and entertaining. Although south facing it is shaded by large surrounding trees - among which is a ginko. The garden features a superb hosta and fern display. No 28 is a well established traditional garden reflecting the charm typical of the era. Mature trees, shrubs, mixed borders and woodland garden creating an oasis of calm just off the bustling Broadway. Live music at No 17 from the Secret Life Sax Quartet, 4:30 - 5:30 pm.

GROUP OPENING

RAILWAY COTTAGES, N22
2 Dorset Road, Alexandra Palace, N22 7SL. *Tube: Wood Green, 10 mins walk. Overground: Alexandra Palace, 3 mins. Buses W3, 184. 3 mins. Free parking in local streets on Suns.* Sun 5 July (2-5.30). Combined adm £4.50, chd free. Home-made teas at 2 Dorset Rd. Also open 11 Park Avenue North.

2 DORSET ROAD
Jane Stevens.

4 DORSET ROAD
Mark Longworth.

14 DORSET ROAD
Cathy Brogan.

22 DORSET ROAD
Mike & Noreen Ainger.

24A DORSET ROAD
Eddie & Jane Wessman.

A row of historical railway cottages, tucked away from the bustle of Wood Green nr Alexandra Palace, takes the visitor back in time.The tranquil country style garden at 2 Dorset Rd flanks three sides of the house. Clipped hedges contrast with climbing roses, clematis, honeysuckle, abutilon, grasses and ferns. Trees incl mulberry, quince, fig, apple and a mature willow creating an interesting

shady corner with a pond. There is an emphasis on scented flowers that attract bees and butterflies and the traditional medicinal plants found in cottage gardens. No 4 is a pretty secluded garden (accessed through the rear of no 2), and sets off the sculptor owners figurative and abstract work. There are three front gardens open for view. No 14 is an informal, organic, bee friendly garden, planted with fragrant and useful herbs, flowers and shrubs. No 22 is nurtured by the grandson of the original railway worker occupant. A lovely place to sit and relax and enjoy the varied planting. No.24a reverts to the potager style cottage garden with raised beds overflowing with vegetables and flowers.

ROOFTOPVEGPLOT, W1
122 Gt Titchfield Street, Wondon, W1W 6ST. Miss Wendy Shillam, 020 7637 0057, coffeeinthesquare@me.com, www.rooftopvegplot.com. *Fitzrovia. Located on the 5th floor, flat roof of a private house. Ring the doorbell marked Shillam & Smith to be let into the building.* Sat 27, Sun 28 June (11-5). Adm £5, chd free. Pre-booking essential, please visit www.ngs.org.uk/events for information & booking. Cream teas. Cakes and drinks using organic and fresh ingredients - cash only. All money goes to NGS charities.

A nutritional garden, where fruit and veg grow amongst complementary flowers in six inches of soil, in raised beds on a flat roof. This is a tiny garden, so tours are restricted to six persons. Home-made cakes and growing and nutritional tips from Wendy Shillam, a keen environmentalist with an extensive knowledge of green nutrition. Tomatoes and cucumber growing in a greenhouse. Grapevine, Apple, Elder, Jasmine, Japanese wineberry. Strawberries, Potatoes. Salads, garlic, annuals, roses, marigolds, nasturtiums, sweet and garden peas, climbing beans and courgettes. 2020 will see us trying Indian (climbing) spinach. Sorry no wheelchair access. 5 flights of stairs to get up to the garden. Resting places on landings and in the studio at the top.

24 Twyford Avenue

ROYAL TRINITY HOSPICE, SW4

30 Clapham Common North Side, SW4 0RN. **Royal Trinity Hospice, www.royaltrinityhospice.org.uk.** *Tube: Clapham Common. Buses: 35, 37, 345,137 (37 + 137 stop outside).* Sun 12 Apr, Sun 31 May, Sun 6 Sept (10.30-4.30). Adm £3.50, chd free. Tea.
Royal Trinity's beautiful, award winning gardens play an important therapeutic role in the life and function of Royal Trinity Hospice. Over the years, many people have enjoyed our gardens and today they continue to be enjoyed by patients, families and visitors alike. Set over nearly 2 acres, they offer space for quiet contemplation, family fun and make a great backdrop for events. Picnics welcome. Ramps and pathways.

7 ST GEORGE'S ROAD, TW1

St Margarets, Twickenham, TW1 1QS. **Richard & Jenny Raworth, 020 8892 3713, jraworth@gmail.com, www.raworthgarden.com.** *1½m SW of Richmond. Off A316 between Twickenham Bridge & St Margarets r'about.* Evening opening Sun 7 June (6-8). Adm £7, chd free. Wine. **Visits also by arrangement May to July for groups of 10 to 30.**
Exuberant displays of Old English roses and vigorous climbers with unusual herbaceous perennials. Massed scented crambe cordifolia. Pond with bridge converted into child safe lush bog garden and waterfall. Large N-facing luxuriant conservatory with rare plants and climbers. Pelargoniums a speciality. Sunken garden Pergola covered with climbing roses and clematis. New white garden. Water feature and fernery. Reading Garden.

87 ST JOHNS ROAD, E17

Walthamstow, Walthamstow, E17 4JH. **Andrew Bliss.** *15 mins walk from W'stow tube/overground or 212/275 bus. Alight at St Johns Rd stop.10 mins walk from Wood St overground. Very close to N Circular.* Sun 26, Mon 27 July (1.30-5.30). Adm £3.50, chd £1. Home-made teas.
My garden epitomises what can be achieved with imagination, design and colour consideration in a small typical terraced outdoor area. Its themes are diverse and incl a fernery, Jardin Majorelle, and 3 individual seating

areas. All enhanced with circles, mirrors and over planting to create an atmosphere of tranquility within an urban environment.

27 ST PETERS SQUARE, W6

W6 9NW. **Oliver & Gabrielle Leigh Wood, oliverleighwood@hotmail.com.** *Tube to Stamford Brook exit station & turn S down Goldhawk Rd. At T-lights cont ahead into British Grove. Entrance to garden at 50 British Grove 100 yds on L.* Sun 26 Apr (2-6). Adm £5, chd free. Home-made teas. **Visits also by arrangement Apr to July.**
This long, secret space, is a plantsman's eclectic semi-tamed wilderness. Created over the last 10yrs it contains lots of camellias, magnolias and fruit trees. Much of the hard landscaping is from skips and the whole garden is full of other people's unconsidered trifles of fancy incl a folly and summer house.

19 ST PETER'S STREET, N1

Islington, N1 8JD. **Adrian Gunning.** *Angel, Islington. Tube: Angel. Bus: Islington Green.* Sun 14 June (2.30-5.30). Adm £3.50, chd free. Also open Arlington Square Gardens. Teas available at St James' Vicarage, 1A Arlington Square, N1 7DS.
Charming secluded town garden with climbing roses, trees, shrubs, climbers, pond, patio with containers, and a gazebo with a trompe l'oeil mural.

Your visits help change lives – your generosity helps Marie Curie fund nurses to care for people night and day in their homes, with donations of more than £9 million

57 ST QUINTIN AVENUE, W10

W10 6NZ. **Mr H Groffman, 020 8969 8292.** *Less than 1m from Ladbroke Grove or White City tube. Buses: 7, 70, 220 all to North Pole Rd. Free parking on Sundays.* Sun 5, Sun 19 July (2-6). Adm £5, chd free. Home-made teas. **Visits also by arrangement July & Aug.**
A 30 x 40 ft garden with a diverse selection of plants incl shrubs for foliage effects. Patio with colour themed bedding material. Focal points throughout. Clever use of mirrors and plant associations. New look, new patio layout, new plantings for 2020 with a good selection of climbers and wall shrubs. Recipient 2018 Mayoral Award for Services to Horticulture. Special theme for 2020 to commemorate 75th anniversary of VE Day and end of WW2.

5 ST REGIS CLOSE, N10

Alexandra Park Road, Muswell Hill, N10 2DE. **Ms S Bennett & Mr E Hyde, 020 8883 8540, suebearlh@yahoo.co.uk.** *Tube: Bounds Green then 102 or 299 bus, or E. Finchley take 102. Alight St Andrews Church. 134 or 43 bus stop at end of Alexandra Pk Rd, follow arrows.* Sun 3 May, Sun 28 June (2-6.30). Sun 26 July (2-6.30), also open 35 Weston Park. Adm £4, chd free. Home-made teas. Gluten free available. Herbal teas. **Visits also by arrangement Apr to Oct for groups of 10+. Short talk on history of the garden. Cost according to catering.**
Cornucopia of sensual delights. Artist's garden famous for architectural features and delicious cakes. New Oriental Tea House. Baroque temple, pagodas, Raku tiled mirrored wall conceals plant nursery. American Gothic shed overlooks Liberace Terrace and stairway to heaven. Maureen Lipman's favourite garden, combines colour, humour, trompe l'oeil with wildlife friendly ponds, waterfalls, weeping willow, lawns, abundant planting. A unique experience awaits! Unusual architectural features including Oriental Tea House overlooking carp pond. Mega plant sale. Open Studio with ceramics and cards. Wheelchair access to all parts of garden unless waterlogged.

West Lodge Park

9 SHORTGATE, N12
**Woodside Park, N12 7JP. John &
Jane Owen.** *Bus: 326, alight at the
green on Southover, follow signs.
Tube: Woodside Park, exit from
northbound platform, follow signs.
Parking: surrounding roads, NOT
Shortgate.* Sun 5 July (1.30-5.30).
Adm £4.50, chd free. Home-made
teas.
A large secluded garden at the
end of a quiet cul-de-sac. Trees
screen surrounding houses,
providing a wooded walkway with
hidden surprises. A large lawn with
herbaceous borders, a rockery and
two small ponds. There is a vegetable
garden and a fruit cage. 19 water
butts help reduce the use of tap
water, and create a naturally fed
irrigation system created by owner
as do drought tolerant plants, both
exotic and traditional. Several steps
and uneven surfaces.

**SOUTH LONDON BOTANICAL
INSTITUTE, SE24**
**323 Norwood Road, SE24 9AQ.
South London Botanical Institute,
www.slbi.org.uk.** *Mainline stn: Tulse
Hill. Buses: 68, 196, 322 & 468 stop
at junction of Norwood & Romola
Rds.* Sun 19 Apr (2-5). Adm £3.50,
chd free. Home-made teas.
Donation to South London Botanical
Institute.

London's smallest botanical garden,
densely planted with 500 labelled
species grown in themed borders.
Wildflowers flourish beside medicinal
herbs. Carnivorous, scented, native
and woodland plants are featured,
growing among rare trees and
shrubs. Spring highlights incl mosses,
unusual bulbs and flowering trees.
The fascinating SLBI building is also
open. Our small cafe serves home-
made teas.

41 SOUTHBROOK ROAD, SE12
**Lee, SE12 8LJ. Barbara & Marek
Polanski.** *Southbrook Rd is situated
off S Circular, off Burnt Ash Rd.
Train: Lee & Hither Green, both
10 mins walk. Bus: P273, 202.*
Sun 31 May (2-5). Adm £4, chd
free. Home-made teas. orange
squash, tea and cakes. Opening
with Blackheath Gardens on Sun
14 June.
Developed over 14yrs, this large
garden has a formal layout, with wide
mixed herbaceous borders full of
colour and interest, surrounded by
mature trees, framing sunny lawns,
a central box parterre and an Indian
pergola. Ancient pear trees festooned
in June with clouds of white Kiftsgate
and Rambling Rector roses. Discover
fish and damselflies in 2 lily ponds.
Many sheltered places to sit and
relax. Enjoy refreshments in a small

classical garden building with interior
wall paintings, almost hidden by
roses climbing way up into the trees.
Orangery. Side access available
for standard wheelchairs. Gravel
driveway, a few steps in sidepath.

131 SOUTHGATE ROAD, N1
**N1 3JZ. John Le Huquet and Vicki
Primm-Sexton.** *East Canonbury.
Bank or Old St tube then 21 or 141
bus to Englefield Rd stop (outside
house). Highbury & Islington tube,
30 bus to Southgate Rd stop, 5 min
wk. Angel tube, 38, 56 or 73 bus to
Ockendon Rd, 5 min walk.* Sun 5
July (12-6). Adm £3.50, chd free.
Light refreshments.
Open for the second time, this
vivacious little walled town garden is
densely planted with over 50 species
of sun-loving perennials, creating
an intense visual experience. The
lush, naturalistic planting showcases
a jamboree of jewel-like blooms
weaving through softly waving
grasses and delicate umbellifers.
Specially commissioned Corten
steel wall screens and a charming
idiosyncratic shed. Garden reached
by staircase.

SOUTHWOOD LODGE, N6

33 Kingsley Place,
Highgate, N6 5EA. Mrs S
Whittington, 020 8348 2785,
suewhittington@hotmail.co.uk.
*Tube: Highgate then 6 mins uphill
walk along Southwood Lane. 4 min
walk from Highgate Village along
Southwood Lane. Buses: 143, 210,
214, 271.* Sun 3 May (2-5.30). Adm
£4, chd free. Home-made teas.
**Visits also by arrangement Apr to
July. Lunch for groups of 10+, or
teas (any number) by arrangement.**
Densely planted garden hidden
behind C18 house (not open). Many
unusual plants, some propagated
for sale. Ponds, waterfall, frogs,
toads, newts. Topiary shapes formed
from self sown yew trees. Sculpture
carved from three trunks of a massive
conifer which became unstable in a
storm. Hard working greenhouse!
Only one open day this year so visits
by appointment especially welcome.
Toffee hunt for children. Secret Life
Sax Quartet will perform in the garden
from 2.30pm.

NEW ◆ SPENCER HOUSE, SW1

27 St James' Place, Westminster,
SW1A 1NR. RIT Capital Partners,
www.spencerhouse.co.uk. *From
Green Park tube: Exit station on
south side, walk down Queen's Walk,
turn L through narrow alleyway.
Turn R & Spencer House will be in
front of you.* **For opening times and
information, please visit garden
website.**
Originally designed in the eighteenth
century by Henry Holland (son-in-law
to Lancelot 'Capability' Brown), the
garden was among the grandest
in the West End. Restored since
1990 under the Chairmanship of
Lord Rothschild, the garden, with a
delightful view of the adjacent Royal
Park, now evokes its original layout
with planting suggested by early
nineteenth-century nursery lists.

GROUP OPENING

SPITALFIELDS GARDENS, E1

E1 6QE. *Nr Spitalfields Market. 10
mins walk from Aldgate E Tube &
5 mins walk from Liverpool St stn.
Overground: Shoreditch High St - 3
mins walk.* Sat 13 June (11-4).
Combined adm £15, chd free.
Home-made teas at Town House,
5 Fournier St, 29 & 30 Fournier St.
Maps available.

26 ELDER STREET

The Future Laboratory.

FLAT 1, 30 CALVIN STREET

Susan Young.

20 FOURNIER STREET

Ms Charlie de Wet.

29 FOURNIER STREET

Juliette Larthe.

31 FOURNIER STREET

Tom Holmes.

21 PRINCELET STREET

Marianne & Nicholas Morse.

37 SPITAL SQUARE

Society for the Protection of
Ancient Buildings.

21 WILKES STREET

Rupert Wheeler.

Discover a selection of courtyard
gardens, some very small, behind fine
C17 French Huguenots merchants'
and weavers' houses in Spitalfields.
Visit the courtyard of 37 Spital
Square, on the site of the C12
priory of St Mary's Spital, now the
Society for the Protection of Ancient
Buildings, founded by William Morris
in 1877. Experience a 'vertical'
garden and roof terrace in nearby
Elder Street, an architect-designed
garden in Wilkes Street, three small
courtyards in Fournier Street, a
larger imaginatively created garden
in Princelet Street, and a 'theatrical'
garden in Calvin St, behind a former
warehouse. Each garden owner
has adapted their particular urban
space to complement an historic
house: vegetables, herbs, vertical and
horizontal beds, ornamental pots,
statuary and architectural artefacts
abound . Plants for sale at SPAB &
Town House.

> Your visits help
> change lives – we
> are the largest
> single funder
> of the Queen's
> Nursing Institute

NEW 1 SPRING PARK AVENUE, CR0

Shirley, Croydon, CR0 5EJ. Mr
Mike Blake. *5m E of Croydon.
Car-Wickham Rd, A232, turn S into
West Way Gardens, R into Spring
Park Av. Public trans- E Croydon
station-fr buses-194,119,198 to
Verdayne Avenue- cross to West
Way Gardens, R into Spring Park Av.*
Sun 12 July (2-5.30). Adm £4, chd
free. Light refreshments.
Open sunny aspect town garden
completely redesigned in 2018. Very
colourful herbaceous planting with
many specimen plants, bulbs and
roses using existing trees and shrubs
to great effect. Easy access to all
parts of garden via curving paths
that lead pass two circular lawns to
custom built oak pergola. Child safe
water feature and raised bedding
areas provide variety, garden access
and interest. A child safe water
feature can be found half way down
the garden, and a patio with seating
is positioned adjacent to the house.
Raised beds, approx 1m high allow
for the less able to plant more easily.
Wheelchair access stone pathway
through garden.

25 SPRINGFIELD AVENUE, N10

Muswell Hill, N10 3SU. Nigel Ragg
& Heather Hampson. *Off Muswell
Hill. Buses 102 299 W7 134 43 From
main r'about at Muswell Hill descend
towards Crouch End . Springfield Av
1st L.* Sun 21 June (2-6). Adm £4,
chd free. Home-made teas.
A mystical and secluded garden
packed with take home ideas. Spread
over 3 atmospheric terraces up to a
backdrop of the trees of Alexandra
Palace. Travel through perennial
planted beds of hydrangeas and
climbing roses shaded by the old
apple tree. The middle terrace is lawn
surrounded by shrubs and climbers.
The south facing paved terrace has
sunny flower beds, water features and
pots. This is a garden full of surprises
from the secluded setting to the
sense of journey from a medium sized
city garden. Three main terraces rising
to a south facing summer house. It
has its challenges as the bottom is
north facing and heavy clay to the top
which is south facing and hot. Uneven
steps.

STOKES HOUSE, TW10
Ham Street, Ham, Richmond, TW10 7HR. Peter & Rachel Lipscomb, 020 8940 2403, rlipscomb@virginmedia.com. *2m S of Richmond off A307. Trains & tube to Richmond & train to Kingston which link with 65 bus stopping at Ham Common every 6 mins.* Sun 7 June (2-5). Adm £4, chd free. Home-made teas. Visits also by arrangement Apr to Sept for groups of 10 to 30.
Originally an orchard, this ½ acre walled country garden surrounding Georgian house (not open) is abundant with roses, clematis and perennials. There are mature trees incl ancient mulberries and wisteria. The yew hedging, pergola and box hedges allow for different planting schemes throughout the year. Supervised children are welcome to play on the slide and swing. Herbaceous borders, brick garden, wild garden, large compost area and interesting trees. Teas, garden tour, history of house and area for group visits. Wheelchair access via double doors from street with 2 wide steps. Unfortunately no access for larger motorised chairs.

  🚲 🐕 ❀ ☕

STONEY HILL HOUSE, SE26
Rock Hill, Sydenham, SE26 6SW. Cinzia & Adam Greaves. *Off Sydenham Hill. Train: Sydenham, Gipsy Hill or Sydenham Hill (closest) stations. Buses: To Crystal Palace, 202 or 363 along Sydenham Hill. House at end of cul-de-sac on L coming from Sydenham Hill.* Sun 24 May (2-6). Adm £5, chd free. Home-made teas. All cakes are home-made and delicious! Prosecco will also be available to enjoy whilst listening to the saxophone quartet.
Garden and woodland of approx 1 acre providing a secluded secret green oasis in the city. Paths meander through mature rhododendron, oak, yew and holly trees, offset by pieces of contemporary sculpture. The garden is on a slope and a number of viewpoints set at different heights provide varied perspectives. The planting in the top part of the garden is fluid and flows seamlessly into the woodland. Fresalca, a wonderful saxophone quartet, will be playing for the afternoon. Swings and woodland tree-house. Access to the main part of the garden is via shallow steps or a grassy slope so assistance will be required.

  🚲 ❀ ☕

SWAKELEYS COTTAGE, 2 THE AVENUE, UB10
Ickenham, Uxbridge, UB10 8NP. Lady Singleton Booth. *Take the B466 to Ickenham from the A40 at Hillingdon Circus. Go 1m into Ickenham village. Coach and Horses PH on R, turn L into Swakeley's Rd. After the shops, The Avenue is on L.* Sun 5 July (2-5). Adm £4, chd free. Home-made teas.
Classic English cottage garden. The garden has been designed by Lady Booth and her late husband Sir Christopher Booth. The garden is charming and wraps around a 600 year old cottage. It consists of herbaceous borders which are dotted with vegetables, garden herbs & fruit trees. There is an abundance of colour and some very interesting plants incorporating different styles.

  ♿ ☕

93 TANFIELD AVENUE, NW2
Dudden Hill, NW2 7SB. Mr James Duncan Mattoon. *Dudden Hill - Neasden. Nearest station: Neasden - Jubilee line then 10 mins walk; or various bus routes to Neasden Parade or Tanfield Ave.* Sun 19 July (2-6). Adm £5, chd free. Home-made teas.
New Chamomile lawn and newly finished Arabic style watercourse, complete an 9 year development of this Plantsman's hillside paradise garden! Raised Deco deck with panoramic views, plunges down steps into Mediterranean and subtropical oasis, overflowing with many rare and exotic plants e.g. Caesalpinia, Hedychium, Puya,! To rear, jungle shade terrace offers cool views of paradise on sunny days. Previous garden was Tropical Kensal Rise (Doyle Gardens), featured on BBC2 Open Gardens and in Sunday Telegraph.

  ❀ ☕

31 TRELAWN ROAD, SW2
SW2 1DH. Mr Mark Simmons. *Brixton. Brixton Tube, turn L along Effra Road towards Sainsbury's. Walk past Halfords and Trelawn Road 1st St on L. Buses 2, 3, 37, 196 & 415.* Sun 7 June (1.30-5). Adm £3.50, chd free. Home-made teas. Also open Brixton Water Lane Gardens. Cakes & biscuits, gluten free/vegan friendly.
A small city garden, only five years old, and designed to give the illusion of space, with a winding path and hidden vistas. Featured in

House Beautiful magazine (06/19). Crammed with plants and dominated by perennials, roses and a crevice garden. There is no lawn, but several seating areas from which to contemplate the space.

  ☕

TRUMPETERS' HOUSE & SARAH'S GARDEN, TW9
Trumpeters' House, Old Palace Yard, Richmond, TW9 1PD. Baroness Van Dedem. *Richmond riverside. 5 mins walk from Richmond Station via Richmond Green in Old Palace Yard. Parking on Richmond Green & Old Deer Park car park only.* Sat 27 June (2-5). Adm £5, chd free. Home-made teas.
The 2 acre garden is on the original site of Richmond Palace. Long lawns stretch from the house to banks of the River Thames. There are clipped yews, a box parterre and many unusual shrubs and trees, a rose garden and oval pond with carp. The ancient Tudor walls are covered with roses and climbers. Discover Sarah's secret gravel garden, orchard, dovecote and mid C18 summerhouse. Wheelchair access on grass and gravel.

  ♿ ☕

24 TWYFORD AVENUE, N2
East Finchley, N2 9NJ. Rachel Lindsay and Jeremy Pratt. *Twyford Ave runs parallel to Fortis Green, between East Finchley & Muswell Hill. Tube: Northern line to East Finchley. Buses 102, 143, 234, 263 to East Finchley. Buses 43, 134, 144, 234 to Muswell Hill. Buses 102 & 234 stop at end of rd. Garden signposted from Fortis Green.* Sun 12 July (2-6). Adm £4, chd free. Home-made teas.
Sunny, 120 foot S facing garden, planted for colour. Brick-edged borders and over-flowing containers packed with masses of traditional herbaceous and perennial cottage garden plants and shrubs. Shady area at rear evolving as much by happy accident as design. Some uneven ground. Water feature. Greenhouse bursting with cuttings. Many places to sit and think, chat or doze. Sale of honey & Bee products.

  🐾 🐕 ❀ ☕

333 VICTORIA PARK ROAD, FLAT 2, E9
Flat 2, Homerton, E9 5DX. Mrs E Cole, 07810 641463, elsacole01@gmail.com.

Overground - 10 mins walk from Homerton Station. Buses 30, 26, 388 alight Wick Road. Tube - Bethnal Green station + 388 bus. Sun 7 June (1.30-5.30). Adm £3, chd free. Home-made teas. Visits also by arrangement May & June for groups of up to 10.

N facing urban garden in which oak sleepers manage a difference in levels equivalent to 1½ floors. Steps lead from a patio to a gravelled landing and then up to a lawn, several borders, a rose arch and a sunny seating area. The geometry is softened by fruit trees, roses, hydrangeas, camellias, ferns and geraniums. Beware: not a garden for people with mobility issues as the steps have no handrails.

✿ ☕

NEW 9 VIEW ROAD, N6

N6 4DJ. Paul and Sophia Davison. *A 9 minute walk (½m) from Highgate Tube. Buses: 134, 43, 263 to Highgate Tube, 143 to North Hill. View Rd is a turning off North Hill. Please enter the garden via the path to the LHS of house.* Sun 14 June (2-5). Adm £4, chd free. Home-made teas.

A well stocked, informally planted front garden leads to a generous rear garden which has been lovingly coaxed back from its wild, overgrown state by the current owners. Large lawn, beautiful hornbeam hedge spanning the garden, mature trees (incl handkerchief trees) bulbs and perennials. Fruit trees, grasses, and a greenhouse plus an enchanting tree house. A garden which continues to evolve. Front garden fully wheelchair accessible, access to the terrace part of the rear garden step free. Steps down to the lawn. Some uneven paths.

♿ ☕

1 WADES GROVE, N21

N21 1BH. C & K Madhvani. *Tube: Southgate then W9 to Winchmore Hill Green then short walk. Train: Winchmore Hill then short walk via Wades Hill.* Sun 5 July (2-6). Adm £3.50, chd free. Home-made teas. Also open 5 Harwood's Yard.

Tiny secluded space in charming peaceful cul-de-sac as featured on the TV series presented by Dee Hart Dyke and Miranda Hart, 'All Gardens Great and Small'. Views divided by selection of mature and young trees. Planting loose and naturalistic. Focus on scented plants, edibles, ground

and wall coverings. Designed to encourage wildlife. Interesting use of recycled materials. Visitors welcome to explore tranquil adjoining Quaker gardens (free) via secret entrance.

✿ ☕

12 WARNER ROAD, N8

N8 7HD. Linnette Ralph. *Nr Alexandra Palace, between Crouch End & Muswell Hill. Turning off Priory Rd. Tube to Finsbury Park then W3 bus to Hornsey Fire Station or bus 144 from Turnpike Lane. Bus W7 to Priory Road.* Sun 31 May (2-5.30). Adm £4, chd free. Home-made teas.

A garden divided into three distinct areas: secluded courtyard area, circular lawn surrounded by mixed planting now with a pond with seating area and a kitchen garden with raised beds, potting shed and a second seating area. Established climbers clothe the tall fences promoting a feeling of seclusion and peace throughout the garden.

✿ ☕

THE WATERGARDENS, KT2

Warren Road, Kingston-upon-Thames, KT2 7LF. The Residents' Association. *1m E of Kingston. From Kingston take A308 (Kingston Hill) towards London; after approx ½m turn R into Warren Rd. No. 57 bus along Coombe Lane West, alight at Warren Rd.* Sun 3 May, Sun 18 Oct (2-5). Adm £5, chd free.

Japanese landscaped garden originally part of Coombe Wood Nursery, planted by the Veitch family in the 1860s. Approx 9 acres with ponds, streams and waterfalls. Many rare trees which, in spring and autumn, provide stunning colour. For the tree lover this is a must see garden. Gardens attractive to wildlife.

GROUP OPENING

NEW WENSLEYDALE ROAD GARDENS, HAMPTON, TW12

Wensleydale Road, Hampton, TW12 2LX. Mr Steve Pickering. *Hampton. From River Thames on A308 in direction of Sunbury, turn R into High St A3008. L into Station Rd. Bear R into Station Approach then R into Wensleydale Rd. At fork bear L to continue on Wensleydale Rd.* Sat 20 June (2.30-5.30). Combined adm £7, chd free. Home-made teas.

 68 WENSLEYDALE ROAD
Julie Melotte.

 70 WENSLEYDALE ROAD
Mr Steve Pickering

 74 WENSLEYDALE ROAD
Mr & Mrs Mike & Andrea Harris.

Three suburban gardens, all different. 68 is a charming garden with abundant and colourful planting and interesting 'found' objects. A round lawn with roses and evergreen borders, leading to a wildlife pond and bog garden. A further lawn path with azaleas, rose trellis and archway to Mediterranean inspired seating area which is surrounded by wild meadow planting and flower cutting plots. This is a garden to sit awhile and hear the bees buzzing! 70 is a traditional garden with classic layout. Greenhouse, summerhouse, pergolas and a rockery. Many evergreen shrubs and perennials.Wisteria clothes pergola and rosa Desdemona repeat flowers on the patio. Greenhouse with succulents and flowering plants for year round colour. 74 is a large traditional garden laid to lawn. Mixed flower borders and shrubs. Feature ginkgo tree. Sunny terraces with pots. Roses & clematis a feature. No 68, access via narrow side entrance not accessible to wheelchairs. No 70 and 74 wheelchair accessible.

♿ ✿ ☕

WEST LODGE PARK, EN4

Cockfosters Road, Hadley Wood, EN4 0PY. Beales Hotels, 020 8216 3904, headoffice@bealeshotels.co.uk, www.bealeshotels.co.uk/westlodgepark/. *1m S of Potters Bar. On A111. J24 from M25 signed Cockfosters.* Sun 10 May (2-5); Sun 25 Oct (1-4). Adm £5, chd free. Light refreshments.

Open for the NGS for over 30yrs, the 35 acre Beale Arboretum consists of over 800 varieties of trees and shrubs, incl National Collection of Hornbeam cultivars (Carpinus betulus) and National collection of Swamp Cypress (Taxodium). Network of paths through good selection of conifers, oaks, maples and mountain ash - all specimens labelled. Beehives and 2 ponds. Stunning collection within the M25. Guided tours available. Breakfasts, morning coffee/biscuits, restaurant lunches, light lunches, dinner all served in the hotel. Please see website.

♿ NPC 🛏 ☕

Railway Cottages, 22 Dorset Road

31 WEST PARK ROAD, TW9
Kew, Richmond, TW9 4DA. Anna Anderson. *Just by Kew Gardens station.* Sun 7 June, Sun 16 Aug (2-5.30). Adm £3.50, chd free. Modern botanical garden with an oriental twist. Emphasis on foliage and an eclectic mix of unusual plants, a reflecting pool and willow screens. Dry bed, shady beds, mature trees and a private paved dining area with dappled light and shade.

12 WESTERN ROAD, E13
Plaistow, E13 9JF. Elaine Fieldhouse. *Stn: Upton Park, 3mins walk.* Buses: 58, 104, 330, 376. No parking restrictions on Suns. Sun 31 May (1-5). Adm £3.50, chd free. Home-made teas. Gluten free/ vegan options available. Urban oasis, 85ft garden designed and planted by owners. Relying heavily on evergreen, ferns, foliage and herbaceous planting. Rear of garden leads directly onto a 110ft allotment and a half allotment adjoining it - part allotment, part extension of the garden - featuring topiary, medlar tree, mulberry tree, 2 ponds, small fruit trees, raised beds and small iris collection.

35 WESTON PARK, N8
N8 9SY. Mrs Theresa & Mr Keith Rutter. *Tube Finsbury Park then W3 bus (Weston Park stop) or W7 (Crouch End Broadway.) Or tube to Archway then 41 bus (Crouch End Broadway).* Short walk from each one. Sun 26 July (2-6). Adm £4, chd free. Delicious home-made teas at 5 St Regis Close N10 2DE open 2-6.30pm. SE facing large garden with a wide range of plants, shrubs and trees suited to varying conditions incl a bog garden. Summer colour in the densely planted beds and pots incl dahlias, cannas and salvias. Elements such as golden bamboo, phormiums, grasses and sculptures provide structure. A curving path leads up to an artists's studio.

WHITE COTTAGE, W7
208 Church Road, Hanwell, W7 3BP. Dawn Keep. *Entrance through side gate. White Cottage is opp Church Fields.* Sun 7, Sun 14 June (2-6). Adm £3.50, chd free. Home-made teas. Tightly packed 20' x 40' north facing garden. Box edged beds brimming with David Austin roses. A mature

wisteria drapes the wall and pergola. The side entrance to the garden features many shade loving plants in pots and hanging baskets. Small water feature.

74 WILLIFIELD WAY, NW11
NW11 6YJ. David Weinberg. *Hampstead Garden Suburb. H2 bus from Golders Green will stop outside or take the 102 or 460 to Hampstead Way & walk up Asmuns Hill and turn R.* Sun 21 June (1.30-5.30). Adm £4.50, chd free. Cream teas. A very peaceful traditional English country cottage garden. Borders full of herbaceous perennials with a central rose bed surrounded by a box parterre. Winner of Suburb In Bloom 2017 and awarded silver gilt by London Garden Society 2019. Wheelchair access to patio area only.

61 WOLSEY ROAD, KT8
East Molesey, KT8 9EW. Jan & Ken Heath, janheath61@gmail.com. *Less than 10 mins walk from Hampton Court Palace & station - very easy to find.* Sun 14 June (2-6). Adm £5, chd free. Home-made teas. Visits also by arrangement

June & July for groups of 20+.
Romantic, secluded and peaceful garden of two halves designed and maintained by the owners. Part is shaded by two large copper beech trees with woodland planting. The second reached through a beech arch has cottage garden planting, pond and wooden obelisks covered with roses. Beautiful octagonal gazebo overlooks pond plus an oak framed summerhouse designed and built by the owners. Extensive seating throughout the garden to sit quietly and enjoy your tea and cake, either in the cool shade of the gazebo under the copper beech trees, relaxing in the summerhouse or enjoying the full sunshine elsewhere in the garden.

33 WOOD VALE, N10
Highgate, N10 3DJ. Mona Abboud, 020 8883 4955, monaabboud@hotmail.com, www.monasgarden.co.uk. *Tube: Highgate, 10 mins walk. Buses: W3, W7 to top of Park Rd.* **Sun 3 May (2-5.30). Adm £4, chd free. Light refreshments. Biscuits and cake, juices and soft drinks. No Teas.**
Visits also by arrangement May to Sept for groups of 5+.
This 100m-long unique and award winning garden is home to the Corokia National Collection along with a great number of other unusual Australasian, Mediterranean and exotic plants complemented by perennials and grasses which thrive thanks to 250 tons of topsoil, gravel and compost brought in by wheelbarrow. Emphasis on structure, texture, foliage and shapes brought alive by distinctive pruning.

7 WOODBINES AVENUE, KT1
Kingston-upon-Thames, KT1 2AZ. Mr Tony Sharples & Mr Paul Cuthbert, 07717 754600, tonysharples@gmail.com. *Take K2, K3, 71 or 281 bus. From Surbiton, bus stop outside Waitrose & exit bus Kingston University Stop. From Kingston, walk or get the bus from Eden Street (opp Heals).* **Sun 19 July (12-6). Combined adm with 15 Catherine Road £7, chd free. Home-made teas. Visits also by arrangement May to Sept.**
We have created a winding path through our 70ft garden with trees, evergreen structure, perennial flowers and grasses. Deep borders create depth, variety, texture and interest

around the garden. We like to create a garden party, so feel welcome to stay as long as you like. We really look forward to seeing you all!

10 WORDSWORTH WALK, NW11
Golders Green, NW11 6AU. Augusta & Laurence Wolff. *Hampstead Garden Suburb. Nr A406 & A1. Tube: Golders Green. H2 Hail & Ride bus from Golders Green to garden, or 13, 102 or 460 buses to Temple Fortune (10 mins walk).* **Sun 7 June (2-6). Adm £4.50, chd free. Also open 48 Erskine Hill.**
Oak Tree Cottage was designed and planted by the owners in 2018. A tranquil woodland front garden contrasts with a structured back garden which is packed with interest: roses, herbs, fruit and vegetables. New for 2020 is the allotment: an example of No Dig. Partial wheelchair access only. Steps at the entrance and in the back garden. Gently sloping paths and access to the back garden and allotment.

1 YORK CLOSE, W7
Hanwell, W7 3JB. Tony Hulme & Eddy Fergusson. *By road only, entrance to York Close via Church Rd. Nearest station Hanwell mainline. Buses E3, 195, 207.* **Sat 27 June (2-6). Adm £6, chd free. Sun 28 June (2-6). Adm £5, chd free.**
Tiny quirky, prize winning garden extensively planted with eclectic mix incl hosta collection, many unusual and tropical plants. Plantaholics paradise. Many surprises in this unique and very personal garden. Pimms Bar available.

10 YORK ROAD, N21
N21 2JL. Androulla & Harry Tsappas. *Winchmore Hill. Buses: 329 and W8 bus routes.* **Sun 28 June (2-6). Adm £4, chd free. Tea. coffee, soft drinks and selection of cakes.**
This suburban garden is full of country perennials canopied with beautiful trees such as Indian bean, olive and acer trees, and has a pretty, dainty look inspired by country cottages. There is a large pond with koi fish which is surrounded by luscious grasses and a rockery. The garden includes a wood choppers' enclave, and an array of wildlife such as frogs, butterflies and bees are prevalent.

ZEN GARDEN AT JAPANESE BUDDHIST CENTRE, W3
Three Wheels, 55 Carbery Avenue, Acton London, W3 9AB. Reverend Prof K T Sato, www.threewheels.org.uk. *Tube: Acton Town 5 mins walk, 200yds off A406.* **Sat 6, Sun 7, Sat 20, Sun 21 June (2-5). Adm £3.50, chd free. Home-made teas. Matcha tea ceremony £3.**
Pure Japanese Zen garden (so no flowers) with 12 large and small rocks of various colours and textures set in islands of moss and surrounded by a sea of grey granite gravel raked in a stylised wave pattern. Garden surrounded by trees and bushes outside a cob wall. Oak framed wattle and daub shelter with Norfolk reed thatched roof. Talk on the Zen garden between 3-4pm. Buddha Room open to public.

24 Grove Park

OPENING DATES

All entries subject to change. For latest information check www.ngs.org.uk

Map locator numbers are shown to the right of each garden name.

February

Snowdrop Festival

Saturday 15th
Horstead House 30

Tuesday 18th
◆ Raveningham Hall 51

Sunday 23rd
Bagthorpe Hall 2
Chestnut Farm 13

Thursday 27th
Chestnut Farm 13

March

Sunday 1st
Chestnut Farm 13

Saturday 14th
◆ East Ruston Old Vicarage 18

Sunday 29th
Gayton Hall 21

April

Sunday 19th
◆ Mannington Estate 39
NEW The Old Rectory 47

Sunday 26th
The Old House 46

May

Saturday 9th
Wretham Lodge 64

Sunday 10th
Wretham Lodge 64

Sunday 17th
Lexham Hall 37

Tuesday 19th
◆ Stody Lodge 54

Saturday 23rd
The Merchants House 42

Sunday 24th
The Old Rectory, Brandon Parva 48
Warborough House 61

Saturday 30th
Sundial Farm 55

Sunday 31st
Bolwick Hall 7
Holme Hale Hall 28

June

Sunday 7th
Barton Bendish Hall 3
Kettle Hill 34
Oulton Hall 50

Sunday 14th
Blickling Lodge 6
NEW Booton Hall 8
High House Gardens 24
Wells-Next-The-Sea Gardens 62

Wednesday 17th
High House Gardens 24

Saturday 20th
NEW Church Cottage 14
NEW La Foray 35

Sunday 21st
Broadway Farm 11
NEW Church Cottage 14
NEW La Foray 35
Manor House Farm, Wellingham 41
Walcott House 59

Thursday 25th
NEW ◆ The Bressingham Gardens 9

Sunday 28th
Bishop's House 4
NEW Felmingham Gardens 19
NEW 14 Mill Hill Road 43
West Barsham Hall 63

July

Saturday 4th
The Firs 20

Sunday 5th
The Firs 20
Manor Farm House, Swannington 40
Swannington Manor 56

Tyger Barn 58

Saturday 11th
Black Horse Cottage 5

Sunday 12th
Black Horse Cottage 5
NEW 26 Ipswich Road 33

Wednesday 15th
The Old Smithy 49

Saturday 18th
NEW Honeysuckle Walk 29

Sunday 19th
Dunbheagan 17

Sunday 26th
Dale Farm 15
30 Hargham Road 23
North Lodge 45

Wednesday 29th
Lexham Hall 37

August

Sunday 2nd
Holme Hale Hall 28
The Long Barn 38
33 Waldemar Avenue 60

Saturday 8th
Greenways 22

Sunday 9th
Brick Kiln House 10
Greenways 22
Highfield House 25
North Lodge 45
Tudor Lodgings 57

Saturday 15th
◆ Severals Grange 53

Sunday 16th
◆ Hoveton Hall Gardens 32

Sunday 23rd
North Corner 44

Sunday 30th
33 Waldemar Avenue 60

September

Sunday 6th
Chapel Cottage 12
7 Holly Close 27

Sunday 13th
High House Gardens 24

Wednesday 16th
High House Gardens 24

Wednesday 30th
◆ Hindringham Hall 26

October

Saturday 17th
◆ East Ruston Old Vicarage 18

By Arrangement

Arrange a personalised garden visit with your club, or group of friends, on a date to suit you. See individual garden entries for full details.

NEW Acre Meadow 1
Black Horse Cottage 5
Brick Kiln House 10
Chestnut Farm 13
Dale Farm 15
NEW Dove Cottage 16
Dunbheagan 17
The Firs 20
Gayton Hall 21
Holme Hale Hall 28
NEW Honeysuckle Walk 29
Horstead House 30
Lake House 36
North Corner 44
Tudor Lodgings 57
Tyger Barn 58
Walcott House 59
West Barsham Hall 63
Wretham Lodge 64

Your visits help change lives – we are the largest single funder of the Queen's Nursing Institute

THE GARDENS

1 NEW ACRE MEADOW

New Road, Bradwell, Great Yarmouth, NR31 9DU. Mr Keith Knights, 07476 197568, kk.acremeadow@tiscali.co.uk, www.acremeadow.co.uk. *Between Bradwell & Belton in Arable surroundings. Take Belton & Burgh Castle turn (New Rd) from r'about at Bradwell on A143 Great Yarmouth to Beccles rd. Then 400 yards on R drive in very wide gateway. For sat nav use NR31 9JW.* **Visits by arrangement July to Sept for groups of 5+. Sun only from July 19 to Sept 13. Groups 5-55. Adm £4, chd free. Light refreshments.** A heady mix of vibrant late summer colour, dark foliage, exotic and insect attracting plants in deep borders on former greenhouses site. Separate areas of interest include Pond area and 60 foot border for pollinators. Main garden unsuitable for wheelchairs as gravel paths throughout. Wheelchair access to main garden limited to viewing area at both ends due to gravel paths.

2 BAGTHORPE HALL

Bagthorpe, Bircham, King's Lynn, PE31 6QY. Mr & Mrs D Morton, 01485 578528, dgmorton@hotmail.com. *3½m N of East Rudham, off A148. Take turning opposite The Crown in East Rudham. Look for white gates in trees, slightly set back from the road.* **Sun 23 Feb (11-4). Adm £5, chd free. Home-made teas. Soups made with organic vegetables from the farm.** A delightful circular walk which meanders through a stunning display of snowdrops naturally carpeting a woodland floor, and returns through a walled-garden. Limited access in the garden, but not the woodland walk.

3 BARTON BENDISH HALL

Fincham Road, Barton Bendish, King's Lynn, PE33 9DL. The Barton Bendish Gardening Team. *5m E of Downham Market off A1122. On entering Barton Bendish follow yellow signs to field parking.* **Sun 7 June (11-5). Adm £6, chd free. Home-made teas in Barton Bendish Hall Court Yard.**

Traditional country estate garden of 10-acres. Woodland drive, orchard, kitchen garden with soft fruits, espaliered fruit trees, vegetables, and a Thomas Messenger style glasshouse full of scented pelargoniums. Walled herb and cut flower garden. Herbaceous borders, south facing terrace. Views of farmland. Sculptures by P. Randall-Page RA and Nigel Hall RA. Some wheelchair access.

4 BISHOP'S HOUSE

Bishopgate, Norwich, NR3 1SB. The Bishop of Norwich, www.dioceseofnorwich.org/gardens. *City centre. Located in the city centre near the Law Courts & The Adam & Eve Pub.* **Sun 28 June (1-5). Adm £4, chd free. Tea.** 4 acre walled garden dating back to the C12. Extensive lawns with specimen trees. Borders with many rare and unusual shrubs. Spectacular herbaceous borders flanked by yew hedges. Rose beds, meadow labyrinth, kitchen garden, woodland walk and long border with hostas and bamboo walk. Popular plant sales. Gravel paths and some slopes.

5 BLACK HORSE COTTAGE

The Green, Hickling, Norwich, NR12 0YA. Yvonne Pugh, 01692 598691, ybp@blackhorsecottage.com. *3m E of Stalham. Turn E off A149 at Catfield, turn L onto Heath Rd, 1½m to centre of Hickling village. Next to The Greyhound Inn (Good food!).* **Sat 11, Sun 12 July (11-5). Adm £5, chd free. Home-made teas. Visits also by arrangement Mar to Oct.** Thatched house close to Hickling Broad and NWT Nature Reserve. Plantsman's garden 2 acres professionally redesigned. Spacious borders and islands with diverse range of characterful planting. Particular emphasis on achieving full year round interest. Wide range of managed mature specimen trees. Many long two-way vistas. Wide mown walkways through large meadow. Various sitting opportunities! Sorry, no dogs allowed.

6 BLICKLING LODGE

Blickling, Norwich, NR11 6PS. Michael & Henrietta Lindsell. *½m N of Aylsham. Leave Aylsham on Old Cromer rd towards Ingworth. Over hump back bridge & house is on R.* **Sun 14 June (11-5). Adm £5, chd free. Home-made teas.** Georgian house (not open) set in 17 acres of parkland including cricket pitch, mixed border, walled kitchen garden, yew garden, woodland/water garden.

The Bressingham Gardens

7 BOLWICK HALL
Marsham, NR10 5PU. Mr & Mrs G C Fisher. *8m N of Norwich off A140. From Norwich, heading N on A140, just past Marsham take 1st R after Plough Pub, signed 'By Road' then next R onto private drive to front of Hall.* **Sun 31 May (1-5). Adm £5, chd free. Home-made teas.**
Landscaped gardens and park surrounding a late Georgian hall. The original garden design is attributed to Humphry Repton. The current owners have rejuvenated the borders, planted gravel and formal gardens and clad the walls of the house in old roses. Enjoy a woodland walk around the lake as well as as stroll through the working vegetable and fruit garden with its double herbaceous border. Please ask at gate for wheelchair directions.

  🐕 ✳ ☕

8 NEW BOOTON HALL
Church Road, Booton, Norwich, NR10 4NZ. Piers & Cecilia Willis. *1m E of Reepham. Drive out of Reepham east on Norwich Rd, after 1m turn L into Church Rd. After 500 metres turn L through white wooden gates just after bendy road sign on L.*

Sun 14 June (11-5). Adm £5, chd free. Home-made teas.
Walled garden with formal layout and tiered lawns re-designed 6 years ago and attached to C17/18 hall. Lawns between the house and parkland meadows, shrub beds, pond planting, small orchard and short woodland walk. Parking in one of the meadows close to drive entrance, prior drop-off by house possible. Wheelchair access, but some gravel quite deep, and some steps, so will require energetic help.

  🐕 🐏 ✳ ☕

9 NEW ◆ THE BRESSINGHAM GARDENS
Low Road, Bressingham, Diss, IP22 2AA. Adrian Bloom, www.thebressinghamgardens.com. *Bressingham Gardens entrance lies to the W of Bressingham Garden Centre & Bressingham Steam Museum, S of the A1066 rd, 2½m W of Diss, 14m E of Thetford.* **For NGS: Evening opening Thur 25 June (6-9). Adm £8.50, chd free. Wine. For other opening times and information, please visit garden website.**
17 acres of gardens which visitors

describe as 'the best they have seen'. Follow the trail around the island beds of the late Alan Bloom's Dell Garden, through the Fragrant Garden, and Adrian's Wood with Giant Redwoods, to famous Foggy Bottom garden, with dramatic rivers of planting. Recent addition of Rosemary's Wood and a new Japanese-inspired garden. A rare opportunity of an evening visit.

  🚌 ☕

10 BRICK KILN HOUSE
Priory Lane, Shotesham, Norwich, NR15 1UJ. Jim & Jenny Clarke, jennyclarke@uwclub.net. *6m S of Norwich. From Shotesham All Saints church Priory Lane is 200m on R on Saxlingham Rd.* **Sun 9 Aug (11-5). Adm £5, chd free. Visits also by arrangement June to Sept.**
2-acre country garden with a large terrace, lawns and colourful herbaceous boarders. There is an intimate rose garden, garden sculptures and a stream running through a diversely planted wood. Parking in field but easy access to brick path.

  🐏 ✳ ☕

The Old Rectory Catford

We help ordinary people open the gates to their extraordinary private gardens to raise impressive amounts of money through admissions, teas and slices of cake!

1 BROADWAY FARM

The Broadway, Scarning, Dereham, NR19 2LQ. Michael & Corinne Steward. *16m W of Norwich. 12m E of Swaffham From A47 W take a R into Fen Rd, opposite Drayton Hall Lane. From A47 E take L into Fen Rd, then immed L at T-junction, immed R into The Broadway.* **Sun 21 June (11-5). Adm £4, chd free. Home-made teas.**
Half acre cottage garden surrounding a C14 clapboard farmhouse. Colourful herbaceous borders with a wide range of perennial and woody plants and a well planted pond, providing habitat for wildlife. A plantswoman's garden ! Wrought Iron display and items for sale.

2 CHAPEL COTTAGE

Rougham, King's Lynn, PE32 2SE. Sarah Butler, 01328 838347, sarahbutler4@gmail.com. *15m E from King's Lynn, 8m SW from Fakenham. On B1145. Parking in the centre of the village. Use map to find the village.* **Sun 6 Sept (11-5). Combined adm with 7 Holly Close £4, chd free. Home-made teas.**
A naturalistic cottage garden that was created by the owner who is interested in the relationship of wildlife to plants, as well as gardens for wellbeing. Divided into charming peaceful areas that include a pond, kitchen garden, herb area. Beehives. Plenty of seating. Set in an attractive rural village with Church open.

3 CHESTNUT FARM

Church Road, West Beckham, Holt, NR25 6NX. Mr & Mrs John McNeil Wilson, 01263 822241, judywilson100@gmail.com. *2½m S of Sheringham. From A148 opp Sheringham Park entrance. Take the rd signed BY WAY TO WEST BECKHAM, about ¾m to the Village Sign and garden.* **Sun 23, Thur 27 Feb, Sun 1 Mar (11-4). Adm £5, chd free. Light refreshments. Visits also by arrangement Feb to Aug for groups of 10 to 30.**
Mature 3 acre garden with collections of many rare and unusual plants and trees. 100+ varieties of snowdrops, drifts of crocus with seasonal flowering shrubs. Later, wood anemones, frittilary meadow, wild flower walk, pond, small arboretum, croquet lawn and colourful herbaceous borders. Display of garden sculpture by local blacksmith Toby Winterbourne Usually visiting nurseries and plants for sale. Wheelchair access tricky if wet.

4 NEW CHURCH COTTAGE

57 White Street, Martham, Great Yarmouth, NR29 4PQ. Jo & Nigel Craske. *Approx 9m N of Gt Yarmouth off A149. Take B1152 signed to Martham & Winterton. On White Street pass Village Hall & Bell Meadow. Garden on L down gravel drive before Church & sharp RH bend.* **Sat 20, Sun 21 June (12-5). Combined adm with La Foray £5, chd free.**
Delightful small cottage garden attached to 200 year old house with views of St Mary's Church. Divided into different areas with lots of plants, many typical but others more unusual. Areas including cool, shady border, hot sunny herbaceous border, small gravel garden, walled garden, sunken area with collection of hostas and greenhouse with pelargoniums and succulents. Unsuitable for wheelchairs.

5 DALE FARM

Sandy Lane, Dereham, NR19 2EA. Graham & Sally Watts, 01362 690065, grahamwatts@dsl.pipex.com. *16m W of Norwich. 12m E of Swaffham. From A47 take B1146 signed to Fakenham, turn R at T-junction, ¼m turn L into Sandy Lane (before pelican crossing).* **Sun 26 July (11-5). Adm £5, chd free. Home-made**

teas. Visits also by arrangement June & July for groups of 10+.
2-acre plant lovers' garden with a large spring-fed pond. Over 1000 plant varieties in exuberantly planted borders with sculptures. Also, gravel, vegetable, nature and waterside gardens. Collection of 130 hydrangeas! Music during the afternoon and remote-controlled model boats on pond for children. Some grass paths and gravel drive. Wide choice of plants for sale.

6 NEW DOVE COTTAGE

Wolferd Green, Shotesham All Saints, Norwich, NR15 1YU. Sarah Cushion, sarah.cushion815@btinternet.com. *From Norwich travel to far end of Poringland, turn R at Poringland rd/Shotesham rd junction by the church, continue along rd for approx 2½m, house pink cottage on L.* **Visits by arrangement June to Aug for groups of up to 30. Adm £4, chd free. Home-made teas.**
⅓ acre densely planted colourful cottage garden including a small pond, summer house, and extensive views across the countryside.

7 DUNBHEAGAN

Dereham Road, Westfield, NR19 1QF. Jean & John Walton, 01362 696163, jandjwalton@btinternet.com. *2m S of Dereham. From Dereham turn L off A1075 into Westfield Rd by the Vauxhall garage/Premier food store. Straight ahead at Xrds into lane which becomes Dereham Rd. Garden on L.* **Sun 19 July (12.30-5). Adm £5, chd free. Home-made teas. Visits also by arrangement June & July for groups of 10+. Up to 17 July.**
Relax and enjoy walking among extensive borders and island beds - a riot of colour all summer. Vast collection of rare, unusual and more recognisable plants in this ever changing plantsman's garden. If you love flowers, you'll love it here. We aim for the WOW factor. Lots of changes for 2020. Featured in Nick Bailey's book 365 Days of Colour. Music during the afternoon. Gravel driveway.

18 ◆ EAST RUSTON OLD VICARAGE
East Ruston, Norwich, NR12 9HN. Alan Gray & Graham Robeson, 01692 650432, erovoffice@btconnect.com, www.eastrustonoldvicarage.co.uk. *3m N of Stalham. Turn off A149 onto B1159 signed Bacton, Happisburgh. After 2m turn R 200yds N of East Ruston Church (ignore sign to East Ruston).* **For NGS: Sat 14 Mar, Sat 17 Oct (12-5.30). Adm £10, chd £1. Light refreshments. For other opening times and information, please phone, email or visit garden website.**
Large garden with traditional borders and modern landscapes inc. Walled Gardens, Rose Garden, Exotic Garden, Topiary and Box Parterres, Water Features, Mediterranean Garden, a monumental Fruit Cage, Containers to die for in spring and summer. Cornfield and Meadow Gardens, Vegetable and Cutting Gardens, Parkland and Heritage Orchard, in all 32 acres. Rare and unusual plants abound. Regional Finalist, The English Garden's The Nation's Favourite Gardens 2019.
  🚻 ✿ 🚗 NPC ☕

GROUP OPENING

19 NEW FELMINGHAM GARDENS
Suffield Road, Felmingham, North Walsham, NR28 0JZ. *16m N of Norwich (towards Cromer), off the B1145 between Felmingham & Banningham.* **Sun 28 June (12-5). Combined adm £5, chd free. Home-made teas.**

  NEW EAST WING
Stephanie Kershaw.
  NEW OAKS FARM COTTAGE
Stephane Lustig.

A converted barn and traditional cottage set in impressive gardens linked by a little gate. A driveway flanked by structural phormiums and ornamental grasses leads to East Wing's open lawns, walled beds and various seating areas including a glass 'pod', as well as bee hives, fruit trees and raised vegetable beds. Leading on into the garden at Oaks Farm Cottage owned by local garden designer (@stephanelustig), which transitions from beautiful pond with delightful summerhouse including well stocked herbaceous borders,

an orchard, terraces and a lawn bordered by mature trees. Look out for the free-range chickens, and stylish fire pit along the way. Both gardens have been created within the last 15 years. Home-made refreshments and plants for sale, with proceeds going to Hospice Ethiopia. Wheelchair access between gardens is via the road - please ask at gate for directions.
  🚻 ✿ ☕

20 THE FIRS
Church Road, Woodton, Nr Bungay, NR35 2NB. Alan & Shirley Steadman, 07903 933667, shirley.steadman@gmail.com. *9m S of A47 (A146 junction). Take B1332 from Norwich. Continue past Woodton sign. Turn R at sign for B1527 to Hempnall. Follow signs for NGS.* **Sat 4, Sun 5 July (11-5). Adm £5, chd free. Home-made teas. Visits also by arrangement July & Aug.**
The field to landscaped garden takes you on a journey of flowers, secrets and fruits. Developed and maintained purely by the owners, the acre garden comprises of secret areas, fish, ornamental and wildlife ponds, an orchard, borders, formal kitchen garden, rose garden, lawn, and much more. Many seating areas.
  🐕 ✿ 🚗 ☕

21 GAYTON HALL
Gayton, King's Lynn, PE32 1PL. Viscount & Viscountess Marsham, 01485 528432, ciciromney@icloud.com. *6m E of King's Lynn. Off the B1145.* **Sun 29 Mar (1-5). Adm £5, chd free. Home-made teas. Visits also by arrangement Feb to Oct for groups of 10 to 30.**
This rambling semi-wild 20-acre water garden, has over 2 miles of paths, and contains lawns, lakes, streams, bridges and woodland. Primulas, astilbes, hostas, lysichiton and gunnera. Spring bulbs. A variety of unusual trees and shrubs, many labelled, have been planted over the years. Wheelchair access to most areas, gravel and grass paths.
  🚻 🐕 🚗 ☕

22 GREENWAYS
Blacksmiths Lane, Hindringham, Fakenham, NR21 0QB. Geraldine Maelzer & Anne Callow. *Close to village centre. A148 Holt to Fakenham Rd, turn by Crawfish*

Pub at Thursford, after 2m turn L Blacksmiths Lane after village hall. Parking at village hall. **Sat 8, Sun 9 Aug (11-4). Adm £4, chd free. Home-made teas.**
A mature 1-acre garden with a meandering stream, developed by the owners with informal planting to give continuous colour and interest; a delight for all gardeners. Sit and listen to birdsong and enjoy the variety of wildlife habitats and the many species of bumble bees and butterflies. Enjoy the late summer colour. Not suitable for wheelchairs.
  ✿ ☕

23 30 HARGHAM ROAD
Attleborough, NR17 2ES. Darren & Karen Spencer. *Turn off A11 at Breckland Lodge, continue 2m into Attleborough, turn R opp Sainsbury's into Hargham Road and we're 200 yds on the R.* **Sun 26 July (11-5). Adm £4, chd free. Home-made teas**
Step into a vibrant, colourful haven in just under a ⅓ acre. Created from scratch with self built structures and home-made water features. Borders filled with perennials and annuals with a variety of exotics. Follow the pathway round to a modern allotment area.
  🚻 ☕

24 HIGH HOUSE GARDENS
Blackmoor Row, Shipdham, Thetford, IP25 7PU. Sue & Fred Nickerson. *6m SW of Dereham. Take the airfield or Cranworth Rd off A1075 in Shipdham. Blackmoor Row is signed.* **Sun 14, Wed 17 June, Sun 13, Wed 16 Sept (2-5.30). Adm £5, chd free. Home-made teas.**
3 acre plantsman's garden developed and maintained by the current owners, over the last 40 years. Garden consists of colour themed herbaceous borders with an extensive range of perennials, box edged rose and shrub borders, woodland garden, pond and bog area, orchard and small arboretum. Plus large vegetable garden. Gravel paths.
  🚻 ✿ ☕

25 HIGHFIELD HOUSE
Back Lane, Castle Acre, King's Lynn, PE32 2AR. David & Jackie Moss. *Off A1065 4m N Swaffham. Follow Signs.* **Sun 9 Aug (11-5). Combined adm with Tudor Lodgings £7, chd free. Light refreshments at Tudor Lodgings.**

La Foray Martham

¾ acre mature plantsman's garden with large herbaceous borders, lawn sloping down to pond, summerhouse and hot border. Terrace with pots, vegetable area and south facing gravel garden. Densely planted and specialising in late summer colour.

26 ♦ HINDRINGHAM HALL

Blacksmiths Lane, Hindringham, NR21 0QA. Mr & Mrs Charles Tucker, 01328 878226, info@hindringhamhall.org, www.hindringhamhall.org. *7m from Holt/Fakenham/Wells. Turn L. off A148 at Crawfish Pub towards Hindringham. L into Blacksmiths Lane after village hall on R.* For NGS: Wed 30 Sept (10-4). Adm £7.50, chd free. Home-made teas on site. For other opening times and information, please phone, email or visit garden website.
Grade 2* Tudor Manor House (not open) surrounded by moat. Medieval site with fishponds. Working walled vegetable garden, Victorian nut walk, formal beds, bog and stream gardens. Something of interest throughout the year continuing well into autumn. Some access for wheelchairs able to cope with gravel paths.

27 7 HOLLY CLOSE

Rougham, King's Lynn, PE32 2SJ. Derek Barker. *15m E of King's Lynn, 8m SW of Fakenham on B1145. Holly Close is ¼ m from the church.* Sun 6 Sept (11-5). Combined adm with Chapel Cottage £4, chd free.
The front garden has a variety of planting, with well stocked borders filled with colour and structure. Rear garden is laid out in potager style, with fruit trees, flowers and vegetables encouraging bees and wildlife. The garden shows how much can be achieved in a small plot providing late summer colour.

28 HOLME HALE HALL

Holme Hale, Swaffham, Thetford, IP25 7ED. Mr & Mrs Simon Broke, 01760 440328, simon.broke@hotmail.co.uk. *2m S of Necton off A47. 1m E of Holme Hale village.* Sun 31 May, Sun 2 Aug (11-4). Adm £6, chd free. Light refreshments in tea room. Visits also by arrangement Apr to Sept.
Walled kitchen garden designed by Arne Maynard in 2000 and replanted in 2016/17. A soft palette of herbaceous plants include some unusual varieties. Topiaries, vegetable

parterres, trained fruits and roses. 130 old wisteria. Wild flower meadow. Long season of interest. Wildlife friendly. Historic buildings including dovecote, coachhouse and barns,. Wheelchair access available to the front garden, kitchen garden and tearoom.

29 NEW HONEYSUCKLE WALK

Litcham Road, Gressenhall, Dereham, NR20 4AR. Simon & Joan Smith, 01362860530, simon.smith@ngs.org.uk. *17m w of Norwich. Follow B1146 & signs to Gressenhall Rural Life Museum then follow Litcham Road into Gressenhall village.* Sat 18 July (10-1). Adm £5, chd free. Home-made teas. Visits also by arrangement June & July for groups of 10+.
2 acre woodland garden featuring two ponds, river and stream boundaries, 80 ornamental trees and a collection of 400 different hydrangeas and 100 hostas. Woodland access is by ¼ m grass track.

30 HORSTEAD HOUSE

Mill Road, Horstead, Norwich, NR12 7AU. Mr & Mrs Matthew Fleming, 07771 655 637, caro.fleming@sky.com. *6m NE of Norwich on North Walsham Road, B1150. Down Mill Rd opp the Recruiting Sergeant pub.* **Sat 15 Feb (11-4). Adm £4, chd free. Home-made teas. We will be serving drinks and cakes. Visits also by arrangement Feb & Mar for groups of up to 20.**
Stunning display of beautiful snowdrops carpet the woodland setting with winter flowering shrubs. A stunning feature are the dogwoods growing on a small island in R. Bure, which flows through the garden. Small walled garden. Wheelchair access to main snowdrop area.

31 ◆ HOUGHTON HALL WALLED GARDEN

Bircham Road, New Houghton, King's Lynn, PE31 6TY. The Cholmondeley Gardens Trust, 01485 528569, info@houghtonhall.com, www.houghtonhall.com. *11m W of Fakenham. 13m E of King's Lynn. Signed from A148.* **For opening times and information, please phone, email or visit garden website.**
The award-winning, 5-acre walled garden includes a spectacular double-sided herbaceous border, rose parterre, wisteria pergola and glasshouses. Mediterranean garden and kitchen garden with arches and espaliers of fruit trees. Antique statues, fountains and contemporary sculptures by Jeppe Hein, Richard Long and Stephen Cox. Plants on sale. Gravel and grass paths. Electric buggies available in the walled garden.

32 ◆ HOVETON HALL GARDENS

Hoveton Hall Estate, Hoveton, Norwich, NR12 8RJ. Mr & Mrs Harry Buxton, 01603 784297, office@hovetonhallestate.co.uk, www.hovetonhallestate.co.uk. *8m N of Norwich. 1m N of Wroxham Bridge. Off A1151 Stalham Rd - follow brown tourist signs.* **For NGS: Sun 16 Aug (10.30-5). Adm £7.50, chd £4. Light refreshments. For other opening times and information, please phone, email or visit garden website.**

15-acre gardens and woodlands taking you through the seasons. Mature walled herbaceous and kitchen gardens. Informal woodlands and lakeside walks. Nature Spy activity trail for our younger visitors. A varied events programme runs throughout the season. Please visit our website for more details. Light lunches and afternoon tea from our on-site Garden Kitchen Cafe. The gardens are approximately 75% accessible to wheelchair users. We offer a reduced entry price for wheelchair users and their carers.

33 NEW 26 IPSWICH ROAD

Norwich, NR2 2LZ. Pat Adcock. *Parking available opposite the garden at Harford Manor School.* **Sun 12 July (11-5). Adm £3.50, chd free. Light refreshments. Tea, coffee, home-made cakes.**
This is no ordinary garden! Only half a mile from Norwich City centre this half acre garden is dedicated to sustainability and biodiversity. Organic and wildlife friendly there are resident chickens, bees, a large wildlife pond, fish pond, vegetables and ornamental plants. The owner is a Master Composter, composting advice available. There is a home-made system of water conservation and storage. Access to rear garden via a gravel area. and may be difficult for some wheelchairs.

34 KETTLE HILL

The Downs, Langham Road, Blakeney, NR25 7PN. Mrs R Winch. *½m from Blakeney off the B1156 to Langham.* **Sun 7 June (11-5). Adm £5, chd free. Home-made teas.**
A garden with herbaceous borders, wild flower meadows and a secret garden. Stunning rose garden and grass paths through woods, a real treat for any garden lover. Excellent views across Morston to the sea, framed by lavender, roses and sky. Gardens have been developed by the owner with design elements from George Carter and Tamara Bridge. Gravel drive way and lawns but hard paving near the house. Ramps are situated around the garden making all except the wood accessible for wheelchairs.

35 NEW LA FORAY

White Street, Martham, Great Yarmouth, NR29 4PQ. Ameesha & Alan Williams. *10m N of Gt Yarmouth approx 2m off A149 follow yellow signs at Martham junction. Parking at Village Hall 2 min walk.* **Sat 20, Sun 21 June (12-5). Combined adm with Church Cottage £5, chd free. Home-made teas.**
A lovely garden with many interesting and unusual features. Mixed herbaceous borders created and maintained by the owners. A bird hide made as a tree house, a wildlife retreat, child's gypsy caravan and friendly pet goats. Several seating areas. Mainly level garden with some wood chip and stone paths. Teas in aid of Donor Family Network.

36 LAKE HOUSE

Postwick Lane, Roman Drive, Brundall, NR13 5LU. Mrs Janet Muter, 01603 712933. *5m E of Norwich. On A47; take Brundall turn at r'about. Turn R into Postwick Lane at T-junction.* **Visits by arrangement Feb to Nov for groups of up to 30. Adm £5, chd free.**
In the centre of Brundall Gardens, a series of ponds descends through a wooded valley to the shore of a lake. Steep paths wind through a variety of shrubs and flowers in season, which attract many kinds of rare birds, dragonflies and mammals.

37 LEXHAM HALL

nr Litcham, PE32 2QJ. Mr & Mrs Neil Foster, www.lexhamestate.co.uk. *6m N of Swaffham off B1145. 2m W of Litcham.* **Sun 17 May, Wed 29 July (11-5). Adm £7, chd free. Home-made teas.**
Parkland with lake and river walks surround C17/18 Hall (not open). Formal garden with terraces, roses and mixed borders. Traditional working kitchen garden with crinkle-crankle wall. Year round interest with rhododendrons, azaleas, camellias and magnolias in the 3-acre woodland garden in May. July sees the walled garden borders at their peak.

38 THE LONG BARN

Flordon Road, Newton Flotman, Norwich, NR15 1QX. Mr & Mrs Mark Bedini. *6m S of Norwich along A140. Leave A140 in Newton Flotman towards Flordon. Exit Newton Flotman & approx 150 yards beyond 'passing place' on L, turn L into drive. Note that SatNav does not bring you to destination.* **Sun 2 Aug (11-4.30). Adm £5, chd free. Home-made teas.**

Beautiful informal garden with new haha creating infinity views across ancient parkland. Strong Mediterranean influence with plenty of seating in large paved courtyard under pollarded Plane trees. Unusual wall-sheltered group of 4 venerably gnarled olive trees, figs and vines, then herbaceous borders, tiered lawns merging northwards into woodland garden. Walks through Parkland the tiny River Tas - serene! Wheelchair drop off at front of house. Gradual lawn slope accesses upper tier of garden. WC requires steps.

&. 🍵

39 ♦ MANNINGTON ESTATE

Mannington, Norwich, NR11 7BB. The Lord & Lady Walpole, 01263 584175, admin@walpoleestate.co.uk, www.manningtonestate.co.uk. *18m NW of Norwich. 2m N of Saxthorpe via B1149 towards Holt. At Saxthorpe/Corpusty follow signs to Mannington.* **For NGS: Sun 19 Apr (12-4). Adm £6, chd free. Light refreshments at Greedy Goose Tearooms. For other opening times and information, please phone, email or visit garden website.**

20 acres feature shrubs, lake and trees. Period gardens. Borders. Sensory garden. Extensive countryside walks and trails. Moated manor house and Saxon church with C19 follies. Wild flowers and birds. The Greedy Goose tearooms offer home-made locally sourced food with light lunches and home-made teas. Gravel paths, one steep slope.

&. 🐑 ❄ 🚗 🛏 🍵

40 MANOR FARM HOUSE, SWANNINGTON

Manor Drive, Swannington, NR9 5NR. Mr & Mrs John Powles. *7m NW of Norwich. Almost halfway between A1067 (to Fakenham) & B1149 (to Holt). In the middle of Swannington village. All parking in next door Romantic Garden Nursery.* **Sun 5 July (10.30-5). Combined adm with Swannington Manor £5, chd free.**

Small garden including knot garden with central lead fountain, topiary and lavender garden enclosed by hornbeam hedging. Terrace with large pots of lavender and agapanthus. Access to the Romantic Garden Nursery, which adjoins the garden.

&. 🐑 ❄ 🍵

41 MANOR HOUSE FARM, WELLINGHAM

Fakenham, Kings Lynn, PE32 2TH. Robin & Elisabeth Ellis, 01328 838227, libbyelliswellingham@gmail.com, www.manor-house-farm.co.uk. *7m W from Fakenham. 8m E from Swaffham, ½ m off A1065. By the Church.* **Sun 21 June (11-5). Adm £6, chd free. Home-made teas.**

Charming 4-acre country garden surrounds an attractive farmhouse. Formal quadrants, 'hot spot' of grasses and gravel, small arboretum, pleached lime walk, vegetable parterre and rose tunnel. Unusual walled 'Taj' garden with old-fashioned roses, tree peonies, lilies and formal pond. A variety of herbaceous plants. Small herd of Formosan Sika deer. Group of South American Rhea. Koi Carp. Some wheelchair access.

🐑 ❄ 🚗 🛏 🍵

42 THE MERCHANTS HOUSE

Blakeney, Holt, NR25 7NT. Mr & Mrs David Marris. *Centre of Blakeney Village. Garden located N of A149 (New Road) up Little Lane in Blakeney.* **Sat 23 May (11.30-4.30). Adm £5, chd free. Home-made teas.**

2 acres of walled 'secret' garden with terrace, woodland walk, parterre, shrub borders, orchard, kitchen garden, herbaceous border and ice house. Dogs on leads. Most of the garden is suitable for wheelchairs.

&. 🐑 ❄ 🍵

Church Cottage

43 NEW 14 MILL HILL ROAD

Norwich, NR2 3DP. Peter Blake & Nick Lodge. *Mill Hill Road is off Earlham Road at the side of the Black Horse pub. Street parking is controlled Monday-Saturday but not on Sunday.* **Sun 28 June (11-5). Adm £3, chd free. Light refreshments.**
This garden surrounds a Victorian town house (not open). The informal front garden has interesting herbaceous plants and shrubs in sun and shade. The shady side garden has ferns and woodland plants. There is a cool fern-house. The rear garden, up some steep steps, has a raised pond, beds, tropical fern house and flowering plants. The owner is a member of the British Pteridological Society. Many ferns! Wheelchair access is not possible. The front garden is on several levels with thirty steps. The back garden is accessed via a further twenty steps.

26 Ipswich Road

44 NORTH CORNER

Market Place, Winterton on Sea, Great Yarmouth, NR29 4BE. David & Julia King, 01493 394953, northcorner14@btinternet.com. *8m N of Great Yarmouth. Enter Winterton on sea by the church & follow Black St until the roads open out into the old market place. North Corner is on the L at the junction between Back Path & North Market Rd.* **Sun 23 Aug (11-5). Adm £3.50, chd free. Visits also by arrangement June to Sept for groups of 5 to 10.**
Constantly evolving small village garden, divided into defined areas to maximise space. Varied planting in beds and pots providing interest throughout the seasons, especially autumn flowering plants. Collections of hostas, agapanthus and bonsai trees. Originally a butcher's shop and half a mile from the beach. There is no designated parking so please park sensitively in the village. Gardening books and magazines available for sale/donation in aid of NGS. The garden is mainly level but has some woodchip paths.

45 NORTH LODGE

51 Bowthorpe Road, Norwich, NR2 3TN. Bruce Bentley & Peter Wilson. *1½ m W of Norwich City Centre. Turn into Bowthorpe Rd off Dereham Rd, garden 150 metres on L. By bus: 21, 22, 23, 23A/B, 24 & 24A from City centre, Old Catton, Heartsease, Thorpe & most of W Norwich. Parking available outside.* **Sun 26 July, Sun 9 Aug (11-5). Adm £4, chd free. Home-made teas.**
Delightful town garden surrounding Victorian Gothic Cemetery Lodge. Full of follies created by current owners, including a classical temple, oriental water garden and formal ponds. Original 80ft-deep well! Predominantly herbaceous planting. House extension won architectural award. Slide show of house and garden history. Wheelchair access possible but difficult. Sloping gravel drive followed by short, steep, narrow, brickweave ramp. WC not easily wheelchair accessible.

46 THE OLD HOUSE

Ranworth, NR13 6HS. The Hon Mrs Jacquetta Cator. *9m NE of Norwich. Nr South Walsham, below historic Ranworth Church.* **Sun 26 Apr (11-4). Adm £5, chd free. Home-made teas.**
Attractive linked and walled gardens alongside Ranworth Inner Broad. Bulbs, shrubs and Villandry inspired potager with interesting sculptures throughout. Mown rides through arboretum with spectacular views of the church and the broad. Some rough grass and gravel. Dogs allowed in arboretum but not in the garden itself. Teas in aid of St Helen's Church Ranworth. Wheelchair access some rough grass and gravel.

47 NEW THE OLD RECTORY

School Road, Catfield, Great Yarmouth, NR29 5DA. Penny Middleditch, middleditch@catfieldoldrectory.co.uk. *A149 to Catfield. ½ m from Catfield village centre turn R by Post Office and L at T junction opposite the Church.* **Sun 19 Apr (11-5). Adm £5, chd free. Light refreshments. home-made cakes, teas and coffees, soup and ploughman light lunches.**
3 acre garden surrounding former Rectory with gate to adjoining 14th century Church. A further 15 acres of Glebe land and paddocks providing circular walk beside small lake and through orchards, woodland and extensive cutting garden. Heavily planted for all year interest but in Spring masses of different species narcissi, species tulips, hellebores, fritillaries and anemone. It is hoped there will be a photographic display at the adjoining Church over the weekend of the garden opening. Teas in aid of All Saints Church will be provided in garden/tent unless weather filthy in which case in adjoining church. There are gravel drives but access should be available through adjoining park field.

48 THE OLD RECTORY, BRANDON PARVA

Stone Lane, Brandon Parva, NR9 4DL. Mr & Mrs S Guest. *9m W of Norwich. Leave Norwich on B1108 towards Watton, turn R at sign for Barnham Broom. L at T-junction, stay on rd approx 3m until L next turn to Yaxham. L at Xrds.* **Sun 24 May (11-5). Adm £5, chd free. Home-made teas.**

4 acre, mature garden with large collection (70) specimen trees, huge variety of shrubs and herbaceous plants combined to make beautiful mixed borders. The garden comprises several formal lawns and borders, woodland garden incl rhododendrons, pond garden, walled garden and pergolas covered in wisteria, roses and clematis which create long shady walkways. Croquet lawn open for visitors to play.

49 THE OLD SMITHY

Mill Road, Marlingford, Norwich, NR9 5HL. Kirsty Reader & David Eagles. *6m W of Norwich. A47 to B1108 Watton Road, take 3rd R Bow Hill, past Mill, along Mill Road, garden on R, parking at village hall, from Easton sign to Marlingford*

opp Des Amis. **Wed 15 July (10-4.30). Adm £4, chd free. Light refreshments at village hall.**

A garden for the family designed by a plantsman, with unusual cottage garden perennials and shrubs. Large north facing border filled with colour for all seasons. Woodland planting, specimen trees, stumpery, vegetables and hens.

50 OULTON HALL

Oulton, Aylsham, NR11 6NU. Bolton Agnew. *4m NW of Aylsham. From Aylsham take B1354. After 4m turn L for Oulton Chapel, Hall ½ m on R. From B1149 (Norwich/Holt rd) take B1354, next R, Hall ½ m on R.* **Sun 7 June (1-5). Adm £5, chd free. Home-made teas.**

C18 manor house (not open) and clocktower set in 6-acre garden with lake and woodland walks. Chelsea designer's own garden - herbaceous, Italian, bog, water, wild, verdant, sunken and parterre gardens all flowing from one tempting vista to another. Developed over 25 yrs with emphasis on structure, height and texture, with a lot of recent replanting in the contemporary manner.

51 ◆ RAVENINGHAM HALL

Raveningham, Norwich, NR14 6NS. Sir Nicholas & Lady Bacon, 01508 548480, sonya@raveningham.com, www.raveningham.com. *14m SE of Norwich. 4m from Beccles off B1136* **A guided walk by Sir Nicholas Bacon of the snowdrops for NGS: Tue 18 Feb (2-4). Adm £20 incl Tea & Cake. Entrance by pre-booking essential, please visit www.ngs.org.uk/events for information & booking. For other opening times and information, please phone, email or visit garden website.**

Traditional country house garden in glorious parkland setting. Restored Victorian conservatory, walled kitchen garden, herbaceous borders, newly planted stumpery. Arboretum established after the 1987 gale, Millennium lake and sculpture by Susan Bacon. February sees large drifts of many different varieties of snowdrops. For general opening times please see garden website www.raveningham.com. Gravel paths allow wheelchair access.

Booton Hall

52 ◆ SANDRINGHAM GARDENS
Sandringham, PE35 6EH. Her
Majesty The Queen, 01485 545408,
visits@sandringhamestate.co.uk,
www.sandringhamestate.co.uk.
*6m NW of King's Lynn. By gracious
permission, the House, Museum &
Gardens will be open.* **For opening
times and information, please
phone, email or visit garden
website.**
Open daily from Fri 3 Apr to Wed 14
Oct inclusive - except Good Friday
10 April and Sat 25 to Friday 31
July inclusive. 60-acres of glorious
gardens and woodland with lakes,
rare plants and trees. Colour and all
year round interest; spring-flowering
bulbs, rhododendrons and azaleas,
lavender and roses. Dazzling autumn
colour. Gravel paths (not deep), long
distances - please tel or visit website
for our Accessibility Guide.

&. ✿ 🚌 ☕

53 ◆ SEVERALS GRANGE
Holt Road B1110, Wood
Norton, NR20 5BL. Jane
Lister, 01362 684206,
hoecroft@hotmail.co.uk,
www.hoecroft.co.uk. *8m S of Holt,
6m E of Fakenham. 2m N of Guist
on L of B1110. Guist is situated 5m
SE of Fakenham on A1067 Norwich
rd.* **For NGS: Sat 15 Aug (2-5).
Adm £5, chd free. Home-made
teas. For other opening times and
information, please phone, email or
visit garden website.**
The gardens surrounding Severals
Grange are a perfect example of
how colour, shape and form can be
created by the use of foliage plants,
from large shrubs to small alpines.
Movement and lightness are achieved
by interspersing these plants with a
wide range of ornamental grasses,
which are at their best in late summer.
Splashes of additional colour are
provided by a variety of herbaceous
plants. Some gravel paths but help
can be provided.

&. 🐄 ✿ 🚌 🛏 ☕

54 ◆ STODY LODGE
Melton Constable,
NR24 2ER. Mr & Mrs Charles
MacNicol, 01263 860572,
enquiries@stodyestate.co.uk,
www.stodylodgegardens.co.uk.
*16m NW of Norwich, 3m S of Holt.
Off B1354. Signed from Melton
Constable on Holt Rd. For SatNav
NR24 2ER. Gardens signed as you
approach.* **For NGS: Tue 19 May (1-
5). Adm £7, chd free. Home-made**

teas. **For other opening times and
information, please phone, email or
visit garden website.**
Spectacular gardens with one
of the largest concentrations of
rhododendrons and azaleas in East
Anglia. Created in the 1920s, the
gardens also feature magnolias,
camellias, a variety of ornamental
and specimen trees, late daffodils,
tulips and bluebells. Expansive
lawns and magnificent yew hedges.
Woodland walks and 4 acre Water
Gardens filled with over 2,000 vividly-
coloured azalea mollis. Home-made
teas provided by selected local and
national charities. Access to most
areas of the garden. Gravel paths
to Azalea Water Gardens with some
uneven ground.

&. 🐄 ✿ 🚌 ☕

55 SUNDIAL FARM
Shelton Green, Shelton, Norwich,
NR15 2SQ. Ally & John Hodgson.
*12m S of Norwich. From A140 take
B1527 towards Hempnall. Turn R
towards Fritton. Cross the common
& take 1st L (Alburgh Rd).* **Sat 30
May (11-5). Adm £5, chd free.
Home-made teas.**
5-acre family garden with charming
features including giant topiary faces,
a secret garden, a grass labyrinth
and a pond. There is an ornamental
cutting and vegetable garden with
raised beds and a greenhouse,
extensive perennial planting, a
hazel walk, orchards and a wood.
Wheelchair access may be difficult
as there are some steps and different
surfaces, but help can be called upon
if needed.

🐄 ✿ ☕

56 SWANNINGTON MANOR
Norwich, NR9 5NR. Gregory &
Sue Darling. *7m NW of Norwich.
Almost halfway between A1067
(to Fakenham) & B1149 (to Holt).
Parking at Romantic Garden Nursery.*
**Sun 5 July (10.30-5). Combined
adm with Manor Farm House,
Swannington £5, chd free. Light
refreshments.**
C17 manor house (not open)
creates a stunning backdrop to this
garden which is framed by 300yr
old hedges, thought to be unique in
this country. 7 acres includes mixed
shrub and herbaceous borders, a
water garden, sunken rose garden,
a recently installed potager style
vegetable garden, specimen trees
and sloping lawns make this garden
both delightful and unusual. Some

access for wheelchairs able to cope
with gravel paths.

&. 🐄 ☕

57 TUDOR LODGINGS
Castle Acre, King's Lynn,
PE32 2AN. Gus & Julia
Stafford Allen, 01760 755334,
jstaffordallen@btinternet.com. *4m
N of Swaffham off A1065. Parking
in the field below the house.* **Sun 9
Aug (11-5). Combined adm with
Highfield House £7, chd free.
Light refreshments in the Barn.
Visits also by arrangement July
& Aug.**
The 2- acre garden fronts a C15 flint
house (not open), and incorporates
part of the Norman earthworks.
C18 dovecote, abstract topiary,
lawn and a 'Mondrian' knot garden.
Ornamental grasses and hot border.
Productive fruit cage and cutting
garden. A natural wild area includes
a shepherd's hut and informal pond.
Bantams and Ducks. Wheelchair
access is limited, please ask for
assistance beforehand. Disabled WC.

&. 🐄 ✿ ☕

58 TYGER BARN
Wood Lane, Aldeby, Beccles,
NR34 0DA. Julianne Fernandez,
www.chasing-arcadia.com. *Approx
1m from Toft Monks. From A143
towards Great Yarmouth at Toft
Monks turn R into Post Office Lane
opp White Lion Pub, after ¼ m
turn L into Wood Lane. After ½ m
Tyger Barn is 2nd house on L.* **Sun
5 July (12-4). Adm £5, chd free.
Light refreshments. Visits also
by arrangement June & July for
groups of up to 20.**
Featured in The English Garden
magazine in February 2019, Tyger
Barn is a modern country garden
started in 2007. It includes extensive
borders with hot, exotic and 'ghost'
themes, a secret cottage garden, wild
flower swathes and colonies of bee
orchids. A traditional hay meadow
and ancient woodland provide a
beautiful setting. Garden is mainly
level, but is divided by a shingle drive.

&. ✿ Ⓓ ☕

59 WALCOTT HOUSE
Walcott Green, Walcott,
Norwich, NR12 0NU. Mr & Mrs
Nick Collier, 07986 607170,
julietcollier1@gmail.com. *3m N of
Stalham. Off the Stalham to Walcott
rd (B1159).* **Sun 21 June (11-5).
Adm £5, chd free. Home-made**

teas. **Visits also by arrangement in July for groups of 20+.**

A 12 acre site with over 1 acre of formal gardens based on model C19 Norfolk farm buildings. Woodland and damp gardens; arboretum; vistas with tree lined avenues; woodland walks. Small single steps to negotiate when moving between gardens in the yards.

60 33 WALDEMAR AVENUE

Hellesdon, Norwich, NR6 6TB. Sonja Gaffer and Alan Beal. *Waldemar Ave is situated about 400 yards off Norwich ring road towards Cromer on the A140.* **Sun 2, Sun 30 Aug (11-5). Adm £4, chd free. Home-made teas.**

A surprising and large suburban garden of many parts with an exciting mix of exotic and tropical plants combined with unusual perennials, many grown from seed. A quirky palm-thatched Tiki hut is an eye catching feature. Teas will be served and you can sit by the pond which is brimming with wildlife and rare plants. A large collection of succulents will be on show and there will be plants to buy. Wheelchair access surfaces are mostly of lawn and concrete and are on one level. Two entrance gates are 33 and 39 inches wide respectively.

61 WARBOROUGH HOUSE

2 Wells Road, Stiffkey, NR23 1QH. Mr & Mrs J Morgan. *13m N of Fakenham, 4m E of Wells-Next-The-Sea on A149 in the centre of village. Parking is available & signed at garden entrance. Coasthopper bus stop outside garden. Please DO NOT park on the main road as this causes congestion.* **Sun 24 May (11-4). Adm £5, chd free. Home-made teas.**

7- acre garden on a steep chalk slope, surrounding C19 house (not open) with views across the Stiffkey valley and to the coast. Woodland walks, formal terraces, shrub borders, lawns and walled garden create a garden of contrasts. Garden slopes steeply in parts. Paths are gravel, bark chip or grass. Disabled parking allows access to garden nearest the house and teas.

GROUP OPENING

62 WELLS-NEXT-THE-SEA GARDENS

Wells-Next -The-Sea, NR23 1DP. *10m N of Fakenham. All gardens near Coasthopper 'Burnt Street' or 'The Buttlands' bus stops. Car-parking for all gardens in Market Lane area.* **Sun 14 June (11-5). Combined adm £5, chd free. Light refreshments at Caprice.**

CAPRICE
Clubbs Lane, Wells-next-the-Sea. David & Joolz Saunders.

HIRAETH
11 Burnt Street, Wells-next-the-Sea. Jen Davies.

7 MARKET LANE
Wells-next-the-Sea. Hazel Ashley.

NORFOLK HOUSE
17 Burnt Street, Wells-next-the-Sea. Katrina & Alan Jackson.

POACHER COTTAGE
15 Burnt Street. Roger & Barbara Oliver.

Wells-next-the-Sea is a small, friendly coastal town on the North Norfolk Coast. Popular with families, walkers and bird watchers. The harbour has shops, cafes, fish and chips. Beach served by a narrow gauge railway. Fine parish church. The five town gardens, though small, demonstrate a variety of design and a wide selection of planting. Wheelchair access except Norfolk House which has limited access.

63 WEST BARSHAM HALL

Fakenham, NR21 9NP. Mr & Mrs Jeremy Soames, 01328 863519, susannasoames@gmail.com. *3m N of Fakenham. From Fakenham take A148 to Cromer then L on B1105 to Wells. After ½ m L again to Wells. After 1½ m R The Barshams & West Barsham Hall.* **Sun 28 June (11-5). Adm £6.50, chd free. Home-made teas. Morning coffee and light refreshments, afternoon cream teas. Visits also by arrangement May to Sept.**

Large garden with lake, approx 10-acres. Mature yew hedging and sunken garden originally laid out by Gertrude Jeykll. Swimming pool garden, shrub borders, kitchen garden with herbaceous borders, fruit cage, cutting garden and bog garden. Separate old fashioned cottage garden also open. Some slopes and gravel paths.

64 WRETHAM LODGE

East Wretham, IP24 1RL. Mr Gordon Alexander & Mr Ian Salter, 01953 498997. *6m NE of Thetford. A11 E from Thetford, L up A1075, L by village sign, R at Xrds then bear L.* **Sat 9, Sun 10 May (11-5). Adm £5, chd free. Tea. Visits also by arrangement Apr to Sept.**

10 acre garden surrounding former Georgian rectory (not open). In spring masses of species tulips, hellebores, fritillaries, daffodils and narcissi; bluebell walk and small woodland walk. Topiary pyramids and yew hedging lead to double herbaceous borders. Shrub borders and rose beds (home of the Wretham Rose). Traditionally maintained walled garden with fruit, vegetables and perennials.

We open the gates to the nation's best gardens, offering a relaxing, memorable and affordable day out. A perfect experience to share with friends and family.

NORTH EAST

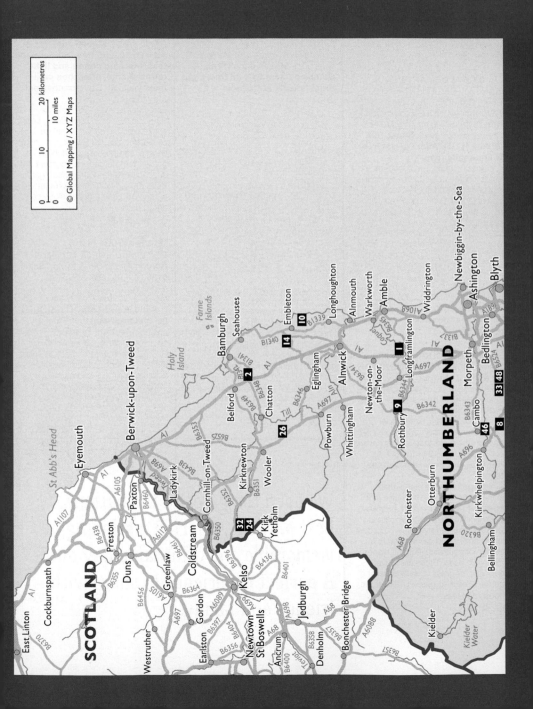

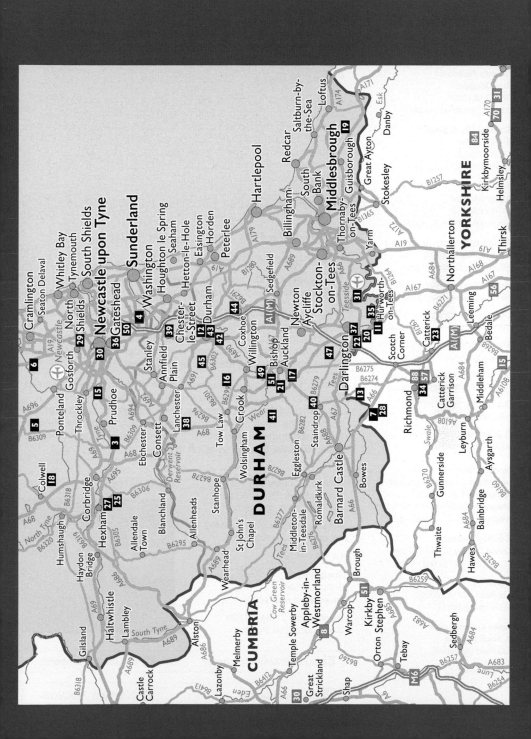

Volunteers

County Durham

County Organiser
Iain Anderson
01325 778446
iain.anderson@ngs.org.uk

County Treasurer
Sue Douglas
07712 461002
sue.douglas@ngs.org.uk

Booklet Co-ordinator
Sheila Walke
07837 764057
sheila.walke@ngs.org.uk

Publicity
Alison Morgan
01913 843842
alison.morgan@ngs.org.uk

Assistant County Organisers
Gill Knights 01325 483210
gillianknights55@gmail.com

Helen Jackson 07985 699960
helen.jackson@ngs.org.uk

Dorothy Matthews 01325 354434
matthews.dorothy@googlemail.com

Monica Spencer 01325 286215
monica.spencer@ngs.org.uk

Margaret Stamper 01325 488911
margaretstamper@tiscali.co.uk

Gill Naisby 01325 381324
gillnaisby@gmail.com

Sue Walker 01325 481881
walker.sdl@gmail.com

Northumberland & Tyne
and Wear County Organiser
& Booklet Coordinator
Maureen Kesteven 01914 135937
maureen.kesteven@ngs.org.uk

County Treasurer
David Oakley 07941 077594
david.oakley@ngs.org.uk

Publicity
Liz Reid 01914 165981
liz.reid@ngs.org.uk

Talks Co-ordinator
& Social Media
Liz Reid (as above)

County Durham: an unsung county.

County Durham lies between the River Wear and the River Tees and is varied and beautiful.

Our National Garden Scheme gardens are to be found in the city, high up in the dales, in the attractive villages of South Durham and outskirts of industrial Teesside. Something different every week.

Choose your old favourites but also check out our wonderful new gardens. Country gardens include an exciting newly developed woodland and garden at The Stables, traditional village gardens at High Bank Farm and Homelands and a wildlife garden at East Middleton. Our town gardens can surprise you too. Oakdene tucked away in Darlington and the must-see quirky new Garden and Studio at 67 in St Helen Auckland.

All our garden owners are looking forward to welcoming you.

Northumberland is a county of ancient castles and wild coastline, of expansive views and big skies.

This beautiful landscape with its picturesque valleys provides the backdrop for a delightful range of gardens.

There's a great variety of styles from the walled vegetable gardens and sumptuous borders of large country houses to exciting contemporary planting. A historic manor house has a Gertrude Jekyll connection whilst a newly made garden is experimental and sustainable and full of ideas for organic growing.

Another unusual garden has been made on an exceptionally steep slope, showing that you can transform even the most difficult of sites. There are city gardens too: a tiny courtyard packed with colour or the landscaped garden rooms around a hospice. From a series of cottage plots in a fishing village to arboreta and dramatic water features, there is so much to inspire.

Assistant County Organisers
Maxine Eaton 077154 60038
acottagegardener@gmail.com

Natasha McEwen 07917 754155
natashamcewengd@aol.co.uk

Liz Reid (as left)

Susie White
07941 077594
susie@susie-white.co.uk

David Young 01434 600699
david.young@ngs.org.uk

Below: Wallington

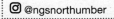 **f** @gardensopenforcharity   **🐦** @NGSNorthumberl1

 **📷** @ngsnorthumber   **🐦** @Durham_TeesNGS

OPENING DATES

All entries subject to change. For latest information check **www.ngs.org.uk**
Map locator numbers are shown to the right of each garden name.

March

Sunday 1st
◆ Crook Hall & Gardens 12

April

Sunday 19th
Adderstone House 2

Saturday 25th
◆ Wallington 46

May

Sunday 17th
Blagdon 6

Sunday 24th
Lilburn Tower 26

Sunday 31st
Croft Hall 11
NEW The Moore House 33

June

Sunday 7th
The Beacon 3
24 Bede Crescent 4
◆ Whalton Manor Gardens 48

Saturday 13th
Acton House 1
Ushaw College 45
◆ Wallington 46

Sunday 14th
Loughbrow House 27
Neasham Abbey 35

Friday 19th
The Fold 16

Saturday 20th
NEW Craster's Hidden Gardens 10
The Fold 16

Sunday 21st
NEW High Bank Farm 20
NEW Holmelands 22
◆ Mindrum Garden 32
Ravensford Farm 41

Saturday 27th
Fallodon Hall 14
Woodlands 50

Sunday 28th
Ferndene House 15
Oliver Ford Garden 38

July

Saturday 4th
NEW East Middleton 13
Kirky Cottage 24

Sunday 5th
Marie Curie Hospice 30
NEW The Stables 44

Saturday 11th
◆ Raby Castle 40

Sunday 12th
Bichfield Tower 5
St Margaret's Allotments 43
Woodbine House 49

Sunday 19th
24 Bede Crescent 4
Kiplin Hall 23
Lambshield 25
NEW The Moore House 33
NEW Oakdene Lodge 37

Sunday 26th
Gardener's Cottage Plants 18
Middleton Hall Retirement Village 31
St Cuthbert's Hospice 42

August

Sunday 2nd
NEW Garden and studio at 67 17
Heather Holm 19

Sunday 9th
Capheaton Hall 8

Sunday 16th
Hillside Cottages 21

Saturday 22nd
Maggie's 29

Sunday 23rd
Walworth Gardens 47

September

Thursday 17th
◆ Crook Hall & Gardens 12

November

Saturday 7th
◆ Cragside 9

Sunday 8th
◆ Cragside 9

By Arrangement

Arrange a personalised garden visit with your club, or group of friends, on a date to suit you. See individual garden entries for full details.

Acton House 1
Adderstone House 2
The Beacon 3
24 Bede Crescent 4
Broaches Farm 7
Ferndene House 15
The Fold 16
Hillside Cottages 21
Kirky Cottage 24
Lambshield 25
Lilburn Tower 26
Loughbrow House 27
Lowbridge House 28
Mr Yorke's Walled Garden 34
25 Park Road South 39
Ravensford Farm 41
St Cuthbert's Hospice 42
Woodlands 50
Woodside House 51

© Susie White

Fallodon Hall

THE GARDENS

◼ ACTON HOUSE

Felton, Morpeth, NE65 9NU.
Mr Alan & Mrs Eileen Ferguson.
Head Gardener 07779 860217,
jane@actonhouseuk.com. *A1 N of
Morpeth. N of Felton. Signed turnoff
on R. Follow signs.* **Sat 13 June (1-
4). Adm £5, chd free. Home-made
teas. Visits also by arrangement
May to Aug for groups of 5+.**
This walled garden has structure,
colour and variety of planting, with
abundant herbaceous perennials
and different grasses. Planted in
the spring of 2011, it has sections
devoted to fruit and vegetables, David
Austin rose borders, standard trees
and climbers spreading over the brick
walls. There are additional mixed
borders, a ha-ha, and developing
woodland planting, in total extending
over 5 acres. Herbaceous perennial
plantings include species and varieties
favoured by butterflies and bees.

◻ ADDERSTONE HOUSE

Adderstone Mains, Belford,
NE70 7HS. John & Pauline
Clough, 07714662520,
John.clough@me.com. *1m S of
Belford off A1. Best approached from
the N off A1 Adderstone Mains is 1m
S of Belford, turn L off A1. From S,
0.7m N of Purdy Lodge on R but turn
dangerous, continue to Belford, turn
& approach from N. Ample parking.*
**Sun 19 Apr (1-4). Adm £6, chd free.
Light refreshments in the Barn
beside the Japanese Garden. Visits
also by arrangement Mar to Oct for
groups of 10+.**
A Victorian house, gardens, millpond
with folly and grounds of 10½ acres.
Established and 'new projects' in
development with Sean Murray (RHS
Chelsea Challenge winner).
New Japanese Garden with cherry
blossom, Walled garden; an orchard
leads to the sunken garden; rose walk
and formal garden, then on to the
mill pond, fruit/vegetable plots and
vineyard. Plant stall, teas and grape
juice from vineyard.

◻ THE BEACON

10 Crabtree Road, Stocksfield,
NE43 7NX. Derek & Patricia
Hodgson, 01661 842518,
patandderek@btinternet.com.
12m W of Newcastle upon Tyne.
*From A69 follow signs into village.
Station & cricket ground on L . Turn
R into Cadehill Rd then 1st R into
Crabtree Rd (cul de sac) Park on
Cadehill.* **Sun 7 June (2-6). Adm £5,
chd free. Cream teas. Visits also
by arrangement Apr to Sept for
groups of 10+.**
This garden illustrates how to make
a cottage garden on a steep site with
loads of interest at different levels.
Planted with acers, roses and a
variety of cottage garden and formal
plants. Water runs gently through
it and there are tranquil places to
sit and talk or just reflect. Stunning
colour and plant combinations.
Wildlife friendly - numerous birds,
frogs, newts, hedgehogs. Haven for
butterflies and bees. Owner available
for entertaining group talks. Steep, so
not wheelchair friendly but wheelchair
users have negotiated the drive and
enjoyed the view of the main garden.

◻ 24 BEDE CRESCENT

Washington, NE38 7JA. Sheila
Brookes, 0191 417 9702,
sheilab24@hotmail.co.uk.
*From A1231 follow directions to
Washington Old Hall, turn L onto
Abbey Rd, then L onto Village
Lane. Turn L into Bede Cres just
before the Black Bush, garden
is the end house at the grassed
oval.* **Sun 7 June, Sun 19 July
(12.30-4.30). Adm £2.50, chd free.
Cold drinks, biscuits & crisps
available if desired. Visits also
by arrangement May to Sept for
groups of up to 20.**
A lesson in how to make a small
shady place colourful and interesting.
Small 'courtyard style' garden, with
central paved area, surrounded by
borders containing shrubs and box
balls for year round structure, and
packed with colourful Astilbes, lilies
and clematis for summer impact.
Small patio front garden, with
gravel border planted with box balls
and containerised shrubs. Light
refreshments available from several
nearby cafes and pubs around our
pretty Village Green, (Village is a multi
Gold medal winner in Northumbria in
Bloom, (part of the Britain in Bloom).
Access into rear paved 'courtyard
garden' via a side gate, (which should
accommodate a small wheelchair,
although not a wide entrance).

◻ BICHFIELD TOWER

Belsay, Newcastle Upon Tyne,
NE20 0JP. Lesley & Stewart
Manners, 075114 39606,
lesleymanners@gmail.com,
www.bitchfieldtower.co.uk. *Private
rd off B6309, 4m N of Stamfordham
and SW of Belsay village.* **Sun 12
July (1-4). Adm £5, chd free.
Home-made teas.**
A 6 acre maturing garden in it's 4th
year of rejuvenation. Set around a
Medieval Pele Tower, there is an
impressive stone water feature, large
trout lake,mature woodland, Pear
Orchard, and 2 Walled gardens.
Extensive herbaceous borders, prairie
borders and contemporary grass
borders. Delicious home-made teas
provided by the 6th Morpeth Scout
Group in the carriage house garden
and building. Historic building, tennis
court, woodlands, fairy walk for kids,
croquet lawn and set, trout lake, pop-
up shops of local businesses.

◻ BLAGDON

Seaton Burn, NE13 6DE. Viscount
Ridley, www.blagdonestate.co.uk.
*5m S of Morpeth on A1. 8m N of
Newcastle on A1, N on B1318, L at
r'about (Holiday Inn) & follow signs
to Blagdon. Entrance to parking area
signed.* **Sun 17 May (1-4.30). Adm
£5, chd free. Home-made teas.**
Unique 27 acre garden encompassing
formal garden with Lutyens designed
'canal', Lutyens structures and walled
kitchen garden. Valley with stream
and various follies, quarry garden and
woodland walks. Large numbers of
ornamental trees and shrubs planted
over many generations. National
Collections of Acer, Alnus and
Sorbus. Trailer rides around the estate
(small additional charge) and stalls
selling local produce/crafts. Partial
wheelchair access.

◻ BROACHES FARM

Dalton, Richmond, DL11 7HW. Mr
& Mrs Hutchinson, 01833 621369,
jude1@myfwi.co.uk. *7m W of
Scotch Corner. From Scotch Corner
on A66 W, 7m turn L at The Rokeby
Inn. After ½m turn L to Dalton.
Farm on L after 1m.* **Visits by
arrangement June to Aug any
number of visitors. Adm £4, chd
free.**
In 1996 this wonderful garden was
a field. It now includes 2 ponds, one
with koi, stream, bog garden and
wooded area. Mixed colourful borders

are full of herbaceous perennials. Informal and naturalistic, this is a rural idyll. Abundant wildlife incl kingfishers, dippers, wagtails, frogs and toads. Lots of seating areas including summerhouse and gazebo.

⑧ CAPHEATON HALL

Capheaton, Newcastle Upon Tyne, NE19 2AB. William & Eliza Browne-Swinburne, 01913758152, capheatonhall@gmail.com, www.capheatonhall.co.uk/accomodation. *24m N of Newcastle off A696. From S turn L onto Silver Hill rd signed Capheaton. From N, past Wallington/Kirkharle junction, turn R.* **Sun 9 Aug (1-5). Adm £5, chd free. Home-made teas.**
Set in parkland, Capheaton Hall has magnificent views over the Northumberland countryside. Formal ponds sit south of the house, which has C19 conservatory, and a walk to a Georgian folly of a chapel. The outstanding feature is the very productive walled kitchen garden, at its height in late summer, mixing colourful vegetables, espaliered fruit with annual and perennial flowering borders. Victorian glasshouse and conservatory. Wheelchair access to the walled garden and teas in the house is limited by steps and gravel paths, but the lawns are closely mown and generally flat.

⑨ ♦ CRAGSIDE

Rothbury, NE65 7PX. National Trust, 01669 620333, cragside@nationaltrust.org.uk, www.nationaltrust.org.uk/cragside. *13m SW of Alnwick. (B6341); 15m NW of Morpeth (A697).* **For NGS: Sat 7, Sun 8 Nov (10-4). Adm £13.60, chd £6.80. Light refreshments at Cragside Tea Rooms or Still Room. For other opening times and information, please phone, email or visit garden website.**
The Formal Garden is in the 'High Victorian' style created by the 1st Lord and Lady Armstrong. Incl orchard house, carpet bedding, ferneries, Italian terrace and Rose borders. The largest sandstone Rock Garden in Europe with its tumbling cascades. Extensive grounds of over 1000 acres famous for rhododendrons in June, large lakes and magnificent conifer landscape. The House, mainly the design of Norman Shaw, with its very fine

Woodlands

© Susie White

arts and crafts interiors is worth a separate visit. Only partial wheelchair access to formal garden.

GROUP OPENING

⑩ NEW CRASTER'S HIDDEN GARDENS

1, 2 and 5 Chapel Row, Craster, Alnwick, NE66 3TU. Sue Chapman, Gill Starkey, June Drage. *Park in the pay & display parking at entrance to village. Walk to the harbour & turn L along Dunstanburgh Rd. Look for NGS sign on L before you reach the castle field. There is no parking in the village. Prebooking essential on this date.* **Sat 20 June (1-4). Combined adm £5, chd £2.50. Home-made teas in village hall, provided by WI.**
Due to visitor numbers to Craster, tickets are limited and must be pre-booked. To reserve 'phone 01665 576512, or email junedrage@btconnect.com. In sight of Dunstanburgh Castle, in the picturesque village of Craster, sit 3 very different cottage gardens showing what can be achieved in a windy seaside setting. Formerly allotments attached to fishermen's cottages - No.1 is still in development, and has two ponds, colour-themed borders and prairie style planting. No. 2 has sea views, bee friendly plants,

roses galore and a lovely herbaceous border. No. 5 is a ¼ acre, divided into several separate areas: woodland garden, pond, fruit and vegetables plus borders featuring many unusual perennials, shrubs, grasses and ferns. The garden is managed to encourage wildlife. Teas in the village hall, proceeds to WI. Access unsuitable for wheelchairs. Steep uneven ground.

⑪ CROFT HALL

Croft-on-Tees, DL2 2TB. Mr & Mrs Trevor Chaytor Norris. *3m S of Darlington. On A167 to Northallerton, 6m from Scotch Corner. Croft Hall is 1st house on R as you enter village from Scotch Corner.* **Sun 31 May (2-5). Adm £5, chd free. Home-made teas.**
A lovely lavender walk leads to a Queen Anne-fronted house (not open) surrounded by a 5 acre garden, comprising a stunning herbaceous border, large fruit and vegetable plot, two ponds and wonderful topiary arched wall. Pretty rose garden and mature box Italianate parterre are beautifully set in this garden offering peaceful, tranquil views of open countryside. No dogs Wheelchair access, some gravel paths.

12 ◆ CROOK HALL & GARDENS
Sidegate, Durham City, DH1 5SZ.
Maggie Bell, 0191 384 8028,
info@crookhallgardens.co.uk,
www.crookhallgardens.co.uk.
*Centre of Durham City. Crook Hall
is short walk from Durham's Market
Place. Follow the tourist info signs.
Pay and display parking available
at entrance.* **For NGS: Sun 1
Mar, Thur 17 Sept (10-5). Adm
£6, chd £3. incl Hall. For other
opening times and information,
please phone, email or visit garden
website.**
Described in Country Life as
having 'history, romance and
beauty'. Intriguing medieval manor
house surrounded by 4 acres of
fine gardens. Visitors can enjoy
magnificent cathedral views from
the 2 walled gardens. Other garden
'rooms' incl the silver and white
garden. An orchard, moat pool,
maze and Sleeping Giant give
added interest! Refreshments in the
Tea Room (main building) and the
Café (entrance building). No dogs
Wheelchair accessible and disabled
WC.

13 NEW EAST MIDDLETON
Caldwell, Richmond, DL11 7QL.
Deny & Dave Holden. *12m W of
Darlington. 9m N of Richmond. 7m
SE of Barnard Castle. Turn off B6274
in Caldwell village towards Hutton
Magna for 1m. Half mile up track
with passing places. Field Parking.
Hard standing parking for wheelchair
users.* **Sat 4 July (1-6). Adm £4,
chd free. Light refreshments.**
Wildlife friendly half acre includes
pond, mixed planting of perennials,
trees and shrubs, vegetables and
courtyard garden with greenhouse.
Additional land with orchard and
small arboretum started in 2000.
Wheelchair friendly. Plants, art and
craft work for sale. Creature trail.
Small exhibit of classic motorbikes.
Dogs on leads welcome.

14 FALLODON HALL
Alnwick, NE66 3HF. Mr & Mrs
Mark Bridgeman, 01665 576252
www.bruntoncottages.co.uk. *5m
N of Alnwick, 2m off A1. From the
A1 turn onto the B6347 signed
Christon Bank & Seahouses. Turn
into the Fallodon gates after exactly
2m, at Xrds. Follow drive for 1m.* **Sat
27 June (2-5). Adm £5, chd free.
Home-made teas in stable yard.**

Neasham Abbey

Extensive, well established garden,
with a hot greenhouse beside the
bog garden. The late C17 walls of
the kitchen garden surround cutting
and vegetable borders and the fruit
greenhouse. Natasha McEwen
replanted the sunken garden from
1898 and the redesigned 30m border
newly planted in 2017. Woodlands,
pond and arboretum over 10 acres
to explore. Renowned home-made
teas in stable yard. Partial wheelchair
access.

15 FERNDENE HOUSE
2 Holburn Lane Court, Holburn
Lane, Ryton, NE40 3PN.
Maureen Kesteven, 0191 413
5937, maureen.kesteven@ngs.
org.uk, www.facebook.com/
northeastgardenopenforcharity/.
*In Ryton Old Village, 8m W of
Gateshead. Off B6317, on Holburn
Lane in Old Ryton Village. Park in
Co-op carpark on High St, cross
rd & walk through Ferndene Park
following yellow signs.* **Sun 28 June
(1-4.30). Adm £5, chd free. Home-
made teas. Light lunch available.
Visits also by arrangement Apr to
Aug for groups of 10+.**
¾ acre garden, developed from
2009, surrounded by trees. Informal
areas of herbaceous perennials, more
formal box bordered area, sedum
roof, wildlife pond, cutting, gravel
and bog gardens. Willow work. Early

interest - hellebores, snowdrops,
daffodils, bluebells and tulips.
Summer interest from wide range of
flowering perennials.1½ acre mixed
broadleaf wood with beck running
through. Driveway, from which main
borders can be seen, is wheelchair
accessible but 'phone for assistance.

16 THE FOLD
High Wooley, Stanley
Crook, DL15 9AP. Mr & Mrs
G Young, 01388 768412,
gfamyoung@gmail.com. *Turn R
at Xrds in Brancepeth, opp turn to
Castle, drive 3m along the single
track rd until you reach the junction
on bend with the main rd. Entrance
100yards on L.* **Fri 19, Sat 20
June (11-4). Adm £4, chd free.
Home-made teas. Visits also
by arrangement May to Sept for
groups of 10 to 30.**
Garden, approx ½ acre created
over 25 years in an area that had
been extensively mined. It stands at
700ft and enjoys splendid views over
countryside. Herbaceous borders,
alpine bed, island beds, ponds,
numerous mature trees and small roof
garden. Wide range of plants, mostly
perennials, many grown from seed
and cuttings. Emphasis on colour,
harmony and texture to create all year
interest. No dogs No disabled access
as steep slopes and gravel paths.

17 NEW GARDEN AND STUDIO AT 67

Manor Road, St. Helen Auckland, Bishop Auckland, DL14 9ER. Mitsi B Kral, www.instagram.com/gardenat67/. *From A68 West Auckland, turn on to station rd towards St Helen Auckland avoiding the by-pass follow the rd over the bridge and on to Manor Rd, garden on R by pedestrian crossing.* **Sun 2 Aug (12-5). Adm £4, chd free. Home-made teas.**
The garden at 67 is at the rear of a Georgian house which was formerly a pub. Artist Mitsi and her partner Nic have landscaped the walled garden over the last 2 years. The garden is a magical eclectic mix of unusual plants, packed with colour. There are wildlife ponds, raised vegetable garden, greenhouse, rose garden, wisteria walk, alpine garden, herb garden and salvaged items. Wheelchair access is to the main feature of the garden, other paths are gravel.

18 GARDENER'S COTTAGE PLANTS

Gardener's Cottage, Bingfield, Newcastle Upon Tyne, NE19 2LE. Andrew Davenport, www.gcplants.co.uk. *6m N of Corbridge. From N turn L off A68 signed Bingfield, after approx 0.6m turn L at T junction, garden on R approx 0.9m. From S turn R off A68 signed Bingfield, garden on R approx 1.8m.* **Sun 26 July (11-4). Adm £4, chd free. Variety of home-made cakes, biscuits and scones.**
This compact (¼ acre) experimental garden and nursery provides an education in organic and sustainable gardening. Organic vegetable, fruit, herb and floral gardens show the use of mulching, composting, growing systems and other ideas from the garden's inventive creator. Wild flowers thrive amongst cultivated varieties in a range of attractive and wildlife friendly ornamental borders. Collection of unusual, historic and rare plants of the mid-Tyne valley.

19 HEATHER HOLM

Stanghow Road, Stanghow, Saltburn-By-The-Sea, TS12 3JU. Arthur & June Murray. *Stanghow is 5 km E of Guisborough on A171. Turn L at Lockwood Beck (signed Stanghow) Heather Holm is on the R past the Xrds.* **Sun 2 Aug (12-4). Adm £4, chd £1. Home-made teas. Home-made cakes and teas.**
At 700 feet above sea level on the edge of the North Yorkshire Moors, Stanghow has won numerous RHS Gold awards for Best Small Village, winning again in 2017, and was a Champion among Champions in the 2013 Britain in Bloom competition. Heather Holm has extensive topiary which adds form and structure to this ¼ acre garden. No dogs Wheelchair access to viewing deck only.

20 NEW HIGH BANK FARM

Cleasby Road, Stapleton, Darlington, DL2 2QE. Lesley Thompson. *e are located on the rd leading to Cleasby & Manfield from the Stapleton Rd. Drive 300 yards. you will see a signpost saying 'Nursery on a Farm', take this turning & park in the car park.* **Sun 21 June (2-5). Combined adm with Holmelands £4, chd free. Home-made teas.**
The front garden has an abundance of roses, leading onto the Orchard. The back garden has a lovely cottage garden, with a secluded summer house to relax in, together with a lovely paved area with beautiful pots and you can sit and listen to the trickling water from our lovely fishpond. Beautiful roses, cottage garden and a secluded summerhouse, with a wonderful water feature. No dogs You can park in the car park and wheelchair access is available.

Your visits help change lives – since 1927, we've donated over £60 million to nursing and caring charities

---

GROUP OPENING

21 HILLSIDE COTTAGES

Low Etherley, Bishop Auckland, DL14 0EZ. Mary Smith, Eric & Delia Ayres, 01388 832727, mary@maryruth.plus.com. *Off the B6282 in Low Etherley, nr Bishop Auckland. To reach the gardens walk down the track opp number 63 Low Etherley. Please park on main rd. Limited disabled parking at the cottages.* **Sun 16 Aug (1.30-5). Combined adm £4, chd free. Home-made teas. Tea coffee and other beverages, cakes and savoury snacks. Visits also by arrangement Feb to Nov for groups of up to 30.**

1 HILLSIDE COTTAGE
Eric & Delia Ayres.

2 HILLSIDE COTTAGE
Mrs M Smith.

The mature gardens of these two C19 cottages offer contrasting styles. At Number 1, grass paths lead you through a layout of trees and shrubs including many interesting specimens. Number 2 is based on island beds and has a cottage garden feel with a variety of perennials among the trees and shrubs and also incl a wild area, vegetables and fruit and a greenhouse with a collection of succulents and cacti. Both gardens have ponds and water features. There are a wide variety of specimen trees in both gardens including a Wollomi pine and a beautiful Monkey Puzzle tree. Children will be able to see pond life close up. At number 2 there are two stone railway sleepers from the nearby 1825 Stockton and Darlington railway line. There are steps in both gardens.

22 NEW HOLMELANDS

Cleasby, Darlington, DL2 2QY. Nicky & Clare Vigors. *1st open yard on R approaching village from Stapleton.* **Sun 21 June (2-5). Combined adm with High Bank Farm £4, chd free. Tea.**
Semi formal garden with orchard and large vegetable patch. Herbaceous beds and climbing roses as well as standard roses. Laid out in a semi formal design to create a harmonious effect. Attractive mixed borders, formal topiary and lavender at the front of the house. No dogs

23 KIPLIN HALL

nr Scorton, Richmond, DL10 6AT. Kiplin Hall Trustees, www.kiplinhall.co.uk. *Between Richmond & Northallerton on B6271. Approx 5m E of A1. Exit at J52 towards Brompton on Swale, & follow signs to Scorton & Kiplin Hall.* **Sun 19 July (10-5). Adm £6.80, chd free. Light refreshments.** Fabulous lake views, gardens, woodland and parkland. These beautiful grounds, once in decline, are being restored to their former beauty in this lovely setting. Topiary surrounds the White and Rose Gardens. Perennial and Hot Borders, Knot and Sensory Gardens. Mayflies dance in the Bog Garden and the Walled Garden is once more productive. From snowdrops to glorious autumn colours, this garden is a joy! Our on site tearoom offers home baked goods, lunches and teas using fresh garden produce. Hot/cold drinks, wine, beer. Wheelchair access. The gardens close to the house and Walled Garden are accessible. Coaches must be booked in advance.

24 KIRKY COTTAGE

12 Mindrum Farm Cottages, Mindrum, TD12 4QN. Mrs Ginny Fairfax, 01890 850246, ginny@mindrumgarden.co.uk, mindrumestate.com/mindrum-garden/kirky-cottage-garden/. *6m SW of Coldstream. 9m NW of Wooler on B6352. 4m N of Yetholm village.* **Sat 4 July (11-5.30). Adm £4, chd free. Home-made teas. Visits also by arrangement for groups of 10+.** It is 6 years since Ginny Fairfax created Kirky Cottage Garden in the beautiful Bowmont Valley surrounded, and protected by, the Border Hills. A gravel garden in cottage garden style, old roses, violas and others jostle with favourites from Mindrum. It is a lovely, abundant garden and, with Ginny's new and creative ideas, ever evolving.

25 LAMBSHIELD

Hexham, NE46 1SF. David Young, 01434 600699, david.young@ngs.org.uk. *2m S of Hexham. Take the B6306 from Hexham. After 1.6m turn R at chevron sign. Lambshield drive is 2nd on L after 0.6m.* **Sun 19 July (12.30-5). Adm £5, chd free. Visits also by arrangement May to July for groups of 10+.**

3 acre country garden begun in 2010 with strong structure and exciting plant combinations. Distinct areas and styles with formal herbaceous, grasses, contemporary planting, cottage garden, pool and orchard. Cloud hedging, pleached trees, and topiary combine with colourful and exuberant planting. Modern sculpture. Oak building and fencing by local craftsmen. New woodland garden being developed. Level ground but gravel paths not suitable for wheelchairs.

26 LILBURN TOWER

Alnwick, NE66 4PQ. Mr & Mrs D Davidson, 01668 217291, lilburntower@outlook.com. *3m S of Wooler. On A697.* **Sun 24 May (2-5). Adm £5, chd free. Home-made teas. Visits also by arrangement May to Sept for groups of 10+.** 10 acres of magnificent walled and formal gardens set above river; rose parterre, topiary, scented garden, Victorian conservatory, wild flower meadow. Extensive fruit and vegetable garden, large glasshouse with vines. 30 acres of woodland with walks. Giant lilies, meconopsis around pond garden. Rhododendrons and azaleas. Also ruins of Pele Tower, and C12 church. Partial wheelchair access.

27 LOUGHBROW HOUSE

Hexham, NE46 1RS. Mrs K A Clark, 01434 603351, patriciaclark351@btinternet.com. *1m S of Hexham on B6306. Dipton Mill Rd. Rd signed Blanchland, ¼ m take R fork; then ¼ m at fork, lodge gates & driveway at intersection.* **Sun 14 June (2-5). Adm £5, chd free. Home-made teas. Visits also by arrangement.** A real country house garden with sweeping, colour themed herbaceous borders set around large lawns. Unique Lutyens inspired rill with grass topped bridges and climbing rose arches. Part walled kitchen garden and paved courtyard. Bog garden with pond. New border and rose bed. Wild flower meadow with specimen trees. Woodland quarry garden with rhododendrons, azaleas, hostas and rare trees. Home-made jams and chutneys for sale.

28 LOWBRIDGE HOUSE

Dalton, Richmond, DL11 7FB. Mrs Clarissa Milbank, 01833 621228, clarissamilbank@btinternet.com. *From W turn R off A66 at Rokeby Inn. In 1½ m turn L to Dalton. Straight over Xrds. 100yds. Lowbridge House is on L. From E 6½ m from Scotch Corner on A66 take L turn to Dalton. L at Xrds 100yds on L is Lowbridge House.* **Visits by arrangement May to Aug for groups of up to 20. Adm £6, chd free. Refreshments to be discussed on booking.** Rural setting with wonderful panoramic views of local countryside. Garden consists of mixed borders, roses and sweet peas. Large pond (small lake) stocked with ghost carp and trout, with natural planting including candelabra primulas and wild flower banks. Island has ducks, coots and moorhens nesting. Patio area suitable for wheelchairs . Woodland and streamside walk with dippers and kingfishers. Most areas are accessible with care.

29 MAGGIE'S

Melville Grove, Newcastle Upon Tyne, NE7 7NU. Christopher Bray, www.maggiescentres.org/newcastle. *Driving into the grounds of the Freeman Hospital, Maggie's can be found opp entrance to the Northern Centre for Cancer Care. Nearest parking the Freeman Hospital multi-storey.* **Sat 22 Aug (11-3). Adm by donation. Home-made teas.** The garden, by Chelsea medal winning designer, Sarah Price, is a sheltered sun trap. There are banked wild flower beds and multiple planters, with seasonal displays, at ground level, plus two roof gardens. This gives a choice of outside spaces for visitors to enjoy. Copper beech, cherry blossom, crocus, bulbs, wild flowers and herbs give a colourful seasonal planting palette. A tranquil oasis. Regional Finalist, The English Garden's The Nation's Favourite Gardens 2019. Home-made cakes and scones. Teas and coffees. Garden inspired mocktails. Partial wheelchair access, gravel in the garden and roof garden, but the main section can be accessed.

30 MARIE CURIE HOSPICE

Marie Curie Hospice, Marie Curie Drive, Newcastle Upon Tyne, NE4 6SS. www.mariecurie.org.uk/help/hospice-care/hospices/newcastle/about. *In West Newcastle just off Elswick rd. At the bottom of a housing estate. Turning is between MA brothers & Dallas Carpets.* **Sun 5 July (2-4.30). Adm £2.50, chd free. Cream teas in our Garden Café.**

The landscaped gardens of the purpose-built Marie Curie Hospice overlook the Tyne and Gateshead and offer a beautiful, tranquil place for patients and visitors to sit and chat. Rooms open onto a patio garden with gazebo and fountain. There are climbing roses, evergreens and herbaceous perennials. The garden is well maintained by volunteers. Come and see the work NGS funding helps make possible. Plant sale and refreshments available. The Hospice and Gardens are wheelchair accessible.

♿ ✿ ☕

31 MIDDLETON HALL RETIREMENT VILLAGE

Middleton St. George, Darlington, DL2 1HA. MHRV, www.middletonhallretirementvillage.co.uk. *From A67 D'ton/Yarm, turn at 2nd r'about signed to Middleton St George. Turn L at the mini r'about & immediately R after the railway bridge, signed Low Middleton. Main entrance is ¼m on L.* **Sun 26 July (10-4). Adm £5, chd free. Light refreshments in The Orangery, on-site.**

Like those in our retirement community, the extensive grounds are gloriously mature, endlessly interesting and with many hidden depths. 45 acres of features beckon; natural woodland and parkland, Japanese, Mediterranean and Butterfly Gardens, croquet lawn, putting green, allotments, ponds, wetland and bird hide. All wheelchair accessible and linked by a series of Woodland Walks.

♿ 🐕 ☕

32 ◆ MINDRUM GARDEN

Mindrum, Northumberland, TD12 4QN. Mr & Mrs T Fairfax, 01890 850228, tpfairfax@gmail.com, www.mindrumestate.com. *6m SW of Coldstream, 9m NW of Wooler. Off B6352, 4m N of Yetholm. 5m from Cornhill on Tweed. Disabled parking close to house.* **For NGS: Sun 21 June (2-5). Adm £5, chd free. For other opening times and information, please phone, email or visit garden website.**

7 acres of romantic planting with old fashioned roses, violas, hardy perennials, lilies, herbs, scented shrubs, and intimate garden areas flanked by woodland and river walks.

Glasshouses with vines, jasmine. Large hillside limestone rock garden with water leading to a pond, delightful stream, woodland and wonderful views across Bowmont valley. Teas in aid of Hospice Care North Northumberland. Large plant sale, mostly home grown. Partial wheelchair access due to landscape. Wheelchair accessible WC available.

♿ 🐕 ✿ 🚗 🚌 ☕

33 NEW THE MOORE HOUSE

Whalton, Morpeth, NE61 3UX. Phillip & Filiz Rodger. *5m W of Morpeth & 4m N of Belsay on B6524. House in middle of village. Park in village. Follow NGS signs.* **Sun 31 May, Sun 19 July (2-5). Adm £6, chd free. Home-made teas in Community Hall.**

2 ½ acre mature garden extensively but sympathetically redesigned by Sean Murray, BBC /RHS Great Chelsea Garden Challenge winner. Garden divided into sections. Wide use and mix of flowering perennials and grasses, also gravel garden and stone rill. Decorative stonework around beds in patio area. Emphasis on scent, colour, texture and form with all year round interest. Tea proceeds to Morpeth Explorer Scouts. Uneven surfaces. Gravel paths and some areas unsuitable for the less able and wheelchairs.

✿ ☕

St Margaret's Allotments

Gardener's Cottage

© Susie White

34 MR YORKE'S WALLED GARDEN

Cravengate, Richmond, DL10 4RE. Mr & Mrs Dennis & Marcia McLuckie, 01748 825525, marcia@yorkshirecountryholidays. co.uk. *5 min walk from Richmond Market Place. Third of way down Cravengate on rd out to Leyburn. From Market Place go up Finkle St, past Black Lion into cobbled Newbiggin. L into Cravengate. Garden on R. No parking at the garden.* **Visits by arrangement Mar to Sept for groups of 10+. No parking for coaches at garden but may park at bottom of hill. Adm £5, chd free. Home-made teas. Pre-ordered home-made cakes, scones, tea and coffee OR wine and nibbles.**

Charming C18 walled garden, redesigned with herbaceous border, ponds, mature trees, standard and climbing roses, vegetable garden, fruit trees, lawns and grassy paths. Yorkshire In Bloom Gold Award 2019. Fabulous views of Billy Banks Woods, Richmond Castle and Culloden Tower. The garden is on a hill. Main grass paths accessible with a wheelchair, but they are quite steep.

♿ 🐕 🛏 🍵

35 NEASHAM ABBEY

Neasham, Near Darlington, DL2 1QW. Barbara-Anne Johnson. *At the Football Stadium r'about on A66 take direction Neasham/ Hurworth. At the end of this rd (approx. 2m) at the T-junction head straight across into the drive of Neasham Abbey.* **Sun 14 June (1-4). Adm £5, chd free. Home-made teas.**

A country house garden with views of the river Tees. Interesting paths lead to different areas including a walled garden of beautiful old red brick surrounding shady borders. A walk between a newly planted orchard and a sunny herbaceous border. A rose garden leads to a shady garden surrounding an old ornamental pond. A new feature of the garden is a rustic children's adventure play area. Regret wheelchair access very limited as all the paths are gravelled.

🐕 ✳ 🍵

36 NEW ◆ NGS BUZZING GARDEN

East Park Road, Gateshead, NE9 5AX. Gateshead Council. *Between Pets' Corner & Saltwell Towers. Pedestrian entrance from East Park Rd or car park in Joicey Road. Open to the public all year as part of the 55 acre Saltwell Park, known as The People's Park*

The Buzzing Garden is a unique collaboration between the National Garden Scheme North East, Trädgårdsresan, Region Västra Götaland and Gateshead Council. Its creation was funded by sponsorship. The garden is a tribute to the importance of international friendship. The Swedish design reflects the landscape of West Sweden, with coast, meadow and woodland areas. Many of the plant species grow wild in Sweden, providing a welcoming vision for visitors and a feast for pollinators. Planted in 2019 the garden is maturing. Visitors can make a Donation to NGS. Dogs on leads.

♿ 🐕 🍵

37 NEW OAKDENE LODGE

Oakdene Avenue, Darlington, DL3 7HR. Tony Inglis & Frances Herschel. *Pedestrian access only from Oakdene Avenue. Find No.1 Oakdene Avenue & walk 40 metres down adjacent alleyway.* **Sun 19 July (1.30-5.30). Adm £5, chd free. Home-made teas.**

Garden established from 2008 and is bordered by large, mature trees within neighbouring Green Park. The garden layout was developed to complement the house (circa 1825), which was originally the boat lodge for a Pease family mansion. Planting includes trees, many shrubs and is ringed by herbaceous borders providing varying flower colours through the growing season. No dogs Paths surrounding the garden are all reasonably level and wheelchair accessible.

♿ 🍵

38 OLIVER FORD GARDEN
Longedge Lane, Rowley, Consett,
DH8 9HG. Bob & Bev Tridgett,
www.gardensanctuaries.co.uk.
*5m NW of Lanchester. Signed from
A68 in Rowley. From Lanchester take
rd towards Sately. Garden will be
signed as you pass Woodlea Manor.*
**Sun 28 June (1-5). Adm £4, chd
free. Home-made teas.**
A peaceful, contemplative 3 acre
garden developed and planted by
the owner and BBC Gardener of the
Year as a space for quiet reflection.
Arboretum specialising in bark,
stream, wildlife pond and bog garden.
Semi-shaded Japanese maple
and dwarf rhododendron garden.
Rock garden and scree bed. Insect
nectar area, orchard and 1½ acre
meadow. Annual wild flower area.
Terrace and ornamental herb garden,.
Has a number of sculptures around
the garden. Managed to maximise
wildlife. Unfortunately not suitable for
wheelchairs.

39 25 PARK ROAD SOUTH
Chester le Street, DH3 3LS. Mrs A
Middleton, 0191 388 3225. *4m N of
Durham. Located at S end of A167
Chester-le-St bypass rd. Precise
directions provided when booking
visit.* **Visits by arrangement May
to Aug. Adm £3, chd free. Light
refreshments.**
A stunning town garden with all year
round interest. Herbaceous borders
with unusual perennials, grasses,
shrubs surrounding lawn and paved
area. Courtyard planted with foliage
and small front gravel garden. The
garden owner is a very knowledgeable
plantswoman who enjoys showing
visitors around her inspiring garden. No
minimum size of group. Plants for sale.

40 ◆ RABY CASTLE
Staindrop, Darlington,
DL2 3AH. Lord Barnard,
01833 660202, admin@raby.co.uk,
www.raby.co.uk/raby-castle.
*12m NW of Darlington, 1m N of
Staindrop. On A688, 8m NE of
Barnard Castle.* **For NGS: Sat
11 July (10-4.30). Adm £7, chd
£3. For other opening times and
information, please phone, email or
visit garden website.**
Raby Castle is one of the founding
gardens of the NGS and has been
opening for charity since 1927. The
18th century Walled Gardens set
within the grounds of Raby Castle.

Designers such as Thomas White
and James Paine have worked
to establish the Gardens, which
now extend to 5 acres, displaying
herbaceous borders, old yew hedges,
formal rose gardens and informal
heather and conifer gardens. The
Stables Cafe and Shop are located in
the Coach Yard at the entrance of the
Walled Gardens. Assistance will be
needed for wheelchairs.

41 RAVENSFORD FARM
Hamsterley, DL13 3NH. Jonathan &
Caroline Peacock, 01388 488305,
caroline@ravensfordfarm.co.uk.
*7m W of Bishop Auckland. From
A68 at Witton-le-Wear turn off W to
Hamsterley. Go through village & turn
L just before tennis courts at west
end.* **Sun 21 June (2-5). Adm £5,
chd free. Home-made teas. Visits
also by arrangement for groups
of up to 30. Single track lane, not
suitable for coaches.**
This 3-acre garden offers colour and
interest throughout the year, but
June is often one of our favourite
months. Beyond the large lawn and
herbaceous beds are two ponds, a
sunken garden, a wood with shade-
loving plants, an orchard and a good
number of unusual plants, shrubs and
trees and on NGS day we sell plants,
serve home-made teas, and have
music in the background. No dogs
Some gravel, so assistance will be
needed for wheelchairs. Assistance
dogs only.

42 ST CUTHBERT'S HOSPICE
Park House Road, Durham,
DH1 3QF. Paul Marriott, CEO,
0191 3861170, paul.hamilton@
stcuthbertshospice.com,
www.stcuthbertshospice.com. *1m
SW of Durham City on A167. Turn
into Park House Rd, the Hospice
is on the L after bowling green car
park. Parking available.* **Sun 26
July (11-4). Adm £4, chd free.
Light refreshments. Visits also by
arrangement Jan to May.**
5 acres of mature gardens surround
this CQC outstanding-rated Hospice.
In development since 1988, the
gardens are cared for by volunteers.
Incl a Victorian-style greenhouse
and large vegetable, fruit and cut
flower area. Lawns surround smaller
scale specialist planting, and areas
for patients and visitors to relax.
Woodland area with walks, sensory
garden, and an 'In Memory' garden

with stream. Plants and produce for
sale. We are active participants in
Northumbria in Bloom and Britain
in Bloom, with several awards in
recent years, including overall winner
in 2015, 2018 & 2019 for the Care/
Residential /Convalescent Homes
/ Day Centre / Hospices category.
Almost all areas are accessible for
wheelchairs. Hot and cold drinks,
home-made cakes and snacks
served in the coffee shop.

ALLOTMENTS

43 ST MARGARET'S ALLOTMENTS
Margery Lane, Durham, DH1 4QU.
*From A1 take A690 to City Centre/
Crook. Straight ahead at T-lights
after 4th r'about. 10mins walk from
bus or rail station.* **Sun 12 July (2-
5). Combined adm £4, chd free.
Home-made teas in St Margaret's
Centre adjacent to allotments.**
5 acres of over 100 allotments
against the spectacular backdrop
of Durham Cathedral. This site has
been cultivated since the Middle
Ages. Enthusiastic gardeners, many
using organic methods, cultivate plots
which display a great variety of fruit,
vegetables and flowers. Guided tour
available. Many unusual vegetables.
Display of creative and fun
competition for plot holders. The site
has some steep and narrow paths.

44 NEW THE STABLES
Old Quarrington, Bowburn,
Durham, DH6 5NN. John and
Claire Little. *All vehicle access via
Crow Trees Lane, Bowburn. Satnav
may be misleading!* **Sun 5 July (11-
5). Adm £4, chd free. Home-made
teas.**
A large family garden full of hidden
surprises and extensive views.
The main garden is about an acre
including gravel garden, vegetable
patch, orchard, play area, lawn and
woodland gardens. There's a further
four acres to explore which include
wildlife ponds, woodlands, walks,
hens, ducks and alpacas. Large play
area available for young children.
Proceeds from refreshments going to
local mountain rescue team. The main
grass paths can be soft and bumpy in
places. Some of the woodland paths
are not accessible to wheelchairs.

45 USHAW COLLEGE

Woodland Road, Durham, DH7 9BJ. The Trustees of Ushaw College, 0191 373 8500, meet@ushaw.org, www.ushaw.org. *3m W of Durham City. From A167 N of Neville's Cross turn on to minor road signed Bearpark & Ushaw College. The College entrance is signed to the R in 2½ m.* **Sat 13 June (10-4). Adm £4, chd free. Light refreshments in the College.** Part of the 50 acre landscape within open countryside around Ushaw College, the gardens were originally laid out in 1840 in front of the Georgian house and feature a formal rhododendron garden with herbaceous borders and rose beds. Extensive renovations to the garden have been under way for the last 5 years and continue, with some wild areas, a former pond, and extensive areas of woodland. Wheelchair access to concentric paths, but not to more overgrown areas.

46 ◆ WALLINGTON

Cambo, NE61 4AR. National Trust, 01670 773600, simon. thompson@nationaltrust.org. uk, www.nationaltrust.org.uk/ wallington. *12m W of Morpeth 20m NW Newcastle. From N B6343; from S via A696 from Newcastle, 6m W of Belsay, B6342 to Cambo.* **For NGS: Sat 25 Apr, Sat 13 June (10-4). Adm £14.80, chd £7.40, family £37. Light refreshments at Courtyard Cafe. For other opening times and information, please phone, email or visit garden website.** Magical walled, terraced garden with herbaceous and mixed borders. Packed with colour. Edwardian conservatory with unusual plants. 100 acres of woodland. Pleasure grounds, river and lakes. Set in a stunning landscape, with opportunities for walking and cycling. House dates from 1688. Wheelchair access limited to top terrace in Walled Garden but elsewhere possible with care and support.

Kirky Cottage

© Susie White

GROUP OPENING

47 WALWORTH GARDENS

Walworth, Darlington, DL2 2LY. *Approx 5m W of Darlington on A68 or ½ m E of Piercebridge on A67. Follow brown signs to Walworth Castle Hotel. Just up the hill from the Castle entrance, follow NGS yellow signs down private track. Tickets & Teas at Quarry End.* **Sun 23 Aug (1-5). Combined adm £5.50, chd free. Home-made teas. Teas at Quarry End.**

THE ARCHES
Stephen & Becky Street-Howard.

CASTLE BARN
Joe & Sheila Storey.

THE DOVECOTE
Tony & Ruth Lamb.

QUARRY END
Iain & Margaret Anderson.

There are 4 gardens to visit in Walworth. Quarry End is a 1.5 acre woodland garden developed over 20 years on the site of an ancient quarry. There is a newly developed woodland in the old quarry, where experimental planting is ongoing. The garden is being continually developed with new plants. It offers an interesting variety of mature trees, shrubs, perennials, a fernery and potager. The site includes an C18 ice house and offers lovely views over South Durham. In contrast Castle Barn, The Dovecote and The Arches are only 8 years old but offer a delightful mix of garden treasures. There are traditional herbaceous borders, extensive vegetable plots and herb gardens, grape vines, a Japanese garden with a Koi pond and a large collection of specimen Acers, an arboretum, an orchard and a wild life pond. There are bee hives and chickens and there is also a large play area available, so bring the family! There is something for everyone in Walworth so do come and join us. Some areas of the Quarry End garden are not accessible for wheelchairs, though the main garden area is.

48 ♦ WHALTON MANOR GARDENS

Whalton, Morpeth, NE61 3UT. Mr T R P S Norton, 01670 775205, gardens@whaltonmanor.co.uk, www.whaltonmanor.co.uk. *5m W of Morpeth. On the B6524, the house is at E end of the village & will be signed.* **For NGS: Sun 7 June (2-5). Adm £5, chd free. Home-made teas. For other opening times and information, please phone, email or visit garden website.**

The historic Whalton Manor, altered by Sir Edwin Lutyens in 1908, is surrounded by 3 acres of magnificent walled gardens, designed by Lutyens with the help of Gertrude Jekyll. The gardens have been developed by the Norton family since the 1920s and incl extensive herbaceous borders, 30yd peony border, rose garden, listed summerhouses, pergolas and walls, festooned with rambling roses and clematis. Partial wheelchair access, some stone steps.

49 WOODBINE HOUSE

22 South View, Hunwick, Crook, DL15 0JW. Stewart Irwin & Colin Purvis. *On main rd through the village opp village green. B6286 off A689 Bishop Auckland - Crook or A690 Durham - Crook. On street parking, entrance to the rear of the property RHS of house.* **Sun 12 July (1-5). Adm £5, chd free. Home-made teas.**

The garden is approx a quarter of an acre, divided into two, one half used as a vegetable garden with large greenhouse. The other half of the garden is lawn with well stocked (and some unusual planting) herbaceous borders and small pond. Bees are kept in the vegetable garden. All refreshments are home-made. No dogs Wheelchair access to refreshment area but paths in garden are not wide enough for wheelchairs.

50 WOODLANDS

Peareth Hall Road, Springwell Village, Gateshead, NE9 7NT. Liz Reid, 07719 875750, liz.reid@ngs.org.uk. *3½ m N Washington Galleries. 4m S Gateshead town centre. On B1288 turn opp Guide Post pub (NE9 7RR) onto Peareth Hall Rd. Continue for ½ m passing 2 bus stops on L. 3rd drive on L past Highbury Ave.* **Sat 27 June (1.30-4.30). Adm £4, chd free. Home-made teas. beer and wine available. Visits also by arrangement June to Aug for groups of 10 to 30. Please confirm near the planned date of visit.**

Mature garden on a site of approx one seventh acre- quirky, with tropical themed planting and Caribbean inspired bar. Also an area of cottage garden planting. A fun garden with colour throughout the year, interesting plants, informal beds and borders, pond area and deck. On the 28 June 2020 Springwell Village has a 'Forties Weekend' with many events and attractions. Eg: 2nd WW battle re-enactments and a military camp are planned on the nearby Bowes Railway (SAM) site. There are also plans for craft and other stalls and live music throughout the village.

51 WOODSIDE HOUSE

Witton Park, Bishop Auckland, DL14 0DU. Charles & Jean Crompton, 01388 609973, ctjcrompton@gmail.com, www.woodsidehousewittonpark. com. *2m N of Bishop Auckland. From Bishop Auckland take A68 to Witton Park. In village DO NOT follow SatNav. park on main st, walk down track next to St Pauls Church.* **Visits by arrangement Apr to Oct. Adm £5, chd free. Light refreshments.**

Stunning 2 acre, mature, undulating garden full of interesting trees, shrubs and plants. Superbly landscaped (by the owners) with island beds, flowing herbaceous borders, an old walled garden, rhododendron beds, fernery, 3 ponds, grass bed and vegetable garden. Delightful garden full of interesting and unusual features: much to fire the imagination. Featured in the Telegraph, Amateur Gardening. Winner of Bishop Auckland in Bloom. Partial wheelchair access.

Your visits help change lives – we've donated over £17 million to Macmillan Cancer Support since 1984

NORTHAMPTONSHIRE

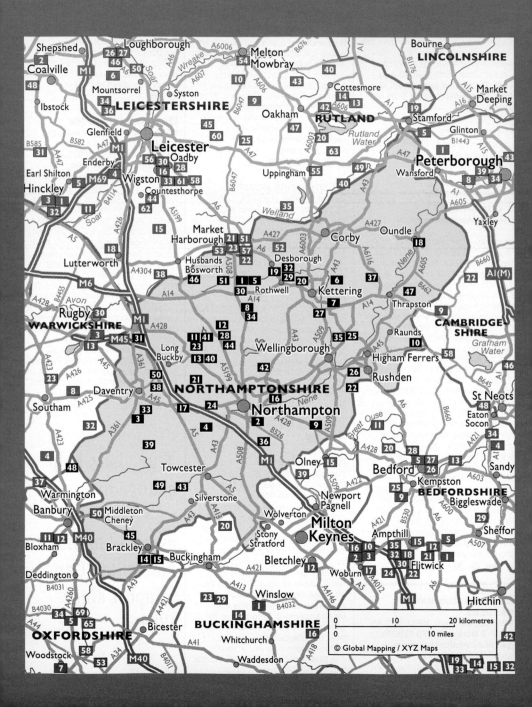

The county of Northamptonshire is famously known as the 'Rose of the Shires', but is also referred to as the 'Shire of Spires and Squires', and lies in the East Midlands area of the country bordered by eight other counties.

Take a gentle stroll around charming villages with thatch and stone cottages and welcoming inns. Wander around stately homes, discovering art treasures and glorious gardens open for the National Garden Scheme: Kelmarsh Hall, Holdenby House, Castle Ashby, Cottesbrooke Hall and Boughton House. In contrast visit some village groups, which include small imaginatively designed gardens.

Explore historic market towns such as Oundle and Brackley in search of fine footwear, antiques and curiosities. Or visit wildlife sanctuaries such as Sulby Gardens with 12 acres of interesting flora and fauna.

The serenity of our waterways will delight, and our winding country lanes and footpaths will guide you around a rural oasis, far from the pressures of modern living, where you can walk knee-deep in bluebells at Boughton House, view hellebores and spring flowers at 67/69 High Street, Finedon or The Old Vicarage at Norton through the seasons, to the late autumn colours of Sulby Gardens.

Our first garden opens in February and the final opening occurs in October, giving a glimpse of gardens throughout the seasons.

Volunteers

County Organisers
David Abbott
01933 680363
david.abbott@ngs.org.uk

Gay Webster
01604 740203
gay.webster@ngs.org.uk

County Treasurer
David Abbott (as above)

Publicity
David Abbott (as above)

Photographer
Snowy Ellson
07508 218320
snowyellson@yahoo.co.uk

Booklet Coordinator
William Portch
01536 522169
william.portch@ngs.org.uk

Talks
Elaine & William Portch
01536 522169
elaine.portch@yahoo.com

Assistant County Organisers
Amanda Bell
01327 860651
asrbell@btinternet.com

Lindsey Cartwright
01327 860056
lindsey@loisweedon.net

Jo Glissmann-Hill
07725 258755
hilljc@hotmail.co.uk

Philippa Heumann
01327 860142
pmheumann@gmail.com

Elaine & William Portch
(as above)

f @northants.ngs
@NorthantsNGS
@northantsngs

Left: Cobblers Cottage

OPENING DATES

All entries subject to change. For latest information check www.ngs.org.uk

Map locator numbers are shown to the right of each garden name.

February

Snowdrop Festival

Sunday 23rd
NEW 32 Back Lane   2
◆ Boughton House   6
67-69 High Street   25

March

Sunday 29th
Woodcote Villa   50

April

Sunday 5th
Flore Gardens   17

Sunday 19th
Briarwood   7
◆ Kelmarsh Hall &
  Gardens   30

Thursday 23rd
Sulby Gardens   46

Sunday 26th
The Old Vicarage   38

May

Sunday 3rd
The Bungalow   8
◆ Cottesbrooke Hall
  Gardens   12
Great Brington
  Gardens   21
NEW Nightingale
  Cottage   34

Sunday 10th
3 Baptists Close   4
Guilsborough Gardens   23
◆ The Old Rectory,
  Sudborough   37
Titchmarsh House   47

Sunday 17th
Badby Gardens   3
Greywalls   22
1 Hinwick Close   27

Sunday 24th
Newnham Gardens   33

Monday 25th
Titchmarsh House   47

Sunday 31st
NEW Nonsuch   35
Old Rectory, Quinton   36
Preston Capes and Little
  Preston Gardens   39
Spratton Gardens   44
Walnut House   48

June

Sunday 7th
Evenley Gardens   14
Harpole Gardens   24
67-69 High Street   25
◆ Kelmarsh Hall &
  Gardens   30

Saturday 13th
Titchmarsh House   47
The Wooden Owl   51

Sunday 14th
3 Baptists Close   4
Foxtail Lilly   18
Hostellarie   29
Kilsby Gardens   31
16 Leys Avenue   32
Weedon Lois & Weston
  Gardens   49
The Wooden Owl   51

Thursday 18th
Sulby Gardens   46

Saturday 20th
Flore Gardens   17

Sunday 21st
NEW Cobblers Cottage   10
Flore Gardens   17
Rosearie-de-la-
  Nymph   42
Slapton Gardens   43

Sunday 28th
Arthingworth Open
  Gardens   1
67-69 High Street   25
Rosearie-de-la-
  Nymph   42

July

Sunday 5th
◆ Castle Ashby
  Gardens   9
NEW East Haddon
  Gardens   13

Sunday 12th
1 Hinwick Close   27
◆ Holdenby House &
  Gardens   28
Ravensthorpe
  Gardens   40
◆ Steane Park   45

Saturday 18th
◆ Evenley Wood
  Garden   15

Sunday 26th
Froggery Cottage   19
Hostellarie   29
Woodcote Villa   50

August

Sunday 16th
The Bungalow   8
NEW Nightingale
  Cottage   34

Thursday 27th
Sulby Gardens   46

September

Sunday 6th
136 High Street   26
16 Leys Avenue   32
Old Rectory, Quinton   36
Woodcote Villa   50

Sunday 13th
Briarwood   7
◆ Coton Manor
  Garden   11
Ravenswood   41

October

Thursday 8th
Sulby Gardens   46

Friday 9th
Sulby Gardens   46

Sunday 18th
◆ Boughton House   6

February 2021

Sunday 28th
67-69 High Street   25

By Arrangement

Arrange a personalised garden visit with your club, or group of friends, on a date to suit you. See individual garden entries for full details.

3 Baptists Close   4
Bosworth House   5
Briarwood   7
The Bungalow   8
The Close, Harpole
  Gardens   24
Dripwell House,
  Guilsborough
  Gardens   23
48 The Fairoaks   16
Foxtail Lilly   18
Froggery Cottage   19
Glendon Hall   20
Greywalls   22
136 High Street   26
67-69 High Street   25
Hostellarie   29
16 Leys Avenue   32
19 Manor Close,
  Harpole Gardens   24
Old West Farm, Preston
  Capes and Little
  Preston Gardens   39
Ravensthorpe Nursery,
  Ravensthorpe
  Gardens   40
Titchmarsh House   47
Woodcote Villa   50

Your visits help change lives – your generosity has supported unpaid carers through donations to Carers Trust totalling over £4 million since 1996

THE GARDENS

GROUP OPENING

1 ARTHINGWORTH OPEN GARDENS

Arthingworth, nr Market Harborough, LE16 8LA. *6m S of Market Harborough. From Market Harborough via A508, after 4m take L to Arthingworth. From Northampton, A508 turn R just after Kelmarsh. Park your car in Arthingworth village & tickets for sale in the village hall.* **Sun 28 June (1-5). Combined adm £6, chd free. Home-made teas at village hall & Bosworth House.**

Arthingworth has been welcoming NGS visitors for a decade. It is a village affair with 8 to 9 gardens opening and 2 pop-up tearooms with home baked cakes. We now have some regulars who keep us on our toes and we love it. Come and enjoy the diversity, we aim to give visitors an afternoon of discovery. Our gardens have been chosen because they are all different in spirit, and tended by young and weathered gardeners. We have gardens with stunning views, traditional with herbaceous borders and vegetables, walled, and artisan. The village is looking forward to welcoming us. St Andrew's Church, Grade II* listed will be open and the village is next to the national cycle path. Wheelchair access to some gardens.

2 NEW 32 BACK LANE

Hardingstone, Northampton, NN4 6BY. Ms H & Mr W Mayes. *From A45 r'about follow High St past church on R, village hall on L, then 1st L into Back Lane or from The Green/War Memorial into other side of Back Lane (loop).* **Sun 23 Feb (11-4). Adm £3.50, chd free.**

Informal, woodland-style, cottage type garden in a ¼ acre plot, underplanted over decades with swathes of snowdrops naturalised throughout the garden. A few hellebores accompany them but the non-specialist collection of snowdrops dominates at this time of year. The garden is on a slope with uneven paths and steps, so care is needed.

GROUP OPENING

3 BADBY GARDENS

Badby, Daventry, NN11 3AR. *3m S of Daventry on E-side of A361.* **Sun 17 May (2-6). Combined adm £5, chd free. Home-made teas in St Mary's Church.**

CHAPEL HOUSE
Moira & Peter Cooper.

THE OLD HOUSE
Mr & Mrs Robert Cain.

SHAKESPEARES COTTAGE
Jocelyn Hartland-Swann.

SOUTHVIEW COTTAGE
Alan & Karen Brown.

Delightful hilly village with attractive old houses of golden coloured Hornton stone, set around a C14 church and two village greens (no through traffic). There are four gardens of differing styles; a wisteria-clad thatched cottage (not open) with a sloping garden and modern sculptures; a traditional garden featuring a spectacular view across fields to Badby Wood; an elevated garden with views over the village; and a secluded garden with five distinct areas, pond and fernery, patio, lawn, small orchard and formal vegetable garden. We look forward to welcoming you to our lovely village!

4 3 BAPTISTS CLOSE

Bugbrooke, Northampton, NN7 3RJ. Claire Smith, 07798 905563, smithsgarden16@gmail.com. *2 mins from A5, 5m from J16 M1. From A5 signs to Bugbrooke, follow road to village that becomes Church St. Park close to Five Bells Pub on L. Baptists Close is on L (no parking in close).* **Sun 10 May, Sun 14 June (1.30-5). Adm £4, chd free. Home-made teas. Visits also by arrangement Apr to Sept for groups of up to 20.**

A medium sized plant lover's garden with tranquil pastoral farmland behind. Designed and planted about 10 yrs ago from a previous farmyard site, the garden has fully mature lime trees down one side and is a mix of shrubs with foliage interest and colourful herbaceous borders. Spring garden under the walnut tree, n-facing potager, traditional borders and short woodland walk. Pathway around

the house (not open) and lawned area. Some large gravel paths and woodland walk not easily accessible.

5 BOSWORTH HOUSE

Oxendon Road, Arthingworth, Nr Market Harborough, LE16 8LA. Mr & Mrs C E Irving-Swift, 01858 525202, irvingswift@btinternet.com. *From the phone box, in Oxendon Rd, take the little lane with no name, 2nd to the R.* **Visits by arrangement May to July for groups of 10 to 20. For groups of 15+ guided tour by Cecile Irving-Swift for 1½ hours.**

Just under 3 acres, almost completely organic garden and paddock with fabulous panoramic views. Early in the season a pleasing display of wood anemones, fritillaries, daffodils, bluebells and tulips. The garden also incl herbaceous borders, orchard, cottage garden with greenhouse, vegetable garden, herbs and strawberries, and little spinney. There is a magnificent Wellingtonia. Partial wheelchair access.

6 ♦ BOUGHTON HOUSE

Geddington, Kettering, NN14 1BJ. Duke of Buccleuch & Queensberry, KT, 01536 515731, info@boughtonhouse.co.uk, www.boughtonhouse.org.uk. *3m NE of Kettering. From A14, 2m along A43 Kettering to Stamford, turn R into Geddington, house entrance 1½m on R.* **For NGS: Sun 23 Feb, Sun 18 Oct (11-3). Adm £6, chd £3. Light refreshments in C18 Stable Block. For other opening times and information, please phone, email or visit garden website.**

The Northamptonshire home of the Duke and Duchess of Buccleuch. The garden opening incl opportunities to see the historic walled kitchen garden and herbaceous border, and the sensory and wildlife gardens. The wilderness woodland will open for visitors to view the spring flowers or the autumn colours. As a special treat the garden originally created by Sir David Scott (cousin of the Duke of Buccleuch) will also be open. Designated disabled parking. Light gravel around house, heavier in walled garden, please see our accessibility document for more information.

24 Bliss Lane, Flore Gardens

7 BRIARWOOD

4 Poplars Farm Road, Barton Seagrave, Kettering, NN15 5AF. William & Elaine Portch, 01536 522169, elaine.portch@yahoo.com, www.elaineportch-gardendesign.co.uk. 1½m SE of Kettering Town Centre. J10 off A14 turn onto Barton Rd (A6) towards Wicksteed Park. R into Warkton Lane, after 200 metres R into Poplars Farm Rd. Sun 19 Apr (10-4); Sun 13 Sept (11-3). Adm £4.50, chd free. Light refreshments. Visits also by arrangement Apr to Sept for groups of 10 to 30.

A garden for all seasons with quirky original sculptures and many faces. Firstly, a south aspect lawn and borders containing bulbs, shrubs, roses and rare trees with yr-round interest; hedging, palms, climbers, a wildlife, fish and lily pond, terrace with potted bulbs and unusual plants in odd containers. Secondly, a secret garden with summerhouse, small orchard, raised bed potager and greenhouse. Crafts for sale and children's quiz.

8 THE BUNGALOW

Harborough Road, Maidwell, NN6 9JA. David & Ann Sharman, 01604 686243. Approx 10m N of Northampton. On A508 between Northampton & Market Harborough, opp Westaways Garage. Sun 3 May, Sun 16 Aug (11-4). Combined adm with Nightingale Cottage £4, chd free. Home-made teas. Visits also by arrangement May to Aug for groups of 10 to 20.

The garden is on a steep, terraced site, which tumbles down to a stream. Bridges lead to a recently acquired wooded area, equally steep. Ann has artistically incorporated a quirky collection of car boot finds, which adds interest to the exuberant planting. Self-seeding is encouraged, giving a natural effect. There are several secluded seating areas for relaxation. A steep site and many steps, sadly not suitable for the less mobile.

9 ◆ CASTLE ASHBY GARDENS

Castle Ashby, Northampton, NN7 1LQ. Earl Compton, 01604 422180, petercox@castleashbygardens.co.uk, www.castleashbygardens.co.uk. 6m E of Northampton. 1½m N of A428, turn off between Denton & Yardley Hastings. Follow brown tourist signs (SatNav will take you to the village, look for brown signs). For NGS: Sun 5 July (10-5.30). Adm £8, chd £2. For other opening times and information, please phone, email or visit garden website.

35 acres within a 10,000 acre estate of both formal and informal gardens, incl Italian gardens with orangery and arboretum with lakes, all dating back to the 1860s, as well as a menagerie which incl meerkats and marmosets. Play area, tearooms and gift shop. Wheelchair access on gravel paths within gardens.

10 NEW COBBLERS COTTAGE

Church Street, Hargrave, Wellingborough, NN9 6BW. Neil & Ros Sheppard. Follow B645 from either Kimbolton or Higham Ferrers, until you see signs for Hargrave. Turn into village onto Church Rd & follow signs (opp north gate of church). Sun 21 June (11-3). Adm £4, chd free. Home-made teas.

Since 1998 we have created a garden with distinctive large borders bursting with flowers, shrubs and trees, linked by gravel paths. There is a pond which is full of life; metal and stone sculptures abound; and there are several seats for relaxation. Vegetables and fruit grow both outside and inside the greenhouse. The garden inspires our grandchildren to play, discover and imagine. There will be two performances by the Hargrave Singers and a display of artworks by local artist. Wheelchair access to majority of garden by gravel paths and a slope which bypasses the entrance steps.

11 ◆ COTON MANOR GARDEN

Coton, Northampton, NN6 8RQ. Mr & Mrs Ian Pasley-Tyler, 01604 740219, www.cotonmanor.co.uk. 10m N of Northampton, 11m SE of Rugby. From A428 & A5199 follow tourist signs. For NGS: Sun 13 Sept (12-5.30). Combined adm with Ravenswood £8, chd free. Light refreshments at Stableyard Cafe. For other opening times and information, please phone or visit garden website.

Winner of The English Garden's The Nation's Favourite Gardens 2019, this 10 acre garden set in peaceful countryside with old yew and holly hedges and extensive herbaceous borders, containing many unusual plants. One of Britain's finest throughout the season, the garden is at its most magnificent in September, and is an inspiration as to what can be achieved in late summer. Adjacent specialist nursery with over 1000 plant varieties propagated from the garden. Partial wheelchair access as some paths are narrow and the site is on a slope.

12 ◆ COTTESBROOKE HALL GARDENS

Cottesbrooke, Northampton, NN6 8PF. Mr & Mrs A R Macdonald-Buchanan, 01604 505808, welcome@cottesbrooke.co.uk, www.cottesbrooke.co.uk. *10m N of Northampton. Signed from J1 on A14. Off A5199 at Creaton, A508 at Brixworth.* **For NGS: Sun 3 May (2-5.30). Adm £7, chd £4. Home-made teas. For other opening times and information, please phone, email or visit garden website.**

Award-winning gardens by Geoffrey Jellicoe, Dame Sylvia Crowe, James Alexander-Sinclair and more recently Arne Maynard. Formal gardens and terraces surround Queen Anne house, with extensive vistas onto the lake and C18 parkland containing many mature trees. Wild and woodland gardens, a short distance from the formal areas, are exceptional in spring. Partial wheelchair access as paths are grass, stone and gravel. Access map identifies best route.

GROUP OPENING

13 NEW EAST HADDON GARDENS

East Haddon, Northampton, NN6 8BT. *A few hundred yards off the A428 (sign posted) between M1 J18 (8m) & Northampton (8m). Parking at Haddonstone Show Gardens & on-road. Strictly no parking in Priestwell Court.* **Sun 5 July (1-5). Combined adm £5, chd free. Home-made teas at St Mary's Church.**

◆ HADDONSTONE SHOW GARDENS
Haddonstone Ltd, 01604 770711, info@haddonstone.co.uk, www.haddonstone.com.

LIMETREES
Barry & Sally Hennessey.

NEW 9 PRIESTWELL COURT
Emma Forbes.

NEW RYEHILLS BARN
Maggie Marsh & Michael Widdowson, 01604 770990, ryehillcountrycottages@gmail.com.

NEW TOWER COTTAGE
John Benson.

The pretty village of East Haddon dates back to the Norman invasion. The oldest surviving building is St Mary's, a C12 church. The village has many thatched cottages built in the local honey-coloured Ironstone. Other features include a thatched village pump and fire station which used to house a hand drawn pump and is now used as the bus shelter. Five gardens of different styles are opening; three for the first time. Partial wheelchair access at Tower Cottage.

GROUP OPENING

14 EVENLEY GARDENS

Evenley, Brackley, NN13 5SG. *From Brackley 1m S on A43. Gardens situated around the village green & Church Lane. Follow signs around the village. Tickets available at each garden, to cover entry to all gardens.* **Sun 7 June (2-6). Combined adm £5, chd free. Home-made teas in St George's Church (2.30-5).**

15 CHURCH LANE
Carrie & Kevin O'Regan.

FINCH COTTAGE
Cathy & Chris Ellis.

14 THE GREEN
Nic Hamblin.

38 THE GREEN
Anna & Matt Brown.

Evenley is a charming village situated approx 1m south of Brackley off the A43. It has a central village green surrounded by many period houses (not open), an excellent village shop and The Red Lion Pub which offers first class food and a warm welcome. Evenley gardens are a mix of established gardens and those being developed over the past 5 yrs. They all have mixed borders with established shrubs and trees. There are also orchards and vegetable gardens in some. Partial wheelchair access to most gardens across gravel drives and narrow paths, with steps to reach some areas.

The Banks, Newnham Gardens

15 ◆ EVENLEY WOOD GARDEN
Evenley, Brackley, NN13 5SH.
Whiteley Family, 07788 207428,
alison@evenleywoodgarden.co.uk,
www.evenleywoodgarden.co.uk.
¾ m S of Brackley. Turn off at
Evenley r'about on A43 & follow
signs within the village to the garden
which is situated off the Evenley &
Mixbury road. **For NGS: Sat 18
July (10-4). Adm £6, chd free.
Light refreshments. For other
opening times and information,
please phone, email or visit garden
website.**
Please come and celebrate summer
in the woods when the roses and
lillies will have taken over from the
azaleas and rhododendrons. A
wonderful opportunity to see all that
has been developed in the woods
since Timothy Whiteley acquired them
in 1980 with the continuation of his
legacy. Morning tea or coffee, lunch
with a glass of wine and home-made
cakes will be available in the café.
Please take care as all paths are
grass.

16 48 THE FAIROAKS
The Fairoaks, Northampton,
NN3 9UZ. Mrs Lucie Oko,
07736 552394,
nanalucie@btinternet.com. A43
Lumbertubs Way, turn onto Standens
Barn Rd, R onto Flaxwell Court, at
r'about 2nd exit onto The Fairoaks.
**Visits by arrangement June to
Aug for groups of 10+. Minimum
donation £3.**
My 'labour of love' is an
unconventional garden that I started
from scratch back in 1993. Since
then I have built up a green sanctuary
for my children and grandchildren
through intuition and a lot of
salvaging! Fellow garden enthusiasts
are most welcome to come and share
banter and tips with me. 'Russian
Vine and Mile a Minute' plant is one of
the expansive features of the garden.
Wheelchair access via side gate.

Your visits help change
lives – we are the largest
single funder of the
Queen's Nursing Institute

GROUP OPENING

17 FLORE GARDENS
Flore, Northampton, NN7 4LQ. Off
A45 2m W of M1 J16. Avoid the new
by-pass. Garden maps provided
at free car park, SatNav NN7 4LS.
Coaches welcome, please phone
01327 341225 for coach parking
information. **Sun 5 Apr (2-6); Sat
20, Sun 21 June (11-6). Combined
adm £6, chd free. Home-made
teas in Chapel School Room
(Apr). Morning coffee & teas in
Church & light lunches & teas
in Chapel School Room (June).**
Donation to All Saints Church &
United Reform Church, Flore (June).

24 BLISS LANE
John & Sally Miller.
Open on all dates

BUTTERCUP COTTAGE
Mrs Elizabeth Chignell.
Open on Sat 20, Sun 21 June

THE CROFT
John & Dorothy Boast.
Open on all dates

THE GARDEN HOUSE
Edward & Penny Aubrey-Fletcher.
Open on Sat 20, Sun 21 June

17 THE GREEN
Mrs Wendy Amos.
Open on Sat 20, Sun 21 June

THE OLD BAKERY
John Amos & Karl Jones,
www.johnnieamos.co.uk.
Open on all dates

**PRIVATE GARDEN OF BLISS
LANE NURSERY**
Christine & Geoffrey Littlewood.
Open on all dates

ROCK SPRINGS
Tom Higginson & David Foster.
Open on all dates

RUSSELL HOUSE
Peter Pickering & Stephen
George, 01327 341734,
peterandstephen@btinternet.
com,
www.RussellHouseFlore.com.
Open on all dates

NEW THE WHITE COTTAGE
Tony & Gill Lomax.
Open on all dates

Flore gardens have been open since
1963 as part of the Flore Flower
Festival. The partnership with the
NGS started in 1992. Flore is an
attractive village with views over

the Upper Nene Valley. We have a
varied mix of gardens including an
impressive new garden and gardens
opening again following a break. They
have all been developed by friendly,
enthusiastic and welcoming owners.
Our gardens range from the traditional
to the eccentric providing yr-round
interest. There are greenhouses,
gazebos and summerhouses, with
seating providing opportunities to rest
while enjoying the gardens. In spring
there are early flowering perennials,
interesting trees, shrubs, and bulbs
in pots and border drifts. There is
planting for all situations from shade
to full sun. June gardens open in
association with Flore Flower Festival.
The gardens incl formal and informal
designs with lots of roses, clematis
and many varieties of trees, shrubs,
perennials, herbs, fruit and some
vegetables. Partial wheelchair access
to most gardens, some assistance
may be required.

18 FOXTAIL LILLY
41 South Road, Oundle, PE8 4BP.
Tracey Mathieson, 01832 274593,
foxtaillilly41@gmail.com,
www.foxtail-lilly.co.uk. 1m from
Oundle town centre. From A605 at
Barnwell Xrds take Barnwell Rd, 1st
R to South Rd. **Sun 14 June (11-5).
Adm £4.50, chd free. Home-made
teas. Visits also by arrangement
June to Sept for groups of 10+.**
A cottage garden where perennials
and grasses are grouped creatively
together amongst gravel paths,
complementing one another to create
a natural look. Some unusual plants
and quirky oddities create a different
and colourful informal garden. Lots
of flowers for cutting and a shop
in the barn. New meadow pasture
turned into new cutting garden. Plant,
flowers and gift shop.

19 FROGGERY COTTAGE
85 Breakleys Road,
Desborough, NN14 2PT.
Mr John Lee, 01536 760002,
www.froggerycottage.com. 6m
N of Kettering. 5m S of Market
Harborough. Signed off A6 & A14.
**Sun 26 July (11.30-5). Combined
adm with Hostellarie £4, chd free.
Home-made teas, a gluten free
option & lunches. Visits also by
arrangement June to Sept.**
1 acre plantsman's garden full of
rare and unusual plants. NCCPG

Collection of 435 varieties of penstemons incl dwarfs and species. Mediterranean and water gardens with large herbaceous borders. Artifacts on display incl old ploughs and garden implements. Penstemon workshops throughout the day.

20 GLENDON HALL
Kettering, NN14 1QE. Rosie Bose, 01536 711732, rosiebose@googlemail.com. *1½ m E of Rothwell. A6003 to Corby (A14 J7) W of Kettering, turn L onto Glendon Rd signed Rothwell, Desborough, Rushton. Entrance 1½ m on L past turn for Rushton.* **Visits by arrangement for groups of up to 30. Adm £4, chd free.** Mature specimen trees, topiary, box hedges and herbaceous borders stocked with many unusual plants. Large walled kitchen gardens with glasshouse and a shaded area, well stocked with ferns. Some gravel and slopes, but wheelchair access via longer route.

GROUP OPENING

21 GREAT BRINGTON GARDENS
Northampton, NN7 4JJ. *7m NW of Northampton. Off A428 Rugby Rd. From Northampton, 1st L turn past main gates of Althorp. Programmes & maps available at free car park.* **Sun 3 May (11-5). Combined adm £5, chd free. Home-made teas & light lunches.**

NEW FAIRVIEW HOUSE
Mrs Angela Evans.

FOLLY HOUSE
Sarah & Joe Sacarello.

NEW 2 HAMILTON LANE
Ruth Hawker.

15 HAMILTON LANE
Mr & Mrs Robin Matthews.

NEW 50 MAIN STREET
Mr Lance Taylor.

NEW THE RECTORY
Rev Andrea Watkins.

ROSE COTTAGE
David Green & Elaine MacKenzie.

THE STABLES
Mrs A George.

THE WICK
Ray & Sandy Crossan.

YEW TREE HOUSE
Mrs Joan Heaps.

Great Brington is proud of over 25 years association with the NGS and arguably one of the most successful one day scheme events in the county. This year we offer ten gardens open to view, they are situated in a circular and virtually flat walk around the village. Our gardens provide inspiration and variety; continuing to evolve each year and designed, planted and maintained by their owners. The village on the Althorp Estate is particularly picturesque, predominately local stone with thatched houses but also well worth a day out in its own right. Visitors will enjoy a warm welcome, plant stalls, and tea and coffee in the church from 11am, lunches in the Reading Room 12-2pm and tea and cakes in the church 2-5pm. The church is of historic interest, and walkers can extend their walk to view Althorp House. Small coaches for groups welcome by prior arrangement only, please email friends_of_stmarys@ btinternet.com.

22 GREYWALLS
Farndish, NN29 7HJ. Mrs P M Anderson, 01933 353495, greywalls@dbshoes.co.uk. *2½ m SE of Wellingborough. A609 from Wellingborough, B570 to Irchester, turn to Farndish by cenotaph. House adjacent to church.* **Sun 17 May (2-5). Adm £3.50, chd free. Light refreshments. Visits also by arrangement for groups of 10 to 30.** A 2 acre mature garden surrounding the old vicarage (not open). The garden features an alpine house with raised alpine beds, stunning water features and natural ponds with views over open countryside. Historic church next door is open.

Old Rectory, Quinton

GROUP OPENING

23 GUILSBOROUGH GARDENS
Guilsborough, NN6 8RA. *10m NW of Northampton. 10m E of Rugby. Between A5199 & A428. J1 off A14. Car parking at Guilsborough Surgery, on West Haddon Rd, NN6 8QE. Information & maps from car park or village hall next to primary school.* **Sun 10 May (1-6). Combined adm £6, chd free. Home-made teas in village hall.**

DRIPWELL HOUSE
Mr J W Langfield & Dr C Moss, 01604 740140, cattimoss@gmail.com.
Visits also by arrangement May & June for groups of 10 to 30. Combined visits with Gower House next door.

FOUR ACRES
Mark & Gay Webster.

FOURWAYS
Phil & Charles Mynard.

THE GATE HOUSE
Mike & Sarah Edwards.

GOWER HOUSE
Ann Moss.

THE OLD HOUSE
Richard & Libby Seaton Evans.

THE OLD VICARAGE
John & Christine Benbow.

PEACE GARDEN
Guilsborough Church of England Primary School.

Enjoy a warm welcome in this village with its very attractive rural setting of rolling hills and reservoirs. Several of us are interested in growing fruit and vegetables, and walled kitchen gardens and a potager are an important part of our gardening. Plants both rare and unusual from our plantsmen's gardens are for sale, a true highlight here. Dripwell House has opened for the NGS since 1986, originally an individual garden and is a destination in its own right. There is thus a lot to see and visitors find that they need the whole afternoon. Competition for children. No wheelchair access at Dripwell House and The Gate House.

&. 🐕 ❀ 🚌 ☕

GROUP OPENING

24 HARPOLE GARDENS
Harpole, NN7 4BX. *On A45 4m W of Northampton towards Weedon. Turn R at The Turnpike Hotel into Harpole. Village maps given to all visitors.* **Sun 7 June (1-6). Combined adm £5, chd free. Home-made teas at The Close.**

BRYTTEN-COLLIER HOUSE
James & Lucy Strickland.

CEDAR COTTAGE
Spencer & Joanne Hannam.

THE CLOSE
Michael Orton-Jones, 07714 896500, michael@orton-jones.com.
Visits also by arrangement Apr to July.

19 MANOR CLOSE
Caroline & Andy Kemshed, 01604 830512, carolinekemshed@live.co.uk.
Visits also by arrangement in June for groups of up to 20.

THE MANOR HOUSE
Mrs Katy Smith.

MILLERS
Mrs M Still.

THE OLD DAIRY
David & Di Ballard.

We welcome everyone to join in the Harpole Gardens experience. Harpole is an attractive village nestling at the foot of the Harpole Hills, with many houses built of the local sandstone. Visit us and delight in a wide variety of gardens of all shapes, sizes and content. We have interesting and quirky artifacts dotted around, a variety of garden structures and plenty of seating for the weary. You will see luxuriant lawns, mixed borders with plants for sun and shade, mature trees, herbs, vegetables and alpines. You can enjoy views over neighbouring farmland and perhaps best of all, enjoy delicious home-made teas at The Close. Wheelchair access at Brytten-Collier House, The Close and The Old Dairy only.

&. ❀ ☕

25 67-69 HIGH STREET
Finedon, NN9 5JN. Mary & Stuart Hendry, 01933 680414, sh_archt@hotmail.com. *6m SE Kettering. Garden signed from A6 & A510 junction.* **Sun 23 Feb (11-3); Sun 7, Sun 28 June (2-6). Adm £3.50, chd free. Soup & roll in Feb (incl in adm). Cream teas in June. 2021: Sun 28 Feb. Visits also by arrangement Feb to Sept.**
⅓ acre rear garden of C17 cottage (not open). Early spring garden with

Ravensthorpe Nursery, Ravensthorpe Gardens

snowdrops and hellebores, summer and autumn mixed borders, many obelisks and containers, kitchen garden, herb bed, rambling roses, and at least 60 different hostas. All giving varied interest from Feb through to Oct. Large selection of home-raised plants for sale (all proceeds to NGS). St Mary's Church open on all dates, with tea & biscuits available in Feb only from 2-4pm.

🐖 ❋ 🚗 ♿

26 136 HIGH STREET
Irchester, Wellingborough, NN29 7AB. Mr & Mrs Ade & Jane Parker, jane692@btinternet.com. *200yds past the church on the bend as you leave the village going towards the A45. Please park on High St. Disabled parking only in driveway.* Sun 6 Sept (11-4). Adm £3.50, chd free. Home-made teas. Visits also by arrangement May to Sept for groups of 10+.
½ acre garden with various different borders including those planted for shade, sun and bee friendly situations. Alpine houses, raised beds and planted stone sinks. Wildlife pond. Seasonally planted tubs. Mostly lawn, some gravel pathways.

♿ ❋ ♿

27 1 HINWICK CLOSE
Kettering, NN15 6GB. Mrs Pat Cole-Ashton. *J9 A14 A509 Kettering. At Park House r'about take 4th exit to Holdenby. Hinwick Close 3rd exit on R. From Kettering A509, at Park House r'about take the 1st exit to Holdenby, Hinwick Close 3rd exit on R.* Sun 17 May, Sun 12 July (12-5). Adm £3.50, chd free. Home-made teas & savouries.
A garden reclaimed from rubble surrounding a new build house (not open). In the past 6 yrs Pat and Snowy have transformed this space into a wildlife haven. The garden has numerous influences; seaside, woodland and English country gardens. Ponds and waterfalls add to the delights. Vintage signs, numerous figures and seating areas at different vantage points are dotted throughout the garden.

♿ ❋ ♿

28 ◆ HOLDENBY HOUSE & GARDENS
Holdenby House, Holdenby, Northampton, NN6 8DJ. Mr & Mrs James Lowther, 01604 770074, office@holdenby.com, www.holdenby.com. *7m NW of*

Northampton. Off A5199 or A428 between East Haddon & Spratton. For NGS: Sun 12 July (11-5). Adm £5, chd £3.50. Cream teas & light refreshments. For other opening times and information, please phone, email or visit garden website.
Holdenby has a historic Grade I listed garden. The inner garden including Rosemary Verey's renowned Elizabethan Garden and Rupert Golby's Pond Garden and long borders. There is also a delightful walled kitchen garden. Away from the formal gardens, the terraces of the original Elizabethan Garden are still visible, one of the best preserved examples of their kind. Wheelchair access over gravelled paths.

♿ 🐖 ♿

29 HOSTELLARIE
78 Breakleys Road, Desborough, NN14 2PT. Stella Freeman, 01536 760124, stelstan78@aol.com. *6m N of Kettering. 5m S of Market Harborough. From church & war memorial turn R into Dunkirk Ave, then 3rd R. From cemetery L into Dunkirk Ave, then 4th L.* Sun 14 June (1-5). Combined adm with 16 Leys Avenue £4, chd free. Sun 26 July (11.30-5). Combined adm with Froggery Cottage £4, chd free. Home-made teas & a gluten free option. Visits also by arrangement June & July for groups of 10 to 30.
Town garden that once was an allotment plot. The length has been divided into different rooms; a courtyard garden with a sculptural clematis providing shade, colour themed flower beds, ponds and water features, cottage garden and gravel borders, clematis and roses, all linked by lawns and grass paths. Collection of over 50 different hostas.

❋ 🚗 ♿

30 ◆ KELMARSH HALL & GARDENS
Main Road, Kelmarsh, Northampton, NN6 9LY. The Kelmarsh Trust, 01604 686543, enquiries@kelmarsh.com, www.kelmarsh.com. *Kelmarsh is 5m S of Market Harborough & 11m N of Northampton. From A14, exit J2 & head N towards Market Harborough on the A508.* For NGS: Sun 19 Apr, Sun 7 June (11-5). Adm £3.50, chd free. The tearoom offers light lunches, cream teas & cakes. For other opening times and information, please phone, email or visit garden website.
Kelmarsh Hall is an elegant Palladian house set in glorious Northamptonshire countryside with highly regarded gardens, which are the work of Nancy Lancaster, Norah Lindsay and Geoffrey Jellicoe. Hidden gems incl an orangery, sunken garden, long border, rose gardens and, at the heart of it all, a historic walled garden. Highlights throughout the seasons incl fritillaries, tulips, roses and dahlias. Beautiful interiors brought together by Nancy Lancaster in the 1930s, in a palladian style hall designed by James Gibbs. The recently restored laundry and servant's quarters in the Hall are open to the public, providing visitors the incredible opportunity to experience life 'below stairs'. Blue badge disabled parking is available close to the Visitor Centre entrance. Paths are loose gravel, wheelchair users advised to bring a companion.

♿ 🐖 ❋ 🚗 ♿

GROUP OPENING

31 KILSBY GARDENS
Middle Street, Kilsby, CV23 8XT.
5m SE of Rugby. 6m N of Daventry on A361. The road through Kilsby village is the B4038. **Sun 14 June (1.30-5.30). Combined adm £6, chd free. Light refreshments at Kilsby Village Hall (1-5).**

12 DAVENTRY ROAD
Julie Bunyan.

17 ESSEN LANE
Emily Beaumont.

GRAFTON HOUSE
Andy & Sally Tomkins.

THE HAVEN
Sarah & Clive Thompson.

LYNN COTTAGE
Alison Harrison.

MANOR COTTAGE
Helen & Tom Jones.

ORCHARD HOUSE
Barbara & Frank Almond.

RAINBOW'S END
Mr & Mrs J Madigan.

SUMMERHILL
Diana & Ron Smith.

SUNDIAL COTTAGE
Richard & Sue Haslett.

Kilsby's name has long been associated with Stephenson's famous railway tunnel and an early skirmish in the Civil War. The houses and gardens of the village offer a mixture of sizes and styles, which reflect its development through time. We welcome you to test the friendliness for which we are renowned. As a special treat, the trail of open gardens in our village will be enlivened by the decorated wheelbarrow competition.

32 16 LEYS AVENUE
Desborough, Kettering, NN14 2PY. Mr & Mrs Keith & Beryl Norman, 01536 760950, bcn@stainer16.plus.com. *6m N of Kettering, 5m S of Market Harborough. From church & War Memorial turn R into Dunkirk Ave & 5th R into Leys Ave.* **Sun 14 June (2-5). Combined adm with Hostellarie £4, chd free. Sun 6 Sept (2-5). Adm £3, chd free. Light refreshments. Visits also by arrangement June to Sept for groups of 10 to 30.**

A town garden with two water features, plus a stream and a pond flanked by a 12ft clinker built boat. There are six raised beds which are planted with vegetables and dahlias. A patio lined with acers has two steps down to a gravel garden with paved paths. Mature trees and acers give the garden yr-round structure and interest. Access by two steps from patio to main garden.

GROUP OPENING

33 NEWNHAM GARDENS
Newnham, Daventry, NN11 3HF.
2m S of Daventry on B4037 between the A361 & A45. Continue to the centre of the village & follow signs for the car park, just off the main village green. **Sun 24 May (11-5). Combined adm £5, chd free. Light refreshments in village hall.**

THE BANKS
Sue & Geoff Chester,
www.suestyles.co.uk.

THE COTTAGE
Jacqueline Minor.

HILLTOP
David & Mercy Messenger.

KEY COTTAGE
David & Janet Woodford.

NEW **STONE HOUSE**
Pat Bannerman.

WREN COTTAGE
Mr & Mrs Judith Dorkins.

Six lovely gardens set in a beautiful old village cradled by the gentle hills of south Northamptonshire. The varied gardens, set around traditional village houses, look enchanting at this special time of year and, for 2020, we are especially pleased to have a new garden opening. Spend the day with us enjoying the gardens, buying at our large plant sale, strolling around the village lanes and visiting our C14 church. Why not treat yourself both to a tasty light lunch and, later, scrumptious cakes and refreshments in the village hall. Please note that the village and gardens are hilly in parts and while most gardens are accessible to wheelchairs, others are more restricted.

34 NEW NIGHTINGALE COTTAGE
Draughton Road, Maidwell, NN6 9JF. Ken & Angela Palmer.
Approx 10m N of Northampton. On A508 between Northampton & Market Harborough, 1st L after Westaways Garage (from A14). **Sun 3 May, Sun 16 Aug (11-4). Combined adm with The Bungalow £4, chd free. Home-made teas.**

A garden designed by the owners over the last 10 yrs, surrounding an old barn. There are many pots and cottage type planting incl some vegetables. There are also some surprises of wooden animals made from prunings, steps and hidden seating areas, but no grass. It is a garden which is always evolving as different species self-seed and are often left to grow. There is a small water feature over rocks into a stones pool where the many garden creatures drink.

35 NEW NONSUCH
Mackworth Drive, Finedon, Wellingborough, NN9 5NL.
David & Carrie Whitworth. *Off Wellingborough Rd (A510) onto Bell Hill, then to Church Hill, 2nd L after church, entrance on the L as you enter Mackworth Drive.* **Sun 31 May (1-5). Adm £3.50, chd free. Drinks, cakes & biscuits.**

⅓ acre country garden, within a conservation boundary stone wall. Mature trees, enhanced by many rare and unusual shrubs and perennial plants. A garden for all seasons with several seating areas. Wheelchair access on a level site with paved and gravel paths.

Your visits help change lives – your generosity helps Marie Curie fund nurses to care for people night and day in their homes, with donations of more than £9 million

36 OLD RECTORY, QUINTON

Preston Deanery Road, Quinton, Northampton, NN7 2ED. Alan Kennedy & Emma Wise, www.garden4good.co.uk. M1 J15, 1m from Wootton towards Salcey Forest. House is next to the church. **Sun 31 May, Sun 6 Sept (10-5). Adm £10, chd free. Pre-booking essential, please visit www.ngs. org.uk/events for information & booking. Light refreshments.** A beautiful contemporary 3 acre rectory garden designed by multi-award-winning designer, Anoushka Feiler. Taking the Old Rectory's C18 history and its religious setting as a key starting point, the main garden at the back of the house has been divided into six parts; a kitchen garden, glasshouse and flower garden, a woodland menagerie, a pleasure garden, a park and an orchard. Elements of C18 design such as formal structures, parterres, topiary, long walks, occasional seating areas and traditional craft work have been introduced, however with a distinctly C21 twist through the inclusion of living walls, modern materials and features, new planting methods and abstract installations. Teas, coffees, cakes & light lunches available. Quinton Old Rectory Poetry Festival (18-21 June 2020). Wheelchair access with gravel paths.

& D ☕

37 ◆ THE OLD RECTORY, SUDBOROUGH

Kettering, NN14 3BX. Mr & Mrs G Toller, 01832 734085, contact@ theoldrectorygardens.co.uk, www.theoldrectorygardens.co.uk. 8m NE of Kettering. Exit 12 off A14. Village just off A6116 between Thrapston & Brigstock. Free private parking in a small paddock adjacent to the house. **For NGS: Sun 10 May (11-5). Adm £7, chd free. Home-made teas. For other opening times and information, please phone, email or visit garden website.** A charming 3 acre village garden situated next to a church, including extensive herbaceous borders, a rose garden, gravel border and highly regarded potager, designed by Rosemary Verey. This is a garden for all seasons with early spring bulbs, a wide variety of old roses, tree peonies, standard Lycianthes Rantonnetii, a small lily pond and charming woodland walk alongside Harpers Brook. Set in a tranquil conservation area with stunning views and setting. Partial wheelchair access as some gravel paths. Guide dogs welcome.

& ✻ ☕ ☕

38 THE OLD VICARAGE

Daventry Road, Norton, Daventry, NN11 2ND. Mr & Mrs Barry & Andrea Coleman. Norton is about 2m E of Daventry, 11m W of Northampton. From Daventry follow signs to Norton for 1m. On A5 N from Weedon follow road for 3m, take L turn signed Norton. On A5 S take R at Xrds signed Norton, 6m from Kilsby. Garden is R of All Saints Church. **Sun 26 Apr (1-5). Adm £4, chd free. Home-made teas in orangery.** The vicarage days bequeathed dramatic and stately trees to the modern garden. The last 40 yrs of evolution and the happy accidents of soil-type, and a striking location with lovely vistas have shaped the garden around all the things that make April so thrilling, including prodigious sweeps of primulas of many kinds and the trees in blossom. The interesting and beautiful C14 church of All Saints will be open to visitors.

🐕 ☕

GROUP OPENING

39 PRESTON CAPES AND LITTLE PRESTON GARDENS

Little Preston, Daventry, NN11 3TF. 6m SW of Daventry. 13m NE of Banbury. 3m N of Canons Ashby. Preston Capes and Little Preston are ½m apart. **Sun 31 May (1-5). Combined adm £5, chd free. Home-made teas at The Old Rectory (1-5).**

CITY COTTAGE
Mrs Gavin Cowen.

THE MANOR
Mr Graham Stanton.

NORTH FARM
Mr & Mrs Tim Coleridge.

THE OLD RECTORY
Luke & Victoria Bridgeman.

OLD WEST FARM
Mr & Mrs G Hoare, caghoare@gmail.com.
Visits also by arrangement in June for groups of 10 to 20.

A selection of five differing gardens in the beautiful unspoilt south Northamptonshire ironstone villages, most with a backdrop of fantastic views of the surrounding countryside. Gardens range from small contemporary, through to classical country style with old fashioned roses and borders. Features include attractive village with local sandstone houses and cottages (not open), Norman church and wonderful views. Partial wheelchair access to some parts of the gardens.

& ✻ ☕

Cottesbrooke Hall Gardens

GROUP OPENING

40 RAVENSTHORPE GARDENS
Ravensthorpe, NN6 8ES. *7m NW of Northampton. Signed from A428. Wigley Cottage is in The Hollows off Bettycroft.* **Sun 12 July (1.30-5.30). Combined adm £5, chd free. Home-made teas at village hall.**

CORNERSTONE
Lorna Jones.

QUIETWAYS
Russ Barringer.

RAVENSTHORPE NURSERY
Mr & Mrs Richard Wiseman, 01604 770548, ravensthorpenursery@hotmail.com.
Visits also by arrangement May to Sept.

TREETOPS
Ros & Gordon Smith.

WIGLEY COTTAGE
Mr & Mrs Dennis Patrick.

Attractive village in Northamptonshire uplands near to Ravensthorpe reservoir and Top Ardles Wood Woodland Trust, which have bird watching and picnic opportunities. Established and developing gardens set in beautiful countryside displaying a wide range of plants, many of which are available from the Nursery. Offering inspirational planting, quiet contemplation, beautiful views, water features, gardens encouraging wildlife and a flower arranger's garden. Partial wheelchair access to Wigley Cottage. Disabled WC at village hall.

41 RAVENSWOOD
Coton, NN6 8RG. Jean & Mike Percival. *1m S of Guilsborough. Follow sign on lane, nr Coton Manor indicating 'Village only' & 'No Through Road', garden 100yds on R. Parking in Coton Manor car park.* **Sun 13 Sept (12-5.30). Combined adm with Coton Manor Garden £8, chd free. Light refreshments at Coton Manor.**
Since purchase, the owners have redeveloped the garden to take advantage of the sloping site overlooking woods and farmland. A wide variety of herbaceous plants, shrubs and maturing trees have been planted to provide colour throughout the gardening year.

42 ROSEARIE-DE-LA-NYMPH
55 The Grove, Moulton, Northampton, NN3 7UE. Peter Hughes, Mary Morris, Irene Kay, Steven Hughes & Jeremy Stanton. *N of Northampton town. Turn off A43 at small r'about to Overstone Rd. Follow NGS signs in village. The garden is on the Holcot Rd out of Moulton.* **Sun 21, Sun 28 June (11-5). Adm £4.50, chd free. Home-made teas & light refreshments.**
We have been developing this romantic garden for about 10 yrs and now have over 1800 roses, incl English, French and Italian varieties. Many unusual water features and specimen trees. Roses, scramblers and ramblers climb into trees, over arbours and arches. Collection of 140 Japanese maples. Mostly flat wheelchair access, but there is a standard width doorway to negotiate.

GROUP OPENING

43 SLAPTON GARDENS
Slapton, Towcester, NN12 8PE. *A hamlet 4m W of Towcester. 1/4 m N of the Towcester to Wappenham road.* **Sun 21 June (2-5.30). Combined adm £6, chd free. Tea at Sowbrook House.**

BRADDEN COTTAGE
Mrs Philippa Heumann.

CORNER HOUSE
Amanda & Stuart Bell.

NEW THE OLD RECTORY
Mr & Mrs Kit James, Kitjames7@gmail.com.

SOWBROOK HOUSE
Mrs Caroline Coke.

Slapton is a very pretty Northamptonshire hamlet with only 30 houses'. Four gardens will be opening for the NGS this year including one new, The Old Rectory a garden originally designed by James Alexander-Sinclair and enhanced by the current owners. Corner House is an established garden with charming rooms and Sowbrook House has shrub and herbaceous borders, as well as a more formal small walled garden. Bradden Cottage is a cottage garden. There is the lovely C12 St Botolph's Chuch with rare Medieval wall paintings which will be open to visitors. Partial wheelchair access with narrow and gravel paths.

The White Cottage, Flore Gardens

Sundial Cottage, Kilsby Gardens

GROUP OPENING

44 SPRATTON GARDENS
Smith Street, Spratton, NN6 8HP.
6½ m NNW of Northampton. On A5199 between Northampton & Welford. S from J1, A14. Car Park at Spratton Hall School with close access to gardens. **Sun 31 May (11-5). Combined adm £7, chd free. Home-made teas.**

THE COTTAGE
Mr & Mrs Andrew Elliott.

FORGE COTTAGE
Daniel & Jo Bailey.

28 GORSE ROAD
Lee Miller.

11 HIGH STREET
Philip & Frances Roseblade.

MULBERRY COTTAGE
Kerry Herd.

NORTHBANK HOUSE
Helen Millichamp.

STONE HOUSE
John Forbear.

VALE VIEW
John Hunt.

WALTHAM COTTAGE
Norma & Allan Simons.

NEW 11 YEW TREE LANE
Niall & Becks O'Brien.

As well as attractive cottage gardens alongside old Northampton stone houses, Spratton also has unusual gardens, including those showing good use of a small area; one dedicated to encouraging wildlife with views of the surrounding countryside; newly renovated gardens and those with new planting; courtyard garden; gravel garden with sculpture; mature gardens with fruit trees and herbaceous borders. There will be a 'Bug Hunt' for children. Tea, cakes and rolls will be available in the Norman St. Andrew's Church, Church Road. The King's Head Pub will be open, lunch reservations recommended.

🚻 🐕 ✿ 🚗 ☕

45 ◆ STEANE PARK
Brackley, NN13 6DP. Lady Connell, 01280 705899, garden@steanepark.co.uk, www.steanepark.co.uk. *2m from Brackley towards Banbury. On A422, 6m E of Banbury.* **For NGS: Sun 12 July (11-5). Adm £4.50, chd free. Cream teas.** For other opening times and information, please phone, email or visit garden website.
The garden was in an extremely dilapidated and overgrown state; over the past 24 yrs we have tried to recapture its original glory. There are beautiful trees in 80 acres of parkland, old waterway and fish ponds, 1620 church in grounds. The gardens are constantly being updated in sympathy with old stone house and church. Amongst many features and attractions there is the The Monet Bridge, built by a craftsman from Suffolk. It was delivered in several pieces and constructed on-site with the aid of a lot of ropes, getting wet and crossed fingers, but the end result looks magnificent! Partial wheelchair access.

🚻 ✿ ☕

We help ordinary people open the gates to their extraordinary private gardens to raise impressive amounts of money through admissions, teas and slices of cake!

Holdenby House & Gardens

© Val Corbett

46 SULBY GARDENS

Sulby, Northampton, NN6 6EZ.
Mrs Alison Lowe. *16m NW of Northampton, 2m NE of Welford off A5199. Past Wharf House Hotel, take 1st R signed Sulby. After R & L bends, turn R at sign for Sulby Hall Farm. Turn R at junction, garden is 1st L. Parking limited, no vans or buses please.* **Thur 23 Apr, Thur 18 June, Thur 27 Aug (2-5); Thur 8 Oct (1-4); Fri 9 Oct (11-4). Adm £4, chd free. Home-made teas.**
Interesting and unusual property, on the Leicestershire border between Welford and Husbands Bosworth, covering 12 acres comprising working Victorian kitchen garden, orchard, and late C18 icehouse, plus species-rich nature reserve incl woodland, feeder stream to River Avon, a variety of ponds and established wild flower meadows. Open Day features incl April: snakeshead fritillaries, cowslips, bluebells. June: wildflower meadows in full bloom. Aug: butterflies, dragonflies, aquatic plants. Oct: a celebration of apples. Plant sales. NB: Children welcome but under strict supervision because of deep water.

47 TITCHMARSH HOUSE

Chapel Street, Titchmarsh, NN14 3DA. Sir Ewan & Lady Harper, 01832 732439, ewan@ewanh.co.uk, www.titchmarsh-house.co.uk. *2m N of Thrapston. 6m S of Oundle. Exit A14 at junction signed A605, Titchmarsh signed as turning E towards Oundle & Peterborough.* **Sun 10, Mon 25 May (2-6); Sat 13 June (12.30-5). Adm £5, chd free. Teas at parish church (May). BBQ lunch & teas at village fete (June). Visits also by arrangement Apr to June for groups of 5+.**
4½ acres extended and laid out since 1972. Special collections of magnolias, spring bulbs, iris, peonies and roses with many rare trees and shrubs. Walled ornamental vegetable garden and ancient yew hedge. Some newly planted areas; please refer to the website. Collections of flowering trees and other unusual plants such as rare Buddleias, Philadelphus, Deutzias and Abelias. Wheelchair access to most of the garden without using steps. No dogs.

48 WALNUT HOUSE

Charlton, Banbury, OX17 3DR.
Sir Paul & Lady Hayter. *In Main St, Charlton, between Banbury and Brackley.* **Sun 31 May (2-5). Adm £5, chd free. Home-made teas.**
Large garden behind C17 farmhouse (not open). Colour themed borders and separate small gardens with beech and yew hedges, each with their own character. Orchard with wild flowers, and an old-fashioned vegetable garden. Wilderness (in C18 sense), and archery lawn. Garden started in 1992 with new hot and gravel garden created in 2011. Wheelchair access to garden with gravel paths.

GROUP OPENING

49 WEEDON LOIS & WESTON GARDENS

Weedon Lois, Towcester, NN12 8PJ. *7m W of Towcester. 7m N of Brackley. Turn off A43 at Towcester towards Abthorpe & Wappenham & turn R for Weedon Lois. Or turn off A43 at Brackley, follow signs to Helmdon & Weston.* **Sun 14 June (1-6). Combined adm £6, chd free. Home-made teas in Baptist Chapel, Weston.**

HILLSIDE
Mrs Karen Wilcox.

LOIS WEEDON HOUSE
Lady Greenaway.

NEW MIDDLETON HOUSE
Mark & Donna Cooper.

OLD BARN
Mr & Mrs John Gregory.

PRIMROSE HILL
Terry & Hugh Tyler.

RIDGEWAY COTTAGE
Jonathan & Elizabeth Carpenter.

NEW STONE HOUSE FARM
Chris Seckington.

4 VICARAGE RISE
Ashley & Lindsey Cartwright.

Two adjacent villages in south Northamptonshire with a handsome Medieval church in Weedon Lois. The extension churchyard contains the grave of the poet Dame Edith Sitwell who lived in Weston Hall (not open), marked with a gravestone by Henry Moore. This year we have two new gardens, both in Weston. One was designed only three years ago by James Alexander-Sinclair, but already well established with lots of unusual planting. The other is an old farmhouse garden with beautiful old trees, herbaceous beds and views across the fields. Our other gardens offer a wonderful mix of colourful perennial beds, vegetables, roses, orchards, woods and even a wavy hedge. We hope you will join us for our open day, enjoy looking round our gardens, and tuck into our famous home-made teas.

50 WOODCOTE VILLA

Old Watling Street (A5), Long Buckby Wharf, Long Buckby, Northampton, NN6 7EW. Sue & Geoff Woodward, geoff.and.sue@btinternet.com. *2m NE of Daventry. From M1 J16, take Flore By-Pass, turn R at A5 r'about for approx 3m. From Daventry follow Long Buckby signs, but turn L at A5 Xrds. From M1 J18/Kilsby follow A5 S for approx 6m.* **Sun 29 Mar, Sun 26 July, Sun 6 Sept (11-6). Adm £5, chd free. Home-made teas. Visits also by arrangement Mar to Sept for groups of 10+.**

In a much admired location, this delightful canalside garden has a large variety of plants, styles, structures and unusual bygones. Bulbs will feature in March, with colourful planting in July and September, all set against a backdrop of trees and shrubs . Lovely places to sit, relax, and watch the boats and wildlife. Admission includes tea, coffee and cold drink. Home-made cake for sale. Sorry, no WC. Wheelchair access over ramp at entrance to garden.

51 THE WOODEN OWL

10A The Green, Clipston, Market Harborough, LE16 9RS. Mrs Julie Connell. *Clipston is on the Daventry, West Haddon, Naseby Market Harborough road. Approx 15m W of Kettering, NW of Northampton & SSE of Leicester. Off A14 J1 take the A5199 to Naseby then Clipston. Off A14 J2 take the A508 to Kelmarsh then Clipston.* **Sat 13 June (2-5.30); Sun 14 June (11-5.30). Adm £4, chd free. Cream teas.**

The garden is within the owner's old plantsman's garden, The Maltings, the garden the owner opened for the NGS for 10 yrs. Full of unusual plants, shrubs and clematis. Many different fruit trees and bushes, vegetables and water garden. A smallish garden with lots of interest. Children's Owl Trail competition. A garden with great interest, especially to people who used to visit The Maltings. Wheelchair access to majority of garden.

Brytten-Collier House, Harpole Gardens

OPENING DATES

All entries subject to change. For latest information check www.ngs.org.uk

Map locator numbers are shown to the right of each garden name.

February

Snowdrop Festival

Sunday 23rd
Church Farm 6
Holmes Villa 19

March

Sunday 1st
Bolham Manor 2

April

Saturday 4th
NEW Oasis Community
Gardens 35

Sunday 19th
◆ Felley Priory 12

Sunday 26th
NEW 1 Highfield Road 17
Normanton Hall 29

May

Sunday 10th
Church House 7

Sunday 17th
Bridge Farm 3
6 Hope Street 21
◆ Norwell Nurseries 31
Nottinghamshire Hospice 33
Upper Grove Farm 47

Sunday 24th
Ivy Bank Cottage 22
Papplewick Hall 38
Patchings Art Centre 40

Monday 25th
Halam Gardens and
Wildflower Meadow 15
Holmes Villa 19
NEW Westmoor House 48

June

Saturday 6th
The Echium Garden 11

Sunday 7th
5 Burton Lane 4
The Chimes 5

NEW Keyworth
Gardens 23
Normanton Hall 29

Saturday 13th
NEW Forge Cottage 13
Piecemeal 41

Sunday 14th
Askham Gardens 1
NEW Forge Cottage 13
NEW Gaunts Hill 14
Piecemeal 41

Saturday 20th
The Old Vicarage 36

Sunday 21st
NEW Hollinside 18
Hopbine Farmhouse,
Ossington 20
Ossington House 37

Saturday 27th
NEW Oasis Community
Gardens 35

Sunday 28th
Lodge Mount 24
Norwell Gardens 30
Thrumpton Hall 45

July

Wednesday 1st
Norwell Gardens 30
Rhubarb Farm 42

Sunday 5th
East Meets West 10
The Manor 26
Norwood Cottage 32
Spring Bank House 44

Sunday 19th
Cornerstones 8
NEW Manor Farm 27
NEW Meadow Farm 28

Sunday 26th
5a High Street 16
The Old Vicarage 36
Park Farm 39

August

Saturday 8th
Oak Barn Exotic
Garden 34

Sunday 9th
The Old Vicarage 36

Sunday 16th
University Park
Gardens 46

Saturday 29th
NEW Oasis Community
Gardens 35

Monday 31st
5 Burton Lane 4
Piecemeal 41

September

Sunday 6th
East Meets West 10
Spring Bank House 44

Sunday 20th
Oak Barn Exotic
Garden 34
Riseholme, 125
Shelford Road 43

October

Sunday 11th
◆ Norwell Nurseries 31

By Arrangement

Arrange a personalised garden visit with your club, or group of friends, on a date to suit you. See individual garden entries for full details.

5 Burton Lane 4
Church Farm 6
Cornerstones 8
Dumbleside 9
5a High Street 16
Holmes Villa 19
NEW Keyworth Gardens 23
Lodge Mount 24
38 Main Street 25
Normanton Hall 29
Norwood Cottage 32
NEW Oasis Community
Gardens 35
The Old Vicarage 36
Park Farm 39
Piecemeal 41
Rhubarb Farm 42
Riseholme, 125
Shelford Road 43
6 Weston Close 49

5a High Street Sutton on Trent

THE GARDENS

GROUP OPENING

❶ ASKHAM GARDENS
Markham Moor, Retford, NG22 0RP.
6m S of Retford. On A638, in Rockley village turn E to Askham or on A57 at East Markham turn N to Askham. **Sun 14 June (2-6). Combined adm £5, chd free. Home-made teas at Manor Lodge.**

DOVECOTE COTTAGE
Mrs C Slack.

MANOR LODGE
Mr & Mrs K Bloom.

NURSERY HOUSE
Mr & Mrs D Bird.

ORCHARD HOUSE
David Garner & Jane Ball.

NEW THE STABLES
Daniel & Ros Barnes.

Variety of pleasant English village gardens, with a flower festival in the church. Nursery House is a plantsman's garden, secluded and private, with every plant meticulously labelled; waterfall and well stocked pond. Dovecote Cottage is an enchanting terraced cottage garden with roses on the walls, perennial beds and attractive raised fish pond. Manor Lodge is a large garden, opposite the church with many summer houses and extensive lawns. The Stables is a south facing, incorporating hedged kitchen garden and large herbaceous bordered koi pond. Deep gravel at Nursery House. Steep slopes at Dovecote Cottage.

& ⌁ ❀ ☕

❷ BOLHAM MANOR
Bolham Way, Bolham, Retford, DN22 9JG. Pam & Butch Barnsdale. *1m from Retford. A620 Gainsborough Rd from Retford, turn L onto Tiln Lane, signed 'A620 avoiding low bridge'. At sharp R bend take rd ahead to Tiln then L Bolham Way.* **Sun 1 Mar (11-3). Adm £3.50, chd free. Light refreshments.**
As you enter this 3 acre mature garden, you are greeted by the 'Dancing willow Ladies' amidst swathes of snowdrops and narcissus. Your eyes are drawn to the occasional well positioned sculpture or topiary feature guiding you through to other areas of the garden and orchard, where even more carpets of snowdrops and early bulbs will greet you. Partial wheelchair access to parts of garden.

& ❀ ☕

❸ BRIDGE FARM
Norwell Woodhouse, Newark, NG23 6NG. Rachel Cook. *If entering the village from Norwell , the property is on the R just after the dairy farm.* **Sun 17 May (1-4). Combined adm with Upper Grove Farm £4, chd free. Home-made teas.**
A large country garden in a quiet village (work in progress) with a wide variety of plants providing flower and foliage colour all year round. A contemporary swimming pond with a tranquil decking area to sit and ponder, views of open fields to the rear. Patio and courtyard, along with raised flower and vegetable beds Plenty of seats available to relax and enjoy tea and a slice of cake.

& ❀ ☕

❹ 5 BURTON LANE
Whatton in the Vale, NG13 9EQ. Ms Faulconbridge, 01949 850942, jpfaulconbridge@hotmail.co.uk, www.ayearinthegardenblog. wordpress.com. *3m E of Bingham. Follow signs to Whatton from A52 between Bingham & Elton. Garden nr Church in old part of village. Follow yellow NGS signs.* **Sun 7 June, Mon 31 Aug (12-4). Adm £3.50, chd free. Home-made teas. Visits also by arrangement May to Sept for groups of up to 30.**
Modern cottage garden which is productive and highly decorative. We garden organically and for wildlife. The garden is full of colour and scent from spring to autumn. Several distinct areas, incl fruit and vegetables. Large beds are filled with over 500 varieties of plants with paths through so you can wander and get close. Also features seating, gravel garden, pond, shade planting and sedum roof. Attractive village with walks.

❀ ☕

❺ THE CHIMES
37 Glenorchy Crescent, Heronridge, NG5 9LG. Stan & Ellen Maddock. *4m N of Nottingham. A611 towards Hucknall on to Bulwell Common. Turn R at Tesco Top Valley up to island. Turn L 100 yds. 1st L then 2nd L onto Glenorchy Crescent to bottom.* **Sun 7 June (1-5). Adm £3, chd free. Home-made teas.**
We would like to invite you to pass through our archway and into our own little oasis on the edge of a busy city. Come and share our well-stocked small garden, full of roses, peonies, lilies and much more. Visit us and be surprised. We look forward to seeing you.

⌁ ☕

❻ CHURCH FARM
Church Lane, West Drayton, Retford, DN22 8EB. Robert & Isobel Adam, robertadam139@btinternet.com. *A1 exit Markham Moor. A638 Retford 500 yds signed West Drayton. 3/4 m, turn R, into Church Lane, 1st R past church. Ample parking in farm yard.* **Sun 23 Feb (10.30-4). Adm £3, chd free. Light refreshments in St Pauls Church. Refreshments served from 11.30am. Visits also by arrangement Feb & Mar for groups of 5 to 20.**
The garden is essentially a spring garden with a small woodland area which is carpeted with many snowdrops, aconites and cyclamen which have seeded into the adjoining churchyard, with approx 180 named snowdrops growing in island beds, along with hellebores and daffodils. Limited amount of snowdrops and miniature iris for sale.

& ⌁ ❀ ☕

❼ CHURCH HOUSE
Hoveringham, NG14 7JH. Alex & Sue Allan. *6 miles east of Nottingham. To the R of the Church and Church Hall in the centre of Hoveringham village.* **Sun 10 May (1-5). Adm £3, chd free. Home-made teas in Hoveringham Village Hall next door to the garden. Tea and cakes served by Hoveringham WI.**
Stunning small gem of a garden, beautifully planted with immaculate hostas which greet you along the gravelled path leading past a mini pseudo-roof garden at eye level. Relax in an oasis of cottage garden style planting where the chickens, small pond, vegetable beds, charming auricula theatre and espalier fruit trees combine to create a delightfully peaceful atmosphere. We warmly welcome you. Deep gravel on driveway and path into the garden so no wheelchair access - sorry.

⌁ ☕

8 CORNERSTONES

15 Lamcote Gardens, Radcliffe-on-Trent, Nottingham, NG12 2BS. Judith & Jeff Coombes, 0115 8458055, judithcoombes@gmail.com, www.cornerstonesgarden.co.uk. *4m E of Nottingham. From A52 take Radcliffe exit at RSPCA junction, then 2nd L just before hairpin bend.* Sun 19 July (1.30-5). Adm £3.50, chd free. Home-made teas. Visits also by arrangement July & Aug for groups of 10+. By arrangement admission price incl cost of refreshments. Plant lovers' garden, approaching ½ acre. Flowing colour themed and specie borders with rare, exotic and unusual plants, provide a wealth of colour and interest, whilst the unique fruit and vegetable garden generates an abundance of produce. Bananas, palms, fernery, fish pond, bog garden, lovely summerhouse area and greenhouse. Enjoy tea and delicious home-made cake in a beautiful setting. Wheelchair access but some bark paths and unfenced ponds.

&. ⛏ ✿ ☊ ☕

9 DUMBLESIDE

17 Bridle Road, Burton Joyce, NG14 5FT. Mr P Bates, 01159 313725, cpbates2015@gmail.com. *5m NE of Nottingham. The Bridle Rd is an unsurfaced, single track, R hand fork off Lambley Ln. Leave passengers at our gate and park 50 yds beyond where the rd branches 3 ways.* Visits by arrangement Feb to Oct for groups of 5+. Adm £6, chd free. Home-made teas incl in adm fee stated.
Gorgeous 2 acres of varied habitat. Stream with primulas, iris, tree ferns and the like; 50yds of mixed herbaceous borders; gardening in grass with wild flowers, Spring and Autumn bulbs; woodland walks of massed cyclamen, snowdrops & anemones and a nice sunny raised gravel bed for alpines and small plants. Plant lovers' delight! Steep slopes towards stream therefore partial access only for wheelchairs.

&. ⛏ ✿ ☊ ☕

10 EAST MEETS WEST

85 Cowpes Close, Sutton-In-Ashfield, NG17 2BU. Kate and Mel Calladine. *Close to Quarrydale School entrance to Carsic Housing Estate. The Cl has limited parking for those with limited mobility. Parking on Stoneyford Rd, NG17 2DU would relieve congestion. Cross on zebra & walk down jitty into Cowpes Cl following NGS signposting.* Sun 5 July, Sun 6 Sept (12-5). Combined adm with Spring Bank House £4, chd free.
East: We have a number of sizable acers, bamboos and Japanese lanterns. A stream flows past a cloud tree into a pond with goldfish and water lilies. West: A trompe d'oeil arch creates a magical garden illusion with an arch shaped 'rainbow' flower bed providing a flamboyant colour arrangement. The front drive has pink/white borders, and 'green' camouflage for bins. No steps from pavement to garden. Cobbled path allows wheelchair access to full length of garden.

&. ✿ ☕

11 THE ECHIUM GARDEN

Walled Garden, Thoresby Park, Nr Ollerton, Newark, NG22 9EP. Linda & Ray Heywood, www.echiumworld.co.uk. *From Nottingham: A614 at Ollerton r'about take turn to A1 in 2m turn L at Thoresby r'about along the County Rd for 1m turn L for Thoresby Courtyard (just before Thoresby Hall Hotel entrance).* Sat 6 June (12-4). Adm £5, chd free.
A short walk to The Echium Garden that occupies a corner of the partially restored five acre walled kitchen garden at Thoresby Park dating from 1700s. Featuring the National Plant Collection of Echium incl the Giant Tree Echium growing to over 14ft, endemic to the Canary Islands. The garden designed in 2018 features herbaceous borders with some unusual & heritage plants grown in Victorian times. Uneven surfaces & gravel paths.

⛏ ✿ ☊ NPC ☕

12 ♦ FELLEY PRIORY

Underwood, NG16 5FJ. Ms Michelle Upchurch for the Brudenell Family, 01773 810230, michelle@felleypriory.co.uk, www.felleypriory.co.uk. *8m SW of Mansfield. Off A608 ½m W M1 J27.* For NGS: Sun 19 Apr (10-4). Adm £5, chd free. Light refreshments. For other opening times and information, please phone, email or visit garden website.
Garden for all seasons with yew hedges and topiary, snowdrops, hellebores, herbaceous borders and rose garden. There are pergolas, a white garden, small arboretum and borders filled with unusual trees, shrubs, plants and bulbs. The grass edged pond is planted with primulas, bamboo, iris, roses and eucomis. Bluebell woodland walk. Orchard with extremely rare daffodils. Regional Finalist, The English Garden's The Nation's Favourite Gardens 2019.

&. ✿ ☊ ☕

Bolham Manor

⬛3 NEW ▶ FORGE COTTAGE

131 Main Street, Sutton Bonington, Loughborough, LE12 5PE. Judith and David Franklin. *3 miles from J24 of M1, and 5 miles NW of Loughborough. Opposite St Michael's Church.* **Sat 13, Sun 14 June (2-6). Combined adm with Piecemeal £5, chd free. Home-made teas.**
A small cottage garden reclaimed from the scrapyard of a Victorian forge and overlooked by a medieval church in the heart of a country village. A leafy, rose-filled passageway leads to a sun-dappled sanctuary looking out over wild meadow, spinney and paddock. Colourful curved herbaceous borders of mixed shrubs and perennials winding around a gnarled Bramley apple tree.

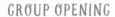

⬛4 NEW ▶ GAUNTS HILL

Bestwood Lodge, Arnold, NG5 8NF. Nigel and Penny Lymn Rose. *5m N of Nottingham. Take Bestwood Lodge Dr up to the Bestwood Lodge Hotel, then turn R & continue until you see a sign saying vehicle access to stables only. Then turn R down the dr.* **Sun 14 June (11-4). Adm £5, chd free. Tea.**
A large country garden with ponds, mature woodlands, greenhouse, borders, lawns and vegetable plot. Car parking available in an adjacent field. Some gravel paths and lawns. There are some steps but these can be avoided.

GROUP OPENING

⬛5 HALAM GARDENS AND WILDFLOWER MEADOW

Nr Southwell, NG22 8AX. *Village gardens within walking distance of one another. Hill's Farm wildflower meadow is a short drive of ½ m towards Edingley village, turn R at brow of hill as signed.* **Mon 25 May (1-5). Combined adm £5.50, chd free. Home-made teas at The Old Vicarage, Halam.**

HILL FARM HOUSE
Victoria Starkey.

HILL'S FARM
John & Margaret Hill.

THE OLD VICARAGE
Mrs Beverley Perks.
(See separate entry)

Hopbine Farmhouse

Lovely mix of a very popular beautiful, well-known, organic, rural plant lovers' garden with clematis, striking viburnums amongst herbaceous borders and sweeping lawns, lots of pond life; contrasting with small wrap-around cottage garden and 6 acre wildflower meadow - part of an organic farm - visitors can be assured of an inspiring discussion with the farmer who is passionate about the benefits of this method of farming for our environment and beef quality. 12th Century Church open - surrounded by freely planted, attractive churchyard - all welcome to enjoy this peaceful haven in English rural village setting. Old Vicarage - gravel entrance to lower flat garden. Further up is on gentle hill. Hill Farm House - gravel entrance. Hill's Farm is flat.

⬛6 5A HIGH STREET

Sutton-on-Trent, NG23 6QA. Kathryn & Ian Saunders, kathrynsaunders.optom@gmail.com. *6m N of Newark. Leave A1 at Sutton on Trent, follow Sutton signs. L at Xrds. 1st R turn (approx 1m) onto Main St. 2nd L onto High St. Garden 50 yds on R. Park on rd.* **Sun 26 July (1-5). Adm £4, chd free. Light refreshments. Visits also by arrangement July & Aug for groups of 10+. Cost for group visits is £5 per head incl refreshments.**
Manicured lawns are the foil for this plantsman's garden. Vistas lead past succulents to tropical areas and vibrant herbaceous beds. Ponds run through the plot, leading to woodland walks and a dedicated fernery (180+ varieties, with magnificent tree ferns). Topiary links all the different planting areas to great effect. Around 1000 named varieties of plants with interesting plant combinations.

17 NEW **1 HIGHFIELD ROAD**
Nuthall, Nottingham, NG16 1BQ.
Richard & Sue Bold. *4mins
from J26 of the M1- 4m NW of
Nottingham City. From J26 of the
M1 take the A610 towards Notts,
R-hand lane at r'about, take turn-
off to Horsendale. Follow rd to
Woodland Dr, then 2nd R is Highfield
Rd.* Sun 26 Apr (1-5). Adm £3, chd
free. Home-made teas.
A corner garden with a large variety
of plants, shrubs, rhodos, azaleas,
bulbs and alpines. Large heuchera
collection gives colour and texture
all year. Espaliered archway, with
apples, plums & pears. Soft fruit
collection. Patio with many pots and
troughs. Greenhouses with tomatoes,
cucumbers and peppers grown
hydroponically. Vegetables incl peas,
beans, root veg and sweetcorn.
Wheelchair access is limited to the
side garden and patio area only.
❀ ☕

18 NEW **HOLLINSIDE**
252 Diamond Avenue,
Kirkby-In-Ashfield, Nottingham,
NG17 7NA. Sue & Bob Chalkley,
rc10@sky.com. *1m E of Kirkby in
Ashfield at the Xrds of the A611
& B6020. Please use the signed
parking 200m on the L towards
Kirkby away from the busy junction.*
Sun 21 June (1-4.30). Adm £3, chd
free. Light refreshments.
A formal front garden with terraced
lawns and borders lead to a shaded
area with ferns, camellias, hydrangeas
and other flowering shrubs. The rear
garden has a wildlife pond, a wild
flower meadow, a summerhouse
and a victorian style greenhouse.
There are topiary box and yews
and a box parterre planted with
roses. The majority of the garden is
suitable for wheelchair use. Limited
disabled parking near house by prior
arrangement.
♿ 🐕 ❀ ☕

*We open the gates to the
nation's best gardens,
offering a relaxing,
memorable and affordable
day out. A perfect
experience to share with
friends and family.*

19 **HOLMES VILLA**
Holmes Lane, Walkeringham,
Gainsborough, DN10 4JP. Peter
& Sheila Clark, 01427 890233,
clarkshaulage@aol.com. *4m NW of
Gainsborough. A620 from Retford or
A631 from Bawtry/Gainsborough &
A161 to Walkeringham then towards
Misterton. Follow NGS signs for 1m.
Plenty of parking. Reserved disabled
parking.* Sun 23 Feb (12-4). Mon 25
May (12-4), also open Westmoor
House. Adm £2.50, chd free.
Home-made teas. Feb opening
offers hot food & soup. Visits also
by arrangement May to July.
1¾ acre plantsman's garden offering
yr-round interest and inspiration
starting with carpets of snowdrops,
mini daffodils, hellebores and spring
bulbs. Unusual collection of plants
and shrubs for winter. Come and
be surprised at the different fragrant
and interesting plants in early spring.
Places to sit and ponder, gazebos,
arbours, wildlife pond, hosta garden,
old tools on display and scarecrows.
A flower arranger's artistic garden.
February opening has home made
soup and hot sausage rolls. Special
parking for those requiring wheelchair
access in yard.
♿ ❀ 🚌 ☕

20 **HOPBINE FARMHOUSE,
OSSINGTON**
Hopbine Farmhouse, Main Street,
Ossington, NG23 6LJ. Mr & Mrs
Geldart. *From A1 N take exit marked
Carlton, Sutton-on-Trent, Weston
etc. At T-Junction turn L to Kneesall.
Drive 2m to Ossington. In village turn
R to Moorhouse & park in field.* Sun
21 June (2-5). Combined adm
with Ossington House £5, chd
free. Home-made teas at The
Hut, Ossington.
A small garden in two parts, the south
garden has a long herbaceous border
with spring, summer and autumn
planting, with clematis, roses and
honeysuckle climbing a brick wall.
The intimate walled north garden has
a full rose bed under-planted with
cranesbill. One wall is covered with
white roses, clematis and hydrangea.
There are shrubs and herbaceous
plants incl many astrantias and
hostas. Some narrow paths.
♿ ❀ ☕

21 **6 HOPE STREET**
Beeston, Nottingham, NG9 1DR.
Elaine Liquorish. *From M1 J25, A52
for Nottm. After 2 r'abouts, turn R for
Beeston at The Nurseryman (B6006).
Beyond hill, turn R into Bramcote Dr.
3rd turn on L into Bramcote Rd, then
immediately R into Hope St.* Sun 17
May (1.30-5.30). Adm £4, chd free.
Home-made teas.
A small garden packed with a wide
variety of plants providing flower
and foliage colour year round.
Collections of alpines, bulbs, mini,
small and medium size hostas (60+),
ferns, grasses, carnivorous plants,
succulents, perennials, shrubs and
trees. A pond and a greenhouse with
subtropical plants. Troughs and pots.
Home-made crafts. Shallow step into
garden, into greenhouse and at rear.
❀ ☕

22 **IVY BANK COTTAGE**
The Green, South Clifton, Newark,
NG23 7AG. David & Ruth Hollands.
*12m N of Newark. From S, exit A46
N of Newark onto A1133 towards
Gainsborough. From N, exit A57
at Newton-on-Trent onto A1133
towards Newark.* Sun 24 May (1-5).
Adm £3.50, chd free. Home-made
teas.
A traditional cottage garden, with
herbaceous borders, fruit trees incl a
Nottinghamshire Medlar, vegetable
plots and many surprises incl a
stumpery, a troughery, dinosaur
footprints and even fairies! Many
original features: pigsties, double privy
and a wash house. Children can search
for animal models and explore inside
the shepherd's van. Seats around and
a covered refreshment area.
❀ ☕

GROUP OPENING

23 NEW **KEYWORTH GARDENS**
Keyworth, Nottingham,
NG12 5AA. Graham & Pippa
Tinsley, 01159 377122,
Graham_Tinsley@yahoo.co.uk.
*Keyworth is a large village between
the A60 & A606 7m S of Nottingham.
Home Farm is near the church,
Rose Cottage about ½m down
Nottingham Rd & The Owls 1m
from both on Stanton Lane. Maps
available to visitors in each garden.*
Sun 7 June (12-5). Combined adm
£6, chd free. Home-made teas
at The Owls and Rose Cottage.
Visits also by arrangement May to
Aug for groups of 10 to 30.

HOME FARM HOUSE, 17 MAIN STREET, NG12 5AA
Graham & Pippa Tinsley, www.homefarmgarden.wordpress.com.

 THE OWLS, NG12 5BD
Anne & Dennis Jones.

ROSE COTTAGE, NG12 5GS
Richard & Julie Fowkes.

Home Farm: Large garden behind old farmhouse. Old orchard, flower and veg gardens, cart shed rebuilt as pergola. Unmown grass planted with perennials, ponds, turf mound, trees and high hedges. Hidden rose and winter gardens. Interesting and unusual perennials for sale by Piecemeal Plants (www.piecemealplants.co.uk). Listed barn open with local history display. Access via gravel yard, some steps and slopes. The Owls: A newly-designed garden with herbaceous borders and colourful mixed planting. Roses, clematis and salvias aiming for year round interest, and a pond and bog garden near the greenhouse. Vegetable plot using raised beds. Two ancient apple trees and productive fig tree from the original garden. Rose Cottage: Small cottage garden informally planted, full of bee-friendly plants. Sedum roof, mosaic and water features add interest. Decked seating area and summerhouse. A wildlife stream meanders down between two ponds and bog gardens. A woodland area leads to fruit, flowers and a herb spiral. Art studio. Paintings and art cards designed by Julie will be on sale at Rose Cottage. Some steps and narrow paths. Disabled parking on the drive at The Owls.

24 LODGE MOUNT
Town Street, South Leverton, Retford, DN22 0BT. Mr A Wootton-Jones, 07730004646, jane1.windsor@gmail.com. *4m E of Retford. Opp Miles Garage on Town Street.* Sun 28 June (12-5). Adm £4, chd free. Light refreshments. Visits also by arrangement June to Aug for groups of 10 to 30.
Lodge Mount Garden is the vision founded and established by Helen just before she died of cancer in 2012. The garden has been open to the public ever since her death. Helen's original plans can be seen through the flourishing growth and development of her plants and trees which now grow strong displaying the vibrant colours which she hoped they

would. Access is via a long sloping driveway. There is one step into the main garden which is flat.

25 38 MAIN STREET
Woodborough, Nottingham, NG14 6EA. Martin Taylor & Deborah Bliss, 07999786097. *Turn off Mapperley Plains Rd at sign for Woodborough. Alternatively, follow signs to Woodborough off A6097 (Epperstone bypass). Property is between Park Av & Bank Hill.* Visits by arrangement May to Aug for groups of up to 10. Adm by donation. Refreshments by arrangement.
Varied 1/3 acre. Bamboo fenced Asian species area with traditional outdoor wood fired Ofuro bath, herbaceous border, raised rhododendron bed, vegetables, greenhouse, pond area and art studio and terrace.

26 THE MANOR
Church Street, East Markham, Newark, NG22 0SA. Ms Christine Aldred. *7m S of Retford. Take A1 Markham Moor r'about exit for A57 Lincoln. Turn at East Markham junction & follow signs for the church. Properties adjacent to the church.* Sun 5 July (1-5). Combined adm with Norwood Cottage £4, chd free. Home-made teas.
An extensive colour themed garden on different levels including a sunken garden and pond surrounded by glorious agapanthus and lavender. Varied levels. Gravel paths.

27 MANOR FARM
Moor Lane, East Stoke, Newark, NG23 5QD. Mr & Mrs Pam and Greg Stevens. *Travelling towards Newark on the A46 exit at East Stoke/Elston slip road follow signs to East Stoke. Travelling towards Nottingham on the A46, exit at Farndon r'about towards East Stoke.* Sun 19 July (1-6). Adm £4, chd free. Home-made teas.
Stunning 1/2 acre country garden planted for colour and perfume - food for the soul. Begun in 2015 still evolving with new secret garden to compliment the packed borders and shrubberies, gravel garden, rose pergola, box parterre and mature trees. Level site. Paved paths throughout the garden.

28 MEADOW FARM
Broadings Lane, Laneham, Retford, DN22 0NF. Maureen Hayward. *10m E of Retford. From A1, take A57 towards Lincoln 5m, L towards Laneham. Village of Laneham, from Main St, L onto Broading Lane, 2nd on R, parking available past gateway.* Sun 19 July (11-4.30). Adm £4, chd free. Home-made teas.
A 1 acre garden that takes you through a hosta garden into a jungle with bananas, tree ferns, cannas. Winding path takes you to a parterre with topiary and sequoiadendron giganteum pendula trees and water features. Also incl a woodland walk, sculptures, wisteria circular walkway, seating throughout, multiple areas of herbaceous planting and unusual specimen trees and plants with Arctic Cabin.

29 NORMANTON HALL
South Street, Normanton-on-Trent, NG23 6RQ. His Honour John & Mrs Machin, 01636822780. *3m SE of Tuxford. Leave A1 at Sutton Carlton/Normanton-on-Trent junction. Turn L onto B1164 in Carlton. In Sutton-on-Trent turn R at Normanton sign. Go through Grassthorpe, turn L at Normanton sign.* Sun 26 Apr, Sun 7 June (2-6). Adm £5, chd free. Home-made teas. Visits also by arrangement.
3 acres with mature oak, lime beech and yew and recently planted trees. Vegetable area. New plantings of bulbs, rhododendrons and a camellia walk. Arboretum planted with unusual, mainly hardwood trees which are between three and twelve years old. Also specimen oaks and beech. New planting of wood anemones. Recently established parkland. All surfaces level from car park.

Your visits help change lives – since 1927, we've donated over £60 million to nursing and caring charities

GROUP OPENING

30 NORWELL GARDENS
Newark, NG23 6JX. *6m N of Newark. Halfway between Newark & Southwell. Off A1 at Cromwell turning, take Norwell Rd at bus shelter. Or off A616 take Caunton turn.* Sun 28 June (1-5). Evening opening Wed 1 July (6.30-9). Combined adm £5, chd free. Home-made teas in Village Hall (28 June) and Norwell Nurseries (1 July).

BRICKYARD COTTAGE
Bernadette McBreen.

FAUNA FOLLIES
Lorraine and Roy Pilgrim.

JUXTA MILL
Janet McFerran.

NORWELL ALLOTMENTS / PARISH GARDENS
Norwell Parish Council.

◆ NORWELL NURSERIES
Andrew & Helen Ward.
(See separate entry)

NEW ROSE COTTAGE
Mr & Mrs Iain and Ann Gibson.

SOUTHVIEW COTTAGE
Margaret & Les Corbett.

This is the 24th yr that Norwell has opened a range of different, very appealing gardens all making superb use of the beautiful backdrop of a quintessentially English countryside village. It incl a garden and nursery of national renown and the rare opportunity to walk around vibrant allotments with a wealth of gardeners from seasoned competition growers to plots that are substitute house gardens, bursting with both flower colour and vegetables in great variety. To top it all there are a plethora of breathtaking village gardens showing the diversity that is achieved under the umbrella of a cottage garden description! The beautiful medieval church and its peaceful churchyard with grass labyrinth will be open for quiet contemplation.

 ♿ ✿ 🚌 ☕

31 ◆ NORWELL NURSERIES
Woodhouse Road, Norwell, NG23 6JX. Andrew & Helen Ward, 01636 636337, wardha@aol.com, www.norwellnurseries.co.uk. *6m N of Newark halfway between Newark & Southwell. Off A1 at Cromwell turning, take rd to Norwell at bus stop. Or from A616 take Caunton turn.* For NGS: Sun 17 May, Sun 11 Oct (2-5). Adm £3.50, chd free.

Home-made teas in the Pavillion, Norwell Nurseries. Opening with Norwell Gardens on Sun 28 June, Wed 1 July. **For other opening times and information, please phone, email or visit garden website.**
Jewel box of over 2,500 different, beautiful and unusual plants sumptuously set out in a one acre plantsman's garden incl shady garden with orchids, woodland gems, cottage garden borders, alpine and scree areas. Pond with opulently planted margins. Extensive herbaceous borders and effervescent colour themed beds. Sand beds showcase Mediterranean, North American and alpine plants. Nationally renowned nursery open with over 1,000 different rare plants for sale. Autumn opening features UK's largest collection of hardy chrysanthemums for sale and the National Collection of Hardy Chrysanthemums. New borders incl the National Collection Of Astrantias. Grass paths, no wheelchair access to woodland paths.

 ♿ ✿ 🚌 NPC ☕

32 NORWOOD COTTAGE
Church Street, East Markham, Newark, NG22 0SA. Anne Beeby, 01777872799, anne.beeby@sky.com. *7m S of*

Hill Farm House

Retford. Take A1 Markham Moor r'about exit for A57 Lincoln. Turn at East Markham junction & follow signs for the church. Property adjacent the church. **Sun 5 July (1-5). Combined adm with The Manor £4, chd free. Home-made teas at The Manor. Visits also by arrangement May to Aug.**
Norwood Cottage is an outstanding example of a plantswoman's take on a cottage garden, combining plants to create a visual feast of texture, colour and form. Partial wheelchair access to parts of garden only. Steps leading to some areas.

33 NOTTINGHAMSHIRE HOSPICE
384 Woodborough Road, Nottingham, NG3 4JF. Nottinghamshire Hospice, www.nottshospice.org. *Located on the B684, Woodborough Rd, served by the bus route no. 45, Sky Blue Line, from the city centre towards Mapperley. No public parking allowed onsite, plenty of on-street parking.* **Sun 17 May (11-4). Adm £3, chd free. Light refreshments.**
Large enclosed area, with various protected trees, shrubs, planting, rockeries and lawn. Within our garden there is a beautiful pond and water feature. There are raised beds, greenhouse and a terraced area. Some sloping areas, with steps. The garden is designed to be a relaxing space and give therapeutic benefit to hospice patients. You are very welcome to bring your own picnic to enjoy.

34 OAK BARN EXOTIC GARDEN
Oak Barn Church Street, East Markham, Newark, NG22 0SA. Simon Bennett & Laura Holmes, www.facebook.com/OakBarn1. *From A1 Markham Moor junction take A57 to Lincoln. Turn R at Xrds into E Markham. L onto High St & R onto Plantation Rd. Enter farm gates at T-Junction, garden located on L.* **Evening opening Sat 8 Aug (5-9). Wine. Sun 20 Sept (1-5). Home-made teas. Adm £3.50, chd free.**
On entering the oak lych-style gate you will be met with the unexpected dense canopy of greenery and tropical foliage. The gravel paths wind under towering palms and bananas which are underplanted with cannas and gingers. On the lowest levels houseplants are bedded out from the large greenhouse to join the summer displays. They surround the Jungle Hut which is used for dining and socialising. Private visits and plant sales by arrangement.

35 NEW OASIS COMMUNITY GARDENS
2a Longfellow Drive, Kilton Estate, Worksop, S81 0DE. Steve Williams, 07795 194957, Stevemark126@hotmail.com, www.oasis-centre.org.uk. *From Kilton Hill (leading to the Worksop hospital), take 1st exit to R (up hill) onto Kilton Cres, Then first exit on right Longfellow Dr. Car Park off Dickens Rd (1st R).* **Sat 4 Apr, Sat 27 June, Sat 29 Aug (10-4). Adm £3, chd free. Cream teas in Oasis Community Centre - 'Food for Life'. Meals can be arranged for group bookings by arrangement. Visits also by arrangement Mar to Oct. We cater for groups, parties and events and corporate groups.**
Oasis Gardens is a community project transformed from abandoned field to an award winning garden. Managed by volunteers the gardens boast over 30 project areas, several garden enterprises and hosts many community events. Take a look in the Cactus Kingdom, the Children's pre-school play village, Wildlife Wonderland or check out a wonderful variety of trees, plants, seasonal flowers and shrubs. The Oasis Gardens hosts the first Liquorice Garden in Worksop for 100 years. The site hosts the 'Flowers for Life' project which is a therapeutic gardening project growing and selling cut flowers and floristry. There is disabled access from Longfellow Drive. From the town end there is a driveway after the first fence on the right next to house number 2.

36 THE OLD VICARAGE
Halam Hill, Halam, NG22 8AX. Mrs Beverley Perks, 01636 812181, perks.family@talk21.com. *1m W of Southwell. Please park diagonally into beech hedge on verge with speed interactive sign or in village - a busy road so no parking on roadside.* **Sat 20 June, Sun 26 July (12-4); Sun 9 Aug (1-5). Adm £4, chd free. Home-made teas. Opening with Halam Gardens and Wildflower Meadow on Mon 25 May (1-5). Visits also by arrangement July & Aug for groups of 10+.**

Likely penultimate garden opening - new build at bottom with new garden - fenced areas.
Single handed labour of love has grown out of 2 acre hillside pony paddocks into much admired landscape gardens. One-time playground for children, a source of shared pleasure for village openings and 18 happy years for NGS. An artful eye for design/texture/colour/ love of unusual plants/trees makes this a welcoming gem to visit/share (see extended website description). Beautiful C12 Church open only a short walk into the village or across field through attractively planted churchyard - rare C14 stained glass window. Gravel drive - undulating levels as on a hillside - plenty of cheerful help available.

37 OSSINGTON HOUSE
Moorhouse Road, Ossington, Newark, NG23 6LD. Georgina Denison. *10m N of Newark, 2m off A1. From A1 N take exit marked Carlton, Sutton-on-Trent, Weston etc. At T-junction turn L to Kneesall. Drive 2m to Ossington. In village turn R to Moorhouse & park in field next to Hopbine Farmhouse.* **Sun 21 June (2-5). Combined adm with Hopbine Farmhouse, Ossington £5, chd free. Home-made teas in The Hut, Ossington.**
Vicarage garden redesigned in 1960 and again in 2014. Chestnuts, lawns, formal beds, woodland walk, poolside planting, orchard. Terraces, yews, grasses. Ferns, herbaceous perennials, roses and a new kitchen garden. Disabled parking available in drive to Ossington House.

38 PAPPLEWICK HALL
Hall Lane, Papplewick, Nottinghamshire, NG15 8FE. Mr & Mrs J R Godwin-Austen, www.papplewickhall.co.uk. *7m N of Nottingham. 300yds out N end of Papplewick village, on B683 (follow signs to Papplewick from A60 & B6011). Free parking at Hall.* **Sun 24 May (2-5). Adm £4, chd free. Donation to St James' Church.**
This historic, mature, 8 acre garden, mostly shaded woodland, abounds with rhododendrons, hostas, ferns, and spring bulbs. Suitable for wheelchair users, but sections of the paths are gravel.

39 PARK FARM

Crink Lane, Southwell, NG25 0TJ. Ian & Vanessa Johnston, 01636 812195, v.johnston100@gmail.com. *1m SE of Southwell. From Southwell town centre go down Church St, turn R on Fiskerton Rd & 200yds up hill turn R into Crink Lane. Park Farm is on 2nd bend.* **Sun 26 July (2-5.30). Adm £4, chd free. Home-made teas. Visits also by arrangement Apr to Aug for groups of 5+. Guided tours offered for groups of 10 or more, at 50p per person extra.**

3 acre garden remarkable for its extensive variety of trees, shrubs and perennials, many rare or unusual. Long colourful herbaceous borders, roses, woodland garden, alpine/scree garden and a large wildlife pond. New for 2020- developing area for acid loving plants, plus additional woodland planting and paths. Spectacular views of the Minster across a wildflower meadow and ha-ha.

40 PATCHINGS ART CENTRE

Oxton Road, Calverton, Nottingham, NG14 6NU. Chas & Pat Wood, www.patchingsartcentre.co.uk. *N of Nottingham city take A614 towards Ollerton. Turn R on to B6386 towards Calverton & Oxton. Patchings is on L before turning to Calverton. Brown tourist directional signs.* **Sun 24 May (10.30-3.30). Adm £3, chd free. Light refreshments at Patchings Cafe.**

Patchings Art Centre celebrated 30 years last year, when we opened new areas and walks in celebration. 50 acres to incl wild flowers, woodland and meadow landscapes. The aim is to inspire and encourage artists to paint in the open, whilst providing enjoyment and tranquillity for visitors. Four exhibition galleries featuring paintings, photography, jewellery, ceramics and glass. Card gallery, gift shop and art materials. Studio artists in residence. New for 2020 Patchings Artists Trail - a unique walk through art history and meeting well known artists from the past. Grass paths, with some undulations and uphill sections accessible to wheelchairs with help. Please enquire for assistance.

41 PIECEMEAL

123 Main Street, Sutton Bonington, Loughborough, LE12 5PE. Mary Thomas, 01509 672056, nursery@piecemealplants.co.uk. *2m SE of Kegworth (M1 J24). 6m NW of Loughborough. Almost opp St Michael's Church the N end of the village.* **Sat 13, Sun 14 June (2-6). Combined adm with Forge Cottage £5, chd free. Mon 31 Aug (2-6). Adm £4, chd free. Visits also by arrangement June to Sept for groups of 5 to 10. For 10+ please contact to discuss.**

Tucked behind early 19th century cottages, a tiny, sheltered walled garden featuring a wide range of unusual shrubs, many flowering and most displayed in around 400 terracotta pots bordering paths. Also climbers, perennials and even a few trees! Focus is on distinctive form, foliage shape and colour combination. Collection of ferns around well. Half-hardy and tender plants fill the conservatory. Plant list available on request.

42 RHUBARB FARM

Hardwick Street, Langwith, Near Mansfield, NG20 9DR. Rhubarb Farm, enquiries@rhubarbfarm.co.uk, , www.rhubarbfarm.co.uk. *On NW border of Nottinghamshire in village of Nether Langwith. From A632 in Langwith, by bridge (single file traffic) turn up steep Devonshire Drive. N.B. Turn off SatNav. Take 2nd L into Hardwick St. Rhubarb Farm at end. Parking to R of gates.* **Wed 1 July (10.30-4). Adm £2.50, chd free. Cream teas made by Rhubarb Farm volunteers available in our on-site cafe. Visits also by arrangement Apr to Nov for groups of 10 to 30.**

52 varieties of fruit and vegetables organically grown not only for sale but for therapeutic benefit. This 2 acre social enterprise provides training and volunteering opportunities to 90 ex offenders, drug and alcohol misusers, and people with mental and physical ill health and learning disability. Optional timed tours at 11am and 2pm. 3x65ft polytunnels, forest school barn, willow dome & arch, 100 hens, flower borders, charity shop, raised beds, comfrey bed and comfrey fertiliser factory, composting toilets. Chance to meet and chat with volunteers with a variety of needs,

who come to gain skills, confidence and training. Main path suitable for wheelchairs but bumpy. Not all site accessible. Cafe & composting toilet wheelchair-accessible. Mobility scooter available.

43 RISEHOLME, 125 SHELFORD ROAD

Radcliffe on Trent, NG12 1AZ. John & Elaine Walker, 01159 119867. *4m E of Nottingham. From A52 follow signs to Radcliffe. In village centre take turning for Shelford (by Co-op). Approx ¾ m on L.* **Sun 20 Sept (1.30-5). Adm £4, chd free. Home-made teas. Visits also by arrangement June to Sept for groups of 20+.**

Imaginative and inspirational is how the garden has been described by visitors. A huge variety of perennials, grasses, shrubs and trees combined with an eye for colour and design. Jungle area with exotic lush planting contrasts with tender perennials particularly salvias thriving in raised beds and in gravel garden with stream. Unique and interesting objects complement planting. Gravel drive and paths.

44 SPRING BANK HOUSE

84 Kirkby Road, Sutton-in-Ashfield, NG17 1GH. Mr Peter Robinson. *From Mansfield take A38 to Sutton-in-Ashfield. Turn R on to Station Rd, turn L on to High Pavement and continue on to Kirkby Rd.* **Sun 5 July, Sun 6 Sept (12-5). Combined adm with East Meets West £4, chd free. Home-made teas.**

Mediterranean planting, a bog garden, a summerhouse and a white garden, a water table from India and lion statues from Nepal, this garden offers much variety. Dug from wasteland in 2012 its clear design displays hundreds of rare plants. Two terraces punctuate its slope and a woodland area with hardy exotics and a wildlife pond offer cobbled paths and mown grass for a choice of garden circuits. Coaches may be possible but will need to park elsewhere.

45 THRUMPTON HALL

Thrumpton, NG11 0AX. Miranda Seymour, www.thrumptonhall.com. *7m S of Nottingham. M1 J24 take A453 towards Nottingham. Turn L to Thrumpton village & cont to*

Thrumpton Hall. **Sun 28 June (1.30-4.30). Adm £5, chd free. Home-made teas.**
2 acres incl. lawns, rare trees, lakeside walks, flower borders, rose garden, new pagoda, and box-bordered sunken herb garden, all enclosed by C18 ha-ha and encircling a Jacobean house. Garden is surrounded by C18 landscaped park and is bordered by a river. Rare opportunity to visit Thrumpton Hall (separate ticket). Jacobean mansion, unique carved staircase, Great Saloon, State Bedroom, Priest's Hole.

46 UNIVERSITY PARK GARDENS

Nottingham, NG7 2RD. University of Nottingham, www.nottingham. ac.uk/estates/grounds/. *Approx 4m SW of Nottingham city centre & opp Queens Medical Centre. NGS visitors: Please purchase admission tickets in the Millennium Garden (in centre of campus), signed from N & W entrances to University Park & within internal road network.*
Sun 16 Aug (12-4). Adm £4, chd free. Light refreshments at The Hemsley near Millennium Garden and Lakeside Arts Centre.
University Park has many beautiful gardens incl the award-winning Millennium garden with its dazzling flower garden, timed fountains and turf maze. Also the huge Lenton Firs rock garden, the dry garden and the Jekyll garden. During summer, the Walled Garden is alive with exotic plantings. In total, 300 acres of landscape and gardens. Picnic area, cafe, walking tours, information desk, workshop, accessible minibus to feature gardens within campus. Plants for sale in Millennium garden. Some gravel paths and steep slopes.

47 UPPER GROVE FARM

Norwell Woodhouse, Newark, NG23 6NG. Kathryn Wiltshire. *A616 either from Newark (10m) or Ollerton (7m) at Xroads turn to Laxton R to Norwell 1st white farmhouse on L, look out for the big chimney pots!* **Sun 17 May (1-4). Combined adm with Bridge Farm £4, chd free.**
We are a country garden around a farmhouse. We have a small orchard and informal beds of spring/summer flowers. Most of garden accessible to wheelchairs, some gravel paths.

48 NEW WESTMOOR HOUSE

West Moor Road, Walkeringham, Doncaster, DN10 4LR. Frances Loates. *Between Bawtry & Gainsborough. At Beckingham take A161N to Walkeringham. L on Sidsaph Hill/High St, then L on West Moor Rd. From Epworth take A161S to Walkeringham. R on Sidsaph Hill/* *High St, then L on West Moor Rd.* **Mon 25 May (1-5). Adm £2, chd free. Light refreshments. Also open Holmes Villa.**
Welcome to our garden, a view from every aspect. A small garden, full of colour and interesting plants. Mature fruit and blossom trees in Spring. Bog and pond area and an aviary with a variety of beautiful birds.

49 6 WESTON CLOSE

Woodthorpe, Nottingham, NG5 4FS. Diane & Steve Harrington, 0115 9857506, mrsdiharrington@gmail.com. *3m N of Nottingham. A60 Mansfield Rd. Turn R at T-lights into Woodthorpe Drive. 2nd L Grange Road. R into The Crescent. R into Weston Close. Please park on The Crescent.* **Visits by arrangement June to Aug for groups of 10 to 30. Minimum group charge £60. Adm £6, chd free. Home-made teas.**
Set on a substantial slope with 3 separate areas surrounding the house. Dense planting creates a full, varied yet relaxed display incl many scented roses, clematis and a collection of over 80 named mature hostas in the impressive colourful rear garden. Walls covered by many climbers. Home propagated plants for sale.

The Manor

OXFORDSHIRE

In Oxfordshire we tend to think of ourselves as one of the most landlocked counties, right in the centre of England and furthest from the sea.

We are surrounded by Warwickshire, Northamptonshire, Buckinghamshire, Berkshire, Wiltshire and Gloucestershire, and, like these counties, we benefit from that perfect British climate which helps us create some of the most beautiful and famous gardens in the world.

Many gardens open in Oxfordshire for the National Garden Scheme between spring and late-autumn. Amongst these are the perfectly groomed college gardens of Oxford University, and the grounds of stately homes and palaces designed by a variety of the famous garden designers such as William Kent, Capability Brown, Rosemary Verey, Tom Stuart-Smith and the Bannermans of more recent fame.

But we are also a popular tourist destination for our honey-coloured mellow Cotswold stone villages, and for the Thames which has its spring near Lechlade. More villages open as 'groups' for the National Garden Scheme in Oxfordshire than in any other county, and offer tea, hospitality, advice and delight with their infinite variety of gardens.

All this enjoyment benefits the excellent causes that the National Garden Scheme supports.

Volunteers

County Organiser
Marina Hamilton-Baillie
01367 710486
marina_hamilton_baillie@hotmail. com

County Treasurer
David White 01295 812679
davidwhite679@btinternet.com

Publicity
Priscilla Frost 01608 811818
info@oxconf.co.uk

Social Media
Lara Cowan
laracowan@icloud.com

Petra Hoyer Millar
petra.hoyermillar@ngs.org.uk

Photographer
Alexandra Davies 07833 461120
alex@alexandrajane.co.uk

Booklet Co-ordinator
Petra Hoyer Millar (as above)

Assistant County Organisers
Lynn Baldwin 01608 642754
elynnbaldwin@gmail.com

Ann Conibear 01865 373494
annconibear494@gmail.com

Lara Cowan (as above)

Dr David & Dr Jill Edwards
07973 129473
drdavidedwards@hotmail.co.uk

Petra Hoyer Millar (as above)

Juliet & Rory Roper-Caldbeck
01608 677866
julietropercaldbeck@hotmail.com

Lyn Sanders
01865 739486
sandersc4@hotmail.com

@NGSOxfordshire

@ngs_oxfordshire

@ngs_oxfordshire

Left: Oak Grove

OPENING DATES

All entries subject to change. For latest information check **www.ngs.org.uk**

Map locator numbers are shown to the right of each garden name.

February

Snowdrop Festival

Sunday 16th

Hollyhocks	37
Monks Head	53
Stonehaven	70

March

Sunday 15th

◆ Waterperry Gardens	74

Sunday 29th

NEW 38 Leckford Road	44

April

Sunday 5th

Ashbrook House	2
Buckland Lakes	14
Wadham College	73

Monday 13th

Kencot Gardens	41
Lime Close	45

Saturday 18th

50 Plantation Road	61

Sunday 19th

Magdalen College	46
50 Plantation Road	61

Saturday 25th

50 Plantation Road	61

Sunday 26th

◆ Broughton Grange	12
The Old Vicarage, Bledington	57
50 Plantation Road	61

May

Sunday 3rd

Old Boars Hill Gardens	56

Wednesday 13th

Kingham Lodge	42

Sunday 17th

The Grove	34
Headington Gardens	35
NEW 38 Leckford Road	44

Sunday 24th

Barton Abbey	5

Monday 25th

Friars Court	28
Meadow Cottage	48

Saturday 30th

NEW Oak Grove	54

Sunday 31st

Broughton Poggs & Filkins Gardens	13
Failford	25
The Grange, Islip	30
Hollyhocks	37
NEW Oak Grove	54
116 Oxford Road	60
Westwell Manor	76

June

Tuesday 2nd

NEW ◆ Stonor Park	71

Wednesday 3rd

Yarnton Manor	80

Saturday 6th

NEW Black Knap House	6
Chivel Farm	16

Sunday 7th

Brize Norton Gardens	9
Cumnor Village Gardens	20
Iffley Gardens	40
The Priory Garden	62
Steeple Aston Gardens	69
Whitehill Farm	78

Saturday 13th

◆ Blenheim Palace	7

Sunday 14th

Langford Gardens	43
The Old Vicarage, Bledington	57

Wednesday 17th

NEW Claridges Barn	18
Midsummer House	51

Thursday 18th

Wootton Gardens	79

Sunday 21st

Bolters Farm	8
◆ Broughton Castle	11
◆ Broughton Grange	12
NEW Claridges Barn	18
NEW 10 Eynsham Road	24
Green and Gorgeous	31
86 Hurst Rise Road	39
Wheatley Gardens	77

Thursday 25th

Rofford Manor	64

Saturday 27th

NEW Oak Grove	54

Sunday 28th

Chalkhouse Green Farm	15
Corpus Christi College	19
NEW Greyhound House	33
NEW Oak Grove	54
NEW Rousham Garden	65
Sibford Gardens	66

July

Sunday 5th

Dorchester Gardens	23
The Filberts	26
Middleton Cheney Gardens	50
Orchard House	59
NEW South Hayes	67
Wadham College	73

Sunday 26th

◆ Broughton Grange	12
Merton College Oxford Fellows' Garden	49

August

Saturday 8th

16 Oakfield Road	55

Sunday 9th

16 Oakfield Road	55

Saturday 22nd

Aston Pottery	3

Sunday 23rd

Aston Pottery	3
Manor House	47

Radcot House	63

Sunday 30th

Bolters Farm	8

September

Sunday 6th

Ashbrook House	2
113 Brize Norton Road	10
◆ Waterperry Gardens	74

Sunday 13th

◆ Broughton Grange	12

October

Sunday 4th

Radcot House	63

February 2021

Sunday 14th

Hollyhocks	37

By Arrangement

Arrange a personalised garden visit with your club, or group of friends, on a date to suit you. See individual garden entries for full details.

Appleton Dene	1
Ashbrook House	2
Bannisters	4
Bolters Farm	8
Carter's Yard, Sibford Gardens	66
Chivel Farm	16
Church Farm Field	17
103 Dene Road	21
Denton House	22
Failford	25
Foxington	27
The Grange	29
The Grange, Islip	30
Greenfield Farm	32
NEW Greyhound House	33
Holly Tree House	36
Hollyhocks	37
Home Close	38
NEW 38 Leckford Road	44
Manor House	47

THE GARDENS

❶ APPLETON DENE

Yarnells Hill, Botley, Oxford, OX2 9BG. Mr & Mrs A Dawson, 07701 000977, annrobe@aol.com. *3m W of Oxford. Take W road out of Oxford, through Botley Rd, pass under A34, turn L into Westminster Way, Yarnells Hill 2nd on R, park at top of hill. Walk 200 metres. Disabled parking at the house.* **Visits by arrangement June to Sept for groups of 5 to 30. No parking for coaches. Adm £4, chd free. Home-made teas. Wine.**
Beautiful secluded garden set in a hidden valley. The ¼ acre garden on a steeply sloping site surrounds a mature tulip tree. There is a skillfully incorporated level lawn area overlooked by deep colour themed borders incl a wide variety of plants for long seasonal interest. Not suitable for wheelchairs as there is a steep slope and steps.

❷ ASHBROOK HOUSE

Blewbury, OX11 9QA. Mr & Mrs S A Barrett, 01235 850810, janembarrett@me.com. *4m SE of Didcot. Turn off A417 in Blewbury into Westbrook St. 1st house on R. Follow yellow signs for parking in Boham's Rd.* **Sun 5 Apr, Sun 6 Sept (2-5.30). Adm £5, chd free. Home-made teas. Visits also by arrangement Apr to Sept for groups of up to 20.**
The garden where Kenneth Grahame read Wind in the Willows to local children and where he took inspiration for his description of the oak doors to Badger's House. Come and see, you may catch a glimpse of Toad and friends in this 3½ acre chalk and water garden, in a beautiful spring line village. In spring the banks are a mass of daffodils and in late summer the borders are full of unusual plants.

❸ ASTON POTTERY

Aston, Bampton, OX18 2BT. Mr Stephen Baughan, www.astonpottery.co.uk. *4m S of Witney. On the B4449 between Bampton & Standlake.* **Sat 22 Aug, Sun 23 Aug (12-5). Adm £5, chd free. Light refreshments in the café on 23 Aug only.**
5 stunning borders set around Aston Pottery. Featuring a 72 metre double hornbeam border full of riotous perennials. An 80 metre long hot bank, a double dahlia border with over 300 dahlias, and 90 metre of over 120 different annuals planted in four giant successive waves of over 5000 plants.

❹ BANNISTERS

Middle Street, Islip, Kidlington, OX5 2SF. Wendy Price, 01865 375418. *2m E of Kidlington & approx 5m N of Oxford. From A34, exit Bletchingdon & Islip. B4027 direction Islip, turn L into Middle St, beside Great Barn.* **Visits by**
arrangement July & Aug for groups of up to 20. Light refreshments.
A hidden garden of perennials and grasses, naturalistic planting contrasted with trained fruit trees and shrubs. A contemporary interpretation of an old garden. Access over gravel paths and some shallow steps.

❺ BARTON ABBEY

Steeple Barton, OX25 4QS. Mr & Mrs P Fleming. *8m E of Chipping Norton. On B4030, ½ m from junction of A4260 & B4030.* **Sun 24 May (2-5). Adm £5, chd free. Home-made teas.**
15 acre garden with views from house (not open) across sweeping lawns and picturesque lake. Walled garden with colourful herbaceous borders, separated by established yew hedges and espalier fruit, contrasts with more informal woodland garden paths with vistas of specimen trees and meadows. Working glasshouses and fine display of fruit and vegetables.

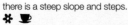

Rofford Manor

© Andrew Lawson

NEW **BLACK KNAP HOUSE**
Priory Road, Heythrop, Chipping Norton, OX7 5TP. Mr Karl Devine. *Follow signs for Heythrop from the A44. We are 1m down the lane on the RH-side. Parking at Black Knap House & Chivel Farm. Please Note: gardens are not in walking distance.* **Sat 6 June (2-5.30). Combined adm with Chivel Farm £10, chd free. Light refreshments.**
A relatively new garden, commenced in 2010, on the site of an ancient quarry. When the garden began, it was no more than a collection of falling down kennels, barns and rough woodland sat on very uneven ground formed of spoil heaps from old stone excavations. The garden now comprises a walled kitchen garden, extensive prairie garden and formal lawn with rill.

7 ◆ **BLENHEIM PALACE**
Woodstock, OX20 1PX. His Grace the Duke of Marlborough, 01993 810530, customerservice@blenheimpalace.com, www.blenheimpalace.com. *8m N of Oxford. The S3 bus runs every 30 mins from Oxford train station & Oxford's Gloucester Green bus station to Blenheim. Oxford Bus Company's 500 leaves from Oxford Parkway & stops at Blenheim.* **For NGS: Sat 13 June (10-6). Adm £5, chd £2. For other opening times and information, please phone, email or visit garden website.**
Blenheim Gardens, originally laid out by Henry Wise, incl the formal Water Terraces and Italian Garden by Achille Duchêne, Rose Garden, Arboretum, and Cascade. The Secret Garden offers a stunning garden paradise in all seasons. Blenheim Lake, created by Capability Brown and spanned by Vanburgh's Grand Bridge, is the focal point of over 2,000 acres of landscaped parkland. The Pleasure Gardens complex incl the Herb and Lavender Garden and Butterfly House. Other activities incl the Marlborough Maze, adventure play area, giant chess and draughts. Wheelchair access with some gravel paths, uneven terrain in places, incl some steep slopes. Dogs allowed in park only.

8 **BOLTERS FARM**
Chilson, Pudlicote Lane, Chipping Norton, OX7 3HU. Robert & Amanda Cooper, art@amandacooper.co.uk. *Centre of Chilson village. On arrival in the hamlet of Chilson, heading N, we are the last in an old row of cottages on R. Please drive past & park considerately on the L in the lane.* **Sun 21 June, Sun 30 Aug (2.30-5.30). Adm £5, chd free. Tea with gluten free options. Visits also by arrangement May to Sept for groups of 5 to 20. No visits in August. Donation to Hands Up Foundation.**
A cherished old cottage garden restored over the last 12 yrs. Tumbly moss covered walls and sloping lawns down to a stream with natural planting and character. Wheelchairs have to negotiate sloping deep gravel and numerous steps.

GROUP OPENING

9 **BRIZE NORTON GARDENS**
Brize Norton, OX18 3LY. www.bncommunity.org/ngs. *3m SW of Witney. Brize Norton Village, S of A40, between Witney & Burford. Parking at Elderbank Hall & Mason Arms in Burford Rd. Coaches welcome with plenty of parking nearby.* **Sun 7 June (1-6).**

Combined adm £5, chd free. Home-made teas at Elderbank Village Hall & Grange Farm.

BARNSTABLE HOUSE
Mr & Mrs P Butcher, www.ourgarden.org.uk.

THE CHAPEL
Chris & Jayne Woodward.

CHURCH FARM HOUSE
Philip & Mary Holmes.

GRANGE FARM
Mark & Lucy Artus.

MIJESHE
Mr & Mrs M Harper.

MILLSTONE
Bev & Phil Tyrell.

PAINSWICK HOUSE
Mr & Mrs T Gush.

RAMSHEAD COTTAGE
Ann Elsmore.

ROOKERY FARM
Ian & Fiona Roberts.

ROSE COTTAGE
Brenda & Brian Trott.

95 STATION ROAD
Mr & Mrs P A Timms.

STONE COTTAGE
Mr & Mrs K Humphris.

Doomsday village on the edge of the Cotswold's offering a number of gardens open for your enjoyment. You can see a wide variety of planting

Claridges Barn

incl ornamental trees and grasses, herbaceous borders, traditional fruit and vegetable gardens. Features incl a Mediterranean style patio, courtyard garden, terraced roof garden, water features; plus gardens where you can just sit, relax and enjoy the day. Tickets and maps available at Elderbank Village Hall and at each garden. Plants for sale at individual gardens. A Flower Festival will take place in the Brize Norton St Britius Church. Partial wheelchair access to some gardens.

10 113 BRIZE NORTON ROAD

Minster Lovell, Witney, OX29 0SQ. **David & Lynn Rogers.** *Approx 2½m W of Witney. On main village road (B4447), ½m N of A40 Witney Bypass intersection on the R.* **Sun 6 Sept (2-5). Adm £3, chd free. Home-made teas.**
Mixed variety garden of over 1 acre including quirky features for added interest. Lawns, meadow grass area, small woodland, native mixed hedging, wildlife pond, fish pond, huge mix of plants and trees with emphasis on yr-round colour. The whole garden has been developed with wildlife in mind.

11 ◆ BROUGHTON CASTLE

Banbury, OX15 5EB. **Martin Fiennes, 01295 276070, info@broughtoncastle.com, www.broughtoncastle.com.** *2½m SW of Banbury. On Shipston-on-Stour road (B4035).* **For NGS: Sun 21 June (2-5). Adm £10, chd free. Cream teas. For other opening times and information, please phone, email or visit garden website.**
1 acre; shrubs, herbaceous borders, walled garden, roses, climbers seen against background of C14-C16 castle surrounded by moat in open parkland. House also open (additional charge).

12 ◆ BROUGHTON GRANGE

Wykham Lane, Broughton, Banbury, OX15 5DS. **S Hester, www.broughtongrange.com.** *¼m out of village. From Banbury take B4035 to Broughton. Turn L at Saye & Sele Arms Pub up Wykham Lane (one way). Follow road out of village for ¼m. Entrance on R.* **For NGS:**

Sun 26 Apr, Sun 21 June, Sun 26 July, Sun 13 Sept (10-5). Adm £9, chd free. Cream teas. For other opening times and information, please visit garden website.
An impressive 25 acres of gardens and light woodland in an attractive Oxfordshire setting. The centrepiece is a large terraced walled garden created by Tom Stuart-Smith in 2001. Vision has been used to blend the gardens into the countryside. Good early displays of bulbs followed by outstanding herbaceous planting in summer. Formal and informal areas combine to make this a special site incl newly laid arboretum with many ongoing projects. Limited access, terraces are accessible from side doors. Garden is on a slope with steps and gravel paths.

GROUP OPENING

13 BROUGHTON POGGS & FILKINS GARDENS

Lechlade, GL7 3JH. **www.filkins.org.uk.** *3m N of Lechlade. 5m S of Burford. Just off A361 between Burford & Lechlade on the B4477. Map of the gardens available.* **Sun 31 May (2-6). Combined adm £6.50, chd free. Home-made teas in Filkins Village Hall.**

BROUGHTON POGGS MILL
Charlie & Avril Payne.

3 THE COACH HOUSE
Peter & Brenda Berners-Price.

THE CORN BARN
Ms Alexis Thompson.

FIELD HOUSE
Peter & Sheila Gray.

FILKINS ALLOTMENTS
Filkins Allotments.

FILKINS HALL
Filkins Hall Residents.

LITTLE PEACOCKS
Colvin & Moggridge.

MERCHANTS COTTAGE
Paul & Corina Floyd.

PEACOCK FARMHOUSE
Pauline & Peter Care.

PIGEON COTTAGE
Lynne Savege.

PIP COTTAGE
G B Woodin.

THE TALLOT
Ms M Swann & Mr Don Stowell.

TAYLOR COTTAGE
Mr & Mrs Ian & Ronnie Bailey.

WELL COTTAGE
Christiaan Richards & Michelle Woodworth.

WILLOW COTTAGE
Emma Sparks.

15 gardens and flourishing allotments in these beautiful and vibrant Cotswold stone twin villages. Scale and character vary from the grand landscape setting of Filkins Hall, to the small but action packed Pigeon Cottage, Taylor Cottage and The Tallot. Broughton Poggs Mill has a rushing mill stream with an exciting bridge; Pip Cottage combines topiary, box hedges and a fine rural view. In these and the other equally exciting and varied gardens horticultural interest abounds. Features incl plant stall by professional local nursery, Swinford Museum of Cotswolds tools and artefacts, and Cotswold Woollen Weavers. Many gardens have gravel driveways, but most are suitable for wheelchair access. Most gardens welcome dogs on leads.

14 BUCKLAND LAKES

Nr Faringdon, SN7 8QW. **The Wellesley Family.** *3m NE of Faringdon. Buckland is midway between Oxford (14m) & Swindon (15m), just off the A420. Faringdon 3m, Witney 8m. Follow the yellow NGS signs which will lead you to driveway & car park by St Mary's Church.* **Sun 5 Apr (2-5). Adm £5, chd free. Home-made teas at Memorial Hall. Donation to RWMT (community bus).**
Descend down wooded path to two large secluded lakes with views over undulating historic parkland, designed by Georgian landscape architect Richard Woods. Picturesque mid C18 rustic icehouse, cascade with iron footbridge, thatched boathouse and round house, and renovated exedra. Many fine mature trees, drifts of spring bulbs and daffodils amongst shrubs. Norman church adjoins. Cotswold village. Children must be supervised due to large expanse of unfenced open water.

15 CHALKHOUSE GREEN FARM
Chalkhouse Green, Kidmore End, Reading, RG4 9AL. Mr & Mrs J Hall, www.chgfarm.com. *2m N of Reading, 5m SW of Henley-on-Thames. Situated between A4074 & B481. From Kidmore End take Chalkhouse Green Rd. Follow NGS yellow signs.* **Sun 28 June (2-6). Adm £4, chd free. Home-made teas.**
1 acre garden and open traditional farmstead. Herbaceous borders, herb garden, shrubs, old fashioned roses, trees incl medlar, quince and mulberries, walled ornamental kitchen garden and cherry orchard. Rare breed farm animals incl British White cattle, Suffolk Punch horses, donkeys, pigs, geese, chickens, ducks and turkeys. Plant and jam stall, donkey and pony rides, swimming in covered pool, grass tennis court, trailer rides, farm trail, WWII bomb shelter, heavy horse and bee display and live music. Partial wheelchair access.

16 CHIVEL FARM
Heythrop, OX7 5TR. Mr & Mrs J D Sword, 01608 683227, rosalind.sword@btinternet.com. *4m E of Chipping Norton. Off A361 or A44. Parking at Chivel Farm & Black Knap House. Please Note: gardens are not in walking distance.* **Sat 6 June (2-5.30). Combined adm with Black Knap House £10, chd free. Light refreshments at Black Knap House. Visits also by arrangement.**
Beautifully designed country garden with extensive views, designed for continuous interest that is always evolving. Colour schemed borders with many unusual trees, shrubs and herbaceous plants. Small formal white garden and a conservatory.

17 CHURCH FARM FIELD
Church Lane, Epwell, Banbury, OX15 6LD. Mrs D V D Castle, 01295 788473. *7½ m W of Banbury on N side of Epwell village.* **Visits by arrangement Apr to Oct. Adm £2, chd free. Tea & cake.**
Woods, arboretum with wild flowers (planting started 1992), over 90 different trees and shrubs in 4½ acres. Paths cut through trees for access to various parts. Lawn tennis court and croquet lawns. Light refreshments (weather permitting).

18 NEW CLARIDGES BARN
Charlbury Road, Chipping Norton, OX7 5XG. Drs David & Jill Edwards. *3m SE of Chipping Norton. Take B4026 from Chipping Norton to Charlbury after 3m turn R to Dean, after 200 metres turn R up track.* **Wed 17, Sun 21 June (10-6). Adm £4, chd free. Home-made teas.**
3½ acres of family garden, wood and meadow hewn from a barleyfield on limestone brash. Situated on top of the Cotswolds, it is open to all weathers, but rewarding views and dog walking opportunities on hand. Large vegetable, fruit, cutting garden and 5 cedar greenhouses, all loved by rabbits, deer and squirrel. Herbaceous borders and woodland gardens with gravel and flagged paths, divided by stone walls. Claridges Barn dates back to the 1600s, the cottage 1860s, converted about 30 yrs ago. Mainly level site with flagstone and gravel paths, flat lawns and some uneven steps.

Your visits help change lives – we are Hospice UK's largest charitable funder donating more than £5.5 million to support hospices in local communities since 1996

19 CORPUS CHRISTI COLLEGE
Merton Street, Oxford, OX1 4JF. Domestic Bursar, www.ccc.ox.ac.uk. *Entrance from Merton St.* **Sun 28 June (6.30-10.30am). Adm £3, chd free. Tea in the Old Lodgings.**
As an experiment, after 27 yrs of NGS afternoon openings, we will open for the second year between 6.30am and 10.30am! Join us for tea and coffee in the Old Lodgings and enjoy our informal, and, I think, beautiful organic garden with the added bonus of great views from the old town wall, across Christ Church gardens, meadows and Cathedral. Wheelchair access with one slope in the garden.

GROUP OPENING

20 CUMNOR VILLAGE GARDENS
Leys Road, Cumnor, Oxford, OX2 9QF. *4m W of central Oxford. From A420, exit for Cumnor & follow B4017 into the village. Parking on road & side roads, behind PO, or behind village hall in Leys Rd. Additional parking in Bertie & Norreys Rd.* **Sun 7 June (2-6). Combined adm £5, chd free. Home-made teas in United Reformed Church Hall, Leys Road.**

36 BERTIE ROAD
Esther & Neil Whiting.

10 LEYS ROAD
Penny & Nick Bingham.

41 LEYS ROAD
Philip & Jennie Powell.

STONEHAVEN
Dr Dianne & Prof Keith Gull.
(See separate entry)

The four gardens feature a wide variety of plants, shrubs, trees, vegetables, fruit and wild flowers. Two of the gardens are cottage style with unusual perennials and many shrubs and trees; one is professionally designed with three structured rooms and relaxed planting; another has a Japanese influence exhibiting unusual plants many with black or bronze foliage and gravel areas. Wheelchair access to 36 Bertie Road and 41 Leys Road. WC facilities in United Reformed Church Hall.

21 103 DENE ROAD
Headington, Oxford, OX3 7EQ.
Mr & Mrs Steve & Mary
Woolliams, 01865 764153,
stevewoolliams@gmail.com. *S
Headington nr Nuffield. Dene Rd
accessed from The Slade from the N,
or from Hollow Way from the S. Both
access roads are B4495. Garden on
sharp bend.* **Visits by arrangement
for groups of up to 10. Adm £3.50,
chd free. Home-made teas.**
A surprising eco-friendly garden with
borrowed view over the Lye Valley
Nature Reserve. Lawns, a wildflower
meadow, pond and large kitchen
garden are incl in a suburban 60ft x
120ft sloping garden. Fruit trees, soft
fruit and mixed borders of shrubs,
hardy perennials, grasses and bulbs,
designed for seasonal colour. This
garden has been noted for its wealth
of wildlife incl a variety of birds,
butterflies and other insects, incl the
rare Brown Hairstreak butterfly, the
rare Currant Clearwing moth and the
Grizzled Skipper.

22 DENTON HOUSE
Denton, Oxford, OX44 9JF. Mr
& Mrs Luke, 01865 874440,
waveney@jandwluke.com. *In
a valley between Garsington &
Cuddesdon.* **Visits by arrangement
Mar to Oct. Home-made teas.**
Large walled garden surrounds a
Georgian mansion (not open) with
shaded areas, walks, topiary and
many interesting mature trees, large
lawns, herbaceous borders and
rose beds. The windows in the wall
were taken in 1864 from Brasenose
College Chapel and Library. Wild
garden and a further walled fruit
garden.

GROUP OPENING

23 DORCHESTER GARDENS
Dorchester-On-Thames,
Wallingford, OX10 7HZ. *Off A4074
or A415 signed to Dorchester.
Parking at Old Bridge Meadow,
at SE end of Dorchester Bridge.
Disabled parking at 26 Manor Farm*

*Road (OX10 7HZ). Tickets available
at each garden.* **Sun 5 July (2-5).
Combined adm £5, chd free. Last
orders for tea at 4.30pm.**

26 MANOR FARM ROAD
David & Judy Parker.
6 MONKS CLOSE
Leif & Petronella Rasmussen.
7 ROTTEN ROW
Michael & Veronica Evans.

Three contrasting gardens in a historic
village surrounding the medieval
Abbey and the scene of many
Midsomer Murders. 26 Manor Farm
Road (OX10 7HZ) was part of an old
larger garden and which now has a
formal lawn and planting, vegetable
garden and greenhouse. Children
should be accompanied. From the
yew hedge down towards the River
Thame, which often floods in winter,
is an apple orchard underplanted with
spring bulbs. 6 Monks Close (OX10
7JA) is idyllic and surprising. A small
spring-fed stream and sloping lawn
surrounded by naturalistic planting
runs down to a monastic fish pond.
Bridges over this deep pond lead to
the River Thame with steep banks;
children should be accompanied.
7 Rotten Row (OX10 7LJ) is
Dorchester's lawless garden, a
terrace with borders leads to a lovely
geometric garden supervised by a
statue of Hebe. Access is from the
allotments. Wheelchair access to 26
Manor Farm Road, partial access to
other gardens. No dogs, please.

24 NEW **10 EYNSHAM ROAD**
Botley, Oxford, OX2 9BP. Jon
Harker. *W side of Oxford. Take
Botley interchange off A34 from
N or S. Follow signs for Oxford &
then turn R at Botley T-lights opp
McDonalds & follow NGS signs.* **Sun
21 June (1-5). Combined adm
with 86 Hurst Rise Road £5, chd
free. Home-made teas.**
Over 15 yrs a New Zealand couple
have established this English style
garden with a nod to their native
land. Gardened organically, with over
100 roses, herbaceous borders, fruit
trees, NZ natives, wildlife pond and
bee hotel combine to create a tranquil
space full of colour. A white garden
and herbaceous border at front of
house were developed within last
couple of yrs.

Failford

25 FAILFORD

118 Oxford Road, Abingdon, OX14 2AG. Miss R Aylward, 01235 523925, aylwardsdooz@hotmail.co.uk. *118 is on the LH-side of Oxford Rd when coming from Abingdon Town, or on the RH-side when approaching from the N. Entrance to this garden is via 116 Oxford Rd.* **Sun 31 May (11-4). Combined adm with 116 Oxford Road £5, chd free. Home-made teas. Visits also by arrangement June to Sept for groups of up to 20.**

A town garden, an extension of the home with many rooms both formal and informal. Features incl walkways through shaded areas, arches, kitchen garden, grasses, roses, topiaries, acers, hostas and heucheras. A wide variety of planting with many quirky features, all within an area 570 sq ft. Partial wheelchair access due to gravel areas, narrow pathways and uneven surfaces.

26 THE FILBERTS

High Street, North Moreton, Didcot, OX11 9AT. Mr & Mrs Prescott. *About 2m from Didcot, signed from the 4130 Didcot-Wallingford road. The Filberts is near The Bear at Home pub, on the opp side of the High St. Parking is on The Croft (Recreation Ground) accessed via Bear Lane.* **Sun 5 July (2-5). Adm £5, chd free. Home-made teas in the village hall.**

1 acre garden used for teaching RHS courses demonstrating many different styles: formal colour themed garden with lily and fish ponds; island beds for old roses, grasses; large informal pond; colourful mixed borders; secluded Japanese area; over 100 varieties of clematis; formal parterre with roses; vegetable garden; fruit cage; orchard. Access via ramp or grass slope through side gate to garden. Many narrow and gravel paths.

27 FOXINGTON

Britwell Salome, Watlington, OX49 5LG. Mrs Mary Roadnight, 01491 612418, mary@foxington.co.uk. *At Red Lion Pub take turning to Britwell Hill. After 350yds turn into drive on L.* **Visits by arrangement Apr to Sept for groups of 5 to 30. Adm £10, chd free. Home-made teas. Special dietary options by prior request.**

Stunning views to the Chiltern Hills provide a wonderful setting for this impressive garden, remodelled in 2009. Patio, heather and gravel gardens enjoy this view, whilst the back and vegetable gardens are more enclosed. The relatively new planting is maturing well and the area around the house (not open) is full of colour. There is an orchard and a flock of white doves. Well behaved dogs are welcome, but they must be kept on a lead at all times as there are many wild animals in the garden, wildflower meadow, wood and neighbouring fields. Wheelchair access throughout the garden on level paths with no steps.

28 FRIARS COURT

Clanfield, OX18 2SU. Charles Willmer, www.friarscourt.com. *4m N of Faringdon. On A4095 Faringdon to Witney. ½m S of Clanfield.* **Mon 25 May (2-6). Adm £4, chd free. Cream teas.**

Over 3 acres of formal and informal gardens with flower beds, borders and specimen trees, lie within the remaining arms of a C16 moat which partially surrounds the large C17 Cotswold stone house. Bridges span the moat with water lily filled ponds to the front whilst beyond the gardens is a woodland walk. A museum about Friars Court is located in the old Coach House. A level path goes around part of the gardens and is suitable for wheelchairs. The museum is accessed over gravel.

29 THE GRANGE

1 Berrick Road, Chalgrove, OX44 7RQ. Mrs Vicky Farren, 01865 400883, vickyfarren@mac.com. *12m E of Oxford & 4m from Watlington, off B480. The entrance to The Grange is at the grass triangle between Berrick Rd & Monument Rd.* **Visits by arrangement June to Oct for groups of 5 to 30. Adm £5, chd free. Home-made teas.**

11 acre plot with an evolving garden including herbaceous borders and a field turned to prairie with many grasses inspired by the Dutch style. There is a lake with bridges and a planted island, a brook running through the garden, wildflower meadow, a further pond, arboretum, an old orchard and partly walled vegetable garden. There is deep water and bridges, which may be slippery when wet. Home-made teas on request (additional £3 per person). Partial wheelchair access on many grass paths, bridges, island and steps.

30 THE GRANGE, ISLIP

Mill Street, Islip, Kidlington, OX5 2SY. Ann & Jon Conibear, 01865 373494 (weekdays only), annconibear494@gmail.com. *2m E of Kidlington & approx 5m N of Oxford. The Grange is 400yds down Mill St on the R. The garden is 200yds from the car park.* **Sun 31 May (1.30-5.30). Adm £4, chd free. Home-made teas. Also open Oak Grove. Combined opening with Hollyhocks on 31 May £6, chd free. Visits also by arrangement Apr to Oct for groups of 10 to 20. Combined visits with Bannisters and/or Hollyhocks can be arranged.**

A 2½ acre garden in a former quarry with landscaped banks and cloud pruned hedges. The garden is naturalistic and combines wild planting with more formal planting of shrubs and perennials. The woodland garden is planted with rare plants and there are wildflower meadows which look especially colourful in the spring. There is a small pond and bog garden edged by a rockery with interesting ferns. The garden has steep gravel paths and is on several levels.

31 GREEN AND GORGEOUS

Little Stoke, Wallingford, OX10 6AX. Rachel Siegfried, www.greenandgorgeousflowers.co.uk. *3m S of Wallingford. Off B4009 between N & S Stoke, follow single track road down to farm.* **Sun 21 June (1-5). Adm £4, chd free. Cream teas.**

6 acre working flower farm next to River Thames. Cut flowers (many unusual varieties) in large plots and polytunnels, planted with combination of annuals, bulbs, perennials, roses and shrubs, plus some herbs, vegetables and fruit to feed the workers! Flowers selected for scent, novelty, nostalgia and naturalistic style. Floristry demonstrations, PYO sweet peas, craft stalls. Wheelchair access on short grass paths, with large concrete areas.

32 GREENFIELD FARM

Christmas Common, Nr Watlington, OX49 5HG. Andrew & Jane Ingram, 01491 612434, andrew@andrewbingram.com. *4m from J5 M40, 7m from Henley. J5 M40, A40 towards Oxford for ½ m, turn L signed Christmas Common. ¾ m past Fox & Hounds Pub, turn L at Tree Barn sign.* **Visits by arrangement June to Sept for groups of up to 30. Adm £4, chd free.**
10 acre wildflower meadow surrounded by woodland, established 22 yrs ago under the Countryside Stewardship Scheme. Traditional Chiltern chalkland meadow in beautiful peaceful setting with 100 species of perennial wild flowers, grasses and 5 species of orchids. ½ m walk from parking area to meadow. Opportunity to return via typical Chiltern beechwood.

33 NEW GREYHOUND HOUSE

The Street, Ewelme, Wallingford, OX10 6HU. Mrs Wendy Robertson, flowerfrond@gmail.com. *Greyhound House is on the main road at the school end of Ewelme. As a courtesy to villagers, please park on the playing field, rather than on the road.* **Sun 28 June (2-5.30). Adm £5, chd free. Home-made teas at Ewelme Primary School. Visits also by arrangement June to Sept. Minimum fee of £40.**
2 acre garden set in historic Chiltern village of Ewelme. Mixed herbaceous borders, ornamental grass walk, walled courtyard with dahlias and late summer flowering perennials, houseplant theatre, fernery, cutting garden, orchard, woodland. Teas will be at the beautiful C15 school located within sight of Greyhound House. It is the oldest school in the county and was built by Alice Chaucer. Partial wheelchair access by a long gravel drive and narrow paths leading to the walled area.

34 THE GROVE

North Street, Middle Barton, Chipping Norton, OX7 7BZ. Ivor & Barbara Hill. *7m E Chipping Norton. On B4030, 2m from junction A4260 & B4030, opp Cinnamon Stick restaurant. Parking in street.* **Sun 17 May (1.30-5). Adm £4, chd free. Home-made teas.**
Mature informal plantsman's ⅓ acre garden, planted for yr-round interest around C19 Cotswold stone cottage (not open). Numerous borders with

wide variety of unusual shrubs, trees and hardy plants; several species weigela, syringe, viburnum and philadelphus. Pond area, well stocked greenhouse. Plant list and garden history available. Home-made preserves for sale. Wheelchair access to most of garden.

GROUP OPENING

35 HEADINGTON GARDENS

Old Headington, Oxford, OX3 9BT. *2m E from centre of Oxford. After T-lights in the centre of Headington, heading towards Oxford, take the 2nd turn on R into Osler Rd. Gardens at end of road in Old Headington & in Beech Rd nearby.* **Sun 17 May (2-6). Combined adm £6, chd free. Home-made teas at Ruskin College.**

11 BEECH ROAD
Lucy & David Lawrence.

THE COACH HOUSE
David & Bryony Rowe.

MONCKTON COTTAGE
Julie Harrod & Peter McCarter, 01865 751471, petermccarter@msn.com.

NEW THE OLD POUND HOUSE
Steve & Jane Cowls.

40 OSLER ROAD
Nicholas & Pam Coote, 07804 932748, pamjcoote@gmail.com.
Visits also by arrangement May to Aug for groups of up to 30.

RUSKIN COLLEGE
Ruskin College, www.ruskincrinklecrankle.org/.

7 ST ANDREWS ROAD
Monique Halloran.

9 STOKE PLACE
Clive Hurst.

Headington Gardens represent an eclectic group of 8 lovely gardens extending from the old Norman village with little lanes, high stone walls and mature trees. The gardens reflect many different styles and eras from the Grade II listed Crinkle Crankle wall in Ruskin College grounds to the exotic and Mediterranean, to high hedged formality with courtyards, cottages and modern gardens. Partial wheelchair access to most gardens due to gravel paths and steps.

36 HOLLY TREE HOUSE

Jarn Way, Boars Hill, Oxford, OX1 5JF. Jillian Morrow, 01865 739486, sandersc4@hotmail.com. *3m S of Oxford. From S ring road towards A34 at r'about follow signs to Wootton & Boars Hill. Up Hinksey Hill take R fork. 1m R into Berkley Rd. Follow road around 1st bend.* **Visits by arrangement in Sept. Combined visit with Uplands.**
A large garden with both formal and free flowing areas of bedding connected by pathways and lawns. This garden features sculpture, ponds and water features and a hidden cottage garden viewed through an archway. Limited wheelchair access. Assistance would be required to see the whole garden.

37 HOLLYHOCKS

North Street, Islip, Kidlington, OX5 2SQ. Avril Hughes, 01865 377104, ahollyhocks@btinternet.com. *3m NE of Kidlington. From A34, exit Bletchingdon & Islip. B4027 direction Islip, turn L into North St.* **Sun 16 Feb (1.30-4.30); Sun 31 May (1.30-5.30). Adm £3, chd free. Home-made teas. Combined adm with Monks Head on 16 Feb £5, chd free. Combined adm with The Grange, Islip on 31 May £6, chd free. 2021: Sun 14 Feb. Visits also by arrangement Feb to Sept for groups of up to 20.**
Plantswoman's small Edwardian garden brimming with yr-round interest, especially planted to provide winter colour, scent and snowdrops. Divided into areas with bulbs, May tulips, herbaceous borders, roses, clematis, shade and woodland planting especially Trillium, Podophyllum and Arisaema, late summer salvias and annuals give colour. Large pots and troughs add seasonal interest and colour. Some steps to access the garden.

Your visits help change lives - we've donated over £17 million to Macmillan Cancer Support since 1984

38 HOME CLOSE
Southend, Garsington,
OX44 9DH. Mrs M Waud & Dr
P Giangrande, 01865 361394,
m.waud@btinternet.com. *3m SE of
Oxford. N of B480, opp Garsington
Manor.* **Visits by arrangement Apr
to Sept. Adm £4.50, chd free.
Refreshments by prior request.**
2 acre garden with listed house (not
open), listed granary and 1 acre
mixed tree plantation with fine views.
Unusual trees and shrubs planted for
yr-round effect. Terraces, stone walls
and hedges divide the garden and
the planting reflects a Mediterranean
interest. Vegetable garden and
orchard.

39 86 HURST RISE ROAD
Cumnor Hill, Oxford, OX2 9HH.
Ms P Guy & Mr L Harris. *W side
of Oxford. Take Botley interchange
off A34 from N or S. Follow signs
for Oxford & then turn R at Botley
T-lights, opp MacDonalds & follow
NGS yellow signs.* **Sun 21 June
(1-5). Combined adm with 10
Eynsham Road £5, chd free.
Home-made teas at 10 Eynsham
Road.**
A small town garden designed and
planted by the owners in 2013. Good
use of a 40ft x 40ft space brimming
with herbaceous perennial plants,
roses, clematis, shrubs and small
trees. Seasonal use of containers
and hanging baskets. An unusual
stone water feature and new for
2020 a metal sculpture. Two raised
beds packed with interesting plants,
rose arch and pergola all add to
a plantaholic's garden. Partial
wheelchair access as path is partly
pebble.

GROUP OPENING

40 IFFLEY GARDENS
Iffley, Oxford, OX4 4EF. *2m S of
Oxford. Within Oxford's ring road,
off A4158 Iffley road, from Magdalen
Bridge to Littlemore r'about, to
Iffley village. Map provided at
each garden.* **Sun 7 June (2-6).
Combined adm £5, chd free.
Home-made teas in village hall.**

17 ABBERBURY ROAD
Mrs Julie Steele.

25 ABBERBURY ROAD
Rob & Bridget Farrands.

86 CHURCH WAY
Helen Beinart & Alex Coren.

122 CHURCH WAY
Sir John & Lady Elliott.

THE MALT HOUSE
Helen Potts.

NEW 4A TREE LANE
Pemma & Nick Spencer-
Chapman.

Secluded old village with renowned
Norman church, featured on cover
of Pevsner's Oxon Guide. Visit 6
gardens ranging in variety and style
from the large Malt House garden
to mixed family gardens with shady
borders and vegetables. Varied
planting throughout the gardens
including herbaceous borders, shade
loving plants, roses, fine specimen
trees and plants in terracing. Features
incl water features, statues, formal
gardens, small lake and Thames
riverbank. Plant Sale at 24 Abberbury
Road (garden not open). Wheelchair
access to some gardens only.

GROUP OPENING

41 KENCOT GARDENS
Kencot, Lechlade, GL7 3QT. *5m
NE of Lechlade. E of A361 between
Burford & Lechlade.* **Mon 13 Apr
(2-6). Combined adm £5, chd free.
Home-made teas at village hall.**

THE ALLOTMENTS
Amelia Carter Charity.

BELHAM HAYES
Mr Joseph Jones.

THE GARDENS
Mark & Jayne Hodds.

HILLVIEW HOUSE
Andrea Moss.

IVY NOOK
Gill & Wally Cox.

KENCOT HOUSE
Tim & Katie Gardner.

THE MALT HOUSE
Hilary & Chris Bradshaw.

MANOR FARM
Henry & Kate Fyson.

WELL HOUSE
Janet & Richard Wheeler.

The 2020 Kencot Gardens group
will consist of 8 gardens and the
allotments. The Allotments, tended
by 8 people, growing a range of
vegetables, flowers and fruit. Ivy
Nook, has spring flowers, shrubs,
rockery, small pond, magnolia
and fruit trees. Belham Hayes, a
mature cottage garden with mixed
herbaceous borders and two old
fruit trees. Emphasis on scent and
colour coordination. The ⅓ acre
garden at The Gardens, has two
old apples trees and newly planted
trees, old well and herbaceous beds.
Plentiful spring bulbs. Manor Farm
has a 2 acre walled garden, bulbs,
wood anemones, fritillaries in mature
orchards, pleached lime walk, 130
yr old yew ball and Black Hamburg
vine. Chickens and occasionally pigs
and lambs. The 2 acre garden at
Kencot House is a haven for wildlife
and incl a gingko tree, shrubs, spring
bulbs, clock house, summerhouse
and a carved C13 archway. Well
House, ⅓ acre garden with mature
trees, hedges, wildlife pond, waterfall,
small bog area, spring bulbs and
rockeries. The Malt House small
enclosed garden has snowdrops,
herbaceous borders, fruit trees and
productive grape vines frame the C17
farmhouse. Also chickens. Hill View, 2
acres with lime tree drive, established
trees, shrubs, perennial borders,
daffodils and aconites. Plant sale at
Manor Farm. No wheelchair access to
The Allotments, other gardens maybe
difficult due to gravel paths.

42 KINGHAM LODGE
West End, Kingham, Chipping Norton, OX7 6YL. Christopher Stockwell, 01608 658226, info@ sculptureatkinghamlodge.com, www.sculptureatkinghamlodge. com. *From Kingham Village, West St turns into West End at tree in middle of road, bear R & you will see black gates for Kingham Lodge immed on L.* **Wed 13 May (10-5). Adm by donation. Home-made lunches & teas.**
Many ericaceous plants not normally seen in the Cotswolds grow on 5 acres of garden, planted over 2 decades. Big display of rhododendron, laburnum arch and azaleas. Formal 150 metre border, backed with trellis, shaded walks with multi-layered planting, an informal quarry pond, formal mirror pond, massive pergola, parterre and unique Islamic garden. Sculpture show from 8-17 May 2020. Islamic pavilion with fountains and rills, pop-up café during the sculpture show. Disabled parking on gravel at the entrance and level access to all areas of the garden.

GROUP OPENING

43 LANGFORD GARDENS
Lechlade, GL7 3LF. *6m S of Burford A361 towards Lechlade. 1½ m E of Filkins. Large free car park in village. Coaches welcome. Map of gardens available.* **Sun 14 June (2-6). Combined adm £7, chd free. Home-made teas at Pember House & village hall.**

BAKERY COTTAGE
Mr & Mrs R Robinson.

THE BARN
Mrs Rachel Range.

BAY TREE COTTAGE
Mr & Mrs R Parsons.

BRIDGEWATER HOUSE
Mr & Mrs T R Redston.

CORKSCREW COTTAGE
Fiona Gilbert.

NEW **CORNER COTTAGE**
Scott Trueman & Ian Burrows.

COTSWOLD BUNGALOW
John & Hilary Dudley.

COTSWOLD COTTAGE
Mr & Mrs Tom Marshall.

THE CROWN
Mr & Mrs D Evans.

THE GRANGE
Mr & Mrs J Johnston.

KEMPS YARD
Mr & Mrs R Kemp.

LIME TREE COTTAGE
Diane & Michael Schultz.

LOCKEY HOUSE
Ms Sophie Hanson.

LOWER FARM HOUSE
Mr & Mrs Templeman.

MEADOW VIEW
Linda Moore.

NEW **PEMBER COTTAGE**
Mrs Jo Edwards.

PEMBER HOUSE
Mr & Mrs J Potter.

ROSEFERN COTTAGE
Mrs D Lowden.

SPRINGFIELD
Mr & Mrs M Harris.

STONECROFT
Christine Apperley.

THE VICARAGE
Mr & Mrs C Smith.

WELLBANK
Sir Brian & Lady Pomeroy.

WELLBANK COTTAGE
Mr & Mrs S Findlay-Wilson.

WELLBANK HOUSE
Mr & Mrs Robert Hill.

Langford is a charming small Cotswold village with both the important Grade I listed St Matthew's Church and a splendid pub, The Bell Inn where lunch is available. 24 gardens will be open, with a delightful mix from large formal to small cottage gardens. Ancient Cotswold stone walls provide a backdrop for many old variety roses. Our plant stall has a large range of local plants and shrubs. Live music in Pember House garden during the afternoon, as well as village teas, and a church floral display add to an enjoyable day for everyone. Most gardens have gravel paths so wheelchair access may vary.

44 NEW **38 LECKFORD ROAD**
Oxford, OX2 6HY. Dinah Adams, 01865 511996, dinah_zwanenberg@fastmail.com. *Central Oxford. North on Woodstock Rd take 3rd L. Coming into Oxford on the Woodstock Rd, 1st R after Farndon Rd. Some 2 hr parking nearby.* **Sun 29 Mar, Sun 17 May (2-4). Adm £4, chd free. Home-made teas in garden loggia. Visits**

also by arrangement Mar to Sept for groups of 5 to 10.
Behind the rather severe facade of a Victorian town house (not open) is a very protected long walled garden with mature trees. The planting reflects the varied levels of shade, and incl rare and unusual plants. The trees in the front garden deserve attention. The back garden is divided into three distinct parts, each with a very different character. Amongst other things there is a hornbeam roof.

45 LIME CLOSE
35 Henleys Lane, Drayton, Abingdon, OX14 4HU. M C de Laubarede, www.mclgardendesign.com. *2m S of Abingdon. Henleys Lane is off main road through Drayton. Please Note: When visiting Lime Close, please respect local residents & park considerately.* **Mon 13 Apr (2-5). Adm £5, chd free. Cream teas. Donation to CLIC Sargent Care for Children.**
4 acre mature plantsman's garden with rare trees, shrubs, roses and bulbs. Mixed borders, raised beds, pergola, topiary and shade borders. Herb garden by Rosemary Verey. Listed C16 house (not open). Cottage garden by MCL Garden Design, planted for colour, an iris garden with 100 varieties of tall bearded irises. Winter bulbs. New arboretum with exotic trees from Asia and USA planted for autumn colour.

46 MAGDALEN COLLEGE
Oxford, OX1 4AU. Magdalen College, www.magd.ox.ac.uk. *Entrance in High St.* **Sun 19 Apr (1-6). Adm £7, chd £6 (chd under 7 yrs free). Light refreshments in the Old Kitchen.**
60 acres incl deer park, college lawns, numerous trees 150-200 yrs old; notable herbaceous and shrub plantings. Magdalen meadow where purple and white snake's head fritillaries can be found is surrounded by Addison's Walk, a tree lined circuit by the River Cherwell developed since the late C18. Ancient herd of 60 deer. Press bell at the lodge for porter to provide wheelchair access.

47 MANOR HOUSE

Manor Farm Road, Dorchester-on-Thames, OX10 7HZ. Simon & Margaret Broadbent, 01865 340101, manor@dotoxon.uk. *8m SSE of Oxford. Off A4074, signed from village centre. Parking at Bridge Meadow (400 metres). Disabled parking at house.* **Sun 23 Aug (2-4.30). Adm £4.50, chd free. Home-made teas in Dorchester Abbey tea room. Visits also by arrangement July & Aug for groups of 10+.**
2 acre garden in beautiful setting around Georgian house (not open) and medieval abbey. Spacious lawn leading to riverside copse of towering poplars with fine views of Dorchester Abbey. Terrace with rose and vine covered pergola around lily pond. Colourful herbaceous borders, small orchard and vegetable garden. Wheelchair access on gravel paths.

48 MEADOW COTTAGE

Christmas Common, Watlington, OX49 5HR. Mrs Zelda Kent-Lemon, 01491 613779, zelda_kl@hotmail.com. *1m from Watlington. Coming from Oxford M40 to J6. Turn R & go to Watlington. Turn L up Hill Rd to top. Turn R after 50yds, turn L into field.* **Mon 25 May (12-5). Adm £5, chd free. Home-made teas. Visits also by arrangement Feb to Oct.**
1¾ acre garden adjoining ancient bluebell woods, created by the owner from 1995 onwards. Many areas to explore including a professionally designed vegetable garden, large composting areas, wild flower garden and pond, old and new fruit trees, many shrubs, much varied hedging and a tall treehouse which children can climb under supervision. Indigenous trees and C17 barn (not open). For visits by arrangement come and see the wonderful snowdrops in Feb and during the month of May visit the bluebell woodland. Partial wheelchair access over gravel driveway and lawns.

49 MERTON COLLEGE OXFORD FELLOWS' GARDEN

Merton Street, Oxford, OX1 4JD. Merton College, 01865 276310. *Merton St runs parallel to High St about half way down.* **Sun 26 July (10-5). Adm £6, chd £6 (chd under 5 free).**
Ancient mulberry, said to have associations with James I. Specimen trees, long mixed border, recently established herbaceous bed. View of Christ Church meadow.

GROUP OPENING

50 MIDDLETON CHENEY GARDENS

Middleton Cheney, Banbury, OX17 2ST. *3m E of Banbury. From M40 J11 follow A422 signed Middleton Cheney. Map available at all gardens.* **Sun 5 July (1-6). Combined adm £5, chd free. Home-made teas at Peartree House.**

CHURCH COTTAGE
David & Sue Thompson.

CROFT HOUSE
Richard & Sandy Walmsley.

NEW THE GABLES
Adam & Wanda Teeuw.

19 GLOVERS LANE
Michael Donohoe & Jane Rixon.

38 MIDWAY
Margaret & David Finch.

PEARTREE HOUSE
Roger & Barbara Charlesworth.

14 QUEEN STREET
Brian & Kathy Goodey, 01295 710554, brian.goodey@btinternet.com. **Visits also by arrangement in July for groups of 5 to 10.**

SPRINGFIELD HOUSE
Lynn & Paul Taylor.

Large village with C13 church with renowned William Morris stained glass. 8 open gardens with a variety of sizes, styles and maturity. Of the smaller gardens, one contemporary garden contrasts formal features with colour-filled beds, borders and exotic plants. Another modern garden has flowing curves that creates an elegant, serene feeling. One features cottage and Mediterranean planting with summerhouse and statuary. A mature small front and back garden is planted profusely with a feel of an intimate haven. A garden that has evolved through family use, feature rooms, and dense planting. One of the larger gardens continues with its renovation of a long lost garden, along with restoring areas of orchard, beds and borders. Another has an air of mystery with hidden corners and an extensive water feature weaving its way throughout the garden. A newly planted garden, opening for the first time, features a mixture of courtyards, pergola, borders and a stunning view of the church.

51 MIDSUMMER HOUSE

Woolstone, Faringdon, SN7 7QL. Penny Spink. *7m W & 7m S of Faringdon. Woolstone is a small village off B4507, below Uffington White Horse Hill. Take the road towards Uffington from the White Horse Pub.* **Wed 17 June (2-6). Adm £4, chd free. Home-made teas.**
On moving to Midsummer House five years ago, the owners created the garden using herbaceous plants brought with them from their previous home at Woolstone Mill House (not open this year). Herbaceous border, parterre with new topiary, and espaliered Malus Everest. The garden designed by owner's son Justin Spink, a renowned garden designer and landscape architect. Wheelchair access over short gravel drive at entrance.

52 MILL BARN

25 Mill Lane, Chalgrove, OX44 7SL. Pat Hougham, 01865 890020, pat@gmec.co.uk. *12m E of Oxford. Chalgrove is 4m from Watlington off B480. Mill Barn is in Mill Lane on the W of Chalgrove, 300yds S of Lamb Pub.* **Visits by arrangement May to Sept for groups of 5+. Adm £4, chd free. Combined visit with The Manor garden £6, chd free. Home-made teas. Wine & canapés for eve visits.**
Mill Barn has an informal cottage garden with a variety of flowers throughout the seasons. Rose arches and a pergola lead to a vegetable plot surrounded by a cordon of fruit trees all set in a mill stream landscape. The Manor garden has a lake and wildlife areas, mixed shrubs and herbaceous beds that surround the C15, Grade 1 listed Manor House (not open).

50 Plantation Road

53 MONKS HEAD

Weston Road,
Bletchingdon, OX5 3DH.
Sue Bedwell, 01869 350155,
bedwell615@btinternet.com.
*Approx 4m N of Kidlington. From
A34 take B4027 to Bletchingdon,
turn R at Xrds into Weston Rd.* **Sun
16 Feb (1.30-4.30). Adm £3, chd
free. Home-made teas. Combined
adm with Hollyhocks £5, chd free.
Visits also by arrangement.**
Plantaholics' garden for all year
interest. Bulb frame and alpine area,
greenhouse. Changes evolving all
the time.

54 NEW OAK GROVE

Brill Road, Horton-Cum-
Studley, Oxford, OX33 1BU.
Sarah Weston, 01865 351655,
sarahweston@maxply.co.uk. *Take
Brill Rd for 1m from the village of
Horton-cum-Studley & Oak Grove will
be on the L. Name clearly displayed
in wall either side of a brown gate.*
**Sat 30, Sun 31 May, Sat 27, Sun
28 June (2-6). Adm £5, chd £1.
Home-made teas. Visits also by
arrangement Apr to Oct for groups
of up to 30.**
A 5 acre garden with colourful and
varied herbaceous and rose borders
and a further 10 acres of wildflower
meadows with mown paths for easy
viewing. Wildlife and butterfly friendly
with interest most of the year. Sorry no
dogs. Wheelchair access to all areas,
providing it is not too wet.

55 16 OAKFIELD ROAD

Carterton, OX18 3QN. Karen &
Jason. *Off A40 Oxford W bound
Carterton & Brize Norton junction.
Go past RAF Brize Norton main
gate, head for town center. Through
T-lights, take 3rd L Foxcroft Dr.
Follow road around to T-junction,
then turn R into Oakfield Rd.* **Sat 8,
Sun 9 Aug (11-5). Adm £3.50, chd
free. Home-made teas.**
A tropical inspired garden that
incorporates good use of the small
space. Overflowing with palms,
bamboo, cannas, tree ferns,
hedychiums, tetrapanax papyrifera
'rex' and colocasia. Small walkway
leading to a decked area with hot tub
and thatched gazebo with its own
Tiki bar. Also small pond, lawn, patio
area and greenhouse, in an area of
10 x 12 metre. Opening over 2 days
to accommodate guests. Partial
wheelchair access on patio area only.

GROUP OPENING

56 OLD BOARS HILL GARDENS
Jarn Way, Boars Hill, Oxford, OX1 5JF. *3m S of Oxford. From S ring road towards A34 at r'about follow signs to Wootton & Boars Hill. Up Hinksey Hill take R fork. 1m R into Berkley Rd to Old Boars Hill.* **Sun 3 May (2-5.30). Combined adm £6, chd free. Home-made teas.**

HEDDERLY HOUSE
Mrs Julia Bennett.

UPLANDS
Lyn Sanders, 01865 739486, sandersc4@hotmail.com. **Visits also by arrangement Mar to Oct for groups of 5+.**

WHITSUN MEADOWS
Jane & Nigel Jones, 07500 722722, jones.oxford@btinternet.com. **Visits also by arrangement in June.**

YEW COTTAGE
Michael Edwards.

Four delightful gardens in a conservation area. Whitsun Meadows has Oxford views with mature Scots pine, English oak, acer and cherry. The numerous herbaceous borders, hosta beds, gravel gardens and a wildflower meadow are on a level site. Hedderly House has a 3 acre terraced hillside garden with wooded walks and ponds with extensive views over the Vale of the White Horse. Yew Cottage is nestled in the hillside with a central magnolia, colourful flower-filled beds with the treat of seeing the owners veteran cars. Uplands is a southerly facing cottage garden with an extensive range of plants for colour for every season and a new formal area.

  ♿ 🐄 🌼 🚗 ☕

57 THE OLD VICARAGE, BLEDINGTON
Main Road, Bledington, Chipping Norton, OX7 6UX. Sue & Tony Windsor, 01608 658525, tony.g.windsor@gmail.com. *6m SW of Chipping Norton. 4m SE of Stow-on-the-Wold. On the main street B4450 through Bledington. Not next to church.* **Sun 26 Apr (11-5). Light refreshments. Sun 14 June (2-6). Adm £4, chd free. Visits also by arrangement May to July. Wine & canapés for evening visits.**
$1\frac{1}{2}$ acre garden around a late Georgian vicarage (1843) not open. Borders and beds filled with spring bulbs, hardy perennials, shrubs and trees. Informal rose garden with over 300 David Austin roses. Small pond and vegetable garden. Paddock with trees, shrubs and herbaceous border. Planted for yr-round interest. Gravel driveway and gently sloped garden can be hard work for wheelchair users.

♿ 🐄 🌼 🚗 ☕

58 OLD WHITEHILL BARN
Old Whitehill, Tackley, Kidlington, OX5 3AB. Gill & Paul Withers, 01865 331097, gillwithers@gmail.com. *10m N of Oxford. 3m from Woodstock. Hamlet $\frac{3}{4}$m S of Tackley. Accessed from either A4260 & A4095.* **Visits by arrangement Mar to Sept for groups of up to 30.**
1 acre country garden on a sloping site around a stone barn conversion. Created by the owners from a farmyard and surrounding field over last 18 yrs. Sunny walled courtyard. Colour themed borders. Field of formal and informal areas, mature hedging, orchard, meadow grass and enclosed vegetable garden.

🌼 ☕

59 ORCHARD HOUSE
Asthall, Burford, OX18 4HH. Dr Elizabeth Maitreyi, 07939 111605, oneconsciousbreath@gmail.com. *3m E of Burford. 1st house on R as you come downhill into Asthall.* **Sun 5 July (2-6). Adm £5, chd free. Home-made cakes & cream teas.** Donation to MS Society.
A 5 acre garden in the making. Formal borders and courtyard. New paths and hedges created in 2018 are developing adding more character and planting opportunities. The whole design is now visible. We are creating an English garden

Pigeon Cottage, Broughton Poggs & Filkins Gardens

finely balanced between the formal and the wild. Beautiful sculptures add to the planting and there is woodland to walk in beyond. The Maytime Inn offers very good food and accommodation if booked well in advance. Dogs on a lead are welcome. Wheelchair access with one step down from the driveway. No WC available.

60 116 OXFORD ROAD
Abingdon, OX14 2AG. Mr & Mrs P Aylward, 01235 523925, aylwardsdooz@hotmail.co.uk. *116 Oxford Rd is on the RH-side if coming from A34 N exit, or on the LH-side after Picklers Hill, turn if approaching from Abingdon town centre.* **Sun 31 May (11-4). Combined adm with Failford £5, chd free. Home-made teas. Visits also by arrangement June to Sept for groups of up to 20.**
New town garden opening for its third year, a creation that started in July 2014. The garden is wedge-shaped, 70ft top, 37ft at the bottom and 80ft in length. The challenge was it had to be interesting and look as though it had been there for many years. It has a folly greenhouse and other unusual features, plus raised beds, lawns, herbaceous borders and a diverse collection of plants and trees. Limited access by gravel driveway. Uneven surfaces and paths.

61 50 PLANTATION ROAD
Oxford, OX2 6JE. Philippa Scoones. *Central Oxford. N on Woodstock Rd take 2nd L. Coming into Oxford on Woodstock Rd turn R after Leckford Rd. Best to park on Leckford Rd. No disabled parking near house.* **Sat 18, Sun 19, Sat 25, Sun 26 Apr (2-5). Adm £3.50, chd free. Home-made teas.**
Surprisingly spacious city garden designed in specific sections. N-facing front garden, side alley filled with shade loving climbers. S-facing rear garden with hundreds of tulips in spring, unusual trees incl Mount Etna Broom, conservatory, terraced area and secluded water garden with water feature, woodland plants and alpines. Good design ideas for small town garden and 100s of pots that add to the overall atmosphere.

62 THE PRIORY GARDEN
Church Lane, Charlbury, OX7 3PX. Dr D El Kabir & Colleagues. *6m SE of Chipping Norton. Large Cotswold village on B4022 Witney-Enstone Rd, near St Mary's Church.* **Sun 7 June (2-5). Adm £5, chd free. Home-made teas.**
1½ acre of formal terraced topiary gardens with Italianate features. Foliage colour schemes, shrubs, parterres with fragrant plants, old roses, water features, sculpture and inscriptions aim to produce a poetic, wistful atmosphere. Formal vegetable and herb garden. Arboretum of over 3 acres borders the River Evenlode and incl wildlife garden and pond. Home-made teas in the new Charlbury Community Centre (limited parking nearby). Partial wheelchair access.

63 RADCOT HOUSE
Radcot, OX18 2SX. Robin & Jeanne Stainer, www.radcothouse.com. *1¼ m S of Clanfield. On A4095 between Witney & Faringdon, 300yds N of Radcot bridge.* **Sun 23 Aug, Sun 4 Oct (2-6). Adm £5, chd free. Home-made teas.**
Approx 3 acres of dramatic yet harmonious planting in light and shade, formal pond, fruit and vegetable cages. Convenient seating at key points enables relaxed observation and reflection. Extensive use of grasses and unusual perennials and interesting sculptural surprises. Spectacular autumn display.

64 ROFFORD MANOR
Rofford Lane, Little Milton, Oxford, OX44 7QQ. Mr & Mrs Jeremy Mogford. *10m SE of Oxford. 1m from Little Milton on Chalgrove Rd. Signposted Rofford only. Parking on verges outside garden.* **Evening opening Thur 25 June (5.30-7.30). Adm £25. Pre-booking essential, please visit www.ngs.org.uk/ events for information & booking. Evening drinks & canapés.**
Discover one of Oxfordshire's secret treasures in this 2 acre garden created since 1985 around the venerable gabled house and within old walls, with some design and planting by Michael Balston. From the cloud-clipped box garden to the burgeoning vegetable garden, and including deep herbaceous borders and herb, rose and swimming pool gardens, it is all designed and planted to an exceptional standard, with the bonus

of many memorable views out over the surrounding countryside. Yew hedges and pleached limes provide enclosures and frame borders and there is a feast of interesting plants to enjoy.

65 NEW ROUSHAM GARDEN
Rousham House, Rousham, Bicester, OX25 4QU. Mr Charles Cottrell-Dormer. *Once you reach Rousham, parking & gardens are clearly signed.* **Sun 28 June (10-5). Adm £10.**
C18 gardens designed by William Kent with ponds, cascades, statuary and rill. Walled gardens with herbaceous borders, pigeon house and kitchen garden, the park is home to a herd of Longhorn cattle. Bring a picnic. Wheelchair access with some parts of garden quite steep.

GROUP OPENING

66 SIBFORD GARDENS

Sibford Gower, OX15 5RX. *7m W of Banbury. Near the Warwickshire border, S of B4035, in centre of village near Wykham Arms Pub.* **Sun 28 June (2-6). Combined adm £7, chd free. Home-made teas at Sibford Gower Village Hall (opp the church).**

BUTTSLADE HOUSE
James & Sarah Garstin.

CARTER'S YARD
Sue & Malcolm Bannister, 01295 780365, sebannister@gmail.com. **Visits also by arrangement May to Oct for groups of 5 to 30.**

HOME CLOSE
Graham & Carolyn White.

HOME FARM
Professor Stephen Kennedy.

LARKSPUR
Ivan & Veronique Tyrrell.

In two charming small villages of Sibford Gower and Sibford Ferris, off the beaten track with thatched stone cottages, five contrasting gardens ranging from an early C20 Arts and Crafts house (not open) and garden, to varied cottage gardens bursting with bloom, interesting planting and some unusual plants. No wheelchair access to Carter's Yard, partial access to Buttslade House, Home Farm and Home Close.

🐂 ✳ ☕

67 NEW SOUTH HAYES

Yarnells Hill, Oxford, OX2 9BG. Mark & Louise Golding. *2m W of Oxford. Take Botley Rd heading W out of Oxford, pass under A34, turn L onto Westminster Way, Yarnells Hill is 2nd road on R. Park at top of hill & walk 100 metres down the lane.* **Sun 5 July (2-6). Adm £4, chd free. Home-made teas.**
One acre garden transformed to make the most of a steeply sloping site. Formal planting close to the house (not open) and a raised decking area which overlooks the garden. Gravel pathways are retained by oak sleepers and pass through swathes of hardy perennials and grasses, leading to the lower garden with natural wildlife pond and fruit trees. Garden once owned by the late Primrose Warburg, an Oxford galanthophile. Not suitable for wheelchairs due to steep slope and gravel filled steps.

🐂 ✳ Ⓓ ☕

68 64 SPRING ROAD

Abingdon, OX14 1AN. Janet Boulton, 01235 524514, j.boulton89@btinternet.com, www.janetboulton.co.uk. *S Abingdon from A34 take L turn after police station into Spring Rd. Minute's drive to number 64 on L.* **Visits by arrangement July to Sept. Adm £5, chd free. Tea.**
A very special small but unique artist's garden (4½ x 30½ metres) behind a Victorian terrace house. Predominantly green with numerous inscribed sculptures relating to art, history and the human spirit. Inspired by gardens the owner has painted, especially Little Sparta in Scotland. Visitors are invited to watch a film about this celebrated garden before walking around the garden itself.

☕

GROUP OPENING

69 STEEPLE ASTON GARDENS

Steeple Aston, OX25 4SP. *14m N of Oxford, 9m S of Banbury. ½m E of A4260.* **Sun 7 June (2-6). Combined adm £5, chd free. Home-made teas in village hall.**

ACACIA COTTAGE
Jane & David Stewart.

CEDAR COTTAGE
Josephine Meddings & Robert Scott.

COMBE PYNE
Chris & Sally Cooper.

KRALINGEN
Mr & Mrs Roderick Nicholson.

THE LONGBYRE
Mr Vaughan Billings.

PRIMROSE GARDENS
Richard & Daphne Preston, 01869 340512, richard.preston5@btopenworld.com. **Visits also by arrangement Apr to July for groups of 10+. We can provide an introductory talk followed by tea and cake!**

Steeple Aston, often considered the most easterly of the Cotswold villages, is a beautiful stone built village with gardens that provide a wide range of interest. A stream meanders down the hill as the landscape changes from sand to clay. The 6 open gardens include small floriferous cottage gardens, large landscaped gardens, natural woodland areas, ponds and bog gardens, and themed borders. Primrose Gardens and Longbyre have gravel and Acacia Cottage also has some steps. Kralingen has slopes to stream and bog garden.

♿ 🐂 ✳ �car ☕

70 STONEHAVEN

6 High Street, Cumnor, Oxford, OX2 9PE. Dr Dianne & Prof Keith Gull. *4m from central Oxford. Exit to Cumnor from the A420. In centre of village opp PO. Parking at back of PO.* **Sun 16 Feb (2-5). Adm £3, chd free. Opening with Cumnor Village Gardens on Sun 7 June (2-6).**
Front, side and rear garden of a thatched cottage (not open). Front is partly gravelled and side courtyard has many pots. Rear garden overlooks meadows with old apple trees underplanted with ferns, wildlife pond, unusual plants, many with black or bronze foliage, planted in drifts and repeated throughout the garden. Planting has mild Japanese influence; rounded, clipped shapes interspersed with verticals. Snowdrops in Feb. There are two pubs in the village serving food; The Bear & Ragged Staff and The Vine. Gravel drive to access garden.

♿ 🐂 ✳ 🚗

71 NEW ◆ STONOR PARK

Stonor, Henley-On-Thames, RG9 6HF. Lady Ailsa Stonor, 01491 638587, administrator@stonor.com, www.stonor.com. *Stonor is located between the M4 (J8/J9) & the M40 (J6) on the B480 Henley-on-Thames to Watlington road. If you are approaching Stonor on the M40 from the E, please exit at J6 only.* **For NGS: Tue 2 June (2-4.30). Adm £6.50, chd free. Home-made teas. For other opening times and information, please phone, email or visit garden website.**
Surrounded by dramatic sweeping valleys and nestled within an ancient deer park, you will find the gardens at Stonor, which date back to Medieval times. Visitors love the serenity of the our C17 walled, Italianate Pleasure Garden and herbaceous perennial borders beyond.

 🚗 ☕

Green and Gorgeous

72 UPPER GREEN
Brill Road, Horton cum Studley, Oxford, OX33 1BU. Susan & Peter Burge, 01865 351310, sue.burge@ndm.ox.ac.uk, www.uppergreengarden.co.uk. *6½m NE of Oxford. Enter village, turn R up Horton Hill. At T-junction turn L into Brill Rd. Upper Green 250yds on R, 2 gates before pillar box. Roadside parking.* **Visits by arrangement Feb to Sept for groups of up to 30. Home-made teas. Donation to British Skin Foundation.**
Mature ½ acre wildlife friendly garden packed with interest and colour throughout the year. Over 1500 plants in garden database. Wildlife friendly. Herbaceous borders, gravel bed, rock bed, ferns, hot border, potager, bog and pond. Snowdrop collection. Alpines. Apple trees support rambling roses. Spectacular views. Great compost! Sorry, no dogs. Gravel drive limits wheelchair access.

73 WADHAM COLLEGE
Parks Road, Oxford, OX1 3PN. The Warden & Fellows. *Central Oxford. Wadham College gardens are accessed through the main entrance of the college on Parks Rd.* **Sun 5 Apr, Sun 5 July (12-5). Adm £2, chd free.**
5 acres, best known for trees, spring bulbs and mixed borders. In Fellows' main garden, fine ginkgo and *Magnolia acuminata*; bamboo plantation; in Back Quadrangle very large *Tilia tomentosa* 'Petiolaris'; in Mallam Court white scented garden est 1994; in Warden's garden an ancient tulip tree; in Fellows' private garden, Civil War embankment with period fruit tree cultivars, recently established shrubbery with unusual trees and ground cover amongst older plantings.
&

74 ◆ WATERPERRY GARDENS
Waterperry, Wheatley, OX33 1JZ. School of Economic Science, 01844 339226, office@waterperrygardens.co.uk, www.waterperrygardens.co.uk. *7½m from Oxford city centre. From*

E M40 J8, from N M40 J8a. Follow brown tourist signs. For SatNav please use OX33 1LA. **For NGS: Sun 15 Mar, Sun 6 Sept (10-5.30). Adm £8.50, chd free. Light refreshments in the teashop (10-5). For other opening times and information, please phone, email or visit garden website.**
Waterperry gardens are extensive, well-maintained and full of interesting plants. From The Virgin's Walk with its shade-loving plants to the long classical herbaceous border, brilliantly colourful from late May until October. The Mary Rose Garden illustrates modern and older roses, and the formal garden is neatly designed and colourful with a small knot garden, herb border and wisteria tunnel. Newly redesigned walled garden, river walk, statues and pear orchard. Riverside walk may be inaccessible to wheelchair users if very wet.

WAYSIDE

82 Banbury Road, Kidlington, OX5 2BX. Margaret & Alistair Urquhart, 01865 460180, alistairurquhart@ntlworld.com. *5m N of Oxford. On R of A4260 travelling N through Kidlington.* **Visits by arrangement May to Sept for groups of up to 30. Adm £3, chd free. Tea.**
¼ acre garden shaded by mature trees. Mixed border with some rare and unusual plants and shrubs. A climber clothed pergola leads past a dry gravel garden to the woodland garden with an extensive collection of hardy ferns. Conservatory and large fern house with a collection of unusual species of tree ferns and tender exotics. Important collection of hardy garden ferns. Partial wheelchair access.

&♿ ❀ ☕ ▶

76 WESTWELL MANOR

Westwell, Nr Burford, OX18 4JT. Mr Thomas Gibson. *2m SW of Burford. From A40 Burford-*
Cheltenham, turn L ½m after Burford r'about signed Westwell. After 1½m at T-junction, turn R & Manor is 2nd house on L. **Sun 31 May (2-6.30). Adm £5, chd free. Donation to Aspire.**
7 acres surrounding old Cotswold manor house (not open) with knot garden, potager, shrub roses, herbaceous borders, topiary, earth works, moonlight garden, auricula ladder, rills and water garden.
❀

GROUP OPENING

77 WHEATLEY GARDENS

High Street, Wheatley, OX33 1XX. *5m E of Oxford. Leave A40 at Wheatley, turn into High St. Gardens at W end of High St, S side.* **Sun 21 June (2-6). Combined adm £5, chd free. Cream teas at The Manor House.**

BREACH HOUSE GARDEN
Liz Parry.

THE MANOR HOUSE
Mrs Elizabeth Hess, 01865 875022, echess@hotmail.co.uk.
Visits also by arrangement Apr to Sept for groups of up to 30.

THE STUDIO
Ann Buckingham.

Three adjoining gardens in historic Wheatley are: Breach House Garden with many shrubs, perennials, a contemporary reflective space and a wild meadow with ponds; The Studio with walled garden and climbing roses, clematis, herbaceous borders, vegetables and fruit trees; The Elizabethan Manor House (not open) a romantic oasis with formal box walk, herb garden, rose arches and old rose shrubbery. Various musical events. Wheelchair access with assistance due to gravel paths, two shallow steps and grass.

&♿ 🐕 ❀ ☕ ▶

Stonehaven

Foxington

78 WHITEHILL FARM

Widford, Burford, OX18 4DT. Mr & Mrs Paul Youngson, 01993 822894, anneyoungson@btinternet.com. *1m E of Burford. From A40 take road signed Widford. Turn R at the bottom of the hill, 1st house on the R with ample car parking.* **Sun 7 June (1.30-6). Adm £4, chd free. Home-made teas. Visits also by arrangement June to Sept.**
2 acres of hillside gardens and woodland with spectacular views overlooking Burford and Windrush valley. Informal plantsman's garden built up by the owners over 25 yrs. Herbaceous and shrub borders, ponds and bog area, old fashioned roses, ground cover, ornamental grasses, bamboos and hardy geraniums. Large cascade water feature, pretty tea patio and wonderful Cotswold views.

GROUP OPENING

79 WOOTTON GARDENS

Wootton, OX13 6DP. *Wootton is 3m SW of Oxford. From the Oxford ring road S, take the turning to Wootton. Parking for all gardens at the Bystander Pub & on the road.* **Thur 18 June (2-6). Combined adm £5, chd free. Home-made teas.**

13 AMEY CRESCENT
Sylv & Liz Gleed.

60 BESSELSLEIGH ROAD
Freda East.

67 BESSELSLEIGH ROAD
Jean Beedell.

14 HOME CLOSE
Kev & Sue Empson.

35 SANDLEIGH ROAD
Hilal Baylav Inkersole.

5 inspirational small gardens, all with very different ways of providing a personal joy. 13 Amey Cresent is a gravel garden with grasses and prairie plants. The garden has a small wildlife pond, alpine house and troughs. 14 Home Close is a garden containing mainly shrubs with an unusually shaped lawn. There is also a pond, raised bed and a vegetable garden. 67 Besselsleigh Road is a compact and vibrant garden. Its deep borders are brimming with a variety of colourful plants shaped around a pathway. 60 Besselsleigh Road is 'The Deadwood Stage' with ornamental wood, sticks, stones, toadstools, many creatures to find in the secret garden; and some green stuff with coloured bits. 35 Sandleigh Road is a mature garden, laid to lawn on two levels. Grown mostly from cuttings the garden is brimming with vibrant flowers, pondside planting and

glass art. Partial wheelchair access.

80 YARNTON MANOR

Church Lane, Yarnton, OX5 1PY. Yarnton Manor, 01865 809400, events@yarntonmanor.com, www. yarntonmanor.com. *From M40 J9, follow A34 towards Oxford for approx 6m until A44 exit. At Peartree Interchange, follow A44 N towards Woodstock, at r'about take 1st L onto Cassington Rd. Follow road for ½m & then take L onto Church Lane. Yarnton Manor signed 500 metres on R.* **Wed 3 June (11-4). Adm £5, chd free. Home-made teas.**
7 acres of gardens incl a large back lawn, walled garden, sunken garden, kitchen garden and lime tree avenue. The gardens feature a large variety of shrubs, herbaceous borders, mature trees, climbers, as well as some new planting and seasonal bedding against a backdrop of a C17 Manor House. The gardens are designed and overseen by Robin Lane Fox. Croquet and garden games available on the lawn (on request). Access via a gravel path with several small steps in the majority of the gardens. No wheelchair accessible facilities.

OPENING DATES

All entries subject to change. For latest information check www.ngs.org.uk

Map locator numbers are shown to the right of each garden name.

February

Snowdrop Festival

Sunday 16th
Millichope Park   38

Friday 21st
NEW The Old Vicarage, Bishops Castle   46

Saturday 22nd
NEW The Old Vicarage, Bishops Castle   46

Sunday 23rd
NEW The Old Vicarage, Bishops Castle   46

April

Sunday 19th
Edge Villa   16

Sunday 26th
Ruthall Manor   51

Tuesday 28th
Brownhill House   7

May

Saturday 2nd
Kinton Grove   32

Sunday 3rd
Kinton Grove   32
Lyndale House   36

Wednesday 6th
NEW Westwood House   61

Saturday 9th
Bowbrook Allotment Community   4

Sunday 10th
Longden Manor   33
Millichope Park   38
Oteley   49

Friday 15th
◆ Wollerton Old Hall   63

Saturday 16th
Ruthall Manor   51
Upper Shelderton House   58

Sunday 17th
◆ Delbury Hall Walled Garden   15
NEW 3 Haye Court   22
Henley Hall   23
Ruthall Manor   51
Upper Shelderton House   58

Wednesday 20th
Goldstone Hall Gardens   19

Sunday 24th
The Gardeners Lodge   18
The Mount   40
Walcot Hall   59

Monday 25th
Walcot Hall   59

Tuesday 26th
Brownhill House   7

Wednesday 27th
Goldstone Hall Gardens   19

Saturday 30th
Beaufort   3

Sunday 31st
Longner Hall   34
Stanley Hall Gardens   54
Windy Ridge   62

June

Tuesday 2nd
NEW Westhope College   60

Sunday 7th
NEW Broadward Hall   6

Wednesday 10th
NEW 1 Oakeley Mynd   43
3 Oakeley Mynd   42

Thursday 11th
Goldstone Hall Gardens   19

Saturday 13th
Ruthall Manor   51

Sunday 14th
NEW 3 Haye Court   22
◆ Hodnet Hall Gardens   25

Morville Hall Gardens   39
Ruthall Manor   51

Saturday 20th
Secret Garden   53

Sunday 21st
◆ Delbury Hall Walled Garden   15
NEW Kingslow Hall   31
Lyndale House   36

Wednesday 24th
Goldstone Hall Gardens   19

Saturday 27th
Cruckfield House   14

Sunday 28th
Windy Ridge   62
NEW Woodlands   64

Tuesday 30th
Brownhill House   7

July

Every day from Monday 27th to Friday 31st
NEW Offcot   45

Wednesday 1st
NEW Hillview   24

Thursday 2nd
Avocet   2
NEW Cheriton   8

Friday 3rd
Avocet   2
NEW Cheriton   8

Sunday 5th
Hargrove   21
The Mount   40
Stottesdon Village Open Gardens   55
Upper Marshes   57

Tuesday 7th
48 Bramble Ridge   5

Thursday 9th
Goldstone Hall Gardens   19

Friday 10th
48 Bramble Ridge   5
NEW 12 Colley Close   10
NEW 74 Conway Drive   11

Saturday 11th
Ruthall Manor   51

Sunday 12th
NEW Hope House Children's Hospice Garden   29
Ruthall Manor   51

Sunday 19th
The Hollies (Welshampton)   27
Holly House   28
Lower Brookshill   35
Sambrook Manor   52

Wednesday 22nd
Goldstone Hall Gardens   19

Saturday 25th
Cruckfield House   14
NEW Oswestry Gatacre Allotments & Gardens Association   48

Sunday 26th
27 Croxon Rise   13
NEW Esme's Garden   17
NEW Nancy's Garden   41
NEW Oswestry Gatacre Allotments & Gardens Association   48

Wednesday 29th
5 Church Street   9
1 Cross Villas   12

August

Sunday 2nd
Merton   37

Sunday 9th
◆ Delbury Hall Walled Garden   15
Windy Ridge   62

Thursday 13th
Goldstone Hall Gardens   19

Wednesday 19th
Goldstone Hall Gardens   19

Sunday 23rd
Edge Villa   16

Sunday 30th
Bowbrook Allotment Community   4
Sambrook Manor   52

THE GARDENS

1 ANCOIREÁN
24 Romsley View, Alveley,
WV15 6PJ. Judy & Peter Creed,
01746 780504, pdjc@me.com. *6m
S Bridgnorth off A442 Bridgnorth
to Kidderminster rd. N from
Kidderminster turn L just after
Royal Oak PH. S from Bridgnorth
turn L after Squirrel pub. Take 3rd
turning on R & follow NGS signs.*
**Visits by arrangement June &
July for groups of 10+. Adm £4,
chd free. Home-made teas by
arrangement.**
Natural garden layout on several
levels, developed over 30yrs, with
a large variety of herbaceous plants
and shrubs, water features, wooded
area with bog garden containing
numerous varieties of ferns and
hostas, and colourful alpine scree.
Features, wooded area, stumpery,
ornamental grass border and Spring
bulb collection, clematis collection,
acer and azalea beds. Selection
of plants for sale. Close to Severn
Valley Railway and Country Park and
Dudmaston Hall NT.

2 AVOCET
3 Main Road, Plealey,
Shrewsbury, SY5 0UZ. Malc &
Jude Mollart, 01743 791743,
malcandjude@btinternet.com.
*6m SW of Shrewsbury. From A5
take A488 signed Bishops Castle,
approx ½ m past Lea Cross Tandoori
turn L signed Plealey. In ¾ m turn
L, garden on R. SatNav unreliable!*
Thur 2, Fri 3 July (10.30-4).

Combined adm with Cheriton £6,
chd free. Home-made teas. **Visits
also by arrangement Apr to July
for groups of up to 30.**
Cottage style garden with modern
twists owned by plantaholics, shared
with wildlife. Designed round series
garden rooms for year round interest:
wildlife pool, mixed borders, seaside
and gravel gardens, succulents,
trained fruit, sculpture. Constantly
evolving. Opportunity to see 2
neighbouring gardens of same size,
with similar organic principles and for
wildlife but different interpretations.
Collection of vintage garden tools.

3 BEAUFORT
Coppice Drive, Moss Road
Wrockwardine Wood,
Telford, TF2 7BP. Mike King,
www.carnivorousplants.uk.com.
*Approx 2m N from Telford town
centre. From Asda Donnington, turn
L at lights on Moss rd, ⅓m, turn L
into Coppice Drive. 4th Bungalow
on L with solar panels.* **Sat 30 May
(10-5). Adm £4, chd free. Light
refreshments.**
If carnivorous plants are your thing,
then come and visit our National
Collection of Sarracenia (pitcher
plants); also over 100 different Venus
flytrap clones (Dionaea muscipula),
Sundews (Drosera) and Butterworts
(Pinguicula.) - over 6000 plants in
total. Large greenhouses at Telford's
first carbon negative house; a
great place to visit - kids will love
it! Not wheelchair accessible into
greenhouses.

ALLOTMENTS

4 BOWBROOK ALLOTMENT COMMUNITY
Mytton Oak Road, Shrewsbury,
SY3 5BT. Bowbrook Allotment
Community, bowbrookallotments.
wordpress.com. *On western edge
of Shrewsbury between A5 Bypass
& Royal Shrewsbury Hospital.
From A5 Shrewsbury Bypass take
B4386 (Mytton Oak Road) towards
Shrewsbury, following signs to Royal
Shrewsbury Hospital. The allotment
entrance is ½ m from A5 r'about, on
R, opp Oak Lane.* **Sat 9 May, Sun
30 Aug (2-6). Adm £5, chd free.
Light refreshments.**
Recipient of RHS National Certificate
of Distinction, this 5 acre site,
comprising 93 plots, displays wide
ranging cultivation methods. The
site has featured on BBC TV, local
radio programmes and in several
magazines. Members cultivate
organically with nature in mind using
companion planting and attracting
natural predators. Green spaces
flourish throughout and include
Gardens of the 4 Seasons, orchards,
and many wildlife features including
wild flower meadows and pond.
Children are encouraged to be part
of the community and have their own
special places such as a story telling
willow dome, willow tunnel, sensory
garden and turf spiral. See how the
Contemplation Garden and the Prairie
Garden have developed. Wheelchair
access possible with care. Generally
flat wide grass paths allow access to
all the main areas of the site, although
paths may be bumpy!

5 48 BRAMBLE RIDGE
Bridgnorth, WV16 4SQ. Chris & Heather, 07572 706706, heatherfran48@gmail.com. *From Bridgnorth N on B4373 signed Broseley. 1st on R Stanley Lane, 1st R Bramble Ridge. From Broseley S on B4373, nr Bridgnorth turn L into Stanley Lane, 1st R Bramble Ridge.* Tue 7, Fri 10 July (12-5). Adm £4, chd free. Home-made teas. Visits also by arrangement May to Sept for groups of up to 20.
Steep garden with many steps, part wild, part cultivated, terraced in places and overlooking the Severn valley with views to High Rock and Queens Parlour. Described by some as fascinating and full of interest; the garden incl shrubs, perennials, small vegetable plot, herbs, wildlife pond and summerhouse. Full of interesting plants. Roughly 88 steps from the front of the house to the very top of the garden.

6 NEW BROADWARD HALL
Broadward, Clungunford, Craven Arms, SY7 0QA. Anthony & Caro Skyrme. *5m from Craven Arms; 9m from Ludlow on A49. Turn off nr Ludlow Food Centre thru Bromfield. Follow rd towards Leintwardine. Just before Leintwardine turn R towards Clungunford before S bend in rd, turn L, cont along lane, over small stone bridge; Gate lodge on L.* Sun 7 June (2-5). Adm £5, chd free. Home-made teas in the Music Room or on the terrace.
The Broadward Hall estate is a site of special scientific interest (SSSI). With well established, extensive, herbaceous borders, ancient trees and a Victorian walled garden (undergoing restoration). Other areas of interest include the magnificent, giant sequoia trees which line an early C19 archery walk; Victorian Pump House. Tea available with a variety of cakes on offer. Disabled access to Music Room via a concrete ramp, disabled WC.

7 BROWNHILL HOUSE
Ruyton XI Towns, Shrewsbury, SY4 1LR. Roger & Yoland Brown, 01939 261121, brownhill@eleventowns.co.uk, www.eleventowns.co.uk. *9m NW of Shrewsbury on B4397. On the B4397 in the village of Ruyton XI Towns.* Tue 28 Apr, Tue 26 May, Tue 30 June (1.30-5). Adm £4, chd

free. Home-made teas. Visits also by arrangement Apr to June.
A unique 2 acre hillside garden with many steps and levels bordering R Perry. Visitors can enjoy a wide variety of plants and styles from formal terraces to woodland paths. The lower areas are for the sure-footed and mobile while the upper levels with a large kitchen garden have many places to sit and enjoy the views. Kit cars on show.

8 NEW CHERITON
Plealey, Pontesbury, Shrewsbury, SY5 0UY. Vicky Wood. *6m SW of Shrewsbury. From A5, take A488 signed Bishops Castle; approx ½ m past Lea Cross Tandoori, turn L signed to Plealey; in ¾ m turn L, garden on R. SatNav unreliable.* Thur 2, Fri 3 July (10.30-4). Combined adm with Avocet £6, chd free. Home-made teas.
Family garden where every space has a function, with annual and perennial cut flower borders, fruit and vegetables, polytunnel, chickens, wildlife pond, outdoor cooking and green woodworking areas. Full of colour with stunning borrowed views to the fields and hill beyond. Opportunity to see 2 neighbouring gardens of same size with similar organic principles and for wildlife with different interpretations.

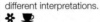

9 5 CHURCH STREET
Ruyton X1 Towns, Shrewsbury, SY4 1LA. Steve & Jill Owen, 01939 261591, eleventowns@outlook.com. *From A5 take B4397 to Ruyton XI Towns. Enter the village, carry straight on passing The Talbot pub on the R. House is on the L. 50m further on, opposite school.* Wed 29 July (1-5). Combined adm with 1 Cross Villas £4, chd free. Light refreshments. Visits also by arrangement June to Oct for groups of 20 to 30.
Long village garden divided into sections affording different styles of planting: herbaceous borders with a wide variety of plants, shrubs and trees giving year-round interest through texture and colour; wild flower area and wildlife pond. Summer house, vegetable area and greenhouse. Not suitable for wheelchairs.

10 NEW 12 COLLEY CLOSE
Shrewsbury, SY2 5YN. Kevin & Karen Scurry. *Off Telford Way near Shrewsbury police st. From r'about by police stn head down Telford Way at next r'about take 2nd exit onto Oswell Rd then 1st R into Colley Close. Please use shuttle bus between gardens as parking limited in Colley Close.* Evening opening Fri 10 July (5-9). Combined adm with 74 Conway Drive £6, chd free. Light refreshments.
This garden has 3 ponds including a large koi pond and waterfall, wildlife pond and goldfish pond all surrounded by interesting planting. A large collection of specimen bonsai trees accent the koi pond giving an oriental feel to the garden. The front garden has a large collection of grasses. The garden has good wheelchair access and many seating areas to view the garden from many different angles.

11 NEW 74 CONWAY DRIVE
Shrewsbury, SY2 5UY. Andrew & Deborah Abel. *Off Monkmoor Rd near Shrewsbury Police Stn. At Lord Hill towards town turn R at T-lights towards Police Stn. At r'about 2nd exit, then 1st R into Conway Drive. Please use free shuttle bus between the gardens as parking is limited in Colley Close.* Evening opening Fri 10 July (5-9). Combined adm with 12 Colley Close £6, chd free. Light refreshments.
A delightful urban garden with extensive use of pots to accentuate various garden rooms. Garden is well planted with many specimen trees and shrubs in a stylish, contemporary setting. Borders contain herbs, herbaceous and tropical planting mingled throughout the garden. Featuring a rockery, waterfall and fish pond. Various seating areas make it a lovely place to spend a summer's evening.

12 1 CROSS VILLAS
School Road, Ruyton XI Towns, SY4 1JZ. Amy Heath & Adrian Thorn. *From A5 take B4397 to Ruyton XI Towns. Enter the village, carry straight on passing The Talbot pub on the R. House is on L after 50 metres & 50 metres from 5 Church Street. Parking in school opposite.* Wed 29 July (1-5). Combined adm with 5 Church Street £4, chd free. Plantswoman's garden being brought

back from the edge of chaos. Small but full to the brim with scented roses, clematis and herbaceous perennials. Open with neighbouring garden at 5 Church Street. Not suitable for wheelchairs.

13 27 CROXON RISE

Oswestry, SY11 2YQ. Natalie & Tony Bainbridge. *Eastern Oswestry. ½ m from A5 Oswestry Bypass. Take B4580 to Oswestry. Take 1st L Harlech Rd, 1st exit r'about Cabin lane. Take 5th L Aston Way, 1st L & 1st L again Croxon Rise. Please park courteously in surrounding rds.* **Sun 26 July (11-4). Adm £4, chd free. Home-made teas.**

Packing a lot into a small space, this secluded, beautifully planted town garden offers interest at every turn. Mixed borders provide colour through to late summer. A raised bed vegetable garden, greenhouse and cut flower garden, soft fruit cage, seating areas, and water features. A rose garden surrounds a mature cherry tree and south facing wall protects step-over and cordon fruits. Open the same day as Oswestry Allotments - why not visit both gardens?

14 CRUCKFIELD HOUSE

Shoothill, Ford, Shrewsbury, SY5 9NR. Geoffrey Cobley, 01743 850222. *5m W of Shrewsbury. A458 from Shrewsbury, turn L towards Shoothill.* **Sat 27 June, Sat 25 July (2-5.30). Adm £6, chd free. Home-made teas. Visits also by arrangement June to Aug for groups of 30+. (Refreshments extra).**

An artists romantic 3 acre garden, formally designed, informally and intensively planted with a great variety of unusual herbaceous plants. Nick's garden, with many species trees, shrubs and wildflower meadow, surrounds a large pond with bog and moisture-loving plants. Ornamental kitchen garden. Rose and peony walk. Courtyard fountain garden, large shrubbery and extensive clematis collection Extensive topiary, and lily pond.

15 ◆ DELBURY HALL WALLED GARDEN

Delbury Hall Estate, Mill Lane, Diddlebury, Craven Arms, SY7 9DH. Mr & Mrs Richard Rallings, 01584 841 222, info@myndhardyplants.co.uk, www.myndhardyplants.co.uk. *8m W of Craven Arms. 1m off B4368, Craven Arms to Bridgnorth, through village of Diddlebury, turn R at Mynd Hardy Plants sign.* **For NGS: Sun 17 May, Sun 21 June, Sun 9 Aug (11-5). Adm £5, chd free. Home-made teas. English wine from our own vineyard. For other opening times and information, please phone, email or visit garden website.**

A two acre early Victorian Walled Garden with large herbaceous borders, a vegetable and a herb garden, shrubbery, vines and very old fruit trees. In addition there is a large Penstemon and Hemerocallis collection. Gravel and grass paths. Dogs are welcome in the Walled Garden but not in the Hall Gardens.

16 EDGE VILLA

Edge, nr Yockleton SY5 9PY. Mr & Mrs W F Neil, 01743 821651, billfneil@me.com. *6m SW of Shrewsbury. From A5 take either A488 signed to Bishops Castle or B4386 to Montgomery for approx 6m then follow NGS signs.* **Sun 19 Apr, Sun 23 Aug (2-5). Adm £5, chd free. Home-made teas. Visits also by arrangement Apr to Sept for groups of 10+. Light lunches for bus groups on request.**

Two acres nestling in South Shropshire hills. Self-sufficient vegetable plot. Chickens in orchard, foxes permitting. Large herbaceous borders. Dewpond surrounded by purple elder, irises, candelabra primulas and dieramas. Large selection of fragrant roses. Teas in sheltered courtyard. Wendy House and Teepee for children. Many unusual plants propagated for sale. Some German and French spoken. Some gravel paths.

17 NEW ESME'S GARDEN

Church Row, Meole Village, Shrewsbury, SY3 9EX. Nancy Estrey & Peter Alltree. *Through wicker gate by No 3 Church Row and follow path to the garden at the top. For Church Row, take next turning on the L; on-street parking on Church Row, Church Road &*

Upper Road or take shuttle bus from Nancy's garden. **Sun 26 July (1-5). Combined adm with Nancy's Garden £6, chd free. Home-made teas in Peace Memorial Hall, Upper Road, Meole Village.**

Esme's Garden is situated in a secluded spot in the centre of Meole Village, with the beautiful Meole Church as a backdrop. Designed purely for its exuberant planting, gravel paths take you on a romantic journey through trees, shrubs and perennials, eventually leading to a central oasis by a tranquil pond. There are also many unexpected features. Both gardens are nurtured by Nancy. On the level, but a lot of gravel paths which might prove difficult for wheelchairs.

18 THE GARDENERS LODGE

2 Roseway, Wellington, Telford, TF1 1JA. Amanda Goode, www.lovegrowshereweb.wordpress.com/. *1½ m (4 mins) from J7 (M54). B5061 Holyhead Rd 2nd L after NT 'Sunnycroft'. (New Church Rd) We are the cream house on corner of NCR & Roseway.* **Sun 24 May (10-4.30). Adm £4, chd free. Home-made teas.**

There was just one tree in the garden when the current owner purchased The Gardener's Lodge, the ground having been cleared, ready to sell as a building plot. However the owner had other plans for it: the garden is now eclectically divided, arranged and planted into areas: Mediterranean, Cottage, Indian etc but, seamlessly, each section merges and leads into the next developing idea. A small urban garden with seating, water features and shade.

Your visits help change lives – we are the largest single funder of the Queen's Nursing Institute

19 GOLDSTONE HALL GARDENS

Goldstone, Market Drayton, TF9 2NA. John Cushing, 01630 661202, enquiries@goldstonehall.com, www.goldstonehall.com. *5m N of Newport on A41. Follow brown & white signs from Hinstock. From Shrewsbury A53, R for A41 Hinstock & follow brown & white signs & NGS signs.* **Wed 20, Wed 27 May, Thur 11, Wed 24 June (2-5). Home-made teas. Evening opening Thur 9 July (4-8). Wine. Wed 22 July, Thur 13, Wed 19 Aug, Wed 2, Wed 9 Sept (2-5). Home-made teas. Adm £6, chd free. Visits also by arrangement Apr to Sept for groups of 10+.**
5 acres with highly productive beautiful kitchen garden. Unusual vegetables and fruits - alpine strawberries; heritage tomatoes, salad, chillies, celeriac. Roses in Walled Garden from May; Double herbaceous in front of old English garden wall at its best July and August; Sedums and Roses stunning in September. Teas served in award winning oak framed pavilion in the midst of the garden with cakes created by our talented chef. Lawn aficionados will enjoy the stripes. Rosetted restaurant, AA Red Star Country House Hotel, Good Hotel Guide listed; As featured in national lifestyle magazines. Majority of garden can be accessed on gravel and lawns.

&. 🚗 🛏 💷

20 GUILDEN DOWN COTTAGE

Guilden Down, Clun, Craven Arms, SY7 8NZ. Mike Black & Sue Wilson, 07795 275557, sue.guilden@gmail.com. *1m from Clun past YHA. Follow signs to YHA from Clun High Street; follow rd for 1m, past cottages on L. At farm bear R through farm buildings. 100yds at end of rd; garden on L.* **Visits by arrangement Apr to July for groups of up to 30. Adm £5, chd free. Home-made teas.**
With spectacular views, this one acre organic garden has been developed over the past 14 years to be in harmony with its surroundings. Divided into many rooms, there are vibrant herbaceous borders and terraces, rose trellises and a large vegetable plot. Our wild garden includes a natural pond, living willow structures, wild flower orchard, trees, shrubs and planted borders. https://m.facebook.com/teaontheway Partial wheelchair access, front garden only but worth it for the views.

&. 🐾 💷

21 HARGROVE

Wall-Under-Heywood, Church Stretton, SY6 7DP. Sally & Gerard Wainwright. *Hargrove - grid ref SO 5013 9286. Approached by a drive directly off B4371 on Wall Bank. Proceed over cattle grid down ⅔m.* **Sun 5 July (1-6). Adm £6, chd free. Home-made teas.**
Approached by a ⅔ m tree lined drive through parkland with meadows either side, bordered by ancient

woodland. Varied 2 acre gardens surround a contemporary country house. Water features, walled herb and soft fruit garden with cascading roses. Orchard and extensive random flower beds created for family, friends and six dogs. Woodland walk bordering lake with swans (and hopefully cygnets). Plant and craft sales.

🐾 🐕 ✳ 🚗 💷

22 NEW 3 HAYE COURT

Lower Forge, Eardington, Bridgnorth, WV16 5LQ. Eileen Paradise, 01746 764884, eileenparadise22@gmail.com. *2½ m S of Bridgnorth on B4555. Continue for 1m past Eardington over railway bridge; do not take next L but carry on for further 200 metres then take L - follow yellow NGS signs.* **Sun 17 May, Sun 14 June (11-5). Adm £5, chd free. Light refreshments. Visits also by arrangement May to July for groups of up to 20.**
Enchanting garden with year round interest; innovative design by plantswoman/floral designer. Started 5 years ago but well established; a stylish, peaceful sanctuary. Contemporary sculpture, elegant statuary; Glorious views across Severn Valley, paved paths, clipped box, cloud pruning, unusual planting schemes in delicate hues; teas served in sheltered courtyard. Not suitable for wheelchairs. Quiche & salad at lunchtime; tea/coffee/cold drinks/ cakes all day.

✳ 💷

23 HENLEY HALL

Henley, Ludlow, SY8 3HD. Helen & Sebastian Phillips. *2m E of Ludlow. 1½ m from the A49. Take the A4117 signed to Clee Hill & Cleobury Mortimer. On reaching Henley, the gates to Henley Hall are on the R when travelling in the direction towards Clee Hill.* **Sun 17 May (12-5). Adm £5, chd free. Home-made teas. Enjoy tea, home-made cakes and light refreshments in the Ball Room.**
Henley Hall offers a mixture of formal and informal gardens. The historic elements include a formal lawn, stone staircase with balustrades and a ha-ha, mature specimen trees, a walled garden, 'pulmonary' water feature and yew hedges. Highlights include walk ways along the banks of the river Ledwyche with decorative weirs and a stone arched bridge, and woodland

Delbury Hall Walled Garden

paths. Some parts of the garden are accessible by wheelchair.

 ♿ 🐕 ☕

24 NEW HILLVIEW

High Street, Clun, Craven Arms, SY7 8JB. Mellie Lewis, 01588 640673, melanie.lane@virgin.net. *On high street in Clun. Please park in Memorial Hall car park, 5 mins walk from garden - follow yellow NGS signs.* Wed 1 July (10-5). Adm £4, chd free. Home-made teas. Visits also by arrangement June to Aug for groups of up to 20.

Pretty, well-planted cottage-style garden in the heart of Clun. Featuring the first and only Aeonium species and cultivar National Plant Collection in the UK, awarded in 2019. A vast array of this fascinating plant collected by the owner over many years. Rare and familiar varieties displayed and labelled for the enthusiast with some on sale.

🌼 NPC ☕

25 ◆ HODNET HALL GARDENS

Hodnet, Market Drayton, TF9 3NN. Sir Algernon & The Hon Lady Heber-Percy, 01630 685786, secretary@hodnethall.com, www.hodnethallgardens.org. *5½m SW of Market Drayton. 12m NE Shrewsbury. At junction of A53 & A442.* For NGS: Sun 14 June (11-5). Adm £8, chd £1. Light refreshments. For other opening times and information, please phone, email or visit garden website.

60 acre landscaped garden with series of lakes and pools; magnificent forest trees, great variety of flowers, shrubs providing colour throughout season. Unique collection of big-game trophies in C17 tearooms. Kitchen garden. For details please see website and Facebook page. Maps are available to show access for our less mobile visitors.

 ♿ 🐎 🚗 NPC ☕

26 THE HOLLIES (CLUN)

Rockhill, Clun, SY7 8LR. Pat & Terry Badham, 01588 640805, patbadham@btinternet.com. *10m W of Craven Arms. 8m S of Bishops Castle. From A49 Craven Arms take B4368 to Clun. Turn L onto A488 continue for 1½m. Bear R signed Treverward. After 50 yards turn R at Xrds, property is 1st on L.* Visits by arrangement June to Aug for

groups of up to 30. Adm £4, chd free.

A garden of approx 2 acres at 1000ft which was started in 2009. Features include a kitchen garden with raised beds and fruit cage. Large island beds and borders with perennials, shrubs and grasses, specimen bamboos and trees. A birch grove and wildlife dingle with stream, rain permitting! Refreshments can be arranged at a local cafe in Clun (daytime hours) Wheelchair access is available to the majority of the garden over gravel and grass.

 ♿ ☕

27 THE HOLLIES (WELSHAMPTON)

Welshampton, SY12 0QA. Andrew & Marie Haydon. *A495 ½m E of Welshampton towards Whitchurch. Located on the A495 east of Welshampton Shropshire. From Welshampton head towards Whitchurch. ½m. Follow Yellow Signs.* Sun 19 July (11-5). Combined adm with Holly House £6, chd free. Home-made teas.

3 acres around Victorian house; mature & new specimen trees, roses, woodland area; old established orchard with some heritage varieties; duck pond with breeding ducks. Please use car parking in the Hollies to access neighbouring garden.

🐎 ☕

28 HOLLY HOUSE

Welshampton, SY12 0QA. Mike & Ruth Dinsdale, 01948710924, ruth.dinsdale@btinternet.com. *On A495 ½m E of Welshampton towards Whitchurch. From Welshampton head towards Whitchurch for ½m; Follow yellow NGS signs.* Sun 19 July (11-5). Combined adm with The Hollies (Welshampton) £6, chd free. Home-made teas. Visits also by arrangement May to Sept for groups of 10 to 30.

A densely planted ⅓ acre plants-woman's country garden featuring some rare and unusual plants, herbaceous borders and ornamental pond. Leading to a 1 acre field with both mature and newly planted specimen trees, a natural wild life pond, wild flower "project", vegetable garden and rural views. A garden trail quiz for children and plant sales. The garden is not suitable for wheelchairs.

🐎 🌼 ☕

29 NEW HOPE HOUSE CHILDREN'S HOSPICE GARDEN

Nant Lane, Morda, Oswestry, SY10 9BX. Simi Epstein, www.hopehouse.org.uk/. *Off A483 (Welshpool to Oswestry Rd) at Morda just S of Oswestry. In Morda, turn L in village at Hope House sign & yellow NGS signs, then L into Nant Lane.* Sun 12 July (12-6). Adm £5, chd free. Light refreshments. Refreshments in aid of the hospice.

Come and visit our peaceful, green landscape with large natural pond full of birdlife and wildlife, reflective garden, secret Fairy Garden, formal and informal borders, wild flowers. Colourful hanging baskets, flower sculptures and humorous statuary. Teenage garden with places to lounge and enjoy the sound of water. Collection of silver birches and other specimen trees. Children's all-abilities play area. Accompanied tours of the hospice (subject to circumstances). Good wheelchair access everywhere.

 ♿ 🐕 🌼 🚗 ☕

30 NEW HORATIO'S GARDEN

The Robert Jones & Agnes Hunt Orthopaedic Hospital, Gobowen, Oswestry, SY10 7AG. Imogen Jackson, www.horatiosgarden.org.uk. *At the spinal unit. From A5 follow signs to Orthopaedic Hospital; parking in pay & display car park by hospital.* Sun 20 Sept (2-5). Adm £5, chd free. Home-made teas.

Beautifully designed by Bunny Guinness and delightfully planted, this garden opened to great acclaim in Sept 2019. Part-funded by the National Garden Scheme, the garden offers a place of peace and therapy for patients at the spinal unit. Raised beds, creative use of space, beautiful specimen trees, potting shed, sculpture, all in soothing hues. A pretty rill runs the length of the garden. Very good access throughout.

 ♿ 🌼 ☕

We help ordinary people open the gates to their extraordinary private gardens to raise impressive amounts of money through admissions, teas and slices of cake!

31 NEW KINGSLOW HALL

Kingslow, Pattingham, Wolverhampton, WV6 7DY. Tony & Belinda Marshall. *Outskirts of Pattingham. 2.3m W of Pattingham, turn off A464 Shifnal to Wolverhampton down Burnhill Green Rd. Follow brown signs for Patshull Park Hotel. Turn R onto Patshull Rd & follow NGS signs.* **Sun 21 June (12-5). Adm £5, chd free. Home-made teas.**
This magnificent estate garden last opened for the Scheme in 1977. The landscape and gardens have been transformed with specimen trees introduced into woodlands; the traditional rose garden has been replanted and enhanced with complementary planting; wildlife and wildflowers encouraged. Kitchen garden completely renovated and is now a vast productive space with many different fruits, flowers and vegetables.

32 KINTON GROVE

Kinton, Nesscliffe, Shrewsbury, SY4 1AZ. Tim & Judy Creyke, 01743 741263, judycreyke@icloud.com. *Off A5, between Shrewsbury & Oswestry, approximately 1m from Nesscliffe. Follow the A5 to the r'about at the Oswestry end, ie NW end, of the Nesscliffe by-pass. Follow the signs to Kinton, approx 1m.* **Sat 2, Sun 3 May (1-5). Adm £5, chd free. Home-made teas. Visits also by arrangement Apr to June for groups of 5 to 30.**
A garden of ¾ acre surrounding a Georgian house. The garden features well-filled herbaceous borders, roses, a gravel area, raised vegetable beds, and a wide range of interesting trees and shrubs. Hedges, including some as old as the house, divide up the garden. Lovely views across the Breidden hills and plenty of pleasant places to sit, whilst enjoying cream tea and cakes.

33 LONGDEN MANOR

Plealey, Pontesbury, Shrewsbury, SY5 0XL. Karen Lovegrove. *From Shrewsbury take Longden Rd from A4380. Through Hook-a-Gate & Annscroft to Longden. Pass Village Shop & Post Office on L & Turn R opposite The Tankerville Arms Car Park.* **Sun 10 May (10-4). Adm £5, chd free. Home-made teas.**
Large estate garden with lots of character and interest: woodland walks and grass paths; humorous topiary; wide variety of specimen trees; rhododendrons and azaleas; wildflowers; restored water garden; panoramic vistas of surrounding countryside; holly garden. Also, children's treasure hunt, giant Jenca, skittles and croquet - a great place for all the family to visit.

34 LONGNER HALL

Atcham, Shrewsbury, SY4 4TG. Mr & Mrs R L Burton. *4m SE of Shrewsbury. From M54 follow A5 to Shrewsbury, then B4380 to Atcham. From Atcham take Uffington Road, entrance ¼m on L.* **Sun 31 May (2-5). Adm £5, chd free. Home-made teas.**
A long drive approach through parkland designed by Humphry Repton. Walks lined with golden yew through extensive lawns, with views over Severn Valley. Borders containing roses, herbaceous and shrubs, also ancient yew wood. Enclosed one acre walled garden open to NGS visitors. Mixed planting, garden buildings, tower and game larder. Short woodland walk around old moat pond which is not suitable for wheelchairs.

35 LOWER BROOKSHILL

Nind, Lydham, (near) Bishops Castle, SY5 0JW. Patricia & Robin Oldfield. *3m N of Lydham on A488. Take signed turn to Nind & after ½m sharp L & follow narrow rd for another ½m. Drive very slowly on single track road & use temporary passing places if needed.* **Sun 19 July (2-6). Adm £5, chd free. Tea.**
10 acres of hillside garden and woods at 950ft within the AONB. Begun in 2010 from a derelict and overgrown site, cultivated areas rub shoulders with the natural landscape using fine borrowed views over and down a valley. Includes brookside walks, a 'pocket' park, four ponds (including a Monet lily pond), mixed borders and lawns, cottage garden and annual wild flowers. Not wheelchair friendly.

36 LYNDALE HOUSE

Astley Abbotts, Bridgnorth, WV16 4SW. Bob & Mary Saunders. *2m out of Bridgnorth off B4373. From High Town Bridgnorth take B4373 Broseley Rd for 1½m, then take lane signed Astley Abbotts & Colemore* Green. **Sun 3 May, Sun 21 June (2-5). Adm £4, chd free. Light refreshments.**
1½ acre garden which has been lovingly tended for 25yrs. Rose terrace under planted with tulips and alliums. Large lawns interspersed with well planted flower beds. New Japanese themed pool with Koi. Courtyard with colourfully planted pots and topiary. Masses of tulips in the spring, and beautiful roses in the summer. Plenty of seating. Water features. Tea on the terrace over looking countryside. Topiary garden, waterfall to pool, many unusual trees. Please ask owner about wheelchair friendly access.

37 MERTON

Shepherds Lane, Bicton, Shrewsbury, SY3 8BT. David & Jessica Pannett, 01743 850773, jessicapannett@hotmail.co.uk. *3m W of Shrewsbury. Follow B4380 from Shrewsbury past Shelton for 1m Shepherd's Lane turn L garden signed on R or from A5 by pass at Churncote r'about turn towards Shrewsbury 2nd turn L Shepherds Lane.* **Sun 2 Aug (1-5). Adm £4, chd free. Tea. provided by local Macmillan group. Visits also by arrangement May to Sept.**
Mature ½ acre botanical garden with a rich collection of trees and shrubs including unusual conifers from around the world. Hardy perennial borders with seasonal flowers and grasses plus an award winning collection of hosta varieties in a woodland setting. Outstanding gunneras in a waterside setting with moisture loving plants. Level paths and lawns.

38 MILLICHOPE PARK

Munslow, Craven Arms, SY7 9HA. Mr & Mrs Frank Bury, www.wildegoosenursery.co.uk. *8m NE of Craven Arms. off B4368 Craven Arms to Bridgnorth Rd. Nr Munslow then follow yellow signs.* **Sun 16 Feb (2-5); Sun 10 May (1-6); Sun 11 Oct (2-5). Adm £6, chd free. Light refreshments in the walled garden tea room.**
Historic landscape gardens covering 14 acres with lakes, cascades dating from C18, woodland walks and wildflowers. Snowdrops in February, Bluebells and Violas in May, Autumn colour in October. Also open the Walled Garden at Millichope, an exciting restoration project bringing

the walled gardens and C19 glasshouses back to life. There is the opportunity to see the Bouts Viola collection the UK's largest collection of hardy, perennial, scented violas with many varieties on sale during the May opening at Wildegoose Nursery in the walled garden.

Sambrook Manor

GROUP OPENING

39 MORVILLE HALL GARDENS

Morville, Bridgnorth, WV16 5NB. *3m W of Bridgnorth. On A458 at junction with B4368.* **Sun 14 June (2-5). Combined adm £6, chd free. Home-made teas in Morville Church.**

THE COTTAGE
Ms A Nichol-Smith.

THE DOWER HOUSE
Dr Katherine Swift.

1 THE GATE HOUSE
Mr & Mrs Rowe.

2 THE GATE HOUSE
Mrs G Medland.

MORVILLE HALL
Mr & Mrs A Lewis & The National Trust.

SOUTH PAVILION
Mrs Joy Jenkinson.

An interesting group of gardens that surround a beautiful Grade I listed mansion (house not open). The Cottage has a pretty walled garden with plenty of colour. The Dower House is a horticultural history lesson about Morville Hall which includes a turf maze, cloister garden, Elizabethan knot garden, C18 canal garden, Edwardian kitchen garden and more. It is the setting of Katherine Swift's bestselling book 'The Morville Hours', and the sequel 'The Morville Year'. 1 and 2 The Gate House are cottage-style gardens with colourful borders, formal areas, lawns and wooded glades. The three acre Morville Hall (NT) garden has a parterre, medieval stew pond, shrub borders and large lawns, all offering glorious views across the Mor Valley. South Pavilion features new thoughts and new designs in a small courtyard garden. Please note that National Trust membership does not give admission to this NGS opening. Mostly level ground, but plenty of gravel paths and lawns to negotiate.

40 THE MOUNT

Bull Lane, Bishops Castle, SY9 5DA. Heather Willis, 01588 638288, adamheather@btopenworld.com. *Bishops Castle off A488 Shrewsbury to Knighton Rd. at the top of the town, 130 metres up Bull Lane on R. No parking at the property itself, but parking is free in Bishops Castle. Sunday 24th May opening is same date as neighbouring Walcot Hall.* **Sun 24 May, Sun 5 July (1-6). Adm £4, chd free. Home-made teas. Visits also by arrangement Apr to Sept for groups of up to 30.**
An acre of garden that has evolved over 24 years, with 4 lawns, a rosebed in the middle of the drive with pink and white English roses, and herbaceous and mixed shrub borders. There are roses planted throughout the garden and in the spring daffodils and tulips abound. Two large beech trees frame the garden with a view that sweeps down the valley over fields and then up to the Long Mynd. Access easy to parts of the garden itself, but not to WC which is in the house up steps.

41 NEW NANCY'S GARDEN

11 Elmfield Road, Shrewsbury, SY2 5PB. Nancy Estrey & Peter Alltree. *Off Belvedere Avenue. Parking is available at Shirehall Council car park off Belvedere Avenue. A free shuttle bus is available between Nancy's Garden & Esme's Garden where there is limited on-street parking.* **Sun 26 July (1-5). Combined adm with Esme's Garden £6, chd free. Home-made**
teas at Peace Memorial Hall on Upper Road, Meole Brace Village.
Nancy's garden is a small suburban garden with lots of form, foliage and colour. Winding paths lead you to a circular lawn, patio and pond. A secluded patio at the top of the garden is surrounded by lush planting that gives a sub tropical feel. A summer house used throughout the summer is a true outside room. A plantswomen's garden featuring a wealth of plants. Beautifully designed to give colour and form all year round. Tranquil seating and pond. Both gardens nurtured by Nancy.

42 3 OAKELEY MYND

Stank Lane, Bishops Castle, SY9 5EX. Derek & Eileen Mattey, 01588 638944, eileenlmattey@gmail.com. *Approx 2m E of Bishop's Castle, off B4385. Follow B4385 for approx ½m, turn L at NGS sign. Garden located on R, 1m up the hill. Limited parking at garden. On open day, please use free shuttle bus from Bishops Castle.* **Wed 10 June (11-5). Combined adm with 1 Oakeley Mynd £6, chd free. Home-made teas. Visits also by arrangement June to Aug for groups of up to 20.**
Just under 1 acre, south facing, wildlife-friendly country garden. Informal planting, with wild flowers, herbaceous perennials, shrubs, small wildlife pond, produce garden, greenhouses and fruit trees. Hillside setting at 935'/285m with lovely views over the Shropshire Hills. Not suitable for wheelchairs.

43 NEW 1 OAKELEY MYND
Stank Lane, Bishops Castle, SY9 5EX. Judith Shone & John Kearins. *Approx 2m E of Bishop's Castle, off B4385. Follow B4385 for approx ½ m, turn L at NGS sign. Garden located on R, 1m up the hill. Limited parking at garden. On open day, please use free shuttle bus from Bishops Castle.* **Wed 10 June (11-5). Combined adm with 3 Oakeley Mynd £6, chd free. Home-made teas.**
A two acre, hillside garden with far reaching views of the surrounding hills. The higher level has a woodland area, mixed shrub and perennial borders and vegetable beds alongside two greenhouses. The lower level has wild flower areas, fruit trees, a fruit and vegetable garden, shade planting under the trees and mixed planting on the bank dividing the two areas.

44 NEW OAKLY PARK
Bromfield, Ludlow, SY8 2JW. Lord & Lady Plymouth. *Off A49 (Shrewsbury to Hereford Rd) opp Ludlow Farm Shop. Take immediate L turn towards Bromfield Church, follow rd over bridge & take L hand fork. Watch for yellow NGS signs.* **Sun 6 Sept (1-5). Adm £10, chd free. Pre-booking essential, please visit www.ngs.org.uk/ events for information & booking. Light refreshments at The Clive Arms and the Ludlow Kitchen, part of the estate.**
One of Shropshire's magnificent estates, rarely open to the public, named after its centuries-old oak trees. At the confluence of the River Onny and Teme, with extensive views to Ludlow and the south Shropshire Hills. Well-planted borders, rose garden, fern grotto, lake, interesting historical buildings and features. 2 acres of productive walled garden supplying produce to Ludlow Farm site. Accommodation available at The Clive Arms. IT IS ESSENTIAL TO PURCHASE TICKETS TO THIS OPENING IN ADVANCE at www.ngs. org.uk. Not suitable for wheelchairs.

45 NEW OFFCOT
Kynaston, Kinnerley, Oswestry, SY10 8EF. Tom Pountney. *Just off A5 on Nesscliffe r'about towards Knockin. Then take the 1st L towards Kinnerley. Follow NGS signs from this road.* **Daily Mon 27 July to Fri 31 July (10-4). Adm £4, chd free.**

Light refreshments. served in the garden bar.
A cottage garden with lots of winding pathways leading to different focal points. The garden is packed with a wide range of evergreen and deciduous trees and shrubs and under planted with herbaceous perennials. There is a natural looking pond with a running stream feeding into it. A haven for wildlife. So many different areas to see and enjoy including the garden bar.

46 NEW THE OLD VICARAGE, BISHOPS CASTLE
Church Lane, Bishops Castle, SY9 5AF. Helen and Jerry Robinson. *Near the junction of Church Street & Kerry Lane, directly behind St John's Church. Pedestrian access through the main gate on Church Lane or through the garden gate to the rear of St John's churchyard.* **Fri 21, Sat 22 Feb (11-4). Sun 23 Feb (11-4). Light refreshments. Adm £3.50, chd free. Teas will only be served on Sunday at the garden.**
Extending to just over one and a half acres, the gardens include lawned areas surrounded by perennial beds and mature shrubs, an ornamental pond, orchard and romantic ruin, fragments of the lost thirteenth century church. Snowdrops abound throughout the garden in February. The garden includes a stained glass studio open as part of the Bishops Castle Arts Festival www.bishopscastleartsfestival.com. Refreshments are widely available in the town of Bishops Castle on the Friday and Saturday. Level access over gravel drive and lawns.

47 THE OLD VICARAGE, CLUN
Vicarage Road, Clun, Craven Arms, SY7 8JG. Peter & Jay Upton, 01588 640775, jay@salopia.plus.com. *16m NW of Ludlow. Over bridge at Clun towards Knighton (parking in public car park by bridge); walk up to church, turn L into Vicarage Rd; house on R next to church.* **Visits by arrangement May to Sept for groups of up to 30. Adm £5, chd free. Home-made teas at Guilden Down Cottage (also open by arrangement).**
A revived, old vicarage garden: a slow retrieval and recovery revealing a wealth of features and plants chosen by plantsmen vicars: buddleia globosa

fascinates bees and butterflies; glorious oriental poppies fascinate visitors. 'The Tree', an enormous Leyland cypress (5th biggest girth in the world); the most dramatic feature is a formal wisteria allee with alliums - a symphony of mauve and purple.

ALLOTMENTS

48 NEW OSWESTRY GATACRE ALLOTMENTS & GARDENS ASSOCIATION
Lloyd Street, Oswestry, SY11 1NL. Graham Mitchell, 01691 654961, gsfmitchell@gmail.com, gatacre.wordpress.com. *2 parts to the allotments either side of Liverpool Road. From Whittington 'r'about on A5 turn towards Oswestry B4580. In ½ m go across staggered junction (L then R). Continue 100y then bear sharp L. After 200y straight over r'about, then 3rd on L.* **Sat 25, Sun 26 July (10.30-3.30). Adm £5, chd free. Home-made teas. Visits also by arrangement July & Aug for groups of 5 to 10.**
Two adjacent, large allotment communities in the heart of Oswestry; well supported and well-loved by local residents. Vast array of fruit, flowers, vegetables in every shape and form grown on the allotments. Allotment holders will be on-hand to talk about their produce and give advice. Entry ticket covers both sides of the allotments. The main pathways are wheelchair friendly, but the small paths tend to be rather steep or narrow. There are disabled WC on one side of the site.

49 OTELEY
Ellesmere, SY12 0PB. Mr R K Mainwaring, 01691 622514. *1m SE of Ellesmere. Entrance out of Ellesmere past Mere, opp Convent nr to A528/495 junction.* **Sun 10 May (2-5). Adm £5, chd free. Light refreshments. Visits also by arrangement May to Oct for groups of 10+. Coaches by Arrangement.**
10 acres running down to The Mere. Walled kitchen garden, architectural features, many old interesting trees. Rhododendrons, azaleas, wild woodland walk and views across Mere to Ellesmere. First opened in 1927 when the National Garden Scheme started. Beautiful setting on the Mere. Wheelchair access if dry.

50 POOH CORNER

6 Laburnum Close, St Martins, Oswestry, SY11 3HU. Sue Napper, 01691 774368, suenapper@talktalk.net. *5m NE of Oswestry in St Martin's village. Follow NGS signs from A5. Please park courteously outside property and in surrounding roads.* **Visits by arrangement Mar to June for groups of up to 30. Adm £4, chd free. Light refreshments.**
A plants-woman's garden giving particular emphasis to shade loving perennials and unusual shrubs and climbers, some of which are rarely grown outdoors. Relatively compact in size and divided into 4 distinct areas providing diverse growing conditions for a wide variety of plants including ferns, primulas and alpines. Partial wheelchair access only but mainly level throughout.

51 RUTHALL MANOR

Ditton Priors, Bridgnorth, WV16 6TN. Mr & Mrs G T Clarke, 01746 712608, clrk608@btinternet.com. *7m SW of Bridgnorth. At Ditton Priors Church take road signed Bridgnorth. then 2nd L. Garden 1m.* **Sun 26 Apr, Sat 16, Sun 17 May, Sat 13, Sun 14 June, Sat 11, Sun 12 July, Sat 19, Sun 20 Sept (1-6). Adm £5, chd free. Home-made teas. Visits also by arrangement Apr to Oct.**
Offset by a mature collection of specimen trees, the garden is divided into intimate sections, carefully linked by winding paths. The front lawn flanked by striking borders, extends to a gravel, art garden and ha-ha. Clematis and roses scramble through an eclectic collection of wrought-iron work, unique pottery and secluded seating. A stunning horse pond features primulas, iris and bog plants. Lots of lovely shrubs to see. Jigsaws for sale bring or buy. Wheelchair access to most parts.

52 SAMBROOK MANOR

Sambrook, Newport, TF10 8AL. Mrs E Mitchell, 01952 550256, eileengran@hotmail.com . *Between Newport & Ternhill, 1m off A41. In the village of Sambrook.* **Sun 19 July, Sun 30 Aug (12.30-5). Adm £5, chd free. Home-made teas. Visits also by arrangement May to Sept for groups of 10+.**
Deep, colourful, well-planted borders offset by sweeping lawns surrounding

an early C18 manor house (not open). Wide ranging herbaceous planting with plenty of roses to enjoy; the arboretum below the garden, with views across the river, has been further extended with new trees. The waterfall and Japanese garden are now linked by a pretty rill. Lovely garden to visit for all the family. Woodland area difficult for wheelchairs.

53 SECRET GARDEN

21 Steventon Terrace, Steventon New Road, Ludlow, SY8 1JZ. Mr & Mrs Wood, 01584 876037, carolynwood2152@yahoo.co.uk. *Park & Ride if needed, stops outside garden.* **Sat 20 June (1-5.30). Adm £3.50, chd free. Home-made teas. Home-made cakes, tea, coffee, ice cream. Visits also by arrangement June to Sept.**
½-acre of very secret south facing garden, Developed over 30yrs with enthusiasm creativity and the love of gardening by the present owners. Divided up into different sections: rose garden, herbaceous borders, koi fish pond with gazebo, summer house, poly tunnel and chickens.

Mediterranean style terrace garden with views of the Shropshire hills. Heart of England in Bloom Chairman's Award. wheelchair friendly can get round all lower parts of garden including seeing the chickens poly tunnel greenhouse some paths /lawns to get around.

54 STANLEY HALL GARDENS

Bridgnorth, WV16 4SP. Mr & Mrs M J Thompson. *½ m N of Bridgnorth. Leave Bridgnorth by N gate B4373; turn R at Stanley Lane. Pass Golf Course Club House on L & turn L at Lodge.* **Sun 31 May (2-5.30). Adm £4, chd free. Home-made teas.**
Georgian landscaped drive with rhododendrons, fine trees in parkland setting, woodland walks and fish ponds. Restored ice house. Dower House (Mr and Mrs C Wells): 4 acres of specimen trees, contemporary sculpture, walled vegetable garden and potager. The Granary (Mr and Mrs J. Major) Fine herbaceous border, hanging baskets and planters. South Lodge (Mr Tim Warren) Hillside cottage garden. Wheelchair access to the main gardens.

Beaufort

GROUP OPENING

55 STOTTESDON VILLAGE OPEN GARDENS

Stottesdon, nr Kidderminster, DY14 8TZ. *In glorious S Shropshire near Cleobury Mortimer (A4117/B4363). 30m from Birmingham (M5/42), 15m E of Ludlow (A49/4117) and 10ml south of Bridgnorth (A458/442) STOTTESDON is between Clee Hill and the Severn Valley. NGS Signed from B4363. SatNav DY14 8TZ.* **Sun 5 July (2-6). Combined adm £5, chd free. Light refreshments in the Parish Church.**

Located in unspoilt countryside near the Clee Hills, up to 10 gardens and the heritage church in Stottesdon village are open to visitors. Several places have stunning views. Some gardens feature spaces for outdoor living. Many are traditional or more modern 'cottage gardens', containing fruit, vegetables and livestock. There are contrasting vegetable gardens including one devoted to permaculture principles and one to growing championship winners. Take teas and refreshments in the Norman church and join a unique guided tour of the historic Tower, Bells and Turret Clock. A garden-related competition to be held and be judged by garden visitors. Dogs on leads please. Heritage Church open - tower tours. Lunches will be available at The Fighting Cocks pub before the 2pm NGS opening - call pub on 01746 718270 to pre-book (essential). Most gardens have some wheelchair access. Those gardens not suitable for wheelchair access will be listed.

56 SUNNINGDALE

9 Mill Street, Wem, Shropshire, SY4 5ED. Mrs Susan Griffiths, 01939 236733, sue.griffiths@btinternet.com. *Town centre. Wem is on B5476. Parking in public car park Barnard St. The property is opp the purple house below the church. There is also some on street free parking on the High Street.* **Sun 27 Sept (11-4). Adm £3, chd free. Home-made teas. Cakes £2 drinks £1. Visits also by arrangement Feb to Nov for groups of 10+.**

A good half acre town garden. A wildlife haven for a huge variety of birds including nesting gold crests. A profusion of excellent nectar rich plants means that butterflies and other pollinators are in abundance. Interesting plantings with carefully collected rare plants and unusual annuals means there is always something new to see, in a garden created for all year round viewing.

Koi pond and natural stone waterfall rockery. Antique and modern sculpture. Sound break yew walkway. Large perennial borders, with rare plants, unusual annuals, exotic climbers, designed by owner as an all year round garden. Why not include a visit by having lunch at the floral Castle Hotel in Wem. Although the garden is on the level there are a number of steps mostly around the pond area; paths are mainly gravel or flags; there is a flat lawn.

57 UPPER MARSHES

Catherton Common, Hopton Wafers, nr Kidderminster, DY14 0JJ. Jo & Chris Bargman. *3m NW of Cleobury Mortimer. From A4117 follow signs to Catherton. Property is on Common land 100yds at end of track.* **Sun 5 July (12-5). Adm £5, chd free. Home-made teas.**

Commoner's stone cottage and 3 acre small holding. 800' high. Garden has been developed to complement its unique location on edge of Catherton common with herbaceous borders, vegetable plot, herb garden. Short walk down to a spring fed wildlife pond. Plenty of seats to stop and take in the tranquillity. Optional circular walk across Wildlife Trust common to SSI field. Various animals and poultry.

58 UPPER SHELDERTON HOUSE

Shelderton, Clungunford, Craven Arms, SY7 0PE. Andrew Benton & Tricia McHaffie. *Between Ludlow & Craven Arms. Heading from Shrewsbury to Ludlow on A49, take 1st R after Onibury railway crossing. Take 3rd R signed Shelderton. After approx 2½m the house is on L. Look out for yellow NGS signs.* **Sat 16, Sun 17 May (1.30-5). Adm £5, chd free. Home-made teas.**

Set in a stunning tranquil position, our naturalistic and evolving 6½ acre garden was originally landscaped in 1962. Most of the trees, azaleas and rhododendrons were planted then. There is a wonderful new kitchen garden designed and planted by Jayne and Norman Grove. Ponds and woodland walk encourage wildlife. A large sweeping lawn leads in various directions revealing a multitude of colourful rhododendron and azalea beds, ponds a varied collection of trees and a very productive kitchen

Horatio's Garden

garden. There are plenty of tranquil seating areas from which to enjoy a moment in our garden. unfortunately our garden isn't flat and there are gravel paths, however if you contact us beforehand we may be able to offer a solution.

59 WALCOT HALL
Lydbury North, SY7 8AZ. Mr & Mrs C R W Parish, 01588 680570, secretary@walcothall.com, www.walcothall.com. *4m SE of Bishop's Castle. B4385 Craven Arms to Bishop's Castle, turn L by Powis Arms, in Lydbury North.* **Sun 24, Mon 25 May (1.30-5.30). Adm £5, chd free. Tea.**
Arboretum planted by Lord Clive of India's son, Edward. Cascades of rhododendrons, azaleas amongst specimen trees and pools. Fine views of Sir William Chambers' Clock Towers, with lake and hills beyond. Walled kitchen garden; dovecote; meat safe; ice house and mile-long lakes. Outstanding ballroom where excellent teas are served. Russian wooden church, grotto and fountain now complete and working; tin chapel. Relaxed borders and rare shrubs. Lakeside replanted, and water garden at western end re-established. The garden adjacent to the ballroom is accessible via a sloping bank, as is the walled garden and arboretum.

60 NEW WESTHOPE COLLEGE
Westhope, Craven Arms, SY7 9JL. Alison Bentley-Price, www.westhope.org.uk/. *At Westhope off the B4368 Craven Arms/Bridgnorth road. From A49 at Craven Arms turn L (from Shrewsbury) or R (from Ludlow). Follow B4368 then signs (on L or R) to Westhope College. Watch for yellow NGS signs.* **Tue 2 June (10-5). Adm £5, chd free. Tea.**
More than 3,500 common orchids live in our meadow: a delight to see. There are wildflowers, wildlife and a lovely woodland walk with stream/pond. The now restored walled garden is full of produce and flowers. The pretty front garden welcomes visitors to the college, part of which opened for the National Garden Scheme in the 1980s. The large main garden has been rewilded for over 30 years. Good wheelchair access throughout.

61 NEW WESTWOOD HOUSE
Oldbury, Bridgnorth, WV16 5LP. Hugh & Carolyn Trevor-Jones. *Take the Ludlow Road B4364 out of Bridgnorth. Past the Punch Bowl Inn and turn 1st L. Westwood House will be sign-posted on the R.* **Wed 6 May (2-5). Adm £5, chd free. Home-made teas. Refreshments in aid of St Nicholas Church, Oldbury.**
A beautiful country garden, well designed and planted around the house, particularly known for its tulips. Sweeping lawns offset by deeply planted mixed borders; newly planted pool garden. Extensive productive kitchen and cutting garden, with everything designed to attract wildlife for organic growth. Far reaching views of this delightful corner of the county and woodland walks to enjoy. Reasonable access around the house, but gravel paths and some steps.

62 WINDY RIDGE
Church Lane, Little Wenlock, Telford, TF6 5BB. George & Fiona Chancellor, 01952 507675, fiona.chancellor@ngs.org.uk. *2m S of Wellington. Follow signs for Little Wenlock from N (J7, M54) or E (off A5223 at Horsehay). Parking signed. Do not rely on SatNav.* **Sun 31 May, Sun 28 June, Sun 9 Aug, Sun 6 Sept (12-5). Adm £6, chd free. Home-made teas. Visits also by arrangement May to Sept for groups of 10+.**
Universally admired for its structure, inspirational planting and balance of texture, form and all-season colour, the garden more than lives up to its award-winning record. Developed over 30 years, 'open plan' garden rooms display over 1000 species (mostly labelled) in a range of colour-themed planting styles, beautifully set off by well-tended lawns, plenty of water and fascinating sculpture. Some gravel paths but help available.

63 ◆ WOLLERTON OLD HALL
Wollerton, Market Drayton, TF9 3NA. Lesley & John Jenkins, 01630 685760, info@wollertonoldhallgarden.com, www.wollertonoldhallgarden.com. *4m SW of Market Drayton. On A53 between Hodnet & A53-A41 junction. Follow brown signs.* **For NGS: Fri 15 May (12-5). Adm £8, chd £1.**

Light refreshments. **For other opening times and information, please phone, email or visit garden website.**
4-acre garden created around C16 house (not open). Formal structure creates variety of gardens each with own colour theme and character. Planting is mainly of perennials, the large range of which results in significant collections of salvias, clematis, crocosmias and roses. Wales & Marches Regional Winner, The English Garden's The Nation's Favourite Gardens 2019. Ongoing lectures by Gardening Celebrities including Chris Beardshaw, and other garden designers and personalities. For refreshments, food is freshly prepared in the Tea Room for each open day. Home-cooked, hot and cold lunches which have a reputation for quality, licensed to sell alcohol. Free Head Gardener's Walks. Partial wheelchair access.

64 NEW WOODLANDS
Brandhill, Onibury, Craven Arms, SY7 0PG. John & Anne Green. *Off A49 at Onibury level crossing. From Shrewsbury direction take 1st R after level crossing (L from Ludlow direction); turn into Green Lane about ½m along; last house on R at top of hill. Watch for NGS signs.* **Sun 28 June (2-5). Adm £5, chd free. Tea.**
A mature garden, with outstanding views across the South Shropshire Hills, which has undergone major transformation; where dense shrubbery and rhododendrons once covered the garden, intimate and cleverly planted spaces have emerged with an interesting range of plants. The woodland garden with its vast array of woodland and shade plants is of particular interest as are the specimen trees.

We open the gates to the nation's best gardens, offering a relaxing, memorable and affordable day out. A perfect experience to share with friends and family.

Somerset, Bristol, Bath and South Gloucestershire make up a National Garden Scheme 'county' of captivating contrasts, with castles and countryside and wildlife and wetlands, from amazing cities to bustling market towns, coastal resorts and picturesque villages.

Bristol's stunning location and famous landmarks offer a wonderful backdrop to our creative and inspiring garden owners who have made tranquil havens and tropical back gardens in urban surroundings. The surrounding countryside is home to gardens featuring contrasting mixtures of formality, woodland, water, orchard and kitchen gardens.

Bath is a world heritage site for its Georgian architecture and renowned for its Roman Baths. Our garden visitors can enjoy the quintessentially English garden of Bath Priory Hotel with its billowing borders and croquet lawn, or venture further afield and explore the hidden gems in nearby villages.

Somerset is a rural county of rolling hills such as the Mendips, the Quantocks and Exmoor National Park contrasted with the low-lying Somerset Levels. Famous for cheddar cheese, strawberries and cider; agriculture is a major occupation. It is home to Wells, the smallest cathedral city in England, and the lively county town of Taunton.

Visitors can explore more than 150 diverse gardens, mostly privately owned and not normally open to the public ranging from small urban plots to country estates.

Somerset Volunteers

County Organiser
Laura Howard 01460 282911
laura.howard@ngs.org.uk

County Treasurer
Jill Wardle 01460 281902
jill.wardle@ngs.org.uk

Publicity
Roger Peacock
roger.peacock@ngs.org.uk

Social Media
Rae Hick 07972 280083
raehick@gmail.com

Photographer
Sue Sayer 07773 181891
suesayer58@hotmail.com

Presentations
Dave & Prue Moon 01373 473381
davidmoon202@btinternet.com

Booklet Co-ordinator
Position vacant. For details please contact Su Mills or Laura Howard (as above)

Booklet Distributor
Ash Warne 07548 889705
ashwarne@btinternet.com

Assistant County Organisers
Liz Anderson 07871 103257
lizandersoncello@gmail.com

Marsha Casely 07854 882616
marsha.casely@ngs.org.uk

Patricia Davies-Gilbert 01823 412187 pdaviesgilbert@gmail.com

Alison Highnam 01258 821576
allies1@btinternet.com

Janet Jones 01749 850509
janet.jones@ngs.org.uk

Nicky Ramsay 01643 862078
nicky.ramsay@ngs.org.uk

Judith Stanford 01761 233045
judithstanford.ngs@hotmail.co.uk

Ash Warne (as above)

Bristol Area Volunteers

County Organiser
Su Mills 01454 615438
su.mills@ngs.org.uk

County Treasurer
Ken Payne 01275 333146
kg.payne@outlook.com

Publicity
Myra Ginns 01454 415396
myra.ginns@ngs.org.uk

Booklet Co-ordinator
Position vacant. For details please contact Su Mills or Laura Howard (as above)

Booklet Distributor
Graham Guest 01275 472393
gandsguest@btinternet.com

John Simmons 07855 944049
john.acheta@btinternet.com

Assistant County Organisers
Angela Conibere 01454 413828
aeconibere@hotmail.com

Graham Guest (as above)

Tracey Halladay 07956 784838
thallada@icloud.com

Christine Healey 01454 612795
christine.healey@uwclub.net

Margaret Jones 01225 891229
ian@weircott.plus.com

Jeanette Parker 01454 299699
jeanette_parker@hotmail.co.uk

Jane Perkins 01454 414570
janekperkins@gmail.com

Irene Randow 01275 857208
irene.randow@sky.com

OPENING DATES

All entries subject to change. For latest information check www.ngs.org.uk

Map locator numbers are shown to the right of each garden name.

February

Snowdrop Festival

Sunday 2nd
Rock House   74
Vine House   93

Sunday 9th
Rock House   74

Saturday 15th
◆ East Lambrook Manor
   Gardens   28

Sunday 16th
◆ Elworthy Cottage   30

Sunday 23rd
Algars Manor   2
Algars Mill   3

Thursday 27th
◆ Elworthy Cottage   30

March

Sunday 1st
NEW Langford Court   53

Tuesday 3rd
◆ Hestercombe
   Gardens   44

Saturday 21st
Lower Shalford Farm   57

Sunday 22nd
Rock House   74

Sunday 29th
◆ Midney Gardens   59
Rock House   74

April

Thursday 9th
◆ Elworthy Cottage   30

Saturday 11th
Weir Cottage   97

Sunday 12th
Hangeridge
   Farmhouse   40
Weir Cottage   97

Monday 13th
◆ Elworthy Cottage   30
Truffles   91

Wednesday 15th
◆ Greencombe
   Gardens   38

Thursday 16th
◆ Elworthy Cottage   30

Friday 17th
NEW The Downs
   Preparatory School   25

Saturday 18th
NEW The Downs
   Preparatory School   25
Westbrook House   99

Sunday 19th
Fairfield   31
Rose Cottage   75
◆ The Yeo Valley Organic
   Garden at Holt
   Farm   101

Saturday 25th
4 Haytor Park   42
◆ The Walled Gardens of
   Cannington   94

Sunday 26th
Algars Manor   2
Algars Mill   3
4 Haytor Park   42
Lucombe House   58
◆ The Walled Gardens of
   Cannington   94
Watcombe   95
Wayford Manor   96

Thursday 30th
Bath Priory Hotel   9

May

Sunday 3rd
◆ East Lambrook Manor
   Gardens   28
Greystones   39

Thursday 7th
◆ Kilver Court
   Gardens   51

Friday 8th
◆ Elworthy Cottage   30

Saturday 9th
Hillcrest   45
Lane End House   52

Sunday 10th
Hillcrest   45
Lane End House   52
◆ Milton Lodge   61

Wednesday 13th
Laughing Water   54

Sunday 17th
Watcombe   95

Thursday 21st
◆ Elworthy Cottage   30

Saturday 23rd
John's Corner   50
Lower Shalford Farm   57

Sunday 24th
Babbs Farm   5
◆ Court House   21
John's Corner   50
NEW Somerset Street
   Display Gardens   81

Monday 25th
Babbs Farm   5
◆ Elworthy Cottage   30
◆ Stoberry Garden   84

Tuesday 26th
Wellfield Barn   98

Sunday 31st
Rendy Farm   72
NEW Somerset Street
   Display Gardens   81

June

Tuesday 2nd
◆ Hestercombe
   Gardens   44

Wednesday 3rd
Wrington Gardens   100

Saturday 6th
NEW Barrow Farm   7
Isle Abbotts Gardens   48
Little Hintock   55
Stoneleigh Down   86

Sunday 7th
Elmcroft   29
Isle Abbotts Gardens   48
◆ Milton Lodge   61
Penny Brohn UK   70
St Arilda's House   77
Stoneleigh Down   86
Wrington Gardens   100

Wednesday 10th
Laughing Water   54
Watcombe   95

Friday 12th
The Miller's House   60

Saturday 13th
The Old Rectory,
   Doynton   66
Westbrook House   99

Sunday 14th
9 Catherston Close   15
Holland Farm   46

Thursday 18th
9 Catherston Close   15
◆ Special Plants   83

Sunday 21st
Batcombe House   8
Crete Hill House   23
◆ Elworthy Cottage   30
Frome Gardens   34
Model Farm   62
Nynehead Court   64
Stogumber Gardens   85
Swift House   89

Thursday 25th
◆ Elworthy Cottage   30

Saturday 27th
NEW 13 Glenarm Walk   36

Sunday 28th
Fernhill   32
NEW 13 Glenarm Walk   36
Laughing Water   54
The Old Rectory,
   Limington   67
Yews Farm   102

July

Thursday 2nd
9 Catherston Close   15

Saturday 4th
Brewery House   12
NEW 165 Newbridge
   Hill   63
NEW The Rib   73

Sunday 5th
Ball Copse Hall   6
Gants Mill & Garden   35
4 Haytor Park   42
Honeyhurst Farm   47
◆ Milton Lodge   61
NEW 165 Newbridge
   Hill   63
Nynehead Court   64
The School Yard   78

By Arrangement

Arrange a personalised garden visit with your club, or group of friends, on a date to suit you. See individual garden entries for full details.

Algars Manor

THE GARDENS

1 ABBEY FARM

Montacute, TA15 6UA. Elizabeth McFarlane, 01935 823556, abbey.farm64@gmail.com. *4m from Yeovil. Follow A3088, take slip rd to Montacute, turn L at T-junction into village. Turn R between Church & King's Arms (no through rd).* Visits by arrangement May & June for groups of 10 to 20. Adm £5.50, chd free. If light refreshments are required please ask for details.
2½ acres of mainly walled gardens on sloping site provide the setting for Cluniac Medieval Priory gatehouse. Interesting plants incl roses, shrubs, grasses, clematis. Herbaceous borders, white garden, gravel garden. Small arboretum. Pond for wildlife - frogs, newts, dragonflies. Fine mulberry, walnut and monkey puzzle trees. Seats for resting. Restored Grade 2 listed dovecote. Gravel area and one steep slope.

2 ALGARS MANOR

Station Rd, Iron Acton, BS37 9TB. Mrs B Naish. *9m N of Bristol, 3m W of Yate/Chipping Sodbury. Turn S off Iron Acton bypass B4059, past village green and past White Hart PH, 200yds, then over level Xing. No access from Frampton Cotterell via lane; ignore SatNav. Parking at Algars Manor.* Sun 23 Feb (1-4). Sun 26 Apr (2-5). Home-made teas. Combined adm with Algars Mill £5, chd free.
2 acres of woodland garden beside River Frome, mill stream, native plants mixed with collections of 60 magnolias and 70 camellias, rhododendrons, azaleas, eucalyptus and other unusual trees and shrubs. Daffodils, snowdrops and other early spring flowers. Teas at Algars Manor in April.(No teas in February). Partial wheelchair access only, gravel paths, some steep and uneven slopes.

3 ALGARS MILL

Frampton End Rd, Iron Acton, Bristol, BS37 9TD. Mr & Mrs John Wright. *9m N of Bristol, 3m W of Yate/Chipping Sodbury. (For directions see Algars Manor).* Sun 23 Feb (1-4). Sun 26 Apr (2-5). Home-made teas. Combined adm with Algars Manor £5, chd free.
2 acre woodland garden bisected by River Frome; spring bulbs, shrubs; very early spring feature (Feb-Mar) of wild Newent daffodils. 300-400yr-old mill house (not open) through which millrace still runs.

4 NEW AVALON

Higher Chillington, Ilminster, TA19 0PT. Dee & Tony Brook, 07506 688191, dee1jones@hotmail.com. *From A30 take turning signed to Chillington opp Swandown Lodges. Take 2nd L down Coley Lane and then 1st L into Moor Lane. Avalon is the large pink house. Parking limited, so car sharing advised if possible* Visits by arrangement Apr to Sept for groups of up to 20. Adm £4, chd £2. Home-made teas.
Secluded hillside garden with wonderful views as far as Wales. The lower garden has large herbaceous borders, a sizeable wildlife pond and 2 greenhouses filled with RSA succulents. The middle garden has mixed borders, a lawn with wild spotted orchids, allotment area and a small orchard. The upper garden has a spring fed water course with ponds, plus many terraces with different planting schemes.

5 BABBS FARM

Westhill Lane, Bason Bridge, Highbridge, TA9 4RF. Sue & Richard O'Brien, www.babbsfarm.co.uk. *1½m E of Highbridge, 1½m SSE of M5 exit 22. Turn into Westhill Lane off B3141 (Church Rd), 100yds S of where it joins B3139 (Wells-Highbridge rd).* Sun 24, Mon 25 May, Sun 30, Mon 31 Aug (2-5). Adm £5, chd free. Home-made teas.
¾ acre plantsman's garden on Somerset Levels, gradually created out of fields surrounding old farmhouse over last 30 yrs and still being developed. Trees, shrubs and herbaceous perennials planted with an eye for form and shape in big flowing borders. Various ponds (formal and informal), box garden, patio area and conservatory.

6 BALL COPSE HALL

Hill Lane, Brent Knoll, Highbridge, TA9 4DF. Mrs S Boss & Mr A J Hill. *From A38 follow signs to Woodlands Hotel then L into car park.* Sun 5 July (2-5). Adm £5, chd free. Home-made teas. Cream teas.
S-facing Edwardian house (not open) on lower slopes of Knoll. Front garden maturing well with curving slopes and paths. Ha-ha, wild area and kitchen garden. Views to Quantock and Polden Hills. Kitchen garden enclosed by crinkle crankle wall. Flock of Soay sheep. The distinctive hill of Brent Knoll, an iron age hill fort, is well worth climbing 449ft for 360° view of surrounding hills incl Glastonbury Tor and Somerset Levels. Lovely C13 church renowned for its bench ends. Partial wheelchair access. Steep gravel paths in places.

165 Newbridge Hill

7 NEW **BARROW FARM**
North Barrow, Yeovil, BA22 7LZ.
Mr Joel Trott. *A359 from Sparkford,
Hearn Lane to North Barrow,
between post box and phone box*
Sat 6 June (2-5). Adm £4, chd
free. Home-made teas.
Young farmhouse garden rammed
full with thousands of plants as the
inexperienced and new to gardening
owners experiment with their ideas
to beautiful effect. All summer
flowers from a large selection of
perennials, box hedging, pergolas,
rose garden with over 100 roses
and large naturalised pond garden.
Wonderful views of rolling Somerset
countryside from meadow orchard A
secret entrance takes you for a stroll
through the field where you can meet
the black Welsh mountain sheep and
alpacas

8 **BATCOMBE HOUSE**
Gold Hill, Batcombe,
Shepton Mallet, BA4 6HF.
Libby Russell, www.
mazzullorusselllandscapedesign.
com. *In centre of Batcombe, 3m
from Bruton. Please park in field just
down from church as signed.* Sun 21
June (2.30-5.30). Adm £6.50, chd
£2.50. Home-made teas.
A designer's garden of two parts
– one a riot of colour through
kitchen terraces, potager leading to
wildflower orchard; the other a calm
contemporary amphitheatre with large
herbaceous borders and interesting
trees and shrubs. Designer garden,
plantswoman's garden. Interesting
herbaceous planting, naturalistic
planting, wildflowers and roses,
interesting pots, always changing.
Wheelchairs are welcome but we are
a steep garden with steps and difficult
access to some of the garden for
wheelchairs.

9 **BATH PRIORY HOTEL**
Weston Rd, Bath, BA1 2XT.
Jane Moore, Head
Gardener, 01225 331922,
info@thebathpriory.co.uk,
www.thebathpriory.co.uk. *Close to
centre of Bath. Metered parking in
Royal Victoria Park. No 4, 14, 39 and
37 buses from City centre. Please
note: Disabled parking only in Hotel
grounds.* Thur 30 Apr (2-5). Adm
£3.50, chd free. Home-made teas.
Discover 3 acres of mature walled
gardens. Quintessentially English, the

garden has billowing borders, croquet
lawn, wild flower meadow and ancient
specimen trees. Spring is bright
with tulips and flowering cherries.
Perennials and tender plants provide
summer highlights while the kitchen
garden supplies herbs, fruit and
vegetables to the restaurant. Gravel
paths and some steps.

GROUP OPENING

10 **BENTER GARDENS**
Benter, Oakhill, Radstock,
BA3 5BJ. *Between the villages of
Chilcompton, Stratton on the Fosse
and Oakhill, narrow lanes. A37 from
Bristol and Shepton Mallet, turn to
gardens by village shop in Gurney
Slade. Follow lane for approx 1m,
turn R at grass triangle before incline.
From Bath A367, after S on F, 2nd
R to Benter.* Sat 18 July (2-6).
Combined adm £5, chd free.
Home-made teas.

COLLEGE BARN
Alex Crossman & Jen Weaver.
(See separate entry)
FIRE ENGINE HOUSE
Patrick & Nicola Crossman.

Two contrasting gardens in a
beautiful, peaceful and tranquil
secluded valley setting, surrounded
by woodland. A profusion of
herbaceous borders add colour with
interest in each garden. The garden
at Fire Engine House is mature and
established, with lawns, generous
borders and narrow, enticing paths;
through a garden door and tumble-
down bothy is a small orchard with
specimen trees. College Barn: (please
see separate entry).

11 **BRADON FARM**
Isle Abbotts, Taunton, TA3 6RX.
Mr & Mrs Thomas Jones,
deborahjstanley@hotmail.com.
*Take turning to Ilton off A358. Bradon
Farm is 1½m out of Ilton on Bradon
Lane.* Visits by arrangement June
to Aug for groups of 10+. Adm £6,
chd free. Home-made teas.
Classic formal garden, demonstrating
the effective use of structure. Much
to see incl parterre, knot garden,
pleached lime walk, formal pond,
herbaceous borders, orchard and
wildflower planting.

12 **BREWERY HOUSE**
Southstoke, Bath, BA2 7DL. John
& Ursula Brooke, 01225 833153,
jbsouthstoke@gmail.com. *2½m
S of Bath. A367 Radstock Rd from
Bath. At top of dual carriageway turn
L onto B3110. Straight on at double
r'about. Next R into Southstoke.*
Sat 4 July (2-5). Adm £4, chd
free. Cream teas. Visits also
by arrangement May to Aug for
groups of 5 to 20. Refreshments
by arrangement.
³⁄₄ acre garden in centre of village.
The garden is all organic. We have
collected over the years a number
of hydrangea species, grasses,
euphorbia, clematis and bamboo.
Splendid views to S over rolling
countryside. Long established walled
garden with fine, mature trees, shrubs
and climbers. The mature planting
gives a sense of mystery as one
explores the contrast of colours and
shapes. Plants for sale. Wheelchair
access restricted to lower part of
garden.

14 **BROOMCLOSE**
off the road to Porlock
Weir, Porlock, Minehead,
TA24 8NU. David & Nicky
Ramsay, 01643 862078,
nickyjramsay@googlemail.com. *Off
A39 on Porlock Weir Rd, between
Porlock and West Porlock. From
Porlock take rd signed to Porlock
Weir. Leave houses of Porlock
behind and after about 500 yards
we are 1st drive on L. NB Some
SatNavs direct wrongly from Porlock
- so beware.* Visits by arrangement
Apr to Sept for groups of up to
30. Adm £4, chd free. Home-
made teas. Gluten-free cake
available.
Large, varied garden set around
early 1900s Arts and Crafts house
overlooking the sea. Original stone
terraces, Mediterranean garden,
pond, long borders, copse, camellia
walk, large orchard with bee hives.
Maritime climate favours trees,
shrubs and herbaceous plants. We
are increasingly looking to plant
drought tolerant species. Mixed
orchard including 37 apple varieties
- many recently grafted from local
heritage collections. Wildlife actively
encouraged.

15 **9 CATHERSTON CLOSE**
Frome, BA11 4HR. Dave & Prue
Moon. *15m S of Bath. Town centre*

W towards Shepton Mallet (A361). R at Sainsbury's r'about, follow lane for ½m. L into Critchill Rd. Over Xrds, 1st L Catherston Close. **Sun 14, Thur 18 June, Thur 2 July (12-5). Adm £4, chd free. Opening with Frome Gardens on Sun 21 June.** Wander around the corner to see the unexpected, a small town garden which has grown to ⅓ acre! Colour-themed shrub and herbaceous borders, patio, pergolas, pond and evolving wild meadow areas lead to wonderful far reaching views. Productive 'no dig' vegetable and fruit garden with greenhouse. Exhibition of garden photography from near and far, by the garden owner, displayed in summerhouse. Gold winner Frome-in-Bloom. Several shallow steps, gravel paths.

&. ✿

Avalon

16 CHERRY BOLBERRY FARM

Furge Lane, Henstridge, BA8 0RN. Mrs Jenny Raymond, 01963 362177, cherrybolberryfarm@tiscali.co.uk. *6m E of Sherborne. In centre of Henstridge, R at small Xrds signed Furge Lane. Continue straight up lane, over 2 cattle grids, garden at top of lane on R.* **Visits by arrangement in June for groups of 5+. Adm £5, chd free.** 40 yr-old award winning, owner designed and maintained, 1 acre garden planted for yr-round interest with wildlife in mind. Colour themed island beds, shrub and herbaceous borders, unusual perennials and shrubs, old roses and an area of specimen trees. Lots of hidden areas, brilliant for hide and seek! Vegetable and flower cutting garden, greenhouses, nature ponds. Wonderful extensive views. Garden surrounded by our dairy farm which has been in the family for over 100 years. We milk Jersey and Jersey cross cows, and also some sheep, horses and hens!

&. 🐄 ✿ 🚌 ☕

17 COLDHARBOUR COTTAGE

Radford Hill, Radford, Radstock, BA3 2XU. Ms Amanda Cranston, 01761 470600, amanda.cranston@yahoo.co.uk. *Bath & NE Somerset. South of Bath, please ask for directions when booking.* **Visits by arrangement Apr to Sept for groups of up to 10. Individual visitors welcome. Adm £5, chd £2.50. Light refreshments.** Please confirm group visitor

numbers 2 weeks prior to visit. An acre rural garden with mature trees, wild areas, cut flower and kitchen garden, greenhouse, open lawns and borders with secluded seating areas. Interesting outbuildings, hen house, small ponds, mini stumpery attracting yr-round wildlife and birds. Spring bulbs, wild primroses in April, colourful tulips later; the white garden gently comes to life before flourishing in summer. Summer long colour of herbaceous borders. Recently planted fern and hosta garden hides behind a shady corner in a dark pool contrasting the green and cream plants. Rose and lavender path lead to a riot of white japanese anemones in August as apple and medlar trees fruit. Wheelchair access to grassed areas may be weather-dependant. Some narrow and uneven paths.

&. ✿ ☕

18 NEW COLEFORD HOUSE

Underhill, Coleford, Radstock, BA3 5LU. Mr James Alexandroff. *Coleford House is opp Kings Head Pub in Lower Coleford with black wrought iron gates just before bridge over river. Parking in field 150 metres up the lane.* **Sun 13 Sept (10.30-4.30). Adm £5, chd free. Light refreshments.** The river Mells flows through this picturesque garden with large lawns, wild flower planting, ornamental pond, woodland, substantial herbaceous borders, walled garden, arboretum/orchard, kitchen garden, bat house, orangery and museum of classic cars. Most of the garden is wheelchair friendly.

&. 🐄 ☕

19 COLLEGE BARN

Benter, Oakhill, Radstock, BA3 5BJ. **Alex Crossman & Jen Weaver.** *Between the villages of Chilcompton, Stratton on the Fosse and Oakhill, narrow lanes. A37, frm Bristol and Shepton Mallet, turn to gardens by village shop in Gurney Slade. Follow lane for approx 1m, turn R at grass triangle before incline. From Bath A367, after S on F, 2nd R to Benter.* **Sat 12 Sept (3-7). Adm £5, chd free. Wine. Opening with Benter Gardens on Sat 18 July (2-6).** Created in the last 6 years, the garden at College Barn draws upon its surroundings of meadows and woodland, with hazel and hornbeam hedges and naturalistic plantings of perennials in large blocks or in matrices with ornamental grasses. Intimate walled garden filled with vegetables, herbs, flowers and fruit. A peaceful and tranquil secluded valley setting, surrounded by woodland. Featured in Gardens Illustrated.

20 COOMBE HOUSE

102 Bove Town, Glastonbury, BA6 8JG. **Mr Alan Gloak MBE, 07860 463647, a.gloak@btinternet.com, www.coombehouse.org.** *½m from town centre. Take shuttle bus from town hall car park. Coombe House in Bove Town is at top of hill which*

is top of the High St. **Sun 12 July (2-6). Adm £5, chd free. Cream teas. Visits also by arrangement June to Aug for groups of 10 to 20. Donation to TS5C.**
2-acre romantic and lavishly-planted garden, incl unusual and tender plants. Dramatic scenes, pools, terraces and Abbots' retreat. Kitchen garden, orchards, nut walk and lots to see and ponder on. An English garden in a mystical town with lots of country views It is a garden of colour, a rich liqueur distilled from the elements that surround it. Partial help at hand to assist.

21 ♦ COURT HOUSE

East Quantoxhead, TA5 1EJ. **East Quantoxhead Estate (Hugh Luttrell Esq), 01278 741271, hugh_luttrell@yahoo.co.uk.** *12m W of Bridgwater. Off A39, house at end of village past duck pond. Enter by Frog Street (Bridgwater/Kilve side from A39). Car park £1 in aid of church.* **For NGS: Sun 24 May, Sun 19 July (2-5). Adm £5, chd free. Cream teas. Discount/prepaid vouchers are not valid on the NGS charity days kindly donated by Court House. For other opening times and information, please phone or email.**
Lovely 5 acre garden, trees, shrubs (many rare and tender), herbaceous

and 3 acre woodland garden with spring interest and late summer borders. Traditional kitchen garden (chemical free). Views to sea and Quantocks. Gravel, stone and some mown grass paths.

22 NEW COX'S HILL HOUSE

Horton, Bristol, BS37 6QT. **Charles Harman.** *Approx 1m W of A46, 4m N of M4 J18. Please see location app what3words: giggle.listen.nicer.* **Sun 12 July (2-5.30). Adm £5, chd free. Teas in aid of the Nelson Trust.**
1 acre garden created by current owners over past 12 yrs and laid out over 2 levels, each backed by a high stone wall, with panoramic views to south and west. Small vegetable/ cutting garden and formal lawn flanked by pleached limes on lower level; upper level has herbaceous, shrub and yellow themed borders and orchard with meadow grass and wild flowers. Garden can largely be accessed step-free, but steep ramps and gravel paths may be problematic for wheelchairs.

23 CRETE HILL HOUSE

Cote House Lane, Durdham Down, Bristol, BS9 3UW. **John Burgess.** *2m N of Bristol city centre/3m S J16 M5. A4018 Westbury Rd from city centre, L at White Tree r'about, R into Cote Rd, continue into Cote House Lane across the Downs. 2nd house on L. Parking on street.* **Sun 21 June (1-5). Adm £4, chd free. Home-made teas.**
C18 house in hidden corner of Bristol. Mainly SW facing garden, 80'x40', with shaped lawn, heavily planted traditional mixed borders - shrub, rose, clematis and herbaceous. Pergola with climbers, terrace with pond, several seating areas. Design changes for 2020. A couple of seating areas not accessible by wheelchair as accessed though borders via stepping stones. Whole garden can be viewed.

24 THE DAIRY, CHURCH LANE

Clevedon Road, Weston-in-Gordano, Bristol, BS20 8PZ. **Mrs Chris Lewis, 01275 849214, chris@dairy.me.uk.** *Weston-in-Gordano is on B3124 Portishead to Clevedon rd. Find Parish Church on main rd and take lane down side*

East Lambrook Manor Gardens

© Ellen Rooney

Coleford House

of churchyard for 200m. *Access by coach involves a walk of 400m* **Visits by arrangement May to Sept for groups of 20+. Adm £6, chd free. Home-made teas.**

The garden surrounds a barn conversion and has been developed from concrete milking yards and derelict land. Once the site of Weston in Gordano Manor House, the ambience owes much to the use of medieval stone which had lain undiscovered in the land for over 2 centuries. Changes of level, with steps and gravel paths, make wheelchair access difficult.

25 NEW THE DOWNS PREPARATORY SCHOOL

Charlton Drive, Wraxall, Bristol, BS48 1PF. The Downs Preparatory School, thedownsschool.co.uk. *4.3m from J19 of the M5 or 8.3m from the centre of Bristol. Follow signs for Noahs Ark Zoo Farm from motorway or centre of Bristol.* **Fri 17,**

Sat 18 Apr, Fri 7, Sat 8 Aug (10-4). Adm £6, chd free. Tea, coffee, home-made cakes and biscuits will be served.

65 acres wrap around the Grade II listed Charlton House, once part of a wider estate including the well-known Tyntesfield National Trust property. Come and discover historic garden features, stumpery, pond and greenhouse. In addition, an edible and medicinal bed and well-presented annual bedding displays framed by beautiful views across open parkland with specimen trees dotted around the estate. Gravel paths and some steps. The majority of the garden is wheelchair accessible.

26 NEW DUNKERY VIEW

Brandish Street, Allerford, Minehead, TA24 8HR. Mr M Harris. *4m from Minehead. Off A39 between Minehead and Porlock.* **Sat 5, Sun 6 Sept (11-5). Adm £3.50, chd free. Light refreshments. Tea, Coffee, home baked cakes.**

½ acre plantsman's garden packed with unusual shrubs, grasses and tender perennials laid out in the cottage garden style. Repeat flowering roses, savias, dahlias and other late season herbaceous plants produce a riot of colour in late summer. A productive vegetable garden adds to the bounty.

27 EAST END FARM

Pitney, Langport, TA10 9AL. Mrs A M Wray, 01458 250598. *2m E of Langport. Please telephone for directions.* **Visits by arrangement in June. Adm £3.50, chd free.** Approx ⅓ acre. Timeless small garden of many old-fashioned roses in beautiful herbaceous borders set amongst ancient listed farm buildings. Mostly wheelchair access - some narrow paths.

28 ◆ EAST LAMBROOK MANOR GARDENS

Silver Street, East Lambrook, TA13 5HH. Mike & Gail Werkmeister, 01460 240328, enquiries@eastlambrook.com, www.eastlambrook.com. *2m N of South Petherton. Follow brown tourist signs from A303 South Petherton r'about or B3165 Xrds with lights N of Martock.* For NGS: Sat 15 Feb, Sun 3 May, Sat 11 July (10-5). Adm £6, chd free. Tea and cakes with gluten free options. Discount/prepaid vouchers are not valid on the NGS charity days kindly donated by East Lambrook Manor. 2021: Sun 14 Feb. For other opening times and information, please phone, email or visit garden website.

The quintessential English cottage garden created by C20 gardening legend Margery Fish. Plantsman's paradise with contemporary and old-fashioned plants grown in a relaxed and informal manner to create a remarkable garden of great beauty and charm. With noted collections of snowdrops, hellebores and geraniums and the excellent specialist Margery Fish Plant Nursery. Also open 1 Feb - 31 Oct, Tues to Sat and BH Mons plus Suns in Feb and May to July; (10-5). Main features not accessible to wheelchair users due to narrow paths and steps.

29 ELMCROFT

11 The Roman Way, Glastonbury, BA6 8AB. Mrs Joanna Cobb. *From Glastonbury town centre take A361 Fishers Hill in direction Shepton Mallet. Turn R at top of hill onto Butleigh Rd and immed R onto Tor View Ave for The Roman Way.* Sun 7 June (11-5). Adm £3, chd free. Light refreshments. Picnics also welcome.

Situated on legendary Wearyall Hill with stunning views of Glastonbury Tor and the Levels, this once neglected garden has been transformed by art historian Joanna into an intriguing and varied series of rooms. Incorporating all the elements and senses, here is space for exploration, inspiration, conversation and contemplation. Artists and photographers welcome. Stay for an hour or the day. Winner of Glastonbury in Bloom since 2017, including Special Award.

Your visits help change lives – since 1927, we've donated over £60 million to nursing and caring charities

30 ◆ ELWORTHY COTTAGE

Elworthy, Taunton, TA4 3PX. Mike & Jenny Spiller, 01984 656427, mike@elworthy-cottage.co.uk, www.elworthy-cottage.co.uk. *12m NW of Taunton. On B3188 between Wiveliscombe and Watchet.* For NGS: Sun 16, Thur 27 Feb, Thur 9, Mon 13, Thur 16 Apr, Fri 8, Thur 21, Mon 25 May, Sun 21, Thur 25 June, Thur 9, Sun 26, Thur 30 July, Sun 16, Mon 31 Aug (11-4). Adm £4, chd free. Home-made teas. Visits also by arrangement Apr – Aug and also Feb for snowdrops. Tea proceeds to Children's Hospice South West. For other opening times and information, please phone, email or visit garden website.

1 acre plantsman's garden in tranquil setting. Island beds, scented plants, clematis, unusual perennials and ornamental trees and shrubs to provide yr-round interest. In spring, pulmonarias, hellebores and more than 350 varieties of snowdrops. Planted to encourage birds, bees and butterflies, lots of birdsong. Wild flower areas and developing wildflower meadow., decorative vegetable garden, living willow screen. Seats for visitors to enjoy views of the surrounding countryside. Garden attached to plantsman's nursery, open at the same time. Discount/prepaid vouchers are not valid on the NGS charity days kindly donated by Elworthy Cottage.

Watcombe

31 FAIRFIELD

Stogursey, Bridgwater, TA5 1PU.
Lady Acland Hood Gass. *7m E of
Williton. 11m W of Bridgwater. From
A39 Bridgwater to Minehead rd turn
N. Garden 1½ m W of Stogursey
on Stringston rd. No coaches.* **Sun
19 Apr (2-5). Adm £5, chd free.
Home-made teas.**
Woodland garden with bulbs, roses
shrubs and fine trees. Paved maze.
Views of Quantocks and sea.

32 FERNHILL

Whiteball, Wellington,
TA21 0LU. Peter Bowler, www.
sampfordarundel.org.uk/fernhill.
*3m W of Wellington. At top of
Whiteball hill on A38 on L going
West, just before dual carriageway,
parking on site, Blue Badge parking
only in front of house please.* **Sun 28
June, Sun 23 Aug (2-5). Adm £4,
chd free. Home-made teas.**
In approx 2 acres, a delightful garden
to stir your senses, with a myriad
of unusual plants and features.
Intriguing almost hidden paths leading
through English roses and banks of
hydrangeas. Scenic views stretching
up to the Blackdowns and its famous
monument. Truly a Hide and Seek
garden ..... for all ages. Well stocked
herbaceous borders, octagonal
pergola and water garden with slightly
wild boggy area and a specimen
Dawn Redwood dating from 1960.
Wheelchair access to the tea terrace
is from the drive and front of house
only.

33 FOREST LODGE

Pen Selwood, BA9 8LL.
Mr & Mrs James and Lucy
Nelson, 07974 701427,
lucillanelson@gmail.com. *1½ m
N of A303, 3m E of Wincanton.
Leave A303 at B3081 (Wincanton
to Gillingham rd), up hill to Pen
Selwood, L towards church. ½ m,
garden on L - low curved wall and
sign saying Forest Lodge Stud.*
**Visits by arrangement Mar to
Oct for groups of 10 to 30. Adm
£6, chd free. Home-made teas.
Donation to Heads Up Wells,
Balsam Centre Wincanton.**
3 acre mature garden with many
camellias and rhododendrons in May.
Lovely views towards Blackmore
Vale. Part formal with pleached
hornbeam allée and rill, part water
garden with lake. Wonderful roses in
June. Unusual spring flowering trees

such as Davidia involucrata, many
beautiful cornus. Interesting garden
sculpture. Wheelchair access to front
garden only, however much of garden
viewable from there.

GROUP OPENING

34 FROME GARDENS

Frome, BA11 4HR. *15m S of Bath.
9 Catherston Cl signed r'about A361
W of town. Elmfield Hse, New Bldgs
Lne, A362 Portway T-light, Locks Hill,
5th L signed. 3 Lynfield Rd, A362
r'about L Badcox, R Nunney Rd,
2nd R Lynfield Rd signed.* **Sun 21
June (12-5). Combined adm £6,
chd free.**

9 CATHERSTON CLOSE
Dave & Prue Moon.
(See separate entry)

NEW ELMFIELD HOUSE
Nigel & Frances Day.

3 LYNFIELD ROAD
Sharon Rossiter & Dinah Randall.

A warm welcome awaits you at each
contrasting town garden developed
to share the lives and character of
the current owners. 9 Catherston
Close will bowl you over on seeing
how this town garden grew into
⅓ acre! Colour themed borders,
pergolas, pond, evolving wild
meadow area with fine far reaching
views. No dig veg and fruit plots.
Exhibition of owner's photography
on display. Elmfield House, entering
via a wicket gate engenders a feeling
of secrecy, surprise and welcome.
Surrounded by high stone walls lies a
60' by 100' secret garden with formal
lawn, mature trees and overflowing
flowerbeds. An elaborately decorated
folly completes the picture. 3 Lynfield
Road, 4 yrs after moving in, 1970's
garden is rejuvenated. Conifer and
rock front garden, fruit and veg
grows midst borders. Themed walled
Mediterranean back garden combines
hard landscaping and soft planting,
water features, pergola with roses
and clematis, gravel paths to paved
terrace. Thriving olive, fig and lemon
trees. Catherston Cl few gravel paths,
slopes, shallow steps. Elmfield Hse
few shallow steps. 3 Lynfield Rd some
gravel, steps in back garden.

35 GANTS MILL & GARDEN

Gants Mill Lane, Bruton,
BA10 0DB. Elaine & Greg Beedle,
gantsmill.co.uk. *½ m SW of Bruton.
From Bruton centre take Yeovil rd,
A359, under railway bridge, 100yds
uphill, fork R down Gants Mill Lane.
Parking for wheelchair users.* **Sun
5 July (2-5). Adm £6, chd free.
Home-made teas.**
¾ acre garden. Clematis, rose
arches and pergolas, streams, ponds,
waterfalls. Riverside walk to top weir,
delphiniums, day lilies, 100+ dahlia
varieties, vegetable, soft fruit and
cutting flower garden. Garden is
overlooked by the historic watermill,
open on NGS day. Firm wide paths
round garden. Narrow entrance to mill
not accessible to wheelchairs. WC.

36 NEW 13 GLENARM WALK

Brislington, Bristol, BS4 4LS.
Martin Fitton. *A4 Bristol to Bath.
A4 Brislington, at Texaco Garage at
bottom of Bristol Hill turn into School
Rd & immediately R into Church
parade. Car Park first turn on R or
take 2nd R into Glenarm Rd, and 2nd
R again for car park.* **Sat 27, Sun
28 June (1-4). Adm £4, chd free.
Home-made teas.**
As you walk through the gate you
will be welcomed by Japanese Koi.
Then take a step to another level to
the relaxing Japanese garden rooms
surrounded by Acers and cloud
trees. Past the fire pit area where
you can embrace the true sound of
Japan, continue through a gate to
a peaceful Zen garden. There you
will find seating to enjoy the serene
atmosphere.

Your visits help
change lives –
we've donated
over £17 million to
Macmillan Cancer
Support since 1984

GROUP OPENING

37 NEW **GOATHURST GARDENS**

Goathurst, Bridgwater, TA7 0AT. *4m SW of Bridgwater or 2½m W of North Petherton. Close to church in village. Park in field at north end village (signed) 500 yds from gardens. Tickets from Old Orchard only.* **Sat 18, Sun 19 July (2-5). Combined adm £5, chd free. Home-made teas at The Lodge.**

NEW **THE LODGE**
Sharon & Richard Piron.

OLD ORCHARD
Mr Peter Evered.

2 beautiful examples of quintessentially English cottage gardens in a rural village setting only 30 yds apart. Old Orchard is a ¼ acre garden planted to complement the cottage with over 100 clematis viticella interplanted with a range of shrubs, herbaceous perennials, annuals and summer bulbs. The Lodge is a ⅓ acre garden surrounding a thatched cottage comprising flower borders packed with shrubs and perennials. Fruit and vegetable beds are also a feature. Both gardens have wheelchair access to most areas.

38 ◆ **GREENCOMBE GARDENS**

Porlock, TA24 8NU. Greencombe Garden Trust, 01643 862363, info@greencombe.org, www.greencombe.org. *Between Porlock and West Porlock, off road to Porlock Weir. Follow A39 W through Porlock and fork R onto B3225 to Porlock Weir. Drive ½m and turn L at Greencombe Gardens sign. Go up drive; parking signed.* **For NGS: Wed 15 Apr, Wed 15 July (2-6). Adm £7, chd £1. Cream teas served on lawn with spectacular view onto Porlock Bay. For other opening times and information, please phone, email or visit garden website.** Donation to Plant Heritage.

Organic woodland garden of international renown, Greencombe stretches along a sheltered hillside and offers outstanding views over Porlock Bay. Moss-covered paths meander through a collection of ornamental plants that flourish beneath a canopy of oaks, hollies, conifers and chestnuts. Camellias, rhododendrons, azaleas, lilies, roses, clematis, and hydrangeas blossom among 4 National Collections. Champion English Holly tree (Ilex aquifolium), the largest and oldest in the UK. A millennium chapel hides in the wood. An ecologically constructed Green Room holds garden records, collection information, and paintings by Exmoor artist Jon Hurford.

NPC

39 **GREYSTONES**

Hollybush Lane, Bristol, BS9 1JB. Mr & Mrs P Townsend. *2m N of Bristol city centre, close to Durdham Down in Bristol, backing onto the Botanic Garden. A4018 Westbury Rd, L at White Tree r'about, L into Saville Rd, Hollybush Lane 2nd on R. Narrow lane, parking limited, recommended to park in Saville Rd.* **Sun 3 May (2-5). Adm £3.50, chd free. Home-made teas.**

Peaceful garden with places to sit and enjoy a quiet corner of Bristol. Interesting courtyard with raised beds and large variety of conifers and shrubs leads to secluded garden of contrasts - from sun drenched beds with olive tree and brightly coloured flowers to shady spots, with acers, hostas and a fern walk. Magnificent rambling roses. Small apple orchard, espaliered pears and koi pond. Paved footpath provides level access to all areas.

&. 🐕 ☕

40 HANGERIDGE FARMHOUSE
Wrangway, Wellington, TA21 9QG. Mrs J M Chave, 07812 648876, hangeridge@hotmail.co.uk. *2m S of Wellington. Off A38 Wellington bypass signed Wrangway. 1st L towards Wellington monument, over motorway bridge 1st R.* **Sun 12 Apr, Sun 26 July (2-5). Adm £3, chd free. Home-made teas. Visits also by arrangement Apr to Aug for groups of 10+.**
Rural fields and mature trees surround this 1 acre informal garden offering views of the Blackdown and Quantock Hills. Magnificent hostas and heathers, colourful flower beds, cascading wisteria and roses and a trickling stream. Relax with home-made refreshments on sunny or shaded seating admiring the views and birdsong.

&. 🐕 ☕

41 THE HAY BARN
Kingstone, Ilminster, TA19 0NS. Philippa Sage. *Kingstone is 1m out of Ilminster on Crewkerne road. Coming from Ilminster take Crewkerne road, at Kingstone Church turn L, road turns to gravel follow round to L. The Haybarn is first house on R.* **Sun 26 July, Sun 13 Sept (1-5.30). Adm £5, chd free. Home-made teas.**
Delightful garden created over past 8 yrs, wrapping around an attractive Moolham stone barn conversion creating a wonderful sense of peace and tranquility. Paths invite you around the garden to view the collection of unusual plants, shrubs and trees providing yr-round colour and interest. Gravel areas provide ideal planting for drought loving plants. Trees link the garden into the countryside. Front of house and driveway gravel, making pushing a wheelchair hard. Please ask for assisted parking. Plants for sale.

&. ✿ ☕

42 4 HAYTOR PARK
Bristol, BS9 2LR. Mr & Mrs C J Prior, 07779 203626, p.l.prior@gmail.com. *3m NW of Bristol city centre. From A4162 Inner Ring Rd take turning into Coombe Bridge Ave, Haytor Park is 1st on L. Please no parking in Haytor Park.* **Sat 25 Apr (2-5). Sun 26 Apr (2-5), also open Lucombe House. Sun 5 July (2-5). Adm £3.50, chd free. Visits also by arrangement May to Aug for groups of 10 to 30.**
Celebrating 20 years for the NGS, this quirky, very personal garden still offers fresh discoveries, along secret paths and in mysterious spaces. Plants for all seasons, down among the dragons, over many arches, around the wildlife pond and framing benches for resting and dreaming. Find a green roofed studio plus pots and more plants. Children's competition'Finding Dragons',with prizes.

✿ ☕

43 HENLEY MILL
Henley Lane, Wookey, Wells, BA5 1AW. Peter & Sally Gregson, 01749 676966, millcottageplants@gmail.com, www.millcottageplants.co.uk. *2m W of Wells, off A371 towards Cheddar. Turn L into Henley Lane, 50 yds turn L through stone pillars, continue to end of drive. Henley Mill is on R of building, visitor entry through garage doors. Limited parking-car sharing advised. Coaches may drop visitors at end of 100yd drive, car available to help* **Visits by arrangement May to Sept. Adm £5, chd free. Home-made teas.**
Beside River Axe, with a zigzag boardwalk at river level, lies 2½ acres of scented garden with roses, hydrangea borders, shady folly garden and late summer borders with grasses and perennials. Kitchen and cutting garden. Deck overhangs mill leat and looks down onto gunneras, Siberian iris and miscanthus. Due to the river children must be accompanied by an adult at all times please. Wild area of native English daffodils, fritillaries and cowslips in spring. Rare Japanese hydrangeas and new Chinese epimediums. We hold a collection of Benton bearded irises by Cedric Morris, some may well be in flower in May/June. Plants, as seen in the garden, for sale. Garden is on 1 level, paths may get a bit muddy after heavy rain.

&. ✿ 🚗 ☕

44 ◆ HESTERCOMBE GARDENS
Cheddon Fitzpaine, Taunton, TA2 8LG. Hestercombe Gardens Trust, 01823 413923, info@hestercombe.com, www.hestercombe.com. *3m N of Taunton, less than 6m from J25 of M5. Follow brown daisy signs. SatNav postcode TA2 8LQ.* **For NGS: Tue 3 Mar, Tue 2 June (10-5). Adm £13.30, chd £6.65. Light refreshments in Stables Café offering light lunches, teas and cakes and covered courtyard seating. Discount/ prepaid vouchers not valid on NGS charity days kindly donated by Hestercombe. For other opening times and information, please phone, email or visit garden website.**
Magnificent Georgian landscape garden designed by artist Coplestone Warre Bampfylde, Victorian terrace and shrubbery and an exquisite example of a Lutyens/Jeykll designed formal garden. Together these comprise of 50 acres of woodland walks, temples, terraces, pergolas, lakes and cascades. Hestercombe House offers a contemporary art gallery, sumptuous restaurant and second-hand book shop. 3 periods of garden design, contemporary art gallery, restaurant and cafe, restored watermill and barn, historic house and family garden trails, special late openings. Gravel paths, steep slopes, steps. All abilities access route marked. Tramper mobility scooter available, booking recommended in advance.

&. 🐕 ✿ 🚗 ☕

Your visits help change lives – your generosity has supported unpaid carers through donations to Carers Trust totalling over £4 million since 1996

45 HILLCREST
Curload, Stoke St Gregory,
Taunton, TA3 6JA. Charles
& Charlotte Sundquist,
01823 490852, chazfix@gmail.com.
*At top of Curload. From A358 turn L
along A378, then branch L to North
Curry and Stoke St. Gregory. L ½ m
after Willows & Wetlands centre.
Hillcrest is 1st on R with parking
directions.* **Sat 9, Sun 10 May (2-5).
Combined adm with Lane End
House £7, chd free. Home-made
teas. Visits also by arrangement
Apr to Sept for groups of 5 to
30. Visits by arrangement to be
booked and paid for in advance.**
The garden boasts stunning views of
the Somerset Levels, Burrow Mump
and Glastonbury Tor, but even on a
hazy day this 6 acre garden offers
plenty of interest. Woodland walks,
varied borders, flowering meadow
and several ponds; also kitchen
garden, greenhouses, orchards and
unique standing stone as focal point.
Most of garden is level. Long gently
sloping path through flower meadow
to lower pond and wood.

46 HOLLAND FARM
South Brewham, Bruton,
BA10 0JZ. Mrs Nickie Gething. *3m
N of Wincanton. From Wincanton:
B3081for 3m toward Bruton. R to S
Brewham. Follow NGS signs. From
Mere: B3092 toward Frome. Under
A303, past Stourhead Hse. L to
Alfred's Tower/Kilmington. Follow
NGS signs.* **Sun 14 June (2-5.30).
Adm £6, chd free. Home-made
teas in the Garden Room.
Delicious home-made cakes,
scones and biscuits.**
The house and garden at Holland
Farm were created from a derelict
farmyard 13 years ago. The garden
now boasts a number of exquisite
rooms, divided by hornbeam and yew
hedging. Some rooms are tranquil,
with a simple water feature or trees,
others burst with a variety of planting.
The house frames a stunning French-
style courtyard where the sound of
water echoes. The hornbeam avenue
leads the visitor to a swimming
lake with lakeside planting. Limited
wheelchair access.

47 HONEYHURST FARM
Honeyhurst Lane, Rodney Stoke,
Cheddar, BS27 3UJ. Don &
Kathy Longhurst, 01749 870322,
donlonghurst@btinternet.com,
www.ciderbarrelcottage.co.uk. *4m
E of Cheddar. From A371 between
Wells and Cheddar, turn into Rodney
Stoke signed Wedmore. Pass
church on L and continue for almost
1m.* **Sun 5, Mon 6 July (2-5).
Adm £4, chd free. Home-made
teas. Cream teas. Visits also
by arrangement Apr to Aug for
groups of 10 to 30.**
⅔ acre part walled rural garden with
babbling brook and 4 acre traditional
cider orchard, with views. Specimen
hollies, copper beech, paulownia,
yew and poplar. Pergolas, arbour
and numerous seats. Mixed informal
shrub and perennial beds with many
unusual plants. Many pots planted
with shrubs, hardy and half-hardy
perennials. Level, grass and some
shingle.

GROUP OPENING

48 ISLE ABBOTTS GARDENS
Church Street, Isle Abbotts,
nr Ilminster, TA3 6RJ. *4m N of
Ilminster. From Ilminster, take New
Road until you cross A303. Take
1st L then 1st R. Follow rd for 2m
to village. From Fivehead (A378)
follow signs to Isle Abbotts Car park,
postcode TA3 6RH.* **Sat 6, Sun 7
June (2-5.30). Combined adm
£6, chd free. Teas, coffees and
delicious home-made cakes in
Village Hall.**

GREGGS
Jenny Byrom.

LAUREL COTTAGE
Ann Cottell.

MONKS ORCHARD
Maureen & David Bradshaw.

NEW PITTS COTTAGE
Lorraine Vaun-Davis.

Historic village dating from Saxon
times, located on edge of Somerset
Levels with many thatched and stone
cottages. C13 Grade I listed church is
described as 'The Jewel in the Crown
of Somerset Churches'. Open church
tower. 4 very different gardens with
many exquisite herbaceous borders.
Laurel Cottge: ⅓ acre garden
developed over 32 yrs. Paths weave
through herbaceous borders where

plants are encouraged to self seed.
Greggs: ⅓ acre garden of many
parts, shrubs and borders joined by
winding paths. Monks Orchard: ¾
acre garden developed over 16 yrs.
Many large mixed borders with lots
of unusual plants. Stunning views.
Plants for sale propagated from
garden. Pitts Cottage: In delightful
setting. This large garden having been
neglected for 10 yrs is now being
developed by the new owner with a
passion for plants and flowers. Before
photos will be on display. Wheelchair
access to 3 gardens (Pitts Cottage
part gravelled).

49 ♦ JEKKA'S HERBETUM
Shellards Lane, Alveston, Bristol,
BS35 3SY. Mrs Jekka McVicar,
01454 418878, sales@jekkas.com,
www.jekkas.com. *7m N of M5 J16
or 6m S from J14 of M5. 1m off A38
signed Itchington. From M5 J16,
A38 to Alveston, past church turn
R at junction signed Itchington. M5
J14 on A38 turn L after T-lights to
Itchington.* **For NGS: Sun 2 Aug
(10-4). Adm £5, chd free. Light
refreshments. Our herb inspired
café will be open offering
seasonal herb-based treats,
home-made cakes and coffee as
well as Jekka's herbal infusions.
For other opening times and
information, please phone, email or
visit garden website.**
Jekka's Herbetum is a living
encyclopaedia of herbs, displaying
the largest collection of culinary herbs
in Europe. A wonderful resource for
plant identification for the gardener
and a gastronomic experience for
chefs and cooks. Wheelchair access
possible however terrain is rough from
car park to Herbetum.

50 JOHN'S CORNER
2 Fitzgerald Road, Bedminster,
Bristol, BS3 5DD. John Hodge,
0117 9720558. *3m from city centre.
S of Bristol, off St.John's Lane,
Totterdown end. 1st house on
R, entrance at side of house. On
number 91 bus route. Parking in
residential street.* **Sat 23, Sun 24
May, Sat 5, Sun 6 Sept (1-5). Adm
£4, chd free. Home-made teas.
Visits also by arrangement May to
Oct for groups of 20 to 30.**
Unusual and interesting city garden
in Bedminster with a mixture of
exciting plants and features. Ponds,

ferns and much more. Eden project style greenhouse with collection of cacti. Paths, no steps. Not all areas accessible by wheelchair.

& ⚘ ☕

51 ◆ KILVER COURT GARDENS
Kilver Street, Shepton Mallet, BA4 5NF. Roger & Monty Saul, 01749 340410, info@kilvercourt.com, www.kilvercourt.com. *Directly off A37 rd to Bath, opp Showerings factory in Shepton Mallet. Disabled parking in lower car park.* **For NGS: Thur 7 May, Thur 10 Sept (10-4). Adm £7.50, chd free. Light refreshments in Sharpham Pantry Restaurant & Harlequin Café. Discount/prepaid vouchers are not valid on the 2 NGS charity days kindly donated by Kilver Court. For other opening times and information, please phone, email or visit garden website.**
Visitors can wander by the millpond, explore the formal and informal gardens and enjoy a replica of the splendid Chelsea Flower Show Gold Medal winning rockery where a gushing recirculated stream flows from pool to pool and waterfalls into the lake. All this set against the stunning backdrop of Charlton Viaduct with the recently planted 100m border beyond. Featured on BBC Gardeners' World and in regional and national press. Some slopes, rockery not accessible for wheelchairs but can be viewed.

& ⚘ 🚗 ☕

52 LANE END HOUSE
Curload, Stoke St Gregory, Taunton, TA3 6JA. Eric & Veronica Martin, 01823491261, va.martin@gmail.com. *Curload, Stoke St Gregory, Taunton TA3 6JA. Taunton A358 turn L on A378, Fork L to North Curry & Stoke St Gregory. L ½ m after Willows & Wetlands Centre. 1st house on L. Parking at Hillcrest garden opp.* **Sat 9, Sun 10 May (2-5). Combined adm with Hillcrest £7, chd free. Visits also by arrangement May to July for groups of up to 10. Limited parking, max 4 vehicles.**
A mature Somerset Levels garden set on heavy clay with mixed borders, orchard, veg patch, greenhouses and free range chickens. The recent introduction of a ½ acre field into the garden sees mature trees and shrubs sharing the garden with newly planted specimen trees, a pond and wildflower areas that support our own honey bees and a variety of wildlife. Unique sculptures enhance the 1 acre plot. Level gardens with gravel courtyard.

& ☕

53 NEW LANGFORD COURT
Langford, BS40 5DA. Sir David & Lady Wills. *11½ m S of Bristol. 150yds S of A38 Bristol to Bridgwater rd. 1½ m N of Churchill T-lights. Signed Upper Langford.* **Sun 1 Mar (2-5). Adm £5, chd free. Home-made teas.**
The formal gardens cover many acres and this provides a rare opportunity to wander around this beautiful country estate in Spring. Number of discrete gardens within this vast space incl cutting garden, large mature pond, woodland, parterre, fernery along with large established herbaceous borders. The gardens have further been developed since its last opening, an old rose garden has been transformed into a tranquil white garden with multi stemmed silver birches, white herbaceous border and fragrant jasmine and the front borders have also been widened and developed.

& ⚘ ☕

Hestercombe Gardens

Your visits help change lives – we are Hospice UK's largest charitable funder donating more than £5.5 million to support hospices in local communities since 1996

54 LAUGHING WATER
Weir Lane, Yeovilton, Yeovil, BA22 8EU. Peter & Joyce Warne, 01935 841933, p.j.warne@btinternet.com. *2m from A303, 7m N of Yeovil. Leave A303 signed Ilchester, take B3151 dir RNAS Yeovilton, take Bineham Lane, signed Yeovilton village, Laughing Water last house on R at end of village. Park at weir just past house.* Wed 13 May, Wed 10 June (1.30-4.30). Adm £3.50, chd free. Sun 28 June (2-5). Combined adm with The Old Rectory, Limington £6, chd free. Home-made teas only at Laughing Water. Visits also by arrangement May to July for groups of 5 to 30. Morning, afternoon or early evening visits welcome, refreshments available.
½ acre+ garden hidden behind Grade II listed house (not open). A maturing garden, with ever changing beds and borders reflecting the owner's love of flowers and foliage. Sweeping grass paths lead through mixed beds packed with shrubs, herbaceous perennials, annuals and bulbs. Floriferous from early spring through to autumn frosts. Large wildlife pond and other ornamental water features. Picturesque weir (after which the house is named) on river 20 mtrs past house. Fleet Air Arm Memorial Church, with C13 Nave, in village worth a visit. Limited wheelchair access.
❋ ☕

55 LITTLE HINTOCK
Higher Vellow, near Stogumber, Taunton, TA4 4JH. Julian Spicer & Christopher Legrove. *Between Taunton (15m) and Minehead (12m): 1½m from A358. On Yellow Road halfway between Stogumber and Lower Vellow.* Sat 6 June (12-6). Adm £3, chd free. Home-made teas.
Quirky and rather wild. Cobbled path to stone cottage, dating from 1600, thick with climbers. Below, a stream winds through the orchard (more climbers) and woodland garden, with undulating grass paths. Above, pockets of unruly garden in steep woodland, with steps and steep paths. Views across the peaceful valley. 1½ acres in all.
🐾 🐕 ☕

56 LITTLE YARFORD FARMHOUSE
Kingston St Mary, Taunton, TA2 8AN. Brian Bradley, 01823 451350, yarford@ic24.net. *1½m W of Hestercombe, 3½m N of Taunton. From Taunton on Kingston St Mary rd. At 30mph sign turn L at Parsonage Lane. Continue 1¼m W, to Yarford sign. Continue 400yds. Turn R up concrete rd.* Visits by arrangement Apr to Sept. Adm £5, chd free. Cream teas/light refreshments by prior arrangement.
Unusual 5 acre garden embracing C17 house (not open) overgrown with climbing plants. 3 ponds and waterlilies. Its special interest are its 300+ rare and unusual tree cultivars: the best collection of broad leaf and conifer cultivars in Somerset West (listed on NGS website); those trees not available to Bampfylde Warre at Hestercombe in C18. An exercise in landscaping and creating views both within the garden and without to the vale and the Quantock Hills. Featured in Somerset Living 2019. On Google map. Mostly wheelchair access.

57 LOWER SHALFORD FARM
Shalford Lane, Charlton Musgrove, Wincanton, BA9 8HE. Mr & Mrs David Posnett. *Lower Shalford is 2m NE of Wincanton. Leave A303 at Wincanton go N on B3081 towards Bruton. Just beyond Otter Garden Centre turn R Shalford Lane, Lower Shalford is ½m on L. Parking opp house.* Sat 21 Mar, Sat 23 May (10-4). Adm £5, chd free. Light refreshments.

Fairly large open garden with extensive lawns and wooded surroundings with drifts of daffodils in spring. Small winterbourne stream running through with several stone bridges. Walled rose/parterre garden, hedged herbaceous garden and several ornamental ponds. Partial wheelchair access.
☕

58 LUCOMBE HOUSE
12 Druid Stoke Ave, Stoke Bishop, Bristol, BS9 1DD. Malcolm Ravenscroft, 01179 682494, famrave@gmail.com. *4m NW of Bristol centre. At top of Druid Hill. Garden on R 200m from junction.* Sun 26 Apr (2-5). Adm £3.50, chd free. Home-made teas. Also open 4 Haytor Park. Visits also by arrangement May to Sept.
For tree lovers of all ages!! In addition to the 250 yr old Lucombe Oak - registered as one of the most significant trees in the SW - there are over 30 mature English trees planted together with ferns and bluebells to create an urban woodland - plus a newly designed Arts & Craft front garden. A new path through the woodland will be completed in time for the NGS opening. It is hoped that a musical group featuring flautists will be present. Rough paths in woodland area, 2 steps to patio.
♿ ❋ ☕

59 ♦ MIDNEY GARDENS
Mill Lane, Midney, Somerton, TA11 7HR. David Chase & Alison Hoghton, 01458 274250, www.midneygardens.co.uk. *1m SE of Somerton. 100yds off B3151. From Podimore r'about on A303 take A372. After 1m R on B3151 towards Street. After 2m L on bend into Mill Lane.* For NGS: Sun 29 Mar, Sun 20 Sept (11-5). Adm £6, chd £1.50. Home-made teas. Discount/ prepaid vouchers not valid on NGS charity days kindly donated by Midney Gardens. For other opening times and information, please phone or visit garden website.
1.4 acre plantsman's garden, where unusual planting combinations, interesting use of colour, subtle themes and a natural flowing style create a garden full of variety and inspiring ideas. Increasingly known for its wildlife friendly planting, it includes a seaside garden, white garden, kitchen garden, woodland walk, wildlife pond and undercover

Glenarm Walk

62 MODEL FARM
Perry Green, Wembdon, Bridgwater, TA5 2BA. Mr & Mrs Dave & Roz Young, 01278 429953, daveandrozontour@hotmail.com, www.modelfarm.com. *4m from J23 of M5. Follow Brown signs from r'about on A39 2m W of Bridgwater.* Sun 21 June (2-5.30). Adm £4, chd free. Home-made teas.
4 acres of flat gardens to S of Victorian country house. Created from a field in last 10 yrs and still being developed. A dozen large mixed flower beds planted in cottage garden style with wildlife in mind. Wooded areas, lawns, wildflower meadows and wildlife pond. Plenty of seating throughout the gardens with various garden sculptures. Lawn games incl croquet and various garden sculptures from Somerset artists.
& 🐴 ✿ 🛏 ☕

63 NEW 165 NEWBRIDGE HILL
Bath, BA1 3PX. Helen Hughesdon, www.thehiddengardensofbath.co.uk. *On the western fringes of Bath (A431), 100m on L after Apsley Road. Several bus routes go to Newbridge Hill.* Sat 4, Sun 5 July (10-5). Adm £4, chd free. Light lunches and home-made cakes served in aid of The Peggy Dodd Centre for those suffering from memory loss.
Incorporating 'Sculpture to Enhance a Garden', an exhibition of outdoor sculpture, this Bath In Bloom award winning garden offers herbaceous borders, vegetable garden, greenhouse, shade garden, treehouse and swing, and a sunny terrace overlooking the garden where the refreshments are served. Pieces of sculpture are for sale. We regret that there is no wheelchair access.
☕

world gardens. The nursery offers a selection of herbaceous perennials, alpines, herbs and grasses.
✿ ☕

60 THE MILLER'S HOUSE
17 Horn Street, Nunney, Frome, BA11 4NP. Caroline Toll. *3m SW of Frome off A361. Nunney Catch, A361 between Frome and Shepton Mallet, follow signs to Nunney (1m) to village, turn L over little bridge, L into Horn St, 100 yards up on L. Please park in Old Quarry Car Park.* Fri 12 June (12.30-4). Adm £4, chd free. Light refreshments. Teas provided by Kilmersdon Gardeners, proceeds shared with NGS.
Garden of person who considers herself to be an untidy planter! Mostly perennial garden, terraced borders, rockeries, large romantic mill pond and wild area designed for bee and butterfly attraction, areas to sit and enjoy views of garden. Don't miss the terraced veg patch and small modern sculptures. Caution needed around mill pond steps and paths, stout footwear advisable. Wild paddock along the valley between the leat and Nunney Brook. There are several corners to rest in from which to enjoy the different views. Partial wheelchair access, small steps to top garden, part of remaining garden and millpond can be viewed here.
 ☕

61 ◆ MILTON LODGE
Old Bristol Road, Wells, BA5 3AQ. Simon Tudway Quilter, 01749 679341, www.miltonlodgegardens.co.uk. *½ m N of Wells. From A39 Bristol-Wells, turn N up Old Bristol Rd; car park 1st gate on L signed.* For NGS: Sun 10 May, Sun 7 June, Sun 5 July (2-5). Adm £5, chd free. Tea. Discount/prepaid vouchers are not valid on the NGS charity days kindly donated by Milton Lodge. For other opening times and information, please phone or visit garden website.
Mature Grade II terraced garden. Architectural terraces transformed from sloping land with profusion of plants capitalising on views of Wells Cathedral and Vale of Avalon. Garden was restored to its former glory by current owner's parents who moved here in 1960, orchard replaced with collection of ornamental trees. Cross Old Bristol Rd to 7 acre woodland garden, the Combe, a natural peaceful contrast to formal garden of Milton Lodge. Now a peaceful, serene and relaxing atmosphere within the garden following the ravages of two World Wars. Unsuitable for wheelchairs/pushchairs or those with limited mobility due to slopes and differing levels.
✿ ☕

Your visits help change lives – your generosity helps Marie Curie fund nurses to care for people night and day in their homes, with donations of more than £9 million

64 NYNEHEAD COURT

Nynehead, Wellington, TA21 0BN. Nynehead Care Ltd, 01823 662481, nyneheadcare@aol.com, www.nyneheadcare@aol.com. 1½m N of Wellington. M5 J26 B3187 towards Wellington. R on r'about marked Nynehead & Poole, follow lane for 1m, take Milverton turning at fork. **Sun 21 June, Sun 5 July (11-4.30). Adm £5, chd free. Light refreshments in Orangery. Visits also by arrangement Mar to Sept for groups of 10 to 30.**
The house is a private residential care home for the elderly, once the home of the Sandford family from 1590-1902. There was a stone house in late C14 but it was rebuilt in 1675 by John Sandford. The gardens are noted for many superb specimen trees, a pinetum and ice house built in 1803. Taunton Deane Borough Council also awarded the gardens an historic landscape award. Garden tour with Head Gardener at 11.30am and 2.30 pm. Partial wheelchair access: cobbled yards, gentle slopes, chipped paths, liable to puddle during or after rain. Please wear suitable footwear.

& ✿ ☕

65 NEW ◆ OLD DOWN MANOR GARDENS

Foxholes Lane, Tockington, Bristol, BS32 4PG. Old Down Estate, 01454 414081, countrypark@olddownestate.co. uk. Between Olveston and Tockington in S. Glos. Old Down Estate is approx 5 mins from M4 & M5 Almondsbury interchange & 5 mins from Severn Bridge at Aust. 10 miles N off Bristol. **For NGS: Tue 7 July (10-5). Adm £5, chd free. Tea and cake in the Manor House. For other opening times and information, please phone or email.**
Old Down Manor is a wonderful example of Victorian architecture; an elaborate setting for its surrounding flora. An old walled garden, framing an abundance of old English roses, flows onto rolling lawns and rockery gardens with views across the Severn Valley. Tempting pathways lead through a choice of woodland or wild flower meadows down to a tranquil lake with its own special node to nature. Very limited access due to the uneven pathways and surfaces.

🐾 🚗 ☕

66 THE OLD RECTORY, DOYNTON

18 Toghill Lane, Doynton, Bristol, BS30 5SY. Edwina & Clive Humby, www.doyntongardens.tumblr.com. At heart of village of Doynton, between Bath and Bristol. Parking in Bury Lane, on L just after the junction with Horsepool Lane. Car parking is signposted and charges may apply as there is another local event being held that day. **Sat 13 June (11-4). Adm £5, chd free. Home-made teas by WI.**
Doynton's Grade II-listed Georgian Rectory's walled garden and extended 15 acre estate. Renovated over 12 yrs, it sits within AONB. Garden has diversity of modern and traditional elements, fused to create an atmospheric series of garden rooms. Large landscaped kitchen garden featuring canal, vegetable plots, fruit cages and tree house. Partial wheelchair access, some narrow gates and uneven surfaces.

🐾 ✿ ☕

67 THE OLD RECTORY, LIMINGTON

Church St, Limington, Yeovil, BA22 8EQ. John Langdon & Paul Vintner, 01935 840127, jdlpv@aol.com. 2m E of Ilchester. From A303 exit on A37 to Yeovil/Ilchester. At 1st r'about L to Ilchester/Limington. 2nd R to Limington. Continue 1½m and house is immediately past church on R. Please park on drive. **Sun 28 June (2-5). Combined adm with Laughing Water £6, chd free. Home-made teas at Laughing Water. Visits also by arrangement Apr to July for groups of 5+. For group visits brief talk on history of Old Rectory.**
For group visits we provide cream teas, ploughman's lunches and wine by prior arrangement. Romantic walled gardens of 2 acres. Formal beds and herbaceous borders. Many unusual shrubs and trees incl 200 yr-old lucombe oak, liriodendron, laburnocytisus, trochdendron, leycesteria and poncirus. New meadow and wildlife pond and trees. A variety of peaceful seating areas where refreshments can be taken. Gravel drive, one gentle slope only into rear garden. No steps.

& 🐾 🚗 ☕

68 PARISH'S HOUSE

Hook Hill, Timsbury, Bath, BA2 0ND. Aisha Bangura. On B3115 North Road to Hook Hill entrance on R or from Camerton/Tunley take Timsbury exit at mini r'about, follow rd bend R. Garden is at E edge of village. **Sun 9 Aug (2-5). Adm £5, chd free. Home-made teas.**
8-acre garden surrounding Regency house (not open) with beautiful views across open countryside. Lawns sweep down to ha-ha. Colour themed herbaceous and shrub borders. Elegant water feature. Arboretum of specimen trees and more recently planted acer glade. New woodland walk taking you from native British woodland to more exotic woodland planting. Walled kitchen garden: vegetables, fan trained and cordoned fruit trees of significant age and cut flower beds. Parts of the garden are being developed so we invite you to share our vision, anticipation and excitement!

& 🐾 ✿ ☕

69 PARK COTTAGE

Wrington Hill, Wrington, Bristol, BS40 5PL. Mr & Mrs J Shepherd. Halfway between Bristol & Weston S Mare. 10m S of Bristol on A370 at Cleeve turn L onto Cleeve Hill Rd (opp sports field). Continue on Cleeve Hill Road for 1½ miles. Car park in paddock on R 50m from garden on L. **Sun 26 July, Sun 2 Aug (2-6). Adm £5, chd free. Home-made teas provided by Wrington Pop-Up Vintage Café.**
Take a colourful journey through 1¼ acres of this 'Alice in Wonderland' garden. Divided by high hedges is an established perennial flower garden developed over 27 yrs. Explore the labyrinth of different areas including a potager, jungle garden, rainbow border, white garden, green gallery, dahlia border & 90 ft of double herbaceous borders. A large Victorian-style greenhouse displays tender plants. Countryside views and plenty of seating. No WC available. Mostly good wheelchair access, some narrow bark chip paths. Narrow flagstone bridge with steps.

& 🐾 ✿ ☕

70 PENNY BROHN UK

Chapel Pill Lane, Pill, North Somerset, BS20 0HH. Penny Brohn UK, 01275 370073, fundraising@pennybrohn.org.uk, www.pennybrohn.org.uk. 4m W of

Bristol. Off A369 Clifton Suspension Bridge to M5 (J19 Gordano Services). Follow signs to Penny Brohn UK and to Pill/Ham Green (5 mins). **Sun 7 June (10-4). Adm £4, chd free. Cakes and light lunches are available.**
3½ acre tranquil garden surrounds Georgian mansion with many mature trees, wild flower meadow, flower garden, cedar summerhouse, fine views from historic gazebo overlooking River Avon, courtyard gardens with water features. Garden is maintained by volunteers and plays an active role in the Charity's Living Well with Cancer approach. Plants, teas, music and plenty of space to enjoy a picnic. Gift shop. Tours of centre to find out more about the work of Penny Brohn UK. Some gravel and grass paths.

71 THE RED POST HOUSE
Fivehead, Taunton, TA3 6PX.
The Rev Mervyn & Mrs Margaret Wilson, 01460 281558, margaretwilson426@gmail.com. *10m E of Taunton. On the corner of A378 and Butcher's Hill, opp garage.*

From M5 J25, take A358 towards Langport, turn L at T-lights at top of hill onto A378. Garden is at Langport end of Fivehead. **Sun 20 Sept (2-5). Adm £4, chd free. Home-made teas. Visits also by arrangement May to Oct for groups of up to 20.**
⅓ acre walled garden with shrubs, borders, trees, circular potager, topiary. We combine beauty and utility. Further 1½ acres, lawn, orchard and vineyard. Plums, 40 apple and 20 pear, walnut, quince, medlar, mulberry, fig. Fruit trees may be in blossom. Mown paths, longer grass. Views aligned on Ham Hill. Summerhouse with sedum roof, belvedere. Garden in its present form developed over last 15 yrs. Paths are gravel and grass, belvedere is not wheelchair accessible. Dogs on leads.

72 RENDY FARM
Oake, Taunton, TA4 1BB. Mr & Mrs N Popplewell. *1m from Oake PO and shop on road from Oake to Nynehead.* **Sun 31 May (2-5.30). Adm £5, chd free. Home-made teas.**

3 acre garden with formal walled front garden, raised vegetable beds and greenhouse enclosed by hornbeam, box and yew hedging. Decorative fruit and cut flower beds, meadow with large wild pond and orchard with stream running through, marked by pollarded willows and small garden surrounding shepherd's hut. Regret no wheelchair access.

73 NEW THE RIB
St. Andrews Street, Wells, BA5 2UR. Paul Dickinson & David Morgan-Hewitt. *Wells City Centre, adjacent to East end of Wells Cathedral and opposite Vicars Close. There is absolutely no parking at or adjacent to this city garden. Visitors should use one of the 5 public car parks and enjoy the 10-15 minutes stroll through the city to The Rib.* **Sat 4 July (1-5). Adm £5, chd free. Cream teas in the magnificent C15 Vicars Hall opp Garden. Unique opportunity - not normally open to the public.**
The Rib is one of the few houses in England that can boast a cathedral and a sacred well in its garden. Whilst the garden is compact, it delivers a unique architectural and historical punch. Long established trees, interesting shrubs and more recently planted mixed borders frame the view in the main garden. Orchard. Cottage garden. Vicars Hall catering provided by cathedral caterers. Vicars Hall is not wheelchair accessible - 30+ uneven steps. Further accessible options in city. Slightly bumpy but short gravel drive and uneven path to main rear garden. 2-3 steps up to orchard and cottage gardens.

74 ROCK HOUSE
Elberton, BS35 4AQ. Mr & Mrs John Gunnery. *10m N of Bristol. 3½m SW Thornbury. From Old Severn Bridge on M48 take B4461 to Alveston. In Elberton, take 1st turning L to Littleton-on-Severn and turn immed R.* **Sun 2, Sun 9 Feb, Sun 22, Sun 29 Mar (11-4). Adm £4, chd free. 2021: Sun 31 Jan, Sun 7 Feb.**
2 acre garden. Pretty woodland vistas with many snowdrops and daffodils, some unusual. Spring flowers, cottage garden plants and roses. Old yew tree and pond. Limited wheelchair access.

Monks Orchard, Isle Abbotts Gardens

75 ROSE COTTAGE

Smithams Hill, East Harptree, Bristol, BS40 6BY. Bev & Jenny Cruse, 01761 221627, bandjcruse@gmail.com. *5m N of Wells, 15m S of Bristol. From B3114 turn into High St in EH. L at Clock Tower and immed R into Middle St, up hill for 1m. From B3134 take EH rd opp Castle of Comfort, continue 1½ m. Car parking in field opp cottage.* **Sun 19 Apr (2-5). Adm £5, chd free. Home-made teas. Visits also by arrangement Apr to June for groups of up to 30.**

This 1-acre hillside cottage garden, carpeted with seasonal bulbs, primroses and hellebores, welcomes spring. Bordered by stream and established mixed hedges. The garden is evolving with new planting. Plenty of seating areas to enjoy panoramic views over Chew Valley, home-made teas and the music of the Congresbury Brass Band. Wildlife area with pond in corner of car pk field develops with interest. Hillside cottage garden with panoramic views over Chew Valley, full of spring and summer colour of roses and hardy geraniums. Organically gardened and planted to encourage wildlife. Limited wheelchair access, hillside setting.

76 NEW THE ROYAL CRESCENT HOTEL & SPA

16 Royal Crescent, Bath, BA1 2LS. The Royal Crescent Hotel & Spa, 01225 823 333, info@royalcrescent.co.uk, www.royalcrescent.co.uk/. *The gardens are behind the hotel. Walk through the front door of the hotel, carry straight on and exit the back door - the gardens will be in front of you. The nearest car park to the hotel is Charlotte Street car park.* **Mon 6, Tue 7 July (11-3.30). Adm £5, chd free. Light refreshments.**

One acre of secluded gardens sits waiting for you behind this iconic hotel, lovingly curated by head gardener John Bennett and his team. Gently winding lavender paths take you across the beautiful lawns, with various stunning floral displays along the route. Century-old trees, glamorous rose bushes, historic buildings and interesting statues; this garden has it all. Garden map available on the website. Wheelchairs can access most pathways in the garden.

The School Yard

77 ST ARILDA'S HOUSE

Kington, Thornbury, Bristol, BS35 1NQ. Carolyn & Tom Frost. *Leave Thornbury out of Castle St turning L into Kington Lane. Continue towards Oldbury, St Arilda's House is approx 1½ m on L. Follow signs for parking.* **Sun 7 June (2-5.30). Adm £5, chd free.**
Approx ¾ -acre garden in traditional English style. Walled garden with many split sections incl rose beds, herbaceous, shrubs and mature trees. Vegetable garden and small orchard outside walled area.

78 THE SCHOOL YARD

2 High Street, Wickwar, Wotton-Under -Edge, GL12 8NE. Jeanette & Tony Parker. *12m N of Bristol. Between T-lights at N end of High Street. If using SatNav please note High Street Wickwar not High Street Wotton under Edge. Parking in village - please park respectfully and consider our neighbours.* **Sun 5 July (1.30-5). Adm £5, chd free. Home-made teas in village hall.**
Garden arranged around a former Victorian school. Vegetable plot with large greenhouse. Raised beds edged by espalier and step-over fruit trees. Terraced flower garden with variety of trees and shrubs. Rockery. Mediterranean courtyard. Ancient yew tree and olive tree in courtyard area. Variety of English apples and pear trees. Limited wheelchair access, gravel paths and steps.

79 SERRIDGE HOUSE

Henfield Rd, Coalpit Heath, BS36 2UY. Mrs J Manning, 01454 773188. *9m N of Bristol. On A432 at Coalpit Heath T-lights (opp church), turn into Henfield Rd. R at PH, ½ m small Xrds, garden on corner with Ruffet Rd, park on Henfield Rd.* **Visits by arrangement July & Aug for groups of 10+. Adm £5, chd free. Cream teas. Home-made teas/glass of wine (evening).**
2½ acre garden with mature trees, heather and conifer beds, island beds mostly of perennials, woodland area with pond. Colourful courtyard with old farm implements. Lake views and lakeside walks. Unique tree carvings. Mostly flat grass and concrete driveway. Wheelchair access to lake difficult.

80 SOLE RETREAT

Haydon Drove, Haydon, nr West Horrington, Wells, BA5 3EH. Jane Clisby, 01749 672648/07790 602906, janeclisby@aol.com, www.soleretreat.co.uk. *3m NE of Wells. From Wells take B3139 towards the Horringtons and keep on main road for 3m. L into Haydon Drove, follow Sole Retreat Reflexology signs, garden 50yds on L. Pls phone if you feel unsure of directions.* **Visits by arrangement June to Aug for groups of up to 20. Car sharing advisable as restricted parking. Adm £4.50, chd free. Home-made teas. Please confirm numbers 2 weeks prior to agreed date.**
Described as "stepping into a piece of paradise". It certainly is a challenge to garden at 1000' on the Mendip Hills AONB. Laid out with tranquillity and healing in mind, the garden is full of old favourites set in ⅓ acre. 10 differing areas within dry stone walls and raw face bedrock incl herbaceous borders, labyrinth, water feature, contemplation garden and recent addition of the Gothic corner. Small pond quietly sits within one of the herbaceous borders. Tranquil, contemplation garden with corners for relaxation and mindfulness. Some gravel, narrow paths.

81 NEW SOMERSET STREET DISPLAY GARDENS

23-25 Somerset Street, Kingsdown, Bristol, BS2 8LZ. John & Heather Frenkel and others. *From Whiteladies Road, go up Cotham Hill. At roundabout, straight ahead. At end turn L, then 2nd R into Fremantle ROAD (not Lane). At end, turn R into Somerset St. Parking limited, find nearest space.* **Sun 24, Sun 31 May (2-5). Adm £3.50, chd free.**
A linked row of walled gardens dating from the 18th century, separated from their houses by a narrow setted street. Designed as display gardens for the enjoyment of passers-by, they form a welcome green space of shrubs and perennials between terraces of Georgian houses. Features include a box parterre, pleached hornbeam hedge, fan-trained apple trees, pond, mature trees and mixed borders. Steps, paths, no wheelchair access.

82 SOUTH KELDING

Brewery Hill, Upton Cheyney, Bristol, BS30 6LY. Barry & Wendy Smale, 0117 9325145, wendy.smale@yahoo.com. *Halfway between Bristol and Bath. Upton Cheyney lies ½ m up Brewery Hill off A431 just outside Bitton. Detailed directions and parking arrangements given when appt made. Restricted access means pre-booking essential.* **Visits by arrangement May to Sept for groups of 5 to 30. Adm £4.50, chd free. Home-made cakes and tea/coffee are an additional £2.50 pp.**
7 acre hillside garden offering panoramic views from its upper levels, with herbaceous and shrub beds, prairie-style scree beds, orchard, native copses and small arboretum grouped by continents. Large wildlife pond, boundary stream and wooded area featuring shade and moisture-loving plants. In view of slopes and uneven terrain this garden is unsuitable for disabled access.

83 ◆ SPECIAL PLANTS

Greenway Lane, Cold Ashton, SN14 8LA. Derry Watkins, 01225 891686, derry@specialplants.net, www.specialplants.net. *6m N of Bath. From Bath on A46, turn L into Greenways Lane just before r'about with A420.* **For NGS: Thur 18 June, Thur 16 July, Thur 20 Aug, Thur 17 Sept, Thur 15 Oct (11-5). Adm £5, chd free. Home-made teas. For other opening times and information, please phone, email or visit garden website.**
Architect-designed ¾ acre hillside garden with stunning views. Started autumn 1996. Exotic plants. Gravel gardens for borderline hardy plants. Black and white (purple and silver) garden. Vegetable garden and orchard. Hot border. Lemon and lime bank. Annual, biennial and tender plants for late summer colour. Spring fed ponds. Bog garden. Woodland walk. Allium alley. Free list of plants in garden.

84 ◆ **STOBERRY GARDEN**
Stoberry Park, Wells,
BA5 3LD. Frances & Tim
Young, 01749 672906,
stay@stoberry-park.co.uk,
www.stoberryhouse.co.uk. ½ m
N of Wells. From Bristol - Wells on
A39, L into College Rd and immed L
through Stoberry Park, signed. **For
NGS: Mon 25 May (2-5.30). Adm
£5, chd free. Light refreshments.
Discount/prepaid vouchers are
not valid on NGS charity day
kindly donated by Stoberry
Garden. For other opening times
and information, please phone,
email or visit garden website.**
With breathtaking views over Wells
Cathedral, this 6 acre family garden
planted sympathetically within
its landscape provides stunning
combinations of vistas accented
with wildlife ponds, water features,
sculpture, 1½ acre walled garden,
gazebo, and lime walk. Colour and
interest every season; spring bulbs,
irises, salvias, wild flower circles,
new wild flower meadow walk
and fernery. Interesting sculpture
artistically integrated. New garden
created with Alan Titchmarsh for
garden programme on ITV. Regret no
wheelchair access. No dogs.

🛏 ☕

GROUP OPENING

85 **STOGUMBER GARDENS**
Station Road, Stogumber,
TA4 3TQ. 11m NW of Taunton. 3m
W of A358. Signed to Stogumber, W
of Crowcombe. Village maps given
to all visitors. **Sun 21 June (2-6).
Combined adm £6, chd free.
Home-made teas in Village Hall.**

HIGHER KINGSWOOD
Fran & Tom Vesey.

KNOLL COTTAGE
Elaine & John Leech,
01984 656689,
john@Leech45.com,
www.knoll-cottage.co.uk.
Visits also by arrangement June
to Sept for groups of 5 to 30.

POUND HOUSE
Barry & Jenny Hibbert.

WICK BARTON
Sara & Russ Coward.

4 delightful and very varied gardens
in picturesque village at edge of
Quantocks. Two surprisingly large
gardens near the village centre,
plus two very large gardens on the
outskirts of the village, with many
rare and unusual plants. Conditions
range from waterlogged clay to
well-drained sand. Features include
a courtyard, ponds, bog gardens,
rockery, vegetable and fruit gardens,
and a collection of over 80 different
roses. Fine views of surrounding
countryside. Wheelchair access to
main features of all gardens.

& 🐄 🌼 🚗 🛏 ☕

86 **STONELEIGH DOWN**
Upper Tockington Road,
Tockington, Bristol, BS32 4LQ.
Su & John Mills, 01454 615438,
susanlmills@gmail.com. 12m N
of Bristol. On LH side of Upper
Tockington Road when travelling
from Tockington towards Olveston.
Set back from the road up a gravel
drive. Parking in village. **Sat 6, Sun
7 June, Sat 5, Sun 6 Sept (2-5).
Adm £5, chd free. Home-made
teas. Visits also by arrangement
Apr to Oct for groups of 10 to 30.
Admission incl tea/coffee/cake
and introduction to the garden.**
Approaching ⅔ acre, the south-
facing garden has curved gravel
pathways around an S-shaped lawn
that connects themed areas. On a
level site, it has been densely planted
with a wide variety of trees, shrubs,
perennials and bulbs for yr-round
interest. Plenty of places to sit. Steps
into courtyard. Look at the website
for pop-up openings. Finalist in BBC
Gardeners' World Magazine 'Gardens
of the Year 2018', and filmed for BBC
Gardeners' World and ITV's 'Love
Your Garden'. Featured in the 2019
March issue of Gardeners' World
magazine.

🐄 🌼 ☕

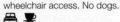

Your visits help
change lives – we
are the largest
single funder
of the Queen's
Nursing Institute

GROUP OPENING

87 **STOWEY GARDENS**
Stowey, Bishop Sutton, Bristol,
BS39 5TL. 10m W of Bath. Stowey
Village on A368 between Bishop
Sutton and Chelwood. From
Chelwood r'about take A368 to
Weston-s-Mare. At Stowey Xrds turn
R to car park, 150yds down lane,
ample off road parking opp Dormers.
Limited disabled parking at each
garden which will be signed. **Sun 19
July (2-6). Combined adm £5, chd
free. Home-made teas at Stowey
Mead, pedestrian entrance for
teas via lower gate at Stowey
Xrds on A368, entrance to R
of seat, diagonally opp lane to
Dormers.**

DORMERS
Mr & Mrs G Nicol.

◆ **MANOR FARM**
Richard Baines & Alison Fawcett,
01275 332297.
🛏

STOWEY MEAD
Mr Victor Pritchard.

3 very different gardens, not to be
missed, each with its individual style
and planting. A broad spectrum of
interest and styles developing year on
year. But there is far more than this
in these gardens, the visitor's senses
will be aroused by the sights, scents
and diversity of these 3 gardens in
the tiny, ancient village of Stowey.
Flower-packed beds, borders and
pots, roses, topiary, hydrangeas,
exotic garden, many unusual trees
and shrubs, orchards, vegetables,
ponds, specialist sweet peas, lawns,
Stowey Henge, and ha ha. An
abundant collection of mature trees
and shrubs. Ample seating areas,
wonderful views from each garden.
Something of interest for everyone,
all within a few minutes walk of car
park at Dormers. Plant sales at
Dormers. Well behaved dogs on short
leads welcome. Wheelchair access
restricted in places, many grassed
areas in each garden.

& 🐄 🌼 🛏 ☕

88 **SUTTON HOSEY MANOR**
Long Sutton, TA10 9NA. Roger
Bramble, 0203 9066213,
rbramble@bdbltd.co.uk. 2m E of
Langport, on A372. Gates N of A372
at E end of Long Sutton. **Sun 26**

July (2.30-6). Adm £6, chd free. **Home-made teas. Visits also by arrangement Aug & Sept for groups of 10 to 30.**
3 acres, of which 2 walled. Lily canal through pleached limes leading to amelanchier walk past duck pond; rose and juniper walk from Italian terrace; judas tree avenue; pteiea walk. Ornamental potager. Drive-side shrubbery. Music by Young Musicians Symphony Orchestra.

89 SWIFT HOUSE

9 Lyndale Avenue, Stoke Bishop, Bristol, BS9 1BS. Mark & Jane Glanville, www.bristolgarden.weebly.com. *NW Bristol - 4m from city centre. 2m from M5 J18 Portway (A4). Turn into Sylvan Way. At lights take R onto Shirehampton Rd. After ¾ m turn R into Sea Mills Lane. Lyndale Ave is 2nd rd on L - we're half way up.* **Sun 21 June (1-4.30). Adm £4, chd free.**
We've designed our city garden to look beautiful, provide fruit and vegetables and to be a haven for wildlife. Plants are grown to provide food and shelter throughout the year with the emphasis on flowers that are nectar rich. We have the largest breeding colony of swifts in Bristol www.bristolswifts.co.uk. See inside our swift boxes via live cameras and learn about swift conservation. Plants and swift boxes for sale.

90 TORMARTON COURT

Church Road, Tormarton, GL9 1HT. Noreen & Bruce Finnamore, 01454 218236, home@thefinnamores.com. *3m E of Chipping Sodbury, off A46 at J18 M4. Follow signs to Tormarton from A46 then follow signs for car parking.* **Visits by arrangement Apr to June for groups of 10+. Adm £5, chd free. Please contact for refreshment arrangements.**
11 acres of formal and natural gardens in stunning Cotswold setting. Features incl roses, herbaceous, kitchen garden, Mediterranean garden, mound and natural pond. Extensive walled garden, spring glade and meadows with young and mature trees.

91 TRUFFLES

Church Lane, Bishop Sutton, Bristol, BS39 5UP. Sally Monkhouse. *10m W of Bath. On A368 Bath to Weston-super-Mare. Take rd opp PO/stores uphill towards Top Sutton/Hinton Blewett. 1st R Church Lane. Please park carefully on nearby rds, level disabled parking places top of drive.* **Mon 13 Apr (11-5). Adm £4, chd free. Home-made teas.**
Over 3 acres, lake views and surprises. Spring bulbs. Formal and wildlife planting linked with meandering paths, lots of sturdy seating. Some changes made in 2019. Magical wooded valley, ephemeral stream, wildflower meadows, hens. Wildlife pond, formal flower beds, some sculpture. Unique ¼ acre kitchen garden with several 21 ft long x 4 ft wide waist high raised beds. Wonderful views. Fairly steep drive up to house, grass and gravel paths for partial wheelchair access.

92 ◆ UNIVERSITY OF BRISTOL BOTANIC GARDEN

Stoke Park Road, Stoke Bishop, Bristol, BS9 1JG. University of Bristol Botanic Garden, 0117 4282041, botanic-gardens@bristol.ac.uk, botanic-garden.bristol.ac.uk/. *¼ m W of Durdham Downs. Located in Stoke Bishop next to Durdham Downs 1m from city centre. After crossing the Downs to Stoke Hill, Stoke Park Rd is 1st on R.* **For NGS: Sun 12 July (10-5). Adm £7, chd free. Light refreshments. Hot and cold drinks, sandwiches, salads, cakes and ice cream provided by local delicatessen Chandos Deli.** For other opening times and information, please phone, email or visit garden website. Donation to University of Bristol Botanic Garden. Exciting and contemporary award winning Botanic Garden with dramatic displays illustrating collections of Mediterranean flora, rare native, useful plants (incl European & Chinese herbs) and those that illustrate plant evolution. Large floral displays illustrating pollination in flowering plant and evolution. Glasshouses, home to giant Amazon waterlily, tropical fruit, medicinal plants, orchids, cacti and unique sacred lotus collection. For other opening times see website. Regional Finalist, The English Garden's The Nation's Favourite Gardens 2019. Special tours of garden throughout day plus sculpture pieces by internationally renowned artist Luke Jerram. Upon request wheelchair available to borrow from Welcome Lodge. Wheelchair friendly primary route through garden incl. glasshouses, accessible WCs.

Fire Engine House, Benter Gardens

93 VINE HOUSE

Henbury Road, Henbury, Bristol, BS10 7AD. Pippa Atkinson. *2m from M5 J17. From M5 J17 head to Bristol Centre. At 3rd r'about, R to Blaise. L at end of Crow Lane. 1st house on R.* **Sun 2 Feb (1.30-4). Adm £3.50, chd free.**
1½ acres of garden behind listed Georgian house. Mature trees, shrubs, herbaceous borders, rock stream and gunnera. Garden originally planted in 1940's for yr-round interest by the Hewer family, and features many unusual plants and trees. Partial wheelchair access, some paths around upper area of garden.

94 ◆ THE WALLED GARDENS OF CANNINGTON

Church Street, Cannington, TA5 2HA. Bridgwater College, 01278 655042, walledgardens@btc.ac.uk, www. canningtonwalledgardens.co.uk. *Part of Bridgwater & Taunton College Cannington Campus, 3m NW of Bridgwater. On A39 Bridgwater-Minehead rd - at 1st r'about in Cannington 2nd exit, through village. War memorial, 1st L into Church Street then 1st L.* **For NGS: Sat 25, Sun 26 Apr, Sat 19, Sun 20 Sept (10-4). Adm £5.95, chd free. Light refreshments. Discount/ prepaid vouchers not valid on NGS charity days kindly donated by Bridgwater College. For other opening times and information, please phone, email or visit garden website.**
Within the grounds of a medieval Priory, the Walled Gardens of Cannington are a gem waiting to be discovered! Classic and contemporary features incl the hot herbaceous border, the blue garden, the sub-tropical walk and a Victorian style fernery, amongst others. Botanical glasshouse where arid, sub-tropical and tropical plants can be seen. 2 smaller gardens within the walls (The Bishop's and Southern Hemisphere Gardens) are areas of real tranquillity. Tea room, plant nursery, gift shop, also events throughout the year. So plenty to see and do for all the family! Gravel paths. Motorised scooter can be borrowed free of charge (only one available).

   NPC

95 WATCOMBE

92 Church Road, Winscombe, BS25 1BP. Peter & Ann Owen, 01934 842666, peterowen449@btinternet.com. *12m SW of Bristol, 3m N of Axbridge. 100 yds after yellow signs on A38 turn L, (from S), or R. (from N) into Winscombe Hill. After 1m reach The Square. Watcombe on L after 150yds.* **Sun 26 Apr, Sun 17 May, Wed 10 June (2-5.30). Adm £4, chd free. Home-made cakes and cream teas, gluten free available. Visits also by arrangement Apr to June.**
¾-acre mature Edwardian garden with colour-themed, informally planted herbaceous borders. Strong framework separating several different areas; pergola with varied wisteria, unusual topiary, box hedging, lime walk, pleached hornbeams, cordon fruit trees, 2 small formal ponds and growing collection of clematis. Many unusual trees and shrubs. Small vegetable plot. Some steps but most areas accessible by wheelchair with minimal assistance.

96 WAYFORD MANOR

Wayford, Crewkerne, TA18 8QG. *3m SW of Crewkerne. Turn N off B3165 at Clapton, signed Wayford or S off A30 Chard to Crewkerne rd, signed Wayford.* **Sun 26 Apr (2-5). Adm £6, chd £3. Home-made teas.**
The mainly Elizabethan manor (not open) mentioned in C17 for its 'fair and pleasant' garden was redesigned by Harold Peto in 1902. Formal terraces with yew hedges and topiary have fine views over W Dorset. Steps down between spring-fed ponds past mature and new plantings of magnolia, rhododendron, maples, cornus and, in season, spring bulbs, cyclamen, giant echium. Primula candelabra, arum lily, gunnera around lower ponds.

97 WEIR COTTAGE

Weir Cottage, Weir Lane, Marshfield, SN14 8NB. Ian & Margaret Jones. *Weir Lane. Opp Weir Farm. 7m NE of Bath. Look for yellow sign on A420 between Cold Ashton & Chippenham. Weir Lane is at the E end of the High St.* **Sat 11, Sun 12 Apr (11-4). Adm £3, chd free. Home-made teas. All refreshment money to PTA Scarecrow Trail for Marshfield Primary Sch. Refreshments in the cottage if wet.**
S facing garden of ¼ of an acre. High stone walls to the N give some protection against Marshfield weather. Well drained limestone soil. Focus on Spring bulbs. Sat. 11th Guided walk by Cotswold Wardens. Meet Market Place 10am. Boots advised. Also, extensive, challenging but fun scarecrow trail organized by PTA of Marshfield Primary Sch. Regret no wheelchair access.

98 WELLFIELD BARN

Walcombe Lane, Wells, BA5 3AG. Virginia Nasmyth, 01749 675129. *½m N of Wells. From A39 Bristol to Wells rd turn R at 30 mph sign into Walcombe Lane. Entrance at 1st cottage on R, parking signed.* **Tue 26 May (11.30-4.30). Adm £5, chd free. Home-made teas. Visits also by arrangement June & July for groups of up to 20. Please confirm numbers two weeks prior to visit.**
Created over 23 yrs from a concrete farmyard into a tranquil ½-acre garden and still progressively developing. Structured design integrates house, lawn and garden with landscape. Wonderful views, ha-ha, pond/bog garden, mixed borders, hydrangea bed, hardy geraniums, formal sunken garden, grass walks with interesting young and semi-mature trees. Moderate slopes in places, some gravel paths

99 WESTBROOK HOUSE

West Bradley, BA6 8LS. Keith Anderson & David Mendel, andersonmendel@aol.com. *4m E of Glastonbury. From A361 at W Pennard follow signs to W Bradley (2m). From A37 at Wraxall Hill follow signs to W Bradley (2m).* **Sat 18 Apr, Sat 13 June (11-5). Adm £5, chd free. Visits also by arrangement Apr to Aug for groups of 10+. Donation to West Bradley Church.**
4 acres comprising 3 distinct gardens around house with mixed herbaceous and shrub borders leading to meadow and orchard with spring bulbs, species roses and lilacs. Planting and layout began 2004 and continues to the present.

GROUP OPENING

100 WRINGTON GARDENS
School Road, Wrington, Bristol, BS40 5NB. *At top of School Rd, by junction with Ropers Lane, Long Lane and Old Hill. 10m SW of Bristol, midway between A38 at Redhill or Lower Langford and A370 at Congresbury. Beware SatNav may take you to Orchard Close. Warfords is opp The Hanging Tree. Car parking in nearby field.* **Wed 3, Sun 7 June (2-5.30). Combined adm £5, chd free. Home-made teas at Mathlin Cottage.**

MATHLIN COTTAGE
Tony & Sally Harden.

WARFORDS
Roger & Susan Vincent.

2 contrasting properties on the edge of a delightful and historic village. Mathlin Cottage: a cottage garden accessed by shallow steps with wonderful views of the Mendip Hills. Border, pergola and walkway in front garden; more cottage-style back garden, full of bee/butterfly plants. Small pond, greenhouse and salad/soft fruit plot. Large specimen of Paul's Himalayan Musk tumbles over beech hedge dividing flower garden from fruit and vegetable areas. Plenty of seating and places to relax. Warfords: pretty garden remodelled since 2015, designed to encompass the wide and wonderful backdrop of the Mendip Hills. Plants of interest for all seasons, including alpines and sub-tropical species such as echiums. S-facing terrace in back garden, shaded by tulip tree. Grapevine. Beyond the greenhouse, with orchids, is a sunken gravel vegetable and fruit garden with raised beds. Plants for sale. Mathlin Cottage: wheelchair access for tea only. Warfords: wheelchair access in most of the garden.

Your visits help change lives – since 1927, we've donated over £60 million to nursing and caring charities

Manor Farm, Stowey Gardens

101 ◆ THE YEO VALLEY ORGANIC GARDEN AT HOLT FARM
Bath Road, Blagdon, BS40 7SQ. Mr & Mrs Tim Mead, 01761 258155, visit@yeovalleyfarms.co.uk, www.yeovalley.co.uk. *12m S of Bristol. Off A368. Entrance approx ½m outside Blagdon towards Bath, on L, then follow garden signs past dairy.* **For NGS: Sun 19 Apr (2-5). Adm £6, chd free. Light refreshments. For other opening times and information, please phone, email or visit garden website.**

One of only a handful of ornamental gardens that is Soil Association accredited, 6½ acres of contemporary planting, quirky sculptures, bulbs in their thousands, purple palace, glorious meadow and posh vegetable patch. Great views, green ideas. Events, workshops and exhibitions held throughout the year - see website for further details. Level access to café, around garden some grass paths, some uneven bark and gravel paths. Accessibility map available at ticket office.

102 YEWS FARM
East Street, Martock, TA12 6NF. Louise & Fergus Dowding, 01935 822202, fergus.dowding@btinternet.com, instagram.dowdinglouise. *Turn off main road through village at Market House, onto East St, past PO, garden 150 yds on R, 50m before Nag's Head.* **Sun 28 June (2-5). Adm £7, chd free. Home-made teas. Glass of fine home-made cider to all with a healthy constitution and aged over 18. Visits also by arrangement May to Aug for groups of 20+.**

Theatrical planting in large walled garden. Sculptural planting for height, shape, leaf and texture, pandemic of box topiary. Self seeded Ligusticum lucidum prairie garden. Low maintenance farmyard garden in cracked concrete, hens do the weeding, and pigs the compost heap. Working organic kitchen garden. Orchard and active cider barn – taste the difference! Mostly wheelchair access if you come in side gate.

OPENING DATES

All entries subject to change. For latest information check www.ngs.org.uk

Extended openings are shown at the beginning of the month.

Map locator numbers are shown to the right of each garden name.

March

Sunday 29th
The Beeches 4

April

Sunday 5th
The Beeches 4

Thursday 9th
23 St Johns Road 44

Sunday 12th
'John's Garden' at
Ashwood Nurseries 28

Sunday 26th
NEW 12 Meres Road 32
Millennium Garden 34

Tuesday 28th
The Upper House 51

May

Saturday 2nd
Yew Tree Cottage 62

Sunday 3rd
Cats Whiskers 11
Hall Green Gardens 26
NEW 12 Meres Road 32

Friday 8th
Keeper's Cottage;
Bluebell Wood 29

Saturday 9th
Keeper's Cottage;
Bluebell Wood 29

Friday 15th
23 St Johns Road 44

Sunday 17th
10 Paget Rise 39
Tanglewood Cottage 47

Wednesday 20th
The Secret Garden 46

Saturday 23rd
Four Seasons 22

Sunday 24th
The Beeches 4
Dorset House 18
Four Seasons 22
The Old Dairy House 37

Monday 25th
Bridge House 7
The Old Dairy House 37

Friday 29th
22 Greenfield Road 25

Saturday 30th
22 Greenfield Road 25

Sunday 31st
NEW Sandon Hall 45

June

Monday 1st
◆ Middleton Hall &
Gardens 33

Tuesday 2nd
◆ Middleton Hall &
Gardens 33

Wednesday 3rd
High Trees 27

Friday 5th
The Secret Garden 46

Sunday 7th
Ashcroft and Claremont 2
NEW Butt Lane Farm 9
Courtwood House 16
The Garth 23
3 Marlows Cottages 31
The Pintles 41
8 Rectory Road 43
49 The Plantation 48
NEW Thornbridge
Allotments 49
12 Waterdale 53
19 Waterdale 54

Wednesday 10th
Bankcroft Farm 3

Friday 12th
23 St Johns Road 44

Saturday 13th
Hall Green Gardens 26

Sunday 14th
Hall Green Gardens 26
The Old Vicarage 38
Priory Farm 42
Wild Wood Lodge 57

Wednesday 17th
Bankcroft Farm 3

Friday 19th
Yarlet House 61

Saturday 20th
Vernon House 52

Sunday 21st
The Beeches 4
Colour Mill 15
198 Eachelhurst Road 19
5 East View Cottages 20
Millennium Garden 34
2 Woodland Crescent 59

Wednesday 24th
Bankcroft Farm 3
5 East View Cottages 20
The Secret Garden 46

Saturday 27th
Tanglewood Cottage 47

Sunday 28th
Brooklyn 8
◆ Castle Bromwich Hall
Gardens 10
NEW Cheadle
Allotments 12
5 East View Cottages 20
The Garth 23
Grafton Cottage 24
15 New Church Road 36
Woodleighton Grove,
Karibu Garden 60

July

**Every Thursday to
Thursday 16th**
Yew Tree Cottage 62

Sunday 5th
21 Alexandra Drive 1
Bournville Village 6
Marie Curie Hospice
Garden 30
◆ Mitton Manor 35
NEW Sandon Hall 45
49 The Plantation 48
91 Tower Road 50
12 Waterdale 53
19 Waterdale 54

Thursday 9th
23 St Johns Road 44

Friday 10th
Grafton Cottage 24

Sunday 12th
21 Alexandra Drive 1
97 Clays Lane 14
Grafton Cottage 24
3 Marlows Cottages 31
2 Woodland Crescent 59

Saturday 18th
NEW Fifty Shades of
Green 21

Sunday 19th
The Beeches 4
NEW Fifty Shades of
Green 21

Saturday 25th
Woodbrooke Quaker
Study Centre 58

Sunday 26th
Grafton Cottage 24
The Wickets 55
Yew Tree Cottage 62

Wednesday 29th
The Secret Garden 46

August

Sunday 9th
97 Clays Lane 14
Grafton Cottage 24
Wild Wood Lodge 57

Thursday 20th
Church Cottage 13
Colour Mill 15

Thursday 27th
The Wickets 55

Sunday 30th
The Wickets 55

September

Sunday 6th
The Beeches 4

Sunday 13th
Bridge House 7

October

Saturday 17th
◆ Dorothy Clive
Garden 17

Sunday 18th
◆ Dorothy Clive
Garden 17

THE GARDENS

1 21 ALEXANDRA DRIVE
Yoxall, Burton-On-Trent, DE13 8PL. Mr & Mrs Paul Shum. *9m SW of Burton On Trent. Located on A515. Easily accessible from A38 at Lichfield or Burton On Trent, can also be accessed via the A50 at Sudbury.* **Sun 5, Sun 12 July (11-5). Adm £3.50, chd free. Home-made teas.**
A plant lovers dream, full of colour and perfume. Every inch packed with wide varieties of roses, clematis, sanguisorba, lilies and thalictrum between many other different plants. Also featuring wooden arches and large Indian sandstone patio. A hidden gem-the more you look, the more you will find. Slightly sloping grassed area.
& 🚗 ☕

GROUP OPENING

2 ASHCROFT AND CLAREMONT
Stafford Road, Eccleshall, ST21 6JP. Mrs G Bertram. *7m W of Stafford. J14 M6. At Eccleshall end of A5013 the garden is 100 metres before junction with A519. On street parking nearby. Note: Some Satnavs give wrong directions.* **Sun 7 June (2-5). Combined adm £4.50, chd free. Home-made teas at Ashcroft.**

ASHCROFT
Peter & Gillian Bertram.

26 CLAREMONT ROAD
Maria Edwards.

Weeping limes hide Ashcroft, a 1 acre garden of green tranquillity, rooms flow seamlessly around the Edwardian house. Covered courtyard with lizard water feature, sunken herb bed, kitchen garden, greenhouse, wildlife boundaries home to five hedgehogs increasing yearly. Deep shade border, woodland area and ruin with stone carvings and stained glass sculpture. Claremont is a master class in clipped perfection. An artist with an artist's eye has blurred the boundaries of this small Italianate influenced garden. Overlooking the aviary, a stone lion surveys the large pots and boarders of vibrant planting, completing the Feng-Shui design of this beautiful all seasons garden. Tickets, teas and plants available at Ashcroft. Wheelchair access at Ashcroft only.
& ❀ ☕

3 BANKCROFT FARM
Tatenhill, Burton-on-Trent, DE13 9SA. Mrs Penelope Adkins. *2m NW of Burton-on-Trent. 2m SW of Burton upon Trent take Tatenhill Rd off A38 on Burton/Branson flyover, 1m 1st house on L after village sign. Parking on farm.* **Wed 10, Wed 17, Wed 24 June (2-5). Adm £3.50, chd free.**
Lose yourself for an afternoon in our 1½-acre organic country garden. Arbour, gazebo and many other seating areas to view ponds and herbaceous borders, backed with shrubs and trees with emphasis on structure, foliage and colour. Productive fruit and vegetable gardens, wildlife areas and adjoining 12 acre native woodland walk. Picnics welcome. Gravel paths.
&

4 THE BEECHES
Mill Street, Rocester, ST14 5JX. Ken & Joy Sutton, 01889 590631, kenandjoy.sutton@ngs.org.uk. *5m N of Uttoxeter. On B5030 from Uttoxeter turn R at 2nd r'about into village by JCB factory. At Red Lion Pub & mini r'about take rd signed Mill Street. Garden 250yds on R. Parking at JCB academy Sundays only.* **Sun 29 Mar, Sun 5 Apr (1-4.30). Tea. Sun 24 May, Sun 21 June, Sun 19 July, Sun 6 Sept (1.30-5). Home-made teas. Adm £4, chd free. Visits also by arrangement May to July for groups of 20+. Min price £80 if less than 20 people, refreshments available at extra cost.**
A stunning plant lover's garden of ⅔ acre with countryside views, box garden, shrubs, rhododendrons and azaleas, vibrant colour-themed herbaceous borders, scented roses, clematis and climbing plants, fruit trees, pools, late flowering perennials, vegetable and soft fruit garden. Perennials cut back and shrubs pruned to reveal an under planting of spring jewels from bulbs, hellebores and early perennials (March & April). Partial wheelchair access.
& ❀ 🚗 ☕

5 BIRCH TREES

Copmere End, Eccleshall, ST21 6HH. Susan & John Weston, 01785 850448, john.weston@ngs.org.uk. *1½ m W of Eccleshall. On B5026, turn at junction signed Copmere End. After ½ m straight across Xrds by Star Inn.* Visits by arrangement June & July for groups of 10 to 30. Adm £5, chd free. Tea & biscuits included.
Surprising ½ acre SW-facing sun trap hidden from the road which takes advantage of the 'borrowed landscape' of the surrounding countryside. Take time to explore the pathways between the island beds which contain many rare & unusual herbaceous plants and shrubs; also vegetable patch, stump bed, alpine house, orchard and water features.
& ❋ ☕ ♨

GROUP OPENING

6 BOURNVILLE VILLAGE

Birmingham, B30 1QY. Bournville Village Trust, www.bvt.org.uk. *Gardens spread across 1,000 acre estate. Walks of up to 30 mins between some. Map supplied on day.* Sun 5 July (10-5). Combined adm £8, chd free. Home-made teas at various locations. Light meals, additional parking & comfort facilities: Wyevale Garden Centre, B30 2AE; Rowheath Pavilion, B30 1HH.

103 BOURNVILLE LANE
B30 1LH. Mrs Jennifer Duffy.

52 ELM ROAD
Mr & Mrs Jackie Twigg.

82 HAY GREEN LANE
B30 1UP. Mr Tony Walpole & Mrs Elsie Wheeler.

21 HIGH HEATH CLOSE
Dr Faint & Ms Dorward.

11 KESTREL GROVE
Mr Julian Stanton.

32 KNIGHTON ROAD
B31 2EH. Mrs Anne Ellis & Mr Lawrence Newman.

 MASEFIELD COMMUNITY GARDEN
Mrs Sally Gopsill.

 8 NEWENT ROAD
Mr & Mrs Edward and Mary Rutledge.

Bournville Village is showcasing 8 gardens - 2 of which are new to the scheme. Bournville is famous for it's large gardens, outstanding open spaces and of course it's chocolate factory! Free information sheet/map available on the day. Gardens spread across the 1,000 acre estate, with walks of up to 30 minutes between sites. For those with a disability, full details of access are available on the NGS website. Visitors with particular concerns with regards to access are welcome to call Bournville Village Trust on 0300 333 6540 or email: CommunityAdmin@bvt.org.uk. Music and singing available across a number of sites. Please check on the day.
& ❋ ☕

Your visits help change lives – we've donated over £17 million to Macmillan Cancer Support since 1984

---

7 BRIDGE HOUSE

Dog Lane, Bodymoor Heath, B76 9JD. Mr & Mrs J Cerone, 01827 873205, janecerone@btinternet.com. *5m S of Tamworth. From A446 at Belfry Island take A4091to Tamworth, after 1m turn R onto Bodymoor Heath Lane & continue 1m into village, parking in field opp garden.* Mon 25 May, Sun 13 Sept (2-5). Adm £4, chd free. Home-made teas. Visits also by arrangement May to Sept for groups of 10 to 30.
1 acre garden surrounding converted public house. Divided into smaller areas with a mix of shrub borders, azalea and fuchsia, herbaceous and bedding, orchard, kitchen garden with large greenhouse. Pergola walk, formal fish pool, pond, bog garden and lawns. Kingsbury Water Park and RSPB Middleton Lakes Reserve located within a mile.
& 🐾 ❋ ☕ ♨

8 BROOKLYN

Gratton Lane, Endon, Stoke-on-Trent, ST9 9AA. Janet & Steve Howell. *4m W of Leek. 6m from Stoke-on-Trent on A53 turn at Black Horse Pub into centre of village, R into Gratton Lane 1st house on R. Parking signed in village.* Sun 28 June (12-5). Adm £3.50, chd free. Cream teas.
A cottage garden in the picturesque old village of Endon. Pretty front garden overflows with roses, geraniums and astrantia, box surrounds a central sundial. Rear garden features shady area with hostas and ferns, small waterfall and pond. Steps lead to rear lawn, large well stocked borders and summerhouse. Several seating areas with village and rural views. Enjoy tea and cake in the potting shed. Traditional cottage garden in rural village location.
❋ ☕

9 NEW BUTT LANE FARM

Butt Lane, Ranton, Stafford, ST18 9JZ. Pete & Claire Pickering, 07975928968, claire-pickering@hotmail.co.uk. *6m W of Stafford. Take A518 to Haughton, turn R Station Rd (signed Ranton) 2m turn L at Butt Ln. Or from Great Bridgeford head W B5405 for 3m. Turn L Moorend Ln, second L Butt Lane.* Sun 7 June (10-4). Adm £3, chd free. Light refreshments. Homemade Pizza and BBQ available. Visits also by arrangement May to Aug for groups of 20+. Pre-booked Homemade Pizzas and BBQ or tea and cake can be offered.
Developing cottage style garden entering from unspoilt farmland through small wooded area onto lawns surrounded by floral beds and productive fruit and vegetable areas. With unusual areas of interest, greenhouse area, well and outside kitchen.

10 ◆ CASTLE BROMWICH HALL GARDENS

Chester Road, Castle Bromwich, Birmingham, B36 9BT. Castle Bromwich Hall & Gardens Trust, 0121 749 4100, admin@cbhgt.org.uk, www.castlebromwichhallgardens.org.uk. *4m East of Birmingham centre. 1m J5 M6 (exit N only).* For NGS: Sun 28 June (12.30-4.30). Adm £5, chd £1. Cream teas. Cafe is also open for light refreshments.

Dorothy Clive Garden

For other opening times and information, please phone, email or visit garden website.
10 acres of restored C17/18 walled gardens attached to a Jacobean manor (now a hotel) just minutes from J5 of M6. Formal yew parterres, wilderness walks, summerhouses, holly maze, espaliered fruit and wild areas. We are opening the Gardens for the Great Get Together (inspired by Jo Cox) #moreincommon. Hopefully people from our wider neighbouring communities will be using the garden and enjoying tea time on the lawn. We will be inviting the community to bring and share food on the day. Paths are either lawn or rough hoggin - sometimes on a slope. Most areas generally accessible, rough areas outside the walls difficult when wet.

🐾 🐈 ✿ 🚗 ☕

🔟 CATS WHISKERS
42 Amesbury Rd, Moseley, Birmingham, B13 8LE. **Dr Alfred & Mrs Michele White.** *Opp back of Moseley Hall Hospital. Past Edgbaston Cricket ground straight on at r'about & up Salisbury Rd. Amesbury Rd, 1st on R.* **Sun 3 May (1.30-5). Adm £3.50, chd free. Wine.**
A plantsman's garden developed over the last 38 years but which has kept its 1923 landscape. The front garden whilst not particularly large is full of interesting trees and shrubs; the rear garden is on 3 levels with steps leading to a small terrace and further steps to the main space. At the end of the garden is a pergola leading to the vegetable garden and greenhouse. Two flights of steps in back garden.

✿ ☕

12 NEW CHEADLE ALLOTMENTS
Delphouse Road, Cheadle, Stoke-On-Trent, ST10 2NN. **Cheadle Allotment Association.** *On the A521 1m to the west of Cheadle town centre.* **Sun 28 June (1-5). Adm £5, chd free. Home-made teas. Refreshments are incl in the adm price.**
The allotments, which were opened in 2015, are located on the western edge of Cheadle (Staffs). There are 29 plots growing a variety of vegetables, fruits and flowers. A new addition in 2019 was a community area, with an adjacent wildlife area. A small community orchard is currently being developed. Wheelchair access on all main paths.

♿ 🐈 ☕

13 CHURCH COTTAGE
Aston, Stone, ST15 0BJ. **Andrew & Anne Worrall, 01785 815239, acworrall@aol.com.** *1m S of Stone, Staffordshire. N side of St Saviour's Church, Aston. Go S 150 metres on A34 after junction with A51. Turn L at Aston Village Hall. 200 metres down lane into churchyard for parking.* **Thur 20 Aug (12-4.30). Adm £3.50, chd free. Home-made teas. Visits also by arrangement July & Aug**

for groups of 10 to 20.
An acre of cottage garden with large pond, waterfall and stream. Trees, sculptures, small orchard and wild flower meadow. Dahlias by award-winning grower Dave Bond. Views across the R Trent. St Saviour's Church and Trent and Mersey Canal nearby.

🐈 ☕

14 97 CLAYS LANE
Branston, Burton-On-Trent, DE14 3HT. **Mrs Jan Wood, 07967 211016, intheframeuk@hotmail.co.uk.** *From A38 Lichfield or Derby, take Branston exit (A5121) into Branston village. Clays Ln is opp the church & Vicarage Restaurant. 97 is a bungalow on the L side.* **Sun 12 July, Sun 9 Aug (11-5). Adm £4, chd free. Home-made teas. Visits also by arrangement July & Aug for groups of 10 to 30.**
'If you go down to the Wood's today be sure of a big surprise!' A garden of rooms, each themed with its own personality, with tantalising glimpses from one into the next. Mature trees, shrubs, tall hedging, make it a haven for wildlife. Bamboo, grasses, topiary, summer bedding, & over 20 mini-landscapes (created by me), strategically displayed, some for sale, plus planter-chairs of alpines & succulents.

✿ ☕

15 COLOUR MILL
Winkhill, Leek, ST13 7PR. **Bob & Jackie Pakes, 01538 308680, jackie.pakes@icloud.com, www.colourmillbandb.co.uk.** *7m E of Leek. Follow A523 from either Leek or Ashbourne, look for NGS signs on the side of the main rd which will direct you down to Colour Mill.* **Sun 21 June, Thur 20 Aug (1.30-5). Adm £3.50, chd free. Home-made teas. Visits also by arrangement June to Sept.**
1½ acre S-facing garden, created in the shadow of a former iron foundry, set beside the delightful R Hamps. Informal planting in a variety of rooms surrounded by beautiful 7ft beech hedges. Large organic vegetable patch complete with greenhouse and polytunnel. Maturing trees provide shade for the interesting seating areas. River walk through woodland and willows. Herbaceous borders. A display of Willow Weaving at our August opening.

✿ 🏠 ☕

16 COURTWOOD HOUSE
3 Court Walk, Betley, CW3 9DP.
Mike Reeves. *6m S of Crewe. On
A531 toward Keele & Newcastle
under Lyme or from J16 off M6,
pickup A531 off A500 on Nantwich
rd, into village by Betley Court.* **Sun
7 June (12-5). Adm £4, chd £2.
Light refreshments.**
Small L-shaped, walled garden,
which is designed as a walk-through
sculpture. Mainly shrubs with
structures and water features, hidden
spaces and seating areas, with strong
shapes and effects utilising a wide
range of materials, incl. a synthetic
lawn. Small art gallery with acrylic
paintings by owner for sale.

17 ◆ DOROTHY CLIVE GARDEN
**Willoughbridge, Market Drayton,
TF9 4EU. Willoughbridge
Garden Trust, 01630 647237,
info@dorothyclivegarden.co.uk,
www.dorothyclivegarden.co.uk.**
*3m SE of Bridgemere Garden World.
From M6 J15 take A53 W bound,
then A51 N bound midway between
Nantwich & Stone, near Woore.*
**For NGS: Sat 17, Sun 18 Oct
(10-4). Adm £5, chd free. Light
refreshments in the Tearooms.
Vintage Afternoon Tea can be
pre-booked. For other opening
times and information, please
phone, email or visit garden
website.**

12 informal acres, incl superb
woodland garden, alpine scree,
gravel garden, fine collection of trees
and spectacular flower borders.
Renowned in May when woodland
quarry is brilliant with rhododendrons.
Waterfall and woodland planting.
Laburnum Arch in June. Creative
planting has produced stunning
summer borders. Large Glasshouse.
Spectacular autumn colour. Much
to see, whatever the season. The
Dorothy Clive Tea Rooms will be open
throughout the weekend during winter
for refreshments, lunch and afternoon
tea. Open all week in summer. Plant
sales, Gift room Picnic area and
children's play area for a wide age
range. Wheelchairs (inc. electric) are
available to book through the tea
rooms . Disabled parking is available.
Toilets on both upper and lower car
parks.

18 DORSET HOUSE
**68 Station Street, Cheslyn Hay,
WS6 7EE. David Blundell.** *2m SE
of Cannock J11 M6 A462 towards
Willenhall. L at island. At next island
R into one way system (Low St),
at T junction L into Station St. A5
Bridgetown L to island, L Coppice
St. R into Station St.* **Sun 24 May
(11-5). Adm £3, chd free. Home-
made teas.**
An inspirational ½ -acre garden with
country cottage planting at its best.

Unusual rhododendrons, acers,
shrubs and perennials planted in
mixed borders. Clematis-covered
arches and hidden corners with water
features all come together to create a
haven of peace and tranquillity.

19 198 EACHELHURST ROAD
**Walmley, Sutton Coldfield,
B76 1EW. Jacqui & Jamie
Whitmore.** *5mins N of Birmingham.
M6 J6, A38 Tyburn Rd to Lichfield,
continue to T-lights at Lidl & continue
on Tyburn Rd, at island take 2nd exit
to destination rd.* **Sun 21 June (1-
4.30). Adm £3, chd free.**
A long garden approx 210ft x 30ft
divided by arches and pathways.
Plenty to explore incl wildlife pond,
corner arbour, cottage garden and
hanging baskets leading to formal
garden with box-lined pathways, well,
stocked borders, gazebo and chicken
house then through to raised seating
area, overlooking Pype Hayes golf
course, with summer house and bar
and Mediterranean plants.

20 5 EAST VIEW COTTAGES
**School Lane, Shuttington, nr
Tamworth, B79 0DX. Cathy
Lyon-Green, 01827 892244,
cathyatcorrabhan@hotmail.com,
www.ramblinginthegarden.
wordpress.com.** *2m NE of
Tamworth. From Tamworth,
Amington Rd or Ashby Rd to
Shuttington. From M42 J11, B5493
for Seckington & Tamworth, 3 mls
L turn to Shuttington. Pink house nr
top of School Lane. Parking signed,
disabled at house.* **Sun 21 June
(1-5); Wed 24 June (1-4); Sun 28
June (1-5), chd free. Adm £4, chd free.
Home-made teas. 2021: Sun 14
Feb. Visits also by arrangement
June & July for groups of up to 30.
Min charge £60 (excl teas) if less
than 15. Groups by appt also in
Feb 2021.**
Deceptive & quirky plantlover's
garden, full of surprises & always
something new. Informally planted
themed borders, cutting beds,
woodland & woodland edge,
stream, water features, sitooterie,
folly, greenhouses & many artefacts.
Roses, clematis, perennials, potted
hostas. Snowdrops & witch hazels
in Feb. Benches & seating areas for
contemplation & enjoying home-made
cake. 'Wonderful hour's wander'.

Vernon House

21 NEW FIFTY SHADES OF GREEN

20 Bevan Close, Shelfield, Walsall, WS4 1AB. Annmarie and Andrew Swift, 07963041402, annmarie.1963@hotmail.co.uk. *Walsall. M6 J10 take A454 to Walsall for 1.6m turn L at Lichfield St for ⅓m, turn L onto A461 Lichfield Rd for 2m, at Co-op T-lights turn L onto Mill rd then follow yellow signs.* **Sat 18 July (2-10.30); Sun 19 July (10-5). Adm £3.50, chd free. Home-made teas. Visits also by arrangement May to Sept for groups of 5 to 10.**
We have a small garden of 15m x 11m taking several years to create & landscape. It has several distinctive areas of interest incl two ponds linked by a stream with a stone waterfall, four unique water features, places to sit, watch & relax. Wildlife is encouraged & welcomed. Our planting style is varied with Ferns, Hostas, Palms, Bananas, Bamboos, architectural plants for foliage & over 40 trees. The garden has a bridge over a stream & deep water. Steps to and from areas. Gravel pathways. Please note: we are located in a cul-de-sac & parking is limited. Please park with consideration. Parking is available on Broad Lane.

22 FOUR SEASONS

26 Buchanan Road, Walsall, WS4 2EN. Marie & Tony Newton, www.fourseasonsgarden.co.uk. *Adjacent to Walsall Arboretum. From Ring Rd A4148 nr Walsall town centre. At large junction take A461 to Lichfield. At 1st island 3rd exit Buchanan Ave, fork R into Buchanan Rd.* **Sat 23, Sun 24 May, Sat 24, Sun 25 Oct (10-5). Adm £4.50, chd free. Tea.**
Stunning in all seasons. Suburban, S-facing ¼ acre, gently sloping to arboretum. 120 acers, 450 azaleas, bulbs, hellebores, camellias, perennials, begonias, bright conifers, topiary and shrubs. Autumn colours, bark and berries. Semi-formal, oriental, woodland-like areas and jungle. Themes incl contrast of red, blue and yellow. Pagoda, bridges, water features, stone ornaments. Some steps. WC. Please note: access into the garden is down 10 steps.

Yew Tree Cottage

23 THE GARTH

2 Broc Hill Way, Milford, Stafford, ST17 0UB. Anita & David Wright, 01785 661182, anitawright1@yahoo.co.uk, www.anitawright.co.uk. *4½m SE of Stafford. A513 Stafford to Rugeley rd; at Barley Mow turn R (S) to Brocton; L after ½m.* **Sun 7, Sun 28 June (2-6). Adm £4, chd free. Cream teas. Visits also by arrangement May to Sept for groups of 20+.**
½ acre garden of many levels on Cannock Chase AONB. Acid soil loving plants. Series of small gardens, water features, raised beds. Rare trees, island beds of unusual shrubs and perennials, many varieties of hosta and ferns. Varied and colourful foliage, summerhouses, arbours and quiet seating to enjoy the garden. Ancient sandstone caves.

24 GRAFTON COTTAGE

Barton-under-Needwood, DE13 8AL. Margaret & Peter Hargreaves, 01283 713639, marpeter1@btinternet.com. *6m N of Lichfield. Leave A38 for Catholme S of Barton, follow sign to Barton Green, L at Royal Oak, ¼m.* **Sun 28 June (11.30-5); Fri 10 July (1.30-5); Sun 12, Sun 26 July, Sun 9 Aug (11.30-5). Adm £4.50, chd free. Home-made teas. Visits also by arrangement June to Aug. Min adm £90 if less than 20 people. Donation to Alzheimer's Research UK.**

Admired over 27 years our aim is to provide a pleasant afternoon. Unusual herbaceous plants with new additions introduced, perfume from old fashioned Roses, Sweet peas, dianthus, phlox and lilies, viticella clematis, salvias and violas. Cottage garden annuals and use of foliage plants play a part in the garden. Coloured themed borders, amphitheatre, brook, parterre to celebrate 25 years of opening.

25 22 GREENFIELD ROAD

Stafford, ST17 0PU. Alison & Peter Jordan, 01785 660819, alison.jordan2@btinternet.com. *3m S of Stafford. Follow the A34 out of Stafford towards Cannock. 2nd L onto Overhill Rd.1st R into Greenfield Rd.* **Evening opening Fri 29 May (6.30-9). Adm £5, chd free. Wine. Sat 30 May (11-4.30). Adm £3, chd free. Cream teas. Visits also by arrangement for groups of 5 to 20.**
Suburban garden created in the last 8 years,working towards all round interest.In spring bulbs and stunning azaleas and rhododendrons.June onwards perennials and grasses. A garden that shows being diagnosed with Parkinson's needn't stop you creating a peaceful place to sit and enjoy. Come in the evening and enjoy a glass of wine while listening to live music. Flat garden but with some gravelled areas.

GROUP OPENING

26 HALL GREEN GARDENS

Hall Green, Birmingham, B28 8SQ. 01216247906. *Off A34, 3m city centre, 6m from M42 J4. From City Centre start at 120 Russell Rd B28 8SQ . From M42 start at 638 Shirley Rd B28 9LB.* **Sun 3 May, Sat 13, Sun 14 June (1-5.30). Combined adm £5, chd free. Home-made teas on May 3rd at 120 Russell Road, on July 13th and 14th at 111 Southam Road. Visits also by arrangement Apr to Sept. Not all our gardens are open by arrangement. Check on NGS website.**

42 BODEN ROAD
Mrs Helen Lycett.
Open on Sat 13, Sun 14 June

36 FERNDALE ROAD
Mrs E A Nicholson, 0121 777 4921.
Open on all dates
Visits also by arrangement Apr to Sept for groups of up to 30.

63 GREEN ROAD
Mr & Mrs A Wilkes, 01217770510.
Open on all dates
Visits also by arrangement Apr to Sept.

120 RUSSELL ROAD
Mr David Worthington, 0121 624 7906, hildave@hotmail.com.
Open on all dates
Visits also by arrangement Apr to Sept for groups of up to 30.

638 SHIRLEY ROAD
Dr. and Mrs. M. Leigh.
Open on Sat 13, Sun 14 June

87 SOUTHAM ROAD
Mrs Sarah Moss,
s.moss720@btinternet.com.
Open on all dates
Visits also by arrangement Apr to Sept.

111 SOUTHAM ROAD
Ms Val Townend & Mr Ian Bate.
Open on Sat 13, Sun 14 June

19 STAPLEHURST ROAD
Mrs Sheena Terrace.
Open on Sun 3 May

A group of diverse suburban gardens. Boden Rd: Large restful garden, mature trees, cottage borders, seating areas and small vegetable area. Ferndale Rd: Florist's large suburban garden, ponds and waterfalls, and fruit garden. Green Rd: Eccentric's north facing wildlife friendly garden.

Russell Rd: Plantsman's garden, formal raised pond and hosta collection and unusual perennials, container planting. 87 Southam Rd: Mature garden with deep, sunny herbaceous borders. 111 Southam Rd: Mature garden with well defined areas incl ponds, white garden, rescue hens and a majestic cedar. Shirley Rd: Large young garden with herbaceous borders, vegetables and greenhouses. Staplehurst Rd: shady suburban garden with mature trees, pond and mixed borders. Some gardens have limited wheelchair access. Telephone for more information or consult the NGS website.

  ♿ ✿ ☕

27 HIGH TREES

Drubbery Lane, nr Longton Park, Stoke-on-Trent, ST3 4BA. Peter & Pat Teggin. *5m S of Stoke-on-Trent. Off A5035, midway between Trentham Gardens & Longton. Opp Longton Park.* **Wed 3 June (1-4). Adm £4, chd free. Cream teas.** A delightful, secluded, inspirational garden. Intensively planted mixed herbaceous borders with bulbs in spring, trillium, climbing roses and clematis with an emphasis on scent and colour combinations. Spires, flats and fluffs interwoven with structure planting and focal points. Planted for year round interest with many unusual plants. Delicious cakes. W.C. And two minutes from a Victorian park.

We help ordinary people open the gates to their extraordinary private gardens to raise impressive amounts of money through admissions, teas and slices of cake!

28 'JOHN'S GARDEN' AT ASHWOOD NURSERIES

Ashwood Lower Lane, Ashwood, nr Kingswinford, DY6 0AE. John Massey, www.ashwoodnurseries.com. *9m S of Wolverhampton. 1m past Wall Heath on A449 turn R to Ashwood along Doctor's Lane. At T-junction turn L. Park at Ashwood Nurseries.* **Sun 12 Apr (10-4). Adm £5, chd free. Light refreshments at adjacent Tea Room at Ashwood Nurseries. An additional mobile catering facility serves drinks and snacks.**
A stunning private garden adjacent to Ashwood Nurseries, it has a huge plant collection and many innovative design features in a beautiful canal-side setting. There are informal beds, woodland dells, a stunning rock garden, a unique ruin garden, an Anemone pavonina meadow and wildlife meadow. Fine displays of bulbs and Spring-flowering plants and a notable collection of Malus and Amelanchier. Tea Room, Garden Centre and Gift Shop at adjacent Ashwood Nurseries. Coaches are by appointment only. Disabled access difficult if very wet.

  ♿ ✿ NPC ☕

29 KEEPER'S COTTAGE; BLUEBELL WOOD

24 Greensforge Lane, Stourton, Stourbridge, DY7 5BB. Peter & Jenny Brookes, 07974 454503, peter@brookesmedia.com. *2m NW of Stourbridge. At junction of A449 & A458 at Stourton, take Bridgnorth Rd (A458) westward, after ½m turn R into Greensforge Ln. Keeper's Cottage ½m on R.* **Fri 8, Sat 9 May (11-3.30). Adm £4, chd free. Home-made teas. Visits also by arrangement Apr & May for groups of 5 to 20.**
This stunning bluebell wood adorns the banks of a river deep in the South Staffordshire countryside, yet only a few miles from the conurbation. In May, the bluebells form a beautiful carpet, sweeping through the natural woodland and down to the river, the site of ancient nail making. It is a quintessentially English landscape which can only be glimpsed for a few short weeks of the year. Special teas & children's games to celebrate the 75th anniversary of VE day. The woods contain steep pathways.

 ☕

Yew Trees

30 MARIE CURIE HOSPICE GARDEN

Marsh Lane, Solihull, B91 2PQ. Mrs Do Connolly, www.mariecurie. org.uk/westmidlands. *Close to J5 M42 to E of Solihull Town Centre. M42 J5, travel towards Solihull on A41. Take slip toward Solihull to join B4025 & after island take 1st R onto Marsh Lane. Hospice is on R. Limited onsite parking - available for blue badge holders.* **Sun 5 July (11-4). Adm £3.50, chd free. Home-made teas, plus light refreshments at the hospice bistro.**

The gardens incl two large, formally laid out patients' gardens incl a ball fountain water feature and large rose/clematis arches, indoor courtyards, a vegetable plot, a long border adjoining the car park and a beautiful wildlife and pond area. The volunteer gardening team hope that the gardens provide a peaceful and comforting place for patients, their visitors and staff.

&

31 3 MARLOWS COTTAGES

Little Hay Lane, Little Hay, WS14 0QD. Phyllis Davies. *4m S of Lichfield. Take A5127, Birmingham Rd. Turn L at Park Lane (opp Tesco Express) then R at T junction into Little Hay Lane, ½m on L.* **Sun 7 June, Sun 12 July (11-4). Adm £3.50, chd free. Home-made teas.**

Long, narrow, gently sloping cottage style garden with borders and beds containing abundant herbaceous perennials and shrubs leading to vegetable patch.

32 NEW 12 MERES ROAD

Halesowen, B63 2EH. Nigel & Samantha Hopes, www.hopesgardenplants.co.uk. *4m from M5 Junction 3. Follow the A458 out of Halesowen heading W for 2m., L turn onto Two Gates Lane just after Round of Beef pub, this becomes Meres Rd, House is on R* **Sun 26 Apr, Sun 3 May (11-4). Adm £3.50, chd free. Home-made teas.**

A little oasis in the heart of the black country, with stunning views across to Shropshire, the borders are filled with interest and colour throughout the year. A garden for plant hunters and collectors, we hold a National Collection of Border Auriculas, with a passion for Snowdrops, Hellebores, Epimedium, Bearded Iris, Roscoea and Kniphofia.

NPC

33 ◆ MIDDLETON HALL & GARDENS

Middleton, Tamworth, B78 2AE. Middleton Hall Trust, 01827 283095, enquiries@middleton-hall.co.uk, www.middleton-hall.co.uk. *4m S of Tamworth, 2m N of J9 M42. On A4091 between The Belfry & Drayton Manor.* **For NGS: Mon 1, Tue 2 June (11-4). Adm £6, chd free. For other opening times and information, please phone, email or visit garden website.**
Our formal gardens form part of the 42 estate of the Grade II* Middleton Hall, the seventeenth-century home of naturalists Francis Willoughby and John Ray. The formal gardens are made up of a Walled Garden, lawns and an orchard. The Walled gardens contain a variety of herbaceous and seasonal planting with specimen plants that have a botanical and/ or historical significance to our site. Bake 180 Coffee Shop will also be open serving lunches and other light refreshments. Wheelchair access - Walled Garden paths are paved, Glade and Orchard paths are grass. No access to 1st floor of the Hall and Nature Trail.

34 MILLENNIUM GARDEN

London Road, Lichfield, WS14 9RB. Carol Cooper. *1m South of Lichfield. Off A38 along A5206 towards Lichfield ¼ m past A38 island towards Lichfield. Park in field on L. Yellow signs on field post.* **Sun 26 Apr, Sun 21 June (1-5). Adm £3.50, chd free. Home-made teas.**
2-acre garden with mixed spring bulbs in the woodland garden and host of golden daffodils fade slowly into the summer borders in this English country garden. Designed with a naturalistic edge and with the environment in mind. A relaxed approach creates a garden of quiet sanctuary with the millennium bridge sitting comfortably, with its surroundings of lush planting and mature trees. Well stocked borders give shots of colour to lift the spirit and the air fills with the scent of wisterias and climbing roses. A stress free environment awaits you at the Millennium Garden. Park in field then footpath round garden. Some uneven surfaces.

Marie Curie Hospice Garden

35 ◆ MITTON MANOR

Mitton, Penkridge, Stafford, ST19 5QW. Mrs E A Gooch, 01785291391, info@mittonmanor.co.uk, www.mittonmanor.co.uk. *2m W of Penkridge. Property is on Whiston Rd. Parking in field before house. No parking for coaches.* **For NGS: Sun 5 July (11-4.30). Adm £7.50, chd free. Cream teas. Full afternoon teas available to pre-order. Please visit www.mittonmanor. co.uk to book. For other opening times and information, please phone, email or visit garden website.**

This 7-acre country garden was started in 2001 and has been developed from an overgrown wilderness. The garden surrounds a Victorian manor (not open) and contains rooms of different styles, formal box/topiary, prairie planting and natural woodland bordered by a stream. Stunning vistas, water features and sculpture. New potager started in 2018. Many levels, narrow and gravel paths.

36 15 NEW CHURCH ROAD

Sutton Coldfield, B73 5RT. Owen & Lloyd Watkins. *4½ m NW of Birmingham city centre. Take A38M then A5127 to 6 Ways r'about, take 2nd exit then bear L Summer Rd then Gravelly Lane over Chester Rd to Boldmere Rd, 5th R New Church Rd.* **Sun 28 June (1-4). Adm £4, chd free. Light refreshments.**

A garden created and recreated, evolving over 9 years. From the new patio an extended pond takes centre stage. A new small stumpery and dry shade area have recently been added. Herbaceous borders, tree ferns and bamboo hedging, a rockery and woodland area. Rear of the garden has raised vegetable beds, fruit trees and chickens. Wheelchair access possible although some areas may not be accessible. Several steps, ramps available.

&. ✿ ☕

37 THE OLD DAIRY HOUSE

Trentham Park, Stoke-on-Trent, ST4 8AE. Philip & Michelle Moore. *S edge of Stoke-on-Trent. Next to Trentham Gardens. Off Whitmore Rd. Please follow NGS signs or signs for Trentham Park Golf Club. Parking in church car park.* **Sun 24 May (1.30-5); Mon 25 May (1-4.30). Adm £3.50, chd free. Home-made teas.**

Grade 2 listed house which originally formed part of the Trentham Estate forms backdrop to this 2-acre garden in parkland setting. Shaded area for rhododendrons, azaleas plus expanding hosta and fern collection. Mature trees, 'cottage garden' and long borders and stumpery. Narrow brick paths in vegetable plot. Large courtyard area for teas. Wheelchair access - some gravel paths but lawns are an option.

&. ✿ ☕

38 THE OLD VICARAGE

Fulford, nr Stone, ST11 9QS. Mike & Cherry Dodson. *4m N of Stone. From Stone A520 (Leek). 1m R turn to Spot Acre & Fulford, turn L down Post Office Terrace, past village green/Pub towards church. Parking signed on L.* **Sun 14 June (11.30-4). Adm £4, chd free. Home-made teas.**

1½ acres of formal sloping garden around Victorian house. Sit on the terrace or in the summerhouse to enjoy home-made cakes and tea amongst mature trees, relaxed herbaceous borders, roses and a small pond. Move to the organic vegetable garden with raised beds, fruit cage and very big compost heaps! In complete contrast, easy walk around the natural setting of a two-acre reclaimed lake planted with native species designed to attract wildlife. Waterfall, jetty, fishing hut, acer and fern glade plus young arboretum provide more interest. Children will enjoy meeting the chickens and horses. A garden of contrasts, with easy formality around the Victorian house and the accent on very natural planting around the lake, managed for wildlife and sustainability. Wheelchair access to most areas.

&. 🐕 ☕

39 10 PAGET RISE

Paget Rise, Abbots Bromley, Rugeley, WS15 3EF. Mr Arthur Tindle. *4m W of Rugeley 6m S of Uttoxeter and 12m N of Lichfield. From Rugeley: B5013 E. At T junc turn R on B5014. From Uttoxeter take the B5013 S then B5014. From Lichfield take A515 N then turn L on B5234. In Abbots Bromley follow NGS yellow signs.* **Sun 17 May (11-5). Adm £3, chd free. Light refreshments.**

This small 2 level garden has a strong Japanese influence. Rhododendrons and a wide range of flowering shrubs. Many bonsai-style Acer trees in shallow bowls occupy a central gravel area with stepping stones. The rear of the garden has a woodland feel with a fairy dell under the pine tree. A little gem of a garden! Arthur hopes visitors will be inspired to take away ideas to use in their own garden. Arthur is a watercolour artist & will be displaying a selection of his paintings for sale.

☕

40 PAUL'S OASIS OF CALM

18 Kings Close, Kings Heath, Birmingham, B14 6TP. Mr Paul Doogan, 0121 444 6943, gardengreen18@hotmail.co.uk. *4m from city centre. 5m from M42 J4. Take A345 to Kings Heath High St then B4122 Vicarage Rd. Turn L onto Kings Rd then R to Kings Close.* **Visits by arrangement May to Aug for groups of up to 20. Evenings and weekends. Adm £2.50, chd free. Home-made teas.**

Garden cultivated from nothing into a little oasis. Measuring 18ft x 70ft. It's small but packed with interesting and unusual plants, water features and 7 seating areas. It's my piece of heaven.

Your visits help change lives – we are Hospice UK's largest charitable funder donating more than £5.5 million to support hospices in local communities since 1996

Yarlet House

41 THE PINTLES

18 Newport Road, Great Bridgeford, Stafford, ST18 9PR. Peter & Leslie Longstaff, 01785 282582, peter.longstaff@ngs.org.uk. *From J14 M6 take A5013 towards Eccleshall, in Great Bridgeford turn L onto B5405 after 600 metres turn L onto Great Bridgeford Village Hall car park The Pintles is opp the hall main doors.* **Sun 7 June (1.30-5). Adm £3.50, chd free. Home-made teas. Visits also by arrangement in June for groups of 10 to 30.**

Located in the village of Great Bridgeford this traditional semi-detached house has a medium sized wildlife friendly garden designed to appeal to many interests. There are two greenhouses, 100s of cacti and succulents, vegetable and fruit plot, wildlife pond, weather station and hidden woodland shady garden. Plenty of outside seating to enjoy the home-made cakes and refreshments. Steps or small ramp into main garden.

✿ ☕

42 PRIORY FARM

Mitton Road, Bradley, Stafford, ST18 9ED. Debbie Farmer. *$3\frac{1}{2}$m W Penkridge. At Texaco island on A449 in Penkridge take Bungham Ln. Continue for $2\frac{1}{2}$m past Swan & Whiston Hall to Mitton. Turn R to Bradley, continue 1m to Priory Farm on L.* **Sun 14 June (10.30-4.30). Adm £5, chd free. Home-made teas. BBQ subject to availability.**

Come and see the changes at Priory Farm where a warm welcome awaits. Sumptuous cakes and weather permitting tasty BBQ. With acres of grounds surrounding the lake and abundance of wildlife. Imaginative planting, dells. Beautiful views from any standpoint.

🐾 ✿ ☕

43 8 RECTORY ROAD

Solihull, B91 3RP. Nigel & Daphne Carter. *Town centre. From M42 J5 follow directions toward Solihull town centre. L into New Rd at T-lights opp Solihull School.1st L after St Alphege Church into Rectory Rd.* **Sun 7 June (11-6). Adm £3, chd free. Home-made teas.**

Stunning town garden divided into areas with different features. A garden with unusual trees and intensively planted borders. Walk to the end of the garden and step into a newly created Japanese garden complete with pond, fish and traditional style bridge. Sit on the shaded decking area and enjoy home-made cakes. A garden to attract bees and butterflies with plenty of places to relax. Japanese features.

 🐾 ☕

44 23 ST JOHNS ROAD

Rowley Park, Stafford, ST17 9AS. Fiona Horwath, 07908 918181, fiona_horwath@yahoo.co.uk. *$\frac{1}{2}$m S of Stafford Town Centre. Just a few mins from J13 M6, towards Stafford. After approx 2m on the A449, turn L into St. John's Rd after bus-stop.* **Thur 9 Apr (2-5). Adm £4, chd free. Home-made teas. Evening opening Fri 15 May (6.30-8.30). Adm £6, chd free. Wine. Fri 12 June, Thur 9 July (2-5). Adm £4, chd free. Home-made teas. Refreshments incl in adm Friday 15th May. Visits also** by arrangement Apr to July for groups of 20+.

Pass through the black and white gate of this Victorian house into a part-walled gardener's haven. Bulbs and shady woodlanders in Spring and masses of herbaceous plants and climbers. Sit and enjoy home-made cakes by the pond or Victorian-style greenhouse. Gardener is keen Hardy Plant Society member and sows far too many seeds, so always something good for sale! Our new outdoor kitchen is great for refreshments! The waterlily wildlife pond remains - with the greenhouses - the beating heart of the garden. A growing interest in alpines is leading to a proliferation of troughs. Whilst ferns, the quiet green stars of shady areas are also increasing in number!

45 NEW SANDON HALL
Sandon, Stafford, ST18 0BZ.
8th Earl of Harrowby. *6m from J14 of M6. From J14 of M6 take A34 to Stafford, take 2nd Exit off r'about onto A5013, turn L onto B5066 Sandon Rd, turn R onto A51 Lichfield/Rugeley, main entrance is on the L.* **Sun 31 May, Sun 5 July (10-5). Adm £5, chd free. Light refreshments in the conservatory.**
Country Estate Garden with Backdrop of Grade II Listed Sandon Hall (Not Open) featured in 1st year of NGS in 1927. 3yrs off a 10yr regeneration plan with emphasis on wildlife conservation using organic practices. Beautiful display of Rhododendrons in May. Formal Terrace planting, Amphitheatre Rose Garden, Friends Garden, Wildlife Areas and a 100m Potager giving stunning displays in July. For other opening times and details of garden tours please see our social media or email grant@sandonhall.co.uk. Main Features accessible, some gravel paths. Disabled Parking and level access entrance available.

46 THE SECRET GARDEN
3 Banktop Cottages, Little Haywood, Stafford, ST18 0UL.
Derek Higgott & David Aston, 01889 883473, poshanddeks@gmail.com. *5m SE of Stafford. A51 from Rugeley or Weston signed Little Haywood A513 Stafford Coley Ln, Back Ln R into Coley Gr. Entrance 50 metres on L.* **Wed 20 May, Fri 5, Wed 24 June, Wed 29 July (11-4). Adm £4, chd**

free. Home-made teas. Visits also by arrangement May to Aug for groups of 10+.
Wander past the other cottage gardens and through the evergreen arch and there before you is a fantasy for the eyes and soul. Stunning garden approx ½ acre, created over the last 30yrs. Strong colour theme of trees and shrubs, underplanted with perennials, 1000 bulbs and laced with clematis; other features incl water, laburnum and rose tunnel and unique buildings. Is this the jewel in the crown? Raised gazebo with wonderful views over untouched meadows and Cannock Chase. Wheelchair access - some slopes.

47 TANGLEWOOD COTTAGE
Crossheads, Colwich, Stafford, ST18 0UG. Dennis & Helen Wood, 01889 882857, shuvitdog@gmail.com. *5m SE of Stafford. A51 Rugeley/Weston R into Colwich. Church on L school on R, under bridge R into Crossheads Ln follow railway approx ¼ m (it does lead somewhere). Parking signed on grass opp Brick Kiln Cottage.* **Sun 17 May (10.30-3.30); Sat 27 June (11-4). Adm £3, chd free. Home-made teas. Visits also by arrangement May to Sept for groups of 20+.**
A country cottage garden incl koi carp pool, vegetables, fruit and an array of wonderful perennials. Meander through the garden rooms, enjoying sights, sounds and fragrances. Many seats to absorb the atmosphere incl the courtyard to enjoy Helen's home-made fayre - cakes and meals. Year on year people spend many hours relaxing with us and don't forget Charlie the parrot. Art/jewellery/crafts/book sales. Annual HPS Plant fair usually on same weekend. Lots of gravel paths, some steps, people with walking sticks seem to manage quite well.

48 49 THE PLANTATION
Pensnett, Brierley Hill, DY5 4RT.
Dave & Kath Baker. *From Russells Hall Hospital, take Pensnett High St (A4101) to Kingswinford. After 1½ m turn L into The Plantation. Please park with consideration.* **Sun 7 June, Sun 5 July (11-3). Adm £3, chd free. Home-made teas.**
Small suburban garden 60 ft x 30 ft with lots of roses, hemerocallis, well stocked borders and fruit trees. Greenhouse with tomatoes,

cucumbers and grape vine. Productive vegetable garden.

49 NEW THORNBRIDGE ALLOTMENTS
Beeches Road, Great Barr, Birmingham, B42 2PT. Thornbridge Allotments. *We are a short walk from the Walsall Road (A34). The nearest bus services are the 51/X51 which stops on the Walsall Rd, or the 28/52 stops over the rd.* **Sun 7 June (11-3). Adm £4, chd free. Cream teas.**
Thornbridge Allotments is a small but perfectly formed allotment garden, which is split into 75 separate plots. We are a very community focused allotment run by a dedicated team of volunteers and we like to welcome members of the public to our site to see the work that goes on, and to have an all-important cup of tea. We have wheelchair access to the whole site, and also wheelchair accessible WC facilities.

50 91 TOWER ROAD
Four Oaks, Sutton Coldfield, B75 5EQ. Heather & Gary Hawkins. *3m N Sutton Coldfield. From A5127 at Mere Green island, turn onto Mere Green Rd towards Sainsburys, L at St James Church, L again onto Tower Rd.* **Sun 5 July (1.30-5.30). Adm £3, chd free. Home-made teas.**
163ft S-facing garden with sweeping borders and island beds planted with an eclectic mix of shrubs and perennials. This year we are opening our garden a month later in July to give our visitors a chance to see a different view of our garden. A vast array of home-made cakes will tempt you during your visit. The ideal setting for sunbathing, children's hide and seek and lively garden parties. Large selection of home-made cream teas to eat in the garden or take away. Plant sale on front drive for garden visitors and passers by. More than just an Open Garden, we like to think of it as a garden party! There are 2 steps up into the garage and 2 steps down to the garden, which is then completely flat.

51 THE UPPER HOUSE

The Green, Barlaston, Stoke-On-Trent, ST12 9AE. Mr Paul Williams, 01782 373790, enquiries@theupperhouse.com, www.theupperhouse.com. *The grounds of The Upper House Hotel. From the A34 enter Barlaston and cross the canal and railway before turning right on The Green.* **Tue 28 Apr (10-4). Adm by donation. Light refreshments. We have a restaurant on site which can be booked in advance if required.**

The gardens at The Upper House were originally created for Francis Wedgwood, the grandson of Josiah, when the house was built around 1850. The house was built to enable the Wedgwood family to escape the pollution of the potteries. The gardens benefit from far ranging views over the Trent valley and are split into distinct areas comprising of woodland, formal gardens and a hay meadow. The woodland has a carpet of bluebells at this time of year, if the weather obliges. The Japanese and marriage gardens come into their own as well. Our restaurant can provide more substantial refreshment such as lunch and afternoon teas if required. Please book in advance. Wheelchair access to the bluebell wood and Japanese garden could prove difficult.

52 VERNON HOUSE

26, Vernon Road, Edgbaston, Birmingham, B16 9SH. Dr & Mrs Steve & Chris Smith. *2m W of Birmingham city centre. Take the A456 (Hagley Rd). If arriving from E (Birmingham) turn R in to Portland Rd, then 2nd R onto Vernon Rd. If arriving from W (M5) turn L in to Rotton Park Rd, then 2nd R (exit 3) onto Vernon Rd.* **Sat 20 June (12-4). Adm £4, chd free. Light refreshments.**

A large (over 1/3 acre) but secluded city garden framed by mature trees. There are extensive lawns and herbaceous borders with a wide range of planting creating several distinct areas. Decks, pergolas and patios offer a variety of places to sit and reflect. Featuring an ornamental koi pond, a wildlife pond with bog garden, a unique holly hedge and an architect designed conservatory. Three small steps up to patio areas and a further 3 steps to access main garden.

Your visits help change lives – we are the largest single funder of the Queen's Nursing Institute

53 12 WATERDALE

Compton, Wolverhampton, WV3 9DY. Mr & Mrs Colin Bennett. *1½ m W of Wolverhampton city centre. From Wolverhampton Ring Rd take A454 towards Bridgnorth for 1m. Waterdale is on the L off A454 Compton Rd West.* **Sun 7 June, Sun 5 July (12.30-5.30). Combined adm with 19 Waterdale £5, chd free.**

A riot of colour welcomes visitors to this quintessentially English garden. The wide central circular bed and side borders overflow with classic summer flowers, incl the tall spires of delphiniums, lupins, irises, campanula, poppies and roses. Clematis tumble over the edge of the decked terrace, where visitors can sit among pots of begonias and geraniums to admire the view over the garden.

54 19 WATERDALE

Compton, Wolverhampton, WV3 9DY. Anne & Brian Bailey, 01902 424867, m.bailey1234@btinternet.com. *1½ m W of Wolverhampton city centre. From Wolverhampton Ring Rd take A454 towards Bridgnorth for 1m. Waterdale is on L off A454 Compton Rd West.* **Sun 7 June, Sun 5 July (12-5.30). Combined adm with 12 Waterdale £5, chd free. Home-made teas. Visits also by arrangement May to July for groups of 10 to 30.**

A romantic garden of surprises, which gradually reveals itself on a journey through deep, lush planting, full of unusual plants. From the sunny, flower filled terrace, a ruined folly emerges from a luxuriant fernery and leads into an oriental garden, complete with tea house. Towering bamboos hide the way to the gothic summerhouse and mysterious shell grotto. Find us on Facebook at 'Garden of Surprises'.

---

55 THE WICKETS

47 Long Street, Wheaton Aston, ST19 9NF. Tony & Kate Bennett, 01785 840233, ajtonyb@talktalk.net. *8m W of Cannock, 10m N of Wolverhampton, 10m E of Telford. M6 J12 W towards Telford on A5; 3m R signed Stretton; 150yds L signed Wheaton Aston; 2m L; over canal, garden on R or at Bradford Arms on A5 follow signs.* **Sun 26 July, Thur 27, Sun 30 Aug (1.30-5). Adm £3.50, chd free. Home-made teas. Visits also by arrangement July & Aug.**

There's a delight around every corner and lots of quirky features in this most innovative garden. Its themed areas incl a fernery, grasses bed, hidden gothic garden, succulent theatre, cottage garden beds and even a cricket match! It will certainly give you ideas for your own garden as you sit and have tea and cake. Afterwards, walk by the canal and enjoy the beautiful surrounding countryside. Wheelchair access - two single steps in garden and 2 gravel paths.

56 WILD THYME COTTAGE

Woodhouses, Barton Under Needwood, Burton-On-Trent, DE13 8BS. Ray & Michele Blundell. *B5016 Midway between villages of Barton & Yoxall. From A38 through Barton Village B5016 towards Yoxall. Or from A513 at Yoxall centre take Town Hill sign for Barton. Garden is at Woodhouses, approx 2m from either village.* **Sun 25 Oct (11-4.30). Adm £4, chd free. Light refreshments.**

The garden surrounds a self built Oak frame house now 20 years old but looks 200 and extends to 1/3 acre. There is a collection of over 120 Japanese Maples with white bark Birch and rare trees, shrubs and herbaceous perennials. Large beds of Ornamental grasses & late flowering perennials. Growers of Zantedeschia (Arum Lily's). Plants sales. Emphasis is on successive interest throughout the year. Newly constructed Lychgate entrance. Ornamental grasses. Rare trees and shrubs. Partial wheelchair access on gravel and grass.

57 WILD WOOD LODGE

Bushton Lane, Anslow, Burton-On-Trent, DE13 9QL. Richard & Dorothy Ward, 01283 812100, poplarsfarm@breathe.com. *Bushton Lane is signed in centre of village. Wild Wood Lodge is ¼ m down Bushton Lane.* **Sun 14 June, Sun 9 Aug (1.30-5). Adm £3.50, chd free. Home-made teas. Visits also by arrangement June to Aug.** Covering approx 2 acres, the garden consists of a productive orchard with apples, pears and plums. A Soft Fruit Garden with Raspberries and Strawberries etc., a wide selection of vegetables on raised beds, colourful herbaceous borders, shrubs, ornamental trees, wild life pond and fishing lake. The Garden was overall winner in the Staffordshire Agricultural Societies Farm Garden Competition 2019. Level garden, wide paths.

58 WOODBROOKE QUAKER STUDY CENTRE
1046 Bristol Road, Selly Oak, B29 6LJ. Woodbrooke Quaker Study Centre, 0121 472 5171, enquiries@woodbrooke.org.uk, www.woodbrooke.org.uk. *6m SW of Birmingham. On A38 Bristol Rd, S of Selly Oak, opp Witherford Way.* **Sat 25 July (12-4). Adm £5, chd free. Home-made teas. Visits also by arrangement for groups of 5+. We offer paid guided tours for groups throughout the year.** George Cadbury's former home, which incl a lake, wild area, herbaceous borders, herb garden and a walled garden, the whole area extending to 10 acres. Very fine variety of trees. Our Head Gardener and other staff will be on hand to help visitors to identify the key garden features and make the most of their visit. Garden tours and short talks will be available. Freshly baked cakes and hot drinks will be available to purchase all day. Some paths may be unsuitable for wheelchair access depending on the weather.

59 2 WOODLAND CRESCENT
Finchfield, Wolverhampton, WV3 8AS. Mr & Mrs Parker, 01902 332392, alisonparker1960@hotmail.co.uk. *2m SW of Wolverhampton City centre. From Inner Ring Rd take A41 W to Tettenhall. At junction with A459 turn L onto Merridale Rd. Straight over Bradwell Xrds then R onto Trysull Rd. 3rd R onto Coppice Rd & 1st R onto Woodland Crescent.* **Sun 21 June, Sun 12 July (11.30-4.30). Adm £3, chd free. Cream teas. Visits also by arrangement June & July for groups of 5 to 30.**

A semi-detached townhouse garden 120 x 25 ft, every inch packed with perennials, trees, acers, shrubs, roses, hostas and clematis. Wildlife pond and nesting boxes to attract birds. Productive vegetable and fruit garden. Informal style but clipped box and topiary animals add some formality.

60 WOODLEIGHTON GROVE, KARIBU GARDEN
9 Woodleighton Grove, Uttoxeter, ST14 8BX. Graham & Judy White, 01889 563930, graham&judy.white@ngs.org.uk. *Take B5017 Marchington Rd from Uttoxeter Town Centre. Go over Railway Bridge, then take 1st exit at r'about, then 3rd exit at next r'about into Highwood Rd, After ¼ m turn R then 1st L.* **Sun 28 June (1-4). Adm £8, chd free. Home-made teas. Price incl refreshments. Pre-booking essential for the Ticketed Opening Day on Sun 28 Jun - please contact the garden owners for tickets. Visits also by arrangement June & July. Groups should be a min 12 people.** A tranquil & intriguing garden informally planted on two levels. Unique landscaping & design features incl a Giant Insect Hotel; Bell Tower; Folly; Dovecote; Boardwalk; Stumpery; Archways; Natural Stream; Bridges & Waterfall. Various collections of Plants & Artefacts incl 400 cacti, succulents, sempervivum & jovibaba plus over 250 vintage and antique horticultural & agricultural hand tools.

61 YARLET HOUSE
Yarlet, Stafford, ST18 9SD. Mr & Mrs Nikolas Tarling. *2m S of Stone. Take A34 from Stone towards Stafford, turn L into Yarlet School & L again into car park.* **Fri 19 June (10-1.30). Adm £4, chd free. Home-made teas. Donation to Staffordshire Wildlife Trust.** 4 acre garden with extensive lawns, walks, lengthy herbaceous borders and traditional Victorian box hedge. Water gardens with fountain and rare lilies. Sweeping views across Trent Valley to Sandon. New peaceful Japanese garden for 2020. Victorian School Chapel. 9 hole putting course. Boules pitch. Yarlet School Art Display. Gravel paths.

62 YEW TREE COTTAGE
Podmores Corner, Long Lane, White Cross, Haughton, ST18 9JR. Clive & Ruth Plant, 07591 886925, pottyplantz@aol.com. *4m W of Stafford. Take A518 W Haughton, turn R Station Rd (signed Ranton) 1m, then turn R at Xrds ¼ m on R.* **Sat 2 May (2-5). Every Thur 2 July to 16 July (11-4). Sun 26 July (2-5). Adm £3.50, chd free. Home-made teas. Visits also by arrangement May to July for groups of 5+.** Hardy Plant Society member's garden brimming with unusual plants. All-yr-round interest incl Meconopsis, Trillium. ½ -acre incl gravel, borders, vegetables and plant sales. National Collection Dierama featured on BBC Gardeners World flowering first half July. Facebook 'Dierama Species in Staffordshire'. Covered vinery for tea if weather is unkind, and seats in the garden for lingering on sunny days. Partial wheelchair access, grass and paved paths, some narrow and some gravel.

63 NEW YEW TREES
Whitley Eaves, Eccleshall, Stafford, ST21 6HR. Mrs Teresa Hancock, 07973432077, hancockteresa@gmail.com. *7m from J14 M6. Situated on A519 between Eccleshall (2.2 m) and Woodseaves, (1m). Traffic cones & signs will highlight the entrance.* **Visits by arrangement June to Aug. Adm £4, chd free. Home-made teas.** 1 acre garden divided into rooms by mature hedging, shrubs & trees enjoying views over the surrounding countryside. Large patio area with containers & seating for refreshments. Other features incl pond, topiary, vegetable plot, hen run & wildlife area. If the garden is visited during June/July there is 8 acres of natural wild flower meadow to enjoy before it is cut for hay.

We open the gates to the nation's best gardens, offering a relaxing, memorable and affordable day out. A perfect experience to share with friends and family.

OPENING DATES

All entries subject to change. For latest information check www.ngs.org.uk

Map locator numbers are shown to the right of each garden name.

February

Snowdrop Festival

Sunday 16th
◆ Blakenham Woodland
   Garden   7
Gable House   20

Sunday 23rd
The Laburnums   32

March

Sunday 1st
The Old Rectory,
   Brinkley   39

April

Saturday 4th
NEW Thornham Walled
   Garden   58

Sunday 5th
Great Thurlow Hall   24
◆ The Place for Plants,
   East Bergholt Place
   Garden   46

Sunday 19th
Helyg   27

Sunday 26th
◆ Blakenham Woodland
   Garden   7
NEW Granary Barn   22
◆ The Place for Plants,
   East Bergholt Place
   Garden   46

May

Sunday 3rd
NEW Finndale House,   17
NEW Grundisburgh
   House   26
Rosedale   53

Sunday 10th
◆ Fullers Mill Garden   19
Street Farm   57

Sunday 17th
Drinkstone Park   15
The Priory   49

Sunday 24th
Bridges   9
Lavenham Hall   34

Monday 25th
Batteleys Cottage   3
Cattishall Farmhouse   12

Saturday 30th
◆ Wyken Hall   66

Sunday 31st
Bay Tree House   4
246 Ferry Road   16
Freston House   18
Ousden House   43
41 Westmorland Road   61
◆ Wyken Hall   66

June

Sunday 7th
Barton Mere   2
Berghersh Place   6
Great Thurlow Hall   24
Lillesley Barn   35
Old Gardens   38
The Old Rectory,
   Nacton   41
◆ Somerleyton Hall
   Gardens   54

Sunday 14th
NEW Ashe Park   1
Becks End Farm   5
Great Bevills   23
5 Parklands Green   45
The Rooks   52
Wenhaston Grange   60
Wood Farm, Gipping   64

Saturday 20th
NEW Brambly Hedge   8
Holm House   31

Sunday 21st
Heron House   29
Hillside   30
NEW The Old Rectory,
   Kirton   40
Priors Oak   48
Wood Farm, Sibton   65

Sunday 28th
◆ Blakenham Woodland
   Garden   7

July

Saturday 4th
NEW Church Cottage   13
NEW Orchard House   42
White House Farm   62

Sunday 5th
White House Farm   62

Sunday 12th
Redisham Hall   51
NEW Squires Barn   55

Sunday 19th
NEW Manor House,   36
The Old Rectory,
   Brinkley   39
Paget House   44

August

Sunday 2nd
Rosedale   53

Saturday 8th
Gislingham Gardens   21

Sunday 9th
Gislingham Gardens   21

Sunday 16th
NEW The Priory, Laxfield
   Rd   50

Sunday 30th
Bridges   9
Henstead Exotic
   Garden   28

September

Sunday 6th
Green Farmhouse   25

Sunday 13th
11 Brookside   10

October

Sunday 4th
◆ Fullers Mill Garden   19

Sunday 11th
◆ The Place for Plants,
   East Bergholt Place
   Garden   46

February 2021

Sunday 21st
Gable House   20

By Arrangement

Arrange a personalised garden visit with your club, or group of friends, on a date to suit you. See individual garden entries for full details.

Berghersh Place   6
By the Crossways   11
Dip-on-the-Hill   14
Drinkstone Park   15
246 Ferry Road   16
Gislingham Gardens   21
Helyg   27
Heron House   29
Holm House   31
Larks' Hill   33
Lillesley Barn   35
Moat House   37
Old Gardens   38
The Old Rectory,
   Nacton   41
Paget House   44
5 Parklands Green   45
Polstead Mill   47
Priors Oak   48
The Priory   49
NEW Stone Cottage   56
41 Westmorland Road   61
White House Farm   62
NEW The Willows   63

Your visits help change lives – your generosity has supported unpaid carers through donations to Carers Trust totalling over £4 million since 1996

THE GARDENS

1 NEW ASHE PARK
Ivy Lodge Road, Campsea
Ashe, Woodbridge, IP13 0QB.
Mr Richard Keeling. *Using the
postcode in Sat Nav will bring you
to the entrance to Ashe Park on Ivy
Lodge Road. Drive through entrance
signed Ashe Park, go past the gate
cottage on left and follow signs to
car park.* **Sun 14 June (10.30-5).
Adm £6, chd free.**
In the 350 years of this 12 acre
garden's existence it has gone
through many changes. Gertrude
Jekyll said of it in 1905 that it was
interesting but it had no coherence
of design. Since then the main house
has been destroyed and the gardens
have been re-aligned, however the
bones of the gardens have been
retained namely canals, massive
cedar trees, yew hedges, walled
garden and many more features.
Partial wheelchair access, some
gravel paths and steps.
&

2 BARTON MERE
Thurston Road, Great Barton,
IP31 2PR. Mr & Mrs C O
Stenderup. *2m E of Bury St
Edmunds. From Bury St Edmunds
on A143 through Gt Barton turn R at
Bunbury Arms PH. Entrance ½m on
L. From Thurston take Gt Barton Rd
from railway bridge. Entrance 1½m
on R.* **Sun 7 June (1-5). Adm £4,
chd free. Tea.**
C16 house (not open) with later
Georgian façade, set in 50 acres
of parkland. Extensive lawns with
views over the Mere.Rose garden
and herbaceous borders mostly
surrounded by C16 walls, two
courtyards and large conservatory.
Productive vegetable garden,old
orchard and beautiful grass tennis
court. Gravel paths.
&

3 BATTELEYS COTTAGE
The Ling, Wortham, Diss,
IP22 1ST. Mr & Mrs Andy & Linda
Simpson. *3m W of Diss. Turn signed
from A143 Diss/Bury Rd at Wortham.
By Church turn R at T-junction.
At top of hill turn L. Go down hill
& round sharp L corner.* **Mon 25
May (11.30-4.30). Adm £5, chd
free. Home-made teas and light
refreshments.**

A varied one acre garden planted for
abundance in all seasons. Formality
and informality, a mix of winding bark
paths, light and shade, secluded
spots to sit, new vistas at every
turn. Fitting into its rural setting, it
supports a wealth of bird life. There
is a diversity of planting in densely
planted borders as well as pots,
sculptures, meadow, ponds, stream
and vegetable areas to inspire you.
Wheelchair access to most parts of
the garden, gravel, grass and bark
paths.
& ✿ 🚗 ☕

4 BAY TREE HOUSE
The Green, Rougham, Bury St.
Edmunds, IP30 9JP. Mrs Claire
Farthing & Mr Chris Farthing.
*Come off A14 J45 & head for
Rougham. At T-junction, turn L
follow road for approx 1 ½m, past
Rougham Sports Hall. Go round 90
degree bend to R. Follow signs for
parking & disabled parking.* **Sun 31
May (10.30-5). Adm £4.50, chd
free. Home-made teas.**
Nearly 2 acres of garden. Patio with
wisteria draped pergola. Decking
with bench overlooking a wildlife
pond and small stream. 100ft long
border, rose arbour, parterre garden.
Green oak arches with wisteria and
Italian pots. Mature trees. Lollipop
hornbeams with curved yew hedging.
3 sculptures, new Himalayan birch
grove and new large autumnal bed.
Lovely country views. Wheelchair
access the garden is mainly flat with
only one small gravel path which can
be avoided.
& 🐕 ✿ ☕

5 BECKS END FARM
School Road, Westhall,
Halesworth, IP19 8QZ. Mr &
Mrs John & Marjorie Milbank. *E
of Halesworth on A144 between
Halesworth & Bungay. From
Halesworth turn R at the Spexhall
Xrds. Continue along & take 3rd
turning L. Becks End Farm is the
first house on L.* **Sun 14 June
(11-5.30). Adm £5, chd free. Light
refreshments. cake and tea/
coffee/soft drinks.**
Set in one and a half acres comprising
lawns, trees, hard landscaping,
wide herbaceous flower borders,
orchard, natural pond, vegetable
garden and central pole fruit cage.
Pleached Hornbeam hedges screen
the paddock and stable block. The
garden surrounds an old Victorian
Schoolhouse on the edge of the

village and has been designed and
developed since 2007 when acquired
by the present owners. No wheelchair
access because of steps.
☕

6 BERGHERSH PLACE
Ashbocking Road, Witnesham,
Ipswich, IP6 9EZ. Mr & Mrs T C
Parkes, wendyparkes@live.com.
*North of Witnesham village, B1077
double bends. Farm entrance,
concrete drive, approx 1m S of
Ashbocking Xrds. Entrance on sharp
bend so please drive slowly. Turn in
between North Lodge & Berghersh
House.* **Sun 7 June (12-5). Adm
£4.50, chd free. Home-made teas.
Visits also by arrangement in June
for groups of 10 to 30.**
Peaceful walled and hedged gardens
surround elegant Regency house (not
open) among fields above the Fynn
Valley. Circular walk from the farm
buildings, around house with lawns
and mature trees to a pretty view of
the valley. Mound, ponds, bog area
and orchard paddock. Informal family
garden with shrub and perennial
beds. Garden created over last 20
years by current owner. Parking
for elderly and disabled at end of
farmyard close to family garden. Most
areas are accessible to disabled
visitors.
& 🐕 ☕

7 ◆ BLAKENHAM WOODLAND GARDEN
Little Blakenham,
Ipswich, IP8 4LZ. M
Blakenham, 07917612355,
blakenham@btinternet.com, www.
blakenhamwoodlandgarden.org.
uk. *4m NW of Ipswich. Follow signs
at Little Blakenham, 1m off B1113
or go to Blakenham Woodland
Garden web-site.* **For NGS: Sun
16 Feb, Sun 26 Apr, Sun 28 June
(9.30-4.30). Adm £5, chd free.
Home-made teas. NGS days
only. For other opening times and
information, please phone, email or
visit garden website.**
Beautiful 6 acre woodland garden
with variety of rare trees and shrubs,
Chinese rocks and landscape
sculpture. Lovely in spring with
snowdrops, daffodils, camellias,
magnolias and bluebells followed by
roses in early summer. Woodland
Garden open from 16 Feb - 28 July.
& ✿ 🚗 ☕

8 NEW BRAMBLY HEDGE

Lowestoft Road, Beccles, NR34 7DE. Lynton & Teresa Cooper. *From town centre head towards Lowestoft, along Ingate - on the R after lights. From Lowestoft direction head through Worlingham on the L before lights. Roadside parking Ellough Rd. NR34 7AA.* **Sat 20 June (11-5). Adm £3.50, chd free. Home-made teas.**

A garden of contrasts and surprises. A modern introduction to a quirky woodland finish, the visitor can explore a huge variety of shrubs and trees with many unusual specimens. Add in a beautiful raised-bed potager and just when you think you have seen it all, and relax with tea and cake on one of the many seats dotted around, tucked away is a gem you missed the first time. Partial wheelchair access.

9 BRIDGES

The Street, Woolpit, Bury St. Edmunds, IP30 9SA. Mr Stanley Bates & Mr Michael Elles. *Through green coach gates marked Deliveries. From A14 take slip rd to Woolpit, follow signs to centre of village, road curves to R. Bridges is on L & covered in Wisteria & opp Co-op.* **Sun 24 May, Sun 30 Aug (11-5). Adm £5, chd free. Home-made teas.**

C15 Grade 11 terraced house in the centre of a C12 Suffolk village with walled garden to the rear of the property. Additional land was acquired 20 years ago, and this garden was developed into formal and informal planting. The main formal feature is the Shakespeare Garden featuring the bust of Shakespeare, and the 'Umbrello' a recently constructed pavillion in an Italianate design. Statue of Shakespeare, The Umbrello, various surprises for children of all ages. Usually a Wind Quintet playing in the main garden. Two public houses The Swan and The Bull in village open for lunch. Teas in aid of St. Mary's Church, Woolpit. Not suitable for wheelchairs.

10 11 BROOKSIDE

Moulton, Newmarket, CB8 8SG. Elizabeth Goodrich & Peter Mavroghenis. *Near the Packhorse Bridge & Pub. 3m due E of Newmarket on B1085.* **Sun 13 Sept (2-5). Adm £5, chd free. Light refreshments.**

1½ acres over 4 levels. Traditional hedges, mature trees and roses at the front while rear garden landscaped in contemporary style. Lower terrace with water feature and fig trees. Terraced beds with ornamental grasses, knot garden, hosta courtyard. Metal retaining wall to former paddock, many specimen trees, apple espalier bordered greenhouse with kitchen garden, apples and vines. Teas in aid of Moulton Village Hall.

11 BY THE CROSSWAYS

Kelsale, Saxmundham, IP17 2PL. Mr & Mrs William Kendall, miranda@bythecrossways.co.uk. *2m NE of Saxmundham, just off Clayhills Rd. ½ m N of town centre, turn R to Theberton on Clayhills Rd. After 1½ m, 1st L to Kelsale, then turn L immed after white cottage.* **Visits by arrangement May to Sept for groups of up to 10. Adm £5, chd free. Home-made teas. Soft drinks, tea and coffee.**

Three acre wildlife garden designed as a garden within a working organic farm where wilderness areas lie next to productive beds. Large semi-walled vegetable and cutting garden and a spectacular crinkle-crankle wall. Extensive perennial planting, grasses and wild areas. This garden is not highly manicured which more traditionally minded gardeners may find alarming! The garden is mostly flat, with paved or gravel pathways around the main house, a few low steps and extensive grass paths and lawns.

12 CATTISHALL FARMHOUSE

Cattishall, Great Barton, Bury St. Edmunds, IP31 2QT. Mrs J Mayer, 07738 936496, joannamayer42@googlemail.com. *3m NE of Bury St Edmunds. Approach Great Barton from Bury on A143 take 1st R turn to church. If travelling towards Bury take last L turn to church as you leave the village. At church bear R & follow lane to Farmhouse on R.* **Mon 25 May (1-5). Adm £4, chd free. Home-made teas.**

Approx 2 acre farmhouse garden enclosed by a flint wall and mature beech hedge laid mainly to lawns with both formal and informal planting and large herbaceous border. There is an abundance of roses, small wildlife pond and recently developed kitchen garden incl a wild flower area and fruit cages. Chickens, bees and a boisterous Labrador also live here. Generally flat with some gravel paths. The occasional small step.

13 NEW CHURCH COTTAGE

Braiseworth Lane, Braiseworth, IP23 7DT. Mr Rajat Jindal. *Enter from A140 on a 1m narrow track road or through Eye.* **Sat 4 July (11-5). Combined adm with Orchard House £6, chd free. Home-made teas at Orchard House.**

A naturalistic garden set in 2.5 acres and developed from scratch over the last 9 years. A combination of formal and informal features including a parterre, cottage garden surrounding an 18th Century thatched cottage, ponds, large prairie style beds, a wildflower meadow, Hornbeam cubes, two copses, pleached limes, raised vegetable beds, a willow dome and specimen trees. Wheelchair accessible with care, mainly on grass.

Finndale House

14 DIP-ON-THE-HILL

Ousden, Newmarket,
CB8 8TW. Geoffrey & Christine
Ingham, 01638 500329,
gki1000@cam.ac.uk. *5m E of
Newmarket; 7m W of Bury St
Edmunds. From Newmarket: 1m
from junction of B1063 & B1085.
From Bury St Edmunds follow signs
for Hargrave. Parking at village hall.
Follow NGS sign at the end of the
lane.* **Visits by arrangement June
to Sept for groups of up to 20.
Max of fifteen visitors. Adm £4.50,
chd free. Light refreshments.**
Approx one acre in a dip on a
S-facing hill based on a wide range
of architectural/sculptural evergreen
trees, shrubs and groundcover:
pines; grove of Phillyrea latifolia;
'cloud pruned' hedges; palms; large
bamboo; ferns; range of kniphofia
and croscosmia. Visitors may wish to
make an appointment when visiting
gardens nearby. No wheelchair
access. No dogs.

15 DRINKSTONE PARK

Park Road, Drinkstone, Bury St.
Edmunds, IP30 9ST. Michael &
Christine Lambert, 01359 272513,
chris@drinkstonepark.co.uk,
www.drinkstonepark.co.uk. *6m
from Bury St Edmunds. E on A14
J46 turn L and the R for Drinkstone.
W on A14 J46 turn R for Drinkstone.
Turn into Park Rd. We are not in the
village. Park Rd is parallel to the road
that runs through the village.* **Sun 17
May (12-5.30). Adm £5, chd free.**
Home-made teas provided by All
Saint Church, Drinkstone. **Visits
also by arrangement May to July.**
Afternoon teas and light lunches
available.
Three acre garden with wildlife and
ornamental ponds, herbaceous
borders, roses, orchard, woodland
and wildlife area, productive
vegetable plot with poly tunnel and
greenhouses. The garden also boasts
an original Ha Ha with views across
the Suffolk landscape. 'Our Folly' is
a sunken garden created from part
of the unearthed cellars of an old
mansion demolished in 1950 now
planted with ferns. Some gravel
paths.

16 246 FERRY ROAD

Felixstowe, IP11 9RU. Mrs
Sally Gallant, 01394 276336,
sallyjag@hotmail.co.uk. *At
Felixstowe Golf Club you will find*
*Ferry Rd opposite, travel up Ferry
Rd & house is 4th on L.* **Sun 31 May
(11.30-5). Combined adm with
41 Westmorland Road £5, chd
free. Light refreshments at 41
Westmorland Road. Visits also
by arrangement May to Oct for
groups of up to 20.**
Newly established garden which
attempts to give year round colour
and interest, places to sit and
ponder. Various walkways lead you
around this secluded coastal garden,
moments from the sea. Some mature
trees, and attractive hedging, shady
walkway and wooden boardwalk,
herbaceous borders and Japanese
themed feature. Sunny sheltered
sitting areas. Not suitable for
wheelchair users due to steps. Well
behaved dogs on a lead.

Your visits help change
lives – your generosity
helps Marie Curie fund
nurses to care for people
night and day in their
homes, with donations of
more than £9 million

17 NEW FINNDALE HOUSE,

Woodbridge Road, Grundisburgh,
Woodbridge, IP13 6UD. Bryan &
Catherine Laxton. *On the B1079,
2m NW of Woodbridge. Parking is in
the field (postcode IP13 6PU) blue
badge parking by the house. Short
walk to Grundisburgh House.* **Sun 3
May (11-5). Combined adm with
Grundisburgh House £6, chd free.
Home-made teas.**
A Georgian house surrounded by 10
acres of garden and meadows which
are bisected by a 'Monet' style bridge
over the River Lark. The garden was
designed 30 years ago and has been
refreshed by recent additions. Many
mature trees, colourful herbaceous
borders, thousands of daffodils
followed by tulips and alliums, roses in
the summer and dahlias to round the
year off. Productive kitchen garden.
Lunches available at The Dog PH in
village. Gravel drive.

18 FRESTON HOUSE

The Street, Freston, Ipswich,
IP9 1AF. Mr & Mrs Andrew & Judith
Whittle, www.frestonhouse.co.uk.
*Go under the Orwell Bridge
from Ipswich towards Holbrook.
At the junction for Holbrook &
Woolverstone, turn sharp R signed
Freston. After 300m, turn L into
a no through road.* **Sun 31 May
(12-5). Adm £5, chd free. Light
refreshments.**
20 acre garden and large Georgian
rectory set in parkland, planted from
2006 onwards by the current owners.
Individual colour-themed, roomed
gardens, cottage garden and formal
long borders with mass plantings of
hundreds of shrubs and perennials.
A one acre kitchen garden, wildlife
pond, winter garden, gravel garden
and woodlands with over 1,000
varieties of hosta and other shade
loving plants. One of the largest
collection of hostas in the country.
Several roomed, coloured-themed
gardens, large winter garden, 200
varieties of bearded iris, large wildlife
pond. Some gravel paths.

19 ♦ FULLERS MILL GARDEN

West Stow, IP28 6HD.
Perennial, 01284 728888,
fullersmillgarden@perennial.org.
uk, www.fullersmillgarden.org.uk.
*6m NW of Bury St Edmunds. Turn
off A1101 Bury to Mildenhall Rd,
signed West Stow Country Park,
go past Country Park continue for
1/4 m, garden entrance on R. Sign at
entrance.* **For NGS: Sun 10 May,
Sun 4 Oct (11-5). Adm £5, chd
free.** Home-made teas. **For other
opening times and information,
please phone, email or visit garden
website.**
An enchanting 7 acre garden on the
banks of the river Lark. A beautiful
site with light dappled woodland
and a plantsman's paradise of rare
and unusual shrubs, perennials
and marginals planted with great
natural charm. Euphorbias and lilies
are a particular feature with the late
flowering colchicums, including many
rare varieties, being of great interest in
Autumn. Tea, coffee and soft drinks.
Home-made cakes. Partial wheelchair
access around garden.

20 GABLE HOUSE
Halesworth Road, Redisham, Beccles, NR34 8NE. John & Brenda Foster. *5m S of Beccles. Signed from A12 at Blythburgh and A144 Bungay/Halesworth Rd.* **Sun 16 Feb (11-4). Adm £4.50, chd free. Light refreshments incl warming soups available in February. 2021: Sun 21 Feb.** Donation to St Peter's Church, Redisham.

We have a large collection of snowdrops, cyclamen, hellebores and other flowering plants for the Snowdrop Day in February. Many bulbs and plants will be for sale. Hot soup and home-made teas available. Greenhouses contain rare bulbs and tender plants. A one acre garden with lawns and scree with water feature. We have a wide range of unusual trees, shrubs, perennials and bulbs collected over the last fifty years.

&. ❋ 🚗 ☕

GROUP OPENING

21 GISLINGHAM GARDENS
Mill Street, Gislingham, IP23 8JT. 01379 788737. *4m W of Eye. Gislingham 2½ m W of A140. 9m N of Stowmarket, 8m S of Diss. Disabled parking at Ivy Chimneys. Parking limited to disabled parking at Chapel Farm Close.* **Sat 8, Sun 9 Aug (11-4.30). Combined adm £5, chd free. Light refreshments at Ivy Chimneys. Visits also by arrangement July to Sept for groups of up to 30. Adm £7 to incl tea and cake. Please contact Ivy Chimneys 01379 788737.**

12 CHAPEL FARM CLOSE
Ross Lee.

IVY CHIMNEYS
Iris & Alan Stanley.

2 varied gardens in a picturesque village with a number of Suffolk timbered houses. Ivy Chimneys is planted for yr round interest with ornamental trees, some topiary, exotic borders and fishpond set in an area of Japanese style. Wisteria draped pergola supports a productive vine. Also a separate ornamental vegetable garden. Small orchard on front lawn. New 12 Chapel Farm Close is a tiny garden, exquisitely planted and an absolute riot of colour. Despite the garden's size, the owner has planted a Catalpa, a Cornus Florida Rubra and many unusual plants. It is a fine example of what can be achieved in a small space. Wheelchair access to Ivy Chimneys. Access for smaller wheelchairs only at 12 Chapel Farm Close.

&. 🐕 ❋ ☕

---

22 NEW GRANARY BARN
Little Green, Burgate, Diss, IP22 1QQ. Wendy Keeble. *23m NE of Bury St Edmunds; 6m SW of Diss; 1m S of A143. On A143 between Wortham & Botesdale, take turning signed Burgate Little Green (Buggs Ln) & follow NGS signs to car park 200 yd walk from garden. No parking on verges or common please.* **Sun 26 Apr (11-5). Adm £4, chd free. Light refreshments. Gluten-free and vegetarian options.**

If re-wilding is the latest trend, we must be high fashion! From 2 acres of mown grass 10 yrs ago, the garden now has formal planting near the house, a box parterre & pergola, herbaceous borders, a productive orchard, vegetable & soft fruit beds, leading to a large perennial wildflower meadow with native trees. This wildlife haven is freshest in Spring with an abundance of blossom and bulbs. Focus on attracting and sustaining wildlife, a copse of 120 native trees, vegetable garden and fruit cages. Partial wheelchair access. Visitors may be dropped at a paved area accessing almost half the garden and vehicles removed to the cark park.

&. ❋ ☕

---

23 GREAT BEVILLS
Sudbury Road, Bures, CO8 5JW. Mr & Mrs G T C Probert. *4m S of Sudbury. Just N of Bures on the Sudbury rd B1508.* **Sun 14 June (2-5.30). Adm £4, chd free. Home-made teas.**

Overlooking the Stour Valley the gardens surrounding an Elizabethan manor house are formal and Italianate in style with Irish yews and mature specimen trees. Terraces, borders, ponds and woodland walks. A short drive away from Great Bevills visitors may wish to also see the C13 St Stephen's Chapel with wonderful views of the Old Bures Dragon recently re-created by the owner. Woodland walks give lovely views over the Stour Valley. Gravel paths.

&. 🐕 ❋ ☕

---

24 GREAT THURLOW HALL
Great Thurlow, Haverhill, CB9 7LF. Mr George Vestey. *12m S of Bury St Edmunds, 4m N of Haverhill. Great Thurlow village on B1061 from Newmarket; 3½ m N of junction with A143 Haverhill/Bury St Edmunds rd.* **Sun 5 Apr, Sun 7 June (2-5). Adm £5, chd free. Home-made teas in the Church.**

13 acres of beautiful gardens set around the River Stour, the banks of which are adorned with stunning displays of daffodil and narcissi together with blossoming trees in spring. Herbaceous borders, rose garden and extensive shrub borders come alive with colour from late spring onwards, there is also a large walled kitchen garden and arboretum.

&. 🐕 ☕

---

25 GREEN FARMHOUSE
The Green, Shelland, Stowmarket, IP14 3JE. Miss Rosemary Roe. *4m NW of Stowmarket, 10m SE of Bury St Edmunds. A14 W-bound. A1308-signed Wetherden, L to Harleston, follow NGS signs. A14 E-bound take Wetherden/Haughley Park turn, then R signed Buxhall. Follow NGS signs.* **Sun 6 Sept (2-5). Adm £5, chd free. Home-made teas.**

2 acre garden created around a thatched cottage commanding wonderful views of Mid-Suffolk countryside. A garden with all-year interest and wide variety of plants. Easy walks through garden rooms with shrubs, herbaceous borders, lawns and vistas, courtyard, stumpery, natural pond and new prairie style border. Garden would be a good subject for photographic/art groups. Partial wheelchair access.

&. ❋ 🚗 ☕

---

26 NEW GRUNDISBURGH HOUSE
Woodbridge Road, Grundisburgh, Woodbridge, IP13 6UD. Mrs Linden Hibbert. *Not, as the postcode claims, at the junction but just off B1079. Search for The Grundisburgh House Gallery (google maps) for precise location. Last house in the village on the left. Disabled parking at house.Main car park in nearby field (IP13 6PU).* **Sun 3 May (11-5). Combined adm with Finndale House, £6, chd free. Home-made teas at Finndale House.**

3-acre garden wrapping around classic Georgian house, highlights include natural swimming pond, formal garden, spring bulbs and fruit blossom, roses, irises and hydrangeas. New projects are

Ashe Park

on-going but include planting more hedging, ornamental trees and pleaching. There is a pop-up art gallery in the old coach house which is open intermittently throughout the year. The Grundisburgh Dog serves hot food. 3m from Woodbridge with numerous restaurants and cafes. Wheelchair access paved terrace and path in the formal garden, decking with two steps on swimming pond terrace. Remainder is gravel path.

♿ 🐕 ❀ ☕

27 HELYG
Thetford Road, Coney Weston, Bury St. Edmunds, IP31 1DN. Jackie & Briant Smith, 01359 220106, briant. broadsspirituality@gmail.com. *From Barningham Xrds/shop turn off the B1111 towards Coney Weston & Knettishall Country Park. After approx 1 mile Helyg will be found on the L behind some large willow trees.* Sun 19 Apr (2-5). Adm £3.50, chd free. Cream teas. Served in conservatory or on trays to take to seats around the garden. Visits also by arrangement Apr to Sept for groups of 10 to 20.
Just under half an acre of garden being developed for ease of maintenance and including new features each year. This relaxing garden, with many secluded seating areas, includes a woodland walk, raised flower beds, rose beds, large vegetable plot, small orchard, chickens, wildlife area, ponds and water features. Most of the garden is wheelchair accessible with a variety of surfaces including concrete slab, gravel and wood-chip paths.

♿ ☕

28 HENSTEAD EXOTIC GARDEN
Church Road, Henstead, Beccles, NR34 7LD. Andrew Brogan, www.hensteadexoticgarden.co.uk. *Equal distance between Beccles, Southwold & Lowestoft approx 5m. 1m from A12 turning after Wrentham (signed Henstead) very close to B1127.* Sun 30 Aug (11-4). Adm £4, chd free. Home-made teas.
2 acre exotic garden featuring 100 large palms, 20+ bananas and 200 bamboo plants. 2 streams, 20ft tiered walkway leading to Thai style wooden covered pavilion. Mediterranean and jungle plants around 3 large ponds with fish. winner Britains best garden 2015 on itv as voted by Alan Titchmarsh. Unique garden buildings, streams, waterfalls, rock walkways, different levels, Victorian grotts, giant compost toilet etc.

🐕 ❀ 🚗 ☕ ☕

29 HERON HOUSE
Aldeburgh, IP15 5EP. Mr & Mrs Jonathan Hale, 01728 452200, jonathanrhhale@aol.com. *At the southeastern junction of Priors Hill Rd & Park Rd. Last house on Priors Hill Rd on south side, at the junction where it rejoins Park Rd.* Sun 21 June (2-5). Adm £5, chd free. Tea. Visits also by arrangement Apr to Oct.
2 acres with superb views over the North Sea, River Alde and marshes. Unusual trees, herbaceous beds, shrubs and ponds with a waterfall in large rock garden, and a stream and bog garden. Some half hardy plants in the coastal micro-climate. Partial wheelchair access.

♿ 🐕 ☕

30 HILLSIDE
Union Hill, Semer, Ipswich, IP7 6HN. Mr & Mrs Neil Mordey. *Car park through field gate off A1141.* Sun 21 June (11-5). Adm £5, chd free. Home-made teas. Home-made sandwiches and cakes.
This garden in its historic setting of 10.5 acres has sweeping lawns running down to a spring fed carp pond. The formal garden has island beds of mixed planting for a long season of interest. The wild area of meadow has been landscaped with extensive tree planting to complement the existing woodland. There is also a small walled kitchen garden. Most areas are accessible although the fruit and vegetable garden is accessed over a deep gravel drive.

❀ ☕

31 HOLM HOUSE
Garden House Lane, Drinkstone, Bury St. Edmunds, IP30 9FJ. Mrs Rebecca Shelley, Rebecca.shelley@hotmail.co.uk. *7m SE of Bury St Edmunds. Coming from the E exit A14 at J47, from the W J46. Follow signs to Drinkstone, then Drinkstone Green. Turn into Rattlesden Road & look for Garden House Lane. Then it is first house on L.* Sat 20 June (11-4.30). Adm £5, chd free. Light refreshments provided by All Saints Church, Drinkstone. Visits also by arrangement May to Sept for groups of 10+.
Around 10 acres, including: orchard and lawns with mature trees and clipped Holm Oaks; formal garden with topiary, parterre and borders; rose garden; woodland walk with hellebores, camellias, rhododendrons and bulbs; new lake, woodland planting and wild flower meadow; cut flower garden with greenhouse; large kitchen garden with impressive greenhouse; Mediterranean courtyard with mature olive tree. Much of the garden is wheelchair accessible, but not the kitchen garden.

☕

Your visits help change lives – we are the largest single funder of the Queen's Nursing Institute

32 THE LABURNUMS

The Street, St James South Elmham, Halesworth, IP19 0HN. Mrs Jane Bastow. *6m W of Halesworth, 7m E of Harleston & 6m S of Bungay. Parking at nearby village hall. For disabled parking please phone to arrange. Yellow signs from 8m out in all directions.* **Sun 23 Feb (10-4). Adm £4.50, chd free. Light refreshments. Hot/Cold drinks, variety of home-made cakes and hot soup with crusty bread. Gluten free will be available.**

Again open for Snowdrops, but also the beautiful Hellebores and other flowering plants and shrubs. More snowdrops will be added to the 20,000 odd Snowdrops already planted in the last few years. The herbaceous beds and borders are always being added to by the 'plantaholic' owner. A garden for wildlife with a large variety of birds and creatures. A haven to relax in and enjoy nature in all forms. Plant stall with a variety of plants and bulbs. Newly restored pond and sunken garden. Thousands of Snowdrops complementing the Hellebores and other plants. Conservatory packed with tender plants. Large glasshouse. Gravel drive. Partial wheelchair access to front garden. Steps to sunken garden. Concrete path in back garden.

33 LARKS' HILL

Clopton Road, Tuddenham St Martin, IP6 9BY. Mr John Lambert, 01473 785248, jrlambert@talktalk.net. *3m NE of Ipswich. From Ipswich take B1077, go through village, take the Clopton Rd to the L, after 300 metres at the brow of the hill you will see the house. Follow the car parking signs.* **Visits by arrangement May to Aug for groups of 20+. Adm £5, chd free. Home-made teas.**

The gardens of eight acres comprise woodland, a newly-planted conifer garden, and formal areas, and fall away from the house to the valley floor. A hill within a garden and in Suffolk at that! Hilly garden with a modern castle keep with an interesting and beautiful site overlooking the gentle Fynn valley and the village beyond. A fossil of a limb bone from a Pliosaur that lived at least sixty million years ago was found in the garden in 2013. The discovery was reported in the national press but

its importance has been recognised world-wide. A booklet is available to purchase giving all the details. Our Big Shed Café can comfortably seat thirty or so and there is additional seating outside. Sit and talk and plan what to do next.

34 LAVENHAM HALL

Hall Road, Lavenham, Sudbury, CO10 9QX. Mr & Mrs Anthony Faulkner, www.katedenton.com. *Next to Lavenham's iconic church & close to High St. From church turn off the main rd down the side of church (Potland Rd). Go down hill. Car Park on R after 100 metres.* **Sun 24 May (11-5). Adm £5, chd free. Teas available in the village.**

5 acre garden built around the ruins of the original ecclesiastical buildings on the site and the village's 1 acre fishpond. The garden incl deep borders of herbaceous planting with sweeping vistas and provides the perfect setting for the sculptures which Kate makes in her studio at the Hall and exhibits both nationally and internationally. 40 garden sculptures on display. There is a gallery in the grounds which displays a similar number of indoor sculptures and working drawings. Many areas wheelchair accessible. However, please note gravel paths and slopes within the garden may limit access to certain areas.

35 LILLESLEY BARN

The Street, Kersey, Ipswich, IP7 6ED. Mr Karl & Mrs Bridget Allen, 07939 866873, bridgetinkerseybarn@gmail.com. *In village of Kersey, 2m NW Hadleigh. Driveway is 200 metres above 'The Bell' pub. Lillesley Barn is situated behind 'The Ancient Houses'.* **Sun 7 June (11-5). Combined adm with Old Gardens £5, chd free. Home-made teas. Visits also by arrangement May to July.**

Dry gravel garden (inspired by the Beth Chatto Garden) including variety of mediterranean plants, ornamental grasses, herbs and collection of succulents. Large herbaceous border, rose arbours and small orchard with poultry. Golden willow hedge and fruit trees. The garden contains various species of birch, elder, amelanchier and willow. All within an acre of garden bordered on two sides by fields. Meals available at The Bell Inn. Not suitable for Wheelchair access

due to gravel, uneven ground and a slope.

36 NEW MANOR HOUSE,

Leiston Road, Middleton, Saxmundham, IP17 3NS. Steve Thorpe & Mandy Beaumont. *See Paget House entry for directions to parking. Once there, Manor House is an 8-minute signed walk.* **Sun 19 July (10.30-4.30). Combined adm with Paget House £5, chd free. Home-made teas at Paget House.**

Just over an acre of garden on a triangular plot. Started from a wilderness in 2015 - now an ambulatory garden with seating to enjoy many new tree plantings, borders, meadows and a vegetable garden created from scratch. Biodiversity encouraged and 'right plant, right place' ethos.

37 MOAT HOUSE

Little Saxham, Bury St. Edmunds, IP29 5LE. Mr & Mrs Richard Mason, 01284 810941, rnm333@live.com. *2m SW of Bury St Edmunds. Leave A14 at J42 – leave r'about towards Westley. Through Westley Village, at Xrds R towards Barrow/Saxham. After 1.3m turn L down track. (follow signs).* **Visits by arrangement May to July for groups of 20+. Entrance price includes tea and cake. Adm £9, chd free. Home-made teas. Suzanne's home-made cakes are renowned. Always a warm welcome at Moat House.**

Set in a 2 acre historic and partially moated site. This tranquil mature garden has been developed over 20yrs. Bordered by mature trees the garden is in various sections incl a sunken garden, rose and clematis arbours, herbaceous borders with hydrangeas and alliums surrounded by box hedging, small arboretum. A Hartley Botanic greenhouse erected and new partere created in 2017. Secluded and peaceful setting, each year new additions and wonderful fencing.

38 OLD GARDENS

The Street, Kersey, Ipswich, IP7 6ED. Mr & Mrs David Anderson, 01473 828044, davidmander15@gmail.com. *10m W of Ipswich. 100 metres from The Bell Inn on the same side of the road.*

Sun 7 June (11-5). Combined adm with Lillesley Barn £5, chd free. Teas available at Lillesley Barn. Visits also by arrangement May to July.

Entered from The Street, a natural garden with wild flowers under a copper beech tree. To the rear, a formal garden designed by Cherry Sandford with a sculpture by David Harbour. Meals available at The Bell Inn.

&. 🐾 ☕

39 THE OLD RECTORY, BRINKLEY

Hall Lane, Brinkley, CB8 0SB. Mr & Mrs Mark Coley. *Hall Lane is a turning off Brinkley High St. At the end of Hall Lane, white gates on the R.* Sun 1 Mar (12-4). Light refreshments in Brinkley Village Hall. Sun 19 July (1.30-5.30). Home-made teas in Brinkley Village Hall. Adm £5, chd free.

Two acre garden started in 1973 when there was nothing there except a few large trees and snowdrops. Interesting trees planted since include a large liriodendron (tulip tree) planted in 1975. In the spring, many snowdrops, helebores and winter flowering shrubs. Mixed herbaceous borders with roses, interesting perennials and pockets of annuals grown from seed. Traditional potager with box hedges. Partial wheelchair access.

🌼 ☕

40 NEW THE OLD RECTORY, KIRTON

Church Lane, Kirton, Ipswich, IP10 0PT. Mr & Mrs N Garnham. *Adjacent to Kirton parish church on corner of Church Lane & Burnt House Lane. Car parking available in Church Hall car park next door.* Sun 21 June (12-6). Adm £5, chd free. Home-made teas.

Open for the first time, this traditional English garden contains mixed flower borders for both sun and shade providing year-round colour, fragrance and succour for bees and butterflies. The 3 acre garden contains many mature trees, including varieties of oak, which give it a park-like feel. Many plants are labelled. Delicious teas served by rose and lavender border. Plant stall. Refreshments in aid of Falkenham Church. Not suitable for disabled.

🌼 ☕

41 THE OLD RECTORY, NACTON

Nacton, IP10 0HY. Mrs Elizabeth & Mr James Wellesley Wesley, 01473 659673, tizyww@gmail.com. *The garden is down the road to Nacton from the first A14 turn off after Orwell bridge going N/E. Parking on Church Rd opp Old Rectory driveway. This will be signed.* Sun 7 June (11-5). Adm £4.50, chd free. Home-made teas. Visits also by arrangement Mar to Oct for groups of up to 20.

Just under 2 acres of garden divided into areas for different seasons: mature trees and herbaceous borders, herb/picking garden, rose garden. Light soil so many self sown flowers. Damp area with emphasis on foliage (Rheum, Darmera, Rodgersia, Hellebores). Most recently a terrace to West side of the house, still a work in progress after 28 years, looking at how to bring in more butterflies. The Ship Inn is 2m up road in Levington and does good pub lunches. Lovely walks on the Orwell Estuary with extensive bird life especially at low tide. Nacton is very accessible from Ipswich and surrounding areas. Most areas are accessible for disabled visitors, however several grassy slopes and various different levels so some energy needed to get everywhere!

&. 🐾 🌼 ☕

42 NEW ORCHARD HOUSE

Braiseworth Road, Braiseworth, Eye, IP23 7DS. Mary Woodin & Andrew Martindale. *2m SW of Eye,*

2m off A140. Sat 4 July (11-5). Combined adm with Church Cottage £6, chd free. Home-made teas. Gluten free will be available.

A tranquil 3 acre garden surrounding a Suffolk farmhouse and artist's studio. Bordered by mature trees and hedges, including Dawn Redwoods, Catalpa, flower borders, knot garden, vegetable/herbs, pond with gunneras, woodland path and orchard. Based on the garden, Mary wrote and illustrated "Drawn to the "Country" which encapsulates living and gardening in Suffolk. The studio will be open to visitors.

&. 🐾 ☕

43 OUSDEN HOUSE

Ousden, Newmarket, CB8 8TN. Mr & Mrs Alastair Robinson. *Newmarket 6m, Bury St Edmunds 8m. Ousden House stands at the west end of the village next to the Church.* Sun 31 May (2-5). Adm £6, chd free. Home-made teas.

A large spectacular garden with fine views over the surrounding country. Herbaceous borders, rose garden and lawns leading to Spring woodland, and lake. Additional special features include a long double crinkle-crankle yew hedge leading from the clock tower and a moat garden densely planted with hellebores, flowering shrubs and moisture loving plants. Tea is served in the house or the courtyard and in aid of St. Peter's Church Ousden. Extensive garden on various levels not suitable for wheelchairs or people who find difficulty in walking.

🌼 ☕

The Priory

44 PAGET HOUSE

Back Road, Middleton, Saxmundham, IP17 3NY. Julian & Fiona Cusack, 01728 649060, julian.cusack@btinternet.com. *From A12 at Yoxford take B1122 towards Leiston. Turn L after 1.2m at Middleton Moor. After 1m enter Middleton village & drive straight ahead into Back Road.* **Sun 19 July (10.30-4.30). Combined adm with Manor House, £5, chd free. Home-made teas. Gluten-free, dairy-free and vegan cake options. Visits also by arrangement Apr to Sept for groups of up to 30. Guided tours.** The garden is designed to be wildlife friendly with wild areas meeting formal planting.There is an orchard and a vegetable plot. There are areas of woodland, laid hedges, a pond supporting amphibians and dragonflies, a wild flower meadow and an abstract garden sculpture by local artist Paul Richardson. We record over 40 bird species each year and a good showing of butterflies, dragonflies and wild flowers including orchids. Gravel drive and mown paths.

♿ 🐄 🌾 ✿ 🅳 ☕

45 5 PARKLANDS GREEN

Fornham St Genevieve, Bury St. Edmunds, IP28 6UH. Mrs Jane Newton, newton.jane@talktalk.net. *2m Northwest of Bury St Edmunds off B1106. Plenty of parking on the green.* **Sun 14 June (11-4). Adm £5, chd free. Home-made teas. Visits also by arrangement May to Sept. Adm incl tea and cake.** 1½ acres of gardens developed since the 1980s for all year interest. There are mature and unusual trees and shrubs and riotous herbaceous borders. Explore the maze of paths to find 4 informal ponds, a tree house, the sunken garden, greenhouses and woodland walks. Partial wheelchair access only.

🐄 ✿ 🚗 ☕

46 ◆ THE PLACE FOR PLANTS, EAST BERGHOLT PLACE GARDEN

East Bergholt, CO7 6UP. Mr & Mrs Rupert Eley, 01206 299224, sales@placeforplants.co.uk, www.placeforplants.co.uk. *2m E of A12, 7m S of Ipswich. On B1070 towards Manningtree, 2m E of A12. Situated on the edge of East Bergholt.* **For NGS: Sun 5, Sun 26 Apr (2-5). Adm £7, chd free.**

Sun 11 Oct (1-4). Adm £6, chd free. Home-made teas. For other opening times and information, please phone, email or visit garden website. 20-acre garden originally laid out at the turn of the last century by the present owner's great grandfather. Full of many fine trees and shrubs, many seldom seen in East Anglia. A fine collection of camellias, magnolias and rhododendrons, topiary, and the National Collection of deciduous Euonymus. Partial Wheelchair access in dry conditions - it is advisable to telephone before visiting.

♿ ✿ 🚗 🅽🅿🅲 ☕

47 POLSTEAD MILL

Mill Lane, Polstead, Colchester, CO6 5AB. Mrs Lucinda Bartlett, 07711 720418, lucyofleisure@hotmail.com. *Between Stoke by Nayland & Polstead on the R Box. From Stoke by Nayland take rd to Polstead - Mill Lane is 1st on L & Polstead Mill is 1st house on R.* **Visits by arrangement May to Sept for groups of 10+. Adm £6, chd free. Home-made teas. Range of refreshments from coffee and biscuits to full cream teas or light lunches.** The garden has been developed since 2002, it has formal and informal areas, a wild flower meadow and a large productive kitchen garden. The R Box runs through the garden and there is a mill pond, which gives opportunity for damp gardening, while much of the rest of the garden is arid and is planted to minimise the need for watering. Featured in Secret Gardens of East Anglia. Partial wheelchair access.

♿ ✿ ☕

48 PRIORS OAK

Leiston Road, Aldeburgh, IP15 5QE. Mrs Trudie Willis, 01728 452580, trudie.willis@ dinkum.free-online.co.uk, www.sites.google.com/site/ priorsoakbutterflygarden. *1m N of Aldeburgh on B1122. Garden on L opp RSPB Reserve.* **Sun 21 June (2-6). Adm £5, chd free. Home-made teas. tea and cake. Visits also by arrangement May to Sept for groups of up to 10.** 10-acre wildlife and butterfly garden. Ornamental salad, herb and vegetable gardens. Herbaceous borders, ferns and Mediterranean and unusual plants. Pond, bogs and acid grassland with small wood. Skirting

the wood are 100 buddleias in 30 varieties forming a perfumed tunnel. Very tranquil and fragrant garden with grass paths and yearly interest. Rich in animal and bird and butterfly life. Specialist butterfly garden, as seen in SAGA magazine,and Horticulture in USA, renovated railway carriages, tortoise breeding, donkeys, wildlife walks. private visits by arrangement.

♿ ✿ ☕

49 THE PRIORY

Stoke by Nayland, Colchester, CO6 4RL. Mrs H F A Engleheart, 01206 262216, victoria. engleheart@btinternet.com. *5m SW of Hadleigh. Entrance on B1068 to Sudbury (NW of Stoke by Nayland).* **Sun 17 May (2-5). Adm £5, chd free. Home-made teas. Visits also by arrangement Apr to Sept for groups of 10+.** Interesting 9 acre garden with fine views over Constable countryside; lawns sloping down to small lakes and water garden; fine trees, rhododendrons and azaleas; walled garden; mixed borders and ornamental greenhouse. Wide variety of plants. Wheelchair access over most of garden, some steps.

♿ 🐄 ✿ 🚗 ☕

50 NEW THE PRIORY, LAXFIELD RD

Badingham, Woodbridge, IP13 8LS. Mr Nick Smith, Ncmsmith@me.com. *A1120 to Badingham. At White Horse pub, turn in Low Street. 0.25m R into Mill Road. Uphill for 0.75m. L at post box onto Laxfield Road. 0.5m past Priory Cottage, follow NGS signs.* **Sun 16 Aug (11-4.30). Adm £5, chd free. Home-made teas. Tea, coffee and locally made cakes available.** Designed by Frederic Whyte - a Chelsea Gold Medal winner - we wanted to create a garden with a contemporary feel, that had clear structure and focused on a refined palette of plants. The challenge was to clearly delineate between Priory Barn's guest areas, the kitchen garden, more formal borders and informal planting leading to the established orchard. Wheelchair access slightly restricted by gravel paths and a limited number of steps.

♿ 🛋 ☕

51 REDISHAM HALL

Redisham Rd, Redisham, nr Beccles, NR34 8LZ.

Philip & Lucy Everington,
www.redishamhallnurseries.co.uk.
*5m S of Beccles. From A145, turn W
on to Ringsfield-Bungay rd. Beccles,
Halesworth or Bungay, all within 5m.*
**Sun 12 July (2-6). Adm £5, chd
free. Home-made teas.**
C18 Georgian house (not open).
6.5 acre garden set in 400 acres
parkland and woods including a
traditional 2-acre Walled kitchen
garden with Peach house, Vinery
and Glasshouses. Large fruit cage,
Espalier fruit trees, many varieties
of vegetables, Herbs and Flower
beds. Lawns, Herbaceous borders,
Shrubberies, Woodland garden,
Ha-Ha wall, Ponds, Arboretum and
Mature trees. SORRY NO DOGS.
On site Plant Nursery & Tearoom.
The Walled Kitchen Garden is open
to the public during the summer
months. NEW FOR 2020 - The Walled
Kitchen Garden has undergone
some major improvements during
the winter months & now has
a 190ft long central path with
Herbaceous borders. Wheelchair
access is possible with assistance,
gravel paths, steps, some slopes
and uneven surfaces. Parking is on
uneven parkland.

52 THE ROOKS
**Old Paper Mill Lane, Claydon,
Ipswich, IP6 0AL. Mrs Marilyn
Gillard.** *Off A14 at J52. From r'about
turn in Claydon & take first available
R, into Old Ipswich Rd where parking
is available. The Rooks is 200m, first
house in Old Paper Mill Lane with
thatched roof.* **Sun 14 June (11-4).
Adm £4, chd free. Home-made
teas. Various home-made cakes.**
The garden surrounds a thatched
cottage built c1600. The garden
has been divided into rooms to give
different feelings of interest, with
seating in most areas. There are
two ponds, mixed borders, trees,
statues and features. Not suitable for
wheelchairs because of slopes and
steps.

53 ROSEDALE
**40 Colchester Road, Bures,
CO8 5AE. Mr & Mrs Colin Lorking.**
*6m SE of Sudbury. From Colchester
take B1508. After 10 metres garden
on L as you enter the village, from
Sudbury B1508 after 5 metres
garden on R.* **Sun 3 May, Sun 2
Aug (12-5). Adm £4, chd free.
Home-made teas.**

Approx one-third of an acre
plantsman's garden developed over
the last 24 years, containing many
unusual plants, herbaceous borders
and pond. For the May opening see
a super collection of peonies and
for the August opening a stunning
collection of approx 60 Agapanthus
in full flower. Pond, Ruin, rare and
unusual plants. Not to mention
homemade cakes & teas.

**54 ♦ SOMERLEYTON HALL
GARDENS**
**Somerleyton, NR32 5QQ. Lord
Somerleyton, 01502 734901,
info@somerleyton.co.uk,
www.somerleyton.co.uk.** *5m
NW of Lowestoft. From Norwich
(30mins) - on the B1074, 7m SE of
Great Yarmouth (A143). Coaches
should follow signs to the rear west
gate entrance.* **For NGS: Sun 7
June (10-5). Adm £6.95, chd
£4.90. Light refreshments in
Cafe. For other opening times and
information, please phone, email or
visit garden website.**
12½ acres of beautiful gardens
contain a wide variety of magnificent
specimen trees, shrubs, borders
and plants providing colour and
interest throughout the yr. Sweeping
lawns and formal gardens combine
with majestic statuary and original
Victorian ornamentation. Highlights
incl the Paxton glasshouses, pergola,

walled garden and famous yew hedge
maze. House and gardens remodelled
in 1840s by Sir Morton Peto. House
created in Anglo-Italian style with
lavish architectural features and fine
state rooms. All areas of the gardens
are accessible, path surfaces are
gravel and can be a little difficult after
heavy rain. Wheelchairs available on
request.

55 NEW SQUIRES BARN
**St. Cross South Elmham,
Harleston, IP20 0PA. Stephen &
Ann Mulligan.** *6m W of Halesworth,
6m E of Harleston & 7m S of Bungay.
On New Road between St Cross &
St James. Parking in field opposite.
Yellow signs from 8m out in all
directions.* **Sun 12 July (10.30-4).
Adm £3.50, chd free. Home-made
teas. Hot/cold drinks, variety of
home-made cakes, some gluten
free.**
A young and evolving garden of 3
acres, including an orchard, cutting
and kitchen garden with greenhouse,
large ornamental pond with water
lilies, fish and waterfall, wildflower
area, island beds of mixed planting
and a growing range of trees .Views
over surrounding countryside. Gravel
drive with pool. Plant stall. The garden
is largely grass with some slight
slopes. Seating is available across the
garden.

Grundisburgh House

56 NEW STONE COTTAGE

34 Main Road, Woolverstone, Ipswich, IP9 1BA. Mrs Jen Young, j_s_young@icloud.com. *Take B1456 towards Shotley. When leaving Woolverstone Village the yellow signs will direct you to Stone Cottage.* **Visits by arrangement Apr to June for groups of 10 to 30. Please email to arrange. Adm £4, chd free. Home-made teas.**

An idyllic Suffolk Country cottage, surrounded by a garden created and maintained by the owner from a derelict space into a beautiful relaxing garden. Over a hundred roses, unusual delphiniums, irises, spring bulbs and many more are planted together in stunning colour combinations that provide year round interest and perfume. A lovely space to sit and enjoy. Areas of gravel paths.

 🐕 ✿ ☕

57 STREET FARM

North Street, Freckenham, IP28 8HY. David & Clodagh Dugdale. *3m W of Mildenhall. Near Chippenham, Fordham & Mildenhall.* **Sun 10 May (11-5). Adm £4, chd free. Light refreshments.**

Approx 1 acre of landscaped garden, with several mature trees. The garden includes a water cascade, pond with island and a number of bridges. Formal rose garden, rose pergola and hornbeam walk. Gravel paths with steps and slopes.

☕

> Your visits help change lives – since 1927, we've donated over £60 million to nursing and caring charities

58 NEW THORNHAM WALLED GARDEN

Thornham Magna, Eye, IP23 8HA. Beyond The Wall, www.beyondthewall.org.uk/our-garden. *3m SW of Eye, off the A140. From the A140 heading N to Norwich, take the L turning at the White Horse pub, Stoke Ash, to Thornham Magna. Take the R turning at the Four Horseshoes pub.* **Sat 4 Apr (11-4). Adm £5, chd free. Home-made teas. Refreshments in aid of Beyond The Wall.**

2-acre Victorian walled garden maintained by adults with disabilities. Layout still based on restoration version designed by Peter Thoday. Boasts an orchard, mirrored rose and double herbaceous border, tropical glasshouse, a vinery with established vines and fruit/vegetable garden. Level site, gravel paths around the garden. Glasshouses are accessible by integrated ramps. Accessible WC facilities. Charity no. 292229.

 🐕 ✿ ☕

Thornham Walled Garden

60 WENHASTON GRANGE

Wenhaston, Halesworth, IP19 9HJ.
Mr & Mrs Bill Barlow. *Turn SW from A144 between Bramfield & Halesworth. Take the single track rd (signed Walpole 2) Wenhaston Grange is approx ½ m, at the bottom of the hill on L.* **Sun 14 June (11-4). Adm £5, chd free. Home-made teas.**
Over 3 acres of varied gardens on a long established site which has been extensively landscaped and enhanced over the last 15 yrs. Long herbaceous borders, old established trees and a series of garden rooms created by beech hedges. Levels and sight lines have been carefully planned. The veg garden is now coming on nicely and there is also a wildflower meadow and woodland garden. The garden is on a number of levels, with steps so wheelchair access would be difficult.

61 41 WESTMORLAND ROAD

Felixstowe, IP11 9TJ.
Mr & Mrs Mick & Diane Elmes, 01394 284647, dianeelmes0@gmail.com. *Enter Felixstowe on A154. At r'about take 1st exit then turn R into Beatrice Avenue. L to High Road East. Proceed to Clifflands Car Park & turn L. Follow signs No. 41 is on the corner of Wrens Park.* **Sun 31 May (11-5). Combined adm with 246 Ferry Road £5, chd free. Light refreshments. Cakes and savouries with a selection of drinks at 41 Westmorland Road. Visits also by arrangement Feb to Oct for groups of up to 20.**
We moved into this house in 2009 since when we have recovered the garden by taking down 21 leylandii trees and various other dead trees.It is now a perennial garden(over 400 different types of perennial plants) with interesting and eclectic features. All main areas wheelchair accessible.

62 WHITE HOUSE FARM

Ringsfield, Beccles, NR34 8JU.
Jan Barlow, Justin 07780 901233, coppertops707@aol.com. *2m SW of Beccles. From Beccles take B1062 to Bungay, after 1¼ turn L signed Ringsfield. Continue for approx 1m. Parking opp church. Garden 300yds on L.* **Sat 4 July (10-4.30); Sun 5 July (2-5.30). Adm £5, chd free. Light refreshments. Cakes and savoury flans. Visits also by arrangement Apr to Sept**

for groups of 10 to 30.
Tranquil park-type garden approx 30 acres, bordered by farmland and with fine views. Comprising formal areas, copses, natural pond, woodland walk, vegetable garden and orchard. Picnickers welcome. NB The pond and beck are unfenced Uneven paving around house. Partial wheelchair access to the areas around the house.

63 NEW THE WILLOWS

Rectory Road, Whepstead, Bury St. Edmunds, IP29 4TE. Ms Vicki Martin, vickimartin52@btinternet.com, , www.vickimartin.co.uk. *5m S of Bury St Edmunds. From the Bury St Edmunds-Glemsford rd (B1066) turn E onto Rectory Road at the top of the hill in Whepstead. The Willows is a yellow-rendered, orange-roofed house visible from the road.* **Visits by arrangement Mar to Oct for groups of up to 30. Individuals and groups welcome, talk or garden tour available. Light refreshments.**
Japanese-inspired garden with multiple areas e.g. tea garden, koi pond, Zen courtyard, dry stream, staggered bridge, stepping stones, rocks/boulders, waterfalls, shade garden, representations of Hokusai's 'Great Wave' and the Tofuku-Ji grid. A personal interpretation, not a cliché! Wide range of often rare/unusual plants including acers, conifers, bamboos and a Mahonia collection. Approx 1 acre. Wheelchair access mostly restricted to lawn and terrace, see plan at vickimartin.co.uk.

64 WOOD FARM, GIPPING

Back Lane, Gipping, Stowmarket, IP14 4RN. Mr & Mrs R Shelley. *From A14 take A1120 to Stowupland, Turn L opp Petrol Station, Turn R at T- junction, follow for approx 1m turn L at Walnut Tree Farm, then imm R & follow for 1m along country lane. Wood Farm is on L.* **Sun 14 June (1-4.30). Adm £5, chd free. Home-made teas. Large Party Barn with Facilities.**
Wood Farm is an old farm with ponds, orchards and a magnificent 8 acre wild flower meadow (with mown paths) bordered with traditional hedging, trees and woodland. The large cottage garden was created in 2011 with a number of beds planted with flowers, vegetables and topiary.

Wildlife is very much encouraged in all parts of the garden (particularly bees and butterflies). In June 2018 used by an International Fashion Brand as their A/W18 Photo Shoot. Partial wheelchair access.

65 WOOD FARM, SIBTON

Halesworth Road, Sibton, Saxmundham, IP17 2JL. Andrew & Amelia Singleton. *4m S of Halesworth. Turn off A12 at Yoxford onto A1120. Turn R after Sibton Nursery towards Halesworth. Take the 2nd drive on R after the White Horse PH.* **Sun 21 June (2-6). Adm £5, chd free. Home-made teas.**
Country garden surrounding old farmhouse, divided into colour themed areas, incl white garden, hot courtyard and blue and yellow border. Large (unfenced) ponds, vegetable garden, wild white flowering shrub area and mown walks. Garden designer owner. Teas in aid of The Friends of St Peter's Church, Sibton. Some gravel paths which are not suitable for wheelchairs.

66 ♦ WYKEN HALL

Stanton, IP31 2DW. Sir Kenneth & Lady Carlisle, 01359 250262, kenneth.carlisle@wykenvineyards. co.uk, www.wykenvineyards.co.uk. *9m NE of Bury St Edmunds. Along A143. Follow signs to Wyken Vineyards on A143 between Ixworth & Stanton.* **For NGS: Sat 30, Sun 31 May (10-6). Adm £5, chd free. For other opening times and information, please phone, email or visit garden website.**
4-acres around the old manor, and an RHS Partner Garden. The gardens include knot and herb gardens, old-fashioned rose garden, kitchen and wild garden, nuttery, pond, gazebo and maze; herbaceous borders and old orchard. Woodland walk and vineyard nearby. Restaurant (booking 01359 250287.) and shop. Vineyard. Farmers' Market Sat 9 - 1.

Your visits help change lives – we've donated over £17 million to Macmillan Cancer Support since 1984

OPENING DATES

All entries subject to change. For latest information check www.ngs.org.uk

Extended openings are shown at the beginning of the month.

Map locator numbers are shown to the right of each garden name.

January

Wednesday 8th
Timber Hill   58

Wednesday 15th
Timber Hill   58

Wednesday 22nd
Timber Hill   58

February

Snowdrop Festival

Sunday 9th
◆ Gatton Park   19

Monday 10th
Timber Hill   58

Tuesday 11th
Timber Hill   58

Wednesday 12th
Timber Hill   58

Thursday 13th
Timber Hill   58

March

Tuesday 10th
◆ The Sculpture Park   47

Sunday 15th
Albury Park   1

Sunday 22nd
Timber Hill   58
◆ Vann   60

Monday 23rd
◆ Vann   60

Tuesday 24th
◆ Vann   60

April

Saturday 4th
11 West Hill   61

Sunday 5th
Caxton House   7
NEW Little Orchards   28
11 West Hill   61

Saturday 11th
The Chalet   8

Sunday 12th
The Chalet   8
Shieling   49

Monday 13th
Coverwood Lakes   14
Timber Hill   58
◆ Vann   60

Tuesday 14th
◆ Vann   60

Wednesday 15th
◆ Vann   60

Sunday 19th
Coverwood Lakes   14
Springwood House   53

Thursday 23rd
◆ Dunsborough Park   15

Sunday 26th
◆ Hatchlands Park   22
Springwood House   53

May

**Daily from
Monday 18th to
Sunday 24th**
Chauffeur's Flat   9

Sunday 3rd
Coverwood Lakes   14
The Garth Pleasure
    Grounds   18

Monday 4th
◆ Vann   60

Tuesday 5th
◆ Vann   60

Wednesday 6th
◆ Vann   60

Sunday 10th
Coverwood Lakes   14
The Garth Pleasure
    Grounds   18
Westways Farm   63

Friday 15th
◆ Ramster   42

Saturday 16th
Hall Grove School   21
NEW Little Orchards   28

Sunday 17th
Chilworth Manor   10
NEW Little Orchards   28
◆ Titsey Place
    Gardens   59

Saturday 23rd
15 The Avenue   4
Shieling   49

Sunday 24th
Lower House   30
The Manor House   31
Shieling   49
57 Westhall Road   62

Monday 25th
15 The Avenue   4
57 Westhall Road   62

Sunday 31st
High Clandon Estate
    Vineyard   25
Monks Lantern   33
The Therapy Garden   57

June

**Daily from
Monday 22nd to
Sunday 28th**
Chauffeur's Flat   9

Wednesday 3rd
NEW Little Orchards   28

Saturday 6th
NEW Orchard House   40

Sunday 7th
Fairmile Lea   17
Moleshill House   32
Norney Wood   34
The Old Rectory   39

Wednesday 10th
Oakleigh   36
Wildwood   64

Saturday 13th
7 Rose Lane   45

Sunday 14th
◆ Loseley Park   29
◆ Titsey Place
    Gardens   59

Tuesday 16th
◆ The Sculpture Park   47

Saturday 20th
The Coach House   12
NEW Little Orchards   28

11 West Hill   61

Sunday 21st
The Coach House   12
NEW Little Orchards   28
Sleepy Hollow   50
◆ Vann   60
11 West Hill   61
NEW Yew Tree Cottage   67

Friday 26th
Ashcombe   2
Ashleigh Grange   3

Sunday 28th
Ashcombe   2
Ashleigh Grange   3

July

Wednesday 1st
Ashleigh Grange   3

Saturday 4th
Woodbury Cottage   65

Sunday 5th
Pratsham Grange   41
Woodbury Cottage   65

Tuesday 7th
Woodland   66

Thursday 9th
Woodland   66

Sunday 12th
NEW Tanhouse Farm   56
Woodland   66

Saturday 18th
Earleywood   16
16 Hurtmore Chase   26
NEW Lambert Road
    Allotments   27

Sunday 19th
Earleywood   16
16 Hurtmore Chase   26
◆ Titsey Place
    Gardens   59

Sunday 26th
The Garth Pleasure
    Grounds   18
NEW Heathlands   23
Heathside   24

August

Sunday 2nd
The Garth Pleasure
    Grounds   18

Sunday 9th
41 Shelvers Way   48

THE GARDENS

1 ALBURY PARK
Albury, GU5 9BH. Trustees of Albury Estate. *5m SE of Guildford. From A25 take A248 towards Albury for ¼m, then up New Rd, entrance to Albury Park immed on L.* Sun 15 Mar, Sun 4 Oct (2-5). Adm £5, chd free. Home-made teas.
14 acre pleasure grounds laid out in 1670s by John Evelyn for Henry Howard, later 6th Duke of Norfolk. ¼m terraces, fine collection of trees, lake and river. Gravel path and slight slope.

2 ASHCOMBE
Chapel Lane, Westhumble, Dorking, RH5 6AY. Vivienne & David Murch. *From A24 at Boxhill/ Burford Bridge follow signs to Westhumble. Through village & L up drive by ruined chapel (1m from A24).* Evening opening Fri 26 June (6-8.30). Combined adm with Ashleigh Grange £8, chd free. Sun 28 June (1-5). Combined adm with Ashleigh Grange £6, chd free. Wine.
Plantaholics 1½ acre wildlife friendly sloping garden on chalk and flint. Enclosed 3rd of acre with large borders of roses, delphiniums & clematis. Amphibian pond. Secluded decking and Patio area with colourful acers and views over garden & Boxhill. Gravel bed of salvia and day lilies. House surrounded by banked flower beds and lawn leading to bee and butterfly garden. Wine and Pimms available. Gravel paths, steps and a sloping site.

3 ASHLEIGH GRANGE
off Chapel Lane, Westhumble, RH5 6AY. Clive & Angela Gilchrist, 01306 884613, ar.gilchrist@btinternet.com. *2m N of Dorking. From A24 at Boxhill/ Burford Bridge follow signs to Westhumble. Through village & L up drive by ruined chapel (1m from A24).* Evening opening Fri 26 June (6-8.30). Combined adm with Ashcombe £8, chd free. Wine. Sun 28 June (1-5). Combined adm with Ashcombe £6, chd free. Home-made teas. Wed 1 July (2-5.30). Adm £3.50, chd free. Home-made teas. Visits also by arrangement May to July for groups of 5+. Sorry no access for coaches. Donation to Barnardo's.
Plant lover's chalk garden on 3½ acre sloping site in charming rural setting with delightful views. Many areas of interest incl rockery and water feature, raised ericaceous bed, prairie style bank, foliage plants, woodland walk, fernery and folly. Large mixed herbaceous and shrub borders planted for dry alkaline soil and widespread interest.

4 15 THE AVENUE
Cheam, Sutton, SM2 7QA. Jan & Nigel Brandon, 020 8643 8686, janmbrandon@outlook.com. *1m SW of Sutton. By car; exit A217 onto Northey Av, 2nd R into The Avenue. By train; 10 mins walk from Cheam station. By bus; use 470.* Evening opening Sat 23 May (6-9). Adm £8, chd £3. Wine. Mon 25 May (1-5). Adm £5, chd free. Home-made teas. Visits also by arrangement May to July for groups of 10 to 30.
A contemporary garden designed by RHS Chelsea Gold Medal Winner, Marcus Barnett. Four levels divided into rooms by beech hedging and columns; formal entertaining area, contemporary outdoor room, lawn and wildflower meadow. Over 100 hostas hug the house. Silver birch, cloud pruned box, ferns, grasses, tall bearded irises, contemporary sculptures. Partial wheelchair access, terraced with steps; sloping path provides view of whole garden but not all accessible.

⑤ BARDSEY
11 Derby Road, Haslemere, GU27 1BS. Maggie & David Boyd, 01428 652283, maggie.boyd@live.co.uk, www.bardseygarden.co.uk. *¼ m N of Haslemere station. Turn off B2131 (which links A287 to A286 through town) 400yds W of station into Weydown Rd, 3rd R into Derby Rd, garden 400yds on R.* **Visits by arrangement June & July for groups of 10+. Home-made teas.** Unexpected 2 acre garden in the heart of Haslemere. Several distinct areas containing scent, colour, texture and movement. Stunning pictorial meadow within an ilex crenata parterre. Prairie planted border provides a modern twist. Large productive fruit and vegetable garden. Natural ponds and bog gardens. Several unusual sculptures. Bee hives and bug hotel. Ducks and chickens supply the eggs for cakes. Classic MGs. First third of garden level, other two thirds sloping.

⑥ THE BOTHY
Tandridge Court, Tandridge Lane, Oxted, RH8 9NJ. Diane & John Hammond, 07785612478, dhammo@hotmail.co.uk. *5 mins from J6 of M25, towards Oxted.*

From N, at r'about on A25 between A22 & Oxted go S to Tandridge after ¼ m follow signs. From S, N up Tandridge Ln from Ray Ln, on exiting Tandridge village follow signs. Do not use Jackass Ln from A25. **Visits by arrangement June & July. Adm £5, chd free.**
A 1½ acre hillside garden on 5 levels. Accessed by steps and slopes, creating varying views, with specimen trees, incl a Sequoia, Acers and Banana. Explore wild banks, perennial beds, woodland and relaxing areas along with a productive kitchen garden with raised beds, fruit trees, fruit cage and large greenhouse. Each level contains either water features, garden artwork, chickens and more. Check NGS website for pop-up openings. The garden entrance is down a number of steps and on different levels and therefore it is unsuitable for people with mobility issues.

⑦ CAXTON HOUSE
67 West Street, Reigate, RH2 9DA. Bob Bushby, 01737 243158 / 07836201740, Bob.bushby@sky.com. *On A25 towards Dorking, approx ¼ m W of Reigate. Parking on Rd or past Black Horse PH on Flanchford Rd.*

Sun 5 Apr (2-5). Adm £5, chd free. **Cream teas. Visits also by arrangement Apr to Sept for groups of 10+.**
Lovely large spring garden with Arboretum, 2 well stocked ponds, large collection of hellebores and spring flowers. Pots planted with colourful displays. Interesting plants. Small Gothic folly built by owner. Herbaceous borders with grasses, perennials, spring bulbs, and parterre. New bed with wild daffodils and prairie style planting in summer. new wild flower garden in arboretum. Wheelchair access to most parts of the garden.

⑧ THE CHALET
Tupwood Lane, Caterham, CR3 6ET. Miss Lesley Manning & Mr David Gold, www.davidgold.co.uk. *½ m N of M25 J6. Exit J6 off M25 onto A22 to N. After ½ m take sharp 1st L, or follow signs from Caterham. Ample free parking. Disabled access via top gate in Tupwood Lane.* **Sat 11, Sun 12 Apr (11-4.30). Adm £6, chd free. Home-made teas.** Donation to St Catherine's Hospice.
A true festival of Spring at The Chalet. 55 acres of stunning grounds incorporating a 19 hole golf course. Spectacular carpets of daffodils, ornamental ponds with magnificent koi fish, ancient woodlands and planted terraces. See Classic cars, Owls Out and About, take the woodland trail and enjoy all-day entertainment. Lots of fun for the children. David and Lesley are there on both days. On view, a limited edition Blue Train Bentley, a Phantom Rolls Royce and a helicopter plus the oldest FA Cup and other trophies. Toilet facilities available. Entrance fee incl parking, list of events and map. Fresh homemade cakes, hot snacks and drinks, ice creams plus a Wine and Beer bar. Partial wheelchair access, some steep slopes. 3 large unfenced ponds.

⑨ CHAUFFEUR'S FLAT
Tandridge Lane, Tandridge, RH8 9NJ. Mr & Mrs Richins, 01883 742983. *2m E of Godstone. 2m W of Oxted. Turn off A25 at r'about for Tandridge. Take 2nd drive on L past church. Follow arrows to circular courtyard. Do not use Jackass Ln even if your SatNav tells you to do so.* **Daily Mon 18 May to**

Titsey Place Gardens

Sun 24 May (10-5). Home-made teas. Daily Mon 22 June to Sun 28 June (10-5). Adm £5, chd free. Home-made teas (Sats & Suns only). **Visits also by arrangement May to Sept.**

Enter a $1\frac{1}{2}$ acre tapestry of magical secret gardens with magnificent views. Touching the senses, all sure footed visitors may explore the many surprises on this constantly evolving exuberant escape from reality. Imaginative use of recycled materials creates an inspired variety of ideas, while wild and specimen plants reveal an ecological haven.

10 CHILWORTH MANOR
Halfpenny Lane, Chilworth, Guildford, GU4 8NN. Mia & Graham Wrigley, www.chilworthmanorsurrey.com. $3\frac{1}{2}$ m SE of Guildford. From centre of Chilworth village turn into Blacksmith Lane. 1st drive on R on Halfpenny Lane. **Sun 17 May (11-5). Adm £6, chd free. Home-made teas.**

The grounds of the C17 Chilworth Manor, create a wonderful tapestry: a jewel of an C18 terraced walled garden, topiary, herbaceous borders, sculptures, mature trees and stew ponds that date back a 1000 years. A fabulous, peaceful garden for all the family to wander and explore or just to relax and enjoy! Perhaps our many visitors describe it best: "Magical", "a sheer delight", 'elegant and tranquil", "a little piece of heaven", "spiffing!". Garden and Tree Walks at 12 noon, 1.30pm, 2.30pm and 4pm. Tasting of Chilworth Manor Rose Wine throughout the day.

11 2 CHINTHURST LODGE
Wonersh Common, Wonersh, Guildford, GU5 0PR. Mr & Mrs M R Goodridge, 01483 535108, michaelgoodridge@ymail.com. 4m S of Guildford. From A281 at Shalford turn E onto B2128 towards Wonersh. Just after Waverley sign, before village, garden on R, via stable entrance opposite Little Tangley. **Visits by arrangement May to July for groups of 10+. Adm £6, chd free. Home-made teas.**

One acre yr-round enthusiast's atmospheric garden, divided into rooms. Herbaceous borders, dramatic white garden, specimen trees and shrubs, gravel garden with water

feature, small kitchen garden, fruit cage, two wells, ornamental ponds, herb parterre and millennium parterre garden. Some gravel paths, which can be avoided.

12 THE COACH HOUSE
The Green, Chiddingfold, Godalming, GU8 4TU. Mr & Mrs S Brooks, bbgardendesign.co.uk. 7M S of Godalming. Eastern corner of village green. Parking around village green or along Pickhurst Rd. **Sat 20 June (11-5). Sun 21 June (11-5), also open Sleepy Hollow. Adm £5, chd free. Home-made teas.**

Garden designer's garden comprising one acre walled garden and additional courtyards, designed by the owners and created since 2013. Lawns divided into areas by trees and borders filled with perennials, shrubs and roses. A courtyard white garden, wildflower meadow, stumpery, serenity pond and kitchen garden provide varied interest. New in 2020 a small courtyard filled with crops in pots!

13 COLDHARBOUR HOUSE
Coldharbour Lane, Bletchingley, Redhill, RH1 4NA. Mr Tony Elias, 01883 742685, eliastony@hotmail.com. Coldharbour Lane off Rabies Heath Rd $\frac{1}{2}$ m from A25 at Bletchingley & 0.9m from Tilburstow Hill Rd. Park in field & walk down to house. **Sat 5, Sun 6 Sept (1-5). Adm £5, chd free. Home-made teas. Visits also by arrangement Apr to Oct for groups of 10+.**

This $1\frac{1}{2}$ acre garden offers breathtaking views to the South Downs. Originally planted in the 1920's, it has since been adapted and enhanced. Several mature trees and shrubs incl a copper beech, a Canadian maple, magnolias, azaleas, rhododendrons, camellias, wisterias, berberis georgeii, vitex agnus-castus, fuschias, hibiscus, potentillas, mahonias, a fig tree and a walnut tree.

14 COVERWOOD LAKES
Peaslake Road, Ewhurst, GU6 7NT. The Metson Family, 01306 731101, farm@coverwoodlakes.co.uk, www.coverwoodlakes.co.uk. 7m SW of Dorking. From A25 follow signs for Peaslake; garden $\frac{1}{2}$ m beyond Peaslake on Ewhurst rd. **Mon 13, Sun 19 Apr, Sun 3, Sun 10 May, Sun 11 Oct (11-5). Adm £6, chd free. Light refreshments. Visits also by arrangement for groups of 20+.**

14 acre landscaped garden in stunning position high in the Surrey Hills with 4 lakes and bog garden. Extensive rhododendrons, azaleas and fine trees. $3\frac{1}{2}$ acre lakeside arboretum. Marked trail through the 180 acre working farm with Hereford cows and calves, sheep and horses, extensive views of the surrounding hills. Light refreshments, incl home produced beef burgers, gourmet coffee and home-made cakes.

15 ♦ DUNSBOROUGH PARK
Ripley, GU23 6AL. Baron & Baroness Sweerts de Landas Wyborgh, 01483 225366, office@sweerts.com, www.dunsboroughpark.com. 6m NE of Guildford. Entrance across Ripley Green via The Milkway past cricket green on R & playground on L, round corner to double brown wooden gates. **For NGS: Thur 23 Apr (1-5). Adm £7, chd free. Home-made teas. For other opening times and information, please phone, email or visit garden website.**

6 acres of garden redesigned by Penelope Hobhouse and Rupert Golby – a box parterre showcase for Tulips and Dahlias. Series of garden rooms; lush herbaceous borders/ standard wisteria; 70ft Gingko hedge; Rose Walk; Secret Garden & ancient Mulberry tree; Italian Garden & stone pine; potager; Water Garden with folly bridge. April: Spectacular tulip displays in meadow/Penelope Hobhouse borders/'hot' border/ Peacock Gate. May: Wisteria. June: Peonies and Roses. 40+ Dahlia varieties in Sept. Produce for sale if available. Teas by invited charities. Cobbled courtyard on entrance. Afterwards gravel paths and grass.

16 EARLEYWOOD

Hamlash Lane, Frensham, Farnham, GU10 3AT. Mrs Penny Drew. *3m S of Farnham just off A287. From A31 Farnham take A287 to Frensham. R lst turn passed Edgeborough School. From A3, N on A287 to Frensham. Parking available, More House School Lower Car Park top of Hamlash Lane.* **Sat 18, Sun 19 July (11-5). Adm £5, chd free. Home-made teas.**

Award winning (2019), ½ acre garden with colourful shrubberies, unusual trees and mixed borders throughout. Summer flowering shrubs, particularly hydrangeas and hardy hibiscus, together with herbaceous perennials in colour themed borders and shade loving plants under the trees. Unusual tender perennials in containers. Productive greenhouse and small pond. New features to be enjoyed in 2020. John Negus, well known horticulturalist, gardening writer and broadcaster will be in the garden to answer gardening questions during the weekend. Also demonstration of lavender weaving and craft items for sale. Disabled drop off at front gate, short gravel drive then level lawns throughout.

& ✿ ☕

17 FAIRMILE LEA

Portsmouth Road, Cobham, KT11 1BG. Steven Kay. *2m NE of Cobham. On Cobham to Esher rd. Access by lane adjacent to Moleshill House & car park for Fairmile Common woods.* **Sun 7 June (2-5). Combined adm with Moleshill House £6.50, chd free. Home-made teas.**

Victorian sunken garden fringed by rose beds and lavender with a pond in the centre. An old acacia tree stands in the midst of the lawn. Interesting planting on a large mound camouflages an old underground air raid shelter. Caged vegetable garden. Formality adjacent to wilderness.

& 🐄 ☕

18 THE GARTH PLEASURE GROUNDS

Newchapel Road, Lingfield, RH7 6BJ. Mr Sherlock & Mrs Stanley, ab_post@yahoo.com, , www.oldworkhouse.webs.com. *From A22 take B2028 by the Mormon Temple to Lingfield. The Garth is on the L after 1½ m, opp Barge Tiles. Parking: Gun Pit Rd in Lingfield & limited space for disabled at Barge Tiles.* **Sun 3, Sun 10 May,**

Sun 26 July, Sun 2 Aug (2-6). Adm £5, chd free. Home-made teas. Visits also by arrangement May & June for groups of 10 to 30.

Mature 9 acre Pleasure Grounds created by Walter Godfrey in 1919 present an idyllic setting surrounding the former parish workhouse refurbished in Edwardian style. The formal gardens, enchanting nuttery, a spinney with many mature trees and a pond attract wildlife. Wonderful bluebells in spring. The woodland gardens and beautiful borders full of colour and fragrance for year round pleasure. Many areas of interest incl pond, woodland garden, formal gardens, spinney w/ large specimen plants incl 500yr old oak, many architectural features designed by Walter H Godfrey. Open 4-9 May and 27 July-1August for Historic Houses Association (2-6 pm). We need clarification when booking - HHA or NGS. Partial wheelchair access in woodland, iris and secret gardens.

& 🐄 ✿ ♿ 🚌 ☕

19 ◆ GATTON PARK

Reigate, RH2 0TW. Royal Alexandra & Albert School, 01737 649068,

events@gatton-park.org.uk,
www.gattonpark.co.uk. *3m NE of
Reigate. 5 mins from M25 J8 (A217)
or from top of Reigate Hill, over
M25 then follow sign to Merstham.
Entrance off Rocky Lane accessible
from Gatton Bottom or A23
Merstham.* **For NGS: Sun 9 Feb
(12-5). Adm £5, chd free. Light
refreshments in Gatton Hall. Soup
and roll lunch and locally baked
cake. For other opening times and
information, please phone, email
or visit garden website.** Donation to
another charity.
Historic 260-acre estate in the Surrey
Hills AONB. 'Capability' Brown
parkland with ancient oaks. Discover
the Japanese garden, Victorian
parterre and breathtaking views over
the lake. Seasonal highlights include
displays of snowdrops and aconites
in February. Ongoing restoration
projects by the Gatton Trust. Bird
hide open to see herons nesting.
Free guided tours and activities for
children.

20 21 GLENAVON CLOSE
Claygate, Esher, KT10 0HP.
Selina & Simon Botham,
www.designsforallseasons.co.uk.
*2m SE of Esher. From A3 S exit
Esher, R at T-lights. Cont straight
through Claygate village bear R at
two mini r'bouts. Past church & rec.
Turn L at bollards into Causeway.
At end straight over to Glenavon Cl.*
**Sun 13 Sept (2-5). Adm £4, chd
free. Home-made teas.**
A relaxing 66ft x 92ft secluded garden
created by garden designer Selina
Botham and her husband Simon.
An awkward shaped suburban
plot with swathes of grasses and
perennials around a spacious lawn
and curving paths invite exploration.
River inspired barefoot walk through
soft blue planting leads to the garden
studio and pond. Sculpted bug hotels
and birdhouses and wildlife-friendly
planting. Guided tours by RHS Gold
medal winning designer, exhibit of
private garden design work and RHS
show garden concepts.

21 HALL GROVE SCHOOL
London Road (A30), Bagshot,
GU19 5HZ. Mr & Mrs A R Graham,
www.hallgrove.co.uk. *6m SW of
Egham. M3 J3, follow A322 1m until
sign for Sunningdale A30, 1m E of
Bagshot, opp Longacres garden
centre, entrance at footbridge.*

Ample car parking. **Sat 16 May
(2-4.30). Adm by donation. Home-
made teas.**
Formerly a small Georgian country
estate, now a co-educational
preparatory school. Grade II listed
house (not open). Mature parkland
with specimen trees. Historical
features incl ice house, old walled
garden under restoration, lake,
woodland walks, rhododendrons and
azaleas. Live music at 3pm.

22 ◆ HATCHLANDS PARK
East Clandon, Guildford, GU4 7RT.
National Trust, 01483 222482,
hatchlands@nationaltrust.org.uk,
www.nationaltrust.org.uk/
hatchlands-park. *4m E of Guildford.
Follow brown signs to Hatchlands
Park (NT).* **For NGS: Sun 26 Apr
(10-5). Adm £8.40, chd £4.20.
Light refreshments. For other
opening times and information,
please phone, email or visit garden
website.**
Garden and park designed by
Repton in 1800. Follow one of the
park walks to the stunning bluebell
wood in spring (2.5km/1.7m round
walk over rough and sometimes
muddy ground). In autumn enjoy the
changing colours on the long walk.
Partial wheelchair access to parkland,
rough, undulating terrain, grass and
gravel paths, dirt tracks, cobbled
courtyard. Tramper booking essential.

23 NEW HEATHLANDS
Oakshade Road, Oxshott,
Leatherhead, KT22 0LE. Mr Glenn
Burnell. *Heathlands is located
directly opp St Andrew's church &
next door to Oxshott Club.* **Sun 26
July (11-5). Adm £3, chd free.
Home-made teas. Also open
Heathside.**
Small, very modern contemporary
courtyard style garden with water
taking centre stage within the design
scheme, whilst achieving a relaxed
mediterranean feel, with planting to
compliment. Immediately backs on
to the Oxshott Bowling Club. fully
accessible all hard surface areas.

24 HEATHSIDE
10 Links Green Way, Cobham,
KT11 2QH. Miss Margaret Arnott
& Mr Terry Bartholomew. *1½m E
of Cobham. Through Cobham A245,
4th L after Esso garage into Fairmile*

*Lane. Straight on into Water Lane.
Links Green Way 3rd turning on L.*
**Sun 26 July (11-5). Adm £4.50,
chd free. Home-made teas. Also
open Heathlands.**
⅓ acre terraced, plants persons
garden, designed for yr-round
interest. Gorgeous plants all set off
by harmonious landscaping. Urns
and obelisks aid the display. Two
ponds and six water features add
tranquil sound. Many topiary shapes
add formality. Stunning colour
combinations excite. Beautiful Griffin
Glasshouse housing the exotic. Many
inspirational ideas. Situated 5m from
RHS Wisley.

**25 HIGH CLANDON ESTATE
VINEYARD**
High Clandon, Off Blakes Lane,
East Clandon, GU4 7RP. Mrs
Sibylla Tindale, 01483 225660,
finewine@highclandon.co.uk,
www.highclandon.co.uk. *A3 Wisley
junction, L for Ockham/Horsley for
2m to A246. R for Guildford for
2m, then 100yds past landmark
Hatchlands NT, turn L into Blakes
Lane straight up hill through gates
High Clandon to vineyard entrance.
Extensive parking in our woodland
area.* **Sun 31 May (11-4). Adm
£6, chd free. Home-made teas
on lawns of High Clandon
Estate Vineyard. Visits also by
arrangement May to Sept for
groups of 5 to 20.**
Vistas, gardens, sculptures, multi-
Gold vineyard in beautiful Surrey
Hills AONB. On 12 acres. Panoramic
views to London, water features,
Japanese garden, wildflower meadow,
truffière, apiary, vineyard, English
sparkling wine High Clandon Cuvée
sold from atmospheric Glass Barn.
Twice winner Cellar Door of Year.
Sculptures in Vineyard exhibition.
Percentage of sales to Cherry Trees
charity. Atmospheric Glass Barn used
for wine tastings and art exhibitions.
Over 150 works of art on show in
gardens and Vineyard. High Clandon
Cuvée multi-gold awarded Sparkling
wine available at £6 per glass.
Available by the bottle. Homemade
teas & cakes. Huge Wildflower
Meadow with rare butterflies. There
is a short stretch of 4 metres of gravel
to cover in one direction. Otherwise
access is on lawned paths all on firm
ground.

Chilworth Manor

26 16 HURTMORE CHASE
Hurtmore, Godalming, GU7 2RT.
Mrs Ann Bellamy. *4m SW of
Guildford. From Godalming follow
signs to Charterhouse & cont about
¼m beyond Charterhouse School.
From A3 take Norney, Shackleford
& Hurtmore turn off & proceed E for
½m.* **Sat 18 July (11-5); Sun 19
July (1-5). Adm £4, chd free. Light
refreshments.**
A secluded medium sized (approx
¼ acre) garden comprised mainly
of a large lawn divided into discrete
areas by shrubs, trees and colourful
flowerbeds. On the bungalow side
of the lawn there is a patio area with
hanging baskets, troughs and planted
pots with fuchsias being a speciality.
In the opposite corner there is a
shaded arbour bordered by hostas.
Award winner - Godalming in Bloom
2019. Kerb height step up from patio
to lawn so minor assistance may be
required for wheelchairs.
ॐ ✿ ☕

**27 NEW LAMBERT ROAD
ALLOTMENTS**
Lambert Road, Banstead,
SM7 2QX. Reigate and Banstead
borough council. *Entrance between
50 & 52. A217. A2022 E bound. R
at 2nd r'about onto B2217. Next
r'about onto Park Rd. Turn R into
Banstead Community Hall. Blue
badge holders may park at allotment
entrance on Lambert Rd.* **Sat 18
July (2-5). Adm £4, chd free.**

Lambert Road Allotments are coming
up to their centenary. The site is not
in clear view to the general public so
this is a perfect opportunity to find
and see local growers. The 31 plots
are tended by a diverse cross section
of the local community. They display
a wide variety of fruit, vegetables
and flowers as well as a range of
approaches to cultivation. Partial
wheelchair access. Some areas are
uneven and will need careful attention.
ॐ

28 NEW LITTLE ORCHARDS
Prince Of Wales Road,
Outwood, Redhill, RH1 5QU.
Nic Howard, 01883744020,
info@we-love-plants.co.uk. *A few
hundred metres N of the Dog and
Duck Pub.* **Sun 5 Apr, Sat 16, Sun
17 May, Wed 3, Sat 20, Sun 21
June, Sat 5, Sun 6 Sept (11-5).
Adm £5, chd free. Home-made
teas. Visits also by arrangement
Apr to Oct for groups of 10 to 30.**
Garden Designer's contemporary
cottage garden that has been planted
for all year round interest using a
tapestry of foliage textures as well
as flower interest. The garden is
arranged as a series of connected
garden areas that flow between
the old gardeners' cottage and the
old stables. The small spaces are
full of character, with paved areas,
brick walls and vintage garden
paraphernalia.
✿ 🚗 🅳 ☕

29 ◆ LOSELEY PARK
Guildford, GU3 1HS. Mr &
Mrs A G More-Molyneux,
01483 304440/405112,
pa@loseleypark.co.uk,
www.loseleypark.co.uk. *4m SW
of Guildford. For SatNav please use
GU3 1HS, Stakescorner Lane Please
note: opens May- end of July -
please check our website for details.*
**For NGS: Sun 14 June (11-5).
Adm by donation. Tea. For other
opening times and information,
please phone, email or visit garden
website.**
Delightful 2½ acre walled garden.
Award winning rose garden (over
1,000 bushes, mainly old fashioned
varieties), extensive herb garden,
fruit/flower garden, white garden with
fountain, and spectacular organic
vegetable garden. Magnificent vine
walk, herbaceous borders, moat
walk, ancient wisteria and mulberry
trees. Refreshments available.
ॐ ✿ 🚗 ☕

30 LOWER HOUSE
Bowlhead Green, Godalming,
GU8 6NW. Georgina Harvey.
*1m from A3 leaving at Thursley/
Bowlhead Green junction. Follow
Bowlhead Green signs. Using A286
leave us at Brook (6m from Haslemere &
3m from Milford). Follow NGS signs
for approx 2m. Field Parking.* **Sun
24 May (11-5). Adm £6, chd free.
Home-made teas.**
The garden has been planted over
the last 30 years with several unusual

trees. Shrubs, ground cover and low hedges add interest and depth of views. Mixed evergreens and deciduous plants give year round interest. Roses add colour and a parterre with only white roses create structure leading to the Standard Ballerina and Lavender walk. Lively kitchen garden with greenhouses and plants for sale. Alternative routes avoiding steps for wheelchairs users, although some paths could be narrow.

31 THE MANOR HOUSE
Three Gates Lane, Haslemere, GU27 2ES. Mr & Mrs Gerard Ralfe.
NE of Haslemere. From Haslemere centre take A286 towards Milford. Turn R after Museum into Three Gates Lane. At T-Junction turn R into Holdfast Lane. Car park on R. **Sun 24 May (12-5). Adm £5, chd free. Home-made teas.**
Described by Country Life as 'The hanging gardens of Haslemere', The Manor House gardens are in a valley of the Surrey Hills. One of Surrey's inaugural NGS gardens, fine views, 6 acres, water gardens.

32 MOLESHILL HOUSE
The Fairmile, Cobham, KT11 1BG. Penny Snell, pennysnellflowers@ btinternet.com, , www.pennysnellflowers.co.uk. *2m NE of Cobham. On A307 Esher to Cobham Rd next to free car park by A3 bridge, at entrance to Waterford Close.* **Sun 7 June (2-5). Combined adm with Fairmile Lea £6.50, chd free. Sun 23 Aug (2-5). Adm £5, chd free. Also open Randalls Allotments (23 Aug only).** Home-made teas at Fairmile Lea (June) and Moleshill House (Aug). **Visits also by arrangement May to Sept for groups of 10+.**
Romantic garden. Short woodland path leads from dovecote to beehives. Informal planting contrasts with formal topiary box and garlanded cisterns. Colourful courtyard and pots, conservatory, pond with fountain, bog garden. Pleached avenue, circular gravel garden replacing most of the lawn. Gipsy caravan garden, green wall and stumpery. Espaliered crab apples. Chickens and Bees. Music at Moleshill House, teas at Fairmile Lea. Garden 5 mins from Claremont Landscape Garden, Painshill Park and Wisley, also adjacent to excellent dog walking woods.

33 MONKS LANTERN
Ruxbury Road, Chertsey, KT16 9NH. Mr & Mrs J Granell, 01932 569578, janicegranell@hotmail.com. *1m NW from Chertsey. M25 J11, signed A320/Woking. R'about 2nd exit A320/Staines, straight over next r'about. L onto Holloway Hill, R Hardwick Lane. ½m, R over motorway bridge, on Almners then Ruxbury Rd.* **Sun 31 May (1-5). Adm £5, chd free. Light refreshments. Visits also by arrangement May to July for groups of up to 20. Entrance price incl a piece of cake and a tea or coffee.**
A delightful garden with borders arranged with colour in mind: silvers and white, olive trees, nicotiana and senecio blend together. Large rockery and an informal pond. A weeping silver birch leads to the oranges and yellows of a tropical bed, with large bottle brush, hardy palms and fatsia japonica. There is a display of hostas, cytisus battandieri and a selection of grasses in an island bed. Aviary with small finches. Workshop with handmade guitars,and paintings. Pond with ornamental ducks and fish. Music and wine. Wheelchairs are welcome and we reserve a couple of parking spaces at the entrance to the garden, as the gravel drive is not easy for wheelchairs.

34 NORNEY WOOD
Elstead Road, Shackleford, Godalming, GU8 6AY. Mr & Mrs R Thompson, www.norneywood.co.uk. *5m SW of Guildford. At Xrds of Elstead rd & Shackleford rd, ½m towards Elstead from A3 Hurtmore/Shackleford junction. Follow signs for parking.* **Sun 7 June (10.30-5). Adm £8, chd free. Home-made teas.**
In the style of Gertrude Jekyll, created over a period of 10 years, the garden is set against a backdrop of mature trees and rhododendrons. The formal lawn terrace garden is surrounded by rose and herbaceous borders. Gertrude Jekyll's love of structures has been recreated with a Thunder house and paths linking the upper lawn terrace with the Tranquility water garden and pleached Lime tree walk. Mixed herbaceous and rose borders; Water features in the form of structured ponds and natural ponds; Woodland backdrop with mature trees and open grassland area; flower

cutting garden. Garden pavilions and structured landscapes. Local arts and crafts being exhibited for the first time and for sale. Wheelchair access possible on upper level only.

35 [NEW] OAKLANDS
Eastbourne Road, Blindley Heath, Lingfield, RH7 6LG. Joy & Justin Greasley, 01342 837369, joy@allaero.com. *S of Blindley Heath Village. From M25 take A22 to East Grinstead. At Blindley Heath T-lights carry straight on, after 800yds take sign on L to Nestledown Boarding Kennels. Oaklands is down the lane on the L.* **Visits by arrangement June to Aug for groups of 5 to 30. Limited parking available, please check with owners. Adm £5, chd free. Home-made teas.**
A contemporary garden of approximately half an acre designed and developed by the owners from new 23 years ago and surrounded by SSSI. Starting from scratch, and with very little gardening experience the garden, like the owners it is maturing nicely. Vibrant colour, large pots, lawn, herbaceous planting with plenty of seating areas complimented by some unusual features. Level access on paths to main features.

36 OAKLEIGH
22 The Hatches, Frimley Green, GU16 6HE. Angela O'Connell, 01252 668645, angela.oconnell@icloud.com. *Frimley Green. 100 metres from village green. On street parking.* **Wed 10 June (2-5). Combined adm with Wildwood £4.50, chd free. Home-made teas at Wildwood. Visits also by arrangement in June for groups of 10 to 20. Opening with Wildwood.**
A magical long garden with a few surprises. There are plenty of colours and textures with a great variety of different plants. Wander past the long borders and under a rose arch and you will find the garden opens up to two large colour themed mixed beds. The style is naturalistic with just a hint of elegance. Fruit and vegetables grow by the summerhouse and pots adorn the top patio. The garden is mostly level but the side alley is narrow and there are two steps up onto the lawn. There are no paths only an uneven lawn.

37 OCKHAM MILL

Mill Lane, Ripley, GU23 6QT. Tina, tffou0@gmail.com. *Off Ockham roundabout on A3 (nr RHS Wisley), down a single-track rd. Parking limited to 5 cars; no coach access. Detailed directions provided at booking.* **Visits by arrangement in June for groups of 5 to 20. Appointments available from 1-21 June. Adm £4, chd free. Home-made teas.**

Working water mill on stream- 2 acre water garden, lake, 5 islands, bridges & gazebo. Herbaceous & shrub borders (gunnera, persicaria) follow natural contours. Summerhouse by perennial bed with roses, grasses, salvia. Mature trees on C13 dam, underplanted with hydrangeas, rhodos & shade-loving plants (hosta, heuchera, ferns). Garden designed by owners and I. Neville. Partial wheelchair access.

&. 🐾 ☕

38 ODSTOCK

Castle Square, Bletchingley, RH1 4LB. Averil & John Trott, 01883 743100. *3m W of Godstone. Just S of A25 in Bletchingley. At top of village nr Red Lion PH. For ramblers we are on the Greensand Way footpath.* **Visits by arrangement May to Sept for groups of 10 to 30. Adm £5. Light refreshments. Refreshments available by prior arrangement.**

²/₃ acre plantsman's garden maintained by owners and developed for yr-round interest. Special interest in grasses, climbers and dahlias. A no dig, low maintenance vegetable garden. Short gravel drive. Main lawn suitable for wheelchairs but some paths may be too narrow.

&. �car ☕

39 THE OLD RECTORY

Sandy Lane, Brewer Street, Bletchingley, RH1 4QW. Mr & Mrs A Procter, 01883 743388 or 07515 394506, trudie.y.procter@googlemail.com. *Top of village nr Red Lion PH, turn R into Little Common Lane then R Cross Rd into Sandy Lane. Parking nr house, disabled parking in courtyard.* **Sun 7 June (11-4). Adm £5, chd free. Home-made teas. Visits also by arrangement Apr to Aug for groups of 10 to 30.**

Georgian Manor House (not open). Quintessential Italianate topiary garden, statuary, box parterres, courtyard with columns, water features, antique terracotta pots. Much of the 4 acre garden is the subject of ongoing reclamation. This incl the ancient moat, woodland with fine specimen trees, one of the largest Tulip trees in the country, a rill, sunken and exotic garden. New water garden. Gravel paths.

&. 🐾 ❁ ☕

40 NEW ORCHARD HOUSE

5 The Mount, Esher, KT10 8LQ. Kathy & Richard Goode. *Outskirts of Esher, off the A307. From the A307 Portsmouth Rd turn into Hawkshill Way, opp the entrance to Claremont School. Take 2nd turning R into The Mount. Orchard House is on L near the top of the rd.* **Sat 6 June (2-6). Adm £5, chd free. Home-made teas.**

Set on a steep hill with a surprising 30 mile view towards Windsor. Almost an acre of terraced cottage garden style planting with banks of roses and paeonies, grasses, clematis and foxgloves and year round interest. Also a small woodland garden and exotic border. Steep paths and lots of steps.

❁ ☕

41 PRATSHAM GRANGE

Tanhurst Lane, Holmbury St Mary, RH5 6LZ. Alan & Felicity Comber, 01306 621116, alancomber@aol.com. *12m SE of Guildford, 8m SW of Dorking. From A25 take B2126, after 4m turn L into Tanhurst Lane. From A29 take B2126, before Forest Green turn R on B2126 then 1st R to Tanhurst Lane.* **Sun 5 July, Sun 23 Aug (1-5). Adm £5, chd free. Home-made teas. Visits also by arrangement July & Aug for groups of 10+.**

5 acre garden overlooked by Holmbury Hill and Leith Hill. Features incl 2 ponds joined by cascading stream, extensive scented rose and blue hydrangea beds. Also herbaceous borders, cutting flower garden, 2 white beds. South garden replanted over last 4 years. Some steps, steep slopes, slippery when wet, gravel paths. Deep ponds and a drop from terrace.

&. ❁ ☕

42 ◆ RAMSTER

Chiddingfold, Surrey, GU8 4SN. Mr & Mrs Paul Gunn, 01428 654167, office@ramsterhall.com, www.ramsterevents.com. *Ramster is on A283 1½m S of Chiddingfold,*
large iron gates on R, the entrance is signed from the road. **For NGS: Fri 15 May (10-5). Adm £7.50, chd free. Light refreshments in the teahouse in the main car park by the garden entrance. For other opening times and information, please phone, email or visit garden website.**

A stunning, mature woodland garden set in over 20 acres, famous for its rhododendron and azalea collection and its carpets of bluebells in Spring. Enjoy a peaceful wander down the grass paths and woodland walk, explore the bog garden with its stepping stones, or relax in the tranquil enclosed tennis court garden. The tea house, found by the entrance to the garden, serves sandwiches, cakes and drinks, and is open every day while the garden is open. The teahouse is wheelchair accessible, some paths in the garden are suitable for wheelchairs.

&. 🐾 ❁ �car ☕

43 RANDALLS ALLOTMENTS

Old Nursery Lane, Cobham, KT11 1JN. Elmbridge Borough Council, www.cobhamgardenclub.com. *1.2m from Moleshill House going towards Cobham, off the A307 Esher to Cobham Rd, on the RHS opp Sheargold Pianos & behind Premier Service Station. Entrance is ½ way down Old Nurseries Lane.* **Sun 23 Aug (2-5). Adm £3.50, chd free. Also open Moleshill House. Home-made teas.**

Well presented allotments in Cobham, growing unusual vegetables, fruit & salad items from different countries. Guided tours are available by the knowledgeable owners of the plots. Green Fingers Garden Shop on site. If you have ever thought about 'Growing Your Own' this will inspire you. The Greenfingers Shop will be open for visitors as a special opportunity, offering plants, garden sundries, composts etc. All at highly competitive prices. We will also have local honey for sale. Tea/coffee and homemade cakes will also be available to enjoy, and the opportunity to join our club. There is wheelchair access, but some areas are uneven and will need careful attention.

&. 🐾 ❁ ☕

44 ROOKERY FARM

Balchins Lane, Westcott, Dorking, RH4 3LL. Mrs Tanya Demaine, tjdemaine101@gmail.com. *Off A25.*

From Dorking, go through Westcott, at bottom of Coast Hill turn R onto Balchins Lane. Parking past garden in field on R. Please turn R when exiting field as rd is single track. **Visits by arrangement May to July for groups of 10 to 30.** This Queen Anne house is set in 3 acres of formal and informal gardens. A white circular garden, roses, old brick paths and scented arbour. Cutting and vegetable garden, with apiary. Herbaceous borders with rose walk. Garden becomes less formal as it radiates from house. The topiary and box hedging of the patio and courtyard, lead to wildflower meadow, mown paths, small orchard, wild pond and views to Ranmore.

45 7 ROSE LANE
Ripley, GU23 6NE. Mindi McLean, 01483 223200, info@broadwaybarn.com, www.broadwaybarn.com. *Just off Ripley High St on Rose Lane. 3rd house on L, next to shoe repair shop.* **Sat 13 June (10-4). Adm £3.50, chd free. Home-made teas.** 7 Rose Lane is a small but perfectly formed village centre garden behind an historic Grade II listed cottage. It has 3 rooms - a traditional perennial flower garden laid to lawn; a vegetable and fruit garden with Agriframe orchard and a working garden with greenhouse, compost bins and shed. It is a perfect example of how to make the most of a cottage garden. Coincides with Ripley Farmers Market and Grapes & Grain Drinks Festival on 13 June (10am-4pm).

46 SAFFRON GATE
Tickners Heath, Alfold, Cranleigh, GU6 8HU. Mr & Mrs D Gibbison, 01483 200219, clematis@talk21.com. *Between Alfold & Dunsfold. A281 between Guildford & Horsham approx 8m turn at Alfold crossways follow signs for Dunsfold. Do not turn at A281 T-lights for Dunsfold (wrong road).* **Visits by arrangement Apr to July for groups of 10+. Adm £5, chd free. Home-made teas.** This garden is a plant lovers paradise, colour for most of the year, many unusual plants and a plethora of clematis of all shapes and sizes as featured in the RHS garden magazine. A new bed with scented roses has been added. Arbor with many

varieties of climbers. A productive vegetable garden. Garden was subject of a lecture given at Great Dixter. Disabled drop off point.

47 ◆ THE SCULPTURE PARK
Tilford Road, Churt, Farnham, GU10 2LH. Eddie Powell, 01428 605453, sian@thesculpturepark.com, www.thesculpturepark.com. *Corner of Jumps and Tilford Rd, Churt. Look out for Bell & The Dragon pub, we are directly opp. You can use our car park or the pub where refreshments are available.* **For NGS: Tue 10 Mar, Tue 16 June (10-5). Adm £5, chd £3. For other opening times and information, please phone, email or visit garden website.** This garden sculpture exhibition is set within an enchanting arboretum and wildlife inhabited water garden. You should set aside between two and four hours for your visit as there are two miles of trail within 10 acres. Our displays evolve and diversify as the seasons pass, with vivid and lush colours of the rhododendrons in May and June to the enchanting frost in the depths of winter. Around one third of The Sculpture Park is accessible to wheelchairs. Disabled toilets are available.

Your visits help change lives – your generosity has supported unpaid carers through donations to Carers Trust totalling over £4 million since 1996

48 41 SHELVERS WAY
Tadworth, KT20 5QJ. Keith & Elizabeth Lewis, 01737 210707, kandelewis@ntlworld.com. *6m S of Sutton off A217. 1st turning on R after Burgh Heath T-lights heading S on A217. 400yds down Shelvers Way on L.* **Sun 9 Aug (2-5.30). Adm £5, chd free. Home-made teas. Visits also by arrangement Apr to Aug for groups of 10+.** Visitors say 'one of the most colourful gardens in Surrey'. In spring, a myriad of small bulbs with specialist daffodils and many pots of colourful tulips. Choice perennials follow. Cobbles

and shingle support grasses and self sown plants with a bubble fountain. Annuals and herbaceous plants ensure colour well into September. A garden for all seasons.

49 SHIELING
The Warren, Kingswood, Tadworth, KT20 6PQ. Drs Sarah & Robin Wilson, 01737 833370, sarahwilson@doctors.org.uk. *Kingswood Warren Estate. Off A217, gated entrance just before church on S-bound side of dual carriageway after Tadworth r'about . ¾ m walk from Station. Parking on The Warren or by church on A217.* **Sun 12 Apr (2-4). Adm £5, chd free. Home-made teas. Evening opening Sat 23 May (6-8). Adm £8, chd free. Wine. Sun 24 May (11-4). Adm £5, chd free. Home-made teas. Visits also by arrangement May & June for groups of 10+.** One acre garden restored to its original 1920s design. Formal front garden with island beds and shrub borders. Unusual large rock garden and mixed borders with collection of beautiful slug free hostas and uncommon woodland perennials. The rest is an interesting woodland garden with acid loving plants, a new shrub border and a stumpery. Play area for children. Plant list provided for visitors. Lots for children to do with swing, slide, sandpit and Wendy house in woodland glade. Some narrow paths in back garden. Otherwise resin drive, grass and paths easy for wheelchairs.

50 SLEEPY HOLLOW
Pook Hill, Chiddingfold, Godalming, GU8 4XR. Mrs Susanna Money. *Exit A3 at Milford, follow A283 towards Petworth for 3m, R into Combe Ln. Proceed 1½ miles then R into Prestwick Ln, bear L into Pook Hill.* **Sun 21 June (11-5). Adm £5, chd free. Home-made teas. Also open The Coach House.** Wander around the formal gardens which incl a knot garden with box hedges, a vegetable garden and greenhouse and a stunning cutting garden. Take a stroll through light woodland along a meandering stream. Incl three paddocks, the garden is just over 15 acres. Enjoy tea on our relaxing terrace looking out over the extensive lawn and summer beds.

51 2 SLYFIELD FARM COTTAGES

Cobham Road, Stoke D'Abernon, Cobham, KT11 3QH. Mr & Mrs Clive and Chrissie Shaw, 01932 863460, chrissieanneshaw@yahoo.co.uk. *2½M SE of Cobham. Take A245 from Cobham towards Fetcham go over M25 and we are 0.2M (325m) on L up a small farm drive & immediately R. (We are not at Slyfield House).* **Visits by arrangement May & June for groups of 10 to 20. Adm £4, chd free. Home-made teas.**
Our tranquil cottage garden has been planted for all year round interest using a tapestry of foliage textures as well as flowers, some of them rare & unusual, lots of them scented. It's planned with nature in mind with plenty of nectar & pollen plants for the bees, butterflies, moths & bats that visit here. Birds also play a big part in the garden with fruit & berry plants for them.

52 SOUTHLANDS LODGE

Southlands Lane, Tandridge, Oxted, RH8 9PH. Colin David & John Barker, 07500009603, colin3d@gmail.com. *3min from J6 of M25. From Tandridge Village head S down hill for ¼ m to T-junction with Southlands Lane. Turn L along Southlands Lane, approx ¼ m to Southlands Lodge entrance gate.* **Visits by arrangement July & Aug for groups of 5 to 20. Parking for 5 cars, if additional space is required a paddock is available. Adm £4, chd free. Home-made teas.**
A surprising garden, on the edge of a woodland, enjoying open views of adjacent fields. Formal and informal areas are scaled to compliment a late Georgian gatehouse. Mass planting offsets selected specimens, mostly chosen for their pollen and nectar that helps sustain the resident honey bees. An enclosed vegetable garden with greenhouse, a flock of Shetland sheep and chickens add interest. The garden contains a working apiary of 10 beehives. Two pairs of Guinea Fowl roam free through the property. An 'insect hotel' features. Gluten free cakes will be available, all cakes will contain nuts and dairy.

Randalls Allotments

53 SPRINGWOOD HOUSE
85 Petworth Road, Haslemere, GU27 3AX. Mr & Mrs Ian Bateson. *1m E of Haslemere. Entrance to property is almost opp junction of Holdfast Lane with Petworth Rd. Postcode for SatNav brings you approx 300yds W entrance.* **Sun 19, Sun 26 Apr (11-4). Adm £5, chd free. Home-made teas.**
Wooded walkway with large amount of native bluebells at the end of April, and 24 small wooden bridges following spring-fed stream. 3 large ponds with further bridges set in parkland type garden, waterfalls connecting the ponds which contain fish and also three small islands. Two large fields with walkways round the perimeter and an orchard. Bridge walkway is narrow and bare earth, step of 2-3 inches at each bridge. At end of walk there is a steep path, return if necessary.

54 SPURFOLD
Radnor Road, Peaslake, Guildford, GU5 9SZ. Mr & Mrs A Barnes, 01306 730196, spurfold@btinternet.com. *8m SE of Guildford. A25 to Shere then through to Peaslake. Pass Village stores & L up Radnor Rd.* **Visits by arrangement May to July for groups of 10+. Home made teas or wine and canapés in evening - all by arrangement.**
2½ acres, large herbaceous and shrub borders, formal pond with Cambodian Buddha head, sunken gravel garden with topiary box and water feature, terraces, beautiful lawns, mature rhododendrons and azaleas, woodland paths, and gazebos. Garden contains a collection of Indian elephants and

Your visits help change lives – we are Hospice UK's largest charitable funder donating more than £5.5 million to support hospices in local communities since 1996

other objets d'art. Topiary garden created 2010 and new formal lawn area created in 2012.

55 STUART COTTAGE
Ripley Road, East Clandon, GU4 7SF. John & Gayle Leader, 01483 222689, gayle@stuartcottage.com, www.stuartcottage.com. *4m E of Guildford. Off A246 or from A3 through Ripley until r'about, turn L & cont through West Clandon until T-lights, then L onto A246. East Clandon 1st L.* **Visits by arrangement June to Sept for groups of 10+. Refreshments can be arranged as suitable for the time of day. Home-made teas.**
Walk in to this tranquil partly walled ½ acre garden to find an oasis of calm. Beds grouped around the central fountain offer floral continuity through the seasons with soft harmonious planting supported by good structure with topiary, a rose/clematis walk and wisteria walk. Outside the wall is the late border with its vibrant colours and fun planting. Just a lovely garden.

56 NEW TANHOUSE FARM
Rusper Road, Newdigate, RH5 5BX. Mrs N Fries. *8m S of Dorking. On A24 turn L at roundabout at Beare Green. R at T-junction in Newdigate 1st farm on R approx 2/3m. Signposted Tanhouse Farm Shop.* **Sun 12 July (2-5.30). Adm £5, chd free. Light refreshments at Tanhouse Farm Shop, next to car park. Lunches and teas served til 5pm.**
Country garden created by owners since 1987. 1 acre of charming rambling gardens surrounding a C16 house (not open). Herbaceous borders; small lake and stream with ducks and geese, and an orchard with wild garden and meadow walk, with plentiful seats and benches to stop for contemplation.

57 THE THERAPY GARDEN
Manor Fruit Farm, Glaziers Lane, Normandy, Guildford, GU3 2DT. The Centre Manager, www.thetherapygarden.org. *SW of Guildford. Take A323 travelling from Guildford towards Aldershot, turn L into Glaziers Ln in centre of Normandy village opp War Memorial. The Therapy Garden is 200yds*

on L. **Sun 31 May, Sun 30 Aug (11-4). Adm £5.50, chd free. Light refreshments.**
The Therapy Garden is a horticulture and education charity that uses gardening to generate positive change for those living with mental health challenges. We are a working garden operating with clients 50 weeks a year, so there is always something new going on and fresh areas being developed. 2020 is our 4 year with NGS - come and see what's new! The Therapy Garden is a registered charity that provides social and therapeutic horticulture to different groups in the local community. We are a working garden full of innovation. Barbecue, salads and sandwiches, teas, coffees and cakes all available. Paved pathways throughout most of the garden, many with substantial handrails.

58 TIMBER HILL
Chertsey Road, Chobham, GU24 8JF. Nick & Lavinia Sealy, www.timberhillgarden.com. *4m N of Woking. 2½m E of Chobham & ⅓m E of Fairoaks aerodrome on A319 (N side). 1¼m W of Ottershaw, J11 M25. (If approaching from Ottershaw the A319 is the Chobham Road). See website for more detail.* **Wed 8, Wed 15, Wed 22 Jan, Mon 10, Tue 11, Wed 12, Thur 13 Feb (11-2). Sun 22 Mar (1.30-5), Mon 13 Apr (11-5). Wed 14 Oct (11-2.30). Adm £7, chd free. Refreshments in conservatory on most days. Home-made teas/refreshments served in beautiful old Surrey Barn on Mothering Sunday (Mar 22) & Easter Monday (Apr 13).**
16 acres of garden, park & woodland giving an undulating walk with views to North Downs. Stunning winter garden available to view most Wednesdays from January - March. Lonicera & witch hazel walk, abundant snowdrops, aconites & a sea of crocuses, spectacular camellias (featured in Surrey Life) followed by magnolias & wild cherries. May brings bluebells, azaleas, rhododendrons. Please call. Nature & wildlife trails for adults & children. For other information, pop up openings & events, see Timber Hill website or please telephone.

59 ◆ TITSEY PLACE GARDENS

Titsey, Oxted, RH8 0SA.
The Trustees of the Titsey
Foundation, 07889052461,
jo@jldmarketing.co.uk,
www.titsey.org. *3m N of Oxted.
A25 between Oxted & Westerham.
Follow brown heritage signs to
Titsey Estate from A25 at Limpsfield
or see website for directions.* **For
NGS: Sun 17 May, Sun 14 June,
Sun 19 July, Sun 16 Aug (1-5).
Adm £5, chd £1. Home-made
teas. For other opening times and
information, please phone, email or
visit garden website.**
One of the largest surviving historic
estates in Surrey. Magnificent
ancestral home and gardens of
the Gresham family since 1534.
Walled kitchen garden restored early
1990s. Golden Jubilee rose garden.
Etruscan summer house adjoining
picturesque lakes and fountains.
15 acres of formal and informal
gardens in an idyllic setting. Highly
Commended in the 2019 Horticulture
Week Custodian Awards. Tea room
serving delicious homemade cakes
and selling local produce is open
from 12.30-5.00 pm on open days.
Walks through the estate woodland
are open all year round. Pedigree herd
of Sussex Cattle roam the park. Last
admissions to gardens at 4pm. Dogs
on leads allowed in picnic area, car
park and woodland walks. Disabled
car park alongside tearooms.

60 ◆ VANN

Hambledon, Godalming,
GU8 4EF. Mrs M Caroe,
01428 683413, vann@caroe.com,
www.vanngarden.co.uk. *6m S
of Godalming. A283 to Lane End,
Hambledon. On NGS days only,
follow yellow Vann signs for 2m.
Please park in the field, not in the
road. At other times follow the
website instructions.* **For NGS: Sun
22, Mon 23, Tue 24 Mar (10-6);
Mon 13 Apr (2-6); Tue 14, Wed 15
Apr (10-6). Wed 6 May (10-6), Thur
7 May (10-6), Fri 8 May (2-5.30).
Home-made teas (on Fri 8 May
only). Sun 21 June (12-6). Adm
£7, chd free. N.B. Group meals/
refreshments by arrangement.
Self service refreshments
available on all NGS Open Days.
For other opening times and
information, please phone, email or
visit garden website.**
5 acre English Heritage registered
garden surrounding Tudor and William
and Mary house (not open) with Arts
and Crafts additions by W D Caröe
incl a Bargate stone pergola. At the
front, brick paved original cottage
garden; to the rear, newly dredged
lake, yew walk with rill and Gertrude
Jekyll water garden. Snowdrops and
hellebores, spring bulbs, spectacular
Fritillaria in Feb/March. Island beds,
crinkle crankle wall, orchard with wild
flowers. Vegetable garden. Gertrude
Jekyll water garden and spring
bulbs. Also open by appointment for

individuals or groups. Water garden
paths not suitable for wheelchairs, but
many others are. Please ring prior to
visit to request disabled parking.

61 11 WEST HILL

Sanderstead, CR2 0SB. Rachel
and Edward Parsons. *M25, J6,
A22, 2.9m r'about 4th exit to
Succombs Hill, R to Westhall Rd, at
r'about 2nd exit to Limpsfield Rd,
r'about 2nd exit on Sanderstead Hill
0.9m a sharp R to West Hill, plse
park on West Hill.* **Sat 4, Sun 5 Apr,
Sat 20, Sun 21 June (2-5). Adm
£5, chd free. Home-made teas.
Donation to British Hen Welfare
Trust.**
A hidden gem tucked away... a
beautiful country cottage style garden
set in ½ acre, designed by Sam
Aldridge of Eden Restored. The
garden flows through pathways, lawn,
vegetable and play areas. Flower
beds showcase outstanding tulips,
informal seating areas throughout
the garden allows you to absorb the
wonderful garden, whilst observing
our rescued chickens and rabbits!

62 57 WESTHALL ROAD

Warlingham, CR6 9BG. Robert
& Wendy Baston. *3m N of M25.
M25, J6, A22 London, at Whyteleafe
r'about, take 3rd R, under railway
bridge, turn immed R into Westhall*

The Coach House

© Leigh Clapp

Rd. **Sun 24, Mon 25 May (2-5). Adm £4, chd free. Home-made teas. Free top ups on tea and coffee. Ice cream in warm weather. Donation to Warlingham Methodist Church.**
Reward for the sure footed – many steps to 3 levels! Swathes of tulips. Mature kiwi and grape vines. Mixed borders. Raised vegetable beds. Box, bay, cork oak and yew topiaries. Amphitheatre of potted plants on lower steps. Stunning views of Caterham and Whyteleafe from top garden. Olive tree floating on a circular 'pond' of white and pink flowers. Flint walls, water spilling onto pebbles in secluded lush setting, vegetable borders, summerhouse, large trampoline for children, apple tree with child swing, gravel garden (new).

63 WESTWAYS FARM
Gracious Pond Road, Chobham, GU24 8HH. Paul & Nicky Biddle, 01276 856163, nicolabiddle@rocketmail.com. *4m N of Woking. From Chobham Church proceed over r'about towards Sunningdale, 1st Xrds R into Red Lion Rd to junction with Mincing Lane.* **Sun 10 May (11-5). Adm £4.50, chd free. Home-made teas. Visits also by arrangement Apr to June for groups of 10+.**
6 acre garden surrounded by woodlands planted in 1930s with mature and some rare rhododendrons, azaleas, camellias and magnolias, underplanted with bluebells, lilies and dogwood; extensive lawns and sunken pond garden. Working stables and sandschool. Lovely Queen Anne House (not open) covered with listed *Magnolia grandiflora.* Victorian design glasshouse. New planting round garden room.

64 WILDWOOD
34 The Hatches, Frimley Green, Camberley, GU16 6HE. Annie Keighley, 01252 838660, annie.keighley12@btinternet.com. *3m S of Camberley. M3 J4 follow A325 to Frimley Centre, towards Frimley Green for 1m. Turn R by the green, R into The Hatches for on street parking.* **Wed 10 June (2-5). Combined adm with Oakleigh £4.50, chd free. Home-made teas. Visits also by arrangement June to Aug for groups of 5 to 20. Please**

email owner to customise your visit & inform of dietary needs.
Visitors love the hidden surprises in this romantic cottage garden with tumbling roses, topiary and towering magnolia grandiflora. Holly hedges hide a secret haven with wildlife pond, dell, fernery and shaded loggia. Quirky organic potager with raised beds, fruit trees, tadpole nursery, greenhouses and composting areas. Surrey Wildlife Trust winner - Large Private Garden category. Wildlife gardening introduction by owner. Gravel drive and paths. Care needed by pond.

Your visits help change lives – your generosity helps Marie Curie fund nurses to care for people night and day in their homes, with donations of more than £9 million

65 WOODBURY COTTAGE
Colley Lane, Reigate, RH2 9JJ. Shirley & Bob Stoneley, 01737 244235. *1m W of Reigate. M25 J8, A217 (Reigate). Immed before level crossing turn R into Somers Rd, cont as Manor Rd. At end turn R into Coppice Ln & follow signs to car park. Do not come up Colley Ln from A25.* **Sat 4, Sun 5 July, Sat 5, Sun 6 Sept (1-5). Adm £4, chd free. Home-made teas. Visits also by arrangement July to Sept for groups of 10 to 20.**
Cottage garden just under ¼ acre. It is stepped on a slope, enhanced by its setting under Colley Hill and the North Downs. We grow a colourful diversity of plants incl perennials, annuals and tender ones. A particular

feature throughout the garden is the use of groups of pots containing unusual and interesting plants. The garden is colour themed and is still rich and vibrant in September.

66 WOODLAND
67 York Rd, Cheam, Sutton, SM2 6HN. Sean Hilton, 07879498654, shilton.shx@gmail.com. *York Rd runs parallel to Belmont Rise, main A217 from Sutton to Banstead. From A217 turn L (from N) or R (from S) at T-lights into Dorset Rd. York Rd is 1st L.* **Evening opening Tue 7, Thur 9 July (4.30-7). Adm £6, chd free. Wine. Sun 12 July (1-5.30). Adm £5, chd free. Home-made teas. Visits also by arrangement June & July for groups of 5 to 30. Timings by negotiation.**
Woodland is a suburban walled garden of approx ⅕ acre with a range of plants shrubs and young trees. Hard landscaping has created terraces, two lawns and four levels from the upward incline of the garden. Good selection of shrubs, perennials, hostas, bamboos and ferns. Central features of the garden are a pond with pergola, a weeping copper beech and a Victorian Plant House. Tea, coffee, cakes and soft drinks Sunday 12th. Wine and soft drinks 7th and 9th July. All but the top level accessible by wheelchair.

67 NEW YEW TREE COTTAGE
Grub Street, Limpsfield, RH8 0SH. Mrs Kathy Thomas. *Mid-way between Westerham and Oxted, just off of the A25. Very limited parking at the garden, for disabled visitors only. Park in the Limpsfield Chart Golf Club car park, and walk to the garden (approx. ½ m). Note, Grub St is a dead end.* **Sun 21 June (1-5). Adm £5, chd free. Home-made teas.**
Large enclosed kitchen garden with glasshouses and chickens. From here a gate opens on to the main garden bordered on either side by mixed borders. Specimen trees are planted in the lawn and the summer house is surrounded by beds packed with succulents and exotics. A grass path leads to the prairie garden and shrubbery. At the front there is a parterre and wildflower meadow. Colourful pots abound.

East & Mid Sussex Volunteers

County Organiser, Booklet & Advertising Co-ordinator
Irene Eltringham-Willson
01323 833770
irene.willson@btinternet.com

County Treasurer
Andrew Ratcliffe 01435 873310
andrew.ratcliffe@ngs.org.uk

Publicity
Geoff Stonebanks 01323 899296
sussexeastpublicity@ngs.org.uk

Twitter
Liz Warner 01273 586050
liz.warner@ngs.org.uk

Photographer
Liz Seeber 01323 639478
lizseeber@btinternet.com

Booklet Distributor
Liz Warner (as above)

Assistant County Organisers
Jane Baker 01273 842805
jane.baker@ngs.org.uk

Michael & Linda Belton
01797 252984
belton.northiam@gmail.com

Victoria Brocklebank 01825 890348
victoria.brocklebank@ngs.org.uk

Shirley Carman-Martin
01444 473520
shirleycarmanmartin@gmail.com

Linda Field 01323 720179
lindafield3@gmail.com

Diane Gould 01825 750300
lavenderdgould@gmail.com

Aideen Jones 01323 899452
sweetpeasa52@gmail.com

Dr Denis Jones 01323 899452
sweetpeasd49@gmail.com

Susan Laing 01444 892500
splaing@btinternet.com

Sarah Ratcliffe 01435 873310
sallyrat@btinternet.com

Geoff Stonebanks (as above)

Liz Warner (as above)

David Wright 01435 883149
david.wright@ngs.org.uk

West Sussex Volunteers

County Organiser, Booklet & Advertising Co-ordinator
Ian Gregory 01903 892433
ian.gregory@ngs.org.uk

County Treasurer
Liz Collison 01903 719245
liz.collison@ngs.org.uk

Publicity
Philip Duly 01428 661089
philipduly@tiscali.co.uk

Social Media
Claudia Pearce 07985 648216
claudiapearce17@gmail.com

Photographer
Judi Lion 07810 317057
judi.lion@ngs.org.uk

Assistant County Organisers
Teresa Barttelot 01798 865690
tbarttelot@gmail.com

Sanda Belcher 01428 723259
sandambelcher@gmail.com

Lesley Chamberlain 07950 105966
chamberlain_lesley@hotmail.com

Patty Christie 01730 813323
sussexwestngs@gmail.com

Elizabeth Gregory 01903 892433
elizabethgregory1@btinternet.com

Peter & Terri Lefevre 01403 256002
teresalefevre@outlook.com

Sue Liassides 07876 452938
sue.liassides@ngs.org.uk

Judi Lion (as above)

Carrie McArdle 01403 820272
carrie.mcardle@btinternet.com

Ann Moss 01243 370048
ann.moss@ngs.org.uk

Claudia Pearce (as above)

Fiona Phillips 07884 398704
fiona.h.phillips@btinternet.com

Susan Pinder 01403 820430
nasus.rednip@gmail.com

Diane Rose 07789 565094
dirose8@me.com

Sussex is a vast county with two county teams, one covering East and Mid Sussex and the other covering West Sussex.

Over 80 miles from west to east, Sussex spans the southern side of the Weald from the exposed sandstone heights of Ashdown Forest, past the broad clay vales with their heavy yet fertile soils and the imposing chalk ridge of the South Downs National Park, to the equable if windy coastal strip.

Away from the chalk, Sussex is a county with a largely wooded landscape with imposing oaks, narrow hedged lanes and picturesque villages. The county offers much variety and our gardens reflect this. There is something for absolutely everyone and we feel sure that you will enjoy your garden visiting experience - from rolling acres of parkland, country and town gardens, to small courtyards and village trails. See the results of the owner's attempts to cope with the various conditions, discover new plants and talk with the owners about their successes.

Many of our gardens are open by arrangement, so do not be afraid to book a visit or organise a visit with your local gardening or U3A group.

Should you need advice, please e-mail sussexeastpublicity@ngs.org.uk for anything relating to East and Mid Sussex or sussexwestngs@gmail.com for anything in West Sussex.

@SussexNGSEast
@SussexNGS
@ngseastsussex

@Sussexwestngs
@SussexWestNGS
@sussexwestngs

OPENING DATES

All entries subject to change. For latest information check www.ngs.org.uk

Extended openings are shown at the beginning of the month.

Map locator numbers are shown to the right of each garden name.

February

Snowdrop Festival

By Arrangement
Pembury House 118
5 Whitemans Close 159

Sunday 2nd
◆ Highdown Gardens 75

Sunday 16th
Manor of Dean 94
The Old Vicarage 114

Friday 28th
The Garden House 57

March

Sunday 8th
NEW The Hamblin Centre 66

Sunday 15th
The Old Vicarage 114

Thursday 19th
◆ Highdown Gardens 75

Sunday 22nd
Manor of Dean 94

Saturday 28th
Butlers Farmhouse 24

Sunday 29th
Butlers Farmhouse 24
◆ King John's Lodge 81

April

Saturday 4th
Down Place 42

Sunday 5th
Down Place 42

Sunday 12th
Peelers Retreat 117

Monday 13th
The Old Vicarage 114

Friday 17th
◆ Great Dixter House, Gardens & Nurseries 62

Saturday 18th
Rymans 127

Sunday 19th
Newtimber Place 102
Penns in the Rocks 119
Rymans 127

Tuesday 21st
Bignor Park 15

Wednesday 22nd
Fittleworth House 51
The Grange 61

Saturday 25th
Banks Farm 10
The Garden House 57
Sandhill Farm House 133
Winchelsea's Secret Gardens 161

Sunday 26th
Banks Farm 10
The Garden House 57
Manor of Dean 94
Offham House 109
Parsonage Farm 115
Sandhill Farm House 133

Wednesday 29th
Fittleworth House 51

May

Saturday 2nd
◆ King John's Lodge 81

Sunday 3rd
◆ Clinton Lodge 32
◆ King John's Lodge 81
Stanley Farm 145

Wednesday 6th
Fittleworth House 51
◆ Sheffield Park and Garden 139

Friday 8th
96 Ashford Road 8

Saturday 9th
Cookscroft 33
Ham Cottage 65
NEW Redriff 124
NEW Silver Springs 142

Sunday 10th
Ham Cottage 65
Hammerwood House 67
Mountfield Court 100
Peelers Retreat 117
NEW Redriff 124
NEW Silver Springs 142
Stone Cross House 146

Monday 11th
Holly House 77

Tuesday 12th
Bignor Park 15

Wednesday 13th
Cookscroft 33
Fittleworth House 51
The Grange 61
The Walled Garden at Tilgate Park 152

Thursday 14th
The Walled Garden at Tilgate Park 152

Friday 15th
Caxton Manor 27
2 Quarry Cottages 123

Saturday 16th
96 Ashford Road 8
Blue Jays 17
Caxton Manor 27
NEW Forest Ridge 55
Limekiln Farm 86
2 Quarry Cottages 123

Sunday 17th
Blue Jays 17
Champs Hill 28
NEW Forest Ridge 55
Garden House, 49 Guillards Oak 58
Hammerwood House 67
Legsheath Farm 85
Limekiln Farm 86
The Moongate Garden 99
The Old Vicarage 114
Penns in the Rocks 119
Sienna Wood 141

Wednesday 20th
Balcombe Gardens 9

Thursday 21st
South Grange 144

Friday 22nd
Great Lywood Farmhouse 63

Saturday 23rd
96 Ashford Road 8
54 Elmleigh 47
NEW 29 Fairlight Avenue 48

◆ Herstmonceux Castle Gardens and Grounds 72
◆ The Priest House 122

Sunday 24th
54 Elmleigh 47
Foxglove Cottage 56
NEW Warnham Park 153

Monday 25th
Copyhold Hollow 34
54 Elmleigh 47
Great Lywood Farmhouse 63
Oaklands Farm 107

Saturday 30th
51 Carlisle Road 26
Lowder Mill 90
NEW Warnham Park 153

Sunday 31st
Aldsworth House 2
The Beeches 12
51 Carlisle Road 26
Lowder Mill 90
Seaford Gardens 135

June

Every Wednesday and Thursday from Wednesday 24th
◆ The Apuldram Centre 5

Tuesday 2nd
Driftwood 43

Wednesday 3rd
Aldsworth House 2

Thursday 4th
Chidmere Gardens 30
NEW Kitchenham Farm 82

Friday 5th
1 Pest Cottage 120

Saturday 6th
12 Ainsworth Avenue 1
NEW 23 Clarence Road 31
54 Elmleigh 47
Harlands Gardens 69
Lordington House 89
Skyscape 143
Waterworks & Friends 155

Sunday 7th
12 Ainsworth Avenue 1
Breanross 20
NEW 23 Clarence Road 31
54 Elmleigh 47
Fairlight End 49

Harlands Gardens 69
Hassocks Village
    Garden Trail 70
◆ High Beeches
    Woodland and
    Water Garden 74
Jacaranda 79
Lordington House 89
Mill Hall Farm 98
1 Pest Cottage 120
Selhurst Park 137
Sennicotts 138
Skyscape 143
Town Place 150

Monday 8th
◆ Clinton Lodge 32

Tuesday 9th
NEW Kitchenham Farm 82

Wednesday 10th
Fittleworth House 51
The Grange 61
4 Hillside Cottages 76
Rolfs Farm 126

Thursday 11th
NEW Bramley 19
Kemp Town Enclosures:
    South Garden 80

Friday 12th
NEW Bramley 19
The Garden House,
    Crowborough 59

Saturday 13th
Cookscroft 33
Durford Abbey Barn 44
The Garden House,
    Crowborough 59
Mayfield Gardens 95
Rymans 127

Sunday 14th
Down Place 42
Durford Abbey Barn 44
NEW The Hamblin
    Centre 66
Mayfield Gardens 95
Old Stonelynk Edge 113
Ringmer Park 125
Rymans 127
NEW St Leonards-on-Sea
    Group 130
Seaford Gardens 135
Town Place 150

Monday 15th
Down Place 42

Tuesday 16th
◆ Alfriston Clergy
    House 3
Driftwood 43

Wednesday 17th
Fittleworth House 51
Rolfs Farm 126

Thursday 18th
NEW Crowborough
    Gardens 35

Friday 19th
NEW The Old House 112
Parsonage Farm 115
NEW Warren Cottage 154

Saturday 20th
Balcombe Gardens 9
54 Elmleigh 47
◆ King John's Lodge 81
Luctons 91
◆ The Priest House 122
Town Place 150
Winchelsea's Secret
    Gardens 161

Sunday 21st
54 Elmleigh 47
Herstmonceux Parish
    Trail 73
◆ King John's Lodge 81
Luctons 91

Monday 22nd
◆ Clinton Lodge 32

Tuesday 23rd
Luctons 91

Saturday 27th
Burwash Hidden
    Gardens 23
Mandalay 93
North Hall 104
NEW St Mary's
    Hospital 131

Sunday 28th
Ashdown Park Hotel 7
NEW Gorselands 60
North Hall 104
North Springs 105
Peelers Retreat 117
NEW Westwell House 156

Tuesday 30th
Bignor Park 15
Driftwood 43
NEW St Mary's
    Hospital 131

July

**Every Wednesday
and Thursday to
Thursday 16th**
◆ The Apuldram Centre 5

Thursday 2nd
Butlers Farmhouse 24
NEW 3 Normandy
    Drive 103

Saturday 4th
NEW The Barn 11
54 Elmleigh 47
NEW Grovelands 64
49 New Road 101

Sunday 5th
NEW Alpines 4
NEW The Barn 11
Bexhill-on-Sea Trail 14
54 Elmleigh 47
NEW Gorselands 60
NEW Grovelands 64
Whithurst Park 160

Thursday 9th
Holly House 77

Saturday 11th
Fletching Secret
    Gardens 53

Sunday 12th
Foxglove Cottage 56
Hellingly Parish Trail 71

Tuesday 14th
Driftwood 43

Wednesday 15th
Fittleworth House 51
The Grange 61
Wych Warren House 163

Friday 17th
◆ St Mary's House
    Gardens 132

Saturday 18th
The Beeches 12
70 Dale View 40
54 Elmleigh 47
The Hundred House 78
The Moongate Garden 99
49 New Road 101
Oaklands Farm 107
NEW Peacehaven &
    Saltdean Trail 116
◆ St Mary's House
    Gardens 132

Sunday 19th
The Beeches 12

70 Dale View 40
54 Elmleigh 47
NEW Field Place Manor
    House & Barns 50
NEW The Hamblin
    Centre 66
4 Hillside Cottages 76
The Hundred House 78
NEW Peacehaven &
    Saltdean Trail 116

Wednesday 22nd
Burgess Hill NGS
    Gardens 22
Fittleworth House 51
Knightsbridge House 83
NEW Thakeham Place
    Farm 149
The Walled Garden at
    Tilgate Park 152

Thursday 23rd
The Walled Garden at
    Tilgate Park 152

Saturday 25th
Knightsbridge House 83

Sunday 26th
NEW D & S Haus 37
NEW Thakeham Place
    Farm 149

Thursday 30th
Driftwood 43

August

Saturday 1st
54 Elmleigh 47

Sunday 2nd
54 Elmleigh 47

Monday 3rd
◆ Clinton Lodge 32

Saturday 8th
Follers Manor 54

Sunday 9th
Champs Hill 28
Follers Manor 54
Garden House,
    49 Guillards Oak 58
Peelers Retreat 117

Wednesday 12th
Fittleworth House 51
◆ Merriments
    Gardens 96

Saturday 15th
Camberlot Hall 25
Holly House 77
Limekiln Farm 86

Saffrons

THE GARDENS

1 12 AINSWORTH AVENUE

Ovingdean, Brighton, BN2 7BG.
Jane & Chris Curtis. *From Brighton
take A259 coast road E, passing
Roedean School on L. Take 1st L at
the r'about into Greenways & 2nd R
into Ainsworth Ave. No 12 on R.* **Sat
6, Sun 7 June (1-5). Combined
adm with Skyscape £5, chd free.
Tea & cake at Skyscape.**
A small (36ft x 46ft at back and 36ft
x 36ft at front) coastal garden that
began in 2014, and is now becoming
established. Pergola, arches and
arbour strategically positioned to
provide privacy and a choice of
places to sit with different aspects,
even a glimpse of the sea. Mixed
planting, mostly new but several
mature trees, incl a large walnut that
creates a focal point.

2 ALDSWORTH HOUSE

Emsworth Common Road,
Aldsworth, PO10 8QT.
Tom & Sarah Williams,
darmady1@btinternet.com. *6m
W of Chichester. From Havant
follow signs to Stansted House
until Emsworth Common Rd,
stay on this road until Aldsworth.
From Chichester B2178/B2146
follow road through Funtington to
Aldsworth.* **Sun 31 May, Wed 3
June (11-5). Adm £5, chd free.
Light refreshments. Visits also by
arrangement May to mid-June for
groups of 10+. Drinks & biscuits.**
A 6 acre garden for plant lovers, set
in gorgeous countryside in the South
Downs National Park, containing
many rare and interesting plants,
shrubs and trees in varied conditions
including 2 gravel gardens, a bog
garden, 2 arboretums, a walled
garden and a mound. It also includes
a wild area and a croquet lawn all set
among beautiful old trees including a
magnificent 200 year old plane tree.
Short DVD showing the garden and
family in the 1930s. Quiz for children.
Majority of the garden is flat, gravel
and slope areas a little difficult. Please
No Dogs.

3 ◆ ALFRISTON CLERGY
HOUSE

Alfriston, BN26 5TL. National
Trust, 01323 871961,
alfriston@nationaltrust.org.uk,
www.nationaltrust.org.uk/alfriston.
*4m NE of Seaford. Just E of B2108,
in Alfriston village, adjoining The
Tye & St Andrew's Church.* **For
NGS: Tue 16 June (10.30-4.30).
Adm £6.20, chd £3.10. For other
opening times and information,
please phone, email or visit garden
website.**
Enjoy the scent of roses; admire the
vegetable garden and orchard in a
tranquil setting with views across
the River Cuckmere. Visit this C14
thatched Wealden hall house, the first
building to be acquired by the NT in
1896. Our gardener will be available
to talk to you about the garden.
Partial wheelchair access.

4 NEW ALPINES

High Street, Maresfield, Uckfield,
TN22 2EG. Ian & Cathy Shaw.
*1½m N of Uckfield. Garden approx
150 metres N of Budletts r'about
towards Maresfield. Blue Badge
parking at garden, other parking in
village.* **Sun 5 July (11.30-5). Adm
£6, chd free. Home-made teas.**
This is a young (6 yrs), 1 acre garden
with large and rampant mixed
borders, each loosely following a
limited colour palette of unusual
combinations. Numerous new trees
incl orchard with beehives and
meadow grasses. Wildlife pond with

Sweet Springs, Crowborough Gardens

bog garden, developing stumpery and fernery. Veggie patch with raised beds, fruit cage, pretty greenhouse, and bee garden. Wheelchair access with a few steps round greenhouse.

5 ♦ THE APULDRAM CENTRE
Appledram Lane South, Apuldram, Chichester, PO20 7PE. The Apuldram Centre, 01243 783370, info@apuldram.org, www.apuldram.org. *1m S of A27. Follow A259 Fishbourne & turn into Appledram Lane South.* **For NGS: Every Wed and Thur 24 June to 16 July (10-3). Adm £4, chd free. Light refreshments. For other opening times and information, please phone, email or visit garden website.**
Award-winning wildlife and sensory garden. Winding pathway sensitively planted with bee loving plants, all grown from seed, which leads to a tranquil pond and garden. Full of surprises, this garden encompasses many interesting features incl sculptures and other art works created by our adult trainees with learning difficulties. Teas, coffees, light lunches and home-made cakes served in the café until 4pm. Local produce incl home-made apple juice, local honey and a large selection of bedding plants and perennials for sale. Wheelchair access throughout sensory garden. Restricted access to working greenhouses and vegetable plots.

6 ♦ ARUNDEL CASTLE & GARDENS - THE COLLECTOR EARL'S GARDEN
Arundel, BN18 9AB. Arundel Castle Trustees Ltd, 01903 882173, visits@arundelcastle.org, www.arundelcastle.org. *In the centre of Arundel, N of A27.* **For opening times and information, please phone, email or visit garden website.**
Ancient castle, family home of the Duke of Norfolk. 40 acres of grounds and gardens which include hot subtropical borders, English herbaceous borders, stumpery, wild flower garden, two glasshouses with exotic fruit and vegetables, walled flower and organic kitchen gardens. C14 Fitzalan Chapel white garden.

7 ASHDOWN PARK HOTEL
Wych Cross, East Grinstead, RH18 5JR. Mr Kevin Sweet, 01342 824988, reservations@ashdownpark.co.uk, www.elitehotels.co.uk. *6m S of East Grinstead. Turn off A22 at Wych Cross T-lights.* **Sun 28 June (1-5). Adm £5, chd free. Light refreshments.**
186 acres of parkland, grounds and gardens surrounding Ashdown Park Hotel. Our Secret Garden is well worth a visit with many new plantings. Large number of deer roam the estate and can often be seen during the day. Enjoy and explore the woodland paths, quiet areas and views. Access over gravel paths and uneven ground with steps.

8 96 ASHFORD ROAD
Hastings, TN34 2HZ. Lynda & Andrew Hayler. *From A21 (Sedlescombe Rd N) towards Hastings, take 1st exit on r'about A2101, then 3rd on L (approx 1m). 2½m from 29 Fairlight Ave.* **Fri 8, Sat 16, Sat 23 May (1-5) May. Adm £3, chd free. Also open 29 Fairlight Avenue on 23 May only.**
Small (100ft x 52ft) Japanese inspired front and back garden. Full of interesting planting with many acers, azaleas and bamboos. Over 100 different hostas, many miniature. Lower garden with greenhouse and raised beds. Also an attractive Japanese Tea House.

GROUP OPENING

9 BALCOMBE GARDENS
Follow B2036 N from Cuckfield for 3m. ¼m N of Balcombe Station, turn L immed before Balcombe Primary School. From N, take J10A from M23 & follow S for 2½m. Gardens signed within village. **Wed 20 May, Sat 20 June (12-5). Combined adm £6, chd free. Home-made teas at Stumlet.**

STUMLET
Oldlands Avenue, RH17 6LW. Max & Nicola Preston Bell.

46 WESTUP FARM COTTAGES
London Road, RH17 6JJ. Chris Cornwell, 01444 811891, chris.westup@btinternet.com. **Visits also by arrangement Apr to Sept.**

WINTERFIELD
Oldlands Avenue, RH17 6LP. Sue & Sarah Howe, 01444 811380, sarahjhowe_uk@yahoo.co.uk. **Visits also by arrangement Apr to June.**

Balcombe is in a designated AONB. Traceable back to the Saxons, the village contains 55 listed buildings incl C15 parish church of St Mary's. Nearby is the famous Ouse Valley Viaduct, ancient woodlands, lake, millpond and reservoir. Within this setting there are three quite different gardens that are full of variety and interest, and will appeal to plant lovers. Set amidst the countryside of the High Weald, No 46 is a classic cottage garden with unique and traditional features linked by intimate paths through lush and subtle planting. There is also a new herb and butterfly garden. In the village, Winterfield is a country garden packed with uncommon shrubs and trees, herbaceous borders, a summerhouse, pond and wildlife area. Nearby Stumlet is a garden in transition, from being a space for boys to play, to becoming a peaceful area with places to sit and relax, plus vegetables in deep beds and a prolific herb garden. Wheelchair access at Winterfield and Stumlet.

10 BANKS FARM
Boast Lane, Barcombe, Lewes, BN8 5DY. Nick & Lucy Addyman. *From Barcombe Cross follow signs to Spithurst & Newick. 1st road on R into Boast Lane towards the Anchor Pub. At sharp bend carry on into Banks Farm.* **Sat 25, Sun 26 Apr (11-5). Adm £5, chd free. Home-made teas.**
9 acre garden set in rural countryside. Extensive lawns and shrub beds merge with the more naturalistic woodland garden set around the lake. An orchard, vegetable garden, ponds and a wide variety of plant species add to an interesting and very tranquil garden. Wheelchair access to the lower part of the garden with sloping grass paths, which may be difficult.

🔟 NEW THE BARN

Burgham Farm, Sheepstreet Lane, Etchingham, TN19 7AZ. Eleanor Knowles & Mary Barnes. *Located off the main Etchingham-Ticehurst road. A farm road leaves Sheepstreet Lane heading E downhill towards the River Limden. The carpark is 400 metres on the R. Partial one-way system operates.* **Sat 4, Sun 5 July, Sat 29, Sun 30 Aug (11-5). Adm £5, chd free. Light refreshments in the courtyard garden.**

Set in approx 1 acre, this former hop garden has evolved using a variety of influences from famous gardens and the interests of the owners. The planting is of semi mature trees and shrubs, underplanted with a variety of herbaceous perennials and large borders of mixed herbaceous plants. The variety of roses and dahlias are of particular interest. Wheelchair access to majority of the garden with uneven grass in places.

🔢 THE BEECHES

Church Road, Barcombe, Lewes, BN8 5TS. Sandy Coppen, 01273 401339, sand@thebeechesbarcombe.com, www.thebeechesbarcombe.com. *From Lewes, A26 towards Uckfield for 3m, turn L signed Barcombe. Follow road for 1½m, turn L signed Hamsey & Church. Follow road for approx ½m & parking on the R in a field.* **Sun 31 May, Sat 18, Sun 19 July (2-5). Adm £6, chd free. Home-made teas. Visits also by arrangement May to Aug for groups of 10 to 20. Home-made teas. Wine & canapés for eve visits.**

C18 walled garden with cut flowers, vegetables, salads and fruit. Separate orchard and rose garden. Herbaceous borders and hot border. There are two ponds, one with a willow house. Extensive lawns and a C18 barn. A hazel walk is being developed and a short woodland walk. An old ditch has been made into a flowing stream with gunnera, ferns, hostas and a few flowers. Wheelchair access without steps, but some ground is a little bumpy. Dogs on lead welcome.

🔢 4 BEN'S ACRE

Horsham, RH13 6LW. Pauline Clark, 01403 266912, brian.clark8850@yahoo.co.uk. *E of Horsham. A281 via Cowfold, after Hilliers Garden Centre, turn R by Tesco on to St Leonards Rd, straight over r'about to Comptons Lane, next R Heron Way, 2nd L Grebe Cres, 1st L Ben's Acre.* **Sat 29 Aug (1-5). Adm £4.50, chd free. Home-made teas. Visits also by arrangement July & Aug for groups of 10 to 30. Garden groups & clubs most welcome.**

Described as inspirational, a visual delight on different levels with ponds, rockery, summerhouse and arbours, all interspersed with colourful containers and statuettes. The compartmentalised layout of the garden lies at the heart of the design. Small themed sections nest within borders full of harmonising perennials, climbers, roses and more. See what a diverse space can be created on a small scale. Seating throughout the garden, a large selection of delicious cakes and tea served on trays from teapots with cosies in fine china. Plant sale. 15 mins from Leonardslee and NT Nymans. Visit us on YouTube Pauline & Brian's Sussex Garden.

GROUP OPENING

🔢 BEXHILL-ON-SEA TRAIL

Bexhill & Little Common. Follow individual NGS signs to gardens from main roads. 5 gardens open, 2 in the same road, others further away. Tickets & maps at all gardens. **Sun 5 July (12-5). Combined adm £5, chd free. Home-made teas & light lunch at Westlands.**

NEW 64 COLLINGTON AVENUE

TN39 3RA. Dr Roger & Ruth Elias.

NEW SMALL HOUSE

Sandhurst Lane, TN39 4RG. Veronika & Terry Rogers.

WESTLANDS

36 Collington Avenue, TN39 3NE. Madeleine Gilbart & David Harding.

NEW 15 WINSTON DRIVE

TN39 3RP. Maureen & Alan Francis.

26 WINSTON DRIVE

TN39 3RP. Ron & Clare Brazier.

Westlands with mature shrubs in the front and a large walled rear garden with shrubs, trees, lawn, fruit and vegetables. 15 Winston Drive is a delightful traditional garden with fruit trees, a vegetable garden and flower beds, framed by mature hedges and trees, clipped box and paths. 26 Winston Drive with sweeping borders, 275 species of shrubs, trees and perennials, topiary balls and structural planting. Small House is a beautiful garden surrounded by trees and extensive flower beds. 64 Collington Avenue is a bit of a surprise as it incorporates the garden next door too. 34 yrs in the making, it has a beautiful mix of herbaceous planting with structural shrubs, vegetables, planting to encourage wildlife and stunning roses. Plant sale at Westlands. Partial wheelchair access to some gardens.

🔢 BIGNOR PARK

Pulborough, RH20 1HG. The Mersey Family, www.bignorpark.co.uk. *5m S of Petworth & Pulborough. Well signed from B2138. Nearest villages Sutton, Bignor & West Burton. Approach from the E, directions & map available on website.* **Tue 21 Apr, Tue 12 May, Tue 30 June (2-5). Adm £5, chd free. Home-made teas.**

11 acres of peaceful garden to explore with magnificent views of the South Downs. Interesting trees, shrubs, wild flower areas, with swathes of daffodils in spring. The walled flower garden has been replanted with herbaceous borders. Temple, Greek loggia, Zen pond and unusual sculptures. Former home of romantic poet Charlotte Smith, whose sonnets were inspired by Bignor Park. Spectacular Cedars of Lebanon and rare Lucombe Oak. Wheelchair access to shrubbery and croquet lawn, gravel paths in rest of garden and steps in stables quadrangle.

🔢 4 BIRCH CLOSE

Arundel, BN18 9HN. Elizabeth & Mike Gammon, 01903 882722, e.gammon@talktalk.net. *1m S of Arundel. From A27 & A284 r'about at W end of Arundel take Ford Rd. Immed turn R & follow Torton Hill Rd to Dalloway Rd (straight on), Birch Close on L after bend. About 1m from r'about.* **Visits by arrangement Apr & May for groups of 10 to 30. Adm £3.50, chd free. Light refreshments on request.**

⅓ acre of woodland garden on edge

of Arundel. Wide range of mature trees and shrubs with many hardy perennials. Emphasis on extensive selection of spring flowers and clematis (incl many montanas). All in a tranquil setting with secluded corners, meandering paths and plenty of seating. Partial wheelchair access to approx half of garden.

17 BLUE JAYS

Chesworth Close, Horsham, RH13 5AL. Stella & Mike Schofield, 01403 251065. *5 mins walk SE of St Mary's Church, Horsham. From A281 (East St) L down Denne Rd, L to Chesworth Lane, R to Chesworth Close. Garden at end of close. 4 disabled spaces, other parking in local streets & Denne Rd car park.* **Sat 16, Sun 17 May (12.30-5). Adm £4, chd free. Home-made teas. Visits also by arrangement Apr to July for groups of 10+. Donation to The Badger Trust.** Wooded 1 acre garden with rhododendrons, camellias and azaleas. Candelabra primulas and ferns edge the River Arun. Primroses and spring bulbs border woodland path and stream. Cordylines, gunneras, flower beds, a pond, a fountain and formal rose garden set in open lawns. Arch leads to a vegetable plot and orchard bounded by the river. Large WW2 pill box in the orchard; visits inside with short talk are available. Wheelchair access to most areas.

18 ◆ BORDE HILL GARDEN

Borde Hill Lane, Haywards Heath, RH16 1XP. Borde Hill Garden Ltd, 01444 450326, info@bordehill.co.uk, www.bordehill.co.uk. *1½ m N of Haywards Heath. 20 mins N of Brighton, or S of Gatwick on A23 taking exit 10a via Balcombe.* **For NGS: Mon 7 Sept (10-5). Adm £9.95, chd £6.70. For other opening times and information, please phone, email or visit garden website.** Rare plants and stunning landscapes make Borde Hill Garden the perfect day out for horticultural enthusiasts, families and those who love beautiful countryside. Enjoy tranquil outdoor rooms, woodland walks, playgrounds, picnic areas, home-cooked food and events throughout the season. Wheelchair access to 17 acres of formal garden. Dogs welcome on leads.

19 NEW BRAMLEY

Lane End Common, North Chailey, Lewes, BN8 4JH. Marcel & Lee Duyvesteyn, www.mulberrycottages.com/cottages/bramley-lodge. *From A272 North Chailey mini-r'abouts take NE turn to A275 signed Bluebell Railway, after 1m turn R signed Fletching. 'Bramley' is 300yds on the R. Free car park opp & roadside parking.* **Thur 11, Fri 12 June (1-5.30). Adm £5, chd free. Home-made teas.** Rural 1 acre garden. Planting began in 2006 and incl an orchard avenue with wild flowers and long grassed areas and beehives. Vegetable garden, numerous formal and informal ornamental flowerbeds and borders. Planted for strong seasonal effect and structure. Interesting planting and design. SSSI nearby.

20 BREANROSS

Pett Road, Pett, Hastings, TN35 4HA. Tim & Libby Rothwell. *4m E of Hastings. From Hastings, take A259 towards Rye. At White Hart/Beefeater turn R into Friars Hill. Descend into Pett village. White boarded house on R. Parking & WC at village hall.* **Sun 7 June (11-5). Adm £3, chd free. Also open Fairlight End.** The steeply, sloping garden offered the new owners a fairly blank canvas when they bought the property in Oct 2014. There were two old espalier apple trees, a mature perimeter hedge and a quirky stone wall, but no borders. Now there is a wealth of planting, a cedar greenhouse with cold frames, a woodland border and an informal water feature. There is a display of before and after photos, and a wealth of ideas for making the most of a steeply sloping site. Sloping front garden. Level terrace with nice views of the steeply, sloping garden.

21 BRIGHTLING DOWN FARM

Observatory Road, Dallington, TN21 9LN. Val & Pete Stephens, 07770 807060 / 01424 838888, valstephens@icloud.com. *1m from Woods Corner. At Swan Pub at Woods Corner, take road opp signed Brightling. Take 1st L signed Burwash & almost immed, turn into 1st driveway on L.* **Visits by arrangement June to Sept for groups of 10 to 30. On Thurs 4,** Fri 5 June & Fri 18, Fri 25 Sept only. **Adm £10, chd free. Home-made teas included.** The garden has several different areas incl a Zen garden, water garden, walled vegetable garden with two large greenhouses, herb garden, herbaceous borders and a new woodland walk. The garden makes clever use of grasses and is set amongst woodland with stunning countryside views. Winner of the Society of Garden Designers award. Most areas can be accessed with the use of temporary ramps.

GROUP OPENING

22 BURGESS HILL NGS GARDENS

10m N of Brighton, off B2113. Good walkers can reach 20 The Ridings first by walking from train station. Bus stops in area. Tickets & maps from any garden. **Wed 22 July (1-5). Combined adm £5, chd free. Home-made teas at 14 Barnside Avenue.**

14 BARNSIDE AVENUE
RH15 0JU. Brian & Sue Knight.

20 THE RIDINGS
RH15 0LW. Rachelle & Malcolm Russell.

30 SYCAMORE DRIVE
RH15 0GH. John Smith & Kieran O'Regan.

59 SYCAMORE DRIVE
RH15 0GG. Steve & Debby Gill.

This diverse group of four gardens is a mixture of established and small new gardens. Two of the group are a great example of what can be achieved over a 10 yr period from a blank canvas in a new development (Sycamore Drive), while close by is 14 Barnside Avenue, a wisteria clad house (pruning advice given) with a more mature garden with family lawn and borders, likewise 20 The Ridings is a mature garden with productive outside grapevine (pruning advice given). Many useful ideas for people living in new build properties with small gardens and heavy clay soil. Partial wheelchair access to some gardens.

GROUP OPENING

23 BURWASH HIDDEN GARDENS
Burwash, TN19 7EN.
www.burwashopengardens.org.uk.
In Burwash village on A265. Burwash is 3m W of junction with A21 at Hurst Green; 6m E of Heathfield. Follow signs for parking from High St. Tickets & maps at all gardens. **Sat 27 June (1-5). Combined adm with Mandalay £6, chd free. Home-made teas in Swan Meadow Sports Pavilion, Ham Lane.**

BRAMDEAN
Fiona & Paul Barkley.

[NEW] IVY HOUSE
Susan & Dom Beddard.

LINDEN COTTAGE
Philip & Anne Cutler.

LONGSTAFFES
Dorothy & Paul Bysouth.

MOUNT HOUSE
Richard & Lynda Maude-Roxby.

Home of Rudyard Kipling who lived at Bateman's near the village for many years. Admire our collection of hidden gardens, many behind centuries old period houses, here in the heart of the High Weald AONB. The six gardens vary in design, style and planting, and range in size from small cottage gardens to three acres. Located on and around the picturesque High St, all are within a level and easy walking distance of each other; dedicated parking close by. Restricted wheelchair access to rear gardens as mainly terraced properties.

※ 🍵

24 BUTLERS FARMHOUSE
Butlers Lane, Herstmonceux, BN27 1QH. Irene Eltringham-Willson, 01323 833770, irene.willson@btinternet.com, www.butlersfarmhouse.co.uk.
3m E of Hailsham. Take A271 from Hailsham, go through village of Herstmonceux, turn R signed Church Rd, then approx 1m turn R. Do not use SatNav! **Sat 28, Sun 29 Mar, Thur 2 July (2-5). Adm £4, chd free. Sat 22, Sun 23 Aug (2-5). Adm £6, chd free. Home-made teas. Jazz in the garden in Aug. Visits also by arrangement Mar to Oct. Refreshments on request.**

Lovely rural setting for 1 acre garden surrounding C16 farmhouse with views of South Downs. Pretty in spring with daffodils, hellebores and primroses. Come and see our meadow in July and perhaps spot an orchid or two. Quite a quirky garden with surprises round every corner including a rainbow border, small pond, Cornish inspired beach corners, a poison garden and secret jungle garden. Relax and listen to live jazz in the garden in Aug. Most of garden accessible by wheelchair.

&. ※ 🚗 🛏 🍵

25 CAMBERLOT HALL
Camberlot Road, Lower Dicker, Hailsham, BN27 3RH. Nicky Kinghorn. *500yds S of A22 at Lower Dicker, 4½ m N of A27 Drusillas r'about. From A27 Drusillas r'about through Berwick Station to Upper Dicker & L into Camberlot Rd after The Plough Pub, we are 1m on the L. From the A22 we are 500yds down Camberlot Rd on the R.* **Sat 15, Sun 16 Aug (2-5). Adm £6, chd free. Home-made teas.**
A 3 acre country garden with a lovely view across fields and hills to the South Downs. Created from scratch over the last 7 yrs with all design, planting and maintenance by the owner. Lavender lined carriage driveway, naturalistic border, vegetable garden, shady garden, 30 metre white border and exotic garden. New part-walled garden and summerhouse with new planting. Wheelchair access over gravel drive and some uneven ground.

&. 🍵

26 51 CARLISLE ROAD
Eastbourne, BN21 4JR. Mr & Mrs N Fraser-Gausden. *200yds inland from seafront (Wish Tower), close to Congress Theatre.* **Sat 30, Sun 31 May (2-5). Adm £4, chd free. Home-made teas.**
Small walled, s-facing garden (82ft x 80ft) with mixed beds intersected by stone paths and incl small pool. Profuse and diverse planting. Wide selection of shrubs, old roses, herbaceous plants and perennials mingle with specimen trees and climbers. Constantly revised planting to maintain the magical and secluded atmosphere.

 ※ 🍵

27 CAXTON MANOR
Wall Hill, Forest Row, RH18 5EG. Adele & Jules Speelman. *1m N of Forest Row, 2m S of East Grinstead. From A22 take turning to Ashurstwood, entrance on L after ⅓ m, or 1m on R from N.* **Fri 15, Sat 16 May (2-5). Adm £5, chd free. Home-made teas.** Donation to St Catherine's Hospice, Crawley.
Delightful 5 acre Japanese inspired gardens planted with mature rhododendrons, azaleas and acers surrounding large pond with boathouse, massive rockery and waterfall, beneath the home of the late Sir Archibald McIndoe (house not open). Japanese tea house and Japanese style courtyard. **Also open 2 Quarry Cottages (separate admission).**

※ 🚗 🍵

28 CHAMPS HILL
Waltham Park Road, Coldwaltham, Pulborough, RH20 1LY. Mr & Mrs David Bowerman, info@thebct.org.uk, www.thebct.org.uk. *3m S of Pulborough. On A29 turn R to Fittleworth into Waltham Park Rd, garden 400 metres on R.* **Sun 17 May, Sun 9 Aug (2-5). Adm £5, chd free. Tea. Visits also by arrangement Apr to Sept for groups of 10+.**
A natural landscape, the garden has been developed around three disused sand quarries, with far-reaching views across the Amberley Wildbrooks to the South Downs. A woodland walk in spring, leads you past beautiful sculptures against a backdrop of colourful rhododendrons and azaleas. In summer the garden is a colourful tapestry of heathers, which are renowned for their abundance and variety.

&. 🚗 🍵

29 CHANNEL VIEW
52 Brook Barn Way, Goring-by-Sea, Worthing, BN12 4DW. Jennie & Trevor Rollings, 01903 242431, tjrollings@gmail.com. *1m W of Worthing, near seafront. Turn S off A259 into Parklands Ave, L at T-junction into Alinora Crescent. Brook Barn Way is immed on L.* **Visits by arrangement May to Sept for groups of 5 to 30. Adm £5, chd free. Home-made teas.**
A seaside Tudor cottage garden, cleverly blending the traditional, antipodean and subtropical with dense planting, secret rooms and intriguing sight-lines. Sunny patios,

insect friendly flowers and unusual structures supporting over 100 roses, clematis and other climbers, as well as brick and flint paths inlaid with thundereggs, radiating from a wildlife pond in the heart of the garden. Numerous planted hanging baskets and containers, sinuous beds packed with flowers and foliage, with underplanting to ensure a 3D experience. Lots of unusual plants for sale. Partial wheelchair access.

30 CHIDMERE GARDENS
Chidham Lane, Chidham, Chichester, PO18 8TD. Jackie & David Russell, www.chidmerefarm.com. *6m W of Chichester on A259. Turn into Chidham Lane, continue until a RH-bend, followed by a 2nd RH-bend. Chidmere Gardens is on the L immed after the large village pond.* **Thur 4 June, Thur 10 Sept (2-5). Adm £5, chd free. Tea.**
Wisteria clad C15 house (not open) surrounded by yew and hornbeam hedges situated next to Chidmere pond; a natural wildlife preserve approx 5 acres. Garden incl formal rose garden, well stocked herbaceous borders, contemporary borders and 8 acres of orchards with wide selection of heritage and modern varieties of apples, pears and plums. Partial wheelchair access.

31 NEW 23 CLARENCE ROAD
Horsham, RH13 5SJ. Caron Gillet. *E of Horsham. From Cowfold A281 turn R on to B2180 Clarence Rd, No 23 is 50yds on L. Street parking free on Sundays. 10 min walk from Horsham station (east exit).* **Sat 6, Sun 7 June (10.30-4.30). Adm £3.50, chd free. Home-made teas. Dairy & gluten free cakes.**
A pretty, mature, 100ft garden full of colourful perennials and shrubs bordering a curvaceous lawn. Slowly moving towards being more wildlife friendly with the recent addition of a natural pond. Good size vegetable plot for fruit and fresh produce. Plenty of seating offered under the shade of a mature grape vine and passion flower. Fragrant, shady seating area near house (not open) with containerised ferns.

32 ◆ CLINTON LODGE
Fletching, TN22 3ST. Lady Collum, 01825 722952, garden@clintonlodge.com, www.clintonlodgegardens.co.uk. *4m NW of Uckfield. Clinton Lodge is situated in Fletching High St, N of Rose & Crown Pub. Off road parking provided. It is important visitors do not park in street. Parking available from 1pm. Gardens open 2pm.* **For NGS: Sun 3 May, Mon 8, Mon 22 June, Mon 3 Aug (2-5.30). Adm £6, chd free. Home-made teas. For other opening times and information, please phone, email or visit garden website.** Donation to local charities.
6 acre formal and romantic garden overlooking parkland with old roses, William Pye water feature, double white and blue herbaceous borders, yew hedges, pleached lime walks, copy of C17 scented herb garden, Medieval style potager, vine and rose allée, wild flower garden. Canal garden, small knot garden, shady glade and orchard. Caroline and Georgian house (not open).

33 COOKSCROFT
Bookers Lane, Earnley, Chichester, PO20 7JG. Mr & Mrs J Williams, 01243 513671, williams. cookscroft330@btinternet.com, www.cookscroft.co.uk. *6m S of Chichester. At end of Birdham Straight A286 from Chichester, take L fork to East Wittering B2198. 1m before sharp bend, turn L into Bookers Lane, 2nd house on L. Parking available.* **Sat 9, Wed 13 May (11-4). Light refreshments. Evening opening Sat 13 June (5-9). Wine. Adm £5, chd free. Visits also by arrangement Apr to Sept for groups of up to 30.**
A garden for all seasons which delights the visitor. Started in 1988, it features cottage, woodland and Japanese style gardens, water features and borders of perennials with a particular emphasis on southern hemisphere plants. Unusual plants for the plantsman to enjoy, many grown from seed. The differing styles of the garden flow together making it easy to wander anywhere. The garden has grass paths and unfenced ponds.

St Mary's House Gardens

© Judi Lion

34 COPYHOLD HOLLOW

Copyhold Lane, Borde Hill, Haywards Heath, RH16 1XU. Frances Druce, 01444 413265, ngs@copyholdhollow.co.uk, *2m N of Haywards Heath. Follow signs for Borde Hill Gardens. With Borde Hill Gardens on L over brow of hill, take 1st R signed Ardingly. Garden ½m. If the drive is full, please park in the lane.* **Mon 25 May (12-4). Adm £4, chd free. Home-made teas. Visits also by arrangement May & June.**
A different NGS experience in 2 n-facing acres. The cottage garden surrounding C16 house (not open) gives way to steep slopes up to woodland garden, a challenge to both visitor and gardener. Species primulas a particular interest of the owner. Stumpery. Not a manicured plot, but with a relaxed attitude to gardening, an inspiration to visitors.

❀ ☕

GROUP OPENING

35 NEW CROWBOROUGH GARDENS

Myrtle Road, Crowborough, TN6 1EY. *Crowborough is 10m S of Tunbridge Wells on A26. All gardens close to town centre. Please park in town centre public car parks.* **Thur 18 June (1-5). Combined adm £6, chd free. Home-made teas.**

NEW **BELLEMARIE**
Glenn & Allison Ford.

NEW **HOATH COTTAGE**
Frances Arrowsmith.

NEW **8 MILL LANE**
Brenda Smart.

NEW **MOLE END**
Pauline Bastick.

NEW **SWEET SPRINGS**
Janet Gamba.

Crowborough is the highest inland town in East Sussex on the edge of Ashdown Forest. Five gardens are opening, four of which are within easy walking distance of the town centre. Please use the central car parks as parking near these gardens is difficult. Hoath Cottage is an informal garden dedicated to encouraging and supporting wildlife and features an extraordinary mature beech tree. 8 Mill Lane is a compact lawned garden with clematis walk, and well stocked borders with shrubs and perennials. Mole End owned by a member of the Hardy Plant Society, is a garden for all seasons, with deep borders, vegetable and fruit garden, and a beehive. Sweet Springs, has an extensively planted large garden wrapped around the cottage, with vastly different soil conditions throughout. The fifth garden is approx 1m from the town centre and does require use of a car; on street parking. Bellemarie is a visual extravaganza, a small garden providing a colourful taste of the Caribbean. Home-made teas in the Gallery Cafe, Crowborough Community Centre, Pine Grove, TN6 1FE

❀ ☕

---

36 CUPANI GARDEN

8 Sandgate Close, Seaford, BN25 3LL. Dr D Jones & Ms A Jones OBE, 01323 899452, sweetpeasa52@gmail.com, www.cupanigarden.com. *From A259 follow signs to Alfriston, E of Seaford. R off the Alfriston Rd onto Hillside Ave, 2nd L,1st R & 1st R. Park in adjoining streets. Bus 12A Brighton/Eastbourne, get off Millberg Rd stop & walk down alley to the garden.* **Visits by arrangement July & Aug for groups of up to 10. Adm £7, chd free. Light refreshments.**
Cupani is a tranquil haven with a delightful mix of trees, shrubs and perennial borders in different themed beds. Courtyard garden, gazebo, summerhouse, water features, sweet pea obelisks, and a huge range of plants. See TripAdvisor reviews. Garden undergoing major renovation in 2020 so closed for open days, but we welcome private visits, for small numbers of visitors. Delicious afternoon tea and a good range of lunches. Vegetarian, vegan and gluten free options. See menu on our website. Plants, jams, and china for sale. Not suitable for wheelchairs, steps to courtyard and steep steps to WC.

🐕 ❀ ♿ ☕

Twyford, 35 Dorset Avenue, East Grinstead Town Gardens

37 NEW **D & S HAUS**
41 Torton Hill Road, Arundel, BN18 9HF. **Darrell Gale & Simon Rose.** *1m SW of Arundel town square. From A27 Ford Rd/ Chichester Rd r'about, take exit to Ford & immed turn R into Torton Hill Rd. Continue uphill & at the large oak tree, keep L & we are on the L going down the hill.* **Sun 26 July (12-5). Adm £4.50, chd free. Home-made teas.**
A lush suburban garden, 25ft x 200ft, which the owners have transformed over the yrs. Both front and rear gardens contain a mass of palms, bananas, bamboos and all manner of spiky and large lush leaves. Rules are not followed, as the delights of colour, shape and texture have driven its design, with desert plants next to bog plants, a pond, stream and raised flint bed. Many quirky sculptures. Lush tropical planting and many unusual plants and features. No wheelchair access as many steps, narrow areas and gravel.
✿ ☕

38 **DACHS**
Spear Hill, Ashington, RH20 3BA. **Bruce Wallace, 01903 892466, wallacebuk@aol.com.** *Approx 6m N of Worthing. From A24 at Ashington onto B2133 Billingshurst Rd, R into Spear Hill. We are the 1st house, garden runs along Billingshurst Rd. Do not go up Spear Hill as we are at the bottom.* **Visits by arrangement Apr to Sept for groups of 10+. Optional talk on the garden & gardening tips. Adm £4.50, chd free. Home-made teas.**
A waterlogged field turned into a beautiful garden of about 2 acres incl white garden, bog area and stream. Over 250 varieties of daffodil and narcissus, with more added each year. AGM varieties for sale. Free gifts for children to encourage them to grow things and a number of plants for sale. Disabled parking by house on tarmac drive and access to the rear patio by ramp. No steps.
 🐄 ✿ 🚗 ☕

39 **DALE PARK HOUSE**
Madehurst, Arundel, BN18 0NP. **Robert & Jane Green, 01243 814260, robertgreen@farming.co.uk.** *4m W of Arundel. Take A27 E from Chichester or W from Arundel, then A29 (London) for 2m, turn L to Madehurst & follow red arrows.* **Visits by arrangement June &**

July for groups of 10+. Adm £4.50, chd free. Home-made teas. Set in parkland, enjoying magnificent views to the sea. Come and relax in the large walled garden which features an impressive 200ft herbaceous border. There is also a sunken gravel garden, mixed borders, a small rose garden, dreamy rose and clematis arches, interesting collection of hostas, foliage plants and shrubs, an orchard and kitchen garden. Wheelchair access not easy.
♿ ✿ 🚗 ☕

40 **70 DALE VIEW**
Hove, BN3 8LB. **Chris & Tony Ashby-Steed.** *1m from Hove junction of A27. From the Hove junction of A27, at the r'about take A2038 towards Hove. Continue down to mini-r'about by Grenadier Pub & take 2nd exit into West Way. Dale View is 1st L after zebra crossing.* **Sat 18, Sun 19 July (11-5). Adm £5, chd free. Home-made teas.**
Star of C4's Gogglebox for 5 yrs, Chris Ashby-Steed and husband Tony have completely re-landscaped their garden (100ft by 40ft) over the last 4 yrs. It shows lush and full planting across several zones and seating areas. Surrounded by mature trees, highlights incl herbaceous borders, fountain, rose garden, shady garden and terraced raised beds, with interest from spring through to late autumn. We will be providing a variety of teas, coffees and soft drinks as well as a fabulous array of home-made cakes, including gluten-free and vegan.
🐄 ✿ ☕

41 **47 DENMANS LANE**
Lindfield, Haywards Heath, RH16 2JN. **Sue & Jim Stockwell, 01444 459363, jamesastockwell@aol.com, www. lindfield-gardens.co.uk/47denmans-lane.** *Approx 1½m NE of Haywards Heath town centre. From Haywards Heath train station follow B2028 signed Lindfield & Ardingly for 1m. At T-lights turn L into Hickmans Lane, then after 100 metres take 1st R into Denmans Lane.* **Visits by arrangement Mar to Sept for groups of 5+. Adm £8, chd free. Home-made teas incl. Call to discuss wine & canapé options, & visits combined with Lindfield Jungle.**
This beautiful and tranquil 1 acre garden was described by Sussex

Life as a 'Garden Where Plants Star'. Created by the owners, Sue and Jim Stockwell, over the past 20 yrs, it is planted for interest throughout the yr. Spring bulbs are followed by azaleas, rhododendrons, roses and herbaceous perennials. The garden also incl ponds, vegetable and fruit gardens. NB: Deep water. Most of the garden accessible by wheelchair, but some steep slopes.
♿ ✿ 🚗 ☕

42 **DOWN PLACE**
South Harting, Petersfield, GU31 5PN. **Mr & Mrs D M Thistleton-Smith, 01730 825374, selina@downplace.co.uk.** *1m SE of South Harting. B2141 to Chichester, turn L down unmarked lane below top of hill.* **Sat 4, Sun 5 Apr, Sun 14, Mon 15 June (1.30-5.30). Adm £5, chd free. Home-made & cream teas. Visits also by arrangement Apr to July for groups of 10+. Refreshments by prior request. Donation to The Friends of Harting Church.**
Set on the South Downs with panoramic views out to the undulating wooded countryside. A garden which merges seamlessly into its surrounding landscape with rose and herbaceous borders that have been moulded into the sloping ground. There is a well stocked vegetable garden and walks shaded by beach trees which surround the natural wild meadow in which various native orchids flourish. Substantial top terrace and borders accessible to wheelchairs.
♿ ✿ ☕

We help ordinary people open the gates to their extraordinary private gardens to raise impressive amounts of money through admissions, teas and slices of cake!

43 DRIFTWOOD

4 Marine Drive, Bishopstone,
Seaford, BN25 2RS.
Geoff Stonebanks & Mark
Glassman, 01323 899296,
geoffstonebanks@gmail.com,
www.driftwoodbysea.co.uk. *A259
between Seaford & Newhaven. Turn
L into Marine Drive from Bishopstone
Rd, 2nd on R. Only park same
side as house please, not on bend
beyond the drive.* Tue 2, Tue 16,
Tue 30 June, Tue 14, Thur 30
July (11-5). Adm £6, chd free.
Light refreshments. Visits also
by arrangement June & July for
groups of up to 20. Guided tour
included. Light refreshments.
Driftwood celebrates its 10th year
opening for NGS. Monty Don
introduced Geoff's garden on BBC
Gardeners' World with these words,
a small garden by the sea, full of
character, with inspired planting and
design. Francine Raymond proclaimed
in the Sunday Telegraph that Geoff's
enthusiasm is catching, he and his
amazing garden deserve every visitor
that makes their way up his enchanting
garden path. Countless amazing
TripAdvisor visitor's comments,
awarded 3rd successive Certificate of
Excellence 2019 for over 100 five-star
reviews. Large selection of Geoff's
home-made cakes and savoury items
available, all served on vintage china,
on trays, in the garden. Access over
steep drive, narrow paths and many
levels with steps. Help readily available
on-site or call ahead before visit.

44 DURFORD ABBEY BARN

Petersfield, GU31 5AU. Mr & Mrs
Lund. *3m from Petersfield. Situated
on the S side of A272 between
Petersfield & Rogate, 1m from the
junction with B2072. Limited parking
by house.* Sat 13, Sun 14 June
(2-5.30). Adm £4, chd free. Home-
made teas.
With lovely views across open
countryside to the South Downs,
this 1 acre garden is set around a
converted barn in the National Park.
It has distinct levels and areas incl
cottage garden with rose arches
and herbaceous borders, a natural
pond, shady vine covered pergola,
productive vegetable terrace, lawns
and shrubberies, prairie border,
and seating placed to enjoy the
surroundings. Partial wheelchair
access as some areas have quite
steep grass slopes to negotiate.

45 DURRANCE MANOR

Smithers Hill Lane, Shipley,
RH13 8PE. Gordon & Joan
Lindsay, 01403 741577,
galindsay@gmail.com. *7m SW
of Horsham. A24 to A272 (S from
Horsham, N from Worthing), turn W
towards Billingshurst. Approx 1¾ m,
2nd L Smithers Hill Lane signed to
Countryman Pub. Garden 2nd on L.*
Mon 31 Aug (12-6). Adm £6, chd
free. Home-made teas. Visits also
by arrangement Apr to Oct.
This 2 acre garden surrounding
a Medieval hall house (not open)
with Horsham stone roof, enjoys
uninterrupted views over a ha-ha of
the South Downs and Chanctonbury
Ring. There are many different
gardens here, Japanese inspired
gardens, a large pond, wildflower
meadow and orchard, colourful long
borders, hosta walk, and vegetable
garden. There is also a Monet style
bridge over a pond with waterlilies.

GROUP OPENING

46 EAST GRINSTEAD TOWN GARDENS

*7m E of Crawley on A264 & 14m N
of Uckfield on A22. Tickets & maps
at each garden. Parking at The
Meads Primary School (RH19 4DD)
for 4 of the gardens. Imberhorne
Lane Public Car Park 75yds away
for Imberhorne Allotments, disabled
parking on-site.* Sun 16 Aug (12-5).
Combined adm £6, chd free.
Home-made teas.

NEW IMBERHORNE ALLOTMENTS

RH19 1TX. Imberhorne
Allotment Association,
www.imberhorneallotments.org.

27 MILL WAY

RH19 4DD. Jeff Dyson.

29 MILL WAY

RH19 4DD. Dee & Richard Doyle.

16 MUSGRAVE AVENUE

RH19 4BS. Carole & Bob Farmer.

7 NIGHTINGALE CLOSE

RH19 4DG. Gail & Andy Peel.

TWYFORD, 35 DORSET AVENUE

RH19 2AB. Norman & Julie
Mockford.

Gardens to lift the spirits and make
you smile! Established gardens,
displaying a mix of planting incl

shrubs, perennials, dahlias and
annuals, tubs and baskets. Three
are past winners of East Grinstead in
Bloom Best Front Garden, the back
gardens have quite different styles.
16 Musgrave Avenue has a thriving
vegetable garden. 7 Nightingale Close
is on heavy clay in a frost pocket
going down to a stream (no access),
plus a potager and collection of
bonsai. Twyford, 35 Dorset Avenue
has an eclectic mix of garden rooms
and soft fruit. Imberhorne Allotments
consist of 80 plots with a diverse
mix of planting incl grape vines, fruit,
flowers and a community orchard.
The enthusiastic owners are keen
propagators, growing from seed,
cuttings and plugs, sharing their
surplus plants. Plenty of advice
available and plants for sale at several
gardens. The Town Council hanging
baskets and planting in the High St
are not to be missed and achieved
a Gold Medal in 2019 from South
and South East in Bloom. For steam
train fans, the Bluebell Railway starts
nearby. Partial wheelchair access at
some gardens.

47 54 ELMLEIGH

Midhurst, GU29 9HA. Wendy
Liddle, 07796 562275,
wendyliddle@btconnect.com. *¼
W of Midhurst off A272. Reserved
disabled parking at the top of the
drive, please phone on arrival for
assistance.* Sat 23, Sun 24, Mon
25 May, Sats & Suns 6, 7, 20, 21
June; 4, 5, 18, 19 July; 1, 2 Aug
(10-5). Adm £4, chd free. Home-
made teas & cream teas. Visits
also by arrangement May to Aug
for groups of 10 to 30. Donation
to Chestnut Tree House, The King's
Arms & Raynaud's Association.
⅕ acre property with terraced front
garden, leading to a heavily planted
rear garden with majestic 100 yr old
Black Pines. Shrubs, perennials,
packed with interest around every
corner, providing all season colours.
Many raised beds, numerous
sculptures, vegetables in boxes, a
greenhouse, pond, and hedgehogs
in residence. A large collection of
tree lilies, growing 8-10ft. Child
friendly. Come and enjoy the peace
and tranquility in this award-winning
garden, our little bit of heaven. Not
suitable for electric buggies.

48 NEW 29 FAIRLIGHT AVENUE

Hastings, TN35 5HS. Peggy Harvey & Barbara Martin. *From Hastings seafront take A259 (Old London Rd) to Ore village. Turn R into Fairlight Rd at Co-op store by T-lights, continue along road, 1st R, 300 metres, into Fairlight Ave. Park on roadside. 2½ m from 96 Ashford Rd.* **Sat 23 May (12-5). Adm £3, chd free. Home-made teas. Also open 96 Ashford Road.**

A stunning, small and interesting low maintenance tropical garden newly created by the owners. Island planting with palms, yuccas and other blade shape leaf plants with shingle walkways throughout. In contrast, a smaller wildlife garden to the rear with pond and varied planting for birds and insects. The front garden is designed as a seascape with slate river run, sandstone rocks and seaside planting.

49 FAIRLIGHT END

Pett Road, Pett, Hastings, TN35 4HB. Chris & Robin Hutt, 07774 863750, chrishutt@fairlightend.co.uk, www.fairlightend.co.uk. *4m E of Hastings. From Hastings take A259 to Rye. At White Hart Beefeater turn R into Friars Hill. Descend into Pett village. Park in village hall car park, opp house.* **Sun 7 June (11-5). Adm £6, chd free. Home-made teas. Also open Breanross.**

Visits also by arrangement May to Sept for groups of 10+. Donation to Pett Village Hall.

Gardens Illustrated said 'The 18th century house is at the highest point in the garden with views down the slope over abundant borders and velvety lawns that are punctuated by clusters of specimen trees and shrubs. Beyond and below are the wildflower meadows and the ponds with a backdrop of the gloriously unspoilt Wealden landscape'. Wheelchair access with steep paths, gravelled areas, and unfenced ponds.

50 NEW FIELD PLACE MANOR HOUSE & BARNS

The Boulevard, Worthing, BN13 1NP. Southdowns Leisure Enterprises, 01903 446401, Events@fieldplace.co.uk, www.fieldplace.co.uk. *Field Place is 5 mins walk from Durrington railway station.* **Sun 19 July (11-4). Adm £4, chd free. Light refreshments.**

Visits also by arrangement in July.

The beautiful new wedding gardens designed by Juliet Sargeant, who won gold at Chelsea Flower Show, will open for the NGS for the first time. There are several rooms, which will bloom at different times of the year, so there will always be something changing in the garden and new plants coming to life. If you are with friends, or just want a quiet moment to yourself, you will be able to find a pleasant spot amongst the colourful plants and scented flowers. Dogs on leads please.

51 FITTLEWORTH HOUSE

Bedham Lane, Fittleworth, Pulborough, RH20 1JH. Edward & Isabel Braham, 01798 865074, marksaunders66.com@gmail.com, www.racingandgreen.com. *2m E, SE of Petworth. Midway between Petworth & Pulborough on the A283 in Fittleworth, turn into lane by sharp bend signed Bedham. Garden is 50yds along on the L.* **Weds 22, 29 Apr; 6, 13 May; 10, 17 June; 15, 22 July; 12, 19 Aug (2-5). Adm £5, chd free. Home-made teas. Also open The Grange (22 Apr, 13 May, 10 June, 15 July). Visits also by arrangement Apr to Aug for groups of 10+. Tours of the garden last approx 1-2 hrs.**

3 acre tranquil, romantic country garden featuring working walled kitchen garden growing a wide range of fruit, vegetables and flowers. Large glasshouse and old potting shed, mixed flower borders, roses, rhododendrons and lawns. Magnificent 115ft tall Cedar overlooks wisteria covered Grade II listed Georgian house (not open). Wild garden and pond, new stream and rock garden. The garden sits on a gentle slope, but is accessible for wheelchairs and buggies. Non-disabled WC.

Field Place Manor, House & Barns

© Judi Lion

52 FIVE OAKS COTTAGE

Petworth, RH20 1HD. Jean & Steve Jackman, 07939 272443, jeanjackman@hotmail.com. *5m S of Pulborough. SatNav does not work! To ensure best route, we will provide printed directions at time of booking.* **Visits by arrangement the first two weeks of July for groups of up to 30. Adm £5, chd free. Home-made teas.**

An acre of delicate jungle surrounding an Arts and Crafts style cottage (not open), with stunning views of the South Downs. Our unconventional garden is designed to encourage maximum wildlife, with a knapweed and hogweed meadow on clay attracting clouds of butterflies in July, plus two small ponds and lots of seating. An award-winning, organic garden with a magical atmosphere. Please call or email us now to arrange!

GROUP OPENING

53 FLETCHING SECRET GARDENS

High Street, Fletching, Uckfield, TN22 3SS. *4m NW of Uckfield. Park at Church Farm, Church St, TN22 3SP for 2 gardens. Head N out of High St for Searles & Holmesdale Oast, after approx 2m take R at junction into Bell Lane, continue approx ½ m, TN22 3YB.* **Sat 11 July (12-5). Combined adm £6, chd free. Home-made teas at Holmesdale Oast.**

> **HOLMESDALE OAST**
> Susanna Martin.
>
> **NEW SEARLES**
> David & Jane Sachon.
>
> **STONES**
> Belinda & David Croft.
>
> **4 WHITES COTTAGES**
> Philip & Joy Burchell.

In the heart of the picturesque village of Fletching, near the historic church there are two small, welcoming cottage style gardens, each with their own character. The garden at Stones is packed with interest in a relatively small space. Colourful hanging baskets and pots, vegetable plot, fruiting kiwi climber, cardoon bed and mistletoe. The edge of the garden is wild to provide habitat for birds and wildlife. 4 Whites Cottages has much packed into it, incl soft fruit,

cottage flowers, shrubs and herbs, plus an observatory. Holmesdale Oast is a pleasant surprise. Situated out of the main village off Bell Lane, down a track, a cottage garden with a difference, with a restored deep Oast pond and a sandstone bridge. Allow plenty of time to explore the nearby garden at Searles. Drive up the long drive, park by the house (not open). There is a large walled garden, vegetable garden, rose beds, large glasshouse, deep ponds and so much more. Both of these Bell Lane gardens come with much history. Partial wheelchair access to some parts of the gardens.

54 FOLLERS MANOR

White Way, Alfriston, BN26 5TT. Geoff & Anne Shaw, www.follersmanor.co.uk. *½ m S of Alfriston. From Alfriston uphill towards Seaford. Park on L in paddock before garden. Garden next door to old Alfriston Youth Hostel, immed before road narrows. Visitors with walking difficulties drop at gate.* **Sat 8, Sun 9 Aug (11-4). Adm £7, chd free. Home-made teas. Donation to Alzheimers Society.**

Contemporary garden designed by Ian Kitson attached to C17 listed historic farmhouse. Entrance courtyard, sunken garden, herbaceous displays, wildlife pond, wildflower meadows, woodland area and beautiful views of the South Downs. Winner of Sussex Heritage Trust Award and three awards from the Society of Garden Designers; Best Medium Residential Garden, Hard Landscaping and, most prestigious, the Judges Award. A newly designed area of the garden by original designer Ian Kitson completed 2019. Please No Dogs.

55 NEW FOREST RIDGE

Paddockhurst Lane, Balcombe, Haywards Heath, RH17 6QZ. Philip & Rosie Wiltshire, 01444 811890, rosiem.wiltshire@btinternet.com. *3m from M23, J10a. M23 J10a take B2036 to Balcombe. After ⅔m take 1st L onto B2110. After Worth School turn R into Back Lane. After 2m it becomes Paddockhurst Lane. Forest Ridge on R after 2¼m. Ignore SatNav to track!* **Sat 16, Sun 17 May (2-5.30). Adm £5, chd free. Home-made teas.**

On a ridge with far-reaching views,

site of the former home of the Balcombe family, a charming 4½ acre Victorian garden, boasting the oldest Atlantic Cedar in Sussex flanking the croquet lawn. Formal and informal planting, ponds, winding paths, woodland dell and mini arboretum. Azaleas, rhododendrons and camelia abound, many rare/unusual species. Owner maintained, restoring and redesigning areas.

56 FOXGLOVE COTTAGE

29 Orchard Road, Horsham, RH13 5NF. Peter & Terri Lefevre, 01403 256002, teresalefevre@outlook.com. *From Horsham station, over bridge, at r'about 3rd exit (signed Crawley),1st R Stirling Way, at end turn L, 1st R Orchard Rd. From A281, take Clarence Rd, at end turn R, at end turn L. Street parking.* **Sun 24 May, Sun 12 July, Sun 30 Aug (1-5). Adm £4.50, chd free. Home-made teas. Vegan, gluten & dairy free cake. Visits also by arrangement June to Aug for groups of 10+. Garden clubs & groups welcome.**

A surprising 150ft x 50ft plantaholic's garden, full of unusual containers, vintage finds and quirky elements. Gravel and bark paths dissect both sun and shade borders bursting with colourful planting. Salvias in abundance! A beach inspired summerhouse and deck are flanked by a water feature in a pebble circle. The end of the garden is dedicated to plant nursery, cut flowers and fruit growing. New wildlife pond for 2020. Plenty of seating in both sun and shade throughout the garden. Member of the Hardy Plant Society. A large selection of unusual plants for sale.

57 THE GARDEN HOUSE

5 Warleigh Road, Brighton, BN1 4NT. Bridgette Saunders & Graham Lee, 07729 037182, contact@gardenhousebrighton.co.uk, www.gardenhousebrighton.co.uk. *1½ m N of Brighton pier, Garden House is 1st L after the Xrds, past the open market. Paid street parking. London Road station nearby. Buses 26 & 46 stopping at Bromley Rd.* **Fri 28 Feb (12.30-3.30); Sat 25, Sun 26 Apr (11.30-4). Adm £5, chd free. Tea, coffee, hot soup & bread (Mar). Home-made teas (Apr). Visits also by arrangement**

Nymans

Mar to July for groups of 10 to 30.
One of Brighton's secret gardens. We
aim is to provide yr-round interest with
trees, shrubs, herbaceous borders
and annuals, fruit and vegetables, two
glasshouses, a pond and rockery. A
friendly garden, always changing with
a touch of magic to delight visitors,
above all it is a slice of the country in
the midst of a bustling city. Garden
produce and plants for sale.

58 GARDEN HOUSE, 49 GUILLARDS OAK

Midhurst, GU29 9JZ. Mr & Mrs
David Christie, 01730 813323,
pattychristie49@gmail.com. *Leave
Midhurst on the A272 towards
Petersfield. Guillards Oak is the wide
opening on the L, halfway up the hill
before the pelican crossing. Entrance
to garden through the green gate.*
**Sun 17 May, Sun 9 Aug (1-5). Adm
£5, chd free. Home-made teas.
Visits also by arrangement Apr to**

Aug for groups of 5 to 20.
This ¼ acre garden was changed in
2012 from an expanse of lawn under
trees to a parterre with clematis,
roses and trained fruit on arches to
become the view from the s-facing
house. Busy greenhouse, grand
design style fruit cage, wendy house
and bug palace, connected by a
small woodland walk under a huge
Swamp Cypress, Banksia rose and
trachelospermum climbing up the
house. Teas will be served on the
terrace overlooking the garden.

59 THE GARDEN HOUSE, CROWBOROUGH

Burnt Oak Road, Burnt Oak,
Nr Crowborough, TN6 3SD.
**Mrs Jane Smith, 01892 654301,
janemanchoo@icloud.com.** *From
Crowborough town centre, turn R
into Croft Rd, continue into Whitehill
Rd. At end of road, straight across
r'about into Alice Bright Lane, this*
*will lead into Burnt Oak Rd. House
¾m on L.* **Fri 12, Sat 13 June
(1-5). Adm £5, chd free. Light
refreshments. Sat 5, Sun 6 Sept
(11-4). Adm by donation. Tea.
Visits also by arrangement June to
Sept for groups of 10 to 30.**
3 acre garden set in rural countryside,
designed by award-winning Juliet
Sergeant. The garden is divided into
different rooms starting at the front
with fun topiary, large trees and a
wildflower meadow, leading to the
white courtyard, formal rose garden,
feature flower beds, rhododendron
walk, and veggies. Mature trees and
hedges and clever sculptures makes
for interesting surprises. Unusual
sculptures and objects placed around
the garden. Water features both
formal and for wildlife. Quiet places to
sit and enjoy the seasons and colours
while enjoying tea, coffee, and home-
made cakes. Crowborough Arts Open
Studios on 5 & 6 Sept.

60 NEW **GORSELANDS**
Common Hill, West Chiltington, Pulborough, RH20 2NL. Philip Maillou. *12m N of Worthing. Approx 1m N of Storrington. Take either School Hill or Old Mill Drive from Storrington. 2nd L on to Fryern Rd to West Chiltington & continue on to Common Hill. Gorselands is on the R. Roadside parking.* **Sun 28 June, Sun 5 July (2-5). Adm £4, chd free. Home-made teas.**
Approx ¾ acre garden featuring mature mixed borders, dahlia garden, fruit area, woodland area with giant Redwood, camellias, azaleas, rhododendrons and two ponds. There will be a small selection of oil paintings for sale by Oxfordshire artist Jackie Hughes, ranging from landscapes to still life. Wheelchair access on sloping garden with short grass.

&♿ 🐄 ✿ ☕

61 **THE GRANGE**
Hesworth Lane, Fittleworth, Pulborough, RH20 1EW. Mr & Mrs W Caldwell. *3m W of Pulborough. From Pulborough or Petworth on reaching Fittleworth turn S onto B2138, then W at Swan Pub. From the S, turn L off A29 onto B2138 at Bury Gate, then L again at Swan Pub. For Satnav use RH20 1EN.* **Wed 22 Apr, Wed 13 May, Wed 10 June, Wed 15 July (2-5). Adm £5, chd free. Home-made teas. Also open Fittleworth House.**
3 acre garden gently sloping to the River Rother surrounding pretty C18 house (not open). Formal areas enclosed by yew hedges comprising colour themed beds, small orchard and herbaceous borders containing a wide variety of interesting plants. A wide variety of tulips planted for 2020. The garden has gravel paths.

&♿ 🐄 ☕

We open the gates to the nation's best gardens, offering a relaxing, memorable and affordable day out. A perfect experience to share with friends and family.

62 ♦ **GREAT DIXTER HOUSE, GARDENS & NURSERIES**
Northiam, TN31 6PH. Great Dixter Charitable Trust, 01797 253107, groupbookings@greatdixter.co.uk, www.greatdixter.co.uk. *8m N of Rye. Off A28 in Northiam, follow brown signs.* **For NGS: Fri 17 Apr (11-5.30). Adm £13, chd free. Light refreshments. For other opening times and information, please phone, email or visit garden website.**
Designed by Edwin Lutyens and Nathaniel Lloyd. Christopher Lloyd made the garden one of the most experimental and constantly changing gardens of our time, a tradition now being carried on by Fergus Garrett. Clipped topiary, wildflower meadows, the famous long border, pot displays, exotic garden and more. Spring bulb displays are of particular note. Regional Finalist, The English Garden's The Nation's Favourite Gardens 2019. Please see garden website for accessibility information.

✿ 🚌 ☕

63 **GREAT LYWOOD FARMHOUSE**
Lindfield Road, Ardingly, RH17 6SW. Richard & Susan Laing, 01444 892500, splaing@btinternet.com. *2½m N of Haywards Heath. Between Lindfield & Ardingly on B2028. From Lindfield, after approx 2m turn L down signed paved track. 1st house on R, car park beyond house.* **Fri 22, Mon 25 May (2-6). Adm £6, chd free. Home-made teas. Visits also by arrangement May & June for groups of 10 to 30.**
Approx 1½ acre garden surrounding C17 Sussex farmhouse (not open). The extensive but accessible and gentle terracing provides immediate views of many different aspects of the garden and distant views towards the South Downs. There are garden seats on every level making this a garden in which to rest and enjoy the countryside. Wheelchair access possible, some slopes and short grass.

&♿ 🐄 ✿ ☕

64 NEW **GROVELANDS**
Wineham Lane, Wineham, Henfield, BN5 9AW. Mrs Amanda Houston. *8m SW Haywards Heath. From Haywards Heath A272 W approx 6m, then L into Wineham Lane. House 1¾m on L after Royal Oak Pub. 3m NE Henfield N on A281, R onto B2116 Wheatsheaf Rd, L into Wineham Lane. House ½m*
on R. **Sat 4, Sun 5 July, Sat 5, Sun 6 Sept (11-5). Adm £5, chd free. Home-made teas.**
A South Downs view welcomes you to this rural garden set in over an acre in the hamlet of Wineham. Created and developed by local landscape designer Sue McLaughlin and the owners, it is designed to delight throughout the seasons. Features include mixed borders, mature shrubs and an orchard. A vegetable garden with greenhouse, cutting flower area and pond hide behind a tall clipped hornbeam hedge.

🐄 🐕 ☕

65 **HAM COTTAGE**
Hammingden Lane, Highbrook, Ardingly, RH17 6SR. Peter & Andrea Browne, 01444 892746, aegbrowne@btinternet.com, hamcottage.com. *5m N of Haywards Heath. On B2028 1m S of Ardingly turn L into Burstow Hill Lane signed Highbrook, then follow NGS signs.* **Sat 9, Sun 10 May (2-5). Adm £5, chd free. Home-made teas. Visits also by arrangement May to Sept for groups of up to 30.**
8 acre garden created during the last 30 yrs by the present owners. There is yr-round interest with colour bursting from the many borders, rhododendrons and winter garden. A stream flows through the bog garden down over waterfalls into a bluebell carpeted wood. There is an amphitheatre within an old sandstone quarry, and sculptures and mechanical contraptions giving added interest.

🐄 ✿ 🛏 ☕

66 NEW **THE HAMBLIN CENTRE**
Main Road, Bosham, Chichester, PO18 8PJ. The Hamblin Trust, 01243 572109, office@thehamblinvision.org.uk, www.hamblincentre.org.uk. *3m W of Chichester. The Hamblin Centre is on the R just after Bosham r'about going W on the A259, just before the r'about on the L going E. 10 mins walk from Bosham station. 700 Stagecoach bus stop is 2 mins walk.* **Sun 8 Mar, Sun 14 June, Sun 19 July (11-4.30). Adm £4.50, chd free. Home-made teas. Visits also by arrangement Mar to Oct for groups of 20 to 30.**
An ornamental and wildlife garden in harmony with the Hamblin Centre's work towards health and wellbeing. Shrubs, perennials, mature specimen

and fruit trees; including tulip tree and mulberry, a wildlife pond with bog garden, a wildflower meadow and a rock garden. Snowdrops, many varieties of daffodil and orchids. Boundary areas are left natural, providing a range of wildlife habitats. Guided garden tours. Plant nursery. Wheelchair access to most areas.

&♿ ❀ 🛏 ☕

67 HAMMERWOOD HOUSE

Iping, Midhurst, GU29 0PF. Mr & Mrs M Lakin. *3m W of Midhurst. Take A272 from Midhurst, approx 2m outside Midhurst turn R for Iping. From A3 leave for Liphook, follow B2070, turn L for Milland & Iping.* Sun 10, Sun 17 May (1.30-5). Adm £5, chd free. Home-made teas. Donation to Iping Church.

Large s-facing garden with lots of mature shrubs incl camellias, rhododendrons and azaleas. An arboretum with a variety of flowering and fruit trees. The old yew and beech hedges give a certain amount of formality to this traditional English garden. Tea on the terrace is a must with the most beautiful view of the South Downs. For the more energetic there is a woodland walk. Partial wheelchair access as garden is set on a slope.

♿ 🐕 ❀ ☕

68 HARBOURSIDE

Prinsted Lane, Prinsted, Southbourne, PO10 8HS. Ann Moss, 01243 370048, ann.moss@ngs.org.uk. *6m W of Chichester, 1m E of Emsworth. Turn L into Prinsted Lane off the A259. Chinese take away on corner. Follow lane until forced to the R past the Scout Hut car park. House is adjacent. Old boat & buoy with house name in front garden.* Visits by arrangement for groups of 10 to 30. Adm £4.50, chd free. Light refreshments.

Award-winning coastal garden takes you on a journey through garden styles from around the world. Visit the Mediterranean, France, Holland, New Zealand and Japan. Enjoy tree ferns, topiary, shady area, secret woodland parlour, potager, containers, unusual shrubs and plants, silver birch walk, herbaceous borders, art, crafts, wildlife, seaside garden, blue and white area. A garden with yr-round

colour and interest. Guided and explanatory tour of garden. Piped music and welcoming fire. Home-made refreshment options incl. lunch, supper, fizz and canapés. Plants and gardening items for sale. Wheelchair access to most of the garden, after 10ft of gravel at entrance.

♿ ❀ ☕

GROUP OPENING

69 HARLANDS GARDENS

Penland Road, Haywards Heath, RH16 1PH. *Follow the yellow signs from Balcombe Rd or Milton Rd & Bannister Way (Sainsbury's). Bus stop on Bannister Way (Route 30, 31, 39 & 80). Gardens within 5 min easy walk from train station & bus stop.* Sat 6, Sun 7 June (12-5). Combined adm £5, chd free. Home-made teas at 5 Sugworth Close.

52 PENLAND ROAD
Karen & Marcel van den Dolder.

55 PENLAND ROAD
Steve & Lisa Williams.

NEW **72 PENLAND ROAD**
Sarah Gray & Graham Delve.

5 SUGWORTH CLOSE
Lucy & Brian McCully.

27 TURNERS MILL ROAD

Sam & Derek Swanson.

We are thrilled to announce a new and additional garden into our trail for 2020. Our eclectic mix of town gardens designed, built and maintained by busy people continue to inspire and delight our visitors. This year we're opening slightly later so visitors can enjoy our summer gardens. We comprise awkward shapes and differing gradients, designed with relaxation and socialisation in mind. Our gardens offer rich cottage-style planting schemes, varied ponds, pretty courtyards, practical kitchen gardens and habitats for wildlife. Look out for interesting pots and carnivorous plants. Please check our Facebook page 'Harlands Gardens' for updated information. Our home-made cakes are always a joy including an outstanding contribution from a 'Bake-off' contestant. Roadside parking is readily available. Park once to visit all gardens. Plants sale at 55 Penland Road. The quaint English villages of Cuckfield and Lindfield are worthy of a visit. Nymans (NT) and Wakehurst (Kew) are also nearby. Partial wheelchair access to all gardens.

♿ ❀ ☕

Fittleworth House

© Julie Skelton

Penns In The Rocks

© Leigh Clapp

GROUP OPENING

70 HASSOCKS VILLAGE GARDEN TRAIL

Hassocks, BN6 8EY. *6m N of Brighton, off A273. Gardens are E of Stonepound Xrds & 2m W of Ditchling, N & S of B2116. Trail can be walked. Hassocks train station nearby. Park on road or in free car parks. No parking in Parklands Rd.* **Sun 7 June (1-5). Combined adm £6, chd free. Home-made teas at United Reformed Church (1.15-5).**

13 CHANCELLORS PARK
Steve Richards & Pierre Voegeli.

2 OCKLEY LANE
Simon & Judith Amey.

PARKLANDS ROAD ALLOTMENTS
Tony Copeland & Jeannie Brooker.

The two gardens on this trail are quite different but each have a wide range of unusual plants and shrubs. One is well established, the other looks established but is relatively new. Excellent examples of use of space to incl seating places, winding paths and wonderful selections of plants. The 55 allotments are not to be missed, where a wide range of classic vegetables, plus some exotic vegetables grow. The allotmenteers will show you their plots and answer questions. There are spectacular views across the Downs and up to Jack and Jill Windmills, and an ancient woodland lies along the north side of the allotments. One of the few remaining chalk streams, the Herring Stream, flows through the village, where flash floods have occurred. Whilst on the trail, you can visit the rain gardens in Adastra Park, BN6 8QH that shows how house holders can reduce flash flooding by holding back rain water. WC also available. Dogs permitted at allotments only.

✿ ☕

GROUP OPENING

71 HELLINGLY PARISH TRAIL

Gardens are close by, Brook Cottage is 500 metres from Priors Grange. Parking field opp Brook Cottage, otherwise park in the roads & lanes around church. Follow yellow signs. Bus 51 from Eastbourne. **Sun 12 July (11-4). Combined adm £5, chd free. Ploughman's lunches & afternoon tea at Brook Cottage.**

BROADVIEW
BN27 4EX. Gill Riches.

BROOK COTTAGE
BN27 4HD. Dr Colin Tourle MBE & Mrs Jane Tourle.

PRIORS GRANGE
BN27 4EZ. Sylvia Stephens.

Three gardens will open in the small village of Hellingly with its Grade I listed church which has the oldest circ in the country. There are two examples of delightful cottage gardens, one of which wraps around a Grade II listed house (not open). The third garden is a green oasis of mature shrubs and trees surrounded by water (children must be supervised at all times) and a mill race. Great plant sale at Priors Grange. The Cuckoo Cycle Trail is nearby.

✿ ☕

72 ◆ HERSTMONCEUX CASTLE GARDENS AND GROUNDS

Herstmonceux, Hailsham, BN27 1RN. Bader International Study Centre, Queen's University (Canada), 01323 833816, c_harber@bisc.queensu.ac.uk, www.herstmonceux-castle.com. *Located between Herstmonceux & Pevensey on the Wartling Rd. From Herstmonceux take A271 to Bexhill, 2nd R signed Castle. Do not use SatNav.* For NGS: Sat 23 May (10-6). Adm £7, chd free. Last admission at 5pm. Cream teas & light lunches in Chestnuts Tearoom. For other opening times and information, please phone, email or visit garden website. Herstmonceux is renowned for its magnificent moated castle set in beautiful parkland and superb Elizabethan walled gardens, leading to delightful discoveries such as our rhododendron, rose and herb gardens and onto our woodland trails. Take a slow stroll past the lily covered lakes to the 1930s folly and admire the sheer magnificence of the castle. The gardens and grounds first opened for the NGS in 1927. Avenue of ancient chestnut trees. Concessions £6. Partial wheelchair access to formal gardens.

GROUP OPENING

73 HERSTMONCEUX PARISH TRAIL

4m NE of Hailsham. Tickets & map available at any garden. Please note this is not a walking trail. Sun 21 June (12-5). Combined adm £6, chd free. Teas & BBQ lunch at The Windmill.

THE ALLOTMENTS, STUNTS GREEN
BN27 4PP. Nicola Beart.

COWBEECH HOUSE
BN27 4JF. Mr Anthony Hepburn.

1 ELM COTTAGES
BN27 4RT. Audrey Jarrett.

MERRIE HARRIERS BARN
BN27 4JQ. Lee Henderson.

THE WINDMILL
BN27 4RT. Windmill Hill Windmill Trust, windmillhillwindmill.org/.

Four gardens and a historic windmill will open as part of the Herstmonceux Parish Trail. Cowbeech House, a place to linger, has an exciting range of water features and sculpture in the garden, dating back to 1731. Vintage car collection available to view. Merrie Harries Barn, is a garden with sweeping lawn and open countryside beyond. Colourful herbaceous planting and a large pond with places to sit and enjoy the view, this is a developing garden that 4 yrs ago was agricultural land. The Allotments comprise 54 allotments growing a huge variety of traditional and unusual crops. Park in the pub across the road from 1 Elm Cottages. 1 Elm Cottages is a stunning cottage garden packed full of edible and flowering plants you cannot afford to miss. From here a short stroll back towards the village will take you the historic Windmill that will be the venue for refreshment and plants for sale.

74 ◆ HIGH BEECHES WOODLAND AND WATER GARDEN

High Beeches Lane, Handcross, Haywards Heath, RH17 6HQ. High Beeches Gardens Conservation Trust, 01444 400589, gardens@highbeeches.com, www.highbeeches.com. *5m NW of Cuckfield. On B2110, 1m E of A23 at Handcross.* For NGS: Sun 7 June, Sun 4 Oct (1-5). Adm £8.50, chd £2. For other opening times and information, please phone, email or visit garden website. Donation to Plant Heritage.
25 acres of enchanting landscaped woodland and water gardens with spring daffodils, bluebells and azalea walks, many rare and beautiful plants, an ancient wildflower meadow and glorious autumn colours. Picnic area. National Collection of Stewartias.

75 ◆ HIGHDOWN GARDENS

33 Highdown Rise, Littlehampton Road, Goring-by-Sea, Worthing, BN12 6FB. Worthing Borough Council, 01903 501054, highdown. gardens@adur-worthing.gov.uk, www.highdowngardens.co.uk. *3m W of Worthing. Off the A259 approx 1m from Goring-by-Sea Train Station.* For NGS: Sun 2 Feb, Thur 19 Mar (10.30-4.30). Adm by donation. For other opening times and information, please phone, email or visit garden website.
Created by Sir Frederick Stern, these unique chalk gardens are situated on downland countryside and are home to a unique collection of rare plants and trees, with many raised from seed brought from China by great collectors like Wilson, Farrer and Kingdon-Ward. A colourful succession of spring bulbs such as snowdrops, crocus, daffodils, anemones and bluebells. We are delighted to again offer our popular spring bulb guided tours by the Head Gardener on 2 Feb only, for £2.50 at 11am, 12pm, 1pm, 2pm and 3pm. Partial wheelchair access to sloping hillside garden with mainly grass paths.

 NPC

76 4 HILLSIDE COTTAGES

Downs Road, West Stoke, Chichester, PO18 9BL. Heather & Chris Lock, 01243 574802, chlock@btinternet.com. *3m NW of Chichester. From A286 at Lavant, head W for 1½ m, nr Kingley Vale.* Wed 10 June (11-4); Sun 19 July (2-5). Adm £4, chd free. Home-made teas. Visits also by arrangement June & July.
Garden 120ft x 27ft in a rural setting, densely planted with mixed borders and shrubs. Large collection of roses, mainly New English shrub roses; walls, fences and arches covered with mid and late season clematis; baskets overflowing with fuchsias. A profusion of colour and scent in a well maintained small garden.

77 HOLLY HOUSE

Beaconsfield Road, Chelwood Gate, Haywards Heath, RH17 7LF. Mrs Deirdre Birchell, 01825 740484, db@hollyhousebnb.co.uk, www.hollyhousebnb.co.uk. *7m E of Haywards Heath. From Nutley village on A22 turn off at Hathi Restaurant signed Chelwood Gate 2m. Chelwood Gate Village Hall on R, Holly House is opp.* Mon 11 May, Thur 9 July, Sat 15, Sun 16 Aug (2-5). Adm £5, chd free. Home-made teas. Visits also by arrangement for groups of up to 30.
An acre of English garden providing views and cameos of plants and trees round every corner with many different areas giving constant interest. A fish pond and a wildlife pond beside a grassy area with many shrubs and flower beds. Among the trees and winding paths there is a cottage garden which is a profusion of colour and peace. Exhibition of paintings and cards by owner. Garden accessible by wheelchair in good weather, but it is not easy.

78 THE HUNDRED HOUSE

Pound Lane, Framfield, TN22 5RU.
Dr & Mrs Michael Gurney. *4m E of
Uckfield. From Uckfield take B2102
through Framfield. 1m from centre of
village turn L into Pound Lane, then
³/₄m on R. Disabled parking is close
by the entrance gate to the garden.*
Sat 18, Sun 19 July (2-5). Adm £5,
chd free. Home-made teas.
Delightful garden with panoramic
views, set in the grounds of the
historic The Hundred House (not
open). Fine stone ha-ha. 1½ acre
garden with mixed herbaceous
borders, productive vegetable garden,
greenhouse, ancient yew tree, pond
area with some subtropical plants,
secret woodland copse and orchard.
Beech hedge, field and butterfly walk,
silver birch (jacquemontii) grove under
development. Home-grown plants,
vegetables and fruit for sale.

& ☙ ✿ ☕

79 JACARANDA

Chalk Road, Ifold, RH14 0UE. Brian
& Barbara McNulty, 01403 751532,
bmcn0409@icloud.com. *1m S of
Loxwood. From A272/A281 take
B2133 (Loxwood). ½m S of Loxwood
take Plaistow Rd, then 3rd R into
Chalk Rd. Follow signs for parking &
garden. Wheelchair users can park in
driveway.* Sun 7 June (2-5). Adm £5,
chd free. Home-made teas. Visits
also by arrangement May to Sept
for groups of up to 20.
A plantaholic's garden created from
scratch over the past 20 yrs. Curved
borders take you on a journey around
a garden full of unusual shrubs, trees
with interesting bark, roses, climbers
and perennials. Hostas in pots are a
particular feature and are displayed
in many areas. In the vegetable
area there is a large raised bed, a
greenhouse and a hanging potting
bench. A garden for all seasons!

& ☙ ✿ ☕

80 KEMP TOWN ENCLOSURES: SOUTH GARDEN

Lewes Crescent, Brighton,
BN2 1FH. Kemp Town Enclosures
Ltd, kte.org.uk. *On S coast, 1m E
of Brighton Palace Pier, ½m W of
Brighton Marina. 2m from Brighton
station. Bus no 7, stop St Mary's
Hall. M23/A23 to Brighton Palace
Pier; L on A259. 5m S A27 on
B2123, R on A259.* Thur 11 June
(12-3.30). Adm £7.50. Tours every
30 mins from 12pm to 3.30pm (2
groups of 15 per tour) included.
Pre-booking essential, please

visit www.ngs.org.uk/events for
information & booking. Light
refreshments.
Unique historic Grade II listed Regency
private town garden in a spectacular
seaside location. Enduring strong
salty winds and thin chalk soil, the
garden balances naturalistic planting
and a more ordered look, relaxed not
manicured. With several distinctive
areas, this wonderful 5 acre garden
combines open lawns, winding paths,
trees, herbaceous and shrub borders
and a shaded woodland garden.
Designed by Henry Phillips in 1820s,
the garden was a central feature of
the Regency Development of the
Kemp Town Estate. Queen Victoria
and Edward VII walked in these
gardens. Lewis Carroll visited many
times and the garden tunnel is said to
have inspired the rabbit hole in 'Alice
in Wonderland'. Ramped gate entry.
Gravel winding paths give access to
most of the garden. Relatively steep
slopes on main lawn and in the garden
tunnel.

& ☕

81 ♦ KING JOHN'S LODGE

Sheepstreet Lane,
Etchingham, TN19 7AZ. Jill
Cunningham, 01580 819220,
harry@kingjohnsnursery.co.uk,
www.kingjohnsnursery.co.uk. *2m
W of Hurst Green. Off A265 near
Etchingham. From Burwash turn L
before Etchingham Church, from
Hurst Green turn R after church,
into Church Lane, which leads into
Sheepstreet Lane after ½m, then
L after 1m.* For NGS: Sun 29 Mar
(11-4); Sat 2, Sun 3 May, Sat 20,
Sun 21 June (11-5). Adm £5, chd
free. Home-made teas & lunches
in the tearoom of King John's
Nursery. For other opening times
and information, please phone,
email or visit garden website.
4 acre romantic garden for all
seasons. An ongoing family project
since 1987. From the eclectic shop,
nursery and tearoom, stroll past
wildlife pond through orchard with
bulbs, meadow, rose walk, and fruit
according to the season. Historic
house (not open) has broad lawn,
fountain, herbaceous border, pond,
and ha-ha. Explore secret woodland
with renovated pond, and admire
majestic trees and 4 acre meadows.
Small children's soft play. Garden
is mainly flat. Stepped areas can
usually be accessed from other areas.
Disabled WC.

& ☙ ✿ 🚗 🛏 ☕

82 NEW KITCHENHAM FARM

Kitchenham Road, Ashburnham,
Battle, TN33 9NP. Amanda &
Monty Worssam. *S of Ashburnham
Place. From A271 Herstmonceaux
to Battle Rd take L, turn ½m after
Boreham St bridge. Kitchenham
Farm is ½m on L. Parking in the
grounds of the Farm.* Thur 4, Tue
9 June (2-5). Adm £5, chd free.
Light lunches & home-made teas.
1 acre country house garden set
amongst traditional farm buildings
with stunning views over the Sussex
countryside. Series of borders around
the house (not open) and lawns, and
mixed herbaceous borders incl roses
and delphiniums. A ha-ha separates
the garden from the fields and sheep.
The garden adjoins a working farm, a
beautiful setting to enjoy a delicious
afternoon tea. Full wheelchair access,
but there is one step to the WC.

& ☙ ☕

83 KNIGHTSBRIDGE HOUSE

Grove Hill, Hellingly, Hailsham,
BN27 4HH. Andrew & Karty
Watson, 07879 407408. *3m N of
Hailsham, 2m S of Horam. From
A22 at Boship r'about take A271,
at 1st set of T-lights turn L into Park
Rd & drive for 2²/₃m, garden on R.*
Wed 22, Sat 25 July, Wed 9, Sat
12 Sept (2-5). Adm £6, chd free.
Home-made teas.
Mature landscaped garden set
in 5 acres of tranquil countryside
surrounding Georgian house (not
open). Several garden rooms,
spectacular herbaceous borders
planted in contemporary style in
traditional setting. Opening July
and Sept for visitors to enjoy a very
different experience. Lots of late
season colour with grasses and
some magnificent specimen trees;
also partly walled garden. Wheelchair
access to most of garden, gravel
paths.

& ☙ ✿ 🚗 ☕

84 LAROCHE, 43 COOMBE DROVE

Bramber, Steyning, BN44 3PW.
Lynne Broome, 01903 814170,
lynnecbroome@gmail.com. *From
Bramber Castle r'about, take Clays
Hill signed Steyning, turn 2nd L into
Maudlin Lane, after 100 metres, turn
R into Coombe Drove. Garden at
top of road.* Visits by arrangement
from 14 Feb to end March & June
for groups of 10 to 30. If group
smaller ask to join another group.

Adm £4.50. Home-made teas. ⅓ acre garden situated on lower slope of the South Downs. Very wide variety of plants, many unusual. Portland stone terracing, with a small but steep woodland path with many snowdrops, hellebores, aconites and cyclamen in spring. In summer the garden bursts into colour with a white bed, hot bed, an array of containers, hanging baskets and a beautiful pergola covered in roses and clematis. Due to steep slope and steps, wheelchair access to lower lawn only.

85 LEGSHEATH FARM

Legsheath Lane, nr Forest Row, RH19 4JN. Mr & Mrs M Neal. *4m S of East Grinstead. 2m W of Forest Row, 1m S of Weirwood Reservoir.* Sun 17 May (1.30-4.30). Adm £5, chd free. Home-made teas. Donation to Holy Trinity Church, Forest Row.
Legsheath was first mentioned in Duchy of Lancaster records in 1545. It was associated with the role of Master of the Ashdown Forest. Set high in the Weald, with far reaching views of East Grinstead and Weirwood Reservoir. The garden covers 11 acres with a spring fed stream feeding ponds. There is a magnificent davidia, rare shrubs, embothrium, and many different varieties of meconopsis, abutilons.

86 LIMEKILN FARM

Chalvington Road, Chalvington, Hailsham, BN27 3TA. Dr J Hester & Mr M Royle. *10m N of Eastbourne. Nr Hailsham. Turn S off A22 at Golden Cross & follow the Chalvington Rd for 1m. The entrance has white gates on the LH-side. Disabled parking space close to the house, 100 metres further along road.* Sat 16, Sun 17 May, Sat 15, Sun 16 Aug (2-5). Adm £5, chd free. Home-made teas in the Oast House.
The garden was designed in the 1930s when the house was owned by Charles Stewart Taylor, MP for Eastbourne. It has not changed in basic layout since then. The planting aims to reflect the age of the C17 property (not open) and original garden design. The house and garden are mentioned in Virginia Woolf's diaries of 1929, depicting a particular charm and peace that still exists today. Flint walls enclose the

main lawn, herbaceous borders and rose garden. Nepeta lined courtyard, Physic garden, informal pond, and specimen trees including a very ancient oak. Talk about the Physic garden at 2.30pm and 3.30pm each day of opening.

87 LINDFIELD JUNGLE

16 Newton Road, Lindfield, Haywards Heath, RH16 2ND. Tim Richardson & Clare Wilson, 01444 484132, info@lindfieldjungle.co.uk, www.lindfieldjungle.co.uk. *Approx 1½m NE of Haywards Heath town centre. Take B2028 into Lindfield. Turn onto Lewes Rd (B2111), turn onto Chaloner Rd & turn R into Chaloner Close (no parking in close or at garden). Garden is located at far end, use postcode RH16 2NH.* Mon 31 Aug (1-5). Combined adm with 5 Whitemans Close £6, chd free. Home-made teas at 5 Whitemans Close. Visits also by arrangement July to Sept for groups of 5 to 10. Visit can be combined with 47 Denmans Lane.
A surprising, intimate garden, approx 17 metres x 8 metres. Transformed since 1999 into an atmospheric jungle oasis planted for tropical effect. Lush and exuberant with emphasis on foliage and hot colours that develop through the seasons. From the planter's terrace enjoy the winding path through lillies, cannas, ginger and bamboo, to the tranquil sundowner's deck over hidden pools. Join Tim & Clare for tiffin and celebrate with them coming 2nd in the Gardener's World magazine Garden of the Year competition 2018!

Your visits help change lives – your generosity has supported unpaid carers through donations to Carers Trust totalling over £4 million since 1996

88 THE LONG HOUSE

The Lane, Westdean, Nr Seaford, BN25 4AL. Robin & Rosie Lloyd, 01323 870432, rosiemlloyd@gmail.com, www.thelonghousegarden.co.uk. *3m E of Seaford, 6m W of Eastbourne. From A27 follow signs to Alfriston then Litlington, Westdean 1m on L. From A259 at Exceat, L on Litlington Rd, ¼m on R. Free parking in the village.* Visits by arrangement May to July for groups of 10+. Owners on hand to guide & answer questions. Adm £10, chd free. Home-made teas included.
The Long House's 1 acre garden has become a favourite for private group visits, being compared for romance, atmosphere and cottage garden planting to Great Dixter and Sissinghurst. Lavenders, hollyhocks, roses, a wildflower meadow, a long perennial border, water folly and pond are just some of the features, and everyone says Rosie's home-made cakes are second to none. Situated on the South Downs Way in the SDNP. Gravel forecourt at entrance, some slopes and steps.

89 LORDINGTON HOUSE

Lordington, Chichester, PO18 9DX. Mr & Mrs John Hamilton, 01243 375862, hamiltonjanda@btinternet.com. *7m W of Chichester. On W side of B2146, ½m S of Walderton, 6m S of South Harting. Enter through white railings.* Sat 6, Sun 7 June (1.30-4.30). Adm £5, chd free. Home-made teas. Visits also by arrangement June & Sept for groups of up to 30.
Early C17 house (not open) and walled gardens in SDNP. Clipped yew and box, lawns, borders and fine views. Vegetables, fruit, poultry in kitchen garden. Carpet of daffodils in spring. 100+ roses planted since 2008. Trees both mature and young. Lime avenue planted in 1973 to replace elms. Wild flowers in field outside walls (accessible on foot). Overlooks Ems valley, farmland and wooded slopes of South Downs, all in AONB. Wheelchair access is possible, but challenging with gravel paths, uneven paving and slopes. No disabled WC.

90 LOWDER MILL

Bell Vale Lane, Fernhurst, Haslemere, GU27 3DJ. Anne & John Denning, 01428 644822, anne@denningconsultancy.co.uk, www.lowdermill.com. *1½m S of Haslemere. Follow A286 out of Midhurst towards Haslemere, through Fernhurst & take 2nd R after Kingsley Green into Bell Vale Lane. Lowder Mill is approx ½m on R.* Sat 30, Sun 31 May (11-5.30). Adm £4.50, chd £2. Home-made teas served overlooking the lake.

C17 mill house and former mill set in 3 acre garden. The garden has been restored with the help of Bunny Guinness. Interesting assortment of container planting, forming a stunning courtyard between house and mill. Streams, waterfalls, innovative and quirky container planting around the potting shed and restored greenhouse. Raised vegetable garden. Rare breed chickens and ducks, as well as resident kingfishers. Extensive plant stall, mainly home propagated.

91 LUCTONS

North Lane, West Hoathly, East Grinstead, RH19 4PP. Drs Hans & Ingrid Sethi, 01342 810085, ingrid@sethis.co.uk. *4m SW of East Grinstead, 6m E of Crawley. In centre of West Hoathly village, near church, Cat Inn & Priest House. Car parks in village.* Sat 20 June (1-5), also open The Priest House. Sun 21, Tue 23 June (1-5). Adm £5, chd free. Home-made teas. Visits also by arrangement June to Sept for groups of 10 to 30.

A 2 acre Gertrude Jekyll style garden with box parterre, topiary, acclaimed herbaceous borders, swathes of spotted orchids, wild flower orchard, pond, chickens, greenhouses, large vegetable and fruit garden, croquet lawn, revamped herb garden, and a huge variety of plants, especially salvias. Admired by overseas garden tour visitors, many people comment on its peaceful atmosphere.

92 MALTHOUSE FARM

Streat Lane, Streat, Hassocks, BN6 8SA. Richard & Helen Keys, 01273 890356, helen.k.keys@btinternet.com. *2m SE of Burgess Hill. From r'about between B2113 & B2112 take Folders Lane & Middleton Common Lane E (away from Burgess Hill); after 1m R into Streat Lane, garden*

is ½m on R. Sun 23, Wed 26 Aug (2-5.30). Adm £6, chd free. Home-made teas. Visits also by arrangement Apr to Sept for groups of 10+.

Rural 5 acre garden with stunning views to South Downs. Garden divided into separate rooms; box parterre and borders with glass sculpture, herbaceous and shrub borders, mixed border for seasonal colour and kitchen garden. Orchard leading to partitioned areas with grass walks, snail mound, birch maze and willow tunnel. Wildlife farm pond with planted surround. Stunning views to the South Downs. Wheelchair access mainly on grass, with some steps (caution if wet).

93 MANDALAY

High Street, Burwash, Etchingham, TN19 7EN. David & Vivienne Wright, 01435 883149, burwashgardener@gmail.com, www.burwashopengardens.org.uk. *Mandalay is not accessed via the High St, the entrance to the garden is off Ham Lane, opp the Rose & Crown Pub.* Sat 27 June (1-5). Combined adm with Burwash Hidden Gardens £6, chd free. Home-made teas. Visits also by arrangement June to Aug for groups of 10 to 16. Tea & cake included.

Contemporary style cottage garden behind C18 listed village house (not open). A narrow garden just 97ft x 21ft and about the size of a main Chelsea Show garden. Extensive and ongoing replanting by owners since 2018 to create more open, vibrant yet secluded space with interesting, unusual planting. Specimen olive trees, roses, clematis, border perennials, harmonious hard landscaping, water feature, and colourful containers complete the scene. Plenty of seating for relaxation and quiet reflection. NB No WC at garden.

94 MANOR OF DEAN

Tillington, Petworth, GU28 9AP. Mr & Mrs James Mitford, 07887 992349, emma@mitford.uk.com. *3m W of Petworth. From Petworth towards Midhurst on A272, pass Tillington & turn R onto Dean Lane following NGS signs. From Midhurst on A272 towards Petworth past Halfway Bridge, turn L following NGS signs.* Sun 16 Feb (2-4); Sun 22 Mar, Sun 26 Apr (2-5). Adm £4.50, chd free. Home-made teas. Visits also

by arrangement Feb to Sept for groups of 20+. Sorry no coaches. Traditional English garden, approx 3 acres with herbaceous borders, a variety of early flowering bulbs, snowdrops, spring bulbs, grass walks and grass steps. Walled kitchen garden with fruit, vegetables and cutting flowers. Lawns, rose garden and informal areas with views of the South Downs. Garden under a long-term programme of improvements. Garden on many levels with old steps and paths making it unsuitable for buggies or wheelchairs.

GROUP OPENING

95 MAYFIELD GARDENS

Mayfield, TN20 6AB. *10m S of Tunbridge Wells. Turn off A267 into Mayfield. Parking is available in the village & field parking at Hoopers Farm, TN20 6BD. A detailed map will be available at each of the gardens.* Sat 13, Sun 14 June (1-5). Combined adm £7, chd free. Home-made teas at Hoopers Farm & The Oast.

HOOPERS FARM
Andrew & Sarah Ratcliffe.

MEADOW COTTAGE
Adrian & Mo Hope.

MULBERRY
M Vernon.

OAKCROFT
Nick & Jennifer Smith.

THE OAST
Mike & Tessa Crowe.

SOUTH STREET PLOTS
Val Buddle.

SUNNYBANK COTTAGE
Eve & Paul Amans.

TEW COT
Jon & Sue Barnes.

Mayfield is a beautiful Wealden village with tearooms, an old pub and many interesting historical connections. The gardens to visit are all within walking distance of the village centre. They vary in size and style, including colour themed, courtyard and cottage garden planting, wildlife meadows and fruit and vegetable plots. There are far reaching, panoramic views over the beautiful High Weald. Partial wheelchair access to some gardens; see leaflet on the day for details.

Sienna Wood

© Leigh Clapp

96 ◆ MERRIMENTS GARDENS
Hawkhurst Road, Hurst Green,
TN19 7RA. Lucy Cross,
01580 860666,
bookings@merriments.co.uk,
www.merriments.co.uk. *Off A21,
1m N of Hurst Green. On A229
Hawkhurst Rd. Situated between
Hurst Green & Hawkhurst 300yds on
R from A21/A229 junction.* **For NGS:
Wed 12 Aug (9-5). Adm £9, chd
free. For other opening times and
information, please phone, email or
visit garden website.**
Our beautiful 4 acre garden with colour
themed borders is set amongst the
rolling countryside of East Sussex.
Seamlessly blending, its large borders
of inspiring planting evolve through the
seasons from spring pastels to the fiery
autumn hues of the many trees, all on
a gently sloping s-facing site with good
parking and easy access. There are a
number of benches in the garden to
allow visitors to enjoy the atmosphere
of this special ever-evolving garden.
There are many unusual plants most of
which are sold in the plant centre; there
is also a great shop and restaurant
serving home-made lunches and teas.
Wheelchairs available from the shop.
Dogs are welcome on leads.

97 ◆ MICHELHAM PRIORY
Upper Dicker, Hailsham,
BN27 3QS. Sussex Archaeological
Society, 01323 844224,
propertymich@sussexpast.co.uk,
www.sussexpast.co.uk. *3m W of
Hailsham. A22 N from Eastbourne,
exit L to Arlington Rd W. 1⅛m turn
R, Priory on R after approx 300yds.*
**For opening times and information,
please phone, email or visit garden
website.**
The stunning 7 acre gardens at
Michelham Priory (open to the
public) are enclosed by England's
longest water-filled moat, which
teams with wildlife and indigenous
waterlilies. Cloister and Physic
gardens weave together features of
medieval gardening. Over 40 yrs of
developments have created a variety
of features incl herbaceous borders,
orchard, kitchen garden and tree lined
Moat Walk. The gardens have 80,000
daffodils that create a blaze of colour
from early spring onwards.

98 MILL HALL FARM
Whitemans Green, Cuckfield,
Haywards Heath, RH17 5HX. Kate
& Jonathan Berry, 01444 455986,
katehod@gmail.com. *2½m E of
A23, junction with B2115. Driveway
on N-side B2115 at W-end of Burrell
Cottages. Parking in paddock at
top of drive on the R.* **Sun 7 June
(12.30-5). Adm £5, chd free.
Home-made teas. Visits also by
arrangement Apr to July. Donation
to Plant Heritage.**
Planting began in March 2012 to
this 2½ acre, n-facing garden with
long view sloping down to pond
with lilies, irises, and sanguisorba.
Long border with young trees and
herbaceous plants incl cercidiphyllum,
catalpa aurea, Metasequoia Gold
Rush, cornus, acers, pulmonarias,
daylilies, phlox, penstemon,
geraniums and brunnera, climbing
roses, and clematis. There is also a
fruit and vegetable garden. Victorian
underground water cistern. Plants for
sale. Deep pond. Sloping lawn and
no hard paths. No wheelchair access
to WC.

Forest Ridge

99 THE MOONGATE GARDEN

6 Elm Avenue, East Preston, Littlehampton, BN16 1HJ. Helen & Derek Harnden, 07870 324654, derek@shiningmylight.plus.com. *Over railway crossing from A259, continue straight onto Golden Ave. Turn R into Elm Ave, within 110 metres.* Sun 17 May, Sat 18 July, Sat 19 Sept (1-4). Adm £5, chd free. Home-made teas. Visits also by arrangement May to Sept for groups of 20+.

One feature is the stunning Purbeck stone wall with a moongate opening bisecting the garden, creating 2 distinct halves. Other features include circular lawns, a Hobbit house, vertical planting, fern/stumpery, 2 ponds with a contemporary stainless steel waterfall, Japanese area, vegetables and fruit raised planters. A haze of purple alliums in May, followed by verbena and persicarias in summer. Unusual grasses and cosmos carry the garden into autumn. Find us on Facebook by searching The Moongate Garden. Wheelchair access through large gate on left side of house, with direct access to garden on flat paving.

100 MOUNTFIELD COURT

Robertsbridge, TN32 5JP. Mr & Mrs Simon Fraser, 07831 642120, Lucinda@mountfield.me.uk. *3m N of Battle. On A21 London-Hastings; ½m NW from Johns Cross.* Sun 10 May (2-5). Adm £5, chd free. Home-made teas. Visits also by arrangement in May.

3 acre wild woodland garden; bluebell lined walkways through exceptional rhododendrons, azaleas, camellias, and other flowering shrubs; fine trees and outstanding views. Stunning paved herb garden. Recently restored unique C18 walled garden.

101 49 NEW ROAD

Durrington, Worthing, BN13 3JG. Ian & Wendy Nicholson, 07881 922312, wendy@housecoach.co.uk. *3m NW of Worthing. From A27 at Worthing turn off into Durrington Hill, take the 3rd turning on the R into New Rd. Number 49 is on the corner of New Rd & Arun Crescent.* Sat 4, Sat 18 July (12-4). Adm £4, chd free. Home-made teas. Visits also by arrangement June & July for

groups of up to 20.

Contemporary town garden. The resourceful owners have carved out a series of garden rooms to create paradise on a shoestring. Ingenious use is made of upcycled materials and gifted plants give the borders a colourful and eclectic feel. The veranda has the best vantage point. The dining area is flanked by a generously proportioned fish pond and sun deck. A slatted screen with moongate opening separates the fire pit seating area from the rest and here, entertaining is key! No wheelchair access and no WC facilities.

102 NEWTIMBER PLACE

Newtimber, BN6 9BU. Mr & Mrs Andrew Clay, 01273 833104, andy@ newtimberholidaycottages.co.uk, www.newtimberplace.co.uk. *7m N of Brighton. From A23 take A281 towards Henfield. Turn R at small Xrds signed Newtimber in approx ½ m. Go down Church Lane, garden is on L at end of lane.* Sun 19 Apr (2-5.30). Adm £5, chd free. Home-made teas.

Beautiful C17 moated house (not open). Gardens and woods full of bulbs and wild flowers in spring. Herbaceous border and lawns. Moat flanked by water plants. Mature trees, wild garden, ducks, chickens and fish. Wheelchair access across lawn to parts of garden, tearoom and WC.

103 NEW 3 NORMANDY DRIVE

East Preston, Littlehampton, BN16 1LT. Sarah Chandler, 07903 400543, sarahchandler@live.co.uk. *From A280/A259 r'about, follow sign to East Preston on B2140. Over railway crossing, take immed L on to North Lane, leading into Sea Rd. Pass the shops on your L then Normandy Drive is 2nd R.* Thur 2 July, Thur 3 Sept (1-5). Adm £4.50, chd free. Home-made teas. Visits also by arrangement June to Sept for groups of 10 to 30.

A self-confessed plantaholic's garden, 45' x 65', just 5 mins from the sea and a true delight. Still in its infancy, designed around a large pergola providing seating areas, borders full of pretty herbaceous perennials, cutting flowers, climbers and a little bit of fruit and veg for good measure. Further interest incl small wildlife pond, corten steel planters, obelisks, pots, water feature and greenhouse.

104 NORTH HALL

North Hall Lane, Sheffield Green, Uckfield, TN22 3SA. Celia & Les Everard, 01825 791103, indigodogs@yahoo.co.uk. *1½ m NW of Fletching village. 6m N of Uckfield. From A272 turn N at Piltdown or N Chailey. From A275 turn E at Sheffield Green into North Hall Lane.* Sat 27, Sun 28 June (2-5.30). Adm £4.50, chd free. Home-made teas. Visits also by arrangement Apr to June for groups of 10+.

A quintessential cottage garden surrounding a C16 house (not open) planted to please the senses. Owner maintained, planting is dense and varied in an informal fusion of soft colours complimented by beautiful shade loving foliage. Flowing themed island beds and a moated terrace add to many other cottage garden features. Wildlife and self-seeding encouraged. Homegrown plants and scrumptious teas.

105 NORTH SPRINGS

Bedham, nr Fittleworth, RH20 1JP. Mr & Mrs R Haythornthwaite. *Between Fittleworth & Wisborough Green. From Wisborough Green take A272 towards Petworth. Turn L into Fittleworth Rd signed Coldharbour & proceed 1½ m. From Fittleworth take Bedham Lane off A283 & proceed for approx 3m NE. Limited parking.* Sun 28 June (1-6). Adm £5, chd free. Home-made teas.

Hillside garden with beautiful views surrounded by mixed woodland. Focus on structure with a wide range of mature trees and shrubs. Stream, pond and bog area. Abundance of roses, clematis, hostas, rhododendrons and azaleas.

106 ◆ NYMANS

Staplefield Road, Handcross, RH17 6EB. National Trust, 01444 405250, nymans@nationaltrust.org.uk, www.nationaltrust.org.uk/nymans. *4m S of Crawley. On B2114 at Handcross signed off M23/A23 London-Brighton road. Metrobus 271 & 273 stop nearby.* For NGS: Sat 12 Sept (10-5). Adm £14.70, chd £7.30. For other opening times

and information, please phone, email or visit garden website.

One of NT's premier gardens with rare and unusual plant collections of national significance. In autumn dramatic shows of native tree colour can be seen in the adjoining woodland, where there are opportunities to spot wildlife. The comfortable yet elegant house, a partial ruin, reflects the personalities of the creative Messel family. Some level pathways. See full access statement on Nymans website.

107 OAKLANDS FARM

Hooklands Lane, Shipley, Horsham, RH13 8PX. Zsa & Stephen Roggendorff, 01403 741270, zedrog@roggendorff.co.uk. *S of A272, R at Countryman Pub, follow yellow signs. Or N of A24 Ashington. Head along Billingshurst Rd, take 1st R signed Shipley, garden 2m up lane, S of Shipley village.* Mon 25 May, Sat 18 July (10.30-5.30). Adm £6, chd free. Home-made teas. Visits also by arrangement Apr to Sept for groups of 5 to 20.

Country garden designed by Nigel Philips. Approached from a small lane, along an oak lined drive leading to the house and farm. The drive opens out to an enclosed courtyard with pleached hornbeam and yew. The herbaceous borders are filled with summer colours. Small orchard beyond the tennis court and wild meadow area with views into the fields. Vegetable garden with raised beds and greenhouse. Gravel and brick paths, large lawn area and grassy fields.

108 OCKLYNGE MANOR

Mill Road, Eastbourne, BN21 2PG. Wendy & David Dugdill, 01323 734121, ocklyngemanor@hotmail.com, www.ocklyngemanor.co.uk. *Close to Eastbourne District General Hospital. Take A22 (Willingdon Rd) towards Old Town, turn L into Mill Rd by Hurst Arms Pub.* Visits by arrangement May to Aug for groups of up to 20.

A welcome return to the scheme for this hidden oasis behind an ancient, flint wall. Informal and tranquil, ½ acre chalk garden with sunny and shaded places to sit. Use of architectural and unusual trees. Rhododendrons, azaleas and acers in raised beds. Garden evolved over 20

yrs, maintained by owners. Georgian house (not open), former home of Mabel Lucie Attwell. Short gravel path before entering garden. Brick path around perimeter.

109 OFFHAM HOUSE

The Street, Offham, Lewes, BN7 3QE. Mr S Goodman and Mr & Mrs P Carminger. *2m N of Lewes on A275. Offham House is on the main road (A275) through Offham between the filling station & the Blacksmiths Arms.* Sun 26 Apr (1-5). Adm £5, chd free. Home-made teas.

Romantic garden with fountains, flowering trees, arboretum, double herbaceous border and long peony bed. 1676 Queen Anne house (not open) with well knapped flint facade. Herb garden and walled kitchen garden with glasshouses, coldframes, chickens, guinea fowl, sheep and ducks. Large selection of pelargoniums for sale.

110 NEW OLD CROSS STREET FARM

West Burton, Pulborough, RH20 1HD. Belinda & David Wilkinson, 01798 839373, belinda@westburton.com. *Centre of the hamlet of West Burton. If travelling S on the A29, continue & turn off at the signs for Bignor, Roman Villa. The house is found in the centre of the village of West Burton, not as indicated by the postcode!* Visits by arrangement May to Oct for groups of 10 to 30. Adm £6, chd £4. Light refreshments.

A modern garden with a nod to traditional planting nestled in the ancient landscape of the South Downs. Despite its ancient buildings the garden was only designed and planted 13 yrs ago and enjoys many of the contemporary twists not usually found in such a landscape. An abundance of mass planting, demonstrates the advantages of a limited planting palate. An enormous circular lawn, cloud hedging, an orchard, cutting garden, transformed farmyard, modern mass planting, all year interest, a cottage garden, use of hedging, a raised formal pond, uses of different hard landscaping materials, planting of over 40 trees.

111 OLD ERRINGHAM COTTAGE

Steyning Road, Shoreham-By-Sea, BN43 5FD. Fiona & Martin Phillips, 07884 398704, fiona.h.phillips@btinternet.com. *2m N of Shoreham by Sea. From A27 Shoreham flyover take A283 towards Steyning. Take 2nd R into private lane. Follow sharp LH-bend at top, house on L.* Visits by arrangement from end of May & June for groups of 10 to 30. Home-made teas.

Plantsman's garden set high on the South Downs with panoramic views overlooking the Adur valley. 1⅓ acres with flower meadow, stream bed and ponds, formal and informal planting areas with over 600 varieties of plants. Very productive fruit and vegetable garden with glasshouses. Many plants grown from seed and coastal climate gives success with tender plants. Part of house dates from 1480 (not open).

112 NEW THE OLD HOUSE

Waldron, Heathfield, TN21 0QX. Jennifer Graham. *In centre of village opp The Star Inn & War Memorial.* Fri 19 June (1-5). Combined adm with Warren Cottage £5, chd free. Home-made teas in Waldron Village Hall.

Total renovation was required on my arrival in 2004. Apart from a long hedge the garden was cleared and levels changed. My plan was to conceal the ordinariness of the garden's shape through a strong landscape plan of my own design, and good structural planting. I wanted numerous pathways, plenty of seating, strong perfume, and a formal water feature. Those key elements are still critical today. Lunches available at the local pub, The Star Inn.

113 OLD STONELYNK EDGE

63 Battery Hill, Fairlight, Hastings, TN35 4AP. Joe & Kerry Gentleman. *5m E of Hastings. On the Ore to Cliff End main road at the junction with Warren Rd. 101 bus stops close by. Parking limited.* Sun 14 June (1.30-5). Adm £5, chd free. Home-made teas.

Large, well established garden with variety of shrubs and borders. Small wildlife pond. Various flower beds and lawn sloping steeply down to sizeable fish pond with a bridge leading to woodland walk and a variety of shady seating areas. Not suitable for wheelchairs or those with reduced mobility.

114 THE OLD VICARAGE

The Street, Washington, RH20 4AS. Sir Peter & Lady Walters, 07766 761926, meryl.walters@me.com. *2½m E of Storrington, 4m W of Steyning. From Washington r'about on A24 take A283 to Steyning. Pass Frankland Arms, R to St Mary's Church.* Sun 16 Feb (10.30-3.30); Sun 15 Mar (10.30-4); Mon 13 Apr, Sun 17 May, Mon 31 Aug (10.30-5); Sun 11 Oct (10.30-4). Adm £6, chd free. Home-made teas. Gluten free cakes & biscuits. Visits also by arrangement Mar to Sept for groups of 10 to 30.

Gardens of 3½ acres set around 1832 Regency house (not open). The front, formally laid out with topiary, wide lawn, mixed border, and contemporary water sculpture. The rear, features new and mature trees from C19, herbaceous borders, water garden and stunning uninterrupted views of the North Downs. Also Japanese garden with waterfall and pond, a large copse, stream, treehouse and stumpery. 2000 tulips have been planted for spring as well as 10,000 mixed bulbs in the meadow area. New in 2018 an Italianate gazebo with green oak columns and lead roof. Wheelchair access to the front garden, but the rear garden is on a slope.

Oaklands Farm

© Judi Lion

115 PARSONAGE FARM
Kirdford, RH14 0NH. David &
Victoria Thomas, 01403 820295,
davidandvictoria.thomas@gmail.
com. *5m NE of Petworth. From
centre of Kirdford (before church)
turn R through village towards Balls
Cross, past Foresters Pub on R.
Entrance on L, just past R turn to
Plaistow. For SatNav use RH14 0NG.*
Sun 26 Apr, Fri 19 June, Sun 13
Sept (2-6). Adm £7.50, chd free.
Home-made teas. Visits also
by arrangement Apr to Sept for
groups of 10+. Coaches can be
accommodated.
Major garden in beautiful setting
developed over 20 yrs with fruit
theme and many unusual plants.
Formally laid out on grand scale with
long vistas; C18 walled garden with
borders in apricot, orange, scarlet and
crimson; topiary walk; pleached lime
allée; tulip tree avenue; rose borders;
large vegetable garden with trained
fruit; turf amphitheatre; lake; informal
autumn shrubbery and jungle walk.

&♿ 🚗 ☕

GROUP OPENING

**116 NEW PEACEHAVEN &
SALTDEAN TRAIL**
*Follow yellow signs on A259 Brighton
to Eastbourne road & the r'abouts
in Saltdean & Peacehaven. Street
parking adjoining these gardens. Not
a walking trail.* Sat 18, Sun 19 July
(11-5). Combined adm £5, chd
free. Light refreshments.

BOXWORTH
21 Tor Road, Peacehaven,
BN10 7SX. Gerard
Rooney & Duncan Ward,
www.boxworthflowers.com.

TOR COTTAGE
8 Tor Road, Peacehaven,
BN10 7SX. Julie & Ron Basham.

NEW 33 WIVELSFIELD ROAD
Saltdean, Brighton, BN2 8FP. Chris
Briggs & Steve Jenner.

33 Wivelsfield Road is a new garden,
cleared in 2016, landscaped during
2017 and planting started later that
year. Split over three levels filled
with colourful perennials, annuals,
grasses, and succulents planted in
the ground and in containers. The
formal garden leads onto a wildflower
meadow extending onto the downs,
giving spectacular views of both
the ocean and SDNP. Boxworth is
a seaside garden developed over

past 7 yrs, packed with colourful and
interesting plants, perennial border,
cutting garden, dahlias, shaded
area with ferns and hostas. Displays
in the greenhouse, floral art in the
summerhouse. Seating areas for
refreshments. Distant sea views from
the terrace. Tor Cottage, is a tranquil
mature garden with trees, shrubs,
plants, bamboo, ornamental grasses
and koi pond. Plenty of colour and
different areas including vegetable
garden, rockeries and woodland.
There are shady areas and seating in
the sun or under the pergola. Artist
studio in the garden.

✿ ☕

117 PEELERS RETREAT
70 Ford Road, Arundel, BN18 9EX.
Tony & Lizzie Gilks, 01903 884981,
timespan70@tiscali.co.uk. *1m S of
Arundel. At Chichester r'about take
exit to Ford & Bognor Regis onto
Ford Rd. We are situated close to
Maxwell Rd, Arundel.* Sun 12 Apr,
Sun 10 May, Sun 28 June, Sun
9 Aug (2-5). Adm £4, chd free.
Home-made teas. Visits also
by arrangement Apr to Oct for
groups of 5 to 30. An amusing talk
'You Reap What You Sow' about
our NGS journey, followed by
afternoon tea.
A stunning garden filled with
imaginative woodland sculptures,
natural features and a flare for the
unusual. This inspirational space is
a delight in which to sit and relax,
enjoying a truly delicious home-
made tea. Set around interlocking
beds packed with colour and scent,
gently shaded by specimen trees,
tinkling water from a pebbled stream
and raised fish pond. Restricted
wheelchair access due to narrow
side entrance. Regret no motorised
wheelchairs.

🐐 🚗 ☕

*Your visits help change
lives – we are Hospice
UK's largest charitable
funder donating more
than £5.5 million to
support hospices in local
communities since 1996*

118 PEMBURY HOUSE
Ditchling Road, Clayton,
Hassocks, BN6 9PH. Nick &
Jane Baker, 01273 842805,
pembury@ngs.org.uk,
www.pemburyhouse.co.uk. *6m
N of Brighton, off A23. On B2112,
110yds from A273. Parking for
groups at house. Please car share.
Overflow parking at village green,
BN6 9PJ; then enter by cinder track
& back gate. Good public transport
service.* Visits by arrangement
Feb & Mar, see dates on own
website. Pre-booking essential
for individuals & groups, please
phone or email. Adm £10, chd
free. Home-made teas included.
Depending on the vagaries of the
season, hellebores and snowdrops
are at their best in Feb and March.
It is a country garden, tidy but not
manicured. Work always in progress
on new areas. Winding paths give
a choice of walks through 3 acres
of owner maintained garden, which
is in and enjoys views of the SDNP.
Wellies, macs and winter woolies
advised. A German visitor observed
'this is the perfect woodland garden'.
Pre-payment required for larger
groups. No concessions.

🐐 ✿ 🚗 ☕

119 PENNS IN THE ROCKS
Groombridge, Tunbridge
Wells, TN3 9PA. Mr & Mrs
Hugh Gibson, 01892 864244,
www.pennsintherocks.co.uk. *7m
SW of Tunbridge Wells. On B2188
Groombridge to Crowborough
road, just S of Xrd to Withyham. For
SatNav use TN6 1UX which takes
you to the white drive gates, through
which you should enter the property.*
Sun 19 Apr, Sun 17 May (2-6).
Adm £6, chd free. Home-made
teas. Visits also by arrangement
Mar to July for groups of 10+.
Large garden with spectacular
outcrop of rocks, 140 million yrs
old. Lake, C18 temple and woods.
Daffodils, bluebells, azaleas,
magnolias and tulips. Old walled
garden with herbaceous borders,
roses and shrubs. Stone sculptures
by Richard Strachey. Part C18 house
(not open) once owned by William
Penn of Pennsylvania. Restricted
wheelchair access. No disabled WC.
Dogs on lead in park only.

&♿ 🐐 ✿ ☕

120 1 PEST COTTAGE
Carron Lane, Midhurst, GU29 9LF. Jennifer Lewin. *W edge of Midhurst behind Carron Lane Cemetery. Free parking at recreation ground at top of Carron Lane. Short walk on woodland track to garden, please follow signs.* **Fri 5 June (2-7); Sun 7 June (2-6). Adm £4, chd free. Light refreshments.**
This edge of woodland, architects' studio garden of approx ³/₄ acre sits on a sloping sandy site. Designed to support wildlife and bio-diversity, a series of outdoor living spaces, connected with informal paths through lightly managed areas, creates a charming secret world tucked into the surrounding common land. The garden spaces have made a very small house (not open) into a hospitable family home. Exhibition of Architects projects. Track access and sloping site makes the garden unsuitable for wheelchairs or restricted mobility.
🐕 ☕

121 6 PLANTATION RISE
Worthing, BN13 2AH. Nigel & Trixie Hall, 01903 262206, trixiehall@btinternet.com. *2m from seafront on outskirts of Worthing. A24 meets A27 at Offington r'about. Turn into Offington Lane, 1st R into The Plantation, 1st R again into Plantation Rise. Parking on The Plantation only, short walk up to 6 Plantation Rise.* **Visits by arrangement Apr to Sept for groups of up to 30. Adm £5, chd free. Home-made teas included.**
Clever use is made of evergreen shrubs, azaleas, rhododendrons and acers enclosing our 70' x 80' garden, enhancing the flower decked pergolas, folly and summerhouse, which overlooks the pond. Planting incl 9 Tristus silver birches, which are semi pendula, plus a lovely combination of primroses, anemones and daffodils in spring and a profusion of roses, clematis and perennials in summer. The garden has some steps. WC available on request.
♿ 🚗 ☕

122 ◆ THE PRIEST HOUSE
North Lane, West Hoathly, RH19 4PP. Sussex Archaeological Society, 01342 810479, priest@sussexpast.co.uk, www.sussexpast.co.uk. *4m SW of East Grinstead, 6m E of Crawley. In centre of West Hoathly village, near church, the Cat Inn & Luctons.*

Car parks in village. For NGS: **Sat 23 May (10.30-5.30). Sat 20 June (10.30-5.30), also open Luctons. Adm £2, chd free. Home-made teas. For other opening times and information, please phone, email or visit garden website.**
C15 timber-framed farmhouse with cottage garden on acid clay. Large collection of culinary and medicinal herbs in a small formal garden and mixed with perennials and shrubs in exuberant borders. Long established yew topiary, box hedges and espalier apple trees provide structural elements. Traditional fernery and stumpery, recently enlarged with a small secluded shrubbery and gravel garden. Be sure to visit the fascinating Priest House Museum, adm £1 for NGS visitors.
🐕 ☀ ☕

123 2 QUARRY COTTAGES
Wall Hill Road, Ashurst Wood, East Grinstead, RH19 3TQ. Mrs Hazel Anne Archibald. *1m S of East Grinstead. From N turn L off A22 from East Grinstead, garden adjoining John Pears Memorial Ground. From S turn R off A22 from Forest Row, garden on R at top of hill.* **Fri 15, Sat 16 May (2-5). Adm £3.50, chd free. Home-made teas.**
Peaceful little garden that has evolved over 40 yrs by present owners. A natural sandstone outcrop hangs over an ornamental pond; mixed borders of perennials and shrubs with specimen trees. Many seating areas tucked into corners. Highly productive vegetable plot. Terrace round house. Florist and gift shop in barn. **Also open Caxton Manor (separate admission).**
🐕 ☀ ☕

124 NEW REDRIFF
Rannoch Road, Crowborough, TN6 1RA. John Mitchell. *1m S of Crowborough. From T-lights at Crowborough Cross, follow A26 (Beacon Rd) W uphill for ¹/₂m, then turn R into Warren Rd. Follow road downhill to Xrd & turn R into Rannoch Rd, Redriff 6th on R.* **Sat 9, Sun 10 May (2-5). Combined adm with Silver Springs £5, chd free. Light refreshments.**
¹/₃ acre garden with a Japanese influence comprising dense planting of rhododendrons, azaleas, camellias, acers, wisteria, bamboo and topiary features. Elevated patio with shady pergola and summerhouse, both affording seating overlooking interesting fish pond, waterfall and views over the rear garden. Light

refreshments in Crowborough Community Centre Cafe, Pine Grove, Crowborough TN6 1UA. Wheelchair access to most parts of the garden.
♿ ☀ ☕

125 RINGMER PARK
Uckfield Road, Ringmer, Lewes, BN8 5RW. Deborah & Michael Bedford, www.ringmerpark.com. *On A26 Lewes to Uckfield road. 1¹/₂m NE of Lewes, 5m S of Uckfield.* **Sun 14 June (2-5). Adm £5, chd free. Home-made teas.**
A welcome return to the NGS for this wonderful garden with its beautiful roses. The garden at Ringmer Park has been developed over the last 33 yrs as the owner's interpretation of a classic English country house garden. It extends over nearly 8 acres and comprises 15 carefully differentiated individual gardens and borders which are presented to optimise the setting of the house (not open), close to the South Downs.
♿ 🐕 🚗 ☕

126 ROLFS FARM
Witherenden Road, Mayfield, TN20 6RP. Tess Hurrell. *2m E of Mayfield (approx 5 mins). On Witherenden Rd, we are ¹/₂m from Mayfield end of road. Do not follow SatNav to postcode. Long, narrow, uneven driveway downhill through woods.* **Wed 10, Wed 17 June (10-3). Adm £5, chd free. Light refreshments.**
Very different from the usual NGS garden! Large wildlife friendly garden (no boundary fences to encourage visiting wildlife) with wildflower meadows, hazel trees, and clipped box hedging. Large orchard next to the garden. Tom Stuart-Smith designed modern meadow garden. Two ponds, small vegetable garden, and informal, naturalistic planting throughout. Uneven grass paths, sensible shoes please. Sorry, no wheelchair access as steep uneven driveway, and many steps in garden.
☕

127 RYMANS
Apuldram, Chichester, PO20 7EG. Mrs Michael Gayford. *1m S of Chichester. Take Witterings Rd, at 1¹/₂m SW turn R signed Dell Quay. Turn 1st R, garden ¹/₂m on L.* **Sat 18, Sun 19 Apr, Sat 13, Sun 14 June, Sat 12, Sun 13 Sept (2-5). Adm £6, chd free. Home-made teas.**
Walled and other gardens surrounding

lovely C15 stone house (not open); bulbs, flowering shrubs, roses, ponds, and potager. Many unusual and rare trees and shrubs. In late spring the wisterias are spectacular. The heady scent of hybrid musk roses fills the walled garden in June. In late summer the garden is ablaze with dahlias, sedums, late roses, sages and Japanese anemones. Newly restored natural pond.

🐕 ❀ 🚗 ☕

128 SAFFRONS
Holland Road, Steyning, BN44 3GJ. Tim Melton & Bernardean Carey, 01903 810082, tim.melton@btinternet.com. *6m NE of Worthing. Exit r'about on A283 at S end of Steyning bypass into Clays Hill Rd. 1st R into Goring Rd, 4th L into Holland Rd. Park in Goring Rd & Holland Rd.* Visits by arrangement in July for groups of 10 to 30. Adm £5, chd free. Home-made teas.
An artist's garden of textural contrasts and complementary colors. Well-furnished late summer flower beds of shrubby salvias, eryngiums, agapanthus, dahlias and lilies. The broad lawn is surrounded by borders with maples, rhododendrons, hydrangeas and mature trees interspersed with ferns and grasses. A large fruit cage and vegetable beds comprise the productive area of the garden. Plant sale. Wheelchair access difficult in very wet conditions.

♿ 🐕 ❀ ☕

129 ST BARNABAS HOUSE
2 Titnore Lane, Goring-By-Sea, Worthing, BN12 6NZ. Rosemarie Finley, www.stbh.org.uk. *W of Worthing & just N of the r'about between the A259 & the A2032. Titnore Lane can be accessed via the A27 from the N, the A259 from the W (Littlehampton) or the A2032 from the E (Worthing).* Sat 12, Sun 20 Sept (2-4.30). Adm £4, chd free. Home-made teas.
Our grounds have a central courtyard garden like an exotic atrium with seating, water features and abundant foliage from tree ferns, magnolias and katsura trees. Outside there is a large pond with fountain-aerator, adding tranquillity with the sound of running water. There is also a lavender maze, meadow and areas depicting roundhouses which were part of a settlement dating back to 800BC. Tea and coffee will be served by St Barnabas House volunteers.

Good access to the site, central courtyard, main surrounding gardens and car park. Pond area paths can be affected by heavy rain.

♿ 🐕 ❀ ☕

GROUP OPENING

130 NEW ST LEONARDS-ON-SEA GROUP
St Leonards-on-Sea, TN38 0UU. *2m W of Hastings. From A259 turn into Harley Shute Rd B2092 towards Battle. Go up the hill, straight over mini r'about, over narrow railway bridge, then take 1st R into Fernside Ave. Park in Gillsmans Park.* Sun 14 June (11-4). Combined adm £5, chd free. Home-made teas at 33 Fernside Avenue.

> NEW CORNERWAYS, 31 FERNSIDE AVENUE
> Greta Romaine.

> NEW 33 FERNSIDE AVENUE
> Dick & Anne Foster.

> NEW 37 FERNSIDE AVENUE
> Barbara Smith.

> NEW 10 WISHING TREE CLOSE
> Glenys Jacques.

Enjoy four very different gardens in this coastal town lying between Bexhill and Hastings. Start your garden safari at 37 Fernside Avenue, enjoy tea during the afternoon at 33 Fernside Avenue, move on to 31 Fernside Avenue, then take a short 10 min walk to 10 Wishing Tree Close. The gardens offer a wealth of scent, colour, interest and ideas. Water features abound with fountains, waterfalls, a beach area with a cabin, and even a pond with friendly fish. The group includes a Hastings in Bloom award-winning garden with a stunning, colourful front garden. There is also a garden in an elevated position with drought-tolerant planting, slate rocks and driftwood. From an intriguing small garden with lots of tiny areas to colourful gardens full of roses, clematis and fuchsias, there is much to see. You can also be sure of a warm welcome! Partial wheelchair access to three gardens, no access to 10 Wishing Tree Close.

♿ ❀ ☕

131 NEW ST MARY'S HOSPITAL
St Martins Square, Chichester, PO19 1NR. St Mary's Trust. *Central Chichester. From East St, turn into St Martin's St adjacent to M&S Food, follow road round RH-bend & you will see the hospital entrance in the corner.* Sat 27, Tue 30 June (11-4). Adm £4, chd free. Home-made teas.
A large formal garden, opened by HRH Princess Alexandra, comprising large rose beds, traditional fruit trees, herb garden, large lawn. Four impressive knot gardens designed by Mr Ray Winnett, our Gardener who based them on medieval designs and planted them in 2015. Visitors can also visit the hospital building, not usually open to the public. A hidden gem in the heart of Chichester. Wheelchair access to garden and hospital, but assistance maybe required for small ridges onsite.

♿ 🐕 ❀ ☕

132 ♦ ST MARY'S HOUSE GARDENS
Bramber, BN44 3WE. Roger Linton & Peter Thorogood, 01903 816205, info@stmarysbramber.co.uk, www.stmarysbramber.co.uk. *1m E of Steyning. 10m NW of Brighton in Bramber village off A283.* For NGS: Fri 17, Sat 18 July (2-5.30). Adm £6, chd free. Light refreshments. For other opening times and information, please phone, email or visit garden website.
5 acres incl formal topiary, large prehistoric *Ginkgo biloba*, and magnificent *Magnolia grandiflora* around enchanting timber-framed Medieval house (not open for NGS). Victorian Secret Gardens incl splendid 140ft fruit wall with pineapple pits, Rural Museum, Terracotta Garden, Jubilee Rose Garden, King's Garden and circular Poetry Garden. Woodland walk and Landscape Water Garden. In the heart of the SDNP. Wheelchair access with level paths throughout.

♿ ❀ 🚗 ☕

Your visits help change lives – your generosity helps Marie Curie fund nurses to care for people night and day in their homes, with donations of more than £9 million

133 SANDHILL FARM HOUSE
Nyewood Road, Rogate,
Petersfield, GU31 5HU.
Rosemary Alexander,
07551 777873, rosemary@
englishgardeningschool.co.uk,
www.rosemaryalexander.co.uk. *4m
SE of Petersfield. From A272 Xrds in
Rogate take road S signed Nyewood
& Harting. Follow road for approx
1m over small bridge. Sandhill Farm
House on R, over cattle grid.* **Sat
25, Sun 26 Apr, Sat 26, Sun 27
Sept (2-5). Adm £5, chd free.
Home-made teas. Visits also by
arrangement Feb to Oct for groups
of 10 to 30.**
Front and rear gardens broken up
into garden rooms incl small kitchen
garden. Front garden incl small
woodland area, planted with early
spring flowering shrubs, ferns and
bulbs including snowdrops. White
garden, large leaf border and terraced
area. Rear garden has rose borders,
small decorative vegetable garden,
red border and grasses border. Home
of author and principal of The English
Gardening School. The garden has
gravel paths and a few steps not
easily negotiated in a wheelchair.
✿ Ⓓ ☕

GROUP OPENING

134 NEW SAXON TRAIL WORTH
Worth, Crawley, RH10 7RG.
*Clayton, Turners Hill Rd RH10 4SW,
500yds E of Balcombe Rd. Osmund
Close RH10 7RG. 1¼m from Three
Bridges Station. Bus stop Nuffield
Park (84). Parking: Hazelhurst Drive
RH10 4SW, Osmund Close & Saxon
Rd RH10 7RG. Tickets & maps
at all gardens.* **Sun 16 Aug (1-5).
Combined adm £5, chd free.
Home-made teas at 7 Osmund
Close.**

NEW **CLAYTON**
Jackie & Graham Chalker.

NEW **3 OSMUND CLOSE**
Ray & Joy Monk.

NEW **4 OSMUND CLOSE**
Brian Partington.

NEW **5 OSMUND CLOSE**
Rose & Alastair Wells.

NEW **7 OSMUND CLOSE**
Kevin & Jo Stokes.

Eclectic range of 5 town gardens,
in easy walking distance, offering a
variety of aspects incl planting, pots,
ornaments and water features. Trees

incl acers, catalpa, cercis, dicksonia.
Clayton, formerly Delft Cottage has
beautiful borders and cottage-style
planting wrapped partly round Arts
and Crafts House (not open), and
courtyard areas for entertaining
and relaxation. The Osmund Close
gardens incl herbaceous perennials,
grasses, roses, shrubs and trees,
plus interesting exotics; aeoniums,
agaves, and banana plants. One
front garden has been transformed,
newly planted in a soft and calming
colour palette. Another is having
a partial facelift with new borders
for 2020. Two gardens are situated
adjacent to woodland providing a
secluded and peaceful backdrop,
with the sound of birds twittering and
water cascading. Like Clayton, all the
gardens have established areas for
quiet contemplation, relaxation and
socialising. 5 min walk from Osmund
Close leads to the Anglo-Saxon St.
Nicholas' Church dating back to AD
950.
✿ ☕

GROUP OPENING

135 SEAFORD GARDENS
*Tickets & maps at each garden. 5
gardens open 31 May & 9 open on
14 June (2 Barons Close & High
Trees open at noon). All signed from
the A259. 12a bus route. Please
note: this is not a walking trail.*
**Sun 31 May (12-5). Combined
adm £5, chd free. Sun 14 June
(11-5). Combined adm £7, chd
free. Home-made teas at various
gardens, see map on the day.**

2 BARONS CLOSE
BN25 2TY. Diane Hicks.
Open on Sun 14 June

34 CHYNGTON ROAD
BN25 4HP. Dr Maggie Wearmouth
& Richard Morland.
Open on all dates

NEW **8 CLAREMONT COURT**
Claremont Road, BN25 2PE.
Ms Carol Adam.
Open on Sun 14 June

NEW **5 CLEMENTINE AVENUE**
BN25 2UU. Joanne Davis.
Open on Sun 14 June

COSY COTTAGE
69 Firle Road, BN25 2JA. Ernie
& Carol Arnold, 07763 196343,
ernie.whitecrane@gmail.com.
Open on all dates
Visits also by arrangement Apr
to Sept.

HIGH TREES
83 Firle Road, BN25 2JA.
Tony & Sue Luckin.
Open on Sun 14 June

LAVENDER COTTAGE
69 Steyne Road, BN25 1QH.
Christina & Steve Machan.
Open on all dates

NEW **MADEHURST**
67 Firle Road, BN25 2JA.
Martin & Palo.
Open on all dates

SEAFORD ALLOTMENTS
Sutton Drove, BN25 3NQ. Peter
Sudell, www.salgs.co.uk.
Open on Sun 14 June

**SEAFORD COMMUNITY
GARDEN**
East Street, BN25 1AD.
Seaford Community Garden,
www.seaford-sussex.
co.uk/scg/.
Open on Sun 31 May

Seaford Gardens is opening twice in
2020. On 31 May, 5 gardens open.
34 Chyngton Road is divided into
garden rooms with pastels, hot beds
and a small meadow. Cosy Cottage, a
cottage garden over 3 levels with
ponds, flowers, vegetables, shrubs
and a Tai Chi Temple. Lavender
Cottage a flint walled garden with
a coastal and kitchen garden.
Madehurst is a garden on different
levels with interesting planting and
seasonal interest. Seaford Community
Garden provides an interesting space
for members of the community
to come together and share the
experience. On 14 June, 9 gardens
will open incl 4 of the above, plus
2 Barons Close (open at noon), a
riot of colour with beautiful roses
weaving in and out, over fences. 5
Clementine slopes upwards over 3
levels and opens out onto the downs.
High Trees (open at noon), a beautiful
garden with plants, ferns and grasses.
8 Claremont Court a small garden,
close to the sea, evoking the seaside.
A good example of what can be
grown so close to the sea. Seaford
Allotments offer a unique chance to
see a variety of planting and colour.
A site of 189 well maintained plots
with a wildlife area, a dye bed and
a compost WC. Wheelchair access
to Seaford Community Garden and
partial access to 34 Chyngton Road.
✿ ☕

136 SEDGWICK PARK HOUSE
Sedgwick Park, Horsham,
RH13 6QQ. Clare Davison,
01403 734930,
clare@sedgwickpark.com,
www.sedgwickpark.co.uk. *1m S
of Horsham off A281. A281 towards
Cowfold, Hillier Garden Center
on R, then 1st R into Sedgwick
Lane. At end of lane enter N gates
of Sedgwick Park or W gate via
Broadwater Lane, from Copsale
or Southwater off A24.* **Visits by
arrangement from end of Mar
to Sept for groups of 10+. Adm
£6, chd free. Home-made teas &
optional tour of house.**
Parkland, meadows and woodland.
Formal gardens by Harold Peto
featuring 20 interlinking ponds,
impressive water garden known as
The White Sea. Large Horsham stone
terraces and lawns look out onto
clipped yew hedging and specimen
trees. Well stocked herbaceous
borders, set in the grounds of Grade II
listed Ernest George Mansion. One of
the finest views of the South Downs,
Chanctonbury Ring and Lancing
Chapel. Turf labyrinth and organic
vegetable garden. Garden has uneven
paving, slippery when wet; unfenced
ponds and swimming pool.

137 SELHURST PARK
Halnaker, Chichester,
PO18 0LZ. Richard & Sarah
Green, 01243 839310,
mail@selhurstparkhouse.co.uk. *8m
S of Petworth. 4m N of Chichester
on A285.* **Sun 7 June (2-5). Adm
£4.50, chd free. Home-made teas.
Visits also by arrangement June &
July for groups of up to 20.**
Come and explore the varied gardens
surrounding a beautiful Georgian
flint house (not open) approached
by a chestnut avenue. The flint
walled garden has a mature 160ft
herbaceous border with unusual
planting along with rose, hellebore
and hydrangea beds. Pool garden
with exotic palms and grasses
divided from a formal knot and herb
garden by Espalier apples. Kitchen
and walled fruit garden. Wheelchair
access to walled garden, partial
access to other areas.

138 SENNICOTTS
West Broyle, Chichester,
PO18 9AJ. Mr & Mrs James
Rank, ngs@sennicotts.com, ,
www.sennicotts.com. *2m NW of*

*Chichester. White gates diagonally
opp & W of the junction between
Salthill Rd & the B2178.* **Sun 7
June (2-6). Adm £5, chd free.
Home-made teas. Visits also
by arrangement May to Sept for
groups of 20+. Large buses cannot
enter our gates.**
Historic gardens set around a
Regency villa (not open) with views
across mature Sussex parkland to
the South Downs. Working walled
kitchen and cutting garden where
refreshments will be available. Lots
of space for children and a warm
welcome for all.

**139 ◆ SHEFFIELD PARK AND
GARDEN**
Uckfield, TN22 3QX. National
Trust, 01825 790231,
sheffieldpark@nationaltrust.
org.uk, www.nationaltrust.org.
uk/sheffieldpark. *10m S of East
Grinstead. 5m NW of Uckfield; E
of A275.* **For NGS: Wed 6 May
(10-5). Adm £11, chd £5.50. Light
refreshments in Coach House
Tearoom. For other opening times
and information, please phone,
email or visit garden website.**
Magnificent 120 acres (40 hectares)
landscaped garden laid out in C18
by Capability Brown and Humphry
Repton. Further development in early
years of this century by its owner
Arthur G Soames. Centrepiece is
original lakes with many rare trees

and shrubs. Beautiful at all times of
the year, but noted for its spring and
autumn colours. National Collection
of Ghent azaleas. Natural play trail for
families on South Park. Large number
of Champion Trees, 87 in total. Garden
largely accessible for wheelchairs,
please call for information.

140 SHEPHERDS COTTAGE
Milberry Lane, Stoughton,
Chichester, PO18 9JJ. Jackie
& Alan Sherling, 07795 388047,
milberrylane@gmail.com. *9⅙m NW
Chichester. Off B2146, next village
after Walderton. Cottage is near
telephone box & beside St Mary's
Church. No parking in lane beside
house.* **Visits by arrangement Apr
to Aug for groups of 10 to 30.**
A compact terraced garden using the
borrowed landscape of Kingley Vale
in the South Downs. The s-facing flint
stone cottage (not open) is surrounded
by a Purbeck stone terrace with lush
planting schemes. The upper beds
are planted with a profusion of tulips,
alliums, roses, verbascum and lilies.
A small orchard (under-planted with
meadow), lawns, yew hedges, ilex
balls and drifts of wind grass provide
structure and yr-round interest. Many
novel design ideas for a small garden.
Ample seating throughout the garden
to enjoy the views. Not suitable for
wheelchairs or people with mobility
issues.

Driftwood

141 SIENNA WOOD

Coombe Hill Road, East Grinstead, RH19 4LY. Belinda & Brian Quarendon, 07970 707015, Belinda222@hotmail.com. *1m W of East Grinstead, off B2110 East Grinstead to Turners Hill. Garden is ½m down Coombe Hill Rd on L.* **Sun 17 May (1-5). Adm £5, chd free. Home-made teas. Visits also by arrangement May & June for groups of 10+.**
Explore our beautiful 3½ acre garden, picturesque lakeside walk and 6 acre ancient woodland behind. Start at the herbaceous borders surrounding the croquet lawn, through the formal rose garden to the lawns and summer borders; then down through the arboretum to the lake and back past the exotic border, orchard and vegetable garden. Many unusual trees and shrubs. Child friendly with children's nature trail, treehouse and play area. Possible sighting of wild deer including white deer. Partial wheelchair access to many parts of the garden.

142 NEW SILVER SPRINGS

Heavegate Road, Crowborough, TN6 1UA. Barbara Diamond. *1m S of Crowborough. From S on A26 turn L, or from N turn R, onto Fielden Rd. Garden on L at junction with Fielden Rd. Parking on Fielden Rd only.* **Sat 9, Sun 10 May (2-5). Combined adm with Redriff £5, chd free. Light refreshments.**
¼ acre garden, developed by the current owner (a keen plantswoman) over the past 25 yrs from a bare site. Shrubs, perennials, rock garden and bulbs in three areas surrounding the house (not open), each with a different character. Yr-round interest with emphasis on spring and a wide range of hydrangeas in the summer. Light refreshments in Crowborough Community Centre Cafe, Pine Grove, Crowborough TN6 1UA.

143 SKYSCAPE

46 Ainsworth Avenue, Ovingdean, Brighton, BN2 7BG. Lorna & John Davies. *From Brighton take A259 coast road E, passing Roedean School on L. Take 1st L at the r'about into Greenways & 2nd R into Ainsworth Ave, Skyscape at the top on R.* **Sat 6, Sun 7 June (1-5). Combined adm with 12 Ainsworth Avenue £5, chd free. Tea & cake served on the patio.**
250ft s-facing rear garden on a sloping site with fantastic views of South Downs and sea. Garden created by owners over past 6 yrs. New orchard, flower beds and planting with bees in mind. Rich variety of plants on each level. Plants for sale. Full access to site via purpose built sloping path.

144 SOUTH GRANGE

Quickbourne Lane, Northiam, Rye, TN31 6QY. Linda & Michael Belton, 01797 252984, belton.northiam@gmail.com. *Between A268 & A28, approx ½m E of Northiam. From Northiam centre follow Beales Lane into Quickbourne Lane, or Quickbourne Lane leaves A286 approx ½m S of A28 & A286 junction. Disabled parking at front of house.* **Thur 21 May (1-5); Sat 5, Sun 6 Sept (11-5). Adm £6, chd free. Home-made teas (May). Teas & light lunches made to order (Sept). Visits also by arrangement Apr to Oct.**
Hardy Plant Society members' garden with wide variety of trees, shrubs, perennials, grasses, pots arranged into a complex garden display for yr-round colour and interest. Raised vegetable beds, wildlife pond, new water features, orchard with rose arbour, soft fruit cage and living gazebo. House roof runoff diverted to storage and pond. Small area of wildwood. An emphasis on planting for insects. We try to maintain nectar and pollen supplies and varied habitats for most of the creatures that we share the garden with, hoping that this variety will keep the garden in good heart. Home propagated plants for sale. Hard paths through much of the garden, but steps up to patio and WC.

145 STANLEY FARM

Highfield Lane, Liphook, GU30 7LW. Bill & Emma Mills. *For SatNav please use GU30 7LN, which takes you to Highfield Lane & then follow NGS signs. Track to Stanley Farm is 1m.* **Sun 3 May (12-5). Adm £5, chd free. Home-made teas served in the courtyard.**
1 acre garden created over the last 15 yrs around an old West Sussex farmhouse (not open), sitting in the midst of its own fields and woods. The formal garden incl a kitchen garden with heated glasshouse, orchard, espaliered wall trained fruit, lawn with ha-ha, and cutting garden. A motley assortment of animals incl sheep, donkeys, chickens, ducks and geese. Bluebells flourish in the woods, so feel free to bring dogs and a picnic, and take a walk after visiting the gardens. Wheelchair access via a ramp to view main part of the garden. Difficult access to woods due to muddy, uneven ground.

146 STONE CROSS HOUSE

Alice Bright Lane, Crowborough, TN6 3SH. Mr & Mrs D A Tate. *1½m S of Crowborough Cross. At Crowborough T-lights (A26) turn S into High St & shortly R onto Croft Rd. Over 3 mini-r'abouts to Alice Bright Lane. Garden on L at next Xrds.* **Sun 10 May (2-5). Adm £5, chd free. Home-made teas.**
Beautiful 9 acre country property (not open) with gardens containing a delightful array of azaleas, acers, rhododendrons and camellias, interplanted with an abundance of spring bulbs. The very pretty cottage garden has interesting examples of topiary and unusual plants. Jacob sheep graze the surrounding pastures. Gravel drive, but mainly flat and no steps. No WC.

147 SULLINGTON OLD RECTORY

Sullington Lane, Storrington, Pulborough, RH20 4AE. Oliver & Mala Haarmann. Mark Dixon, Head Gardener, 07749 394012, mark@sullingtonoldrectory.com. *Traveling S on A24 take 3rd exit on Washington r'about. Proceed to Xrds on A283 for Sullington Lane & Water Lane. Take L onto Sullington Lane & garden located at the top.* **Visits by arrangement for groups of up to 30 on 8, 9, 15 & 16 July. Adm £12, chd free. Tour with Head Gardener at 10am or 2pm & home-made teas included. If group smaller ask to join another group.**
With a backdrop of stunning views of the South Downs, the naturalistic style of this beautiful country garden sits perfectly into the surrounding landscape. The garden includes a potager, orchard, herb garden, established trees and shrubs, a pleached lime walk, new colour themed perennial borders, a profusion of grasses and an experimental planting in the moist meadow. Refreshments at The Workshop Café, Sullington Manor Farm. Wheelchair access to most areas.

148 ◆ SUSSEX PRAIRIES
Morlands Farm, Wheatsheaf Road
(B2116), Henfield, BN5 9AT. Paul &
Pauline McBride, 01273 495902,
morlandsfarm@btinternet.com,
www.sussexprairies.co.uk. *2m NE
of Henfield on B2116 Wheatsheaf
Rd (also known as Albourne Rd).
Follow Brown Tourist signs indicating
Sussex Prairie Garden.* For NGS:
Sun 13 Sept (11-5). Adm £9, chd
free. Home-made teas. For other
opening times and information,
please phone, email or visit garden
website.
Exciting prairie garden of approx 8
acres planted in the naturalistic style
using 60,000 plants and over 1,600
different varieties. A colourful garden
featuring a huge variety of unusual
ornamental grasses. Expect layers
of colour, texture and architectural
splendour. Surrounded by mature oak
trees with views of Chanctonbury Ring
and Devil's Dyke on the South Downs.
Permanent sculpture collection
and exhibited sculpture throughout
the season. Rare breed sheep and
pigs. New tropical entrance garden
planted in 2018. Woodchip pathway
at entrance. Soft woodchip paths in
borders not accessible, but flat garden
for wheelchairs and mobility scooters.
Disabled WC.

**149 NEW THAKEHAM PLACE
FARM**
The Street, Thakeham,
Pulborough, RH20 3EP. Mr &
Mrs T Binnington. *In the village of
Thakeham, 3m N of Storrington. The
farm is at the E end of The Street,
where it turns into Crays Lane.
Follow signs down the farm drive to
Thakeham Place.* Wed 22, Sun 26
July (2-5). Adm £3.50, chd free.
Home-made teas.
Set in the middle of a working dairy
farm, the garden has evolved over
the last 30 yrs. Taking advantage of
its sunny position on free draining
greensand, the borders are full of
sun loving plants and grasses, with
a more formal area surrounding the
farmhouse (not open) and lovely views
across the farm to Warminghurst from
the orchard.

150 TOWN PLACE
Ketches Lane, Freshfield, Sheffield
Park, RH17 7NR. Anthony &
Maggie McGrath, 01825 790221,
mcgrathsussex@hotmail.com,
www.townplacegarden.org.uk.

*5m E of Haywards Heath. From
A275 turn W at Sheffield Green into
Ketches Lane for Lindfield. 1¾m on
L.* Sun 7, Sun 14, Sat 20 June (2-
6). Adm £6, chd free. Cream teas.
Visits also by arrangement in June
for groups of 20+.
A stunning 3 acre garden with a
growing international reputation for
the quality of its design, planting and
gardening. Set round a C17 Sussex
farmhouse (not open), the garden
has over 700 roses, herbaceous
borders, herb garden, topiary
inspired by the sculptures of Henry
Moore, ornamental grasses, an 800
yr old oak, potager, and a unique
ruined Priory Church and Cloisters
in hornbeam. There are steps in the
garden, but all areas can be viewed
from a wheelchair.
&♿ ✿ ☕ ⬤

151 UPWALTHAM BARNS
Upwaltham, GU28 0LX. Roger
& Sue Kearsey, 01798 343145,
suekearsey39@gmail.com. *6m S
of Petworth. 6m N of Chichester
on A285.* Visits by arrangement
Apr to Sept for groups of up to
25. Garden Clubs welcome. Adm
£4.50, chd free. Home-made teas.
Unique farm setting transformed into
a garden of many rooms. Entrance
is a tapestry of perennial planting to
set off C17 flint barns. At the rear is a
walled, terraced garden redeveloped
and planted with an abundance of
unusual plants, we are always adding
something new. Beautiful inner
courtyard and seating area for tea,
coffee and great home-made cakes.
Extensive vegetable garden. Roam
at leisure, relax and enjoy. Features
incl lovely views of the South Downs
and a C12 Shepherds Church (open
to visitors). Partial wheelchair access
with some gravel paths.
&♿ ✿ ☕ ⬤

**152 THE WALLED GARDEN AT
TILGATE PARK**
Tilgate Drive, Tilgate, Crawley,
RH10 5PQ. Nick Hagon,
www.friendsoftilgatepark.co.uk.
*SE Crawley. Leave M23 at J11. From
r'about follow A23 Brighton Rd for
short distance. At T-lights turn R
at sign to Tilgate Park onto Tilgate
Drive. Follow signs in Park for parking
incl disabled parking.* Evening
opening Wed 13, Thur 14 May,
Wed 22, Thur 23 July (6.30-9).
Adm £5, accompanied children
under 16 free. No concessions.
Cash only. Light refreshments

included.
There is much more to know about
the award-winning Tilgate Park than is
realised on a family visit. Why not join
a tour with Park Manager, Nick Hagon
to discover more about this special
environment? In spring learn about
the azaleas, camellias, candelabra
primulas and rhododendrons and
in July the walled garden and the
centuries old specimen trees. Talk
and tour begins at 7pm, near the
Walled Garden. For more information
please phone 01293 521168.
Wheelchair access within the walled
garden only.
&♿ ✿ ☕

153 NEW WARNHAM PARK
Robin Hood Lane, Warnham,
Horsham, RH12 3RP. Mrs Caroline
Lucas. *Turn in off A24 end of Robin
Hood Lane by the large poster. Turn
immed L through the hedge & then
the arch, over the grid & into the
Deer Park. Follow signs for parking.*
Sun 24, Sat 30 May (2-5.30). Adm
£5, chd free. Cream teas.
The garden is situated in the middle
of a 200 acre Deer Park, which has
a very special herd of Red Deer
husbanded by the Lucas Family for
over 150 yrs. Borders with traditional
planting and a kitchen garden that is
prolific most of the yr. The rest of the
garden comprises of different spaces,
including a small white garden, a
Moroccan courtyard and a walled
garden. There is also a woodland
walk. Disabled WC.
&♿ ✿ ☕ ⬤

154 NEW WARREN COTTAGE
Warren Lane, Cross In Hand,
Heathfield, TN21 0TB. Mr & Mrs
Allcorn. *2½m E of Heathfield; 2M W
of Blackboys. At junction of B2102
Lewes Rd & Warren Lane. Follow
signs for parking near garden.* Fri
19 June (1-5). Combined adm
with The Old House £5, chd free.
Home-made teas in Waldron
Village Hall.
½ acre mature, secluded garden
being redeveloped by the owners
and using many reclaimed materials.
Includes 60ft herbaceous border with
oak frame support, long grass area
with specimen shrubs and mown
paths, wildlife pond and borders,
vegetable patch with raised beds,
greenhouses and potting shed, a pub
shed and magical fairy/woodland
garden.
&♿ ✿ ☕

GROUP OPENING

155 WATERWORKS & FRIENDS

Broad Oak & Brede, TN31 6HG.
*Waterworks Cots Brede, off A28
by church & opp Red Lion Pub,
³/₄m at end of lane. Woodlands &
Sculdown on B2089 Chitcombe Rd,
W off A28 at Broad Oak Xrds. Start
at any garden, directions given.* **Sat
6 June (10.30-4). Combined adm
£5, chd free. Light refreshments
at Sculdown.**

SCULDOWN
TN31 6EX. Mrs Christine Buckland.

4 WATERWORKS COTTAGES
TN31 6HG. Mrs Kristina
Clode, 07950 748097,
kristinaclode@gmail.com, www.
kristinaclodegardendesign.co.uk.
**Visits also by arrangement June
to Nov for groups of 10 to 30.
Please car share if possible,
parking limited.**

WOODLANDS
TN31 6EU. Mr George Terry.

An opportunity to visit 3 unique
gardens and discover the Brede
Steam Giants 35ft Edwardian water
pumping engines, and Grade II
listed pump house located behind
4 Waterworks Cottages. Garden
designer Kristina Clode has created
her wildlife friendly garden at 4
Waterworks Cottages over the last
10 yrs. Delightful perennial wildflower
meadow, pond, wisteria covered
pergola and mixed borders packed
full of unusual specimens with yr-
round interest and colour. Woodlands
is an intensely colourful back garden
in 3 sections, also designed by
Kristina Clode. Mixed borders, lawn
and pleached hornbeam hedge,
leading to a formal quartered box
edged garden with filigree gazebo and
vibrant planting. Framed view to the
perennial wildflower meadow beyond.
Sculdown's garden is dominated by
a very large wildlife pond formed as
a result of iron-ore mining over 100
yrs ago. The stunning traditional
cottage (not open) provides a superb
backdrop for several colourful
herbaceous borders and poplar
trees. Plants for sale at 4 Waterworks
Cottages. At Brede Steam Giants,
WC available, but regret no disabled
facilities and assistance dogs only
(free entry, donations encouraged).
Wheelchair access at Sculdown

(park in flat area at top of field) and
in the front garden of 4 Waterworks
Cottages only.

156 NEW WESTWELL HOUSE

Main Street, Northiam, Rye,
TN31 6NB. J Hull & P Beale. *Just
off Main St, opp the GP Surgery,
Northiam. Down gravel drive on opp
side of road to GP Surgery & village
car park. Park in village car park or
on road only (no vehicles at house).*
**Sun 28 June (11-5). Adm £4, chd
£1. Light refreshments.**
Our garden is a multicoloured journey,
past the magnolias and azaleas at the
entrance and you can start to explore
the more intimate areas. Whether
finding a shady spot by the pond
(perhaps take a seat in the boathouse),
gazing at the meandering laburnum
and wisteria over the pergola, or sitting
under the wellingtonia in the paddock,
there are many places to sit and enjoy.
We hope you do.

157 WHITEHANGER

Marley Lane, Haslemere,
GU27 3PY. David & Lynn
Paynter, 07774 010901,
lynn@whitehanger.co.uk. *3m S of
Haslemere. Take the A286 Midhurst
road from Haslemere & after approx
2m turn R into Marley Lane (opp
Hatch Lane). After 1m turn into drive
shared with Rosemary Park Nursing
Home.* **Visits by arrangement
June to Sept for groups of 5 to
30. Refreshments incl tea & cake
(day), wine (eve).**
Set in 6 acres on the edge of the
SDNP surrounded by NT woodland,
this rural garden was started in 2012
when a new Huf house was built
on a derelict site. Now there are
lawned areas with beds of perennials,
a serenity pool with Koi carp, a
wildflower meadow, a Japanese
garden, a sculpture garden, a
woodland walk and a large rockery.

158 3 WHITEMANS CLOSE

Cuckfield, Haywards
Heath, RH17 5DE. David &
Christine Hart, 01444 473520,
shirleycarmanmartin@gmail.com.
*1m N of Cuckfield. On B2036
signed Balcombe, Whitemans
Close is 250yds from r'about on
LH-side. Park on road, no parking
in Whitemans Close. Buses stop*

*at Whitemans Green, where there
is also a large car park.* **Visits by
arrangement for groups of up
to 20. Combined visit with 5
Whitemans Close on 21 May &
11 June. Home-made teas at 5
Whitemans Close.**
A new garden recently planted with
some very special perennials, grasses,
shrubs and trees. The small back
garden has been a challenge! The
plantaholic owner has packed every
square inch with real gems and then
more, likewise the front area with its
treasures. The enthusiastic owner will
explain her planting ideas. A garden
to follow from its newness now, to
becoming established in the future.

159 5 WHITEMANS CLOSE

Cuckfield, Haywards Heath,
RH17 5DE. Shirley Carman-
Martin, 01444 473520,
shirleycarmanmartin@gmail.com.
*1m N of Cuckfield. On B2036 signed
Balcombe Whitemans Close is
250yds from r'about on LH-side. Park
on road, no parking in Whitemans
Close. Buses stop at Whitemans
Green, where there is also a large car
park.* **Mon 31 Aug (1-5). Combined
adm with Lindfield Jungle £6, chd
free. Home-made teas. Visits also
by arrangement for Snowdrop Visits
on 15, 16 & 17 Feb for groups of
up to 20. Combined visit with 3
Whitemans Close on 21 May & 11
June.**
A garden visit for snowdrop and
plant lovers. Individuals welcome to
pre-book. A relatively small cottage
garden packed full of exciting and
unusual plants, plus a large snowdrop
collection. Flower beds overflow with
gorgeous plants in colour schemed
borders, small but productive
vegetable garden, collection of
echeveria and sempervivum and
half hardy plants too. A plantsman's
garden not to miss. Our delicious
home-made teas, served on vintage
china have been very much enjoyed
by our garden visitors.

160 WHITHURST PARK

Plaistow Road, Kirdford, near
Billingshurst, RH14 0JW. Mr
Richard Taylor & Mr Rick Englert,
www.whithurst.com. *7m NW of
Billingshurst. A272 to Wisborough
Green, follow sign to Kirdford, turn R
at 1st T-junction through village, then
R again, 1m on Plaistow Rd, look
for the white Whithurst Park sign at*

roadside. **Sun 5 July (11-5). Adm £5, chd free. Home-made teas.** 10 yr old walled kitchen garden, many espaliered fruit trees. Herb beds, vegetable beds, flower borders and cutting beds. Central greenhouse and potting shed with interesting behind the wall support buildings, incl extensive compost area close to beehives and the bee border and bee wildflower meadow. Sustainability through permaculture principles. Dogs allowed in main grounds, but not in walled garden. Wheelchair access via ramp up a 3 inch step onto garden paths.

 ♿ 🐕 ✿ ☕

GROUP OPENING

161 WINCHELSEA'S SECRET GARDENS
Winchelsea, TN36 4EJ. *2m W of Rye, 8m E of Hastings. Purchase ticket for all gardens at first garden visited; a map will be provided showing gardens & location of refreshments.* **Sat 25 Apr (1-5.30); Sat 20 June (11-5). Combined adm £6, chd free. Home-made teas at Winchelsea New Hall.**

THE ARMOURY
Mr & Mrs A Jasper.
Open on all dates

BACKFIELDS END
Sandra & Peter Mackenzie Smith.
Open on Sat 20 June

CLEVELAND HOUSE
Mr & Mrs J Jempson.
Open on all dates

CLEVELAND PLACE
Sally & Graham Rhodda.
Open on all dates

EVENS
Judith & James Payne.
Open on Sat 20 June

NEW **GILES POINT**
Ant Parker & Tom Ashmore.
Open on all dates

KING'S LEAP
Philip Kent.
Open on all dates

LOOKOUT COTTAGE
Mary & Roger Tidyman.
Open on Sat 20 June

MAGAZINE HOUSE
Susan Stradling.
Open on Sat 20 June

PERITEAU HOUSE
Dr & Mrs Lawrence Youlten.
Open on all dates

RYE VIEW
Howard Norton & David Page.
Open on all dates

SOUTH MARITEAU
Robert & Sheila Holland.
Open on Sat 20 June

Many styles, large and small, secret walled gardens, spring bulbs, tulips, roses, herbaceous borders and more, in the beautiful setting of the Cinque Port of Winchelsea. Explore the town with its magnificent church and famous medieval merchants' cellars. Guided tours of cellars, booking essential 07596 182874. Information at winchelsea.com. For enquiries, or if you are bringing a coach please contact david@ryeview.net, 01797 226524. Wheelchair access to six gardens in April and nine in June; see map provided on the day for details.

♿ ✿ 🚗 ☕

162 2 WOODSIDE
Lewes Road, Laughton, Lewes, BN8 6BL. Dick & Kathy Boland, 01323 811507, kathy.boland01@btinternet.com. *Approx 6m E of Lewes on B2124. In Laughton village 300yds E of Roebuck Pub.* **Visits by arrangement June & July for groups of 5 to 20.** The garden was designed for summer living by its retired owners. It is approx

⅓ acre and comprises a herb garden, a rockery and pond with fish, lawn and herbaceous borders, a small stream and wildlife pond, fruit trees, fruit cage, rose garden and vegetables in raised beds, a shaded area in a less formal setting among trees, planted with shade loving plants.

🐕 ✿

163 WYCH WARREN HOUSE
Wych Warren, Forest Row, RH18 5LF. Colin King & Mary Franck. *1m S of Forest Row. Proceed S on A22, track turning on L, 100 metres past 45mph warning triangle sign. Or 1m N of Wych Cross T-lights track turning on R. Go 400 metres across golf course till the end.* **Wed 15 July (2-8). Adm £5, chd free. Home-made teas.** 6 acre garden in Ashdown Forest, AONB, much of it mixed woodland. Perimeter walk around property (not open). Delightful and tranquil setting with various aspects of interest providing a sensory and relaxing visit. Lovely stonework, specimen trees, exotic bed, three ponds, herbaceous borders, greenhouse and always something new on the go, but above all plenty of space to roam and enjoy. From the terrace, overlooking beautiful views, refreshments will be available. Partial wheelchair access by tarmac track to the kitchen side gate.

♿ 🐕 ✿ ☕

St Mary's Hospital

© Judi Lion

OPENING DATES

All entries subject to change. For latest information check www.ngs.org.uk

Extended openings are shown at the beginning of the month

Map locator numbers are shown to the right of each garden name.

February

Snowdrop Festival

Saturday 8th
Elm Close 15

Sunday 9th
Elm Close 15

Saturday 15th
◆ Hill Close Gardens 17

April

Every Saturday and Sunday from Saturday 11th
◆ Bridge Nursery 8

Monday 13th
◆ Bridge Nursery 8

Sunday 19th
Broadacre 9
Dunchurch Park Hotel 13

May

Every Saturday and Sunday
◆ Bridge Nursery 8

Friday 8th
◆ Bridge Nursery 8
Earlsdon Gardens 14

Saturday 23rd
Ilmington Gardens 21

Sunday 24th
Ilmington Gardens 21
Pebworth Gardens 31

Monday 25th
◆ Bridge Nursery 8
Pebworth Gardens 31

June

Every Saturday and Sunday
◆ Bridge Nursery 8

Saturday 6th
Tysoe Gardens 36

Sunday 7th
Maxstoke Castle 26
Tysoe Gardens 36

Saturday 13th
NEW 6 Canon Price
Road 11
Hunningham Gardens 20

Sunday 14th
NEW 6 Canon Price
Road 11
Hunningham Gardens 20
Lighthorne Gardens 24
Packington Hall 29
Styvechale Gardens 35

Sunday 21st
Honington Gardens 19
Kenilworth Gardens 22
Warmington Gardens 37
Whichford & Ascott
Gardens 40

Saturday 27th
Welford-on-Avon
Gardens 38

Sunday 28th
NEW Ansley Gardens 2
Berkswell Gardens 6
NEW Stoneleigh Village
Gardens 34
Welford-on-Avon
Gardens 38
Wellesbourne
Allotments 39

Tuesday 30th
Dunchurch Park Hotel 13

July

Every Saturday and Sunday
◆ Bridge Nursery 8

Sunday 5th
Avon Dassett Gardens 4
Blacksmiths Cottage 7

Saturday 11th
NEW 6 Canon Price
Road 11

The Old Rectory, Lighthorne Gardens

Sunday 12th
NEW 6 Canon Price
Road 11

Saturday 18th
Guy's Cliffe Walled
Garden 16

Sunday 19th
◆ Avondale Nursery 5

Sunday 26th
NEW The Malt House 25

Friday 31st
Anya Court Care Home 3

August

Every Saturday and Sunday
◆ Bridge Nursery 8

Saturday 1st
Anya Court Care Home 3

Sunday 23rd
◆ Avondale Nursery 5

Monday 31st
◆ Bridge Nursery 8

September

Every Saturday and Sunday
◆ Bridge Nursery 8

Saturday 5th
Squab Hall Farm 33

Sunday 6th
Burmington Grange 10
Squab Hall Farm 33

October

Saturday 24th
◆ Hill Close Gardens 17

By Arrangement

Arrange a personalised garden visit with your club, or group of friends, on a date to suit you. See individual garden entries for full details.

Admington Hall 1
10 Avon Carrow, Avon
Dassett Gardens 4
Broadacre 9
NEW 6 Canon Price
Road 11
The Croft House 12
16 Delaware Road,
Styvechale Gardens 35
Elm Close 15
Fieldgate, Kenilworth
Gardens 22
The Hill Cottage 18
2 The Hiron, Styvechale
Gardens 35
19 Leigh Crescent 23
The Motte, Hunningham
Gardens 20
Oak House 28
NEW 3 Park Walk 30
Priors Marston Manor 32
Squab Hall Farm 33

THE GARDENS

1 ADMINGTON HALL

Admington, Shipston-on-Stour, CV36 4JN. Mark & Antonia Davies, 01789 450279, adhall@admington.com. *6m NW of Shipston-on-Stour. From Ilmington, follow signs to Admington. Approx 2m, turn R to Admington by Polo Ground. Continue for 1m.* **Visits by arrangement May to Sept for groups of 10+. Home-made teas. Dietary requirements can be catered for by prior request.**
A continually evolving 10 acre garden with an established structure of innovative planning and planting. An extensive collection of fine and mature specimen trees provide the essential core structure to this traditional country garden. Features incl a lush broad lawn, orchard, water garden, large walled garden, wildflower meadows and extensive modern topiary. This is a garden in motion. Wheelchair access to most parts of garden, albeit some routes will take slightly longer.

GROUP OPENING

2 NEW ANSLEY GARDENS

Ansley, CV10 0QR. *Ansley is situated W of Nuneaton, adjacent to Arley. Ansley is directly off the B4114.* **Sun 28 June (1.30-6). Combined adm £5, chd free. Light refreshments & home-made cakes in Ansley Village Hall.**

NEW **1A BIRMINGHAM ROAD**
Adrian & Heather Norgrove.

NEW **25 BIRMINGHAM ROAD**
Pat & David Arrowsmith.

NEW **59 BIRMINGHAM ROAD**
Joan & Peter McParland.

NEW **35 NUTHURST CRESCENT**
Roger & Heather Greaves.

NEW **THE OLD POLICE HOUSE**
Mike & Hilary Ward.

NEW **1 PARK COTTAGES**
Janet & Andy Down.

Ansley is a small ex-mining village situated in North Warwickshire. The six gardens open are a selection of different styles and offerings. They range from a very small traditional cottage garden crammed with flowers and pots to larger gardens maximising the amazing views of the countryside. There is one that has been transformed into a walled garden, one with a large range of unusual plants and a country garden with mature plants and ancient roses. They each offer something different to the garden visitor. Five of the gardens are in close proximity with the opportunity to walk across the fields on public footpaths to the sixth garden for those who are able. The local Norman church will be open and the Morris Dancing Group will be entertaining visitors during the day. Wheelchair access to some gardens.
☕

3 ANYA COURT CARE HOME

286 Dunchurch Road, Rugby, CV22 6JA. Karen Handley. *Opp Sainsbury's on the Dunchurch Rd. If our car park is busy please use their car park as an alternative. Please go to Anya Court reception, who will guide you to garden.* **Fri 31 July, Sat 1 Aug (10.30-3.30). Adm £5, chd free. Cream teas.**
A large landscaped garden with an abundance of trees, shrubs, lawns and planting beds. Sensory perennial planting and annual displays meander alongside paths leading to the residents garden club with raised vegetable beds. Café patio area to have a cup of tea and home-made cake whilst enjoying the garden. New for 2020: a wildflower meadow, host plant butterfly border and butterfly breeding house. Fully accessible to wheelchairs.

The Old House, Honington Gardens

GROUP OPENING

4 AVON DASSETT GARDENS
Southam, CV47 2AE. *7m N of Banbury. From M40 J12 turn L & L again onto the B4100, following signs to Herb Centre & Gaydon. Take 2nd L into village (signed). Park in cemetery car park at the top of the hill.* **Sun 5 July (2-6). Combined adm £7, chd free. Home-made teas at The Thatches.**

10 AVON CARROW
Anna Prosser,
annaatthecarrow@btopenworld.com.
Visits also by arrangement Apr to Oct for groups of 5 to 30. Refreshments on request.
🛏

11 AVON CARROW
Mick & Avis Forbes.

THE COACH HOUSE
Diana & Peter Biddlestone.

THE EAST WING, AVON CARROW
Christine Fisher & Terry Gladwin.

HILL TOP FARM
Mr D Hicks.

OLD MILL COTTAGE
Mike & Jill Lewis.

THE OLD RECTORY
Lily Hope-Frost.

POPPY COTTAGE
Audrey Butler.

THE SNUG
Mrs Deb Watts.

THE THATCHES
Trevor & Michele Gill.

Pretty Hornton stone village sheltering in the lee of the Burton Dassett hills, well wooded with parkland setting and The Old Rectory mentioned in Domesday Book. Wide variety of gardens including kitchen gardens, cottage, gravel and tropical gardens. Range of plants incl alpines, herbaceous, perennials, roses, climbers and shrubs. The gardens are on/off the main road through the village. For 2020, we expect to run a shuttle service from top to bottom of the village. Features incl book sale, plant sales, tombola and historic church open. Wheelchair access to most gardens.
 & 🐕 🌼 🚐 ☕

5 ◆ AVONDALE NURSERY
at Russell's Nursery, Mill Hill, Baginton, CV8 3AG.
Gary Leaver, 07367 590620, enquiries@avondalenursery.co.uk, www.avondalenursery.co.uk. *3m S of Coventry. At junction of A45 & A46 take slip road to Baginton, 1st L to Mill Hill, opp Old Mill Inn.* **For NGS: Sun 19 July, Sun 23 Aug (10.30-4.30). Adm £3, chd free. For other opening times and information, please phone, email or visit garden website.** Donation to Plant Heritage. Vast array of flowers and ornamental grasses, incl National Collections of *Anemone nemorosa*, *Sanguisorba* and *Aster novae-angliae*. Choc-a-bloc with plants, our Library Garden is a well labelled reference book illustrating the unusual, exciting and even some long-lost treasures. Adjacent nursery is a plantaholic's delight! Big collections of *Helenium, Crocosmia, Agapanthus, Sanguisorba* and ornamental grasses. The garden will be looking at its best in July and August.
& 🐕 🌼 🚐 NPC ☕

GROUP OPENING

6 BERKSWELL GARDENS
Berkswell, Coventry, CV7 7BB.
7m W of Coventry. A452 to Balsall Common & follow signs to Berkswell. Tickets & maps available at the village Reading Room (CV7 7BB) & also at each garden. Car necessary to visit all gardens. **Sun 28 June (11-6). Combined adm £6, chd free. Light refreshments.**

NEW **2 AGRICULTURAL COTTAGES**
Mrs Jane Edwards.

BEEHIVE COTTAGE
Sophie & Graham Lock.

BROOKSIDE HOUSE
Shirley & Frank Rounthwaite.

145 DUGGINS LANE
Mary & Edward Cotterrell.

NEW **SPENCER'S END**
Mr Gordon Clark.

SQUIRRELS JUMP
Brian & Jenny Harris.

248 STATION ROAD
Caroline & Paul Joyner.

THE TOWER HOUSE
Penny & David Stableforth.

YEW TREE BARN
Angela & Ken Shaw.

Berkswell is a beautiful village dating back to Saxon times with a C12 Norman church and has several C16 and C17 buildings including the pub and old Museum. In 2014 and 2015 the village was awarded Gold in the RHS Britain in Bloom campaign, plus a special RHS award in 2014 for the Best Large Village in the Heart of England. The gardens provide great variety with fine examples of small and large, formal and informal, wild, imaginatively planted herbaceous borders and productive vegetable gardens. Something for everyone and plenty of ideas to take home. Light refreshments at Beehive Cottage, Berkswell Reading Room, 248 Station Road and Yew Tree Barn. Also open to visitors is the C12 Norman church and garden. Wheelchair access to some gardens.
🐕 🌼 ☕

7 BLACKSMITHS COTTAGE
Little Compton, Moreton-in-Marsh, GL56 0SE. Mrs Andrew Lukas.
Garden entrance is opp the village hall car park. Please park at village hall or in Reed College car park nearby. **Sun 5 July (1.30-5.30). Adm £5, chd free. Home-made teas at village hall.**
This walled garden has been created in the last 5 yrs for all seasons with many fine and unusual trees, shrubs, plants and bulbs set around a large lawn with a beautiful Aqualens fountain at its centre. Unusual varieties of clematis climb through shrubs and up walls. There is a productive vegetable garden, greenhouse and summerhouse. All designed and made by the owners to create a sense of magic.
 ☕

8 ◆ BRIDGE NURSERY
Tomlow Road, Napton, Southam, CV47 8HX. Christine Dakin & Philip Martino, 01926 812737, chris.dakin25@yahoo.com, www.bridge-nursery.co.uk. *3m E of Southam. Brown tourist sign at Napton Xrds on A425 Southam to Daventry road.* **For NGS: Every Sat and Sun 11 Apr to 27 Sept (10-4). Mon 13 Apr, Fri 8, Mon 25 May, Mon 31 Aug (10-4). Light refreshments. Adm £3, chd free. For other opening times and information, please phone, email or visit garden website.**
Clay soil? Don't despair. Here is an acre of garden full of an exciting

range of plants which thrive in hostile conditions. Grass paths lead you round borders filled with many unusual plants. Features incl a pond and a bamboo grove complete with panda! A peaceful haven for wildlife and visitors. A recent comment from a visitor is that the garden is comfortable with itself. Christine and Philip will gladly provide coffee or tea and biscuits on request. Visits also by arrangement, groups welcome, all proceeds to the NGS.

⁹ BROADACRE
Grange Road, Dorridge, Solihull, B93 8QA. John Woolman, 07818 082885, jw234567@gmail.com, www.broadacregarden.org. *Approx 3m SE of Solihull. On B4101 opp The Railway Inn. Plenty of parking.* **Sun 19 Apr (2-6). Adm £5, chd free. Home-made teas. Visits also by arrangement.**
Broadacre is a semi-wild garden, managed organically. Attractively landscaped with pools, lawns and trees, beehives, and adjoining stream and wildflower meadows. Bring stout footwear to follow the nature trail. Dorridge Cricket Club is on-site (the bar will be open). Lovely venue for a picnic. Dogs and children are welcome. Excellent country pub, The Railway Inn, at the bottom of the drive.

🔟 BURMINGTON GRANGE
Cherington, Shipston-on-Stour, CV36 5HZ. Mr & Mrs Patrick Ramsay. *2m E of Shipston-on-Stour. Take Oxford Rd (A3400) from Shipston-on-Stour, after 2m turn L to Burmington, go through village & continue for 1m, turn L to Willington & Barcheston, on sharp L bend turn R over cattle grid.* **Sun 6 Sept (2-6). Adm £5, chd free. Home-made teas.**
Interesting plantsman's garden extending to about 1½ acres, set in the rolling hills of the North Cotswolds with wonderful views over unspoilt countryside. The garden is well developed considering it was planted 18 years ago. Small vegetable garden, beautiful sunken rose garden with herbaceous and shrub borders. Orchard and tree walk with unusual trees.
☕

🔟🔟 NEW 6 CANON PRICE ROAD
Nursery Meadow, Barford, Warwick, CV35 8EQ. Mrs Marie-Jane Roberts, 07775 584336. *From A429 turn into Barford. Park on Wellesbourne Rd & walk into Nursery Meadow by red phone box. No 6 is R in 1st close.* **Sat 13, Sun 14 June, Sat 11, Sun 12 July (2-5.30). Adm £5, chd free. Light refreshments in the garden room. Visits also by arrangement Apr to Sept for visitors up to 60 max. Refreshments on request.**
A new build garden of 4 yrs adjoining a ½ acre mixed garden including a pond, rockery, colour themed shrubs and perennials, a nature garden and herb garden. There are areas of flowers for cutting and drying and 180 dahlias grown for exhibition, plus 7 vegetable beds and 9 types of fruit including fan trained peaches and cordon pears. 7 seating areas and colourful planted containers. Access via a single slab path that joins a wide path through the garden. No WC.
♿ ✻ 🚗 ☕

🔟🔢 THE CROFT HOUSE
Haselor, Alcester, B49 6LU. Isobel & Patrick Somers, 07767 306673, ifas1010@aol.com. *6m W of Stratford-upon-Avon, 2m E of Alcester, off A46. From A46 take Haselor turn. From Alcester take old Stratford Rd, turn L signed Haselor, then R at Xrds. Garden in centre of village. Please park considerately.* **Visits by arrangement May & June**

for groups of 5 to 30. Adm £4, chd free. Home-made teas.
Wander through an acre of trees, shrubs and herbaceous borders densely planted with a designer's passion for colour and texture. Hidden areas invite you to linger. Gorgeous scented wisteria on two sides of the house. Organically managed, providing a haven for birds and other wildlife. Frog pond, treehouse, small vegetable plot and a few venerable old fruit trees from its days as a market garden. Garden is on a gentle slope. Step-free access, but too narrow for most wheelchairs.
✻ ☕

🔢🔟 DUNCHURCH PARK HOTEL
Rugby Road, Dunchurch, Rugby, CV22 6QW. Dunchurch Park Hotel, 01788 810656, reservations@dunchurch.co.uk, www.dunchurch.co.uk. *Just S of Rugby on the A426 & just N of the A45/M45 J1.* **Sun 19 Apr, Tue 30 June (10-3). Adm £4, chd free. Light refreshments. Tue 30 June incl an indoor Bonhams Valuation Day (11-2), suggested donation £2 per item, proceeds to NGS.**
Dunchurch Park Hotel is set in beautiful Grade II* listed grounds and gardens, a perfect setting in which to explore and unwind. Bar 1823 will be offering a selection of refreshments on the day which can be enjoyed in the bar itself or on our terrace overlooking the gardens. Partial wheelchair access to some areas of the grounds.
♿ 🐄 🚗 🚌 ☕

Admington Hall

GROUP OPENING

🔢 EARLSDON GARDENS
Coventry, CV5 6FS. *Turn towards Coventry at A45 & A429 T-lights. Take 3rd L into Beechwood Ave, continue ½m to St Barbara's Church at Xrds with Rochester Rd. Maps & tickets at St Barbara's Church Hall.* **Fri 8 May (11-4). Combined adm £5, chd free. Light refreshments at St Barbara's Church Hall.**

43 ARMORIAL ROAD
Gary & Jane Flanagan.

3 BATES ROAD
Victor Keene MBE.

28 CLARENDON STREET
Ruth & Symon Whitehouse.

NEW 26 CONISTON ROAD
Judith & Colin Yates.

NEW 38 CONISTON ROAD
Louise & Martin Prue.

27 HARTINGTON CRESCENT
David & Judith Bogle.

40 HARTINGTON CRESCENT
Viv & George Buss.

114 HARTINGTON CRESCENT
Liz Campbell & Denis Crowley.

40 RANULF CROFT
Spencer & Sue Swain.

15 ROCHESTER ROAD
Professor Jane Hutton.

54 SALISBURY AVENUE
Pam Moffit.

2 SHAFTESBURY ROAD
Ann Thomson & Bruce Walker.

23 SPENCER AVENUE
Susan & Keith Darwood.

84 SPENCER AVENUE
Chris & Ruth Winters.

Varied selection of town gardens from small to more formal with interest for all tastes incl a mature garden with deep borders bursting with spring colour; a large garden with extensive lawns and an array of rhododendrons, azaleas and large mature trees; densely planted town garden with sheltered patio area and wilder woodland; and a surprisingly large garden offering interest to all ages! There is also a pretty garden set on several levels with hidden aspect; a large peaceful garden with water features and vegetable plot; a large mature garden in peaceful surroundings; and a plantaholic's garden with a large variety of plants, clematis and small trees.

🐕 ❀ ☕

🔢 ELM CLOSE
Welford-on-Avon, CV37 8PT. Eric & Glenis Dyer, 01789 750793, glenisdyer@gmail.com. *5m SW of Stratford, off B4390. Elm Close is between Welford Garage & The Bell Inn, roadside parking.* **Sat 8, Sun 9 Feb (11-3). Adm £4, chd free. Home-made teas. Opening with Welford-on-Avon Gardens on Sat 27, Sun 28 June (1-5). Visits also by arrangement Feb to Sept for groups of 10 to 30.**
Drifts of snowdrops, aconites, erythroniums and hellebores in spring are followed by species peonies, sumptuous tree peonies, herbaceous peonies and delphiniums. Colourful Japanese maples, daphnes and cornus are underplanted with hostas, heucheras and brunneras. Then agapanthus, salvias and hydrangeas extend the seasons, with hundreds of clematis providing yr-round colour. Wheelchair access over slightly sloping front gravel drive. Garden mainly flat with two very shallow steps.

ぇ ❀ ☕

🔢 GUY'S CLIFFE WALLED GARDEN
Coventry Road, Guy's Cliffe, Warwick, CV34 5FJ. Sarah Ridgeway, www.guyscliffewalledgarden.org.uk. *Behind Hintons Nursery in Guy's Cliffe. Guy's Cliffe is on the A429, between North Warwick & Leek Wootton.* **Sat 18 July (10-3.30). Adm £3.50, chd free. Home-made teas.**
A Grade II listed garden of special historic interest, having been the kitchen garden for Guy's Cliffe House. The garden dates back to the mid-1700s. Restoration work started 6 yrs ago; using plans from the early C19, the garden layout has already been reinstated and the beds, once more, planted with fruit, flowers and vegetables incl many heritage varieties. Glasshouses awaiting restoration. Original C18 walls. Exhibition of artefacts discovered during restoration. Wheelchair access through entrance of Hintons Nursery and paths through garden. WC with disabled access.

ぇ 🐕 ❀ ☕

1 The Wheelwrights, Warmington Gardens

17 ◆ **HILL CLOSE GARDENS**
Bread and Meat Close,
Warwick, CV34 6HF. Hill Close
Gardens Trust, 01926 493339,
centremanager@hcgt.org.uk,
www.hillclosegardens.com. *Town
centre. Follow signs to Warwick
racecourse. Entry from Friars St onto
Bread and Meat Close. Car park
by entrance next to racecourse. 2
hrs free parking. Disabled parking
outside the gates.* **For NGS: Sat 15
Feb (11-4); Sat 24 Oct (11-5). Adm
£4.50, chd £1. Light refreshments
in Visitor Centre. Gluten free
options. For other opening times
and information, please phone,
email or visit garden website.**
Restored Grade II* Victorian
leisure gardens comprising 16
individual hedged gardens, 8 brick
summerhouses. Herbaceous borders,
heritage apple and pear trees,
C19 daffodils, over 100 varieties of
snowdrops, many varieties of asters
and chrysanthemums. Heritage
vegetables. Plant Heritage border,
auricula theatre, and Victorian style
glasshouse. Children's garden.
Wheelchair available, please phone to
book in advance.
🚻 ❀ 🚗 NPC 🍵

18 **THE HILL COTTAGE**
Kings Lane, Snitterfield, Stratford-
upon-Avon, CV37 0QA. Gillie &
Paul Waldron, 07895 369387,
info@thehillcottage.co.uk,
www.thehillcottage.co.uk. *5 mins
from M40 J15. Take A46 Stratford,
1m take 2nd exit at r'about, ½m R
into Kings Lane, over A46, 1st R,
2nd house on L. From Village: up
White Horse Hill, R at T-junction, over
A46, R into Kings Lane, 2nd house
on L.* **Visits by arrangement Apr to
Sept for groups of 5 to 20. Adm
£5, chd free. Home-made teas
£3.50 per person.**
High on a ridge overlooking orchards
and golf course with fabulous
views to distant hills, this 2¼ acre
garden, full of surprises, offers varied
planting; sunny gravel with exotic
specimens; cool, shady woodland with
relaxed perennial groups; romantic
green oak pond garden and stone
summerhouse; pool with newts and
dragonflies. The big project in 2019, a
traditional walled kitchen garden and
glasshouse. Bluebell wood best in late
April. Gazebo, pergolas, lavender walk,
lilies, clematis, and too many pots to
count! Not suitable for wheelchairs or
scooters as many steps and slopes.
❀ 🏠 🍵

GROUP OPENING

19 **HONINGTON GARDENS**
Shipston-on-Stour, CV36 5AA.
*1½ m N of Shipston-on-Stour. Take
A3400 towards Stratford-upon-Avon,
then turn R signed Honington.* **Sun
21 June (2-5.30). Combined adm
£6, chd free. Home-made teas.**

HONINGTON GLEBE
Mr & Mrs J C Orchard.

HONINGTON HALL
B H E Wiggin.

MALT HOUSE RISE
Mr P Weston.

THE MALTHOUSE
Mr & Mrs R Hunt.

THE OLD HOUSE
Mr & Mrs I F Beaumont.

ORCHARD HOUSE
Mr & Mrs Monnington.

C17 village, recorded in Domesday,
entered by old toll gate. Ornamental
stone bridge over the River Stour and
interesting church with C13 tower and
late C17 nave after Wren. Six super
gardens. 2 acre plantsman's garden
consisting of rooms planted informally
with yr-round interest in contrasting
foliage and texture, lily pool and
parterre. Extensive lawns and fine
mature trees with river and garden
monuments. Secluded walled cottage
garden with roses, and a structured
cottage garden formally laid out with
box hedging and small fountain.
Small, developing garden created by
the owners with informal mixed beds
and borders. Wheelchair access to
most gardens.
🚻 🐾 ❀ 🚗 🍵

GROUP OPENING

20 **HUNNINGHAM GARDENS**
Hunningham, Leamington Spa,
CV33 9DS. Margaret & Peter
Green. *6m NE of Leamington Spa,
8m SW of Rugby, 7m S of Coventry.
Just off the Fosse Way (B4455),
or take B4453 from Leamington
through Weston-under-Wetherley,
then turn R to Hunningham. Parking
in village at CV33 9DS & at Sandy
Acre at CV47 9QE.* **Sat 13, Sun 14
June (1-5.30). Combined adm £6,
chd free. Home-made teas in St
Margaret's Church Parish Room
from 1pm.**

NEW **3 ELM FARM COTTAGES**
David & Moira Rawlings.

GLENCOVE
Simon & Annabel Shackleton.

NEW **HUNNINGHAM CROFT**
Mark & Joanne Wardle.

HUNNINGHAM HILL FARM
Jonathan Hofstetter.

THE MOTTE
Margaret & Peter Green,
01926 632903,
margaretegreen100@gmail.com.
Visits also by arrangement May
to Aug for groups of up to 20.

THE OLD HALL
Nicholas & Rona Horler.

SANDY ACRE
David & Janis Tait.

NEW **THE VICARAGE**
Rev & Mrs Hugh & Carole
Priestner.

Hunningham, a hamlet nestling in the
countryside close to the River Leam
with St Margaret's Church dating
in part to the C13. Eight gardens in
varied styles, with more possibly open
on the day. A plant lover's garden
brimming with woodland plants,
tender perennials, unusual shrubs
and trees, new fruit and vegetable
plot and a plant filled conservatory.
Newly formed garden with pleached
hornbeam avenue, parterre with
feature sculpture, panoramic views,
wooded areas, cut flower garden
and new holm oak circle. Large
partly walled garden with mature
shrubs and trees surrounding the
Old Hall. Hedged cottage garden
with herbaceous perennials, fruit and
vegetable areas. A garden set high on
the hill with views across the Shire,
with herbaceous planting, walled
vegetable garden, natural pond,
orchard and wildflower meadow. New
for 2020 are a bijou cottage front
garden ablaze with colour, a large
garden featuring many mature trees
providing a haven for birds, and a
garden under redevelopment. Some
gardens have views across the River
Leam. Good plant sale.
🚻 🐾 ❀ 🍵

*Your visits help change lives
– since 1927, we've donated
over £60 million to nursing
and caring charities*

GROUP OPENING

21 ILMINGTON GARDENS
Ilmington, CV36 4LA.
01608 682230. *8m S of Stratford-upon-Avon. 8m N of Moreton-in-Marsh. 4m NW of Shipston-on-Stour off A3400. 3m NE of Chipping Campden.* Sat 23, Sun 24 May (12.30-6). Combined adm £7, chd free. Home-made teas in Ilmington Community Shop, Upper Green (Sat) & at the village hall (Sun). Donation to Shipston Home Nursing.

THE BEVINGTONS
Mr & Mrs N Tustain.

CHERRY ORCHARD
Mr Angus Chambers.

COMPTON SCORPION FARM
Mrs Karlsen.

THE DOWER HOUSE
Mr & Mrs M Tremellen.

FOXCOTE HILL
Mr & Mrs Michael Dingley.

FROG ORCHARD
Mr & Mrs Jeremy Snowden.

GRUMP COTTAGE
Mr & Mrs Martin Underwood.

ILMINGTON MANOR
Mr Martin Taylor.

OLD FOX HOUSE
Rob & Sarah Beebee.

RAVENSCROFT
Mr & Mrs Clasper.

STUDIO COTTAGE
Sarah Hobson.

Ilmington is an ancient hillside Cotswold village 2m from the Fosse Way with two good pubs and splendid teas. Buy your ticket at Ilmington Manor (next to the Red Lion Pub); wander the 3 acre gardens with fish pond. Then walk to the upper green behind the village hall to Foxcote Hill's large gardens and Old Fox House (new in 2019), then tiny Grump Cottage's small stone terraced suntrap. Up Grump St to Ravenscroft's large sculpture filled sloping vistas commanding the hilltop. Walk to nearby Frog Lane, view cottage gardens of Cherry Orchard, Frog Orchard, and Studio Cottage. Then to the Bevingtons many-chambered cottage garden at the bottom of Valanders Lane near the church and manor ponds and beyond to the Dower House in Back Street. Also, visit the delightful Compton Scorpion Farmhouse's magic garden a mile way. The Ilmington Morris Men performing round the village on Sun 24th May only.

GROUP OPENING

22 KENILWORTH GARDENS
Kenilworth, CV8 1BT. *Fieldgate Lane, off A452. Tickets & maps available at most gardens. Parking available at Abbey Fields. Street parking on Fieldgate Lane (limited), Siddley Avenue & Beehive Hill.* Sun 21 June (12-5). Combined adm £6, chd free. Home-made teas at St Nicholas Parochial Hall from 1pm.

BEEHIVE HILL ALLOTMENTS
Kenilworth Allotment Association.

FIELDGATE
Liz & Bob Watson, 01926 512307, liz.watson@ngs.org.uk.
Visits also by arrangement May to Sept for groups of 5 to 30. Home-made teas by prior request.

14C FIELDGATE LANE
Sandra & Bob Aulton.

7 FIELDGATE LAWN
Simon Cockell.

65 RANDALL ROAD
Mrs Jan Kenyon.

2 ST NICHOLAS AVENUE
Mr Ian Roberts.

ST NICHOLAS PAROCHIAL HALL
St Nicholas Church.

1 SIDDELEY AVENUE
Clare Wightman.

THE STABLES, 3 FIELDGATE LAWN
Gerry Rutter.

NEW TREE TOPS
Joanna & George Illingworth.

Kenilworth was historically a very important town in Warwickshire. It has one of England's best castle ruins, Abbey Fields and plenty of pubs and good restaurants. The gardens open this year are very varied. There are small and large gardens, formal, contemporary and cottage styles with trees, shrubs, herbaceous borders, ponds and more intimate, wildlife friendly areas, plus plenty of vegetables at the allotments. Many of the gardens have won Gold in the Kenilworth in Bloom garden competition. Partial wheelchair access to most of the gardens.

23 19 LEIGH CRESCENT
Long Itchington, Southam, Warwickshire, CV47 9QS. Tony Shorthouse, 01926 817192, Tonyshorthouse19@gmail.com.
Leigh Crescent off the Stockton Rd in Long Itchington village. Visits by arrangement July to Sept for groups of 5 to 10. Adm £5, chd free. Tea. Discover a tropical garden where dappled sunlight filters through the green canopy above and sounds of a waterfall fill the air. A tropical garden, hidden in a Warwickshire village, densely packed with rare and unusual species, many raised from seed.

The Croft House

GROUP OPENING

24 LIGHTHORNE GARDENS
Lighthorne, Warwick, CV35 0AR.
10m S of Warwick. Lighthorne will be signed from the Fosse Way & B4100. **Sun 14 June (2-5.30). Combined adm £6, chd free. Home-made teas at the village hall.**

NEW **BISHOPS HILL HOUSE**
Sheila Barrett.

1 CHURCH HILL COURT
Irene Proudman.

NEW **3 CHURCH HILL COURT**
Nick & Marie.

4 CHURCH HILL COURT
Carol Schofield & Martin Preedy.

NEW **6 CHURCH HILL COURT**
Rachel Edgington.

THE OLD RECTORY
The Hon Lady Butler.

THE PADDOCK
Martin & Lesley Thornton.

NEW **ST CLEMENTS**
Mike & Carol Smith.

Lighthorne is a compact, pretty village between the Fosse Way and the B4100, with a charming church (open), pub, cafe and village hall. Featuring the spectacular walled garden of The Old Rectory to smaller, designer, contemporary and traditional gardens; there is plenty to interest the visitor. A total of eight gardens will be open. Car parking at the sports ground with free shuttle service into the village and back. Disabled car parking at the village hall. Partial wheelchair access to some of the gardens.
&. 🐕 ☕

25 NEW THE MALT HOUSE
Charlecote, Warwick, CV35 9EW.
Katriona & Rupert Collins. *10 mins from J15 of the M40 taking the A429. About 2m along the A429 take R turn to Charlecote. Enter the village passing telephone box on L. The Malt House is approx 100 metres past this on L.* **Sun 26 July (12-5.30). Adm £5, chd free. Home-made teas.**
Lovely Grade II listed house (not open) set in charming hamlet of Charlecote, on the edge of Charlecote House and deer park. Beautiful borders offering interest and colour throughout the year and featuring a small pond which attracts an abundance of wildlife.

Dinsdale House, Tysoe Gardens

Enjoy mixed borders brimming with agapanthus and beautiful pots. Walk around the vegetable plot and cutting patch and admire a large variety of dahlias. There will be tea and delicious cake for sale, plus hand tied bunches of flowers. Access over gravel drive and 2 steps to the main border area.
🐕 ☕

26 MAXSTOKE CASTLE
Coleshill, B46 2RD. G M Fetherston-Dilke. *2½ m E of Coleshill. E of Birmingham, on B4114. Take R turn down Castle Lane, Castle drive 1¼ m on R.* **Sun 7 June (11-5). Adm £7.50, chd £5. Home-made teas.**
Approx 5 acres of garden and grounds with herbaceous, shrubs and trees in the immediate surroundings of this C14 moated castle. No wheelchair access to house.
&. ❀ ☕

27 ◆ THE MILL GARDEN
55 Mill Street, Warwick, CV34 4HB.
Julia (née Measures) Russell & David Russell, www.visitwarwick.co.uk/placeofinterest/the-mill-garden. *Off A425 beside old castle gate, at the bottom of Mill St. Disabled parking & drop only, use nearby St Nicholas car park.* **For opening times and information, please visit garden website.**
This garden lies in a magical setting on the banks of the River Avon, beneath the walls of Warwick Castle. Winding paths lead round every corner to dramatic views of the castle and ruined Medieval bridge. This informal cottage garden is a profusion of plants, shrubs and trees. Beautiful all year. In 2019 the

garden won Gold in Warwick in Bloom and the owners received an Outstanding Achievement Award for their charitable fundraising. The garden was also awarded Certificate of Excellence from TripAdvisor. Open daily 1st April to 31st October 9am-6pm £3. Partial wheelchair access. Not suitable for electric wheelchairs or large pushchairs. Sorry no dogs.
&. ❀

28 OAK HOUSE
Waverley Edge, Bubbenhall, Coventry, CV8 3LW. Helena Grant, 07731 419685, helena.grant@btinternet.com. *15 mins from Leamington Spa via the Oxford Rd/A423 & the Leamington Rd/A445 & the A46. Spaces for 4 cars only.* **Visits by arrangement May to Nov for groups of up to 20. Adm £5, chd free. Tea & cake £3 per person.**
Tucked away next to Waverley Woods, Oak House enjoys a walled garden that has been landscaped and extended over 30 yrs. The garden is split on 2 levels with 7 seating areas allowing for relaxed appreciation of every aspect of the garden, with peaceful places to sit, ponder and enjoy. A focal point is the large terracotta urn, over 60 yrs old, which delivers vertical interest and the summerhouse and arbour which face each other diagonally across the garden. The curved borders have a wide range of planting creating distinct areas which surround the lawn. There are over 80 different plant varieties giving yr-round interest which is a haven for birds and other wildlife. Wheelchair access only on level path which runs round the house.
&. ❀ ☕

29 PACKINGTON HALL
Meriden, nr Coventry, CV7 7HF.
Lord & Lady Guernsey,
www.packingtonestate.co.uk.
*Midway between Coventry &
Birmingham on A45. Entrance
400yds from Stonebridge Island
towards Coventry. For SatNav please
use CV7 7HE.* **Sun 14 June (2-5).
Adm £6, chd free. Home-made
teas.**
Packington is the setting for an
elegant Capability Brown landscape.
Designed from 1751, the gardens
include sweeping lawns down to a
serpentine lake, impressive cedars of
Lebanon, wellingtonias and various
other trees, a 1762 Japanese bridge,
a millennium rose garden, wildflower
meadow and mixed terrace borders.
Home-made teas on the terrace or
in The Pompeiin Room if wet. No
wheelchair access to gardens.

30 NEW **3 PARK WALK**
Rugby, CV21 2QP. Mr David
Wadsworth, 07769 907642,
Slingates2003@aol.com.
*Rugby town centre. Park Walk
is pedestrian only access & runs
alongside Caldecott Park. Parking
is available on Lancaster Rd (free,
2 hrs no return) or adjacent to the
Benn Hall on Newbold Rd.* **Visits
by arrangement June to Aug
for groups of 5 to 20. Light
refreshments.**
A smallish residential garden in Rugby
town centre with a cottage garden
style. It has evolved gradually over the
last 6 yrs, structured around mature
old fashioned shrubs and a good
collection of English and old roses,
with a wide range of herbaceous
perennials taking centre stage amidst
this back drop. Wheelchair access to
narrow, level garden with one step.

The Malt House

GROUP OPENING

31 PEBWORTH GARDENS

Stratford-upon-Avon, CV37 8XZ. www.pebworth.org/ngs-open-gardens. *7m SW of Stratford-upon-Avon.* **Sun 24, Mon 25 May (1-5). Combined adm £7, chd free. Home-made teas at Pebworth Village Hall.**

BANK HOUSE
Clive & Caroline Warren.

FAR VIEW
Mr & Mrs Adrian Carus.

FELLY LODGE
Maz & Barrie Clatworthy.

IVYBANK
Mr & Mrs R Davis.
NPC

THE KNOLL
Mr & Mrs K Wood.

MAPLE BARN
Richard & Wendi Weller.

MEON COTTAGE
David & Sally Donnison.

OAK HOUSE
Sue & Oz Jordan.

THE OLD BARN
Kevin & Tracey Morley.

PEBWORTH ALLOTMENTS
Les Madden.

PETTIFER HOUSE
Mr & Mrs Michael Veal.

Pebworth is a delightful village with thatched cottages and properties young and old. There are a variety of garden styles from cottage gardens to modern, walled and terraced gardens. Pebworth is topped by St Peter's Church, which has a large ring of ten bells, unusual for a small rural church. This year we have 10 gardens and the Pebworth Allotments opening, with scrumptious tea and cakes provided by the Pebworth WI in the village hall. The Pebworth Allotments have only been in existence a few years and residents have lovingly tended to them. They are smart and productive! Some of the Allotmentiers are real characters. Do visit and have chat, they have a wealth of knowledge. Please ask for the ramp for wheelchair access to village hall. Wheelchair access is limited in some gardens. Guide and Assistance dogs welcome.

32 PRIORS MARSTON MANOR

The Green, Priors Marston, CV47 7RH. Dr & Mrs Mark Cecil, 07934 440949, whewitt15@yahoo.co.uk. *8m SW of Daventry. Off A361 between Daventry & Banbury at Charwelton. Follow sign to Priors Marston approx 2m. Arrive at T-junction with war memorial on R. Manor on L.* **Visits by arrangement June to Sept. Mon-Thurs only (excl BH). Adm £6, chd free.**

Arrive in Priors Marston village and explore the manor gardens. Greatly enhanced by present owners to relate back to a Georgian manor garden and pleasure grounds. Wonderful walled kitchen garden provides seasonal produce and cut flowers for the house (not open). Herbaceous flower beds and a sunken terrace with water feature by William Pye. Lawns lead down to the lake around which you can walk amongst the trees and wildlife, with stunning views up to the house and garden aviary. Sculpture on display. Partial wheelchair access.
&

33 SQUAB HALL FARM

Harbury Lane, Bishops Tachbrook, Leamington Spa, CV33 9QB. Mrs Bec Evans, bec@squab.co.uk. *10 mins from J13/14 M40. From the Tachbrook Rd/Harbury Lane junction, head towards Harbury on Harbury Lane, 300 metres past the entrance to Mallory Court Hotel on the same side of the road.* **Sat 5, Sun 6 Sept (11-4.30). Adm £5, chd free. Light refreshments. Visits also by arrangement Apr to Sept.**

In many respects this is a secret garden, in touch with the surrounding countryside. Once discovered never forgotten. It is the result of over 40 yrs of loving attention and natural evolution and provides a space for family to enjoy whilst reflecting the owners unique creativity and magical sparkle. Suitable for wheelchair users. Assistance dogs only.
& 💭

GROUP OPENING

34 NEW STONELEIGH VILLAGE GARDENS

Stoneleigh, CV8 3DP. *The village is situated 5m N of Leamington Spa & 5m S of Coventry off the A46. Car parking will be signed in the centre of the village.* **Sun 28 June (2-5). Combined adm £5, chd free. Light refreshments at Stoneleigh Village Club.**

NEW BRIDGE END
Tim & Nicky Sawdon.

NEW HOLLY HOUSE
Janet & David Gibson.

NEW THE OLD POST OFFICE
Peter & Jan Whitehouse.

NEW 3 WALKERS ORCHARD
Keith & Julie Walker.

Opening its gardens for the first time in 2020, Stoneleigh is an ancient village. Cistercian monks founded nearby Stoneleigh Abbey in the middle of the C12. After the dissolution of the monasteries, in 1561 the Abbey passed to the Leigh family and the Estate remained in their possession for 400 yrs. The development of the Estate into a thriving agricultural community led to the need for housing for workers, and the almshouses in the village date back to 1594. Teas will be served in the village club, originally a Reading Room founded in 1856 to promote knowledge and learning in the community. The gardens open in the village reflect different styles and are all interesting in their own unique way. There are mature shrubs, and perennials in herbaceous borders, as well as small vegetable plots, and some greenhouses and summerhouses.
✿ 💭

We help ordinary people open the gates to their extraordinary private gardens to raise impressive amounts of money through admissions, teas and slices of cake!

GROUP OPENING

35 STYVECHALE GARDENS

Baginton Road, Coventry, CV3 6FP. *The gardens are located on the s-side of Coventry close to A45. Tickets & map available on the day from West Orchard United Reformed Church, The Chesils, CV3 6FP. Advance tickets available from suepountney@btinternet.com.* **Sun 14 June (11-5). Combined adm £5, chd free. Light refreshments throughout the day & hot bacon or sausage batches from 11-2. Donation to Coventry Myton Hospice.**

11 BAGINTON ROAD
Ken & Pauline Bond.

164 BAGINTON ROAD
Fran & Jeff Gaught.

16 DELAWARE ROAD
Val & Roy Howells, 02476 419485, valshouse@hotmail.co.uk.
Visits also by arrangement May to Sept for groups of 10 to 30. Combined visit with 2 The Hiron.

2 THE HIRON
Sue & Graham Pountney, 02476 502044, suepountney@btinternet.com.
Visits also by arrangement May to Sept for groups of 10 to 30. Combined visit with 16 Delaware Road.

177 LEAMINGTON ROAD
Barry & Ann Suddens.

27 RODYARD WAY
Jon & Karen Venables.

A collection of lovely, mature, suburban gardens, each one different in style and size. Come and enjoy the imaginatively planted herbaceous borders, spectacular roses, water features, fruit and vegetable patches, cottage garden planting and shady areas, something for everyone and plenty of ideas for you to take home. Relax in the gardens and enjoy the warm, friendly welcome you will receive from us all. Plants for sale in some gardens. Several other gardens will be open on the day, including 40 Ranulf Croft.

GROUP OPENING

36 TYSOE GARDENS

Tysoe, Warwick, CV35 0SE. *W of A422, N of Banbury (9m). E of A3400 & Shipston-on-Stour (4m). N of A4035 & Brailes (3m). Parking on recreation ground CV35 0SE. Entrance tickets & maps at village hall. Free bus.* **Sat 6, Sun 7 June (2-6). Combined adm £7, chd free. Home-made teas in Tysoe Village Hall & cold drinks at Garden Cottage.**

DINSDALE HOUSE
Julia & David Sewell.

GARDEN COTTAGE & WALLED KITCHEN GARDEN
Sue & Mike Sanderson, www.twkg.co.uk.

NEW HONEYCOTE FARMHOUSE
Alastair & Alexandra Murdie.

IVYDALE
Sam & Malcolm Littlewood.

7 JEFFS CLOSE
Emma & Tom Moffatt.

KERNEL COTTAGE
Christine Duke.

THE OLD POLICE HOUSE
Bridget & Digby Norton.

NEW TIW BARN
Robert & Nicola Rexton.

THE WILLOWS
Alan & Ethel Birkbeck.

Tysoe, an original Hornton stone village stands on the north-east foothills of the Cotswolds. For 2020 we are introducing two new gardens in Lower Tysoe. We thought it would be nice to incorporate all parts of Tysoe, Upper, Middle and Lower for our visitors to get a full picture of our community. Our gardens and houses are diverse in character, size and in their planting. Our courtesy bus will be available to all areas of Tysoe. We are opening slightly later than in 2019 so have a few extra days in early June and hope that the weather is kind and encourages the slothful summer plants to come out early! However, you can be sure that Tysoe will offer a happy atmosphere, some glorious gardens, a good walk round the village or, if you prefer, a free bus ride, and a jolly good tea made by the large band of WI bakers and other cooking enthusiasts living in the village. A warm welcome awaits you in this buzzy, energetic, friendly village and gardening community. Come and check us out! Partial wheelchair access.

GROUP OPENING

37 WARMINGTON GARDENS

Banbury, OX17 1BU. *5m NW of Banbury. Take B4100 N from Banbury, after 5m turn R across short dual carriageway into Warmington. From N take J12 off M40 onto B4100.* **Sun 21 June (1-5). Combined adm £6, chd free. Home-made teas at village hall.**

2 CHAPEL STREET
c/o Mark Broadbent, Group Coordinator.

3 COURT CLOSE
Mr & Mrs C J Crocker.

GOURDON
Jenny Deeming.

GREENWAYS
Mark Broadbent.

LANTERN HOUSE
Peter & Tessa Harborne.

THE MANOR HOUSE
Mr & Mrs G Lewis.

THE ORCHARD
Mike Cable.

SPRINGFIELD HOUSE
Jenny & Roger Handscombe, 01295 690286, jehandscombe@btinternet.com.

1 THE WHEELWRIGHTS
Ms E Bunn.

Warmington is a charming historic village, mentioned in the Doomsday Book, situated at the north-east edge of the Cotswolds in a designated AONB. There is a large village green with a pond overlooked by an Elizabethan Manor House (not open). There are other historic buildings including St Michael's Church, The Plough Inn and Springfield House all dating from the C16 or before. There is a mixed and varied selection of gardens to enjoy during your visit to Warmington. These include the formal knot gardens and topiary of The Manor House, cottage and courtyard gardens, terraced gardens on the slopes of Warmington Hill and orchards containing local varieties of apple trees. Some gardens will be selling home-grown plants. WC at village hall, along with delicious home-made cakes, and hot and cold drinks. Warmington is on a hill with many steps and gravel driveways which could be difficult for wheelchair access.

GROUP OPENING

38 WELFORD-ON-AVON GARDENS

Welford-on-Avon, CV37 8PT. *5m SW of Stratford-upon-Avon. Off B439 towards Bidford-on-Avon from Stratford upon Avon.* **Sat 27, Sun 28 June (1-5). Combined adm £6, chd free. Home-made teas in the Village Memorial Hall.**

Blacksmiths Cottage

NEW ALCOVE
Peter & Carole Deakin.

ASH COTTAGE
Peter & Sue Hook.

ELM CLOSE
Eric & Glenis Dyer.
(See separate entry)

NEW THE OLD FORGE
Karen Dickinson.

THE OLD RECTORY
Frank Kennedy.

6 QUINEYS LEYS
Gordon & Penny Whitehurst.

9 QUINEYS LEYS
Ann Raff.

NEW ROWAN HOUSE
Lynne & Dave Smith.

5 WILLOWBANK
Mrs Jane Badcock.

Welford-on-Avon has a superb position on the river with serene swans, dabbling ducks and resident herons. It also has a beautiful C12 church and a selection of pubs serving great food. There are many different house styles and an abundance of beautiful cottages with thatched roofs, some dating from C17. The village has chocolate-box charisma! Welford also has many keen gardeners. The gardens that are opening range from small to large, from established to newly designed and planted, and include some with fruit and vegetable plots.

39 WELLESBOURNE ALLOTMENTS

Kineton Road, Wellesbourne, Warwick, CV35 9NE. Wellesbourne Allotments, www. wellesbourneallotments.co.uk. *5m E of Stratford-upon-Avon. On LH-side of Kineton Rd (B4086) E of Wellesbourne, 400 metres from shops in precinct.* **Sun 28 June (2-5). Adm £4, chd free. Home-made teas.**

Follow the history of Wellesbourne Allotments dating from 1838 and discover the importance of the Joseph Arch story featured in BBC's Countryfile. Find out how allotments contribute to wellbeing today and can help people living with dementia. Impressive vegetables, delicious fruits and beautiful flowers abound on the site offering interest to novice and experienced gardeners of all ages. A large, lush and lovely rural site growing a huge range of crops. Meet enthusiastic gardeners and sample delicious home-made teas. Plants and produce for sale, scarecrows, children's questionnaire, bee-keepers tent, a landscaped dementia-friendly plot, music, stalls, vintage ice cream. Level site with hard surface entrance and roadway.

GROUP OPENING

40 WHICHFORD & ASCOTT GARDENS

Whichford & Ascott, Shipston-on-Stour, CV36 5PG. *6m SE of Shipston-on-Stour. For parking please use CV36 5PG. We have a large car park.* **Sun 21 June (1-5). Combined adm £6, chd free. Home-made teas.**

ASCOTT LODGE
Charlotte Copley.

BELMONT HOUSE
Robert & Yoko Ward.

MULBERRY HOUSE
Mr Richard Thomas.

THE OLD RECTORY
Peter & Caroline O'Kane.

PLUM TREE COTTAGE
Janet Knight.

WHICHFORD HILL HOUSE
Mr & Mrs John Melvin.

THE WHICHFORD POTTERY
Jim & Dominique Keeling,
www.whichfordpottery.com.

The gardens in this group reflect many different styles. The two villages are in an AONB, nestled within a dramatic landscape of hills, pasture and woodland, which is used to picturesque effect by the garden owners. Fine lawns, mature shrub planting and much interest to plantsmen provide a peaceful visit to a series of beautiful gardens. Many incorporate the inventive use of natural springs, forming ponds, pools and other water features. Classic cottage gardens contrast with larger and more classical gardens which adopt variations on the traditional English garden of herbaceous borders, climbing roses, yew hedges and walled enclosures. Partial wheelchair access as some gardens are on sloping sites.

OPENING DATES

All entries subject to change. For latest information check www.ngs.org.uk

Map locator numbers are shown to the right of each garden name.

January

Thursday 16th
Westcroft 54

Thursday 23rd
Westcroft 54

Thursday 30th
Westcroft 54

February

Snowdrop Festival

Thursday 6th
Westcroft 54

Friday 7th
Westcroft 54

Sunday 9th
Westcroft 54

Thursday 13th
Westcroft 54

Thursday 20th
Westcroft 54

Saturday 22nd
◆ Lacock Abbey
  Gardens 34

Sunday 23rd
Westcroft 54

Thursday 27th
Westcroft 54

March

Thursday 5th
Westcroft 54

Sunday 22nd
Broadleas House
  Gardens 9
◆ Corsham Court 13
Fonthill House 19

April

Friday 17th
◆ Bowood Woodland
  Gardens 8

Sunday 19th
Allington Grange 2
Foxley Manor 21

Saturday 25th
◆ Iford Manor
  Gardens 31

Sunday 26th
◆ Corsham Court 13
Cottage in the Trees 15
Oare House 41

May

Friday 1st
Blackland House 6

Sunday 3rd
◆ Waterdale House 52

Sunday 10th
Broadleas House
  Gardens 9
Manor Farm House 39

Sunday 17th
◆ Twigs Community
  Garden 50

Wednesday 20th
Hazelbury Manor
  Gardens 25

Thursday 21st
Windmill Cottage 56

Friday 22nd
Windmill Cottage 56

Saturday 23rd
Job's Mill 32

Sunday 24th
Cottage in the Trees 15
Little Durnford Manor 36

Sunday 31st
1 Southview 48

June

Thursday 4th
Cadenham Manor 10
Trantor House 49
Windmill Cottage 56

Friday 5th
Windmill Cottage 56

Saturday 6th
West Lavington Manor 53

Sunday 7th
NEW Abbotstone House 1
Ark Farm 3
NEW Bluebells 7
Chisenbury Priory 11
Cottage in the Trees 15
NEW Fovant House 20
Hazelbury Manor
  Gardens 25
Hyde's House 30
◆ Lydiard Park Walled
  Garden 37
The Old Rectory,
  Boscombe 43
Purton House 44
Trantor House 49

Saturday 13th
Help for Heroes 26
NEW Wadswick Green 51

Sunday 14th
Dauntsey Gardens 17
NEW Howe Mill 29
NEW Wadswick Green 51

Saturday 20th
Hilperton House 27
NEW Seend House 46
NEW Seend Manor 47

Sunday 21st
Hannington Village
  Gardens 24
Hilperton House 27
Manor Farm 38

Thursday 25th
Whatley Manor 55

Sunday 28th
Broadleas House
  Gardens 9
NEW Cortington Manor 14
Duck Pond Barn 18
Oare House 41

July

Thursday 2nd
Windmill Cottage 56

Friday 3rd
Windmill Cottage 56

Sunday 5th
Gold Hill 23
Horatio's Garden 28

Saturday 11th
Dane Brook 16

Sunday 12th
Dane Brook 16

Sunday 19th
◆ Twigs Community
  Garden 50

Sunday 26th
130 Ladyfield Road &
  Allotments 35
The Old Mill 42

August

Sunday 16th
Gasper Cottage 22

Sunday 23rd
Broadleas House
  Gardens 9

Sunday 30th
Wudston House 57

September

Thursday 10th
Pythouse Kitchen
  Garden 45

Sunday 13th
1 Southview 48

Wednesday 16th
Hazelbury Manor
  Gardens 25

We open the gates to the nation's best gardens, offering a relaxing, memorable and affordable day out. A perfect experience to share with friends and family.

Seend Manor

THE GARDENS

⬛ NEW ABBOTSTONE HOUSE
Whiteparish, Salisbury, SP5 2SH. Mrs Andrew Lax. *On A27 in The Street Whiteparish. 100yds from shop and church on A27 heading towards Salisbury. Large box hedge with iron gates, parking in field along driveway.* Sun 7 June (2-6). Adm £4, chd free. Home-made teas. Also open Bluebells.
Large garden surrounding 400 year old Jacobean house with many roses, herbaceous and shady borders, pond, vegetable garden, walled garden surrounding the swimming pool. Variety of mature trees. Wide gates and gravel driveway and paving.

⬛ ALLINGTON GRANGE
Allington, Chippenham, SN14 6LW. Mrs Rhyddian Roper, www.allingtongrange.com. *2m W of Chippenham. Take A420 W from Chippenham. 1st R signed Allington Village, entrance 1m up lane on L.* Sun 19 Apr (2-5). Adm £5, chd free. Home-made teas.
Informal country garden of approx 1½ acres, around C17 farmhouse (not open), with yr-round interest and a diverse range of plants. Many early spring bulbs. Mixed and herbaceous borders, colour themed; white garden with water fountain. Pergola lined with clematis and roses. Walled potager. Small orchard with chickens. Wildlife pond with natural planting. Mainly level with ramp into potager. Dogs on leads.

⬛ ARK FARM
Old Wardour, Tisbury, Salisbury, SP3 6RP. Mrs Miranda Thomas. *Old Wardour is 2m from Tisbury. Drive down High Street and on, past station, take 1st R. Follow signs to Old Wardour Castle.* Sun 7 June (2-5). Adm £5, chd free. Home-made teas.
Informal hidden gardens in beautiful setting with small wooded area, pond, water plants, lakeside walk, views of Old Wardour castle. This is a very difficult garden for wheelchairs. Not advised!

⬛ BEGGARS KNOLL CHINESE GARDEN
Newtown, Westbury, BA13 3ED. Colin Little & Penny Stirling, 01373 823383, silkendalliance@talktalk.net. *1m SE of Westbury. Turn off B3098 at White Horse Pottery, up hill towards the White Horse for ¾m. Parking at end of drive for 10-12 cars.* Visits by arrangement in July for groups of 10 to 20. Adm £5.50, chd free. Tea and home-made cake £3.50.
Entry to this Chinese-style garden with several rooms in one acre of chalk hillside includes a guided tour. Chinese pavilions and gateways are surrounded by colourful plantings of rare Chinese trees, shrubs and flowers making it a plantsman's garden. Intricate mosaic pavements wind around ponds and rocks. Potager, with chickens, incl new rose path. Spectacular views to the Mendips. We already have quite a reputation for the home-made cakes - especially the walnut and coffee cake.

⬛ BIDDESTONE MANOR
Chippenham Lane, Biddestone, SN14 7DJ. Rosie Harris, Head Gardener, 01249 713211. *5m W of Chippenham. On A4 between Chippenham & Corsham turn N. From A420, 5m W of Chippenham, turn S.* Visits by arrangement May & June for groups of 5+. Daytime or evening. Adm £5, chd free.
Cotswold stone C17 manor house, not open, with 5 acres of garden to enjoy. Lake, ponds and streams, arboretum, vegetable and cutting gardens. Formal front garden and natural plantings for wildlife around watersides. Refreshments as requested on booking. Guided walks with Rosie Harris. Wheelchair access to most parts, a few steps, help always available.

6 BLACKLAND HOUSE
Quemerford, Calne, SN11 8UQ.
Polly & Edward Nicholson,
www.bayntunflowers.co.uk.
*Situated just off A4. We will be
operating a one-way system,
entering the grounds through the
entrance to St. Peter's Church and
exiting through our main gate.* **Fri
1 May (2-4.30). Adm £10, chd
free. Home-made teas incl in
admission. Donation to Dorothy
House Hospice.**
A wonderfully varied 4½ acre garden
adjacent to River Marden. (House
not open). Formal walled productive
and cutting garden, traditional
glasshouses, rose garden and wide
herbaceous borders. Interesting
topiary, trained fruit trees and
specialist displays of historic tulips
and unusual spring bulbs. Hand-tied
bunches of flowers for sale. Partial
wheelchair access, steps, grass and
cobbles.

7 NEW BLUEBELLS
Cowesfield, Whiteparish,
Salisbury, SP5 2RB.
Hilary Mathison,
hilary.mathison@icloud.com. *SW
of Salisbury. On main A27 road from
Salisbury to Romsey. 1½ m SW of
Whiteparish, 100-200 metres inside
county boundary.* **Sun 7 June (2-6).
Adm £4, chd free. Home-made
teas. Also open Abbotstone
House. Visits also by arrangement
Apr to Aug for groups of 10 to 20.**
Relatively new garden on established
1½ acre plot, with deciduous
woodland incl bluebells in season.
Adjoining new build contemporary
house, so rear courtyard reflects this;
other areas incl shady border and
wildlife pond. Large lawn surrounded
by differing beds and borders with
some newly planted areas. Large
feature bed planted with white birch
and cornus. Wheelchair access
to part of garden with paving and
compacted stone.

**8 ♦ BOWOOD WOODLAND
GARDENS**
Calne, SN11 9PG. The Marquis
of Lansdowne, 01249 812102,
houseandgardens@bowood.org,
www.bowood.org. *3½ m SE of
Chippenham. Located off J17 M4
nr Bath & Chippenham. Entrance
off A342 between Sandy Lane &
Derry Hill Villages. Follow brown
tourist signs. For SatNav please*
use SN11 9PG. **For NGS: Fri 17
Apr (11-6). Adm £7.25, chd free.
Light refreshments. For other
opening times and information,
please phone, email or visit garden
website.**
This 60 acre woodland garden of
azaleas, magnolias, rhododendrons
and bluebells is one of the most
exciting of its type in the country.
From the individual flowers to
the breathtaking sweep of colour
formed by hundreds of shrubs, this
is a garden not to be missed. The
Woodland Gardens are located 2m
from Bowood House & Garden.
Access is limited for wheelchairs due
to rough terrain.

**9 BROADLEAS HOUSE
GARDENS**
Devizes, SN10 5JQ.
Mr & Mrs Cardiff, 07884 340103,
broadbridge_jon@hotmail.com.
*1m S of Devizes. From Hartmoor
Rd turn L into Broadleas Park,
follow rd for 350 metres then turn
R into estate. Please note, there is
no access from A360 Potterne Rd.
Easy access for cars, minibuses and
coaches, large coaches may park
off site* **Sun 22 Mar, Sun 10 May,
Sun 28 June, Sun 23 Aug (2-5).
Adm £7, chd free. Teas, coffees,
cakes and soft drinks. Visits also
by arrangement Mar to Oct for
groups of 10+.**
6 acre garden of hedges, herbaceous
borders, rose arches, bee garden and
orchard stuffed with good plants. Well
stocked kitchen and herb gardens.
Mature collection of specimen trees
incl magnolia, handkerchief, redwood,
dogwood. Overlooked by the house
and arranged above the small valley
garden which is crowded with
magnolias, camellias, rhododendrons,
azaleas, cornus and hydrangeas.
Wheelchair access to upper garden
only, some gravel and narrow grass
paths.

10 CADENHAM MANOR
Foxham, Chippenham,
SN15 4NH. Victoria & Martin
Nye, garden@cadenham.com.
*B4069 from Chippenham or M4
J17 through Sutton Benger, turn
R in Christian Malford and L in
Foxham. From A3102 turn L from
Calne or R from Lyneham (NW)
at Xrds between Hilmarton and
Goatacre.* **Thur 4 June (2-5.30).
Adm £10, chd free. Pre-booking**
essential, please visit www.ngs.
org.uk/events for information
& booking. Home-made teas.
Visits also by arrangement Mar
to Sept for groups of 10 to 30,
please email Victoria at garden@
cadenham.com. Refreshments by
arrangement.**
This glorious 4 acre garden comprises
a series of rooms around a listed
manor and dovecote. Divided by
yew hedges and moats, the garden's
rooms are furnished with specimen
trees, mixed borders with stunning
displays of old roses, plus fountains
and statues to focus the eye. Water
garden in old canal, well-stocked
vegetable garden, herb garden and
lavender garden.

11 CHISENBURY PRIORY
East Chisenbury, SN9 6AQ.
Mr & Mrs John Manser,
peterjohnmanser@yahoo.com. *3m
SW of Pewsey. Turn E from A345 at
Enford then N to E Chisenbury, main
gates 1m on R.* **Sun 7 June (2-6).
Adm £5, chd free. Home-made
teas. Visits also by arrangement
May & June.**
Medieval Priory with Queen Anne
face and early C17 rear (not open)
in middle of 5 acre garden on chalk.
Mature garden with fine trees within
clump and flint walls, herbaceous
borders, shrubs, roses. Moisture
loving plants along mill leat, carp
pond, orchard and wild garden, many
unusual plants.

12 COCKSPUR THORNS
Berwick St James, Salisbury,
SP3 4TS. Stephen & Ailsa Bush,
01722 790445,
stephenjdbush@gmail.com. *8m
NW of Salisbury. 1m S of A303, on
B3083 at S end of village of Berwick
St James.* **Visits by arrangement
May to July for groups of 10 to
20. Adm £5, chd free. Home-
made teas.**
2¼ acre garden, completely
redesigned 20 yrs ago and
developments since, featuring
roses (particularly colourful in June),
herbaceous border, shrubbery, small
walled kitchen garden, secret pond
garden, mature and new unusual
small trees, fruit trees and areas
of wild flowers. Beech, yew and
thuja hedgings planted to divide
the garden. Small number of vines
planted during early 2016.

13 ◆ CORSHAM COURT
Corsham, SN13 0BZ.
Lord Methuen, 01249 701610,
staterooms@corsham-court.co.uk,
www.corsham-court.co.uk. *4m
W of Chippenham. Signed off A4 at
Corsham.* For NGS: Sun 22 Mar,
Sun 26 Apr (2-5.30). Adm £5, chd
£2.50. For other opening times and
information, please phone, email or
visit garden website.
Park and gardens laid out by
Capability Brown and Repton.
Large lawns with fine specimens
of ornamental trees surround the
Elizabethan mansion. C18 bath house
hidden in the grounds. Spring bulbs,
beautiful lily pond with Indian bean
trees, young arboretum and stunning
collection of magnolias. Wheelchair
(not motorised) access to house,
gravel paths in garden.
&

14 NEW ▶ CORTINGTON MANOR
Corton, Warminster, BA12 0SY.
Mr & Mrs Simon Berry. *5m S of
Warminster. From Warminster, take
rd thro Sutton Veny to Corton. Do
not bear L into Corton but continue
for ½ m. From A303, take A36, L
to Boyton, cross railway and R at T
jnct. Continue for ¾ m.* Sun 28 June
(2-5). Adm £7, chd free. Home-
made teas.
4 acres of wild and formal gardens
surround rose clad C18 manor house.
Herbaceous border, yew bays with
Portuguese laurel line main lawn.
Bank of white roses and foxgloves
edges swimming pool. Sweet pea
arch opens to cutting garden, veg
garden and orchard divided by yew
hedges. Lime avenue leads to river
and pond from walled herb garden.
Stable yard features pleached
hornbeams and beech hedges.
❀ ☕ 🍷

15 ◆ COTTAGE IN THE TREES
Tidworth Rd, Boscombe Village,
nr Salisbury, SP4 0AD. Karen &
Richard Robertson, 01980 610921,
robertson909@btinternet.com.
*7m N of Salisbury. Turn L off A338
just before Social Club. Continue
past church, turn R after bridge to
Queen Manor, cottage 150yds on R.*
Sun 26 Apr, Sun 24 May (1.30-5).
Adm £3.50, chd free. Sun 7 June
(12-5). Combined adm with The
Old Rectory, Boscombe £6, chd
free. Also open Trantor House.
Home-made teas. Visits also
by arrangement Mar to Sept for
groups of 10+.

Enchanting ½ acre cottage garden,
immaculately planted with water
feature, raised vegetable beds,
small wildlife pond and gravel
garden. Spring bulbs, hellebores and
pulmonarias give a welcome start to
the season, with pots and baskets,
roses and clematis. Mixed borders of
herbaceous plants, dahlias, grasses
and shrubs giving all-yr interest. Large
variety of cottage plants for sale,
grown from the garden.
🌱 🐄 ❀ 🚗 ☕

16 DANE BROOK
Milkhouse Water, Pewsey,
SN9 5JX. Mr & Mrs P Sharpe. *1m
NE of Pewsey. From Pewsey take
B3087 Burbage Rd. After approx
¾ m turn L to Milkhouse Water.
Dane Brook is 1st on R after railway
bridge.* Sat 11, Sun 12 July (12.30-
5.30). Adm £5, chd free. Home-
made teas. Gluten free available.
Donation to SSAFA.
Approx 1 acre of gardens, incl
herbaceous beds, shrubs, trees, semi
formal garden, roses, oxbow pond
with planted banks and thatched
summerhouse. Tree lined river walk
runs the length of the garden, leading
to shrubbery. Also lawns and paved
areas with planted containers. Far
reaching views from paddocks. Free
range fresh laid eggs. Rare breed
sheep, horses and vintage tractor,
hopefully honey on sale from our
bees. Wheelchair accessible in dry
weather with exception of pond and
stream areas.
& 🐄 ❀ ☕ 🍷

Westcroft

GROUP OPENING

17 DAUNTSEY GARDENS
Church Lane, Dauntsey,
Malmesbury, SN15 4HW. *5m SE of
Malmesbury. Approach via Dauntsey
Rd from Gt Somerford, 1¼m from
Volunteer Inn Great Somerford.* Sun
14 June (1-5). Combined adm
£7.50, chd free. Home-made teas
at Idover House.

THE COACH HOUSE
Col & Mrs J Seddon-Brown.

DAUNTSEY PARK
Mr & Mrs Giovanni Amati,
01249 721777, enquiries@
dauntseyparkhouse.co.uk.

THE GARDEN COTTAGE
Miss Ann Sturgis.

IDOVER HOUSE
Mr & Mrs Christopher Jerram.

THE OLD COACH HOUSE
Tony & Janette Yates.

THE OLD POND HOUSE
Mr & Mrs Stephen Love.

This group of 6 gardens, centred
around the historic Dauntsey Park
Estate, ranges from the Classical C18
country house setting of Dauntsey
Park, with spacious lawns, old trees
and views over the River Avon, to
mature country house gardens and
traditional walled gardens. Enjoy the
formal rose garden in pink and white,
old fashioned borders and duck
ponds at Idover House, and the quiet
seclusion of The Coach House with its
thyme terrace and gazebos, climbing
roses and clematis. Here, mop-
headed pruned crataegus prunifolia
line the drive. The Garden Cottage
has a traditional walled kitchen
garden with organic vegetables, apple
orchard, woodland walk and yew
topiary. Meanwhile the 2 acres at The
Old Pond House are both clipped and
unclipped! Large pond with lilies and
fat carp, and look out for the giraffe
and turtle. The Old Coach House is
a small garden with perennial plants,
shrubs and climbers.

18 DUCK POND BARN
Church Lane, Wingfield,
Trowbridge, BA14 9LW. Janet
& Marc Berlin, 01225 777764,
janet@berlinfamily.co.uk. *On
B3109 from Frome to Bradford on
Avon, turn opp Poplars PH into
Church Lane. Duck Pond Barn is at
end of lane. Big field for parking.* Sun
28 June (2-5). Adm £4, chd free.
Light refreshments. Visits also by
arrangement June & July.
Garden of 1.6 acres with large duck
pond, lawns, ericaceous beds,
orchard, vegetable garden, big
greenhouse, spinney and wild area
of grass and trees with many wild
flowers. Large dry stone wall topped
with flower beds with rose arbour. 3
ponds linked by a rill in flower garden
and large pergola in orchard. Set in
farmland and mainly flat. Music on
open day. Coach parties please ring
in advance for catering purposes.

19 FONTHILL HOUSE
Tisbury, SP3 5SA.
The Lord Margadale of Islay,
www.fonthill.co.uk/gardens. *13m
W of Salisbury. Via B3089 in Fonthill
Bishop. 3m N of Tisbury.* Sun 22
Mar (12-5). Adm £7, chd free.
Sandwiches, quiches and cakes,
soft drinks, tea and coffee. All
proceeds to NGS.
Wonderful woodland walks with
daffodils, rhododendrons, azaleas,
shrubs, bulbs; magnificent views;
formal gardens. The gardens have
been extensively redeveloped under
the direction of Tania Compton and
Marie-Louise Agius. The formal
gardens are being continuously
improved with new designs, exciting
trees, shrubs and plants. Gorgeous
William Pye fountain and other
sculptures. Partial wheelchair access.

20 NEW FOVANT HOUSE
Church Lane, Fovant, Salisbury,
SP3 5LA. Amanda & Noel Flint.
*Fovant House is located approx.
6½m W of Wilton and 9.3m E of
Shaftesbury. Take A30 to Fovant
then head N through village and
follow signs to St Georges Church.*
Sun 7 June (2-5.30). Adm £5, chd
free. Home-made teas.
Fovant House is a former Rectory set
in about 3 acres of formal garden.
(House not open). In 2016 the
garden was redesigned by Arabella
Lennox Boyd. Garden includes 60m
herbaceous border, terraces and
parterre. A range of mature trees
include Cedars , Copper Beech and
Ash. Majority of garden has easy
wheelchair access subject to ground
conditions being dry.

21 FOXLEY MANOR
Foxley, Malmesbury, SN16 0JJ.
Richard & Louisa Turnor. *2m W
of Malmesbury. 10 mins from J17
on M4. Turn towards Malmesbury/
Cirencester, then towards Norton
and follow signs for the Vine Tree,
yellow signs from here.* Sun 19 Apr
(10.30-4.30). Adm £5, chd free.
Cream teas.
Yew hedges divide lawns, borders,
rose garden, lily pond and a newer
wild area with a natural swimming
pond shaded by a Liriodendron.
Views through large Turkey Oaks to
farmland beyond. Small courtyard
gravel garden. Sculptures are sited
throughout the gardens. Regret steps
and gravel paths make this unsuitable
for wheelchairs.

22 GASPER COTTAGE
Gasper Street, Gasper Stourton,
Warminster, BA12 6PY.
Bella Hoare & Johnnie Gallop.
*Near Stourhead Gardens, 4m from
Mere, off A303. Turn off A303 at
B3092 Mere. Follow Stourhead
signs. Go through Stourton. After
1m, turn R after phone box, signed
Gasper. House 2nd on R going up
hill. Parking past house on L, in field.*
Sun 16 Aug (11-5). Adm £5, chd
free. Home-made teas.
1½ acre garden, with views to
glorious countryside. Luxurious
planting of dahlias, grasses, asters,
cardoons and more, incl new
perennial planting. Orchard with
wildlife pond. Artist studio surrounded
by colour balanced planting with
formal pond. Pergola with herb
terrace. Several seating areas.
Garden model railway. 1 step into
studio garden, 3 steps to access
garden by house. Orchard accessible
if not too wet.

23 GOLD HILL
Hindon Lane, Tisbury, Salisbury,
SP3 6PZ. Anne Ralphs. *On Hindon
Lane, 500 yds up on R from top of
Tisbury High street. From Hindon, on
L 500yds after road narrows. Parking
down the lane in field beside the
garden.* Sun 5 July (2-5). Adm £5,
chd free. Home-made teas.
Overlooking the Nadder Valley the
house and garden, which are Arts
and Crafts inspired, were created
on a 1.2-acre derelict builder's
yard and field between 2015 and
2017. Formal garden with mixed
shrub and perennial planting giving

interest throughout the year. Sunken garden, rose garden, fruit trees, walled garden, pond and fountain, parterre beds. Regret not suitable for wheelchairs.

GROUP OPENING

24 HANNINGTON VILLAGE GARDENS
Hannington, Swindon, SN6 7RP. *Off B4019 Blunsdon to Highworth Rd by the Freke Arms. Park behind the Jolly Tar PH, or opp Lushill House.* **Sun 21 June (11-5.30). Combined adm £7, chd free. Home-made teas in Hannington Village Hall.**

BUTLER'S COTTAGE
Mr & Mrs John & Karen Mayell.

GLEBE HOUSE
Charlie & Tory Barne.

LUSHILL HOUSE
John & Sasha Kennedy.

QUARRY BANK
Paul Minter & Michael Weldon.

ROSE COTTAGE
Mr & Mrs Keith & Ruth Scholes.

YORKE HOUSE GARDEN
Mrs Catherine Bozeat.

Hannington has a dramatic hilltop position and the views into and out of the village resulted in it being made a very large conservation area. The C12 church stands apart from the settlement which has a Jacobean Manor House and many other listed buildings. Large and small gardens in a variety of styles. Many of the gardens follow the brow of the hill and afford stunning views of the upper Thames Valley and the surrounding farm land which is crossed by footpaths and bridleways. Please check the website as numerous other gardens will be added nearer the opening date. Limited wheelchair access as many gardens are on steep hills and feature steps.

25 HAZELBURY MANOR GARDENS
Wadswick, Box, Corsham, SN13 8HX. Mr L Lacroix. *5m SW of Chippenham, 5m NE of Bath. From A4 at Box, A365 to Melksham, at Five Ways junction L onto B3109 towards Corsham; 1st L in ¼m,*

drive immed on R. **Wed 20 May (10-4). Home-made teas. Sun 7 June (1-5). Cream teas. Wed 16 Sept (10-4). Home-made teas. Adm £5, chd free.**
The C15 Manor house comes into view as you descend along the drive and into the Grade II landscaped Edwardian gardens. The extensive plantings that surround the house are undergoing considerable redevelopment by the owners and their Head Gardener. A wide range of organic horticulture is practiced in 8 acres of relaxed yet playful gardens. Regret much of garden inaccessible to wheelchair users.

26 HELP FOR HEROES
Tedworth House Recovery Centre, Arcot Road, Tidworth, SP9 7AJ. Help for Heroes, www.helpforheroes.org.uk. *Located off A338 just S of Tidworth and 3m N of A303.* **Sat 13 June (1-4). Adm by donation. Home-made teas. Refreshments made by volunteers with donations to Help for Heroes.**
Help for Heroes run Tedworth House Recovery Centre to provide Recovery and Rehabilitation for wounded, injured and sick service personnel, Veterans and their families. The grounds include a fruit and vegetable garden which is used as a therapeutic gardening space for horticultural activities and further woodlands with an Iron-Age style roundhouse where Veterans can learn woodworking skills.

27 HILPERTON HOUSE
The Knap, Hilperton, Trowbridge, BA14 7RJ. Chris & Ros Brown. *1½m NE of Trowbridge. Follow A361 towards Trowbridge and turn R at r'about signed Hilperton. House is next door to St Michael's Church in the Knapp off Church St.* **Sat 20, Sun 21 June (2-6). Adm £5, chd free. Home-made teas.**
2½ acres well stocked borders, small stream leading to large pond with fish, water lilies, waterfall and fountain. Fine mature trees incl unusual specimens. Walled fruit and vegetable garden, small woodland area. Rose walk with roses and clematis. Interesting wood carvings, mainly teak. 160yr old vine in conservatory of Grade II listed house, circa 1705 (not open). Activity sheets for children. Some gravel and lawns. Conservatory not wheelchair

accessible. Path from front gate has uneven paving but can be bypassed on lawn.

28 HORATIO'S GARDEN
Duke of Cornwall Spinal Treatment Centre, Salisbury Hospital NHS Foundation Trust, Odstock Road, Salisbury, SP2 8BJ. Horatio's Garden Charity, www.horatiosgarden.org.uk. *1m from centre of Salisbury. Follow signs for Salisbury District Hospital. Please park in car park 10 (which will be free to NGS visitors on the day).* **Sun 5 July (1-4). Adm £5, chd free. Tea and delicious cakes - made by Horatio's Garden volunteers - will be served in the Garden Room.**
Award winning hospital garden, opened in Sept 2012 and designed by Cleve West for patients with spinal cord injury at the Duke of Cornwall Spinal Treatment Centre. Built from donations given in memory of Horatio Chapple who was a volunteer at the centre in his school holidays. Low limestone walls, which represent the form of the spine, divide densely planted herbaceous beds. Everything in the garden designed to benefit patients during their long stays in hospital. Garden is run by Head Gardener and team of volunteers. South West Regional Winner, The English Garden's The Nation's Favourite Gardens 2019. 3 Society of Garden Designers Awards 2015, BALI Award 2014. Designer Cleve West has 8 RHS gold medals, incl Best in Show at RHS Chelsea Flower Show in 2011 & 2012. 3pm - short talk about therapeutic gardens and the work of Horatio's Garden, Salisbury. Fully accessible to wheelchairs.

Your visits help change lives - your generosity has supported unpaid carers through donations to Carers Trust totalling over £4 million since 1996

29 NEW HOWE MILL
Newton Road, Ramsbury, Marlborough, SN8 2PP. *½ m from B4192. Drive through Chilton Foliat from Hungerford on B4192. Take 1st turning L signed to Ramsbury (Newtown Road), Howe Mill is 1st property on L.* **Sun 14 June (2-5.30). Adm £10. Ticketed event, no admission on day, pre-booking essential. Please visit www.ngs.org.uk/events for information & booking. Home-made teas.**

Idyllic waterside garden set in about 5 acres with an apt balance of nature and horticulture. A medley of bridges and walkways transporting you over streams and leats into a wonder of secrecy and hidden gems. Colourful herbaceous borders with some less common planting. Lime and Hornbeam avenues leading the eye to statued vistas. Admirable selection of sculpture adorning the less formal areas of the garden. Box edged vegetable garden with an established steel framed greenhouse. Overall an exciting variety of trees, shrubs, planting and outbuildings with the odd grotto. Limited wheelchair access, dependent on weather. Soft ground and deep water.

30 HYDE'S HOUSE
Dinton, SP3 5HH. Mr George Cruddas. *9m W of Salisbury. Off B3089 nr Dinton Church on St Mary's Rd.* **Sun 7 June (2-5). Adm £6, chd free. Home-made teas at Thatched Old School Room with outside tea tables.**

3 acres of wild and formal garden in beautiful situation with series of hedged garden rooms. Numerous shrubs, flowers and borders, all allowing tolerated wild flowers and preferred weeds, while others creep in. Large walled kitchen garden, herb garden and C13 dovecote (open). Charming C16/18 Grade I listed house (not open), with lovely courtyard. Every year varies. Free walks around park and lake. Steps, slopes, gravel paths and driveway.

31 ♦ IFORD MANOR GARDENS
Bradford-on-Avon, BA15 2BA. Mr Cartwright-Hignett, 01225 863146, info@ifordmanor.co.uk, www.ifordmanor.co.uk. *7m S of Bath. Off A36, brown tourist sign to Iford 1m. Or from Bradford-on-Avon or Trowbridge via Lower Westwood Village (brown signs). Please note all approaches via narrow, single track lanes with passing places.* **For NGS: Sat 25 Apr (11-4). Adm £7.50, chd £6.50. Home-made teas. Please see website for details. For other opening times and information, please phone, email or visit garden website.**

An exemplar of Harold Peto's garden design at his former home, this 2½ acre romantic garden provides inspiration to many and was used as a key location in The Secret Garden (2020). Restored and extended by the current owners, Troy Scott Smith was recently appointed Head Gardener. Steep flights of steps link the terraces with pools, fountains, urns, colonnades and statues. Last garden entry at 3.30pm. As the garden is on a steeply terraced hillside, characterised by steep flights of steps, wheelchair access is limited. Please call for details.

32 JOB'S MILL
Five Ash Lane, Crockerton, Warminster, BA12 8BB. Lady Silvy McQuiston. *1½ m S of Warminster. Down lane E of A350, S of A36 r'about.* **Sat 23 May (2-5.30). Adm £4.50, chd free. Home-made teas.**

Delightful 5 acre garden through which River Wylye flows. Laid out on many levels surrounding old converted water mill. Water garden, herbaceous border, vegetable garden, orchard, riverside and woodland walks and secret garden. Grass terraces designed by Russell Page. Bulbs and erythronium in the spring and perhaps the tallest growing wisteria?

33 KETTLE FARM COTTAGE
Kettle Lane, West Ashton, Trowbridge, BA14 6AW. Tim & Jenny Woodall, 01225 753474, trwwoodall@outlook.com. *Kettle Lane is halfway between West Ashton T-lights and Yarnbrook r'about on S side of A350. Garden ½ m down end of lane.* **Visits by arrangement May to Sept for groups of up to 20. Adm £4.50, chd free. Light refreshments incl tea and coffee.**

Previously of Priory House, Bradford on Avon, the garden of which was on Gardeners World, September 2017, we have now created a new cottage garden, full of colour and style, flowering from May to Oct. Bring a loved one/friend to see the garden and have some refreshment. One or two steps.

34 ♦ LACOCK ABBEY GARDENS
High Street, Lacock, Chippenham, SN15 2LG. National Trust, 01249 730459, lacockabbey@ nationaltrust.org.uk, www.nationaltrust.org.uk/lacock. *3m S of Chippenham. Off A350. Follow NT signs. Use public car park (parking fee).* **For NGS: Sat 22 Feb (10.30-5.30). Adm £6, chd £3. Light refreshments in courtyard tea room. Several pubs and tea rooms in village. For other opening times and information, please phone, email or visit garden website.**

Woodland garden with carpets of aconites, snowdrops, crocuses and daffodils. Botanic garden with greenhouse, medieval cloisters and magnificent trees. Mostly level site, some gravel paths.

35 130 LADYFIELD ROAD & ALLOTMENTS
Ladyfield Road, Chippenham, SN14 0AP. Philip & Pat Canter and Chippenham Town Council. *1m SW of Chippenham. Between A4 Bath and A420 Bristol rds. Signed off B4528 Hungerdown Lane which runs between A4 & A420.* **Sun 26 July (1.30-5.30). Adm £4, chd free. Home-made teas. Cream teas.**

Very pretty small garden with more than 40 clematis, climbing roses and small fish pond. Curved neat edges packed with colourful herbaceous plants and small trees. 2 patio areas with lush lawn, pagoda and garden arbour. Also Hungerdown Allotments, 15 allotments owned by Chippenham Town Council. Wheelchair access to main path and lawn in garden and to allotments on main drive only.

36 LITTLE DURNFORD MANOR
Little Durnford, Salisbury, SP4 6AH. The Earl & Countess of Chichester. *3m N of Salisbury. Just N beyond Stratford-sub-Castle. Remain to E of R Avon at road junction at Stratford Bridge and continue towards Salterton for ½ m heading N. Entrance on L just past Little Durnford sign.* **Sun 24 May (2-**

5). Adm £4, chd free. Home-made teas in cricket pavilion within grounds.

Extensive lawns with cedars, walled gardens, fruit trees, large vegetable garden, small knot and herb gardens. Terraces, borders, sunken garden, water garden, lake with islands, river walks, labyrinth walk. Little Durnford Manor is a substantial grade II listed, C18 private country residence (not open) built of an attractive mix of Chilmark stone and flint. Camels, alpacas, llama, pigs, pygmy goats, donkeys and sheep are all grazing next to the gardens.

🐕 ✤ ☕

37 ✦ LYDIARD PARK WALLED GARDEN

Lydiard Tregoze, Swindon, SN5 3PA. Swindon Borough Council, 01793 466664, lydiardpark@swindon.gov.uk, www.lydiardpark.org.uk. *3m W Swindon, 1m from J16 M4. Follow brown signs from W Swindon.* **For NGS: Sun 7 June (11-4). Adm £3, chd £2. Light refreshments in Coach House Tea Rooms. For other opening times and information, please phone, email or visit garden website.**

Beautiful ornamental C18 walled garden. Trimmed shrubs alternating with individually planted flowers and bulbs incl rare daffodils and tulips, sweet peas, annuals and wall-trained fruit trees. Unique features incl well and sundial. Wide level paths, no steps.

♿ ✤ 🐕 🛏 ☕

38 MANOR FARM

Crudwell, Malmesbury, SN16 9ER. Mr & Mrs J Blanch. *4m N of Malmesbury on A429. Heading N on A429 in Crudwell, turn R signed to Eastcourt. Farm entrance is on L 200m after end of speed limit sign.* **Sun 21 June (11-5). Adm £5, chd free. Home-made teas. Gluten free options available.**

The garden is set within Cotswold stone walls and a backdrop of Crudwell church with a further 5 acres of parkland featuring Japanese maples and a Roman style summerhouse. The garden is divided by box and yew hedges to create different areas both formal and informal. Herbaceous borders with old fashioned roses are grown among fountains and extensive lawns.

♿ 🐕 ✤ ☕

39 MANOR FARM HOUSE

Manor Farm Lane, Patney, Devizes, SN10 3RB. Mr & Mrs Mark Alsop. *Between Pewsey and Devizes. Take 3rd entrance on L going up Manor Farm Lane from village green. Parking available in paddock.* **Sun 10 May (2-5). Adm £5, chd free. Home-made teas.**

2-acre plantsman's garden designed in 1980s and updated by us over the past 8 yrs. Lawned areas with borders surrounded by yew hedging, large border by tennis court, formal vegetable garden with buxus parterres and meadow with spring bulbs, box mound and new moist plants garden. Limited wheelchair access due to upward slope and gravel paths. No toilets.

♿ ☕

40 MANOR HOUSE, STRATFORD TONY

Stratford Tony, Salisbury, SP5 4AT. Mr & Mrs Hugh Cookson, 01722 718496, lucindacookson@stratfordtony.co.uk, www.stratfordtony.co.uk. *4m SW of Salisbury. Take minor rd W off A354 at Coombe Bissett. Garden on S after 1m. Or take minor rd off A3094 from Wilton signed Stratford Tony and racecourse.* **Visits by arrangement June to Sept for groups of 5 to 30. Adm £5, chd free. Refreshments by arrangement.**

Varied 4 acre garden with all yr interest. Formal and informal areas. Small lake fed from R Ebble. Pergola-covered vegetable garden, parterre garden, orchard, shrubberies, roses,

Help for Heroes

specimen trees, waterside planting, winter colour and structure, many original contemporary features and places to sit and enjoy the downland views. Herbaceous beds undergoing renovation in 2020. Some gravel.

♿ 🚗 ☕

41 OARE HOUSE

Rudge Lane, Oare, nr Pewsey, SN8 4JQ. Sir Henry Keswick. *2m N of Pewsey. On Marlborough Rd (A345).* **Sun 26 Apr, Sun 28 June (2-6). Adm £6, chd free. Cream teas. Home-made cakes. Donation to The Order of St John.**

1740s mansion house later extended by Clough Williams Ellis in 1920s (not open). The original formal gardens around the house have been developed over the years to create a wonderful garden full of many unusual plants. Current owner is very passionate and has developed a fine collection of rarities. Garden is undergoing a renaissance but still maintains split compartments each with its own individual charm; traditional walled garden with fine herbaceous borders, vegetable areas, trained fruit, roses and grand mixed borders surrounding formal lawns. The Magnolia garden is wonderful in spring with some trees dating from 1920s, together with strong bulb plantings. Large arboretum and woodland with many unusual and champion trees. In spring and summer there is always something of interest, with the glorious Pewsey Vale as a backdrop. Partial wheelchair access.

♿ 🐕 ✤ ☕

42 THE OLD MILL
Ramsbury, SN8 2PN.
Annabel & James Dallas. *8m NE of Marlborough. From Marlborough head to Ramsbury. At The Bell PH follow sign to Hungerford. Garden behind yew hedge on R 100yds beyond The Bell.* Sun 26 July (2-6). Adm £6, chd free. Tea.
Water running through a multitude of channels no longer drives the mill but provides a backdrop for whimsical garden of pollarded limes and naturalistic planting. Paths meander by streams and over small bridges. Vistas give dramatic views of downs beyond. Potager style kitchen garden and separate cutting garden provide a more formal contrast to the relaxed style elsewhere. Limited wheelchair access as gravel paths and bridges and very soft ground in places.

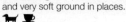

43 THE OLD RECTORY, BOSCOMBE
Tidworth Road, Boscombe, Salisbury, SP4 0AB. Helen & Peter Sheridan, 07712 004797, helen.sheridan@uwclub.net. *7m N of Salisbury on A338. From Salisbury, 2nd L turning after Earl of Normanton PH, just S of Boscombe Social Club and Black Barn.* Sun 7 June (1.30-5). Combined adm with Cottage in the Trees £6, chd free. Home-made teas. Visits also by arrangement May to July for groups of 10 to 30.
The elegant gardens of this period property feature a traditional walled garden with herbaceous borders and vegetable beds, contrasting with a parkland of sweeping lawns, mature trees and flowering shrubs. Wheelchair access, though ground may be soft after rain. Gravel paths.

44 PURTON HOUSE
Church End, Purton, Swindon, SN5 4EB. Mrs Myf Barker. *Turn off Purton High St towards St Mary Church into Church St. At tithe barn L into Church End, after about 300 metres car park on R opp Purton Organics sign (shop open).* Sun 7 June (1-5). Adm £5, chd free. Home-made teas.
This is something different. A large organically managed garden with beautiful specimen trees and Georgian house. Used as wedding venue. The huge ancient plane tree by the lake (formerly monastic carp ponds) is home to a fairy garden.

Walled garden with many old varieties of fruit trees, soft fruit and vegetables. NB some weeds as garden is in mid restoration. Interesting sculptures, dove cote, boat house, Italian style garden, fernery, large ancient carp pond, huge plane tree along with many other interesting specimen trees. Possible wheelchair access to lawn areas although some rough ground.

45 PYTHOUSE KITCHEN GARDEN
West Hatch, Tisbury, SP3 6PA. Mr Piers Milburn, 01747 870444, info@pythousekitchengarden.co.uk, www.pythousekitchengarden.co.uk. *A350 S of E Knoyle, follow brown signs to Walled Garden approx 3m. From Tisbury take Newtown road past church, stay on it 2½ m, garden on R. Check map on www.pythousekitchengarden.co.uk.* Thur 10 Sept (10-4). Adm £5, chd free. Light refreshments. Visits also by arrangement May to Oct.
3 acres of working kitchen garden, in largely continuous use since C18, with fruit-lined walls and gnarled apple trees leading down to an orchard via ravishing, rosa rugosa-edged, beds of flowers, soft fruit, vegetables and beehives. A restaurant now occupies the old potting shed and conservatory, with terraces for tea on open days. Abundant herbs, kiwis and apricots, as well as the deliciously scented 1920s HT rose, Mrs Oakley Fisher, growing by the kitchen door. Restaurant opens 10am for delicious home-made food at coffee, lunch and teatime, served both inside and out on terrace, open until 4pm on open days. Grass paths across slope.

46 NEW SEEND HOUSE
High Street, Seend, Melksham, SN12 6NR. Maud Peters. *In Seend village, near church and opp post office.* Sat 20 June (1-6). Combined adm with Seend Manor £10, chd free. Home-made teas.
Seend House is a Georgian house with 6 acres of gardens and paddocks. Framed with yew and box. Highlights include: a rose garden, a stream lavender, a view of a knot garden from above, a walled garden as well as formal borders. There is also an amazing view across the valley to Salisbury Plain.

47 NEW SEEND MANOR
High Street, Seend, Melksham, SN12 6NX. Stephen & Amanda Clark. *In centre of village, opp village green with car parking for garden visitors.* Sat 20 June (1-6). Combined adm with Seend House £10, chd free. Home-made teas.
Created over 20 yrs, a stunning walled garden with 4 quadrants evoking important parts of the owners lives - England, China, Africa and Italy, with extensive trelliage, hornbeam hedges on stilts, cottage orne, temple, Chinese ting, grotto, fern walk, fountains, parterres, stone loggia and more. Wonderful views. Kitchen garden. Folly ruin in woods. Courtyard garden. Extensive walled gardens, water features, garden structures, topiary and hedging, fountains and one of the best views in Wiltshire! Many gravel paths, so wheelchairs with thick tyres are best.

48 1 SOUTHVIEW
Wick Lane, Devizes, SN10 5DR. Teresa Garraud, 01380 722936, tl.garraud@hotmail.co.uk. *From Devizes Mkt Pl go S (Long St). At r'about go straight over, at mini r'about turn L into Wick Lane. Continue to end of Wick Lane. End of terrace on L. Park in road or roads nearby.* Sun 31 May, Sun 13 Sept (2-5). Adm £4, chd free. Light refreshments. Visits also by arrangement May to Sept for groups of up to 10.
An atmospheric and very long town garden, full of wonderful planting surprises at every turn. Densely planted with both pots near the house and large borders farther up, it houses a collection of beautiful and often unusual plants, shrubs and trees many with striking foliage. Colour from seasonal flowers is interwoven with this textural tapestry. 'Truly inspirational' is often heard from visitors.

49 TRANTOR HOUSE
Hackthorne Road, Durrington, SP4 8AS. Mrs Jane Turner, 01980 655101, sjcturner@talktalk.net. *9 m N of Salisbury. Turn off A345 (signed Village Centre) onto Hackthorne Rd. Approx 200 yds on L.* Thur 4 June (12-5). Sun 7 June (12-5), also open Cottage in the Trees. Adm £4, chd free. Refreshments

available at Cottage in the Trees **7 June. Visits also by arrangement May to July.** Border Oak timber framed house on country lane surrounded by approx ⅔ acre of both formal and informal gardens. Attractive mixed and herbaceous colour themed borders, rose garden, wildlife pond and stream. Summerhouse, raised vegetable beds and wildflower meadow. Chickens. Sloping garden with steps

50 ◆ TWIGS COMMUNITY GARDEN

Manor Garden Centre, Cheney Manor, Swindon, SN2 2QJ. TWIGS, 01793 523294, twigs.reception@gmail.com, www. twigscommunitygardens.org. uk. *From Gt Western Way, under Bruce St Bridges onto Rodbourne Rd. 1st L at r'about, Cheney Manor Industrial Est. Through estate, 2nd exit at r'about. Opp Pitch & Putt. Signs on R to Manor Garden Centre.* **For NGS: Sun 17 May, Sun 19 July (12-4). Adm £3, chd free. Home-made teas. Excellent hot and cold lunches available at Olive Tree café within Manor Garden centre adj to Twigs. For other opening times and information, please phone, email or visit garden website.** Delightful 2 acre community garden, created and maintained by volunteers. Features incl 7 individual display gardens, ornamental pond, plant nursery, Iron Age round house, artwork, fitness trail, separate kitchen garden site, Swindon beekeepers and the haven, overflowing with wild flowers. Featured in Garden Answers & Wiltshire Life magazine and on Great British Gardens website. In Top 100 Attractions in SW England. Most areas wheelchair accessible. Disabled WC.

Your visits help change lives – we are the largest single funder of the Queen's Nursing Institute

Biddestone Manor

Wudston House

51 NEW **WADSWICK GREEN**
Corsham, SN13 9RD.
Rangeford Villages,
www.wadswickgreen.co.uk.
Signed from Bradford on Avon and Corsham, directions off B3109. Please use Westwells Road entrance, Neston, Corsham. **Sat 13, Sun 14 June (11-4). Adm £5, chd free. Light refreshments.**
Wadswick Green Retirement Village's parkland landscape of formal, informal and wild gardens has interest throughout the year. Seasonal bulbs, flowering shrubs and perennial borders contrast with clipped hedges, mature trees and lawns, attracting the welcomed wildlife. Relax in the Italian Terrace Garden. Refreshments from The Greenhouse Restaurant & Coffee Shop. Dogs must be on leads.

52 ◆ **WATERDALE HOUSE**
East Knoyle, SP3 6BL. Mr & Mrs Julian Seymour, 01747 830262. *8m S of Warminster. N of East Knoyle, garden signed from A350. Do not use SatNav.* **For NGS: Sun 3 May (2-6). Adm £5, chd free. Home-made teas. For other opening times and information, please phone.**
In the event of inclement weather, before visiting, please check www.ngs.org.uk. 4 acre mature woodland garden with rhododendrons, azaleas, camellias, maples, magnolias, ornamental water, bog garden, herbaceous borders. Bluebell walk. Shrub border created by storm damage, mixed with agapanthus and half hardy salvias. Difficult surfaces, sensible footwear essential, parts of garden very wet. Please keep to raked and marked paths in woodland. Partial wheelchair access.

53 **WEST LAVINGTON MANOR**
1 Church Street, West Lavington, SN10 4LA. Andrew Doman, andrewdoman01@gmail.com. *6m S of Devizes, on A360. House opp White St, where parking is available.* **Sat 6 June (11-6). Adm £10, chd free. Home-made teas and lunch provided by West Lavington Youth Club. Visits also by arrangement. Donation to West Lavington Youth Club.**
5 acre walled garden first established in C17 by John Danvers who brought Italianate gardens to the UK. Herbaceous border, Japanese garden, rose garden, orchard and arboretum with some outstanding specimen trees all centred around a trout stream and duck pond. White Birch grove and walk along southern bank of the stream. Picnics welcome. Only limited areas of garden accessible by wheelchair.

54 WESTCROFT

Boscombe Village, nr
Salisbury, SP4 0AB. Lyn
Miles, 01980 610877,
lynmiles@icloud.com,
www.westcroftgarden.co.uk.
*7m N/E Salisbury. On A338 from
Salisbury, just past Boscombe &
District Social Club, park there or
in field opp house, signed on day.
Disabled parking only on drive.*
**Thurs 16, 23, 30 Jan; Thur 6, Fri
7, Sun 9, Thurs 13, 20, Sun 23,
Thur 27 Feb; Thur 5 Mar (11-4).
Adm £3, chd free. Home-made
soups, scrummy teas inside the
house. Visits also by arrangement
Jan to Mar for groups of 20+ on
weekdays only except Thursdays.**
Whilst overflowing with roses in
June, in Jan and Feb the bones of
this ⅔ acre galanthophile's garden
on chalk are on show. Brick and flint
walls, terraces, rustic arches, gates
and pond add character. Drifts of
snowdrops carpet the floor whilst
throughout is a growing collection
of over 400 named varieties. Many
hellebores, pulmonarias, grasses
and seedheads add interest.
Snowdrops (weather dependent) and
snowdrop sundries for sale, greetings
cards, mugs, bags, serviettes etc.
Wheelchair access is limited to lower
levels and not easy when the ground
is soft in mild or wet weather.

55 WHATLEY MANOR

Easton Grey,
Malmesbury, SN16 0RB.
Christian & Alix Landolt,
01666 822888,
reservations@whatleymanor.com,
www.whatleymanor.com. *4m
W of Malmesbury. From A429 at
Malmesbury take B4040 signed
Sherston. Manor 2m on L.* **Thur
25 June (2-7). Adm £5, chd free.
Home-made teas in The Loggia
Garden. Hotel also open for lunch
and full afternoon tea.**
12 acres of English country gardens
with 26 distinct rooms each with a
strong theme based on colour, scent
or style. Original 1920s plan inspired
the design and combines classic style
with more contemporary touches; incl
specially commissioned sculpture.
Dogs must be on a lead at all times.

56 WINDMILL COTTAGE

Kings Road, Market Lavington,
SN10 4QB. Rupert & Gill Wade,
01380 813527. *5m S of Devizes.*

Duck Pond Barn

*Turn E off A360 1m N of W.
Lavington, signed Market Lavington
& Easterton. At top of hill turn L into
Kings Rd, L into Windmill Lane after
200yds. Limited parking on site,
more parking nearby.* **Thur 21, Fri
22 May, Thur 4, Fri 5 June, Thur
2, Fri 3 July (2-5). Adm £4, chd
free. Home-made teas. Visits also
by arrangement May to July for
groups of 5 to 30.**
1 acre cottage style, wildlife friendly
garden on greensand. Mixed beds
and borders with long season of
interest. Roses on pagoda, large
vegetable patch for kitchen and
exhibition at local shows, greenhouse,
polytunnel and fruit cage. Whole
garden virtually pesticide free for last
20 yrs. Small bog garden by wildlife
pond. Secret glade with prairie.
Grandchildren's little wood and wild
place. Mostly accessible, some soft
and gravel paths.

57 WUDSTON HOUSE

High Street, Wedhampton,
Devizes, SN10 3QE. David
Morrison, 07881 943213,
djm@piml.co.uk. *Wedhampton lies
on N side of A342 approx 4m E of
Devizes. House is set back on E side
of village street at end of drive with
beech hedge on either side.* **Sun
30 Aug (2-6). Adm £12, chd free.
Light refreshments. Visits also
by arrangement June to Sept for
groups of 10+. Refreshments by
arrangement.**
The garden of Wudston House was
started in 2010, following completion
of the house. It consists, inter alia, of
formal gardens round the house, a
perennial meadow, pinetum and an
arboretum. Nick Macer and James
Hitchmough, who has pioneered
the concept of perennial meadows,
have been extensively involved in
aspects of the garden, which is still
developing. Partial wheelchair access.

OPENING DATES

All entries subject to change. For latest information check www.ngs.org.uk

Map locator numbers are shown to the right of each garden name.

24 Croft Bank

August

Saturday 1st
The River School 40

Sunday 2nd
Hiraeth 22

Saturday 8th
Offenham Gardens 34

Sunday 9th
Offenham Gardens 34

Saturday 15th
Westacres 50

Sunday 16th
Cowleigh Lodge 14
NEW The Firs 19
Westacres 50

Saturday 22nd
Oak Tree House 32

Saturday 29th
Morton Hall Gardens 29

Sunday 30th
1 Church Cottage 11
3 Oakhampton Road 33
Pear Tree Cottage 36

Monday 31st
1 Church Cottage 11
3 Oakhampton Road 33

September

Saturday 5th
◆ Whitlenge Gardens 55

Sunday 6th
◆ Whitlenge Gardens 55

Sunday 13th
White Cottage &
Nursery 53

Saturday 19th
NEW Ravelin 39

Sunday 20th
Brockamin 8
NEW Ravelin 39

By Arrangement

Arrange a personalised garden visit with your club, or group of friends, on a date to suit you. See individual garden entries for full details.

NEW Acorns Children's
Hospice 1
24 Alexander Avenue 2
Badge Court 4
Barnard's Green House 5
Brockamin 8
NEW Buckland Manor 9
1 Church Cottage 11
Conderton Manor 13
Cowleigh Lodge 14
24 Croft Bank 15
The Dell House 16
6 Dingle End 17
The Folly 20
Hanley Swan NGS
Gardens 21

Hilltop Farm, Eckington
Gardens 18
Hiraeth 22
Long Hyde House 25
Mantoft, Eckington
Gardens 18
74 Meadow Road 27
Millbrook Lodge 28
New House Farm 30
Oak Tree House 32
3 Oakhampton Road 33
Overbury Court 35
Pear Tree Cottage 36
NEW Primrose Hospice
Bromsgrove 38
NEW Ravelin 39
The River School 40
The Tynings 46
Westacres 50
Wharf House 51
Whitcombe House 52
White Cottage &
Nursery 53

THE GARDENS

1 NEW ACORNS CHILDREN'S HOSPICE
350 Bath Road, Worcester,
WR5 3EZ. *On A38 approx 1¼m south of Worcester. From M5 J7 towards Worcester then L at first island onto A4440. R at 2nd island onto A38 towards city centre for approx ½m* Sun 14 June (11-4). Adm £4, chd free. Light refreshments. **Visits also by arrangement in June for groups 6 to 15. Refreshments as agreed in advance.**

1½ acres designed for the benefit of children and young people with life limiting illnesses and their families. Incl play areas, raised beds for young people to plant vegetables, tranquil memorial garden with gentle stream and memorial pebbles for children who have passed away and an enclosed bedroom garden set aside for recently bereaved families. Acers, silver birch and other trees and shrubs feature This is not a traditional National Garden Scheme garden but one that shows how gardens can have a positive effect on peoples' wellbeing. Coffee, tea and cakes morning and afternoon. Soup and roll available at lunchtime All areas wheelchair accessible.
🅰 ✿ ☕

2 24 ALEXANDER AVENUE
Droitwich Spa, WR9 8NH. Malley & David Terry, 01905 774907, terrydroit@aol.com. *1m S of Droitwich. Droitwich Spa towards Worcester A38. Or from M5 J6 to Droitwich Town centre.* Visits by arrangement Apr to Aug. Adm £3.50, chd free. Refreshments available by arrangement only. Beautifully designed, now with mature plantings and giving feeling of space and tranquillity, many varieties of clematis growing through shrubs and high hedges. Borders with rare plants and shrubs. Sweeping curves of lawns and paths to woodland area with shade-loving plants. Drought-tolerant plants in S-facing gravel front garden. Alpine filled troughs. April spring bulbs including good variety of snowdrops, erythroniums, specie tulips and alpines, July/August clematis, colourful mixed shrub and herbaceous borders. Partial wheelchair access.
🅰 🚗 ☕

Wychwood House

GROUP OPENING

3 ALVECHURCH GARDENS

Red Lion Street, Alvechurch, B48 7LF. Group Co-ordinator Jason Turner. *3m N of Redditch, 3m NE of Bromsgrove. NGS Gardens are signed from all roads into Alvechurch village. Pick up your map when you pay for your ticket at the first garden you visit.* **Sat 20, Sun 21 June (1-6). Combined adm £6, chd free. Light refreshments at The Shrubbery, Bear Hill, Alvechurch, B48 7JX.**

18 BEAR HILL
Alexandra & Nicholas Wood.

69 BIRMINGHAM ROAD
Anna and Andy Ingram.

28 CALLOW HILL ROAD
Martin & Janet Wright.

CORNER HOUSE
Janice Wiltshire.

NEW **THE MOAT HOUSE**
Mike and Tracy Fallon.

THE OLD SWAN
Ray & Norma Yarnell.

RECTORY COTTAGE
Celia Hitch, 0121 445 4824, celia@rectorycottage-alvechurch.co.uk.

THE SHRUBBERY
Chris Thompson & Liz Fox.

4 SNAKE LANE
Jason Turner & Paul Emery.

76 TANYARD LANE
Dianne & Barry Court.

NEW **WYCHWOOD HOUSE**
Chris & Stephanie Miall.

Large village with new development and historically interesting core with buildings spanning medieval to Edwardian and St Laurence church dedicated in 1239. There is a selection of lovely open gardens ranging from a riverside previous rectory with waterfall to a corner plot gardened for wildlife. There are a professionally landscaped terraced garden and a cottage garden with lots of colour in pots and a wrap-around informal garden. Also a large garden on the old site of the Bishop of Worcester's Summer Palace and a sloped garden with potted plants and shrubs and a garden with wooden bridge, decking and pebbled areas. Around the gardens there are rose beds, shrubberies, herbaceous beds and fruit and vegetable gardens. Last but not least some gardens include sculptures. Not all gardens are wheelchair accessible or they may have partial access.

4 BADGE COURT

Purshull Green Lane, Elmbridge, Droitwich, WR9 0NJ. Stuart & Diana Glendenning, 01299 851216, dianaglendenning1@gmail.com. *5m N of Droitwich Spa. 2½m from J5 M5. Turn off A38 at Wychbold down side of the Swan Inn. Turn R into Berry Lane. Take next L into Cooksey Green Lane. Turn R into Purshull Green Lane. Garden is on L.* **Visits by arrangement May to July for groups of 10 to 30. Tour takes 1 hour and includes history of house. Adm £5, chd free. Home-made teas. Tea/coffee/juice and home-made cakes.**
The 2½ acre garden at Badge Court is divided into a series of uniquely different areas and contains a large selection of specimen trees and over 80 varieties of roses and clematis. Areas within the garden include a large pool with fish, stumpery, walled garden with aviary, Mediterranean garden (new), large vegetable garden, orchard, cherry tunnel, herbaceous and specialist borders.

&. ❀ ☕

5 BARNARD'S GREEN HOUSE

Hastings Pool, Poolbrook Road, Malvern, WR14 3NQ. Mrs Sue Nicholls, 01684 574446. *1m E of Malvern. At junction of B4211 & B4208.* **Visits by arrangement Feb**

Ravelin

to Sept for groups of up to 20. Adm £4, chd free.

With a magnificent backdrop of the Malvern Hills, this $1\frac{1}{2}$ acre old-fashioned garden is a plantsman's paradise. The main feature is a magnificent cedar. 3 herbaceous and 2 shrub borders, rose garden, red and white and yellow borders, an evergreen and hydrangea bed, 2 rockeries, pond, sculptures and vegetable garden. Good garden colour throughout the year. Was the home of Charles Hastings - founder of the British Medical Association (1794-1866). Dogs on leads.

6 BIRTSMORTON COURT

Birtsmorton, nr Malvern, WR13 6JS. Mr & Mrs N G K Dawes. *7m E of Ledbury. Off A438 Ledbury/Tewkesbury rd.* Sun 7 June (2-5.30). Adm £7, chd free. Home-made teas. Teas provided by Castlemorton School.

10 acre garden surrounding beautiful medieval moated manor house (not open). White garden, built and planted in 1997 surrounded on all sides by old topiary. Potager, vegetable garden and working greenhouses, all beautifully maintained. Rare double working moat and waterways including Westminster Pool laid down in Henry VII's reign to mark the consecration of the knave of Westminster Abbey. Ancient yew tree under which Cardinal Wolsey reputedly slept in the legend of the Shadow of the Ragged Stone. No dogs.

7 BRIDGES STONE MILL

Alfrick Pound, WR6 5HR. Sir Michael & Lady Perry. *6m NW of Malvern. A4103 from Worcester to Bransford r'about, then Suckley Rd for 3m to Alfrick Pound.* Sun 19 Apr (2-5.30). Adm £6, chd free. Home-made teas.

Once a cherry orchard adjoining the mainly C19 flour mill, this is now a $2\frac{1}{2}$ acre all-year-round garden laid out with trees, shrubs, mixed beds and borders. The garden is bounded by a stretch of Leigh Brook (an SSSI), from which the mill's own weir feeds a mill leat and small lake. A rose parterre and a traditional Japanese garden complete the scene. Wheelchair access by car to courtyard.

8 BROCKAMIN

Old Hills, Callow End, Worcester, WR2 4TQ. Margaret Stone, 01905 830370, stone.brockamin@btinternet.com. *5m S of Worcester. $\frac{1}{2}$m S of Callow End on the B4424, on an unfenced bend, turn R into the car-park signed Old Hills. Walk towards the houses keeping R.* Sun 9 Feb (11-4); Sun 22 Mar, Sun 7 June, Sun 20 Sept (2-5). Adm £4, chd free. Home-made teas. Visits also by arrangement Feb to Oct for groups of 10+.

This is a plant specialist's $1\frac{1}{2}$ acre informal working garden, parts of which are used for plant production rather than for show. Situated next to common land. Mixed borders with wide variety of hardy perennials where plants are allowed to self seed. Includes Plant Heritage National Collections of Symphyotrichum (Aster) novae-angliae and some Hardy Geraniums. Unusual plants for sale. Open for snowdrops in Feb, daffodils in March, geraniums in June and asters in September. Good collection of Pulmonarias. Seasonal pond/bog garden and kitchen garden. Teas with home-made cakes from Malvern Country Markets. An access path reaches a large part of the garden.

9 NEW BUCKLAND MANOR

Buckland, Broadway, WR12 7LY. Mr Mike Dron, 01386 852626, info@bucklandmanor.co.uk. *In the village of Buckland approximately halfway between Broadway and Toddington.* Tue 5 May (10-3). Adm £7, chd £5. Light refreshments. Teas, coffee and cake. Visits also by arrangement May to Oct for groups of up to 30. Refreshments arranged in advance through the hotel.

10 acre semi formal English country garden under redevelopment, serving a luxury hotel and restaurant in a C13 Cotswold mansion. Herbaceous and mixed borders, herb garden, extensive lawns, croquet lawn, bluebell wood, wildflowers, newly planted specimen trees and fruit trees. Spring fed streams and ponds. Views across Severn Valley of Bredon Hill and the Malvern Hills. Cider mill, streams, specimen trees, fruit trees, spring bulbs, Wisteria, herb garden, lawns and beautiful beds and borders. All areas of the gardens and grounds can be accessed. There are various steps near to the building but there are longer routes around them.

10 BYLANE

Worcester Road, Earls Croome, WR8 9DA. Shirley & Fred Bloxsome. *1m N of Upton on Severn turning. On main A38 directly past Garden Centre, signed Bridle Way turn down bridle way to park.* Sun 5 Apr, Sun 17 May, Sun 12 July (1-5). Adm £3.50, chd free. Light refreshments.

Herbaceous garden, paddock with wildlife pond, vegetable garden, and chickens, woodland walk with mature trees and wild flowers, approximately 2 acres in all. Plenty of seating areas and shelter if needed, very quiet and secluded. Children welcome.

11 1 CHURCH COTTAGE

Church Road, Defford, WR8 9BJ. John Taylor & Ann Sheppard, 01386 750863, ann98sheppard@btinternet.com. *3m SW of Pershore. A4104 Pershore to Upton rd, turn into Harpley Rd, Defford, black & white cottage at side of church. Parking in village hall car park.* Sun 24, Mon 25 May, Sun 30, Mon 31 Aug (11-5). Adm £3.50, chd free. Home-made teas. Visits also by arrangement May to Aug for groups of 10 to 30.

True countryman's $\frac{1}{3}$ acre garden. Interesting layout. Japanese - style feature with 'dragons den'. Specimen trees; water features; perennial garden, vegetable garden; poultry; stream side bog garden. New features in progress. Wheelchair access to most areas.

12 NEW 6, CHURCHDOWN ROAD

Malvern, WR14 3JX. Mr & Mrs B Bradford. *In the Poolbrook area of Malvern close to Barnards Green & St Andrews Church; Churchdown Rd is a cul de sac turning directly off the A4208 (Barnards Green to Welland Rd.).* **Sat 23, Sun 24 May (1.30-5). Adm £3.50, chd free. Light refreshments.**
4 years ago this was a neglected space with old fruit trees overgrown conifers and crumbling walls. Much hard work and many garden centre visits has resulted in a colourful and productive artists garden with well stocked borders, specimen trees and a feature rockery. A pond, waterfall, a decked seating area with views of the Malverns and a sale of Irises complete a garden we hope you will enjoy. Wheelchair users would only be able to visit the terrace and view the extensive rockery. There is seating on the terrace.

🐕 ✤ ☕

13 CONDERTON MANOR

Conderton, nr Tewkesbury, GL20 7PR. Mr & Mrs W Carr, 01386 725389, carrs@conderton.com. *5½ m NE of Tewkesbury. From M5 - A46 to Beckford - L for Overbury/ Conderton. From Tewkesbury B4079 to Bredon - then follow signs to Overbury. Conderton from B4077 follow A46 directions from Teddington r'about.* **Visits by arrangement Mar to Nov for groups of up to 30. Light refreshments. Coffee and biscuits in the morning. Tea and biscuits/ cakes in the afternoon Wine and snacks in the evening.**
7 acre garden with magnificent views of Cotswolds. Flowering cherries and bulbs in spring. Formal terrace with clipped box parterre; huge rose and clematis arches, mixed borders of roses and herbaceous plants, bog bank and quarry garden. Many unusual trees and shrubs make this a garden to visit at all seasons. Visitors are particularly encouraged to come in spring and autumn when the trees are at their best. This is a garden/ small arboretum of particular interest for tree lovers. The views towards the Cotswolds are spectacular and it provides a peaceful walk of about an hour. Some gravel paths and steps - no disabled WC.

♿ 🚌 ☕

14 COWLEIGH LODGE

16 Cowleigh Bank, Malvern, WR14 1QP. Jane & Mic Schuster, 01684 439054, dalyan@hotmail.co.uk. *7m SW from Worcester, on the slopes of the Malvern Hills. From Worcester or Ledbury follow the A449 to Link Top. Take North Malvern Rd (behind Holy Trinity church), follow yellow signs. From Hereford take B4219 after Storridge church, follow yellow signs.* **Sun 14 June, Sun 16 Aug (11-5). Adm £5, chd free. Home-made teas. Visits also by arrangement June to Aug for groups of 10 to 30. An additional charge of £2.50 for home-made teas.**
The garden on the slopes of the Malvern Hills has been described as 'quirky'! Formal rose garden, grass beds, bamboo walk, colour themed beds, nature path leading to a pond, Acer bank, chickens. Large vegetable plot and orchard with views overlooking the Severn Valley. Explore the poly tunnel and then relax with a cuppa and slice of home-made cake served with a smile. This is the 6th year of opening of a developing and expanding garden - visitors from previous years will be able to see the difference! Lots of added interest with staddle stones, troughs, signs and other interesting artefacts. Slopes and steps throughout the garden. WC and refreshments.

🐕 ✤ ☕

15 24 CROFT BANK

Malvern, WR14 4DU. Andy & Cathy Adams, 01684 899405, andrewadams2005@yahoo.co.uk. *From Worcester on A449 to Gt Malvern. R onto B4232 signed Bromyard & West Malvern. Continue approx 1½ m. Turn R at Elim College Conference centre onto Croft Bank. No 24 is on R.* **Visits by arrangement July & Aug for groups of up to 30. Refreshments on request. Adm £4, chd free. Home-made teas.**
This half acre garden enjoys wonderful far reaching south and westerly views from high on the Malvern Hills. It has evolved over the past ten years.There are colourful flower borders for all seasons, a wide variety of roses and feature lavender beds in summer. There is a woodland area, bog garden and pond. There are places to sit in sun, shade and shelter, to take in the view or retreat in nature. Morning coffee, lunches, afternoon tea, home-made cakes,

wine, pimms or soft drinks can be discussed and catered for. Sloping areas and woodland walk not suitable for wheelchairs. Some steps.

♿ ☕

16 THE DELL HOUSE

2 Green Lane, Malvern Wells, WR14 4HU. Kevin & Elizabeth Rolph, 01684 564448, stay@thedellhouse.co.uk, www.dellhousemalvern.uk. *2m S of Gt.Malvern. Behind former church on corner of A449 Wells Rd & Green Lane. NB Satnavs / Google don't work with postcode.* **Visits by arrangement Mar to Nov. Short notice visits possible. Adm £4, chd £2. Light refreshments.**
Two acre wooded hillside garden of the 1820s former rectory, now a B&B. In the latter stages of recovery and development by the current owners. Peaceful and natural, the garden contains many magnificent specimen trees including a Wellingtonia Redwood. Informal in style with meandering bark paths, historic garden buildings, garden railway and a paved terrace with outstanding views. Spectacular tree carvings by Steve Elsby, and other sculptures by various artists. Featured in 'A survey of Historic Parks & Gardens in Worcestershire'. Partial wheelchair access but good views from the level paved terrace. Parking is on gravel. Sloping bark paths, some quite steep.

🐕 🛏 ☕

17 6 DINGLE END

Inkberrow, WR7 4EY. Mr & Mrs Glenn & Gabriel Allison, 01386 792039. *12m E of Worcester. A422 from Worcester. At the 30 sign in Inkberrow turn R down Appletree Lane then 1st L up Pepper St. Dingle End is 4th on R of Pepper St. Limited parking in Dingle End but street parking on Pepper St.* **Visits by arrangement Mar to Sept for groups of 5 to 20. Adm £3, chd free. Soup and sandwiches if required and arranged in advance.**
Over 1 acre garden with formal area close to the house opening into a flat area featuring a large pond, stream and weir with apple orchard and woodland area. Large vegetable garden incl an interesting variety of fruits. Garden designed for wildlife and attractive to birds on account of water and trees. Refreshments for pre arranged groups can be tailored by arrangement e.g. soup

and sandwiches, tea and cakes etc. Wheelchair access - slopes alongside every terrace.

 ♿ 🐕 ☕

GROUP OPENING

18 ECKINGTON GARDENS

Hilltop, Nafford Road, Eckington, WR10 3DH. Group Coordinator Richard Bateman. *2 gardens - 1 in Nafford Rd the other in Upper End. A4104 Pershore to Upton & Defford, L turn B4080 to Eckington. In centre, by war memorial turn L into New Road (becomes Nafford Road).* **Sat 6, Sun 7 June (11-5). Combined adm £5, chd free. Home-made teas at Mantoft.**

HILLTOP FARM
Richard & Margaret Bateman, 01386 750667, richard. bateman111@btinternet.com. **Visits also by arrangement May to Sept for groups of 5 to 30. Refreshments by prior arrangement.**

MANTOFT
Mr & Mrs M J Tupper, 01386 750819. **Visits also by arrangement May to Sept for groups of 5 to 30. Refreshments by prior arrangement.**

2 very diverse gardens set in/ close to lovely village of Eckington. Hilltop - 1 acre garden designed by owners from a field 35yrs ago, with sunken garden/pond, rose garden, herbaceous borders, interesting topiary incl. cloud pruning and formal hedging designed to reduce the effect of wind and having 'windows' linking to extensive views over the beautiful Worcestershire countryside. Sculptures made by owner. Vegetable yurt (added 2018) has been successful in allowing pollination and preventing damage to young plants from pigeons, rabbits, butterflies and deer. Mantoft (formerly The Croft) - Wonderful ancient thatched cottage with 1½ acres of magical gardens. Fish pond with ghost koi, Cotswold and red brick walls, large topiary, treehouse with seating, summer house and dovecote, pathways, vistas and stone statues, urns and herbaceous borders. Recently featured in Cotswold Life - should not be missed. Some wheelchair access issues.

 ♿ 🐕 ☕

19 NEW THE FIRS

Brickyard Lane, Drakes Broughton, Pershore, WR10 2AH. Ann & Ken Mein. *From J7 M5 take the B4084 towards Pershore. At Drakes Broughton turn L to Stonebow Road. First R into Walcot Lane then second R into Brickyard Lane. The Firs is 200 yds on L.* **Sun 26 July, Sun 16 Aug (2-5). Adm £3.50, chd free. Light refreshments.**
This new 2 acre garden on heavy clay is a work in progress and constantly evolving as new ideas and plans are introduced. Over 200 trees have been planted and mixed borders have been established around the house and barn. Birch trees, Roses and Hydrangeas create a real wow factor in the garden landscape. A new kitchen garden focused on edible perennials is being established amongst young fruit trees.

 ☕

20 THE FOLLY

87 Wells Road, Malvern, WR14 4PB. David & Lesley Robbins, 01684 567253, lesleycmedley@btinternet.com. *1½ m S of Great Malvern & 9m S of Worcester. Approx 8m from M5 via J7 or J8 exits. Situated in Malvern Wells on A449, 0.7m N of B4209 and 0.2m S of Malvern Common. Parking off A449 0.25m N on lay-by or side road, or in 0.1m N turn E on Peachfield Road which runs by Malvern Common.* **Sun 5 July (1.30-5.30). Adm £4, chd free. Light refreshments. Tea, coffee and home baking available. Visits also by arrangement June to Sept for groups of 5 to 20. Visits in August excluded.**
Steeply sloping garden on Malvern Hills with views over Severn Vale. 3 levels accessed by steps, paved/ gravel paths and ramps. Potager and greenhouse, courtyard, formal terrace and lawn, pergola, mature cedars, ornaments and sculpture in landscaped beds and borders. Climbers, small trees, shrubs, hostas, grasses and ferns, with new areas developing. Seating on each level. Gravel and rockery gardens, small cottage garden, stumpery and shrubbery linked by winding paths with an intimate atmosphere as views are concealed and revealed.

 ☕

Walnut Cottage

GROUP OPENING

21 HANLEY SWAN NGS GARDENS

Hanley Swan, WR8 0DJ.
Group Co-ordinator Brian
Skeys, 01684 311297,
brimfields@icloud.com. *5m E of
Malvern, 3m NW of Upton upon
Severn, 9m S of Worcester & M5.
From Worcester/Callow End take
B4424 to Hanley Castle then turn R.
From Upton upon Severn B4211 to
Hanley Castle turn L. From Malvern/
Ledbury from A449 take B4209.
Signed from village Xrds.* Sat 6,
Sun 7 June (1-5). Combined adm
£6, chd free. Cream teas at 19
Winnington Gardens. **Visits also
by arrangement July to Sept for
groups of 5 to 30. Number of
gardens available and admission
cost agreed at time of booking.**

CHASEWOOD
Mrs Sydney Harrison,
01684 310527, Sydneyharrison@
btinternet.com.

MEADOW BANK
Mrs Lesley Stroud & Mr Dave
Horrobin, 01684 310917,
djhorrobin@gmail.com.

THE PADDOCKS
Mr & Mrs N Fowler.

19 WINNINGTON GARDENS
Brian & Irene Skeys.

20 WINNINGTON GARDENS
Mr & Mrs Pete & Tina Sauntson.

YEW TREE COTTAGE
Mr & Mrs David & Margaret Read.

6 gardens different in style in Hanley
Swan. Chasewood has lavender,
old fashioned roses. A gravel garden
with an iris and thyme walk, new
trees, bonsai and collection of coach
built prams. Meadow Bank is a
modern interpretation of a cottage
garden with a hot border, dedicated
iris bed. The Paddocks is a wildlife
garden with ponds, mixed borders,
new greenhouse with cacti and
succulents. Yew Tree Cottage, C17
cottage, within a cottage garden,
a vegetable garden at the rear.
Developed since 2011 when their son
'gave them back the football pitch', a
curved patio was built, 20 Winnington
Gardens has an octagonal
greenhouse, water features,
decorative details, colourful beds and
planters provide year round colour.

19 Winnington Gardens is a garden
of rooms. Mixed borders enclosed
with climbing roses, a small oriental
garden, fruit trees, raised herb bed
with a special standard gooseberry,
collection vintage garden tools.
Wildlife photos. 6 gardens different
in size & style. Entrance tickets from
Chasewood. Four gardens access
too narrow for wheelchairs and
Mobility scooters. One with access
and one partial access with gravel
paths.

22 HIRAETH

30 Showell Road, Droitwich,
WR9 8UY. Sue & John Fletcher,
07752 717243 or 01905 778390,
sueandjohn99@yahoo.com. *1m
S of Droitwich. On The Ridings
estate. Turn off A38 r'about into
Addyes Way, 2nd R into Showell
Rd, 500yds on R. Follow the yellow
signs!* Sun 3 May, Sun 28 June,
Sun 2 Aug (2-5). Adm £3.50, chd
free. Home-made teas. **Visits also
by arrangement May to Aug for
groups of 10 to 30.**
Third acre gardens, front, rear
contain many plant species, cottage,
herbaceous, hostas, ferns, acer trees,
300yr old Olive Tree, pool, waterfall,
oak sculptures, metal animals etc inc
giraffes, elephant, birds. New patio
last year and rear lawn removed, but
still an oasis of colours in a garden
not to be missed described by visitor
as 'A haven on the way to Heaven'.
Excellent tea, coffee, cold drinks,
home-made cakes and scones
served with china cups, saucers,
plates, tea-pots and coffee-pots
- silver service! Partial wheelchair
access.

23 ◆ LITTLE MALVERN COURT

Little Malvern, WR14 4JN. Mrs
T M Berington, 01684 892988,
littlemalverncourt@hotmail.com,
www.littlemalverncourt.co.uk.
*3m S of Malvern. On A4104 S of
junction with A449.* For NGS: Every
Fri 13 Mar to 27 Mar (2-5). Adm
£5, chd free. Mon 25 May (2-5).
Adm £8, chd £1. Tea & biscuits
(March). Home-made teas (May
BH). **For other opening times and
information, please phone, email or
visit garden website.**
10 acres attached to former
Benedictine Priory, magnificent views
over Severn Valley. Garden rooms and
terrace around house designed and

planted in early 1980's; chain of lakes;
wide variety of spring bulbs, flowering
trees and shrubs. Notable collection
of old-fashioned roses. Topiary hedge
and fine trees. The May Bank Holiday
- Flower Festival in the Priory Church.
Partial wheelchair access.

24 THE LODGE

off Holmes Lane, Dodderhill
Common, Hanbury, Bromsgrove,
B60 4AU. Mark & Lesley Jackson.
*1m N of Hanbury Village. 3½m E
from M5 J5, on A38 at the Hanbury
Turn Xrds take A4091 S towards
Hanbury. After 2½m turn L into
Holmes Lane, then IMMEDIATE L
again into dirt track. Car Park (Worcs
Woodland Trust) on L.* Sat 27, Sun
28 June (11-4). Adm £4, chd free.
Cream teas.
A one and half acre garden attached
to a part c16 black and white house
(not open) with 3 lawned areas,
traditional greenhouse, various
beds plus stunning views from
Dodderhill Common over the North
Worcestershire countryside. Small
display of classic cars plus other
cars of interest. Tea, coffee, soft
drinks, cream teas and home-made
cakes served 11am - 4pm. Garden
is wheelchair accessible, disabled
parking within grounds, toilets not
wheelchair accessible. No dogs.

25 LONG HYDE HOUSE

Long Hyde Road, South Littleton,
Evesham, WR11 8TH. David
& Linda Lamb, 01386 834697,
davidlamb1943@gmail.com. *From
the Badsey r'about on A46, follow
B4035 towards Bretforton, then L
on B4085 to The Littletons approx
1.7m. L onto Long Hyde Rd. Garden
on L opp playing field.* Sat 27, Sun
28 June (2-5). Adm £5, chd free.
Home-made teas. **Visits also
by arrangement June & July for
groups of 10 to 30.**
Beautiful 1 acre traditional garden
in Vale of Evesham with stunning
views of Cotswolds. Formal rose
garden, clipped box hedging, parterre
garden, herb garden with 2 ponds,
large vegetable area, extensive
borders, giant chess set with dark
planting , lavender bed, and variety of
baskets and tubs. Honey locust tree
dominates main lawn, raised patios
and seating areas. Wide paths and
disabled parking.

GROUP OPENING

26 MARLBROOK GARDENS

Braces Lane, Marlbrook, Bromsgrove, B60 1DY. Group Co-ordinator David Morgan. *2m N of Bromsgrove. 1m N of M42 J1, follow B4096 signed Rednal, turn L at Xrds into Braces Lane. 1m S of M5 J4, follow A38 signed Bromsgrove, turn L at T-lights into Braces Lane. Parking available.* Sun 31 May (1.30-5.30). Combined adm £5, chd free. Home-made teas. Refreshments in both gardens.

OAK TREE HOUSE
Di & Dave Morgan.
(See separate entry)

SARANACRIS
John & Janet Morgan.

2 unique and stunning gardens with contrasting styles. Saranacris unusual steeply sloping garden in former sand quarry designed and built by owners over 20 yrs. Dense jungle style planting with eclectic mix of plants including the rare, unusual and exotic laced with garden favourites. Homage to Japanese gardens with Koi pond, a stream sparkles and glistens over a waterfall, a shady glade dominated by a large weeping willow all populated

by scrap metal artworks from road side artists in Zimbabwe. When all is done relax on the roof terrace with home-made cakes and a cup of tea. Oak Tree House plantswoman's cottage garden overflowing with plants, pots and interesting artifacts. Secluded patio with plants and shrubs for Spring, small pond and waterfall. Plenty of seating, wildlife pond, water features, alpine area, rear open vista. Scented plants, hostas, dahlias and lilies. Conservatory with art by owners. Also 'Wynn's Patch' - part of next door's garden maintained on behalf of the owner. Garden Quiz for children.

27 74 MEADOW ROAD

Wythall, B47 6EQ. Joe Manchester, 01564 829589, joe@cogentscreenprint.co.uk. *4m E of Alvechurch. 2m N from J3 M42. On A435 at Becketts Farm r'about take rd signed Earlswood/Solihull. Approx 250 metres turn L into School Drive, then L into Meadow Rd.* Visits by arrangement May to Aug. Adm £3.50, chd free. Home-made teas.

Has been described one of the most unusual urban garden dedicated to woodland, shade-loving plants. 'Expect the unexpected' in a few tropical and foreign species. Meander

through the garden under the majestic pine, eucalyptus and silver birch. Sit and enjoy the peaceful surroundings and see how many different ferns and hostas you can find. As seen on BBC Gardeners' World.

28 MILLBROOK LODGE

Millham Lane, Alfrick, Worcester, WR6 5HS. Andrea & Doug Bright, andreabright@hotmail.co.uk. *11m from M5 J7. A4103 from Worcester to Bransford r'about, then Suckley Rd for 3m to Alfrick Pound to find car park on L for Nature Reserve.* Sat 6, Sun 7 June (1-5). Adm £5, chd free. Home-made teas. Visits also by arrangement Mar to June for groups of 10+. Tea, coffee and home-made cakes available.

A 3½ acre garden and woodland developed by current owners over 23 years. Large informal flowerbeds planted for all year round interest, contains camellias, magnolias and acers. Spring flowering bulbs through to asters and dahlias. Pond with stream and bog garden. Fruit and vegetable garden and gravel garden. Situated in an area of outstanding natural beauty and opposite a nature reserve. Refreshments in aid of Save the Children. Slopes and grass/woodland paths.

29 MORTON HALL GARDENS

Morton Hall Lane, Holberrow Green, Redditch, B96 6SJ. Mrs A Olivieri, www.mortonhallgardens.co.uk. *In the centre of Holberrow Green, at a wooden bench around a tree, turn up Morton Hall Lane. Follow the NGS signs to the gate opposite Morton Hall Farm.* Sat 29 Aug (10-4). Adm £9, chd free. Home-made teas. Tea, coffee, soft drinks & a selection of cakes.

One of Worcestershire's best kept secrets. Perched atop an escarpment with breath taking views, hidden behind a tall hedge, lies a unique garden of outstanding beauty. A garden for all seasons, it features one of the country's largest fritillary spring meadows, sumptuous herbaceous summer borders, a striking potager, a majestic woodland rockery and an elegant Japanese Stroll Garden with tea house. For other garden openings please see website. Unsuitable for wheelchairs due to uneven ground and gravel pathways.

Rothbury

30 NEW HOUSE FARM

Elmbridge Lane, Elmbridge, WR9 0DA. Charles & Carlo Caddick, 01299 851249, Carlocaddick@hotmail.com. *2½m N of Droitwich Spa. A442 from Droitwich to Cutnall Green. Take lane opp Chequers Pub. Go 1m to T-junction. L towards Elmbridge Green/Elmbridge (past church & hall). At T-junction go R into Elmbridge Lane, garden on L.* **Sat 2, Sun 3 May (2-4.30). Adm £4.50, chd free. Home-made teas. Visits also by arrangement May to Sept for groups of 10 - max 20.**

This charming one acre garden surrounding an early C19 farm house (not open) has a wealth of rare trees and shrubs under planted with unusual bulbs and herbaceous plants. Special features are the topiary and perry wheel, natural pond, dry garden, rose garden, and small courtyard retreat. Plants for sale in aid of Alzheimer's. Partial wheelchair access due to steps.

GROUP OPENING

31 NORTH WORCESTER GARDENS

5 Beckett Drive, Worcester, WR3 7BZ. Jacki & Pete Ager. *Northwick, Worcester. Five town gardens off A449, Ombersley Rd, south of Claines r'about. Look for NGS Yellow signs from the main road.* **Sat 27, Sun 28 June (11-5). Combined adm £5, chd free. Home-made teas at 27 Sheldon Park Road. Home-made ice cream at 5 Beckett Drive. Cold drinks at 14 Beckett Road.**

5 BECKETT DRIVE
Jacki & Pete Ager.

NEW 14 BECKETT ROAD
Mr & Mrs Mike & Julia Roberts.

NEW 19 BEVERE CLOSE
Mr & Mrs Malcolm & Diane Styles.

10 LUCERNE CLOSE
Mark & Karen Askwith.

NEW 27 SHELDON PARK ROAD
Mr & Mrs Alan & Helen Kirby.

Five town gardens on the northern edge of Worcester each having its own identity. The diversity of this quintet of gardens would satisfy anyone from a dedicated plantsman to an enthusiastic amateur while

also offering plenty of ideas for landscaping, planting and structures. The landscaped garden at 5 Beckett Drive includes borders planted at different levels using palettes of harmonising or contrasting colours complemented by innovative features. 10 Lucerne Close is a cottage-style garden literally packed with a wide variety of plants with secluded seating areas. 27 Sheldon Park Road is a contemporary style garden planned with low maintenance in mind and expertly planted with many different foliage plants. The hard landscaping set amongst colourful borders with vegetables planted amongst the flowers are significant features at 14 Beckett Road. And by no means least, 19 Bevere Drive with a stunning collection of bonsai trees planted in an oriental setting. Tickets can be purchased from any of the gardens. Maps showing driving and walking routes available. Wheelchair access at Beckett Drive and Lucerne Close is restricted.

32 OAK TREE HOUSE

504 Birmingham Road, Marlbrook, Bromsgrove, B61 0HS. Di & Dave Morgan, 0121 445 3595, meandi@btinternet.com. *On A38 midway between M42 J1 & M5 J4. When open individually park in old A38 - R fork 250 yds N of garden or small area in front of Marlbrook Pub car park 200 yds S.* **Evening opening Sat 22 Aug (5-9). Adm £5, chd free. Wine. Opening with Marlbrook Gardens on Sun 31 May. Visits also by arrangement May to Aug for groups of 10+.**

Plantswoman's cottage garden overflowing with plants, pots and interesting artifacts. Secluded patio with plants and shrubs for Spring, small pond and waterfall. Plenty of seating, separate wildlife pond, water features, alpine area, rear open vista. Scented plants, hostas, dahlias and lilies. Conservatory with art by owners. Visitor HS said: "Such a wonderful peaceful oasis". Also: 'Wynn's Patch' - part of next door's garden being maintained on behalf of the owner. Oak Tree House open as single garden by arrangement May to August.

33 3 OAKHAMPTON ROAD

Stourport-On-Severn, DY13 0NR. Sandra & David Traynor, 07970 014295, traynor007@btinternet.com. *Between Astley Cross & Kings Arms PHs. From Stourport take A451 Dunley Rd towards Worcester. 1600 yds turn L into Pearl Lane. 4th R into Red House Rd, past the Kings Arms Pub, and next L to Oakhampton Rd. Extra parking at Kings Arms Pub.* **Sun 31 May, Sun 28 June, Sun 19 July, Sun 30, Mon 31 Aug (10-5). Adm £3.50, chd free. Home-made teas. Visits also by arrangement May to Aug for groups of up to 30.**

Beginning in March 2016 our plan was to put together a garden with a decidedly tropical feel to include palms from around the world, with tree ferns, bananas and as many other strange and unusual plants from warmer climes that would normally be considered difficult to grow here, as well as a pond and small waterfall. Not a large garden but you'll be surprised what can be done with a small space! Some narrow paths.

GROUP OPENING

34 OFFENHAM GARDENS

Main Street, Offenham, WR11 8QD. *Approaching Offenham on B4510 from Evesham, L into village signed Offenham & ferry ¾m. Follow road round into village. Parking in Village Hall car park opp Church. Walk to gardens from car park.* **Sat 8, Sun 9 Aug (11-5). Combined adm £5, chd free. Home-made teas. Light savoury snacks around lunch time, home-made teas and strawberries & cream.**

BROADWAY VIEW
Brett Pillinger & Rachel Bates.

DECHMONT
Angela & Paul Gash.

LANGDALE
Sheila & Adrian James, www.langdalegarden.uk.

ROSELEA
Mike & Linda Ansell.

WILLOWAY
Stephen & Linda Pitts.

Offenham is a picturesque village in the heart of the Vale of Evesham, with thatched cottages and traditional maypole. Five gardens of diverse styles from plantsman to exotic, including Langdale a Daily Mail 2019 National Garden Competition Finalist. Broadway View has a formal front garden. In the rear courtyard garden peaceful water features together with lush big leaf plants, olives and lemon trees make for a very tranquil space. With a mature walnut tree Dechmont features box topiary, conifers, shrubs and acers, colour from bulbs, perennials, annuals, clematis and roses set within curved borders. Langdale is a plant lover's garden designed for all year round interest. Surrounding a tranquil rill are garden rooms in a variety of styles with many unusual plants. Roselea is a lovely new garden with added interest of an aviary, some sheep and goats in the smallholding to the rear of the garden, and a good size vegetable and fruit garden. At Willoway, a corridor of Hostas leads to a lush carpet of lawn, then to an oriental area containing 2 well stocked ponds, waterfalls, many varieties of Acer and Hydrangea.

35 OVERBURY COURT

Overbury, GL20 7NP. Sir Bruce & Lady Bossom, 01386 725111(office), pa@overburyenterprises.co.uk. *5m NE of Tewkesbury. Village signed off A46. Turn off village rd beside the church. Park by the gates & walk up the drive.* Visits by arrangement Mar to Oct for groups of 10+. No refreshments available. Adm £5, chd free.

Georgian house 1740 (not open); landscaped garden of same date with stream and pools; daffodil bank and grotto. Plane trees, yew hedges; shrubs; cut flowers; coloured foliage; gold and silver, shrub rose borders. Norman church adjoins garden. Close to Whitcombe and Conderton Manor. Some slopes, while all the garden can be viewed, parts are not accessible to wheelchairs.

36 PEAR TREE COTTAGE

Witton Hill, Wichenford, Worcester, WR6 6YX. Pamela & Alistair Thompson, 01886 888295, peartree.pam@gmail.com, www.peartreecottage.me. *13m NW of Worcester & 2m NE of Martley.*

From Martley, take B4197. Turn R into Horn Lane then take 2nd L signed Witton Hill. Keep L & Pear Tree Cottage is on R at top of hill. Sun 31 May (11-6); Sun 30 Aug (3.30-10). Adm £5, chd free. Home-made teas. Sun 30 August 2020 - wine & Pimms served after 6pm!. Visits also by arrangement May to Sept. Small groups - even couples very welcome.

A Grade II listed black and white cottage (not open) SW-facing gardens and far reaching views across orchards to Abberley Clock Tower. The ¾ acre gardens comprise of gently sloping lawns with mixed and woodland borders, shade and plenty of strategically placed seating. The garden exudes a quirky and humorous character with the odd surprise and even includes a Shed of the Year Runner Up 2017! 'Garden by Twilight' evenings are very popular. Trees, shrubs and sculptures are softly uplit and the garden is filled with 100's of candles and nightlights (weather permitting!) Visitors are invited to listen to the owls and watch the bats whilst enjoying a glass of wine. Partial wheelchair access.

Cowleigh Lodge

GROUP OPENING

37 PERSHORE GARDENS
Pershore, WR10 1BG. Group Co-ordinator Jan Garratt, www.visitpershore.co.uk. *On B4084 between Worcester & Evesham, & 6m from exit 7 on M5. There is also a train station to the north of the town.* **Sat 6, Sun 7 June (1-5). Combined adm £6, chd free. Home-made teas at Holy Redeemer Primary School, Number 8 Community Arts Centre in the High Street and at pubs and cafes in the town. Also refreshments at some individual gardens. These will be indicated on the map/description sheet.**
Most years about twenty gardens open in Pershore. This small town has been opening gardens as part of the NGS for 50 years, almost continuously. In those days the open gardens were in the Georgian heart of the town but now, gardens open from all over the town. Some gardens are surprisingly large, well over an acre, while others are courtyard gardens. All have their individual appeal and present great variety. The wealth of pubs, restaurants and cafes offer ample opportunities for refreshment while the Abbey and the River Avon are some of the many points of interest in this market town. Tickets with a map are valid for both days and are available in advance from the Tourist Information in the library and 'Blue' in Broad Street and on the day at Number 8 Community Arts Centre in the High Street and any open garden. Refreshments available in pubs, hotels and cafes in the town, at Holy Redeemer School and in Number 8 Community Arts Centre in the High Street. Some individual gardens may provide teas on the day and this will be indicated on the map/description sheet handed out with tickets. Wheelchair access to some gardens.

🐄 ✤ 🚗 🚌 🍵

38 NEW PRIMROSE HOSPICE BROMSGROVE
St Godwalds Road, Bromsgrove, B60 3BW. Emma Williams, 01527889796, info@primrosehospice.org. *From A38 North L to B4184 to Aston Fields then L at 1st island. From A38 South R filter signed Aston Fields then over 1st island. After island R into St. Godwalds Rd. Entrance after*
last house on L. **Sun 12 July (12-4). Adm £3, chd free. Cream teas. Visits also by arrangement July & Aug.**
Tranquil hospice garden maintained solely by volunteers offering a safe, relaxing space to patients, their families, staff and volunteers. Not a traditional National Garden Scheme garden but one that shows how gardens can benefit those with life limiting illnesses and their families. It's the stories behind this garden that make it interesting and important.

& 🐄 ✤ 🍵

39 NEW RAVELIN
Gilberts End, Hanley Castle, WR8 0AS. Mrs Christine Peer, 01684 310215, cvpeer55@btinternet.com. *From Worcester/Callow End B4424 or from Upton B4211 to Hanley Castle then B4209 to Hanley Swan. From Malvern B4209 to Hanley Swan. At pond/Xrds turn to Welland. ½ m turn L opp Hall to Gilberts End.* **Sat 23, Sun 24 May (12.30-5); Sat 19, Sun 20 Sept (11.30-4). Adm £5, chd free. Light refreshments. Visits also by arrangement Apr to Oct.**
A ½ acre mature yet ever changing garden with a wide range of unusual plants full of colour and texture. Of interest to plant lovers and flower arrangers alike with views overlooking the fields and the Malvern Hills. Seasonal interest provided by a wide variety of hellebores, hardy geraniums, aconitums, heucharas, Michaelmas daisies, grasses and dahlias and a fifty-year-old silver pear tree. Thought to be built on medieval clay works in the royal hunting forest. Garden containing herbaceous and perennial planting with gravel garden, woodland area, pond, summer house and plenty of seating areas around the garden. A quiz for children. Largely flat, partial access for disabled- regret no mobility scooters.

🐄 ✤ 🚗 🍵

40 THE RIVER SCHOOL
Oakfield House, Droitwich Road, Worcester, WR3 7ST. Christian Education Trust-Worcester, 01905 451309, lacerta@btinternet.com, www.riverschool.co.uk. *2.4m N of Worcester City Centre on A38 towards Droitwich. At J6 M5, take A449 signed for Kidderminster, turn off at 1st turning marked for Blackpole. Turn R to Fernhill Heath & at T- junction with A38*
turn L. The school is ½ m on R. **Sat 25 Apr, Sat 1 Aug (10.30-3.30). Adm £5, chd free. Light refreshments in the Lewis Room near garden entrance. Visits also by arrangement Apr to Sept for groups of 10 to 30. Outside school hours and not Sunday.**
Worcester's lost garden. A Horticultural College garden being brought back to life. For 35 years after WW2 it was known as Oakfield Teacher Training College for Horticulture. With its reputation visitors came from 58 countries and at least 8 other Horticultural Colleges were founded by people inspired by it. The Estate features many less common shrubs and trees as well as a Forest School pond area. These are working school grounds being recovered mainly by volunteers, with children encouraged to garden in term time. A historically important but not traditional NGS garden! No dogs allowed. Teas. coffees, cold drinks, cakes and savouries available.

🍵

41 ◆ RIVERSIDE GARDENS AT WEBBS
Wychbold, Droitwich, WR9 0DG. Webbs of Wychbold, 01527 860000, www.webbsdirect.co.uk. *2m N of Droitwich Spa. 1m N of M5 J5 on A38. Follow tourism signs from M5.* **For opening times and information, please phone or visit garden website.**
2½ acres. Themed gardens incl Colour spectrum, tropical and dry garden, Rose garden, vegetable garden, National Collection of Harvington Hellebores, seaside garden, bamboozelum and self sufficient Garden. New Wave gardens opened 2004 includes natural seasonal interest with grasses and perennials. This area is also home to our Hobbit House and beehives which produce honey for our own food hall. The New Wave Garden was slightly changed over 2014 to become more of a natural wildlife area. There are willow wigwams and wooden tepees made for children to play in. This area now incl a bird hide and the Hobbit house. Open all yr except Christmas, Boxing Day and Easter Sun. Our New Wave Gardens area has grass paths which are underlaid with mesh so people with heavy duty wheelchairs can be taken around.

& ✤ 🚗 NPC 🍵

42 ROTHBURY

5 St Peter's Road, North Malvern, WR14 1QS. John Bryson, Philippa Lowe & David. *7m W of M5 J7 (Worcester). Turn off A449 Worcester to Ledbury Rd at B4503, signed Leigh Sinton. Almost immed take the middle rd (Hornyold Rd). St Peter's Rd is ¼m uphill, 2nd R.* Sun 19 Apr (2-5). Home-made teas. Mon 25 May (11-5); Sun 21 June (11-4.30); Sun 26 July (11-5). Light refreshments. Adm £3.50, chd free.

Set on slopes of Malvern Hills, ⅓ acre plant-lovers' garden surrounding Arts and Crafts house (not open), created by owners since 1999. Herbaceous borders, rockery, wildlife pond, vegetables, small orchard, containers. Magnificent Eucryphia glutinosa in July. A series of hand-excavated terraces accessed by sloping paths and steps. Views and seats. http:// www.facebook.com/RothburyNGS/. Fresh coffee, pots of tea, filled rolls, (except 19 April) home-made cakes, cream teas. Gluten free cake and rolls available. Partial wheelchair access. One very low step at entry, one standard step to main lawn and one to WC. Decking slope to top lawn. Dogs on leads.

🕿 🐄 🌸 🍵

43 ◆ SPETCHLEY PARK GARDENS

Th Estate Office, Spetchley Park, Worcester, WR5 1RS. Mr Henry Berkeley, 01905 345106, enquiries@ spetchleygardens.co.uk, www.spetchleygardens.co.uk. *2m E of Worcester. On A44, follow brown signs.* For NGS: Fri 3 Apr, Sun 5 July (10.30-5). Adm £8, chd £2.50. Light refreshments. For other opening times and information, please phone, email or visit garden website.

Surrounded by glorious countryside lays one of Britain's best-kept secrets. Spetchley is a garden for all tastes and ages, containing one of the biggest private collections of plant varieties outside the major botanical gardens and weaving a magical trail for younger visitors. Spetchley is not a formal paradise of neatly manicured lawns or beds but rather a wondrous display of plants, shrubs and trees woven into a garden of many rooms and vistas. Plant sales, gift shop and tea room. Annual Specialist Plant Fair will be held on Sat 18 April. Gravel paths.

🕿 🌸 🚗 🍵

44 ◆ STONE HOUSE COTTAGE GARDENS

Church Lane, Stone, DY10 4BG. Louisa Arbuthnott, 07817 921146, louisa@shcn.co.uk, www.shcn.co.uk. *2m SE of Kidderminster. Via A448 towards Bromsgrove, next to church, turn up drive.* For opening times and information, please phone, email or visit garden website.

A beautiful and romantic walled garden adorned with unusual brick follies. This acclaimed garden is exuberantly planted and holds one of the largest collections of rare plants in the country. It acts as a shop window for the adjoining nursery. Open Wed to Sat late March to early Sept 10-5. Partial wheelchair access.

🕿 🌸 🚗

45 NEW 12 THREE SPRINGS ROAD

Pershore, WR10 1HH. Mr & Mrs Roger Smith. *From M5 J6 take B4084 towards Pershore. Turn R onto A4104 towards Upton. No 12 is 300 yds on R (1st house in layby opp BP garage). 12 on gatepost. Please park in local roads ensuring no obstruction.* Thur 23 July (10-4). Adm £3, chd free. Light refreshments. Tea / coffee and cakes.

Garden has well defined areas with mature and young trees, perennial shrubs, 4 formal colour themed parterres, informal planting and young and mature trees. Easy access for wheelchairs. Major part of garden is behind house and is gently sloping from top to bottom, about 25 by 45 yards. New projects most years. Enthusiastic amateur. Access to all garden on paving slabs (and lawn).

🕿 🐄 🍵

46 THE TYNINGS

Church Lane, Stoulton, Worcester, WR7 4RE. John & Leslie Bryant, 01905 840189, johnlesbryant@btinternet.com. *Stoulton is 5m S of Worcester; 3m N of Pershore. On the B4084 between M5 J7 & Pershore. The Tynings lies beyond the church at the extreme end of Church Lane. Ample parking.* Visits by arrangement June to Sept. Adm £4, chd free. Light refreshments.

Acclaimed plantsman's ½-acre garden, generously planted with a large selection of rare trees and shrubs. Features incl specialist collection of lilies, many unusual climbers and rare ferns. The colour continues into late summer with cannas, dahlias, berberis, euonymus and tree colour. Surprises around every corner. Lovely views of adjacent Norman Church and surrounding countryside. Plants labelled and plant lists available.

🕿 🐄 🌸 🚗 🍵

47 THE WALLED GARDEN

6 Rose Terrace, off Fort Royal Hill, Worcester, WR5 1BU. William & Julia Scott. *Close to the City centre. ½m from Cathedral. Via Fort Royal Hill, off London Rd (A44). Park on 1st section of Rose Terrace & walk the last 20yds down track.* Sat 18, Wed 22 July (1-5). Adm £4, chd free. Tea. This C19 Walled Kitchen Garden, reawakened in 1995 by the present owners is a quiet garden evolving through the seasons. This productive tapestry includes culinary and medicinal herbs, fruit and vegetables, espaliered fruit trees, as well as medlar, mulberry and quince trees, chickens and bees. History is at the centre of the rescue and evolution of this enclosed garden which is chemical free. Historic garden with a focus on herbs and their uses.

🌸 🍵

48 NEW WALNUT COTTAGE

Lower End, Bricklehampton, Pershore, WR10 3HL. Mr & Mrs Richard & Janet Williams. *2½ m S of Pershore on A4084, then R into Bricklehampton Lane to T-junction, then L. Cottage is on R.* Sun 21 June, Sun 5 July (3-7). Adm £6, chd free. Wine. incl glass of wine or soft drink.

One and a half acre garden with views of Bredon Hill, designed into rooms, many of which have been created using high formal hedging of beech, hornbeam, copper beech and yew. There is a small "front garden" with a circular gravel path, a well stocked original garden area with pond and arches to the side of the house, a magnolia garden with several species of the plant, a magnificent tree garden with specimen trees from around the world, many of which are quite uncommon, over 200 roses, some in colour themed beds, others climbing over a long pergola or up other trees, a greenhouse, raised Koi Carp pond and a metal stairway leading to a roof based viewing platform surrounded by more roses. The garden continues to evolve and a Japanese garden is next planned. Plenty of seating and interesting artefacts add to the appeal.

🍵

49 NEW **WARNDON COURT**
St. Nicholas Lane, Worcester,
WR4 0SL. Doctors Rachel & David
Pryke. 1/3 m from J6 M5. Take
A4440 (towards Blackpole), over
island onto B4639, Berkeley Way.
1st L (Hastings Dr) then immediate
L again (St Nicholas Lane) Warndon
Court at end next to St Nicholas
Church. **Sun 17 May, Sun 14 June
(1-5.30). Adm £5, chd free. Home-
made teas in St Nicholas Church
barn, next door.**
Warndon Court is a 2 acre family
garden surrounding a Grade 2 listed
farmhouse (not open) featuring a
circular route taking in formal rose
gardens and terraces, two ponds,
pergolas, topiary (including a dragon
dressed as The Gruffalo!) a potager
and a woodland walk along the dry
moat and through the secret garden.
It has bee-friendly wildlife areas and
is home to great-crested newts and
slow-worms. Grade 1 listed St Nicholas
Church will also be open to visitors.
There will be an art exhibition of original
oil paintings in the barn. Tea and cakes
will be available in the church barn
next door, for a separate charity. The
gardens around the house can be
accessed across the lawn. The potager
is accessible but the woodland walk is
bumpy with slopes at each end.
  ♿ 🐕 ✿ 🍵

50 **WESTACRES**
Wolverhampton Road, Prestwood,
Stourbridge, DY7 5AN. Mrs
Joyce Williams, 01384 877496,
Koijoy62@yahoo.co.uk. 3m W
of Stourbridge. A449 in between
Wall Heath (2m) & Kidderminster
(6m). Ample parking Prestwood
Nurseries (next door). **Sat 15, Sun
16 Aug (11-4). Adm £5, chd free.
Home-made teas. Visits also by
arrangement June to Sept.**
3/4 -acre plant collector's garden with
unusual plants and many different
varieties of acers, hostas, shrubs.
Woodland walk, large fish pool.
Covered tea area with home-made
cakes. Come and see for yourselves,
you won't be disappointed. Described
by a visitor in the visitors book as 'A
garden which we all wished we could
have, at least once in our lifetime'.
Garden is flat. Disabled parking.
  ♿ 🐕 ✿ 🚌 🍵

51 **WHARF HOUSE**
Newnham Bridge, Tenbury
Wells, WR15 8NY. Gareth
Compton & Matthew Bartlett,
01584 781966, gco@no5.com,

www.wharfhousegardener.blog. Off
the A456 in hamlet of Broombank,
between Mamble & Newnham
Bridge. Garden signed. Do not rely
on SatNav. **Visits by arrangement
May to Sept. Adm £5, chd free.
Home-made teas.**
A 2 acre country garden, set around
an C18 house and out-buildings (not
open). Mixed herbaceous borders with
some colour theming: White Garden;
Bright Garden; Spring Garden; long
double borders; courtyards; stream
with little bridge to an island; vegetable
garden. The garden is on several
levels, with limited wheelchair access
and some uneven paths.
  🐕 ✿ 🍵

52 **WHITCOMBE HOUSE**
Overbury, Tewkesbury,
GL20 7NZ. Faith & Anthony
Hallett, 01386 725206,
faith.hallett1@gmail.com. 9m S of
Evesham, 5m NE Tewkesbury. Leave
A46 at Beckford to Overbury (2m).
Or B4080 from Tewkesbury through
Bredon/Kemerton (5m). Or small lane
signed Overbury at r'about junction
A46, A435 & B4077. Approx 5m
from J9 M5. **Visits by arrangement
Apr to Aug for groups of 5 to 30.
Adm £4, chd free.**
English cottage garden, (1 acre) set
in Cotswold village, Overbury. Long
borders of herbaceous, climbers and
shrubs, stone walls, gravel stream
flanked primula, astilbe and geranium.
Hydrangea, lavender and rose. Pastel
colours merge with cool blue and late
hot planting framed under canopy
of acer, and beech.and catalpa.
Nooks and crannies, a bridge and a
vegetable parterre adjoin surrounding
Yew.
  ♿ 🐕 ✿ 🚌 🍵

53 **WHITE COTTAGE &
NURSERY**
Earls Common Road, Stock
Green, Inkberrow, B96 6SZ. Mr
& Mrs S M Bates, 01386 792414,
smandjbates@aol.com,
whitecottage.garden. 2m W
of Inkberrow, 2m E of Upton
Snodsbury. A422 Worcester to
Alcester, turn at sign for Stock
Green by Red Hart Pub, 1 1/2 m to
T- junction, turn L 500 yds on the L.
**Mon 13 Apr, Sun 3, Sun 24, Mon
25 May, Sun 7, Sun 21 June, Sun
19 July, Sun 13 Sept (11-4.30).
Adm £4, chd free. Refreshments
are on a commercial basis. Visits
also by arrangement Apr to Sept
for groups of 10+. Individuals and**

groups welcome.
2 acre garden with large herbaceous
and shrub borders, island beds,
stream and bog area. Spring meadow
with 1000's of snakes head fritillaries.
Formal area with lily pond and circular
rose garden. Alpine rockery and
new fern area. Large collection of
interesting trees incl Nyssa Sylvatica,
Parrotia persica, and Acer 'October
Glory' for magnificent Autumn colour
and many others. Nursery and
Garden open most Thursdays from
10.30-5pm, please check before
visiting. For other opening times and
information please phone, email or
visit garden website and Facebook.
Wheelchair access.
  ♿ ✿ 🚌 🍵

54 **THE WHITE HOUSE**
Seedgreen Lane, Astley Burf,
DY13 0SA. John & Joanna Daniels,
www.talesfromacountrygarden.
wordpress.com. 3m SW of
Stourport on Severn. Off B4196 Holt
Heath/Stourport Rd. From Stourport
L towards Larford Fishing Lakes,
garden 1.8m. From Holt Heath R
onto Crundles Lane towards Astley
Burf, R in village then 1st L into
Seedgreen Lane. **Sun 17 May, Sun
5 July (2-5). Adm £3.50, chd free.
Home-made teas.**
Informal 1 acre constantly evolving
country garden and orchard in peaceful
surrounding. Large mixed borders
with shrubs, roses and cottage garden
plants. Orchard has ornamental and
productive trees and veg garden. Large
Victorian style greenhouse with scented
leaved pelargoniums. New feature in
the orchard is an 'autumn bed' planted
with perennial Helianthus, Rudbeckia,
Echinops and ornamental grasses. A
collection of vintage garden tools is
exhibited in an outbuilding. Gardened
with wildlife in mind leaving areas of
long grass in the orchard with paths
mown through.
  ♿ ✿ 🍵

55 ◆ **WHITLENGE GARDENS**
Whitlenge Lane, Hartlebury,
DY10 4HD. Mr & Mrs K J
Southall, 01299 250720, keith.
southall@creativelandscapes.
co.uk, www.whitlenge.co.uk. 5m
S of Kidderminster, on A442. A449
Kidderminster to Worcester L at
T-lights, A442 signed Droitwich, over
island, 1/4 m, 1st R into Whitlenge
Lane. Follow brown signs. **For
NGS: Sat 4, Sun 5 Apr, Sat 27,
Sun 28 June, Sat 5, Sun 6 Sept
(10-5). Adm £4.50, chd £2. Light**

refreshments in the adjacent Tea rooms. **For other opening times and information, please phone, email or visit garden website.**

3 acre show garden of a professional Garden designer incorporating a large variety of trees, shrubs etc. features include a Twisted brick pillar pergola, Moongate as featured on TV, waterfalls, ponds and streams. Mystic features of the Green Man, 'Sword in the Stone' and cave fernery. Walk the turf labyrinth and take refreshments in The Garden 'Design Studio' tearoom. Extensive plant nursery. 2½ metre high solid Oak Moongate set into reclaim brickwork with 4 cascading waterfalls, deck walk through giant Gunnera leaves, herb garden, 400 sq metre grass labyrinth, 'Garden of Thyme/time' plus children's play/pet corner. Locally sourced home-made food in tearoom, light snacks to hot meals. Wheelchair access mix of hard pathways, gravel pathways and lawn.

♿ ✿ 🚗 ☕

GROUP OPENING

56 WICK VILLAGE

School Lane, Wick, Pershore, WR10 3PD. Co-ordinator Mark Heath. *1m E of Pershore on B4084. Signed to Wick is almost opposite Pershore Horticultural College. Tickets for gardens at car park next to St Marys.* **Sun 14 June (1.30-6). Combined adm £7, chd free. Home-made teas in the field where cars are parked, which is next to St Marys.**

LAMBOURNE HOUSE
Mr & Mrs G Power.

NEW MERRYWAY, OWLETTS LANE
Mrs Clair Meikle-Taylor.

THE OLD FORGE
Sean & Elaine Young.

NEW THE OLD STABLES, YOCK LANE
Mr & Mrs Tony & Amalia Knight.

NEW TIMBERCROFT, TIMBER LANE
Mrs Carol Woolliscroft.

NEW 12 TIMBERDOWN
Mr Cyril Hagley.

NEW 13 WICK HOUSE CLOSE
Mr & Mrs Nigel & Gill Barker.

NEW 14 WICK HOUSE CLOSE
Mrs Joy Dodgson.

WYKE MANOR
Charles Hudson.

Langdale

Wick village gardens for 2020 offer the visitor a range of extraordinary garden experiences from modern gardens with superb views over towards Pershore, gardens undergoing development, small cottage gardens which contain delicious vegetables and the larger modern gardens. We last opened in 2015 and since then gardens in the village have developed and new gardens have and are still emerging. You can visit the romantic and picturesque Wyke Manor garden, gardens with plenty of well-stocked herbaceous borders, productive fruit and vegetable plots and magical ponds teeming with wildlife. You can also visit gardens that have been recently redesigned to meet todays horticultural challenges and proving that 'low maintenance' gardening is not synonymous with a lack of creativity or beautiful planting. Wick is a historic village just on the edge of Pershore with attractive well maintained gardens and a historic 4km circular walk. Ice creams and cold drinks also available in the village as advertised on the day. The Confetti Fields are not opening for the NGS 2020 Many of the gardens are suitable for wheelchair access.

♿ ✿ 🚗 ☕

57 68 WINDSOR AVENUE

St.Johns, Worcester, WR2 5NB. Roger & Barbara Parker. *W area of Worcester, W side of R Severn. Off the A44 to Bromyard. Into Comer Rd, 3rd L Into Laugherne Rd, 3rd L into Windsor Ave, at bottom in Cul-de-sac. Limited parking, please park courteously on road sides, car share if possible.* **Sun 24, Mon 25 May (1-5). Adm £4.50, chd free. Light refreshments. Tea, Coffee and Cake. Soft drinks also available.** "Our 10th year of opening." Almost one acre garden divided into three areas, situated behind a 1930's semi detached house in a cul-de-sac. Visitors are amazed and comment on size of garden and the tranquility! The garden includes bog gardens, flower beds, 'oriental' area, vegetable patch, five greenhouses and a Koi pond plus three other ponds each in very different styles. We also have Ornamental Pheasants and other birds! Gravel paths are everywhere.

✿ ☕

Volunteers

County Organisers

East Yorks
Helen Marsden
01430 860222
helen.marsden@ngs.org.uk

North Yorks – Cleveland, Hambleton, Richmond, Rydale & Scarborough
Hugh Norton
01653 628604
hughnorton0@gmail.com

South & West Yorks & North Yorks – Craven, Harrogate, Selby & York
Veronica Brook
01423 340875
veronica.brook@ngs.org.uk

County Treasurer
Angela Pugh
01423 330456
angela.pugh@ngs.org.uk

Publicity & Social Media
Jane Cooper 01484 604232
jane.cooper@ngs.org.uk

Sally Roberts 01423 871419
sally.roberts@ngs.org.uk

Booklet Advertising
John Plant
01347 888125
rewelacottage@gmail.com

By Arrangement Visits
Penny Phillips
01937 834970
penny.phillips@ngs.org.uk

Clubs & Societies
Penny Phillips (as above)

Assistant County Organisers

East Yorks
Ian & Linda McGowan
01482 896492
ianandlinda.mcgowan@ngs.org.uk

Hazel Rowe 01430 861439
hazel.rowe@ngs.org.uk

Natalie Verow 01759 368444
natalieverow@aol.com

North Yorks
David Lis 01439 788846
david.lis@ngs.org.uk

Gillian Mellor 01723 891636
gill.mellor@ngs.org.uk

David Morgan 07827 958103
david.j.morgan@ngs.org.uk

Judi Smith 01845 567518
judi.smith@ngs.org.uk

West & South Yorks
Deborah Bigley 01423 330727
debsandbobbigley@btinternet.com

Felicity Bowring 01729 823551
felicity.bowring@ngs.org.uk

Jane Hudson 01924 840980
jane.hudson@ngs.org.uk

Chris & Fiona Royffe
01937 530306
plantsbydesign@btinternet.com

Elizabeth & David Smith
01484 644320
elizabethanddavidsmith@ngs.org.uk

Bridget Marshall BEM
01423 330474
biddy.marshall@ngs.org.uk

f @YorkshireNGS

 @YorkshireNGS

 @ngsyorkshire

Yorkshire, England's largest county, stretches from the Pennines in the west to the rugged coast and sandy beaches of the east: a rural landscape of moors, dales, vales and rolling wolds.

Nestling on riverbanks lie many historic market towns, and in the deep valleys of the west and south others retain their 19th century industrial heritage of coal, steel and textiles.

The wealth generated by these industries supported the many great estates, houses and gardens throughout the county. From Hull in the east, a complex network of canals weaves its way across the county, connecting cities to the sea and beyond.

The Victorian spa town of Harrogate with the RHS garden at Harlow Carr, or the historic city of York with a minster encircled by Roman walls, are both ideal centres from which to explore the gardens and cultural heritage of the county.

We look forward to welcoming you to our private gardens – you will find that many of them open not only on a specific day, but also 'by arrangement' for groups and individuals - we can help you to get in touch.

Left: Jackson's Wold

OPENING DATES

All entries subject to change. For latest information check **www.ngs.org.uk**

Map locator numbers are shown to the right of each garden name.

February

Snowdrop Festival

Sunday 16th
Bridge Farm House	7
Devonshire Mill	21

Sunday 23rd
Bridge Farm House	7
72 Church Street	13

March

Sunday 15th
Fawley House	27

Saturday 28th
Primrose Bank Garden and Nursery	72

Sunday 29th
Clifton Castle	15
Goldsborough Hall	34
Primrose Bank Garden and Nursery	72

April

Sunday 5th
Ellerker House	25

Sunday 19th
The Circles Garden	14
Fawley House	27

Saturday 25th
249 Barnsley Road	1

Sunday 26th
249 Barnsley Road	1

May

Saturday 2nd
Linden Lodge	50

Sunday 3rd
Linden Lodge	50
Well House	94

Whixley Gardens	96

Friday 8th
Highfield Cottage	41
Well House	94
Whixley Gardens	96

Sunday 10th
Barnville	2
◆ Jackson's Wold	48
Low Hall	51
Scape Lodge	79
◆ Stillingfleet Lodge	85
Warley House Garden	93
Woodlands Cottage	98

Tuesday 12th
◆ Himalayan Garden & Sculpture Park	44

Wednesday 13th
Warley House Garden	93

Sunday 17th
Millrace Garden	59
The Orchard	67
◆ RHS Garden Harlow Carr	75

Wednesday 20th
Land Farm	49

Saturday 23rd
The Red House	73
Tamarind	89

Sunday 24th
Penny Piece Cottages	70
The Red House	73
The Ridings	76
Tamarind	89

Monday 25th
Bridge Farm House	7
Holmfield	45

Wednesday 27th
Glencoe House	33

Sunday 31st
Bramblewood Cottage	6
Rewela Cottage	74
1 School Lane	80
The Villa	91

June

Wednesday 3rd
5 Hill Top	42

Friday 5th
◆ Shandy Hall Gardens	81

Saturday 6th
Hunmanby Grange	47
Old Sleningford Hall	65

Shiptonthorpe Gardens	83

Sunday 7th
5 Hill Top	42
Hunmanby Grange	47
◆ Norton Conyers	62
Old Sleningford Hall	65
Shiptonthorpe Gardens	83
◆ The Yorkshire Arboretum	101

Friday 12th
Markenfield Hall	55

Sunday 14th
Bramblewood Cottage	6
Brookfield	8
Clifton Castle	15
Cobble Cottage	16
NEW Grafton Gardens	35
White Wynn	95
Willow Cottage	97

Wednesday 17th
Glencoe House	33

Sunday 21st
Birstwith Hall	5
Havoc Hall	40
◆ Jackson's Wold	48
The Old Vicarage	66
Tythe Farm House	90
Yorke House & White Rose Cottage	100

Wednesday 24th
NEW The Cottage	17
East Morton Gardens	23

Thursday 25th
Land Farm	49

Friday 26th
◆ Shandy Hall Gardens	81

Sunday 28th
3 Embankment Road	26
Fernleigh	28
Highfield Cottage	41
Millgate House	57
Mr Nick's	60
23 The Paddock	68

July

Wednesday 1st
The Grange	36
Sleightholmedale Lodge	84

Saturday 4th
Beechcroft Farmhouse	3

Sue Proctor Plants Nursery Garden	87

Sunday 5th
Bugthorpe Gardens	9
72 Church Street	13
◆ Dove Cottage Nursery Garden	22
Honey Head	46
Low Stonehills Farm	52
NEW Maunby Hall	56
Millgate House	57
The Ridings	76
Sue Proctor Plants Nursery Garden	87

Wednesday 8th
Brookfield	8

Saturday 11th
249 Barnsley Road	1
Cawood Gardens	11
NEW Galehouse Barn	32

Sunday 12th
249 Barnsley Road	1
Cawood Gardens	11
Dacre Banks & Summerbridge Gardens	19
Daneswell House	20
NEW Five Small Town Gardens	30
NEW Galehouse Barn	32
Sheffield Gardens	82

Wednesday 15th
NEW The Cottage	17
◆ Parcevall Hall Gardens	69

Saturday 18th
Stonefield Cottage	86

Sunday 19th
East Wing, Newton Kyme Hall	24
Goldsborough Hall	34
The Manor House	53
115 Millhouses Lane	58
The Nursery	63
Stonefield Cottage	86
NEW The Vines	92

Wednesday 22nd
The Nursery	63

Sunday 26th
Fernleigh	28

Wednesday 29th
The Grange	36

1 School Lane

THE GARDENS

1 249 BARNSLEY ROAD

Flockton, Wakefield, WF4 4AL. Nigel & Anne Marie Booth, 01924 848967, nigel.booth1@btopenworld.com. *On A637 Barnsley Road. M1 J38 or 39 follow the signs for Huddersfield. Parking on Manor House Rd (WF4 4AL for Sat Nav) & Hardcastle Lane (WF4 4AR for Sat Nav).* Sat 25, Sun 26 Apr, Sat 11, Sun 12 July (1-5). Adm £4, chd free. Home-made teas. Visits also by arrangement Apr to Sept.

An elevated garden with fantastic panoramic views. 1/3 acre south facing garden packed with an abundance of spring colour, created from 1000's of bulbs, perennials, shrubs and trees. Make a return visit in the summer to view the transformation, displaying up to 60 hanging baskets and over 150 pots, creating the 'wow factor' garden. Limited wheelchair access. Disabled drop off point. Ukulele group playing live in the garden at the July opening.

2 BARNVILLE

Wilton, Nr Pickering, YO18 7LE. Bill & Liz Craven, 07867 503242, lizcraven40@gmail.com. *4m E of Pickering. On main A170, travelling from Pickering towards Scarborough, enter village of Wilton. Turn R. House on L in 200yrds.* Sun 10 May (12-5). Adm £4, chd free. Home-made teas. Visits also by arrangement May and Aug for groups of 10+ incl cream teas. We welcome both daytime and evening visits.

Over an acre of hidden gardens on edge of North York Moors lovingly designed and maintained by the current owners, featuring a myriad of unusual plants and trees. Magnolia, camellia and azalea shelter naturalised bulbs, trillium and erythronium. Summer's cool green foliage highlights agapanthus, ornamental grasses, hydrangeas, species lilies and carpets of cyclamen. Lower garden unsuitable for wheelchairs in wet, but level stone paths in upper gardens. Access to sunken garden via steps - can be viewed from above.

3 BEECHCROFT FARMHOUSE

Aldwark, nr Alne, York, YO61 1UB. Alison Pollock. *14m NW of York, 17m E of Harrogate, 7m SW of Easingwold. Follow signs for Aldwark Manor hotel & golf course for village. Approach from A1(M) and W is via Aldwark Toll Bridge (40p toll for cars).* Sat 4 July (1-5). Adm £4, chd free. Home-made teas.

Country garden surrounding Georgian farmhouse (not open). Winding paths lead through series of smaller gardens with different planting themes. Cottage borders with old roses, tulips, clematis. Hidden areas with seating give a secluded feel. Gravel courtyard with small formal pond, late perennials and grasses.

4 90 BENTS ROAD

Bents Green, Sheffield, S11 9RL. Mrs Hilary Hutson, 011422 58570, h.hutson@paradiseregained.net. *3m SW of Sheffield. From Moore St r'about in Sheffield Centre (nr Waitrose), follow A625. After approx 3m turn R on to Bents Rd.* Visits by arrangement July & Aug for groups of up to 30. Adm £4, chd free. Light refreshments.

Plantswoman's NE facing garden. Patio with alpine troughs for year-round interest, plus pots of colourful tropical plants in summer. Mixed borders surround a lawn which leads to mature trees underplanted with shade-loving plants at end of garden. Many unusual and borderline-hardy species. Front garden peaks in summer with hot-coloured blooms. Front garden and patio flat and accessible. Remainder of back garden accessed via 6 steps (with handrail), so unsuitable for wheelchairs.

5 BIRSTWITH HALL

High Birstwith, Harrogate, HG3 2JW. Sir James & Lady Aykroyd, 01423 770250, ladya@birstwithhall.co.uk. *5m NW of Harrogate. Between Hampsthwaite & Birstwith villages, close to A59 Harrogate/Skipton Rd.* Sun 21 June (2-5). Adm £5, chd free. Home-made teas. Visits also by arrangement Apr to July for groups of 10 to 30.

Charming and varied 4 acre garden nestling in secluded Yorkshire dale. Formal garden and ornamental orchard, extensive lawns leading to picturesque stream. Large pond and

Victorian greenhouse. Also home-made teas and refreshments for large groups.

6 BRAMBLEWOOD COTTAGE

Old Coach Road, Bradfield, Sheffield, S6 6HX. Nigel Dunnett. *6m from Sheffield City centre. From Sheffield follow Loxley Road (B6077) turn L onto New Road just before Damflask reservoir. Follow alongside reservoir until Old Coach Road.* Sun 31 May, Sun 14 June, Sun 13 Sept (2-5). Adm £5, chd free. Home-made teas. Opening with Sheffield Gardens on Sun 12 July.

Experimental hillside garden with extensive areas of naturalistic perennial planting and large-scale log-pile and habitat sculptures. A range of different types of designed annual and perennial meadows and a bluebell woodland. Strong ecological and sustainable gardening theme. A front garden pool, rain gardens and bioswales. Pennine views. Signed copies of books by Nigel Dunnett available. The garden is an experimental working environment for the owner, testing out different methods of planting and combinations that might be used more widely. No wheelchair access possible.

7 BRIDGE FARM HOUSE

Long Lane, Great Heck, Selby, DN14 0BE. Barbara & Richard Ferrari. *6m S of Selby, 3m E M62 J34. At M62 J34 take A19 to Selby, at r'about turn E towards Snaith on A645. After level crossing turn R at T-lights, L at T-junction onto Main St, past Church, to T-junction, cross to car park.* Sun 16, Sun 23 Feb (1-4). Adm £3, chd free. Mon 25 May (12-4). Adm £4, chd free. Home-made teas in church opp (May only).

2 acre garden divided by hedges into separate areas planted with unusual and interesting plants. All yr interest starts with hellebores, winter shrubs and over 150 named snowdrops. Long double mixed borders, bog and gravel gardens, interesting trees. Hens, compost heaps and wildlife areas. Please note, no refreshments available at Feb openings. Wheelchair access easiest by front gate, please ask.

8 BROOKFIELD

Jew Lane, Oxenhope, Keighley, BD22 9HS. Mrs R L Belsey, 01535 643070. *5m SW of Keighley. From Keighley take A629 (Halifax) Fork R A6033 towards Haworth & Oxenhope turn L at Xrds into village. Turn R (Jew Lane) at bottom of hill.* **Sun 14 June, Wed 8 July (1.30-5.30). Adm £4, chd free. Home-made teas. Visits also by arrangement May to July for groups of 5 to 10.**

An intimate 1 acre sloping garden with steps and paths leading down to a large pond with an island, mallards, wild geese and greylags. Many varieties of primula candelabra and florindae and dactylorrhiza majalis which have seeded into the lower lawn around a small pond with stream; azaleas and rhododendrons. Unusual trees and shrubs in a series of island beds, screes, greenhouses and conservatory. 'Round and round the garden' children's quiz. Steep narrow paths, not suitable for wheelchairs.

GROUP OPENING

9 BUGTHORPE GARDENS

Bugthorpe, York, YO41 1QG. *Bugthorpe. 4m E of Stamford Bridge, A166, village of Bugthorpe.* **Sun 5 July (10-4). Combined adm £6, chd free. Light refreshments.**

3 CHURCH WALK
Barrie Creaser & David Fielding, 01759 368152, barriecreaser@gmail.com. **Visits also by arrangement June & July for groups of up to 20.**

THE OLD RECTORY
Dr & Mrs P W Verow.

Two contrasting gardens situated in the small village of Bugthorpe. 3 Church Walk: a garden created in 2000, surprisingly mature, with mixed borders and trees, water feature and pond. Raised vegetable garden and greenhouse. The lawn leads onto a paddock with views of open countryside. The Old Rectory: ¾ acre country garden with views of the Yorkshire Wolds. Mixed borders, ponds, terrace, summerhouse, courtyard and many mature trees. Raised vegetable beds.

10 NEW CALF HEY FARM

Barkisland, Halifax, HX4 0ET. Anthea Thornber, 07771 357752, calfhey@icloud.com. *Between Barkisland, Krumlin & Stainland villages. Set Sat Nav to Barkisland Village FIRST, then use garden post code. Do not approach from Sonoco Paper Mill.* **Sun 20 Sept (11-3). Adm £5, chd free. Home-made teas.**

A young, evolving garden around a West Yorkshire farmhouse with fine views. The owners are creating a relaxing space to enjoy an eclectic mix of colourful scented garden borders and the surrounding views of Krumlin. The garden features 320ft of stone walls, trees, stone sculptures, nature ponds, raised beds, wildlife areas, cobbled paths, lawns, native hedges and most recently a cut flower paddock.

GROUP OPENING

11 CAWOOD GARDENS

Cawood, nr Selby, YO8 3UG. 01757 268571, dave-judyjones@hotmail.co.uk. *On B1223 5m N of Selby & 7m SE of Tadcaster. Between York & A1 on B1222. Village maps given at all gardens.* **Sat 11, Sun 12 July (12-5). Combined adm £5, chd free. Home-made teas at both gardens. Also open Galehouse Barn. Visits also by arrangement June to July**

9 ANSON GROVE
Tony & Brenda Finnigan, 01757 268888, beeart@ansongrove.co.uk. **Visits also by arrangement June & July for groups of 10 to 20.**

21 GREAT CLOSE
David & Judy Jones, 01757 268571, dave-judyjones@hotmail.co.uk. **Visits also by arrangement June & July for groups of 10 to 20.**

Two contrasting gardens in an attractive historic village are linked by a pretty riverside walk to the C11 church and memorial garden and across the Castle Garth to the remains of Cawood Castle. 9 Anson Grove is a small garden with tranquil pools and secluded sitting places. Narrow winding paths and raised areas give views over oriental-style pagoda, bridge and Zen garden. 21 Great Close is a flower arranger's garden,

designed and built by the owners. Interesting trees and shrubs combine with herbaceous borders incl many grasses. Two ponds are joined by a stream, winding paths take you to the vegetable garden and summerhouse, then back to the colourful terrace for views across the garden and countryside beyond. Crafts and paintings on sale at 9 Anson Grove. Cards on sale at 21 Great Close. Limited wheelchair access.

13 72 CHURCH STREET

Oughtibridge, Sheffield, S35 0FW. Linda & Peter Stewart. *6m N of Sheffield. M1 (J36) A61 (Sheffield). Turn R at Norfolk Arms pub. In Oughtibridge follow one-way system turning L immed after zebra crossing. On 57 bus route and short walk up hill from tram link bus.* **Sun 23 Feb (11-2); Sun 5 July (11-4). Adm £3.50, chd free. Light refreshments.**

Hidden from the busy street is our peaceful country garden with naturalistic planting leading down to Coumes Brook and backed by native woodland. In February the garden bursts into life with a stunning display of snowdrops. The garden railway next door will be open to garden visitors on 5 July.

14 THE CIRCLES GARDEN

8 Stocksmoor Road, Midgley, nr Wakefield, WF4 4JQ. Joan Gaunt. *Equidistant from Huddersfield, Wakefield & Barnsley, W of M1. Turn off A637 in Midgley at the Black Bull Pub (sharp bend) onto B6117 (Stocksmoor Rd). Please park on L adjacent to houses.* **Sun 19 Apr (1.30-4.30). Adm £4, chd free. Home-made teas.**

An organic and self-sustaining plantswoman's ½ acre garden on gently sloping site overlooking fields, woods and nature reserve opposite. Designed and maintained by owner. Herbaceous, bulb and shrub plantings linked by grass and gravel paths, woodland area with mature trees, meadows, fernery, greenhouse, fruit trees, viewing terrace with pots. About 100 hellebores grown from my seed. Hellebores South African plants, hollies, and small bulbs of particular interest.

15 CLIFTON CASTLE
Ripon, HG4 4AB. Lord & Lady Downshire. *2m N of Masham. On rd to Newton-le-Willows & Richmond. Gates on L next to red telephone box.* **Sun 29 Mar, Sun 14 June (2-5). Adm £5, chd free. Home-made teas.**
Breathtaking views over lower Wensleydale; the gardens include formal walks through the wooded 'pleasure grounds' with abundant wild flowers, affording views over the river from the top path and returning at river level. The walled kitchen garden is similar to how it was set out in the C19. New wild flower meadows have been laid out with modern sculptures. Gravel paths and steep slopes to river.

16 COBBLE COTTAGE
Rudgate, Whixley, YO26 8AL. John Hawkridge & Barry Atkinson, 01423 331419, john_barry44@outlook.com. *8m W of York, 8m E of Harrogate, 6m N of Wetherby. From High St, L at Anchor Inn onto Station Rd, on L.* **Sun 14 June (1-5). Combined adm with Grafton Gardens £7, chd free. Opening with Whixley Gardens on Sun 3, Fri 8 May (12-5). Visits also by arrangement May to July for groups of 20+.**
Imaginatively designed, constantly changing, small cottage garden full of decorative architectural plants and old family favourites. Interesting water garden, containers and use of natural materials. Black and white courtyard garden and Japanese - style garden with growing willow screen.

17 NEW THE COTTAGE
55 Bradway Road, Bradway, Sheffield, S17 4QR. Jane Holbrey. *6m S Sheffield City Centre. Follow Greenhill Parkway (B6054) towards Derbyshire, cottage set back just before Dore & Totley Golf Club.* **Wed 24 June, Wed 15 July (12-5). Adm £3.50, chd free. Light refreshments.**
Cottage garden with specimen fruit trees including step-over apples. Herbaceous borders, vegetable plot, wild flower area, auricula theatre. Contemporary shepherd's hut and open pond. Garden has steps and uneven York stone paving. Many seating areas. No wheelchair access possible.

18 COW CLOSE COTTAGE
Stripe Lane, Hartwith, Harrogate, HG3 3EY. William Moore & John Wilson, 01423 779813, cowclose1@btinternet.com. *8m NW of Harrogate. From A61(Harrogate-Ripon) at Ripley take B6165 to Pateley Bridge. 2m beyond Burnt Yates turn R, signed Hartwith/ Brimham Rocks onto Stripe Lane. Parking available.* **Visits by arrangement for groups of 10+. Adm £5, chd free. Light refreshments.**
2/3 acre country garden on sloping site with stream and far reaching views. Large borders with drifts of interesting, well-chosen, later flowering summer perennials and some grasses contrasting with woodland shade and streamside plantings. Gravel path leading to vegetable area. Courtyard area, terrace and seating with views of the garden. Orchard and ha-ha with steps leading to wild flower meadow. The lower part of the garden can be accessed via the orchard.

GROUP OPENING

19 DACRE BANKS & SUMMERBRIDGE GARDENS
Nidderdale, HG3 4EW. Tony & Pat Hutchinson and Mark & Amy Hutchinson, www.yorkehouse.co.uk. *4m SE Pateley Bridge, 10m NW Harrogate,10m N Otley, on B6451 & B6165. Parking at each garden. Maps available to show garden locations.* **Sun 12 July (12-5). Combined adm £8, chd free. Home-made teas at Yorke House, Low Hall and Woodlands Cottage.**

LOW HALL
Mrs P A Holliday.
(See separate entry)

RIVERSIDE HOUSE
Joy Stanton, 07815695233, joy.stanton21@gmail.com.
Visits also by arrangement May to July for groups of 5 to 20.

WOODLANDS COTTAGE
Mr & Mrs Stark.
(See separate entry)

YORKE HOUSE & WHITE ROSE COTTAGE
Tony & Pat Hutchinson & Mark & Amy Hutchinson.
(See separate entry)

Dacre Banks and Summerbridge Gardens are situated in the beautiful countryside of Nidderdale and designed to take advantage of the scenic Dales landscape. The gardens are linked by attractive walks along the valley, but each may be accessed individually by car. Low Hall has a romantic walled garden set on different levels around the historic C17 family home (not open) with herbaceous borders, shrubs, climbing roses and tranquil water garden. Riverside House is an atmospheric waterside garden on many levels, supporting shade-loving plants and features a Victorian folly, fernery, courtyard and naturalistic riverside plantings. Woodlands Cottage is a garden of many rooms, with exquisite formal and informal plantings, and an attractive wild flower meadow which harmonises with mature woodland. Yorke House has extensive colour-themed borders and water features with beautiful waterside plantings. The newly developed garden at White Rose Cottage is specifically designed for wheelchair users. Visitors welcome to use orchard picnic area at Yorke House. Partial wheelchair access at some gardens. Full wheelchair access at White Rose Cottage.

27 FAWLEY HOUSE

7 Nordham, North Cave, nr Brough, Hull, HU15 2LT. Mr & Mrs T Martin, 01430 422266, louisem200@hotmail.co.uk, www.nordhamcottages.co.uk. *15m W of Hull. L at J38 on M62E. L at '30' & signs: Wetlands & Polo. At L bend, R into Nordham. Fawley's on R. From Beverley, B1230 to N Cave. R after church. Over bridge.* **Sun 15 Mar, Sun 19 Apr (12-5). Adm £5, chd free. Home-made teas. Visits also by arrangement Jan to June for groups of 10+. Adm incls teas, please liaise if not required.**
Tiered, 2½ acre garden with lawns, mature trees, formal hedging and gravel pathways. Lavender beds, mixed shrub/herbaceous borders, and hot double herbaceous borders. Apple espaliers, pears, soft fruit, produce and herb gardens. Terrace with pergola and vines. Sunken garden with white border. Woodland with naturalistic planting and spring bulbs. Quaker well, stream and spring area with 3 bridges, ferns and hellebores near mill stream. Beautiful snowdrops and aconites early in year. Treasure hunt for children, art exhibition and cards for sale. Self catering accommodation at Nordham Cottages - see website. Refreshments in the stone cottage with log fires in March and also in April if cold. Partial wheelchair access to top of garden and terrace on pea gravel, sloping paths thereafter.
& 🐎 ✿ 🚗 🚐 ☕ 💷

28 FERNLEIGH

9 Meadowhead Avenue, Meadowhead, Sheffield, S8 7RT. Mr & Mrs C Littlewood, 01142 747234, littlewoodchristine@gmail.com. *4m S of Sheffield city centre. From Sheffield city centre. A61, A6102, B6054 r'about, exit B6054. 1st R Greenhill Ave, 2nd R. From M1 J33, A630 to A6102, then as above.* **Sun 28 June, Sun 26 July, Sun 30 Aug (11-5). Adm £3.50, chd free. Home-made teas and cakes. Visits also by arrangement May to Aug for groups of 10 to 30.**
Plantswoman's ⅓ acre cottage style suburban garden. Large variety of unusual plants set in differently planted sections to provide all-yr interest. Seating areas to view different aspects of garden. Auricula theatre, patio, gazebo and greenhouse. Miniature log cabin with living roof and cobbled area with

unusual plants in pots. Sempervivum, alpine displays and wildlife 'hotel'. Wide selection of home grown plants for sale. Animal Search for children.
✿ ☕ 💷

ALLOTMENTS

29 FIRVALE ALLOTMENT GARDEN

Winney Hill, Harthill, nr Worksop, S26 7YN. Don & Dot Witton, 01909 771366, donshardyeuphorbias@btopenworld.com, www.euphorbias.co.uk. *12m SE of Sheffield, 6m W of Worksop. M1 J31 A57 to Worksop. Turn R to Harthill. Allotments at S end of village, 26 Casson Drive at N end on Northlands Estate.* **Visits by arrangement Apr to June. Adm £3, chd free. Home-made teas at 26 Casson Drive Harthill (S26 7WA).**
Large allotment with 13 island beds displaying 500+ herbaceous perennials including the National Collection of hardy euphorbias with over 100 varieties flowering between March and October. Organic vegetable garden. Refreshments, WC, plant sales at 26 Casson Drive – small garden with mixed borders, shade and seaside garden.
✿ 🚗 NPC ☕

GROUP OPENING

30 NEW FIVE SMALL TOWN GARDENS

Bishops Croft, Beverley, HU17 8JY. Jonathan & Kath Roe. *Bishops Croft is a turning off The Leases / Albert Terrace in central Beverley. East on A1174 to T Lights (Rose & Crown on L) straight over onto A164 at r'about L onto Manor Rd. No 19 on L. Grayburn Lane car park is nearby. Access Willow Grove via Pasture Terrace from A1079/via Tiger Lane, off North Bar Within. York Rd N end of Beverley on A1079 leading from Beverley to York. 100yds from North Bar, opp gates leading to Netherd's yard* **Sun 12 July (1-5). Combined adm £6, chd free. Home-made teas at 6 York Road.**

NEW 2 BISHOPS CROFT
Jonathan & Kath Roe.

NEW 19 MANOR ROAD
Rosemary Dyason.

5 WILLOW GROVE
Tim Cartwright Taylor.

NEW 5 YORK ROAD
Pam & Jeremy Cridlan.

6 YORK ROAD
Pamela Hopkins.

Five gardens in central Beverley that show what can be done with creative approaches to small spaces. Garden styles range from the relatively traditional to relatively experimental and many points in between.
☕

31 FRIARS HILL

Sinnington, YO62 6SL. Mr & Mrs C J Baldwin, 01751 432179, friars.hill@abelgratis.co.uk. *4m W of Pickering. On A170.* **Visits by arrangement Mar to July. Adm £5, chd free.**
Plantswoman's 1¾ acre garden with year round colour. Early interest with hellebores, bulbs and woodland plants. Herbaceous beds, hostas, delphiniums, old roses and stone troughs. Excellent autumn colour.
& 🐎 ✿ 🚗 ☕ 💷

32 NEW GALEHOUSE BARN

Bishopdyke Road, Cawood, Selby, YO8 3UB. Mr & Mrs J Lloyd, 07768 405642, junelloyd042@gmail.com. *On B1222 1m out of Cawood towards Sherburn in Elmet.* **Sat 11, Sun 12 July (12-5). Adm £3.50, chd free. Also open Cawood Gardens. Home-made teas at Cawood Gardens. Visits also by arrangement Apr to Sept for groups of 5 to 20.**
The Barn: A plantaholic's informal cottage garden, created in 2015, to encourage birds and insects. Raised beds with tranquil seating area. The Farm: S facing partly shaded varied herbaceous border. N facing exposed shaded border redeveloped 2017 and ongoing for spring and autumn interest. Small new experimental 50 shades of white garden. Raised beds for vegetables. Partial wheelchair access.
& 🐎 💷

33 GLENCOE HOUSE

Main Street, Bainton, Driffield, YO25 9NE. Liz Dewsbury, 01377 217592, efdewsbury@gmail.com. *6m SW of Driffield on A614. 10m N of Beverley on B1248 Malton Rd. The house is on the W side of A614 in centre of the village. Parking is around village or in lay-by 280m N of house*

towards the Bainton r'about. **Wed 27 May, Wed 17 June (12-5). Adm £4, chd free. Home-made teas. Visits also by arrangement in June for groups of 5 to 30.**
A tranquil 3 acre garden developed from a small-holding over 40+ years and continually evolving. Trees, shrubs, roses, clematis and masses of herbaceous perennials grow in the cottage garden, which is next to an area of parkland planted with specimen trees and an orchard. Furthest from the house, there is a naturalistic established planting of native and unusual trees plus large wildlife pond. Wheelchair access to paved area in cottage garden but difficult elsewhere.

34 GOLDSBOROUGH HALL
Church Street, Goldsborough, HG5 8NR. Mr & Mrs M Oglesby, 01423 867321, info@goldsboroughhall.com, www.goldsboroughhall.com. *2m SE of Knaresborough. 3m W of A1M. Off A59 (York-Harrogate) car park 300yds past pub on R.* **Sun 29 Mar (11-4); Sun 19 July (11-5). Adm £5, chd free. Light lunches, cream teas, sandwiches and cakes. Visits also by arrangement. Donation to St Mary's Church.**

Previously opened for NGS from 1928-30 and now beautifully restored by present owners (re-opened in 2010). 12 acre garden and formal landscaped grounds in parkland setting and Grade II*, C17 house, former residence of HRH Princess Mary, daughter of George V and Queen Mary. Gertrude Jekyll inspired replanted 120ft double herbaceous borders and rose garden. Quarter-mile Lime Tree Walk planted by royalty in the 1920s, orchard, restored kitchen garden and new glasshouse, flower borders featuring 'Yorkshire Princess' rose, named after Princess Mary and a new wild flower meadow. Gravel paths and some steep slopes.

GROUP OPENING

35 NEW GRAFTON GARDENS
Marton Cum Grafton, York, YO51 9QJ. Mrs Glen Garnett. *2 ½ m S of Boroughbridge. Turn off the A168 or B6265 to Marton or Grafton (South of Boroughbridge).* **Sun 14 June (12-5). Combined adm with Cobble Cottage £7, chd free. Tea at Well House.**

NEW **PADDOCK HOUSE**
Tim & Jill Smith.

WELL HOUSE
Glen Garnett.
(See separate entry.)

These two gardens in adjacent rural villages are also connected by a public footpath. Overlooking open fields, close to The Punch Bowl PH in Marton, Paddock House is elevated with extensive views down a large sloping lawn to a wildlife pond and the Hambleton Hills. A plant lover's garden where the house is encircled by a profusion of pots and extensive plant collections combining cottage gardening with the Mediterranean and Tropical. A curved terrace of York stone and steps using gravel and wood sleepers leads to many seating areas culminating in a cutting garden and small greenhouse. Well House in Grafton nestles under the hillside, also with long views to the White Horse. This 1½ acre garden was begun 39 years ago and is under constant change. A traditional English cottage garden with herbaceous borders, climbing roses and ornamental shrubs with a variety of interesting species. Paths meander through the borders to an orchard with geese and chickens.

Parcevall Hall Gardens

Dove Cottage Nursery Garden

36 THE GRANGE

Carla Beck Lane, Carleton in Craven, Skipton, BD23 3BU. Mr & Mrs R N Wooler, 07740 639135, margaret.wooler@hotmail.com. 1½ m SW of Skipton. Turn off A56 (Skipton-Clitheroe) into Carleton. Keep L at Swan Pub, continue to end of village then turn R into Carla Beck Lane. **Wed 1, Wed 29 July (12-4.30). Adm £5, chd free. Cream teas. Visits also by arrangement June & July for groups of 30+. Incls tour and refreshments (min charge). Donation to Sue Ryder Care Manorlands Hospice.**
Over 4 acres set in the grounds of Victorian house (not open) with mature trees and panoramic views towards The Gateway to the Dales. The garden has been restored by the owners over the last 2 decades with many areas of interest being added to the original footprint. Bountiful herbaceous borders with many unusual species, rose walk, parterre, mini-meadows and water features. Large greenhouse and raised vegetable beds. Oak seating placed throughout the garden invites quiet contemplation - a place to 'lift the spirits'. Gravel paths and steps.

37 GREAT CLIFF EXOTIC GARDEN

Cliff Drive, Crigglestone, Wakefield, WF4 3EN. Kristofer Swaine, yorkshirekris@hotmail.co.uk, , www.facebook.com/yorkshirekris. 1m from J39 M1. From M1 (J39) take A636 towards Denby Dale, past Cedar Court Hotel then L at British Oak pub onto Blacker Lane. Parking on Cliff Road motorway bridge. **Visits by arrangement July to Sept for groups of 10 to 30. £4, chd free. £6.50 incl garden visit, tea/coffee/juice and home-made cakes.**
An exotic garden on a long narrow plot. Possibly the largest collection of palm species planted out in Northern England including a large Chilean wine palm. Colourful and exciting borders with zinnias, cannas, ensete, bananas, tree ferns, agaves, aloes, colcasias and bamboos. Jungle hut, winding paths, pond that traverses the full width of the garden and vegetable plot. Unsuitable for wheelchairs.

38 GREENCROFT

Pottery Lane, Littlethorpe, Ripon, HG4 3LS. David & Sally Walden, 01765 602487, s-walden@outlook.com. 1½ m SE of Ripon town centre. Off A61 Ripon bypass follow signs to Littlethorpe, turn R at Church. From Bishop Monkton take Knaresborough Road towards Ripon then R to Littlethorpe. **Sun 2 Aug (12-4). Adm £5, chd free. Home-made teas. Visits also by arrangement July & Aug for groups of 20+.**
½ acre informal garden made by the owners with long herbaceous borders packed with colourful late summer perennials, annuals and exotics culminating in a circular garden with views through to large wildlife pond and surrounding countryside. Special ornamental features incl gazebo, temple pavilions, formal pool, stone wall with mullions and gate to pergola and cascade water feature.

39 GREENWICK FARM

Huggate, York, YO42 1YR. Fran & Owen Pearson, 01377 288122, greenwickfarm@hotmail.com. *2m W of Huggate. From York on A166, turn R 1m after Garrowby Hill, at brown sign for picnic area & scenic route. White wind turbine on drive.* **Sun 16 Aug (12-5). Adm £4.50, chd free. Home-made teas. Tea tables in conservatory & outside. Visits also by arrangement July & Aug.**

1 acre woodland garden created in 2010 from disused area of the farm. Set in a large dell with mature trees. Paths up the hillside through borders lead to terrace and woodland planting. Many seating areas with spectacular views across wooded valley and the Wolds. Stumpery and hot border. New summerhouse, water feature and brushed steel sculpture. Described by guests as a graceful and tranquil garden. Access for wheelchairs difficult, but good view of garden from hard standing outside house/tea area.

40 HAVOC HALL

York Rd, Oswaldkirk, York, YO62 5XY. David & Maggie Lis, 01439 788846, Davidglis@me.com, www.havochall.co.uk. *21m N of York. On B1363, 1st house on R as you enter Oswaldkirk from S & last house on L as you leave village from N.* **Sun 21 June (1-5). Adm £5.50, chd free. Home-made teas. Visits also by arrangement May to Oct for groups of 10+.**

Started in 2009, comprising 12 areas incl knot, herbaceous, mixed shrub and flower gardens, courtyard, vegetable area and orchard, woodland walk and large lawned area with hornbeam trees and hedging. To the S is a 2 acre wild flower meadow and small lake. Extensive collection of roses, herbaceous perennials and grasses. See website for other opening times. Wheelchair access: some steps but these can be avoided.

41 HIGHFIELD COTTAGE

North Street, Driffield, YO25 6AS. Debbie Simpson, 01377 256562, debbie@simpsonhighfield.karoo.co.uk. *30m E of York, 29m E of M62. Exit at A614/A166 r'about onto York Rd into Driffield. Straight on until you reach the park with the Indian takeaway opp. Highfield*

Cottage is the white detached house next to park. **Fri 8 May, Sun 28 June (10.30-4.30). Adm £4, chd free. Cream teas. Visits also by arrangement May to Nov.**

A ¾ acre suburban garden bordered by mature trees and stream. Structure is provided by numerous yew and box topiary, a pergola and sculptures. Constantly evolving, the garden has something for everyone; lawns with island beds, mixed shrubs, fruit trees and herbaceous borders. The garden has been described as 'magical' and a 'hidden gem' by NGS visitors. Refreshments weather permitting, if raining there are alternative cafes in town centre about 600 metres from garden. No WC. The garden is not suited to wheelchairs and access is uneven.

42 5 HILL TOP

Westwood Drive, Ilkley, LS29 9RS. Lyn & Phil Short. *½m S of Ilkley town centre, steep uphill. Turn S at town centre T-lights up Brook St, cross The Grove taking Wells Rd up to the Moors and follow NGS signs.* **Wed 3, Sun 7 June (11-4.30). Adm £3.50, chd free. Home-made teas.**

Delightful ⅔ acre steep garden on edge of Ilkley Moor. Sheltered woodland underplanted with naturalistic, flowing tapestry of foliage, shade-loving flowers, shrubs and ferns amongst large moss covered boulders. Many Japanese maples. Natural stream, bridges, meandering gravel paths and steps lend magic to 'Dingley Dell'. Lawns, large rockery and summerhouse with stunning views. Some steep steps.

43 HILLSIDE

West End, Ampleforth, York, YO62 4DY. Sue Shepherd & Jon Borgia, 01439 788993, sue@sueandjon.net. *West End of Ampleforth village, 4m S of Helmsley. From A19, follow brown sign to Byland Abbey & continue to Ampleforth. From A170 take B1257 to Malton, after 1m turn R to Ampleforth. Roadside parking only. Please be considerate.* **Sat 5, Sun 6 Sept (10.30-4.30). Adm £4, chd free. Light refreshments. Visits also by arrangement June to Oct for groups of 10 to 30.**

Half acre garden on a south facing slope, and half acre field. The design is evolving, based on informal planting and a wildlife friendly approach.

Woodland and meadow areas. Ponds and boggy areas. Lawn rising up to summer house and deck with fine views of the Coxwold - Gilling Gap. Fruit trees and kitchen garden. Wild garden in field. All year round interest with an emphasis on autumn colour.

44 ♦ HIMALAYAN GARDEN & SCULPTURE PARK

The Hutts, Hutts Lane, Grewelthorpe, Ripon, HG4 3DA. Mr & Mrs Roberts, 01765 658009, info@himalayangarden.com, www.himalayangarden.com. *5m NW of Ripon. From N: A1(M) J51 A684 (Bedale) then B6268 (Masham). From S: A1M J50 (Ripon) then A6108 (Masham) after North Stainley turn L (Mickley & Grewelthorpe). Follow AA & garden signs.* **For NGS evening opening Tue 12 May (4-8.30). Adm £10, chd £4. Light refreshments.**

Winner of Yorkshire in Bloom Tourist Attractions Award 2018 & 2019. 45 acres of garden inspired by the Himalayas. Widely considered to have the North's largest collection of rhododendrons, azaleas and magnolias, and a haven for plants. There are almost 20,000 plants including some 1,400 rhododendron varieties, 250 azalea varieties and 150 different magnolias; and a newly planted 20-acre arboretum. Over 80 contemporary sculptures, Himalayan shelter, lakeside pagoda, thatched summer house, Buddha garden, Norse shelter, contemplation circle and three lakes. Sturdy footwear required. Only partial Wheelchair Access.

We help ordinary people open the gates to their extraordinary private gardens to raise impressive amounts of money through admissions, teas and slices of cake!

45 HOLMFIELD

Fridaythorpe, YO25 9RZ. Susan & Robert Nichols, 01377 236627, susan@wiresculptures.net. *9m W of Driffield. From York A166 through Fridaythorpe. 1m turn R signed Holmfield. 1st house on lane.* **Mon 25 May (12-5). Adm £4.50, chd free. Home-made teas. Visits also by arrangement May to July for groups of 10+. Minimum notice 2 weeks for group visits.**
Informal 2 acre country garden on gentle S-facing slope. Developed from a field over last 30yrs. Large mixed borders, bespoke octagonal gazebo, family friendly garden with 'Hobbit House', sunken trampoline, large lawn, tennis court, hidden paths for hide and seek. Productive fruit cage, vegetable and cut flower area. Collection of phlomis. Display of wire sculptures. Bee friendly planting. Some gravel areas, sloping lawns. Wheelchair access possible with help.
& ❀ ⌂ ☕ 🍴

46 HONEY HEAD

Wood Nook, Meltham, Holmfirth, HD9 4DU. Susan & Andrew Brass. *6m S of Huddersfield. Turn from A616 to Honley, through village then follow Meltham rd for 1m, turn L on Wood Nook Lane.* **Sun 5 July (10-4). Adm £4, chd free. Home-made teas.**
Set high on a Pennine hillside with panoramic views, Honey Head aspires to provide year round interest whilst attempting to be self sufficient in fruit, vegetables, cut flowers and plants. Formal gardens with interconnecting ponds lead to extensive kitchen gardens with greenhouses complemented by areas planted to encourage wildlife. Weather permitting we will have "The Saxpots" playing an assortment of music, a local ensemble who are keen to support our event.
🐕 ❀ ☕ 🍴

We open the gates to the nation's best gardens, offering a relaxing, memorable and affordable day out. A perfect experience to share with friends and family.

47 HUNMANBY GRANGE

Wold Newton, Driffield, YO25 3HS. Tom & Gill Mellor, 01723 891636, gill.mellor234@gmail.com. *12½m SE of Scarborough. Hunmanby Grange home of Wold Top Brewery, between Wold Newton & Hunmanby on rd from Burton Fleming to Fordon.* **Sat 6, Sun 7 June (11-5). Adm £5, chd free. Light refreshments in Wold Top Brewery bar area. Field and Forage will also be catering in courtyard. Visits also by arrangement June to Sept for groups of 10+. Please contact Wold Top Brewery on 01723 892222 for details.**
Hunmanby Grange sits high on the Yorkshire Wolds where the power of the wind and the shallow chalk wolds soils have dictated the garden design. A series of gardens surround the house giving scope for changes in design and planting. In the Brewery courtyard is the water feature from The Welcome to Yorkshire Chelsea Garden - The Brewers Yard. The Wold Top Brewery will also be open. Children are very welcome in the garden. There is plenty of space in the woodland with mown and bark paths for exploration, garden games are stored in the tennis house and picnics are welcome in this area too. Steps can be avoided by using grass paths and lawns. Pond garden not completely accessible to wheelchairs but can be viewed from gateway.
& 🐕 ❀ ⌂ ☕ 🍴

48 ◆ JACKSON'S WOLD

Sherburn, Malton, YO17 8QJ. Mr & Mrs Richard Cundall, 07966 531995, jacksonswoldgarden@gmail.com, www.jacksonswoldgarden.com. *11m E of Malton, 10m SW of Scarborough. Signs only from A64. A64 Eastbound to Scarborough. R at T-lights in Sherburn, take the Weaverthorpe rd, after 100 metres R fork to Helperthorpe & Luttons. 1m to top of hill, turn L at garden sign.* **For NGS: Sun 10 May, Sun 21 June (1-5). Adm £4, chd free. Home-made teas. For other opening times and information, please phone, email or visit garden website.**
2 acre garden with stunning views of the Vale of Pickering. Walled garden with mixed borders, numerous old shrub roses underplanted with unusual perennials. Woodland paths lead to further shrub and perennial borders. Lime avenue with wild flower meadow. Traditional vegetable garden

with roses, flowers and framed by a Victorian greenhouse. Adjoining nursery. Tours by appointment.
& ❀ ⌂ ☕

49 LAND FARM

Edge Lane, Colden, Hebden Bridge, HX7 7PJ. Mr J Williams. *8m W of Halifax. At Hebden Bridge (A646) after 2 sets of T-lights take turning circle to Heptonstall & Colden. After 2¾m in Colden village turn R at Edge Lane 'no through rd'. In ¾m turn L down lane.* **Wed 20 May, Thur 25 June (10-5). Adm £5.50, chd free. Home-made teas.**
An intriguing 6 acre upland garden within a sheltered valley, created entirely by the present owner over a period of 40 years. In that time the valley has been planted with 20,000 trees by friends, neighbours and myself, which has encouraged a habitat rich in bird and wildlife. Within the garden, vistas have been created around thought provoking sculpture. Meconopsis and cardiocrimum lilies. Recently developed ½ acre moss garden. Partial wheelchair access, please telephone 01422 842260.
& 🐕 ☕

50 LINDEN LODGE

Newbridge Lane, nr Wilberfoss, York, YO41 5RB. Robert Scott & Jarrod Marsden, 07900 003538, rdsjsm@gmail.com. *10m E of York. From York on the A1079, ignore signs for Wilberfoss, take next turning signed Bolton village, after 1m at the Xrds, turn L onto Newbridge Lane, Linden Lodge is on R in 200m.* **Sat 2, Sun 3 May (12-5). Adm £4.50, chd free. Light refreshments. cakes & cream teas. Visits also by arrangement Apr & May for groups of 20+. Cream teas or wine, juice & nibbles offered.**
6 acres in all. 1 acre garden, owner designed and constructed since 2000. Gravel paths edged with brick or lavender, many borders with unusual mixed herbaceous perennials, shrubs and feature trees. A wildlife pond, summer house, nursery, glasshouse & fruit cage. Orchard and woodland area. Formal garden with pond/water feature. 5 acres of developing meadow, trees, pathways, hens and Shetland sheep. New vegetable garden. Plant sales. Gravel paths and shallow steps.
& 🐕 ❀ ⌂ ☕ 🍴

51 LOW HALL
Dacre Banks, Nidderdale, HG3 4AA. Mrs P A Holliday, 01423 780230, 1pamelaholliday@gmail.com. *10m NW of Harrogate. On B6451 between Dacre Banks & Darley.* **Sun 10 May (1-5). Adm £4.50, chd free. Home-made teas. Also open Woodlands Cottage. Opening with Dacre Banks & Summerbridge Gardens on Sun 12 July (12-5). Visits also by arrangement May to Sept for groups of 5 to 30.**
Romantic walled garden set on differing levels designed to complement historic C17 family home (not open). Spring bulbs, rhododendrons; azaleas round tranquil water garden. Asymmetric rose pergola underplanted with auriculas and lithodora links orchard to the garden. Extensive herbaceous borders, shrubs and climbing roses give later interest. Bluebell woods and lovely countryside of the farm all round overlooking the R Nidd. 80% of garden can be seen from a wheelchair but access involves three stone steps.

52 LOW STONEHILLS FARM
Fraisthorpe, Bridlington, YO15 3QR. Jackie Riby, 07751 257420, jackieriby@hotmail.com. *On main A165, 4m S of Bridlington. ½m from Fraisthorpe village on opposite side of the main rd.* **Sun 5 July (10.30-5.30). Adm £4.50, chd free. Home-made teas. Visits also by arrangement June & July.**
1½ acre site in a rural setting. Various mixed borders including herbaceous, pretty rose bed, vegetable garden surrounding sweeping lawns. Beyond the garden is a wildlife area and young orchard, home to chickens and ducks. A meandering path around a large ancient ash tree is a riot of colour in spring, and home to The Bug Hotel. The front yard has a large, naturally fed, well stocked pond. The garden is developing for the benefit of my family and to encourage wildlife and insects.

53 THE MANOR HOUSE
Holme-On-Swale, Thirsk, YO7 4JE. Mr & Mrs Steve & Judi Smith, 01845 567518, judiandsteve@outlook.com. *7m S/W from Thirsk. From A1 J50 onto A6055 N, onto B6267 E from Ripon/*

Thirsk A61 onto B6267. **Sun 19 July (1-5). Adm £4.50, chd free. Home-made teas. Variety of home baked refreshments and drinks. Visits also by arrangement Feb to Sept for groups of up to 30.**
Almost two acres of mature, well established gardens with level lawns, a variety of specimen trees and shrubs, magnolias, rhododendrons, camellias. Sweeping herbaceous beds with many seasonal bulbs, and perennial planting, peonies, roses, rambling clematis. Restored walled kitchen garden with vegetables, herbs and fruit, greenhouse and potting shed, newly planted orchard and woody wild areas. Access by gravelled path onto large level lawns.

54 MANSION COTTAGE
8 Gillus Lane, Bempton, Bridlington, YO15 1HW. Polly & Chris Myers, 01262 851404, chrismyers0807@gmail.com. *2m NE of Bridlington. From Bridlington take B1255 to Flamborough. 1st L at T-lights - Bempton Lane, turn 1st R into Short Lane then L at end. Continue - L fork at Church.* **Sat 8, Sun 9 Aug (10-4). Adm £4, chd free. Light refreshments. Visits also by arrangement June to Sept for groups of 10+. Refreshments possible by arrangement.**
Exuberant, lush, vibrant borders with late perennial planting in this peaceful, surprising hidden garden. Visitors' book says 'A veritable oasis', 'The garden is inspirational'. Areas incl a globe garden, mini hosta walk, Japanese themed area, 100ft border, summerhouse, vegetable plot, cuttery, late summer hot border, bee and butterfly border, deck and lawns. New for 2020 a garden art studio. Delicious sweet and savoury bakes, produce, plants and hand made soaps. No wheelchair access.

55 MARKENFIELD HALL
Ripon, HG4 3AD. Lady Deirdre & Mr Ian Curteis, 01765 692303, info@markenfield.com, www.markenfield.com. *3m S of Ripon. A61 between Ripon & Ripley. Turning between two low stone gateposts. Beware Sat Navs.* **Fri 12 June (2-5). Adm £4, chd free. Cream teas. Visits also by arrangement May to Sept for groups of 10 to 20. Tea and cake can be arranged. Tours combine the Hall and Garden.**

The work of the Hall's owner Lady Deirdre Curteis and gardener Giles Gilbey. Mature planting combines with newly-designed areas, where walls with espaliered apricots and figs frame a mix of hardy perennials. The final phase of restoration started in 2017 when the Farmhouse-wing's garden was re-planted to eventually blend seamlessly with the Hall's main East Border. The gardens surround Markenfield Hall - a moated, medieval manor house - one of the oldest, continuously inhabited houses in the country. Partial wheelchair access.

56 NEW MAUNBY HALL
Maunby, Thirsk, YO7 4HA. Mr Peter Hill Walker. *5m NW of Thirsk, 5m S of Northallerton From Northallerton follow A167 South. From A1(M) Junction 50 take A61 towards Thirsk. Turn L at r'about (A167-Northallerton). Parking at farm opp* **Sun 5 July (2-5). Adm £5, chd free. Home-made teas.**
An established country garden overlooking parkland with fine trees. Long mixed herbaceous border, box parterre, lawns and ha-ha. Large shrubs, nut walk, rose arches and clipped yews. Limited wheelchair access

57 MILLGATE HOUSE
Millgate, Richmond, DL10 4JN. Tim Culkin & Austin Lynch, 01748 823571, Millgate1@me.com, www.millgatehouse.com. *Centre of Richmond. House located at bottom of Market Place opp Barclays Bank. Just off corner of Market Place. Park in the Market Place no restrictions on Sunday.* **Sun 28 June, Sun 5 July (10-6). Adm £3.50, chd free.**
SE walled town garden overlooking R Swale. Although small, the garden is full of character, enchantingly secluded with plants and shrubs. Foliage plants incl ferns and hostas. Old roses, interesting selection of clematis, small trees and shrubs. RHS associate garden. Immensely stylish, national award-winning garden. Specialist collections of clematis, ferns, hostas and roses. Featured in Gardeners' World and The English Garden 2019. Many steps and steep slopes. Slippery surfaces not suitable for wheelchairs.

58 115 MILLHOUSES LANE
Sheffield, S7 2HD. Sue & Phil Stockdale. *Approx 4m SW of Sheffield City Centre. Follow A625 Castleton/Dore Road, 4th L after Prince of Wales Pub, 2nd L. OR take A621 Baslow Rd; after Tesco garage take 2nd R, then 1st L.* **Sun 19 July (1-5). Adm £3.50, chd free. Home-made teas.**
Plantswoman's ⅓ acre south facing level cottage style garden, containing many choice and unusual perennials and bulbs, providing year round colour and interest. Large collection of 50+hostas, roses, peonies and clematis, together with unusual, tender and exotic plants - aeoniums, echeverias, bananas etc. Seating areas throughout the garden. Wide range of home propagated plants for sale.

59 MILLRACE GARDEN
84 Selby Road, Garforth, Leeds, LS25 1LP. Mr & Mrs Carthy, 0113 2869233, carolcarthy.millrace@gmail.com, www.millrace-plants.co.uk. *5m E of Leeds. On A63 in Garforth. 1m from M1 J46, 3m from A1.* **Sun 17 May (1-5). Adm £5, chd free. Home-made teas. Visits also by arrangement on first Wed of the month between March and Sept 1-4pm.**
Overlooking a secluded valley, garden incl large herbaceous borders containing over 3000 varieties of perennials, shrubs and trees, many of which are unusual and drought tolerant. Ornamental pond, vegetable garden and walled terraces leading to wild flower meadow, small woodland, bog garden and wildlife lakes. Propagation opportunity depending on season (cuttings, seeds, divisions). Art exhibition at May 17 opening with The Illuminate Choir singing during the afternoon. Most of the garden is accessible for wheelchairs. Although there are steps in places there is generally an alternative ramp.

60 MR NICK'S
Linden House, 16 Northgate, Cottingham, HU16 4HH. Eric Nicklas & Mrs Pat Plaxton, 01482 847788, mrnick@mrnick.karoo.co.uk. *4m NW of Hull. A164, onto B1233 to Cottingham. Garden on L 50yds before rail crossing. From A1079, take B1233, past bowling club, over crossing. 50 yds on R.* **Sun 28 June (10-4.30). Adm £3.50, chd free. Home-made teas. Also open 23 The Paddock. Visits also by arrangement for groups of 5 to 30. Refreshments by arrangement. Donation to Hospice in Hull.**
A hidden gem of a garden. There are different areas of interest which are thoughtfully laid out. The garden features a mixture of lawned areas as well as borders and a greenhouse. There are many seating areas to relax and enjoy the wonderful atmosphere that this garden provides, never far away from the sound of running water; there is plenty to interest and entertain you during your visit. Home-made wine free when entering the museum. Homebrew demonstration and wine tasting.

61 ◆ NEWBY HALL & GARDENS
Ripon, HG4 5AE. Mr R C Compton, 01423 322583, info@newbyhall.com, www.newbyhall.com. *4m SE of Ripon. (HG4 5AJ for Sat Nav). Follow brown tourist signs from A1(M) or from Ripon town centre.* **For opening times and information, please phone, email or visit garden website.**
40 acres of extensive gardens and woodland laid out in 1920s. Full of rare and beautiful plants. Formal seasonal gardens, stunning double herbaceous borders to R Ure and National Collection of Cornus. Miniature railway and adventure gardens for children. Sculpture exhibition (open June - Sept). Free parking. Licensed restaurant. Shop and plant nursery. Wheelchair map available. Disabled parking. Manual and electric wheelchairs available on loan, please call to reserve.

62 ◆ NORTON CONYERS
Wath, Ripon, HG4 5EQ. Sir James & Lady Graham, 01765 640333, info@nortonconyers.org.uk, www.nortonconyers.org.uk. *4m NW of Ripon. Take Melmerby & Wath sign off A61 Ripon-Thirsk. Go through both villages to boundary wall. Signed entry 300 metres on R, follow track to our car park.* **For NGS: Sun 7 June (2-5). Adm £6, chd free. Home-made teas. For other opening times and information, please phone, email or visit garden website.**
Romantic mid C18 walled garden of interest to garden historians. Lawns, herbaceous borders, yew hedges, and Orangery with attractive pond. The garden retains essential features of its original C18th design with sympathetic planting in the English style. There are borders of gold and silver plants, of old fashioned peonies and irises in season. Visitors frequently comment on the tranquil and romantic atmosphere. For House opening dates and times see website. Unusual hardy plants for sale. Most areas wheelchair accessible, gravel paths.

63 THE NURSERY
15 Knapton Lane, Acomb, York, YO26 5PX. Tony Chalcraft & Jane Thurlow, 01904 781691, janeandtonyatthenursery@hotmail.co.uk. *2½ m W of York. From A1237 take B1224 direction Acomb. At r'about turn L (Beckfield Ln.), after 150 metres Turn L.* **Sun 19, Wed 22 July (1-6). Adm £3.50, chd free. Home-made teas. Visits also by arrangement May to Aug for groups of 10+.**
A former suburban commercial nursery, now an attractive and productive 1acre organic, private garden. Wide range of fruit with over 100 fruit trees, many in trained form. Many different vegetables grown both outside and under cover incl a large 20m greenhouse. Productive areas interspersed with informal ornamental plantings provide colour and habitat for wildlife. The extensive planting of different forms and varieties of fruit trees make this an interesting garden for groups to visit by appointment at blossom and fruiting times in addition to the main summer openings.

64 THE OLD RECTORY
Arram Road, Leconfield, Beverley, HU17 7NP. David Baxendale, 01964 502037, davidbax@newbax.co.uk. *On entering Arram Rd you will see a double bend sign approx 80yds on L. The entrance to the Old Rectory is by the sign. If you reach the church you have missed it.* **Visits by arrangement Jan to June for groups of up to 10. Adm £5, chd free.**
Approx 3 acres of garden and paddock. The garden is particularly attractive from early spring until mid summer. Notable for aconites, snowdrops, crocuses, daffodils and bluebells. Later hostas, irises, lilies and roses. There is a small wildlife

pond with all the usual residents incl grass snakes. Well established trees and shrubs, with new trees planted when required.

65 OLD SLENINGFORD HALL

Mickley, nr Ripon, HG4 3JD. Jane & Tom Ramsden. *5m NW of Ripon. Off A6108. After N Stainley turn L, follow signs to Mickley. Gates on R after 1½m opp cottage.* **Sat 6, Sun 7 June (12-4). Adm £5, chd free. Home-made teas.**
A large English country garden and award winning permaculture forest garden. Early C19 house (not open) and garden with original layout; wonderful mature trees, woodland walk and Victorian fernery; romantic lake with islands, watermill, walled kitchen garden; beautiful long herbaceous border, yew and huge beech hedges. Several plant and other stalls. Picnics very welcome. Reasonable wheelchair access to most parts of garden. Disabled WC at Old Sleningford Farm next to the garden.

66 THE OLD VICARAGE

North Frodingham, Driffield, YO25 8JT. Professor Ann Mortimer. *6m E of Driffield on B1249. From Driffield take B1249 E for approx 6m. The church is on L. Garden is opp. Entrance is on T-junction of rd to Emmotland & B1249. From North Frodingham take the B1249 W for ½m.* **Sun 21 June (10.30-5). Adm £4.50, chd free. Light refreshments. Also open Tythe Farm House.**
1½ acre plantsman's garden, owner developed over 23 years. Many themed areas e.g. rose garden, jungle, desert, fountain, scented, kitchen gardens, glasshouses. Numerous classical statues, unusual trees and shrubs, large and small ponds, orchard, nuttery. Children's interest with 'jungle book' and wild animal statues. Neo-Jacobean revival house, built 1837, mentioned in Pevsner (not open). The land now occupied by the house and garden was historically owned by the family of William Wilberforce. Visitors are welcome to pick produce from the fruit cage and kitchen garden. Parking in farmyard opp. Parts of the garden are inaccessible but can be viewed from above.

67 THE ORCHARD

4a Blackwood Rise, Cookridge, Leeds, LS16 7BG. Carol & Michael Abbott, 0113 2676764, michaei. john.abbott@hotmail.co.uk. *5m N of Leeds centre, 5 minutes from York Gate garden. Off A660 (Leeds-Otley) N of A6120 Ring Rd. Turn L up Otley Old Rd. At top of hill turn L at T-lights (Tinshill Lane). Please park in Tinshill Lane.* **Sun 17 May (12-4.30). Adm £3.50, chd free. Home-made teas. Pop up cafe and cover for inclement weather. Visits also by arrangement May & June for groups of 10+.**
⅓ acre plantswoman's hidden oasis. A wrap around garden of differing levels made by owners using stone found on site, planted for yr-round interest. Extensive rockery, unusual fruit tree arbour, oriental style seating area and tea house, linked by grass paths, lawns and steps. Mixed perennials, hostas, ferns, shrubs, bulbs and pots amongst paved and pebbled areas. Best in area award Leeds in Bloom.

68 23 THE PADDOCK

Cottingham, HU16 4RA. Jill & Keith Stubbs, 07932 713 281, Keith@cottconsult.karoo.co.uk. *Half way between Beverley & Hull. From Humber Bridge signs to Beverley. Castle Rd on R past hospital & follow NGS signs. From Beverley signs to Humber Bridge. Harland Way on L at 1st r'about & follow NGS signs. Garden at S end of village.* **Sun 28 June (10-4.30). Adm £3.50, chd free. Cream teas. Visits also by arrangement in June.**
A secret garden found behind a small mixed frontage. Archway to themed areas within garden created and maintained by current owners - Japanese, Mediterranean, fairy, mixed herbaceous, patios and lawns. Also two differing ponds, ornamental and tree sculptures. Plants for sale along with blacksmith's garden ornaments and sculptures. Assisted access for disabled only for 23 The Paddock through front gate.

Norton Conyers

69 ◆ PARCEVALL HALL GARDENS
Skyreholme, Skipton,
BD23 6DE. Walsingham
College, 01756 720311,
parcevallhall@btconnect.com,
www.parcevallhallgardens.co.uk.
*9m N of Skipton. Signs from B6160
Bolton Abbey-Burnsall rd or off
B6265 Grassington-Pateley Bridge
& at A59 Bolton Abbey r'about.* **For
NGS: Wed 15 July (10-5). Adm
£7, chd free. Light refreshments.
For other opening times and
information, please phone, email or
visit garden website.**
The only garden open daily in the
Yorkshire Dales National Park. 24
acres in Wharfedale sheltered by
mixed woodland; terrace garden,
rose garden, rock garden, ponds.
Mixed borders, spring bulbs, tender
shrubs and autumn colour. Tea rooms
(contact no. 01756 720630) at the foot
of the gardens. There is no wheelchair
access in the garden as it is set on a
steep hillside with uneven paths.

🐕 ✿ ☕

70 PENNY PIECE COTTAGES
41/43 Piercy End, Kirkbymoorside,
York, YO62 6DQ. Mick &
Ann Potter. *Follow A170 to
Kirkbymoorside at r'about turn up
into Kirkby Main St approx 300yds
on R. Street parking plus council car
park at top of Main St.* **Sun 24 May
(11-5). Adm £4, chd free. Home-
made teas.**
Hidden away off the main street in
Kirkbymoorside is a romantic cottage
garden. Now fully matured it offers a
sunny circular gravel garden, lawns
with island beds planted with mixed
shrubs and border perennials. Gravel
pathway leads to a brick garden,
informal pond, bog garden and
colourful herbaceous border. Wildlife
pond and pretty wild flower meadow.
Lots of places to sit and relax.

🐕 ✿ 🚗 ☕

71 PILMOOR COTTAGES
Pilmoor, nr Helperby,
YO61 2QQ. Wendy & Chris
Jakeman, 01845 501848,
cnjakeman@aol.com. *20m N of
York. From A1M J48. N end B'bridge
follow rd towards Easingwold.
From A19 follow signs to Hutton
Sessay then Helperby. Garden next
to mainline railway.* **Sun 30 Aug
(12-5). Adm £4, chd free. Light
refreshments. Visits also by
arrangement May to Sept.**
A year round garden for rail
enthusiasts and garden visitors.
A ride on the 7¼' Gauge railway
runs through 2 acres of gardens and
gives you the opportunity to view the
garden from a different perspective.
The journey takes you across water,
through a little woodland area, past
flower filled borders, and through
a tunnel behind the rockery and
water cascade. 1½ acre wild flower
meadow and pond. Clock-golf
putting green. Refreshments by two
local WIs with donation to NGS.

♿ 🐕 ✿ ☕

**72 PRIMROSE BANK GARDEN
AND NURSERY**
Dauby Lane, Kexby, York,
YO41 5LH. Sue Goodwill & Terry
Marran, www.primrosebank.co.uk.
*4m E of York. At J of A64 & A1079
take rd signed to Hull, travel 3m &
just as entering Kexby, turn R onto
Dauby Lane, signed for Elvington.
From the E travel on A1079 towards
York. Turn L in Kexby.* **Sat 28, Sun
29 Mar (11-4). Adm £4, chd free.
Home-made teas. Includes
designated area for dogs outside
the tearoom.**
Over an acre of rare and unusual
plants, shrubs and trees. Bulbs,
hellebores and flowering shrubs in
spring, followed by planting for yr
round interest. Courtyard garden,
mixed borders, summer house
and pond. Lawns, contemporary
rock garden, shade and woodland

Scampston Walled Garden

garden with pond, stumpery, and shepherd's hut. Poultry and Hebridean sheep. Dogs allowed in car park and designated tables outside the tearoom. Our eranthis collection has been inspected and we are hoping for accreditation for National Collection status. Certified Location Caravan Site adjoining the nursery, opening Easter 2020. Most areas of the garden are level and are easily accessible for wheelchairs, accessible WC.

73 THE RED HOUSE
17 Whin Hill Road, Bessacarr, Doncaster, DN4 7AF. Rosie Hamlin. *2m S of Doncaster. A638 South, L at T-lights for B1396, Whin Hill Rd is 2nd R. A638 North, R signed Branton B1396 onto Whin Hill.* **Sat 23, Sun 24 May (1-5). Combined adm with Tamarind £5, chd free. Home-made teas.**
Mature ⅔ acre garden. Dry shade a challenge but acid loving plants a joy. Fine acers, camellia, daphne, rhododendrons, skimmia and eucryphia. Alpine terrace, rockery, small woodland garden through to lawn with modern rotating summerhouse, shrubs and young trees. White border conceals pond, compost and hens. Woodland being restored: planting large leaved rhododendrons and new trees.

74 REWELA COTTAGE
Skewsby, YO61 4SG. John Plant & Daphne Ellis, 01347 888125, rewelacottage@gmail.com. *4m N of Sheriff Hutton, 15m N of York. After Sheriff Hutton, towards Terrington, turn L towards Whenby & Brandsby. Turn R just past Whenby to Skewsby. Turn L into village. 400yds on R.* **Sun 31 May (11-5). Adm £5, chd free. Great cakes & scones, teas & coffees, soft drinks. Plus BBQ serving 100% Angus beef-burgers & Lincolnshire sausages. Visits also by arrangement May to July for groups of 20+.**
Situated in a lovely quiet country village this is one of Yorkshire's little hidden treasures. Rewela Cottage was designed from an empty paddock, to be as labour saving as possible, using unusual trees and shrubs to offer interest all year. Their foliage, bark and berries, enhance the well designed structure of the garden. Unusual trees and shrubs have labels giving full descriptions, a picture and

cultivation notes incl propagation. Plant sales are specimens from garden. Many varieties of heuchera, heucherella and tiarellas, penstemon, hostas, ferns and herbs for sale. WC. Some gravel paths may be an effort for a wheelchair.

75 ◆ RHS GARDEN HARLOW CARR
Crag Lane, Harrogate, HG3 1QB. Royal Horticultural Society, 01423 565418, harlowcarr@rhs.org.uk, www.rhs.org.uk/harlowcarr. *1½m W of Harrogate town centre. On B6162 (Harrogate - Otley).* **For NGS: Sun 17 May (9.30-5). Adm £12.15, chd £6.10. For other opening times and information, please phone, email or visit garden website.**
One of Yorkshire's most relaxing yet inspiring locations. Highlights include spectacular herbaceous borders, streamside garden, alpines, scented and kitchen gardens. Lakeside gardens, woodland and wild flower meadows. Betty's Cafe Tearooms, gift shop, plant centre and children's play area incl tree house and log ness monster. Wheelchairs and mobility scooters available, advanced booking recommended.

76 THE RIDINGS
South Street, Burton Fleming, Driffield, YO25 3PE. Roy & Ruth Allerston, 01262 470489. *11m NE of Driffield. 11m SW of Scarborough. 7m NW of Bridlington. From Driffield B1249, before Foxholes turn R to Burton Fleming. From Scarborough A165 turn R to Burton Fleming.* **Sun 24 May, Sun 5 July (1-5). Adm £3.50, chd free. Home-made teas. Visits also by arrangement Apr to July.**
Secluded cottage garden with colour-themed borders surrounding neat lawns. Grass and paved paths lead to formal and informal areas through rose and clematis covered pergolas and arbours. Box hedging defines well stocked borders with roses, herbaceous plants and trees. Seating in sun and shade offer vistas and views. Potager, greenhouse and summerhouse. Terrace with water feature and farming bygones. Terrace, tea area and main lawn accessible via ramp.

77 RUSTIC COTTAGE
Front Street, Wold Newton, nr Driffield, YO25 3YQ. Jan Joyce, 01262 470710, janetmjoyce@icloud.com. *13m N of Driffield. From Driffield take B1249 to Foxholes (12m), take R turning signed Wold Newton. Turn L onto Front St, opp village pond, continue up hill, garden on L.* **Visits by arrangement Apr to Oct for groups of up to 20. Adm £4, chd free.**
Plantswoman's cottage garden of much interest with many choice and unusual plants. Hellebores and bulbs are treats for colder months. Old-fashioned roses, fragrant perennials, herbs and wild flowers, all grown together provide habitat for birds, bees, butterflies and small mammals. It has been described as 'organised chaos'! The owner's 2nd NGS garden. Small dogs only.

78 ◆ SCAMPSTON WALLED GARDEN
Scampston Hall, Scampston, Malton, YO17 8NG. The Legard Family, 01944 759111, info@scampston.co.uk, www.scampston.co.uk/gardens. *5m E of Malton. ½m N of A64, nr the village of Rillington & signed Scampston only.* **For opening times and information, please phone, email or visit garden website.**
An exciting modern garden designed by Piet Oudolf. The 4-acre walled garden contains a series of hedged enclosures designed to look good throughout the year. The garden contains many unusual species and is a must for any keen plant lover. The Walled Garden is set within the grounds and parkland surrounding Scampston Hall. The Hall opens to visitors for a short period during the summer months. A restored Richardson conservatory at the heart of the Walled Garden is used as a Heritage and Learning Centre. The Walled Garden, cafe and facilities are accessible by wheelchair. Some areas of the parkland and the first floor of the Hall are harder to access.

79 SCAPE LODGE

11 Grand Stand, Scapegoat Hill, Golcar, Huddersfield, HD7 4NQ. Elizabeth & David Smith, 01484 644320, elizabethanddavid. smith@ngs.org.uk. *5m W of Huddersfield. From J23 or 24 M62 follow signs to Rochdale. After Outlane village, 1st L. At top of hill, 2nd L. Parking at Scapegoat Hill Baptist Church (HD7 4NU) or in village. 5 mins walk to garden. 303/304 bus.* **Sun 10 May, Sun 23 Aug (1.30-4.30). Adm £4.50, chd free. Home-made teas. Visits also by arrangement May to Aug. Donation to Mayor of Kirklees Charity Appeal.**

⅓ acre contemporary country garden at 1000ft in the Pennines on a steeply sloping site with far-reaching views. Gravel paths lead between mixed borders on many levels. Colour themed informal planting chosen to sit comfortably in the landscape and give year round interest. Steps lead to terraced kitchen and cutting garden. Gazebo, pond, shade garden, collection of pots and tender plants.

❀ 🚗 ☕

80 1 SCHOOL LANE

Bempton, Bridlington, YO15 1JA. Robert & Elizabeth Tyas, rktyas10@gmail.com. *Close to the centre of village. 3m N of Bridlington. From Brid take B1255 toward Flamborough. L at 1st T-lights. Follow Bempton Lane out of residential area then 2nd R onto Bolam Lane. Continue to end and garden is facing.* **Sun 31 May (10-4). Adm £4, chd free. Home-made teas. Visits also by arrangement May to July for groups of 5 to 20.**

A short distance from award winning Bempton Cliffs this village garden provides year round interest. Mixed planting in beds and borders offers a cottage garden feel enhanced by container planting, a crevice rockery, troughs planted with unusual alpines, a small collection of bonsai, miniature hostas, fruit trees, and a growing display of lewisia. Many additional garden features. All areas of the garden can be viewed from a wheelchair.

 ♿ 🐄 ❀ ☕

81 ◆ SHANDY HALL GARDENS

Coxwold, YO61 4AD. The Laurence Sterne Trust, 01347 868465, www.laurencesternetrust.org.uk/ shandy-hall-garden.php. *N of York. From A19, 7m from both Easingwold & Thirsk, turn E signed Coxwold.*

For NGS: Evening opening Fri 5, Fri 26 June (6.30-8). Adm £3, chd free. For other opening times and information, please phone or visit garden website.

Home of C18 author Laurence Sterne. 2 walled gardens, 1 acre of unusual perennials interplanted with tulips and old roses in low walled beds. In old quarry, another acre of trees, shrubs, bulbs, climbers and wild flowers encouraging wildlife, incl over 430 recorded species of moths. Moth trap, identification and release. Wildlife garden. Wheelchair access to wild garden by arrangement.

♿ 🐄 ❀

GROUP OPENING

82 SHEFFIELD GARDENS

Crookes, Sheffield, S10 1UZ. *Two city centre gardens and one at Bradfield. See individual listings for directions.* **Sun 12 July (2-5). Combined adm £8, chd free to two city centre gardens only. Single adm Bramblewood Cottage £5 chd free. Home-made teas at Bramblewood Cottage and 68 Tasker Road.**

BRAMBLEWOOD COTTAGE
Nigel Dunnett.
(See separate entry)

19 FIR STREET
S6 3TG. James Hitchmough.

68 TASKER ROAD
S10 1UZ. Andy Clayden.

Three inspiring gardens designed and owned by members of 'The Sheffield School' of planting design at The University of Sheffield who are at the forefront of current ideas in naturalistic planting design, creating sustainable landscapes and gardening for a changing planet. Their work includes Queen Elizabeth Olympic Park and Pictorial Meadows. Bramblewood Cottage, a one acre garden six miles from Sheffield centre has areas of naturalistic perennial planting, large log-pile sculptures and designed annual and perennial hillside meadows, rain gardens and bioswales. 68 Tasker Road is a family garden using reclaimed materials, managing water through green roofs, ponds and soakaways. 19 Fir Street explores a meadow aesthetic using many plants usually considered too tender for a northern city to mantain colour and foliage interest from February to November.

☕

GROUP OPENING

83 SHIPTONTHORPE GARDENS

Shiptonthorpe, York, YO43 3PQ. *2m NW of Market Weighton. Both gardens are in the main village on the N of A1079.* **Sat 6, Sun 7 June (11-5). Combined adm £5, chd free. Home-made teas in the village hall.**

6 ALL SAINTS DRIVE
Di Thompson.

WAYSIDE
Susan Sellars.

Two contrasting gardens offering different approaches to gardening style. 6 All Saints Drive is an eclectic 'maze-like' garden with a mix of contemporary and cottage garden features; hidden corners, water features and pond. Wayside has interesting planting in different areas of the garden. Developing vegetable & fruit growing areas with greenhouse. Proceeds for teas to go to the village hall and church. Wheelchairs possible with help at Wayside.

♿ 🚗 ☕

84 SLEIGHTHOLMEDALE LODGE

Fadmoor, YO62 7JG. Patrick & Natasha James. *6m NE of Helmsley. Parking can be limited in wet weather. Garden is 1st property in Sleightholmedale, 1m from Fadmoor.* **Wed 1 July, Sun 9 Aug (2-6). Adm £5, chd free. Home-made teas.**

A south facing, 3 acre hillside garden with views over a peaceful valley in the North York Moors. Cultivated for over 100 years, wide borders and descending terraces lead down the valley with beautiful, informal planting within the formal structure of walls and paths. In July and August, the garden features roses, delphiniums and verbascums.

 🐄

85 ◆ STILLINGFLEET LODGE

Stewart Lane, Stillingfleet, York, YO19 6HP. Mr & Mrs J Cook, 01904 728506, vanessa.cook@ stillingfleetlodgenurseries.co.uk, www.stillingfleetlodgenurseries. co.uk. *6m S of York. From A19 York-Selby take B1222 towards Sherburn in Elmet. In village turn opp church.* **For NGS: Sun 10 May, Sun 13 Sept (1-5). Adm £6, chd**

£1. Home-made teas. For other opening times and information, please phone, email or visit garden website.

Organic, wildlife garden subdivided into smaller gardens, each based on a colour theme with emphasis on use of foliage plants. Wild flower meadow and natural pond, 55yd double herbaceous borders. Modern rill garden. Rare breeds of poultry wander freely in garden. Adjacent nursery. Garden Courses run all summer see website. Art exhibitions in the cafe. Gravel paths and lawn. Ramp to cafe if needed. No disabled WC.

86 STONEFIELD COTTAGE
27 Nordham, North Cave, Brough, HU15 2LT. Nicola Lyte. *15m W of Hull. M62 E, J38 towards N Cave. Turn L towards N Cave Wetlands, then R at LH bend. Stonefield Cottage is on R, ¼ m along Nordham.* **Sat 18, Sun 19 July (11-5). Adm £4, chd free. Home-made teas.**

A hidden and surprising 1-acre garden, with an emphasis throughout on strong, dramatic colours and sweeping vistas. Rose beds, mixed borders, vegetables, a riotous hot bed, boggy woodland, wildlife pond, and jacquemontii under-planted with red hydrangeas. Collections of hellebores, primulas, ferns, astilbes, hostas, heucheras, dahlias, hemerocallis and hydrangeas.

87 SUE PROCTOR PLANTS NURSERY GARDEN
69 Ings Mill Avenue, Clayton West, Huddersfield, HD8 9QG. Sue & Richard Proctor, www.sueproctorplants.co.uk. *9m NE of Holmfirth, 10m SW of Wakefield, West Yorkshire. Off A636 Wakefield/Holmfirth. From M1 J39, in Clayton West village turn L signed Clayton West, High Hoyland, then R signed Kaye's F & N School. Turn 1st R to Ings Mill Avenue. Park by conifer hedge.* **Sat 4, Sun 5 July (11-4). Adm £3.50, chd free. Light refreshments. Gluten and lactose free, de-caff tea and coffee available.**

Small, mainly sloping, suburban garden packed full of interest. Summer highlights include over 300 varieties of hostas and close plantings of flowering perennials with some rare and unusual plants. Shaded

gravel and rock gardens show off acers, ferns and miniature hostas, the nursery specialism. Many southern hemisphere and half/borderline hardy plants, includes gingers, salvias and echiums. Our collection of hostas, one of the largest in the North of England, including the smallest, less than 4" in height, to the world's largest 'Empress Wu'. A variety of half-hardy plants, especially climbers, flower throughout the summer. Partial wheelchair access and a graded path to the top of the garden.

88 SWALE COTTAGE
Station Road, Richmond, DL10 4LU. Julie Martin & Dave Dalton, 01748 829452, jmalandplan@btinternet.com. *Richmond town centre. On foot, facing bottom of Market Place, turn L onto Frenchgate, then R onto Station Rd. House 1st on R.* **Visits by arrangement May to Sept for groups of 10+. Teas and refreshments available in town centre nearby. Adm £5, chd free.**

½ -acre urban oasis on steep site, with sweeping views and hidden corners. Several enclosed garden rooms on different levels. Mature herbaceous, rose and shrub garden with strong foliage interest. Magnificent yew and cedar. Organic vegetables and soft fruit and pond. Adjacent orchard and paddock with sheep.

89 TAMARIND
2 Whin Hill Road, Bessacarr, Doncaster, DN4 7AE. Ken & Carol Kilvington. *2m S of Doncaster. Through Lakeside, pass Dome on R turn R at Bawtry Rd T-lights, through pedestrian crossing & T-lights then 1st L. Or - A638 - North from Bawtry to Doncaster turn R signed Cantley-Branton (B1396).* **Sat 23 May (1-5). Cream teas. Sun 24 May (1-5). Combined adm with The Red House £5, chd free. Home-made teas on Sat at Tamarind; Sun at The Red House. The gardens are within easy walking distance of each other.**

A ⅔ acre garden, changing each year, level at the front with acers and varied planting. Shaped lawn leads to a steeply terraced rear garden full of colour and differing styles. White border with dovecote and doves; hot border, rose garden, herbaceous embankment, fern garden and rhododendron garden. Stream with

waterfalls, ponds, rockery and bog garden, thatched summerhouse, patio. Steep steps. The front garden and rear lower patio are accessible to wheelchairs, from which most of the rear garden can be viewed. Steps to the rest of the garden.

90 TYTHE FARM HOUSE
Carr Lane, Wansford, Driffield, YO25 8NP. Terry & Susanne Hardcastle, 07951 126588, susanannhardcastle@gmail.com, www.tythefarmgardens.com. *3m E of Driffield, E Yorkshire. Wansford is 3m E of Driffield on B1249. Turn L at mini r'about onto Nafferton Rd. Carr Lane is opposite the Church. Approx 600 yds on R.* **Sun 21 June (10-5). Adm £5, chd free. Home-made teas. Visits also by arrangement Feb to Sept for groups of 5+. Cold buffet lunch available on request or teas. Please specify at booking.**

Terry and Susanne welcome you to their secret garden that extends to 10 acres. Deciduous woodlands, orchards, lake, courtyard garden, herbaceous, rose garden and Italian sculptures. Formerly a working farm with traditional buildings now renovated. A planting scheme 25 years ago is now maturing. Excavation of the lake and landscaping projects have created something very special as you will see. Only the second public opening of our very private garden. We have ample parking space on site and easy access to most areas. An optional short hike through the woods will prepare you for Susanne's home-made refreshments in the courtyard garden or the garden room as the weather dictates. Access to many parts of the garden is via a few paved paths and level lawns that can become boggy in wet weather.

Your visits help change lives – since 1927, we've donated over £60 million to nursing and caring charities

91 THE VILLA

High Street, Hook, Goole, DN14 5PJ. Penny & John Settle.
Close to M62 J36 & J37. Approach Hook from A614 Boothferry Road along Westfield Lane around 'z' bend to Xrds where the village hall stands. Turn L, garden approx. 300yds down on R. Park on High St. **Sun 31 May (12-4.30). Adm £3.50, chd free. Light refreshments.**
Acquired by the current owners in 2011 in a derelict state, the garden now offers a stunning variety of different areas incl. Mediterranean, an extensive Bonsai display, an oriental area featuring Asian sculptures, a pergola walkway, a paved terrace and a large lawned area. The garden also features a collection of statues, alongside a large variety of perennial shrubs, bamboos and ornamental grasses, bearded irises and hostas. The garden offers plenty of seating for visitors to sit and take in the tranquillity of this hidden gem. Sorry, no wheelchair access.

92 NEW THE VINES

Waplington Hall, Allerthorpe, York, YO42 4RS. Penny & Bill Simmons.
Leave A1079 at Pocklington r'about, SW through Allerthorpe, turn R signed 'Waplington only'. Coming from Melbourne turn L at start of Allerthorpe village. **Sun 19 July (12-4). Adm £4.50, chd free. Home-made teas at Allerthorpe Village Hall. Teas in aid of Village Hall Fund.**
This spacious 1¾ acre English country garden is traditionally planted with varied herbaceous borders of perennials, shrubs and climbers. Walk through an unusual vinehouse full of fruiting grapevines to a thriving walled kitchen garden with fruit trees, vegetables, soft fruit and productive greenhouse. A plantsman's garden also featuring extensive grassed areas with mature and ornamental trees. Most areas of the garden, apart from greenhouses, are grassed and mainly level and accessible for wheelchairs.

93 WARLEY HOUSE GARDEN

Stock Lane, Warley, Halifax, HX2 7RU. Dr & Mrs P J Hinton, 01422 831431, warleyhousegardens@yahoo.com, www.warleyhousegardens.com.
2m W of Halifax. Take A646 (towards Burnley) from Halifax centre. Go through large intersection after

approx 1m. After further 1m take R turn up Windle Royd Lane. Signs will direct you from there. There is disabled parking on site, but limited to 4/5 vehicles. **Sun 10, Wed 13 May (1-5). Adm £5, chd free. Home-made teas. A wide range of home-made cakes. Visits also by arrangement May to July for groups of 10 to 30. 4 weeks notice required please.**
Partly walled 2½ acre garden of demolished C18 House, renovated by the present owners. Rocky paths and Japanese style planting lead to lawns and lovely S-facing views. Alpine ravine planted with ferns and fine trees give structure to the woodland area. Drifts of shrubs, herbaceous plantings, wild flowers and heathers maintain constant seasonal interest. This is an historic garden, renovated after total neglect from 1945 to 1995. Spring planting is enhanced by many new rhododendrons and woodland. A lengthy rockery, alpine ravine and the Japanese Garden are areas of special interest. Most of the garden is accessible to wheelchairs. Lawns usually suitable - unless very wet. Disabled access to WCs and tea-room.

94 WELL HOUSE

Grafton, YO51 9QJ. Glen Garnett.
2½m S of Boroughbridge. Turn off B6265 or A168 S of Boroughbridge. **Sun 3, Fri 8 May (12-5). Combined adm with Whixley Gardens £7, chd free. Opening with Grafton Gardens on Sun 14 June.**
On the outskirts of Grafton village, nestling under a hillside with long views to the White Horse and Hambleton hills, extending to 1½ acres, this garden was begun 39 years ago and is constantly changing. A traditional English cottage garden, with herbaceous borders, climbing and rambling roses, and ornamental shrubs with a variety of interesting species. Paths lead to orchard with ducks and chickens.

95 WHITE WYNN

Ellerton, York, YO42 4PN. Cindy & Richard Hutchinson, 01757 289495, richardahutchinson@btinternet.com.
½m up Shortacre lane, no through road. From York B1228 through Sutton, turning R towards Howden, NGS signs from here. From Selby A19 north. Turn R along A163 towards Market Weighton. Turn L

at Bubwith Xrds follow NGS signs. **Sun 14 June (2-5). Adm £4, chd free. Light refreshments. Also open Willow Cottage. Visits also by arrangement May to Sept for groups of 5 to 30.**
1½ acres developed over 10 years. Front garden and gravel areas. Lawns and patios adjoining 60m long border, wildflower meadow, heather bed, orchard, rose garden with arbour, vegetable beds, woodland and shade beds. A secret garden contains less usual plantings to give a tropical feel. Wildlife friendly with 2 ponds, blackthorn and damson copses, stored logs provide shelter for hedgehogs and toads. Very good, level access, mostly on grass.

GROUP OPENING

96 WHIXLEY GARDENS

York, YO26 8AR. 01423 330474, biddymarshall@btinternet.com.
8m W of York, 8m E of Harrogate, 6m N of Wetherby. 3m E of A1(M) off A59 York-Harrogate. Signed Whixley. **Sun 3, Fri 8 May (12-5). Combined adm with Well House £7, chd free. Home-made teas at The Old Vicarage. Visits also by arrangement for groups of 20+.**

COBBLE COTTAGE
John Hawkridge & Barry Atkinson.
(See separate entry.)

THE OLD VICARAGE
Mr & Mrs Roger Marshall.

Attractive rural yet accessible village nestling on the edge of the York Plain with beautiful historic church and Queen Anne Hall (not open). The gardens are at opposite ends of the village with good footpaths. A plantsman's and flower arranger's garden at Cobble Cottage, Rudgate, has views to the Hambleton Hills. Close to the church, The Old Vicarage, with a ¾-acre walled flower garden, overlooks the old deer park. The walls, house and various structures are festooned with climbers. Gravel and old brick paths lead to hidden seating areas creating the atmosphere of a romantic English garden. Wheelchair access only to The Old Vicarage.

97 WILLOW COTTAGE

Beck Side, Barmby Moor, York, YO42 4HA. Mrs Tez McCloskey, 07790 825110 or 07962 225600. *8m E of York just off A1079, 2m from Pocklington. Centre of village on village green. Parking is on Main St. Cut through church yard & turn R onto Beck Side.* **Sun 14 June (10.30-4). Adm £4, chd free. Light refreshments in the church or garden. Also open White Wynn. Visits also by arrangement May to July for groups of up to 20.**

An all white garden, north facing, perfectly formed with several seating areas giving time to absorb the garden. A secret garden atmosphere, calm and peaceful. Split into three sections and planted for scent. Patio with raised beds, shade area, and sunny lawn with borders, summerhouse and home-made greenhouse. Also of interest, pretty beck, village green with wild flower meadow. Wheelchair access, gravel drive and single step up to lawn.

 ♿ 🐕 ✿ ☕

98 WOODLANDS COTTAGE

Summerbridge, HG3 4BT. Mr & Mrs Stark, 01423 780765, annstark@btinternet.com, www. woodlandscottagegarden.co.uk. *10m NW of Harrogate. On the B6165 W of Summerbridge.* **Sun 10 May (1-5). Adm £4, chd free. Home-made teas. Also open Low Hall. Opening with Dacre Banks & Summerbridge Gardens on Sun 12 July (12-5). Visits also by arrangement May to Aug.**

A 1 acre country garden in Nidderdale, created by its owners and making full use of its setting, which includes natural woodland with wild bluebells and gritstone boulders. There are several gardens within the garden, from a wild flower meadow and woodland rock-garden to a formal herb garden and herbaceous areas. Also a productive fruit and vegetable garden. Gravel paths, steps and grassy slopes.

 ♿ 🐕 ☕

99 ◆ YORK GATE

Back Church Lane, Adel, Leeds, LS16 8DW. Perennial, 0113 267 8240, yorkgate@perennial.org.uk, www.yorkgate.org.uk. *5m N of Leeds. A660 from to Adel, turn R at lights a few meters before 'Divino' restaurant, L on to Church Lane. After the church, turn R onto Back Church Lane then entrance to the garden is on the left.* **For opening times and information, please phone, email or visit garden website.**

An internationally acclaimed one-acre jewel. A garden of immense style divided into 14 garden rooms. Many unusual plants and architectural evergreens. 2020 sees an extension to the garden with new facilities incl a new cafe and gift shop as well as exciting new gardens and plant nursery. Owned by Perennial, the charity that looks after horticulturists and their families in times of need. Narrow gravel and cobbled paths make most of the original garden inaccessible to wheelchairs. The new gardens, tea room, shop and WC are accessible.

 ✿ 🚌 ☕

100 YORKE HOUSE & WHITE ROSE COTTAGE

Dacre Banks, Nidderdale, HG3 4EW. Tony & Pat Hutchinson & Mark & Amy Hutchinson, 01423 780456, pat@yorkehouse.co.uk, www.yorkehouse.co.uk. *4m SE of Pateley Bridge, 10m NW of Harrogate, 10m N of Otley. On B6451 near centre of Dacre Banks. Car park.* **Sun 21 June (11-5). Adm £5, chd free. Cream teas. Opening with Dacre Banks & Summerbridge Gardens on Sun 12 July (12-5). Visits also by arrangement June to Aug for groups of 10+.**

Award-winning English country garden in the heart of Nidderdale. Designed as a series of distinct areas which flow through 2 acres of ornamental garden. Colour-themed borders, natural pond & stream with delightful waterside plantings. Secluded seating areas & attractive views. Adjacent cottage has newly developed garden designed for wheelchair access. Large collection of hostas. Orchard picnic area. Winner Harrogate's Glorious Gardens. All main features accessible to wheelchair users.

 ♿ 🐕 ✿ 🚌 ☕

101 ◆ THE YORKSHIRE ARBORETUM

Castle Howard, York, YO60 7BY. The Castle Howard Arboretum Trust, 01653 648598, marketing@ yorkshirearboretum.org, www.yorkshirearboretum.org. *15m NE of York. Off A64. Follow signs to Castle Howard then look for Yorkshire Arboretum signs at the obelisk r'about.* **For NGS: Sun 7 June (10-4). Adm £7, chd £3.50. For other opening times and information, please phone, email or visit garden website.**

A glorious, 120 acre garden of trees from around the world set in a stunning landscape of parkland, lakes and ponds. Walks and lakeside trails, tours, family activities. We welcome visitors of all ages wanting to enjoy the space, serenity and beauty of this sheltered valley as well as those interested in our extensive collection of trees and shrubs. Internationally renowned collection of trees in a beautiful setting, accompanied by a diversity of wild flowers, birds, insects and other wildlife. Children's playground, cafe and gift shop. Dogs on leads welcome. Not suitable for wheelchairs. Motorised all-terrain buggies are available on loan, please book 24hrs in advance on 01653 648598.

 🐕 🚌 ☕

Wayside

OPENING DATES

All entries subject to change. For latest information check www.ngs.org.uk

Map locator numbers are shown to the right of each garden name.

April

Monday 13th
Llwyngarreg   10

May

Saturday 9th
◆ Colby Woodland Garden   1

Sunday 10th
◆ Colby Woodland Garden   1
◆ Dyffryn Fernant   3
Treffgarne Hall   24

Sunday 24th
Norchard   12
Panteg   15

Wednesday 27th
NEW Pont Trecynny   19

June

Sunday 7th
Llwyngarreg   10

Saturday 13th
Rhyd-y-Groes   20

Sunday 14th
Rhyd-y-Groes   20

Saturday 20th
Glangwili Lodges   6

Sunday 21st
Glangwili Lodges   6
Tradewinds   23

Wednesday 24th
NEW Pont Trecynny   19

Saturday 27th
NEW The Grange   7

Sunday 28th
NEW The Grange   7
◆ Upton Castle Gardens   26

July

Saturday 4th
Glandwr   5

Sunday 5th
Glandwr   5

Saturday 11th
Pen-y-Garn   18

Sunday 12th
Pentresite   17
Pen-y-Garn   18
Treffgarne Hall   24

Saturday 18th
Rhyd-y-Groes   20

Sunday 19th
Rhyd-y-Groes   20

Sunday 26th
Greenacre   8
NEW Lamphey Walled Garden   9

Wednesday 29th
NEW Pont Trecynny   19

August

Sunday 2nd
◆ Dyffryn Fernant   3
Tradewinds   23

Saturday 15th
◆ Norwood Gardens & Tea Rooms   13

Saturday 22nd
NEW The Grange   7

Sunday 23rd
NEW The Grange   7
Llwyngarreg   10

September

Sunday 20th
Pentresite   17

By Arrangement

Arrange a personalised garden visit with your club, or group of friends, on a date to suit you. See individual garden entries for full details.

NEW Dwynant   2
Gelli Uchaf   4
Glandwr   5
Llwyngarreg   10
Nantyietau   11
Norchard   12
The Old Rectory   14
Panteg   15
Pencwm   16
Pentresite   17
Pen-y-Garn   18
NEW Pont Trecynny   19
Rhyd-y-Groes   20
Scotsborough House   21
Stable Cottage   22
Treffgarne Hall   24
Ty'r Maes   25

THE GARDENS

1 ◆ COLBY WOODLAND GARDEN

Amroth, Narberth, Pembrokeshire SA67 8PP. National Trust, 01834 811885, colby@nationaltrust.org.uk, www.nationaltrust.org.uk. *6m N of Tenby, 5m SE of Narberth. Follow brown tourist signs on coast rd & A477.* **For NGS: Sat 9, Sun 10 May (10-5). Adm £10.20, chd £5.10. For other opening times and information, please phone, email or visit garden website.**
8 acre woodland garden in a secluded valley with fine collection of rhododendrons and azaleas.

Wildflower meadow and stream with rope swings and stepping stones for children to explore and play. Ornamental walled garden incl unusual gazebo, designed by Wyn Jones, with internal tromp l'oeil. Incl in the *Register of Historic Parks and Gardens: Pembrokeshire.* Children's play encouraged, incl den building and climbing. Free family activities incl pooh sticks, pond dipping, etc. Children under 5, free entry. Full range of refreshments incl lunches. Partial access for wheelchair users.

♿ 🐔 ❄ 🚌 ☕

2 NEW DWYNANT

Golden Grove, Carmarthen, Carmarthenshire, SA32 8LT. Mrs Sian Griffiths, 01558 668727, sian.41@btinternet.com, www.airbnb.co.uk/rooms/31081717. *14m east of Carmarthen, 3m from Llandeilo. Take B4300 Llandeilo to Carmarthen. Take L turning to Gelli Aur, pass the church and vicarage then take first R onto Old Coach Road. Dwynant is approximately 1/4 m on R.* **Visits by arrangement May & June for groups of up to 10. Following dates only Sun 10 and Sun 24 May, Sun 7 June. Adm £3.50, chd free. Teas on request when booking.**
A ³⁄₄ acre garden set on a steep slope designed to sit comfortably within a verdant countryside environment with beautiful scenery and tranquil woodland setting. A spring garden with lily pond, selection of plants and shrubs incl. azaleas, rhododendrons, rambling roses

set amongst a carpet of bluebells. Seating in appropriate areas to enjoy the panoramic view and flowers.

3 ◆ DYFFRYN FERNANT
Llanychaer, Fishguard, Pembrokeshire SA65 9SP. Christina Shand & David Allum, 01348 811282, christina@dyffrynfernant.co.uk, www.dyffrynfernant.co.uk. *3m E of Fishguard, then ½ m inland. A487 E 2m from Fishguard turn R towards Llanychaer at garden signs. ½ m entrance is on L. Coming from direction of Dinas/Newport Pemb, look for L turn off A487.* **For NGS: Sun 10 May (12-5), also open Treffgarne Hall. Sun 2 Aug (12-5). Adm £7, chd free. Home-made teas. For other opening times and information, please phone, email or visit garden website.**
A 6 acre modern garden which has grown out of its ancient landscape. It is a conversation between its creator, Christina Shand, and the spirit of the place. A profusion of choice plants and shrubs coexist to create a journey which unfolds. 'The best domestic garden in Wales' according to The Times. RHS Partner Garden. A library for garden visitors incl a wide selection of books on gardening and art. Walks, talks and guided tours available-see website. Wheelchair access is difficult but please contact us directly to discuss how we can help you to enjoy the garden.

4 GELLI UCHAF
Rhydcymerau, Llandeilo, Carmarthenshire SA19 7PY. Julian & Fiona Wormald, 01558 685119, thegardenimpressionists@gmail.com, www. thegardenimpressionists. com/visiting-the-garden/. *5m SE of Llanybydder. 1m NW of Rhydcymerau. Please view our website for detailed directions to the garden. Parking v. limited, it is essential to phone or email first.* **Short notice pop-up openings, details on our or NGS website. Booking essential. Also visits by arrangement Jan to Oct. Adm £5, chd free. Home-made teas on request.**
Complementing a C17 Longhouse and 11 acre smallholding this 1½ acre garden is mainly organic. Trees & shrubs are underplanted with hundreds of thousands of

snowdrops, crocus, cyclamen, daffodils, woodland shrubs, clematis, rambling roses, hydrangeas & autumn flowering perennials. Extensive views, shepherd's hut & seats to enjoy them. Snowdrops, daffodils & other spring bulbs, year round flower interest with naturalistic plantings. 6 acres of wildflower meadows, 2 ponds and stream. Please phone first before visiting!

5 GLANDWR
Pentrecwrt, Llandysul, Carmarthenshire SA44 5DA. Mrs Jo Hicks, 01559 363729, leehicks@btinternet.com. *15m N of Carmarthen, 2m S of Llandysul, 7m E of Newcastle Emlyn. On A486. At Pentrecwrt village, take minor rd opp Black Horse PH. After bridge keep L for ¼ m. Glandwr is on R.* **Sat 4, Sun 5 July (11-5). Adm £3.50, chd free. Home-made teas. Visits also by arrangement June to Aug. Teas on request when booking.**
Delightful easily accessed 1 acre cottage garden, bordered by a natural stream. Incl a rockery and colour themed beds. Enter the mature woodland, transformed into an adventurous wander with plenty of shade loving plants, ground cover, interesting trees, shrubs and many surprises.

6 GLANGWILI LODGES
Llanllawddog, Carmarthen, Carmarthenshire SA32 7JE. Chris & Christine Blower. *7m NE of Carmarthen. Take A485 from Carmarthen. ¼ m after Gwili Pottery on L in Pontarsais, turn R for Llanllawddog and Brechfa. ½ m*

after Llanllawddog Chapel, rd bears sharply R, Glangwili Lodges 100yds on R. **Sat 20, Sun 21 June (11-5). Adm £4, chd free. Teas & Light refreshments.**
Our 16 acre estate has a one acre enclosed walled garden, with rockeries, water features, flower and shrub beds, a wisteria arbour, maples, magnolias and espalier fruit trees. Areas outside the wall incl one acre of woodland, with stream, an orchard, 2 acre wildlife area and a hedge tunnel containing a diverse collection of trees. There is also a productive vegetable garden and polytunnels. Wheelchair access within the walled garden, but outside this is more limited.

7 NEW THE GRANGE
Manorbier, Tenby, Pembrokeshire, SA70 7TY. Joan Stace. *4m W of Tenby. From Tenby, take the A4239 for Pembroke. 1/2 mile after Lydstep, The Grange is on L, at the Xrds, adjacent to the main turning for Manorbier. Parking limited.* **Sat 27, Sun 28 June, Sat 22, Sun 23 Aug (1-5). Adm £4, chd free.**
5 acre country garden of two parts. Older established garden around Grade II listed house (not open) has colourful herbaceous borders, rose garden, outdoor chess set and swimming pool (private). Newer garden was reclaimed from a heavy clay bog field which was drained and now consists of a lake with islands, ponds and dry river bed, newly-planted with wide variety of grasses as a 'prairie' garden.

Norchard

Stable Cottage

8 GREENACRE
Deer Park Lane, Nr Milton, Tenby, Pembrokeshire SA70 8PR. Andrew and Jill Baxter. *7m W of Tenby. From A477 at Milton, take turning signposted Lamphey (Stephens Green Lane). Continue to brow of hill then turn R onto Deer Park Lane. Garden ½ m along rd on L.* **Sun 26 July (12-5). Adm £4, chd free. Home-made teas. Also open Lamphey Walled Garden.** Plantaholic's garden of around ⅔ acre intensively planted and developed into a lush, colourful, exotic plant packed haven. Shady jungle garden, raised arid bed, scree garden, tender Tropicals in pots, greenhouse with carnivorous plants. Meandering paths leading to lots of different areas; be prepared for surprises around every corner. Uneven paths unsuitable for wheelchairs.
❀ ☕

9 NEW LAMPHEY WALLED GARDEN
Lamphey, Pembroke, Pembrokeshire SA71 5PD. Mr Simon Richards, 07503 976766, ullapoolsi@hotmail.co.uk. 07503 976766. *½ m from Lamphey village off the Ridgeway at Lower Lamphey*

Park. *Turn off A477 at Milton towards Lamphey for 1m. At T-junction, turn R to Lamphey (signposted), after 1m take R up farm track signed Lower Lamphey Park. Parking behind cottages.* **Sun 26 July (10-5). Adm £3.50, chd free. Also open Greenacre. Donation to The Bumblebee Conservation Trust.** Built in late 1700's an acre with 12 ft-high walls. Renovated 2005, extensive plantings from 2015. Several hundred different species, a plantsperson's garden with a natural feel. Over 30 *Salvia* species, old roses, lavender, sunflowers, grasses and ferns. Espalier apples and pears plus fan-trained stone fruit. Heritage vegetable garden. Wide firm grassed paths slope gently uphill and allow wheelchair access to the majority of garden.
♿ 🐕 ❀

10 LLWYNGARREG
Llanfallteg, Whitland, Carmarthenshire, SA34 0XH. Paul & Liz O'Neill, 01994 240717, lizpaulfarm@yahoo.co.uk, www.llwyngarreg.co.uk. *19m W of Carmarthen. A40 W from Carmarthen, turn R at Llandewi Velfrey, 2½ m to Llanfallteg. Go through village, garden ½ m further*

on: *2nd farm on R. Disabled car park in bottom yard on R.* **Mon 13 Apr, Sun 7 June, Sun 23 Aug (1.30-6). Adm £5, chd free. Home-made teas. Visits also by arrangement. Visitors welcome most days: phone prior to visiting to avoid disappointment.**
Llwyngarreg continues to develop further, delighting plant lovers with its many rarities incl species Primulas, many bamboos incl *Roscoeas, Hedychiums* and *Salvias* extending the season through to riotous autumn colour. Trees and rhododendrons have been underplanted with perennials. The sunken garden for tender/exotic gems and gravel terraces with formal pool continues to mature. Springs form a series of linked ponds across the main garden, providing colourful bog gardens. Wildlife ponds, fruit and veg, composting, twig piles, numerous living willow structures, swings, chickens, goldfish. Partial wheelchair access.
♿ 🐕 ❀ 🚗 ☕

11 NANTYIETAU
New Mill Road, St Clears, Carmarthenshire SA33 4HF. Matt Richards, 01994 231345, mattrichards320@gmail.com. *10m W of Carmarthen. Take the Laugharne turning off A40 then A4066 to Lower St Clears. Take first R after river bridge, continue for ½ m along country lane, passing junction to R. Nantyietau is next house on L.* **Visits by arrangement July & Aug. Adm £5, chd free.**
A one acre garden with a surprising and eclectic mix of the unusual and seldom seen that reflects a passion for plants. Tropical, tender and traditional planting with poultry, fish and other pets to complete the quirky mix. Polytunnel and outbuildings with exotic and spiky plants squeezed into every corner.

12 NORCHARD
The Ridgeway, Manorbier, Tenby, Pembrokeshire SA70 8LD. Ms H Davies, 07790 040278, h.norchard@hotmail.co.uk. *4m W of Tenby. From Tenby, take A4139 for Pembroke. ½ m after Lydstep, take R at Xrds. Proceed down lane for ¾ m. Norchard on R.* **Sun 24 May (1-6). Adm £5, chd free. Home-made teas. Also open Panteg. Visits also by arrangement Apr to July for groups of 10+.**
Historic gardens at medieval residence. Nestled in tranquil and

sheltered location with ancient oak woodland backdrop. Strong structure with formal and informal areas incl early walled gardens with restored Elizabethan parterre and potager. 1½ acre orchard with old (many local) apple varieties. Mill and millpond. Range of wildlife habitats. Extensive collections of roses, daffodils and tulips. Partial wheelchair access. Access to potager via steps only.

& ✿ 🚗 ☕

13 ◆ NORWOOD GARDENS & TEA ROOMS
Llanllwni, Pencader, Carmarthenshire SA39 9DU. The Norwood Gardens Partnership, 07774772314, gerddinorwood@gmail.com. *8m SW of Lampeter. On A485 Carmarthen to Lampeter rd in village of Llanllwni between Talardd Arms and Belle Vue PH. Tourist signs on approaches.* For NGS: Sat 15 Aug (10-4). Adm £5, chd free. Teas available in Tea Rooms. For other opening times and information, please phone or email.
A 3-acre garden under restoration. Wide range of unusual specimens, both herbaceous and woody, incorporated into discrete themed areas, each with own character and linked by paths and borders. New cottage garden and rose garden. Many beautiful and unusual sculptures enhance planting of yr-round interest.

& 🐎 ✿ 🚗 ☕

14 THE OLD RECTORY
Lampeter Velfrey, Narberth, Pembrokeshire, SA67 8UH. Jane & Stephen Fletcher, 01834 831444, jane_e_fletcher@hotmail.com. *3m E of Narbeth. The Old Rectory is next to the church in the middle of Lampeter Velfrey. Parking in the church yard car park.* Visits by arrangement Apr to July. Home-made teas on request when booking. Adm £3.50, chd free.
Historic approx 2 acre garden, sympathetically redesigned and replanted since 2009 and still being restored. Many unique trees, some over 300yrs old, wide variety of planting and several unique, architecturally designed buildings. Formal beds, mature woodland surrounding an old quarry with recently planted terraces and rhododendron bank. Meadow, fernery and orchard.

🐎 🚗 🛏 ☕

15 PANTEG
Llanddewi Velfrey, Narberth, Pembrokeshire SA67 8UU. Mr & Mrs D Pryse Lloyd, 01834 860081, d.pryselloyd@btinternet.com. *Situated off main A40 in village of Llanddewi Velfrey. A40 from Carmarthen, after garage take 1st L. At next T-junction turn L. On R gateway with stone gate pillars which is ½m drive to Panteg.* Sun 24 May (11-5). Adm £4, chd free. Also open Norchard. Visits also by arrangement Mar to Sept.
Approached down a woodland drive, this tranquil, S-facing, large garden, surrounding a Georgian house (not open), has been developed since early 1990s. Plantsman's garden set off by lawns on different levels. Walled garden, wisteria covered pergola. Vegetable garden, camellia and azalea bank, wildflower woodland. Many rare shrubs and plants incl, *Embothrium, Eucryphia* and *Hoheria.*

16 PENCWM
Hebron, Whitland, Pembrokeshire SA34 0JP. Lorna Brown, 01994 419471, lornambrown@hotmail.com. *10m N of Whitland. From A40 take St Clears exit & head N to Llangynin then on to Blaenwaun. Through village, after speed limit signs take 1st L. Over Xrds, 1¼m then 2nd lane on L marked Pencwm.* Visits by arrangement Apr to Oct for groups of 5 to 30. Adm £4, chd free. Teas on request when booking.
A secluded garden of about one acre set among large native trees, designed for year round interest and for benefit of wildlife. A wide variety of exotic specimen trees and shrubs incl magnolias, rhododendrons, hydrangeas, bamboos and acers. Drifts of bluebells and other spring bulbs and good autumn colour. Incl boggy area and pond with appropriate planting. Wellies recommended at most times.

🐎 🛏 ☕

Your visits help change lives – we've donated over £17 million to Macmillan Cancer Support since 1984

17 PENTRESITE
Rhydgaraeau Road, Carmarthen, Carmarthenshire SA32 7AJ. Gayle & Ron Mounsey, 01267 253928, gayle.mounsey@gmail.com. *4m N of Carmarthen. Take A485 heading N out of Carmarthen, once out of village of Peniel take 1st R to Horeb & cont for 1m. Turn R at NGS sign, 2nd house down lane.* Sun 12 July (2-5), also open Pen-y-Garn. Sun 20 Sept (2-5). Adm £4, chd free. Tea and home-made cakes (under cover). Visits also by arrangement May to Sept.
Approx. 2 acre garden developed over the last 13 yrs with extensive lawns, colour filled herbaceous and mixed borders, on several levels. A bog garden and magnificent views of the surrounding countryside. There is now a new area planted with trees and herbaceous plants. This garden is south facing and catches the south westerly winds from the sea. Steep in places but possible for wheelchairs with assistance and care.

& ✿ ☕

18 PEN-Y-GARN
Foelgastell, Cefneithin, Carmarthen, Carmarthenshire SA14 7EU. Mary-Ann Nossent & Mike Wood, 07985077022, ma@penygarncottage.co.uk, www.penygarncottage.co.uk. *10m SE Carmarthen. A48 N from Cross Hands take 1st L to Foelgastell R at T junction, 300m sharp L, 300m 1st gateway on L. A48 S Botanic Gdns turning r'about R to Porthythyd 1st L before T junction. 1m 1st R & 300m on L.* Sat 11 July (11-5). Sun 12 July (11-5), also open Pentresite. Adm £4, chd free. Home-made teas. Visits also by arrangement July to Sept for groups of up to 10. Teas on request when booking.
1⅓ acres unusual setting within a former old limestone quarry, the garden is on several levels with slopes and steps. Sympathetically developed to sit within the landscape, there are 5 distinct areas with a mixture of wild and cultivated plants. A shady area with woodland planting & wild ponds; kitchen garden; terraced borders with shrubs and herbaceous planting; lawns and pond; and a wild garden. This site is a challenge for people who are ambulant disabled as it is on many levels with slopes, steps and narrow paths.

✿ 🛏 ☕

19 NEW **PONT TRECYNNY**
Fishguard, Pembrokeshire, SA65 9SR. Wendy Kinver, 01348873040, wendykinver@icloud.com. *1½m N of Fishguard. Driving up the hill from Fishguard to Dinas turn R ½way up the rd & follow signs. Satnav will take you to a lay-by opp the garden.* **Wed 27 May, Wed 24 June, Wed 29 July (1-6). Adm £4.50, chd free. Visits also by arrangement June to Aug for groups of 5 to 10.**
A diverse garden of 3½ acres. Meander through the meadow planted with native trees, pass the pond and over a bridge which takes you along a path, through an arboretum, orchard and gravel garden and into the formal garden full of cloud trees, exotic plants and pots,which then leads you to the stream and vegetable garden.

20 **RHYD-Y-GROES**
Brynberian, Crymych, Pembrokeshire SA41 3TT. Jennifer & Kevin Matthews, 01239 891363, rhydygroesgardeners@gmail.com. *12m SW of Cardigan. 5m W of Crymych, 16m NE of Haverfordwest, on B4329, ¾m downhill from cattlegrid (from Haverfordwest) & 1m uphill from signpost to Brynberian (from Cardigan).* **Sat 13, Sun 14 June, Sat 18, Sun 19 July (1-5). Adm £4.50, chd £1.50. Home-made teas. Visits also by arrangement May to Aug for groups of 20+.**
Colourful 4 acre country garden at 200m on exposed NE hillside. Dramatic, extensive views across upland bogs and moorland may be enjoyed from strategically placed seating. Exuberantly and skilfully planted to suit the varied conditions. Formal herbaceous borders, shrubbery, woodland area, bog, prairie and natural meadow. Diverse plantings show what is possible without chemicals in this challenging environment. Beautiful, mollusc-proof planting demonstrates what can be achieved without using slug killer, pesticides and fungicides, resulting in a garden that is full of wildlife.

21 **SCOTSBOROUGH HOUSE**
Heywood Lane, Tenby, Pembrokeshire SA70 8BZ. John and Shari Argent, 01834 842 077, shari.argent@gmail.com. *½m W of Tenby. From N (A478) bear R onto A4218, turn R into Serpentine Rd, turn R into Heywood Lane. From S (B4318) turn L into Heywood Lane.* **Visits by arrangement May to Sept. Adm £4, chd free.**
This is a large garden with greenhouses laid out in 1910. It has lovely newly added borders with many original Edwardian trees and a tennis court which has become a formal lawn for Scotsborough House which was built in the 1950s. The orchard area now is left as long grass and this is encouraging wildflowers to make the area more beneficial to wildlife. Garden sheltered by mature trees, Blue Atlantic Cedar, mixed borders of shrubs, roses and herbaceous plants. Former greenhouses with climbing and semi-tropical plants; a very fine old Japanese maple; S-facing walled area and informal lawns around a central formal lawn. Newly restored veg garden. Partial wheelchair access.

22 **STABLE COTTAGE**
Rhoslanog Fawr, Mathry, Haverfordwest, Pembrokeshire SA62 5HG. Mr Michael & Mrs Jane Bayliss, 01348 837712, michaelandjane1954@michaelandjane.plus.com. *Between Fishguard & St David's. Head W on A487 turn R at Square & Compass sign. ½m, at hairpin take track L. Stable Cottage on L with block paved drive.* **Visits by arrangement May to Aug for groups of up to 20. Teas on request when booking. Adm £3, chd free.**
Garden extends to approx ⅓ of an acre. It is divided into several smaller garden types, with a seaside garden, small orchard and wildlife area, scented garden, small vegetable/kitchen garden, and two Japanese areas - a stroll garden and courtyard area.

23 **TRADEWINDS**
Ffynnonwen, Pen-y-Bont, nr Trelech, Carmarthenshire SA33 6PX. Stuart & Eve Kemp-Gee. *10m NW of Carmarthen. From A40 W of Carmarthen, take B4298 to Meidrim, then R onto B4299 towards Trelech. After 5m turn R at Tradewinds sign.* **Sun 21 June, Sun 2 Aug (11-5). Adm £4, chd free. Home-made teas.**
This 3 acre plantsman garden is for the gardener who wants to see unusual and rare plants in a tranquil setting. A garden that is good for the senses, whether it is the scents, sounds of the countryside or the dazzling displays of vivid colour, plant harmonies coupled with textual contrast. The large herbaceous borders, trees, shrubs, roses and shade borders are in abundance. With natural streams flowing through the garden it is a garden for all seasons whatever the weather. Art studio open.

Glangwili Lodges

Colby Woodland Garden

24 TREFFGARNE HALL
Treffgarne, Haverfordwest,
Pembrokeshire SA62 5PJ. Martin
& Jackie Batty, 01437 741115,
jackie.batty@ngs.org.uk. *7m N
of Haverfordwest, signed off A40.
Proceed up through village & follow
rd round sharply to L, Hall ¼m
further on L.* **Sun 10 May (1-5), also
open Dyffryn Fernant. Sun 12
July (1-5). Adm £4.50, chd free.
Home-made teas. Visits also by
arrangement. Teas on request
when booking.**
Stunning hilltop location with
panoramic views: handsome Grade
II listed Georgian house (not open)
provides formal backdrop to garden
of 4 acres with wide lawns and
themed beds. A walled garden, with
double rill and pergolas, is planted
with a multitude of borderline hardy
exotics. Also large scale sculptures,
summer broadwalk, meadow
patch, gravel garden, heather bed
and stumpery. Planted for yr-round
interest. The planting schemes seek
to challenge the boundaries of what
can be grown in Pembrokeshire.

25 TY'R MAES
Ffarmers, Carmarthenshire
SA19 8JP. John & Helen
Brooks, 01558 650541,
johnhelen140@gmail.com. *7m SE
of Lampeter. 8m NW of Llanwrda.
1½m N of Pumsaint on A482, opp
turn to Ffarmers (please ignore
satnav).* **Visits by arrangement Apr
to Oct. See NGS website for pop-
up opening in late Spring. Adm
£4, chd free. Home-made teas on
request when booking.**
4 acre garden with splendid views.
Herbaceous and shrub beds – formal
design, exuberantly informal planting,
full of cottage garden favourites and
many unusual plants. Woodland
garden with over 200 types of tree;
wildlife and lily ponds; pergola,
gazebos, post and rope arcade
covered in climbers. Gloriously
colourful from early spring till late
autumn. Wheelchair note: Some
gravel paths.

**26 ✦ UPTON CASTLE
GARDENS**
Cosheston, Pembroke Dock,
Pembrokeshire SA72 4SE. Prue &
Stephen Barlow, 01646 689996,
info@uptoncastle.com,
www.uptoncastlegardens.com.
*4m E of Pembroke Dock. 2m N of
A477 between Carew & Pembroke
Dock. Follow brown signs to Upton
Castle Gardens through Cosheston.*
**For NGS: Sun 28 June (10-4.30).
Adm £5, chd free. Home-made
teas. For other opening times and
information, please phone, email or
visit garden website.**
Privately owned listed historic gardens
with an exceptional collection of
mature trees and plants extending to
over 35 acres. Rare rhododendrons,
camellias and magnolias abound.
Formal rose garden contains over 150
roses of many varieties and colours.
Fully stocked herbaceous borders
provide constant interest. Traditional
walled, productive kitchen garden.
Arboretum with 15 champion trees.
Walk on the Wild Side: Woodland
walks funded by C.C.W. and Welsh
Assembly Government. Medieval
chapel as featured on Time Team.
Partial wheelchair access.

OPENING DATES

All entries subject to change. For latest information check www.ngs.org.uk

Map locator numbers are shown to the right of each garden name.

April

Saturday 25th
NEW The Flower
Meadow 9

Sunday 26th
NEW The Flower
Meadow 9

May

Friday 8th
Bryngwyn 3

Saturday 9th
Bryngwyn 3

Sunday 17th
Bwlch y Geuffordd 5

Sunday 24th
Arnant House 2

Monday 25th
Arnant House 2

Sunday 31st
NEW Rhos Villa 14

June

Wednesday 3rd
NEW Rhos Villa 14

Sunday 7th
Marlais 11

Sunday 14th
Ysgoldy'r Cwrt 18

Friday 19th
Bryngwyn 3

Saturday 20th
Bryngwyn 3

Sunday 21st
Llanllyr 10

Saturday 27th
Pantygorlan 12

Sunday 28th
Pantygorlan 12

July

Sunday 5th
NEW Rhos Villa 14

Wednesday 8th
NEW Rhos Villa 14

Sunday 12th
Penybont 13

Sunday 19th
Aberystwyth Allotments 1
◆ Cae Hir Gardens 6

Sunday 26th
Penybont 13

August

Sunday 2nd
◆ Ty Glyn Walled
Garden 15

Saturday 8th
NEW The Flower
Meadow 9

Sunday 9th
NEW The Flower
Meadow 9

September

Sunday 6th
Cwrt Mawr Garden 7

By Arrangement

Arrange a personalised garden visit with your club, or group of friends, on a date to suit you. See individual garden entries for full details.

Arnant House 2
Bryngwyn 3
Bwlch y Geuffordd
Gardens 4
NEW Felin Ganol
Watermill 8
Llanllyr 10
Penybont 13
NEW Tynyffordd Isaf 16
Yr Efail 17
Ysgoldy'r Cwrt 18

Arnant House

THE GARDENS

1 ABERYSTWYTH ALLOTMENTS
5th Avenue, Penparcau, Aberystwyth, SY23 1QT. **Aberystwyth Town Council.** *On S side of R Rheidol on Aberystwyth by-pass. From N or E, take A4120 between Llanbadarn & Penparcau. Cross bridge then take 1st R into Minyddol. Allotments ¼ m on R.* **Sun 19 July (1-5). Adm £4, chd free. Home-made teas.**
There are 37 plots in total on 2 sites just a few yards from each other. The allotments are situated in a lovely setting alongside River Rheidol close to Aberystwyth. Wide variety of produce grown, vegetables, soft fruit, top fruit, flowers, herbs. Car parking available. For more information contact Brian Heath 01970 617112. Sample tastings from allotment produce. Grass and gravel paths.

ᏝᏝ

Your visits help change lives – your generosity has supported unpaid carers through donations to Carers Trust totalling over £4 million since 1996

2 ARNANT HOUSE
Llwyncelyn, Aberaeron, SA46 0HF. **Pam & Ron Maddox,** 01545 580083. *On A487, 2m S of Aberaeron. Next to Llwyncelyn Village Hall. Parking in lay-by opp house.* **Sun 24 May (12-5); Mon 25 May (1-5). Adm £4, chd free. Home-made teas. Visits also by arrangement Apr to Sept.**
Garden created 18yrs ago from derelict ground. 1 acre, in Victorian style and divided into rooms and themes. Laburnum arch, wildlife ponds, rotunda and tea house. Wide, long borders full of perennial planting with a good variety of species, numerous statues and

oddities to be discovered. Many attractive ornamental shrubs incl acers, magnolias and rhododendrons in May, plus about 50 different types of clematis. Also a good selection of hellebores, primulas and fritillaries. Partial wheelchair access. Garden is level, but help may be needed on gravel paths. Some paths are very narrow.

ᏝᏝ

3 BRYNGWYN
Capel Seion, Aberystwyth, SY23 4EE. **Mr & Mrs Sue and Terry Reeves,** 01970880760, sueterr02@btinternet.com. *On A4120 between the villages of Capel Seion & Pant y Crug.* **Fri 8, Sat 9 May, Fri 19, Sat 20 June (1-5.30). Adm £4, chd free. Home-made teas. Visits also by arrangement May & June for groups of up to 20.**
Bluebells in May. Traditional wildflower rich hay meadows managed for wildlife. As a result of conservation grazing, hedgerow renovation and tree planting, habitat has been restored such that numbers and diversity of wild flowers and wildlife have increased. Pond for wildlife. Meander along mown paths through the meadows. Small orchard containing Welsh heritage apples and pears. Wild flower seed sales. Some areas accessible by standard wheelchair. Most paths are sloping mown grass, access at users discretion.

4 BWLCH Y GEUFFORDD GARDENS
Bronant, Aberystwyth, SY23 4JD. **Mr & Mrs J Acres,** 01974 251559, gayacres@aol.com, bwlch-y-geuffordd-gardens.myfreesites.net. *12m SE of Aberystwyth, 6m NW of Tregaron off A485. Take turning opp Bronant school for 1½ m then L up ½ m uneven track.* **Visits by arrangement all year round. Adm £5, chd £2. Tea. Please beforehand to book and arrange cake. For a Mad Hatter's Tea Party, please see details on website.** 1000ft high, 3 acre, constantly evolving wildlife and water garden. An adventure garden for children. There are a number of themed gardens, incl Mediterranean, cottage garden, woodland, oriental, memorial and jungle. Plenty of seating. Unique garden sculptures and buildings, incl a cave, temple, gazebo, jungle hut, tree house and

willow den. Children's adventure garden, Musical instruments, Pond dipping, Treasure hunt, Beautiful lake, Temple and labyrinth, Tree house, Sculptures, wildlife rich, particularly insects and birds. Paths are gravel, and there are some steps. There is a shorter route covering the main features, without steps.

ᏝᏝ

5 BWLCH Y GEUFFORDD
New Cross, Aberystwyth, SY23 4LY. **Manuel & Elaine Grande.** *5m SE of Aberystwyth. Off A487, take B4340 to New Cross. Garden on R at bottom of small dip. Parking in lay-bys opp house.* **Sun 17 May (10.30-4.30). Adm £4, chd free. Home-made teas.**
Landscaped hillside 1½ acre garden, fine views of Cambrian mountains. Embraces its natural features with different levels, 3 ponds, mixed borders merging into carefully managed informal areas. Banks of rhododendrons, azaleas, bluebells in spring. Full of unusual shade & damp-loving plants, flowering shrubs, mature trees, clematis & climbing roses scrambling up the walls of the old stone buildings. Partial wheelchair access only to lower levels around house. Some steps and steep paths further up.

ᏝᏝ

6 ♦ CAE HIR GARDENS
Cribyn, Lampeter, SA48 7NG. **Julie and Stuart Akkermans,** 01570 471116, caehirgardens.com. *5m W of Lampeter. Take A482 from Lampeter towards Aberaeron. After 5m turn S on B4337. Cae Hir Gardens are 2m down the road in Cribyn.* **For NGS: Sun 19 July (10-5). Adm £5, chd free. Home-made teas. For other opening times and information, please phone or visit garden website.**
A Welsh Garden with a Dutch History, Cae Hir is a true family garden of unassuming beauty, made tenable by its innovative mix of ordinary garden plants and wildflowers growing in swathes of perceived abandonment. At Cae Hir the natural meets the formal and riotous planting meets structure and form. A garden not just for plant lovers, but also for design enthusiasts. 5 acres of fully landscaped gardens. Tea room serving a selection of homemade cakes and scones and a 'Soup of the Day'. Limited wheelchair access.

ᏝᏝ

7 CWRT MAWR GARDEN

Tregaron, Llangeitho, SY25 6QJ.
Pauline Gorissen. *From Llangeitho take rd to Aberystwyth past Three Horse Shoe PH. Take 1st L, drive for approx. 1m, Cwrt Mawr entrance is on R.* Sun 6 Sept (10-5). Adm £4, chd free. Cream teas. Pizzas, made to order, baked in the wood fired pizza oven will be available.
Beautiful gardens surround a listed Georgian manor in a wonderful rural setting. Centrepiece of the garden is a large stairway, bordered by terraced gardens full of seasonal colour. Newly planted flower beds mix with existing mature areas of rhododendrons, and forest paths wind through ancient woodland. 4 acres of flowing beds, ponds and interesting features make this garden unmissable. Beautifully crafted retaining walls on the terraces constructed from local stone.

8 NEW FELIN GANOL WATERMILL

Llanrhystud, SY23 5AL. Andrew and Anne Parry, 01974 202272, miller@felinganol.co.uk, www.felinganol.co.uk. *8m S of Aberystywyth in Llanrhystud. Approx 8m S of Aberystywyth on the A487 turn L just after the Llanrhystud Village sign. 1st L after the school, narrow lane (unsuitable for heavy vehicles). Felin Ganol in 200m.* Visits by arrangement Apr to Sept for groups of up to 15. Adm £4, chd free.
Informal and relaxed garden bounded by the river Wyre, incorporating lawns, flower borders, herb garden, no-dig vegetable beds surrounding a working watermill. There is a mill pond and orchard and an area of woodland with paths running through. Stone ground flour produced by the mill will be for sale. Access may be restricted for people with limited mobility.

9 NEW THE FLOWER MEADOW

Llain Manal, Rhydlewis, Llandysul, SA44 5QH. Mrs Sarah Redman, www.theflowermeadow.co.uk. *We are located on the B4571. From Newcastle Emlyn we are the last house in Penrhiwpal before the Xrd with the coach garage on it. From Ffostrasol we are the 1st house after Xrd.* Sat 25, Sun 26 Apr, Sat 8, Sun 9 Aug (12-5). Adm £4, chd free. Home-made teas.
Three acre small holding specialising in growing both exotic and wild flowers for cutting. Large hay meadow with many different native species, vegetable garden, greenhouse and poly tunnel for more tender vegetables and fruit. Interesting and attractive courtyard garden with herbaceous perennials, shrubs and young trees. Extensive views over beautiful countryside. Terrain is level. Grass paths.

10 LLANLLYR

Talsarn, Lampeter, SA48 8QB. Mr & Mrs Robert Gee, 01570 470900, lgllanllyr@aol.com. *6m NW of Lampeter. On B4337 to Llanrhystud. From Lampeter, entrance to garden on L, just before village of Talsarn.* Sun 21 June (2-5). Adm £4.50, chd free. Home-made teas. Visits also by arrangement Apr to Oct.
Large early C19 garden on site of medieval nunnery, renovated and replanted since 1989. Large pool, bog garden, formal water garden, rose and shrub borders, gravel gardens, rose arbour, allegorical labyrinth and mount, all exhibiting fine plantsmanship. Yr-round appeal, interesting and unusual plants. Spectacular rose garden planted with fragrant old fashioned shrub and climbing roses. Specialist Plant Fair by Ceredigion Growers Association.

11 MARLAIS

Ffosyffin, Aberaeron, SA46 0EY. Dr & Mrs David Shepherd. *From Aberaeron take A487 S to Henfynyw and bear L at green past bus stop, then L again past single storey cottages. Marlais is second bungalow on R at junction of Parc Ffos.* Sun 7 June (11-5). Adm £3, chd free. Home-made teas.
The garden at Marlais has been created in only 3 years and was designed for easy access and maintenance to suit more mature gardeners with some disability. To the front we have planted a mini orchard with many varieties of top fruit on dwarfing rootstock. The rear garden has raised flower beds with an exceptional variety of unusual plants. The raised vegetable and soft fruit beds are screened by trellis with Tayberry, Loganberry, Blackberry and Wineberry giving over 40 varieties of fruit. A hand built 15 room, 1:12 scale model doll's house will be on show. Only central part of rear garden accessible by wheelchair. Hanging basket workshop, choose your own bespoke basket.

12 PANTYGORLAN

Ystumtuen, Aberystwyth, SY23 3AE. Mr & Mrs Winter, 01970 890224. *12m E of Aberystwyth. On A44, 1m W of Ponterwyd, turn L for Ystumtuen. At top of hill turn R by parking areas. Disabled parking close to house; phone ahead to secure a space.* Sat 27, Sun 28 June (10.30-5). Adm £4, chd free. Home-made teas.
3½ acre garden high in Cambrian mountains, comprising small formal garden with pond, rockery, vegetable plot and shrubbery, encompassed by large mixed woodland with walks, carefully sited sculptures and seating. 2 established lakes with waterfalls accommodating a variety of water plants. Steep slopes make part of the garden unsuitable for wheelchair users and people with mobility issues.

13 PENYBONT

Llanafan, Aberystwyth, SY23 4BJ. Norman & Brenda Jones, 01974 261737, tobrenorm@gmail.com. *9m SE of Aberystwyth. Ystwyth Valley B4340 from Aberystwyth. Stay on B4340 for 9m via Trawscoed towards Pontrhydfendigaid. Curve R over stone bridge. ¼m up hill, R by row of cream houses.* Sun 12, Sun 26 July (11-5). Adm £4, chd free. Home-made teas. Visits also by arrangement May to Sept for groups of up to 30. Open anytime we are home, please ring or email to check first.
Penybont in Wild Wales shows what can be achieved from a green field sloping site in just a few years. This exciting garden (about an acre) extended in 2017 is designed to complement the modern building, its forest backdrop and panoramic views. Lots of Lavender, roses and Hydrangeas. The pond has around 50 good sized Orfe and Koi Carp. Original design, see Red Kites & Buzzards with stunning views of the Ystwyth valley and hill forts. Colour throughout the season. Partial wheelchair access only. Sloping ground, gravel paths and lawn.

14 NEW RHOS VILLA

Llanddewi Brefi, Tregaron, SY25 6PA. Andrew & Sam Buchanan. *From Lampeter take the A485 towards Tregaron. After driving through Llangybi turn R opp the junction for Olmarch, The property*

can be found on the RHS after
1½ m. **Sun 31 May, Wed 3 June,
Sun 5, Wed 8 July (11-4.30). Adm
£3.50, chd free. Home-made teas.**
A ¾ acre garden creatively utilising
local materials. Secret pathways
meander through sun and shade, dry
and damp. A variety of perennials
and shrubs are inter-planted to
create interest throughout the year. A
productive vegetable and fruit garden
with semi formal structure contrasts
the looser planting through the rest of
the garden.

✿ ☕

**15 ◆ TY GLYN WALLED
GARDEN**
Ciliau Aeron, Lampeter, SA48 8DE.
Ty Glyn Davis Trust, 07832970896,
gardener@tyglyndavistrust.co.uk,
www.tyglyndavistrust.co.uk. *3m
SE of Aberaeron. Turn off A482
Aberaeron to Lampeter at Ciliau
Aeron signed to Pennant. Entrance
700 metres on L.* **For NGS: Sun
2 Aug (12-5). Adm £4, chd free.
Home-made teas. For other
opening times and information,
please phone, email or visit garden
website.**
Secluded walled garden in beautiful
woodland setting alongside River
Aeron, developed specifically for
special needs children. Terraced
kitchen garden overlooks herbaceous
borders, orchard and ponds with
child orientated features and
surprises amidst unusual shrubs and
perennials. Planted fruit trees selected
from former gardener's notebook of
C19. Children's play area. Access
paths to lower garden and woodland
walk accessible to wheelchairs.

♿ ✿ ☕

16 NEW TYNYFFORDD ISAF
Capel Bangor, Aberystwyth,
SY23 3NW. Vicky Lines &
Jim Palmer, 01970880534,
vickysweetland@googlemail.com.
*Capel Bangor. From Aberystwth
take L turn off A44 at east end of
Capel Bangor. Follow this rd round
to R until you see sign with Melindwr
Valley Bees.* **Visits by arrangement
July to Sept for groups of up to
15. Adm £3.50, chd free. Light
refreshments.**
A bee farm dedicated to wildlife with
permaculture and forest garden
ethos. Fruit, vegetables, culinary and
medicinal herbs and bee friendly
plants within our wildlife zones.
Beehives are situated in dedicated
areas and can be observed from a

distance. Ornamental and wildflower
areas in a cottage garden theme.
Formal and wildlife ponds. Grass
paths. Not suitable for wheelchairs.
Vintage tractors and other machinery.
Subtropical greenhouse with
carnivorous plants, orchids, exotic
fruits.

🐕 ✿ ☕

17 YR EFAIL
Llanio Road, Tregaron,
SY25 6PU. Mrs Shelagh
Yeomans, 01974 299370,
shelagh.yeomans@ngs.org.uk.
*3m SW of Tregaron. A485 from
Lampeter. L at Llanio to B4578
or A487 from Aberystwyth, L at
Llanfarian (A485) towards Tregaron.
At Tyncelyn B4578, 4m on R.*
**Visits by arrangement Feb to
Oct for groups of up to 30.
Adm £4, chd free. Home-made
teas. Refreshments served in
conservatory with garden views.**
Savour one of the many quiet
spaces to sit and reflect amongst the
informal gardens of relaxed perennial
planting, incl a wildlife pond, shaded
areas, bog and gravel gardens. Be
inspired by the large productive
vegetable plots, three polytunnels
and greenhouse. Wander along grass
paths through the maturing, mostly

native, woodland. Enjoy home-made
teas incorporating homegrown fruit
and veg. Bilingual quiz sheet for
children. Seasonal vegetables for sale.
Gravel and grass paths accessible to
wheelchairs with pneumatic wheels.

♿ 🐕 ✿ 🚌 ☕

18 YSGOLDY'R CWRT
Llangeitho, Tregaron, SY25 6QJ.
Mrs Brenda Woodley,
01974 821542. *1½ m N of
Llangeitho. From Llangeitho, turn L
at school signed Penuwch. Garden
1½ m on R. From Cross Inn take
B4577 past Penuwch Inn, R after
brown sculptures in field. Garden
¾ m on L.* **Sun 14 June (11-5).
Adm £4, chd free. Home-made
teas. Visits also by arrangement
May to Aug.**
One acre hillside garden, with 4
natural ponds which are a magnet
for wildlife plus a fish pond. Areas
of wildflower meadow, bog, dry and
woodland gardens. Established
rose walk. Large Iris ensata and Iris
laevigata collections in a variety of
colours. Regional Finalist, The English
Garden's The Nation's Favourite
Gardens 2019. Unsuitable for
wheelchairs.

🐕 ✿ 🚌 ☕

Aberystwyth Allotments

OPENING DATES

All entries subject to change. For latest information check www.ngs.org.uk

Map locator numbers are shown to the right of each garden name.

By Arrangement

Arrange a personalised garden visit with your club, or group of friends, on a date to suit you. See individual garden entries for full details.

Brookleigh

THE GARDENS

② ◆ BORDERVALE PLANTS

Sandy Lane, Ystradowen, Cowbridge, CF71 7SX. Mrs Claire Jenkins, 01446 774036, bordervaleplants@gmail.com, www.bordervale.co.uk. *8m W of Cardiff. 10 mins from M4 or take A4222 from Cowbridge. Turn at Ystradowen postbox, then 3rd L & proceed ½m, follow brown signs. Garden on R. Parking in rd.* **For NGS: Sun 3 May, Sat 6 June, Sun 5 July, Mon 31 Aug (11-4). Adm £3.50, chd free. For other opening times and information, please phone, email or visit garden website.**

Within mature woodland valley (semi-tamed), with stream and bog garden, extensive mixed borders. Children must be supervised. The Nursery specialises in unusual perennials and cottage garden plants. Nursery opening information can be found on our website. Coach parties welcome by arrangement. Awarded Silver Gilt Medal (for Unusual Welsh grown trees, shrubs & perennials) RHS Flower Show Cardiff. Wheelchair access to top third of garden as well as Nursery.

&. ❊ 🚐

Your visits help change lives – we are Hospice UK's largest charitable funder donating more than £5.5 million to support hospices in local communities since 1996

③ THE CEDARS

20A Slade Road, Newton, Swansea, SA3 4UF. Mr & Mrs Ian and Madelene Scott. *Take the A4067 to Oystermouth, turn right at White Rose PH continue along Newton Rd keeping R at fork to T-junction, turn R & 1st R into Slade Rd, follow yellow signs.* **Sun 29 Mar (2-5). Adm £4, chd free. Home-made teas.**

South facing garden on a sloping site consisting of rooms subdivided by large shrubs and trees. Small kitchen garden with greenhouse. Ornamental pond. Herbaceous perennials, number of fruit trees. It is a garden which affords all year interest with azalea camellias rhododendrons magnolias hydrangeas. Limited number of plants for sale.

❊

GROUP OPENING

④ CEFN CRIBWR GARDEN CLUB

Cefn Cribwr, Bridgend, CF32 0AP. www.cefncribwrgardeningclub. com. *5m W of Bridgend on B4281.* **Sun 28 June (11-5). Combined adm £5, chd free. Home-made teas.**

> **6 BEDFORD ROAD**
> Carole & John Mason.
>
> **13 BEDFORD ROAD**
> Mr John Loveluck.
>
> **2 BRYN TERRACE**
> Alan & Tracy Birch.
>
> **CEFN CRIBWR GARDEN CLUB ALLOTMENTS**
> Cefn Cribwr Garden Club.
>
> **CEFN METHODIST CHURCH**
> Cefn Cribwr Methodist Church.
>
> **77 CEFN ROAD**
> Peter & Veronica Davies & Mr Fai Lee.
>
> **25 EAST AVENUE**
> Mr & Mrs D Colbridge.
>
> **15 GREEN MEADOW**
> Tom & Helen.
>
> **6 TAI THORN**
> Mr Kevin Burnell.

Cefn Cribwr is an old mining village atop a ridge with views to Swansea in the west, Somerset to the south and home to Bedford Park and the Cefn Cribwr Iron Works. The village hall is at the centre with teas, cakes and plants for sale. The allotments

are to be found behind the hall. Children, art and relaxation are just some of the themes to be found in the gardens besides the flower beds and vegetables. There are also water features, fish ponds, wildlife ponds, summerhouses and hens adding to the diverse mix. Themed colour borders, roses, greenhouses, recycling, composting and much more. The chapel grounds are peaceful with a meandering woodland trail. For more information please see our website.

❊

GROUP OPENING

⑤ CORNTOWN GARDENS

Corntown, Bridgend, CF35 5BB. *Take B4265 from Bridgend to Ewenny. Take L in Ewenny on B4525 to Corntown follow yellow NGS signs. From A48 take B4525 to Corntown.* **Sat 27 June (11-4). Combined adm £4, chd free. Home-made teas at Y Bwthyn.**

> **RHOS GELER**
> Bob Priddle & Marie D Robson.
>
> **Y BWTHYN**
> Mrs Joyce Pegg.

Y Bwythyn has had over 30yrs of hard labour, some guesswork and considerable good luck resulting in a delightful garden. The area at the front of the house is a mixture of hot colour combinations whilst at the rear of this modest sized garden the themes are of a more traditional cottage garden style which incl colour themed borders as well as soft fruit, herbs and vegetables. Rhos Geler's garden has a lavender hedge at the front and subjects to attract butterflies. The main garden area at the back of the house is a long narrow garden that is in a series of themed areas. These incl an herbaceous border, shade loving plants, an Elizabethan style knot garden and a Japanese influenced area. Containers hold a range of subjects incl a collection of sempervivums.

❊

The Cedars

⑥ THE COTTAGE

Cwmpennar, Mountain Ash, CF45 4DB. Helen & Hugh Jones, 01443 472784, hhjones1966@yahoo.co.uk. *18m N of Cardiff. A470 from N or S. Then follow B4059 to Mountain Ash. Follow signs for Cefnpennar then turn R before bus shelter into village of Cwmpennar & to top of lane at end of Middle Row.* **Visits by arrangement May to Aug for groups of up to 20. Adm £4, chd free. Home-made teas.**

4 acres and 40yrs of amateur muddling have produced what it is hoped is an interesting garden incl bluebell wood, rhododendron and camellia shrubbery, herbaceous borders, rose garden, small arboretum, many uncommon trees and shrubs. Garden slopes NE/SW.

GROUP OPENING

⑦ CREIGIAU VILLAGE GARDENS

Maes Y Nant, Creigiau, CF15 9EJ. *W of Cardiff (J34 M4). From M4 J34 follow A4119 to T-lights, turn R by Castell Mynach Pub, pass through Groes Faen & turn L to Creigiau. Follow NGS signs.* **Sun 14 June (12-5). Combined adm £6, chd free. Home-made teas at 28 Maes y Nant.**

28 MAES Y NANT
Mike & Lesley Sherwood.

31 MAES Y NANT
Frances Bowyer.

WAUNWYLLT
John Hughes & Richard Shaw.

On the NW side of Cardiff and with easy access from the M4 J34, Creigiau Village Gardens includes three vibrant and innovative gardens. Each quite different, they combine some of the best characteristics of design and planting for modern town gardens as well as cottage gardens. Each has its own forte; Waunwyllt has incorporated next door's garden and this new project will be complete for 2020. At 28 Maes y Nant, cottage garden planting reigns. This is in complete contrast to the strong architecture of 31 Maes y Nant, where the design coordinates water, the garden room and planting, incl a small scale prairie. Anyone looking for ideas for a garden in an urban setting will not go away disappointed; enjoy a warm welcome, home-made teas and plant sales.

⑧ 7 CRESSY ROAD

Penylan, Cardiff, CF23 5BE. Victoria Thornton. *Penylan Cardiff. Approaching from Wellfield Rd, turn R at the T-lights into Marlborough Rd & Cressy Rd is the 3rd turning on the L. From Newport Rd follow Marlborough Rd to Thomas Court, turn L.* **Sun 2 Aug (2-6). Adm £3.50, chd free. Home-made teas.**

Enjoy a warm welcome at No 7. Small subtropical garden, creating an illusion of a much larger space. Lush tropical planting, alive with colour and texture. With an emphasis on wildlife, nectar rich planting, barrel pond, attracting frogs, dragonflies and damselflies. Bug hotel. Ever changing,new plantings to be seen every year. Silver medal, Cardiff in Bloom 2014.

⑨ 22 DAN-Y-COED ROAD

Cyncoed, Cardiff, CF23 6NA. Alan & Miranda Workman, 029 2076 6225, miranda.parsons@talktalk.net. *Dan y Coed Rd leads off Cyncoed Rd at the top and Rhydypenau Rd at the bottom. No 22 is at the bottom of Dan y Coed Rd. There is street parking and level access to the R of the property.* **Sun 5 July (2-6). Adm £4, chd free. Home-made teas. Visits also by arrangement May to Sept for groups of 5 to 20.**

A medium sized, much loved garden. Owners share a passion for plants and structure, each yr the lawn gets smaller to allow for the acquisition of new plants and features! Hostas, ferns, Acers and other trees form the central woodland theme as there is a backdrop provided by the Nant Fawr woods. Year round interest has been created for the owner's and visitor's greater pleasure. There is a wildlife pond, many climbing plants and a greenhouse with a cactus and succulent collection. There is wheelchair access to the garden, patio area only.

GROUP OPENING

⑩ DINAS POWYS

Dinas Powys, CF64 4TL. *Approx 6m SW of Cardiff. Exit M4 at J33, follow A4232 to Leckwith, onto B4267 & follow to Merry Harrier T-lights. Turn R & enter Dinas Powys. Follow yellow NGS signs.* **Sat 11, Sun 12 July (11-5). Combined adm £5, chd free. Home-made teas at Ashgrove and the community gardens incl gluten free and vegan cakes. Donation to Dinas Powys Voluntary Concern and Dinas Powys Community Library.**

1 ASHGROVE
Sara Bentley.
Open on all dates

BROOKLEIGH
Melanie Syme.
Open on Sun 12 July

32 LONGMEADOW DRIVE
Julie & Nigel Barnes.
Open on all dates

30 MILLBROOK ROAD
Mr & Mrs R Golding.
Open on all dates

32 MILLBROOK ROAD
Mrs G Marsh.
Open on all dates

NIGHTINGALE COMMUNITY GARDENS
Keith Hatton.
Open on all dates

There are six gardens to visit in this small friendly village, all with something different to offer, plus the village church. The gardens at 1 Ashgrove, has a large variety of different plants and trees in sweeping beds, with many hidden nooks and places to sit. The community garden features lovely displays of vegetable and fruit. 30 Millbrook Road, a large and beautiful garden, established over 25 years, with lovely pond and waterfall. Brookleigh is a large garden with beautiful mature trees, a sweeping lawn and large ornamental pond. 32 Millbrook Road is a lovely family garden with interesting touches. 32 Longmeadow is full of gorgeous and colourful plants with an unusual water feature. Our village church, St Peters, is also opening with displays of flowers, classic cars and other attractions. Delicious home-made teas will be served, incl vegan and gluten free options, and there will be plants for sale also. There are many restful and beautiful areas to sit and relax. Good wheelchair access at the community gardens. Partial access elsewhere.

11 105 HEATH PARK AVENUE
Heath, Cardiff, CF14 3RG.
Mr and Mrs Gambles,
beverly_gambles@hotmail.com. *Approx 1m from University Hospital. From Gabalfa R'about into Birchgrove turn R into Heathwood Rd. At top of Rd turn R at T-lights into Heath Park Ave. Follow NGS signs.* Sun 23 Aug (12-5). Adm £4, chd free. Home-made teas.
A South facing family garden that is constantly evolving. Perennial borders and plenty of pots surrounding a central lawn give lots of colour throughout the year. A small vegetable plot and greenhouse to grow a variety of plants and vegetables. Small fishpond with lots of frogs and newts.

GROUP OPENING

12 HEN FELIN & SWALLOW BARNS
Vale of Glamorgan, Dyffryn, CF5 6SU. 02920 593082, rozanne5@icloud.com.

3m from Culverhouse. Cross r'about. Sun 5 July (10-5). Combined adm £6, chd free. Home-made teas.
Dyffryn hamlet is a hidden gem in the Vale of Glamorgan; despite the lack of a PH there is a fantastic community spirit. Wheelchair access possible to most of the two gardens. Unprotected river access, children must be supervised in both gardens. Yr Hen Felin: Beautiful cottage garden with stunning borders, breathtaking wildflower meadows, oak tree with surrounding bench, 200yr old pig sty, wishing well, secret garden with steps to river, lovingly tended vegetable garden and chickens. Mill stream running through garden with adjacent wild flowers. Swallow Barns: Cross the bridge over the river and pass under the weeping ash to enter Swallow Barns garden, a 19yr old garden with packed herbaceous borders - formal and informal, orchard, hens, herb garden, lavender patio, willow arches leading to woodland walk and deep secluded pond. We welcome all visitors - old and new. Home-made jams, Pimm's at the pond, cheese and wine, artists' stall, face painting, white elephant stall, jewellery stall and plant stall.

13 16 HENDY CLOSE
Derwen Fawr, Swansea, SA2 8BB.
Peter & Wendy Robinson. *Approx 3m W of Swansea. A4067 Mumbles Rd follow sign for Singleton Hospital. Then R onto Sketty Lane at mini r'about, turn L then 2nd R onto Saunders Way. Follow yellow NGS signs. Please park on Saunders Way if possible.* Sat 5 Sept (1.30-5). Adm £5, chd free. Light refreshments.
Originally the garden was covered with 40ft conifers. Cottage style, some unusual and mainly perennial plants which provide colour in spring, summer and autumn. Hopefully the garden is an example of how to plan for all seasons. Visitors say it is like a secret garden because there are a number of hidden places. Plants to encourage all types of wildlife in to the garden.

14 23 HENLLYS ROAD
Cyncoed, Cardiff, CF23 6NL.
Mrs Jill Evans, 07870654205,
jilltreenut@uwclub.net. *Turn off Cyncoed Rd, in Cyncoed Village down Bettws y Coed Rd. Take 2nd*

L onto Llangorse Rd and 2nd R into Henllys Rd. Garden is halfway down on the R. Visits by arrangement May to Sept for groups of 5 to 10. Adm £4, chd free. Home-made teas.
Urban garden with cottage style planting, with some unusual shrubs, perennials, and bulbs, which try to provide all year round colour. The garden has various seating areas with different aspects incl a summerhouse. There are two lawns, a pergola with wisteria, roses and clematis, with garden sculptures and water features. In the Spring the many containers are filled with dozens of varieties of tulips, which are followed by Agapanthus and Dahlias. Autumn colour is provided by late flowering perennials and shrubs incl Acers, Viburnams, and Cercis. The garden is constantly evolving with new plants and ideas. There are some steps and gravel paths but most of the garden can be viewed from the terrace which is wheelchair friendly. Garden entered via side gate on tarmac drive. Paved ramp down to terrace. Elsewhere there are gravel paths.

15 110 HERITAGE PARK
St Mellons, Cardiff, CF3 0DS.
Sarah Boorman, 07969499967,
sarahbooam@me.com. *Leave A48 at St Mellons junction, take 2nd exit at r'about. Turn R to Willowdene Way & R to Willowbrook Drive. Heritage Park is 1st R. Park outside the cul-de-sac.* Sat 11, Sun 12 July (1-5.30). Adm £3.50, chd free. Home-made teas. Gluten free available. Visits also by arrangement May to Aug for groups of 5 to 10. Up to 15.
An unexpected gem within a modern housing estate. Opening in July instead of May. Evergreen shrubs, herbaceous borders, box topiary and terracotta pots make for a mix between cottage garden and Italian style. With numerous seating areas and a few quirky surprises this small garden is described by neighbours as a calm oasis.

16 NEW 4 HILLCREST

Langland, Swansea, SA3 4PW.
Mr & Mrs Gareth & Penny Cross.
Approach from L, turn at Langland corner on Langland Rd Mumbles; take first L. off Higher Lane; take 3rd L. up Worcester Rd and bungalow faces you at top. **Sun 28 June (2-5). Adm £5, chd free. Home-made teas.**
Redesigned and developed over the last 5 years, our hilltop garden backs onto woodland overlooking Swansea bay and attracts many birds. We have planted large herbaceous borders with mainly perennial plants/shrubs to provide interest and colour through the seasons. The old roses are at their peak June/July. A wildlife pond and fruit/veg garden add to interest.

17 NEW LADY MARY ALLOTMENTS

Lady Mary Road, Cardiff, CF23 5NT. City of Cardiff Council, www.ladymaryallotments.org.uk.
Very close to Roath Park. The allotments are on Lady Mary Rd, just off Lake Rd East. If you enter Lady Mary Rd from the end of the road nearest the lake, the gates to the allotment site will be in front of you. **Sun 12 July (2-4.30). Adm £4, chd free. Light refreshments.**
A stone's throw from the beautiful Roath Park Lake, this group of 120 allotments is a real hidden gem. With a wide variety of fruit, vegetable and flowers cultivated by a mix of experienced and novice plot holders, there's a wealth of friendly advice on growing your own. Plants and some produce available for sale. Street parking available in nearby roads around the lake. Great views from the top of the site across Cardiff towards Caerphilly. The site is very steep so wheelchair access is difficult.

18 LLANDOUGH CASTLE

Llandough, Cowbridge, CF71 7LR.
Mrs Rhian Rees. *1½m outside Cowbridge. At the T- lights in Cowbridge turn onto the St Athan Rd. Continue then turn R to Llandough. Drive into the village follow the car park signs. Walk up a short lane and into the gardens.* **Sat 25, Sun 26 Apr (10-4.30). Adm £5, chd free. Home-made teas.**
Set within castle grounds and with a backdrop of an ancient monument, the 3½ acres of garden incl a potager

with a hint of the Mediterranean, formal lawns and herbaceous beds, a wildlife pond with waterfall and a woodland garden with stumpery and sculpture. Over 60,000 Spring bulbs have been planted including snowdrops, narcissi and tulips. Although some of the gardens are flat, areas like the woodland and gravel drive may be difficult for wheelchair access.

19 NEW LLANGAN PRIMARY SCHOOL

Llangan, Bridgend, CF35 5DR.
Llangan Primary School. *Situated on road leading from Pentre Meyrick junction towards M4 motorway just outside Llangan village. Signs for school carpark. 3m outside town of Cowbridge in Vale of Glamorgan.* **Sun 28 June (12-5). Adm £4, chd free. Home-made teas.**
We are a small primary school in the heart of beautiful countryside just ten minutes from J35 of the M4. This kitchen garden has been transformed from farmland through the vision of children, staff, parents and donations from the local community. Made up of raised vegetable/fruit beds and a sensory herb bed together with a poly tunnel, small hand planted arboretum and wildlife area. Flat paths, no steps.

20 LLANMAES GARDENS

Llanmaes, Llantwit Major, CF61 2XR. 01446796676, oldfroglands@btinternet.com. *5m S of Cowbridge. At T-lights on the B4265 turn off towards Llanmaes to Westwinds, Travel to Church House before the Church & continue down lane to Brown Lion House & on for about 1km to Old Froglands.* **Sun 26 Apr (12.30-5.30). Combined adm £5, chd free. Home-made teas at Old Froglands.**

BROWN LION HOUSE
Mrs Wendy Hewitt-Sayer.

CHURCH COTTAGE
Annie Grujic.

OLD FROGLANDS
Dorne & David Harris, 07702502950, dorneharris@hotmail.co.uk.

WESTWINDS
Ms Jackie Simpson.

Llanmaes, 1m from Llantwit Major, is a pretty village with attractive village green, stream running through and C13 church. Old Froglands is an historic farmhouse with streams and

Bordervale Plants

woodland areas linked by bridges. Ducks swim and chickens roam free. Plantings are varied with interesting foliage. Westwinds, a much loved and continuously developed cottage garden Church Cottage has a pretty garden to the rear, is newly acquired and the owner is still discovering its unknown delights. . Brown Lion House is a newly renovated garden with mature trees and shrubs, patios and pathways and a well established fish pond.

21 LLANTWIT GARDEN
21 Monmouth Way, Boverton, Llantwit Major, CF61 2GT. Don & Ann Knight. *At Llanmaes Rd, T-lights turn onto Eagleswell Rd, next L into Monmouth Way, garden ½ way down on R.* **Sun 7 June (11-5). Adm £4, chd free. Home-made teas.**
This is a Japanese style garden with a Zen gate, Torri gate and Japanese lanterns featuring a large collection of Japanese style trees, a pagoda and 3 water features which incl the great Amazon waterfall along with large Buddha's head and new Koi pond.

22 17 MAES Y DRAENOG
Maes Y Draenog, Tongwynlais, Cardiff, CF15 7JL. Mr Derek Price. *N of M4. From S: M4 , J32, take A4054 into village. R at Lewis Arms pub, up Mill Rd. 2nd R into Catherine Drive, park in signed area (no parking in Maesydraenog). Follow signs to 17 Maesydraenog.* **Sat 30, Sun 31 May (12.30-5.30). Adm £4, chd free. Light refreshments.**
A hidden gem of a garden, in the shadow of Castell Coch, fed by a mountain stream over a footbridge to naturalised areas and small woodland area. Set against a woodland backdrop. Developed over 10 yrs with a good variety of plants, filling two main borders, herbaceous plants for spring and summer displays. Garden structures, summer house, patios, greenhouse and small veg area. Natural mountain stream with wooden footbridge, Summer house, greenhouse and a good variety of plants in borders around house. Rear of house is set against woodland. Not suitable for young children and partial access for wheelchair users.

23 MAES-Y-WERTHA FARM
Bryncethin, CF32 9YJ. Stella & Tony Leyshon. *3m N of Bridgend. Follow*

sign for Bryncethin, turn R at Masons Arms. Follow sign for Heol-y-Cyw garden about 1m outside Bryncethin on R. **Sun 26 July (12-7). Adm £5, chd free. Home-made teas.**
A 3 acre hidden gem outside Bridgend. Entering the garden you find a small Japanese garden fed by a stream, this leads you to informal mixed beds & enclosed herbaceous borders. Ponds & rill are fed by a natural spring. A meadow with large lawns under new planting gives wonderful vistas over surrounding countryside. Mural in the summerhouse by contemporary artist Daniel Llewelyn Hall. His work is represented in the Royal Collection and House of Lords. Fresh hand made sandwiches available.

24 MAGGIE'S SWANSEA
Singleton Hospital, Sketty Lane, Sketty, Swansea, SA2 8QL. Miss Leanne Jennett, www.maggiescentres.org/swansea. *On the grounds of Singleton Hospital. They are next to the Genetic Building & close to the chemotherapy day unit at the back of the main hospital. Please follow yellow signs.* **Visits by arrangement May to Dec. Adm by donation.**
Maggie's Swansea's gardens wrap around the building, and overlook into Swansea Bay. The garden, designed by Kim Wilkie, attracts wildlife, heightening the natural and tranquil feel, and there is also a fully functional allotment. The Centre sits among a small wooded area, and the wings of the design also help to shelter the outside seating areas, meaning that visitors can enjoy sitting out for as much of the year as possible. Decking all the way around the building.

25 NEW 3 MONKSLAND ROAD
Scurlage, Reynoldston, Swansea, SA3 1AY. Mrs Vhairi Cotter, vhairi.cotter@btinternet.com. *From Swansea follow A4118 signed to Port Eynon. Continue until turning R onto B4247 signed to Rhossili. At Medical Centre on the L, turn into Monksland Rd, continue to 3rd house along on R.* **Sun 7 June (1.30-6). Combined adm with Overton and Port Eynon Gardens £5, chd free. Home-made teas. Tea and home-made cakes.**
This small garden, formerly mostly grass, is just 5 years old and still evolving. However it has surprisingly

mature and diverse planting that, within seven distinct areas, features everything from coastal varieties and grasses to roses, perennials and shrubs. Water features encourage wildlife, while plants and shrubs attract bees and butterflies as well as providing year-round interest. Pergola, several seating areas. An ornamental bee hunt for children.

GROUP OPENING

26 OVERTON AND PORT EYNON GARDENS
Overton Lane, Port Eynon, Swansea, SA3 1NR. Solinge22@yahoo.co.uk. *16.8m W of Swansea on Gower Peninsula. From Swansea follow A4118 to Port Eynon. Parking in public car park in Port Eynon. Yellow NGS signs showing gardens.* **Sun 7 June (2-5.30). Combined adm with 3 Monksland Road £5, chd free. Sat 11 July (2-5.30). Combined adm £5, chd free. Tea.**

THE BAYS FARM
Sol Blytt Jordens, Solinge22@yahoo.co.uk.
Open on all dates

6 THE BOARLANDS
Robert & Annette Dyer.
Open on Sun 7 June

BOX BOAT COTTAGE
Ms Christine Williams.
Open on Sun 7 June

WESTCLIFFE HOUSE
David Carlsen-Browne.
Open on Sat 11 July

The Overton gardens offer great views over the Bristol Channel. Port Eynon is the most southerly point on the Gower. Set in the heart of Port Eynon is the charming, sheltered Box Boat Cottage. The other gardens are exposed to strong winds as well as salt laden air. 6 The Boarlands is a plantsman's paradise! A gently sloping garden designed for yr-round interest .Westcliffe House is a fascinating Italian inspired garden.Gardens within gardens.The Bays Farm is an ever developing garden worked on organic principles , created for inspiration and contemplation. Great views over the Bristol Channel. Many rare and unusual plants. Lovely views over the sea. Partial wheelchair access.

Slade

27 50 PEN Y DRE
Rhiwbina, Cardiff, CF14 6EQ. Ann Franklin. *N Cardiff. M4 J32, A470 to Cardiff, 1st L to mini r'about, turn R. At T-lights in village, turn R to Pen-y-Dre.* **Sun 19 July (11-4.30). Adm £3, chd free. Home-made teas.**
Situated in the heart of the conservation area of Rhiwbina Garden Village, this north facing garden features deep herbaceous borders with a variety of cottage garden style plants and shrubs, some rare and unusual. Small pond for wildlife and veg plot. It provides a peaceful haven with year round interest. Home-made refreshments are available in the conservatory and plants for sale by the veg plot.

28 PLAS Y COED
Bonvilston, CF5 6TR. Hugh & Gwenda Child. *Plas y Coed is just off the A48 at Bonvilston. Find the Church & you will find us. Parking will be clearly marked at the Reading Rooms.* **Sat 16, Sun 17 May (10-6). Adm £5, chd free. Home-made teas.**
The garden at Plas y Coed has become more than 'just a garden' in the fifteen years we have lived here. The field that extends beyond the pond and folly is now an arboretum with close on fifty trees - trees chosen for their form, bark and colour. The garden is an interesting marriage of architecture, artwork and landscape. Partial wheelchair access.

29 164 REDLANDS ROAD
Penarth, CF64 2QR. Mrs Jane Starling. *Approx 5m SW of Cardiff. Exit M4 at J33 follow A4232 to Leckwith onto B4267 to Merry Harrier. Turn R & 1st L onto Redlands Rd. Over brow of hill on RHS. Follow NGS yellow signs.* **Sat 25, Sun 26 Apr (10-5). Light refreshments. Sat 8, Sun 9 Aug (10-5). Home-made teas. Adm £4.50, chd free.**
What you find behind the garden gate is not what you are expecting. There is a vibrant oasis at this seaside town garden. The owner cheerfully admits the garden has not really been designed, it has evolved to accommodate the now wonderful variety of plants that are its main feature. The spring garden brings hundreds of tulips and seasonal flowers into bloom. Followed by spectacular summer colour.

31 ST PETER'S COMMUNITY GARDEN
St Fagans Road, Fairwater, Cardiff, CF5 3DW. St Peter's Church. www.stpeterschurchfairwater.org.uk. *On the St Fagans Rd opp Gorse Place. Next Door to Church. A48 to Culverhousecross r'bout take A48 Cowbridge Rd West to Ely r'bout 1st L. At T-lights go L B4488 to Fairwater Green, follow yellow NGS signs.* **Sat 27, Sun 28 June (10-4). Adm £3, chd free. Home-made teas. Visits also by arrangement.**
Secret garden in city suburb. Unusual combination of flower beds, raised vegetable beds and nature reserve, all created by volunteers. Features incl a large natural pond surrounded by wild plants, Welsh heritage apple trees, long herb border and wild flower meadow. This year our major attractions will be our Quiet Garden with a zen feel - water features and monoliths. Craft, book browsing area, tasting. All day refreshments, mostly home-made, and specialist quality plant sales from various growers in South Wales. Disabled WC available. Most of the Garden wheelchair access friendly.

32 SLADE
Southerndown, CF32 0RP. Rosamund & Peter Davies, 01656 880048, rosamund.davies@ngs.org.uk, www.sladeholidaycottages.co.uk. *5m S of Bridgend. M4 J35 Follow A473 to Bridgend. Take B4265 to St. Brides Major. Turn R in St. Brides Major for Southerndown, then follow yellow NGS signs.* **Sun 16, Sun 23 Feb (2-4.30); Sat 4, Sun 5 Apr (2-5). Adm £5, chd free. Home-made teas. 2021: Sun 14, Sun 21 Feb.**
Hidden away Slade garden is an unexpected jewel to discover next to the sea with views overlooking the Bristol Channel. The garden tumbles down a valley protected by a belt of woodland. In front of the house are delightful formal areas a rose and clematis pergola and herbaceous borders. From terraced lawns great sweeps of grass stretch down the

hill enlivened by spring bulbs and fritillaries. Heritage Coast wardens will give guided tours of adjacent Dunraven Gardens with slide shows every hour from 2pm (Apr opening only). Partial wheelchair access.

33 NEW **28 SLADE GARDENS**
West Cross, Swansea, SA3 5QP. Peter and Helen Sheterline. *At the end of Slade Gardens facing Oystermouth Cemetery. Access from Mumbles Rd. Turn R at the r'about into Fairwood Rd, by Dick Bartons & then 1st L into West Cross Lane. Turn L into Bellevue Rd then straight across into Slade Gdns.* **Sun 14 June (1-5). Combined adm with 19 Slade Gardens £5, chd free. Home-made teas. Refreshments will be available both at No 19 Slade Gardens and at No 28. The two gardens are 50m apart.**
This is a recent (2 years) renovation of the old garden of the original Lodge to Oystermouth Cemetery. It is tucked under the steep limestone woodland at the eastern end of the cemetery valley and faces south overlooking the Victorian part of the cemetery. It is planted in cottage garden style with perennials and selected shrubs on the side of the hill separated from a lawn by a limestone wall. The garden can be enjoyed from the terrace of the house which is reached without climbing steps and where tea and cakes can be enjoyed. The view over the garden and 'hidden Valley' of the cemetery is a lovely surprise even for those who know Mumbles well. The scented roses should be in full bloom.

34 **19 SLADE GARDENS**
West Cross, Swansea, SA3 5QP. Norma Stephen. *5m SW of Swansea. At mini r'about on Mumbles Rd A4067 take 2nd exit (Fairwood Rd), 1st L onto West Cross Lane & follow yellow NGS signs.* **Sun 14 June (2-5). Combined adm with 28 Slade Gardens £5, chd free. Home-made teas. Refreshments will be available both at No 19 Slade Gardens and at No 28.**
A very small enclosed front and rear garden, designed to lead you around its informal planting of over 200 species. A garden to sit in! Narrow paths and steps make access difficult for less mobile visitors.

35 **38 SOUTH RISE**
Lanishen, Cardiff, CF14 0RH. Dr Khalida Hasan, 07798925320, khasan38@yahoo.co.uk. *N of Cardiff, from Llanishen Village Station Rd past Train Stn go R down The Rise or further down onto S Rise directly. Following yellow signs.* **Sat 18, Sun 19 July (11-5). Adm £4, chd free. Home-made teas. South Asian savouries and ice cream available. Visits also by arrangement in July.**
A relatively new garden backing on to Llanishen Reservoir gradually establishing with something of interest and colour all yr round. Herbaceous borders, vegetables and fruit plants surround central lawn. Wildlife friendly; variety of climbers and exotics. In front shrubs and herbaceous borders to a lawn. Stepping stones leading to children's play area and vegetable plot also at the back. Variety of home made cakes and Asian savouries such as samosas, yoghurt and chick peas chat. Wheelchair access to rear from the side of the house.

36 **SUNNY COTTAGE**
Mountain Road, Bedwas, Caerphilly, CF83 8ES. Mr & Mrs Paul & Carol Edwards. *Head E from Caerphilly to Bedwas on A468. Turn L at T-lights into village onto Church St follow rd up to St Barrwgs Church. Turn R after bridge then 1st l onto Mountain Rd. Follow NGS signs.* **Sat 6, Sun 7 June (11-4). Adm £3.50, chd free. Home-made teas.**
Terraced garden surrounded by wildlife friendly hedges. Hidden areas on the terraces are linked by paths and arches. Each level is very well stocked with a multitude of flowers, shrubs & trees. Something of interest for every season. 2 lawn areas provide a welcome splash of green. One is shaded by 2 mature apple trees. Seating areas to relax and enjoy the vistas can be found on most levels.

37 **9 WILLOWBROOK GARDENS**
Mayals, Swansea, SA3 5EB. Gislinde Macphereson, 01792 403268, gislinde@ willowgardens.idps.co.uk. *Nr Clyne Gardens. Go along Mumbles Rd to Blackpill. Turn R at Texaco garage up Mails Rd. 1st R along top of Clyne Park, at mini r'about into Westport Ave. 1st L into Willowbrook gardens.* **Sat 9 May (1-6). Sun 10 May (1-5). Adm £5, chd free. Visits also by arrangement Apr to Sept for groups of up to 30.**
Informal ½ acre mature garden on acid soil, designed to give natural effect with balance of form and colour between various areas linked by lawns; unusual trees suited to small suburban garden, especially conifers and maples; rock and water garden. Sculptures, ponds and waterfall.

GROUP OPENING

38 NEW **YSTALYFERA GARDENS**
Ystalyfera, Swansea, SA9 2AJ. *13m N of Swansea. M4 J45 take A4067. Follow signs for Dan yr Ogof caves across 5 r'abouts. After T-lights follow yellow NGS signs.* **Sat 13, Sun 14 June (12-4.30). Combined adm £5, chd free. Home-made teas at Rhosybedw and 4 Clyngwyn Road.**

4 CLYNGWYN ROAD
Paul Steer, www.artinacorner.blogspot. com.

RHOS Y BEDW
Robert & Helen Davies.

Inspiring and eclectic collection of three village gardens. Each with something different to offer visitors: a mature hillside plot with hidden treasures in every corner, a green and peaceful oasis for relaxation and a newly developed garden with garden rooms. Majestic views of the Darren Mountain and the Brecon National Park in the backgrounds. Teas and refreshments available (incl Gluten free option) to be enjoyed in restful and beautiful surroundings. Plant sales are also an attraction. Limited access for those with mobility issues.

OPENING DATES

All entries subject to change. For latest information check **www.ngs.org.uk**
Map locator numbers are shown to the right of each garden name.

March

Sunday 22nd
Llanover 16

April

Saturday 25th
Glebe House 8

Sunday 26th
Glebe House 8
NEW Pilstone House 25

May

Sunday 3rd
High House 11
The Old Vicarage 23

Saturday 9th
Park House 24

Sunday 10th
High Glanau Manor 10

Sunday 17th
The Alma 1

Saturday 23rd
Hillcrest 15

Sunday 24th
Hillcrest 15
◆ Nant y Bedd 21
Wenallt Isaf 30

Monday 25th
Hillcrest 15
◆ Nant y Bedd 21

Saturday 30th
Rockfield Park 26

Sunday 31st
Rockfield Park 26

June

Thursday 4th
Wyndcliffe Court 32

Sunday 7th
Castell Cwrt 4
Middle Ninfa Farm & Bunkhouse 19

Sunday 14th
Trengrove House 28

Saturday 20th
Longhouse Farm 17

Sunday 21st
Longhouse Farm 17

Saturday 27th
Usk Open Gardens 29

Sunday 28th
Usk Open Gardens 29

July

Friday 3rd
Mione 20

Saturday 4th
Hill House 14

Sunday 5th
Hill House 14
NEW Lynbrook 18
Mione 20

Sunday 12th
Clytha Park 6
Mione 20

Saturday 18th
14 Gwerthonor Lane 9

Sunday 19th
Birch Tree Well 2
14 Gwerthonor Lane 9
Highfield Farm 13

August

Saturday 1st
32/33 High Street 12

Sunday 2nd
32/33 High Street 12

Sunday 23rd
Croesllanfro Farm 7

September

Sunday 6th
Highfield Farm 13

Sunday 13th
Old Llangattock Farm 22

Saturday 26th
Sunnyside 27

Sunday 27th
Sunnyside 27

October

Sunday 11th
Castell Cwrt 4

By Arrangement

Arrange a personalised garden visit with your club, or group of friends, on a date to suit you. See individual garden entries for full details.

Birch Tree Well 2
Bryngwyn Manor 3
Castle House 5
Croesllanfro Farm 7
Glebe House 8
Highfield Farm 13
Hillcrest 15
Llanover 16
Longhouse Farm 17
NEW Lynbrook 18
Old Llangattock Farm 22
Sunnyside 27
Wenallt Isaf 30
Woodlands Farm 31
Wyndcliffe Court 32

Nant y Bedd

© Caroline Purvis

THE GARDENS

1 THE ALMA

Bully Hole Bottom, Usk Road, Shirenewton, NP16 6SA. Dr Pauline Ruth. *S-west facing slope overlooking valley. B4235 Usk to Chepstow signposted Bully Hole Bottom. Down hill over bridge up to T junction. Drive straight ahead along track signposted The Alma. Parking in meadow on L.* **Sun 17 May (12-6). Adm £5, chd free. Home-made teas.**
Large and beautiful sheltered SW facing garden, uncommon trees, wisteria, roses and acid loving shrubs. Long border, hot border, productive vegetable garden, old brick outbuildings, fruit cage and vines, wildlife pond, sunset arbour and stream side walk. Drive packed with native daffodils, snowdrops and bluebells in the spring. Wildflower meadow and orchard in development. Sunny terrace for teas. Wheelchair access to level terrace.
ė 🐎 ☕

2 BIRCH TREE WELL

Upper Ferry Road, Penallt, Monmouth, NP25 4AN. Jill Bourchier, 01600 775327, gillian. bourchier@btinternet.com. *4m SW of Monmouth. Approx 1m from Monmouth on B4293, turn L for Penallt & Trelleck. After 2m turn L to Penallt. On entering village turn L at Xrds & follow yellow signs.* **Sun 19 July (2-5.30). Adm £4, chd free. Home-made teas. Visits also by arrangement May to Sept for groups of up to 30.**
Situated in the heart of the Lower Wye Valley, amongst the ancient habitat of woodland, rocks and streams. These 3 acres are shared with deer, badgers and foxes. A woodland setting with streams and boulders which can be viewed from a lookout tower and a butterfly garden planted with specialist hydrangeas incl many plants to also attract bees and insects. Live music will be played (harp and cello), as well as local actors performing famous scenes from Shakespeare. Children are very welcome (under supervision) with plenty of activities in the form of treasure hunts. Not all areas of garden suitable for wheelchairs but refreshments certainly are!
ė ✿ ☕

3 BRYNGWYN MANOR

Raglan, NP15 2JH. Peter and Louise Maunder, 01291 691485, louiseviola@live.co.uk. *2m W of Raglan. Turn S (between the two garden centres) off B4598 (old A40) Abergavenny-Raglan road at Croes Bychan. House ¼ m up lane on left.* **Visits by arrangement Feb to Aug for groups of 5 to 30. Afternoon tea or light refreshments can be arranged. Please contact to discuss requirements for your group.**
3 acres. Winter Snowdrops, Daffodil walk, mature trees, walled parterre garden, mixed borders, lawns, ponds and shrubbery. All areas of the garden can be accessed without using the steps however ground is uneven and many areas consist of grass paths.
ė 🐎 ☕

4 CASTELL CWRT

Llanelen, Abergavenny, NP7 9LE. Lorna & John McGlynn. *1m S of Abergavenny. From Llanfoist B4629 signed Llanelen. ½ m R up single track rd. Approx 500yds past canal, garden entrance 2nd on L. Disabled parking. On combined opening day (June) main parking at Castell Cwrt.* **Sun 7 June (1-6). Combined adm with Middle Ninfa Farm & Bunkhouse £5, chd free. Sun 11 Oct (2-5.30). Adm £3.50, chd free. Home-made teas.**
Large informal wildlife friendly, family garden on 10 acre small holding with fine views overlooking Abergavenny. Lawns with established trees, shrubs and perennial borders. Soft fruit and vegetable gardens. Woodland and hay meadow walks, chickens and geese, bees, livestock in fields and family pets. Children very welcome, animals to see and space to let off steam. Farm Shop with own produce. Hay meadow in bloom in June, Autumn colour in October. Canal & hill Walking on the doorstep! Some gravel paths.
ė 🐎 ✿ ☕

5 CASTLE HOUSE

Castle Parade, Usk, NP15 1SD. Mr & Mrs J H L Humphreys, 01291 672563, info@uskcastle. com, www.uskcastle.com. *200yds NE from Usk centre. Access on foot signed to Usk Castle 300yds E from town square, opp Fire Station. Vehicles 400yds (next L) on Castle Parade in Usk.* **Visits by arrangement May to July for groups of 10 to 30. Also opening as part of Usk Open Gardens.**
Adm £4.50, chd free. Tea in Conservatory or Tithe Barn.
Overlooked by the romantic ruins of Usk Castle which is also open, the gardens were established over 100 years ago, with yew hedges and topiary, long border planted as a pictorial meadow, a croquet lawn and pond. The herb garden has plants that would have been used when the castle was last lived in c.1469. Most areas accessible to wheelchair users
ė 🐎 ✿ �car ☕

6 CLYTHA PARK

Abergavenny, NP7 9BW. Jack and Susannah Tenison. *Between Abergavenny (5m) & Raglan (3m). On old A40 signed Clytha at r'abouts either end.* **Sun 12 July (2-5). Adm £5, chd free. Home-made teas.**
Large C18/19 garden around lake with wide lawns and specimen trees, original layout by John Davenport, with C19 arboretum, and H. Avray Tipping influence. Visit the 1790 walled garden and the newly restored greenhouses. Lots of stalls – gundogs, crafts, plants, walking sticks, local museums, National Trust display, cider demo, Gwent Valley Commandos Motorbicycle Club, and many more. Something for everyone! Gravel and grass paths.
ė 🐎 ✿ ☕

7 CROESLLANFRO FARM

Groes Road, Rogerstone, Newport, NP10 9GP. Barry & Liz Davies, lizplants@gmail.com. *3m W of Newport. From M4 J27 take B4591 towards Risca. Take 3rd R, Cefn Walk (also signed 14 Locks Canal Centre). Proceed over bridge, cont ½ m to island in middle of rd.* **Sun 23 Aug (1.30-5). Adm £5, chd free. Home-made teas. Visits also by arrangement May to Sept.**
An informal two acre garden featuring mass planted perennials, grasses, wildflower meadow and exotic garden. Spring and early summer is a tapestry of green concentrating on leaf form and texture. Late summer, early autumn brings the the garden to a finale with an explosion of colour. A formal garden designed on 6 different levels for easy maintenance. Large barn open to the public, 'fabulous folly' and grotto. Some gravel paths and shallow steps to main area of garden.
ė ✿ 🚗 ☕

8 GLEBE HOUSE

Llanvair Kilgeddin, Abergavenny, NP7 9BE. Mr & Mrs Murray Kerr, 01873 840422, joanna@amknet.com. *Midway between Abergavenny (5m) & Usk (5m) on B4598.* **Sat 25, Sun 26 Apr (2-6). Home-made teas. Visits also by arrangement Apr to Sept. Not suitable for large coaches.**
Borders bursting with spring colour including tulips,narcissi and camassias . South facing terrace with wisteria and honeysuckle, decorative veg garden and orchard underplanted with succession of bulbs. Some topiary and formal hedging in 1½ acre garden set in AONB in Usk valley. Old rectory of St Mary's, Llanfair Kilgeddin which will also be open to view famous Victorian Scraffito Murals. Some gravel and gently sloping lawns.

& 🌼 ☕

9 14 GWERTHONOR LANE

Gilfach, Bargoed, CF81 8JT. Suzanne & Philip George. *8m N of Caerphilly. A469 to Bargoed, through the T-lights next to school then L filterlane at next T-lights onto Cardiff Rd. First L into Gwerthonor Rd, 4th R into Gwerthonor Lane.* **Sat 18, Sun 19 July (11-6). Adm £3.50, chd free. Light refreshments.**
The garden has a beautiful panoramic view of the Rhymney Valley. A real plantswoman's garden with over 800 varieties of perennials, annuals, bulbs, shrubs and trees. There are numerous rare, unusual and tropical plants combined with traditional and well loved favourites (many available for sale). A pond with a small waterfall adds to the tranquil feel of the garden.

& 🌼 ☕

10 HIGH GLANAU MANOR

Lydart, Monmouth, NP25 4AD. Mr & Mrs Hilary Gerrish, 01600 860005, helenagerrish@gmail.com. *4m SW of Monmouth. Situated on B4293 between Monmouth & Chepstow. Turn R into private rd, ¼m after Craig-y-Dorth turn on B4293.* **Sun 10 May (2-5.30). Adm £6, chd free. Home-made teas.**
Listed Arts and Crafts garden laid out by H Avray Tipping in 1922. Original features incl impressive stone terraces with far reaching views over the Vale of Usk to Blorenge, Skirrid, Sugar Loaf and Brecon Beacons. Pergola, herbaceous borders, Edwardian glasshouse, rhododendrons, azaleas,

tulips, orchard with wild flowers. Originally open for the NGS in 1927. Garden guidebook by owner, Helena Gerrish, available to purchase. Gardens lovers cottage to rent.

🌼 🚐 🛏 ☕

11 HIGH HOUSE

Penrhos, NP15 2DJ. Mr & Mrs R Cleeve. *4m N of Raglan. From r'about on A40 at Raglan take exit to Clytha. After 50yds turn R at Llantilio Crossenny. Follow NGS signs, 10mins through lanes.* **Sun 3 May (2-6). Combined adm with The Old Vicarage £6.50, chd free. Home-made teas.**
3 acres of spacious lawns and trees surrounding C16 house (not open) in a beautiful, hidden part of Monmouthshire. South facing terrace and extensive bed of old roses. Swathes of grass with tulips, camassias, wild flowers and far reaching views. Espaliered cherries, pears and scented evergreens in courtyard. Large extended pond, orchard with chickens and ducks, large vegetable garden. Partial wheelchair access, some shallow steps, sloping lawn, gravel courtyard.

& 🌼 ☕

12 32/33 HIGH STREET

Argoed, Blackwood, NP12 0HG. Graeme & Sue Moore. *2m N of Blackwood on A4048 Blackwood to Tredegar Rd, turn E into High St, Argoed.* **Sat 1, Sun 2 Aug (10-5). Adm £3.50, chd free. Home-made teas.**
This tiny gem of a garden in the village high street, packed with interesting plants, has an Italianate air with a little gravel terrace and carefully planned miniature vistas. Inspiration for anyone with a really small plot. Steepish steps make the garden unsuitable for people with limited mobility.

🐄 🌼 ☕

13 HIGHFIELD FARM

Penperlleni, Goytre, NP4 0AA. Dr Roger and Mrs Jenny Lloyd, 01873 880030, jenny.plants@btinternet.com. *4m W of Usk, 6m S of Abergavenny. Turn off the A4042 at the Goytre Arms, over railway bridge, bear L. Garden ½m on R. From Usk off B4598, turn L after Chain Bridge, then L at crossroads. Garden 1m on L.* **Sun 19 July, Sun 6 Sept (2-5). Adm £5, chd free. Home-made teas. Visits also by arrangement May to Sept**

for groups of 5+.
The garden project now is 3 years in and is starting to mature. So it's time for reconfiguration. This 3 acre garden must remain dynamic through the seasons and the years if it is to stay stimulating and rewarding. However it will remain densely planted and intimate, with narrow walks through very tall perennials and shrubs, and will contain a wide array of interesting and rare subjects. Access to almost all garden without steps.

& 🌼 🚐 ☕

14 HILL HOUSE

Church Lane, Glascoed, Pontypool, NP4 0UA. Susan & John Wright. *Between Usk & Pontypool. Approx 2m W of Usk via A472 turn L before Beaufort Arms into Glascoed Lane. Bear L up hill, Church Lane 1st turn on R. House at the very end of narrow lane, do not turn off.* **Sat 4, Sun 5 July (2-6). Adm £5, chd free. Light refreshments.**
Developing garden surrounding a modest 17thC farmhouse with fine views. Small orchard, reflecting pond, herbaceous borders, grasses, farmyard garden with standard parrotia and massed crocosmia and picket beds. Many seats. 30 mins walk through fields, steep return climb. Restricted parking, marshals in attendance. Some gravel paths. No disabled WC.

& ☕

15 HILLCREST

Waunborfa Road, Cefn Fforest, Blackwood, NP12 3LB. Mr M O'Leary & Mr B Price, 01443 837029, bev.price@mclweb.net. *3m W of Newbridge. Follow A4048 to Blackwood town centre or A469 to Pengam (Glan-y-Nant) T-lights, then NGS signs.* **Sat 23, Sun 24, Mon 25 May (11-6). Adm £4, chd free. Cream teas. Visits also by arrangement Apr to Oct for groups of up to 30.**
A cascade of secluded gardens of distinct character, all within 1½ acres. Magnificent, unusual trees with interesting shrubs,ferns and perennials. With choices at every turn, visitors exploring the gardens are well rewarded as hidden delights and surprises are revealed. Well placed seats encourage a relaxed pace to fully appreciate the garden's treasures. Delicious cream teas to be enjoyed. Tulips in April, glorious

blooms of the Chilean Firebushes, Handkerchief Tree and cornuses in May and many trees in their autumnal splendour in October. Lowest parts of garden not accessible to wheelchairs.

 ♿ 🐕 ❀ ☕

16 LLANOVER
nr Abergavenny, NP7 9EF. Mr & Mrs M R Murray, 07753 423635, www.llanovergarden.co.uk. *4m S of Abergavenny, 15m N of Newport, 20m SW Hereford. On A4042 Abergavenny - Cwmbran Rd, in village of Llanover.* **Sun 22 Mar (2-5). Adm £6, chd free. Home-made teas. Visits also by arrangement Mar to Oct for groups of 20+.**
Stunning 15 acre garden laid out in C18. The Rhyd-y-Meirch stream creates sound and movement throughout the garden as it flows into ponds, through the round garden, over cascades and beneath flagstone bridges. Children can run on the lawns, play pooh-sticks along the stream and rills or hide and seek amongst the trees, particularly the numerous early flowering magnolias. The house (not open) is the birthplace of Augusta Waddington, Lady Llanover, C19 patriot, supporter of the Welsh language and traditions. Gwerinyr Gwent will be performing Welsh folk dances during the afternoon in traditional Welsh costume. Lawns, spring bulbs, shrubs and trees. Gravel and grass paths and lawns. No disabled WC.

 ♿ 🐕 ❀ 🚗 ☕

17 LONGHOUSE FARM
Penrhos, Raglan, NP15 2DE. Mr & Mrs M H C Anderson, 01600 780389, m.anderson666@btinternet.com. *Midway between Monmouth & Abergavenny. 4m from Raglan. Off Old Raglan/Abergavenny rd signed Clytha. At Bryngwyn/Great Oak Xrds turn towards Great Oak - follow yellow NGS signs from red phone box down narrow lane.* **Sat 20, Sun 21 June (2-6). Adm £5, chd free. Home-made teas. Visits also by arrangement May to Oct for groups of 5+.**
Over the past 10 years this hidden garden with extensive views and spacious lawns has matured. The woodland walk and its series of ponds and stream will continue to develop. The productive vegetable garden has an additional fruit cage and potting shed. The avenue of malus trees seen from the south-

facing terrace are still a feature supported by borders planted with year-round colourful plants.

 ♿ ❀ ☕

18 NEW LYNBROOK
20A Castle Rise, Llanvaches, Caldicot, NP26 3BS. Gaynor & Andy Sinton, 01633 400269, sintona@hotmail.co.uk. *The house is ½ m N of Penhow on the A48. From Newport turn L off A48 at the Rock & Fountain pub. From Chepstow turn R off A48 by the Tabernacle Church.* **Sun 5 July (1-5). Adm £3, chd free. Home-made teas. Visits also by arrangement July to Sept for groups of up to 10.**
Situated in about a third of an acre this garden has been transformed over the last 15 years from a simple rectangular lawn totally surrounded by conifers to one with many contrasting features in colour, texture and shape. It has numerous shrubs and flowers some of which are quite rare, a variety of stone and metal sculptures, winding pathways, a gazebo and a cascading waterfall.

 🐕 ☕

19 MIDDLE NINFA FARM & BUNKHOUSE
Llanelen, Abergavenny, NP7 9LE. Richard Lewis, 01873 854662, bookings@middleninfa.co.uk, www.middleninfa.co.uk. *2½ m SSW Abergavenny. At A465/ B4246 junction, S for Llanfoist, L at mini r'about, B4269 towards Llanelen, ½ m R turn up steep lane, over canal. ¾ m to Middle Ninfa on R. Main parking at Castel Cwrt.* **Sun 7**

June (1-6). Combined adm with Castell Cwrt £5, chd free.
Large terraced eco-garden on east slopes of the Blorenge mountain. Vegetable beds, polytunnel, 3 greenhouses, orchard, flower borders, wild flowers. Great views, woodland walks, cascading water and ponds. Paths steep in places, unsuitable for less able. Campsite and small bunkhouse on farm. 5 mins walk uphill to scenic Punchbowl Lake and walks on the Blorenge. Wheelchairs can reach only a very limited area on sloping grass from which some of the flower beds and the general view can be seen.

 ❀ 🛏 ☕

20 MIONE
Old Hereford Road, Llanvihangel Crucorney, Abergavenny, NP7 7LB. Yvonne & John O'Neil. *5m N of Abergavenny. From Abergavenny take A465 to Hereford. After 4.8m turn L - signed Pantygelli. Mione is ½ m on L.* **Fri 3, Sun 5, Sun 12 July (10.30-6). Adm £4, chd free. Home-made teas.**
Beautiful garden with a wide variety of established plants, many rare and unusual. Pergola with climbing roses and clematis. Wildlife pond with many newts, insects and frogs. Numerous containers with diverse range of planting. Several seating areas, each with a different atmosphere.Enjoy our new benches in a secret hideaway under th pergola. Lovely home-made cakes, biscuits and scones to be enjoyed sitting in the garden or pretty summerhouse.

 ❀ ☕

Wyndcliffe Court

21 ◆ NANT Y BEDD

Grwyne Fawr, Fforest Coal Pit, Abergavenny, NP7 7LY. Sue & Ian Mabberley, 01873 890219, garden@nantybedd.com, www.nantybedd.com. *In Grwyne Fawr valley. From A465 Llanvair Crucorney, direction Llanthony, then L to Fforest Coal Pit. At grey telephone box cont for 4½ m towards Grwyne Fawr Reservoir.* For NGS: **Sun 24, Mon 25 May (2-6). Adm £5, chd free. Home-made teas.** For other opening times and information, please phone, email or visit garden website.

Blending wild and tame, 6½ acre garden described as 'Absolutely enchanting', 'of the place'. Set high in the Black Mountains by the Grwyne Fawr river with places to sit & enjoy the tranquility. An 'amazing mixture and riot of interest' with vegetables and fruit, mature trees and water. 'A lesson in working with the land and listening to what she tells you'. Productive organic vegetable and fruit gardens, stream, forest and river walk, wildflowers, natural swimming pond, treehouse, tree sculpture, shepherd's hut and eco-features. Ducks, chickens, sheep, pigs, cats. Plants and garden accessories for sale. See www.nantybedd.com for details. Important note: access for visitors with mobility issues is limited by topography and terrain. See www.nantybedd.com for full access audit.

22 OLD LLANGATTOCK FARM

Llangattock Vibon-Avel, Monmouth, NP25 5NG. Dr Cherry Taylor, 07803 853681. *4m W of Monmouth. Follow B4233 Monmouth to Abergavenny rd, turn R after approx 3m, signposted Llangattock. Follow rd for 1m. Garden is down a dirt track on the L by a lodge & pillared entrance.* **Sun 13 Sept (1-5). Adm £5, chd free. Home-made teas.** Visits also by arrangement Mar to Oct for groups of 10 to 20, due to parking being limited to 5 cars.

This is a bit different! Since 2015, it's been created from scratch using no-dig methods & is a showcase for these techniques. It's organic, wildlife rich & constantly evolving, with copious flower beds, herb terraces, vegetable gardens, greenhouses, & it's a hedgehog hotspot in 1¾ acres. Used by Charles Dowding for no-dig courses. Far-reaching views. Steps, slopes, uneven gravel & woodchip paths. By arrangement bookings will incl an explanation of the development of the garden.

23 THE OLD VICARAGE

Penrhos, Raglan, Usk, NP15 2LE. Mrs Georgina Herrmann. *3m N of Raglan. From A449 take Raglan exit, join A40 & move immed into R lane & turn R across dual carriageway. Follow yellow NGS signs. One way traffic system between Old Vicarage and High House,.* **Sun 3 May (2-6). Combined adm with High House £6.50, chd free.**

Set in the rolling Monmouthshire countryside, the Old Vicarage, a 153yr old (1867) Victorian Gothic house, is surrounded by sweeping lawns with young, mature and unusual trees. In addition to traditional and kitchen gardens, there is a parterre with a charming gazebo and a pond area. Range of spring flowers and bee friendly areas. This gem is not one to be rushed and gets better each year.

24 PARK HOUSE

School Lane, Itton, Chepstow, NP16 6BZ. Professor Bruce & Dr Cynthia Matthews. *From M48 take A466 Tintern. At 2nd r'about turn L B4293 After blue sign Itton turn R Park House is at end of lane. Parking 200m before house. From Devauden B4293 1st L in Itton.* **Sat 9 May (10-5). Adm £5, chd free. Home-made teas.**

Approx one acre garden with large vegetable areas and many mature trees, rhododendrons, azaleas, camellias in a woodland setting. Bordering on Chepstow Park Wood. Magnificent views over open country. A few small steps. and irregular paths too narrow for wheelchairs. Disabled parking adjacent to house.

25 NEW PILSTONE HOUSE

Llandogo, Monmouth, NP25 4TH. Nick and Anthea Prest. *Take A466 between Monmouth and Chepstow. Turn off at Bigsweir bridge, which is signed to Whitebrook and The Narth. follow the road for a short distance, the drive entrance is the 2nd on the left and will be indicated with NGS signs.* **Sun 26 Apr (2-5). Adm £5, chd free. Home-made teas.**

19th century garden over several acres in a spectacular south facing position, overlooking the River Wye. Surrounding the house are lawns, terraces with mixed herbaceous planting and established trees and shrubs. There is a large pond with a cascade of water spilling over millstones and the remains of an original cider mill. Some wheelchair access would be problematic, but there is access to some areas of the garden via gravel paths and stone paving.

26 ROCKFIELD PARK

Rockfield, Monmouth, NP25 5QB. Mark & Melanie Molyneux. *On arriving in Rockfield village from Monmouth, turn R by phone box. After approx 400yds, church on L. Entrance to Rockfield Park on R, opp church, via private bridge over river.* **Sat 30, Sun 31 May (10.30-4). Adm £5, chd free. Home-made teas.**

Sunnyside

Rockfield Park dates from C17 and is situated in the heart of the Monmouthshire countryside on the banks of the River Monnow. The extensive grounds comprise formal gardens, meadows and orchard, complemented by riverside and woodland walks. Possible to picnic on riverside walks. Main part of gardens can be accessed by wheelchair but not steep garden leading down to river.

♿ 🐕 ❀ ☕

27 SUNNYSIDE

The Hendre, Monmouth, NP25 5HQ. Helen & Ralph Fergusson-Kelly, 01600 714928, helen_fk@hotmail.com. *4m W of Monmouth. On B4233 Monmouth to Abergavenny rd.* **Sat 26, Sun 27 Sept (12-5). Adm £4.50, chd free. Home-made teas. Visits also by arrangement May to Oct for groups of up to 30.**
A sloping ⅓ acre garden on the old Rolls estate. There is much to be enjoyed throughout the year with formal plant and topiary structure. The garden builds to a profusion of colour towards the end of the summer from russet tones of grasses, then bold injections of scarlet, cerise, violet and gold from bulbs, perennials and trees. Quiet seating areas to enjoy views of the Monmouthshire countryside. Topiary and use of terracing. Some gravel paths.

🐕 ❀ ☕

28 TRENGROVE HOUSE

Nantyderry, Abergavenny, NP7 9DP. Guin Vaughan and Chris Jofeh. *Approx 4m N of Usk , 6m SE of Abergavenny. From Abergavenny, L off the A4042 after Llanover, signed to Nantyderry. From Usk, B4598 N to Chainbridge, then immediately L after bridge.* **Sun 14 June (1-5.30). Adm £5, chd free. Home-made teas in the garden. Gluten free and vegan cakes available.**
Garden designer's own 2½ acre country garden developed over 15 yrs along 'right plant, right place' lines. Informal borders planted for a range of conditions with interesting and some unusual shrubs, trees, perennials and grasses. The garden is managed more or less single handed. I acre meadow, managed to encourage only naturally occurring species and now supporting many wildflowers and grasses.

☕

GROUP OPENING

29 USK OPEN GARDENS

Twyn Square, Usk, NP15 1BH. 07944 616448, UskOpenGardens@gmail.com, www.uskopengardens.com. *From M4 J24 take A449, proceed 8m N to Usk exit. Free parking signposted in town. Blue badge car parking in main car parks & at Usk Castle. Map of gardens provided with ticket.* **Sat 27, Sun 28 June (10-5). Combined adm £7.50, chd free.**
Winner of Wales in Bloom for over 35yrs, Usk is full of hanging baskets and boxes and a wonderful backdrop to around 20 gardens from small cottages packed with colourful and unusual plants to large gardens with brimming herbaceous borders. Romantic garden around the ramparts of Usk Castle. Gardeners' Market with interesting plants. Great day out for all the family with lots of places to eat and drink incl places to picnic. Various cafes, PH and restaurants available for refreshments, plus volunteer groups offering teas and cakes; usually one of the gardens has a pop up Pimms, Prosecco and ice cream bar with a picnic and children's play area by their lake. Gardens allowing well-behaved dogs on leads noted on ticket/map. Usk Castle and School fully accessible but some gardens/areas of gardens are partially wheelchair accessible. Accessibility noted on ticket/map.

♿ ❀ 🚗 🏠 ☕

30 WENALLT ISAF

Twyn Wenallt, Gilwern, Abergavenny, NP7 0HP. Tim & Debbie Field, 01873832753, wenalltisaf@gmail.com. *3m W of Abergavenny. Between Abergavenny and Brynmawr. Leave the A465 at Gilwern & follow yellow NGS signs through the village. Sat navs may not be accurate due to recent road changes.* **Sun 24 May (2-5.30). Adm £5, chd free. Home-made teas. Gluten free and lactose free cakes available. Visits also by arrangement May to Sept for groups of 10+.**
A garden of nearly 3 acres designed in sympathy with its surroundings and the challenges of being 650ft up on a N facing hillside. Far reaching views of the magnificent Black Mountains, mature trees, shrubs, borders, productive vegetable garden, small polytunnel, orchard, pigs, chickens, bee hives. Child friendly with plenty of space to run about.

☕

31 WOODLANDS FARM

Penrhos, NP15 2LE. Craig Loane & Charles Horsfield, 01600 780203, Woodlandsfarmwales@gmail.com, www.woodlandsfarmwales.com. *3m N of Raglan. From A449 take Raglan exit, join A40 & move immed into R lane & turn R across dual carriageway towards Tregare. Follow NGS signs or check website for directions.* **Visits by arrangement Apr to Oct for groups of 10+. Ample parking - cars/small buses. Adm £5, chd free. Home-made teas in the Pavilion at Woodlands Farm Barns. Teas and/or wine by arrangement.**
A design led garden that's built to entertain, even your reluctant partner. The garden has opened for 11 years under the NGS. In 2020 we're opening by appointment only whilst undertaking several new projects in the garden. The 4 acre garden currently contains rooms & hidden spaces which draw you in, with buildings, ponds, viewing platforms, jetty, hard landscaping & sculptures. More next year. Beginner pottery classes and floristry classes available by arrangement. See our website for details.

🚗 🏠 ☕

32 ◆ WYNDCLIFFE COURT

St Arvans, NP16 6EY. Mr and Mrs Anthony Clay, 07710 138972, sarah@wyndcliffecourt.com, www.wyndcliffecourt.com. *3m N of Chepstow. Off A466, turn at Wyndcliffe signpost coming from the Chepstow direction.* **Thur 4 June (2-6). Adm £10. Pre-booking essential, please visit www.ngs. org.uk/events for information & booking. Home-made teas. Visits also by arrangement Apr to Sept for groups of 10+.**
Exceptional and unaltered garden designed by H. Avray Tipping and Sir Eric Francis in 1922. Arts and Crafts 'Italianate' style. Stone summerhouse, terracing and steps with lily pond. Yew hedging and topiary, sunken garden, rose garden, bowling green and woodland. Walled garden and double tennis court lawn under refurbishment. Rose garden completely replanted to a new design by Sarah Price in 2017. Not suitable for children under 12.

☕

OPENING DATES

All entries subject to change. For latest information check www.ngs.org.uk

Extended openings are shown at the beginning of the month.

Map locator numbers are shown to the right of each garden name.

April

Every day from Sunday 12th to Sunday 19th
Llyn Rhaeadr   10

Saturday 18th
NEW Plas Llwynonn   18

Saturday 25th
Llanidan Hall   9

Wednesday 29th
◆ Plas Cadnant Hidden Gardens   17

May

Every day from Sunday 24th to Sunday 31st
Llyn Rhaeadr   10

Sunday 3rd
Gilfach   5
Maenan Hall   12

Sunday 17th
Bryn Gwern   1
Llys-y-Gwynt   11

Saturday 23rd
Cae Newydd   2
Mynydd Heulog   13

Sunday 24th
Cae Newydd   2
Mynydd Heulog   13

Monday 25th
Cae Newydd   2

Saturday 30th
Gwaelod Mawr   6

Sunday 31st
Gwaelod Mawr   6

June

Sunday 7th
◆ Pensychnant   15

Saturday 13th
Crowrach Isaf   4
Pentir Gardens   16

Sunday 14th
Crowrach Isaf   4

Saturday 20th
Llanidan Hall   9

Sunday 21st
NEW Plas Llwynonn   18

Saturday 27th
Pen y Bryn   14

Sunday 28th
Llys-y-Gwynt   11
Pen y Bryn   14

July

Saturday 4th
Llanidan Hall   9

Sunday 5th
Gilfach   5
Gwyndy Bach   7

Saturday 11th
Swn-Y-Gwynt   19

Saturday 18th
NEW Cae Rhydau   3

Sunday 19th
NEW Cae Rhydau   3
Maenan Hall   12
◆ Pensychnant   15

Sunday 26th
Bryn Gwern   1

August

Sunday 2nd
Llanfechell Allotments 8

Saturday 29th
Llyn Rhaeadr   10

Sunday 30th
Llyn Rhaeadr   10

Monday 31st
Llyn Rhaeadr   10

September

Saturday 19th
Treborth Botanic Garden, Bangor University   20

By Arrangement

Arrange a personalised garden visit with your club, or group of friends, on a date to suit you. See individual garden entries for full details.

Bryn Gwern   1
Crowrach Isaf   4
Gilfach   5
Gwyndy Bach   7
Llyn Rhaeadr   10
Llys-y-Gwynt   11
Mynydd Heulog   13
Pen y Bryn   14
Ty Capel Ffrwd   21

Tan Raalt

THE GARDENS

1 BRYN GWERN

Llanfachreth, Dolgellau, LL40 2DH. H O & P D Nurse, 01341 450 255, antique_pete@btinternet.com. *5m NE of Dolgellau. Do not go to Llanfachreth, stay on Bala rd, A 494, 5m from Dolgellau, 14m from Bala.* Sun 17 May, Sun 26 July (10-5). Adm £4, chd free. Cream teas. **Visits also by arrangement May to Sept.**

Sloping 2 acre garden in the hills overlooking Dolgellau with views to Cader Idris, originally wooded but redesigned to enhance its natural features with streams, ponds and imaginative and extensive planting and vibrant planting. The garden is now a haven for wildlife with hedgehogs and 26 species of birds feeding last winter as well as being home to ducks, dogs and cats. Dogs must be on a lead. Stone mason at work and items for sale or orders taken.

2 CAE NEWYDD

Rhosgoch, Anglesey, LL66 0BG. Hazel & Nigel Bond. *3m SW of Amlwch. A5025 from Benllech to Amlwch, follow signs for leisure centre & Lastra Farm. Follow yellow NGS signs (approx 3m), car park on L.* Sat 23, Sun 24, Mon 25 May (11-4). Adm £4, chd free. Light refreshments. Bank Holiday Mon may be DIY teas.

A mature country garden of 2½ acres which blends seamlessly into the open landscape with stunning views of Snowdonia and Llyn Alaw. Variety of shrubs, trees and herbaceous areas, large wildlife pond, polytunnel, greenhouses, raised vegetable beds. Collections of fuchsia, pelargonium, cacti & succulents. An emphasis on gardening for wildlife throughout the garden. Hay meadow. Lots of seating throughout the garden, visitors are welcome to bring a picnic. Garden area closest to house suitable for wheelchairs.

3 NEW CAE RHYDAU

Caeathro, Caernarfon, LL55 2TN. Ms Lieneke van der Veen & Mr Victor van Daal. *4m E of Caernarfon. Take A4086 from Caernarfon to Llanberis. After narrow bridge take R to Bontnewydd and* then immed L. Follow signs Lieneke's Flowers. Take the 2nd track on R. Sat 18, Sun 19 July (11-4.30). Adm £3.50, chd free. Home-made teas.

Formerly a dairy mill. A Dutch couple started in 2000 redesigning the gardens of a 14 acre smallholding. One acre garden contains a variety of plants, shrubs, trees and grasses. Garden accessed along an 800 metres footpath through woodlands and fields. The garden is bordered on one side by a stream. Sitting areas in the sun and shade in several places. Very peaceful, no through road. Free flower arranging workshop by Award winning florist who will help you to make a buttonhole using flowers from the garden.

4 CROWRACH ISAF

Bwlchtocyn, LL53 7BY. Margaret & Graham Cook, 01758 712860, crowrach_isaf@hotmail.com. *1½m SW of Abersoch. Follow rd through Abersoch & Sarn Bach, L at sign for Bwlchtocyn for ½m until junction & no-through rd - TG Holiday Complex. Turn R, parking 50 metres on R.* Sat 13, Sun 14 June (1-5). Adm £4, chd free. Cream teas. **Visits also by arrangement May to Sept for groups of 20+.**

2 acre plot developed from 2000, incl island beds, windbreak hedges, vegetable garden, wild flower area and wide range of geraniums, unusual shrubs and herbaceous perennials. Views over Cardigan Bay and Snowdonia. Grass and gravel paths, some gentle slopes. Parking at garden for disabled visitors.

5 GILFACH

Rowen, Conwy, LL32 8TS. James & Isoline Greenhalgh, 01492 650216, isolinegreenhalgh@ btinternet.com. *4m S of Conwy. At Xrds 100yds E of Rowen S towards Llanrwst, past Rowen School on L, turn up 2nd drive on L.* Sun 3 May, Sun 5 July (2-5.30). Adm £3.50, chd free. Home-made teas. **Visits also by arrangement Apr to Aug.**

1 acre country garden on S-facing slope with magnificent views of the River Conwy and mountains; set in 35 acres of farm and woodland. Collection of mature shrubs is added to yearly; woodland garden, herbaceous border and small pool. Spectacular panoramic view of the Conwy Valley and the mountain range of the Carneddau. Classic cars. Large coaches can park at bottom of steep drive, disabled visitors can be driven to garden by the owner.

6 GWAELOD MAWR

Caergeiliog, Anglesey, LL65 3YL. Tricia Coates. *6m E of Holyhead. ½m E of Caergeiliog. From A55 J4. r'about 2nd exit signed Caergeiliog. 300yds, Gwaelod Mawr is 1st house on L.* Sat 30, Sun 31 May (11-4). Adm £4, chd free. Home-made teas.

2 acre garden created by owners over 20 yrs with lake, large rock outcrops and palm tree area. Spanish style patio and laburnum arch lead to sunken garden and wooden bridge over lily pond with fountain and waterfall. Peaceful Chinese orientated garden offering contemplation. Separate Koi carp pond. Abundant seating throughout. Mainly flat, with gravel and stone paths, no wheelchair access to sunken lily pond area.

7 GWYNDY BACH

Tynlon, Llandrygarn, LL65 3AJ. Keith & Rosa Andrew, 01407 720651, keithandrew.art@gmail.com. *5m W of Llangefni. From Llangefni take B5109 towards Bodedern, cottage exactly 5m out on L. Postcode good for SatNav.* Sun 5 July (11-4.30). Adm £4. Home-made teas. **Visits also by arrangement May to July for groups of 5 to 30.**

¾ acre artist's garden, set amidst rugged Anglesey landscape. Romantically planted in informal intimate rooms with interesting rare plants and shrubs, box and yew topiary, old roses and Japanese garden with large Koi pond (deep water, children must be supervised). Gravel entrance to garden.

Your visits help change lives – your generosity helps Marie Curie fund nurses to care for people night and day in their homes, with donations of more than £9 million

Plas Cadnant Garden

© Val Corbett

8 LLANFECHELL ALLOTMENTS
Brynddu Road, Llanfechell, Amlwch, LL68 0PU. Mike Harris, Secretary. *5m NW of Amlwch, 1m S of Cemaes on Anglesey. From Amlwch on A5025 take L just before Cemaes: from Holyhead on A5025 take R just before Cemaes: from Llangefni, take R at Sportsman's Lodge in Rhosgoch then follow NGS signs.* Sun 2 Aug (10-3). Adm £3.50, chd free. Tea in nearby community cafe.

Established just a few years ago and building on initial success, we now have 18 plots with sheds/greenhouses, and grow a variety of vegetables, soft fruit and flowers. Visit Llanfechell church and/or take a short local walk (maps available at the community shop/cafe) to complete your visit! Cafe open 11am to 3pm, off rd parking in field adj to allotments.

9 LLANIDAN HALL
Brynsiencyn, LL61 6HJ. Mr J W Beverley (Head Gardener). *5m E of Llanfair PwII. From Llanfair PG follow A4080 towards Brynsiencyn for 4m. After Hooton's farm shop on R take next L, follow lane to gardens.* Sat 25 Apr, Sat 20 June, Sat 4 July (10-4). Adm £4, chd free. Home-made teas. Donation to CAFOD.
Walled garden of 1¾ acres. Physic

and herb gardens, ornamental vegetable garden, herbaceous borders, water features and many varieties of old roses. Sheep, rabbits and hens to see. Children must be kept under supervision. Well behaved dogs on leads welcome. Llanidan Church will be open for viewing. The walled garden will be open early in the season for viewing of the spring bulbs. No plant sale at spring opening. Hard gravel paths, gentle slopes.

10 LLYN RHAEADR
15 Parc Bron-y-Graig, Centre of Harlech, LL46 2SR. Mr D R Hewitt & Miss J Sharp, 01766 780224. *From A496 take B4573 into Harlech, take turning to main car parks S of town, L past overspill car park, garden 75yds on R.* Daily Sun 12 Apr to Sun 19 Apr (2-5). Daily Sun 24 May to Sun 31 May (2-5). Sat 29, Sun 30, Mon 31 Aug (2-5). Adm £3.50, chd free. Visits also by arrangement Mar to Sept. Donation to W.W.F.

Landscaped hillside garden blending natural areas with garden plants, shrubs and trees with wildlife, small lake with many species of unusual ducks, fish and wildlife ponds, waterfalls, woodland, gazebos, rockeries, lawns, borders, snowdrops,

daffodils, bluebells, ferns, heathers, camellias, azaleas, rhododendrons, wild flowers. Good paths and seating views of Tremadog Bay, Lleyn Peninsula. Waterfowl collection, dogs allowed on a lead.

11 LLYS-Y-GWYNT
Pentir Road, Llandygai, Bangor, LL57 4BG. Jennifer Rickards & John Evans, 01248 353863. *3m S of Bangor. 300yds from Llandygai r'about at J11, A5 & A55, just off A4244. Follow signs for services (Gwasanaethau). Turn off at no through rd sign, 50yds beyond. Do not use SatNav.* Sun 17 May, Sun 28 June (11-4). Adm £4, chd free. Home-made teas. Visits also by arrangement. £5 to incl tea/coffee & biscuits.

Interesting, harmonious and very varied 2 acre garden incl magnificent views of Snowdonia. An exposed site incl Bronze Age burial cairn. Winding paths and varied levels planted to create shelter, yr-round interest, microclimates and varied rooms. Ponds, waterfall, bridge and other features use local materials and craftspeople. Wildlife encouraged, well organised compost. Good family garden.

12 MAENAN HALL

Maenan, Llanrwst, LL26 0UL.
The Hon Mr & Mrs Christopher
Mclaren. *2m N of Llanrwst. On E
side of A470, ¼ m S of Maenan
Abbey Hotel.* Sun 3 May, Sun 19
July (10.30-4.30). Adm £4, chd
free. Home-made teas. Donation
to Wales Air Ambulance.
A superbly beautiful 4 hectares on
the slopes of the Conwy Valley, with
dramatic views of Snowdonia, set
amongst mature hardwoods. Both
the upper part, with sweeping lawns,
ornamental ponds and retaining walls,
and the bluebell carpeted woodland
dell contain copious specimen
shrubs and trees, many originating at
Bodnant. Magnolias, rhododendrons,
camellias, pieris, cherries and
hydrangeas, amongst many others,
make a breathtaking display. Upper
part of garden accessible but with
fairly steep slopes.

13 MYNYDD HEULOG

Llithfaen, Pwllheli, LL53 6PA. Mrs
Christine Jackson, 01758 750400,
christine.jackson007@btinternet.
com. *From A499 take B4417 road
at r'about signed Nefyn, approx
3m enter Llithfaen, 1st R turn opp
chapel. Follow NGS signs, garden
last property on R, limited parking.*
Sat 23, Sun 24 May (10.30-4.30).
Adm £3.50, chd free. Cream teas.
Visits also by arrangement in May.
Donation to Dog's Trust.

Mynydd Heulog is an C18 stone
cottage set in approx. 1 acre of
sloping garden with amazing views
over the Lleyn and Cardigan Bay.
Gradually being developed over
25 years, the garden is now an
eclectic mix of mature trees, shrubs,
perennials and exotics. Features incl
arches, statues, bridges, summer
house and shepherds hut. Large
terrace and verandah with views and
secret seating areas. narrow paths.

14 PEN Y BRYN

Boduan, Pwllheli, LL53 8UY.
Sandra and Stephen
Deer, 07967101328,
stevedeer@hotmail.com. *4½ m
NW of Pwllheli. A497 Pwllheli to
Nefyn, in 4m pass lay by & AA box
on R. 200yds on take L turn. Signs
will be situated approx 300 yards
along lane. B4354 from Y Ffor, L at
T junction, turn 1st R & follow signs.*
Sat 27, Sun 28 June (11-5). Adm
£3.50, chd free. Home-made teas.
Visits also by arrangement Apr to
July for groups of 5 to 30.
A ¾ acre garden with eclectic mix of
wildlife & lily ponds, gravel gardens,
mixed borders, small orchard,
dell & bog garden, new potager
garden & fountain, interlaced with
meandering gravel paths & brick
steps to accommodate the gentle
slope. Mature shrubs & trees create
secluded, intimate seating areas
to enjoy the tranquillity & glimpses

of distant views to the coast, Garn
Fadryn & Garn Boduan. Partial
wheelchair access to part of the
garden but only if the ground is dry.
Please contact us beforehand and we
will do our best to accommodate.

15 ♦ PENSYCHNANT

Sychnant Pass, Conwy, LL32 8BJ.
Pensychnant Foundation; Warden
Julian Thompson, 01492 592595,
jpt.pensychnant@btinternet.com,
www.pensychnant.co.uk. *2½ m W
of Conwy at top of Sychnant Pass.
From Conwy: L into Upper Gate St;
after 2½ m Pensychnant's Dr signed
on R. From Penmaenmawr: fork R,
up Pass, after walls U turn L into
drive.* For NGS: Sun 7 June, Sun
19 July (10-5). Adm £3.50, chd
free. Home-made teas. For other
opening times and information,
please phone, email or visit garden
website.
Wildlife Garden. Diverse herbaceous
cottage garden borders surrounded
by mature shrubs, banks of
rhododendrons, ancient and Victorian
woodlands. 12 acre woodland walks
with views of Conwy Mountain
and Sychnant. Woodland birds.
Picnic tables, archaeological trail on
mountain. A peaceful little gem. Large
Victorian Arts and Crafts house (open)
with art exhibition. Partial wheelchair
access, please phone for advice.

Maenan Hall

© Carole Drake

GROUP OPENING

PENTIR GARDENS

Pentir, Bangor, LL57 4YA. *Pentir 3m S of Bangor, Gwynedd. A4244 from J11 of A55/A5, continue for 1.7m to Pentir. Either turn L, follow car park signs to field (LL574YB), or proceed, turn R signed Caerhun to car park opp church (LL574EA).* **Sat 13 June (12-5). Combined adm £5, chd free. Home-made teas at Bryn Meddyg.** Donation to Ogwen Valley Mountain Rescue, Llanberis Mountain Rescue.

NEW   BRYN HYFRYD
Mr John Turner.

BRYN MEDDYG
Mr Wyn James.

TAN RALLT
John Lewis & Gary Carvalho.

TY UCHAF
Sian Lewis.

Starting from Pentir square, Ty Uchaf: a small densely packed garden with a wide variety of cottage favourites, plus raised beds and willow lattice. It enjoys a romantic-feel, prioritising colour and texture. The secret gate takes visitors to neighbouring Bryn Meddyg, serving refreshments within a large garden comprising mature shrubs, with several island beds, vegetable garden, soft fruit and secluded seating. A 600-yard walk takes you to Bryn Hyfryd, a front garden set to lawn, borders and pond, and via archway to rear garden with stunning views of Snowdonia and owner's champion Shetland sheep, with kitchen garden and mixed planting. Continue along the lane, a few minutes' walk, to Tan Rallt, backing onto Moel y Ci, the one acre stunningly diverse garden includes a range of mature trees and shrubs, vegetable and soft fruit, herbaceous borders and areas of lawn. Diversely planted pond with tree ferns, bog plants, and giant Gunnera. Adjacent to the Field car park (LL57 4YB), there is an attractive large lake (with safety restrictions). Alongside, is the Village Vicarage, with a small Prayer Garden, that you are welcome to visit for quiet contemplation, and with access to a toilet. There is an alternative access to Bryn Meddyg for wheelchair access. There is restricted disabled access at Ty Uchaf and Bryn Hyfryd.

  ♿ 🐄 ✿ ☕ 🌿

⬛ ◆ PLAS CADNANT HIDDEN GARDENS

Cadnant Road, Menai Bridge, LL59 5NH. Mr Anthony Tavernor, 01248 717174, plascadnantgardens@gmail.com, www.plascadnantgardens.co.uk. *½ m E of Menai Bridge. Take A545 & leave Menai Bridge heading for Beaumaris, then follow brown tourist information signs. Sat Nav not always reliable.* **For NGS: Wed 29 Apr (12-5). Adm £7.50, chd £2. Light refreshments in traditional Tea Room.** For other opening times and information, please phone, email or visit garden website. Donation to Wales Air Ambulance; Anglesey Red Squirrel Trust; Menai Bridge Community Heritage Trust.

Early C19 picturesque garden undergoing restoration since 1996. Valley gardens with waterfalls, large ornamental walled garden, woodland and early pit house. Recently created Alpheus water feature and Ceunant (Ravine) which gives visitors a more interesting walk featuring unusual moisture loving Alpines. Restored area following flood damage. Guidebook available. Visitor centre open. Partial wheelchair access to

Cae Rhydau

parts of gardens. Some steps, gravel paths, slopes. Access statement available. Accessible Tea Room and WC.

 ♿ 🐕 ✿ 🚐 ☕

18 NEW PLAS LLWYNONN
Llanedwen, Llanfairpwllgwyngyll, LL61 6DQ. The Marquis of Anglesey. *2m E of Llanfairpwll. From Llanfairpwll follow A4080 towards Brynsiencyn for 2m. 100yds after Plas Newydd National Trust entrance, turn R at lodge house. Over cattle grid and follow track through parkland for 500yds.* Sat 18 Apr, Sun 21 June (11-4). Adm £4, chd free. Home-made teas.
A Plas Newydd Estate grade 2 listed building. 3 acres semi formal and wild gardens. Espalier pears, grapes, kiwi and Welsh Heritage apple orchard. Surrounded by 12 acres of woodland - snowdrops, wild garlic, bluebells and daffodils until late spring. Picnic areas and benches throughout the gardens and woods. Abundance of birdlife and red squirrels. Walled kitchen garden with Victorian Peach House. Bee hives. If wet, ground can be very soft.

 ♿ 🐕 ✿ ☕

19 SWN-Y-GWYNT
High Street, Llanberis, Caernarfon, LL55 4EN. Keith & Olwen Chadwick. *Llanberis, at the foot of Snowdon. From all directions head towards the village of Llanberis. Turn off the A4086, follow NGS sign onto Llanberis High St then a green sign for Swn-y-Gwynt with the driveway entrance and private car park.* Sat 11 July (11-4.30). Adm £3.50, chd free. Home-made teas.
A S-facing terraced garden with dramatic views of Snowdon and surrounding hills. Steep slate steps lead to the garden comprising of a variety of conifers, mature acers, azaleas, rose bed and herbaceous perennial border with a variety of spring bulbs complemented by hellebores and ferns. There is also a secluded small pond area leading onto slate steps towards a Scots pine terraced area. Children must be supervised at all times.

 🐕 ✿ ☕

20 TREBORTH BOTANIC GARDEN, BANGOR UNIVERSITY
Treborth, Bangor, LL57 2RQ. Natalie Chivers, treborth.bangor.ac.uk. *On the outskirts of Bangor towards Anglesey. Approach Menai Bridge either from Upper Bangor on A5 or leave A55 J9 & travel towards Bangor for 2m. At Antelope Inn r'bout turn L just before entering Menai Bridge.* Sat 19 Sept (10-1). Adm £4, chd free. Home-made teas.
Owned by Bangor University and used as a resource for teaching, research, public education and enjoyment. Treborth comprises planted borders, species rich natural grassland, ponds, arboretum, Chinese garden, ancient woodland, and a rocky shoreline habitat. Six glasshouses provide specialised environments for tropical, temperate, orchid and carnivorous plant collections. Partnered with National Botanic Garden of Wales to champion Welsh horticulture, protect wildlife and extol the virtues of growing plants for food, fun, health and wellbeing. Glasshouse and garden Q&As. Wheelchair access to some glasshouses and part of the garden. Woodland path is surfaced but most

of the borders only accessed over grass.

 ♿ 🐕 ✿ 🚐 ☕

21 TY CAPEL FFRWD
Llanfachreth, Dolgellau, LL40 2NR. Revs Mary & George Bolt, 01341 422006, maryboltminstrel@gmail.com. *4m NE of Dolgellau, 18m SW of Bala. From Dolgellau 4m up hill to Llanfachreth. Turn L at War Memorial. Follow lane ½ m to chapel on R. Park & walk down lane past chapel to cottage.* Visits by arrangement Apr to Sept for groups of 5 to 10. Individual visitors or groups welcome. Adm £4, chd free. Home-made teas.
True cottage garden in Welsh mountains. Azaleas, rhododendrons, acers; large collection of aquilegia. Many different hostas give added strength to spring bulbs and corms. Stream flowing through the garden, 10ft waterfall and on through a small woodland bluebell carpet. For summer visitors there is a continuous show of colour with herbaceous plants, roses, clematis and lilies, incl Cardiocrinum giganteum. Harp will be played in the garden.

 🐕 ✿ ☕

Gwyndy Bach

© Fiona Lea

OPENING DATES

All entries subject to change. For latest information check **www.ngs.org.uk**

Map locator numbers are shown to the right of each garden name.

February

Snowdrop Festival
Wednesday 19th
Aberclwyd Manor   1
Clwydfryn   8

March

Wednesday 11th
Aberclwyd Manor   1

Wednesday 25th
Aberclwyd Manor   1

April

Wednesday 8th
Aberclwyd Manor   1

Wednesday 22nd
Aberclwyd Manor   1

May

Wednesday 6th
Aberclwyd Manor   1

Wednesday 20th
Aberclwyd Manor   1

Saturday 23rd
Hafodunos Hall   16

Monday 25th
Garthewin   14

Sunday 31st
Brynkinalt Hall   5

June

Wednesday 3rd
Aberclwyd Manor   1

Saturday 6th
The Laundry   18

Sunday 7th
The Laundry   18

Saturday 13th
Plas Coch   22

Sunday 14th
Plas Coch   22

Wednesday 17th
Aberclwyd Manor   1

Sunday 21st
Tal-y-Bryn Farm   25

Saturday 27th
Llanarmon-yn-Ial Village
  Gardens   19

Sunday 28th
The Beeches   2
White Croft   28

July

Wednesday 1st
Aberclwyd Manor   1

Saturday 4th
33 Bryn Twr and Lynton 4
Plas Ashpool   21

Sunday 5th
33 Bryn Twr and Lynton 4
The Cottage Nursing
  Home   9

Wednesday 8th
Firgrove   13

Wednesday 15th
Aberclwyd Manor   1

Wednesday 22nd
Firgrove   13

Sunday 26th
Caereuni   6

Wednesday 29th
Aberclwyd Manor   1

August

Wednesday 5th
Firgrove   13

Wednesday 12th
Aberclwyd Manor   1

Saturday 15th
NEW 1 Pen y Bont
  Cottage   20

Wednesday 19th
Firgrove   13

Sunday 23rd
NEW Cedar Gardens   7

Wednesday 26th
Aberclwyd Manor   1

Sunday 30th
Caereuni   6
NEW 1 Pen y Bont
  Cottage   20

Monday 31st
Caereuni   6
NEW 1 Pen y Bont
  Cottage   20

September

Wednesday 2nd
Firgrove   13

Sunday 6th
NEW Saith Ffynnon
  Farm   24

Wednesday 9th
Aberclwyd Manor   1

Thursday 10th
Brynkinalt Hall   5

Sunday 13th
◆ Erlas Victorian Walled
  Garden   12

Wednesday 23rd
Aberclwyd Manor   1

Sunday 27th
Caereuni   6

By Arrangement

Arrange a personalised garden visit with your club, or group of friends, on a date to suit you. See individual garden entries for full details.

Aberclwyd Manor   1
5 Birch Grove   3
33 Bryn Twr and Lynton 4
Brynkinalt Hall   5
Dolhyfryd   10
Dove Cottage   11
Garthewin   14
Gwel Yr Ynys   15
Hilbre, Manor Close   17
Plas Ashpool   21
Plas Y Nant   23
Tal-y-Bryn Farm   25
Ty Brombil   26
Ty Hwnt Yr Afon   27
White Croft   28

Plas Ashpool

THE GARDENS

1 ABERCLWYD MANOR

Derwen, Corwen, LL21 9SF.
**Miss Irene Brown & Mr G
Sparvoli, 01824 750431,
irene662010@live.com.** *7m from
Ruthin. Travelling on A494 from
Ruthin to Corwen. At Bryn SM
Service Station turn R, follow sign
to Derwen. Aberclwyd gates on L
before Derwen. Do not follow sat nav
directions .* **Wed 19 Feb, Wed 11,
Wed 25 Mar, Wed 8, Wed 22 Apr,
Wed 6, Wed 20 May, Wed 3, Wed
17 June, Wed 1, Wed 15, Wed 29
July, Wed 12, Wed 26 Aug, Wed
9, Wed 23 Sept (11-4). Adm £3.50,
chd free. Cream teas. Visits also
by arrangement for groups of 10
to 30.**
4 acre garden on a sloping hillside
overlooking the Upper Clwyd Valley.
The garden has many mature trees
underplanted with snowdrops,
fritillaries and cyclamen. An Italianate
garden of box hedging lies below
the house and shrubs, ponds,
perennials, roses and an orchard are
also to be enjoyed within this cleverly
structured area. Mass of cyclamen in
Sept. Abundance of spring flowers.
Cyclamen in August/September.
Snowdrops in February. Mostly flat
with some steps and slopes.

2 THE BEECHES

Vicarage Lane, Penley, LL13 0NH.
Stuart & Sue Hamon. *Western edge
of village. From Overton 1st L after
20mph sign towards Adrefelyn. From
Whitchurch go along A539 through
village & turn R just after church, to
Adrefelyn. N.B. SatNavs may show
Vicarage Lane as Hollybush Lane.*
**Sun 28 June (1-5). Adm £4, chd
free. Home-made teas.**
The garden surrounds an 1841 former
vicarage and extends to 3½ acres.
It has been redesigned to create an
attractive open garden laid mainly to
lawn with a mixture of over 40 mature
and younger specimen trees. There
are shrub, rose and herbaceous
beds together with a productive
vegetable and fruit area. The walled
courtyard has tender plants incl many
varieties of agapanthus and hostas.
We are delighted to announce that
Bernard Porter, The Head Gardener
at Bridgemere Nursery in south
Cheshire, will be on hand to answer
visitors gardening questions. Bernard

Bronallt

has over 30yrs professional gardening
experience incl running the 6 acre,
award winning, garden at Bridgemere.
A mostly flat garden with gravelled
paths. Grass is usually firm allowing
easy access. Courtyard access has
three very shallow steps.

3 5 BIRCH GROVE

Woodland Park, Prestatyn,
LL19 9RH. **Mrs Iris
Dobbie, 01745 886730,
iris.dobbie@ngs.org.uk.** *A547
from Rhuddlan turn up The Avenue,
Woodland Park after railway bridge
1st R into Calthorpe Dr, 1st L Birch
Gr. 10 mins walk from town centre
- at top of High St, turn R & L onto
The Avenue.* **Visits by arrangement
May to Sept for groups of up to
20. Adm £3, chd free.**
A well established town garden
on three sides of this property.
The gardens consist of a variety
of borders incl woodland, grass,
herbaceous, alpine, shrub, drought,
tropical and a simulated bog garden
with a small pond. The more formal
front garden is lawned with borders

of mixed colourful planting and box
balls. A small greenhouse is fully used
for propagation and storing tender
plants. Gravel drive, few steps.

4 33 BRYN TWR AND LYNTON

Lynton, Highfield Park, Abergele,
LL22 7AU. **Mr & Mrs Colin
Knowlson and Bryn Roberts
& Emma Knowlson-Roberts,
07712 623836, apk@slaters.ltd.**
*From A55 heading W take slip rd into
Abergele town centre. Turn L at 2nd
set of T-lights signed Llanfair TH, 3rd
rd on L. For SatNav use LL22 8DD.*
**Sat 4, Sun 5 July (1-5). Adm £4.50,
chd free. Home-made teas. Visits
also by arrangement in July.**
Bryn Twr is a family garden with
chickens, shrubs ,roses, pots & Lawn.
Lynton completely different , intense
cottage style garden. Veg, Trees,
shrub, roses, ornamental grasses &
lots of pots. Garage with interesting
fire engine; cars and memorabilia;
greenhouse over water capture
system. Partial wheelchair access.

5 BRYNKINALT HALL

Brynkinalt, Chirk, Wrexham, LL14 5NS. Iain & Kate Hill-Trevor, 01691 773425, kate@brynkinalt.co.uk, www.brynkinalt.co.uk. *6m N of Oswestry, 10m S of Wrexham. Come off A5/A483 and take B5070 into Chirk village. Turn into Trevor Rd (beside St Mary's Church). Continue past houses on R. Turn R on bend into Estate Gates. N.B. Do not use postcode with SatNav.* **Sun 31 May, Thur 10 Sept (12-4). Adm £5, chd free. Home-made teas. Visits also by arrangement for groups of 20 to 30.**
5 acre ornamental woodland shrubbery, overgrown until recently, now cleared and replanted, rhododendron walk, historic ponds, well, grottos, ha-ha and battlements, new stumpery, ancient redwoods and yews. Also 2 acre garden beside Grade II* house (see website for opening), with modern rose and formal beds, deep herbaceous borders, pond with shrub/mixed beds, pleached limes and hedge patterns. Home of the first Duke of Wellington's grandmother and Sir John Trevor, Speaker of House of Commons. Stunning Rhododendrons and formal West Garden. Partial wheelchair access. Gravel paths in West Garden and grass paths and slopes in shrubbery.

6 CAEREUNI

Ffordd Ty Cerrig, Godre'r Gaer, Corwen, LL21 9YA. Mr S Williams. *1m N of Corwen. A5 Corwen to Bala rd, turn R at T-lights onto A494 to Chester. 1st R after lay by. House ¼m on L.* **Sun 26 July (2-5). Sun 30, Mon 31 Aug (2-5), also open 1 Pen y Bont Cottage. Sun 27 Sept (2-5). Adm £4.50, chd free.**
A plants man's garden of rare trees, shrubs, topiary and containers of tender plants set in a quirky themed much loved ⅓ acre garden, incl a Japanese smoke water feature & Italian Tuscany conifers. Also a seaside beach with wild grass sand plumes, a welsh gold mine, old ruin & a Chinese peace garden. There is a Mexican Chapel, 1950's petrol garage, wood mans lodge & a new Harry Potter Tower. No teas at Caeruni but Glyndwr Plant Centre and Coffee Shop LL12 9BU approx 1m from garden.

7 NEW CEDAR GARDENS

Llanbedr Hall, Llanbedr Dyffryn Clwyd, Ruthin, LL15 1YD. Mr Peter Jones. *For directions please go to cedargardens.co.uk & click map to download a copy. Also there will be the usual yellow signs to follow.* **Sun 23 Aug (11-4). Adm £3.50, chd free. Light refreshments.**
This tranquil garden is made up of two gardens with the top one featuring a 300 year old Cedar of Lebanon tree. As you wander along to the lower secret garden, there is a rill running through the lower part of the large lawn. At the end of the path is a garden room where refreshments will be served, and adjoining this there are two patios on different levels with beds full of colourful planting. Jacket potatoes and homemade cakes available.

8 CLWYDFRYN

Bodfari, LL16 4HU. Keith & Susan Watson. *5m outside Denbigh. ½ way between Bodfari & Llandyrnog on B5429. Yellow signs at bottom of lane.* **Wed 19 Feb (11-4). Adm £4, chd free. Home-made teas.**
¾ acre garden developed from a field, which has had many changes over the past 30 years. Extensive collection of snowdrops. Orchard with various fruit trees now well established. Vegetable and colourful garden planting below the orchard. Alpine garden with sand plunge beds for alpines and bulbs. Greenhouse with many interesting succulents. Garden access to a paved area at back of house for wheelchair users.

9 THE COTTAGE NURSING HOME

54 Hendy Road, Mold, CH7 1QS. Mr. A.G. Lanini. *12m W of Chester. From Mold town centre take A494 towards Ruthin then follow yellow NGS signs.* **Sun 5 July (2-5). Adm £2, chd £0.50. Light refreshments.** Donation to British Heart Foundation.

The Laundry

© Joe Wainwright

Beautiful garden set in approx 1 acre. Well-established shrubs, herbaceous plants and abundance of colourful window boxes and tubs. Recently re-modelled garden we have now added a waterfall feature incl a fish pond and small area to grow vegetables. The central courtyard has two water features. At the bottom of the garden lies a wooden summer house and extended seating.

♿ ⊞ ✿ ☕

10 DOLHYFRYD
Lawnt, Denbigh, LL16 4SU. Captain & Mrs Michael Cunningham, 01745 814805, virginia@dolhyfryd.com. *1m SW of Denbigh. On B4501 to Nantglyn, from Denbigh - 1m from town centre.* Visits by arrangement Mar to Oct for groups of up to 30. Adm £5, chd free.
Established garden set in small valley of River Ystrad. Acres of crocuses in late Feb/early Mar. Paths through wildflower meadows and woodland of magnificent trees, shade loving plants and azaleas; mixed borders; walled kitchen garden. Many woodland and riverside birds, incl dippers, kingfishers, grey wagtails. Many species of butterfly encouraged by new planting. Much winter interest, exceptional display of crocuses. Gravel paths, some steep slopes.

♿ ⊞ ✿ ☕

11 DOVE COTTAGE
Rhos Road, Penyffordd, Chester, CH4 0JR. Chris & Denise Wallis, 01244 547539, dovecottage@supanet.com. *6m SW of Chester. Leave A55 at J35 take A550 to Wrexham. Drive 2m, turn R onto A5104. From A541 Wrexham/Mold Rd in Pontblyddyn take A5104 to Chester. Garden opp train stn.* Visits by arrangement May to Aug for groups of 5+. Adm £4, chd free. Home-made teas.
Approx 1½ acre garden, shrubs and herbaceous plants set informally around lawns. Established vegetable area, 2 ponds (1 wildlife), summerhouse and woodland planted area. Gravel paths.

♿ ✿ ☕ ⊞ ☕

12 ◆ ERLAS VICTORIAN WALLED GARDEN
Bryn Estyn Road, Wrexham, LL13 9TY. Richard Lewis, 01978 265058, info@erlas.org, www.erlas.org. *From A483 follow signs for the Wrexham Ind Est. From*

A5156 follow signs to Wrexham on A534 (Holt Rd). At 2nd r'about on Holt Rd take 1st L on to Brynestyn Rd, for ½ m. For NGS: Sun 13 Sept (10.30-3.30). Adm £3.50, chd free. Light refreshments. For other opening times and information, please phone, email or visit garden website.
Home of the Erlas Victorian Walled Garden charity, our garden is a place of work, solace & inspiration for adults of all abilities. A garden of 4 parts: The Walled Garden has many delights including a centuries-old Mulberry tree; The West Garden is full of fruit, veg, herbs & our Roundhouse; The Orchard has a mixture of Apple & Pear varieties. Our ecology area provides a haven for flora & fauna. We have wheelchair access throughout the garden, however it is on a slope, but the gradient is not too extreme.

♿ ⊞ ✿ ☕

13 FIRGROVE
Llanfwrog, Ruthin, LL15 2LL. Philip & Anna Meadway, 01824 702677, meadway@ firgrovecountryhouse.co.uk, www.firgrovecountryhouse.co.uk. *1½ m SW of Ruthin. Take the A494 out of Ruthin. At mini r'about go straight onto B5105 to Cerrig y Drudion. Pass St. Mwrog Church on your R & follow road for approx ½ m. Firgrove is on the R.* Wed 8, Wed 22 July, Wed 5, Wed 19 Aug, Wed 2 Sept (11.30-3.30). Adm £4, chd free. Light refreshments.
1½ acre garden with a variety of mature trees and shrubs giving structure with under planting of unusual and colourful plants. A wide variety of clematis climbing trees and shrubs add splashes of colour all through the season. Brugmansias and exotic plants are scattered around the garden in a variety of planters. Lawns and gravel paths offer walks to discover areas to rest and look at the view. Only a very small area of garden is on level ground and care must be taken on slippery sloping lawns,and uneven narrow paths with gravel surfaces.

⊞ 🛏 ☕

14 GARTHEWIN
Llanfairtalhaiarn, LL22 8YR. Mr Michael Grime, 01745 720288, michaelgrime12@btinternet.com. *6m S of Abergele & A55. From Abergele take A548 to Llanfair TH & Llanrwst. Entrance to Garthewin 300yds W of Llanfair TH on A548 to Llanrwst. SatNav misleading.* Mon 25 May (2-6). Adm £5, chd free. Home-made

teas. Visits also by arrangement Apr to Oct for groups of up to 30.
Valley garden with ponds and woodland areas. Much of the 8 acres have been reclaimed and redesigned providing a younger garden with a great variety of azaleas, rhododendrons and young trees, all within a framework of mature shrubs and trees. Teas in old theatre. Chapel open. Some stalls to promote local arts, crafts and foods.

⊞ ☕

15 GWEL YR YNYS
Parc Moel Lus, Penmaenmawr, LL34 6DN. Mr Dafydd Lloyd-Borland, 01492 621319, lloydborland@gwelyrynys.com, www.gwelyrynys.com. *Full directions will be given on booking.* Visits by arrangement Apr to Sept for groups of 10+. Adm £4, chd free. Refreshments to be agreed upon booking.
A dynamic and exciting ¾ acre hillside garden 650ft above sea level. Imaginative landscaping has been undertaken to complement and blend with the countryside beyond. Natural planting incl a large range of herbaceous plants shrubs and trees. Garden structure benefits from streams, freshwater pond, woodland 'dell' area, bog garden and many ferns and hostas. Excellent views out to sea. Chickens. Most areas accessible for wheelchair users.

♿ ⊞ ✿ ☕ ☕

16 HAFODUNOS HALL
Llangernyw, Abergele, Conwy, LL22 8TY. Dr Richard Wood, www.hafodunoshall.co.uk. *1m W of Llangernyw. ½ way between Abergele & Llanrwst on A548. Signed from opp Old Stag Public House. Parking available on site.* Sat 23 May (12-5). Adm £5, chd free. Home-made teas in Victorian conservatory.
Historic garden undergoing restoration after 30yrs of neglect surrounds a Sir George Gilbert Scott Grade I listed Hall, derelict after arson attack. Unique setting. ½ m tree-lined drive, formal terraces, woodland walks with ancient redwoods, laurels, yews, lake, streams, waterfalls and a gorge. Wonderful rhododendrons. Uneven paths and steep steps. Children must have adult supervision at all times. Most areas around the hall accessible to wheelchairs by gravel pathways. Some gardens are set on slopes.

♿ ⊞ ✿ ☕ ☕

17 HILBRE, MANOR CLOSE
Manor Close, Bishop Wood Rd, Prestatyn, LL19 9PH. Robert & Margaret Smith, 01745853628, margaret.smith810@btinternet.com. *From A458 turn N at T-lights up Ffordd Las, turn 2nd R before top of the hill into Stoneby Dr, 1st L onto Orme View Dr then first L Manor Close. Park anywhere near here. Walk up grass track.* **Visits by arrangement Mar to Aug for groups of up to 20. Adm £3, chd free. Home-made teas. Teas may be arranged when booking.**
Hilbre is surrounded by a cottage garden with fish pond and soft fruit. One side has hostas, heucheras and geraniums, the other side has hellebores, cyclamen and fuchsias. In spring the garden is full of daffodils and tulips. In the last few yrs it has been steeply terraced with different narrow levels featuring a woodland walk, orchard, wild flower garden and climbing roses. Sea views from top. Wheelchair access to front garden. Steep steps lead to the terraces and are unsuitable for people with walking difficulties.

🐾 ✿ ☕

18 THE LAUNDRY
Llanrhaeadr, Denbigh, LL16 4NL. Mr & Mrs T Williams, 01745 890515, tomjenny@btinternet.com, thelaundryretreat.co.uk. *3m SE of Denbigh. Entrance off A525 Denbigh to Ruthin Rd.* **Sat 6, Sun 7 June (2-6). Adm £5, chd free. Home-made teas. Visits also by arrangement May to Sept.**
Terraced courtyard garden developed since 2009 surrounded by old stone walls enclosing cottage style planting and formal hedging. 7yrs ago work started on the old kitchen walled garden with a view to incorporating it within the whole garden plan. A chance to see a new garden evolving within an old setting. Woodland walk, roses, pleached limes, peonies and herbaceous planting. Some deep gravel areas, may prove difficult for wheelchair users.

♿ ✿ 🚗 🛏 ☕

GROUP OPENING

19 LLANARMON-YN-IAL VILLAGE GARDENS
Ffordd Rhiw Ial, Llanarmon-Yn-Ial, Mold, CH7 4QE. *6m SW of Mold. From Mold to Ruthin Rd (A494) turn into B5430. After 2 miles turn R to B5431 into Llanarmon. Or 3m from*

A525 & A5104, join B5430 and turn L to Llanarmon. Drop off at Raven Inn. Follow carpark signs. **Sat 27 June (11-4). Combined adm £6, chd free. Light refreshments at The Old Schoolroom. Donation to Church of St Garmon.**

ARDWYN
Gill & Pete Hodson.

BRONALLT
Brenda & Tony Rigby.

NEW FIELDFARE
Peter & Vicky O'Neill.

12A MAES IAL
Beryl Campbell.

Entering Llanarmon-yn-Ial from the B5430 drive over the ancient stone bridge, up the hill to The Old Schoolroom - Yr Hen Ysgoldy. Tickets & refreshments available here & limited disabled parking. Some parking in the village or follow signs for main car park 350 yards out of village on Llandegla Road. Maps of gardens incl with ticket. The gardens are all close to the heart of the village and tickets will also be available at some gardens and main car park. The people of Llanarmon-yn-Ial have been successfully running the Raven Inn and Village Shop as community ventures for many years now.

✿ ☕

20 NEW 1 PEN Y BONT COTTAGE
Llanfihangel Glyn Myfyr, Corwen, LL21 9UH. Ms Suryiah Evans. *Between Cerrigydrudion and Clawddnewydd on the B5105. Follow the B5105 towards Ruthin or Cerrigydrudion (depending on direction of travel). When you reach Llanfihangel Glyn Myfyr, garden is located by the village bridge & Crown Inn.* **Sat 15 Aug (12-4.30). Sun 30, Mon 31 Aug (12-4.30), also open Caereuni. Adm £2.50, chd free. Cream teas.**
This quirky north-facing garden is set against the beautiful backdrop of the Hiraethog moors. It features ornamental shrubs, perennial borders and unusual design features that have been developed to accommodate the challenging landscape. Visitors can explore the ¼-acre garden via a circular route. Delicious cakes and refreshments are available.

🐾 🚗 ☕

21 PLAS ASHPOOL
Llandyrnog, LL16 4HP. Fiona Bell, 07813087797. *5m outside Denbigh. ½ way between Bodfari & Llandyrnog on B5429.* **Sat 4 July (1.30-5.30). Adm £5, chd free. Home-made teas. Visits also by arrangement June to Sept for groups of up to 20.**
This country house garden with views of the Clwydian hills and Vale of Clwyd was developed over 40yrs ago by present owner's family and is now undergoing restoration. The herbaceous and shrub borders, orchard, vegetable garden and sunken rose garden are surrounded by historic farm buildings, now being rescued from disrepair. Wild flowers, hens, bees and pigs complete this rural picture. Partial wheelchair access.

♿ ✿ ☕

22 PLAS COCH
Llanychan, Ruthin, LL15 1UF. Sir David & Lady Henshaw, Enquiries@annedd.com. *Situated on B5429 between villages of Llandyrnog & Llanbedr DC.* **Sat 13, Sun 14 June (10.30-4). Adm £4.50, chd free. Home-made teas.**
Well established country garden with deep and varied herbaceous borders, vegetable garden and fruit trees with recently planted heritage variety small orchard. Other sections incl small yard garden, pond areas, three seater tybach (outside privy) MG TC 1949, all in the centre of the vale of Clwyd with extensive views towards the Clwydian Hills. Wheelchair access but gravel paths.

✿ 🛏 ☕

23 PLAS Y NANT
Llanbedr Dyffryn Clwyd, Ruthin, LL15 1YF. Lesley & Ian, 01824 705444, lesley.callister@ngs.org.uk. *From A494 turn onto B5429 Graigfechan, a pprox 1m, 4th turning L private rd. If using Satnav follow postcode LL15 2YA. Proceed through farmyard continue & keep L, uphill to cottage on R, go straight onto forest track. Travel 0.8m on track, drive on R.* **Visits by arrangement. Adm £4, chd free. Light refreshments. To be discussed when booking.**
Listed Gothic Villa in a serene upland valley (AONB) amid seven acres of gardens, bluebell woods and stream. Rhododendrons, magnolia and specimen trees abound, formal parterre of clipped box and yew. Embryonic Dragon's Head rose garden and trelliage. Procession of seasonal

colour led by snowdrops, primroses and daffodils. Other aspects incl water features, loggia, summer and greenhouses, beehives. Dragon Head carved into fallen tree trunk that has formed an archway over Ha-Ha.

White Croft

24 NEW SAITH FFYNNON FARM

Downing Road, Whitford, Holywell, CH8 9EN. Mrs Jan Miller-Klein, www.7wells.co.uk. *1m outside Whitford village. from Holywell follow signs for Pennant Park Golf Course. Turn R just past the Halfway House. Take 2nd lane on R (signed for Downing & Trout Farm) & Saith Ffynnon Farm is the 1st house on R.* **Sun 6 Sept (12-4). Adm £4, chd free. Home-made teas.** Donation to Plant Heritage.
Wildlife Garden 1 acre and re-wilded meadows of 8 acres, incl ponds, woods, wildflower meadows, butterfly and bee gardens, Medieval herbal knot garden, natural dye garden and the Plant Heritage National Collection of Eupatorium. Guided walks with ID charts of wildflowers, trees, butterflies and other wildlife, and collecting seed to take home. NWWT stands with Reptiles, remote cameras and other displays. Moth trap from night before to be opened when enough visitors are watching. All children must be accompanied by an adult. Hard surface from gate to patio and 2 sections of the garden. No wheelchair access on the damp meadows.

25 TAL-Y-BRYN FARM
Llannefydd, Denbigh, LL16 5DR. Mr & Mrs Gareth Roberts, 01745 540256, falmai@villagedairy.co.uk, www.villagedairy.co.uk. *3m W of Henllan. From Henllan take rd signed Llannefydd. After 2½m turn R signed Llaeth y Llan. Garden ½m on L.* **Sun 21 June (2-5). Adm £5, chd free. Tea/coffee and a piece of Bara Brith incl in adm. Visits also by arrangement Apr to Sept. Refreshments to be discussed when booking.**
Medium sized working farmhouse cottage garden. Ancient farm machinery. Incorporating ancient privy festooned with honeysuckle, clematis and roses. Terraced arches, sunken garden pool and bog garden, fountains and old water pumps. Herb wheels, shrubs and other interesting features. Lovely views of the Clwydian range. Water feature, new rose tunnel,

vegetable tunnel and small garden summer house.

26 TY BROMBIL
Broomhill Lane, Denbigh, LL16 3NH. Mr & Mrs Christopher Sanders, 01745 813852, c-sanders@btconnect.com. *Denbigh Town Centre. Closest council car park LL16 3TS. Walk up alley to High St. Garden Gate is next door to Halifax BS. Entry phone button for House.* **Visits by arrangement Apr to Sept for groups of up to 20. Adm £3, chd free. Refreshments to be arranged upon booking.**
Open the gate to a unique hidden garden below a striking contemporary home. The house and garden are located on a very steep and rocky site. The garden consists of several outdoor 'rooms' at various levels linked by short flights of steps between the buildings. Stone walls, architectural planting, fruit trees, vines and pots make for a rare and very interesting private urban garden. Steep steps could make access difficult for less mobile visitors.

27 TY HWNT YR AFON
Rowen, Conwy, LL32 8YT. Ian & Margaret Trevette, 01492 650871, ian.trevette@btopenworld.com. *Take B5106 from Conwy, R at Groes Inn. Follow signs. Park on rd below Ty Gwyn Hotel, garden 500yds thru village on L fork in rd. Disabled parking on drive.* **Visits by**

arrangement May to Aug. Adm £3, chd free. Home-made teas.
¾ acre garden re-landscaped by owners over last 7yrs. With the backdrop of R Ro and preserved woodland beyond have used the gardens natural features of glacial stone, stream and springs to create an amphitheatre of garden shrubs and plants incl spring bulbs, acers, azaleas, camellias, rhododendrons and a multitude of other favourite perennials. Wheelchair access to view most of garden and for home-made teas on the sun terrace provided by Friends of Llandudno Rotary Club. Some steps.

28 WHITE CROFT
19 Ffordd Walwen, Lixwm, Holywell, CH8 8LW. Mr & Mrs John & Mary Jones, 01352781829, fforddwalwen1@talktalk.net. *From A541 turn onto the B5121 for Lixwm, From A55 come off at J32 or J32A. Drive South, follow Lixwm signs.* **Sun 28 June (1-5). Adm £4, chd free. Home-made teas. Visits also by arrangement May to Sept for groups of 10 to 20.**
Wrap around garden incl Cottage style planting, Dahlia bed, Rock garden, Vegetable plot, Fruit trees. Greenhouse, Stream and Fish pond, Pergola, Balcony views over Clwydian Range and Japanese style garden. The garden has been established over the last 8 yrs. It was originally just lawn and conifer trees. A double garage containing a Westfield Kit Car and a sports car. Car park available.

OPENING DATES

All entries subject to change. For latest information check www.ngs.org.uk

Map locator numbers are shown to the right of each garden name.

April

Saturday 4th
Gorsty House   23

Sunday 5th
Gorsty House   23

Saturday 18th
NEW Abercamlais
House   1

Tuesday 21st
NEW Bryngwyn Hall   7

Sunday 26th
Little House,
Llandinam   29

May

Sunday 3rd
Llangoed Hall Hotel   30

Saturday 9th
◆ Dingle Nurseries &
Garden   14

Sunday 10th
◆ Dingle Nurseries &
Garden   14

Saturday 16th
Rock Mill   46

Sunday 17th
◆ Gregynog Hall &
Garden   25
Penmyarth House -
Glanusk Estate   39
Rock Mill   46

Sunday 24th
Glanwye   21

Monday 25th
Llwyn Madoc   31
Llysdinam   33

Wednesday 27th
◆ Grandma's Garden   24

Thursday 28th
White Hopton Farm   55

Saturday 30th
NEW Celynfa   11
◆ Milebrook House
Garden   35

Sunday 31st
NEW Celynfa   11
◆ Milebrook House
Garden   35
The Rock House   45

June

Saturday 6th
Bryncelyn   6
Tranquillity Haven   50

Sunday 7th
Bryncelyn   6
The Neuadd   37
Tranquillity Haven   50

Tuesday 9th
White Hopton Farm   55

Friday 12th
The Rock House   45

Saturday 13th
Stockton Mill   48

Sunday 14th
Hurdley Hall   27

Saturday 20th
Church House   12
Tremynfa   52
1 Ystrad House   56

Sunday 21st
Church House   12
Tremynfa   52
1 Ystrad House   56

Saturday 27th
Little House,
Llandinam   29

Sunday 28th
Pen-y-Maes   40
NEW Pontrobert
Gardens   44

July

Saturday 4th
Hurdley Hall   27
NEW Llys Celyn   32

Sunday 5th
Cwm-Weeg   13
Hurdley Hall   27
NEW Llys Celyn   32

NEW South Street
Gardens   47
Talgarth Mill   49
Treberfydd House   51

Saturday 11th
Bachie Uchaf   3

Sunday 12th
Bachie Uchaf   3
The Hymns   28

Saturday 18th
NEW 1 Glanrafon   19

Sunday 19th
Fraithwen   15
NEW 1 Glanrafon   19

Wednesday 22nd
White Hopton Farm   55

Saturday 25th
Blaen-y-Cwm   4
Bryn Teg   5
Ponthafren   43

Sunday 26th
Blaen-y-Cwm   4
Bryn Teg   5

August

Saturday 1st
Caebardd   9
◆ Welsh Lavender   54
1 Ystrad House   56

Sunday 2nd
Caebardd   9
Hurdley Hall   27
◆ Welsh Lavender   54
1 Ystrad House   56

Sunday 9th
Garthmyl Hall   17

Saturday 15th
NEW Cefnsuran Farm   10

Sunday 16th
NEW Cefnsuran Farm   10

Saturday 22nd
Ponthafren   43

September

Saturday 5th
Little House,
Llandinam   29

Sunday 13th
Llangoed Hall Hotel   30

Wednesday 16th
◆ Glansevern Hall
Gardens   20

Thursday 17th
◆ Glansevern Hall
Gardens   20

October

Saturday 10th
Tranquillity Haven   50

Sunday 11th
Tranquillity Haven   50

Saturday 17th
◆ Dingle Nurseries &
Garden   14

Sunday 18th
◆ Dingle Nurseries &
Garden   14

Sunday 25th
Gliffaes Country House
Hotel   22

By Arrangement

Arrange a personalised garden visit with your club, or group of friends, on a date to suit you. See individual garden entries for full details.

Abernant   2
NEW Brynteg   8
Caebardd   9
Fraithwen   15
NEW Fron Heulog   16
Gilwern Barn   18
Hebron   26
Hurdley Hall   27
The Hymns   28
Llysdinam   33
Maesfron Hall and
Gardens   34
NEW Nant y Cyff   36
The Neuadd   37
NEW Osprey Studios   38
Pen-y-Maes   40
Plas Dinam   41
Pont Faen House   42
Ponthafren   43
Rock Mill   46
Tranquillity Haven   50
Tremynfa   52
Tyn y Cwm   53
White Hopton Farm   55
1 Ystrad House   56

THE GARDENS

1 NEW **ABERCAMLAIS HOUSE**
Abercamlais, Brecon, LD3 8EY. Mr
Anthony and Mrs Andrea Ballance,
www.abercamlais.com. *6m W of
Brecon. Take the A40 from Brecon
towards Sennybridge. After 6m turn
R immed after the bus stop and
follow yellow NGS signs to the car
park.* **Sat 18 Apr (11-4). Adm £6,
chd free. Home-made teas.**
Abercamlais is a splendid Grade 1
listed mansion house set in extensive
grounds. At the entrance is a lodge
and a beautiful drive contains a
Wellingtonia, a Metasequoia and
some fine Oak trees. There is a fine
octagonal dovecote which used to
be a privy. The grounds also contain
a unique Victorian suspension bridge
that leads to a large walled garden
which is currently being restored.
Easy access to some parts of the
garden. No wheelchair access over
the suspension bridge, however, there
is an alternative route via a stone
bridge.

2 **ABERNANT**
Garthmyl, SY15 6RZ. Mrs
B M Gleave, 01686 640494,
john.gleave@mac.com. *1½ m S of
Garthmyl. On A483 midway between
Welshpool & Newtown (both 8m).
Approached over steep humpback
bridge with wooden statue of a
workman to one side, then straight
ahead to the house & parking.* **Visits
by arrangement Mar to Aug for
groups of 5 to 30. Adm £4, chd
free. Home-made teas.**
Approx 3 acres incl orchard with
stunning display of cherry blossom
in April (85 trees). Knot garden,
box hedging, roses, rockery, pond,
shrubs, ornamental trees, examples
of archaic sundials, fossilised
wood and stone heads. Additional
woodland of 9 acres with borrowed
views of the Severn Valley. Formal
rose garden recently replanted. 85
cherry trees in blossom in late April.
Roses in late June. Picnics welcome
from 12pm.

3 **BACHIE UCHAF**
Bachie Road, Llanfyllin, SY22 5NF.
Glyn & Glenys Lloyd. *S of Llanfyllin.
Going towards Welshpool on A490
turn R onto Bachie Rd after Llanfyllin
primary school. Keep straight for*
*0.8m. Take drive R uphill at cottage
on L.* **Sat 11, Sun 12 July (1.30-5).
Adm £4.50, chd free. Home-made
teas.**
Inspiring, colourful hillside country
garden. Gravel paths meander
around extensive planting & over
streams cascading down into ponds.
Specimen trees, shrubs & vegetable
garden. Enjoy the wonderful views
from one of the many seats; your
senses will be rewarded. Winner Best
Flower & Shrub Garden, Llanfyllin
Show and Winner Montgomeryshire
Agricultural Assoc Best Garden
Competition 2019.

4 **BLAEN-Y-CWM**
Llanbister Road, Llandrindod
Wells, LD1 6SR. Brian and Glyn
Allez. *Take A483 N from Llandrindod
Wells to Llanbister, turn R on
B4356 for 2.5 miles to crossroads
at Crossways Farm, turn R signed
Cantal and follow yellow signs for
1m.* **Sat 25, Sun 26 July (1-5). Adm
£4.50, chd free. Home-made teas.**
4 acre oasis in middle of common
land at 1100' started in 2011 and
ongoing. Extensive lawns with mature
trees, orchard with large duck pond,
streams with bridges, very productive
fruit & vegetable garden, polytunnels
with olives, fig, cape gooseberries;
raised veg beds, fruit cage. Gravel
garden and formal borders, large
rockery, lawns. Free range Indian
Runner ducks, hens, quail, beehives.

Plants, jams, preserves, chutney,
honey and eggs for sale. Greetings
cards for sale. Partial wheelchair
access. Featured in County Times &
Welsh Country magazine.

5 **BRYN TEG**
Bryn Lane, Newtown, SY16 2DP.
Novlet Childs. *N side of Newtown.
Take Llanfair Caereinion Rd towards
Bettws Cedewain and turn L before
hospital. Up hill on L.* **Sat 25 July
(10-5), also open Ponthafren. Sun
26 July (1-5). Adm £3.50, chd free.
Home-made tea and cakes at
Ponthafren on Saturday only.**
Amazing exotic secret Caribbean
garden in centre of Newtown planted
to remind me of my childhood in
Jamaica. An exciting walk through
the jungle. High above the head are
banana leaves & colourful climbers. A
winding path takes you on a journey
through another land. Sounds of
water fill the air; explosion of colourful
intermingling flowers & plants with
giant leaves -paulownia, bamboos,
tetrapanex,. A huge number of plants
on many levels. All shapes, sizes and
colours mixed together as found in
tropical jungles. Feel transported to
another continent. Even in the rain
you will get that jungle experience.
Manual wheelchair access to most of
the garden. Not suitable for mobility
scooters.

Bryncelyn

© Caroline Pears

6 BRYNCELYN
Lluest Lane, Cwmnantymeichaid, Llanfyllin, SY22 5NE. Rosemary Clarke. *Going towards Welshpool on A490 turn R onto Bachie Rd after Llanfyllin primary school. Follow the NGS signs, keep on the Bachie Road for 1½ m. Turn L where the road widens at top of rise.* **Sat 6, Sun 7 June (1-5). Adm £4.50, chd free. Home-made teas.**
3 acre country garden and paddocks. Spectacular backdrop of near hills with views to Cefn Coch & Berwyns. Deep beds of perennial planting with mature trees & shrubs chosen to attract birds and insects; circular walk beside the lake and stream. Meet the resident donkeys and peacocks, find a seat and indulge in your own thoughts and lose yourself in the tranquillity of this achingly special place. Children's play area (supervision required) and children's garden quiz. Partial wheelchair access over gravel area then brick path and grass; excellent views.
& 🐕 ✿ ☕

7 NEW BRYNGWYN HALL
Bwlch-y-Cibau, Llanfyllin, SY22 5LJ. Lady A Linlithgow, www.bryngwyn.com. *3m SE Llanfyllin. From Llanfyllin take A490 towards Welshpool for 3m turn L up drive just before Bwlch-y-Cibau.* **Tue 21 Apr (10-4). Adm £5, chd free. Home-made teas.**
Stunning grade 11* listed 9 acre garden with 60 acres parkland design inspired by William Emes. Prunus subhirtella 'Autumnalis', varieties of hamamelis, mahonia, early flowering daphnes, corylopsis and chimonanthus. Woodland garden carpeted with snowdrops then stunning show of thousands of daffodils, camassias and fritillaries in the long grass down to serpentine lake. Unusual trees and shrubs & unique Poison Garden.
& 🐕 🏠 ☕

8 NEW BRYNTEG
Old Road, Bwlch, Brecon, LD3 7NJ. Maria Pritchard, 01874 730582, m-pritchard@live.co.uk. *4m NW of Crickhowell. Access to Old Rd entrance situated next to the only village public house, The New Inn. Brynteg is situated 300m from the main A40.* **Visits by arrangement Mar to Oct for groups of up to 20. Adm £4, chd free. Light refreshments. please contact**

prior to visit to discuss dietary requirements.
Brynteg, built 1887 with an interesting background & unique garden, situated in the Brecon Beacons National Park with unobstructed views of the Black Mountains. Herbaceous Borders, herb beds fruit & specimen trees. Spend the day at a creative or wellbeing workshop offered to small groups within the beautiful setting of Brynteg. Contact me for info and booking. We look forward to welcoming you. An established Magnolia welcomes all who visit Brynteg. Half of the garden is accessible.
& ✿ 🏠 ☕

9 CAEBARDD
Guilsfield, Welshpool, SY21 9DJ. Sandy Jones, 07816 527344. *From Londis petrol station on A490 nr Guilsfield continue towards Llanfyllin for approx 2m & turn L following NGS signs on single track lane.* **Sat 1, Sun 2 Aug (1-6). Adm £4, chd free. Home-made teas. Visits also by arrangement July to Sept for groups of up to 30.**
A meandering garden with established trees & shrubs circling large pond. Dry stone walls support banks of herbs, wild & herbaceous flowers. Paths lead to hidden Japanese corner with waterfall, bamboos, acers & bridge. Short walk across farmyard to wild meadow full of wildflowers with interlacing paths to raised bed veg plot between orchard & walnut grove. 10 mins hike to top of farm boasts magnificent 100 degree views of Long Mountain, Rodney's Pillar, Shropshire plains around to Berwyns. Cadair Berwen and Allt y Main. Seat at summit to sit and catch your breath. Children's Quiz/treasure hunt. Most of main garden has wheelchair access but paths in wild meadow are too narrow.
& 🐕 ✿ 🏠 ☕

10 NEW CEFNSURAN FARM
Llangunllo, Knighton, LD7 1SL. Gill and Gordon Morgan, cefnsuran@hotmail.com, www.cefnsuran.co.uk. *6m west Knighton. A488 from Knighton towards Llandrindod Wells. After 4m turn R B4356. After 1m turn R sign post Cefnsuran/Rally School follow track 3/4 m.* **Sat 15, Sun 16 Aug (1-5). Adm £4.50, chd free. Home-made teas.**
1 acre sheltered farmhouse garden set in hollow at 1000 ft in beautiful

secluded location. Surrounded by fields, ponds and woodland with wonderful selection of shrubs, trees & flowers plus a wild flower area & an ancient hollow oak. Easy access to all of the garden. Walks can be taken around the two large ponds, along farm trails and also the Glyndwr Way which passes through our garden. Wildlife haven with bees, house martins and swallows. sloping paths mainly level lawns.
& 🏠 ☕

11 NEW CELYNFA
Pen-Y-Bont, Oswestry, SY10 9FN. Joanne Dale. *9m SW Oswestry. From Oswestry S on A483 to Llynclys Xrds (3.4m from A5) turn R on A495 for 4½ m signed Llansantffraid, turn R on B4396 signed Bala then R signed Llansilin & follow yellow NGS signs.* **Sat 30, Sun 31 May (2-5). Adm £4, chd free. Home-made teas. Gluten Free cake options will be available.**
Garden established around 10 years ago & wraps around a stone barn. Set in the stunning Tanat Valley with superb views it has a little bit of everything. Beautifully designed with deep herbaceous borders, a mixture of formal & naturalistic planting, kitchen garden, fruit trees, soft fruits and vegetables. There are plenty of places to sit & enjoy the views with a cup of tea and home-made cake. My Artist studio will be open for visitors to see original artwork.
🐕 ☕

12 CHURCH HOUSE
Llandefalle, Brecon, LD3 0ND. Mr & Mrs Chris & Anne Taylor. *Between Brecon and Llyswen, off A470, signposted Llandefalle, then single track lane for ½ mile. Parking is next to Church.* **Sat 20, Sun 21 June (2-5.30). Adm £4, chd free. Home-made teas.**
One acre garden, subdivided into different areas, each with its own character incl orchard. Skilfully landscaped in the 1980s to provide terraces, generous borders and year round interest. New owners have added small pond, herb garden and rill. Tranquil places to sit and enjoy refreshments with fine views to Black Mts. Next to St Matthew's 15th century Church with notable earlier features. Some steps. Wheelchair access to terraces over sloping lawns but only if ground is dry.
& ✿ ☕

I3 CWM-WEEG

Dolfor, Newtown, SY16 4AT. Dr W Schaefer & Mr K D George, 01686 628992, wolfgang@cwmweeg.co.uk, www.cwmweeg.co.uk. *4½m SE of Newtown. Off Bypass, take A489 E from Newtown for 1½m, turn R towards Dolfor. After 2m turn L down asphalted farm track, signed at entrance. Do not rely on SatNav. Also signed from Dolfor village on NGS days.* **Sun 5 July (2-5). Adm £5, chd free. Home-made teas.** 2½ acre garden set within 24 acres of wildflower meadows and bluebell woodland with stream centred around C15 farmhouse (open by prior arrangement). Formal garden in English landscape tradition with vistas, grottos, sculptures, stumpery, lawns and extensive borders terraced with stone walls. Translates older garden vocabulary into an innovative C21 concept. Extensive under cover seating area in the new Garden Pavilion. Partial wheelchair access. For further information please see garden website.

I4 ◆ DINGLE NURSERIES & GARDEN

Welshpool, SY21 9JD. Mr & Mrs D Hamer, 01938 555145, info@ dinglenurseriesandgarden.co.uk, www.dinglenurseries.co.uk. *2m NW of Welshpool. Take A490 towards Llanfyllin & Guilsfield. After 1m turn L at sign for Dingle Nurseries & Garden. Follow signs and enter the Garden from adjacent plant centre.* **For NGS: Sat 9, Sun 10 May, Sat 17, Sun 18 Oct (9-5). Adm £3.50, chd free. Tea and coffee. For other opening times and information, please phone, email or visit garden website.** RHS recommended 4½ acre garden on S-facing site, sloping down to lakes surrounded by yr-round interest. Beds mostly colour themed with a huge variety of rare and unusual trees, ornamental shrubs and herbaceous plants. Set in hills of mid Wales this beautiful and well known garden attracts visitors from Britain and abroad. Open all yr except 24 Dec - 2 Jan. Partial access to top areas of garden over gravel path for those with mobility issues.

I5 FRAITHWEN

Tregynon, Newtown, SY16 3EW. Sydney Thomas, 01686 650307.

6m N of Newtown. On B4389 midway between villages of Bettws Cedewain & Tregynon. **Sun 19 July (2-5). Adm £4, chd free. Home-made teas. Visits also by arrangement Feb to Oct.** 1½ acre plantswoman's garden with herbaceous borders, rockeries and ponds. Planted with rare plants for yr-round interest and for pollinators. Plants in flower every day of the year: spring bulbs, alpines, alstroemeria collection, lilies, vegetable plot and pool. Collection of unusual snowdrops. Beautiful views. New designs for 2020 incl more autumn colour and bog garden. Snowdrops and hellebores in flower Feb and carpets of cyclamen in Sept. Partial wheelchair access. Some steps, gravel and slopes.

I6 NEW FRON HEULOG

Pentre Llifior, Berriew, Welshpool, SY21 8QJ. Annis Bratt & Tim Ward, 01686 640544, FronHeulogGardens@outlook. com. *8 miles SW from Welshpool. From Berriew take B4389 towards Bettws Cedewain. After 3m pass Methodist chapel. Continue for 300 yds & turn sharp R up small lane. Entrance 300yds on R.* **Visits by arrangement Mar to Sept for groups of 10 to 20. Restricted parking on site. 8 cars maximum. Adm £5, chd free. Home-made teas.** 1½ acre stunning landscaped garden in beautiful setting within 8 acres. Colourful garden with exceptional range of plants divided into different contrasting gardens with unusual shrubs & trees, terraced rockery, dingle garden, potager. Meadow managed for wildlife can be explored via network of paths & includes wildlife pond & shepherd's hut with magnificent views of the surrounding countryside.

I7 GARTHMYL HALL

Garthmyl, Montgomery, SY15 6RS. Julia Pugh, 07716 763567, hello@garthmylhall.co.uk, www.garthmylhall.co.uk. *On A483 midway between Welshpool & Newtown (both 8m). Turn R 200yds S of Nag's Head Pub.* **Sun 9 Aug (12-5). Adm £4.50, chd free. Home-made teas.** Grade II listed Georgian manor house (not open) surrounded by 5 acres of grounds. Long 100 metres

herbaceous borders, newly restored 1 acre walled garden with gazebo, circular flowerbeds, lavender beds, two fire pits and gravel paths. Fountain, 3 magnificent Cedar of Lebanon and giant redwood. Partial wheelchair access. Accessible WC.

I8 GILWERN BARN

Beulah, LD5 4YG. Mrs Penelope Bourdillon, 01591 620203, pbourdillon@gmail.com, www.gilwerngarden.co.uk. *2m N of Beulah. Turn L exactly ¾m from Beulah on B4358. Follow rd for over 1m. Past Cefnhafdref Farm. L at T junction. In 600 yds fork L through stone gateposts.* **Visits by arrangement May to July for groups of 5 to 30. Thursdays only. Adm £4, chd free. Home-made teas.** Terraced garden in the making, on very challenging site situated on steep rocky hillside in the beautiful and secluded Cammarch Valley. Roses, herbaceous and shrub borders. Fine walling and gate posts making use of stone and slate found in the garden. Man-made waterfall and rill. The situation, on a steep rocky slope, is fairly dramatic and makes it interesting. Also perhaps the fact that work is still in progress. The waterfall is quite a feature. Late flowering roses. The peonies should be worth seeing in late May. A new rill, recently planted. Easy access to tearoom up a ramp.

Bryngwyn Hall

vegetable garden, original potting shed, Victorian grotto and orangery. Wysteria scented fountain walk, 4 acre lake with shady seating areas, folly island and wildfowl. Birdhide on banks of R Severn and R Rhiw. Stunning Autumnal colour with a cosy cafe for warming treats. Children's nature trail, Artisan gift shop. Family ticket = 2 adults and three chd for £20 Moon in a Box by Gemma Hughes an 8' lakeside installation. Some parts of the garden will be difficult for wheelchairs.

♿ 🐕 ✳ 🚐 🛏 ☕

21 GLANWYE

Builth Wells, LD2 3YP. Mr & Mrs H Kidston. *2m SE Builth Wells. From Builth Wells on A470, after 2m R at Lodge Gate. From Llyswen on A470, after 6m L at Lodge Gate. Will be signposted. Suggest not using SatNav as unreliable.* **Sun 24 May (2-5). Adm £4, chd free. Home-made teas.**

Large Victorian garden, spectacular rhododendrons, azaleas. Herbaceous borders, extensive yew hedges, lawns, long woodland walk with bluebells and other woodland flowers. Magnificent views of upper Wye Valley.

🐕 ☕

22 GLIFFAES COUNTRY HOUSE HOTEL

Gliffaes Rd, Crickhowell, NP8 1RH. Mrs N Brabner & Mr & Mrs J C Suter, 01874 730371, calls@gliffaeshotel.com, www.gliffaes.com. *3½ m W of Crickhowell. From Crickhowell, drive W for 2½ m, L off A40 and continue for 1m.* **Sun 25 Oct (2-5). Adm £6.50, chd free. Cream teas.**

Gliffaes Hotel has, within its 33 acres of grounds, one of the best small arboretums in Wales with an enviable collection of specimen trees from around the globe planted by far sighted Victorian collectors. It also has numbers of much older trees shedding light on how the woodlands were used and managed in past times. There will be a guided Autumn colours Tree Walk at 2pm. Gliffaes is a country house hotel and is open for lunch, bar snacks, afternoon tea and dinner to non residents and garden visitors. Wheelchair ramp to the west side of the hotel. In dry weather main lawns accessible, but more difficult if wet.

♿ 🐕 🛏 ☕

19 NEW 1 GLANRAFON

Llanwddyn, Oswestry, SY10 0LU. Margaret Herbert. *24m west of Oswestry. From Llanfyllin, follow brown signs to Lake Vyrnwy. Through village of Llanwddyn & turn L across dam then L past Artisans Cafe & park in public car park by playground. Follow yellow signs to garden.* **Sat 18, Sun 19 July (11.30-4). Adm £4, chd free. Home-made teas.**

1 acre secluded garden under development. As a keen plantsperson, I have been establishing this steeply sloping, densely planted wildlife garden with hundreds of varieties of shrubs & perennials over the past 5 years. Very productive raised veg beds, fruit cages and polytunnels, large pond. Lower level floods to depth 30cm, slopes to upper levels free draining sheltered & south-facing. Large greenhouse with ornamental & edible crops. Fruit trees, bushes and vegetables, many of which are unusual varieties. Yard with chickens and ducks. Wheelchairs can access the upper & lower levels via the access road & separate gates. Disabled car park down access road by house.

♿ 🚐 ☕

20 ♦ GLANSEVERN HALL GARDENS

Berriew, Welshpool, SY21 8AH. The Owen Family, 01686 640644, gardens@glansevern.co.uk, www.glansevern.co.uk. *5m SW of Welshpool. On A483 between Newtown & Welshpool, clearly marked on brown tourist signs.* **For NGS: Wed 16, Thur 17 Sept (10.30-4.30). Adm £7.50, chd £3.50. Light refreshments in Potting Shed Cafe or beautiful courtyard. For other opening times and information, please phone, email or visit garden website.**

Beautiful Greek revival house (not open) set in mature parkland with rare and ancient trees. 25 acres of gardens incl walled garden of rooms,

23 GORSTY HOUSE

Hyssington, Montgomery,
SY15 6AT. Gary & Annie Frost.
*A488 N from Bishop's Castle.
Approx 3½ m, turn L to Hyssington,
follow NGS signs. From Churchstoke
towards Bishop's Castle 1m then
turn L to Hyssington, follow NGS
signs. 230yd walk from Village
carpark, disabled parking at house.*
**Sat 4, Sun 5 Apr (1.30-5). Adm £4,
chd free. Home-made teas.**
A renovation, started late in 2014,
of a long neglected garden. 2¼
acres, one acre of which is meadow
with introduced native daffodils
in spring. There are thousands of
daffodils and other spring flowering
bulbs throughout the garden giving
a wonderful uplifting experience
after the dull days of winter. Beautiful
views. A haven for wildlife.

24 ◆ GRANDMA'S GARDEN

Dolguog Estates, Felingerrig,
Machynlleth, SY20 8UJ.
Richard Rhodes, 01654 702244,
info@plasdolguog.co.uk, www.
plasdolguog.co.uk/grandmasgarden.
*1½ m E of Machynlleth. Turn L off
A489 Machynlleth to Newtown rd.
Follow brown tourist signs to Plas
Dolguog Hotel.* **For NGS: Wed
27 May (10.30-4.30). Adm £5,
chd free. Cream teas. For other
opening times and information,
please phone, email or visit garden
website.**
Inspiration for the senses, unique,
fascinating, educational and fun.
Strategic seating, continuous new
attractions, wildlife abundant, 9
acres of peace. Sculptures, poetry
arboretum. Seven sensory gardens,
wildlife pond, riverside boardwalk,
stone circle, labyrinth. Azaleas and
bluebells in May. Children welcome.
Plas Dolguog Hotel open their café
in the conservatory - the hotel is the
admission point - serving inside and
out on patio overlooking gardens.

25 ◆ GREGYNOG HALL & GARDEN

Tregynon, Newtown, SY16 3PL.
Gregynog Trust, 01686 650224,
enquiries@gregynog.org,
www.gregynog.org. *5m N of
Newtown. From main A483, take
turning for Berriew. In Berriew follow
sign for Bettws then for Tregynon
(£2.50 car parking charge applies).*
**For NGS: Sun 17 May (10-4). Adm
£5, chd free. Light refreshments**
at Courtyard Cafe. **For other
opening times and information,
please phone, email or visit garden
website.**
Gardens are Listed Grade I and
some features of William Emes,
18th Century landscape architect,
still remain. Set within 750 acres
of Gregynog Estate a designated
National Nature Reserve in 2013.
Parkland with fountains, lily lake and
water garden. A mass display of
rhododendrons & azaleas & unique
yew hedge create a spectacular
backdrop to the sunken lawns.
Unusual trees. David Austin roses.
Courtyard cafe serving morning
coffee, light lunches and Welsh
afternoon teas. Some gravel paths.

26 HEBRON

Ludlow Road, Knighton,
LD7 1HP. Kevin Collins &
Anita Lewis, 01547 529576,
kd.collins@hotmail.co.uk. *From
Knighton, take A4113 towards
Ludlow, house on R opp playing
fields where parking is available.*
**Visits by arrangement Feb to Oct
for groups of up to 20. Adm £3.50,
chd free. Home-made teas.**
½ acre Victorian town garden.
Surprises await the visitor: garden
divided into distinct rooms by yew
& beech hedges with box topiary
and willow arches. Variety of trees
incl large silver birches, magnolia,
weeping willow and cherry. Many
shrubs provide colour throughout the
season. Heathers, herbs, vegetables
and flower beds. Plenty of seating.
Beehives and garden art.

27 HURDLEY HALL

Hurdley, Churchstoke, SY15 6DY.
Simon Cain & Simon Quin,
07958 915115, simon.cain@
westbourneconsulting.com. *2m
from Churchstoke. Take turning
for Hurdley off A489, 1m E of
Churchstoke. Garden is a further 1m
up the lane.* **Sun 14 June, Sat 4,
Sun 5 July, Sun 2 Aug (11-5). Adm
£5, chd free. Home-made teas.
Visits also by arrangement June to
Aug for groups of 10 to 30.**
Shortlisted in the 'Nation's Favourite
Garden Competition' 2019, 2 acre
garden incl herbaceous and mixed
borders leading to 18 acres of
Coronation Meadows, woodland and
an orchard. Visit in June for meadow
flowers and roses; in July for lavender
and herbaceous borders; or in August
for hot and white borders. Uneven
ground and steep slopes give wide
ranging views but may restrict access.
Live music by Bishops Castle Swing
Band on Sun 5 July from 2pm.

28 THE HYMNS

Walton, Presteigne, LD8 2RA.
E Passey, 07958 762362,
thehymns@hotmail.com,
www.thehymns.co.uk. *5m W of
Kington. Take A44 W, then 1st R
for Kinnerton. After approx 1m, at
the top of small hill, turn L (W).* **Sun
12 July (11-5). Adm £4, chd free.
Visits also by arrangement.**
In a beautiful setting in the heart of the
Radnor valley, the garden is part of
a restored C16 farmstead, with long
views to the hills, and The Radnor
Forest. It is a traditional garden
reclaimed from the wild, using locally
grown plants and seeds, and with a
herb patio, wildflower meadows and
a short woodland walk. It is designed
for all the senses: sight, sound and
smell.

29 LITTLE HOUSE

Llandinam, Newtown,
SY17 5BH. Peter & Pat Ashcroft,
www.littlehouse1692.uk. *1m from
Llandinam Village Hall. Cross river at
statue of David Davies on A470 in
Llandinam. Follow rd for just under
1m, Little House is black & white
cottage on roadside. Limited parking.*
**Sun 26 Apr, Sat 27 June, Sat 5
Sept (1-5). Adm £3.50, chd free.
Home-made teas.**
⅓ acre plantswoman's garden on
a quiet lane surrounded by fields,
woodland & stream. Slate & bark
paths give access to the many
features incl fish & wildlife ponds,
conifer, azalea, grass & mixed beds,
vegetable garden, woodland, mini
meadow, sensory garden, carnivorous
plant & grotto water features, auricula
theatre & alpine/cactus house. 500+
different plants, many propagated for
sale. Spring; auricula theatre will be
at its best with other primulas, winter
heathers & hellebores. Summer; the
garden in full bloom & the sensory
garden alive with colour & wonderful
scents. Autumn; cyclamen, grasses,
crocosmia, michaelmas daisies &
interesting seed heads on show. New
features for 2020.

30 LLANGOED HALL HOTEL

Llangoed Hall Hotel, Llyswen, Brecon, LD3 0YP. Sergio Martinez-Rios, 01874 754525, Mandy_hobbs@live.co.uk, www.llangoedhall.com. *9m S of Builth Wells. 9m W of Hay-on-Wye. From Brecon and Hay-on-Wye follow signs to Builth Wells. In Llyswen follow A470 the hotel is situated on the right down a long drive.* **Sun 3 May, Sun 13 Sept (2-4.30). Adm £4, chd free. Home-made teas.**
Large organic garden with encouragement of wildlife surrounding one of the finest hotels in Wales. Shrub and mixed borders, walled area incl formal herb and rose gardens, soft fruit and fruit trees, cutting border and maze. Croquet lawn (learn to play), superb views of the Black Mountains and Upper Wye Valley. Ducks and chickens. Unusual vegetables grown in the kitchen garden. Steps down to croquet lawn, some gravel paths.

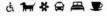

31 LLWYN MADOC

Beulah, Llanwrtyd Wells, LD5 4TU. Patrick & Miranda Bourdillon, 01591 620564, miranda.bourdillon@gmail.com. *8m W of Builth Wells. On A483 at Beulah take rd towards Abergwesyn for 1m. Drive on R. Parking on field below drive - follow signs.* **Mon 25 May (2-5.30). Adm £4, chd free. Cream teas.**
Terraced garden in attractive wooded valley overlooking newly restored lake; yew hedges; rose garden with pergola; kitchen garden and small orchard; azaleas and rhododendrons. As the garden is situated on a slope, it is quite steep in parts.

32 NEW LLYS CELYN

Llanwnog, Caersws, SY17 5JG. Lesley & Tony Geary. *9m W of Newtown. From Newtown A489 W to A470, turn R to Machynlleth & Caersws. After 3m turn R on B4589. Follow signs. Alternative route: from Newtown B4589 from McDonalds direct to Llanwnog.* **Sat 4, Sun 5 July (2-5). Adm £4, chd free. Home-made teas.**
1 acre garden renovated and developed over the last 9 years. Evolving garden packed with many features. Extensive vegetable garden with fruit cage, polytunnel and greenhouse. Newly created herbaceous borders and bog garden.

Wildlife areas incl ponds & habitats, rockery & courtyard garden. Fabulous views of the surrounding countryside and village church steeple.

33 LLYSDINAM

Newbridge-on-Wye, LD1 6NB. Sir John & Lady Venables-Llewelyn & Llysdinam Charitable Trust, 01597 860190/07748 492025, llysdinamgardens@gmail.com, llysdinamgardens.co.uk. *5m SW of Llandrindod Wells. Turn W off A470 at Newbridge-on-Wye; turn R immed after crossing R Wye; entrance up hill.* **Mon 25 May (2-5). Adm £5, chd free. Cream teas. Visits also by arrangement.**
Llysdinam Gardens are among the loveliest in mid Wales, especially noted for a magnificent display of rhododendrons and azaleas in May. Covering some 6 acres in all, they command sweeping views down the Wye Valley. Successive family members have developed the gardens over the last 150yrs to incl woodland with specimen trees, large herbaceous and shrub borders and a water garden, all of which provide varied and colourful planting throughout the yr. The Victorian walled kitchen garden and extensive greenhouses grow a wide variety of vegetables, hothouse fruit and exotic plants. Gravel paths.

34 MAESFRON HALL AND GARDENS

Trewern, Welshpool, SY21 8EA. Dr & Mrs TD Owen, 01938 570600, maesfron@aol.com, www.maesfron.co.uk. *4m E of Welshpool. On N side of A458 Welshpool to Shrewsbury Rd.* **Visits by arrangement for groups of 10+. Adm £5, chd free. Home-made teas. Open all year round. Wide range of refreshments available by prior arrangement.**
Largely intact Georgian estate of 6 acres. House (partly open) built in Italian villa style set in South-facing gardens on lower slopes of Moel-y-Golfa with panoramic views of The Long Mountain. Terraces, Walled Kitchen Garden, Chapel, Display Beds, Restored Victorian Conservatories, Tower, Shell Grotto and gardens below tower. Explore ground floor, wine cellar, old kitchen and servants quarters. Parkland walks with a wide variety of trees. Adjacent paddock and stables. Refreshments

served in the reception rooms or on the terrace. Some gravel, steps and slopes.

35 ◆ MILEBROOK HOUSE GARDEN

Ludlow Road, Knighton, LD7 1LT. James and Zoe Sheehan, 01547 528632, hotel@milebrookhouse.co.uk, www.milebrookhouse.co.uk. *2½m E of Knighton. From Knighton A 4113 E towards Ludlow on L after 2½m.* **For NGS: Sat 30, Sun 31 May (11.30-4.30). Adm £4, chd free. Home-made teas on the terrace or in the hotel. For other opening times and information, please phone, email or visit garden website.**
3 acre traditional garden & woodland surrounding C18 hotel. Flower garden divided into rooms with clipped yew hedges. Bountiful borders with peonies & herbaceous perennials, long rose pergola, giant wisteria, espaliered fruit trees, soft fruit & vegetable area, woodland walk. Watch the red kites soar over the beautiful Teme Valley. Family home of explorer Sir Wilfred Thesiger until 2003 Try a game of croquet, badminton or table tennis.

36 NEW NANT Y CYFF

Aberangell, Machynlleth, SY20 9NJ. Ant and Cathy Brown, 07763 458152, ant.brown58@googlemail.com. *Midway between Dolgellau/Machynlleth. From A470 follow sign Aberangell, past caravan park to Xrds. Turn L approx ½m past all houses and Aberangell sign next house on R in ¼m.* **Visits by arrangement May to Aug individuals/groups max 15. Adm £4, chd free. Refreshments to be arranged prior to visit.**
Large garden divided into areas with different conditions: dry shade to full sun & bog. Lawns, mature trees, mixed borders, hedges, enclosed fruit & vegetable plot. Paths & steps lead to terraced bank, seating & viewing spots, streamside planting. Mature & new plantings for shelter & interest around the garden. Polytunnel & cut flower beds. Developed from original layout using on site materials. Beautiful views over Dovey valley. Wide gravel path to main lawn area and front of house borders.

37 THE NEUADD

Llanbedr, Crickhowell, NP8 1SP. Robin & Philippa Herbert, 01873 812164, philippahherbert@gmail.com. *1m NE of Crickhowell. Leave Crickhowell by Llanbedr Rd. At junction with Great Oak Rd bear L, cont up hill for approx 1m, garden on L. Ample parking.* Sun 7 June (2-6). Adm £5, chd free. Home-made teas. Visits also by arrangement May to July for groups of 5 to 10. Tea is available at £3.50 per head.
Robin and Philippa Herbert have worked on the restoration of the garden at The Neuadd since 1999 and have planted many unusual trees and shrubs in the dramatic setting of the Brecon Beacons National Park. One of the major features is the walled garden, which has both traditional and decorative planting of fruit, vegetables and flowers. There is also a woodland walk with ponds and streams and a formal garden with flowering terraces. Spectacular views, water feature, rare trees and shrubs, plant stall and teas. The owner uses a wheelchair and most of the garden is accessible, but some steep paths.

   🚾 ❀ ☕

38 NEW OSPREY STUDIOS

57 Ynyswen, Penycae, Swansea, SA9 1YT. Rebecca Buck, 07913743457, osprey.studios@btinternet.com, www.ospreystudios.org. *20m from Swansea. M4 exit 45, 15m on A4067 towards Brecon. L after Ynyswen rd sign. L at T junction, Blue house on R, no. 57. 13m from A40/A4067 junction, Sennybridge.* Visits by arrangement June to Aug for groups of up to 10. Adm £4, chd free. Home-made teas.
Wild-life, sculpture and fruit in compact front and back gardens. Blending into the wet meadow at the base of Cribarth, Sleeping Giant Mountain on the SW corner of the Brecon Beacons National Park. Specialising in slug-proof planting! Ceramic sculpture studio on site, sculptures and planters for sale. Teas and home-made cake. Toilet. Easy parking in front. Annual Sculpture Sale and Open Studio held for 1 week in the Summer. Unique Sculpture for sale or commission. Access to front garden and the back garden patio that offers good views.

   🚾 🛏 ☕

39 PENMYARTH HOUSE - GLANUSK ESTATE

The Glanusk Estate, Crickhowell, NP8 1SH. Mrs Harry Legge-Bourke, 01873 810414, info@glanuskestate.com, www.glanuskestate.com. *2m NW of Crickhowell. Please access the Glanusk Estate via the Main Entrance (NP8 1SH) on the A40 and follow signs to car park. There is no access from the B4558 Cwm Crawnon Road.* Sun 17 May (11-4). Adm £7.50, chd free. Light refreshments.
The garden is adorned with many established plant species such as rhododendrons, azaleas, acers, camelia, magnolia, prunus and dogwood giving a vast array of colour in the spring and summer months and over 300 cultivars of Oaks. Alongside the Open Garden, we will be holding the annual Estate Fayre, showcasing over 30 artisans with exhibits of works for sale. Penmyarth Church, a short distance from the gardens, will be open. For more information see our website and social media channels. Historic gardens, Oaks, Cottage Orné, Artisan stands, home-made cakes, coffee, tea and gourmet catering, licensed bar, talks, garden tours, plant sale, activities and demonstrations. The gardens contain some historic features, incl paths and steps which are not suitable for access by wheelchairs or pushchairs.

   ♿ 🚾 ❀ 🚗 🚌 ☕

40 PEN-Y-MAES

Hay-on-Wye, HR3 5PP. Shân Egerton, 01497 820423, penymaes.hay@gmail.com. *1m SW of Hay-on-Wye. On B4350 towards Hay from Brecon. 2½m from Glasbury.* Sun 28 June (2-5). Adm £5, chd free. Home-made teas. Visits also by arrangement July to Sept for groups of 10+.
2 acre garden incl mixed and herbaceous borders; orchard, topiary; walled formal kitchen garden; shrub, modern and climbing roses, peony borders, espaliered pears. Fine mulberry. Beautiful dry stone walling and mature trees. Great double view of Black Mountains and the Brecon Beacons. Emphasis on foliage and shape. Artist's garden.

   ♿ 🚾 ❀ 🚗 ☕

Cefnsuran

Llysdinam

41 PLAS DINAM

Llandinam, SY17 5DQ.
Eldrydd Lamp, 07415 503554,
eldrydd@plasdinam.co.uk,
www.plasdinamcountryhouse.
co.uk. *7½ m SW Newtown. on
A470.* **Visits by arrangement Apr
to Nov for groups of 10+. Adm £8
incl tea, coffee and cake.**
12 acres of parkland, gardens, lawns
and woodland set at the foot of
glorious rolling hills with spectacular
views across the Severn Valley. A
host of daffodils followed by one
of the best wildflower meadows in
Montgomeryshire with 36 species of
flowers and grasses incl hundreds of
wild orchids; Glorious autumn colour
with parrotias, liriodendrons, cotinus
etc. Millennium wood. From 1884
until recently the home of Lord Davies
and his family (house not open).

& 🐐 🚗 🚘 ☕

42 PONT FAEN HOUSE

**Farrington Lane, Knighton,
LD7 1LA. Mr John & Mrs Brenda
Morgan, 01547 520847.** *S of
Knighton off Ludlow Rd. W from
Ludlow on A4113 into Knighton. 1st
L after 20mph sign before school.*
**Visits by arrangement May to Aug
for groups of up to 30. Adm £4,
chd free. Home-made teas.**
Colourful ¾ acre flat garden
brimming with flowers on edge of
town. Arches lead from shady ferny
corners to deep borders filled with
large range of colourful perennials,
annuals & fish pond. Stunning
wisteria, 10 varieties of alstromeria,
rhododendrons & azaleas followed
by colourful perennials, shrubs, and
40 varieties roses. Good late summer
colour. Enjoy views of hills from the
many seats. Yr round colour: tulips,
clematis, rudbeckias, inulas. Disabled
parking in garden.

& 🐕 ✻ ☕

43 PONTHAFREN

**Long Bridge Street, Newtown,
SY16 2DY. Janet Rogers (volunteer
gardener), 01686 621586,
www.ponthafren.org.uk.** *Park in
main car park in town centre, 5 mins
walk. Turn L out of car park, turn L
over bridge, garden on L. Limited
disabled parking, please phone for
details.* **Sat 25 July (10-5); Sat 22
Aug (10-4). Adm by donation.
Home-made teas. Visits also by
arrangement. Individuals/large
groups.**
Ponthafren is a registered charity
for people with mental health issues

or those that feel lonely or isolated. Open door policy so everyone is welcome. Interesting community garden on banks of R Severn run and maintained totally by volunteers: sensory garden with long grasses, herbs, scented plants and shrubs, quirky objects like Guy the Gorilla. Productive vegetable plot. Lots of plants for sale. Covered seating areas positioned around the garden to enjoy the views. Partial wheelchair access.

GROUP OPENING

44 NEW PONTROBERT GARDENS

Pontrobert, Meifod, SY22 6JN. *10m W of Welshpool. A458 W from Welshpool towards Dolgellau for 7m. Turn R B4389 Meifod. L at A495 then immed R to Pontrobert. In village turn L over bridge to Community Centre car park. Map & Admission tickets at Car Park.* Sun 28 June (1-5). Combined adm £5, chd free. Home-made teas in Community Centre.

NEW **3 LON YR YWEN**
Colin and Christine Illstone.

NEW **5 LON YR YWEN**
Mrs Margaret and Revd Mark Hill-Tout.

NEW **6 LON YR YWEN**
Marilyn and Michael Booth.

NEW **MIN Y NANT**
Jane & Roy McGuffin.

The delightful village of Pontrobert is on R Vyrnwy in glorious countryside on both The Glyndwr Way and Ann Griffiths Walk. Home to the historic John Hughes Chapel specially open for visits today. Four very different gardens planted in the last 13 yrs full of colour with different styles of planting and character. Discover rose & clematis arbours, a host of hostas, flowerbeds bursting with colour, stunning sambuccus nigra, raised veg beds. Enjoy the tranquillity of this beautiful village.

45 THE ROCK HOUSE

Llanbister, LD1 6TN. Jude Boutle & Sue Cox. *10m N of Llandrindod Wells. Off B4356 just above Llanbister village.* Sun 31 May (1-5). Adm £4.50, chd free. Home-made teas. Evening opening Fri 12 June

(6.30-9). Adm £6, chd free. Light refreshments.
About an acre of informal hillside garden, 1000ft up with sweeping views over the Radnorshire Hills. Hardy perennials, wildlife ponds, a bluebell meadow, and a laburnum arch, it's a bit of a battle with nature so come and visit and see who you think is winning! Sunday 31st May children's quiz/treasure hunt to keep small people busy. Jimmi Tutti's delicious taster sized cocktails/mocktails available on Friday 12th June, plus music from Welsh folk harpist Joe Botting. Minimal wheelchair access.

46 ROCK MILL

Abermule, Montgomery, SY15 6NN. Rufus & Cherry Fairweather, 01686 630664, fairweathers66@btinternet.com. *1m S of Abermule on B4368 towards Kerry. Best approached from Abermule village as there is an angled entrance into field for parking.* Sat 16, Sun 17 May (2-5). Adm £5, chd free. Home-made teas. Visits also by arrangement in May for groups of up to 30.
2 acre riverside garden on different levels in wooded valley. Colourful borders & shrubberies, specimen trees, terraces, woodland walks, bridges, extensive lawns, fishponds, orchard, herb & vegetable gardens, beehives, dovecote, heather thatch roundhouse, remnants of industrial past (corn mill & railway line). Child and adult friendly activities (supervision required) incl sunken trampoline, croquet and badminton, animal treasure hunt, interactive quiz, wilderness trails, cockleshell tunnel. Sensible shoes and a sense of fun/adventure recommended.

GROUP OPENING

47 NEW SOUTH STREET GARDENS

Beechcroft, South Street, Rhayader, LD6 5BH. Gwyneth Rose & Steve Harley, 01597 811868, info@penralleyhouse.com. *All gardens are 100 metres S of the centre of Rhayder on A470. Parking is in the Smithfield (market) car park in North St. Penralley House and Beechcroft gardens are in South St on the right hand side and the*

Toll house is opp, approx 100m from town clock. Sun 5 July (2-5). Combined adm £5, chd free. Home-made teas in Penralley garden.
Three very different gardens close to the centre of town. The Toll House shows what can be done in a tiny space, with raised beds of annuals, troughs and traditional roses around the door. Penralley House has a large terraced garden with flower borders, mature trees, orchard, chicken coop, fruit garden and lawns. Beechcroft, the largest of the three, has an herbaceous border, fruit garden with green house and compost area, raised vegetable garden, pond and wild flower meadow. Steps lead to a sloped woodland garden with zig zag paths and natural spring at the bottom. All gardens have views of the lovely Gwastedyn Hill at the edge of town. Some parts of Beechcroft are not wheelchair accessible. Tea and cake available in Penralley garden. Plant sales and open textile studio in Beechcroft garden. The upper garden at Beechcroft garden is accessible. Penralley garden is mostly flat and accessible. Disabled parking in Beechcroft.

48 STOCKTON MILL

Marton, Welshpool, SY21 8JL. Stephen & Caroline Cox, 01938 561990, carolinecox74@gmail.com, www.stocktonmill.wordpress.com. *6m SE Welshpool. From Welshpool take A483 S. Turn L on A490 for 3.3m (rd takes L turn 200m after The Cock Inn, Forden) then turn L signed Marton. Continue 1.2m & turn R before pink building. Park in field.* **Sat 13 June (10-5). Adm £4, chd free. Home-made teas.**

Peaceful 3 acre garden by R Camlad in Vale of Montgomery with lovely views. House next to C19 Grade II listed mill (not open). Now a holiday let. Trees mainly planted 30 yrs ago now matured into striking woodland including Himalayan Birch, Himalayan Cherry, Dogwoods and varieties of unusual conifers. Extensive shrub & herbaceous borders, lawns, veg patch & walks by the river. Two wildlife ponds.

♿ 🐕 ❄ 🛏 ☕

49 TALGARTH MILL

The Square, Talgarth, Brecon, LD3 0BW. Talgarth Mill, www.talgarthmill.com. *In centre of Talgarth. Park in free car park opp rugby club, turn L out of car park entrance, follow High St to end, cross bridge, the Mill is on your R.* **Sun 5 July (10-4). Adm £4, chd free. Refreshments available from The Bakers' Table.**

A pretty riverside garden, maintained by volunteers. Along the riverside there is mixed herbaceous planting, a shady area, and steps up to a productive garden with espalier fruit trees, vegetables, soft fruits and a wildlife area. Places to sit and watch the river and its bird life (dippers, wagtails, kingfishers, herons) and the mill wheel turning. Garden is part of a working water mill that produces high quality flour (Great Taste 1 and 2 star), with our staple bread wheat grown just 7m away. Award winning cafe and bakery which champions local, seasonal produce, gourmet coffee and tea. Garden can be accessed by lift. Wide, flat paths for wheelchair access.

♿ ❄ 🚗 ☕

50 TRANQUILLITY HAVEN

7 Lords Land, Whitton, Knighton, LD7 1NJ. Val Brown, 01547 560070, valerie.brown1502@gmail.com. *approx 3m from Knighton and 5m Presteigne. From Knighton take B4355 after approx. 2m turn R on B4357 to Whitton. Car park on L by yellow NGS signs.* **Sat 6, Sun 7 June (2-5); Sat 10, Sun 11 Oct (2-4.30). Adm £4, chd free. Home-made teas. Visits also by arrangement May to Sept for groups of 5 to 20. Refreshments in aid of Knighton Macmillan Cancer Support.**

Amazing Japanese Stroll Garden with borrowed views to Offa's Dyke. Winding paths pass small pools and lead to Japanese bridges over natural stream with dippers and kingfishers. Sounds of water fill the air. Enjoy peace and tranquillity from one of the seats or the Japanese Tea House. Dense oriental planting with Cornus kousa satomi, acers, azaleas, unusual bamboos and wonderful cloud pruning,. New features for 2020.

☕

51 TREBERFYDD HOUSE

Llangasty, Bwlch, Brecon, LD3 7PX. David Raikes & Carla Rapoport, www.treberfydd.com. *6m E of Brecon. From Abergavenny on A40, turn R in Bwlch on B5460. Take 1st turning L towards Pennorth & cont 2m along lane. From Brecon, turn L off A40 towards Pennorth in Llanhamlach.* **Sun 5 July (1-5.30). Adm £5, chd free. Home-made teas.**

Grade I listed Victorian Gothic house with 10 acres of grounds designed by W A Nesfield. Magnificent Cedar of Lebanon, avenue of mature Beech, towering Atlantic Cedars, Victorian rockery, herbaceous border and manicured lawns ideal for a picnic. Wonderful views of the Black Mountains. Plants available from Commercial Nursery in grounds - Walled Garden Treberfydd. House tours every half hour (additional £3), last tour 4pm. Easy wheelchair access to areas around the house, but herbaceous border only accessible via steps.

♿ 🐕 ❄ ☕

52 TREMYNFA

Carreghofa Lane, Llanymynech, SY22 6LA. Jon & Gillian Fynes, 01691 839471, gillianfynes@btinternet.com. *Edge*

Fron Heulog

of Llanymynech village. From N leave Oswestry on A483 to Welshpool. In Llanymynech turn R at Xrds (car wash on corner). Take 2nd R then follow yellow NGS signs. 300yds park signed field, limited disabled parking nr garden. **Sat 20, Sun 21 June (1-5). Adm £4, chd free. Home-made teas. Visits also by arrangement for groups of 10 to 30. Afternoon or evening 15-26 June only. Coach accessible.** S-facing 1 acre garden developed over 14yrs. Old railway cottage set in herbaceous and raised borders, patio with many pots of colourful and unusual plants. Garden slopes to productive fruit and vegetable area, ponds, spinney, unusual trees, wild areas and peat bog. Patio and seats to enjoy extensive views incl Llanymynech Rocks. Pet ducks on site, Montgomery canal close by. 100s of home grown plants and home-made jams for sale. Wheelchairs can access most areas but users will need to walk up/down 2/3 shallow steps, please ring to discuss if concerned.

53 TYN Y CWM
Beulah, Llanwrtyd Wells, LD5 4TS. Steve & Christine Carrow, 01591 620461, stevetynycwm@hotmail.co.uk. 10m W of Builth Wells. On A483 at Beulah take rd towards Abergwesyn for 2m. Drive drops down to L. **Visits by arrangement May to Sept for groups of up to 30. Adm £4, chd free.**
Garden mainly started 18yrs ago, lower garden has spring/woodland area, raised beds mixed with vegetables, fruit trees, fruit and flowers. Perennial borders, summer house gravel paths through rose and clematis pergola. Upper garden, partly sloped, incl bog, winter, water gardens and perennial beds with unusual slate steps. Beautiful views. Property bounded by small river. Children's quiz.

54 ◆ WELSH LAVENDER
Cefnperfedd Uchaf, Maesmynis, Builth Wells, LD2 3HU. Nancy Durham & Bill Newton-Smith, 01982 552467, farmers@welshlavender.com, www.welshlavender.com. Approx 4½ m S of Builth Wells & 13m from Brecon Cathedral off B4520. The farm is 1⅓ m from turn signed

Farmers' Welsh Lavender. **For NGS: Sat 1, Sun 2 Aug (10-6). Adm £5, chd free. Light refreshments. For other opening times and information, please phone, email or visit garden website.**
Welsh Lavender's fields of blue will be at their peak on this weekend. The surrounding gardens continue to develop with Jeni Arnold's stylish wild planting of the steep bank above the ever popular wild swimming pond. This year an improvisational dance troupe lead by the acclaimed Kirstie Simsin will perform. Delicious food will be on offer alongside a vibrant makers' market. The farm, situated at 1100ft high in the hills of mid-Wales, offers spectacular views. Walk in the lavender fields, learn how the distillation process works, and visit the farm shop to try body creams and balms made with lavender oil distilled on the farm. 5% of sales go to the NGS. Coffee, tea, wine and light refreshments available. Partial wheelchair access. Large paved area adjacent to teas and shop area easy to negotiate.

55 WHITE HOPTON FARM
Wern Lane, Sarn, Newtown, SY16 4EN. Claire Austin, 01686 670 342, enquiries@ claireaustin-hardyplants.co.uk, www.claireaustin-hardyplants. co.uk. From Newtown A489, E towards Churchstoke for 7m & turn R in Sarn follow yellow NGS signs. **Thur 28 May, Tue 9 June, Wed 22 July (11-3). Adm £5, chd free. All open day visits must be pre-booked by phone. Light lunches and plants for sale at The Sarn. Visits also by arrangement May to Sept for groups of 15 to 30.**

Horticulturist and author Claire Austin's private 1½ acre plant collector's garden designed along the lines of a cottage garden with hundreds of different perennials. Front garden mainly full of May blooming perennials, back garden, which is split into various areas, has a June and July garden, a small woodland walk, a Victorian fountain and mixed rose borders. Fabulous views over the Kerry Vale. Wide range of Claire Austin's Hardy Plants for sale at The Sarn.

56 1 YSTRAD HOUSE
1 Church Road, Knighton, LD7 1EB. John & Margaret Davis, 01547 528154, jamdavis@ystradhouse.plus.com. At junction of Church Rd & Station Rd. Take the turning opp Knighton Hotel (A488 Clun) travel 225yds along Station Rd. Yellow House at junction with Church Rd. **Sat 20, Sun 21 June, Sat 1, Sun 2 Aug (2-5). Adm £4, chd free. Home-made teas incl gluten free cakes. Visits also by arrangement June to Sept for groups of up to 30.**
A town garden behind a Regency Villa of earlier origins. A narrow entrance door opens revealing unexpected calm and timelessness. A small walled garden with box hedging & greenhouse lead to broad lawns, wide borders with soft colour schemes and mature trees. More intimate features: pots, urns and pools add interest and surprise. The formal areas merge with wooded glades leading to a riverside walk. Lawns and gravelled paths mostly flat, except access to riverside walk.

Hurdley Hall

Early Openings 2021

Plan your garden visiting well ahead – put these dates in your diary!

Gardens across the country open early – before the next year's guide is published – with glorious displays of colour including hellebores, aconites, snowdrops and carpets of spring bulbs.

Bedfordshire
Sun 28 February (2-4)
King's Arms Garden

Cheshire & Wirral
Sat 20, Sun 21 February (1-4)
Briarfield, Burton Village Gardens

Sun 28 February (12.30-4)
Bucklow Farm

By arrangement in February
Rosewood
The Well House

Devon
Fri 5, Fri 12, Sat 20 February (2-5)
Higher Cherubeer

Essex
Sun 24 January (10-4)
Green Island

Glamorgan
Sun 14, Sun 21 February (2-4.30)
Slade

Gloucestershire
Sun 31 January, Sun 14 February (11-3)
Home Farm

Sun 7, Sun 14 February (11-5)
Trench Hill

Hampshire
Sun 14, Mon 15, Sun 21, Mon 22 February (2-5)
Little Court

Kent
Sat 13, Sun 21 February (12-4)
Copton Ash

Sat 6, Sun 7, Mon 8 February (11-3)
Knowle Hill Farm

By arrangement in February
The Old Rectory

Leicestershire & Rutland
Sat 27, Sun 28 February (12-4)
Westview

Northamptonshire
Sun 28 February (11-3)
67-69 High Street

Oxfordshire
Sun 14 February (1.30-4.30)
Hollyhocks

Somerset, Bristol & South Gloucestershire
Sun 31 January, Sun 7 February (11-4)
Rock House

Sun 14 February (10-5)
East Lambrook Manor Gardens

Staffordshire, Birmingham & West Midlands
Sun 14 February (11-3)
5 East View Cottages

Suffolk
Sun 21 February (11-4)
Gable House

Surrey
Wed 13, Wed 20 January, Mon 15, Tue 16, Wed 17, Thur 18 February (11-2)
Timber Hill

Sussex
By arrangement in February
Pembury House

Yorkshire
Sun 21 February (11-4.30)
Devonshire Mill

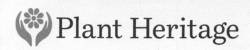 Plant Heritage

Over 70 gardens that open for the National Garden Scheme are holders of a Plant Heritage National Plant Collection although this may not always be noted in the garden description. These gardens carry the [NPC] symbol.

Plant Heritage, 12 Home Farm, Loseley Park, Guildford, Surrey GU3 1HS.
01483 447540 www.plantheritage.org.uk

Acer (excl. japonicum, palmatum cvs.)
Norwell Nurseries, Norwell Gardens, Nottinghamshire

Acer (excl. palmatum cvs.)
Blagdon, North East

Aeoniums
Hillview, Shropshire

Alnus
Ness Botanic Gardens, Cheshire
Stone Lane Gardens, Devon
Blagdon, North East

Anemone nemorosa
Avondale Nursery, Warwickshire

Anemone nemorosa cvs.
Kingston Lacy, Dorset

Araliaceae (excl. Hedera)
Meon Orchard, Hampshire

Aruncus
Windy Hall, Cumbria

Asplenium scolopendrium
Sizergh Castle, Cumbria

Aster & related genera
(autumn flowering)
The Picton Garden, Herefordshire

Aster (Symphyotrichum)
novae-angliae
Avondale Nursery, Warwickshire
Brockamin, Worcestershire

Astilbe
Marwood Hill Garden, Devon

Astrantia
Norwell Nurseries, Norwell Gardens, Nottinghamshire

Betula
Ness Botanic Gardens, Cheshire
Stone Lane Gardens, Devon

Buddleja davidii cvs. & hybrids
Shapcott Barton Knowstone Estate, Devon

Camellia, (autumn and winter flowering)
Green Island, Essex

Camellias & Rhododendrons introduced to Heligan pre-1920
The Lost Gardens of Heligan, Cornwall

Carpinus
Sir Harold Hillier Gardens, Hampshire

Carpinus betulus cvs.
West Lodge Park, London

Ceanothus
Eccleston Square, London

Cercidiphyllum
Sir Harold Hillier Gardens, Hampshire
Hodnet Hall Gardens, Shropshire

Chrysanthemum (Hardy)
Dispersed
Norwell Nurseries, Norwell Gardens, Nottinghamshire
Hill Close Gardens, Warwickshire

Clematis viticella
Longstock Park, Hampshire

Clematis viticella cvs.
Roseland House, Cornwall

Codonopsis & related genera
Woodlands, Fotherby Gardens, Lincolnshire

Colchicum
East Ruston Old Vicarage, Norfolk

Cornus
Sir Harold Hillier Gardens, Hampshire

Cornus (excl. C. florida cvs.)
Newby Hall & Gardens, Yorkshire

Corokia
33 Wood Vale, London

Corylus
Sir Harold Hillier Gardens, Hampshire

Cotoneaster
Sir Harold Hillier Gardens, Hampshire

Cyclamen (excl persicum cvs.)
Higher Cherubeer, Devon

Cystopteris
Sizergh Castle, Cumbria

Daffodil Dispersed
Noel Burr Cultivars
Mill Hall Farm, Sussex

Dierama spp.
Yew Tree Cottage, Staffordshire

Dryopteris
Sizergh Castle, Cumbria

Echium spp., & cvs. from
Macaronesian Islands
The Echium Garden,
Nottinghamshire

Erica & Calluna - Sussex
heather cvs.
Nymans, Sussex

Erythronium
Greencombe Gardens, Somerset

Eucalyptus
Meon Orchard, Hampshire

Eucalyptus spp.
The World Garden at
Lullingstone Castle, Kent

Eucryphia
Whitstone Farm, Devon

Euonymus (deciduous)
The Place for Plants, East
Bergholt Place Garden, Suffolk

Eupatorium
Saith Ffynnon Farm, North East
Wales

Euphorbia (hardy)
Firvale Allotment Garden,
Yorkshire

Fuchsia hardy spp. & cvs.
Croxteth Park Walled Garden,
Lancashire

Galanthus
127 Stoke Road, Bedfordshire

Gaultheria (incl Pernettya)
Greencombe Gardens, Somerset

Geranium sanguineum,
macrorrhizum & x
cantabrigiense
Brockamin, Worcestershire

Geranium sylvaticum
& renardii - forms, cvs.
& hybrids
Wren's Nest, Cheshire & Wirral

Hamamelis
Sir Harold Hillier Gardens,
Hampshire

Hamamelis cvs.
Green Island, Essex

Hedera
Ivybank, Pebworth Gardens,
Warwickshire

Heliotropium
Hampton Court Palace, London

Helleborus (Harvington
hybrids)
Riverside Gardens at Webbs,
Worcestershire

Hilliers (Plants raised by)
Sir Harold Hillier Gardens,
Hampshire

Hoheria
Abbotsbury Gardens, Dorset

Hosta (European and Asiatic)
Hanging Hosta Garden,
Hampshire

Hypericum
Sir Harold Hillier Gardens,
Hampshire

Iris ensata
Marwood Hill Garden, Devon

Juglans
Upton Wold, Gloucestershire

Lapageria rosea
(& named cvs.)
Roseland House, Cornwall

Leucanthemum x Superbum
(Chrysanthemum maximum)
Shapcott Barton Knowstone
Estate, Devon

Lewisia
'John's Garden' at Ashwood
Nurseries, Staffordshire

Ligustrum
Sir Harold Hillier Gardens,
Hampshire

Lithocarpus
Sir Harold Hillier Gardens,
Hampshire

Malus (ornamental)
Barnards Farm, Essex

Metasequoia
Sir Harold Hillier Gardens,
Hampshire

Narcissus (Springfields)
Collection
Springfields Festival Gardens,
Lincolnshire

Nerine sarniensis cvs.
Bickham Cottage, Devon

Osmunda
Sizergh Castle, Cumbria

Paeonia (hybrid herbaceous)
White Hopton Farm, Powys

Pelargonium
Ivybank, Pebworth Gardens,
Warwickshire

Pennisetum spp.
& cvs. (hardy)
Knoll Gardens, Dorset

Penstemon
Froggery Cottage,
Northamptonshire

Peperomia cvs.
Dewsnaps, Derbyshire

Photinia
Sir Harold Hillier Gardens,
Hampshire

Picea spp.
The Yorkshire Arboretum,
Yorkshire

Pinus
Sir Harold Hillier Gardens,
Hampshire

Pinus (excl dwarf cvs.)
The Lovell Quinta Arboretum,
Cheshire & Wirral

Podocarpaceae
Meon Orchard, Hampshire

Polystichum
Greencombe Gardens, Somerset

Primula auricula (Border)
12 Meres Road, Staffordshire

Pterocarya
Upton Wold, Gloucestershire

Quercus
Chevithrone Barton, Devon
Sir Harold Hillier Gardens,
Hampshire

Rhododendron
(Ghent Azaleas)
Sheffield Park and Garden,
Sussex

Rhododendron (Kurume
Azalea Wilson 50)
Trewidden Garden, Cornwall

Rhododendron subsect.
Fortunea
Himalayan Garden & Sculpture
Park, Yorkshire

Rhus
The Place for Plants, East
Bergholt Place Garden, Suffolk

Rodgersia
The Gate House, Devon

Rosa - Hybrid Musk intro by
Pemberton & Bentall 1912-
1939
Dutton Hall, Lancashire

Rosa (rambling)
Moor Wood, Gloucestershire

Sanguisorba
Avondale Nursery, Warwickshire

Santolina
The Walled Gardens of
Cannington, Somerset

Sarracenia
Beaufort, Shropshire

Saxifraga sect.
Ligulatae: spp. & cvs.
Waterperry Gardens, Oxfordshire

Saxifraga sect. Porphyrion
subsect. Porophyllum
Waterperry Gardens, Oxfordshire

Siberian Iris cvs.
British Award Winners
& historically significant
Aulden Farm, Herefordshire

Sorbus
Ness Botanic Gardens, Cheshire
& Wirral

Sorbus (British endemic spp.)
Blagdon, North East

Stern, Sir F
(plants selected by)
Highdown Gardens, Sussex

Stewartia - Asian spp.
High Beeches Woodland and
Water Garden, Sussex

Styracaceae (incl Halesia,
Pterostyrax, Styrax,
Sinojackia)
Holker Hall Gardens, Cumbria

Taxodium spp. & cvs.
West Lodge Park, London

Toxicodendron
The Place for Plants, East
Bergholt Place Garden, Suffolk

Tulbaghia spp. & subsp.
Marwood Hill Garden, Devon

Vaccinium
Greencombe Gardens, Somerset

Yucca
Renishaw Hall & Gardens,
Derbyshire

Society of Garden Designers

The 🅳 symbol at the end of a garden description indicates that the garden has been designed by a Fellow, Member, Pre-Registered Member, Student or Friend of the Society of Garden Designers.

Fellow of the Society of Garden Designers (FSGD) is awarded to Members for exceptional contributions to the Society or to the profession

Rosemary Alexander FSGD
Roderick Griffin FSGD
Sarah Massey FSGD
Juliet Sargeant FSGD
David Stevens FSGD
Robin Templar Williams FSGD
Julie Toll FSGD

Member of the Society of Garden Designers (MSGD) is awarded after passing adjudication

Cheryl Cummings MSGD
Peter Eustance MSGD
Jill Fenwick MSGD
Kate Gould MSGD
Nic Howard MSGD
Barbara Hunt MSGD (retired)
Ian Kitson MSGD
Arabella Lennox-Boyd MSGD
Emma Mazzullo MSGD
Robert Myers MSGD
Chris Parsons MSGD
Dan Pearson MSGD
Emma Plunket MSGD

Jilayne Rickards MSGD
Debbie Roberts MSGD
Libby Russell MSGD
Charles Rutherfoord MSGD
Ian Smith MSGD
Tom Stuart-Smith MSGD
Joe Swift MSGD
Jo Thompson MSGD
Sue Townsend MSGD
Cleve West MSGD
Rebecca Winship MSGD

Pre-Registered Member is a member working towards gaining Registered Membership

Joanne Bernstein
Tamara Bridge
Barbara Brooks
Fiona Cadwallader
Alasdair Cameron
Kristina Clode
Linsey Evans
Anoushka Feiler
Louise Hardwick
Sarah Naybour
Anne-Marie Powell
Faith Ramsay
Caz Renshaw
Judy Shardlow
Virginia von Celsing
Julia Whiteaway

Students
Julianne Fernandez
Tom Gadsby
Jonathan Venables
Adam Vetere

Friend
Paul Kimberley